THE OXFORD HANDBOOK OF

MUSIC CENSORSHIP

THE OXFORD HANDBOOK OF

MUSIC CENSORSHIP

Edited by
PATRICIA HALL

Oxford University Press is a department of the University of Oxford. It furthers
the University's objective of excellence in research, scholarship, and education
by publishing worldwide. Oxford is a registered trade mark of Oxford University
Press in the UK and certain other countries.

Published in the United States of America by Oxford University Press
198 Madison Avenue, New York, NY 10016, United States of America.

© Oxford University Press 2018

All rights reserved. No part of this publication may be reproduced, stored in
a retrieval system, or transmitted, in any form or by any means, without the
prior permission in writing of Oxford University Press, or as expressly permitted
by law, by license, or under terms agreed with the appropriate reproduction
rights organization. Inquiries concerning reproduction outside the scope of the
above should be sent to the Rights Department, Oxford University Press, at the
address above.

You must not circulate this work in any other form
and you must impose this same condition on any acquirer.

Library of Congress Cataloging-in-Publication Data
Names: Hall, Patricia (Patricia Ann)
Title: The Oxford handbook of music censorship / edited by Patricia Hall.
Description: New York, NY : Oxford University Press, [2018] |
Series: Oxford handbooks | Includes bibliographical references and index.
Identifiers: LCCN 2017034683 | ISBN 9780199733163 (cloth : alk. paper) |
ISBN 9780199984183 (oxford handbooks online)
Subjects: LCSH: Music—Censorship. | Music—Political aspects.
Classification: LCC ML3916 .O965 2018 | DDC 363.31—dc23
LC record available at https://lccn.loc.gov/2017034683

1 3 5 7 9 8 6 4 2

Printed by Sheridan Books, Inc., United States of America

Contents

Acknowledgments   ix
Contributors   xi

Introduction   1
PATRICIA HALL

I CENSORSHIP AND RELIGION

1. In the Quest of Gallican Remnants in Gregorian Manuscripts: Archaisms in the Masses for the Holy Cross in Aquitanian Chant Books   7
   LUISA NARDINI

2. The English Kyrie   39
   ALEJANDRO ENRIQUE PLANCHART

3. Governmental Interference as a Shaping Force in Elizabethan Printed Music   69
   JEREMY L. SMITH

4. The Sounds of Indigenous Ancestors: Music, Corporality, and Memory in the Jesuit Missions of Colonial South America   87
   GUILLERMO WILDE

5. "We Should Not Sing of Heaven and Angels": Performing Western Sacred Music in Soviet Russia, 1917–1964   109
   PAULINE FAIRCLOUGH

6. A Strident Silencing: The Ban on Richard Wagner in Israel   131
   NA'AMA SHEFFI

II CENSORSHIP DURING THE ENLIGHTENMENT

7. Harpocrates at Work: How the God of Silence Protected Eighteenth-Century French Iconoclasts — 153
   HEDY LAW

8. Sex, Politics, and Censorship in Mozart's *Don Giovanni/Don Juan* — 175
   MARTIN NEDBAL

9. The Depoliticized Drama: Mozart's *Figaro* and the Depths of Enlightenment — 203
   LAURENZ LÜTTEKEN

10. The Curious Incident of *Fidelio* and the Censors — 221
    ROBIN WALLACE

III CENSORSHIP IN TRANSITIONAL GOVERNMENTS

11. "Years in Prison": Giuseppe Verdi and Censorship in Pre-Unification Italy — 237
    FRANCESCO IZZO

12. Micronarratives of Music and (Self-) Censorship in Socialist Yugoslavia — 259
    ANA HOFMANN

13. Popular Music as a Barometer of Political Change: Evidence from Taiwan — 275
    NANCY GUY

14. Music and Censorship in Vietnam Since 1954 — 303
    BARLEY NORTON

IV CENSORSHIP IN TOTALITARIAN STATES

15. Miguel Ángel Estrella (Classical) Music for the People, Dictatorship, and Memory — 333
    CAROL A. HESS

16. A Case Study of Brazilian Popular Music and Censorship:
    Ivan Lins's Music during Dictatorship in Brazil   355
    THAIS LIMA NICODEMO

17. Alban Berg's "Guilt" by Association   377
    PATRICIA HALL

18. Slow Dissolves, Full Stops, and Interruptions: Terezín, Censorship,
    and the Summer of 1944   389
    MICHAEL BECKERMAN

19. Selling Schnittke: Late Soviet Censorship and the Cold
    War Marketplace   413
    PETER J. SCHMELZ

20. Curb that Enticing Tone: Music Censorship in the PRC   453
    HON-LUN YANG

V CENSORSHIP IN DEMOCRACIES

21. Censorship and the Politics of Reception: The Filmic Afterlife of
    Marc Blitzstein's *The Cradle Will Rock*   477
    DAVID C. PAUL

22. Pete Seeger's Project   499
    DICK FLACKS

23. Government Censorship and Aaron Copland's *Lincoln Portrait*
    during the Second Red Scare   511
    JENNIFER DELAPP-BIRKETT

24. "A Day in the Life": The Beatles and the BBC, May 1967   535
    GORDON THOMPSON

VI CENSORING RACE, GENDER, AND SEXUAL ORIENTATION

25. Composing in Black and White: Code-Switching in the Songs
    of Sam Lucas   559
    SANDRA JEAN GRAHAM

26. Exploring Transitions in Popular Music: Censorship
    from Apartheid to Post-Apartheid South Africa 593
    MICHAEL DREWETT

27. Rap Music and Rap Audiences Revisited: How Race Matters in
    the Perception of Rap Music 609
    TRAVIS L. DIXON

28. Deaths and Silences: Coding and Defiance in Music About AIDS 623
    PAUL ATTINELLO

29. Teaching Silence in the Twenty-First Century: Where Are
    the Missing Women Composers? 637
    ROXANE PREVOST AND KIMBERLY FRANCIS

30. Veiled Voices: Music and Censorship in Post-Revolutionary Iran 657
    AMENEH YOUSSEFZADEH

Index 675

Acknowledgments

I would like to thank Suzanne Ryan for her continued support and enthusiasm for this project. Lauralee Yeary, Assistant Editor at Oxford University Press, was always a pleasure to work with, and an invaluable help in moving the *Handbook* to publication.

An Interdisciplinary Humanities Center Grant from the University of California, Santa Barbara, and a Faculty Block Award from the University of Michigan, Ann Arbor, helped defray the costs of copyediting and translations.

Above all, I am grateful to the authors of this *Handbook* for their patience during the long process of gathering, editing, and translating chapters.

Contributors

Paul Attinello is Senior Lecturer in the International Centre for Music Studies at Newcastle University.

Michael Beckerman is Professor of Music at New York University.

Jennifer DeLapp-Birkett is an independent scholar in musicology.

Travis L. Dixon is Communication Alumni Professorial Scholar and Associate Professor of Communication Studies and African American Studies at the University of Illinois, Urbana-Champaign.

Michael Drewett is Associate Professor of Sociology at Rhodes University.

Pauline Fairclough is Reader in Music at the University of Bristol.

Dick Flacks is Professor of Sociology at University of California, Santa Barbara.

Kimberly Francis is Assistant Professor of Music at the University of Guelph.

Sandra Jean Graham is Associate Professor of Ethnomusicology in the Arts & Humanities division at Babson College.

Nancy Guy is Professor of Integrative Studies in the Department of Music at the University of California, San Diego.

Patricia Hall is Professor of Music Theory for the School of Music, Theatre & Dance at the University of Michigan.

Carol A. Hess is Professor and Chair of the Department of Music at the University of California, Davis.

Ana Hofmann is Senior Research Fellow and Assistant Professor at the Slovenian Academy of Sciences and Arts.

Francesco Izzo is Professor and Head of Music at the University of Southampton.

Hedy Law is Assistant Professor of Musicology at the University of British Columbia.

Laurenz Lütteken is Professor of Musicology at the University of Zurich.

Luisa Nardini is Associate Professor of Musicology at the University of Texas, Austin.

Martin Nedbal is Assistant Professor of Musicology at the University of Kansas.

Thais Lima Nicodemo is Researcher in Music at the University of Campinas.

Barley Norton is Reader in Ethnomusicology at Goldsmiths, University of London.

David C. Paul is Associate Professor of Musicology at the University of California, Santa Barbara.

Alejandro Enrique Planchart is Professor Emeritus of Music at the University of California, Santa Barbera.

Roxane Prevost is Associate Professor of Music at the University of Ottawa.

Peter J. Schmelz is Associate Professor of Music at Arizona State University.

Na'ama Sheffi teaches at the School of Communication at Sapir College in Israel.

Jeremy L. Smith is Professor of Musicology at the University of Colorado Boulder.

Gordon Thompson is Professor and Chair of the Department of Music at Skidmore College.

Robin Wallace is Professor of Musicology at Baylor University.

Guillermo Wilde is Senior Researcher for the National Council for Scientific and Technical Research (CONICET), Argentina.

Hon-Lun Yang is Professor of Music History at Hong Kong Baptist University.

Ameneh Youssefzadeh is Co-consulting Editor of Music at Encyclopedia Iranica, and Visiting Scholar at the City University of New York (CUNY) Graduate Center.

THE OXFORD HANDBOOK OF

MUSIC CENSORSHIP

INTRODUCTION

PATRICIA HALL

"In order to eliminate every cultural and economic peculiarity, no Polish corporation, union or association can exist ... Polish restaurants and cafes are not permitted ... There shall be no Polish newspapers, nor production of Polish books, nor publication of Polish journals. For the same reasons, Poles shall have no right to own radio receivers or phonographs."

Fragment of Wetzel and Hecht's Memorandum, November 25, 1939

DURING a recent visit to Auschwitz-Birkenau, I was particularly struck by the text of this memorandum posted in Block 15, now the site of an exhibition on Poland during World War II. It describes a level of censorship applying not only to music, but Polish life in general. As Halik Kochanski, the author of *The Eagle Unbowed: Poland and the Poles in the Second World War* clarifies, "Nazi ideology demanded the total subjugation of Poland and erasure of all evidence of her statehood" (Kochanski, 98).

Music censorship in Poland, alluded to at the end of the quote (Poles shall have no rights to radio receivers or phonographs), is made explicit in the film *The Pianist*: Wladyslaw Szpilman's performance of Chopin's Nocturne No. 20 in C Sharp Minor, Opus Posthumus, is interrupted by the dramatic bombing of the Polish National Radio. Polish life (and music) does not resume until the end of the war, signified by the 1945 broadcast of Szpilman playing the same Chopin nocturne.

While this could be cited as an extreme and total form of censorship, occurring during a world war and initial invasion of a country, there are equally extreme forms taking place today. Freemuse, established in 1998, "advocating and defending freedom of expression for musicians and composers worldwide," maintains a website in which instances of music censorship are literally posted as they occur, for instance, the blurring of musicians playing instruments in a broadcast by the Islam Republic of Iran Broadcasting in February 2016. Moreover, even a cursory glance online reveals other shocking instances of music censorship: the public beheading of an Iraqi teenager by ISIS in February 2016 for listening to "Western pop music."

In its most elemental form, music censorship requires an agent capable of affecting negative outcomes on a musician. These negative outcomes may take the form of execution, imprisonment, torture, fines, or cancellation of performances and the resulting loss of income. It is not surprising that as a result, many musicians resort to self-censorship. Conflicts between the censoring agent and the musician arise when music does not project the ideals of the agent, whether religious, governmental, or otherwise. In their extensive study of the history of music censorship, Marie Korpe, Ole Retov, and Martin Cloonan list possible censoring agents as "governments, mass media, religious authorities, industries, business firms, school systems, retailers, musical groups, parents, and even individual musicians" (Korpe et al., 240).

This Handbook presents thirty in-depth studies of music censorship from the eighth century to the present. The range of music presented is also very broad, from Gregorian chant to eighteenth-century opera to present-day pop music. Since censorship is a worldwide phenomenon, this volume includes studies from every continent. At the same time, these chapters are representative examples, since it would be impossible to discuss every type of music censorship, a fluid phenomenon that can change daily.

Section I focuses on religion as an object of censorship, but also as a censoring agent. In Chapter 1, Luisa Nardini describes the result of Pepin the Short (714–768) and his son Charlemagne's program to enforce liturgical homogeneity in Western Europe. In Chapter 2, Alejandro Planchart traces the evolution of the English Kyrie, and its transformations in continental sources. Jeremy L. Smith explains the variability of governmental control on printed music during the Protestant/Catholic conflicts of the Elizabethan era in Chapter 3. In Chapter 4, Guillermo Wilde discusses the imposition of Jesuit ideals on the native population of South America, and their resistance to these ideals. Chapter 5, by Pauline Fairclough, elucidates the complex topic of suppressing Western sacred music in Soviet Russia. And finally, Chapter 6, by Na'ama Sheffi, explains the opposition to performing Wagner in Israel after *Kristallnacht*.

Section II, in contrast, focuses on a particular era: the Enlightenment in France and Austria. Beginning with Hedy Law's ingenious study of the role of Harpocrate in eighteenth-century France (Chapter 7), we move to three iconic operas of the period: Martin Nedbal's study of censorship in *Don Giovanni* (Chapter 8), Laurence L Lütteken's of *The Marriage of Figaro* (Chapter 9), and Robin Wallace's reexamination of censorship associated with Beethoven's *Fidelio*. (Chapter 10).

Section III, studies censorship in transitional governments, from nineteenth-century Italy to present-day Taiwan. No volume on censorship would be complete without a discussion of Verdi's operas in pre-Unification Italy, and Francesco Izzo details the many struggles with text censorship that Verdi endured (Chapter 11). The remaining chapters in this section deal with broad periods of censorship in twentieth-century nations: the former Yugoslavia, with an emphasis on the censorship of folk music (Ana Hofmann, Chapter 12), Nancy Guy's study of the censorship of popular music in Taiwan (Chapter 13), and Barley Norton's study of censorship in Vietnam from 1954 to the present (Chapter 14).

Section IV describes censorship in totalitarian governments during the twentieth century. Four of these chapters focus on an individual artist. Chapters 15 and 16 by

Carol Hess and Thais Lima Nicodermo, respectively, discuss the composers Estrella in Argentina and Lins in Brazil. My own chapter traces Berg's attempts at the end of his life to counteract censorship of his opera *Wozzeck* in Nazi Germany (Chapter 17). Michael Beckerman describes the unique censorial conditions of the concentration camp Theresianstadt in 1944 (Chapter 18). Peter Schmelz examines the saga of censorship that has evolved around Schnittke (Chapter 19). And Hon-Lun Yang explains different phases of censorship in the Peoples Republic of China, both in terms of native performers and visiting musicians (Chapter 20).

One might initially imagine that less censorship occurred in democracies, the topic of Section V, however, three of the contributions derive from particularly fraught periods of US history: the labor battles of the 1930s (David Paul's study of the filmic reception of *The Cradle Will Rock*, Chapter 21); the Second Red Scare (Jennifer DeLapp's chapter on Copland's *Lincoln Portrait*, Chapter 23, and Dick Flack's chapter on Pete Seeger during the Vietnam War (Chapter 22). Our final chapter (Chapter 24 by Gordon Thompson) deals with the censorship of a Beatles song by the BBC, but also the entire history of BBC censorship.

Finally, in Section VI we examine race, gender, and sexual orientation as objects of censorship. Beginning with Sandra Graham's study (Chapter 25) tracing the long career and racial code-switching of Sam Lucas, three of these chapters examine censorship of African Americans. Michael Drewett (Chapter 26) compares censorship during the Apartheid and post-Apartheid era of popular songs. Travis L. Dixon examines audience perception of rap music based on race, gender, and other factors (Chapter 27). Two chapters discuss the ongoing censorship of women in both the United States and post-revolutionary Iran. Roxane Prevost and Kimberly Francis (Chapter 29) explore the reasons why women are a distinct minority among composers of classical music. Ameneh Youseffzadeh discusses the suppression of women musicians in the male-dominated state of Iran (Chapter 30). Paul Attinello (Chapter 28) traces music about AIDS, from the first public awareness in 1981 in the repertory of "classical, popular, and avant-garde musics of the Anglophone West."

While Plato's *Republic* is frequently cited as the first extensive discussion of music censorship, music censorship has probably existed as long as music, and will continue to exist in one form or another. I hope this volume makes clear the tremendous complexity, variability, and changing nature of music censorship, as well as the many strategies that musicians have used to counteract it.

References

Kochanski, Halik. 2012. *The Eagle Unbowed. Poland and the Poles in the Second World War*. Cambridge, Mass.: Harvard University Press.

Korpe, Marie, Reitov, Ole and Cloonan, Martin. 2016. "Music Censorship from Plato to the Present." In *Music and Manipulation: On the Social Uses and Social Control of Music*, edited by Steven Brown and Ulrik Volgsten. New York: Berghahn Books.

I

CENSORSHIP AND RELIGION

CHAPTER 1

IN THE QUEST OF GALLICAN REMNANTS IN GREGORIAN MANUSCRIPTS

Archaisms in the Masses for the Holy Cross in Aquitanian Chant Books

LUISA NARDINI

When Pepin the Short (714–768) and his son Charlemagne (742–814) envisioned a program of cultural unification of western Europe, they promoted a series of actions devoted to endorse liturgical homogeneity within the territories of their kingdom and beyond. This program entailed the suppression of regional liturgical traditions and the superimposition of Roman use to Francia and the rest of the Europe. That this was not a straightforward process, however, is attested by the melodic contamination of Roman chant that resulted from the attempt to domesticate the foreign (Roman) musical idiom to the local (Frankish or Gallican) taste. Therefore Gregorian chant—the repertory of chant that emerged from the eighth-century liturgical and musical exchanges between Rome and Francia—can be described as an aesthetic compromise, where compromise refers to the stylistic synthesis operated by Frankish cantors who, while adopting ritual structures and liturgical texts and genres from Rome, preserved some elements and their own liturgical practices and musical language.

Although the contamination of Roman chant with elements of Gallican style and repertory pervaded the whole body of liturgical chant, there are some feasts and ceremonies in which the preservation of Gallican elements was more pervasive and that therefore can be used as a means to reconstructing elements of the Gallican style. Among these there are feasts that were either not included in the Roman chant books or that were already present in the Gallican calendar before the arrival of Roman chant. In their effort to provide texts and melodies for these celebrations, Frankish cantors often conflated the general framework of Roman liturgy with components derived from local, preexisting devotional materials. In some such cases cantors simply reused older pieces and adapted them to the formal structure of Roman chant, while in others they composed new chants that would fit, structurally and stylistically, the recently Romanized arrangement of the mass. These last examples are generally defined as Romano-Frankish chants (Huglo et al. 2013).

In order to identify Gallican chants in extant Gregorian manuscripts, a method of double comparison has been proposed by scholars, the first between Roman and Gregorian books, to isolate chants of non-Roman origins, and the second among manuscripts of the Mozarabic, Ambrosian, and Celtic traditions to narrow down the geographical origins of pieces. After the double process of comparison has been accomplished, it is necessary to test the pieces according to "three main criteria ... (individually or in combination): the evidence of liturgical books and other literary evidence, the literary style of the texts, and the musical style" (Huglo et al. 2013).

Within the repertory of the mass, in particular, one phenomenon has been noticed, the liturgical transformation of chants. This consists in refitting preexisting Gallican chants into Gregorian genres. This way a processional antiphon, or a piece from the ordinary, could change its original function and become an offertory, a communion, or an introit. There are instances of cognate chants in various Western chant traditions that bear more remote pre-Gregorian (Gallican) origins. These were made compatible with the structure of the Gregorian liturgy by way of genre switching (Nardini 2007). These are some of the methodologies that led scholars to identify a number of Gallican chants and to compile lists of extant exemplars (See Leclercq 1924; Huglo et al. 2013; Stäblein 1955, for a lists of individual pieces and bibliographical references; Huglo 1955a,b; Schäfer 1956; de Clerck 1977; Levy 1958–1963; Brockett 2006, for examples of studies of specific repertories).

This chapter analyzes a group of chants for the masses for the Holy Cross copied in manuscripts from Aquitaine that bear signs of more remote pre-Gregorian roots. These roots can be recognized in some textual and musical features, in aspects related to their liturgical collocation, and in the theological arguments they unfold. A comprehensive analysis embracing all constituents of liturgical chants is the only way to attempt the identification of Gallican components in chants copied in Gregorian manuscripts. Rather than proposing the discovery of new pieces, then, this chapter speculates on issues of persistence and change in the transmission of liturgical repertories and the role of music censorship on the practice of liturgical chant.

There is a group of masses for feasts of more remote Gallican origins that include, among others, the Chair of St. Peter, the Finding of the Cross, and the Beheading of St. John the Baptist (Hesbert 1935; Righetti 1950; Ropa 1993) to name just a few. Some of them are alternative masses to others found in Roman chant books for the same calendric day. For instance, in Roman chant books May 3 (Finding of the Cross) is also dedicated to St. Alexander, and August 29 (Beheading of the Baptist) to St. Sabine. Some of the pieces provided for these feasts may contain Gallican components that were filtered through the process of Romanization of chant and ended up being transcribed into Gregorian chant books. Ultimately, they made their way into the uses of other regions of Europe in the Middle Ages.

Reasons for focusing on the mass reside on the consideration that this is the best-documented rite of the Gallican tradition. We can learn about the structure of the Gallican mass from a number of documents, the most descriptive of which are the letters of the pseudo-Germanus. Texts for prayers and scriptural references are included in sacramentaries and lectionaries, the liturgical books used by the celebrant. These include the *Missale gothicum* (a Gallican sacramentary), the *Missale gallicanum vetus*, the Bobbio missal, and the *Missale francorum* (from the north of France), the so-called Mone masses (a group of masses described and published by the German historian F. J. Mone), plus a number of other, fragmentary documents. Lectionaries are preserved in a more scattered series of manuscripts, including the lectionary of Luxeuil, the lectionnaire d'Aniane, the lectionary of Wolfenbüttel, and other incomplete documents (see bibliography). Studies and editions of these documents allow us to advance more solid hypotheses about how Gallican remnants were sifted through the process of Romanization of Francia and entered the Gregorian tradition of chant. However, the identification of individual Gallican chants that were sung at mass is problematic both because they are very rarely listed in sacramentaries and lectionaries and because, when we do have occasional mentions of actual chants, they are generally limited to textual incipits and lack musical notation. This makes it necessary to recur to the method of multiple comparisons mentioned above to overcome the difficulties in the identification of chants. However problematic, a study of the Gallican mass may avail itself of larger and more reliable resources than the office. The divine office, in fact, not only is scarcely documented in extant Gallican sources but also shows stronger signs of regional fragmentation, thus rendering the comparison between the Gallican and Roman, or Gregorian, versions of chants an even more challenging task (Huglo et al. 2013).

The choice of Aquitaine for the present study, finally, is due to the consideration that this region, because of its greater geographical distance from the center of the kingdom, was characterized by a higher degree of retention of non-standardized chants (Huglo et al. 2013). Among Aquitanian manuscripts, graduals Pa903 and Pa776, both published in facsimile editions, will be privileged for this discussion (manuscript sigla are expanded in Appendix 2). Moreover, given the frequent political and cultural exchanges between Aquitaine and various territories of the Italian peninsula, some of these Gallican-influenced chants were later transmitted to Italy and were incorporated into the local liturgical manuscripts (Nardini 2015). Interestingly enough, some of the chants for the Holy Cross analyzed here ultimately reached the city of Rome. As explained below, some of the chants copied in the Roman gradual Bod74 were imported from outside of Rome. This circumstance, while pointing to the multidirectionality of chant transmission in medieval Europe, confirms what other scholars have also suggested: that the special kind of liturgical hybridism that resulted from the process of Romanization of Frankish liturgy—Gregorian chant—ultimately permeated some portions of the Roman rite, the very model to which Carolingian liturgists aimed to conform (Levy 1984; 2000–2001; 2003).

Before digging into the analysis of specific examples, however, it is important to contextualize the process of standardization of chant within the projects of cultural reform of the Carolingians and, previously, the Merovingians in order to define to what extent royal decrees influenced chant practices in Carolingian and post-Carolingian Europe. As mentioned above, the quest for liturgical uniformity was instrumental to the Carolingians' broader plans of political and cultural unification of Europe. Carolingian monarchs knew that the political cohesiveness of their vast domain could only be attained through a project of cultural reform that would help holding together territories that were otherwise characterized by profound geographical, economic, ethnic, and cultural differences. Rosamond McKitterick observes, "with their steady series of conquests during the eighth century, adding Alemannia, Frisia, Aquitaine, the Lombard kingdom in northern Italy, Septimania, Bavaria, Saxony, and Brittany to the Frankish heartlands in Gaul, the Carolingians created what Ganshof regarded as an unwieldy empire" (McKitterick 1996, 59; see also Ganshof 1968).

Of course, any attempt at cultural unification in the medieval West had to go hand in hand with the pursuit of religious concord. With this in mind, Carolingians promoted a series of actions aimed to define and achieve correctness and uniformity in church rituals. We know that before the reign of Pippin III (714–768), not only did Gallican liturgy differ from that of Rome, but there was also no such thing as a prescribed set of approved texts even within the territories of Francia (McKitterick 1996, 61, 59). Indeed, because of the political fragmentation of Europe and the lack of a standard of liturgical uniformity on the part of ecclesiastical and temporal authorities, liturgical practices were substantially heterogeneous from region to region and sometimes from dioceses to dioceses up the eighth century.

Within the territory of pre-Carolingian Gaul, liturgical uses varied greatly from place to place, if not necessarily in the structure of rites, at least in the choice of texts. It is for this reason that scholars have referred to a plurality of liturgical Gallican uses. It was to favor a process of uniformity and ritual correctness that Carolingians pursued fidelity to Roman practices. McKitterick reminds us that "from the reign of Pippin III . . . (714–768), onwards, statements concerning the organization and ritual of the church within the Frankish realms of western Europe reveal a preoccupation with correctness, authority, and concord with the holy see" and also that "unity of law, administration, and ritual was not only required but also swiftly established within the Frankish Church." In synthesis, it was a matter of "production and dissemination of authorized texts" (McKitterick 1996, 61, 62).[1] In fact, in pre-Carolingian Gaul as in the rest of Christian Europe, ritual practices were often simply regulated by bishoprics or, as can be evinced by missionary uses in the sixth century, by whatever texts were at a cleric's hand (for a more recent discussion and additional bibliography, see Hornby 2004).

It was because of the aim to overcome liturgical discordance among churches of the realm that Carolingians envisioned that a successful strategy for liturgical reform could only be attained by pursuing ritual concordance with the Roman (meaning papal) practices. This plan had a three-fold advantage: first, it could be easily recognized as authoritative by subject populations; secondly, it could benefit from the efficient network of papal bureaucracy and canonic tradition and therefore could be more easily spread throughout the territories of medieval Europe; finally and foremost, it was the reflex of a wider program of assimilation of the reign of Francia to Rome, because of the notion—intrinsic to the Carolingian political agenda—that "(Christian) Rome had to be reborn or revived in Francia" (Brown 1994, 14).

In her study on unity and diversity in the Carolingian church, McKitterick underlines that what Carolingians were really seeking was not identity of ritual practices, but a more general sense of concord. In other words, rituals had to be compatible with the uses of Rome in order and structure, but not necessarily exactly identical to them. For example, mass had to be organized according to the practice of Rome with two sets of chants (Proper and Ordinary) intertwined with prayers and readings. Moreover, each genre had to follow the structure of Roman models. Yet there were still margins for variants that consisted in additions and modification to the core repertory to suit the cultic needs of local churches.

The main instrument to promote "'peace, concord, and unanimity' among the whole Christian people" was the *Admonitio generalis*, an articulated body of legislation issued by Charlemagne in 789 that was composed of eighty-two clauses and was mostly devoted to ecclesiastical and spiritual matters (King 1987; Brown 1994). Main concern of the *Admonitio* was the pursuit of the spiritual salvation of humanity. The *Admonitio* stresses the importance of the true doctrine to instill religious piety and to control heresy. The production and availability of correct texts was crucial in this endeavor. Emphasis is given to the necessity of having well-trained scribes and reliable sources in scriptoria, so that only texts in accordance with religious orthodoxy would be produced. As for liturgical practice, the *Admonitio* stresses the urgency for uniformity of practice and concordance with the Roman See (Brown 1994, 20). Pippin's intervention toward the suppression of Gallican and the adoption of Roman chant is defined as instrumental in attaining liturgical uniformity. However, reference to chant is very brief in the *Admonitio*, and more specific details about what the adoption of Roman chant specifically entailed are not included.

There is no doubt, though, that Frankish liturgists succeeded in Romanizing the order and structure of the mass. In fact, they not only acquired the overall organization of the Roman mass but also adopted the formal structure and textual selections of Roman liturgical genres for both the Ordinary and the Proper. For example, introits copied in post-Carolingian chant books conform to Roman uses in their being articulated in antiphon, psalm, and Doxology, as well as, in the majority of cases, in their textual selection. This can be verified for all other genres of the Proper of the mass, although there are repertories, such as alleluias and offertories, that, because of their later period of formation, display greater degrees of variability and inconsistency with more markedly local differentiations.

Table 1.1 compares the rite of mass in the Roman and Gallican liturgies. The table does not aim to imply a deterministic correspondence between Gallican and Roman genres (there are liturgical genres for which, because of formal and stylistic incompatibilities, the comparison cannot be made), but simply to show the order of chants, prayers, and readings and their position in relation to the central event of the Eucharist.

Table 1.1 Confrontation between the structure of the Mass in the Gallican and Gregorian uses. The correspondence is not necessarily liturgical but reflects the order of chants and their position in relation to the main events of the celebration

Gallican Mass	Roman (Gregorian) Mass
1. Antiphona ad prelegendum (with psalm verse)	Introit (with psalm verse)
Call for silence	
Aius (Trisagion) followed by the Kyrie eleison	Kyrie
Benedictus (Prophetia). Replaced during Lent by the Sanctus Deus archangelorum	Gloria
Reading from the Old Testament	
Hymnus trium puerorum	Collect
Reading from the Epistles, the Acts, Revelation, or the martyrologium.	Epistle
Responsorium	Gradual
Antiphona ante evangelium	Alleluia. (Sequence) Alleluia is replaced by the Tract during penitential times.
Aius before the Gospel	
Gospel	Gospel
Sanctus post evangelium	Credo
Preces	
Dismissal of the catechumens	
Sonus	Offertory
Immolatio Missae	Preface
Sanctus	Sanctus
Eucharist	
Fraction antiphon	Eucharistic Prayer
Lord's prayer	Pater noster
Episcopal benediction	Agnus Dei
Trecanum (probably sung during communion)	Communion
	Post-Communion
	Ite Missa est

The earliest Frankish liturgical books, as those published by Hesbert, all conform to the Roman order shown in Table 1.1. Conformity not only pertains to the overall structure of the rite, but also, for the most part, to the texts of Proper and Ordinary chants. Although complete homologation was never completely attained (and probably not even sought after), it is easy to understand that the changes introduced were substantial. Furthermore, the adoption of these changes by the majority of western churches following the Latin rite (with the exception of the churches of the Ambrosian and Old Hispanic rites) is a phenomenon of unprecedented import in the history of Western liturgy.

Even within the mass, however, we can find pockets of localisms in the otherwise standardized structure of the rite. Among these pockets of localism there are the texts for prayers and the selection of readings from the scriptures, for instance, which, studies have demonstrated, show lesser signs of super-regional standardization (McKitterick 1996).

But there were also other elements from the Gallican musico-liturgical practice that were retained in Gregorian chant books. Among these there are a group of ceremonies that were not part of the Roman liturgy. These include the processional antiphons sung during the Rogation days, the three days that preceded the Ascension, or the preces transcribed among the Minor Litanies in Gregorian books (Huglo 1955; de Clerck 1977; Capelle 1925), the translation of the relics at the dedication of a church, or the washing of feet at the baptism of neophytes (Huglo et al. 2013; Schäfer 1956). The tradition of Rogation was not known in Rome, but, through the intermediary role of Frankish manuscripts, was ultimately spread throughout Europe. It is for this circumstance that the chants for Rogation days are a privileged repository of Gallican remnants. Some of these antiphons were re-employed as mass Proper items in some Frankish and Italian manuscripts (Nardini 2007). They are characterized by more florid melodies and imaginative texts that make them differ from the majority of Roman antiphons (Huglo et al. 2013).

As for the forms of localism in the rite of the mass, these may pertain to either musical style, textual features, or the observance of feasts that predate the Romanization of the rite. However, they are difficult to identify because of the lack of extant notated Gallican liturgical books and because of the elapse of about four centuries between the creation of Roman chant (later seventh century) and its transcription in manuscripts. The earliest substantial Roman manuscript, Bod74, dates not earlier than the second half of the eleventh century. These circumstances, therefore, prevent the direct reconstruction of the Gallican (and Roman) archetypes of Gregorian chant, as underlined in the vast bibliography on the subject (see, most recently, McKinnon 2000, 375–403; and Levy 2000–2001; 2003). Localisms in Frankish manuscripts, however, should not be interpreted as forms of inobservance to royal mandates. In all liturgical chant repertories of the Latin Church, in fact, occasional divergences from standardized practices were simply a natural consequence of the need for a continuous balance between uniformity of rituals, realized through dogmatic and liturgical concord, and preservation of feasts, ceremonials, and textual and musical elements belonging to peripheral uses.

One of the main characteristics of Gallican chant that has been underlined in previous studies is the very special style of texts that veers from the psalm-like simplicity of

Roman texts. Even when newly composed, Roman texts mimic the succinct and immediate language of the Scriptures and have plain prose that generally avoids subordinate clauses and complex theological discourses. This is typical of both the texts for Proper chants and liturgical prayers. In particular, Roman texts for prayers are

> rigorously precise in theological formulation and concise in vocabulary: prayer is always addressed to the Father through the Son, and petitions are concisely expressed. By contrast, Gallican prayers develop various aspects of a theme, with an accumulation of rhetorical figures such as repetitions, redundancies, antitheses, and metaphors; and the rich and colorful vocabulary contrasts strongly with that of the Roman liturgy.... Prayers in the Gallican rite were frequently addressed to the Son and the Holy Spirit. (Huglo et al. 2013; see also Manz 1941)

The furbished style of Gallican prayers very likely derived from the intense stream of liturgical composition of sixth-century Merovingian Gaul (Hen 1996; 2001). It eventually affected the style of Romano-Frankish mass Proper texts (Steiner 1993). In this way, Frankish liturgists were able to reemploy imagery, theological concepts, and phraseology typical of Gallican texts within the recently acquired structure of the Roman liturgy.

The masses for the feasts of the Holy Cross copied in the Aquitanian manuscripts Pa776 and Pa903, have Proper texts that resemble, in content and style, more ancient prayers found in Gallican sacramentaries for the mass of the Finding of the Cross. Before proceeding in the analysis of these texts, however, it is useful to briefly trace the history of the introduction of these feasts into the liturgical calendar.

There are two major feasts dedicated to the celebration of the Holy Cross in the liturgical calendar, the Finding (May 3) and the Exaltation (September 14). Both feasts were known in Rome by the seventh century. In Francia observation of the Finding predates the arrival of Roman chant, while the Exaltation was imported with the rest of the repertory. Arguably, it is because of this circumstance that the mass Propers copied in Aquitanian manuscripts have a composite nature whereas chants of Roman and Romano-Frankish origins are intermingled with others displaying signs of Gallican influence.

Although both feasts had been established in Rome before the end of the seventh century, it was not until the second half of the eleventh century that we have a record of notated chants for the Proper of the mass in Roman liturgical books, when the earliest extant Roman book with chants for the Holy Cross, Bod74, is dated. This and the other two mass manuscripts, Vat5319 and F22, provide complete formularies. Examination of these formularies, notwithstanding the late date of compilation of the manuscripts, leads to the identification of the core Roman liturgical repertory for the Holy Cross predating the exportation of chant to Francia. Although the original, seventh-century profile of chants cannot be reconstructed and although the Roman mass Propers do reveal signs of conflation of local (Roman) and foreign (Frankish) influences, it is possible to identify the pieces that belong to the original Roman setting for the Holy Cross. Let us take a closer look at these formularies.

Table 1.2 compares the masses for the Finding of the Cross in extant Roman manuscripts. The chants that are "local" and reflect the pre-Gregorian practice were simply adapted from other masses of the liturgical year. These are the introit *Nos autem* and the gradual *Christus factus est* borrowed from Passion week; the alleluia *Dominus regnavit* and the offertory *Deus enim firmavit* both from Christmas day; and the communion *Spiritus ubi vult* from the week after Pentecost. (In the manuscripts, pieces borrowed from other feasts are provided with rubrics referencing their original liturgical collocation. These rubrics are transcribed in all caps in Table 1.2, as in Cutter 1979). The rest of the formulary of Bod74 and Vat5319 was imported to Rome from elsewhere: the

Table 1.2 Chants for the Proper of the mass of the Finding of the Cross in Roman chant books (Cutter 1979)

Bod74	Vat5319	F22
Processional Antiphon Nos autem gloriari oportet in cruce Domini nostri Jesu Christi in quo est salus vita et resurrectio nostra per quem salvati et liberati sumus	**Processional Antiphon** Nos autem gloriari oportet in cruce Domini nostri Hiesu Christi in quo es salus vita et resurrectio nostra per quem salvati et liberati sumus	
Introit Nos autem gloriari. [REQUIRE IN EBDOMADA DE PASSIONE FERIA III]	**Introit** Nos autem [REQUIRE AD SANCTAM PRISCA]	
	Gradual Christus factus est. IN CENA DOMINI	
	Alleluia Dominus re[gnavit]. NATALE DOMINI MISSAM	
Alleluia Dulce lignum dulces clavos dulcia ferens pondera quae sola fuisti digna sustinere regem caelorum et Dominum		
Prosula Omnipotens Rex aeterne Jesu Nazarene Populi suscipe preces Clemens atque benigne		
Prosula Animas quas redemisti ex Spiritu Sancto gratias quas suscepisti eas a saeculo custody		
Prosula O alma crux nostra salus Christi per cruore te obnixe collaudamus omnes propter Dominum		

(*continued*)

Table 1.2 Continued

Bod74	Vat5319	F22
Sequence Alma fulgens lux praeclara splendidior cunctis gloriosa desiderabilis atque dilecta membrorum Christi et honodrara. Tu sola fuisti digna nobilis triumphata ad caelis es exaltata super omnia ligna cedrorum es collaudata. Catenis infernorum per te sunt destructae animae Sanctorum sunt absolutae. Tartaris legions sunt obligatae per tuum sanctum signum manus armata. Libera nos semper crux gloriosa. Amen		
Offertory Deus enim firmavit	**Offertory** Deus enim. [IN NATALE DOMINI]	
Communion Spiritus ubi vult spirat et vocem ejus audis alleluia dicit Dominus et nescis unde veniat aut quo vadat alleluia alleluia	**Communion** Spiritus ubi vult spirat et vocem ejus audis alleluia. Dicit Dominus et nexcis unde veniat aut quo vadat alleluia alleluia	

Chants for the Proper of the mass of the Exaltation of the Cross in Roman chant books (Cutter 1979)

Bod74	Vat5319	F22
	Introit Nos autem REQUIRE AD SANCTAM PRISCA	**Introit** Nos autem [FERIA III POST DOMINICA IN PALMIS]
	Gradual Christus factus est. REQUIRE IN CENA DOMINI	**Gradual** Christus fac[tus] [CENA DOMINI]
	Alleluia Dominus regna[vit] IN NATALE DOMINI	**Alleluia** Dominus regnavit [NATIVITATE]
	Offertory Deus enim fir[mavit]. MISSA MANE PRIMO	**Offertory** Deus enim fir[mavit]. [IBIDEM]
	Communion Spiritus ubi vult. REQUIRE IN INVENTIONE SANCTE CRUCIS	**Communion** Spiritus ubi vult [FERIA V POST PENTECOSTEN]

processional antiphon *Nos autem gloriari* came from Aquitaine and bears more remote Gallican origins (Nardini 2007); the alleluia *Dulce lignum* is a Romano-Frankish addition to the Roman fund of chants for the Holy Cross that is also copied in a number of manuscripts of French, Italian, German, and English origin (Schlager 1965, 182). The prosulas *Omnipotens rex eterne* and *Animas quas redemisti* and the sequence *Alma fulget lux preclara* are shared with manuscripts from southern Italy. The prosula *O alma crux* is an original piece that was probably composed *in loco* in imitation of the imported prosulas. Given the repertorial similarities for part of the Mass in Bod 74 with Beneventan manuscripts, especially with Ben35 and MC318, it is very likely that *Omnipotens rex eterne, Animas quas redemisti,* and *Alma fulget lux preclara* were imported in Bod 74 from southern Italy (Levy 1971; Planchart 2001; Kelly 1994; Kartsovnik 1998; Nardini 2004). Finally, Table 1.2 shows the interchangeability of liturgical material between the Finding and the Exaltation of the Cross in Roman manuscripts, with Vat5319 being the only one with both formularies.

That *Dulce lignum* was a Romano-Frankish import in an otherwise mostly Roman formulary is proved by a simple and, indeed, unique circumstance. The melodic profile of *Dulce lignum* in Bod 74 is Gregorian, not Roman, since it corresponds to all other European versions of this piece. The melodic incipit provided for the other chants—the introit *Nos autem*, the gradual *Christus factus*, the alleluia *Dominus regnavit*, the offertory *Deus enim firmavit*, and the communion *Spiritus ubi vult*—on the other hand, all coincide with the Roman rendition of the same melodies copied in previous sections of the manuscripts. This circumstance points to a Roman origin for the core formulary for the Holy Cross. After all, the feast of the Exaltation was already known in Rome before the exportation of Roman chant to Francia since "the prayers and readings of the Roman mass-sets for the Exaltation of the Cross belong to the feast's oldest layer in the West" (van Tongeren 2000, 81).

The majority of tenth- to twelfth-century European manuscripts follow the model of Roman manuscripts in that they show an interchange between textual and melodic materials for the two feasts. The formulary for the Exaltation is often transcribed in an abridged form with rubrics referring to the chants for the Finding, since it comes later in the liturgical year, and therefore is copied in a subsequent section of mass books. Besides these repertorial and thematic links, the two feasts have different liturgical histories, are connected to separate cultic traditions, and pertain to distinct spheres of meaning related to the Cross. Both feasts, besides their seventh- and eighth-century institution in the Roman and Frankish calendars, bear more remote Palestinian origins (van Tongeren 2000, 4). The Exaltation commemorates the victory of the Byzantine emperor Heraclius and overthrow of Persian reign in 628. This victory allowed the return to Jerusalem of the relics of the True Cross, which had been previously removed by the Persians. In the spring of 629 the Cross was borne to Jerusalem in triumph by Heraclius himself.

The feast of the Finding derives from a duplex Palestinian tradition later imported by Constantinople, the dedication of the Constantinian basilicas on the Sacred Sepulcher and the Calvary and the remembrance of the finding of the Cross by St. Helena, mother of the emperor Constantine, commonly dated to the year 325. This latter episode (which gives the name to the feast of May 3) prompted the development of a rich literary tradition that was equally cultivated in both the Eastern and Western Christian world. This hagiographic tradition about the Cross also affects some of the Aquitanian Proper texts analyzed below.

The outburst of historical narratives in both Greek and Latin about the legendary events connected with the Holy Cross—the dream of Constantine, St. Helena's recovery, and Heraclius's return of the Holy Wood in Jerusalem—is not surprising, given the centrality of the Cross in Christian spirituality. The wealth of production of hagiographical accounts and theological discourses on the Holy Cross are generally referred to in specialized literature as staurology, from the Greek *stauros* (σταυρός), "cross." Notwithstanding the flourishing of staurological writings since the fourth century, liturgical formularies for the two feasts were created at a much later age (not earlier than the seventh century), were scant in newly composed chants (as we have seen in Roman manuscripts), and poor in staurological contents.

Among Sextuplex manuscripts (Hesbert), which include manuscripts belonging to the earliest Gregorian generation, only the Compendienses (from Compiègne, ninth century) has the Finding of the Cross, while the Corbienses (from Corbie, ninth-tenth century) and the Silvanectensis (from Senlis, ninth century) the Exaltation. All their formularies are aligned with the core Roman repertory with the addition of the alleluias *Dominus regnavit a ligno* in the Compendiensis and *Redemptionem* in the Corbienses (cf. Cutter 1979; Hesbert 1935; and Table 1.3). While the first of these alleluias has a specific staurological focus, "The Lord ruled from the wood (of the Cross)," the alleluia *Redemptionem* is another example of chant borrowed from a pre-existing feast. *Redemptionem* in fact comes from the periods after Easter and Pentecost.

Manuscripts belonging to about one generation later than the Sextuplex sources enrich this basic formulary with a few items. These new items were not borrowed from other masses, but were newly composed for the Holy Cross. For this reason they characterize the formulary with themes and imagery more explicitly referring to the Cross, the events of the crucifixion, and the passion of Christ. The most frequent Frankish additions usually include the offertory *Protege domine*, the alleluia *Dulce lignum*, and the communion *Per signum crucis* (Table 1.3). Content of these pieces will be discussed below together with the other pieces of the Aquitanian tradition.

To synthesize, we can say that in the majority of early Gregorian manuscripts the formularies for the Holy Cross include the basic Roman set of chants (in the Frankish adaptation)—all of which borrowed from other Christological feasts—and a handful of chants that were composed in Francia possibly soon after the arrival of Roman chant in the eighth century. These Romano-Frankish additions are more noticeably focused on the crucifixion, the theology of the Cross, and the role of Christ in the divine design of the human salvation.

It is in eleventh-century Aquitanian manuscripts, however, that we find a much richer repertory of chants with a stronger staurological emphasis. These chants reflect the Gallican tradition of liturgical prayers for the Holy Cross. Pa776, a gradual from Gaillac, and Pa903, a gradual copied at St Yriex of Limoges, have formularies displaying

Table 1.3 Formularies for the Holy Cross in Sextuplex sources and Cambrai 75 (76)

Inventio (May 3rd) M 97 bis—Compendiensis	Exaltatio (September 14th)—Corbiensis
In Nobis autem glori[ari] oporte Ps Deus miseratur nostri Gr Christus factus est/Propter quod et Deus Al Dominus regnavit a ligno Of Dextera Domini V Inpulsus Co Nos autem gloriari … Iesu Christi Ps Deus miseratur nostri	In Nos autem gloriari Ps Dominus regnavit Gr Christus factus est pro nobis Al Redemptionem Of Deus enim firmavit Co Nos autem gloriari … Ihesu Christi. Ps Annunciate inter gentes

Of *Deus enim firmavit* belongs to the second Sunday after Christmas, Al *Redemptiones* to the Tuesday in Easter Week, and Of *Dextera Domini* to the Easter mass.

Cambrai 75 (76).

Inventio (May 3rd)	Exaltatio (September 14th)
In Nos autem* (nn) Al Sancti tui domine Al Dulce lignum Of Protege domine V. Salus omnium Co O crux splendidior	In Nos autem* (nn) Gr Christus factus est* (nn) Al Dicite in gentibus Of Protege domine* (nn) Co Crux benedicta Co Per lignum crucis

an unprecedented richness and originality. Both of them have one formulary for the Finding, while Pa776 has two different formularies for the Exaltation. For the most part these formularies have multiple alleluias and double offertories occasionally embellished with prosulas. Tropes and proses will not be considered here, while prosulas will be only incidentally mentioned (Appendix 1).

The masses combine some of the standard Gregorian chants we have already encountered in Roman and early Gregorian manuscripts, with some newly composed pieces. These newly composed pieces are compatible with the overall structure of Gregorian chant, but were likely composed locally after the standardization of the practices of chant. As is the case with similar repertories developed in various regions of medieval Europe after the diffusion of Gregorian chant (Planchart 1993; Nardini 2006), neo-Gregorian chants often conceal elements of older pre-Gregorian traditions. In the case of the Proper chants for the Holy Cross in Aquitanian manuscripts, it is the thematic analysis of Proper texts that leads toward the recognition of archaic Gallican elements. Table 1.4 lists the incipits of chants for the masses of the Holy Cross in Pa776 and Pa903, and Appendix 1 provides textual transcriptions.

All newly composed Proper chants copied in Pa776 and Pa903 are embroidered with theological concepts and literary metaphors that are derived from the liturgical prayers

Table 1.4 List of Proper chants in the Aquitanian graduals Pa 903 and Pa 776

Pa776

Inventio (May 3rd)	Exaltatio (September 14th)
In Nos autem gloriari*	In Christus pro nobis*
Al Dicite in gentibus	Gr Michi autem/Per quem michi mundus
Ps Laudetur omnis tibi	Al Benedictus sit Ihesus Christus
Ps O quam lignum pretiosum	Of Deus enim firma*
Pr Dicite cori cuncti	Of Dextera domini*
Al Benedictus sit Ihesus	Co Tuam crucem adoramus
Al Salua nos Christe	Alio
Al Tuam crucem adoramus	In Dum esset gens congregata Ps Aspice in orientem
Al Dulce lignum	
Pr Hic vir dux polorum	Gr Pro pio filio*
Of Veniens uir splendidissimus	Al Adoramus te Christe
V. Cumque in sopore	Al Nos autem gloriari
Pr Protege dominarot	Al O crux benedicta
Of Protege domine	Al Tuam crucem*
V. In conspectu tuo	Pr Et lignum crucis
V. Salvator mundi	Al O crux veneranda
Co Tuam crucem adoramus	Of Salva presentem catervam
Co Per signum crucis	V. Salus omnium populorum
Co Crux Ihesu Christi	Co Nobis autem gloriari
	Co Redemptor mundi
	Co Per lignum salui facti sumus

Pa 903

Inventio (May 3rd)	Exaltatio (September 14th)
In *Dum esset gens congregata Ps Aspice in oriente*	
Al Dicite in gentibus	
Al Salua nos christe salvator	
Al Tuam crucem adoramus	
Al Dulce lignum dulces clavos	
Al Per signum sancte crucis	
Of Veniens vir splendidissimus	
V Cumque in sopore somni	
Of Protege domine plebem tuam	
V In conspectu tuo domine	
V Salvator mundi salua nos omnes	
Co Per lignum serui facti sumus	

copied in Gallican sacramentaries for the Finding of the Cross. Although the theological kernel of the Cross is common to all Christian traditions, there are some clusters of meanings that are more geographically characterized, so that we can speak of Roman, Hispanic, or Gallican staurological traditions.

centralto all these [Roman, Hispanic, and Gallican] traditions is the commemoration of the Cross, and the celebration of the feast of the Cross in the perspective of salvation. This central theme is developed and concretized in various motifs ... through the incarnation, which issued into the crucifixion, Jesus emptied and humbled himself, and is elevated by God. In this way, through his precious blood (that is to say, his death on the Cross) the redemption of the world was brought about .... The Cross marks this salvation and refers to both this salutary deliverance and to Christ (van Tongeren 2000, 260; 253–274).

Besides this common thematic focus, Roman and Gallican prayers are differently characterized in contents and literary styles. Gallican texts "are full of metaphor, effusive, lyric in tone and content and narrative in nature: they develop themes and motifs elaborately, richly engaging in associations from Scripture while doing so" (van Tongeren 2000, 260; 253–274). Also, while Roman prayers identify God, the Father, as the principal responsible for the human salvation and Christ as the mediator, Gallican prayers are generally addressed to Christ who is defined as lord, king, redeemer, and savior. This way Christ doesn't assume a simple intermediary role, but is the primary entity in the plan of redemption of the human kind. This Christological emphasis in Gallican texts derived from the urgency to defeat heretical beliefs that denied the divine nature of Christ. The Cross is instrumental in both the Roman and Gallican traditions, but Gallican texts are more lyrical and make an extensive use of metaphors when referring to it.

There are seven main theological motifs associated with the cross in liturgical prayers (van Tongeren 2000). These are: (a) redemption, (b) recirculation, (c) content of salvation, (d) Cross and Eucharist, (e) historical references, (f) the present and eschatology, (g) the Cross characterized. The ways in which these categories are developed, though, reveal a different attitude of Roman and Gallican liturgical composers and illuminates the devotional influences exerted on Aquitanian mass Propers. The categorization proposed by van Tongeren is useful to sort through the different concepts unfolded by the Aquitanian Proper texts and therefore will be used here as a guideline for textual analysis. Pieces are referred to through their order of appearance in Appendix 1. Preexisting chants borrowed from other feasts of the liturgical year are not examined.

Redemption. Redemption is the underlying theme of the entire formularies; however, it is explicitly mentioned in the alleluias *Adoramus te Christe* (6), *Benedictus sit Ihesus* (7), and *Per signum sancte crucis* (12) and in the communion *Redemptor mundi* (24). Jesus is defined as the deviser of the divine design of human salvation and the Cross as his instrument. Christ is adored and blessed in nos. 6 and 7 ("we adore you, Christe, we bless you who redeemed the world through the Cross"; "Blessed be Jesus Christ, our Lord redeemer, and blessed be the wood for which there will be justice"). More concise is no. 12 with: "Through the sign of the Cross make us free, o God, you who redeemed us." No. 24 also mentions the sign of the Cross and the episode of Jesus saving Peter from drowning: "Redeemer of the world, through the sign of the Cross, save us against all adversity, you who saved Peter in the sea, have mercy on us." In no. 24 the underlying reference to Christ's role in the redemption is further defined as a defense against adversity ("ad omni adversitate custodi").

This last example is particularly relevant in a discussion of Gallican influences on Aquitanian mass Propers, since its content and vocabulary strongly resembles a prece of Gallican origins, "Miserere, miserere, miserere illi Deus" (Pa776, 138; see Huglo 1955 [*preces* and *antifone*], Huglo et al. 2013; Brockett (2000), "Have mercy . . . on him, God, o Christ redeemer, let he come (to you); holder and redeemer of the world, Jesus Christ, author of things"). There is also an interesting musical connection between the two pieces, since the communion, a unicum in Aquitanian manuscripts, appears to be mimicking the melodic conduct of the Gallican prece. The scalar motion alternating between descending and ascending movements and concluding on the lowest notes of the melodic range characterize both the prece and the communion. A major difference is a more neumatic, and occasionally melismatic, style (especially on the conclusive *Miserere nobis*, but also on *mundi* and *crucis*) for the communion. Other Gallican-derived elements of this and other melodies will be discussed below.

Recirculation. This theme is about the relation—according to medieval theologians—between the wood of the Tree of Good and Evil in Paradise and the wood of the Cross. While Adam and Eve closed the doors of Heaven to humankind by eating from the Tree of Paradise, the wood of the Cross reignites the hopes of salvation. Recirculation is only marginally present in Roman prayers but is recurrent in Gallican prayers. In the communion *Per lignum* (22) this concept is expressed in a very concise but effective manner, where an obvious reference to redemption is also included: "We were made slaves through the wood and were made free through your Holy Cross; the fruit of the tree seduced us, the Son of God redeemed us." The version in Pa776 that substitutes "servi" with "salvi" (saved) appears to be corrupted. In the communion *Crux Ihesu Christi* (20) the reference to recirculation is more hermetic: "The cross of Jesus Christ opened the door of heaven for us, the cross annulled the constraints of death . . . ."

Content of salvation. This is arguably the most pervasive theme in the Aquitanian masses for the Holy Cross. It is by and large related to the "accessibility of paradise," "the protective function of the Cross," and "the struggle against the enemies." Salvation, "the attainability of Paradise," is "restored by God" in Roman prayers and by Jesus in Gallican ones (cf. van Tongeren 2000, 108–110, 147–148). In the alleluia *O crux benedicta* (11)—a prayer addressed directly to the Cross ("O blessed Cross")—Jesus is defined as the "savior of the world" and the "king of angels." The alleluia *Salva nos Christe* (13) but even more so the offertories *Protege domine* (17) and *Salva presentem catervam* (18) are all centered on salvation. No. 13 also reiterates the episode of Peter saved from the waters ("Save us Christ, savior, through the virtue of the Cross, you who saved Peter in the sea, have mercy on us") and insists for three times—a possible Trinitarian allusion—on morphological variants of "save": "salva," "salvator," and "salvasti." The same text is also found in an antiphon for the adoration of the Holy Cross at Good Friday, "Salva nos Christe, salvator, per virtutem crucis qui salvasti Petrum in mare Miserere nobis" also copied in Pa776, 65v.

But it is with the offertories that we find a stronger emphasis on salvation. No. 17 has two verses centered on it: *In conspectu tuo*, "At your conspectus, o Lord, shall our prayers be acceptable through the sign and virtue of the holy Cross for which we are saved and freed, alleluia"; and *Salvator mundi*, "Savior of the world, save us all and drive all the dangerous things afar from us, and extend the right of your majesty to protect us." Besides the common Gallican-derived notion of Jesus as the savior, *In conspectu tuo* concludes with a string of words—per quem salvati et liberati sumus alleluia—that coincides with another chant of Gallican origins, *Nos autem gloriari . . . alleluia alleluia* a chant that assumes different liturgical functions (antiphon, offertory, and communion) in manuscripts of the Gregorian traditions (Nardini 2007). And it is in the form of an antiphon that is incorporated in the Roman manuscripts Bod74 and Vat5319 as mentioned above (Table 1.2).

No. 16 and its verse *Salus omnium polorum* are also imbedded with salvific themes that echo the main contents just analyzed. As a matter of fact, some Aquitanian and Italian manuscripts have these texts as additional verses for *Protege domine* (see Hankeln, vol. 3, 143–154). In addition to the usual characterizations for Christ and the Cross we have already seen, *Salus omnium polorum* adds a sense of rejoicing "the peoples of believers rejoice and applaud with their hands," possibly in reference to inner meaning of the feast—the Exaltation—that is the joyful celebration of the Cross, the happiness of men in the perspective of the salvation.

Cross and Eucharist. As with Frankish prayers, Aquitanian Proper chants do not make a direct link between the Cross and Eucharist, a theme that is instead present in the Roman euchology. Brief Eucharistic accents appear in nos. 17, 25, and 26 (*Tuam crucem*), since they refer to the sacrifice of mass and the passion of Christ: "would our sacrifice be acceptable to you, alleluia" in no. 17 and "we recall your glorious passion, have mercy on us" in nos. 25 and 26. Nos. 25 and 26 have very similar texts, but different melodies. No. 25 is also copied in Pa903 as a communion for Maundy Thursday.

Historical references. Historical references are quite rare in the Roman euchology and are generally limited to the definition of the historicity of the event of the Crucifixion or to Scriptural quotes, while they are more extensive in Gallican manuscripts. During Gallican services excerpts from the legend of the Finding were included in readings, prayers, and chants. Most of these historical references are about Heraclius's recovery and Helena's finding of the Cross. While such texts are completely absent from Roman and Frankish mass Propers, they are reintroduced in the Aquitanian masses where there are at least two historicizing texts: the introit *Dum esset* (1) and the offertory *Veniens vir* (19) mention the episode of the so-called dream of Constantine. The antiphon of the introit says: "While the people were gathering on the Danube, behold, a splendid man has appeared in the night to the king Constantine saying: alleluia"; and the verse, "Cast your eyes to the east and see a sign for which you will obtain virtue." This is a citation of the legend of Judas Cyriacus's *Inventio crucis*, a text that was in circulation in the West from the sixth century (Borgehammar 1991, 202). The legend narrates "the motif of the River Danube, where Constantine contended with the 'barbarians'" (Baert 2004, 86). In staurological texts the episode of the dream of Constantine on the Danube is interpreted as the anticipation of three other crucial events for the history of Christianity: the conversion of Constantine, the official recognition of the Christian religion, and

Constantine's request to his mother, St. Helena, to depart for Jerusalem to find the wood of the Cross.

No. 19 presents an even more extensive narrative:

> At night a very radiant man came to the king Constantine, woke him saying: look up in the sky and see a sign of the Lord's Cross for which you will gain virtue and strength; after having seen the sign, the king made a replica of the Cross that he had seen in the sky and glorified God, alleluia.

The verse simply reiterates the concept: "While the king Constantine was sound asleep, behold, a man appeared to him through a vision and said: look up in the sky."

References to the legend of the Cross in Gallican prayers should be interpreted with respect to the adoration of relics during the celebrations for the Cross. It appears likely that these two historicizing texts meant to emphasize the physicality of the Cross. The Cross—dreamt by Constantine, found by Helena, and recovered by Heraclius—is the objectified instrument of the human salvation. The reference to Constantine's victory can be explained not simply as a prelude to the victory of Christianity over paganism, but foremost, as the heavenly victory of God over evil. "Salvation as a military victory" is another typical element of Gallican prayers (van Tongeren 2000, 260).

The present and eschatology. Nos. 17 and 18 also bring the actuality of the religious service within the context of Proper texts. In the verse *In conspectu tuo* there is an explicit reference to the prayers offered to God, while no. 18 opens with the words "save the present crowd, which is congregated for your praise."

The Cross characterized. In Gallican texts the Cross is defined as a foundation of faith and an aid to prosperity and against adversity. The cross is defined as a weapon, but also as protection. It is a trophy and the holder of the ransom, Christ. These elements also recur in Aquitanian Proper chants, some of which are structured as prayers directly addressed to the Cross in the second person. In these chants, therefore, the Cross is personified as an active agent of salvation. In the alleluia *Dulce lignum* (9), the Cross is defined as "sweet" and the only one to be worthy to bear Christ, the Lord and king of Heaven, while in no. 11 the cross is "blessed" and the instrument of Christ's triumph. This alleluia also cites excerpts from the *Pange lingua* ("dulce lignum dulce clavo dulce pondus sustines ... sola digna tu fuisti ferre pretium saeculi"). The *Pange lingua* and the other two hymns by Venantius Fortunatus on the Cross became well known toward the end of the sixth century. They therefore predate the institution of the feasts in Rome and Gaul and may have influenced "the selection and composition of textual materials for the formularies of the feast" (van Tongeren 2000, 236).

In conclusion, this textual analysis shows that there are many links, in imagery and vocabulary, between the Aquitanian Proper texts and the Gallican prayers for the Holy Cross. Not all the chants included in the Aquitanian formularies were locally composed, but it is worth noticing that the combination of original and imported pieces stressed religious themes and mimicked phraseology and vocabulary of the Gallican devotional and liturgical Gallican traditions.

The analysis of these masses in Pa776 and Pa903 also reinforces the notion that liturgical materials for the Finding and the Exaltation were interchangeable. Although the two feasts had different histories and only the Finding predates the arrival of Roman chant in Francia, the circumstance that Pa776 has two distinct formularies for the Exaltation with chants that are mostly shared with the feast of the Finding in Pa903 demonstrates that Aquitanian liturgists, when in the process of providing texts and music for the Exaltation, re-employed chants for the Finding that would also reflect the main contents of Gallican staurological thought.

The explicit Christological emphasis in Gallican texts resulted from the need to convey fundamental dogmas to defeat heresies—especially Arianism and adoptionism—that disputed the divine nature of Jesus. In particular, adoptionism, according to which Jesus was God's adoptive son, started to spread throughout Western Europe before the sixth century and encountered a revival in Spain and Gaul during the eighth century (van Tongeren 2000, 264–265). It is not surprising, therefore, that Gallican liturgical compositions for the Holy Cross posed the accent on the divinity of Christ to rebut adoptionism and reinforce the orthodoxy of faith.

Aquitanian Proper texts for the Holy Cross, however, were probably composed not earlier than the eleventh century. Explaining why they are so heavily embedded with Gallican-derived themes may have multiple explanations. One of the factors could have been an archaizing aim to restore aspects of the Gallican compositions that were compatible with the religious sensibility of the Aquitanian people. It is likely that when composing these mass Propers, Aquitanian clerics found immediate inspirations from the collection of prayers of the Gallican traditions and decided to imitate their theological discourse, poetic imagery, and phraseology. This archaizing attitude also characterizes other neo-Gregorian repertories from other regions of medieval Europe, as we have seen.

In the case of southern Italy the archaizing attitude of neo-Gregorian chants also informs the musical style. This is an aspect that is more difficult to ascertain for Aquitanian chants because of the lack of Gallican notated chant books that could be used for comparison. However, there are some neumatic and melodic patterns that may be recognized as Gallican, as, for instance, the "exhuberant melismas ... on the penultimate or antepenultimate syllable," "sequential patterns for a descent" of the type (c-b-a b-a G a-G), and the *pes stratus*, a special neume that "occurs only in chants composed in Gaul (whether Gallican or Romano-Frankish)" (C-D-D, D-E-E, F-G-G-, etc.). These are some of the specifically musical characteristics that scholars have identified as typical of Gallican chant (Huglo et al., 2013) and that also recur in the Aquitanian chants for the Holy Cross. Besides a more generally ornate and melismatic style in all the chants (including communions and introits) a melisma on the penultimate syllable is found in the verse *Salvator mundi* of the offertory *Protege domine* (17), and in the communion *Per signum crucis* (23) (marked with no. 1 in Examples 1.1, and 1.2.). Sequential descending patterns (marked with no. 2 in the examples) appear in many melismatic passages as, for instance, in the alleluia *Per signum sancte crucis* (12, Example 1.3), where the pattern a-G-E F-F-E-D is employed three times in the alleluia. In the verse of the same

EXAMPLE 1.1. Excerpts from the offertories *Protege domine*, Pa903, 77v-78 and *Veniens vir*, Pa903, 77v.

EXAMPLE 1.2. Communion, *Per signum crucis*, Pa776, 82.

EXAMPLE 1.3. Alleluia, *Per signum sancte crucis*, Pa903, 77v.

piece we find others on the syllable *cru*-cis (b-a-G a-G-E F-E-D) and on -*de*-us (G-F-E F-E-D). Others occur in the verse *Salvator mundi* of the offertory *Protege domine* (17) on nocenti-*a* and on prote-*gen*-dum (both with the sequence F-F-E-D E-D-C). The pes stratus (marked with no. 3 in the examples) occurs three times in the alleluia *Per signum sancte crucis*, twice on *ce*-lum in the offertory *Veniens vir* (19) (G-a-a G-a-a), and once on *sa*-crificium in the offertory *Protege domine*, and on *cunc*-ta and *ma*-iestatis of the verse *Salvator mundi*, among others.

Of course, these examples are not sufficient to claim that the chants for the Holy Cross found in Aquitanian manuscripts are of Gallican origins. Indeed they belong to the Romano-Frankish repertory. Although composed or acquired in Aquitaine after the diffusion of Gregorian chant according to the general structure of the Gregorian compositions, they do retain archaic traits belonging to the musical language of Gallican chant. Here, rather than speaking of chants of Gallican origins, we should speak of Romano-Frankish chants incorporating Gallican elements of melodic style as part of the archaizing attitude of these masses.

Archaism, however, may not be the only explanation for the use of these specific textual and musical features. The centrality of Christ and the Cross in the liturgical narrative of these masses can also be viewed in the context of renewed devotion to the figure of Christ and his earthly life during the eleventh century. In particular, the Crucifixion and the passion of Christ were the subject of a renovated exegesis of the scriptures and the writings of the church fathers, which is at the basis of a significant part of the literary and artistic production of the time. "It was in fact, around the turn of the millennium that crucifixion imagery . . . became widespread in the Latin West" (Landes 1995, 301). This restored interest in the figure of Christ was reflected in the development of new pictorial cycles in western churches in which the crucifixion occupied a larger space than any other episode of sacred history (Tronzo 1985) and in the renewed relevance of the cult of relics of the Cross. We know that the relics of the Cross in Aquitaine, for instance, increased significantly in number between the end of the tenth and the beginning of the eleventh centuries (Frolow 1961, 44–45, 133–143).

Even the mention of Constantine the Great in the introit *Dum esset* and the offertory *Veniens vir* may have been a very special way to convey elements of the contemporary Aquitanian society that was characterized by a cultural identification with imperial Rome (Remensnyder, 9 and 108–109). Constantine the Great, the emperor who reunited the eastern and western sides of the Roman empire and who was deemed to be the originator of the rediscovery of the Holy Cross, could have well been considered as the most suitable historical figure to be mentioned within the mass formularies of the Finding and Exaltation of the Cross. As for the music, it is likely that the persistence of Gallican-derived musical features in pieces that otherwise perfectly fit the structure of the Gregorian (or Romanized) mass demonstrates the flexibility of the liturgical repertories of medieval Europe. Religious communities of medieval Europe were continuously negotiating between fidelity to the centralized power of the church and the empire and the preservation of localisms and archaisms in rituals and ceremonies.

We have seen that Carolingian interventions in matters of liturgical practices were intended to pursue concord, not identity, of liturgical practices. This entailed the maintenance of forms of localisms in an otherwise standardized ritual use. As mentioned above, the *Admonitio generalis* stresses the importance of adopting Roman chant and, in doing so, mentions Pippin's involvement in the pursuing of this goal. The historical narratives by Notker Balbulus and Paul the Deacon, though, tell us that the transmission of chant from Rome to Gaul was not a straightforward process. Aside from the sometimes harsh comments about the difficulty to accomplish this goal, these texts do not provide us with sufficient elements to reconstruct precisely the process of transmission, and possibly manipulation, of Roman chant in Francia. Scholars have proposed different views reaching at times radically opposite theses, such as, for instance Gregorian chant being the closest possible rendition of alternatively Roman or Gallican archetypes (McKinnon 2000; Levy, 2000–2001; 2003). Given the impossibility of reconstructing the Roman and Gallican ancestors of Gregorian chant, this problem will probably have to remain unsolved. What is certain, though, is that the study of peripheral chant traditions may lead toward a recognition of additional examples of Gallican, or in general, pre-Gregorian influences in extant European chant manuscripts.

APPENDIX 1

Introits

1. Dum esset gens congregata super danubium ecce vir in nocte splendidus apparuit Constantino regi dicens alleluia

V. Aspice in oriente et vide signum per quod accipiens virtutem

Finding: Pa903, 87
Exaltation: Pa776, 114 (2nd formulary)

2. Christus pro nobis

Exaltation: Pa776, 114 (1st formulary)

3. Nos autem

Finding: Pa776, 81

Graduals

4. Michi autem absit gloriari nisi in cruce domini nostri ihesu Christi
V. Per quem michi mundus crucifixus est et ego mundo

Exaltation: Pa776, 114 (1st formulary)

5. Proprio filio*

Exaltation: Pa776, 114 (2nd formulary) – borrowed from the second formulary of Maundy Tursday in Pa776, 60

Alleluias

6. Adoramus te Christe benedicimus tibi quia per crucem tuam redemisti mundum

Exaltation: Pa 776, 114 (2nd formulary)

7. Benedictus sit Ihesus Christus redemptor noster dominus et benedictum sit lignum per quod sid [!] iusticia

Finding: Pa776, 81
Exaltation: Pa776, 114 (1st formulary)

8. Dicite in gentibus quia dominus regnavit a lingo

Finding: Pa776, 81; Pa903, 87

   Pr Laudetur omnis tibi caterva cunctipotens qui condidisti caelorum astra et regnas per secula

Finding: Pa776, 81; Pa903, 87

   Pr O quam lignum pretiosum ubi salvator mortis cruore crucem pro nobis pependit
Finding: Pa776, 81
   Pr Dicite cori cuncti et psallite in gentibus quia magna domini clementia suis respiciens ovibus regnant omnia sacra et imperavit a ligno proprio filio suo crucifixo qui surrexit et sedet in trono dei conculcato tabulo
Finding: Pa776, 81; Pa903, 87

9. Dulce lignum dulces clavos dulcia ferens pondera quae sola fuisti digna sustinere regem celorum et dominum

Finding: Pa776, 81v, Pa903, 87v
   Pr Hic vir dux polorum viscera victor ascendit ex eculeo manu tenta tendes o membra
Finding: Pa776, 81v; Pa903, 87v

10. Nos autem gloriari oportet in cruce domini nostri ihesu Christi

Exaltation: Pa776, 114-114v

11. O crux benedicta quia in te pependit salvator mundi et in te triumphavit rex angelorum

Exaltation: Pa776, 114v

12. Per signum sancte crucis libera nos deus noster qui per crucem nos redemisti

Pa903, 87v

13. Salva nos Christe salvator per virtutem crucis qui salvasti petrum in mare Miserere nobis

Finding: Pa776, 81; Pa903, 87
Exaltation: Pa776, 114 (1st formulary)

14. Tuam crucem adoramus domine tuam gloriosam recolimus passionem

Finding: Pa776, 81v; Pa903, 87-87v

Exaltation: Pa776, 114v*

Pr. Et lignum crucis benedictum in quo deus pependit et ihesu nazarenus hoc signum apparebit cum dominus venerit iudicare seculum autem per ignem vitam vivamus cum deo semper recolimus

Exaltation: Pa776, 114v

Offertories

15. Deus enim firmavit*

Exaltation: Pa776, 114 (1st formulary)

16. Dextera domini*

Exaltation: Pa776, 114 (1st formulary)

17. Protege domine plebem tuam per signum sancto crucis ab ominibus insidiis inimicorum omnium ut tibi gratiam exubeamus servitutem et acceptabile tibi fiat sacrificium nostrum alleluia

Finding: Pa776, 82; Pa903, 88

V In conspectu tuo domine sint acceptabile preces nostra per signum et virtutem sancte crucis per quem salvati et liberati sumus alleluia

Finding: Pa776, 82; Pa903, 88

V Salvator mundi salva nos omnes et cuncta nocentia a nobis procul repelle atque ad protegendum nos dexteram tuae maiestatis extende

Finding: Pa776, 82; Pa903, 88

18. Salva presentem catervam tuis laudibus congregatum ut sancte crucis vexillum defensor liberis tibi famulemur obsequiis et acceptis votis muniamur auxiliis

Exaltation: Pa776, 114v

V. Salus omnium populorum per crucem Christi factus est letentur per gentes plaudent manibus credentes quia rex noster per crucem suam seculum triumphavit et infernum vicit

Exaltation: Pa776, 114v

19. Veniens vir splendidissimus ad Constantinum regem nocte suscitavit eum dicens aspice in caelum et vide signum crucis domini per quod accipies virtutem et fortitudinem viso autem signo rex fecit similitudinem crucis quam viderat in celum et glorificavit Deum alleluia

Finding: Pa776, 81v; Pa903, 87v

V. Cumque in sopore sommasset Constantinus rex ecce vir per visionem apparuit ei dicens. Aspiciens in ce.

Finding: Pa776, 81v; Pa903, 87v

Prosa Protege dominator domine tuis que famulis et cunctum plebem tuam per virtutem domini signum sanctissimum lignum vite salvatorem crucis ab omini malo libera nos ab hominibus insidiis impiis iniquitatis malorum dolor omnium cunctis delens haec nos tibi gratuita exibetimus sanctum + servitutem qui nos per crucem redemit felicem prius secundum promissionem verbum et accepta tibi sit et amabile tibi fiat sanctum et immaculatum sacrificium nostrum alle proclamet pater lu filius ia spiritus sanctus

Finding: Pa776, 81v-82; Pa903, 87v-88

Communions

20. Crux Ihesu Christi adaperuit nobis ianuam caeli crux solvit vinculo mortis per hoc signum ligni vite sit salutis nostre defende nos Ihesu Christe hic et in futurum

Finding: Pa776, 82

21. Nobis autem gloriari oportet in cruce domini nostri Ihesu Christi

Exaltation: Pa776, 114v-115

22. Per lignum servi (salvi) facti sumus et per sanctam crucem tuam liberati sumus fructus arboris seduxit nos filius dei redemit nos alleluia

Exaltation: Pa776, 115; Pa903, 88

23. Per signum crucis de inimicis nostri libera nos Deus noster

Finding: Pa776, 82; Pa903, 88

24. Redemptor mundi signo crucis ab omni nos adversitate custodi qui salvasti petrum in mare miserere nobis

Exaltation: Pa776, 115

25. Tuam crucem adoramus domine tuam gloriosam recolimus passionem, miserere nostri qui passus est pro nobis alleluia
V. Adoramus Christe redemisti mundum

Finding: Pa776, 82

26. Tuam crucem adoramus domine tuamque gloriosam recolimus passionem, miserere nobis qui passus es pro nobis

Exaltation: Pa776, 114

APPENDIX 2

List of cited manuscripts

Ben35   Benevento, Biblioteca Capitolare, 35. Gradual with tropes and proses, Benevento, saec. XII*in*.

Bod74   Cologny-Genève, Bibliotheca Bodmeriana, Bodmer 74. Gradual with Roman chant, Rome, Santa Cecilia in Transtevere, 1071. Facsimile edition in *Das Graduale von Santa Cecilia in Trastevere (Cod. Bodmer 74)*, ed. by M. Lütolf, Fondation Martin Bodmer, Cologny-Genève 1987.

Cai75   Bibliothèque Municipale, ms 75 (76). Troper, Kyriale, gradual. Arras, St. Vaast, middle 11th cent.

F22   Vatican City, Biblioteca Apostolica Vaticana, Archivio di San Pietro F 22. Gradual with Roman chant. Rome, San Peter's, early 13th cent.

MC318   Montecassino, Archivio dell'Abbazia, 318. Theo-retical writings, region of Benevento, saec. XI.

Pa776   Paris, Bibliothèque Nationale de France, lat. 776. Gradual with tropes, proses, and processional, Gaillac, beginning of 11th cent. Facsimile edition: *Gaillac: Il cod. Paris Bibliothèque Nationale de France lat. 776 sec. XI Graduale*, eds. Nino Albarosa, Heinrich Rumphorst, Alberto Turco (Padova: La Linea Editrice, 2001).

Pa903   Paris, Bibliothèque Nationale de France, lat. 903. Gradual, tropes and proser, Saint Yriex, before 1031. Facsimile edition: *Le Codex 903 de la Bibliothèque Nationale de Paris. Graduel de Saint Yrieix*, Paleographie Musicale, vol. 13/2 (Tournai: Lang, 1930).

Vat5319   Roma, Biblioteca Apostolica Vaticana, Vat. lat. 5319. Gradual with Roman chant-Kyrial-Proser, Rome, San Giovanni in Laterano, late 11th–beginning of 12th cent. Transcription published in *Monumenta Monodica Medii Aevi*, vol. 2, ed. Bruno Stäblein and Margareta Landwehr-Melnicki (Kassel: Bärenreiter, 1970).

Note

1. And I would add also "of acquisition," where this term refers to imports from Roman practice.

References

Editions of Sources of the Gallican Liturgy (for more complete references see Huglo et al. 2013)

Bannister, Henry Marriott, ed. 1917–1919. *Missale Gothicum: A Gallican Sacramentary*. London: Henry Bradshaw Society.

Loew. E. A., ed. 1917–1924. *The Bobbio Missal: A Gallican Mass-Book (MS. Paris, Lat. 13246)*. London: Henry Bradshaw Society.

Mabillion, J., ed. 1685. *De liturgica gallicana libri tres*. Paris. (Reprinted in *Patrologiae cursus completus. Series Latina*. Vol. 72. Paris: Migne, 1844–1891).

Mabillon, J 1687. *Museum italicum seu collectio veterum scriptorum ex bibliothecis italicis*. Paris: J. Boudot, & S. Martin.

Mannister, H. M., ed. 1917–1919. *Missale Gothicum: A Gallican Sacramentary, ms. Vatican. Regin. Lat. 317*. London: Henry Bradwhaw Society.

Missale Francorum. In *Patrologia Latina*, 52, 317ff.

Mohlberg, Leo Cunibert, ed. 1961. *Missale Gothicum*. Rerum ecclesisticarum documenta, ser. maior, *Fontes*, 5. Rome: Herder.

Mohlberg, L. C., L. Eizenhöfer, and P. Siffrin, eds. 1958. *Missale Gallicanum vetus*. Rerum ecclesiasticarum documenta, ser. maior, *Fontes*, 3. Rome: Herder.

Mohlberg, L. C., L. Eizenhöfer, and P. Siffrin, eds. 1957. *Missale Francorum*. Rerum ecclesiasticarum documenta, ser. maior, Fontes, 2. Rome: Herder.

Mone, Franz Joseph, ed. 1850. *Lateinische und griechische Messen aus dem zweiten bis sechsten Jahrhundert*. Frankfurt: Carl Bernhard Lizius.

Ratcliff, E. C. 1971. *Expositio antiquae liturgiae gallicanae*. London: Henry Bradshaw Society.

Rose, Els, ed. 2005. *Missale Gothicum: e codice Vaticano Reginensi Latino 317 editum*. Corpus Christianorum. Series Latina, 159D. Turnhout, Belgium: Brepols.

Sancti Germani, parisiensis episcopi, expositio brevis antiquary liturgiar gallicanae. Ex ms. Codice sancti Martini Augustodunensis a D. Martene exscripta Thes. anecdot. t. V. In *Patrologiae cursus completus. Series Latina*. Vol. 72, cols. 55–78. (An English translation appears in: James McKinnon, ed. 1998. *The Early Christian Period and the Latin Middle Ages*, 54–61. Source Readings in Music History 2. 2d ed. New York: Norton.)

Editions of Texts and Documents of Non-Gallican Liturgies

Cutter, Paul F. 1979. *Musical Sources of the Old-Roman Mass*. Musicological Studies & Documents 36. Neuhausen, Switzerland, and Stuttgart: American Institute of Musicology-Hänssler-Verlag.

Hesbert, René-Jean, ed. 1935. *Antiphonale missarum sextuplex*. Brussels: Vromant. (Reprint, Rome: Herder, 1967.)

Secondary Sources

Baert, Barbara. 2004. *A Heritage of Holy Wood: The Legend of the True Cross in Texts and Image*. Translated by Lee Preedy. Cultures, Beliefs, and Traditions: Medieval and Early Modern People 22. Leiden: Brill.

Baumstark, Anton. 1958. *Comparative Liturgy*. London: A. R. Mowbray, 1958.

Borgehammar, Stephan. 1991. *How the Holy Cross Was Found: From the Event to Medieval Legend with an Appendix of Texts*. Stockholm: Almqvist & Wiksell.

Brockett, Clyde. 2000. "The Easter Processional Antiphon Series at Ravenna." In *Srednjovjekovne glazbene kulture Jadrana. Mediaeval Music Cultures on the Eastern and Western Shores of the Adriatic until the beginning of the 15th Century: Proceedings of the International Musicological Symposium, Split, 1997*, edited by Stanislav Tuksar, 241–257. Zagreb: Croatian Musicological Society.

Brockett, Clyde. 2006. *Letania and Preces: Music for Lenten and Rogation Litanies*. Ottawa: The Institute of Mediaeval Studies.

Brown, Giles. 1994. "Introduction: The Carolingian Renaissance." In *Carolingian Culture: Emulation and Innovation*. Edited by Rosamond McKitterick, 1–51. Cambridge: Cambridge University Press.

Cahn, Peter, and Ann-Katrin Heimer. 1993. *De musica et cantu: Studien zur Geschicthe der Kirkenmusik und der Oper. Helmuth Hucke zum 60. Geburstag*. Hildesheim: Olms.

Capelle, Bernard. 1925. "Deux psautiers gaulois dans le Cod. Aug. CCLIII." *Revue bénédictine* 37: 215–223.

De Clerck, Paul. 1977. *La prière universelle dans les liturgies latines anciennes*. Münster, Germany: Aschendorff.

Cullin, Olivier. 1982. "Une pièce gallicane conservé par la liturgie de Gaillac." *Liturgie et musique (IXe—XIVe s.). Cahiers de Fanjeaux* 17: 287–297.

Deshusses, Jean. 1963. "Le bénédictionnaire gallican du VIIIe siècle." *Ephemerides liturgicae* 77: 169–187.

Duchesne, Louis. (1889) 1920. *Origines du culte chrétien: Étude sur la liturige latine avan Charlemagne*. Paris: De Boccard.

Ecclesiastical History Society. 1996. *Unity and Diversity in the Church: Papers Read at the 1994 Summer Meeting and the 1995 Winter Meeting of the Ecclesiastical History Society*. Studies in Church History 32. Oxford: Ecclesiastical History Society.

Frolow, A. 1961. *Le relique de la Vrai Croix: Recherches sur le développement d'un culte*. Paris: Institute français d'études byzantines.

Ganshof, François Louis. 1968. *Frankish Institutions under Charlemagne*. Translated by Bryce Lyon and Mary Lyon. Providence, R.I.: Brown University Press.

Gastoué, Amedeé. 1937–1939. "Le chant gallican." *Revue du chant grégorien* 41–43.

Griffe, Élie. 1951. "Aux origines de la liturgie gallicane." *Bulletin de litérature ecclésiastique* 52: 17.

Hankeln, Roman. 1999. *Die Offertoriumsprosuln der aquitanischen Handschriften: Vorunte rsuchungen zur Edition des aquitanischen Offertoriumscorpus und seiner Erweiterungen*. Regensburger Studies zur Musikgeschichte 2. Tutzing, Germany: Schneider.

Hen, Yitzhak. 1996. "Unity in Diversity: The Liturgy of Frankish Gaul before the Carolingians." In *Unity and Diversity in the Church: Papers Read at the 1994 Summer Meeting and the 1995 Winter Meeting of the Ecclesiastical History Society*. Studies in Church History Edited by R. N. Swanson, 32. 19–30. Oxford: Ecclesiastical History Society.

Hen, Yitzhak. 2001. *The Royal Patronage of Liturgy in Frankish Gaul: To the Death of Charles the Bald (877)*. London: Henry Bradshaw Society.

Hen, Yitzhak, and Rob Meens, eds. 2004. *The Bobbio Missal: Liturgy and Religious Culture in Merovingian Gaul*. Cambridge: Cambridge University Press.

Hesbert, René-Jean. 1963. "Un antique offertoire de la Pentecôte: 'Factus est repente.'" In *Organicae voces: Festschrift Joseph Smits van Waesberge*. Amsterdam: I.M.M.

Hornby, Emma. 2004. "The Transmission of Western Chant in the 8th and 9th Centuries: Evaluating Kenneth Levy's Reading of the Evidence." *Journal of Musicology* 21 (2004): 418–457. (Reprinted in *Oral and Written Transmission in Chant*, ed. Thomas F. Kelly, 319–358. Burlington, VT: Ashgate, 2009.)

Huglo, Michel. 1955a. "Antifone antiche per la fractio panis." *Ambrosius* 31: 85.

Huglo, Michel. 1955b. "Les preces hispaniques des graduels aquitains empruntées à la liturgie hispanique." *Hispania sacra* 8: 361–383.

Huglo, Michel. 1966. "Les chants de la *missa greca* de Saint-Denis." In *Essays Presented to Egon Wellesz*, edited by Jack Westrup, 74–83. Oxford: Clarendon Press.

Huglo, Michel. 1972. "Altgallikanische Liturgie." In *Geschichte der katholischen Kirckenmusik*, edited by K.G. Fellerer. Kassel: Bärenreiter.

Huglo, Michel. 1982. "La tradition musical aquitaine: Répertoire et notation." In *Liturgie et musique (IXe—XIVe s.), Cahiers de Fanjoux* 17: 253–268.

Huglo, Michel, Jane Bellingham, and Marcel Zijlstra. 2013. "Gallican Chant." In *Grove Music Online*. Oxford Music Online. Accessed January 2008. http://www.oxfordmusiconline.com/subscriber/article/grove/music/10559.

Jungmann, Joseph A. 1986. *Missarum sollemnia: Eine genetische Erklärung der römischen Messe*. Translated by Francis A. Brunner. Westminster, Md: Christian Classic. (Original edition: Vienna: Herder, 1928.)

King, P.D., ed. 1987. *Charlemagne: Translated Sources*. Lambrigg, Australia: King, 1987.

Kartsovnik, Vietscheslav. 1998. *Proper Tropes in the Old Roman Gradual of Santa Cecilia in Trastevere (A.D. 1071)*. In *Chant and Its Peripheries: Essays in Honor of Terence Bailey*, edited by Bryan Gillingham and Paul Merkley, 62–109. Ottawa: Institute of Medieval Music.

Kelly, Thomas F. 1994. "A Beneventan Borrowing in the Saint Cecilia Gradual." In *Max Lütolf zum 60. Geburstag: Festschrift*, edited by B. Hangartener and Urs Fischer, 11–20. Basel: Wiese Verlag, 1994.

Landes, Richard. 1995. *Relics, Apocalypse, and the Deceits of History: Ademar de Chabannes, 989–1034*. Cambridge, Mass.: Harvard University Press.

Leclercq, Henri. 1924. "Gallicane (liturgie)." In *Dictionnaire d'archéologie chrétienne et de liturgie*, edited by Fernand Cabrol and Henri Leclercq. Vol. 6/1, 473–596. Paris: Letouzey et Ané.

Levy, Kenneth. 1958–1963. "The Byzantine Sanctus and its Modal Tradition in East and West." *Annales Musicologiques* 6: 7–67.

Levy, Kenneth. 1971. "Lux de luce. The Origin of an Italian Sequence." *The Musical Quarterly* 57: 40–61.

Levy, Kenneth. 1984. "Toledo, Rome and the Legacy of Gaul." *Early Music History* 4: 49–99.

Levy, Kenneth. 2000–2001. "A New Look at Old Roman Chant I and II." *Early Music History* 19–20: 81–104, 173–198.

Levy, Kenneth. 2003. "Gregorian Chant and the Romans." *Journal of the American Musicological Society* 56: 5–41.

Mabillon, Jean, ed. 1685. *De Liturgia Gallicana Libri III*. Paris: Luteciae Parisiorum–Edmunti Martin et Johannem Boudot.

Manz, George. 1941. *Ausdruckformen der lateinischen Liturgiesprache*. Beuron, Germany: Beuroner Kunstverlag.

McKinnon, James. 2000. *The Advent Project: The Later Seventh-Century Creation of the Roman Mass Proper*. Berkeley: University of California Press.

McKitterick, Rosamond. 1996. "Unity and Diversity in the Carolingian Church." In *Unity and Diversity in the Church: Papers Read at the 1994 Summer Meeting and the 1995 Winter Meeting of the Ecclesiastical History Society*, edited by R. N. Swanson, 59–82. Studies in Church History 32. Oxford: Ecclesiastical History Society.

Nardini, Luisa. 2001. "Il repertori neo-gregoriano del Proprium Missae in area beneventana." Ph.D. diss., Università degli Studi di Roma.

Nardini, Luisa. 2004. "Montecassino, Archivio della Badia, ms 318: Observations on the Second Tonary Mass Repertory." In "… *Et facciam dolçi canti*": *Studi in onore di Agostino Ziino in occasione del suo 65 compleanno*, edited by Bianca Maria Antolini, Teresa Maria Gialdroni, and Annunziato Pugliese, 47–61. Lucca, Italy: LIM.

Nardini, Luisa. 2006. "Non-Standard Introits in Beneventan Manuscripts: Compositional Strategies and Transmission in the Sources." In *Cantus Planus: Papers Read at the 12th Meeting of the IMS Study Group, Lillafüred/Hungary, Aug. 2004*, 345–369. Budapest: Institute for Musicology of the Hungarian Academy of Sciences.

Nardini, Luisa. 2007. "Aliens in Disguise: Byzantine and Gallican Chants in the Latin Liturgy." *Plainsong and Medieval Music* 16: 145–172.

Nardini, Luisa. 2015. "The Masses for the Holy Cross in Some Italian Manuscripts." in Qui musicam in se habet. Studies in Honor of Alejandro Enrique Planchart, edited by Anna Zayaruznaya, Bonnie J. Blackburn, and Stanley Boorman, 41–69. Middleton, WI: American Institute of Musicology.

Planchart, Alejandro E. 1993. "Old Wine in New Bottles." In *De musica et cantu*, edited by Peter Cahn and Ann-Katrin Heimer, 41–64. Hildesheim: G. Olms.

Planchart, Alejandro E.. 2001. "Proses in the Sources of Roman Chant, and Their Alleluias." In *The Study of Medieval Chant: Paths and Bridges, East and West*, edited by Peter Jeffery, 313–339. Cambridge: Boydell.

Porter, Willian Stevens. 1958. *The Gallican Rite*. Studies in Eucharistic Faith and Practice 4. London: Mowbray.

Quasten, Johannes. 1943. "Oriental Influence in the Gallican Liturgy." *Traditio* 1: 55.

Remensnyder, Amy G. 1995. *Remembering Kings Past: Monastic Foundation Legends in Medieval Southern France*. Ithaca, N.Y.: Cornell University Press.

Righetti, Mario. 1950. *Manuale di storia liturgica*. 5 vols. Milan: Àncora.

Ropa, Giampaolo. 1993. "La tradizione marciana e le consuetudini liturgiche dell'area emiliano-romagnola (Ravenna, Bologna e Nonantola)." In *Da Bisanzio a San Marco: Musica e Liturgia*, edited by Giulio Cattin, 239–269. Quaderni di Musica e Storia (presented at the La musica nella storia della civiltà bisantina, Venezia, Fondazione Levi, 6-8 msggio 1993). Venice: Fondazione Ugo e Olga Levy.

Schäfer, Thomas. 1956. *Die Fusswaschung im monastischen Brauchtum und in der lateinischen Liturgie*. Beuron, Germany: Beuroner Kunstverlag.

Schlager, Karl-Heinz. 1965. *Thematischer Katalog der ältesten Alleluia-Melodien aus Handschriften des 10. und 11. Jahrhunderts, ausgenommen das ambrosianische, alt-römische und alt-spanische Repertoire*. Erlanger Arbeiten zur Musikwissenschaft 2. Munich: W. Ricke.

Stäblein, Bruno. 1955. "Gallicanische Liturgie." In *Die Musik in Geschichte und Gegenwart*, vol. 4, cols. 1299–1325. Kassel, Germany: Bärenreiter-Verlag.

Steiner, Ruth. 1993. "Holocausta medullata: An Offertory for St Saturninus." In *De Musica et Cantu*, edited by Peter Cahn and Ann-Katrin Heimer, 263–274. Hildesheim: G. Olms.

Tronzo, William. 1985. "The Prestige of Saint Peter's: Observations on the Function of Monumental Narrative Cycles in Italy." In *Pictorial Narrative in Antiquity and the Middle Ages*, edited by H.L. Kessler and Shreve Simpson, 93–112. Studies in the History of the Art 16.

Vogel, Cyrille. 1960. "Les échanges liturgiques entre Rome et les pays francs jusqu'à l'époque de Charlemagne." In *Le chiese nei regni dell'Europa occidentale* 7, 185–295, 236. Spoleto, Italy: Centro di Studi sull'Alto Medioevo.

Van Tongeren, Louis. 2000. *Exaltation of the Cross: Toward the Origins of the Feast of the Cross and the Meaning of the Cross in Early Medieval Latin*. Leuven, Belgium: Peeters.

CHAPTER 2

THE ENGLISH KYRIE

ALEJANDRO ENRIQUE PLANCHART

The Kyrie eleison as a choral refrain to a series of petitions (a litany) can be traced to fourth-century Jerusalem, according to the testimony of Egeria, who visited the Holy Land between 381 and 384 (Egeria 1999, 124). The Kyrie had reached Rome in the fifth century, and from the letter Gregory the Great (d. 604) wrote to Bishop John of Syracuse, we can gather that it was still essentially a litany at this time. Gregory took care to deny that he was introducing Greek practices into Rome, and in this connection he mentioned that in Rome, unlike in the East, *Kyrie eleison* is sung as often as *Christe eleison* and that on nonfestal days the Greek text was sung without the longer verses that were sung on other occasions (*in quotidianis autem missis aliqua quae dici solent tacemus*). In Gregory's time the Kyrie was still sung by the clergy with the congregation responding (*a clericis dicitur et a populo respondetur*) (Gregory 1862, 956–957). The connection between the Eastern Kyrie litany and the Kyrie of the mass, however, is not straightforward, and it now appears more likely that the Kyrie of the mass was introduced in the West independently of the litanies (De Clerck 1977, 282–295). By the early eighth century, the Kyrie's position after the introit of the mass was fixed; the Kyrie was no longer sung by the people but by the *schola cantorum*; and it consisted of any number of repetitions of the invocation "Kyrie eleison," until the pope signaled a change to "Christe eleison" (Andrieu 1974, 2:84: "*schola vero, finita antiphona, inponit Kyrie eleison*"). By the late eighth century the Kyrie was restricted to nine invocations—three *Kyrie eleison*, three *Christe eleison*, three *Kyrie eleison*—sung antiphonally between the *schola cantorum* and the *regionarii* (subdeacons) (Andrieu 1974, 1:159). There is no reference in either of these *ordines* to any other text, so it is possible that in the eighth century, as the Kyrie was incorporated into the mass, its text was reduced to the nine short Greek acclamations, each possibly sung twice (once by the *schola* and once by the *regionarii*).

Nonetheless, when the Kyrie eleison emerges in the earliest manuscripts with music for the ordinary of the mass in the early tenth century, the manuscripts show a number of versions. Some of the versions look at first sight like the older litany, but these probably derive from developments that took place in the course of the ninth century and had already crystallized not only as different approaches to the performance of the Kyrie

EXAMPLE 2.1 Kyrie XVI of the Vatican editions (Graduale Romanum, Liber Usualis), Melnicki 1954, no. 217. Melnicki reports sources from all over Europe going from the tenth to the eighteenth century, but did not inventory the tenth-century manuscripts with non-diastematic notation. Transcription is from F-Pn *lat.* MS 887, fol. 59v (Limoges, ca. 1030), one of the earliest transcribable copies of the Kyrie. The different sources transmit a considerable number of small variants (cf. Bjork 2003, 359–362).

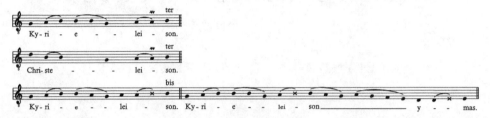

eleison but also into what might be called regional variants (Bjork 2003, 4–7). For some of these regions we have sources from the tenth century, while for others (for example, southern Italy) the earliest surviving sources are from the eleventh century. The early sources already show some international as well as regional melodies and approaches. By the early eleventh century, there are, roughly, five "manners" of singing the Kyrie eleison. These are as follows:

1. Nine Greek invocations, usually sung to a relatively simple melody: aaa, bbb, ccc' or aaa, bbb, aaa'.

This manner is found throughout Europe beginning in the early tenth century. Some very simple Kyries found in the earliest sources with neumes, which do not survive in transcribable form, follow this pattern and appear to be even less ornamented.[1]

2. The first invocation in Greek, and then each of the following invocations preceded by a Latin text with a melody different from that of the Greek invocation. The Latin texts are what modern scholarship calls Kyrie tropes, but only when their melody is different from that of the Greek invocation (Bjork 1980, 2–3).

This manner is found almost exclusively in East Francia, although some of these Kyries were also sung in Italy, where they arrived most likely with the East Frankish repertory, including the Notkerian proses. The piece in Example 2.2 is the only one of these Kyries that was used west of the Rhine, albeit with a different Kyrie melody (Bjork 2003, 12).

3. Each Greek invocation is preceded by a Latin verse with the same melody as the Greek invocation. The melodic pattern can be as simple as aaa, bbb, ccc' or as elaborate as aba, cdc, efe', with the alternation between Greek and Latin in the last pair being broken up phrase by phrase. Scholars from the late nineteenth century to the third quarter of the twentieth century referred to these Latin verses as tropes, but they are not tropes. Rather, they are Latin invocations set to the Kyrie melody,

EXAMPLE 2.2 This transcription is a reconstruction of the version in CH-SGs 484, 209–211, with the help of F-Pn *lat.* 1118, fol. 19v for the trope verses and F-Pn *nouv. acqu. lat.* 1235, fol. 214v, and D-Bs Mus. ms. 40078 (Z. 78), fol. 247r, for the Kyrie. Melnicki 1954, no. 144.

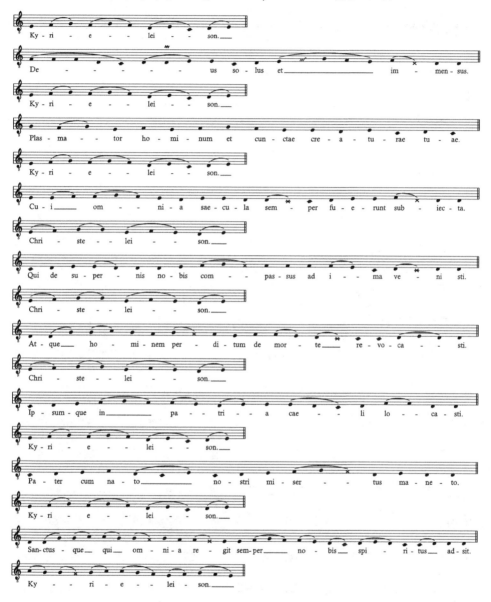

and many of them were composed simultaneously with the melody. They are best called Latin Kyries (Bjork 2003, 171).

This manner of singing the Kyrie was the most widespread one in the lands west of the Rhine. Some of these Kyrie melodies were known east of the Rhine and were sung occasionally in this manner in the tenth century and with increased frequency after the

EXAMPLE 2.3 This is Kyrie XIV of the Vatican editions, Melnicki 1954, no. 64; Source, GB-Ob Rawl. Lit. D 3, fol. 49r.

(a)

eleventh, but in some instances they were sung with separate Latin verses in the second manner listed above.[2]

4. The Greek invocations were sung by themselves, but each set of invocations was introduced by a Latin verse with a separate melody, that is a trope, sometimes with an introductory verse for the entire piece as well.

EXAMPLE 2.3 Continued

EXAMPLE 2.4 Kyrie Vatican *ad lib.* VI, Melnicki 1954, no. 55, from F-Pn *lat.* 903, fols. 166v–167r, the initial E of many of the Greek invocations is uniquely found in this MS.

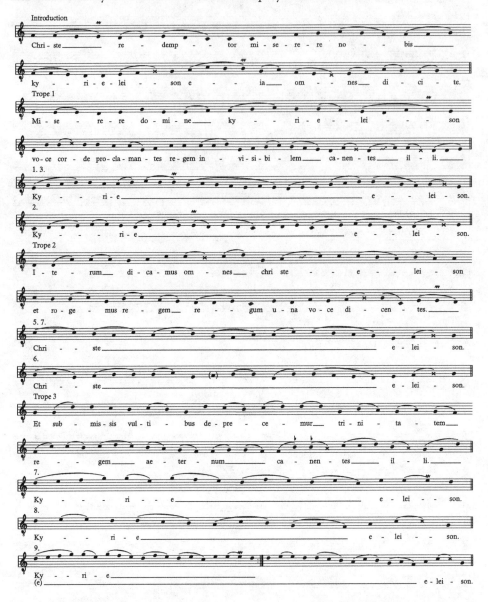

This practice is related to that in Example 2.2. It was also connected, in France and parts of Italy, with Kyries sung in the manner of Example 2.3, so that the introductory verses led not just to sets of Greek invocations but rather to Latin-Greek Kyries with each melodic strain of the Kyrie itself sung twice. This is the way in which the Kyrie in Example 2.4 appears in F-Pn lat. 11118, fol. 12r (Bjork 2003, 261–264). The repertory of these introductions is the smallest and most unstable of the medieval Kyrie repertories. Instances vary from a single introduction to two, three, or four, in different

EXAMPLE 2.5 Melnicki 1954, no. 52, transcribed from I-Bc 40, fols. 21r-v. See also Boe, 28–39.

Ky - ri - e - - - - - - - - lei - - - son.
Auc - - tor___ cae - lo - - rum___ de - us e - ter - ne.
Ky - ri - e - - - - - - - - lei - - - son.
Qui___ po - - lum for - - mas - - ti___ nec - ne so - lum.
Ky - ri - e - - - - - - - - lei - - - son.
Ab___ om - - ni ma - - lo___ tu___ nos___ de - fen - de.
Chris - - te - - - - - - lei - - - son.
Chris - te___ de cae - - lis___ suc - - cur - re___ no - bis.
Chris - - te - - - - - - lei - - - son.
Per___ cru - - cem qui___ cun - - cta___ ad te___ tra - sis - ti.
Chris - - te - - - - - - lei - - - son.
In - - fer - - ni mors___ e - - xis - - tens___ et___ mor - su.
Ky - ri - e - - - - - - - - lei - - - son.
Spi - - ri - - tus cor - - di - - um___ il - lus - tra - tor.
Ky - ri - e - - - - - - - - lei - - - son.
Pu - - ri - - fi - ca___ sanc - te___ cor - da___ nos - tra.
Ky - ri - e - - - - - - - - lei - - - son.
Qui___ tri - - nus reg - - nas___ de - - us___ et___ u - nus.
A - - - - - men.___

combinations and placed at different points in the sequence of the Kyrie invocations. Virtually all instances are unique, so it is hard to determine what a "normal practice" was anywhere. Judging from the very small number of surviving sources, this might have been the predominant manner of ornamenting the Kyrie in pre-conquest England, but it disappears in all post-conquest sources. This might not be just a case of the Norman invaders bringing their own liturgical traditions with them (though they did that), but of the fact that by the early twelfth century this manner of singing the Kyrie was dying all over Europe.

5. Greek and Latin invocations sung in alternation as in the third manner listed above, but in this case the Latin invocation follows the Greek invocation. Thus, textually this manner of singing the Kyrie resembles that of the second manner listed above. The difference, however, is that all nine Latin invocations are sung to the same melody, without any change, and all Greek invocations are sung either to that same melody or a very close variant of it. The entire Kyrie ends with an "amen" or an "alleluia" set to part of the music for the invocations.

This manner was restricted to Italy, largely south of Rome. The earliest southern examples are from the middle of the eleventh century, but we have no earlier sources from the region. Concordances of a few pieces from northern Italy, however, demonstrate that this repertory went back to the tenth century (this Kyrie appears also in I-Vc CVII [100], fols. 32v-33r, copied ca. 1000). It survived in southern Italy, mixed with Kyries imported from both east and west Francia until the thirteenth century.

Two of these manners of singing the Kyrie—those involving actual tropes (Examples 2.2 and 2.4 above)—fell into disuse in the course of the twelfth century. Kyries such as those in Example 2.5 were used largely in southern Italy, while in the north they were adapted to the Frankish manner presented in Example 2.3—that is, with the Latin text preceding the Greek invocation. Thus, north of the Alps, only the Kyries such as those given in Examples 2.1 and 2.3 continued to be sung into the thirteenth century. The same Kyrie melodies, including a relatively large repertory of new melodies and Latin texts composed in the eleventh century and early twelfth century, continued to be sung, either as Greek invocations or with the Latin texts depending on the solemnity of a given feast and the local traditions. If the surviving chant books are a guide, when the Kyries were sung with the Latin texts in the course of the thirteenth century, they were no longer sung in alternation with the Greek invocations.[3]

This was essentially the situation that obtained in continental Europe during the thirteenth century. In the course of the thirteenth and fourteenth centuries, the singing of the Latin verses was gradually abandoned throughout most of the Continent. The abandonment of the Latin verses has never been studied systematically and can only be deduced by comparison of the hundreds of missals and graduals of the thirteenth, fourteenth, and fifteenth centuries that have survived. This is an immense task that has never been attempted, although a foundation for it exists in the critical notes to the edition of the Latin Kyries in *AH* 47. A number of Latin Kyries continued to be copied into the fifteenth century, although there is little evidence that they were sung, since their melodies also appeared just as often with just the Greek invocations. Moreover, there are instances of Kyries with newly composed Latin texts in fourteenth- and fifteenth-century missals (in these cases usually without music, so we cannot tell if the Kyrie melody was newly composed or an old melody was provided with a new Latin text) (*AH* 47, 140–145 and 166–167). A few of the old Latin Kyries (for example, *Clemens rector aeterne*) continued to be copied and possibly sung with their Latin text, but often what we encounter in many sources are vestigial copies of the Latin verses, where only verses 1, 4, and 7 are entered below the music. When the ordinary of the mass began to be set in polyphony in the fourteenth century, a number of such late Latin Kyrie texts were used in a few of the settings. Of the twenty-two surviving polyphonic Kyries of the fourteenth century (these include those edited in Cattin, Stäblein-Harder, and the Kyrie of Machaut's *La messe de Nostre Dame*), eleven have no Latin texts. Of the other eleven, one has a fragment of one of the traditional Latin Kyries, seven other have newly composed metric poems modeled on the conductus and motet poetry of the time, and three have multiple texts in the manner of the contemporary motets. In other words, virtually all the Kyries with Latin texts in this repertory are *sui generis* works, either strophic conductus settings or motet-like works related not to the traditions of plainsong Latin Kyries but rather to the new polyphonic genres of the thirteenth and fourteenth centuries.

The situation in England, however, was quite different. After what David Hiley calls "the heroic age of Anglo-Saxon monasticism" (Hiley 1993, 581), in the seventh and eighth centuries, the time of the Venerable Bede, Benedict Biscop, Boniface, and Alcuin, the English church was virtually destroyed by the Scandinavian invasions of the ninth century. When England began to recover in the tenth century under King Ælfred and his successors, the religious, liturgical, and musical life of the island drew both inspiration and some of its key personnel from the monastic establishments of northeastern France and the Netherlands; the major English establishments were led by three great bishops, Dunstan, Oswald, and Æthelwold. All three were monks and converted the cathedrals over which they presided—Canterbury (Dunstan), Worcester and York (Oswald), and Winchester (Æthelwold)—into monastic cathedrals. In 972 Æthelwold and King Edgar called up a council to lay down guides for the conduct of the English church, which resulted in the *Regularis Concordia* (Symons 1953), with a description of many of the liturgical practices then in use. At the council, advice was sought from monks of St. Peters in Ghent and Saint-Benoit-sur-Loire at Fleury. Earlier in the century Æthelwold had brought monks from Corbie to Abingdon to provide instruction in writing and singing. Unfortunately, the written record of the Anglo Saxon liturgy of the tenth century is extremely fragmentary: there are about thirty books or fragments, a third of which come from Winchester (see Rankin 1987). The surviving Kyrie repertory of pre-conquest England consists of seventeen melodies: nine of them are international in the sense that one finds them in sources from all over Europe between the tenth and the thirteenth centuries; four were found elsewhere in north French (including Norman) and Rhenish sources; four survive only in the Anglo-Saxon manuscripts. There were four Kyrie tropes, one with an international concordance, one with a fairly extensive French concordance, and two found only in England. And there was one Latin Kyrie, a late addition to the pre-conquest repertory but one with a wide distribution in France and the Rhineland. This repertory, in comparison to the Kyrie repertory found in sources from France and the Rhineland in the tenth and eleventh centuries, is anomalous. It has Kyrie tropes of the West Frankish variety but no Latin Kyries except for the addition, in the eleventh century, of *Cunctipotens genitor deus* in one of the surviving manuscripts.

The fall of the Anglo-Saxon Kingdom to William the Conqueror in 1066 produced the first large wave of suppression in England itself. One consequence of the conquest is that virtually none of the English repertory of tropes and proses survives in post-conquest sources. (This loss, however, pales in comparison to the cultural genocide perpetrated on the Spanish nation and its liturgical tradition by the treachery and imperial hubris of Pope Gregory VII, one of the most unappealing figures of the medieval papacy, with his insistence that Spain abandon its traditional liturgy and chant entirely, essentially erasing several centuries of the cultural memory of a nation.) William did replace the entire English hierarchy, including archbishops, bishops, and abbots, with Normans (or, in the case of the first two post-conquest Archbishops of Canterbury, with Italian monks who had been important officers of Norman monasteries), and this change brought with it a revision of the order or service itself. The pieces of the mass and office that were established throughout Europe were of course not changed, but the change is quite noticeable (although not entirely clear-cut) where there was the possibility of choice: in the Alleluias of the Sundays after Pentecost, in the responsories for certain offices, and particularly in the Kyries and other pieces of the ordinary of the mass, as well as in the use of tropes and proses. When one compares the pre-conquest chant books with those from after the conquest and those from Normandy itself, it is clear that even though pieces were sung at different feasts, the versions of the Gregorian melodies sung after the conquest remain those that were sung before the conquest, and the variants found in Norman sources were largely not adopted. But the trope repertory, particularly the tropes for the proper of the mass, does not survive in the post-conquest sources. It might be that by this time this was a dying repertory all over Europe, but it is also true that among French sources proper tropes survive into the twelfth century in central and northeastern manuscripts, but disappear rather early among the Norman and northwestern manuscripts, suggesting that there might have been a Norman antagonism to tropes. Unfortunately, no English sources with transcribable notation existed by 1066, so an entire repertory of tropes—not only those for the local English saints but also adaptations of French and Rhenish pieces reworked in the highly ornamental language of the Anglo Latin poets of tenth century Winchester—are now beyond our reach as music. Among the proses for the local saints, those that were set to French or international melodies can be recovered by comparing their neumation with that of Continental versions that can be transcribed, but a number of proses of insular origin remain also irrecoverable as music. In the case of the Kyries, two of the tropes can be recovered by comparison with French and Rhenish sources, two others, however, are irrecoverable, and none survived in post-conquest manuscripts. The same applies to four of the Kyrie melodies, which were clearly insular in origin. The early Kyrie repertory of post-conquest England becomes almost entirely northern French in character, with a large number of the kinds of Latin Kyries that were sung in northern France at the end of the eleventh century. Many of them, of course, were set to the international melodies that had been sung before in England but only with the Greek invocations.

The liturgy of post-conquest England also took a slightly different direction than on the Continent, including Normandy. The great revival of the tenth century had been carried out primarily by monk-bishops who had turned out the clerks in their cathedral and established monks. The primatial see of England, Canterbury, was a monastic

Table 2.1 The Latin Kyries of the Sarum Use in Liturgical Order

1. Deus creator omnium	Mel 68 (Vat. XIV)
2. Cunctipotens genitor deus	Mel 18 (Vat. IV)
3. Kyrie omnipotens pater	Mel 67 (Vat. no)
4. Kyrie rex splendens	Mel 24 (Vat. VII)
5. Lux et origo lucis	Mel 39 (Vat. I)
6. Kyrie rex genitor	Mel 47 (Vat. VI)
7. Kyrie fons bonitatis	Mel 48 (Vat. II)
8. Orbis factor rex aeterne	Mel 16 (Vat XI)
9. Conditor Kyrie omnium	Mel 70 (Vat V)
10. Rex virginum amator	Mel 18 (Vat IV)

institution, as were Winchester and Worcester. Thus, their liturgical use could not well serve as a model for secular cathedrals or parish churches. Salisbury Cathedral, which was founded by St. Osmund in the late eleventh century and grew to prominence under Bishop Richard Poore (who changed the site of the cathedral in 1218), became essentially the model for the secular liturgy of England, particularly since the Chapel Royal appears to have adopted the Salisbury liturgy. From the thirteenth century onward, professional bookshops in Oxford, London, and Cambridge were able to produce numerous books of the Salisbury use on demand, which made it easier for all the churches on the island to use the Salisbury rite, known as the "use of Sarum," which became largely the English national rite of the later middle ages until the Reformation (Hiley 1993, 584).

The manuscripts (and eventually the printed books) of the use of Sarum established what became a relatively consistent series of Kyries for use in the major feasts of the year and usually presented them in an order of descending liturgical solemnity. With some small variations of order here and there in the sources, the order is as follows (Table 2.1).

These were followed by between ten and thirty other settings (sometimes of the same melodies as those of the Latin Kyries listed above) for less solemn feasts. The melodies, even without the Latin texts, were used as a form of liturgical reference indicating their appropriateness for a given feast. For example, a melody that in more solemn contexts had always a Marian Latin text, could be used without the Latin text for less solemn Marian feasts such as the octaves. The order of the Latin Kyries at the outset was always considered as a general guide to their solemnity, with those at the beginning of the list serving for the more solemn feasts. The placing of the Kyrie for the masses of the Virgin at the end of the list was a traditional feature of such ordered lists, even though the feasts of the Virgin were often among the most solemn (Wickham Legg 1916, 1–6).

The manner in which the Kyries were copied in England began as an analog of the manner in which they were copied across the Channel. In the twelfth- and early-thirteenth-century manuscripts, the Latin Kyries were copied with the melismatic setting of the Greek invocation following each Latin verse. In manuscripts of the later thirteenth century and the fourteenth century, the Latin Kyries were copied with only the Latin text and without the double versicle structure. Throughout the fourteenth and fifteenth centuries, England differed from the Continent by continuing to sing the Latin Kyries as a normal part of the celebration in most feasts above the *simplex* rank.

The English polyphonic repertory of the thirteenth and fourteenth centuries was also qualitatively different from the Continental repertory. There was very little secular polyphony in England, and the English motets of the thirteenth and fourteenth centuries are almost uniformly in Latin with liturgical and devotional texts. Although the English developed their own notational system, derived largely from the Franconian notation of the thirteenth century (as was the French *Ars nova* notation), English music shows an awareness of French polyphony and its notation throughout the fourteenth century, but the converse appears not to be the case. Continental music does not seem to have had much contact with English music at that time. Sometime around 1400, English composers came upon a novel manner of organizing the music for the ordinary of the mass. As on the Continent, English mass music consisted largely of isolated movements, Kyries, Glorias, Credos, and so on, written in different styles that ranged from simple simultaneous declamation of the text in the manner of a *conductus*—but often with the appropriate plainsong in the middle voice of the texture, what modern scholars call "discant style"—to elaborate motet-like compositions based not always on a preexisting cantus firmus but on a voice, the *pes*, that had a repeating melodic and rhythmic pattern and served as the base and guide for the contrapuntal combinations, and to canonic settings supported by one or more slow moving parts. Toward the end of the fourteenth century, English composers, like some of their Continental counterparts, began pairing movements together, primarily Glorias and Credos, and Sanctus and Agnus, by means of similar clefs, mensurations, order of textures (alternation of duos and trios or alternation of sections in different mensurations) and some motivic work. By around 1400, however, one or more English composers came upon a considerably more radical idea when writing mass movements based on the more elaborate motet technique, and it was to organize all five movements of the ordinary of the mass into a cycle where all the movements were motet-like settings based on the same tenor, almost always a preexisting chant that was, however, *not* a mass chant but an antiphon, a responsory, or another kind of chant often chosen, as in the case of motets, for the emblematic and symbolic meaning of the chant itself. This had two immediate consequences: first, it tied the newly composed mass to some liturgical or ceremonial occasion, a coronation, the feasts of the Virgin, the feast of a Saint; second, the repeated use of the same cantus firmus throughout each movement of the mass created a set of contrapuntal constraints and preconditions that in many cases eased (though not necessarily ensured) a *musical* rather than purely *liturgical* sense that the five movements belonged together as a work. It might not be a historical coincidence that such a procedure arose in England rather than on the Continent. This was usually accompanied by a similar structuring of the polyphonic texture of all the movements, with changes of mensuration duplicated from one movement to the next, and the distribution of passages in reduced scoring (usually duos) falling at corresponding places in each movement. All of these traits add up to a completely musical solution to something that would have been important primarily to musicians—the musical and formal structure of the cycle. On the Continent, virtually all singers and composers of sacred polyphony were at this time clerics, while in England they were largely choral vicars—that is, musically trained laymen contracted by the clerics of a given church to take their place in the choral services of that church.

This shift in the manner of organizing all five movements of the ordinary of the mass would prove eventually to be immensely influential, but when it was being accomplished in England in 1400–1410, there is little evidence that anyone across the Channel was paying attention. That was to change in a few years. In 1414 King Sigismund pressured Pope John XXIII into calling an ecumenical council to end the Great Schism of the West, which divided Western Christendom into obediences to three rival popes: Gregory XII, Benedict XIII, and John XXIII. The council met in Constance in southern Germany from 1414 to 1418, and was attended by several hundred cardinals, bishops, abbots, as well as representatives of the universities and the secular rulers. Many of the cardinals and bishops came with considerable retinues including their chapels and musicians. All in all, some eighteen thousand clerics descended upon the city, which at the time had about eight thousand inhabitants (Schuler 1966, 150). Among them came the retinues of the bishops of Lichfield and Norwich, who traveled through Germany. On September 8, 1414, they stopped in Cologne and celebrated the feast of the Nativity of the Virgin, and a local chronicler reported not having heard such splendid singing in thirty years (Schuler 1966, 158). Having arrived in Constance on November 16, the English singers and instrumentalists celebrated the feast of St. Thomas of Canterbury on December 29 with singing and instrumental playing that elicited the most extraordinary admiration from the listeners (Schuler 1966, 159). The memory of these performances and of the music itself clearly lingered on the Continent and was surely renewed by the presence of English musicians among the retinues of the English delegation to the Council of Constance in the 1430s as well. In the 1440s Martin le Franc, in a widely cited passage in his poem *Les champion des dames*, explains part of the new style cultivated by Gilles de Bins, called Binchois, and Guillaume Du Fay by commenting that "they took on the English countenance and followed [John] Dunstaple," (Le Franc (1999), 4:67–69; cf. Fallows 1987 and Strohm 2001). Iohannes Tinctoris, in the *Liber de arte contrapuncti*, written in the 1470s, again places the *fons et origo* of the new style of European music in the 1430s and with the English generation of John Dunstaple (Tinctoris 1975–1978, 2:12). And it is indeed Dunstaple and his slightly older contemporary Leonel Power who provide us with the earliest mass ordinary cycles built on a recurring *cantus firmus* in the tenor (Curtis and Whatey 1994, and 2. Musica Britannica 8).

Evidence of this interest in English music is also provided by the rather large quantity of English pieces that appear in Continental music manuscripts copied between 1420 and 1460. These include mass ordinary movements, either isolated or grouped into cycles, motets, hymns, and songs. In manuscripts from the early part of this period composer attributions are relatively frequent, but for some reason they drop off dramatically in manuscripts copied after about 1450. Given this circumstance, however, it is remarkable to find a considerable number of pieces in the earlier manuscripts identified not by a composer's name but by the remarks "Anglicanus, Anglicus, or De Anglia." This may not mean that the copyist of the manuscript did not know the name of the composer but rather that the nationality of the composer was more important than the name itself—that the work was valued for being English.

Continental copies of English music throughout this period are plagued by small inaccuracies, which Margaret Bent, with her characteristic acuity, has pinned on two factors working independently of each other. First, the exemplars were available to the Continental scribes for only a limited and possibly a short time at any given time (Bent 1979, 1–7.). Second, Continental scribes were at a disadvantage when transcribing some of the more complex English works. English music continued to use full-black notation well into the fifteenth century. This tradition gave the composers four colors to notate the rhythmic subtleties of their music: full black, full red, void black, and void red. Continental notation in the early part of the century, even when using full black notation was restricted to two colors: full black and full red or else full black and void black. After ca. 1430, when void black notation became the norm (with black full as the color notation) the Continental notation remained a two-color notation. Thus Continental scribes had to resort to a different mensuration sign or to a numerical proportion to render some of the rhythmic complications of English music into their notation, a process that they did not always control properly.

Nonetheless, a large repertory of English mass music was copied in northern Italy and southern Germany in these decades, and this is particularly fortunate because the English themselves discarded their own choirbooks with damnable efficiency when their contents became outmoded, no matter how splendidly copied the books had been, and a large number of these books were also destroyed during the upheavals that followed the English Reformation. As a result, the only music for the mass we have from the entire fifteenth century in England is one incomplete choirbook from about 1415–1421 (E-Lbl Add. 57950, Old Hall) and a much smaller, also incomplete choirbook from about 1459–1465 (E-Cmc Pepys 1236). Beyond these, only scattered fragments remain, the most substantial being a collection of twenty-two pages from a choirbook with music for the mass copied around 1490–1515 (E-Ybi Mus 1). The first of these choirbooks was largely devoted to music for the mass, and the movements were copied section by section. It is probably missing one or more gatherings at the beginning, so that it starts partway through one of the Gloria settings and all the Kyries are lost. The second is primarily a collection of motets that includes two Glorias; the only Kyrie in the manuscript is a setting of the litany Kyrie during Holy Week. The extended fragment has fourteen mass movements, among them four Kyries (all with only the Greek text), but only one "cycle" (Gloria, Credo, Sanctus) (Curtis and Whatey 1994).

Table 2.2 English Mass Cycles in Continental Sources (fragmentary movements are denoted by *)

	Mass	Attributions	Sources
01	[Ad fugam]	Standley	I-TRmp 88 (K, G, C, S, A), 314v–322v
02	[De Beata Virgine]	Tik	CZ-Ps D.G.IV 47 (S), 84v–85r I-Las 238 (K*, G*, C*, S*, A*), 1v–10v I-TRmp 89 (K, G, C, S, A), 366v–374r I-TRmp 90 (S), 348v–349r
03	[Sancta Maria Virgo]	Anonymous	I-Las 238 (G*, C*, S*), 37.1r–37.6v
04	Alma redemptoris mater	Power	I-AOs 15 (G, C, S, A), 219v–226r I-TRmp 87 (G, C, S, A), 3v–8v I-TRmp 90 (G), 112v–114r I-TRmd 93 (G), 142v–144r
05	Alma redemptoris mater 1	Anonymous	I-TRmp 87 (K, G), 146v–149v
06	Alma redemptoris mater 2	Anonymous	I-Las 238 (C*, S*, A*), 31r–35r
07	Caput	[Du Fay][1]	I-Las 238 (K*, G*, A*), 17v–20v I-TRmp 88 (K, A), 31v–35v I-TRmp 89 (K, G, C, S, A), 246v–256r I-Trmp 90 (G, C, S), 96v–98r, 168r–170v, 228v–230r I-Trmp 92 (G, C, S), 126v–128r, 236v–238r, 297v–299r
08	Da gaudiorum praemia	Dunstaple	D-LEu 1084 (G*), 230r I-AOs 15 (C, S), 226v–230r US-CA Houghton, Inc. 8948 (G*), flyleaf
09	Deuil angoisseux	Bedingham	I-Trmp 88 (G, C, S, A), 17v–21v, 27v–31v, 214r–216r I-Trmp 90 (G, C), 383v–389r
10	Flos regalis	Frye	I-Br 5557 (G, C, S, A), 30v–38r
11	Fuit homo missus	Anonymous	I-TRmp 88 (K, A), 35v–38v I-TRmp 90 (G, C, S), 103v–105r, 175v–177r, 239v–241r I-TRmd 93 (G, C, S), 133v–135r, 243v–245r, 308v–310r
12	Hilf und gib Rat	Anonymous	CZ-Ps D.G.IV 47 (G, C, S, A), 105v–112r CZ-Ps D.G.IV 57 (motet: O gloriosa mater), 112v–114r I-Trmp 89 (Motet: Salve regina), 354v–356r
13	Iacet granum	Anonymous	I-AOs 15 (G, S), 82v–84r, 214v–216r I-TRmp 87 (G, copied twice), 31v–33v, 141v–142v I-TRmp 90 (G, S), 123v–125r, 271r–272r I-TRmp 92 (S)18v–19 I-TRmd 93 (G, S twice), 153v–155r, 344r–345r, 359v–361r

(continued)

Table 2.2 Continued

	Mass	Attributions	Sources
14	*Meditatio cordis*	Anonymous	CZ-Ps D.G.IV 47 (G, C, S, A), 85v-92r I-TRmp 88 (motet: *Gaude Maria*), 284v-286r
15	*Nobilis et pulchra*	Frye	B-Br 5557 (K, G, C, S, A), 38v-48r
16	*Puisuqe m'amour*	Anonymous	I-TRmp 88 (G, C, S), 85v-93r
17	*Quem malignus spiritus*	Anonymous check TR 93	I-Las 238 (G*), 24 bis r-v I-TRmp 90 (G, C, S, A), 100v-103r, 172v-174r, 234v-239r I-TRmd 93 (G, C, S, A), 130v-133r, 240v-242r, 303v-308r
18	*Rex dabit mercedem*	Anonymous	I-VEbc 755 (G, C, S, A), 54v-63r
19	*Rex saeculorum*	Power Dunstaple	D-Mbs Lat.14274 (G), 121v0123r I-AOs 15 (G, C), 39v-40r, 72v-74r I-TRmp 90 (G, S), 110v-112r, 274v-275v I-TRmp 92 (G, C, S, A), 39r-40r, 46v-49r, 94v-95r I-TRmd 93 (G, S), 140v-142r, 347v-348v,
20	*Salve sancta parens*	Anonymous	I-TRmp 90 (G, C, S, A), 98v-100r, 170v-172r, 230v-234r I-TRmd 93 (G, C, S, A), 128v-130r, 238v-240r, 299v-303r
21	*Sine nomine*	Plummer	B-Br 5557 (K, G, C, S, A), 10v-20r
22	*Sine nomine*	Benet Dunstaple Power	F-CA 11 (G), 20v-22r I-AOs 15 (G, S, A), 194v-195r, 207r-210r I-Mb AD.XIV.49 (S, A*), 74v-80r I-TRmp 87 (C, S, A), 37v-39r, 103v-104v, 106v-107r I-TRmp 90 (G, C, S, A), 118v-120r, 193v-195r, 254v-257r I-TRmp 92 (S*), 98r I-TRmd 93 (G, C, S, A), 148v-150r, 263v-265r, 326v-329v
23	*Sine nomine*	Bedingham	I-TRmp 88 (K, G, C, S, A), 46v-54r I-Trmd 93 (G, C, S, A), 30v-36r
24	*Sine nomine*	Anonymous	I-Bsp frag. E (K*, G*, C*, S*, A*), 1v-10r
25	*Sine nomine*	Dunster (?)	I-TRmp 88 (K), 26v-27r
26	*Sine nomine*	Cox	I-Br 5557 (K, G, C, S, A), 20v-30r
27	*Sine nomine*	Anonymous	I-Br 5557 (K, G, C, S, A), 90v-99r
28	*Sine nomine*	Standley	CZ-Ps D.G.IV 47 (K, G, C, S, A), 53r-v, 164r-165r, 167v-171r

(*continued*)

Table 2.2 Continued

	Mass	Attributions	Sources
29	*Sine nomine*	Benet	I-Bc Q15 (S, A), 24v-26r I-TRmp 87 (G), 165v-167v
30	*Sine nomine*	Anonymous	I-Las 238 (C*, S*), 30 bis r-v I-Rvat CS 14 (K, G, C, S, A), 65v-75r
31	*Sine nomine*	Anonymous	I-Rvat SP B80 (K, G, C, S, A), 61v-70v I-Trmp 88 (K, G, C, S, A), 253v-260r I-TRmp 90 (G), 430v-432r I-VEbc 759 (K, G, C, S, A), 20v-25r
32	*Sine nomine*	Anonymous	I-TRmp 88 (A), 21v-22r I-TRmp 90 (G, C, S), 250v-254r, 318v-324r I-TRmp 93 (S), 322v-326r
33	*So ys emprentid*	Frye	I-Las 238 (K*), 21v
34	*Summae trinitati*	Frye	B-Br 5557 (G, C, S, A), 2v-10r I-TRmp 88 (motet: *Salve virgo*), 70v-71r
35	*Te gloriosus*	Anonymous	I-Las 238 (K*, G*), 25r-26v
36	*Thomas caesus*	Anonymous	I-Rvas SP B 80 (K, G, C, S, A), 166v-181r
37	*Veterem hominem*	Anonymous	CS-Ps D.G.IV 47 (G, C, S, A*), 140v-147r I-TRmp 88 (K, G, C, S, A), 1v-9r, 264v-266r

[1]Attributions in I-TRmp88 and in I-TRmp89, the one in I-TRmp89 erased.

It is possible to postulate three things from the surviving English fragments and the manner English masses are transmitted in continental sources. First, the early English cantus firmus masses were sometimes copied as complete cycles, but most likely the sources from the first half of the fifteenth century were, like the Old Hall manuscript, copied by groups of movements, that is, all the Kyries, then all the Glorias, and so on. Second, English composers, like their Continental counterparts, continued to write isolated mass movements or mass pairs for some time into the fifteenth century and these included isolated Kyrie for nonfestal occasions, which set only the Greek invocations. Third, some shorter mass cycles intended for feasts of lesser rank included Kyries that set only the Greek invocation, but the cycles based on cantus firmi (which were at this time almost uniformly composed either for special occasions or for the feasts of the highest rank) surely set, virtually without exception, the Latin-texted Kyries prescribed by the Sarum use in their fourteenth- and fifteenth-century version—that is, the Latin verses without the Greek invocations (unless the Greek text was part of the Latin verse as is the case in Kyries 3–4 and 6–7 above).

This view, of course, depends on much of what has been found about English masses in the last quarter of the twentieth century. For nearly five hundred years, the view, at least from the standpoint of Continental sources, was quite different. As noted above, English music was eagerly copied and imitated on the Continent between 1420 and 1470. In terms of the mass these copies go from isolated mass movements to complete or near complete masses, and the frequency with which isolated Glorias, Credos, Sanctus, or Agnus Dei that clearly belonged to complete cycles were copied suggests that, in some cases, the exemplars available to Continental scribes were choirbooks organized like Old Hall. But there were surely also what Charles Hamm has called "fascicle manuscripts," which sometimes transmitted a complete mass cycle rather than a group of Kyries, Glorias, or motets. The transmission of the English cantus firmus masses in Continental manuscripts is detailed in Table 2.2.

This list is a conservative one; it includes, with one exception to be discussed later, only those pieces for which a general scholarly consensus has evolved about their English provenance, either because parts of them survive in English manuscripts (since the English generally did not copy Continental works into their choirbooks) or because they present traits that are stylistic or notational mannerisms of English music in the fifteenth century that were rarely used by Continental composers (Hamm 1960, 211–215; 1968, 57–64). Three more expansive lists have been published by Charles Hamm (1968), Rob Wegman (1989), and Gareth Curtis and Andrew Whatey (1994). The first was drafted at a time when our knowledge of central European music was very limited and scholars were unaware of how enthusiastically German and Austrian composers, nowadays mostly anonymous, adopted certain aspects of the English approach to mass composition. The other two are deliberately over-inclusive, and justifiably so, on account of the purpose of each of these studies, particularly in the case of Curtis and Whatey, where they listed every work that any scholar had suggested could be English.

A glance at the fourth column of Table 2.2, which deliberately excludes any surviving English copies of these works, will show that Continental copies of these pieces are rarely complete. It is more than likely that, for the early part of the century, the English choirbooks were copied in the manner of the Old Hall Manuscript, that is, with all the Kyries, then all the Glorias, and so on. Still, the movement most frequently missing from Continental copies is the Kyrie. The copies of English masses in Table 2.2 fall into four categories:

1. Masses copied without the Kyrie: 18 (nos. 3, 4, 6, 8, 9, 10, 12, 13, 14, 16, 17, 18, 19, 20, 22, 29, 32, 34)
1a. Masses from group 1 where a "motet" appears to be a "re-texted" Latin Kyrie: 3 (nos. 12, 14, 34)
2. Masses with long Kyries where the Kyrie verses were eliminated on the Continent: 4 (nos. 11, 30, 31, 36)
3. Masses with short Kyries that fitted the Continental practice: 8 (nos. 1, 2, 23, 24, 25, 27, 28, 33)
4. Masses with long Latin Kyries that retained them in Continental copies: 7 (nos. 5, 7, 15, 21, 26, 35, 37)

Before we proceed, a word about what I called the exceptional entry in Table 2.2: it is the *Missa Hilf und gib rat*, preserved in CZ-Ps D.G.IV 47 (G, C, S, A, motet), with the motet preserved in I-TRmp 89. Every movement and the accompanying motet has a typically English bipartite structure with a section in o and a section in ¢(probably originally c), with long introductory duets. Further, the motet has one text in CZ-Ps D.G.IV 47, *O gloriosa mater Christi*, and two texts in I-TRmp 89, *Salve regina misericordiae* in Wiser's hand, and *Gaude rosa speciosa*, added in a large and coarse later hand, which suggest that all texts are probably contrafacts. What has given pause to a number of scholars is that the cantus firmus in both copies of the motet (but not in the mass) is identified with a German incipit, "Hilf und gib rat," presumably a *Leise*, which would make this piece an improbable combination of an English work and a German cantus firmus, possibly a secular tune, at a time when virtually all English cantus firmus masses used plainsong cantus firmi. The problem is that no source survives for the entire *Leise*, only a quotation in the tenor voice of a quodlibet on *O rosa bella* in the Glogauer Liederbuch (PL-Kj Mus ms 40098), no. 117, consisting of four notes: d, d, c, d, set to the four words (Ringman and Väterlein 1936–1981, I, 40–41). As Andrew Kirkman notes, this is an extremely common melodic pattern, and it is just as likely that somewhere in the transmission German scribes might have identified the opening gesture with a *Leise* they knew (Kirkman 1994, 196). A number of scholars ascribe the mass to one "Philippus" on the basis of a single word under the tenor of the Gloria in CZ-Ps D.G.IV 47, "Philipi," but this is an extremely unlikely position for an ascription, and Kirkman (1994, 196) reports that Rob Wegman suggested that this might be a residual piece of a cantus firmus motto. No such chant has surfaced, and indeed the Cantus database reports no chant beginning in that manner and only one beginning with "Philippus," which indicates how rare such an incipit is. Two chants beginning with this word are reported among medieval rhymed offices: *Philippi imperatoris ille*, the second antiphon in the first nocturn of matins for St. Quirinus (AH 28, no. 56), and *Philippi viridarium sanctorum*, antiphon for matins of SS Felix and Nabor, by the Milanese Franciscan Origo Scaccabarabozzi (AH 14b, no. 3). But neither chant looks like a promising source for the cantus firmus. Still, the tenor of the mass shows not *Hilf und gib Rat* but rather *Philippi* as its incipit. The melodic opening is a commonplace, and the structure of the work is entirely congruent with that of English masses with re-texted Kyries.

There are some aspects in which the raw statistics given above are deceptive. Of the seven pieces in the last category, five are transmitted in two Continental choirbooks that deliberately do not follow Continental practice, the earliest being I-Las 238. This manuscript, as it exists today, is the remnants of a once very luxurious choirbook given to Lucca Cathedral around 1467 by Giovanni Arnolfini, a Lucchese merchant active in Bruges and a cousin of the Giovanni Arnolfini in Van Eyck's famous painting. The manuscript surely came to Lucca with the English theorist John Hothby, a Carmelite friar who was appointed in 1467 as *magiscolus* of the cathedral, where he taught until he returned to England in 1486. Sometime after 1600 the choirbook was dismantled and its leaves were used as binding for notarial registers. By 2007 about forty bifolios had been identified and were separated from the registers, restored as much as possible, and brought back together. The choirbook, as Reinhard Strohm has shown, was most likely produced between 1462 and 1464 for the Chapel of St. Thomas Becket in the Carmelite Friary in Bruges, which was the chapel for the wealthiest English group in that city—the Brotherhood of the Merchant Adventurers—meaning that the English liturgy rather than the Continental one was followed there (Strohm 2008, 38–34).

The other manuscript is B-Br 5777, copied for the Burgundian chapel around 1468 in connection with the marriage of Charles the Bold to Margaret of York (Wegman 1989, 5; 1986). It was surely intended to provide a number of masses for a rite that would be familiar to the new English-born duchess. Thus only three masses with Latin Kyries survive in other Continental manuscripts. There is one overlap in these numbers because the Kyrie of the *Missa Caput* was eventually copied by Hans Wiser in two of his collections, I-TRmp 88 and 89, written ca. 1460 and 1464, respectively. If the leaves with the Kyries of all the masses surviving in I-Las 238 could be recovered, surely nos. 6 and 17 would have to be moved from the first to the fourth category, but this would not change things very much since the nucleus of B-Br 5777 and all of I-Las 238 are, for all intents and purposes, "English manuscripts" copied on the other side of the Channel (though they are in fact, Flemish manuscripts).

The conclusion remains, however, that by and large Continental copyists, who were eager to acquire English works, when faced with the very long and elaborate settings of the English Kyries with Latin verses, mostly left them out. The two manuscripts that are an exception to this policy are both late and either for an English congregation in the case of Lucca 238 or for a chapel that had now an English princess as the wife of the ruler. This leaves only three instances in the entire fifteenth century where we have an English Kyrie with its Latin verses copied in a Continental source: the Kyrie of the *Missa Alma redemptoris 2* in Trent 87, the Kyrie of the *Missa Caput* in Trent 88 and 89, and the Kyrie of the *Missa Veterem hominem* in Trent 88. The possibility of simply removing the Latin verses was used only very sparingly, since Kyries treated that way remained inordinately long. Interestingly enough only one of the really solemn English Kyries was treated that way: that of the *Missa Fuit homo missus*, which surely used the verses of *Deus creator omnium*, since as Margaret Bent notes, the opening of the cantus paraphrases the plainsong of that Kyrie (Bent 1979, 171). The Kyrie of the *Missa Sine nomine* in I-Rvat CS 14 (Hogg 1988, 53–54) and that of I-Rvat SP B 80 probably used one of the shorter sets of verses, since they are not inordinately long. And in the case of no. 31, the *Missa Sine nomine* found in Rome, Trent, and Verona Andrew Kirkman has shown that in every place the mass was copied the Kyrie was not only stripped of its Latin verses but drastically recomposed and shortened in a different way in all three centers (Kirkman 1994, 182–183).

One explanation often used for the elimination of the long English Kyries when the masses were copied on the Continent is that, of course, Latin Kyries were no longer used in most liturgies across the Channel, and thus the English Kyries were essentially useless. But this cannot be the entire explanation since the vast majority of the manuscripts listed in Table 2.2 above were not institutional manuscripts—that is, manuscripts intended to serve a church choir or a princely chapel. Most belonged to private collections compiled by individual musicians either for their own use and edification or as material to teach music (not just liturgical music) to their charges. This was the case with Hans Wiser, whose collection of manuscripts—some copied by himself and his students and some acquired during his years as schoolmaster in the cathedral in Trent—form the largest surviving cache of mid-fifteenth-century music that survives from anywhere (Ward 1975; Wright 1986; Leverett 1990; Gerber 2007). Ironically, of the five exceptions to this statement (B-Br 5557, I-AOs-15, I-Las 238, I-Rvat CS 14, and I-Rvat SP B80), two are for institutions where English liturgical traditions were cultivated, and those are our main Continental sources for the English Kyries with Latin verses. One of the personal collections, I-TRmd 93, which was written by Hans Wiser perhaps around 1453 in Munich (Wright 1996, 31–53; 2003, 247–332), is also arranged like an institutional collection: a series of introits, then Kyries, Glorias, proses, Sanctus, Agnus, and an appendix of motets. Each of the sections of Glorias, Credos, and Sanctus begins with a block of four movements from large-scale English cantus firmus masses, but none of their Kyries appear in the Kyrie section, and some of the Agnus were left out as well.

This suggests that, with the exception of a very small number of collectors, the English Kyries, with their Latin verses, appeared to be too strange a category to warrant copying into their anthologies, even if the music itself was magnificent. One possible explanation for this would be what would have appeared to Continental scribes of the second and third quarters of the fifteenth century to be the irrational nature of the English Kyries in term of their text distribution. A typical Continental Kyrie at the time consisted of three sections of music, with the text "Kyrie eleison," "Christe eleison," and "Kyrie eleison" set to each. Internal repetition of the text within each section was left to the discretion of the performers and was not considered a necessity. When each invocation had separate music, which was extremely rare, the Kyrie consisted of nine sections of music, as in Guillaume Du Fay's *Missa Sancti Iacobi* (Planchart 1976, 30–31). The English Kyries had to have separate music for all nine invocations, since each had a Latin verse, but their distribution was asymmetrical in a manner that must have struck Continental musicians as irrational. The two most common schemes for English Kyries were as follows:

1. Two sections of music, one in triple meter (O) and one in duple meter (C), with the invocations distributed as follows: I (O): K1, K2, K3, X4, X5 || II (C): X6, K7, K8, K9 (cf. *Missa Caput*).
2. Three sections of music, one in triple meter (O), one in duple meter (C), and one in triple meter. On the surface this would be similar to the structure of Continental Kyries, but in the English Kyries divided in this manner the verses are usually distributed as follows: I (O): K1, K2, K3, X4 X5 || II (C): X6, K7, K8 || III (O): K9 (cf. *Missa Fuit homo, Missa Quem malignus*), although in some cases the first division takes place between X4 and X5 (cf. *Missa Nobilis et pulchra*).

Clearly such pieces might have appeared as more than passing strange even to collectors avidly compiling their own anthologies of sacred music for personal reasons. In fact, among Continental manuscripts of the first half of the fifteenth century, the only English

Kyrie with Latin verses that we encounter is the setting of *Deus creator omnium* in the fragmentary *Missa Alma redemptoris mater1* in I-TRmp 87. Later in the century three more English Kyries were copied stripped of their verses. The one we can be certain of is that of the *Missa Fuit homo missus* in I-TRmp 88, not only because of its immense length, but also on account of the extreme asymmetry of the three sections (I in O 68 breves, II in C 88 breves, III in O 24breves) and, as noted above, the fact that the beginning of the cantus paraphrases the plainsong of *Deus creator omnium*. The Kyrie of the *Missa sine nomine* in I-Rvat CS 14 divides the Kyrie in two sections: I in O, 73 breves; II in ¢, 114 breves), the Kyrie of the *Missa sine nomine* in I-Rvat SP B80, TRmp 88, and I-VEbc 759 presents a different situation since the Kyrie was drastically recomposed to produce a shorter movement, which in I-Rvat SP B80 yielded two alternate short Kyries, hence the name Kirkman (1994, 181) has given the piece, "The Two Kyries Mass."

Later in the century some scribes attempted to salvage the English Kyries by transforming them into motets, that is, by applying to them an extended sacred text not connected with the old Kyrie verses such as antiphon, responsory, or a freely composed devotional text. Three of the pieces in Table 2.2 show this: the anonymous *Missa Meditatio cordis* survives only in Prague, CZ-Ps D.G.IV. 47, without a Kyrie, but I-TRmp 88, a manuscript that shows a considerable number of concordances with the Strahov manuscript, transmits a motet, *Gaude Maria Virgo*, with the cantus firmus *Meditatio cordis*, which shares the structural traits of the surviving movements of the mass and is most likely a contrafact of the original Kyrie of that work. Similarly, Walter Frye's *Missa Summae trinitati*, which, exceptionally, is transmitted in I-Br 5557 (one of the few choirbooks that transmits English Kyries with some consistency), without a Kyrie, is clearly related to the motet *Salve Virgo* with the cantus firmus *Summae trinitati*, found in I-TRmp 88 (Snow 1969). The third instance, that of the *Missa Hilf und gib Rat*, has been detailed above.

Indeed, I-Trmp 88, copied by Hans Wiser around 1460 in some ways represents Wiser's attempt at collecting the missing movements from a number of English masses. It contains the Kyrie and Agnus of the *Missa Caput* and of the *Missa Fuit homo missus*, which were missing from his copies in Trent 93 and 90; the Kyrie of the *Missa Veterem hominem*, separated by several dozen folios from the other movements of the mass, which opens the manuscript (as though he was able to obtain a copy of it only after he copied the last four movements of the mass); and the two contrafact Kyries just mentioned. Apart from the two "Continental-English" choirbooks, I-Br 5557 and I-Las 238, I-TRmp 88 is our only purely Continental copy of most of the long English Kyries that survive.

Simply stripping the English Kyries of their Latin verses and singing only the Greek invocations to the music was apparently not considered a viable solution for the most part. The Kyrie of the *Missa Fuit homo missus* sounds very eccentric when sung as it is copied in I-TRmp 88, and the text distribution for the Kyrie in the *Missa sine nomine* in I-Rvat CS 14 also must have struck singers and listeners in the fifteenth century as eccentric. And then there is the matter of the length of the movements. One of the earliest Continental cantus firmus masses is a direct imitation of an English work, Jehan de

Ockeghem's *Missa Caput*, where, beginning with the Gloria, he takes the double statement of the cantus firmus from the English mass movement by movement and duplicates the structure of the model. He did not do so for the Kyrie, and instead used a single statement of the cantus firmus to construct a Kyrie in the usual Continental manner (Bukofzer 1950, 263–264, 266–268). The dimensions of his Kyrie provide a convenient point of comparison with those of the model: Ockeghem's Kyrie is 74 breves long (in three sections of 23, 30, and 21 breves), while the Kyrie of the English mass is 255 breves (in two sections of 105 and 150 breves). The latter is almost as long as the Credo of the mass, and this must have struck Continental musicians as absurd. The asymmetric text setting also apparently made little sense to them, and, for example, Hans Wiser, when he copied the Kyrie of the English *Missa Caput* with text incipits implying the presence of the Latin verses, he redistributed the Kyrie verses (or had an exemplar where they were already so redistributed): verses 1–3 are sung to the first section, verses 4–6 to the second, and the last three verses were left out.

All of this apparently had a number of consequences. The first is that this might be a factor in the fact that, for all the admiration that English music elicited on the Continent in the first half of the fifteenth century, apparently there are virtually no attempts to emulate the English cantus firmus mass (and it was the cantus firmus masses that, as big festal works had long Latin Kyries) until after the mid-century, at a time when a work like Leonel's *Missa Alma redemptoris mater* was nearly fifty years old. The earliest Continental cantus firmus masses we have are Ockeghem's *Missa Caput*, a direct imitation of the English mass; Du Fay's *Missa Se la face ay pale*, which is in many ways his own reaction to the English *Missa Caput*; and Joan Ximeno de Cornago's *Missa Ayo visto lo mappamundi*, which in terms of its structure is related to works such as the Dunstaple/Leonel *Missa Rex saeculorum*. Although all three works date from the early 1450s, the

Table 2.3 Continental Mass–Motet Cycles

	Mass	Attributions	Sources of the complete work
1	*Ad fugam* Motet: *Quae est ista*	Standley Anonymous (Standley?)	I-TRmp 88, I-TRmp 89
2	*Esclave puist il* Motet: *Gaude Maria*	Anonymous	I-TRmp88, 388v-399r I-TRmp 88, 399v-401r
3	*O rosa bella I* Motet: *O pater aeterne*	Anonymous (Joye?)	I-TRmp 88, 363v-372r CZ-Ps D.G.IV 47, 160v-161r, I-Md 2269, 123v-124r
4	*Sine nomine* Motet: *Flos de spina*	Puyllois	I-TRmp 87, 167v-174r, I-TRmp 90 I-TRmp 90, 434v-436r.
5	*Soyez apprantiz* Motet: *Stella caeli*	Le Rouge	I-Rvat SP B80, 71r-80r, I-TRmp 90, 310v-318r I-TRmp 88, 11v-13r

earliest copy we have of them is I-TRmp 88, copied in about 1460, which is also the manuscript where Hans Wiser copied the three long English Kyries of the masses *Caput*, *Fuit homo missus*, and *Veterem hominem*.

A second consequence, which has a number of ramifications, was the spread of a misunderstanding among Continental composers and scribes who had only second-hand knowledge of the English repertory, and came to think that English cantus firmus masses were primarily four-movement cycles beginning with the Gloria. This may be the case with a number of anonymous eastern European masses that are also among the earliest imitations of the English-style cantus firmus mass. The *Missa Christus surrexit*, which Laurence Feininger (1951) once ascribed to Du Fay, survives only in I-TRmp 89, fols. 342v-346v, without a Kyrie or an Agnus, and shows a polyphonic structure resembling the *Missa Caput* and the extraordinary *divisi* in the last sonority of each section found in the *Missa Fuit homo missus*. These divided final notes led Charles Hamm (1968, 72) to consider it an English work. But Reinhard Strohm (1989) has shown that the cantus firmus of the work is actually the German Leise, *Christ ist erstanden*, which virtually assures that it is the work of a German or Austrian composer eagerly imitating the English style. The lack of the Kyrie here might be an accident of transmission, since the Agnus is also missing.

This misunderstanding of the nature of English mass cycles by their near contemporaries also took another form. The efforts to rework the Latin Kyries as motets apparently prompted some imitation as well. Robert Snow (1969) has identified six "Mass-motet cycles," in central European sources. Three of these, listed in Table 2.2, nos. 12, 14, and 34, are surely English masses where the Kyrie was transmitted separately and provided with a contrafact text so it could be used as a motet. But then there are a number of masses that are full five-movement masses with the short Kyries normally used on the Continent but which are clearly related to a motet, and in one instance at least the mass is copied together (Table 2.3) with the related motet following it immediately:

Three of the cases have been generally accepted. The mass by Standley, most likely an English composer, is entirely canonic, and the motet is composed using the same procedures as the mass and is generally considered to be by him. The unusual manner of notating both works clearly ties them together. A more tenuous case is that of Jehan Puyllois, whose *Missa sine nomine* has been associated to his motet *Flos de spina* by Reinhard Strohm (1991, 428–429).

In any case, both the suppression of the English Kyries on the Continent and at the attempt, particularly in the later fifteenth century to recover some of these Kyries in a different guise, appear to have sparked a small tradition of producing mass-motet cycles, which in this case includes at least one English composer, Standley, although it is worth noting that his nationality is assumed on account of his name and some of the traits of his music, all of which survives in central European sources (Bent, New Grove online).

The final step in this story, at least in terms of the evolution of the English polyphonic mass in the fifteenth and sixteenth centuries, is that *sometime*, either at the end of the fifteenth century or the beginning of the sixteenth, English composers *did* stop writing polyphonic Kyries for their festal masses. The early stages of this development

Table 2.4 English Sources for English Kyries

Date reported	Source	Mass	Composer
1970	GB-Cec 300, 1r	*Rex saeculorum* (K*)	Dunstaple/Leonel
1970	GB-Cec 300, 1v–2r	*Sine nomine* (K*)	Dunstaple/Leonel/Benet
1970	GB-Cec 300, 2v	*Da gaudiorum praemia* (K*)	Dunstaple
1955	GB-Cu Ii.V.18, 219v–228r	*Quem malignus* (K, G, C, S*, A*)	Anonymous
1969	GB-Lbl Add 54324, 6r–v	*Caput* (K*)	Anonymous
1969	GB-Lbl Add 54324, 1r	*Alma redemptoris 2* (K*)	Anonymous
1979	GB-Tar DD/L P29/29, 2v	*Salve sancta parens* (K*)	Anonymous

can be gleaned from what survives of E-Yb Mus 1, where we encounter an apparently Continental choirbook where the large-scale settings of the ordinary have no Kyries and a series of Kyries without the Latin verses is copied separately (Baillie and Obussier 1954, 22–24). In the English choirbooks that do survive from the first quarter of the sixteenth century, GB-Llp 1 and GB-CAgc 667 (Skinner 1997, 245–255; Bowers 2005, 659–664), all the large scale polyphonic festal masses begin with the Gloria, there are only a few isolated settings of the Kyrie without the Latin verses, and only the smaller votive masses for the Virgin include a setting of the Kyrie (for example, the Ludford Lady Masses; cf. Bergsagel, I). The reason for this development apparently has to do with the increased use of polyphony in the liturgy in the later part of the fifteenth century and into the sixteenth. By their nature the Latin Kyries, given the assignations in the Sarum use, inhabited a world halfway between the ordinary and the proper, and their presence in any polyphonic setting had the effect of restricting the number of occasions when such a setting could be sung, and composers and choirmasters, each for their own reasons, would have had an interest in making the immensely elaborate polyphonic settings of the mass that became the norm in Tudor England be available for performance on as many feasts as possible.

The almost complete disappearance of English fifteenth-century choirbooks, however, meant that as interest in this repertory arose at the end of the nineteenth century and during the first three quarters of the twentieth, scholars were restricted to the continental copies of nearly all of the English festal masses. An added factor in this was that the large majority of the works that were ascribed to English composers in the sources had no Kyries, or the Kyries survived as what at the time were considered independent motets. Among the few masses that survived with their Latin Kyries on the Continent, most of them, apart from those in B-Br 5557, were anonymous (I-Las 238 was not discovered and reported until 1968) (Strohm 1968), and one of the central works of this repertory, the *Missa Caput*, was regarded as the work of Guillaume Du Fay on the basis of the spurious ascriptions in I-TRmp 88 and 89. It was not until Charles Hamm's 1968 study that a systematic attempt was made at detecting English stylistic traits in the vast repertory of anonymous works in fifteenth-century Continental manuscripts, an attempt that required some time to be refined and digested, so to speak. Two other developments took place precisely around that time. The first was removal of the *Missa Caput* from Du Fay's canon and its identification as an English work, a process that began with Bukofzer's (1950) report of the discovery of part of the Agnus Dei in GB-CO A 3. This was followed by Strohm's (1968) discovery of I-Las 238. Then Ian Bent and Margaret's (1969) report of another English source with parts of the Kyrie led Thomas Walker (1969) to question Du Fay's authorship of the last four movements and culminated in the removal of the entire work from Du Fay's canon (Planchart 1972). The second development was the gradual discovery of fragmentary English sources with the Kyries of a number of the masses that were known from Continental manuscript only as four-movement works (first reported in MB VIII). These are shown in Table 2.4 (including *Caput* as well).

Although the Kyries in Table 2.4 are not very numerous, they are crucial in that they correspond to virtually every major English mass prior to 1450 that survived in Continental sources, including every mass ascribed to Dunstaple in any source. The only Kyrie still missing is that of Leonel Power's *Missa Alma redemptoris mater*. Most of the recovered Kyries are too fragmentary and cannot be entirely reconstructed. Only those of the *Missa sine nomine*, variously ascribed to Dunstaple, Power, and Benet (and most likely by Benet), and that of the *Missa Quem malignus spiritus* survive in complete form. The structure of what survives of GB-CAec 300 indicates that early on these masses, cyclic though they were, were still copied as in The Old Hall manuscript, with the movements grouped by genre, a practice that might have continued in England after it was abandoned on the Continent.

More Kyries might eventually turn up, although one despairs of ever finding complete movements, much less complete masses, in the English archives. Seldom has the destruction of an impressive repertory been quite as thorough. The list published by Curtis and Whatey (1994) includes a considerable number of works that never crossed the Channel and survive only as fragments. They cautiously classify some of them as Gloria-Credo pairs, or Sanctus-Agnus pairs, but pieces such as the impressive Gloria and Credo on *Tu es Petrus* (or perhaps *Puer natus*) that survive as fragments in the same English source as the Agnus of *Caput* (GB-CO A3) were almost certainly part of a full-scale cyclic mass.

Today we can catch bare glimpses of an enormous repertory that was immensely influential outside of England in the early fifteenth century, and eventually evolved into the extraordinary works of early Tudor England. The half dozen or so complete examples that survive, particularly the *Missa Caput*, are among the most impressive fifteenth-century works that have come down to us from anywhere. The attempts to salvage some of these Kyries as motets also produced an interesting if short-lived tradition of mass-motet cycles among Continental composers, both in northern Flanders, which was surely the most frequent point of entry of English music onto the Continent, and for reasons still not entirely clear, in the Germanic areas of central Europe. With the rediscovery of the English Kyries as fragments in insular sources we have recovered not so much a repertory as an understanding of a lost tradition.

Notes

1. Arlt and Rankin 1996, 3:208, 3:295.
2. For example, Vatican Kyrie *ad lib.* VI, Melnicki 1954, no. 55, was widely sung in the West with the Latin text *Tibi Christe supplices*, and in the East with the Latin text *O theos Christus*.
3. The large majority of Kyrie collections from the late twelfth century on, when they transmit Latin Kyries, transmit only the melodies with the Latin text and not in alternation with the melismatic Greek invocation; and when the melodies are copied with the melismatic Greek invocations, the Latin texts are absent entirely. A number of manuscripts will transmit the same melody with and without the Latin texts, but as separate pieces.

References

Andrieu, Michel. 1961–1974. *Les ordines romani du haut moyen âge*. 5 vols. Louvain: Spicilegium Sacrum Lovaniense.

Arlt, Wulf, and Susan Rankin, eds. 1966. *Stiftsbibliothek Sankt Gallen Codices 484 & 381*. 3 vols. Winterthur, Switzerland: Amadeus.

Baillie, Hugh, and Philippe Obussier. 1954. "The York Masses." *Music and Letters* 35: 19–30.

Bent, Ian, and Margaret Bent. 1969. "Dufay, Dunstable, Plummer—A New Source." *Journal of the American Musicological Society* 22: 394–429

Bent, Margaret, ed. 1979. *Fifteenth-Century Liturgical Music II: Four Anonymous Masses*. Early English Church Music 22. London: Stainer and Bell.

Bent, Margaret. 2004. "The Musical Stanzas in Martin Le Franc's *Le Champion des Dames*." In *Music and Medieval Manuscripts, Paleography and Performance. Essays dedicated to Andrew Hughes*, edited by John Haines and Randall Rosenfeld, 91–127. Hants, UK: Ashgate.

Bjork, David. 1980. "The Kyrie Trope." *Journal of the American Musicological Society* 33: 1–41.

Bjork, David. 2003. *The Aquitanian Kyrie Repertory of the Tenth and Eleventh Centuries*, edited by Richard L. Crocker. Burlington, VT: Ashgate.

Blume, Clemens, and Guido Maria Dreves, eds. (1905) 1961. *Tropi Graduales. Tropen des Missale im Mittelalter*. Analecta Hymnica 47. Leipzig: Riesland. Reprint, New York: Johnson Reprint.

Boe, John. 1989. *Beneventanum Troporum Corpus II, Ordinary Chants and Tropes for the Mass from Southern Italy, A. D. 1000–1250, Part 1: Kyrie eleison*. Recent Researches in the Music of the Middle Ages and Early Renaissance 20–21. Madison, WI: A-R Editions.

Bowers, Roger. 2005. "More on the Lambeth Choirbook." *Early Music* 33: 659–664.

Bukofzer, Manfred. 1950. *Studies in Medieval and Renaissance Music*. New York: W. W. Norton.

Cattin, Guilio, et al., eds. 1989. *French Sacred Music*. Polyphonic Music of the Fourteenth Century XXIIIA. Monaco: Éditions de l'Oissau-Lyre.

Curtis, Garteth, and Andrew Whatey. 1994. "Fifteenth-Century English Liturgical Music: A List of the Surviving Repertory." *Research Chronicle of the Royal Musical Association* 27: 1–69.

De Clerck, Paul. 1977. *La prière universelle dans les liturgies latines anciennes, témoinages patristiques et textes liturgiques*. Liturgiewissenschaftliche Quellen und Forschungen 62. Münster in Westfalen: Aschendorff.

Dunstable, John. 1970. "Complete Works." In *Musica Britannica 8*, ed. Manfred Bukofzer, 2nd ed. rev. Margaret Bent and BrianTrowell. London: Stainer and Bell.

Egeria. 1999. *Egeria's Travels*. 3rd ed. Edited and translated by John Wilkinson. Warminster, UK: Aris & Phillips.

Fallows, David. 1987. *Dufay*. Rev. ed. London: Dent.

Feininger, Laurence. 1951. *Missa Caput auctore Gulielmo Dufay cum aliis duabus missis anonymis. Veterem hominem et Christus Surrexit eidem auctori adscribendis.* Monumenta Polyphoniae Liturgicae Sanctae Ecclesiae Romanae. Ser. 1/2. Rome: Societas Universalis Sanctae Caeciliae.

Gerber, Rebecca L., ed. 2007. *Sacred Music from the Cathedral at Trent: Trent, Museo Provinciale D'arte, Codex 1375 (olim 88)*. Monuments of Renaissance Music 12. Chicago: University of Chicago Press.

Graduale Sacrosanctae Romanae Ecclesiae de Tempore et de Sanctis. 1908. Vatican: Vatican Press.

Gregory the Great. 1862. *Sancti Gregorii Papae cognomento Magni Opera Omnia. Vol. 3. Patrologia Latina 77*, edited by J. P. Migne. Paris: Migne.

Charles, Hamm. 1968. "A Catalogue of Anonymous English Music in Fifteenth-Century Continental Manuscripts." *Musica Disciplina* 22: 49–76.

Charles, Hamm. 1960. "A Group of Anonymous English Pieces in Trent 87." *Music and Letters* 41: 211–215.

Hiley, David. 1993. *Western Plainchant: A Handbook*. Oxford: Clarendon Press.

Hogg, Katherine. 1988. "The 'Caput' School: Anglo-Flemish Style in the mid 15th Century." Master's Thesis, University of Manchester.

Kirkman, Andrew. 1994. "The Transmission of English Mass Cycles in Mid to Late Fifteenth Century: A Case Study in Context." *Music and Letters* 75: 180–199.

Le Franc, Martin. 1999. "*Le champion des dame*." In *Classiques français du Moyen Age*, 4 vols, edited by Robert Deshaux, 127–131. Paris. H. Champion.

Leverett, Adelyn Peck. 1990 "A Paleographic and Repertorial Study of the Manuscript Trento, Castello de Buon Consiglio, 91 (1478)," 2 vols. Ph.D. diss., Princeton University.

Liber Usualis Missae et Officii. No. 780. 1954. Tournai, Belgium: Desclée.

Melnicki, Margareta. 1954. *Das einstimmige Kyrie des lateinischen Mittelalters.* Forschungbeiträge zur Musikwissenschaft 1. Regensburg: Bosse.

Planchart, Alejandro Enrique. 1972. "Guillaume Dufay's Masses: Notes and Revisions." *The Musical Quarterly* 58: 1–23.

Planchart, Alejandro Enrique. 1976. "Guillaume Dufay's Masses: A View of the Manuscript Traditions." In *Papers Read at the Dufay Quincentenary Conference, Brooklyn Vollege, December 6-7, 1974*, edited by Allan W. Atlas, 26–60. New York: Departmemy of Music Brooklyn College.

Rankin, Susan. 1987. "Neumatic Notations in Anglo-Saxon England." In *Musicologie medievale: Notations et Séquences, Table ronde du CNRS à l'IRHT d'Orléans-La Source, 10–12 Septembre 1982*, edited by Michel Huglo, 129–144. Paris: Champion.

Ringman, Heribert, and Christian Väterlein, eds. 1936–1981. *Das Glogauer Liederbuch*. 4 vols. Das Erbe deutscher Musik 4, 8, 85–86. Kassel: Bärenreiter.

Schuler, Manfred. 1966. "Die Musik in Konstanz während des Konzils 1414–1418." *Acta Musicologica* 38: 150–168.

Skinner, David. 1997. "Discovering the Provenance and History of the Caius and Lambeth Books." *Early Music* 25: 245–266.

Snow, Robert J. 1969. "The Mass-Motet Cycle: A Mid-Fifteenth-Century Experiment." In *Essays in Musicology in Honor of Dragan Plamenac on His 70th Birthday*, edited by Gustave Reese and Robert J. Snow, 301–320. Pittsburgh: University of Pittsburgh Press.

Stäblein-Harder, Hanna. 1962. *Fourteenth-Century Mass Music in France.* Corpus Mensurabilis Musicae 29. Rome: American Institute of Musicology.

Strohm, Reinhard. 2001."Music, Humanism, and the Idea of a 'Rebirth of the Arts'." In *Music as Concept and Practice in the Late Middle Ages*, edited by Reinhard Strohm and Bonnie J. Blackburn, 346–405. *The New Oxford History of Music 3*, pt. 1. Oxford: Oxford University Press.

Strohm, Reinhard. 1968. "Ein unbekannter Chorbuch des 15. Jahrhunderts," *Die Musikforschung* 21: 40–42.

Strohm, Reinhard. 1989. "Meßzyklen über deutsche Lieder in Trienter Codices," *Liedstudien. Festschrift für Wolfgang Osthoff zum 60. Geburtstag.* Tutzing: Schneider, 77–106.

Strohm, Reinhard. 2008. The Lucca Choirbook: Lucca, Archivio di Stato, MS 238; Lucca, Archivio Arcivescovile, MS 97; Pisa, Archivo Arcivescovile, Biblioteca Maffi, Cartella 11/III. Late Medieval and Early Renaissance Music in Facsimile 2. Chicago: University of Chicago Press.

Symons, Thomas. 1953. *Regularis Concordia: The Monastic Agreement of Monks and Nuns of the English Nation.* London: Thomas Nelson.

Tinctoris, Iohannes. 1975–1978. *Opera Theoretica.* 2 vols. Edited by Albert Seay. Corpus scriptorum de musica 22. Rome: American Institute of Musicology.

Walker, Thomas. 1969. "A Severed Head: Notes on a Lost English Caput Mass." In *Abstracts of Papers Read at the Thirty-Fifth Annual Meeting of the American Musicological Society, Saint Louis, 1969.* N. P.: American Musicological Society.

Ward, Tom. 1975. "The Structure of the Manuscript Trent 92-1." *Musica Disciplina* 29: 127–147

Wegman, Rob. 1986. "New Data Concerning the Origins and Chronology of Brussels, Koninklijke Bibliotheek, MS 5777." *Tijdschrift van de Vereniging voor Nederlandse Muziekgeschiedenis* 36: 5–25.

Wegman, Rob. 1989. Choirbook of the Burgundian Chapel, Brussel, Koninklijke Bibliotheek, MS 5777. Peer: Alamire.

Wickham Legg, John. 1916. *The Sarum Missal Edited from the Early Manuscripts.* Oxford: Clarendon Press.

Wright, Peter. 1986 "On the Origins of Trent 87^1 and 92^2." *Early Music History* 6: 245–270.

Wright, Peter. 1996. "Johannes Wiser's Paper and the Copying of His Manuscripts." In *I codici musicali trentini: Nuove scoperte e nuovi orientamenti della ricerca*, edited by Peter Wright and Carlo Andreotti, 31–53. Trento: Servizio Beni Librari e Archivistici.

Wright, Peter. 2003 "Watermarks and Musicology: The Genesis of Johannes Wiser's Collection." *Early Music History* 22: 217–332.

CHAPTER 3

GOVERNMENTAL INTERFERENCE AS A SHAPING FORCE IN ELIZABETHAN PRINTED MUSIC

JEREMY L. SMITH

The Elizabethan era was arguably the first in English history when governmental forces took such an interest in the new media of print as to inspire some direct precursors of modern-day forms of press censorship. It was also an era that famously witnessed an outpouring of motets, anthems, consort songs, madrigals, keyboard and lute music in print as well as a great rise in British popular forms, including especially the broadside ballad, which was in certain ways rightly treated as a poetic type, but from which stem such famous tunes as "Greensleeves." In this chapter two exemplary events—a governmental admonition and the granting of a royal patent of monopoly—will be shown to have special significance in shaping the ballad and the art music of this era. The admonition, discussed first, involves William Elderton, one of the era's most celebrated and most castigated ballad writers. The monopoly concerned many composers of the art-music tradition. That both events had a lasting effect on the music of this era, particularly in its politicization, has thus far gone unnoticed.

On or about September 8, 1570—some ten years before he would make significant use of "Greensleeves" in a ballad—Elderton received important feedback about his latest publication. It came from the queen's own privy council, which conveyed the following to their "lovinge friends, the *Masters*, Wardens and Companye, Printers and Stationers of London":

> After our hartye commendations we perceave of late a certeene Ballett hath bin sett forthe in prynt by one *William Elderton* intituled *Doctor Stories Stumblinge into Englonde* ymprinted in fflete Strete by *Thomas Colwell*. And albeit the substance thereof seemede to cause therewith a certeene zeale and good meaninge towardes

the ffurtherance of trewe Religion and defaceinge of Papistrye; yet do we find that some partes of the same do particularlye touche by name certeyne personages of honour and reputation tending also to the descreditt of some prences with whom the Queene's Matie standeth presently in terms of amytie.

And therefore we have thoughte wele not onlye to give yowe knowledge thereof and to require and chardge yowe in her M^{tes} name that yowe do forthwith give order that none of the said ballets be uttered or solde abroade and that such of them as have been alredie dispersed may be called in againe with as moche dylligence as may be but also do will and commande yowe that from hence forthe yowe suffer neither booke ballett nor any other matter to be published in print whatsoever the argument thereof shalbe until the same be first seene and allowed either by us of her M^{tes} pryvie cownsell or by thee Commissioners for cawses eccleyasticall there at London. Whereunto wee earnestlye requyer yowe to have speciall regarde as yowe tender her M^{tes} pleasure and will answer for the contrary. So fare yowe well from Rycote the viij of September 1570.

Yor Lovinge ffreindes
R Leycester. E Clynton. F. Knollyes. W. Cecill
(Arber 1875–1894, 5:lxxvi; quoted in Rollins 1920, 212–213)

After hearing this news, presumably from a fellow freeman at Stationers' Hall, Elderton's publisher Thomas Colwell surely wasted little time in notifying his author about the matter. Indeed, Colwell probably went combing through London's livelier taverns and Inn Yards (a theatrical venue that Elderton apparently frequented) that night in a search of the colorful ballad writer and actor who was soon to be widely known for his "ale-crammed nose" (Goldring 2004). Both men had been singled out in this report, which came from the very highest level of government. To have one's name associated with this act of censorship—the wholesale suppression of a printed ballad—was no doubt the cause of some consternation for Colwell. Elderton probably regarded it as one of his more sobering experiences as a professional writer.

Aware of this privy council report and similar documents, such as those concerning the famous 1599 Bishop's Ban on satire, Elizabethan scholars have long operated under the assumption that censorship of print in the late-Tudor era was extraordinarily oppressive and all-encompassing. Pointing to the kind of interaction outlined above—among the privy council, high commission, and Stationers' Company—the traditional view finds Elizabeth's closest advisors painstakingly checking for and rooting out any offensive printable material before it entered the era's English and foreign book markets, which thanks to the presses were larger than ever before (Siebert 1965, 98).

Bibliographers familiar with the Stationers' Company archives, however, have long been wary about such assertions of how well this system actually worked. Studies of the so-called Stationers' Registers, which reflect when and why publishers brought in books for a pre-publication review, showed a haphazard treatment of seditious and immoral texts (Greg 1944). From this perspective, censorship efforts on the whole seemed more often directed toward the protection of a publisher's copyright than the protection of a nation's policies, politicians, and moral fiber. And now literary historians, who once seemed almost uniformly to relish the notion that a government's administration could act so repressively as to inspire an ingenious evasiveness, have also begun to question the efficiency of the system. In studying censorship practices in the realm of poetry and prose, Cyndia Susan Clegg, for example, found them to be so sporadic and ad hoc as to render the whole enterprise inept. She suggests they did relatively little to help Elizabeth with her political needs beyond the encouragement of a limited kind of propaganda that favored the views of her establishment (Clegg 1997, 5).

In this chapter it will be argued, to the contrary, that the politically shaped products that stemmed from this kind of censorship could be seen, at least in music, as an achievement of note, one that should be credited to the effectiveness of the government's actions. But whether or not the system was effective and whether or not the propaganda was indeed limited, ballads were, in any case, one of the most watched of all printed genres, and for good reason. In 1912 Herbert L. Collmann suggested that the "prolificacy, and the audacity with which [Protestants of Mary Tudor's era] leveled their verses against those in authority, explain the reason why the ballad-writers were the objects of decrees made with a view to their suppression." He concluded, however, that "the incorporation of the [Stationers'] Company ... in 1557, ... aided largely by the restoration of the Protestant religion, brought about a rapid change in the tone of the ballads, until at length their language closely reflected the opinions of nine-tenths of the population of London at the time of their issue" (Collmann 1912, ix–x). After a comprehensive review of the extant broadsides material in 1991, Carole Livingston went even further in her appreciative assessment of the effectiveness of the government's control of the press. In her view there was no period of "audaciousness" in the pre-Elizabethan history of the broadside ballad. Governmental interference was a "key formative influence on the ... genre [from] its inception" (Livingston 1991, 849). However contradictory their views of the situation in earlier periods, these authors agree that Elizabethan ballads, at the least, were effectively watched over with care.

That broadside ballads were relatively short works, easy to check over for offensive content, makes the censorship process seem at least feasible for this particular genre. (It is perhaps no accident that we have no extant copies of Elderton's offending verses.) On the other hand, these same broadside ballads were just as unstable as any other kind of literature when it came to the matter of their reception. Many of these ballads were designed by their authors to be read from a pro-establishment perspective and with a particular moral in mind. No matter what the author's intention, what happened when people got them in hand, heard them sung, or sang them, however, was surely not so easy to control. At that point, with so much as a sneer, anyone wishing to do so could shift a reading from what the government might encourage and condone to something they would not wish anyone to hear or accept.

Such hermeneutic instability notwithstanding, the privy council's admonition toward Elderton opens a useful window into the government's point of view and expectations. That the council voiced its appreciation of Elderton's "good meaninge" and "certeene zeale" helps establish what they sought from the ballad press. It is also useful that they condemned the way he "touched" upon the wrong matters in various ways, as this points to what in the ballad might cause anxiety. The most instructive aspect of this admonition, however, was the general direction it gave for the future writers of ballads to take care as they served "her M^{tes} pleasure" (Arber 1875–1894, 5:lxxvi).

Even with only the title to go by, it is easy to see why the privy council made an effort to commend Elderton for his good intentions in writing "Doctor Stories Stumblinge into Englonde" before they pointed out its problems and suppressed it. The title assures us of two things: (1) that Elderton's ballad was of a journalistic type; and (2) that he had spared his anticipated audiences none of his famous black humor—as indicated by the word "Stumblinge." This facetious text suggests that Elderton had engaged in an ad hominem treatment of what turns out to be a Catholic figure of some prominence, and an attack on John Story would likely have pleased the privy council, which had applauded Elderton's efforts to "the ffurtherance of trewe Religion and defaceinge of Papistrye" (Arber 1875–1894, 5:lxxvi).

If once esteemed as a distinguished lawyer, chancellor of the diocese of Oxford (and London), and a Member of Parliament, by the end of Mary's reign Story had earned an infamous reputation as a ruthless persecutor of Protestants. After a period in and out of Elizabethan prisons, he eventually settled in the Netherlands, where he served officially as a customs officer, checking through the cargoes of English ships in an effort to stop the importation of Protestant propaganda into Antwerp and other tenuously Catholic Habsburg areas (Lock 2004). Overseas, Story stood as a thorn in England's side. In 1570 William Cecil, privy councilor, principal secretary, and England's most powerful politician under Elizabeth in his lifetime, masterminded a secret operation to bring him back for a grim accounting (Pollitt 1983, 140–141).

Cecil may well have had personal reasons to pursue the abduction project. In 1568 he had sponsored the seizure of a set of Spanish pay ships that had taken refuge in English harbors (Read 1933, 447). When this led to a trade embargo, it caused some serious economic hardships for English merchants, which temporarily but dangerously weakened Cecil's political position (MacCaffrey 1993, 121). A coup on the order of the abduction of Story would help Cecil regain his former standing as the queen's most trusted collaborator and confidant.

Despite a major glitch—the original crew deserted the mission and a set of last-minute replacements had to be found—the secret operation worked out quite well. Cecil had enlisted and recruited a number of agents for the enterprise, including the exiled William Parker, who was somehow able to convince Story that he was a trustworthy Catholic (Parker had himself been working as a customs agent before he was "turned"). It was at Parker's side that Story unsuspectingly walked onto a ship where a newly recruited crew was poised to detain him and sail back to home shores (Pollitt 1983, 144). When Story arrived in England, Catholic friends were there to help him orchestrate an escape from his latest captors. But Story was promptly recaptured. Then, in what turned out to be a clever piece of political theater, Cecil arranged for Story to be locked up in the same Lollards' Tower that the former Marian chancellor had himself used to imprison (and torture) Protestants some years before (Lock 2004). All told, by the time he stumbled back into England, Story's story had all the markings of the kind of "true-to-life" episode that would attract the interest of the English public at large.

The whole escapade made terrific fodder for a journalistic ballad, but, in telling the tale, could Elderton have blown Parker's cover? Could he have potentially spoiled certain aspects of the trade negotiations? The former seems possible and the latter seems likely. For the sake of resuming trade relations, Cecil was in contact with the Catholic Duke of Alva, the Spanish viceroy of the Netherlands. Alva controlled ports vital to English trading interests (Read 1933, 447). He was also committed to some famously oppressive operations against Protestant rebels in the Netherlands. Leveling invective against a figure such as Alva was surely what the Elizabethan ballad writer must have thought one was supposed to do, given the right opportunity. Yet in the elaborate game that Cecil and the queen were now playing with nearly all the major Catholic powers (Italian, Spanish, and French), this was clearly not the time to do it.

The international perspective on the Story case is significant, as even to disinterested foreigners the whole incident could have seemed as much a breach of international law as any great coup for the Protestant cause. In 1572, Philip II's ambassador baldly accused Cecil (and the queen) of kidnapping (Pollitt 1983, 140). Philip even tried to blackmail Cecil with the information. By 1572 Cecil would probably not have felt much threatened by such an action. But two years earlier the privy council may have been worried that Elderton might have unintentionally served the kind of purposes Philip had proposed.

So, in the end, an ambivalent privy council—one condoning Elderton's intentions but concerned about unintended results—suppressed what was surely a potent journalistic ballad. As Elderton came to terms with this, he must have pondered the implications. He had been commended for his religious zealotry. He was probably also aware that he was told (obliquely, if rather firmly) that he should serve the queen's pleasure. Yet if he learned anything from the privy council's admonition, it was that he could easily get in over his head if he dabbled too strongly in political affairs he did not fully understand.

To continue on as a ballad writer, Elderton faced a daunting set of new conditions. On the one hand, he needed to find subject matter that would interest the public at large and still serve his queen and council. On the other, he needed to be sure to avoid hidden pitfalls, like exposing the identity of any secret agents or besmirching the reputations of special allies, no matter how short the period of diplomatic amity might last. In his subsequent work Elderton demonstrated in various ways that he had taken the gist of this lesson to heart.

After suffering the public humility of what a colleague sarcastically described as an "ell [ill] Fortune" (Rollins 1920, 123), Elderton returned to the trade with a fine work commemorating the bishop of Salisbury, John Jewel, who had died in 1571 (Elderton 1571). Jewel had lived only to middle age, but he had achieved great distinction in his lifetime as an anti-papist controversialist. Jewel had also supported the use of vestments, however, taking a position that was decidedly more conservative than that of his more puritan colleagues (Craig 2004).

Wisely refraining from any discussion of Jewel's positions, Elderton described his subject simply as a "jewel" among religious men, a "Bishopp of so good grace, wher good men be so skant" (Elderton 1571, li. 8). As he considerately added, however, "there [were] some behinde, . . . [on whom Jewel's] Talents did bestowe" (li. 12). In 1920 Hyder Rollins suggested this work was essentially an exercise, an "attempt at pure elegiac poetry" (Rollins 1920, 215). This assessment seems fair, yet it is possible to detect a special political sensitivity in Elderton's approach. Certainly the ballad writer showed an allegiance to the "trewe religion" (Arber 1875–1894, 5:lxxvi) of the kind Elizabeth herself would have appreciated. Perhaps just as importantly, though, as much as he bemoaned Jewel's loss for the sake of his "sheep," Elderton wisely left room for others among the living to become "shepherds" in his place (li. 26).

Jewel's death was not the only event of interest to ballad audiences in 1571. Story died that year too. But Elderton—who presumably did not want to call attention to his prior troubles—passed over the chance to have a last word on that subject. Instead it was yet another political death, that of Thomas Howard, 4th Duke of Norfolk, that inspired a new ballad from Elderton.

Before his fall, Norfolk was an exemplary "personage of reputation and honour" (Arber 1875–1894, 5:lxxvi). He had stood closest to the queen herself in noble rank, as the nation's only living duke. By 1572, however, Norfolk became prominently associated with the very matters that most deeply threatened Elizabeth as she entered her second decade of rule: the Northern Rising; the Ridolfi Plot; and the uncertain status of the Catholic contender for the English crown, Mary Queen of Scots, whom Norfolk had intended to marry. Ultimately Norfolk, who claimed he had never veered from his Protestantism, was little more than a figurehead for the rebels. He was noncommittal with Ridolfi and he seemed all along to have thought his queen would eventually approve of his plan to marry her cousin. But as far as Elizabeth's chief counselors were concerned, this all added up in the end to treachery, and Elizabeth's own consternation was roused in particular by Norfolk's plans to marry a serious rival. Ultimately, the duke was executed as a traitor (Graves 2004).

With newfound restraint in his "A balad intituled the dekaye of the Duke," Elderton responded to Norfolk's execution rather than to his capture and imprisonment (Elderton 1572). As he had done before with Story, Elderton found a title phrase to succinctly summarize the narrative thrust. This time it was a "dekaye" not a demeaning stumble. But Norfolk was described therein as "Duke of high honor" (Elderton 1572, li. 70), and the ballad overall was notably devoid of irony or sarcasm. In marked deference to the duke's former status as the highest peer of the realm, the central theme, his "fall to highe Treason" (li. 70), was recounted not with vengeful relish but as a cautionary tale warning that others may also "lose all" if they do not look to their "dueties" to "Queene and countrie" (li. 78–79).

Rather than vilify Norfolk, Elderton described the pope rather viciously as a "pestilence" (Elderton 1572, li. 11). The hero, so to speak, was the "Triall," which was applauded in the stanzas and had its "good[ness]" emphasized with musical and poetic repetition in Elderton's well-crafted refrain (li. 1). Otherwise, not a single particular offense of Norfolk's was mentioned in this ballad. Yet Elderton managed still to put forth a complex message, at least in terms of self-positioning. In casting Norfolk as a tragic dupe of the pope, Elderton, through his poetic voice, could show his respectful views of Norfolk, as a man of such high rank. In applauding the trial Elderton showed too, however, that he was not questioning the court's findings. It was a restrained and sympathetic stance, which may not have been exactly what Norfolk's prosecutors would have wished to find in this commemorative ballad for someone they prosecuted for a capital offense. But it probably well suited the queen.

In cases such as Norfolk's, Elizabeth faced a delicate political situation. It was abundantly clear that she had to make an example of Norfolk despite his high rank. But to eliminate him would suggest that the hierarchical system that buttressed her position could be dismantled. This was Elizabeth's classic political dilemma (MacCaffrey 1993, 139). The solution was to allow an execution like this to go forward but then to respond to it with marked distaste. Thus the queen got to have it both ways: to show her respect for the monarchical system she embodied as well as to rid herself of its most dangerous element.

Elderton's expressed ambivalence to Norfolk's fate was not unlike his queen's, although his expressive scope was much narrower. Faced with the possibility of further criticism from his superiors, Elderton (unlike Elizabeth) must have felt compelled to praise the efforts of those who had sent Norfolk to his death. Even though the duke was ripe for special disparagement as a convicted traitor, Elderton refrained from embarking on a straightforward attack. However risky, the ambivalent stance he struck in this "good night" for Norfolk was an inspired piece of Tudor political sensitivity.

All told, Elderton's first answers to the privy council seemed well to prove that he had heard their comments and would act upon them. He amply showed a renewed willingness, for example, to write ballads with "good meaninge" and to serve at Elizabeth's pleasure. He also took steps to make sure he did not "touch" upon the wrong matters (Arber 1875–1894, 5:lxxvi). Omitting all facts surrounding Norfolk's treason seems to have been the means to this end. As far as Elderton's future as political writer for the establishment was concerned, all of this might have been tallied up on the credit side.

Yet when forced to reconcile his efforts with the needs of a formidable political body like the privy council, Elderton, it seems, had deprived himself of an important narrative device, the use of telling detail. Thus the new, "politically correct" Elderton may have been something of a disappointment to his audiences. This condition was only temporary, however. In two ballads Elderton would publish in 1579 and 1581, he managed to accomplish a rather formidable political and artistic compromise: to stay the course of service to a royalist agenda without sacrificing the kind of material that made for an engaging story.

In "A newe Ballade, declaryng the daungerous shootyng of the Gunne at the Courte. To the tune of Sicke and sicke," Elderton cast the queen as his main subject (Elderton 1579). Here he reveled in all the story's details to such an extent that reports by Tudor historians and chroniclers, such as John Stow, mesh closely with Elderton's account (Stow 1580, 1196–1204). The backdrop was a diplomatic meeting with the French ambassador at a point when the queen had taken the opportunity to venture out on a barge into the Thames. On the river some "weighty causes" were discussed for a while, but eventually the queen decided simply to relax and royally unwind with a book (Elderton 1579, li. 1–12). Meanwhile, a courtier's servant, Thomas Appleton, drifting by on a nearby scull, had come upon a gun and fired it off (presumably accidentally). Unfortunately, the barrel was aimed at Elizabeth's boating party. Disastrously, a bullet went through both arms of an oarsman who was sitting next to the queen.

However tragic his fate, Elderton did not commiserate with the actual victim of this shooting. His main concern was the queen and her reactions. She apparently spoke to the victim when all others were still recoiling in shock. Later, when the privy council had rashly sentenced Applegate to death for nearly killing their ruler, Elizabeth, again uniquely, heard well his appeal for mercy and stayed the execution (Stow 1580, 1203–1204).

Significantly, the queen's role in the whole affair could easily have been de-emphasized. The real victim of this dramatic episode was the injured waterman, of course, not the monarch; the queen's coolness under fire, however noteworthy, was essentially reactive in nature. But it was only Elizabeth who could see through the passions of the moment to arrive at a humanistic judgment on the side of mercy when it came to Appletree. Elderton's poetic speaker described him as a "wilful beast" (Elderton 1572, li. 58), and it was the "councilors' grave regard [that the] vilest death were fit for his reward" (li. 52–53). For courtiers to be trumped by the wisdom of the queen in this kind of matter was not so problematic for a general populace who would be expected simply to embrace any moral instruction they received from their ruler. But it is more difficult to see how the men who reacted to the violence Elderton depicted on the barge itself could ever have been happy with Elderton's characterization. Even the "nobles two or three" reacted without bravery at the sight of blood (li. 9). Elderton stated baldy that "she [Elizabeth] was readier to give helpe, then all the noble men" (li. 38). It seems that, even with an event as ready-made for a ballad as this, Elderton could get caught up with problems in the details.

Elderton's ultimate solution was an ingenious move to fiction, which would be featured in a work he would publish in 1581: "A new Ballad, declaring the great Treason conspired against the young King of Scots, and how one *Andrew Browne* an Englishman, which was the Kings Chamberlaine, prevented the same. To the tune of Mildred, or else to 'Greensleeves'" (Elderton 1581). As the title suggests, a great English hero, "Andrew Browne," triumphantly saves the "young King of Scots" from imminent danger. Specifically, Browne thwarts this attempt at regicide only to deliver his own form of grim justice in the end: forcing an unnamed "Bishop" to drink the same poison he had murderously intended for the king (Elderton 1581, li. 53–54). Browne is then "knighted ... with gallant gear ... [and given] livings great / For doing such a manly feat" (li. 77–78).

At the time of this ballad's publication, James VI, Scotland's king, had recently declared his majority (in the summer of 1578). The appearance of other historical figures in Elderton's story, such as the "Ladie Nurse" (the countess of Mar) and the "Earl of Morton," help establish that this ballad was of fairly recent vintage (Elderton 1581, li. 18, 97). Although James had been threatened by poisoning attempts earlier in his youth, such a threat was never recorded in the era of his early majority. Nor is there any record at all of any Englishman named Sir Andrew Browne working in Scotland at the time. Pending some unusual and unlikely discovery, it seems quite safe to assume that the attempted crime and the hero who saved the king were products of Elderton's imagination.

After the character Browne is ceremoniously knighted, the ballad goes on to describe a further attempt on James's life, this time from a mysterious source "beyond the seas." Now the saviors are "three noble Earls," one of whom turns out to be an historical figure, the "Earl of Morton" (Elderton 1581, li. 91–97). In the ballad Morton issues a powerful warning to those who might choose to "offend the King," noting that James's "Godmother will not see, / Her Noble Child misused to be" (li. 101–104). Significantly, this is a pointed allusion to another historical character, namely Elizabeth, who had stood as James's godmother at the time of his birth.

Elderton emphasized his "Elizabethan" message in his masterful handling of a subtly varying refrain. The first five stanzas end, "Alas for woe, why would it be so, / This makes a sorrowful heigh ho." But Elderton altered the refrain rather effectively in the penultimate stanza, ending things with a chilling note that if Morton's warning is not heeded, "*She* [i.e., Elizabeth] will make a sorrowful heigh ho [emphasis mine]" (Elderton 1581, li. 103–104). In addition to its use of the "Greensleeves" tune, the ballad's story type and emphasis on Elizabeth are also significant. As with all the other works of Elderton's discussed in this chapter, the piece was strikingly political in nature and could definitely be seen to serve the needs of the queen. Unlike all the others, however, this one was a work of fiction.

This story of Elderton's ballad writing would have come to a more fitting end had "A new Ballad" proven completely devoid of any conceivable political indiscretion. But this was probably not the case. Morton, the one actual historical character besides Elizabeth whom Elderton chose to lionize, had stepped down from a position as the Regent of Scotland when James had declared his majority. Intriguingly, at that point, Morton's days were numbered. Encouraged by a suddenly empowered Catholic faction, James would eventually see to the execution of Morton for his role in the prosecution of his mother, Mary Queen of Scots (Lee 1956, 124–129). Since Mary was imprisoned in England at the time of the ballad's publication, it would seem that Elderton's work might not have been sensitive to James's feelings. Morton, however, was the one in Scotland that the English wished to see remain in power. Although it would have probably been controversial in Scotland, the link that Elderton makes between Elizabeth and Morton may not have caused any problems for the English ballad writer at the time.

In her exhaustive study of "the fabric of Elizabethan press censorship and control," Susan Clegg found that it all added up to "a crazy quilt . . . patched together by the sometimes common and sometimes competing threads of religious, economic, political and private interests" (Clegg 1997, 5). Clegg's findings are undeniably important. But a look at Elderton's output calls into question the value of measuring censorship results by empirical data alone. The admonition Elderton received from the privy council, as argued above, had a clear and important shaping effect on his career.

The Byrd/Tallis Patent of Monopoly

Five years after Elderton was admonished for producing a single controversial work, Elizabeth granted to William Byrd and Thomas Tallis a patent of monopoly that basically protected them from any and all governmental interference. Thus, at the same time that popular ballads were implicitly shaped, if not always closely monitored, by the English government, much of the published art music of the time was explicitly shielded, at least in principle, from inspection.

The wording of the 1575 music patent suggests, in effect, that Tallis and Byrd had been appointed to a new crown commission, one whose purview was restricted to music but was otherwise apparently limitless. Elizabeth stated:

> that we for the especiall affection and good wil that we have and beare to the science of musicke and for the aduauncement thereof, by our letters patents dated the xxii. of January in the xvii. y.re of our raigne, have granted full priviledge and licence unto our welbeloued seruants Thomas Tallis and William Birde Gent. of our Chappell ... for the xxi. yeares next ensuing, to imprint any and so many as they will of set songe or songes in paertes, either in English, Latine, French, Italian, or other tongues that may serue for musicke either in Churche or chamber, or otherwise to be either plaid or soonge. (Byrd and Tallis 1575, f.H4r)

Perhaps it is not surprising that one apparent result of this monopoly was that some of these composers, among the most prominent of the time, discovered that they could use the music press for special political purposes.

The patent makes it clear that Elizabeth awarded this monopoly to Byrd and Tallis in recognition of their exalted status in the musical field. But they, it turns out, were arguably as motivated to serve the Catholic "right" as Elderton had been to serve the Protestant "left"—Byrd was a well-documented Catholic and both composers were allied with Catholic nobles in England who often stood opposed to Cecil (Kerman 2000, 276–278). Literary historians have offered interesting generalizations that seem quite applicable to the case of Byrd and Tallis, given their religious and political interests and status. In briefly reviewing the Elizabethan situation, Alfred Somans concludes, "it was the *highest placed author* who was capable of *giving the greatest offense*, but who was at the same time the least vulnerable to the sanctions of censorship" (Soman 1976, 456; emphasis added). After quoting this passage with approval, Annabel Patterson suggests that such authors effectively escaped "reprisal from officials reluctant to transform *rebels into martyrs*" (Patterson 1984, 29; emphasis added).

Thanks in part to the patent itself, no one aware of the situation in England, then or now, could really dispute that Byrd and Tallis were highly placed. Even the notion that Byrd and Tallis were famous enough to emerge as effective martyrs is germane. No known evidence exists to suggest that Tallis was ever thought of as a Catholic rebel or a potential martyr. In Byrd's case, however, there are indicators, both positive and negative, that his status was a matter of political concern. William Weston, an English Jesuit missionary, set this out clearly with a statement that Byrd "sacrifice[d] ... everything for [his] faith—his position, the court, and all those aspirations common to men who seek preferment in royal circles as a means of improving their fortunes" (Weston 1955, 71). Indeed, the government did keep a sharp eye on Byrd and his family. They even investigated the music performed at the household of Byrd's patron, Thomas Paget (Smith 2010, 1–2).

To follow Patterson and Soman's reasoning, Byrd and Tallis had the wherewithal to publish whatever they chose to, including controversial material. Working together at one point, but mostly with Byrd acting on his own, they published an extensive series of Latin-texted works that have been shown to be glaring in political content (Monson 1997; Kerman 2000). What the composers did with their privileged press is indeed suggestive.

But a closer look at the situation suggests some problems with Patterson's "high placed" theory. Byrd and Tallis likely found that their Latin texts acted as a shielding force (in a less and less Latin-oriented England), but they refrained from publishing some (though not all) of their most controversial works. Furthermore, the composers conspicuously manipulated their titles, prefatory remarks, headings, and so on, to hide, or mute the effect of, certain individual compositions (Smith 2007, 7–8; Smith 2008, 26–28). At two points Byrd allowed editions to go through the very inspection process that the monopoly he owned at the time was supposed to allow him to forgo (Arber 1875–1894, 2:477; 3:279). Most prominently (if particularly), finally, the absence of a title page with the printer's name on Byrd's editions of Catholic masses suggests that these masses, at least, were not even placed before the general public in the composer's lifetime (i.e., they were printed but not exactly published) (Smith 2003, 98–99).

Thus, at first blush—that is, when isolated from contexts, paratextual shielding methods, and conditions of publication—the very presence of politically charged pieces of music in print suggests that, as royally appointed monopolists, Byrd and Tallis were operating without restraint. A closer look reveals, however, that they had taken steps to hide or obscure their actions. Did the royal source of Byrd and Tallis's grant affect their choices along these lines?

Elsewhere I have suggested that Byrd and Tallis, as publishers, were highly sensitive to Elizabeth's (and her successor's) needs, even when voicing conceivably dissenting views (Smith 2008, 39–40). Projecting an image of themselves as royal servants in print, they mixed pointed ideals with royal flattery, coaxing the queen (and king) while keeping her informed about non-majority opinions. Byrd and Tallis's *Cantiones quae ab argumento sacrae vocantur* (1575) may be best understood as part of a sophisticated form of this kind of intimate political communication (Smith 2008, 30). Dealing with English texts or with the queen's counselors presented even greater challenges for the composers.

Among the most provocative English-texted works to pass through the music press was a setting of Chidiok Tichborne's "My prime of youth is but a frost of cares." Tichborne wrote these verses the night before he was executed for participation in the so-called Babington plot of 1586 (Miola 2007, 180). Since this plot was ultimately viewed as a scheme to murder Elizabeth and place Mary Queen of Scots upon her vacated throne, Tichborne's verses were indubitably associated to some extent with the most radical element of the Catholic cause. Although several composers published settings of this poem, the version John Mundy published in 1594 will be the focus of discussion here, as it was produced under the obvious auspices of the Byrd/Tallis music patent (when it was run by Byrd alone).

Like so many music editions of this era, including especially those created by Byrd and Tallis themselves, the music patent played an important role in the shaping of Mundy's edition. The most obvious references to Byrd and his monopoly appear on Mundy's title page, where the composer announced Byrd's patent and used a title, *Songs and psalms* . . . (1594), that closely resembled one of Byrd's, namely his *Psalmes, sonets and songs* . . . (1588) (cf. Mundy 1594, [A]1r and Byrd 1588, [A]1r). Within Mundy's set there is further evidence of Byrd's influence. In one case Mundy set the same poem as Byrd ("Penelope that longed" from another of Byrd's published sets), and many of Mundy's works may be paired with a Byrd model (Kerman 1962, 118–119).

Mundy's "My prime" is in many ways similar to Byrd's "Why do I use my paper, ink and pen" of the *Psalmes*, which contains a stanza from a poem that Henry Walpole had reportedly composed to commemorate the 1581 English execution of Edmund Campion SJ (Kerman 2000, 278). Both songs celebrate a figure that the government treated as a treacherous enemy but that Catholics viewed as a martyr. Both songs had been widely promulgated via surreptitious publication and also thanks to a government-sponsored attempt to counter their Catholic messages with published Protestant "answers" (Tichborne 1586, [A]2r–3v; Munday 1582, D7r–E2v).

The same two works were politically sanitized in various ways before they went to press. Byrd set only one of Walpole's stanzas and two others on the general topic of martyrdom. He left out all direct reference to Campion (Byrd 1588, F4v). Mundy set only the first stanza on Tichborne's poem (Mundy 1594, D1r). Although the poem was not otherwise changed, it appeared in full alongside its answer in a government-sponsored edition (Tichborne 1586, [A]2r–3v). Thus Mundy, who left the verses unattributed in his edition (in keeping with the general practice in music publishing), might have viably claimed in any case that he was not introducing anything new to the public when he reproduced "My prime." All this suggests that these composers had found (or simply enjoyed) the means to protect themselves. But this went only so far. Neither composer presented any text or context that could be read as anti-Catholic and both associated their works with Protestant leaders.

At the same time that Byrd published his partially disguised tribute to Campion, he, in collaboration with the poet Thomas Watson (who was likely Catholic too), published musical tributes to a special group of prominent Protestants, including Elizabeth's principal secretary, Francis Walsingham; Walsingham's former son-in-law, Sir Philip Sidney; and Robert Devereux, 2nd Earl of Essex, who became Walsingham's son-in-law, too, after Sidney's demise (when Essex married Sidney's widow) (Ruff and Wilson 1969, 12–13). Essex, significantly, was also the dedicatee of Mundy's set.

Byrd drew Sidney close to Campion by putting their tributes side by side in his *Psalmes* editions. Rather than use song placement to make the connection, Mundy spoke directly to Essex. In a thinly disguised metaphor, Mundy claimed in his dedication to the earl that the protection Essex provided for him was something Mundy viewed as akin to a "religious sanctuarii" (Mundy 1594, [A]2r). Thanks to the inclusion of "My prime" in his set, no one would have likely thought that Mundy was attempting to associate Essex with any religion other than the Catholicism for which Tichborne was willing to make such grave sacrifices (Hammer 1999, 175–176; Ruff and Wilson 1969, 16–17).

Whether Mundy's edition was cause for concern to Essex is unknown. But Essex was definitely drawn into dangerous associations by Catholic activists and a Catholic press. Most revealingly, in 1595 he was the unauthorized dedicatee of *A conference about the next succession to the crowne of England* (Doleman 1595, *2r–3v). This was a book surreptitiously published on the continent, probably in 1595, by an exiled Englishman writing under the pseudonym "R. Doleman." (The true author is generally thought to be the leading English Jesuit activist, Robert Persons, who was closely associated with his former mission partner, Campion.) The foremost Essex authority, Paul C. Hammer, has suggested that *A conference* was dedicated to Essex for no purpose other than to do damage to Essex's reputation (Hammer 1999, 139, 145, 177).

A conference was also the last of a series of editions, mainly musical, that refer flatteringly to Essex as they associate him with Catholic causes (Ruff and Wilson, 1969, 17–18). And Doleman's edition stands out, in this light, as an extreme case. There can be no real question that Doleman was disingenuous here. To suggest in print that any Englishman held views on the succession was essentially to draw him into something as politically dangerous as providing the wrong answer to the "Bloody Question" (favoring the pope's authority over Elizabeth's). Byrd and Mundy, however, had gone to special trouble to associate Sidney and Essex with Catholic ideas in a manner that would seem, at least by contrast, rather subtle and positive.

Sympathy for Campion and Tichborne was palpable at the time of Byrd and Mundy's publications. To some, such as the influential nominally Protestant John Harington, poems like these resonated with the idea that brave Englishmen had been brutally executed while admirably holding on to their beliefs (Kilroy 2005, 2–3). The efforts of the government to posthumously attack the reputations of Tichborne and Campion would seem now to indicate that Byrd and Mundy were taking special risks in bringing the poems back into public view, especially as they did so while casting them again in a positive light. But perhaps the musicians knew, better than Doleman, that the reputations of these men had gained public support. In any case, with Byrd and Mundy representing one group and Doleman another, it would seem clear that two sets of Catholics were using the same tactic to pursue different goals.

As a privileged English subject, Byrd had the capacity to assess ideas that were developing *within* England and react to them in print. Writing from exile, Doleman enjoyed many more freedoms than did Byrd, but Doleman may not have understood the local conditions. (Or, more ominously, perhaps, Doleman knew the situation all too well and had grasped that Mundy's 1594 effort would be the last of its kind, as Byrd had retired from London and had essentially left music publishing to his future successor, Thomas Morley [Smith 2003, 65].) Admittedly, it is not possible now to determine Byrd's or Doleman's perspectives or motivations. But to gain a sense of the sheer political power involved here it is useful to note that Essex was indeed hurt by Doleman's "association" tactic.

The disfavor Essex felt from his queen at the time was palpable (he claimed he was seriously ill), and his reactions began at this point to seem to many to become more and more extreme and desperate (Hammer 1999, 145 n179). In the end, when he was tried and executed for treason, it was Essex who was personally to feel the most devastating effects of truly falling afoul of the queen and "her pleasure." Things fell out quite differently for the musicians discussed in this chapter. Unless Byrd's retirement was indeed forced upon him and Elderton was to suffer more than the evidence suggests from his "ell fortune," these privileged musicians apparently found that they might continue to represent (in moderated form) some of the more extreme views of their respective factions, as long as they remained sensitive to the needs of their queen.

From the perspective of the cases discussed in this chapter, it appears that the government handled the ballad much differently than it did the music of Byrd, Tallis, and their contemporaries. But, as I have attempted to show, the effect was the same, or at least it was similar in the sense that reflections in a mirror appear to resemble their objects, even though the images are reversed. In the ballad trade, as exemplified by Elderton's efforts, a puritanical force that could quickly drift too far from center thanks to its zeal was pulled to the right, and within the music trade, as defined by Tallis and Byrd's patent, a Catholic position that could be taken to extremes on the continent was pulled to the left. All of this movement might have seemed foreordained (or predetermined perhaps), at least to the student of Elizabethan history, thanks to the fame of Elizabeth's favored political stance of the *via media* or "middle way" (Shagan 2010, 490). But even if the political results were perhaps predictable, the artistic ones were not.

In an ongoing search for the best means of answering the privy council's admonition without losing his audience's interest, Elderton, as I have argued, discovered the potency of propagandized fiction. His discovery deserves special note in the history of the ballad, for over the years Elderton's "Browne" ballads quickly became the basis for many new works, while many other ballads passed into obsolescence (Livingston 1991, 882–901). Of course, few would be likely to ignore any ballad that was sung to the tune of "Greensleeves," but with his move into fiction, Elderton stepped away from the ephemeral position of newsmonger toward the more lasting place of a recognized artist. In their more exalted sphere, Byrd and his fellow composers, who were already comfortably situated as esteemed authors in their day, were political actors of some import. Thanks to the privileged status they had gained from the queen, they had the wherewithal to do just as much as Elderton to infuse music into the political affairs of the day. A study such as this suggests that it is apparently premature to offer a sweeping generalization about the scope and effectiveness of Elizabethan censorship. The foregoing examples of the role of Elizabethan censorship in the music field would seem to demonstrate that until we can discover an all-encompassing general rule it might be best to focus on the careful study of the context and purpose of individuals and individual works of music.

References

Arber, Edward, ed. 1875–1894. *A Transcript of the Registers of the Company of Stationers 1554–1640 AD.* 5 vols. London and Birmingham: privately printed.

Byrd, William. 1588. *Psalmes, sonets, & songs of sadnes and pietie.* London: Thomas East.

Byrd, William, and Thomas Tallis. 1575. *Cantiones, quae ab argumento sacrae vocantur.* London: Thomas Vautrollier.

Clegg, Cyndia Susan. 1997. *Press Censorship in Elizabethan England.* Cambridge: Cambridge University Press.

Collmann, Herbert L., ed. 1912. *Ballads and Broadsides Chiefly of the Elizabethan Period and Printed in Black-Letter.* Oxford: Roxburghe Club.

Craig, John. 2004. "Jewel, John (1522–1571)." In *Oxford Dictionary of National Biography*, edited by H. C. G. Matthew and Brian Harrison. Oxford: Oxford University Press. Online ed., edited by Lawrence Goldman, January 2008. http://www.oxforddnb.com/view/article/14810.

Doleman, R. [pseud.]. 1594 [1595]. *A Conference about the Next Succession to the Crown of Ingland.* Imprinted at N. [i.e., Antwerp: By A. Conincx].

Elderton, William. 1571. *An epytaphe vppon the death of the right reuerend and learned father in God I. Iuell.* London: Thomas Colwell.

Elderton, William. 1572. *A balad intituled, the dekaye of the Duke.* [London]: Thomas Colwell.

Elderton, William. 1579. *A newe Ballade, declaryng the daungerons [sic] shootynge of the Gunne at the Courte.* London: Edward White.

Elderton, William. 1581. *A new Ballad, declaring the great Treason conspired against the young King of Scots, and how one Andrew Browne an Englishman, which was the Kings Chamberlaine, prevented the same.* London: Yarathe James.

Goldring, Elizabeth. 2004. "Elderton, William (d. in or before 1592)." In *Oxford Dictionary of National Biography*, online ed., edited by Lawrence Goldman. Oxford: Oxford University Press. http://www.oxforddnb.com/view/article/8614 (accessed December 26, 2010).

Graves, Michael A. R. 2004. "Howard, Thomas, Fourth Duke of Norfolk (1538–1572)." In *Oxford Dictionary of National Biography*, edited by H. C. G. Matthew and Brian Harrison. Oxford: Oxford University Press. Online ed., edited by Lawrence Goldman, January 2008. http://www.oxforddnb.com/view/article/13941 (accessed December 27, 2010).

Greg, W. W. 1944. "Entrance, Licence and Publication." *The Library*, 4th ser., 25: 1–22.

Hammer, Paul E. J. 1999. *The Polarisation of Elizabethan Politics: The Political Career of Robert Devereux, 2nd Earl of Essex, 1585–1597.* Cambridge: Cambridge University Press.

Kerman, Joseph. 1962. *The Elizabethan Madrigal: A Comparative Study.* Studies and Documents, no. 4. New York: American Musicological Society.

Kerman, Joseph. 2000. "Music and Politics: The Case of William Byrd (1540–1623)." *Proceedings of the American Philosophical Society* 144, no. 3: 275–287.

Kilroy, Gerard. 2005. *Edmund Campion: Memory and Transcription.* Aldershot, U.K.: Ashgate.

Livingston, Carole Rose. 1991. *British Broadside Ballads of the Sixteenth Century: A Catalogue of the Extant Sheets and an Essay.* New York: Garland.

Lee, Maurice Jr. 1956. "The Fall of the Regent Morton: A Problem in Satellite Diplomacy." *Journal of Modern History* 28, no. 2: 111–129.

Lock, Julian. 2004. "Story, John (1503/4?–1571)." In *Oxford Dictionary of National Biography*, edited by H. C. G. Matthew and Brian Harrison. Oxford: Oxford University Press. Online ed., edited by Lawrence Goldman, January 2008. http://www.oxforddnb.com/view/article/26598 (accessed December 27, 2010).

MacCaffrey, Wallace. 1993. *Elizabeth I*. London: Edward Arnold.

Miola, Robert S., ed. 2007. *Early Modern Catholicism: An Anthology of Primary Sources*. Oxford: Oxford University Press.

Monson, Craig. 1997. "Byrd, the Catholics and the Motet: The Hearing Reopened." In *Hearing the Motet: Essays on the Motet of the Middle Ages and the Renaissance*, ed. Dolores Pesce, 348–374. New York and Oxford: Oxford University Press.

Munday, Anthony. 1582. *A breefe aunswer made vnto two seditious pamphlets*. London: [John Charlewood] for Edward White.

Mundy, John. 1594. *Songs and Psalmes composed into 3.4. and 5. parts*. London: Thomas Est [East].

Patterson, Annabel M. 1984. *Censorship and Interpretation: The Conditions of Writing and Reading in Early Modern England, with a New Introduction*. Madison: University of Wisconsin Press.

Pollitt, Ronald. 1983. "The Abduction of Dr John Story and the Evolution of Elizabethan Intelligence Operations." *Sixteenth Century Journal* 14, no. 2: 131–156.

Read, Conyers. 1933. "Queen Elizabeth's Seizure of the Duke of Alva's Pay-Ships." *Journal of Modern History* 5, no. 4: 443–464.

Rollins, Hyder E. 1920. "William Elderton: Elizabethan Actor and Ballad-Writer." *Studies in Philology* 17, no. 2: 199–245.

Ruff, Lillian, and Arnold Wilson. 1969. "The Madrigal, the Lute Song and Elizabethan Politics." *Past and Present* 44: 3–51.

Shagan, Ethan. 2010. "Beyond Good and Evil: Thinking with Moderates in Early Modern England." *Journal of British Studies* 49, no. 3: 488–513.

Siebert, Fredrick S. 1965. *Freedom of the Press in England, 1476–1776: The Rise and Decline of Government Control*. Urbana: University of Illinois Press.

Smith, Jeremy L. 2003. *Thomas East and Music Publishing in Renaissance England*. New York: Oxford University Press.

Smith, Jeremy L. 2007. "William Byrd's Fall from Grace and his First Solo Publication of 1588: A Shostakovian 'Response to Just Criticism?'" *Music & Politics* 1, no. 1: 1–29. www.music.ucsb.edu/projects/musicandpolitics/archive/2007-1/smith.html (accessed 27 December 2010).

Smith, Jeremy L. 2008. "'Turning a New leaf': William Byrd, the East Music-Publishing Firm and the Jacobean Succession." In *Music and the Book Trade, from the Sixteenth to the Twentieth Centuries*, ed. Robin Myers, Michael Harris, and Giles Mandebrote, 25–43. London: Oak Knoll.

Smith, Jeremy L. 2010. "'Unlawful Song': Byrd, the Babington Plot and the Paget Choir." *Early Music* 38, no. 4: 1–13.

Soman, Alfred. 1976. "Press, Pulpit and Censorship in France before Richelieu." *Proceedings, American Philosophical Society* 120, no. 6: 439–463.

Stow, John. 1580. *The chronicles of England from Brute vnto this present yeare of Christ. 1580.* London: [Henry Bynneman for] Ralphe Newberie.

Tichborne, Chidiok [and Thomas Kyd or Thomas Knell]. 1586. *Verses of prayse and ioye written vpon her Maiesties preseruation. Whereunto is annexed Tychbornes lamentation, written in the towre with his own hand, and an aunswere to the same.* London: John Wolfe.

Weston, William. 1955. *The Autobiography of an Elizabethan.* Translated by Philip Caraman. London: Longmans.

CHAPTER 4

THE SOUNDS OF INDIGENOUS ANCESTORS

Music, Corporality, and Memory in the Jesuit Missions of Colonial SouthAmerica

GUILLERMO WILDE
TRANSLATED BY JESSICA POWELL

IN the final scene of the film *The Mission* a group of indigenous children are seen combing through the ruins of a destroyed village. They pull an abandoned violin from the remains, a symbol of the bygone musical splendor of the missions, and set off in a canoe, disappearing down a serene river. These images eloquently convey some of the predominant ideas about the place of European music in the lives of South American indigenous peoples, a theme widely discussed in literature from the eighteenth century to the present day. According to the Jesuit priests, music was a powerful instrument of conversion, capable of seducing indigenous peoples into adopting Christian ways of life, transforming them into "meek lambs."

In various colonial-era chronicles examples of mission art are compared to the best European art of the time, which led to the perception of evangelization as a fertile encounter between homogenous cultures: on the one hand, a handful of priests determined to bring "European culture" to the jungle; on the other, an indigenous population disposed to docilely accept the splendorous Catholic liturgy. In the twentieth century, this idealized image of evangelization was crystallized on an artistic level through the creation of a unique style, the "colonial baroque," conceived as a visible and audible result of the symbiosis between European and Amerindian cultures. In parallel fashion, new theories about "indigenous agency" have attempted to recognize the originality of the baroque style in indigenous creations *sui generis*, identifying "works" and "original creators" in local archives. Nevertheless, recent studies demonstrate that the musical ambit that characterized the missions was open, flexible, plural, and fluid, as well as tied to a functionality less aesthetic than religious in which individuality tended to dissolve into anonymity. Such interpretations have generally ignored the political and cosmological tensions involved in the evangelization process, many of which were directly expressed on the auditory and visual plane (Waisman 1998; Wilde 2007).

Upon their arrival in the sixteenth century, the Jesuits immediately discovered the existence, within the indigenous cultures, of a relationship between musical practices and religious traditions that would make their project of "conversion of souls" impossible. This led them to develop a program whose objective was to impose sonorities upon the Indians that would better correspond to the foundations of Christian civilization while suppressing and adapting any indigenous musical manifestations that were contrary to it. The urban planning structure of the mission imposed a hierarchical and rational spatial and temporal order in which music and sound were fundamental elements. This order defined an official sonority, strictly controlled by the priests, in which, increasingly, formal aspects related to the church and the liturgy predominated over more profane elements linked to the "dangerous" use of the body in festivals. The indigenous people, for their part, either continued with their own sonorous practices in secret or, with the passing of the generations, forgot or assigned them new meanings that allowed them to preserve a space of relative autonomy within the mission.

In this chapter, I intend to analyze the imposition of European music and the censure of traditional indigenous musical traditions as components of a larger project of political and cultural domination that, although culminating in the clear supremacy of the dominant canons, was not completely unilateral. I suggest that both censure and the mechanisms of adaptation employed by the Jesuits in various regions of South America were intended to sever the link between musical expression and corporality that had characterized preexisting native rituals. Music or, more broadly, sound, together with dance and movement, constituted the foundation of personal and collective identity in these societies, as well as of their notions of space and temporality. This complex, which we could characterize as the "erotic dimension" of sound, steadily lost ground with the establishment of a new sonorous order, characterized by regularity, restraint, and hierarchy—that is, stripped of any corporal or sensual connotation.

The first part of the chapter analyzes the characteristics of the music imposed in the missions, highlighting the devices the Jesuits employed to distribute sound spatially and to construct a characteristic tempo for the mission. The second part analyzes the available information about indigenous music at the moment of the missionaries' arrival, emphasizing the role that sound played in the construction of an indigenous subjectivity. The third, and final, part analyzes the significance and persistence of indigenous musical traditions within the mission context.

Order, Sound, and Civility

The Jesuits were engaged in intense missionary activity in various regions of South America beginning in the second half of the sixteenth century. Although their evangelization efforts came much later than those of other religious orders, they were carried out with the zeal of the post–Council of Trent period and, in particular, of the Third Council of Lima, in which the Jesuit church played a crucial role. The Jesuits created the first mission towns, also known as "reducciones," at the beginning of the seventeenth century among the Guaraní of colonial Paraguay and, in the last decades of the same century, in the Chiquitos and Mojos regions. Several years earlier they had developed mission programs in Brazil and Peru with the intent of expanding toward the "border" zones. Despite great cultural and linguistic differences among the integrated native societies and the large geographical distances that separated them, the mission teams obeyed a common political and urban-development plan and, as recent studies demonstrate, also employed many shared musical characteristics, at least during certain time periods. This fact is explained by the high degree of centralization and hierarchy maintained by the Jesuit administration in all of their affairs and areas of influence, which allowed them to maintain strict control over the activities being carried out in distant regions.

The Jesuits were expelled from America in 1767, but even so, thousands of indigenous peoples continued to live in the more than fifty mission towns that had been created in various regions. These towns engendered a true process of "ethnogenesis," that is, the formation of new ethnic groups that, even while they obeyed, in many respects, the Hispanic Civil Canon, were a direct result of missionary activity and of a long process of adaptation and negotiation among priests and indigenous leaders. Populations from quite diverse geographical areas and, typically, speakers of different languages, were congregated and mixed together in "reduction villages," where they became accustomed to dominant political, economic, and linguistic systems and, no less importantly, to common visual and sonorous standards. In this way, a "mission culture" gradually took shape, in which certain figures, such as the indigenous elite (which included musicians), played the crucial role of translators and mediators (Block 1994).[1] This situation raises several questions, which this chapter will attempt to answer: What role did music play in the process of the creation and consolidation of the missions? What was the attitude of the Indians toward European music? What happened to native musical traditions? Were the Indians capable of composing their own works? What instruments did they learn to play? What happened after the Jesuits were expelled?

Speaking generally, the attitude of the Jesuit Church toward musical practices was marked by a series of contradictions. From the time of its founding, the order had prohibited certain musical activities, such as sung masses and the chanting of the choir during the canonical hours. This inclination had both practical and ideological explanations. On the one hand, the apostolic character of the order was in conflict with the special dedication and cloistering that choral activity required. On the other hand, music invited ambiguity, as it both allowed for the elevation of the soul toward God and inspired dangerous emotional states that were to be avoided. The Jesuit pedagogical and spiritual system was based on a rationalist equation, and the practice of spiritual exercises had, specifically, the aim of purifying and elevating the senses, allowing the brothers to discern the goodness or wickedness of acts and thoughts (Kennedy 2005).

After a series of debates carried out within congregations, councils, and synods, the Jesuits relaxed their initial attitude toward music, particularly with regard to chanting.

Especially in the period of the Counter-Reformation, music was transformed into an ally of evangelization, and moving forward, the Jesuits discovered that music could be used as a highly effective evangelical tool. It was in the missions, among the Indians, that the Jesuits began to perceive the efficacy of musical practice in their catechistic and pedagogical work. This efficacy was linked to the creation of a civil order, a rationality that, of necessity, stood in radical opposition to the jungle, that wild space par excellence, in which untamed noises and sounds predominated.

Indeed, the Jesuits' principal efforts went toward creating a civic order among the indigenous peoples that would radically change the way these populations had previously been living in the jungle. The Jesuits typically illustrated the contrast between the time of "heathenism" and the new Christian era, ushered in through conversion, in terms of sonorous metaphors. As one Jesuit wrote, for example: "Whereas before one would hear the din of the howling barbarians," the Jesuits managed to introduce "hymns to God and the Saints." To this end, they created villages with structures based upon a rational and hierarchical urban plan that facilitated the implementation of their religious, political, and musical projects. The church, cemetery, workshops, and priests' residence were located on one side of the village plaza. On the other three sides of the plaza were the Indians' houses, lined up uniformly, one beside the other. A large proportion of the economic activity (crops and cattle raising) took place outside of the villages. Festive demonstrations, which occasionally called together all residents of the village, were carried out in the enormous central plaza.

This principle of urban planning—in which the church and the large central plaza occupied the most prominent place—influenced the development of musical and ceremonial activities. As the Jesuit Peramás explained, in the church, the music was "devout and solemn," avoiding any type of profane melody, even when it was of peninsular origin (Peramás [1791] 1946). The same author described how the mass was sung each morning, accompanied by an organ and other instruments. In the afternoons, the rosary was recited, and, in honor of the Holy Sacrament and the Virgin, a "motet . . . to which the entire village responded" was sung. The conclusion was the Prayer of Contrition. The daily routine was strict regarding these activities, and many of the chronicles of the eighteenth century describe the routine in a more or less uniform fashion. Even a document that dates from after the Jesuits were expelled relates that the Indians maintained the habit of attending daily mass, their work, and the recital of the rosary when they were called at regular intervals throughout the day by the sound of the bells, drums, and voice of the town crier (Doblas [1785] 1836).

Festivities featuring less formal musical expressions tended to unfold in the open spaces outside the church. Companies of soldiers that formed in the villages publically displayed their flags and insignias, accompanied by the sounds of bugles and drums. Drummers and flutists (or fife players) were highly regarded by the Indians, and each village could boast several of them. The Jesuit Anton Sepp provides testimonies from the end of the seventeenth century that refer to the use of these instruments in order to encourage the Indians to participate in collective labors:

> I set about thinking of ways to incite my lazy Indians to work: since they particularly enjoy the drums and fifes, I order that they always be played when I charge them with a difficult task. If, for example, a thick, heavy and particularly tall beam must be raised in the church, my people shall set to work to the festive sounds of their favorite instruments. And if I want the Indians to maintain good humor while working, there is no better method than to sound the drums and fifes all day long. When the bricks are taken from the oven, the drums precede the file of workers; when they go into the countryside to pull weeds, three musicians march at the head of the line, playing their fifes; when they plant the cotton or the corn, kidney beans or garbanzos, they go off to work and return to their homes to the sound of drums and fifes. Even the women have their little drummer-girl.
>
> (Sepp [1709] 1973, 222)

European sonorities were predominant in the most central areas of the village. The Jesuit Joseph Cardiel makes reference to groups, formed in each village, of up to forty musicians, including violins, bassoons, shawms, harps, organs, and clarinets in addition to the singers. The same priest notes that everything was done in the manner of the Spanish cathedrals, adding that among the Indians there were no master musicians who knew how to compose music, so they were content to read and sing what was already written without augmenting or embellishing the melodies in any way, since "they were not able to comprehend anything more" (Cardiel [1747] 1919, 558). This opinion on the Indians' lack of creativity agrees with one expressed a century before by the aforementioned Jesuit, Sepp:

> Our Indians, in truth, have no knack for anything that is invisible or that doesn't appear plainly before our eyes, that is, for the spiritual and the abstract, but they are quite skilled in all mechanical arts: like monkeys, they imitate everything they see, and persist in doing so despite one's patience, magnanimity or indefatigable spirit. Whatever the Paraguayan Indian takes on, he brings to a happy conclusion, and in doing so, does not require a teacher; he must simply have an example always present that he may follow.
>
> (Sepp [1709] 1973, 270)

It should be noted that the comparison of mission music with that practiced in Europe during the same epoch has, in general, tended to confirm this lack of originality and the paucity of native expressions or, in the best of cases, the simplified character that these acquired in the South American territories. In other paragraphs, Sepp highlights the Indians' skill as performers and makers of instruments, and he affirms that, when he arrived in that country, they had a variety of dances, although he gives no precise details about them: "They also have a natural skill for dancing, as they are quite agile and flexible and I do not doubt that they would be greatly honored in any European royal court were they to perform their Indian dances that no one over there has ever seen" (Sepp [1714] 1974, 181).

It is clear from these writings that the appreciation expressed for any limited indigenous abilities for musical creation should be taken cautiously, as they are subject to extreme ethnocentric prejudices. Nevertheless, Sepp is sufficiently convincing in his assertion that the Indians were highly receptive to European sounds, quickly picking up the musical instruments brought over from Europe. Sources indicate that the incorporation of local elements, resulting from the transactions and negotiations between ancient and new musical traditions, were manifest in the realm of *performance* or musical practice, as opposed to in composition. What was the indigenous attitude toward European musical genres and sonorities at different points in time? Was it uniform? What parameters defined its incorporation? Did some type of cultural, psychological, or political motivation determine the selection and preference of some forms in particular? What factors or causes contributed to the continuity of its usage? Most of these questions remain unanswered, and available information has, to date, not allowed for a detailed reconstruction of the characteristics of the music of the missions over a protracted period of time.

Nevertheless, there are some indications that the indigenous peoples were not passive subjects of a hegemonic process. The production and diffusion of various musical genres appeared to be an effective tool in the formation of new indigenous identities, linked directly to religious activity. Such is the case of the "congregations" or brotherhoods (*hermandades* or *cofradías*) formed in various villages in honor of the Virgin Mary. These congregations had a specific repertoire that formed an important part of the Marian liturgy sung in different languages, both in the Guaraní and Chiquitano regions (Waisman 1992). Adults of both sexes, carefully selected on the basis of their "good behavior," were admitted into these associations. Their ceremonies were accompanied by the sounds of shawms and trumpets, and each year on their dedication day they played "solemn vespers" and masses accompanied by music and dance (Cardiel [1770] 1913, 563).

Each space, whether solemn or profane, had its corresponding and differentiated sonorous configurations, strictly controlled by the Jesuits. It should be noted that the Society of Jesus, perhaps more than any other religious order, had an internal structure based upon a strict hierarchy of offices with well-established functions. The limits to what was permitted and what was prohibited were determined by a meticulous discipline based upon the control of one's body and feelings, and upon the criteria of prudence and restraint. As part of this dynamic, the church dictated instructions and created rulebooks intended to regulate every aspect of daily life in the villages. The rules prescribed everything from the formal organization of time based on the liturgical calendar and the utilization of space, to the proper manner of writing, speaking, eating, and, of course, making music.

One of these rulebooks provides abundant information about the restrictions imposed on musical practices. One order issued by the Visiting Father prohibited the playing of shawms and drums while eating in the refectory, a place in which only certain stringed instruments were permitted to play for brief periods. On occasions when priests would visit from other villages, receiving them with the clamor of trumpets, *cajas* (snare drums), shawms, dances, games, flags, or any type of military display was forbidden, as these types of receptions were reserved for bishops, governors, and other high-ranking authorities. Also prohibited was any sort of ostentatious dress as well as the use of fireworks. Skits and plays were also to be avoided, especially where women were present. These types of performances, along with certain dances, were only permitted in the patio of the Jesuit school but not in the plaza, and they were especially forbidden at night.

Another rule stipulated that musicians from other villages not be invited to festivals. A maximum of three singers with good voices could be brought in if the village hosting the festival lacked them. Villages were forbidden to have more than forty singers, and smaller villages were urged to reduce this number even further. We should remember that musicians formed part of the indigenous elite of the missions and were particularly close to the Jesuit priests' spheres of action. This status provided them with a certain margin of freedom in terms of daily obligations within the village, and the rules were enforced less strictly with them than with the rest of the population. This latitude appears to have given rise, especially among the congregants and the singers, to some "scandals," the perpetrators of which were ordered by the precepts to be punished through expulsion from the congregation or the chapel.

With the goal of avoiding disorder, spaces dedicated to purely festive events were increasingly restricted in the missions. Saints' feast days were the only festive occasions authorized by the church's superiors during the eighteenth century, and even these festivals were limited to a certain number of dances, since these tended to cause "scandals" among the Indians. As one of the Jesuits' orders nervously noted:

> Now, once again, an offshoot of the [dance] of the *matachines* has resurfaced, which they call *botargas*, in which they go upside down, one on top of the other: all of these and similar dances depart from the doctrines . . . . Let the dances we see be serious and clean, and may they not offend our modesty.[2]

One paragraph stipulates that neither women, be they juveniles or adults, "nor men dressed in women's clothing" be permitted to attend the dances. Apparently, during the skits, it was common for male Indians to appear "dressed as Indian women," which was considered highly "indecent" by the Jesuits. Wigs and hairpieces were to be sold or burned immediately.

The continual tightening of control over the realms of the festive and the profane is exemplified by the adaptation to the mission context of a Hispanic genre such as the *villancico*. The *villancico*, despite the fact that the chronicles of the period tend to elide it, was actually introduced early on in the missions. As is well known, *villancicos* were compositions of Hispanic origin that included profane elements and were composed by the chapel *maestro* to be sung during feast days such as Christmas, Corpus Christi, and the day of the patron saint, among others. These compositions, sung during specific times, tended to blur the line between the sacred and the profane. According to recent research, what made the mission *villancicos* unique was that they were used for purposes of evangelization, eliminating all profane elements from the indigenous religious traditions and creating a strict separation between merriment and worship. From a formal perspective, the *villancicos* were assimilated into motets sung by multiple, uniformly solemn, voices. Although the songs were happy and had celebratory elements, the lyrics avoided any hint of the profane. In this way, the *villancico* sung by the indigenous converts was transformed into an eminently religious product, in which all traces of profane elements were excluded. This ultimately had the effect of severing the preexisting link between sound and corporality (Illari 2005).[3]

What role did this link play in indigenous religious traditions? Did the domination of the solemn Christian liturgical tradition herald the complete suppression of all performances that involved the use of the body? In the sections that follow, I will explore some elements of the indigenous music traditions encountered by the Jesuits and discuss the ways in which some of these were readapted to the mission context.

Mission Style

To date, we still do not have a complete general history of musical practices within the missions. Eighteenth-century chronicles offer an overly broad and uniform picture that fails to encompass the Reductions as a whole. More precise, yet sparse, details exist for the seventeenth century, which indicate that the missions were, as yet, quite far from establishing a "musical state," such as those described by chroniclers from later periods. Local documentation, which is coming increasingly to light, reveals a much more complex and nuanced reality. We may infer from recently discovered documents that it was common practice, within the mission context, to adapt available resources for use in musical practices. Indigenous musicians did not possess uniform skills, and only some of the villages distinguished themselves musically, depending to great extent upon the individual priests that were in charge of them. In general, there existed a basic repertory, known by the majority of indigenous musicians, which made it possible to address the common needs of all of the villages. Among the Jesuits, generally speaking, the practical aspects of music were valued above artistic mastery. In other words, unlike those figures consecrated by the official history of mission music (Jean Vaisseau, Louis Berger, Sepp, Domenico Zipoli, Martin Schmid, Julian Knogler, and others), they tended to rely on a "basic didactic musical knowledge" while never becoming "experts." While it is likely that the so-called experts indicate general tendencies, in truth, it was the circulation of practical knowledge that was of primary importance (Illari 2006).

One likely exception to this quotidian reality were the celebrations that were occasionally held to commemorate noteworthy events, such as visits from bishops and governors, saints' days, Holy Week, and Corpus Christi, among others. These celebrations frequently required the use of great economic resources as well as the mobilization of people from various villages. In this regard, one of the most interesting descriptions we have encountered details the festivities held to celebrate the centennial of the Society of Jesus held in the Guaraní Reductions in 1649, a year that coincides with the overthrow of the Portuguese troops who had attempted to invade the villages in order to capture indigenous slaves. An annual letter from this period relates that in San Francisco de Javier they celebrated a solemn vespers in which priests invited from other villages participated, choirs sang, the Ave Maria was played, harquebuses were fired, and, alternating from the four corners of the plaza, the sound of bells and shawms rang out. The celebration continued the following morning with more bells, shawms, and harquebuses, followed by the celebration of the mass. In the village of Concepción, they took advantage of the occasion in order to pass the baton of captain of the Reduction on to the chief, Don Alonso Nienguirú, whose father had died. Afterwards they held "a very solemn procession through the plaza, in which one group after another held aloft up to six hundred arches, decorated with fragrant branches and a variety of other natural local items" (*Cartas Anuas* [1641–1643] 1996, 139). Particularly noteworthy were the celebrations carried out in the village of San Ignacio, in which "choir groups" from all of the Reductions of the region came together and sang for the solemn vespers. Before holding mass, companies of ostentatiously attired soldiers were formed to put on showy displays. The procession passed by four altars decorated with motifs and figures from the Old Testament—in this case, a scene of Abraham preparing to sacrifice his son, Isaac. The letter adds that the Indians in San Ignacio performed various dances, among them, an ingenious one with "letters on shields that, through various loops and encounters, came together to spell out the name of San Ignacio." In the aforementioned villages, they took advantage of the festivities to present plays about the battle against the Portuguese in which numerous lantern-lit canoes set out upon the river at night. They also recited poems and songs in multiple languages.

These descriptions point to the well-known contrast between the daily liturgical routine, characterized by the homogeneity of its musical practices, and festive occasions, associated with enormous scenographic displays. In neither case do we see the presence of indigenous musical elements, and the canon was defined by practices brought by the European Jesuits on successive trips to South America. In fact, the stages of mission music recognized by musicology generally coincide with the names of specific Jesuits. The period initiated by the Tyrolean Sepp, who introduced new styles from central Europe, is considered particularly relevant (Lange 1986; Nawrot 2000; Herczog 2001). Before Sepp's arrival, Hispanic musical trends predominated. As Sepp himself writes, the Indians knew nothing of organ music, *basso continuo*, time or measure, the different types of treble, minor steps of notes, music sung in multiple voices, or the poly-choral tradition, since these things were also not known in the Iberian musical traditions in which their teachers had been trained. As Sepp explained, "Not a single mass and nary a psalm had *basso continuo*, despite the fact that it constitutes their essential foundation." According to Sepp, the first Jesuits that taught the Indians to sing were the Dutch priests; after which, he writes, "a Spanish priest arrived" who promoted music and composed masses, vespers, offertories, and litanies" (Sepp [1696] 1971, 203).

In light of existing information, to attempt to determine the "baroque-ness" of mission art based upon its authors, repertories, and original works would only lead to a dead-end that would render impossible any understanding of the socio-cultural reality in question. On the other hand, the definition of a "Jesuit baroque style" fails to encompass the multiplicity of national trends and adaptations that were gestating in Europe during any single epoch. In any event, if we consider the cannon established in Italy toward the end of the seventeenth century, it would be difficult to label the art of the missions by the same designation. The great majority of the missionaries that arrived in South America were unfamiliar with "the style," either because they had not completed their training or because they favored the use of multiple resources that would allow them to better adapt to local situations and pastoral necessities. To this we should add the many material and technical limitations that the Jesuits confronted in their interactions with the Indigenous peoples, whose visual and musical traditions were radically different from their own.

The Erotic Dimensions of Sound

In 1626 three Jesuits were assassinated in the Tape region by a group of Indians led by the religious leader Ñeezú. In later testimonies, some witnesses recounted that one of the rebels had ordered the capture of one of the Jesuits with the cry, "We will kill this priest: we will have only our chief, Ñeezú. In our land, you will hear the sound of our *calabazos* and *tacuaras*" (Blanco 1929, 447–452). Ñeezú had warned the rebels that the Jesuits had forced them to hide these musical instruments and wanted to take their women away from them. During the most important of Guaraní religious rituals, *calabazos* (maracas, gourd rattles) and *tacuaras* (stamping tubes) were used by men and women, respectively. Their sounds were associated with the mythical ancestors and, more broadly, with the native conception of the "being" (*teko*), whose most ideal expression was represented by the shamanic pair (the religious leader and his wife). The reference to these native instruments is highly significant within the context of native resistance to evangelization. Other interpretations suggest that, within the indigenous mindset, the playing of these instruments was charged with sexual symbolism and was linked to the regeneration of the ancient "being." In their rituals, the sound of these instruments was combined with songs and dances in which men and women played symmetrical roles. The Jesuits understood immediately that the conception of the cosmos that served as the basis of these musical practices constituted a very real threat to the installation of the mission regime, since that conception had room only for their principal foes, the indigenous "sorcerers."

The Jesuits were also disquieted by the intimate link that this music proposed between corporality and women, whose roles in these rituals always cast them as the instigators of sexual promiscuity and, therefore, of disorder and disobedience. Descriptions by Jesuits from different regions of mission activity always highlight the ambiguous and promiscuous character of the indigenous rituals performed by local chiefs, for which a large number of people congregated (Lozano [1754] 1874, 3:213–214). Among some indigenous groups, drunkenness was a central element of the celebrations and banquets. One

Jesuit remarked that the Guaraní got up every morning in order to start drinking and that their drunken revelries lasted several days. They would fill their gourds with *chicha* or *guarapo*, fermented drinks made from corn, carob beans, or wild honey. According to Cardiel, the natives ate the enemies they captured and then cleaned out their skulls in order to use them as vessels from which to drink *chicha*.

The drunken revels are most clearly documented among the Indians of Chaco, groups of hunter-gatherers that spoke various languages within the Guaycurú family, and among whom the Jesuit missionaries were active during the eighteenth century. During these festivities, the sonorous elements appear to be completely integrated into the collective celebrations, which functioned to commemorate the arrival of carob bean season, the collection of wild honey, the dissolution of alliances, or the deposition of a leader or to celebrate military victories, female initiation rites, and matrimonial unions. According to the Jesuit priest Lozano, the Guaycurúes carried out their drinking sprees "to the sound of flutes, fifes, drums, and hollow gourds with stones inside them, ordinary instruments used by the sorcerers to worship and invoke the devil" (Lozano [1733] 1941, 5).

The use of gourds along with other native instruments is amply documented in Jesuit records from various regions. In Chaco, they were used for all types of ceremonies, from small receptions, to healing sessions, to funerals. The Jesuit priest Sánchez Labrador writes that the Indians' method of healing consists of "singing, shaking the gourd, and sucking on various parts of the sick person." Along with the gourd, which they called *Lotani*, the Guaycurúes used a type of drum, made from a clay pot filled with water and covered with "deer hide." During funeral ceremonies, an old woman would beat the drum with a stick throughout the entire night "and would sing to the deceased, not a sad song, but rather a happy and lively one." Afterward she would take up the gourd and play it while singing and performing a waggling dancing in front of the deceased (Furlong 1953; see also Charleboix [1757] 1915, 138). On one occasion, Sánchez Labrador asked the Indians if the monotony of that instrument bothered them, and they responded that it did not, clarifying that they were "their own bells." Resigned, the Jesuit determined to accustom himself to sleeping with such a "disagreeable noise" (Sánchez Labrador [1767] 1910, 36–37).

Beyond the notable differences among the aforementioned groups, a series of common traits stand out in the sonorous expressions we have discussed. The first of these is that the instruments used were frequently thought to possess a degree of agency that could dispose them to being used as symbols of the power of native leaders or being treated as though they were people. According to some narratives, among the Tupi-Guaraní, instruments such as maracas were considered to be "oracles" with whom it was possible to communicate; in other instances, special powers capable of regenerating time were attributed to them. The musical instrument was frequently inseparable from its bearer, who transmitted subjective qualities to it. One story from the Guaraní region makes reference to a "sorcerer" who arrived at a Reduction accompanied by his concubine. He appeared before the public covered by a feathered cape and playing "castanets" made from goats' skulls. As he danced, he said he was the true master of death, women, and cornfields and that he could destroy and recreate the world anew with his breath (Becker 1992, 49).[4] Other sources from the period link the sonorous experience to the presence of beings beyond the sphere of human control, with whom it was possible to communicate by means of certain chants, or whose voices were clearly recognizable in "natural" sounds such as the echo of thunder.

Another feature from the written sources that is worth noting is that sonorous expressions, both instrumental and vocal, were inseparable from dance and, therefore, necessitated the use of the body. As confirmed in the majority of ethno-historical and ethnographic literature, this feature was widespread in the Amerindian religious traditions of South America. Sonorous and corporeal practices, as components of ritual, play a role in the formation of native subjectivity. In these societies, the notion of the person (the being) is intimately linked to the creation of the body, which, in turn, gives rise to the observation of a series of activities to keep the body healthy. Song and dance, like body ornamentation and diet, are some of these activities. Humans, it is thought, must sing and dance in order to remember the time of the gods and to assure the reproduction of present time. The dimension of pleasure implied by these practices does not recognize a separation between the body and the mind, nor does it distinguish between a sacred sphere and a profane one. In their most intense moments, the collective native celebrations exacerbated social, political, and sexual ambiguity, an attribute that could be associated with the regenerative character of a ritual in its liminary phase, as defined by Victor Turner (1995). It should be noted that in these practices the feminine element plays a fundamental role.

The Jesuits went to great lengths to break down the underlying basis of native performances, introducing mechanisms of control designed either to eliminate certain sonorities from the natives' sonorous landscape or to divorce them from any meaning linked to traditional religions and impose upon them a solemn character linked to the Christian liturgy. At the same time, they developed mechanisms meant to regiment the use of the body, clearly separating the roles of men and women into a configuration in which the latter remained marginalized from socially and politically relevant practices.

The chronicles from the period provide us with various examples of how this policy of *gender segregation* was carried out. Upon marrying, a woman went to live in her husband's father's home until she learned how to keep house. Women were not permitted to hold official posts in the administration of the villages, and their functions were limited to the domestic realm. From girlhood, they were taught to spin, weave, and sew, while the boys were taught to read and write. Musicians by trade were exclusively men, as were the dancers.[5] Each village had a special area for unmarried women and widows called the *cotiguazú*, from which they were forbidden to leave without supervision. This space could also house women who had committed a crime, and even these were obliged to attend daily masses and the recital of the rosary, accompanied by a warden of the same sex (Cardiel [1747] 1919, 543).

Relations between men and women were strictly controlled, in both public and private spaces. On Sundays, the population gathered in the village plaza. When the church opened, men and women entered by separate doors. Once inside, the sexes remained separate during the service, and were strictly controlled by their respective guardians (Cardiel [1770] 1913).[6] Sexual relations were monitored and, eventually, overseen by the priests, with the aim of maintaining monogamous marriages, the demographic growth of the villages, and proper sexual customs. An interesting excerpt, written by a Spanish functionary some years after the expulsion of the Jesuits, illustrates the extent to which the sex lives of the Indians were controlled, as well as the role sound played in that control:

> Having noticed that the drums were played at various points during the night, and particularly at dawn, curiosity moved me to inquire as to what purpose the drumbeat served. [The Indians] told me that the Jesuits, familiar with the lazy temperament of the Indians who, exhausted after working all day..., arrive home, eat dinner, and then sleep until morning, made them arise at dawn to go to church, and from there, go on to work. Because of this, the husbands were not spending much time with their wives, and the population was diminishing. And so, they decided that, at certain hours of the night, they would remind them, so that they would fulfill their obligations as married people.
>
> (Doblas [1785] 1836: 39)

Readaptation, Duplicity, and Hybridization

The "capture of the sacred," as defined by Christian Duverger (1993) in the Mesoamerican context, consists of adapting the Christian message to local populations. With a pragmatic spirit, the Jesuits took this premise to its maximum expression, guided by the motto: "Indigenize Christianity." This is clearly demonstrated, for example, in the *Natural History of the Indies*, in which José Acosta dedicated a lengthy paragraph to the dances found in Peru and Mexico, known as *taquis* and *mitotes*. In reference to them, the Jesuit concludes the following: "many of these dances are performed in honor of their idols, but were not used for religious purposes, but rather, as a form of recreation and merriment for the village, and so, it is not right to take them away from the Indians, but rather, it should be ensured that no superstition be mixed in with them" (Acosta [1590] 1979, 318). These words may be interpreted as support for the conservation of native musical expressions, but only when they were stripped of their link to traditional beliefs and imbued with Christian meaning; in other words, it is a proposal for cultural adaptation. The important thing was, at first, to know how to distinguish between music that was good for the spirit and music that was bad for the spirit or, expressed another way, between music that elevated the spirit and music that was contaminated by superstition. It appears that the members of the church did not always agree on where to draw the line between the two. They debated as to whether certain native practices should be maintained or eradicated completely. One early example is the debate that began in Brazil in the sixteenth century between Bishop Sardinha and the Jesuit Manuel de Nobrega. The latter defended the Jesuits from criticism that the Europeans were using indigenous music and instruments in Christian celebrations. In other contexts, such as in Acosta's Peru, it was debated whether it was possible to separate music from the religious demonstrations with which they were associated. In this case, the central concern was less the music than the content of the sung texts that were to be used in the indoctrination of the Indians (Estenssoro Fuchs 2003).

A program of cultural adaptation was carried out in various regions with mixed results. The mission strategy consisted of incorporating local elements into the liturgy, especially in the most important celebrations on the religious calendar. The festival was the space par excellence for this type of transaction. In his chronicle, the Jesuit Charlevoix refers to the presence of natural elements in the Corpus festival: flowers, tree branches, birds of all colors tied by the feet, tigers on chains, fish in vessels of water. Charlevoix writes: "The chirping of the birds, the roaring of the lions, the bellowing of the tigers, the sound of the musicians and the singing of the choir, all are heard clearly and combine to form a unique concert" (Charlevoix [1757] 1915, 2:88).

Descriptions of the use of gourds in official celebrations exist for regions such as Chaco and Chiquitos. For example, the Jesuit Florian Paucke notes that, during a celebration honoring the arrival of a royal ensign among the Chaqueños, some women waited in the center of the plaza with "hollow gourds filled with grains of *curucús* [corn] that made noise; some held the heads of dead enemies in their hands or on pikes, and danced at the entrance and sang *victory* in their language, especially when the *Royal Ensign*, who was dressed in boots and "German-style" spurs, arrived, riding with two companions who held the standard aloft on either side of him (Paucke [1780] 1942–1944, 14). For his part, the Jesuit Julian Knogler writes that the Chiquitanos organized dances in the main plaza in which many boys participated, forming circles and playing "pan flutes, made of various tubes of different lengths that the musician plays by moving it from one side of the mouth to the other." This was dance music in which they also played "hollow gourds filled with small stones that the musician shook with his hands," while the rest sang in a chorus or hummed a wordless melody. As for the musicians, the Jesuit concluded the following:

> It would seem exhausting to dance in this way, shouting and constantly moving the body to the rhythm of that monotonous music, especially when it is very hot; nevertheless, it provides a diversion for our Indians and we tolerate it, in light of the fact that there is nothing harmful or objectionable in the pastime. Because, were there any element of this nature in that custom, it could not be a true and permanent pleasure, according to the principles of right and honest judgment.
>
> (Hoffman 1979, 119–185)

The festive character of these occasions is made clear in the above quotation. He writes of a "pastime" that brings the Indians an incomprehensible yet inoffensive pleasure.

Martin Schmid, another Jesuit active in the same region, expresses high praise for these dances and songs, from which he himself derives much happiness (Matthei and Moreno Jeria 1997, 223).

In the second half of the eighteenth century, the Jesuit Escandón provides testimony of what we may consider hybridized musical practices among the Guaraní. In one interesting letter about daily life in the mission, he describes the way in which funerals were carried out in the missions of Paraguay. The musicians and altar boys accompanied the priest, who was dressed in black, to the church, where he sang a requiem. After the body had been placed in the sepulcher, the mother, wife, and relatives of the deceased would begin with a "sort of song, so mournful and out-of-tune, that it is impossible to explain its dissonance." This song, which the Indians called *guahú*, was sung exclusively by women, and it spoke of the dead, saying, "not only what he had been, but also what it was hoped he would have become, had he not died" (Furlong 1965).

The document makes clear reference to the easy coexistence of traditional and new musical expressions in which women's positions were clearly defined, though marginalized and, most likely, misunderstood. In this case, traditional expressions are absorbed into the solemn context of the Christian funereal liturgy. Earlier documents reflect that these songs were also used in festive contexts but that the priests had progressively restricted their performance. In 1679 the Jesuit Provincial Agustín de Aragón complained that immodest songs of foreign provenance had been introduced in the Reductions in Paraguay. He asserted that, on the eve of feast days and continuing throughout most of the night, the Indians went around "the entire area with drums and flutes, singing the *guahú*, men and women all together, necessarily putting the soul at risk." He went on to prohibit these songs and flutes during said celebrations, except in front of the church, without the participation of women, and on a designated schedule (Illari 2005, 455).[7] Nevertheless, we know from later documents that these practices continued in spite of the complaints of the authorities. The Jesuit Carlos Noyelle wrote in 1684 that many errors against the holy religion were committed in the villages, and that the orders of his predecessors had not been able to prevent them. As he explains, "It is said that in our Church they sing words and play tunes that are beyond profane, even during the mass and at Lent." Noyelle goes on to say that the priests themselves applauded these transgressions, turning their backs on the altars in order to watch the dancing (Leonhardt 1924, 207).

Apparently, festive occasions were employed as privileged spaces for the expression and actualization of cultural elements as well as for the recuperation of an erotic dimension associated with the use of the body, which was generally censured within solemn spaces. This erotic dimension allowed for the expression of a certain level of freedom and pleasure, opening a space for the possible coexistence of instruments and musical forms of diverse origins.

The complicity of the priests with regard to these performances raises questions about the possible permeability of the official ideology of conversion, at least at certain moments. One bit of evidence that would seem to offer clues about this permeability is the unique iconography found in the Jesuit village of Santísima Trinidad, located in present-day Paraguay. Inside the enormous church, swaths of an astounding frieze remain, revealing a series of angels playing musical instruments. Four stand out among them, holding curious spherical instruments that look like indigenous maracas. Their body language and the pleats in their clothing suggest the movements of a dance. These figures, carved in the 1760s—that is, just a few years before the expulsion of the Jesuits— may offer clues to the native experience of the Christian liturgy that has remained obscured to us. How can we explain the presence of a symbol of the indigenous ancestors in such a late representation of mission "style?" What meaning is transmitted through the intrinsic ambiguity of those dancing angels? Is there some organizing principle or hierarchization of the musical instruments depicted in the frieze? Is it dependent on some sort of visual or ritual logic?

It is not possible to answer many of these questions. It does seem clear that the sexual, specifically genital, connotations of traditional rituals frequently alluded to in the chronicles have disappeared completely within the unique stylization of the frieze. Among the asexual figures of the angels, the only identifiably feminine figure is the Virgin Mary, represented in two opposing manners—with child and immaculate—both of which serve as a reminder that she is always a virgin and, as such, unbound by the sins of the flesh.[8]

It is difficult to know if this visual evidence points to some kind of duplicity, such as that perceived in the performance of the songs of the *guahú*; to the complete domination of the Christian liturgy over indigenous sonorities; or to something in between. What is certain is that it presents an ambiguity that is, to a certain degree, indecipherable. The Jesuits' motives for including maracas in the ritual and daily lives of the villages appear reasonable. They made it possible for indigenous religious values to be co-opted and reassigned with Christian meanings. But their inclusion also caused the Indians to think differently about the very idea of religious life in the mission, a life strictly controlled by men, and to participate in the power structure that the mission defined. The priests knew how to use the meanings they conveyed to sway political advantage in their favor. But the Indians also knew how to rework those meanings into a discourse of resistance, or, more simply, to stake out a space of autonomy.

Epilogue: After the Expulsion of the Jesuits

The creation of Jesuit missions among the indigenous peoples of South America was marked by a progressive disarticulation of the nexus between the body and sound, a link that had been a hallmark of native religious traditions. The Jesuits discovered that the erotic dimension of sound held a place for indigenous memory: the songs, sonorities, and dances served as a means to remember ancestors and to pass on knowledge and traditions. These practices also constituted modalities for the (re)production of the natives' social and political lives, at the center of which were the religious leaders. Hegemonic mechanisms were oriented toward vigilance and regulation of the use of the body, imposing a rational and hierarchical spatial and temporal regime in which sound ceased to have the function of "fabricating" the person and remembering the ancestors and, instead, was utilized in the service of the reproduction of Christian civil order. Women, whom the Jesuits identified as detrimental to the development of this new temperament, were marginalized and kept strictly separate from places of social relevance. Some traditional sonorities were incorporated into the Christian liturgy, but were stripped of any hint of sensuality.

Despite these efforts, some sources indicate that the indigenous peoples continued to perform some of the sonorous and corporal practices that had supposedly been repressed outside of official zones. The same Jesuits revealed an ambiguous attitude toward these practices, allowing them only when they were not considered to pose a risk to the stability of the mission regime. It is also likely that the priests opted to omit references to these practices in their most widely circulated documents and, in this way, kept them out of sight from foreigners.

The situation changed with the expulsion of the Jesuits in 1767. The Reductions, which until then had maintained a state of relative cultural isolation, began to incorporate external elements through increasing contact with the *criollo* population—that is, with people of mixed indigenous and black ancestry who lived out in the countryside without set borders. In the Guaraní region, the new period was characterized by an abandonment of controls, the increasing incorporation of secular elements, and the gradual decline of ceremonial activity. Many musicians and transcribers were forced to migrate to the region's more important cities, where they acquired a certain renown. Such was the case of Cristobal Pirioby, a Guaraní maestro who, shortly after marrying, abandoned his native village of San Carlos in order to set up shop in Buenos Aires. There, he changed his name to José Antonio Ortiz and established himself as a teacher of voice, violin, spinet, guitar, and harpsichord. His will made reference to various musical instruments and a collection of works of the epoch, evidence of his social position and knowledge of the repertoire (Monzón 1947).

Until the middle of the nineteenth century, mission music retained a solemn character associated with the principle religious celebrations. As late as the 1820s, the French traveler Auguste Saint Hilaire relates that, one afternoon, he saw an indigenous boy kneeling before a lantern and uttering a Guaraní prayer followed by the intonation of "a canticle in everyday language" (Saint Hilaire [1820–1821] 1939, 224). But the predominant tendency was that musical practices tended to incorporate recreational elements and were popular among the middle and lower sectors of the countryside (Susnik 1966, 104; Susnik and Chase-Sardi 1992, 164). During a visit to the villages of Chiquitos, another French traveler, Alcides D'Orbugny, describes festivals that the Indians of that region held during the 1820s. For these celebrations, they would perform dances of an "imitative character," accompanied by festive, "though repetitive," music. In one dance that he found particularly noteworthy, he observed an old man dancing and singing with a gourd full of corn in his hand, surrounded by women who imitated everything he did. Together, they advanced in lines, jumping, with their bodies leaning to one side and the other, "as though they were sowing seeds or plowing," forming expressive shapes and complaining, in their songs, of man-eating ants. At times, the women would raise their dresses, "revealing much of their bodies." The participants did everything with great naturalness and were so engrossed in their dance that they seemed to have forgotten where they were (D'Orbigny [1847] 1945, 1152–1153).

It is difficult to determine the origin and meaning of these celebrations. What is clear is that they recuperated a space for corporality that had supposedly been lost during the long period of Jesuit activity. This apparent return of the repressed may also be interpreted as an attempt by the native population to recreate an autonomous space of expression, through sound, song, and dance, that would reestablish the lost time of their ancestors.

Notes

1. In this context, the concept of "middle ground" or "culture of contact," posited by the historian Richard White, is also useful. For more about the notion of "mission ethnogenesis" see Wilde 2009.
2. Preceptos (s/a, 25) "*Matachines*" refers to a dance in which ancient warrior dances are parodied, while "*botarga*" may be translated as: "ridiculous, multi-colored clothing."
3. For a study on *villancicos* in Spain, see Laird 1997.
4. I have more thoroughly developed the historico-anthropological significance of the maraca in the Guaraní culture in Wilde 2008. On the use of musical instruments as Guaraní gender markers, see Ruiz 2008.
5. The dances: "were performed after the solemn vespers of the celebration. Each village had a dance teacher who taught the steps to a select group of children, composed exclusively of boys" (Nawrot 2000, 24).
6. In his description of the Easter celebration, Cardiel notes: "Once the priest had finished incensing the statues, the congregants joined in a procession around the plaza; on one side, the men and the missionary, carrying the Resurrected One, and, on the other side, the women, carrying the Holy Mother . . . all the while the bugles and the shawms were played with such skill it was as though they were being made to speak" (quoted in Nawrot 2000, 25).
7. Among the present-day *Kaiová*, the *guahú* is a serious song in which the men begin singing first and are joined later by the women. It is accompanied by a dance, always performed in the house of prayer, and always executed in a circular pattern. As a point of contrast, the *kotyhu* is inclusive and danced for pleasure, and may be performed anywhere. According to Chamorro: "While the *kotyhu* provokes laughter, shouts, escapades and 'disorder,' the *guahu* is capable of reminding the *Kaiová* of the saddest episodes of the myth of the Twins . . ." (Chamorro 1995, 86).
8. For an analysis of the meaning of the maracas in the frieze, see Wilde 2008. See also, Wilde 2009.

References

Acosta, José. 1979 (1590). *Historia natural y moral de las Indias*. México: Fondo de Cultura Económica.

Becker, Itala. 1992. "Lideranças indígenas no começo das reducões jesuiticas da provincia do Paraguai." *Pesquisas Antropológicas*, no. 47.

Blanco, José M. 1929. *Historia documentada de la vida y gloriosa muerte de los padres Roque González de Santa Cruz, Alonso Rodríguez y Juan del Castillo*. Buenos Aires: Sebastián Amorrortu.

Block, David. 1994. *Mission Culture on the Upper Amazon: Native Tradition, Jesuit Enterprise, and Secular Policy in Moxos, 1660–1880*. Lincoln: University of Nebraska Press.

Cardiel, José. 1919 (1747). "Costumbres de los Guaraníes." In *Historia del Paraguay desde 1747 hasta 1767*, by Domingo Muriel. Madrid: V. Suárez.

Cardiel, José. 1913 (1770). "Breve Relación de las Misiones del Paraguay." In *Organización social de las doctrinas guaraníes de la Compañía de Jesús*, by Pablo Hernandez. Edited by Gustavo Gilli, 2:514–614. Barcelona.

Cartas Anuas de la Provincia Jesuítica del Paraguay, 1641 a 1643. 1996 (1641–1643). Documentos de Geohistoria Regional Nro 11. Resistencia: Instituto de investigaciones Geohistóricas (CONICET).

Chamorro, Graciela. 1995. *Kurusu Ñe´Ëngatu. Palabras que la historia no podría olvidar*. Asunción: Centro de Estudios Antropológicos de la Universidad Católica.

Charlevoix, François Xavier. 1915 (1757). *Historia del Paraguay*. 6 vols. Madrid: Librería General de Victoriano Suarez.

D'Orbigny, Alcides. 1945 (1847). *Viaje a la América Meridional [. . .] realizado de 1826 a 1833*. Translated by Alfredo Cepeda. 4 vols. Buenos Aires: Editorial Futuro.

Doblas, Gonzalo de. 1836 (1785). "Memoria histórica, Geográfica, política y económica sobre la Provincia de Misiones de indios guaraníes." Buenos Aires: Imprenta del Estado.

Duverger, Christian. 1993. *La conversión de los indios de Nueva España*. México: Fondo de Cultura económica.

Estenssoro Fuchs, Juan Carlos. 2003. *Del paganismo a la santidad. La incorporación de los indios del Perú al catolicismo, 1532–1750*. Lima: Instituto Frances de Estudios Andinos.

Furlong, Guillermo. 1953. *José Cardiel y su Carta-Relación (1747)*. Buenos Aires: Librería del Plata.

Furlong, Guillermo. 1965. *Juan Escandón y su carta a Burriel (1760)*. Buenos Aires: Ediciones Theoria.

Herczog, Johann. 2001. *Orfeo nelle Indie. I Gesuiti e la Musica in Paraguay (1609–1767)*. Galatina: Mario Congedo Editore.

Hoffman, Werner. 1979. *Las misiones jesuíticas entre los chiquitanos*. Buenos Aires: FECIC.

Illari, Bernardo. 2005. "Villancicos, guaraníes y chiquitos: hispanidad, control y resistencia." In *Educación y Evangelización. La experiencia de un Mundo Mejor. X Jornadas Internacionales sobre Misiones Jesuíticas*, edited by Carlos Page, 447–459. Córdoba: Universidad Católica de Córdoba/Agencia Nacional de Promoción Científica y Tecnológica.

Illari, Bernardo. 2006. "Carta de Misiones: sobre la música jesuítico-guaraní en 1651 y su investigación actual." *Revista del Instituto de Investigación Musicológica "Carlos Vega"* 20: 97–113.

Kennedy, T. Frank. 2005. "Jesuits and Music." In *Jesuits and the Arts (1540–1773)*, edited by John W. O´Malley and Gauvin Alexander Bailey, 413–426. Philadelphia: Saint Joseph's Press.

Laird, Paul. 1997. *Towards a History of the Spanish Villancico*. Warren, Mich.: Harmonie Park Press.

Lange, Francisco Curt. 1986. "El Extrañamiento de la Compañía de Jesús del Río de la Plata (1767)." *Revista Musical Chilena* 40 (165): 4–14.

Leonhardt, Carlos. 1924. Datos históricos sobre el teatro misional. *Estudios. Revista Mensual redactada por la Academia Literaria del Plata* 26: 46–59.

Lozano, Pedro. 1874 (1754). *Historia de la Conquista del Paraguay, Río de la Plata y Tucumán*. 5 vols. Buenos Aires: Casa Editora "Imprenta popular."

Lozano, Pedro. 1941 (1733). *Descripción corográfica del Gran Chaco Gualamba*. Tucumán, Argentina: Instituto de antropología, Universidad Nacional de Tucumán.

Matthei, Mauro, and Rodrigo Moreno Jeria. 1997. *Cartas e informes de misioneros jesuítas extranjeros en hispanoamérica*. Cuarta parte(1731–1751). Anales de la Facultad de Teología, vol. 48. Santiago: Pontifícia Universidad Católica de Chile.

Monzón, Antonio. 1947. "Un profesor indígena de música en el Buenos Aires del siglo XVIII." *Estudios* 78 (422): 142–146.

Nawrot, Piotr. 2000. *Indígenas y Cultura Musical de las Reducciones Jesuíticas. Guaraníes, Chiquitos, Moxos*. Cochabamba, Bolivia: Editorial Verbo Divino.

Paucke, Florián. 1942–1944 (1780). *Hacia allá y para acá (una estadía entre los indios Mocobíes, 1749-1767)*. 3 vols. Tucumán and Buenos Aires: Universidad Nacional del Tucumán e Institución Cultural Argentino-Germánica.

Peramás, José Manuel. 1946 (1791). *La república de Platón y los guaraníes*. Buenos Aires: Emece Editores.

Preceptos s/a. "Gobierno de los jesuitas en los pueblos de misiones. Preceptos de nuestros Padres Generales y Provinciales que tocan inmediatamente a los Padres que viven en las Doctrinas en varias materias con sus declaraciones." Archivo General de la Nación (Argentina), Colección Biblioteca Nacional, Legajo 140.

Ruiz, Irma. 2008. "En pos de la dilucidación de un doble enigma: los marcadores sagrados de género de los *mbyá-guaraní*." In *Estudios en lingüística y antropología. Homenaje a Ana Gerzenstein*, edited by C. Messineo, M. Malvestitti, and R. Bein, 323–338. Buenos Aires: Facultad de Filosofía y Letras, Universidad de Buenos Aires.

Saint Hilaire, Auguste. 1939 (1820–1821). *Viaje ao Rio Grande do Sul (1820–1821)*. São Paulo: Companhia Editora Nacional.

Sánchez Labrador, José. 1910 (1767). *El Paraguay católico*. 3 vols. Buenos Aires: Imprenta de Coni Hermanos.

Sepp, Anton. 1971 (1696). *Relación de viaje a las misiones jesuíticas*. Buenos Aires: EUDEBA.

Sepp, Anton. 1973 (1709). *Continuación de las labores apostólicas*. Buenos Aires: EUDEBA.

Sepp, Anton. 1974 (1714). *Jardín de flores Paracuario*. Buenos Aires: EUDEBA.

Susnik, Branislava. 1966.*El indio colonial del Paraguay II: Los trece pueblos guaraníes de las Misiones (1767-1803)*. 3 vols. Asunción: MEAB.

Susnik, Branislava, and Miguel Chase-Sardi. 1992. *Los indios del Paraguay*. Madrid: MAPFRE.

Turner, Victor. 1995. *The Ritual Process: Structure and Anti-Structure*. New York: Aldine de Gruyter.

Waisman, Leonardo. 1992. "'!Viva María!' La música para la Virgen en las misiones de Chiquitos." *Latin American Music Review* 13, no. 2: 213–225.

Waisman, Leonardo. 1998. "¿Cómo escuchar música colonial latinoamericana?" *Música e investigación* 1, no. 2: 99–107.

White, Richard. 1991. *The Middle Ground: Indians, Empires and Republics in the Great Lakes Region, 1650–1815*. Cambridge: Cambridge University Press.

Wilde, Guillermo. 2007. "Toward a Political Anthropology of Mission Sound: Paraguay in the 17th and 18th Centuries." *Music & Politics* 1, no. 2: 1–29. http://www.music.ucsb.edu/projects/musicandpolitics/archive/2007-2.

Wilde, Guillermo. 2008. "El enigma sonoro de Trinidad: Ensayo de Etnomusicología Histórica." *Revista Resonancias*, no. 23: 41–67. http://www.resonancias.cl/resonancias-no-23.

Wilde, Guillermo. 2009. *Religión y Poder en las Misiones de guaraníes*. Buenos Aires: Editorial SB.

CHAPTER 5

"WE SHOULD NOT SING OF HEAVEN AND ANGELS"

Performing Western Sacred Music in Soviet Russia, 1917–1964

PAULINE FAIRCLOUGH

The performance of Western sacred music in Russia during the Soviet period remains an obscure topic in the West. Knowledge of what was played is almost nonexistent outside Russia; within Russian musical circles much is known and remembered from personal experience, but as is often the case with events comfortably within living memory, it has not yet been a subject for research. With regard to Russian sacred music, links with Russian Orthodoxy mean that its fate was bound up with official Soviet attitudes to the church itself, which were themselves shifting and contradictory over the seventy-four-year Soviet period. In effect, between around 1928 and 1965, very little Russian sacred music was publicly performed, and so contemporary Russian scholarship has, not surprisingly, concentrated mainly on the rich performance traditions of the prerevolutionary years.[1] My focus therefore is not on Russian sacred music performance in the Soviet Union but rather on Western sacred music in the concert practice of the major cultural centers of Moscow and Petrograd-Leningrad. I have chosen to end my study at the point of Khrushchev's fall from power in 1964, since despite the ensuing so-called stagnation under Brezhnev, patterns of musical life had changed permanently since the end of the Stalin years and would never return to the pre-Thaw climate of repression.[2]

Lenin's new administration set as one of its early objectives the discrediting and near-elimination of Russian Orthodoxy. It would not be unreasonable, therefore, to expect suspicion toward those musical institutions whose work was closely involved with the church and its music. Nor would it be unreasonable to expect sacred repertoire to be purged from concert schedules. Religious communities were persecuted, churches demolished, and priests discredited and even arrested in vicious campaigns against the Church, so at first glance there seems no reason why the singing of sacred texts should have been permissible in a concert hall—especially in venues so blatantly emblematic of tsarist times as the Imperial Capella in Leningrad or in former churches.[3] However, Western sacred works were an established part of concert repertoire, particularly the large-scale oratorios, requiems, and masses. They therefore belonged to the canon of "bourgeois" works that Lenin's administration wished to bring within reach of the proletariat. To place bans on performing Bach, Handel, and Mozart's sacred works was unthinkable, and was in fact never seriously proposed. Many of these works were, however, set to Latin texts, which meant they would not be understood by the new Soviet working classes. But it was this very fact that helped to ensure their survival: by the mid-1920s, texts would not be presented, translated or otherwise, in program notes. As presented to audiences, Western requiems and masses were religious only in name: their textual content was rendered no more significant than the orchestral parts. Those sacred works that were in vernacular languages such as German were more problematic, and different strategies for accommodating those works were eventually found, as will be seen.

While there was never any ban as such on performing Western sacred music in concerts, artists did not have carte blanche to perform exactly what they liked, when they liked. Tracing the various twists and turns through Soviet music policy to determine what was and was not permissible at any given time does not always give straightforward answers. Evidence of direct party interference in the selection of repertoire does not necessarily mean a document issued by the Kremlin, but can be located in low- and middle-ranking committee decisions that reflect the leadership's taste or opinion at that time. In the case of official or top-down attitudes to religion in Soviet society, prejudice can clearly be seen in decisions made by Narkompros (Commissariat of Enlightenment) and its repertoire committee, Glavrepertkom, in the 1920s; in 1936, the newly formed All-Union Committee on Arts Affairs replaced all previous intermediary committees and was directly answerable to the Central Committee of the Communist Party. As an organization, it was also considerably more interventionist and aggressive than Narkompros had been, but that should not be surprising. During the second half of the 1930s the Stalinist repressions created a climate of such fear and paranoia that whole musical institutions suffered purges thanks to the Committee's desire to demonstrate its own zeal; in such extreme conditions, it is not surprising that repertoire selection became more cautious. A huge upsurge in national feeling during the war years (1941–1945) cemented the xenophobia that was already making its mark on repertoire selection, and this insularity was completely entrenched by the late Stalin period. Russia's musical life was able to refresh itself only after 1953, and though it was a long time before it returned fully to the internationalism of the 1920s and 1930s, by 1964 the process of normalization was well underway. Therefore, the selection of repertoire can be regarded as an evolving process, with influence from the top exerting a greater or lesser influence at certain times, the personal tastes of musicians and artistic advisors initiating important decisions, and repertoire and arts committees performing an intermediary role as interpreters and guardians of the leadership's position.

First Steps: Mikhail Klimov and the Leningrad Capella

As is well documented, the Bolshevik coup of October 1917 did not result in the immediate closure of cultural institutions.[4] The most distinguished prerevolutionary musical bodies (for example, the Bolshoy and Mariinsky Theatres) were generously supported by the new government; indeed, despite the many difficulties and privations of the first decade, multiple new music groups sprang up in response to the revolution's new creative spirit.[5] Two notable prerevolutionary survivors in Petrograd-Leningrad who were given the chance to remodel themselves were the former Imperial orchestra and capella, both organizations which were given priority funding on a level with the big opera houses. After donning various different names throughout the 1920s, they were eventually called the Leningrad Philharmonia and Leningrad State Academic Capella.[6] From the perspective of performing both Russian and Western sacred repertoire, the Leningrad Capella makes an ideal case study for the first half of this chapter because, unlike many other Soviet choirs, it never specialized in folk or popular song repertoire: it had been based in Saint Petersburg since the time of Peter the Great and was protective of its distinguished classical heritage. The Capella therefore took responsibility for maintaining prerevolutionary performance traditions, and the very fact that it did this with government blessing is significant. Its repertoire over the period of this study is a good barometer of broader Soviet cultural policy, echoing changing positions on mass and bourgeois culture, the Russian Orthodox Church, the rise of nationalism under Stalin and the "Thaw" years that followed. Through all these chapters of Soviet cultural history, the performance of Western sacred music is a consistent indicator of official policy.

The conductors and artistic directors of both the Capella and the Philharmonia during the first two decades of the Soviet state were crucial in establishing Leningrad's repertoire traditions, some of which survived for the whole Soviet period and beyond. The body with overall responsibility for musical institutions was Narkompros, headed by Anatoly Lunacharsky[7]: initially, at least, nothing in the musical world happened without the support and permission of this organization.[8] The first conductors of the Philharmonia were Sergey Koussevitsky, Emil Cooper, and Albert Coates; though all would soon emigrate to the West, they played a major role in establishing a high-quality, international concert life under the new Bolshevik government. The Capella, however, maintained Mikhail Klimov as conductor and director from 1918 through 1935, ensuring a remarkable continuity over nearly two decades of dramatic upheaval. Like most musicians in important roles during these years, Klimov was well trained and highly professional. He had been taught composition and conducting at the Petersburg Conservatory by Rimsky Korsakov, Liadov, and Tcherepnin. In addition to this, he seems to have been a gifted administrator and an astute diplomat, traits that were valued highly in the changeable years of the 1920s and 1930s. From the time of the Capella's first concert in

February 1918, Klimov's relationship with Lunacharsky proved critical to the Capella's survival during the 1920s and had a clear impact on their programming.

The Capella's repertoire before 1917 was not confined only to sacred works. Among the secular pieces performed were nineteenth-century romances (Arensky, Glinka, Gounod, and others), choruses from Russian and Western operas (*Prince Igor, Khovanshchina, Orfeo, Tannhauser*, and others) as well as major Western sacred works like Palestrina's *Missa Papae Marcelli* and Handel's *Messiah*.[9] Both sacred and secular repertoire would be retained and further developed after 1917, but initially Klimov had no assurance that the Capella's sacred repertoire would be acceptable to the new Soviet government. Their first postrevolutionary concert—at which they sang sacred music as well as Russian folk songs—was in February 1918, at the House of the Red Army, prefaced by a lecture by Lunacharsky on "The separation of the Church from the State and the art of church singing" in which he argued for the historical value of Russian church singing independently of its religious context.[10] Lunacharsky supported the Capella as a worthy musical institution which could play a full role in the early revolutionary project to bring bourgeois culture to the masses, and he valued Klimov as a talented professional who could be entrusted with the *perestroika* of the Capella from an imperial, private choir to a public one. Moreover, Klimov's talents as an administrator were useful to Lunacharsky beyond his work in the Capella. From 1925, Klimov, at Lunacharsky's behest, joined the administration of the Leningrad Philharmonia, and the two organizations maintained a close relationship, with the Capella acting as the Philharmonia's official choir.[11]

Between 1918 and 1935 (when he stopped conducting due to illness, which proved fatal in 1937), Klimov performed the following major sacred or biblical works, some of which had not previously been in the Capella's repertoire: Mozart Requiem; Beethoven *Missa Solemnis*; Rachmaninoff *All-Night Vigil*; Tchaikovsky *Liturgy*; Berlioz *Damnation of Faust*, Requiem, and *Te Deum*; Verdi Requiem; Bach St. Matthew Passion, B Minor Mass, St. John Passion, Cantata no. 80; Handel *Samson, Judas Maccabeus*; and Brahms Requiem.[12] Not all gained equal status throughout the 1920s and 1930s, and some were quickly deemed problematic: Tchaikovsky's *Liturgy* and Rachmaninoff's *All-Night Vigil* were early casualties of the Repertoire Committee's zeal to ban anything redolent of prerevolutionary Orthodoxy. By 1922 Klimov was required to submit repertoire plans to the repertoire section (Glavrepertkom) of Narkompros for inspection, and those for the forthcoming year were set out on the following lines: (1) Russian folk song, four concerts; (2) Russian choral music, eleven concerts; (3) Russian choral literature of the fifteenth through seventeenth century, one concert; (4) Western choral literature, five programs; (5) works for choir, soloists, and orchestra, five concerts. The single concert devoted to fifteenth- through seventeenth-century Russian choral music was not allowed to go ahead; Klimov would not perform this repertoire again until after 1932. On the Narkompros repertoire committee that year were three highly respected cultural and musical figures: Lunacharsky himself, the music education specialist Nadezhda Briusova, and the theoretician Boleslav Yavorsky. All evidently respected Klimov and the Capella but felt unable to permit them to perform what was self-evidently Orthodox choral liturgy. Tension would simmer over the Capella's retention of sacred works, both

Russian and Western, over several years; by 1926 Lunacharsky had to intervene in their defence. In his address to the presidium of the scientific-artistic section of GUS (The State Academic Council), "On the repertoire of the Leningrad State Capella," he concluded that "[this section] believes that, notwithstanding those political considerations which have been brought to its attention, the best repertoire for the Capella is classical; it is undoubtedly essential for the future of our musical culture." (Sheremet'yeva 1983, 46) By "classical" Lunacharsky almost certainly meant Bach, Handel, Mozart, Haydn, and Beethoven, since Russian sacred music was rapidly becoming a lost cause. A directive from Glavrepertkom in July 1928 states:

> there is no objection to the inclusion in the State Academic Capella's work plan of Bach's 'Passions' and Mass, on the condition that they will not be performed more than twice a year, and not on any day coinciding with the church calendar ... [regarding] concerts of choral Russian music of the 17th and 18th centuries, Glavrepertkom considers these unsuitable and does not permit them.[13]

Tchaikovsky's *Liturgy* had already vanished from the Capella's schedules four years earlier, and Rachmaninoff's *All-Night Vigil* was dropped after 1928, having been performed annually by the Capella from 1923. Neither work would be sung by a major state choir again until the mid 1960s.[14]

Russian sacred music, then, made a fairly swift exit from the Soviet concert stage. But works by Western composers were consistently treated more leniently. Of the above list of Klimov's premieres, a few were dropped quickly: Berlioz's *Te Deum* doesn't appear again in schedules during my time-frame of research; Brahms's Requiem was not heard again after its Soviet premiere (under Klemperer) in 1929 until 1960, and the St. John Passion was only performed a few times in the late 1920s and 1930s before disappearing altogether for twenty years. Both the Passions drop out of the repertoire in the so-called High Stalin period from around 1940 to 1954, as does Beethoven's *Missa Solemnis*. The Leningrad Philharmonia performed the St. John Passion under Kurt Sanderling in 1954–1955, the first time since the 1934–1935 season, but though the Latvian Philharmonic and Capella brought it to Leningrad in 1958, the Leningrad Philharmonia did not perform either Passion again during the period of this study. Bach's B Minor Mass and the Requiems by Mozart, Berlioz, and Verdi, however, attained the rare status of Soviet classics and were the only major sacred works to comfortably maintain their place in the repertoire during the entire Stalin period.

RAPM, THE CULTURAL REVOLUTION, AND THE RISE OF STALINISM

The rise of the Russian Association of Proletarian Musicians (RAPM) and its deleterious effect on Soviet musical life is by now well documented.[15] But the period of its greatest influence in the late 1920s and early 1930s has a broader context: that of the so-called

Cultural Revolution. Catastrophe in the countryside as the result of forced collectivization, industrial unrest, and personal disagreements within the Politburo all fed into what proved to be the first stage of Stalin's consolidation of totalitarian power. The feared charges of saboteur, spy, and Trotskyite now became weapons in this process. Although apparently remote from the musical world, the increased climate of repression and bullying had a powerful effect on all aspects of Soviet life. The press, whose naming-and-shaming campaigns now began to hound victims to their eventual destruction or banishment to the Gulag camps, was an extremely potent force where accusations could be publicly made. Lenin's New Economic Policy was rejected in favor of Stalin's First Five-Year Plan, a blueprint for massive industrial expansion and social reconstruction. During the launch of this process, proletarian organizations did receive some official support, and the stoking of class warfare could only emphasize this.[16] Now that they were indirectly reinforced from above, proletarian music organizations, whose influence had been limited before, felt empowered to attack icons of the musical establishment such as the conservatories and orchestras, certain that their voice echoed government policy.

Leading figures in proletarian groups such as Prokoll and RAPM had never been marginalized, as is clear from the fact that their names appear regularly on committee meeting lists of Narkompros and the Philharmonia throughout the 1920s. RAPM began in 1923 as a small group of like-minded colleagues with no significant influence, but from 1928 their ranks were significantly increased, which, together with the aggressive climate fostered by the Cultural Revolution, also made them much more influential.[17] They seized the opportunity to dominate musical life and attacked their ideological enemies ruthlessly. In a long-winded controversy over the Moscow Conservatory that was encouraged and whipped up by RAPM, a Communist named Boleslav Pshibïshevsky was given the post of rector in 1929 (in preference to the composer Mikhail Ippolitov-Ivanov, the conservatory's own choice), and the conservatory was promptly renamed the Felix Kon Higher Music School.[18] RAPM certainly aimed to extend their influence to the repertoire of the orchestras, and archival evidence shows that they were partially successful, at least in the sphere of sacred music. RAPM managed to create a stifling atmosphere within musical circles, publishing aggressive articles in the mass press and their own journals, *Proletarsky muzïkant* (Proletarian musician, published from 1929) and *Za proletarskuyu muzïku* (Towards a proletarian music, published from 1930). Professors of the stature of Nikolay Myaskovsky preferred to resign their Conservatory posts rather than endure RAPM's constant hounding of their teaching methods and systematic dumbing-down of the curriculum (Hakobian 2010, 266). Attacks on religious music do appear in these journals, and religion itself was one of their targets, even if the religious music they attacked was less that of the concert hall than that sung for worship by Christian groups.[19] That being said, minutes from meetings of Glaviskusstvo (Main administration of arts affairs) between 1929 and 1931 show clearly that the Capella and Leningrad Philharmonia were in RAPM's sights. In a meeting dedicated to antireligious propaganda on April 9, 1929, the Mass [work] Department of Glavisskustvo included among their aims to "ban the sale of religious musical literature," to "examine concert, opera and radio repertoire with the aim of banning religious music and any works saturated with religion," and "to exclude any operas saturated with religion."[20] A worker at the All-Russian Conference on Amateur Musical Art, Moscow, March 1931, angrily declared: "We still have to pose the problem of the liquidation of musical illiteracy as a political question. Because this illiteracy is used by our class enemies—priests, precentors, papists and vermin who shove their own music at us, because we are not literate enough."[21] The tenacity of religion in the Soviet Union is frequently classed with social problems such as alcoholism in documents of this kind.

Stenogrammes from the 1931 conference at which the angry worker spoke out yield further evidence of a burgeoning campaign against the Capella and its sacred repertoire. A representative from Glavisskustvo (possibly the RAPM-based conductor Alexey Sergeyev) declared that the Capella's work was "alien" to the contemporary Soviet listener and the delegation from Leningrad grouped the Capella together with their other targets, the "white émigré" composer Rachmaninoff (especially his composition *The Bells*, to texts by Edgar Allen Poe) and the jazz band leader Leonid Utyesov, as "class enemies."[22] Alexander Davidenko, a leading RAPM composer, complained in 1931 that on the radio workers' choirs were performing Rachmaninov's *All-Night Vigil* while church choirs (meaning the Capella) sang works by proletarian composers (Edmunds 2000, 171). The notion that proletarian choirs, subject to far lighter scrutiny than the big state-sponsored institutions, were still singing the *All-Night Vigil* in 1931 is certainly intriguing, but it is unlikely that this practice was very widespread, and in any case it could surely not have survived much beyond that date.

Unbeknown to RAPM, their days were numbered. Only a year after this conference, the group was dissolved along with all other cultural organizations, and their manifestos and policies themselves became targets for high-level criticism. By the end of 1931, RAPM were already on the defensive, having been publicly attacked and their members openly mocked at a meeting of the All-Russian Drama Committee in December.[23] Mikhail Gnesin's file in the State Archive of Literature and Art contains drafts of his speech––probably written in November 1931 and delivered at the December All-Russian Drama Committee meeting––robustly attacking not only the impoverishment of Soviet musical life, but also the RAPM pamphlet by Viktor Vinogradov "Against the influence of the church in music."[24] Gnesin ridicules Vinogradov's claim that the best antidote to "church influence" (*tserkovshchina*) was the singing of mass songs composed by RAPM.[25] Add this to Shostakovich's scornful description in his All-Russian Drama Committee speech of the works of the RAPM luminaries Koval and Davidenko as "helpless" and "illiterate" and one cannot escape the conclusion that by late 1931 the period of RAPM's intimidation of composers and musicians was nearing its end.[26] This renders its total period of real power a mere three or four years; all the more reason, then, to conclude that its influence during that time must have been exceedingly potent. No one knew in 1928 that its power would be short-lived; and taken together with the social and political background over the period 1927–1932, there was every reason to suppose that its strident antireligious, antibourgeois, and antimodern platforms and bullying tactics would continue indefinitely with the blessing of the State.[27]

During the five years that RAPM exerted real influence on musical life, there is a perceptible drop in the numbers of sacred works performed by the Capella. Handel's *Judas Maccabeus* was done in the Leningrad Philharmonia's 1929–1930 season, to critical acclaim; but it is noticeable that Ivan Sollertinsky's *Leningradskaya Pravda* review took great pains to stress that it was not really a religious work at all but rather a Shakespearean drama (Sollertinsky,1939, 3). In a poignant echo of RAPM's insistence on the importance of mass songs, Klimov's work plans show a marked increase in popular Soviet song repertoire as early as the 1929–1930 season plan. His plans for the 1931–1932 season included the major themes Songs of the Peoples of the USSR (five concerts) and Russian choral literature (four concerts)[28]; other themed concerts included "Humour and satire," a Lenin memorial concert, and "Antireligious choral literature." This last category is clearly extraordinary for the Capella, and it was happily never repeated, since the political pressure to gratify RAPM tastes vanished after the resolution that was issued during that very season.[29]

As already noted, major works of Russian sacred music (Tchaikovsky's *Liturgy* and Rachmaninoff's *All-Night Vigil*) vanished from the Capella's programs after 1928; but after 1932 they did begin once again to perform Russian liturgical music in closed educational concerts in music technicums and conservatories. In Klimov's work plan for 1932–1933, under the heading "Educational-illustrative programs," the following works are listed: Lassus madrigals and motets; Josquin *Stabat mater*; Palestrina madrigals and motets; Lotti *Crucifixus*; Bach "Der Geist hilft under Schwachheit auf"; Russian *raspevi* from the fourteenth century onwards[30]; *kantï* on texts by Simeon Podotsky[31]; polyphonic sacred compositions of Russian eighteenth-century composers (Vasily Titov, Nikolay Bavïkin, Vasily Redrikov); sonatas and sacred concertos for a capella choir and choir with instrumental accompaniment by Italian composers who had worked in Russia such as Baldassare Galuppi, Antonio Sapientsa, Giuseppe Sarti, and their Russian students Artemy Vedel and Stepan Degtyarev; Bach B Minor Mass and Passions; Mozart Requiem. Klimov's plans for the following years up to 1936 additionally include, in standard (noneducational) repertoire: Handel *Samson*; Bach B Minor Mass, St. Matthew Passion, *Magnificat,* and Cantata No. 80; Mozart Requiem; Verdi Requiem; Josquin "Agnus Dei" from *Missa l'homme arme*; Lassus motets; Palestrina movements from a Mass (probably *Missa Papae Marcelli*, which was already in their repertoire); and a Gabrieli 12-part motet. By 1935, Klimov's plans for the next season (which, sadly, he was unable to direct owing to illness) placed eighteenth- and nineteenth-century Russian sacred music in the very first programs.[32] Klimov evidently began cautiously, only performing the treasured early Russian sacred music in special closed concerts, but it seems that he soon brought them back into public view and intended doing so more and more.[33] It is a shame that it is not possible to see what the Capella actually *did* perform in that 1935–1936 season but only Klimov's work plans; but in any case, the change in the Capella's leadership during that year coincided with much deeper shifts in Soviet cultural life that would affect all musical organizations, including the Capella. Tragically, this flowering of sacred music performance would be all too brief.

The Capella after Klimov

Following a brief interval during which E. P. Kudryatseva directed the Capella (from the autumn of 1935), Alexander Sveshnikov was invited to become the Capella's next conductor and artistic director, and he assumed this position from 1937 until the onset of Russia's entry into the war, when Kudryatseva stepped in once more. It was not an easy time to accept such a role; Sveshnikov was a proven choral conductor but his political credentials were nonexistent and he could easily have been vulnerable to attack.[34] The Committee on Arts Affairs, formed in 1936, was soon to launch an aggressive investigation into the organization and affairs of the Leningrad Philharmonia and it was obvious that the Capella would at some point undergo the same process. There is a gap in the Capella's repertoire record-keeping between around 1936–1938 and so it is not currently possible to judge the speed and scale of the changes either of the new conductors instigated. Records resume in the 1938–1939 season, and one important event in 1938 was particularly well documented: the Capella's tour to Moscow in December as part of their 225-year anniversary celebrations. Bach's *Magnificat* formed the big showpiece of their celebrations, and in fact its success in Moscow was cited in documents from the Committee on Arts Affairs to the Kremlin successfully recommending Sveshnikov and select members of the Capella for awards.[35] The Capella's repertoire for 1938–1939, as submitted to the Committee on Arts Affairs in May 1938, ran as follows[36]:

Degtyarev: Minin i Pozharsky
Tchaikovsky: To Joy
Josquin: Canzona
Palestrina: Canzona
Janequin: Song of the Birds
Lasso: Ekho
Schutz: Students' song
Hassler: Madrigal
Bach: Magnificat
Folk songs: Ukrainian, Belarussian, Tartar, Czech, German, Italian, Norwegian, French.
Viktor Beliy: Chuvash song; Golubev: Kuznets; Dunaevsky: mass songs

As can be seen from this list, Sveshnikov had retained Klimov's legacy of blending contemporary Soviet music, folk song, Western sacred music, and even old Russian music (even if the eighteenth-century composer Stepan Degtyarev was the sole representative). It is noticeable, though, that Sveshnikov's selection eschews works that would be listed as obviously sacred: for example, the canzonas by Josquin and Palestrina presumably replace previous sacred works by them. Sacred Russian music has once again vanished, and this time it would not return to public view until Khrushchev's Thaw was well underway.

What does this list tell reveal about repertoire politics between 1935–1938? In the first place, it shows that the Capella's conductor did not judge it safe to perform Russian sacred music, which in itself does not necessarily point to a more aggressive state policy on religion, but more likely reflects the enormously increased climate of repression at the peak of Stalin's mass arrests between 1937 and 1938. Any repertoire that carried even a hint of unacceptability was best avoided when the stakes were so high, and though I have not found any voices raised publicly against Klimov for his attempts to rehabilitate that repertoire in the mid-1930s, it surely seemed safer to Sveshnikov to steer well clear of it. The wide choice of folk songs (including Western ones) strikes a boldly internationalist note that was actually slightly at odds with Stalin's move away from cordial cultural relations with the West, and in particular the openly hostile attitude to Germany until the sudden signing of the Molotov-Ribbentrop pact in 1939. However, the embracing of Ukrainian, Belarussian, and Tartar culture was very much in line with the current policy of what Marina Frolova-Walker has termed Stalin's "national-culture project" of the mid-late 1930s, whereby the supposedly indigenous culture of the Soviet republics was fostered under the control and supervision of Moscow.[37]

In this risky and fragile climate, Sveshnikov had judged Bach's *Magnificat* to be a safe option, and this fact is remarkable in itself. Documents in the Capella file at the Central State Archive of Literature and Art in Saint Petersburg show that Svehsnikov's intention to continue performing Bach's sacred music was not only very short-lived but may have been problematic even at the time. Apart from the big *Magnificat* performances in the anniversary tour, the Capella performed its five-voice fugue "Fecit potentiam" separately, the full text of which is typed up in the Committee repertoire submission.[38] Presenting the Latin in typed Cyrillic on this document raises the distant possibility that it was typed as an aid to avoid censorship and draw attention away from the fact that they were performing in a foreign language. Normally, if not typed in Latin characters, foreign text in such documents was inserted, hand-written. Precisely why anyone should have been at pains to disguise the text is not obvious: the English translation makes no explicit reference to God, though perhaps the biblical source is obvious enough to require veiling: "He has shown strength with his arm / and has scattered the proud in their conceit, / Casting down the mighty from their thrones / and lifting up the lowly." Subsequent references to Bach fugues in the Capella's program lists to the Committee offer no text at all and merely read "Five-voice fugue," or "Fugue." In concert programs, this text would never be reproduced and the audience was thus invited to "hear past" the words and enjoy a purely musical experience. The same, of course, held true for performances during the Stalin period of any Western sacred work.

Regardless of the *Magnificat*'s success, documents for the forthcoming 1939–1940 season show a gradual change of repertoire direction, especially in its a capella listings. The Capella performed an increased number of Soviet popular classics and fewer Western sacred works, retaining only Lotti's *Crucifixus*, Purcell "Evening Hymn," and an unspecified Bach fugue (presumably "Fecit potentiam" from the *Magnificat*). They still did the big classics with the Philharmonia: in March 1939 they performed Handel's *Judas Maccabeus* and in December the same year they gave the Soviet premiere of

Israel in Egypt—a rare example of Sveshnikov enlarging Klimov's portfolio of Western sacred works. Despite positive reviews, this work was dropped and not repeated in the whole period examined here. The years immediately preceding the war, then, saw a shift in emphasis in concert practice from Western to Soviet works, but even the short-lived appearance of the *Magnificat* and *Israel in Egypt* at such a tense period of Soviet history—the peak years of the Stalinist repressions—suggests that the sacred content of these works was not considered a bar to their performance. Rather, if some Western music was dropped in favor of Soviet works in the late 1930s, this was because of a determined drive to demonstrate support for Soviet culture over and above accommodating distinguished foreign conductors and musicians (who had been performing more or less what they wanted) and maintaining an international performance culture. In short, it had to do with the much-vaunted Soviet policy of "national in form, socialist in content," not with any decrees on banning Western music. Within Stalin's "socialism in one country," internationalism had gone out of fashion, while showcasing the "national" art of the Soviet Republics was a matter of urgency. Notwithstanding these pressures, the Capella's repertoire on the eve of the Soviet Union's entry into the war in 1941 was still rich in Western music. It also shows that some sacred (or religious-themed) works were still in the Capella's repertoire. I reproduce here the full repertoire listings submitted to the Committee on Arts Affairs for the 1941–1942 season, prepared before the war[39]:

Russian classics
Taneyev *St John of Damascus* plus smaller works
Glinka "Lullaby"
Rimsky Korsakov Songs ("Venetian Night," "Fields of Tartary," "Old Song," "Oleg")
Cui Two songs
Borodin Polovtsian chorus
Tchaikovsky songs
Arensky "Anchor"
Rachmaninoff "Spring"
Musorgsky "Jesus of Nazareth"
Grechaninov "Lullaby"

Soviet works [not fully listed here] by Alexander Alexandrov, Tomilin, Yegorov, Isaak Dunaevsky, Sergey Vasilenko, Alexander Kastalsky ("Troika"—text by Gogol).
Russian and National folk songs
Prokofiev *Alexander Nevsky*
Khachaturian *Song about Stalin*
Shaporin *On the Field of Kulikovo*

West European classics:
Haydn *Seasons*
Handel *Israel in Egypt, Judas Maccabeus*
Mozart Requiem

Beethoven Ninth Symphony, *Missa Solemnis, Fidelio*
Berlioz Requiem
Grieg *Peer Gynt*
Bach 5-voice Fugue, Motet No. 1, "The Night Falls," chorus [unspecified] from B minor mass, Fugue No. 1 from *Magnificat* ("sicut locutus est")
Janequin [illegible]
Lotti *Crucifixus*
Lasso "Ekho"
Palestrina Kyrie (from Canonic Mass)
Purcell "Evening Hymn"
Rossini Tyrolean chorus from *William Tell*
Saint-Saens *Bolero*
Fogel *Valse*
Verdi *Te Deum*, Requiem
Telemann motet [not named]
Schutz madrigal [non-sacred]
Schumann [sic—should read Verdi] "Rataplan"

With the outset of war, everything changed. In 1941, the Capella was evacuated to Kirov, where it spent the war years singing morale-boosting Soviet and folk songs for soldiers and local people in small venues like schools and hospitals. The shift toward favoring Soviet and Russian repertoire before the war intensified during the war itself, largely owing to Russian musicians' genuine desire to serve the national cause at a time of foreign threat, and also as a result of the sheer volume of new patriotic works produced after 1941: there was simply a lot more Soviet repertoire to choose from, some of it of high quality (cantatas by Khachaturian, Shostakovich, Prokofiev, Shaporin, and others). This change in emphasis was confirmed in the post-war years and became deeply entrenched in Soviet concert practice until after 1953. A typical late-wartime Capella program, given in Tallin, April 4, 1947, illustrates well how things had changed[40]:

Khachaturian *Poem about Stalin*[41]
Grechaninov "Lullaby"
Taneyev "Sunrise," "See such darkness," "Evening"
Lotti *Crucifixus*
Schumann "Gryozi"[42]
Lasso "Ekho"
Davidovsky on Ukrainian folk songs (skita?)
Voloshinov "Winter Morning"
Yegorov "Taiga," "Rodina"
Folk song "Taiga"
Novikov "Evening Bells," Suite on Russian folk themes

Little, apart from Lotti's *Crucifixus*, remained of the Capella's rich prewar Western sacred legacy. As happened a decade earlier, sacred works were more or less entirely confined to large-scale orchestral concerts with the Philharmonia, and even this arrangement could not be sustained. The 1948–1949 season included Bach's B minor mass, Handel's *Samson*, the Berlioz and Verdi requiems and Beethoven's Ninth Symphony. So far, there is no substantial change from the 1938–1939 season. But in February 1948 the musical world suffered a crippling blow that was to have very wide-reaching consequences. After a pugnacious three-day conference of composers, performers, and critics chaired by the Minister of Culture, Andrey Zhdanov, the Central Committee of the Communist Party issued a resolution. It condemned by name five Soviet composers—Shostakovich, Prokofiev, Myaskovsky, Shebalin, and Popov. Their work was criticized for its adherence to Western formalist tendencies, a list of banned works was circulated, and all those with teaching posts at the conservatories were dismissed.[43] Though there was nothing in Zhdanov's resolution that specifically criticized the presence of Western classical music in Soviet schedules, he did place a strong emphasis on the importance of nineteenth-century Russian classics, to the point of instructing Soviet composers to return to that style. Even if there was no ban on Western music as such, the enforced emphasis on Soviet and Russian national music meant that Western repertoire was simply squeezed out. Sacred music was just another casualty of this, rather than a direct target. Programs for the 1949–1950 season show a near-total absence of any Western sacred music: Lotti's *Crucifixus* is the sole survivor in the Capella's prewar sacred a capella repertoire, and when it came to orchestral concerts, in the five seasons between 1948 and 1953 (Moscow and Leningrad combined), they performed only Bach's B Minor Mass (four times), Mozart's Requiem (four times), and Verdi's Requiem (twice) with the Philharmonia. These are all that remained of the Western sacred works in the Capella's repertoire until after Stalin's death in 1953.

The resurrection of sacred music after Stalin's death occurred in various ways. One of the quickest moves to revive a long-neglected work was made by the young conductor Kurt Sanderling. Sanderling, who had moved to the Soviet Union in 1935, became Yevgeny Mravinsky's assistant to the Leningrad Philharmonic during their evacuation in Novosibirsk. In the 1954–1955 season, he conducted the first performance of Bach's St. John Passion since the 1935–1936 Leningrad season (both with the Capella). This seems to have been something of a one-off event, since it was not performed again until the Bach Ensemble from the German Democratic Republic did it on a tour to the Soviet Union in 1968. Other choirs from Soviet-bloc countries played a small part in bringing Bach and others back to Moscow and Leningrad, but mainly outside the boundaries of the period I am investigating here: the Latvian Philharmonia and choir performed Handel's *Messiah* on their tour in 1964, while two tours to Moscow in 1967 by the Estonian male voice choir and the Armenian Capella saw the revival of Cherubini's Requiem and Rossini's *Stabat Mater*. By this time, however, Soviet concert programming was radically altered, and it would be fair to say that Soviet-bloc choirs played a role no more significant than that of visiting Western performers who began to arrive in 1964, when the New York period group Pro Musica first visited the USSR.

Once Western groups began regular visits to the Soviet Union, bringing with them music, new performance techniques and trends, and even instruments, the veil was finally lifted from the wealth of European sacred music from the last half-millennium. The impact of these visits was literally revolutionary. Andrey Volkonsky, then a young composer living in Moscow, knew members of Pro Musica, and learned about their new approaches to performing medieval and Renaissance music. In 1965, he began his own early music ensemble, Madrigal, supplied with recorders and some music from Pro Musica, who had also given Volkonsky recent Western scholarship on music of that period.[44] Also active at that time was Rudolf Barshai's Moscow Chamber Ensemble, which performed a lot of Baroque music during the 1960s, including many sacred works. In the years 1963–64, the final season of this study, there was a series of important revivals: the Latvian Academic Choir gave what may have been the first Soviet performance of Handel's *Messiah*, Barshai conducted Pergolesi's *Stabat Mater*, Sveshnikov performed Stravinsky's *Symphony of Psalms*,[45] and several Western choirs made their first visits. The choir and orchestra of Oberlin College in the United States (directed by Robert Fountain) performed Bach Cantata No. 150, Brahms motet op. 29 no. 2, Palestrina "Hodie Christus natus est," Lotti *Crucifixus*, Lassus "Ekho," Wilkes "Hosanna to the Son of David," and a Mozart's Missa Brevis. Pro Musica's concerts were themed: for example, English Elizabethans, Italian early Baroque, Josquin and his contemporaries, and so on. Soviet musical life was utterly transformed by these visits, and by the growing musical freedoms they were experiencing, in however constrained circumstances. Sveshnikov's State Russian Choir also enjoyed the freedom to expand their repertoire beyond the set pieces they had continually repeated since 1955: Lotti's *Crucifixus* and Iomelli's *Miserere*. From 1958, Lassus, Monteverdi, Josquin, and others returned to the Russian Choir's regular repertoire. But there remained the problem of European vernacular languages: though Western groups might sing in English and medieval French, and even the Latvians could sing the *Messiah*, major Soviet choirs in Moscow were more cautious. This leads us to a bizarre chapter in Soviet sacred performance that lasted a very long time: the Sovietization of J. S. Bach.

Bach à la Stalin: The Sovietization of the Sacred Songs

Bach's sacred songs had been an early part of the Capella's repertoire under Klimov: programs preserved in his archive show that in April 1921 the Capella performed "Der Geist hilft unsrer Schwachheit auf," "Ich liebe Jesum," "Komm, süsser Tod," "Mein Jesu was für Seelnweh," "Vergiss mein nicht," and "Komm, Jesu, komm."[46] One of Sveshnikov's notable, though controversial, achievements was the preservation of part of Bach's a capella legacy through setting the music to Soviet texts. This was not something he did with the Capella; rather, this particular tradition seems to have begun with the choir he formed during the war: the State Academic Russian Choir of the USSR (and its youth section, the Boys' Choir), usually called simply the Russian Choir or even

Sveshnikov's Choir. The first year that one of these songs was performed seems to have been 1949: "Come, people" with words by Alexander Preis. Sveshnikov's Russian Choir regularly sang these bowdlerized versions, with a range of titles such as "Night departs"; "When the sun shines over us"; "Who carries proudly the banner of victory"; "Spring hopes"; "Joy of life"; "Who carries a sad burden"; "Let us sing a festive song," "Heart, be silent," "Consolation"; "Song of Triumph." All of these titles were first performed in 1951; over the years more were added, and indeed, choirs were still singing these words well into the 1980s. New editions of choral music published in the late 1980s reprinted them, and some as early as 1966 gave both the original German *and* the Soviet texts, so that the choir could select which version to sing for themselves.[47] The Soviet texts therefore became completely embedded in Soviet choral performance long after their original purpose (to provide politically safe alternatives to the original texts) had become irrelevant.

One example from these songs will suffice to illustrate the kind of texts that were set. "Gimn likovaniya" (Hymn of rejoicing) was "Dir, dir Jehova, will ich singen" (BWV 452) with new words by Ya. Rodionov. The opening lines of its text are as follows: "I praise great deeds and bravery / For the truly brave there are no obstacles! / I praise valour and might / A hero leads us on to greatness."[48] The ingratiating nature of such words is obvious, but not all Soviet Bach texts were like this: many were innocuous poems about spring, nature, and sunshine. The same fate befell Russian sacred works by Dmitry Bortniansky, Maxim Berezovsky, and others (Sveshnikov performed their music again from 1965, and Yurlov made it a specialty of his from around that time), though that particular line of inquiry goes beyond the scope of this chapter. Sometimes textual changes to the originals could be quite minor: substituting "sun" for "God," for example, or describing a hymn to God as a hymn to nature. Writing about this aspect of Sveshnikov's career, S. Kalinin defends this practice as a necessary evil:

> Sveshnikov, brought up in this culture [that of Church training] . . . bravely performed the sacred music of Russian composers, often skilfully manoeuvering, sometimes compromising, but always preserving the highest humanitarian spirituality and philosophical ideas. The circumstances of those times required certain sacrifices for the sake of saving music. In the 1940s and 50s, and in the last years of the choir, Sveshnikov performed a lot of Russian sacred music—famous concertos by Bortniansky and Berezovsky, works by Balakirev, Rachmaninoff, Kastalsky. Often he had to alter the texts, but it was worth doing so; these good words, which we remember from those unkind years, meant that this imperishable part of Russian choral culture was not consigned to oblivion (Kalinin 1998,153).

Final Thoughts

There was never any period in Soviet history when no Western sacred music was performed. Despite many limitations and restrictions, a handful of solo and orchestral works always remained in the repertoire. Any attempt to analyze why it was, for example, that Bach's *Magnificat* was dropped while the B Minor Mass was consistently performed would be fruitless. It is easy to understand why major concert works like the Romantic requiems retained their place: these were popular dramatic works that, despite their "bourgeois" origins, fit the grandiose style that was so much a part of Stalinist culture. Brahms's German Requiem, which set biblical texts in the vernacular, was an equally obvious candidate for omission, despite the fact that Bach's Passions were performed several times in the 1930s. Clearly, it was Russian sacred music that fared the worst. But though it would be correct to point out that almost no Renaissance or medieval sacred music had been heard in Moscow or Leningrad for thirty years or more, this has more to do with that fact that such repertoire did not form a strong part of the imperial Capella's traditions, and so it is not surprising that Klimov did not seek to make a special place for it after 1917. And though Volkonsky was indeed a pioneer of Soviet times in establishing a performing tradition for early music, he himself stated bluntly that he simply got the music from libraries:

> I always find it strange when people ask me where I got the music from for "Madrigal." What dreadfully lazy people! In any decent library, say for example that of the Conservatory, you can find the complete Palestrina edition. I simply took them into the reading room and copied them. I don't know why no one else had thought of doing it, because the music was all there! The Philharmonia in Peter [Saint Petersburg] has a wonderful library. They have the complete works of Schutz and Palestrina. Probably, these 19th-century editions contain many mistakes, but the scores are accessible. (Dubinets 2010, 62)

It is tempting to attribute neglect of all corners of repertoire during the Soviet period to political repression. But in fact there are a great many causes, among which simple lack of interest and awareness ranks just as highly as any ban from Narkompros or the Kremlin. In fact, as I hope to have shown, such bans were few and far between, and most gaps in performance practice occurred because of general caution, not because any committee or politician decreed that certain works could not be played. After all, the West's own traditions of performing early music were reinforced, even rejuvenated, in the 1960s, so it was not the case that musicians in Europe and America reliably knew and played such music while those behind the Iron Curtain were oblivious to it.[49] The supposed "discovery" of early music by Soviet audiences and composers in the 1960s must be set in the context of a staid, but nevertheless palpable tradition of performing a small handful of Baroque and Renaissance works throughout the entire Stalin period (quickly expanded to a slightly more generous handful after 1953): while it is likely that not a soul in the audience at Pro Musica's first concert had ever heard music by Dowland, Morley, or Wilkes, it is very likely that many knew at least one work by Lotti (*Crucifixus*) or Josquin (the likely candidate being "Et incarnatus est"), and practically everyone would have known Lassus's "Ekho" or "Tik-tak," perennial favorites with Soviet choirs. There was, therefore, a small performance tradition of singing early music that had clung on throughout the Stalin years, almost fading in the late 1940s and early 1950s, but reviving soon after that. It took only inspiration and encouragement from visiting choirs for the old Soviet choral conductors to take up the cause for their own national early music culture—not just the performance of Western works, but also the music of the Orthodox liturgy and the works that it produced in the eighteenth and nineteenth centuries.

[Parts of this chapter derive from my earlier article "'Don't Sing It on a Feast Day': The Reception and Performance of Western Sacred Music in Soviet Russia, 1917–1953," Journal of the American Musicological Society, Vol. 65, No. 1 (Spring 2012), pp. 67–111.]

Notes

1. See, for example, the monumental six-volume study *Dukhovnaya muzika v dokumentakh i materialakh* [Russian Sacred Music in Documents and Materials], edited by Marina Rakhmanova et al. (Moscow: Yazïki slavyanskoy kul'turï, 2002–2010). The last date I have traced of a public performance of Rachmaninoff's *All-Night Vigil* is 1928, and 1965 marks the year of Alexander Sveshnikov's recording of that work by Melodiya.
2. Dates for the ending of the "Thaw" period do vary among historians because it was never a seamless process, even under Khrushchev; Peter Schmelz has recently extended the period to 1974, thereby arguing for the longest Thaw period currently on record, a whole decade later than the earliest cut-off point of 1964. See Peter Schmelz, *Such Freedom, If Only Musical: Unofficial Soviet Music during the Thaw* (New York: Oxford University Press, 2009).
3. Churches were used as concert venues in the early Soviet period: in 1918, Moscow Conservatory students performed a three-concert series of Western sacred works (Mozart Requiem, Bach sacred songs, and other works by Corelli, Haydn, and Bach) at the Church of St. Peter and Paul, Moscow. It is worth noting that at this early stage, Latin texts were still translated for Russian audiences: the entire Requiem text is given in Russian in the program. See RGALI fund 2985, inventory 1, file 640. The latest date I have traced for this practice of translating or summarizing the Latin Requiem text is 1922, with extensive summaries by Igor Glebov (Boris Asafiev) placed alongside the Latin original. See RGALI fund 2685, inventory 1, file 244.
4. The best account of this is still to be found in Schwarz, *Music and Musical Life*, 11–37.
5. In the first half-decade after 1917, new orchestras included Persimfans, the famous conductorless orchestra founded by Lev Tseitlin in 1922. There is a short list of post-1917 ensembles in Schwarz (1983, 32–33).
6. The Leningrad Philharmonia was first called the (Petrograd) State Symphony Orchestra, then the State Philamonic Orchestra, and finally the Leningrad Philharmonia—a huge musical and educational organization founded formally in 1921, of which the orchestra itself was just one part. The Moscow Philharmonia was founded in 1925, with similar

wide-reaching structures. The Leningrad Capella was initially renamed the Petrograd People's Choral Academy (1918), gaining the appellation "Academic" in 1922, becoming the Leningrad State Academic Capella, then from 1954 the Glinka State Academic Capella. It is known today simply as the Glinka Academic Capella.

7. Lunacharsky occupies an honorable place in the annals of early Soviet history. He was well educated and a respected writer and lecturer on the arts. Stalin demoted him to the post of Soviet ambassador to Spain in 1933: a clear signal that his liberal role in Soviet cultural life was at a definitive end. In poor health at the time, Lunacharsky died of natural causes on the way to his new post—a fate that almost certainly saved him from being purged with his Bolshevik colleague Nikolay Bukharin and others in the show trials of the 1930s.

8. For a good account of Narkompros's membership and policies as well as an excellent picture of musical life during the first five years after 1917, see Amy Nelson, *Music for the Revolution. Musicians and Power in Early Soviet Russia* (University Park: Pennsylvania University Press, 2004), 13–40.

9. A complete list of pre- and post-revolutionary repertoire up to 1957 is given in D. V. Tkachev and I. L. Gusin, *Leningradskaya akademicheskaya kapella imeni M. I. Glinki* [The Leningrad Academic Glinka Capella. (Leningrad: 1957), 139–161.

10. The concert was reviewed in *Izvestiya*, February 21, 1918. See Nadezhda Sheremet'yeva, *M. G. Klimov. Dirizher Leningradskiy akademicheskoy kapelli* [M. G. Klimov. Director of the Leningrad Academic Capella] (Leningrad: Muzïka, 1983), 20–21.

11. They had been merged briefly under Narkompros but from July 1922 the Capella was independent. Records show that a merger was again broached in the summer of 1941, but was vigorously opposed by the Capella management. See TsGALI fund 77, inventory 2, file 242, pp. 4–7. Its independence saved it from the purge that followed the Committee on Arts Affairs investigation of the Philharmonia in late 1937, which resulted in several arrests. When the Capella's turn came to be investigated in 1941, its affairs were judged to be in good order. The investigation seems to have taken place actually during the first few months of the war: by the time the report was sent to the Committee on Arts Affairs (September 1941) the Capella had already been evacuated to Kirov.

12. He performed many other smaller sacred works, including sacred songs and motets by Lassus, Palestrina, and Bach, in addition to early Russian liturgical music (from the fourteenth century on). After 1932, when the proletarian organizations that campaigned against religious music were dissolved, the Capella again performed Russian liturgical music for a brief period until around 1935–1936.

13. See RGALI fund 645 inventory 1, file 524, p. 55. The document is signed by the secretary of Glavrepertkom, Sokolov.

14. The director of the Respublika choir and Alexander Sveshnikov's pupil, Alexander Yurlov, first discovered this repertoire in the 1950s. See the reminiscences of his choristers A. Ushkarov, I. Veprintsev, and Ye. Buneyeva in *Alexander Yurlov*, edited by Irina Marisova (Moscow: Sovetskiy Kompozitor, 1983), 65 and 103–108. All remember the upsurge in interest in Russian choral music of the sixteenth and seventeenth centuries and how Yurlov was a passionate advocate of this repertoire very early on. Sveshnikov finally recorded Rachmaninoff's *All-Night Vigil* with Melodiya in 1965.

15. See for example Nelson, *Music for the Revolution*, 207–240.

16. See Nelson, *Music for the Revolution*, 207–210.

17. In 1928 the membership of Prokoll was partially absorbed into that of RAPM. Neil Edmunds reports that even in 1928 RAPM's Moscow membership was only fifty, though

unfortunately it is unclear whether this count took place before or after Prokoll members joined. It is likely (in my opinion) that the figure of fifty represents the extended membership after Prokoll's partial absorption. See Neil Edmunds, *The Soviet Proletarian Music Movement* (Bern: Peter Lang, 2000), 12.

18. Felix Kon was a political activist with no links to music so far as is currently known. For an excellent discussion of the proletarian groups' activities in music from 1917 to 1932, see Edmunds, *The Soviet Proletarian Music Movement*. For a useful brief summary of the extent of RAPM's influence at this time, see Nelson, *Music for the Revolution*, especially 213–220.

19. See for example G. Anisimov, "Na bor'ba s tserkovshchinoy v muzïke" [On the struggle with the church's influence in music] *Za proletarskuyu muzïku* 6 (40) (1932), 6–9, where the writer indignantly quotes from the 1927 plenum of the All-Union Society of Evangelical Christians, who reported seven Evangelical choirs in Leningrad. Religion, along with the so-called "kulaks" (rich peasants), was a target of the Cultural Revolution, which extended the attacks upon priests and worshippers that Lenin had initiated, but informal small-scale meetings of worshippers were never fully stamped out. The toleration of this Soviet "Christian Union" typified the more liberal years of the New Economic Policy (approximately 1921–1928).

20. RGALI fund 645 (Glavisskustvo), inventory 1, file 121, pp. 87–88.

21. RGALI fund 645, inventory 1, file 344. Stenogramme of All-Russian Conference on Amateur Musical Art, p. 12.

22. See RGALI fund 645 inventory 1, file 344. Stenogramme of All-Russian Conference on Amateur Musical Art, p. 28.

23. See transcripts in Gnesin's file: RGALI fund 2954, inventory 1, file 176, pp. 87–124. For a discussion of this chapter in Soviet musical life, and of Gnesin's contribution to debates at this point, see Marina Frolova Walker and Jonathan Walker, *Music and Soviet Power 1917-1932*, pp. 314–321; and Yekaterina Vlasova, *1948 god v sovetskoy muzïke* [The year 1948 in Soviet music] (Moscow: Klassica XXI, 2010), 122–141.

24. Viktor Vinogradov, *Protiv tserkovshchina v muzïke*. Moscow: State Music Publishers, 1931.

25. See RGALI fund 2954, inventory 1, file 176, p. 56.

26. RGALI fund 2954, inventory 1, file 176, pp. 91–92 verso, 111 (recto and verso).

27. Modernism was also a RAPM target, despite the fact that earlier in the 1920s, proletarian groups like Proletkul't had included major figures of Soviet modernism. By the late 1920s, this attitude had changed, and an aggressive anti-intellectualism prevailed in RAPM music circles.

28. Works in this category range from Glinka's "Lullaby" to songs by the RAPM composers Davidenko and Koval.

29. See Russian National Library, manuscript department. Fund 1127 (Klimov), file 26.

30. A *raspev* is basically the same as plainchant.

31. *Kant* in Russian simply means "song," but *kantï* in this context denotes a capella sacred songs that could be sung in church.

32. See Russian National Library, manuscript department. Fund 1127 (Klimov), file 26 (Klimov's work diary).

33. Whether the Capella really did perform this repertoire publicly is impossible to verify. Klimov's work diary shows that it was certainly his intention, but Sheremet'yeva's excellent book (which, like my own study, includes study of Klimov's personal papers as well as the Capella fund in TsGALI) states that it was only sung in closed educational concerts. See Sheremet'yeva, *M. G. Klimov*, 69.

34. Sveshnikov did not join the Communist Party until 1948, the year when he was asked to take up the post of rector at the Moscow Conservatory. Unfortunately, this was in replacement for Vissarion Shebalin, sacked in the wake of the 1948 attacks on him and other distinguished figures in Soviet musical life: Shostakovich, Prokofiev, Myaskovsky, and Gavriil Popov.
35. See especially the letter from the Presidium of the Committee on Arts Affairs to the Kremlin in RGALI fund 962, inventory 16, file 15, p. 136.
36. I retain the Russian spelling convention of Lasso rather than Lassus in citations and quotations from Russian documents and published sources.
37. The limitations of this "fostering" (for example, requiring every nation to have Russian as their first language, and being directly under Moscow's command) are discussed by Frolova-Walker in her seminal article "National in Form, Socialist in Content: Musical Nation-Building in the Soviet Republics." *Journal of the American Musicological Society*, 51/2, 1998, pp. 331–371.
38. See TsGALI fund 77 inventory 2, file 166.
39. TsGALI fund 77, inventory 2, file 229. This plan was, of course, unrealized.
40. TsGALI fund 77, inventory 2, file 346, p. 20.
41. This would have been the chorus part only, sung without orchestra.
42. This work, which remained very popular not only in the Capella's repertoire but in that of numerous Soviet choirs, was a wordless choral arrangement of the piano piece "Traumerei."
43. For a concise account of this episode in Soviet musical life, see Schwarz 1983, pp. 204–248
44. Namely, Gustav Reese, *Music of the Renaissance*. New York, W.W. Norton & Co., Inc., 1954. For a discussion of Madrigal, see Elena Dubinets, *Knyaz Andrey Volkonsky: Partitura zhizni* [Prince Andrey Volkonsky: the score of life] (Moscow: Ripol Klassik, 2010), 61–73.
45. He had already recorded this work with Melodiya in 1962.
46. See Russian National Library, manuscript department. Fund 1127 (Klimov), file 21 (concert programmes).
47. See J. S. Bach, 10 songs for voice and piano, Moscow: Muzïka, 1966; but the multi-volume "The State academic Russian Choir of the USSR sings" edited by Sveshnikov only gives Soviet-period texts.
48. The song is available online at http://www.notarhiv.ru/zarubkomp/bah/noti/1%20%286%29.pdf
49. I would like to take this opportunity to thank David Fallows for several enlightening conversations on this topic, especially for sharing his own performance experiences as an early music performer in California during the 1960s.

References

Archival Sources

Committee on Arts Affairs. Rossiyskiy Gosudarstvennïy Arkhiv Literaturï i Iskusstva [Russian State Archive of Literature and Art], Moscow. (RGALI fund 962)

Asaf'yev. Rossiyskiy Gosudarstvennïy Arkhiv Literaturï i Iskusstva [Russian State Archive of Literature and Art], Moscow. (RGALI fund 2658)

Glaviskusstvo and Narkompros. Rossiyskiy Gosudarstvennïy Arkhiv Literaturï I Iskusstva [Russian State Archive of Literature and Art], Moscow. (RGALI fund 645)

Glavrepertkom. Rossiyskiy Gosudarstvennïy Arkhiv Literaturï i Iskusstva [Russian State Archive of Literature and Art], Moscow. (RGALI fund 656)
Gnesin. Rossiyskiy Gosudarstvennïy Arkhiv Literaturï i Iskusstva [Russian State Archive of Literature and Art], Moscow. (RGALI fund 2954)
Ippolitov-Ivanov. Gosudarstvenniy tsentral'niy muzey muzïkal'noy kul'turï imenni M. I. Glinki [Glinka State Central Museum of Musical Culture], Moscow. (GTsMMK fund 2)
Kiselev. Rossiyskiy Gosudarstvennïy Arkhiv Literaturï i Iskusstva [Russian State Archive of Literature and Art], Moscow. (RGALI fund 2985)
Klimov. Manuscript Department, National Library of Russia, St. Petersburg.
Leningrad Capella. Tsentral'niy Gosudarstvennïy Arkhiv Literaturï i Iskusstva, St. Petersburg. (TsGALI fund 77)
Moscow Philharmonia. Rossiyskiy Gosudarstvennïy Arkhiv Literaturï i Iskusstva [Russian State Archive of Literature and Art], Moscow. (RGALI fund 2922)
Program archive of the Leningrad Philharmonia. Philharmonia Library, St Petersburg.
Sveshnikov. Gosudarstvenniy tsentral'niy muzey muzïkal'noy kul'turï imenni M. I. Glinki [Glinka State central museum of musical culture], Moscow. (GTsMMK fund 448)

Published Primary Sources

Anisimov, G. 1932. "Na bor'ba s tserkovshchinoy v muzïke" [On the struggle with the church's influence in music]. *Za proletarskuyu muzïku* 6, no. 40: 6–9.
Dubinets, Elena. 2010. *Knyaz Andrey Volkonsky: Partitura zhizni* [Prince Andrey Volkonsky: the score of life]. Moscow: Ripol Klassik.
Sollertinsky, Ivan. 1939. Untitled review. *Leningradskaya Pravda*, 22 April, 3.
Vinogradov, Viktor. 1931. *Protiv tserkovshchina v muzïke* [Against church influence in music]. Moscow: State Music Publishers.

Secondary Sources

Edmunds, Neil. 2000. *The Soviet Proletarian Music Movement*. Bern: Peter Lang.
Frolova-Walker, Marina and Walker, Jonathan. 2012. *Music and Soviet Power 1917–1932*, Woodbridge: Boydell Press.
Frolova-Walker, Marina. 1998. "National in Form, Socialist in Content: Musical Nation-Building in the Soviet Republics." *Journal of the American Musicological Society* 51, no. 2: 331–371.
Hakobian, Levon. 2010. "Shostakovich, Proletkul't and RAPM." In *Shostakovich Studies* 2, edited by Pauline Fairclough, 263–271. Cambridge: Cambridge University Press.
Kalinin, Stanislav, ed. 1998. *Pamyati Alexandra Vasil'evicha Sveshnikova* [In memory of Alexander Vasil'evich Sveshnikov]. Moscow: Muzïka.
Marisova, Irina, ed. 1983. *Alexander Yurlov*. Moscow: Sovetskiy Kompozitor.
Muzalevsky, Vladimir. 1938. *Stareyshiy russkiy khor* [The oldest Russian choir]. Leningrad and Moscow: Iskusstvo.
Muzalevsky, Vladimir. 1960. *Mikhail Georgevich Klimov: Ocherk zhizni i tvorcheskoy deyatel'nosti* [Mikhail Georgevich Klimov: Essays on his life and work]. Leningrad: Sovetskiy Kompozitor.
Nelson, Amy. 2004. *Music for the Revolution: Musicians and Power in Early Soviet Russia*. University Park: Pennsylvania State University Press.

Schmelz, Peter. 2009. *Such Freedom, if Only Musical: Unofficial Soviet Music During the Thaw*. New York: Oxford University Press.

Schwarz, Boris. 1983. *Music and Musical Life in Soviet Russia, 1917–1981*. Enl. ed. Bloomington: Indiana University Press.

Sheremet'yeva, Nadezhda. 1983. *M. G. Klimov. Dirizher Leningradskiy akademicheskoy kapellï* [M. G. Klimov. Director of the Leningrad academic capella]. Leningrad: Muzïka.

Tkachev, D. V. and Gusin, I. L. 1957. *Leningradskaya akademicheskaya kapella imeni M. I. Glinki* [The Leningrad Academic Glinka Capella]. Leningrad.

Vlasova, Yekaterina. 2010. *1948 god v sovetskoy muzïke* [The year 1948 in Soviet music]. Moscow: Klassika XXI.

CHAPTER 6

A STRIDENT SILENCING
The Ban on Richard Wagner in Israel

NA'AMA SHEFFI

FOLLOWING *Kristallnacht*, the anti-Jewish pogrom that took place in Germany in November 1938, Richard Wagner (1813–1883) became persona non grata in Israel's concert halls. Several days after the pogrom a work by Wagner was removed from the concert program of the Palestine Symphony Orchestra—which would become the Israel Philharmonic Orchestra (henceforth, "IPO")—for ideological reasons. After the establishment of the state of Israel in 1948, Wagner became identified with the racist views of National Socialism and vicious anti-Semitism and his musical oeuvre turned into one of the explicit symbols of the Holocaust and its atrocities. No one, however, from the legislative and judicial authorities to the Board for Film and Theater Review (the censorship board) and the broadcasting and orchestra institutions ever publicly banned the performance of Wagner's work.

Since the 1990s Wagner has been the only composer whose performance in Israel has stirred up bitter resentment. The ban on other composers, whom the orchestras and broadcasting authorities refrained from performing, was lifted. Franz Lehar, Carl Orff, and Richard Strauss—all composers who collaborated with the Nazi regime—are not frequently included in the programs of Israel's large orchestras, but they no longer arouse public controversy. Recordings of performers who collaborated with the Nazis to one degree or another—including conductors Wilhelm Furtwängler, Herbert von Karajan, and Karl Böhm and singers such as German soprano Elizabeth Schwartzkopf and Norwegian soproano Kirsten Flagstad—are broadcast. From the outset Richard Strauss was the only musician who generated as much discontent as Wagner. As the founding director of the music chamber in the Nazi Ministry of Propaganda, Strauss was perceived as an ideological ally of the Nazis.

The gradual lifting of the ban on composers and performers identified with National Socialism gave birth to the most profound statement against playing the music of these artists. In January 1994, after several sessions of the Knesset debating the performance of works by anti-Semitic composers identified with National

Socialism, its Education and Culture Committee came up with a document supporting the status quo. Its statement that freedom of expression is a supreme value in Israel was accompanied by an appeal "from the heart," requesting the cultural institutions to refrain from performing the works of the anti-Semitic composers, should these hurt the feelings of the public (Lahav 2001, 3). The public in question was specific—Holocaust survivors who associated the music of the anti-Semitic composers with their lives in the labor, concentration, and death camps. This was the first time the Knesset had ever formulated such a clear-cut directive. Until then the ministers of education and culture were guided by a uniform line regardless of their political affinity: all believed that there was no room for the state to intervene in a matter that was essentially artistic. Particularly lucid on this point was Minister of Education Zalman Aran who in 1956 replied to a parliamentary question: "Once sounds are born, they have an independent existence, and I don't think there is any point in forbidding the existence of sound."[1]

In this chapter, I will analyze the fundamental reasons for the opposition to performing Wagner's work in Israel in a broad cultural and political context. I believe that Wagner became a symbol, the representative of the wrongdoings perpetrated by National Socialism, thus making him a tool in the hands of those who created the memory of the Holocaust in the then young Israeli society. Consequently, in Israel Wagner's music became a memorial site for the Holocaust of European Jewry, and banning him was perceived as a cultural act with an educational angle. Public discourse was charged with emotional context, having to handle the trauma that the Holocaust imprinted not only upon the survivors and their families, but on the Israeli public in its entirety.[2] The Wagner controversy relates not only to historical events but to the political context of the time as well. The Reparations Agreement (1952), the establishment of full diplomatic relations with the Federal Republic of Germany (1965), normalization of West Germany's status in the 1970s, the crisis of trust between Prime Minister Menachem Begin and Chancellor Helmut Schmidt (1981), and the breakdown of trust between Israelis and Germans over the Gulf War (1991) permeated the public discourse over Wagner.

Numerous Israelis regarded the ban on Wagner as an opportunity to underscore their objection to the atrocities committed by the National Socialists even as their government was warming up relations with the Federal Republic of Germany. Similar motivation encouraged others to support the performance of Wagner: according to their worldview, Israel should adopt a liberal approach that would swiftly counteract what the Nazis had sought to do to Jewish culture. A fundamental discussion of Wagner's role as one of the formulators of nineteenth-century intellectual anti-Semitism was almost non-existent in Israel. The majority of references to anti-Semitic context were confined to populist statements. An assortment of social groups participated in the discussion: Holocaust survivors whose presence in the discourse increased the older they became and their relative presence in society diminished; those who had left Europe, and Germany in particular, prior to the Holocaust; and, as of the 1980s, younger generations who had not experienced the Holocaust.

In interpreting the discourse I will refer to articles and reports that appeared in the Israeli press, which was the main stage for the public debate, as well as the Israel Philharmonic Orchestra's concert programs, public appeals to musical and governmental institutions, debates in the Knesset and its Education and Culture Committee, and additional literature regarding Israeli society and the controversy surrounding Wagner within and outside Israel. It is no simple matter to characterize the public discussion of the Wagner affair by partisan and socioeconomic or generational characteristics. Even if some characteristics can be identified, the most notable of them is the lack of significant cross-sections of position-holders in the discussion.

The Birth of a Symbol

The Wagner affair in Israel was openly defined only fifty years after the end of World War II. In 1994, the Knesset's Education and Culture Committee discussed the composers associated with National Socialism in Israeli consciousness. As is customary in the brief history of the discourse on Wagner in Israeli society, in this case too the committee refrained from establishing hard and fast rules regarding composers in general and Wagner in particular. Nonetheless, the committee approached musical bodies with the objective of having them accept their request "from the heart," and refrain from playing the works of composers that aroused stormy emotions in some Israelis. Seven years later the committee considered including a piece by Wagner in a concert at the annual Israel Festival. Shaul Yahalom, a National Religious Party Knesset member associated with a cultural and national standpoint, defined the essential problem well:

> No need for fine distinctions here. There is no doubt that in the popular mind Wagner has become the classic symbol of anti-Semitism and the spiritual father of Nazism. There is nothing to argue about here, and we could line up a thousand proofs, but even if we don't agree, this is what happened and it is an inalienable part of the culture of the State of Israel. The first boycott of Wagner was begun by the people in the art world themselves, by the Palestine Philharmonic Orchestra, when, after *Kristallnacht*, it canceled its performance of a Wagner piece. This means that the musicians themselves felt they just could not do it.[3]

Seventy years later it became obvious that the emotional element of the Wagner boycott was its main characteristic. The discussion was not motivated by legislation, ideology, or rational arguments, but rather by emotions that filtered down through the generations and were internalized as part of the collective memory of Israelis. Moreover, Wagner's place in Israeli society is not only a symbol of Nazi crimes. Many believe the debate serves as a platform for examining the morality of Israeli society and its willingness to express a critical viewpoint when politics dictates otherwise. Indeed, from the moment the overture to *Die Meistersinger von Nürnberg* was removed from the program in November 1938, Wagner was viewed as not only an artist but a complete idea.

Like other important European artists since the nineteenth century, Wagner's musical works were incorporated into the Palestine Symphonic Orchestra's repertoire. The orchestra was established in 1936 by violinist Bronislaw Huberman for ideological reasons. As a political personality, Huberman was aware of the negative changes affecting German Jews since the Nazis' rise to power. He refused an invitation sent by Wilhelm Furtwängler to appear in Nazi Germany and wrote him harsh letters in 1933. After the Nazi race laws came into effect in February 1936, he published an open and critical letter to German intellectuals in the *Manchester Guardian* (Huberman 2005). The orchestra he established in Palestine became the home of Jews who had previously performed in well-known European orchestras and had decided to leave their country due to anti-Semitic persecution and the enforcement of Germany's racist laws. The conductor of the opening concert was Arturo Toscanini, a no less political personality. After refusing to appear in his homeland, Italy, upon realizing the future course of action of Benito Mussolini's regime, he also refused to conduct a concert in Wagner's city, Bayreuth, which was the first of the German cities to be adopted by the Nazis at the end of the 1920s (Sachs 1988).

The extensive repertoire of the orchestra was ideologically challenged following the organized pogrom against Germany's Jews on the night between November 9 and 10, 1938. Within a day, reports on the events of *Kristallnacht* reached the Jewish *Yishuv* in Palestine. The opening concert in the series was planned for the following Saturday evening, November 12. It might well be that the total silence of the German intellectuals prompted Huberman to respond immediately by removing *Die Meistersinger von Nürnberg* from the program. The circumstances were obvious: the plot was associated with medieval German culture, now compared with the belligerent Nazi regime of the time; the composer, Richard Wagner, was a renowned member of anti-Semitic circles despite the fact that he was helped by Jews in his work.[4] The chairperson of the management of the orchestra, Moshe Chelouche, one of Tel Aviv's notable figures, approached Eugen Szenkár who was to conduct the concert that evening. Szenkár could easily relate to the sentiments as he was on the list of 108 artists who had been banned by the Nazi propaganda minister, Joseph Goebbels (Geiger 2002). He replaced Wagner's piece with the overture to *Oberon*, written by an earlier German composer, Carl Maria von Weber, who was, among other things, the object of Wagner's admiration. In February 1939 Szenkár himself conducted pieces by Wagner during the orchestra's tour of Cairo and Alexandria.

Thus, the same people who had staunchly supported social liberalism and intellectual pluralism in Europe and who had refused to cooperate with the standard-bearers of totalitarianism now used a cultural artifact to express an ideological position. The protest against racist legislation in Nazi Germany, and the connection between Wagner's music and the events of the times which the *Yishuv* intellectuals and artists suggested, framed Wagner's work of art as a symbol of evil. At the time, it was impossible to foresee that this momentary act would be perpetuated as voluntary censorship that would be repeated time and again.

The circumstances that brought about the first cancellation of a performance of Wagner's music became part of the public discourse that followed. Ideological context, political weakness replaced by a moral response, and strong emotions—all these appeared in different permutations in all stages of the public controversy in Israel. The institutions of the Jewish *Yishuv* did not intervene in the decision taken in 1938. When later questioned on this issue, the state institutions also refused to act and made do with outlining a pluralistic line of action. The demand to enforce voluntary censorship filtered upward from below, from the public. Only at the end of the twentieth century, when the boycott on composers and performers who collaborated with the Nazis (with the exception of Wagner who was perceived as a factor that influenced the Nazis) was lifted, did the state institutions modify their approach somewhat. It was then established that since the matter was emotional, it was appropriate to be mindful of the feelings of the survivors, but again the institutions refrained from enforcing censorship on Wagner's works in Israel. Nonetheless, publications regarding Hitler's admiration of Wagner, the Wagner family's admiration of Hitler, the early Nazification of Bayreuth, and the statements of survivors that Wagner's music was played in the concentration camps, transformed the sounds into a monument for the Holocaust and the outcasts in Israeli society alike. Arguments for and against performing Wagner's music only intensified the symbolization process and the choice not to publicly perform Wagner's works. Until the 1990s Richard Strauss was also associated with this process.

The Foundations of Internal Censorship

The 1950s and 1960s were formative years in Israeli society that witnessed a huge increase in population—the result of mass immigration. The population grew from 650,000 in 1948 when the state was established to three million at the end of the 1960s. As an immigrant society, the cultural roots and ideational approaches of Israelis are wide-ranging. Despite its diversity, the political, economic, social, and cultural patterns that shaped its infrastructure were consolidated during the first twenty years of the state's existence; and some were later altered.[5] Configuration of the country's foreign policy and the ways of preserving the memory of the Holocaust were consolidated. These two issues are of cardinal importance in interpreting the responses to attempts to perform Wagner's music in Israel.

Examination of the reports on the Wagner affair in Israel's daily papers in the 1950s and 1960s is surprising. Not only Wagner was in the eye of the storm, but so was Richard Strauss. Differentiating between the opposition to each of them is not entirely clear and may well be one of the causes of the vagueness about Wagner's role in the Third Reich. The extensive place accorded to discussion of this issue is also somewhat surprising. A handful of newspapers were published in those years in Israel and can be divided into three main categories: those belonging to political bodies; foreign-language newspapers printed for new immigrants that were in most cases labeled politically; and those that acted according to market forces, had political affiliations, albeit were not owned by any party. Other types of media were limited: The Voice of Israel, the state radio station broadcast on two networks during part of the day; and Galei Zahal, the army station, which broadcast only a few hours of the day. State television was founded in 1968, and multiple channels have existed since the 1990s. The electronic media joined the discussion of the boycotted composers as of the 1980s.

The Wagner-Strauss issue was raised for discussion five times during the 1950s and 1960s. On all these occasions the desire to perform their music was bound up with political issues, and none of them served for setting hard and fast rules regarding the future. The only context in which an unequivocal regulation regarding German culture was determined related to holding public performances in the German language. In November 1950, the Board for Film and Theater Review (the censorship board) published an announcement according to which no further performances in German would be allowed in Israel.[6] Since this was a decree the public could not follow, it was observed only in part. Thus, for example, when mezzo-soprano Jennie Tourel demanded to sing Mahler's *Das Lied von der Erde* in German, her request was granted; and Marlene Dietrich, who had two performances in Israel, sang several songs in German (after making it clear that if anyone objected she would sing in English).[7] The IPO management discussed the matter in 1963, leaving matters to an ad hoc decision when the time came. In the same debate the matter of the orchestra playing liturgical music was also raised, a sign of the degree of sensitivity to cultural-national issues in the young country. In November 1966 a group of World War II partisans asked the orchestra to refrain from performing musical works in German.[8]

Debates on Wagner and Strauss in the press, the Knesset, and the public arena in general were responses to the intention to perform or the actual performance of their music. In most cases the public debate related to Strauss, but Wagner was mentioned in the same breath, as if the two represented the same challenge to Israel's nation and culture. November 1952 was the first time the papers published reports on the intention to play the music of the two composers. In fact, the IPO intended to play a piece from *Till Eulenspiegel*. The immense interest aroused was a counter reaction to the warming of Israel's foreign relations with West Germany. At the beginning of that year, Prime Minister David Ben-Gurion announced the signing of the Reparation Agreement between Israel and West Germany, which was accompanied by a heated demonstration in Jerusalem and a trenchant public debate in which the parties—both right-wing and left-wing—attacked the government (Segev 1993, 211–252). By now many were opposed to the idea of playing the music of Strauss, "who had perpetuated the memory of the fallen in his *In Memoriam*, wrote a hymn to [Hans] Frank, arch-executioner of Poland, and frequently panegyrized his leaders in works of praise of the Nazi party."[9]

Public discussion at this stage of the controversy revealed not only the rage over reestablishing relations with Germany, but also historical pain. The IPO had no intention whatsoever of playing any of Wagner's music, but once his name came up in the debate, the complexity that Israelis felt vis-à-vis the sounds of his music became clear:

In Leipzig they stopped playing Mendelssohn, in Vienna they didn't play Mahler. We continued to play Wagner until the new immigrants arrived as they felt terrified when hearing his sounds. These were living people who had experienced on their own skin the atrocities of the influence of Wagner's music on the German savages. And we ceased performing the music of the father of anti-Semitic ideology in music, and in art in general.[10]

In just a few words the *Davar* writer decoded the core of the problem: sounds. Aversion to the emotional connotation associated with playing specific sounds had been discussed in the nineteenth century in Freidrich Neitzche's insightful essay "Twilight of the Idols." His argument regarding the power of motifs which Wagner constantly used and which trigger the emotions of listeners, were developed by intellectuals and researchers in the following centuries as well.[11] Despite the emotional complexity, the state of Israel preferred to preserve the democratic-liberal values that were at the basis of its guidelines and refrain from enlisting censorship as a response to these fervent emotions.

In the spring of 1953 the issue was inflamed even more as a result of a series of recitals by violinist Jascha Heifetz, which included Strauss' Violin Sonata in E-flat major, Op. 18. The aggravation was, among other things, the result of Heifetz's resolute resistance to censorship on music and his refusal to comply with the repeated request of the Minister of Education, Professor Ben-Zion Dinur, and the Minister of Justice, Dr. Pinchas Rosen, who also served as the IPO chairperson. The intervention of these two deserves special attention. Dinur initiated the Holocaust Martyrs' and Heroes' Remembrance—Yad va-Shem Law (1953) and was the motivating force for establishing the Yad va-Shem institution (Dinur 2009). Several years later Rosen became the influential political figure that outlined the application of the Nazis and Nazi Collaborators Punishment Law (1950) in the course of the hearing of the matter of Israel (Rudolf) Kastner, who had negotiated with the Nazis to save Hungarian Jews (September 1954 to June 1955; Kastner was murdered in 1957 and was exonerated a year later); and, in a completely different vein, he was involved in the matter of the senior Nazi official Adolf Eichmann from May 1960 to May 1962 (Bondy 1990). It was clear that the two ministers were sensitive to the reservations felt by numerous Israelis about the penetration of German culture into their society. The increasingly hostile expressions toward Heifetz were also directed at the IPO, which hosted him in a concert series. Finally, on April 16, 1953, a few days after Holocaust and Heroism Remembrance Day in Israel, Heifetz was attacked at the end of a recital in Jerusalem. Even in face of this brutal act, however, censorship was not applied to Strauss in Israel.[12]

The IPO attempt to incorporate pieces from Strauss' *Don Juan* at the end of 1956 was thwarted due to a harsh public response and the fact that the subject was raised for debate in the Knesset. Minister of Education Zalman Aran refused to enforce censorship on music, arguing that "once sounds are born, they have an independent existence." Members of the IPO and Chairperson Rosen published a manifesto announcing their intention to implement their right to make artistic decisions (Bondy 1990, 489; Interpellation 670, Nov. 26, 1956). By the end of that decade the issue of problematic composers was raised several times for discussion in the IPO management, but no real results emerged.

A full-blown storm broke out in June 1966 with the publication of an article dealing with the concluding series of the 1965/6 season in which the orchestra declared its intention of incorporating some of Wagner's and Strauss's pieces in the following season. The chapter opened with the words, "A change has taken place in the nation's attitude towards the exterminators of our people." This wording stirred up anger among many, including public figures who participated in the public debate on Wagner and Strauss in its early stages. The following day the problematic sentence was removed, but the fundamental explanation remained unchanged:

> We feel the time has come for a change, not only because of the paramount demands of artistic freedom, but also because the opposition to Wagner has become a mere gesture. Why should we go on denying ourselves some of the greatest music by forbidding the playing of Wagner, a loss that cannot be replaced by the works of any other composer, while a mere convenience like the German Volkswagen, with all its associations with the Hitler era, is allowed to crowd our streets? [. . .] Accordingly, this time we must take a rational and courageous stand and allow Wagner's music to be played, thereby reopening the door to works included among the best of the music composed in the nineteenth century.[13]

In complete antithesis to the emotional public atmosphere surrounding the subject, Uri Toeplitz, the orchestra's first flautist and member of the management, argued rationally in his article about the hypocrisy of the attempt to differentiate between commodities and cultural symbols. He totally rejected the voluntary censorship which had been implemented over the years only because it was so easy to do so. The timing of the announcement was not accidental. Since the early 1960s West Germany had been increasingly present in Israeli public life. In 1960 an allegedly chance meeting took place between Prime Minister David Ben-Gurion and German Chancellor Konrad Adenauer in New York. Five years later the two countries established full diplomatic relations (Romberg 2005). In 1960 Adolf Eichmann was abducted and taken to Israel, and his trial opened a year later. This was the first time that the general public in Israel was exposed to life in the labor, concentration, and death camps. Overt emotional handling of the charged past was a breakthrough. Until then it was obvious that public discussion of the Holocaust was limited to dealing with the courage of the few who rose up against the Nazis, courage compatible with the Zionist ethos (Yablonka 2004). The emotional change vis-à-vis the past that took place in Israeli society as a collective was doubtlessly the backdrop for accepting the decision to incorporate Wagner and Strauss into the repertoire.

In the summer of 1966 Israelis found themselves in a taxing situation: alongside the deep economic recession, they were concerned that the Syrians would divert the waters of the Jordan River, thus drying out the country. Nevertheless, the dispute over the musicians identified with National Socialism was promptly inflamed, drawing in more politicians than in the past. They felt that the non-interventional policy of the Ministry of Education and Culture was the core of the ambiguity, but in fact, it had made a totally clear statement of its refusal to take an unambiguous stand on the issue: the ministry refused to deal with cultural censorship or any other measure that would dictate cultural life in Israel. Between the lines, moreover, an argument emerged that would become paramount in the following decades: the fact that a foreign conductor, Zubin Mehta, wanted to perform *Tristan und Isolde,* incited Israelis who felt that the issue was "Jewish" and "internal to Israel."[14] In the fall of 1969 Mehta attempted to violate the cultural taboo by performing a piece from *Till Eulenspiegel* but reconsidered due to the opposition.

In contrast to the music of Wagner and Strauss, which generated fierce opposition, Carl Orff's music was performed freely. The Israeli Opera produced *Carmina Burana,* a composition designed to serve as an antithesis to the atonality employed by the Jewish composer Arnold Schönberg. The works of Orff, a notorious collaborator with the Nazi regime, were also broadcast on state radio.[15]

The very existence of these detailed discussions on the place of the collaborating composers is surprising. Only a small part of Israeli society grew up on classical music. The complexity of the works of Wagner and Strauss doubtlessly limited their appeal to the Israeli public. But their significance, and moreover their instrumentality, made them familiar to Israeli society. The instrumentalization of both was twofold: on the one hand they served as a lightning rod for Israelis' opposition to renewing ties with Germany. On the other, Israel's refraining from censoring them proved the loyalty of Israel's leadership to cultural pluralism. In the following decades the place of the "banned composers" underwent a change in Israeli society.

Between Fasting and Memory

Discussions of the collaborating composers continued in the following decades. By the end of the century the attitude toward them softened, and they were accepted in the concert halls and radio stations, but with one exception: Richard Wagner. The relative calm that characterized the 1970s in this context should not mislead us. It was a deceptive decade in Israeli society. From a sense of power accorded by the achievements of the Six-Day War (1967), the overall mood changed dramatically following the losses of the 1973 Arab-Israeli War. That decade also witnessed a political upheaval beginning with a series of resignations in politics and the military after the war, and ending in the historical replacement of the hegemonic party in 1977. The Likud party took up the reins of power and formed a coalition with the religious parties, and this political change also marked a shift in attitudes toward Wagner.

At the end of 1981 the IPO played *Liebestod* from *Tristan and Isolde.* It was the first time in forty-three years that Wagner's music had been performed in an Israeli concert hall. But this was not a genuine breakthrough since a heated argument that took place in the hall cast a pall over the performance. The piece was performed as an encore after Zubin Mehta, the orchestra's musical director, made a preliminary announcement, suggesting that those who objected to the piece leave the hall. A breakthrough vis-à-vis Wagner came from a different direction: it was the first time that a meaningful debate about Wagner's place in the history of music and his worldview was conducted in Israel.[16] In this case, too, the force of emotions related to political events. A party traditionally opposed to ties with Germany, insisting on preventing the performance of composers identified with National Socialism, had come into power. When the controversy resumed, Prime Minister Menachem Begin was involved in an open conflict with Chancellor Helmut Schmidt regarding the latter's statement that Germany was indirectly responsible for the Palestinian refugees. In addition, despite their advanced years Holocaust survivors joined the discussion with a vengeance. It may well be that the relative openness of Israeli society regarding the survivors spurred them to do so, or perhaps they were investing special efforts, under the assumption that it was one of their last opportunities to leave their mark on the debate.

One of the statements made by Avraham Melamed, a Holocaust survivor and violinist in the orchestra, is worthy of note:

> Some time ago I saw the film *Apocalypse Now*, and in one of the scenes helicopters came down and bombed to the sound of music that made my stomach turn over. At first I didn't understand what was wrong with me, but afterwards I suddenly realized that it was Wagner's music.[17]

Melamed's words once more bear witness to the fact that sounds can generate resistance. Furthermore, his statement clarifies why it was impossible to impose censorship at this stage. In previous decades Israeli society could conduct internal debates on the issue of composers, as it was a closed society with meager resources. Israelis hardly ever traveled abroad, cultural import to Israel was insignificant, and exposure to international media was limited. Ever since the 1967 War, and particularly since the beginning of the 1980s, a crucial change had taken place. The economic situation of the country and its citizens improved and thus it was no longer possible to control the cultural abundance experienced by Israelis. Consequently, Melamed, inadvertently watching an American war film, was ill-prepared for the emotional turmoil that stemmed from his personal history as a Holocaust survivor.

In the 1980s the Israeli press was in its heyday and included newspapers that were affiliated with national, religious, and ultra-Orthodox groups as well as thriving local papers. Accordingly, the public debate took on a considerably sectarian and cultural nature. At this stage two interconnected issues concerning Israeli society were particularly notable. One of these issues related to individual freedom. As a result of growing exposure to the outside world through increased travel abroad and television watching, Israelis were becoming more aware of their own personal freedom. Now the moral question of playing Wagner went beyond the question of possible insult to the feelings of the Holocaust survivors. Israelis also asked themselves if it was permissible to prohibit the consumption of cultural works.[18]

Together with this fundamental debate, other questions relating to national belonging in the context of listening to Wagner were raised for discussion. Right-wingers raised questions with a national flavor, believing that Israelis should not listen to Wagner as he was the symbol of anti-Semitism and was identified with the catastrophe that had befallen the Jews. Left-wingers believed that the evil and racism represented by Wagner mandated that he should remain outside Israel's accepted cultural works. One of the responses merits particular attention. Knesset Member Shevach Weiss (Labor Alignment), a Holocaust survivor himself, explained in his column in *Davar*: "It is an un-Jewish act by an orchestra that was founded by survivors of Nazism, by the indirect victims of Wagnerism. It is a narrowness of spirit in Jews, a sort of embracing of the oppressive seigneur. This time the seigneur comes in the form of a German musician."[19] In other words, Weiss sought to refrain from any possible identification of the victim with the hangman, a common phenomenon, the analysis of which is still in its early stages (see, e.g., LaCapra 2001).

The question of nationalism also sharpened another observation. Things that had been barely mentioned in the 1960s were now particularly notable: the demand that the Wagner issue be discussed within Israeli society (from the point of view of the good of the society) and not by outsiders. This approach was characteristic of quite a few op-ed articles—including those written by secular people—in which the following type of dilemmas were interwoven:

> How would Zubin Mehta and his people react if, for example, they were brought together in some place where there were sacred cows. Suppose someone got up and said: 'We are about to slaughter the cows. Those who do not want to watch, should leave.' Would that seem right to Zubin Mehta?[20]

Dov Shilansky, deputy minister in the prime minister's office, was far more outspoken. In a radio interview he suggested that Mehta "go back to India." Later he claimed that he had meant that the Israelis alone should decide upon the Wagner issue. As in the early days of the controversy, now too the debate drew journalists from right and left, politicians, intellectuals, and musicians. No one demanded that the state impose censorship.

The issue of Wagner and Strauss was raised again several times in the 1980s. In November 1982 conductor Igor Markevitch recorded *Till Eulenspiegel* with the Israel Broadcasting Authority Symphony Orchestra. His request to include the piece in the season's repertoire was denied, but it spurred the Broadcasting Authority's management to decide to permit playing musical pieces by collaborators with National Socialism, with the exception of Wagner and Strauss, who would be played for didactic purposes only. Two years later, the collection *Who's Afraid of Richard Wagner,* which comprised articles by Wagner, and studies about him, was published (Litvin and Shelach 1984). This was the first time Israelis were offered comprehensive material on Wagner and his perceptions. A year earlier, in 1983, the Western world marked the centennial of Wagner's death, an event that was completely ignored in Israel.

At the end of the decade it seemed that the attitude toward Wagner had softened. In 1988 a recital series performed by the Israeli pianist Gilead Mishory included Franz Liszt's adaptation of Wagner's *Liebestod*. This was reported only after the event and did not engender a storm. In the summer of that year the only channel of Israel television broadcast a report on the opening of the Bayreuth festival. In the press there were attempts to entitle it "Last Night Israeli Television Broke the Ban," but the television people did not attribute much importance to the report.[21] In the fall of 1989 the IPO played two pieces from *Tristan und Isolde* and *Götterdämmerung* during a rehearsal. Despite the fact that it was only a rehearsal, a Labor Party Knesset Member raised a parliamentary question. This was not the first time the subject was raised in the Knesset plenum. Right-wing Knesset members had raised parliamentary questions in 1956, 1957, and 1981, and in this context demanded cutting the IPO budget. In all these cases the ministers of education refrained from intervening. This time the minister replied that the orchestra did not plan to play Wagner's music in public, and those musicians who did not want to participate were excused from rehearsals. It seems that as long as Wagner's music was not performed by the principal musical body in Israel, participants in the debate preserved a measure of restraint.[22]

The same dichotomy between a passionate flood of emotions and a measure of softening toward musicians identified with National Socialism also characterized the 1990s. With the dawn of the new decade, for the first time a short piece by Strauss was included in a concert given by the Rishon Letzion Symphony Orchestra. The Israeli conductor, Noam Sheriff, conducted *Metamorphosis*, and the response was moderate. In 1994 the same kind of compliant acceptance characterized the broadcasting of an opera series by Strauss on Channel 8 (the culture and science channel which was part of the basic channel package in Israel) and the ever-increasing broadcasting of his music on The Voice of Music, the national classical music program. Strauss also became part of the repertoire of the IPO, which was perceived as representing the nation. Initially, his music was incorporated in the 1993/4 season in a special program for youth; the following year a series of his *Lieder* was included at the opening of the season, and a year later pieces from *Salome* and *Don Quixote* were performed. At this stage, additional information on Strauss was published. He had acted for the Nazis but had refused to cut off his ties with Stephan Zweig, a Jew who had written the libretto for some of his operas; his son had married a Jew and thus his grandchildren were Jewish, and Strauss had used his connections in order to protect his family. By the end of the decade Lehar and Orff, who until then were part of the group of collaborators boycotted in Israel, were also included in the repertoire of Israeli orchestras.

This public acceptance, however, was not the fate of Wagner, who remained controversial despite the fact that his music was now played freely on public broadcasting channels. Channel 8 broadcast *Der fliegende Holländer* in 1994 and a more extensive series of his works—including, *Der Ring des Nibelungen*, *Tannhäuser*, and *Die Meistersinger von Nürnberg*—in 1997 and 1998. The Voice of Music devoted more and more time to Wagner. At the beginning of 1995 a series of documentaries was broadcast, exploring the complexity of Wagner's views, including the deep anti-Semitism he often expressed. The same year the station broadcast *Der fliegende Holländer* in full for the first time. Seemingly, it may be said that Israelis had accepted the idea that problematic as it may be, Wagner was part of the history of music and therefore his music was worthy of being broadcast and studied. Those for whom his music caused emotional distress could choose not to listen to specific programs, but there was no reason to ban his music entirely. It may well be that willingness to accept Wagner and other collaborator musicians as part of the broadcasting schedule was bound up with changes that took place in the Israeli broadcasting bodies: the transition to multi-channel television enabled people to watch "forbidden" works of art on international cultural channels, such as ARTE, the German-French channel, and 3-SAT, the German-Austrian-Swiss channel.

In contrast to the liberal approach characteristic of the radio and television broadcasts, live performances of Wagner by the IPO still had the power to rekindle the dispute. The pretext for the 1990s debate was a special IPO concert conducted by Daniel Barenboim, which included pieces by Wagner, and like the events of the 1960s and 1980s, it provoked a passionate confrontation from outspoken opponents of the music. The orchestra's management tried to avoid two impediments. The first was to steer clear of playing Wagner in a subscription concert for members of the audience who had purchased tickets in advance, as they might feel that they were a captive audience. The other impediment was raised by the publicists and politicians in the 1980s: the fact that Zubin Mehta was a foreigner. This time the choice fell on Barenboim, a Jew who had lived for several years in Israel and grounded an attempt to prevent the debate from turning into a national issue. But all this was of no avail.

Directly after the announcement of the special concert, the debate flared up and many of those who had participated in it in the 1980s joined in again. Avraham Melamed, the IPO violinist, believed that this time public reaction would be restrained: "I do not assume there will be the same public reaction there once was, because to use a phrase, the arms with the numbers tattooed on them, well, the skin has shrunk a lot."[23] He himself was proof that the picture was otherwise. As his colleagues performed Wagner inside the hall, Melamed stood at the entrance to the Mann Auditorium and played "Kaddish."[24] Moreover, as will be seen a decade later, the smaller the influence of the (now elderly) Holocaust survivors on society, the greater and more significant was their role in the debate. This time as well, quotidian life fueled the fire. The special concert took place in December 1991, ten months after the end of the Gulf War, during which Iraq had launched missiles at Israel. The threat of chemical warheads, the knowledge that a German company had supplied Iraq with toxic chemicals, the dictatorship in Iraq, the incitement of religious and racist sentiment against Israel and Zionism, and the seclusion of Israelis inside their homes—somewhat reminiscent of the ghetto experience—all these revived memories of historical experiences. The comparisons between the present and the Holocaust, between Saddam Hussein and Adolf Hitler, and between contemporary Germany and twelve years of the Nazi regime were not late in coming (Zuckermann 1998). The fact that this time the events related to a united and larger Germany only added fuel to the flames. That National Socialism was experienced so vividly in Israeli society almost fifty years after it had collapsed can illuminate why Wagner remained an icon in Israeli culture.

As in previous cases, this time too the debate dealt not only with historical connotations and definitely not with the issue of censorship. Three interesting grounds were raised as a pretext for the prohibition that should be voluntarily—and not legally—imposed on performing Wagner. One was Barenboim's age. He was born in 1942 and was perceived by Holocaust survivors as a person who would never be able to understand them. If in the past Mehta had been rejected entirely due to his different nationality, now Barenboim's age served as a reason for his ineligibility to decide the matter.[25] Barenboim's foreign origin, in fact, fueled the nationalistic arguments of ultra-Orthodox groups. The ultra-Orthodox press published several articles that expressed strong opposition to the non-Jewish customs of secular Israelis, and as an example they gave the performance of Wagner's music which, they believed, divided the nation.[26] Arguments against performing Wagner were also voiced by the left, but from the opposite perspective. From the outset, Ariel Hirschfeld, researcher and critic, disqualified the argument regarding the contradiction between the willingness to consume German products and the resolute rejection of Wagner. He argued that in this matter Israeli society should act independently and not in accordance with the Western world:

> Abstaining from Wagner is one of the few truly cosmopolitan acts carried out here in the musical field, an act that does not resemble the provincial, imitative sycophancy typical of musical life here and of the Philharmonic in particular.[27]

At the end of the 1990s the picture was ambiguous. On the one hand, there was no genuine objection to the inclusion of composers who were associated with National Socialism in the public's consciousness on radio and television broadcasts. The majority of these composers were also accepted in the concert halls. Wagner, on the other hand, remained a clear-cut symbol of all that Israelis condemned: totalitarianism, anti-Semitism, and National Socialism. Paradoxically, from a symbol of Social Nationalism Wagner became an identifying label of the Holocaust survivors themselves. The choice of voluntary censorship vis-à-vis public performance of his music left him a significant factor in Israeli culture.

THE TWENTY-FIRST CENTURY—VOLUNTARY CENSORSHIP—THE NEXT GENERATION

A decade later, Barenboim was again caught in the eye of the storm. In the summer of 2001 matters reached a climax when the Committee of Education and Culture declared him "a cultural persona non grata."[28] Although this statement had no real potency, it manifested the extent of injury felt by the committee members in view of the conductor's activities in Israel. As on previous occasions, the committee did not demand the total avoidance of playing Wagner's music—that aroused discontent in large parts of Israeli society. But now they chose to directly attack and punish the person who defied them and their opinion. It may be assumed that they perceived Barenboim as a serial violator of civil order. At the time he was involved in the West-Eastern Divan Orchestra project, which he promoted together with his friend, the Palestinian intellectual Edward Said, and also performed in the West Bank as a sign of solidarity with the Palestinians.[29]

The affair began with an invitation to the Berlin State Orchestra and its conductor, Barenboim, to the Israel Festival. Reports on the orchestra's intention to incorporate a piece by Wagner were raised for debate in the Knesset plenum in April, and in May, the Education, Culture and Sports Committee convened for a special debate on the matter. Managers of the Israel Festival, active and retired politicians, representatives of the Holocaust survivors and second-generation Holocaust survivors, and experts in music and history all participated in the discussion, at the conclusion of which the festival organizers were asked to revoke the program that included the first act of *Die Walküre* (the second opera of *Der Ring des Nibelungen*) and replace it with a different one. Together with Barenboim, the festival organizers agreed to the change despite the fact that tickets to the concert had been quickly sold.[30] However, at the end of the revised concert, the finale of the entire festival, Barenboim asked to discuss the Wagner issue with the audience and play a piece. Like Mehta before him, Barenboim suggested that those who were opposed could leave the hall. The restraint in the hall enabled the orchestra to play the piece from *Tristan und Isolde* in relative peace and quiet. But it was the quiet before a great storm which evolved several days later and ended with Barenboim's condemnation.

About six months earlier, the Wagner issue had been discussed extensively. The Rishon LeZion Symphony Orchestra, which was the first to perform Strauss publicly, performed Wagner's *Siegfried Idyll* during a Friday noon concert. The orchestra's announcement of the concert met with a lukewarm response, and outside the hall only a handful of people demonstrated. It may well be that they realized that they would not be able to stir up a debate as in the past, since the Tel Aviv district court had rejected a petition submitted by two Holocaust survivors, residents of Rishon LeZion, requesting a permanent injunction instructing the orchestra to refrain from performing any musical pieces by Wagner or Strauss. This was the first time the Wagner affair reached an Israeli court, but the stance of the institutions in Israel remained unchanged. Like the education ministers in the past, the court also adopted the pluralistic liberal position. In the hearing Judge Yehuda Zaft determined:

> The controversy over the question of performing Wagner and Strauss in Israel is basically an ethical controversy and a matter of worldview. [. . .] In a democratic pluralistic society, and such is Israeli society, a variety of opinions and beliefs, competitive in ways of persuasion and public struggle, should be allowed, while the court should not use its power to favor one side or the other.[31]

In this case too the calm was misleading. As the first notes were heard, an older member of the audience silenced the orchestra by rattling deafening clappers. Response in the media was scant and relatively moderate. Noam Ben-Zeev, the musical critic of *Ha'aretz*, used the clappers as a metaphor for interpreting the standpoint of Israelis toward Wagner, drawing upon the story of Haman the Wicked from the Book of Esther. Haman's plan to slaughter all the Jews was foiled; in the case of Wagner there were other executioners.[32]

Both these cases can be interpreted in different ways. On the institutional level it was obvious that the state institutions in Israel preferred to leave the Wagner issue open for ad hoc decisions. This preference was based on a pluralistic standpoint that respects the choice of individuals in society to listen to Wagner in public or refrain from doing so. On the social level, two connected changes were evident: an increase in intervention by Holocaust survivors and a similar response from the younger generations. The increasingly adverse reaction of the survivors can be largely attributed to their understanding that the state institutions held fast to the policy of nonintervention that began in the 1950s. This understanding, along with their recognition of the calm acceptance of broadcasting the music of Wagner and Strauss on state radio and the culture channel, which were received in numerous households in Israel, led the survivors to conclude that, if they wished to maintain their opposition to the public performance of Wagner, they must take action.

The circumstances of that time also prompted the direct intervention of the survivors: their advancing years and the late realization in Israeli society of the depth of the survivors' emotions doubtlessly contributed to their lucid voices. It is reasonable to assume that their willingness to open up and act toward making the opposition to Wagner permanent was designed to preserve their standpoint in Israel even after their demise. In this context it is important to remember that in the concert conducted by Barenboim many of the people who left the hall were in their thirties and forties, in other words, young people who had not experienced the Holocaust and were most probably not members of the second generation. The second possible interpretation is that perhaps the opposition to Wagner had become a symbol, and therefore the choice of refraining from performing his music in public no longer depended on the times or the generational belonging of those who were opposed to performing his music in public.

The state of Israel and its official bodies never boycotted Wagner and never imposed censorship on the public performance of his music in concert halls or over the broadcasting systems, including state bodies. Any parliamentary question raised in the Knesset or any individual appeal in court yielded the same result: adherence to the pluralistic approach that considers the wishes of one person and the opposition of the other, and seeks to find peaceful social ways in which to resolve the tension between the two. However, the wish to keep a balance between contradictory wishes did not pacify the debate itself. Whenever musical pieces by Wagner (and in the beginning, those by Strauss as well) were included in the repertoire or actually performed, heated controversy arose. Despite the repeated presence of some participants in the discourse, it is hard to characterize the discourse by explicit traits. Blatant condemnations of the playing of Wagner in Israel were expressed by survivors, members of the second generation, and ultra-Orthodox groups—each for their own reasons. More moderate words were voiced by left-wing publicists, shedding light on the intrinsic anti-Semitism of Wagner's views and his totalitarian approach, which perhaps had a significant influence over the Nazis. Many of those who defended performing his music had come to Israel from Germany before the Holocaust; for them, preserving cultural pluralism and a liberal approach was a key to protecting a society from the rise of extremism.

The case of Wagner in Israeli society is a clear example of the capacity of a society to cope with potent controversy and choose non-solution as a solution. The aspiration of some to preserve democratic-liberal values and cultural pluralism was challenged by the deep desire of others to totally avoid public performance of Wagner, which resembles voluntary censorship. Despite the years that have passed since the Holocaust, the generational change, and the changes in the composition of society and its elected members, the controversy over Wagner has persisted in Israel for over seventy years.

Notes

1. Interpellation 670, November 26, 1956. This chapter is based on an extensive work, see: Sheffi, Na'ama. 2013. *The Ring of Myths: The Israelis, Wagner and the Nazis*, rev. ed. Sussex, UK: Sussex Academic Press.
2. On the ways of commemorating the Holocaust in Israel, see Young 1990 and Shapira 1998. On processing trauma, see LaCapra 2001, 86–113.
3. Minutes no. 268, meeting of the Knesset Education, Culture and Sport Committee, May 8, 2001.
4. Controversy regarding the political-ideational belonging of Wagner has continued for decades. Vaget 1993.
5. On the main characteristics in Israeli society, see Shapira 2004 and Eisenstadt et al. 1970.
6. On the censorship board's request, see letter from the Film and Theater Review Board to the IPO management, May 6, 1952, IPO Archives, "miscellaneous" file.
7. W. Levy to the editor of *Ha-Emet*, June 8, 1952, IPO Archives, Wagner and Strauss file.
8. Minutes of meeting of the public board of the Israeli Philharmonic Orchestra, Jerusalem, January 8, 1963, IPO Archives, internal affairs file.
9. Y. Admon to Minister of Education and Culture, December 1, 1952, IPO Archives, Wagner and Strauss file.
10. "With or Without the Richards" [Hebrew], *Davar*, December 1.
11. On the intensive use of motifs, see, for example, Donington 1974, 20–25. Wagner's contemporaries and intellectuals recognized the power of the use of motifs. Nietzsche 1911, 16–56, 57–58; and Mann [1933] 1985. For contemporary interpretation of the effect of music on consciousness, see Sacks 2007, 3–93.
12. A. Carlebach, "Manners of a Guest" [Hebrew], *Ma'ariv*, April 13, 1953. Most of the Hebrew press in Israel reported the occurrence (*Davar, Ha'aretz, Herut, Haolam Hazeh, Ma'ariv, Haboker, Hador,* and *Yedioth Ahronoth*), as had the foreign-language press (*Jediot Hadashot, Emeth, Jerusalem Post, Yediot Hayom*). Reports had also appeared in the foreign press, including the *New York Post*, the *New York Herald Tribune*, the *Herald Tribune* (Paris), and the *Buenos Aires Herald*.

13. U. Toeplitz, "On the Importance of Wagner," *IPO program*, June 1966.
14. After he was attacked in *Ma'ariv*, Adv. Haim Korngold defended Mehta. "The Voice of Everywhere: Are You a Fan of Strauss?" [Hebrew]. *Ma'ariv*, June 27, 1966; Haim Kornglold to editor of *Ma'ariv*, June 28, 1966, IPO Archives, local press file. Mehta raged in view of the orchestra's retreating from its intention and called it, "Chicken means and lack of guts." The contents of this telegram was reported in a letter sent by orchestra member Wolfgang Levi to the management chairman, Attorney Haim Korngold, June 10, 1966, IPO Archives, Wagner and Strauss file.
15. I was told about Orff's being played on the Voice of Israel by the manager of the Voice of Music, Avi Hanani, in a personal interview in Jerusalem (February 11, 1996). According to him, the reason had been the personal acquaintance between Orff and one of the senior officials of Kol Yisrael, Kar-El Salmon, who had been at school with Orff. A fascinating documentary film has been made of Orff's life under the Nazi regime and afterwards: *O Fortuna*, directed by Tony Palmer, Bayerischer Rundfunk, WDR Köln, Ladbroke Productions, LWT Productions, and RM Arts, 1996.
16. See, for example, "An Ignoble Genius, Not a Symbol but a Spiritual Father [Hebrew], *Ma'ariv*, November 3, 1981, and "Agenda Proposal 1699, submitted by M.K. Haggai Merom *Ha'aretz*, May 22, 1987 and *Divrei Ha-Knesset*, session 110, Twelfth Knesset, 1990, 1: 334–336. There were references to the composer's anti-Semitic views in previous decades as well.
17. "A Matter of Sensitivity" [Hebrew], *Ma'ariv*, October 18, 1981.
18. Basic Law: Human Dignity and Liberty, 1992, which indirectly deals with this type of issue, was passed only in the following decade.
19. "A Musical Ear and an Impervious Heart" [Hebrew], *Davar*, October 25, 1981.
20. "Consideration for Feelings" [Hebrew], *Yedioth Ahronoth*, October 21, 1981.
21. On the concerts of Mishory, see "Three Times Gilead" [Hebrew], *Ma'ariv*, January 29, 1988; "Not Only Wagner" [Hebrew], *Davar*, February 15, 1988; and "For the First Time: A Work by Wagner Was Played in Israel" [Hebrew], *Yedioth Ahronot*, February 6, 1988. On the television broadcast, see "Last Night Television Broke the Ban on Wagner" [Hebrew], *Yedioth Ahronoth*, August 21, 1988.
22. See, for example: Interpellation 670, November 26, 1956 (Esther Raziel-Naor); Agenda Proposal 1699, submitted by M.K. Haggai Merom, *Divrei Ha-Knesset*, Session 110, Twelfth Knesset (1990) I: 334–336.
23. Avraham Melamed in an interview on *Good Morning Israel* [Hebrew], Galei Zahal (Army Radio), December 15, 1991, 8:43 A.M.
24. "Kaddish in Front of the Mann Auditorium" [Hebrew], *Globes*, December 27, 1991.
25. "The Time Has Come for Wagner to Be Just Music Again" [Hebrew], *Ha'aretz*, December 16, 1991.
26. "Life without Wagner . . ." [Hebrew], *Yom Hashishi*, December 27, 1991; and "Now the Feelings of Secular Jews Are Being Hurt, Too" [Hebrew], *Yated Ne'eman*, December 20, 1991.
27. "The Overt Simplicity of that Honor" [Hebrew], *Ha'aretz*, December 27, 1991.
28. Minutes no. 316, meeting of the Knesset Education, Culture and Sport Committee, July 24, 2001.
29. Anger at Barenboim also remained unchanged three years later, when his name came up for the Wolf Prize. Caspi, Michal. 2004. Background document on: Wolf Foundation Prize awarded to Daniel Barenboim, submitted to the Knesset Education and Culture Committee, 29.2.2004.

30. Minutes no. 268, meeting of the Knesset Education, Culture and Sport Committee, May 8, 2001.
31. Alther Podlowsky, Gedaliahu Appel and Israel Silberberg vs. Rishon LeZion Symphony Orchestra, CMA 27228/00, October 24 [Hebrew]. On the struggle of Holocaust survivors versus Wagner performances via legal appeals, see: Sheffi, Na'ama. 2004. "Between Collective Memory and Manipulation: The Holocaust, Wagner and the Israelis." *Journal of Israeli History* 23, no. 1: 65–77.
32. "A Holocaust survivor took out clappers, and the orchestra continued to play Wagner," *Ha'aretz*, October 29, 2000.

References

Archives

Hanani, Avi. 1996. Personal interview, Jerusalem, February 11.
Israel Philharmonic Orchestra Archive, Tel Aviv.
Knesset Education, Culture and Sport Committee (prints and online protocols).
Knesset Plenum Protocols (*Divrei Ha-Kneseet* and online protocols).

Literature

Bondy, Ruth. 1990. *Felix: Pinchas Rosen and His Time*. Tel Aviv: Zmora-Bitan [Hebrew].
Dinur, Ben Zion. 2009. *Ben Zion Dinur: Posthumous and Other Writings*, edited by Ariel Rein. Jerusalem: The Dinur Center for Research in Jewish History and The Zalman Shazar Center for Jewish History [Hebrew].
Donington, Robert. 1974. *Wagner's "Ring" and Its Symbols: The Music and the Myth* New York: St. Martin's Press.
Eisenstadt, Shmuel Noah, Rivkah Bar Yosef, and Chaim Adler. 1970. *Integration and Development in Israel*. New York: Praeger.
Geiger, Friedrich. 2002. "Die 'Goebbels-Liste' vom 1. September 1935. Eine Quelle zur Komponistenverfolgung im NS-Staat." *Archiv für Musikwissenschaft* 59, no. 2: 104–112.
Huberman, Bronislaw. [1933 and 1936] 2005. "Huberman and Nazi Germany." http://www.huberman.info/literature/articles/nazi_germany/
LaCapra, Dominick. 2001. *Writing History, Writing Trauma*. Baltimore: Johns Hopkins University Press.
Lahav, Dan. 2001. "Background document on the subject: Performing Wagner's music at the 2001 Israel Festival." Submitted to the Knesset Education and Culture Committee, May 7 [Hebrew].
Litvin, Rina, and Hezi Shelach, eds. 1984. *Who's Afraid of Richard Wagner: Different Aspects of the Controversial Figure*. Jerusalem: Keter [Hebrew].
Mann, Thomas. [1933] 1985. "The Sorrows and Grandeur of Richard Wagner." In *Pro and Contra Wagner*, translated by A. Blunden. Chicago: University of Chicago Press.
Nietzsche, Friedriech. 1911. *The Case of Wagner, Nietzsche Contra Wagner, and Selected Aphorisms*, translated by Anthony M. Ludovici. Edinburgh and London: T.N. Foulis.
Romberg, Otto R. 2005. *Forty Years of Diplomatic Relations between the Federal Republic of Germany and Israel*. Frankfurt: Tribune Books.

Sachs, Harvey. 1988. *Toscanini*. New York: Harper & Row.
Sacks, Oliver W. 2007. *Musicophilia: Tales of Music and the Brain*. New York: Alfred A. Knopf.
Segev, Tom. 1993. *The Seventh Million: The Israelis and the Holocaust*. New York: Hill & Wang.
Shapira, Anita, ed. 2004. *Israeli Identity in Transition*. Westport, Conn.: Praeger.
Shapira, Anita. 1998. "The Holocaust: Private Memory and Public Memory." *Jewish Social Studies* 4, no. 2: 40–58.
Sheffi, Na'ama. 2004. "Between Collective Memory and Manipulation: The Holocaust, Wagner and the Israelis." *Journal of Israeli History* 23, no. 1: 65–77.
Sheffi, Na'ama. 2013. *The Ring of Myths: The Israelis, Wagner and the Nazis*, rev. ed. Sussex, UK: Sussex Academic Press.
Vaget, Hans-Rudolf. 1993. "Anti-Semitism, and Mr. Rose: Merkwurd'ger Fall!" *The German Quarterly* 66, no. 2: 222–236.
Yablonka, Hanna. 2004. *The State of Israel vs. Adolf Eichmann*. New York: Schocken Books.
Young, James E. 1990. "When a Day Remembers: A Performative History of Yom Ha'Shoah." *History and Memory* 2, no. 2: 54–75.
Zuckermann, Moshe. 1998. *Zweierlei Holocaust: der Holocaust in den politischen Kulturen Israels und Deutschlands*. Göttingen, Germany: Wallstein.

11
CENSORSHIP DURING THE ENLIGHTENMENT

CHAPTER 7

HARPOCRATES AT WORK
How the God of Silence Protected Eighteenth-Century French Iconoclasts

HEDY LAW

CLASSIC studies of censorship often frame censorship in negative terms (Post 1998, 2). The Old Regime, portrayed as an oppressive state, regulated the circulation of books and ideas (Cerf 1967, 2). On one level, some evidence supports this view. The book industry expanded throughout the eighteenth century, from fewer than a thousand titles per year in 1715 to four thousand per year by the end of century (Roche 1998, 508). Between 1659 and 1789, 942 individuals were imprisoned at the Bastille due to offenses related to the book trade, and more than three hundred of them were authors (Roche 1984, 88, 91). François-Marie Arouet, or Voltaire, was kept there twice, for a total of eleven months, and Denis Diderot spent prison time at Vincennes. These incidents might lead one to see a broad trajectory from the oppressive Old Regime to the freedoms proclaimed in the 1789 *Declaration of the Rights of Man and of the Citizen*. This progression makes eighteenth-century France an exemplary period for the study of censorship.

Studies of eighteenth-century censorship in France have examined how books transmitted ideas. In the strictest sense, censorship laws in France required that all books obtain official approval called *privilège*, which was a formal right for publication and for authors to receive what we now call copyright of their work. Since a *privilège* had to be obtained before publication of a work, this form of censorship is called preventive censorship (Hanley 1980, 266). These laws had roots in a royal ordinance passed in 1563, during the reign of Charles IX. They were revised in August 1686, when Louis XIV issued a press law that regulated censorship and book trading in Paris, and reissued on February 28, 1723. The law was not always strictly enforced, but after Robert-François Damiens attempted to assassinate Louis XV on January 5, 1757, the law was reinstated and remained practically unchanged through the Revolution. The law states that no printed words should undermine the authority of the king, the church, or conventional morality. As a result, anticlerical publication, subversive work, and pornography were banned. Claude Adrien Helvétius's atheist book *De l'Esprit* (1758) was initially approved by the censor, Jean-Pierre Tercier, but was subsequently condemned by the Parlement and was burned on February 10, 1759. Tercier subsequently lost his position as royal censor (Martin 1984, 78–79).

Yet the ban did not stop the circulation of ideas. In an attempt to understand the relationships between iconoclast authors such as Voltaire and Jean-Jacques Rousseau and the French Revolution, historians have studied how their ideas reached eighteenth-century audiences. Since the 1960s, historian Robert Darnton has investigated eighteenth-century France as an "information age" of its own. He has asked the basic question of how ideas that led to the collapse of the Old Regime spread in eighteenth-century France. Over the years, he has discovered from the archives of the Société typographique de Neuchâtel illegal books that received special treatments in the book trade; he has identified what books counted as "clandestine" literature and developed a list of 720 forbidden "best-sellers" of the French Enlightenment; he has examined the publication history of the *Encyclopédie* and argued that the Enlightenment was best understood in terms of the business of the book trade (Darnton 1996). His work has shown that the books eighteenth-century people read on a daily basis were not necessarily those we now consider influential in our history of social thought. Louis-Sébastien Mercier's utopic novel *An l'2440* (1771), for example, comes first on his list of the 720 clandestine best-sellers. Yet Rousseau's collected work—which by common consensus has had enormous political significance—came a distant twenty-third on the same list (Darnton 1995b, 195). This fact indicates that the popularity of a book was not proportionally related to the influence of the ideas there. To understand how censorship functioned in eighteenth-century France means that one cannot simply examine the publication of ideas but also must investigate how booksellers, printers, and peddlers worked together to spread those ideas. At the very least, the impact of ideas was contingent upon the material resources through which readers encountered them (Chartier 2011, 3).

The more historians understand the circulation of ideas in eighteenth century France, the more they discover that ideas were transmitted via different channels and different media in various ways. To be sure, with the rise of the reading population, books were crucial to the dissemination of ideas, especially in the two decades leading up to the French Revolution. But unpublished materials also played important roles in the dissemination of ideas. Given that censorship restricted the content and circulation of printed matter, it also indirectly encouraged the transmission of unpublished materials. Frédéric-Melchior Grimm's *Correspondance littéraire*, one of the most cited unpublished journals documenting an extensive period of Parisian culture from 1753 to 1789, was circulated in the form of manuscript to no more than fifteen wealthy subscribers who could afford the steep annual subscription fees. In addition to the latest chronicles, epigrams, anecdotes, and reviews of recently published literature, *Correspondance littéraire* frequently included unpublished works, including almost a third of Voltaire's work from 1750 through 1778. Like unpublished material, oral communication had long helped disseminate ideas in France. Gossips, which could easily be dismissed as quotidian and therefore insignificant, in effect formed a crucial link in the eighteenth-century communicative network. Some of them even found their way in the printed form. In a fascinating study of the papers kept at the archives of the Bastille, Darnton discusses how a chambermaid was convicted of slander for having turned details of Louis XV's private life, which she overheard in informal talk at court, into a fairy tale. Talking and reading, Darnton has argued, amplified each other in ways that spread information (Darnton 2004, 102). An examination of books while neglecting other forms of communication would underestimate the complexity of the eighteenth-century information age in which books form a part (Darnton 2010, 1–5).

It is true that edicts allowed the state to control the circulation of ideas, but in reality authors and censors worked together to make the system more elastic than it appears. The number of censors grew from less than 10 before 1660 to 178 by the Revolution (Roche 1984, 82). Censors could grant tacit permission (*permissions tacites*) or oral *tolèrances* to authors for publication of their works. Works could be printed outside of France and then smuggled back into France via underground channels. Some censors were more lenient than others. Less than twelve percent of the censors were nobles who held administrative, military, or judiciary positions; 60 percent of the censors were physicians, lawyers, or similar functionaries; 40 percent of them had been members of the academies. Some were editors of journals. In 1757, for example, nine of the ten editors of the *Journal des Savants* were censors. Since many censors had considerable political or ecclesiastical power, they could readily enforce the ideology of the monarchy (Roche 1984, 82). Yet the reality was more complex than this hypothetical scenario. Censors had to approve a large volume of works, from about two hundred to four hundred per year around 1700, to more than five hundred per year between 1750 and 1763, and to more than one thousand in 1780. The rejection rate of a given year was between 10 and 30 percent (Roche 1984, 83). A recent biographical dictionary by William Hanley provides information on royal censors' lives and—more importantly—the works they censored. This multivolume biographical dictionary (though only the first two of the projected five volumes have been published) already provides crucial details. The playwright Antoine Bret (1717–1792), for example, wrote some verses Madame de Pompadour found offensive and was ordered by Louis XV to be imprisoned at the Bastille in 1749. He spent three months in jail. But about a decade later, he was recruited in October 1758 as royal censor. He was dismissed as a royal censor a few years later in 1767, but he was reinstated in 1774 and remained as a censor for literature and history from 1775 to 1790. His personal experience made him a sympathetic censor (Hanley 2005, 1:315–317). Some administrators were also directly responsible for lowering the censorship standard. The censor Chrétien-Guillaume de Lamoignon de Malesherbes, the royally appointed director of the Librairie from 1750 to 1763 who administered the system that oversaw all book and journal trades in France, made significant use of *permissions*. Although he did not tolerate critiques of the monarchy, he relaxed the stringent standard of censorship during his tenure. He criticized the incoherence of the system and even helped authors evade censorship laws. He helped bring the monumental *Encyclopédie, ou dictionnaire raisonné des sciences, des arts, et des métiers* and Rousseau's *Émile* to print (Darnton

1979, 9–14; Roche 1984, 82). Other censors worked with authors. The liberal censor Christophe Piquet, who censored Rousseau's *La Nouvelle Héloïse*, made twenty-three suggestions on the manuscripts, and twenty-one of them are about nuances of ideas. Only in two instances did Piquet eliminate passages that offended God and the king (Roche 1984, 83). These instances show that censorship in Old Regime France does not have to be understood in the negative terms of oppression against freedom. Rather, it can be understood in the positive terms of complicity and collaboration among knowing practitioners. Primary sources provide revealing details about these censors. Louis-Sébastian Mercier noted in his *Tableau de Paris* that the "trembling, spineless, nitpicking royal censors made the foreign presses Holland, the Netherlands, and the Switzerland wealthy. They only approved insignificant works. Sometimes they managed to give a little passport to silly remarks." Mercier observed that the kings could no longer annihilate printing (Mercier 1782, 2:51–52). Scholars agree: by 1789, the system of censorship was basically dysfunctional (Roche 1984, 82–83).

We have seen that the scholarship of censorship in France has turned from books to a broadly defined network of communication. This trend in scholarship also broadens the range of sources historians consult. Darnton's recent work on slander examines a wide range of sources, including traditional ones such as published books and police reports, and nontraditional ones including epigrams, slander and libel cases, puns and poems, and even popular songs such as vaudevilles, romances, and chansons. Investigating the ways information spread in the Old Regime has led historians to think across modern disciplinary boundaries and to treat songs as historical sources that are as revealing as standard sources including edicts, account books, censorship records, and book catalogs (Brown 1999, 307–308; Darnton 2010, 66–78).

Yet if songs took part in the communication network, then what about music in general? Historians who study censorship in the Old Regime admit that they rarely think about music (Chartier 2000, 325). This neglect is, in a sense, defendable. None of the 720 examples of clandestine literature identified by Darnton in France from 1769 to 1789 have the word "music" in the title, and the identified genres from this body of work have little to do with music (Darnton 1995b, 201–208). That is to say, none of the underground literature identified was published exclusively in the form of books on music or music scores, even though some of the banned literature, such as Diderot's *Lettres sur les sourds et muets,* include brief musical examples. If music books were not banned as illegal literature, then according to the methods developed by social historians, there would seem to be no reason to pay attention to music in discussions of Old Regime censorship. Historians have disagreed with this assumption (Bartlet 1992, 16; Hemmings 1994, 44–49; Darlow 2012, 36). Censorship reports kept in the Archives Nationales show that printed music, like all the other printed materials, was also subject to a type of censorship. The composer André-Ernest-Modeste Grétry, as music historian M. Elizabeth C. Bartlet pointed out, had a censor created for him (Bartlet 1984, 130–131). But because censorship was primarily designed to study words in print, the nonverbal medium of music made it difficult for eighteenth-century censors to detect subversive content. For a discussion of music censorship in the Old Regime, we need to see beyond the lack of music books in the identified clandestine literature and reframe censorship in terms not of printed or non-printed materials, but more broadly, of verbal and nonverbal communication. The question, therefore, is not just to identify the musical pieces that were censored but, following Darnton's reasoning, also to investigate the ways the nonverbal medium of music took part in the policed communicative circuits.

It is a challenge to uncover communicative circuits that involve both verbal and nonverbal elements. In a general sense, oral communication by definition often left little textual evidence. More specifically, popular tunes such as vaudevilles often created double meanings for audiences. When old tunes were set to new lyrics, audiences who knew the original tunes and lyrics would be able to detect new meanings (Brown 1986, 261).

Another approach to study music and censorship is to study the suppression of unofficial theaters called Théâtres de la Foire (known generally as the "Forains"). The Forains produced popular entertainment loosely called *opéra comique* that threatened the official theaters of the Académie Royale de Musique (or the Opéra in short), the Comédie-Française, and at times the Comédie-Italienne. The Comédie-Française and the Opéra had official privileges to employ spoken dialogues, music, and dance in their spectacles. After February 22, 1707, when dialogues were forbidden at any Parisian theaters except the official ones, Charles Alard and the widow Maurice (née Jeanne Godefroy) bought royal privilege from the director of Opéra Pierre Guyenet the next year, a purchase that enabled his troupe to use instrumentalists, singers, and dancers at the Forains. Alard subsequently invented the genre of *pièces en écriteaux* and had the audiences sing the verses displayed on large placards to popular vaudeville tunes. Increasingly threatened by the growing popularity of the Forains, the Comédie-Italienne and the Comédie-Française forbade in 1745 all performances of *opéra comique* except for pantomimes, but this ban did not diminish the popularity of vaudevilles. The Opéra-Comique and the Comédie-Italienne merged in 1762, easing the decades-long tension between these two theaters (Martin, 2002, 34–43).

Studies of institutional history have separated official repertory from popular repertory, as well as works performed under the Old Regime from those performed during the Revolution. In his study of works performed at the popular theaters in Paris in the Old Regime, Robert Isherwood decided not to explore the political impact of the popular repertory, for he feared that his study would come across as teleological (Isherwood 1986, vii). Consequently his book *Farce and Fantasy* (1986) succeeds in giving a non-teleological account of popular entertainment in the Old Regime, but his work also stops short of exploring the political significance of popular theatrical works in the Old Regime. Likewise, scholars working on musical works performed at the Opéra show that these works had gone through rounds of censorship before they could perform there. Bartlet identified not the censored materials per se but the process through which works were censored. Not only did she rediscover Voltaire's *Samson*, but she also explained how it was censored before it was performed. Her work has forged a path that brings together institutional and repertory histories. We now know how a work for the Opéra was approved. A libretto for an opera had to be approved by the lieutenant general of police and the Opéra before a composer was allowed to set it to music. The author could propose a composer, and his finished score had to go through a round of audition before production could be approved (Bartlet 1982, 34–35).

Another category of studies focuses not directly on music but more generally on theater and politics. Inspired by Jürgen Habermas's *The Structural Transformation of the Public*, a number of scholars have analyzed the political implications of theater. Cultural historian Sarah Maza has argued that the Paris public extended their interest from the theater to the courtroom as they read trial briefs in the 1770s and 1780s (Maza 1993, 17). More recently, Jeffrey Ravel has questioned the supposed transformation from the theatrical to the textual in the second half of eighteenth-century France. The fact that Parisians read more in the 1770s and 1780s does not mean that the theater became less influential in the same period. On the contrary, Ravel's study of inattentive, noisy spectator behaviors in the parterres of three major official theaters (Comédie-Française, Comédie-Italienne, and the Opéra) shows that public opinion was formed within confined spaces throughout the Old Regime. By studying the behaviors of the parterre spectators and their political significance, Ravel complements Darnton's work on communicative circuits. Not only did talking and reading amplify each other, as Darnton has shown, but the locations in which talking and reading took place, including the parterre, also allowed for the formation, consolidation, and circulation of public opinion (Ravel 1999, 13–66).

Examination of suppressed theaters introduces the issue of silence. Inspired by Michel Foucault's work on power and resistance, most notably in *Discipline and Punish*, political scientist Wendy Brown's work on silences provides a helpful theoretical paradigm for analyzing different modalities of power generated by silence. Silence is a political position, she argues. It presents freedom from oppression, but not yet power to effect social change (Brown 1998, 324). Her theorization of silence may help explain the workings of power and resistance in eighteenth-century French music.

What follows is an analysis of the politics of silence in eighteenth-century pantomime, which was a type of theatrical dumb show made popular by the Forains. Rather than treating silence simply as a theatrical effect, I examine how this type of theatricalized silence functioned as a political tool. Within the context of theater rivalry, political suppression of the troupe of Opéra-Comique was represented onstage as the silencing of the personification of Opéra-Comique. More specifically, I offer an analysis of one pantomime, *Les Oracles d'Harpocrate, ou le dieu du silence à la foire* by Charles-François Pannard, performed by the troupe Nouveau Spectacle-Pantomime on August 15, 1746, a year after one of the many rounds of suppression in the history of the Forains. Among the roughly forty pantomimes performed between 1746 and 1749, *Les Oracles d'Harpocrate* was unusual in that its synopsis was published (Campardon 1877, 2:180). Its music is not extant, but its synopsis is preserved at the Bibliothèque-Musée de l'Opéra in Paris (F-Po, Liv 18 [2348]; Rizzoni 2000, 471). I shall demonstrate how this pantomime politicizes silence by featuring the rarely discussed Egyptian god of silence Harpocrates.

Harpocrates and the Politics of Silence

On August 10, 1746, the pantomime *Les Oracles d'Harpocrate, ou le dieu du silence à la foire* by Charles-François Pannard (1689–1765), known generally as the Racine of vaudeville, was performed at the Théâtre de St. Saint-Laurent in Paris. In contrast to the Comédie-Française, which staged standard repertories, the Opéra-Comique continually staged small genres, including standard and current repertory. In addition to stock commedia dell'arte works and parodies, Pannard produced a set of self-reflexive works from the late 1720s through the 1740s about the history of popular entertainment in Paris, a category of works that followed a convention of works such as *La Querelle des théâtres* (1718) by his predecessors Alain-René Lesage and Louis Fuzelier. Pannard joined the Opéra-Comique in 1731 and was prolific in the 1730s and 1740s. His major works include *L'Impromptu du Pont-Neuf* (1729), *Momus à Paris* (1732), *La Comédie sans paroles ou Le Pot pourri comique, ou L'Acte pantomime* (1732), *Le Départ de l'Opéra-Comique* (1733), *La Répétition interrompue ou le petit-maître malgré lui* (1735), *L'Histoire de l'Opéra-Comique ou les Métamorphoses de la foire* (1736), *La Critique de l'Opéra-Comique* (1742), and *L' Impromptu des acteurs* (1745). Having strived for survival for decades, Pannard produced works, including *Le Temple du sommeil* (1731), *L'Absence* (1734), and *Le Rien* (1737), that brought to surface the suggestive themes of inactivity and nonexistence. Some of Pannard's works have self-reflective properties. These works include *Le Vaudeville* (1737, 1743), *Le Concerto pantomime* (1734), *La Muse pantomime* (1737), and *La Pantomime* (1738). Among the plays he wrote, his *Compliment de clôture*, an example of the genre of compliment, received multiple revivals. It was first performed September 30, 1731, the last day of the Saint-Laurent fair and was performed annually from 1735 to 1742, and was last performed in 1749. Pannard was not an ungrateful iconoclast. In 1745, when the Forains gained permission to perform again after being suppressed, Pannard produced *Compliment de rentrée*, evidently as a sequel to his *Compliment de clôture* (Rizzoni 2000, 104–105; Martin 2002, 238–241).

Pannard's repertories offer a chronicle of the Opéra-Comique from the perspective of the suppressed. As shown from the collection of works as outlined above, we can analyze *Les Oracles d'Harpocrate, ou le dieu du silence à la foire* in terms of the politics of silence. This approach, I suggest, helps explain the workings of silence in theatrical works written later by Pierre-Augustin Caron de Beaumarchais, who frequented the Forains in his formative years and should have been familiar with Pannard's plays. We can then take Beaumarchais's theatrical works as a point of departure when we revisit musical settings of his Figaro plays in a new light. This approach helps explain moments when authors and composers collaborated with censors and audiences. In this way, we can use Harpocrates, the god of silence, as a gateway to obtain a glimpse of music in the censorship environment of Old Regime France.

The Egyptian god of silence, though little known in the twentieth century, was a common theme in seventeenth-century and eighteenth-century arts. Ever since Gisbertus Cuperus (1644–1713) published his *Gisberti Cuperi consulis, & professoris Daventriensis Harpocrates seu explicatio imagunculae argenteae antiquissimae* in 1676, there were continual interests in this Egyptian god, son of Isis and Osiris, who appeared in iconography as a man pressing a finger against his lips. Indeed, this book, though written in Latin, includes images of Harpocrates wearing a basket on his hat, surrounded by lotus leaves, lentils, fish, vegetable seeds, and birds, which symbolize abundance. In the frontispiece of his *Gisb. Cuperi Harpocrates, sive explicatio imaginculae argenteae perantiquae* (1687), Harpocrates is shown standing on top of a monument, holding a cane decorated by leaves shaped like tongues—which, according to the 1755 *Dictionnaire universel des arts et des sciences*, represent language—and fruits that look like hearts (Figure 7.1) (Dyche 1758, 1:527). The Egyptians used Harpocrates to represent the balance between language and heart, or reason and emotion. Harpocrates was commonly found in palaces to remind Egyptian kings to exercise judgment and empathy. Sculptures of Harpocrates were placed at the entrances of temples, monuments, and other public locations. The Romans used Harpocrates more generally to symbolize the ability to guard secrets. He represents in broad terms diplomacy and discretion.

Cuperus's book influenced artists and composers in different countries. It was published in Amsterdam and it might have motivated the prolific Italian poet Count Nicolò Minato (1630–1698) to write a three-act *dramma per musica* titled *Il silentio di Harpocrate*, first set to music by the Viennese court composer Antonia Draghi for performance in the Hofburgtheater of Vienna on February 27, 1677, and later by Bernardo Pasquini for the Palazzo Colonna in Rome in 1686. These works on Harpocrates must have stimulated considerable interest. A richly illustrated edition was published in Utrecht in 1687 and was reissued in 1694. Inspired by Cuperus, French physician and archaeologist Jacob Spon (1647–1685) translated Cuperus's work into the French and wrote on Harpocrates extensively in his *Recherches curieuses d'antiquité* (1683). In addition to Cuperus's research, Spon also consulted classics such as Augustine's *The City of God against the Pagans* and Varron's *De langua Latina*. Even though Harpocrates was not as well known as other mythological figures such as Orpheus, the work of Cuperus and Spon indicates that he was a literary topic in Western classics (Spon 1683, 120–133).

Based on Cuperus's historical survey on Harpocrates, Spon applied Cuperus's historical research to the social contexts of late seventeenth-century France, and his approach, I would argue, could be applied to musical works by the end of the Old Regime as well. Instead of simply translating Cuperus into French, Spon added that Harpocrates was a symbol of suppression. Following Spon's work, a number of writers and artists adopted the theme of Harpocrate in their works. In his twenty-third *Satire* (1646) on censorship, Jacques Du Lorens claims, "Harpocrates has shown that it is not necessary to say everything" (Du Lorens 1869, 203). Likewise, the abbé Noël Antoine Pluche (1688–1761) connected Harpocrates to the eighteenth-century police, who played an important role in censoring materials. In "Harpocrate, ou la police" in chapter 15 of his two-volume *Histoire du ciel* (1739), he reminds viewers to hold back quarrels for the sake of societal

FIGURE 7.1 Frontispiece of *Gisb. Cuperi Harpocrates, sive explicatio imagunculae argenteae perantiquae; quae in figuram Harpocratis formata repraesentat solem. Ejusdem monumenta antiqua inedita . . . Accedit Stephani Le Moine epistola de Melanophoris* (Trajecti ad Rhenum, apud F. Halma, 1687).

Reproduced by permission of the Special Collections Research Center of the University of Chicago Library.

peace (Pluche 1739, 1:90–97). Possibly inspired by these literary works, sculptor Maurice Falconet made a model of Cupid for the Salon exhibition of 1755 in an attempt to fulfill a commission by Madame de Pompadour. As with Harpocrates, this Cupid's right index finger presses against his lips (Salmon 2002, 311–313).

Harpocrates also represents the state of contemplation. Chevalier Ramsay, or Andrew Michael (1686–1743), stages a scene of absorption in his *Les Voyages de Cyrus* (1728). As Cyrus contemplates the meaning of language in a temple, an old man enters the same temple. He kneels in front of the statue of Harpocrates and remains for a long time in a state of profound silence (Ramsay 1727, 6; Fried 1980, 10). In Lesage's *Histoire de Gil Blas* (1732), the protagonist (or whichever character is speaking) invokes the name of Harpocrates to represent reticence: "I assured my mistress that she could stay tranquil and that I was Harpocrates among the trusting valets" (Lesage 1960, 1:693–694). In Abbé Jean-Baptiste Dubos's *Réflexions critiques sur la poésie et sur la peinture* (1733), Harpocrates is described as exerting social influence by silencing a person next to him. In literature, when Harpocrates is placed next to a major figure such as a prince, the physical proximity between these two figures indicates the major figure's prudence (Dubos 1733, 1:186). In *La Valise trouvée* (1740), Lesage makes a direct connection between absorption and Harpocrates in the coffeehouse he frequented in the province. There he saw chess players who were so focused on their games that they appeared to be oblivious to their richly ornamented surroundings and to their spectators. The observers similarly watched in profound silence. There was no sound except the noises made by the players when they moved the pieces. The effect was so unforgettable that Lesage found it appropriate to call this coffeehouse the "café of Harpocrate" (Lesage 1821, 12:210).

Though Harpocrates may often represent the suppressor, he also offers protection to the suppressed and promotes self-censorship. Voltaire, in his forbidden book *Le Taureau blanc* of 1772, sets the stage in an Egyptian setting, in which a twenty-four-year-old princess Amaside is forbidden to speak by her guardian, the thirteen-hundred-year-old eunuch Mambrès. She is only allowed to worship Harpocrates and can only talk to a white bull, which was once a man and later becomes her lover when he returns to human form. Here Harpocrates indicates suppression on the one hand and protection of the silenced on the other. Voltaire's *Le Taureau blanc* shows that Harpocrates was a cultural icon in 1772, and he continued to be one through the 1780s. In *Les Fables égyptiennes et grecques* (1786), Antoine-Joseph Pernety (1716–1801) used Harpocrates to emphasize that wise men know how to be silent. This is why, Pernety argued, ancient men including Salomon used enigmas, parables, hieroglyphs, and symbols to communicate with those wise enough to understand them (Pernety 1786, 1:330). The painter Jean-Jacque Lequeu (1757–1825?) drew an image of Harpocrates in 1786 in order to warn spectators to "stop speaking in the second anti-chamber located in front of the cabinet of Mr. Montholon" (BnF, Département Estampes et photographie, EST VE-92). This painting shows that Harpocrates was no longer only a topic in Egyptology, a literary trope, a mythological figure in sculpture, or an exotic marker but now served a practical function. Much like a modern stop sign, he warned spectators to behave themselves. Harpocrates in this instance neither represents the suppressor nor the suppressed. Rather, he promotes self-restraint as a form of civic virtue.

If the image of Harpocrates became widespread, then the meanings of this image changed from the scholarly study of Egyptian religion in the late seventeenth century to the representation of suppression and the promotion of self-censorship in late eighteenth-century France. In addition to these various types of meanings, Harpocrates conveys above all a type of politicized silence. Harpocrates highlights silence as a form of resistance. This type of silence dislocates the opposition between defiance and compliance by emphasizing the refusal to take a side. Because of its nonverbal nature, this type of silence escapes the mechanism of censorship in Old Regime France, which was based on verbal evidence. How does the politics of silence operate in *Les Oracles d'Harpocrate*?

In *Les Oracles d'Harpocrate*, the politics of silence is closely intertwined with the rise of pantomime, which communicates a narrative primarily by gestures, including spontaneous bodily movements, with the support of acting, music, social dance, and other unspoken means of communication such as animals, costumes, props, and stage sets. As shown from the extant pantomime synopses for eighteenth-century theater and dance, pantomime is an effective genre for demonstrating feelings such as envy, love, and hate and for presenting scenes of recognition and confrontation. Bound by its basically nonverbal nature, it is less effective for conveying complex narrative and logical argument. Yet this limitation did not restrict choreographers and playwrights from producing pantomimes. Rather, the limitation prompted them to explore the expressive potential of nonverbal communication. As we shall see in the case of *Les Oracles d'Harpocrate*, Pannard used a wide range of sounds and gestures to compensate for a lack of spoken dialogue. In so doing, he prioritized the live performance over the written text and conveyed to the audience his criticisms of censorship during the performance while not leaving tangible textual residues that might jeopardize the livelihood of his troupe. Even though the ban on spoken dialogue did pose some obstacles to performances in the Forains, it succeeded in relativizing the dominance of verbal language and amplifying the domain of nonverbal communication. By working within legal limits, Pannard turned pantomime into a laboratory of human expression and communication.

The literature on Harpocrates published in the late seventeenth and eighteenth centuries helps explain the plot of *Les Oracles d'Harpocrate*. As its title suggests, this pantomime is about the Egyptian god Harpocrates who oversees the Forains. In scene 1, Harpocrates sits on his throne with two fingers of his left hand pressing against his lip. Without saying a word, Harpocrates's gesture would instantly communicate to the audiences that the play belongs to the self-reflexive repertories that Pannard had been producing. Audiences familiar with Pannard's works would expect the play to be about the perennial theater rivalry in Paris, unreasonable theater censorship, the reopening of the Forains in 1746, the rise of pantomime as a defensive genre, and the politics of silence. Some audiences might also expect a play about victimizing the Forains and criticisms of the censors. But what is remarkable about this pantomime is that Pannard stayed away from a victim narrative and offered more broadly an overview of the diverse theatrical scene in contemporary Paris. The nine scenes of the pantomime form a loosely connected narrative that explains how the Egyptian god of silence turns into the Genie of Pantomime, a transformation that indicates the rise of pantomime as action ballet in the Opéra (Winter 1974, 161–180; Guest 1996, 25–42).

The beginning of *Les Oracles d'Harpocrate* distances itself from a predictable victim narrative. The first scene opens with the God of Silence sitting on the throne, surrounded by four mutes, who perform a ceremonial dance and bring an urn onto the stage. Harpocrates invites consultation of the oracle. From the second scene onward, the play does not show exotic elements. Instead it uses Harpocrates as an abstract cultural symbol. Scene 2 opens with an old and joyful man who wants to marry a young girl, who attempts to stay away from him. They ask Harpocrates for advice. Harpocrates hits the urn, which shows certain results that annoy the old man and please the girl. While they are leaving the stage, Harpocrates mocks one and applauds the other. There is no sign in the synopsis that indicates which one Harpocrates mocks and which he applauds. This ambiguity demonstrates that Pannard was careful enough not to assign a political position to Harpocrates. If Harpocrates refuses to take any single side, he then appears to represent neither the suppressed nor the suppressor. The third scene is about the confrontation between a charlatan and a student surgeon. Whereas in scene 2 Harpocrates mocks one and applauds another, here he mocks both the charlatan and a student surgeon. By the end of scene 3, Harpocrates assumes the role of an impartial judge. Contrary to the expected victim narrative, this pantomime sends mixed messages that distance Harpocrates from an icon of the oppressor, and thereby avoids pitting the Forains against the censors. Even though *Les Oracles d'Harpocrate* was performed in a time when the Opéra-Comique had just regained privileges to perform, Harpocrates symbolizes anything but sheer oppression.

If the first scene sets the stage and the following two scenes illustrate what Harpocrates does by acting as an impartial judge, then from scenes four to nine, the pantomime gets into the heart of the matter by delineating the rivalry among the Paris theaters. Scene 4 starts with the personified character Opéra who complains how he struggles to survive and approaches Harpocrates for advice. Harpocrates strikes the urn. He then takes out some unspecified objects that represent ballets. The Opéra dismisses his solution as ineffective. Harpocrates neglects him. He strikes the urn again and a little girl comes out and performs a *dance entrée*. Scene 5 shows an unhappy poet, whose hat has three feathers representing tragedies-comedies, parody, and opera. His costumes are revealing as well. On his sleeves and clothes are epigrams, madrigals, sonnets, rondeaux, rhapsodies, anagrams, and enigmas that represent the range of literary works he writes for a living. He shows Harpocrates his empty wallet and his works. Harpocrates strikes the urn. He then takes out a guidon and suggests that he start making military weapons. The poet refuses and leaves the scene. Scene 6 features Arlequin as a shopkeeper, who carries with him an ell and a balance and asks Harpocrates how to make more money. Harpocrates suggests that he cheat by shortening the ell. Scene 7 demonstrates rivalry between the Comédie-Française and Comédie-Italienne. They first congratulate each other and then reveal their contempt for one another, and end by debating among themselves who is better. They ask Harpocrates what they should do in order to attract more audiences. In scene 8 the Opéra-Comique, represented by Pierrot, reveals to Harpocrates its struggle to survive. Harpocrates tells him again about the resources in dance and pantomime. He begins to "sing" the following lines with gestures: "The language of the eyes has a charming function, / its support helps get you out of trouble." The climax of the pantomime is the end of scene 8, when all characters disappeared, and the Genie of Pantomime, dressed in a pastoral outfit, replaces Harpocrates. He offers Opéra-Comique his "protection" and invites everyone to join in a ballet. The final scene concludes by asserting the power of nonverbal communication (Rizzoni 2000, 171, n. 378).

Even though Pannard was reluctant to politicize Harpocrates, he politicized his pantomime, which shows an overall structure with loosely connected episodes that climaxes on the success of Opéra-Comique. Seeing in this light, the pantomime made a self-congratulatory statement about the return of the Opéra-Comique. Using Harpocrates as an allegorical figure, *Les Oracles d'Harpocrate* turns theater rivalry into a comedy. This pantomime demonstrates how the ossification of ballets at the Opéra coincided with the politicization of silence, which led to the success of the Opéra-Comique. Such a progression from the trivial to the serious, from ancient Egypt to contemporary France, from myth to current cultural criticism, and from the farcical to the serious turns this pantomime into one about theater politics. The triple functions Harpocrates plays—as an icon of oppressor, a protector of silence, and a predecessor of the Genie of Pantomime—make the pantomime less confrontational and more diplomatic than it appears. A common theme that runs through all the nine scenes is not how the official theaters silenced the Opéra-Comique, but more generally, the effectiveness of nonverbal communication.

The triumph of nonverbal communication brings out differences between the printed synopsis and the performance. In scene 2, although it is probable that Harpocrates mocks the old man and applauds the girl, it could be interpreted otherwise, depending on the performance. Despite the emphasis on the God of Silence, the pantomime is not at all about silence as an abstract concept, but about showing various types of nonverbal communication, including music. Throughout the pantomime music takes on an increasingly significant role. In scene 1, a dance is accompanied by musical instruments. Scene 4 begins with the entrance of the character Opéra, accompanied by a bass and a bassoon. In scene 7, the personified Comédie-Française, dressed as a Roman actor, enters with two pantomime dancers. His gestures are accompanied by a bassoon, which imitates the vocal inflection of French spoken tragedy. This bassoon solo captures the spoken declamation at the Comédie-Française to a melody with rhythmic stresses that suggest operatic declamation (Wentz 2013, 1). The end of this scene presents Comédie-Française, who asks an actress to sing "by gesture." Again it is not clear from the synopsis how gestures could communicate a couplet. In the final scene, the abstract singing is made concrete when a parrot comes out and sings "with a squeaker." By the end of the pantomime, music takes on a primary role. And singing makes silence communicative.

The synopsis indicates interaction between actors and the audience. Audiences at the beginning of the pantomime take a passive role. But in the last scene, scene 9, a canary comes out and addresses the audience directly. Breaking the fourth wall of the theater, it says "lower, lower" and tells the moral of the pantomime directly to the spectators. Once the noisy spectators become attentive, a parrot comes out of a tree and sings a vaudeville: "The parrot and the actor, / both learn by rote / Here is their similarity; / In front of the audiences, / One hisses and another is hissed; / Here is the difference." This is a remarkable moment because the song shows how the oral culture and the print media intersected and how the Forains encouraged active interaction between activities onstage and audiences. It provides a snapshot of a multimedia work that incorporated music, dance, commedia dell'arte slapstick comedy, social dance, gesture, fake animal talk, and a parrot's song. This pantomime synopsis provides telling textual evidence showing exchanges between performers and audiences.

Few men of letters in Paris took performances at the Forains seriously. But these works influenced the young Pierre Augustin Caron de Beaumarchais (1732–1799), who reportedly attempted to be a juggler at the Forains in 1750, when he was eighteen, and decades later wrote the influential Figaro plays that anticipated the fall of the Old Regime (Loménie 1873, 1:72). If Pannard's self-reflexive repertories were performed continually from the late 1720s through 1740s, Beaumarchais should have known of this convention. Despite this circumstantial biographical link between *Les Oracles d'Harpocrate* and Beaumarchais's plays, we see more generally how iconoclasts Pannard and Beaumarchais used nonverbal communication strategically in order to circumvent censorship.

Unlike the other unpublished pantomimes performed by the Nouveau Spectacle-Pantomime, *Les Oracles d'Harpocrate* was read and approved August 8, 1746, by the royal censor Prosper Jolycot de Crébillon and approved for publication three days later by the lieutenant general of police, Claude Henri Feydeau de Marville. The case of *Les Oracles d'Harpocrate* shows a facet of tolerance that has seldom been discussed in studies of censorship. Censors could easily have taken Harpocrates to be a representation of France and the play as criticism of the Old Regime. But both Crébillon and Marville did not do so. Instead of criticizing it as potentially subversive, they gave Pannard their approval for performance and publication. We can guess why censors approved the work. In addition to the potentially subversive themes, *Les Oracles d'Harpocrate* centers on the relationship between the ballet convention and the rise of pantomime in the history of French dance. The Egyptian setting provides a mythic context that explains the birth of the Genie of Pantomime. From this angle, *Les Oracles d'Harpocrate* is in fact a type of historical account of the emergence of pantomime in Paris. One should note that the birth of the God of Pantomime did not replace the celebratory ballets that were essential to the French culture, for as soon as Harpocrates turned into the God of Pantomime, the ballets were summoned to celebrate this event. What is gained, as shown in this pantomime, is a new type of dance called pantomime that coexisted with and enriched—and not replaced and annulled—the noble dance convention (Harris-Warrick and Brown 2005, 231). *Les Oracles d'Harpocrate* therefore documents the integration of ballet into French opera in the 1730s and 1740s, most notably in the flower scene of Jean-Philippe Rameau's *Les Indes galantes* (1735). It chronicles the rise of action ballets performed by Marie Sallé from the 1730s, the employment of librettist Louis de Cahusac at the Opéra in 1745, and the young dancer Jean-Georges Noverre at the Forains in 1743. It also unveils a new age of action ballet in Paris and in Europe. It predates Cahusac's important dance treatise *La Danse ancienne et moderne* (1754), Noverre's influential *Lettres sur la danse* (1760), and writings on action ballet by choreographer Gasparo Angiolini in the 1770s. Even though *Les Oracles d'Harpocrate* conveys mild criticism, it succeeds overall in explaining the rise of pantomime against the contexts of the history of ballet and theater rivalry in eighteenth-century France.

How Harpocrates Protected Musicians

Based on the meanings of Harpocrates as outlined above, we can assess the importance of silence in our putative history of music censorship. No librettists used Harpocrates as a character in French opera, but we should refrain from making hasty conclusions. Jacqueline Waeber has discussed the significance of Beaumarchais in the development of pantomime in France (Waeber 2000). Inspired by her work, I propose using Beaumarchais as a helpful link between the Forains and the official theaters in Paris. As a playwright, Beaumarchais had experience working with censors including François Louis Claude Marin, and Claude-Prosper Jolyot de Crébillon, or Crébillon junior, and Antoine Bret. His plays *Le Barbier de Séville* and *Le Mariage de Figaro* were censored multiple times. He finally wrote an operatic libretto *Tarare*, set to music by Salieri, which was also censored twice. One of its censors was the sympathetic Bret, who, as mentioned above, started out as a Bastille veteran. These biographical details, I suggest, help explain how Beaumarchais adopted music as a form of nonverbal communication. This new picture may help us explain parts of *Il Barbiere di Siviglia* (1782), set by Giovanni Paisiello (1740–1816), and by extension, of *Le Nozze di Figaro* (1786), set to music by Wolfgang Amadeus Mozart (1756–1791). When we put all these pieces together, we can make a claim that Harpocrates symbolically protected such iconoclasts as Pannard in 1746, Voltaire in 1772, Beaumarchais, Paisiello, and by extension, even Mozart well into the late 1780s.

Of all of Beaumarchais theatrical works, his early parades were not published, and therefore they were not censored. As shown in his other theatrical works, we see a three-stage censorship process. The play first gained approval from a royal censor. Then it had to obtain approval for performance. After the performance, he needed to obtain approval for the publication of his play. But at every stage a play could be censored. His first theatrical work, *Eugénie,* passed the censor Marin the first time on December 30, 1766, and was approved for performance by Antoine Gabriel de Sartines the next day. But the first day the play was performed, January 29, 1767, he received a letter from Marin who asked him to make changes. Marin approved the libretto, with the preface *Essai sur le genre dramatique sérieux,* for publication on June 27 of the same year. His next play, *Les Deux amis,* was approved by Marin on April 18, 1769, and gained approval for performance again from de Sartines on April 28. The premiere was on January 13, 1770, and the play was approved for publication by Marin three and a half months later, on April 30 (Beaumarchais 1988, 1241–1242).

Despite Beaumarchais's favorable experience working with Marin and de Sartines, he ran into censorship troubles with his *Le Barbier de Séville*. The four-act play was rejected by the Comédie-Italienne in 1772. Marin approved it on February 12, 1773, and the next day, de Sartines approved it for performance. On February 5, 1774, the play was approved by the second censor, Antonin Artaud, and was approved for performance a week later, on February 12. On December 29, 1774, the play was approved by the third censor, Crébillon, *fils*. Beaumarchais expanded it to five acts. It was permitted for publication on January 31, 1775, by the new prefect of police, Jean Charles Pierre Lenoir. It was finally premiered February 23, 1775. The second performance on February 26 restored the four-act approved version. This is the version we use today (Beaumarchais 1988, 1300–1301).

The case of *Le Mariage de Figaro* was different because Beaumarchais finished the play in 1778. It received favorable comments in October 1781 from the first censor, Coqueley de Chaussepierre, who demanded only minor modifications. Meanwhile, Beaumarchais read the script in various private locations of Paris. In July 1782, the new censor Jean Baptiste Antoine Suard was hostile to the play. On June 13, 1783, Louis XVI banned the scheduled performance of the play at the Théâtre des Menus-Plaisirs at the last moment. Between June and September 1783, the third censor, Malesherbes's friend Gabriel Henri Gaillard, supported it. At the end of 1783, the fourth censor, a certain Guidi, approved it. This approval was followed by two more. The fifth censor, Abbé Pierre-Françoise Desfontaines, approved it on January 15, 1784 and the sixth censor, Bret, approved it again on February 22. Six days later, on February 28, Coqueley de Chaussepierre gave him approval for publication and performance. His approval was followed by those of Bret on March 21 and Lenoir on March 29. After these rounds of approval, the play had its first performance at the Comédie-Française on April 27, 1784. Its preface was approved later by Bret on January 25, 1785, and gained approval for publication by Lenoir on January 31 (Beaumarchais 1988, 1364–1366; Hanley 2005, 1:321–322).

Beaumarchais finished the libretto of *Tarare* in 1784 and was adopted by the Opéra for performance. Having learned from issues of censorship surrounding *Le Mariage de Figaro*, Beaumarchais started to read the libretto in front of his friends and in the salons while Salieri was working on the music at his home in Paris. Beaumarchais sent the manuscript of his work to the censor Bret on March 26, 1786, who approved it for the first time on March 28 and the second time on December 21, 1786. As soon as it was approved, Salieri returned to Paris to finish the music for rehearsal. It was premiered on June 8, 1787 (Beaumarchais 1988, 1434–1435).

From the perspective of Pannard's *Les Oracles d'Harpocrate*, Harpocrates could be said to have protected Beaumarchais in several ways. Beaumarchais took advantage of oral culture and he spent three years reading his *Le Mariage de Figaro* and *Tarare* in the Paris salons when he was trying to the get his plays approved. No laws banned him from *reading* his plays in private settings before or after they were published. His action indicates that he knew well in advance how his censors would read his work and how he could circumvent censorship by means of oral communication. In his readings, he might have brought his audiences' attention to his uses of popular tunes in the play (Brown 1986, 261–265; Carter 1987, 42). Although he did not refer to Harpocrates explicitly, he should have at least heard of the tried-and-true lesson from the Forains that nonverbal materials could very likely circumvent censorship. In this general sense, at least, one could claim that he was symbolically protected by Harpocrates by exercising self-censorship.

Harpocrates could also be said to protect Beaumarchais in a second way. Beaumarchais charged songs in his plays with political meanings. In a letter he wrote to his father when he was in Spain, he said: "We say here, like in Italy, 'words are nothing, music is everything'" (Beaumarchais 1969, 1:145). If Beaumarchais was making what we now call anthropological observations when he traveled in Spain, then he turned his observation into a political statement in his plays. In his first Figaro play *Le Barbier de Séville*, Beaumarchais assigned Figaro to sing the following lines in act 1, scene 2, the first scene in which he appears onstage: "These days what is not worth saying gets set to music." Figaro politicizes singing by singing a song, but then he tones down the political criticism by giving it a comical guise, drawing a casual connection between singing and conviviality. Like Pannard, Beaumarchais politicized songs in his plays, making them accessible to audiences and at the same time communicating criticisms through them. Tellingly, in act 1, scene 2, of Paisiello's *Il Barbiere di Siviglia*, Figaro starts with a strophic song, "Diamo alla noja il bando." Paisiello interrupted the second stanza of the song with a recitative. "Whatever goes badly in verses, / either sets to music, / or sets as a burlesque comedy." Contrary to Pannard, who set political commentaries to songs, Paisiello offers suggestive criticism in his recitative and frames the criticism with a song. Here Harpocrates could be said to protect Figaro's song in a spoken play, and separately, a recitative-within-a-song in an opera.

In the case of *Le Mariage de Figaro*, Beaumarchais concluded the play with a song that conveys political criticism. In the last scene of the play, Suzanne sings in the refrain of the second stanza, "laws are written by the most powerful people." In the seventh stanza Figaro sings about the temporary impact of kings, as opposed to the long-lasting significance of Voltaire's work: "Of twenty kings we praise, / death shatters the altar, / And Voltaire is immortal." The most obviously subversive meanings are sung by the minor character Brid'oison in the last stanza of the same song, which concludes the play: "When good people are oppressed / they kick and shout; they are restless in a hundred ways. / Everything finishes with songs." As in the ending in Pannard's *Les Oracles d'Harpocrate* and the beginning of Beaumarchais's *Le Barbier de Séville*, a song lightens the potentially subversive meaning in the text. Indeed, Mozart's librettist Lorenzo Da Ponte must have noticed the subversive subtext in Beaumarchais's play. As if he were to feel the power of Harpocrates, he exercised self-censorship and revised the ending of it. The lyrics retain the conviviality of dancing and singing and are rid of political criticisms (Carter 1987, 37).

Similarly, Beaumarchais in his opéra *Tarare* (1787) criticized the dominance of verbal communication as parochial. In scene 2 of the prologue, the allegorical figure of Nature says, "It is their [human beings'] language. We must smile at it: / a noble pride makes them almost sure of it / but see how nature / pours them out by the thousands, / without choice and without moderation." These few verses reveal the different effectiveness of verbal and nonverbal communication. Unlike Paisiello, who showed the difference between recitative and song in his *Il Barbiere di Siviglia*, Antonio Salieri, who set the libretto to music at Beaumarchais's home, designed an instrumental interlude for a dangerous encounter. In act 3, scene 5, the hero Tarare is disguised as a deaf-mute. As with the princess Amaside in Voltaire's *Le Taureau blanc*, Tarare is advised not to speak, for "a word is a crime." As if protected by Harpocrates, Tarare, who is described elsewhere in the opera as an eloquent man, becomes a mute. When he sees Atar, Tarare kneels in front of him and exercises discretion. This high-risk encounter is accompanied by an instrumental interlude.

We have seen from this study different ways in which Harpocrates, the god of silence, could be said to protect French iconoclasts symbolically in the Old Regime from the 1740s through 1780s. Other than examining censors' reports and seeing from them what words or phrases were considered subversive, this paper demonstrates how playwrights and composers communicated potentially sensitive meanings in their work while working within boundaries of censorship. Within this context, a song, a short recitative, a musical interlude may communicate criticisms to those ready to notice them.

In a comparative study between censorship in France of 1789 and in Berlin of 1989, Darnton concludes that readers in Berlin before the revolution in 1989 read critically and aggressively for hidden meanings (Darnton 1995a, 57). Even a hint of suppression in the text could communicate hidden meanings to readers. As shown from the above analyses, Pannard and Beaumarchais seem to feed on similar aggressive reading and viewing practices by offering in their plays cues that suggest instances of self-restraint. But in the case of Paisiello and Mozart, their Figaro operas tone down markers of potentially subversive content in the places Beaumarchais had originally included them in his plays. The important issue concerning nonverbal communication and censorship is not when and where rules were enforced, but how authors and composers got across potentially politically sensitive commentaries by navigating around these rules. The gray area negotiated by censors and playwrights thus demonstrates the real effectiveness of censorship in the Old Regime.

In conclusion, this essay uses the Egyptian god Harpocrates as a means through which we obtain a glimpse of music censorship in Old Regime France. As with gesture, animal talk, and dance in *Les Oracles d'Harpocrate*, music could be used to circumvent censorship. Instead of a unidirectional oppression-toward-freedom narrative, this essay has identified forms of complicity and collaboration among parties of practitioners in Old Regime France. Although the censorship laws of the Old Regime were written primarily to control words in print, one can still find ways to detect instances of music censorship in the unevenly regulated world of prerevolutionary France.

References

Bartlet, M. Elizabeth C. 1982. "Beaumarchais and Voltaire's *Samson*." *Studies in Eighteenth-Century Culture* 11: 33–49.

Bartlet, M. Elizabeth C. 1984. "Politics and the Fate of 'Roger et Olivier,' a Newly Discovered Opera by Grétry." *Journal of the American Musicological Society* 37, no. 1: 98–138.

Bartlet, M. Elizabeth C. 1992. "On the Freedom of Theater and Censorship: The *Adrien* Controversy (1792)." In *1789–1989: Musique, Histoire, Démocratie*, edited by Antoine Hennion, 3 vols. 1:15–30. Paris: Éditions de la maison des sciences de l'homme.

Beaumarchais, Pierre Augustin Caron de. 1969. *Correspondance*. Edited by Brian N. Morton. 5 vols. Paris: Nizet.

Beaumarchais, Pierre Augustin Caron de. 1988. *Oeuvres*. Edited by Pierre Larthomas with the collaboration of Jacqueline Larthomas. Paris: Gallimard.

Brown, Bruce Alan. 1986. "Beaumarchais, Mozart, and the Vaudeville: Two Examples from 'The Marriage of Figaro.'" *The Musical Times* 127, no. 1718: 261–265.

Brown, Bruce Alan. 1999. "*Les Rêveries renouvelées des Grecs*: Facture, Function and Performance Practice in a Vaudeville Parody of Gluck's *Iphigénie en Tauride* (1779)." In *Timbre und Vaudeville: zur Geschichte und Problematik einer populären Gattung im 17. Und 18. Jahrhundert: Bericht über den Kongress in Bad Homburg 1996*, edited by Herbert Schneider, 308–343. Hildesheim: Olms, 1999.

Brown, Wendy. 1998. "Freedom's Silences." In *Censorship and Silencing: Practices of Cultural Regulation*, edited by Robert C. Post, 313–327. Los Angeles: The Getty Research Institute for the History of Art and the Humanities.

Carter, Tim. 1987. *W. A. Mozart: Le nozze di Figaro*. Cambridge: Cambridge University Press.

Cerf, Madeleine. 1967. "La Censure royale à la fin du XVIIIe siècle." *Communications* 9: 2–27.

Chartier, Roger. 2000. "Afterword: Music in Print." In *Music and the Cultures of Print*, edited by Kate van Orden, 325–341. New York: Garland.

Chartier, Roger. 2011. "*Un Garçon plein d'esprit mais extrêmement dangereux*: The Darnton Subversion." In *Into Print: Limits and Legacies of the Enlightenment. Essays in Honor of Robert Darnton*, edited by Charles Walton, 1–14. University Park: Pennsylvania State University Press.

Campardon, Émile. 1877. *Les Spectacles de la foire. Théâtres, acteurs, sauteurs, et danseurs de corde, monstres, géants . . . des foires Saint-Germain et Saint-Laurent, des boulevards et du Palais-Royal depuis 1595 jusqu'à 1791*. 2 vols. Paris: Berger-Levrault.

Darlow, Mark. 2012. *Staging the French Revolution: Cultural Politics and the Paris Opéra, 1789–1794*. Oxford: Oxford University Press.

Darnton, Robert. 1979. *The Business of Enlightenment: A Publication History of the Encyclopédie 1775–1800*. Cambridge, Mass.: Harvard University Press.

Darnton, Robert. 1995a. "Censorship, a Comparative View: France, 1789–East Germany, 1989." *Representations* 49: 40–60.

Darnton, Robert. 1995b. *The Corpus of Clandestine Literature in France, 1769–1789*. New York: W. W. Norton.

Darnton, Robert. 1996. *The Forbidden Best-Sellers of Pre-Revolutionary France*. New York: W. W. Norton.

Darnton, Robert. 2004. "Mademoiselle Bonafon and the Private Life of Louis XV: Communication Circuits in Eighteenth-Century France." *Representations* 87, no. 1: 102–124.

Darnton, Robert. 2010. *Poetry and Police: Communication Networks in Eighteenth-Century Paris*. Cambridge, Mass.: Harvard University Press.

Dubos, Jean-Baptiste. 1733. *Réflexions critiques sur la poésie et sur la peinture*. 3 vols. Paris: P. J. Mariette.

Du Lorens, Jacques. 1869. *Satires de Dulorens*. Édition de 1646 Contenant de vingt-six Satires. Paris: D. Jouaust.

Dyche, Thomas. 1758. *Dictionnaire universel des arts et sciences, françois, latin et anglois*. 3 vols. Amsterdam: Jean Neaulme.

Foucault, Michel. 1977. *Discipline and Punish: The Birth of the Prison*. Translated by Alan Sheridan. New York: Pantheon Books.

Fried, Michael. 1980. *Absorption and Theatricality: Painting and Beholder in the Age of Diderot*. Berkeley: University of California Press.

Guest, Ivor. 1996. *The Ballet of the Enlightenment: The Establishment of the Ballet d'Action in France, 1770–1793*. London: Dance Books.

Habermas, Jürgen. 1989. *The Structural Transformation of the Public Sphere: An Inquiry into a Category of Bourgeois Society*. Translated by Thomas Burger with the assistance of Frederick Lawrence. Cambridge, MA: MIT Press.

Hanley, William. 1980. "The Policing of Thought: Censorship in Eighteenth-Century France." *Studies on Voltaire and the Eighteenth Century* 183: 265–295.

Hanley, William. 2005, 2016. *A Biographical Dictionary of French Censors, 1742–1789*. Vols. 1 and 2. Ferney-Voltaire, France: Centre internationale d'étude du XVIIIe siècle.

Harris-Warrick, Rebecca, and Bruce Alan Brown, eds. 2005. *The Grotesque Dancer on the Eighteenth-Century Stage: Gennaro Magri and His World*. Madison: University of Wisconsin Press.

Hemmings, Frederick William John. 1994. *Theatre and State in France, 1760–1905*. Cambridge: Cambridge University Press.

Isherwood, Robert. 1986. *Farce and Fantasy: Popular Entertainment in Eighteenth-Century Paris*. New York: Oxford University Press.

Lesage, Alain René. 1821. *Oeuvres de Le Sage*. 12 vols. Paris: A.A. Renouard.

Lesage, Alain René. 1960. *Histoire de Gil Blas de Santillane*. In *Romanciers du XVIIIe siècles*, edited by René Etiemble. 5 vols. Paris: Gallimard.

Loménie, Louis de. 1873. *Beaumarchais et son temps: Études sur la société en France au XVIIIe siècle d'après des documents inédits*. 2 vols. Paris: Michel Lévy.

Martin, Henri-Jean. 1984. "L'Affaire de *De l'Esprit*." In *Histoire de l'édition française, vol. 2, Le Livre triumphant, 1660–1830*, edited by Henri-Jean Martin and Daniel Roche with the collaboration of Jean-Pierre Vivet, 78–79. Paris: Promodis.

Martin, Isabelle. 2002. *Le Théâtre de la foire: des tréteaux aux boulevards*. Oxford: Voltaire Foundation.

Maza, Sarah. 1993. *Private Lives and Public Affairs: The Causes Célèbres of Prerevolutionary France*. Berkeley: University of California Press.

Mercier, Louis-Sébastian. 1782. *Tableau de Paris*. Nouvelle éd. 8 vols. Amsterdam.

Pernety, Antoine Joseph. 1786. *Les Fables égyptiennes et grecques*. 2 vols. Paris: Bauche.

Pluche, Noël Antoine. 1739. *Histoire du ciel considérée selon les idées des poëtes, des philosophes, et de Moïse*. 2 vols. Paris: La Veuve Estienne.

Post, Robert C., ed. 1998. *Censorship and Silencing: Practices of Cultural Regulation*. Los Angeles: Getty Research Institute.

Ramsay, Chevalier. 1727. *Les Voyages de Cyrus: avec un discours sur la mythologie*. Paris: G.F. Quillau.

Ravel, Jeffrey. 1999. *The Contested Parterre: Public Theater and French Political Culture, 1680–1791*. Ithaca, N.Y.: Cornell University Press.

Rizzoni, Nathalie. 2000. *Charles-François Pannard et l'esthétique du 'petit.'* Oxford: Voltaire Foundation.

Roche, Daniel. 1984. "La Censure;" "La Police du livre;" In *L'Histoire de l'édition française, vol. 2, Le livre triumphant 1660–1830*, edited by Henri-Jean Martin et Roger Chartier with the collaboration of Jean-Pierre Vivet, 76–93. Paris: Promodis.

Roche, Daniel. 1998. *France in the Enlightenment*. Translated by Arthur Goldhammer. Cambridge, MA: Harvard University Press.

Salmon, Xavier. 2002. *Madame de Pompadour et les arts*. Paris: Réunion des musées nationaux.

Spon, Jacob. 1683. *Recherches curieuses d'antiquité; contenues plusieurs dissertations, sur des médailles, bas-reliefs, statuës, mosaïques & inscriptions antiques*. Lyon: Thomas Amaulry.

Waeber, Jacqueline. 2000. "Beaumarchais et Rousseau: Sur quelques aspects du renouveau de la pantomime et de l'avènement du mélodrame." *French Studies of the Eighteenth and Ninteenth Centuries* 8: 205–224.

Wentz, Jed. 2013. "An Annotated livret of Lully's Roland as a Source for Seventeenth-Century Declamation." *Cambridge Opera Journal* 2013:1–36.

Winter, Marian Hannah. 1974. *The Pre-Romantic Ballet*. London: Pitman.

CHAPTER 8

SEX, POLITICS, AND CENSORSHIP IN MOZART'S *DON GIOVANNI/DON JUAN*

MARTIN NEDBAL

NUMEROUS studies of Mozart's operas touch on the relationship between Mozart, his librettists, and the notoriously strict Viennese censors. Censorship figures prominently in discussions of the earliest printed libretto of Mozart's *Don Giovanni*, published in Vienna in the spring or summer of 1787 (before the premiere of the opera in Prague in the fall of that year). According to the theory first articulated by Alfred Einstein (1956, 220), the libretto was published for inspection by the censors, and in order to avoid a censorial ban, Mozart and his librettist Lorenzo da Ponte left out the most risqué numbers in the first act, including the famous "Champagne" aria and the whole first-act finale containing Don Giovanni's attempted rape of the peasant girl Zerlina.[1] Similarly, several scholars have suggested that various aspects of Mozart's other operas, such as *The Magic Flute*, also reflect the restrictive Viennese censorship of the period.[2] These theories and studies are often based on the assumption that composers and librettists in Mozart's Vienna had to curb their creative desires in order to avoid a censorial ban, and that even then their authorial vision was frequently altered during the process of inspection. Moreover, many scholars search for traces of various methods through which the opera authors attempted to circumvent the censors.[3]

These perspectives certainly reflect important aspects of Viennese theater from the late eighteenth century onward. Vienna was one of the first cities in the German-speaking world with an official system of theater censorship, established in 1770. As a result, large portions of theatrical pieces were excised, entire works were prohibited from performance, and various Viennese intellectuals expressed frustration with censorship. But, as more detailed studies of theater and opera censorship have shown (Holquist 1994; Giger 1999; Höyng 2003; Izzo 2007), late eighteenth- and nineteenth-century systems of theatrical control were complex and often arbitrary; they did not necessarily incorporate a unidirectional chain of command emanating from the censor in order to restrict the creative urges of the author, the rules according to which the censors judged their works were not permanently fixed, and the process of approval or banning was far from straightforward. Michael Holquist (1994) and Peter Höyng (2003) have proposed instead that censorship be viewed as a bundle of multidirectional and often contradictory negotiations stretching beyond censors and authors. In this essay I explore what Holquist (1994, 21) calls the "dialogic aspects of censorship" with the example of institutional supervision over the content of Mozart's *Don Giovanni*. First, I reevaluate the issues surrounding the 1787 Vienna libretto, and second, I discuss the role of censorship in several performances from around 1800 of a German adaptation of Mozart's opera, titled *Don Juan*, at the Vienna court theater.

As mentioned earlier, the office of the theater censor was established in Vienna in 1770. That same year, Empress Maria Theresia appointed Franz Karl Hägelin to that office, which he held for the next thirty-four years, retiring in December of 1804.[4] Hägelin was officially responsible for supervising the content of any German-language opera and spoken play to be performed in any Viennese theater. Throughout most of his tenure, Hägelin was especially strict with the works presented at the Viennese court theater (consisting throughout this period of the Burgtheater and Kärntnertortheater) due to its association with the imperial government and its representative function as an exemplary institution of German national culture.

The strictness with which Hägelin and other court theater personnel approached the content of German-language works to be presented at the institution in the early 1780s becomes obvious when we compare Viennese versions of plays and libretti written for foreign stages to the originals. The opening of the first-act aria of Prince Alwin, the main hero of the 1782 opera *Das Irrlicht*, provides a concise example. The libretto by Christoph Friedrich Bretzner was originally published in 1779 in North Germany and set to music by several local composers. In 1782, Gottlieb Stephanie the Younger adapted it for the Viennese court theater where it appeared in a musical setting by Ignaz Umlauf. Stephanie's revision of the opening of Alwin's aria aims at reducing sexual innuendo in the prince's account of his first encounter with his future bride Blanka. Bretzner's Alwin sings (Bretzner 1776, 12):

Solch ein Mädgen sah ich nirgends,	I have never seen a maiden like this,
so voll himmlischer Gefühle,	so full of heavenly sentiments,
so gemacht zu Amors Spiele,	so ready for amorous games,
so voll holder Zärtlichkeit.	so full of charming tenderness.

The Viennese Alwin sings (Stephanie 1781, 9):

Solch ein Mädchen sah' ich nirgends,	I have never seen a maiden like this,
so voll unschuldvoller Sitte,	so full of innocent morals,
so voll Reiz und so voll Güte,	so full of beauty and kindness,
so voll sanfter Zärtlichkeit.	so full of gentle tenderness.

It is likely that Stephanie understood Bretzner's image of "Amors Spiele" as signifying Alwin's erotic fantasies and feared that the passage might incite similar fantasies in the audience. The Viennese Alwin, then, expresses non-sexual interest in Blanka and her unspoiled personal character. The excision or revision of suggestive passages was, as I show below, an important aspect of Hägelin's approach to theatrical works, and the censor would certainly have to approve the libretto of *Das Irrlicht* for publication and performance. Although it is difficult to say with any certainty whether Stephanie changed the aria due to his own aesthetic sensibilities or because he anticipated objections by Hägelin, the aria's revision exemplifies the uptight transformations commonly executed in *Singspiel* libretti adapted for presentations at the Viennese court theater around 1780.[5]

Due at least partially to Hägelin's supervision, most of the strictly censored German-language repertoire of the Viennese court theater from the early 1780s avoided any depictions of behavior that could be considered offensive to the moral sensibilities of audiences. Had the Italian comic operas (such as *Don Giovanni*) that Mozart produced in Vienna during his last decade originated as German *Singspiele*, they would have hardly been admitted for performance alongside the German-language works presented at the court theater. This is in fact what happened during Mozart's lifetime in Munich, where the censors forbid a German version of *Don Giovanni*, purportedly (that is, according to the official report) due to Don Giovanni's attempted abduction of Zerlina in the first-act finale (see Weidinger 2002, 832–833). Besides the attempted rape, numerous other elements in *Don Giovanni* also would have contradicted censorial and editorial principles applied to German works throughout the 1780s. Weidinger (2002, 876) lists some of these: hedonism, adultery, the willingness of female characters to engage in sexual relations with men outside of marriage, celebrations of orgiastic excess, hints at sexual acts that occur behind the scene, and the generalized criticism of nobility.

The original Mozart/Da Ponte operas, however, were in Italian, and their language might account for why they were allowed to appear on the stages of the court theater. Throughout the late eighteenth century, German and non-German theatrical works were censored separately by different personnel, and non-German works were most likely approached with greater leniency presumably because only the educated elites could understand Italian or French and any potential immoral content was therefore incomprehensible for the uneducated masses.[6]

Little is known about the censorship of Italian opera in Vienna during the 1780s beyond the possibility that it was not as strict as German censorship.[7] It might have been this lack of information that led to the assumptions, mentioned earlier, that Mozart and Da Ponte feared the censors so much that they deleted crucial scenes from the 1787 libretto of *Don Giovanni*. But even the few scattered sources show that Italian opera censorship was indeed much less organized and rigorous than the German institution, led by Hägelin. Notably, the person who had the final say in the approval of a libretto was not a special censor but most likely Emperor Joseph II himself (Beales 2009, 2: 465–469). In letters from his travels to Italy in 1784, the emperor talks about the libretti of operas he heard there—he even sent some of those libretti to Vienna, accompanied by his personal evaluations—but nowhere does he show much concern for moral or political issues (Thurn 1920, 44, 47, 48). The only instance when he mentions censorship is in connection with the German translation of Beaumarchais' *The Marriage of Figaro*: in a letter from January 31, 1785, the emperor points out that there are many offensive passages in it but delegates the censor (Hägelin) to do the necessary corrections or prohibit the piece altogether (Thurn 1920, 60). According to Da Ponte, when it came to evaluating the appropriateness of his Italian adaptation of Beaumarchais' play, it was the emperor himself who was the arbiter and let the opera pass into performance (Da Ponte 2000, 128–130). One can imagine that the emperor and his officials were not as prudish in their theatrical tastes as the German censor, especially considering the widely rooted understanding of Italian theater as an exclusive form of entertainment for the nobility. As a result, it is likely that the 1787 Vienna libretto was not published for the censors but for some other reason. Tomislav Volek (1987, 55) has proposed that the libretto might have served as promotion material for potential sponsors, whereas Ian Woodfield (2010, 35) has treated the libretto simply as a working draft without speculating on its purpose. The most extensive discussion of the libretto to date is in Hans Ernst Weidinger's sixteen-volume dissertation (2002, esp. 833–839), in which the author largely rejects the censorship hypothesis and suggests that the opera might have been originally commissioned in Vienna (not Prague) to celebrate dynastic marriages in the Habsburg family, and thus the 1787 Vienna libretto was published in connection to that Viennese commission.

That the *Don Giovanni* libretto was probably not under as much moralistic scrutiny as *Das Irrlicht* does not mean, however, that there was absolutely no supervision of content in Italian operas during the Josephine period. In his creation of the *Don Giovanni* libretto, Da Ponte did make certain choices that parallel principles embraced by the censors of German theater. One such principle seems to have been at work in the conception of scene 10 in the first act, which immediately follows the love duet "Là ci darem la mano" and ends with Donna Elvira's aria "Ah fuggi il traditor." As Weidinger has pointed out (2012, 876–877), the aria and the whole scene in which Elvira prevents Don Giovanni and Zerlina from departing the stage to consummate their passion for one another did not exist in Giovanni Bertati and Giuseppe Gazzaniga's 1787 opera *Don Giovanni, o sia Il convitato di pietra* that Da Ponte used as a model. In the earlier opera, Don Giovanni seduces the peasant girl Maturina, she sings an aria, and eventually the two depart for Maturina's house. In having Donna Elvira prevent the couple's departure, Da Ponte might be following the principle—later articulated and enforced in German works by Hägelin—that no two lovers be allowed to depart the stage together for an enclosed space, since such a departure would prompt the spectators to imagine that they will engage in sexual activity once off the stage.[8]

To interpret the addition of Elvira's aria as a result of some censorial sensibilities would be simplistic, however, because we do not know the exact reasons behind Da Ponte's decision to include the scene. There could have been some morally conscious censor of Italian operas during the late 1780s in Vienna (though there is no indication as to who, and there is also no indication that Hägelin was reading works in languages other than German). Or Da Ponte might have anticipated that the censor (or the emperor himself) would object to Don Giovanni and Zerlina's departure and therefore introduced the Elvira scene. It is equally possible, nevertheless, that Da Ponte, who was the official poet of the Italian company at the court theater at the time and whose task it was to supervise the adaptation of any outside libretto for the Viennese stage, sought to censor certain aspects of the adapted texts himself due to his own views on what standards of propriety should be upheld in works performed at the imperial theater.[9] Yet another possibility is that Da Ponte's addition of Elvira's interruption had nothing to do with censorship or moralistic standards but resulted from the need to expand Bertati's one-act work into a much larger form.

The ambiguous encounters between *Don Giovanni* and the nebulous institution of Viennese theater censorship continued after Mozart's death. Following the opera's initial run at the court theater in 1788, *Don Giovanni* disappeared from that stage for a whole decade. It was revived in 1798 under the title *Don Juan* in a four-act German adaptation with interpolated scenes and spoken dialogue instead of recitative. The author of the adaptation was Friedrich Karl Lippert, a baritone actor-singer who also performed the role of Don Juan until his death in May of 1803. After Lippert's death, the opera was shortened and converted back to two acts in December of 1803. The new version received two more performances in late December of 1803 (afterwards the opera would not be revived until 1817—in a slightly revised version; see Hadamowsky 1966, 28). It would seem that the court theater adaptation of *Don Giovanni* into *Don Juan* would take into consideration the stricter censorial supervision of the German theater and mainly focus on revisions of the original operas' political and moral content. Yet the adaptation process was in fact more convoluted than that, and censorship played a significant but not a decisive or strictly suppressive or prohibitive role in it.

Handwritten copies of the German texts and scores associated with the 1798 and 1803 performances of *Don Juan* survive in the Austrian National Library. One of these manuscripts (*Don Juan*, A-Wn, Mus. Hs. 32702) contains black-ink entries in Hägelin's hand as well as his permit allowing the publication and performance of the work with the suggested changes. The manuscript was written in 1798, and Hägelin most likely first read the libretto that year, executing a few changes and giving his written permission for performance and publication on the penultimate page. The permission is not dated—as Lisa de Alwis (2012, 94) has explained, "Hägelin . . . only began adding dates in 1801." The manuscript was later used to record the revision of the four-act version into the two-act version, and after that revision, Hägelin read it once again in December of 1803.[10] After his initial inspection on December 16, 1803, Hägelin returned the libretto to the theater directorship with an explanatory note in which he asks for changes in scenes 16 and 18:

> Im Folge hoher Weißung vom / heutigen Dato wird gegenwärtiges / Oper der Direction / mit der Erinnerung / zurückgestellt, daß die roth / angestrichene im 16. Auftritte, / dann die Scene zwischen Don / Juan und Zerlina im 18. Auf- / tritte des ersten Aktes als höchst- / unanständig umzuarbeiten, / sodann nachmahls vorzulegen sey. / Den 16. Xber 1803 / Hägelin

Following a high request [i.e., by a higher instance] from today's date, the present opera is being returned to the directorship [of the court theater] with the reminder, that the [passages] marked in red in Scene 16, then the encounter between Don Juan and Zerlina in Scene 18 of the first act are highly indecent and need to be revised and submitted once again. On December 16, 1803, Hägelin.

The corrections Hägelin asked for were executed within two days, and so, on December 18, 1803, the censor gave the permission for the opera's performance and publication (Figure 8.1).[11] Upon initial examination, the libretto suggests a straightforward process of gradually tightening control, so dutiful as to prompt the musicologist Otto Erich Deutsch (1993, 69), who examined the libretto in the early twentieth century, to imagine that Mozart would have turned in his grave and cursed in an indecent manner had he known what Hägelin and other censors did to his opera.

Many of the black-ink changes entered into the libretto by Hägelin and other reviewers (the comments and rewrites are in multiple hands) either in 1798 or 1803 conform to the principles that Hägelin himself spelled out earlier in his career. In 1795 Hägelin wrote a collection of guidelines on the matters of theater censorship for his colleagues in Hungary, in which he listed specific elements of theatrical works that other censors should be particularly vigilant about.[12] He divides the sources of problematic content into three areas—religion, politics, and morals. All three appear in the *Don Juan* libretto.

In a section from the 1795 guidelines discussing content impermissible in a theatrical piece out of religious considerations (Glossy 1897, 320), Hägelin warns against using any words or phrases that are related to Biblical passages or catechism, and thus many such passages are rewritten in the *Don Juan* libretto. Throughout the opera, for example, various characters exhort others to "confess" (*beitchten*) their crimes, and the verb is always changed into a form of "to admit" (*bekennen*), so that it no longer alludes explicitly to religious practices and texts.

Another group of problematic expressions discussed by Hägelin in his guidelines are those connected to social and political issues. An element that the censor specifically warns about and is then corrected numerous times throughout the *Don Juan* libretto is the criticism of nobility (Glossy 1897, 325). Throughout the *Don Juan* manuscript, we find corrections in statements where various characters make a connection between Don Juan's evil deeds and his noble status. In the second-act conversation (within the four acts of 1798) between Zerlina and Don Juan, the peasant girl at first refuses to trust Don Juan's marriage proposal since her parents have warned her not to trust "highborn gentlemen" (*vornehmen Herren*) and their intentions. Don Juan responds that when a "highborn gentleman" is in love he always has good intentions. The phrase "highborn gentleman" appears a few more times throughout the manuscript, and every time it is rewritten to omit references to social class; for example, Zerlina ends up talking about "such gentlemen as you" (*solche Herren wie Sie sind*) and Don Juan about "a man like me" (*Herr meines gleichen*).

Hägelin devotes the most substantial portion of his guidelines to a description of various ways in which a theatrical text can be immoral (Glossy 1897, 317–320, 326–328),

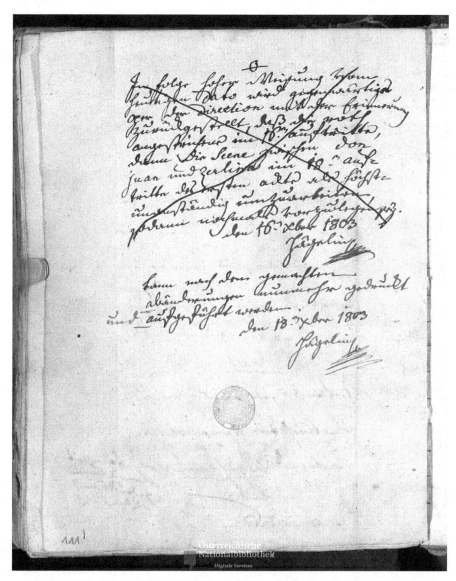

FIGURE 8.1 The final page of the censor's copy of Lippert's *Don Juan* adaptation with two notes by Hägelin from December of 1803.

and, conspicuously, most of the rewrites within the *Don Juan* manuscript can be interpreted as having to do with moral issues. For example, whenever the word "seducer" (*Verführer*) appears in the manuscript, it is changed into "Betrüger" (*deceiver*), and the verb "to seduce" (*verführen*) transforms into "to abduct" (*entführen*). These revisions change the meaning of the speeches to which they are applied. The fact that in the censored document Donna Elvira accuses Don Juan of "abducting" not "seducing" her, makes less explicit the possibility that the two had sexual relations. Squeamishness also dominates the censors' approach to the ending of the first act (within the original Italian opera and the revised two-act version of 1803), where Hägelin and his superiors were especially concerned about the few lines that follow Zerlina's cries for help after Don Juan drags her out of the dancing hall. In his note from December 16, Hägelin mentions that the most problematic passages in scene 18 of the first-act finale have been marked with red crayon, and a section of that scene is indeed highlighted with a red line on the left (Figure 8.2). Numerous passages within that section are crossed out and rewritten in brown ink, and the following illustration shows the most substantial changes (the revisions are shown in boldface):

(Don Juan führt Zerlina sträubend ~~in ein Seiten Kabinet~~ **ab**.)	(Don Juan leads the struggling Zerlina ~~into a side chamber~~ **away**.)
ZERLINA	ZERLINA
O Himmel! Ich bin verrathen.	O heavens! I am lost.
LEPORELLO	LEPORELLO
Sie ~~riecht~~ **merkt** schon ~~den Braten~~ **die Posse**.	~~She can smell the roast.~~ **She now has figured out the joke**.
	...
DONNA ANNA. ELVIRA. OCTAVIO.	DONNA ANNA. ELVIRA. OCTAVIO.
Laß uns schnell ~~ins Zimmer~~ **in den Vorsaal** dringen,	Let us hurry and break into the ~~room~~ **hallway**.
Sie ~~entreißen seinen Schlingen~~ **hierher zurück** bringen.	Let us ~~tear her away from his snares~~ **bring her back here**.
MASETTO	MASETTO
~~Ach Zerlina. Möchts gelingen~~ **Ja sie schnell zurücke bringen**.	~~Ach, Zerlina. What if he succeeds~~ **Yes bring her back here**.

By requesting such systematically aligned revisions, Hägelin clearly sought to avoid explicit references to Don Juan's sexual assault on Zerlina and followed the aforementioned principle, articulated in the 1795 guidelines, that no two characters of the opposite sex should be allowed to depart the stage to an enclosed space (see also De Alwis 2012, 99–100).

As restrictive and straightforward as the revisions in the *Don Juan* manuscript seem, it is difficult to ascertain to what extent the censor himself was in control of the opera's content. Although the handwriting of numerous comments in the manuscript is similar to that of Hägelin's concluding note and can therefore safely be ascribed to the censor, other, often more substantial revisions have clearly been entered or influenced by other reviewers. At the beginning of his December 16 note, Hägelin talks about following a "high request," which indicates that a superior censorial institution evaluated theatrical pieces independently from him. This might have been the *Polizeihofstelle* (police court office), a division of the Ministry of Police, which was appointed in 1801 by Emperor

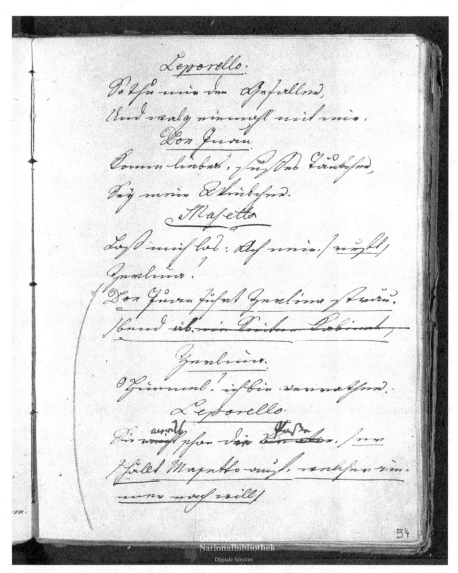

FIGURE 8.2 The beginning of the section in the first-act finale of *Don Juan* deemed indecent by Hägelin (in his note from December 16, 1803) and highlighted in red crayon. Visible are also the subsequent cut in stage direction and the revision of Leporello's line.

Francis II to review theatrical works independent from Hägelin (see De Alwis 2012, 59). The opening of the note also makes it seem as if Hägelin were trying to distance himself from the ruling of the higher institution (presumably the *Polizeihofstelle*), which suggests that the decisions and rules about what was permissible and what was considered indecent were adjustable and not always completely clear, and that opinions of different censors and state officials could conflict with each other.[13]

Another set of 1803 revisions must have come from the court theater personnel, as we can see in the series of scenes involving the Hermit and the murder of Don Octavio.[14]

These scenes do not exist in the original Italian opera and were interpolated only into the 1798 adaptation where they opened the fourth act (the third act in this version concludes with the famous sextet). Don Juan and Leporello reconvene in front of a statue of the murdered Komthur (Commendatore) that happens to stand next to a hermit's abode. Suddenly Don Octavio arrives to pray in front of the statue. Don Juan murders the hermit, dons his clothes, assumes his identity, persuades Octavio to lay aside his weapons, and murders him as well. The vile actions outrage the Komthur's spirit, who reproofs Don Juan, at which point the 1798 plot returns to that of the Italian opera. Hägelin passed the scene into performance in 1798 with minor alterations.[15] The scene became popular with audiences, mainly due to the humorous episodes associated with Leporello—this becomes obvious from a review of the court theater production published in the May 25, 1803, issue of the *Allgemeine musikalische Zeitung* (translated and annotated in Albrecht 2008, 145).

In December 1803, the scene was cut and replaced with a conversation in which Leporello recounts previous events to Don Juan. That this cut must have occurred only in December 1803 is clear from the theater posters that list the Hermit as one of the characters up until March 1803 (the last performances before the revision) but drop him in December (*Theaterzettel Burgtheater* 1798, 1799, 1803). The replacement dialogue was written in between the lines of the 1798 Hermit scene that were crossed out in brown ink. Afterwards further changes were added by several reviewers, one of whom must have been Hägelin, judging by the handwriting.[16] The revised replacement text was later written on separate sheets that were inserted into the manuscript, probably to make it easier for copyists to decipher the final form of the new scene. Although the chronology of the revision is more or less clear (the 1798 scene with the Hermit was censored, then crossed out and replaced with the 1803 version without the Hermit that was censored and written on a separate sheet), the reasons for its execution are not. It is tempting to interpret the excision and replacement of the Hermit scenes as an act of censorial strictness and the tightening of restrictions between 1798 and 1803: perhaps by late 1803 the double murder (including that of a religious person) became problematic for the authorities supervising Viennese theaters or for someone from the court theater staff anticipating objections from the censors (scholars usually refer to such an act of anticipation as self-censorship). But it is also quite possible that the revision had nothing to do with censorship and simply aimed at shortening the opera (the *Allgemeine musikalische Zeitung* critic did complain about excessive length of Lippert's adaptation prior to revision).

Even in those revisions within the *Don Juan* libretto that were clearly executed at the censors' request, it is problematic and simplistic to think, as Deutsch (1993) did, of Hägelin or the Viennese authorities as destroying the spirit of the original Mozartian work. Many of the scenes that were heavily revised by the censors usually differ quite a bit from the Italian original. The scenes depicting the murders of the Hermit and Don Octavio do not exist in Da Ponte's original story; instead they closely copy the Don Juan traditions of the Viennese popular theater, especially the 1783 play *Dom Juan* written by Karl Marinelli for the Leopoldstadt Theater.[17]

The censoring of scenes that have parallels in Da Ponte's libretto did not necessarily impinge on the content of the original *Don Giovanni* either, as becomes clear in the two sections that Hägelin specifically mentions in his 1803 report. The mollification of the language and stage directions associated with Don Juan's abduction of Zerlina that Hägelin requested and that was entered into the manuscript afterwards would not have been necessary in the Italian original (Table 8.1). Only one of the rewrites within Lippert's adaptation of scene 18 changes a phrase, a form of which was already present in Da Ponte's original Italian libretto. Da Ponte had Zerlina defend herself from Don Giovanni with the word "scoundrel" (Scellerato), and Lippert translated it as "no, traitor" (*Nein, Verräther*). In 1803 the phrase was changed (most likely at Hägelin's or the *Polizeihofstelle*'s urging) to "Help, Masetto" (*Hilf, Masetto*)—perhaps to make Zerlina's references to Don Juan's sexual advances less direct. All the other changes in Lippert's translation of the scene, however, were executed in sentences through which the German adaptation had brought an element of crass sexual humor into Da Ponte's libretto. Lippert, for example, transformed the admonishing remark "This will lead to ruin" with which the Italian Leporello reacts to Zerlina's abduction into the raucous "[Zerlina] can smell the roast." Lippert also expanded Masetto's exclamations "Oh Zerlina" into the more suggestive "Oh, Zerlina. What if [Don Juan] succeeds." After the censor's 1803 call for revision, Leporello's remark was changed to the more neutral "[Zerlina] now has figured out the joke," and Masetto's exclamation into "Bring [Zerlina] quickly back." Both revisions, therefore, curtail not the content of Da Ponte and Mozart's original but rather that of Lippert's translation. Another rewrite in fact brings the German adaptation closer to Da Ponte's original. According to the stage directions in Lippert's adaptation, Don Juan was to lead Zerlina into a "side chamber" (*Seiten Kabinet*); after the 1803 revision, he simply "leads her away," which is closer to Da Ponte's "leads Zerlina to a door" (*conduce Zerlina presso una porta*).

The German text of the second scene that Hägelin wanted changed in 1803 also differs significantly from Da Ponte's original. The scene roughly corresponds to act 1, scene 15 of *Don Giovanni*: it ends with the famous "Champagne" aria but opens with a newly devised monologue for Don Juan in which he threatens the absent Elvira for interrupting his tryst with Zerlina and declares his resolve to possess the peasant girl at any cost. The censorial manuscript contains three distinct versions of the aria and the preceding monologue, two on the original pages and one on inserted sheets (Table 8.2). Alongside the two aria texts on the original pages runs a double line in red crayon that Hägelin mentions in his note from December 16, 1803; one of these two texts therefore must have been used during the earlier performances of the opera, whereas the third text was likely the one added at the censors' request (Figure 8.3).[18] The two earlier versions of the aria significantly alter the meaning of the Italian original. In the first version, Lippert replaces the list of dances that Don Giovanni envisions for the party with a list of anonymous women he will encounter: instead of "Let the dance be without any order, a minuet, a folia, and an allemande you shall lead" (*Senza alcun ordine / la danza sia, / chi 'l minuetto / chi la follia / chi l' alemanna / farai ballar*), we find "Quite nameless [i.e., so numerous that their names cannot all be made known] are the damsels here, English

Table 8.1 A comparison of Da Ponte's Italian text for Zerlina's abduction scene from the 1788 Vienna *Don Giovanni* libretto to the censored passages from Lippert's 1798 translation

1788 VIENNA TEXT		LIPPERT'S TRANSLATION	
DON GIOVANNI Vieni con me mia vita...	DON GIOVANNI Come with me my life...	DON JUAN Komm liebes, süßes Täubchen, Sey mein Weibchen. ...	DON JUAN Come my dear, sweet dove, Be my little wife. ...
(*Ballando conduce Zerlina presso una porta e la fa entrare quasi per forza.*)	(*Dancing, he leads Zerlina to a door and makes her enter, almost with force.*)	(*Don Juan führt Zerlina sträubend in ein Seiten Kabinet ab.*)	(*Don Juan leads Zerlina struggling into a side chamber away.*)
ZERLINA Oh Numi! son tradita! ...	ZERLINA O gods! I am lost! ...	ZERLINA O Himmel! Ich bin verrathen.	ZERLINA O heavens! I am lost.
LEPORELLO Qui nasce una ruina ...	LEPORELLO This will lead to ruin ...	LEPORELLO Sie ~~riecht~~ merkt schon ~~den Braten~~ die Posse. ...	LEPORELLO She ~~can smell~~ has figured out ~~the roast~~ the joke now. ...
ZERLINA Gente ajuto, ajuto gente: ...	ZERLINA Help people, help people: ...	ZERLINA (*inwendig.*) ~~Hülfe! Hülfe! Hülfe!~~	ZERLINA (*from the inside.*) ~~Help! Help! Help!~~
D. AN., D. ELV., D. OTT. Soccorriamo l'innocente! ...	D.AN, D.ELV., D. OTT. Let's help the innocent! ...	D. ANNA. ELVIRA. OCT. Laß uns schnell ~~ins Zimmer~~ in den Vorsaal dringen, Sie ~~entreißen seinen Schlingen~~ hierher zurück bringen.	D. ANNA. ELVIRA. OCT. Let us hurry and break into the ~~room~~ hallway. Let us ~~tear her away from his snares~~ bring her back here.
MASETTO Ah Zerlina! ...	MASETTO Oh Zerlina! ...	MASETTO ~~Ach Zerlina. Möchts gelingen~~ Ja, sie schnell zurücke bringen.	MASETTO ~~Oh, Zerlina. What if he succeeds~~ Yes bring her quickly back.
ZERLINA Scellerato!	ZERLINA Scoundrel!	ZERLINA ~~Nein Verräther~~ Hilf Masetto!	ZERLINA ~~No, you traitor!~~ Help Masetto!

(*continued*)

Table 8.1 Continued

1788 VIENNA TEXT		LIPPERT'S TRANSLATION	
D. AN., D. ELV., D. OTT.	D. AN., D. ELV., D. OTT.	D. ANNA. ELVIRA. OCTAVIO	D. ANNA. ELVIRA. OCTAVIO
Ora grida da quel lato: *(si sente il grido e lo strepito dalla parte opposta.)* Ah gittiamo giù la porta: *(gettano giù la porta!)*	Now cries come from that side: *(the cries and noise are coming from the opposite side.)* Let's break down the door: *(they break through the door.)*	~~Ja, das war~~ Sprengt die Thür auf jener Seite.	~~Yes that was~~ break down the door on that side.

ones and Styrian ones, Schwabian ones and Bavarian ones, Everything according to one's taste, that is beautiful" (*Ganz ohne Nahmen sind hier die Damen / Englisch und steurisch, / Schwäbisch und bäurisch, / Alle nach Gusto, das ist nur schön*). The insistent rhythms and *sforzandi* setting the list of dances in Mozart's musical setting of Da Ponte's Italian text (mm. 33–42) now accompany a list of anonymous women and thus acquire a more explicitly sexual undertone.[19]

The second version of the aria text, written in between the crossed-out lines of the first (Figure 8.3), would be even more problematic from a censor's point of view since it replaces the stanza in which Don Juan enumerates women of various nationalities with a list of physical attributes: "One can take the blonde one or the brunette, the slim one or the fat one—every one of them is mine!" (*Faßt man die Blonde / Wie die Brunette / Schlanke und fette—jede ist mein!*). In connection with these new stanzas, Mozart's pounding music must have sounded even more violently sexual. This second version also introduces the image of a violent assisted rape into the aria: "Friend Leporello covers my back, shares my delight, and stops the screams, and calms them down" (*Freund Leporello deckt mir den Rücken, / Theilt mein Entzücken, / Und hindert das Schreyn, / Und schläfert sie ein*).

It is not clear which of the first two versions Hägelin and the other officials read in December 1803 and which text Hägelin was speaking against in his note from December 16. The second version of the monologue and aria contains some small-scale revisions some of which bear resemblance to Hägelin's handwriting: for example, someone (likely Hägelin) rewrote the phrase in which Don Juan refers to Zerlina as a "tasty treat" (*Leckerbissen*) into one that refers to her as a "treasure" (*Schatz*), thus probably attempting to downplay the monologue's sensuality.[20] It is possible that these revisions already originated in 1798 and that Hägelin passed the more risqué (second) version of the monologue and aria by then. By the 1803 censoring, Hägelin either became stricter or he was ordered to become stricter (by the higher censorial instance mentioned in the December 16 note), and demanded that the second version be cut. This course of events would indicate that around 1800 censorial rules were being renegotiated, it was not clear

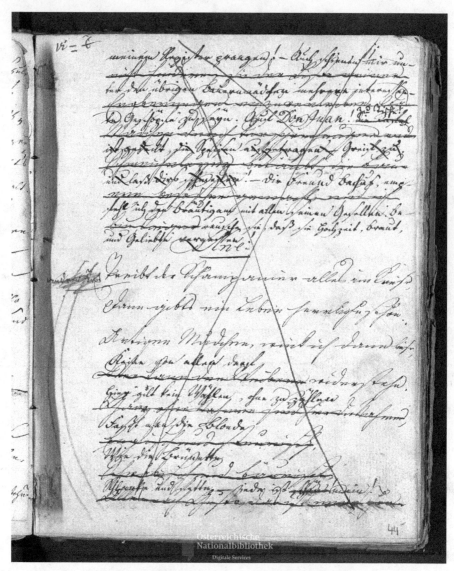

FIGURE 8.3 The opening of the "Champagne" aria in the manuscript of *Don Juan*. The first version of the preceding monologue and aria text is crossed out in brown ink and replaced with the second version (also in brown ink). Both versions are also crossed out in brown ink. The remark "Vi=o" in the left-hand corner points to the inserted sheet that contains the third version. On the left side of the aria text, there is a double line in red crayon that Hägelin mentions in his note from December 16, 1803.

what exactly should be deemed problematic in a theatrical piece, and various officials often arrived at conflicting conclusions.

Another possibility is that the second version of the aria was written into the libretto after Hägelin's 1798 review, but before the December 1803 censoring. Perhaps Lippert invented the second version at some point during the opera's runs in the previous years to make the role more burlesque, or it was written by the person revising the opera in December 1803. This would suggest that either Lippert got away with an unsanctioned, more explicitly sexual version of the aria that he performed at some point between 1798 and his death in the spring of 1803, or that the person revising the opera in December of 1803 thought the second version could pass the censors. Again, all of these scenarios show the censorial process as unclear and ambiguous.

In any case, a final (third) version of the aria was inserted into the libretto after the 1803 censorial intervention, and this final version was probably supposed to be used during the performances in late December 1803. Instead of impinging on the spirit of Da Ponte's *Don Giovanni*, however, the third version in fact restored some elements of Da Ponte's text back into *Don Juan*. The revision returns to the third stanza a list of dances to be presented at the party: "Now as I dance, the English and the Styrian one, the Schwabian and the Bavarian one, I am whirling around, I can see it already, how beautiful!" (*Jetzo im Tanze, / Englisch und steyrisch, / Schwäbisch und bayrisch, / Dreh' ich mich wirbelnd schon seh' ichs, wie schön!*). The new aria also does not talk about any specific physical interactions between Don Juan and the females—like Da Ponte's Italian text and unlike Lippert's translation, it is suggestive but no longer crude. It is hard to imagine that Mozart would turn and curse in his grave had he come across this eventual outcome of the censorial intervention against Lippert's text; if anything, he would probably have been more surprised by the new monologue and the crude second version of the aria. As in the first-act finale, Hägelin's intervention in the "Champagne" aria certainly involved a great deal of prudishness, yet far from going against the spirit of the original Mozartian work, it in fact partially washed away the farce and crudeness that the opera accrued throughout the multiple German adaptations.

Complicating matters further is the fact that the censorial copy of the *Don Juan* libretto is only one out of several documents associated with the court theater production of the opera between 1798 and 1803, and the other documents feature additional variants of the "Champagne" aria. One of the documents that must have been used in the theater during the opera's performances is the prompter's book dated 1798 that survives in the Austrian National Library (*Don Juan*, A-Wn., Mus. Hs. 32706).[21] The prompter's book contains Lippert's original translation and the 1803 revisions entered into the censorial libretto. Yet, the prompter's book at times deviates from the censorial manuscript. For example, in the "Champagne" scene, we find only the first version of the monologue and aria together with an inserted sheet containing the third version of the monologue and a completely new version of the aria (see Table 8.2). The new aria text is clearly related to the third version from the censor's book (it also returns to a list of dances) but many lines differ from it—apparently the text continued to be revised after the final censorial endorsement.

Also the rendition of Zerlina's abduction scene as it appears in the prompter's book deviates from the censorial manuscript. While some of the revisions from the censorial manuscript are entered into the prompter's book in red crayon, others are not (Figure 8.4). The stage direction about Don Juan leading Zerlina "into

Table 8.2 Four versions of Don Juan's "Champagne" aria from the manuscript materials associated with the 1798–1803 performances of Lippert's adaptation of Mozart's *Don Giovanni* at the Viennese court theater

Original 1798 Version	Later Version (between 1798 and 1803—text written between the lines of the previous version)	December 1803 Version (on an inserted sheet)	The Prompter's Book Version (most probably based on the December 1803 version; I have left out the repetitions of phrases)
[folio 44, recto]	[folio 44, recto]	[folio 43, verso]	[folio 33, recto]
Treibt der Schampanier alles im Kreise,	Treibt der Schampanier alles im Kreise,	Treibt der Champagnier alles im Kreise,	Treibt der Champagner alles im Kreise
Dann gibts ein Leben herrlich und schön.	Dann gibts ein Leben herrlich und schön.	Dann gibt's ein Leben herrlich und schön.	Dann giebts ein Leben herrlich und schön.
Artigen Mädchen wink ich dann leise,	Artigen Mädchen wink ich dann leise,	Artigen Mädchen wink' ich dann leise:	Artigen Mädchen wink ich dann leise
Wer kann den Weibern wohl widerstehn.	Keine von allen darf widerstehn.	Wer kann den Schönen wohl kalt widerstehn?	Keine von allen darf widerstehn.
		[folio 43, recto]	
Ganz ohne Nahmen sind hier die Damen,	Hier gilt kein Wählen, ohne zu zählen,	Jetzo im Tanze, Englisch und steyrisch,	Hier gilt kein Wählen Ohne zu zählen.

Englisch und steurisch,
Schwäbisch und bäurisch,
Alle nach Gusto, das ist nur schön.

[folio 44, verso]

Ich unterdessen nach alter Weise,
Führe mein Liebchen ins Seitengemach.
Trotz Weh und Ach!
Blonde, Brunette,
Schwarze ich wette,
Zählt mein Register Morgen noch zehn.

Faßt man die Blonde
Wie die Brunette
Schlanke und Fette—jede ist mein!

[folio 44, verso]

Freund Leporello deckt mir den Rüken,
Theilt mein Entzücken,
Und hindert das Schreyn,
Und schläfert sie ein—
Morgen, beim Teufel!
Muß mein Register
Wohl um ein Dutzend, Stärker noch seyn!

Schwäbisch und bayrisch,
Dreh' ich mich wirbelnd schon
seh' ichs, wie schön!

Freund Leporello theilt mein Entzücken,

Ließt mir in Blicken,
Und die mich geflohn,
Die nahen mir schon.
Morgen, ja morgen,
Muß mein Register
Größer als heute,—
Glänzender seyn.

Tanzet wird englisch,
Deutsch und französisch,
Schwäbisch und steyrisch,
Alles ist schön.

Man wird im rauschenden Walzer sich drehn

Freund Leporello dekt mir den Rüken,

Theilt mein Entzüken,
Und ordnet die Reihen.
Morgen, beim Henker
Muß mein Register
Um ein beträchtliches stärker noch seyn.

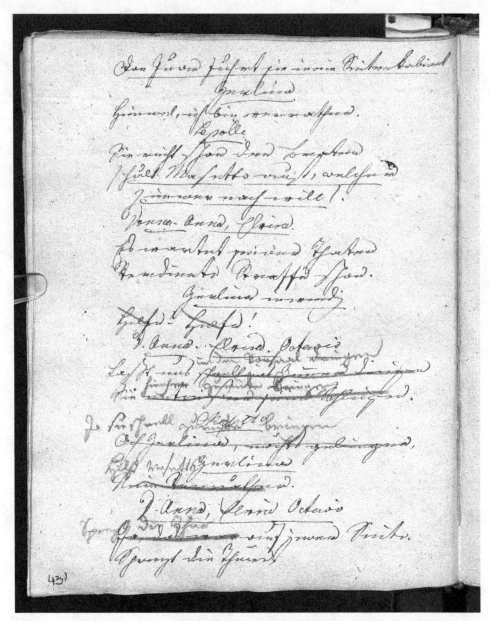

FIGURE 8.4 The abduction of Zerlina in the first-act finale of *Don Juan* as presented in the prompter's book from 1798. Certain revisions from the censorial manuscript are entered into the 1798 text in red crayon, others are not.

a side chamber" is not cut, and understandably so: stage directions in a libretto are often only tentatively associated with what actually happens in a production and they have no significance for a prompter. Another line that remains uncorrected in the prompter's book is a little more puzzling: the prompter's book leaves intact

Leporello's reaction to Zerlina's screams "*Sie riecht schon den Braten*" (She can smell the roast), although the censor or some other reviewer changed it to "*Sie merkt schon die Posse*" (She now has figured out the joke) in the censorial manuscript. Perhaps the reason for the omission was simply an oversight. But it is also possible that the court theater personnel took a critical stance toward the change: the revised line no longer rhymes with the previous one ("*Himmel ich bin verrathen*"), and furthermore, it does not necessarily transform Lippert's portrayal of Leporello taking an ironic stance to Zerlina's distress. Whatever the reason for ignoring certain rewrites demanded by the censor, the two lines (standing in for several other unchanged ones within the prompter's book) suggest that the theater personnel had some leeway to ignore certain censorial commands.

As I have shown, certain aspects of the 1803 revision of *Don Juan* (especially the revisions of scenes 16 and 18) suggest that the supervision of the court theater by the authorities became stricter in the early nineteenth century despite the fact that the process was extremely convoluted. But the concept of a gradually strengthening control of Viennese theaters becomes problematic when we consider the 1798 version in connection to the supervision over the content of German operas written for the court theater in the 1780s. The example of Prince Alwin's aria from *Das Irrlicht* illustrates the tendency to eliminate even the slightest hints at a sexual subtext in preparing the texts of court theater *Singspiele* in the early 1780s. This clearly does not happen in the 1798 *Don Juan*, which subsumes elements from Da Ponte's Italian opera that would never be permitted into the German productions from the 1780s and adds new burlesque elements (such as the Hermit scene or Masetto's and Leporello's suggestive comments about Zerlina's abduction).

The discrepancy between the supervision of content in operas such as *Das Irrlicht* and that of the 1798 *Don Juan* corresponds to a series of changes in the constitution of the court theater's *Singspiel* company between the early 1780s and late 1790s. Between 1778 and 1783, *Singspiele* were produced as part of the prestigious National Theater directly supervised by Emperor Joseph II. As Oscar Teuber (1903, 37–47) has shown, the process of choosing, adapting, and approving the German works to be performed at the National Theater during Joseph II's lifetime involved not only the censor, but also various court bureaucrats, theater personnel, and the emperor himself, all of whom wanted to ensure that the pieces performed at the national institution held up the highest artistic and also moral standards. The *Singspiele* ultimately proved unsuccessful, and so in 1783 the emperor disbanded the German opera troupe and replaced it with an Italian opera company. Another attempt at producing *Singspiele* at the court theater occurred between 1785 and 1788, when the emperor engaged another German opera company. The venture was also short-lived, due to the financial problems called forth by the Turkish War of 1788 (see Albrecht, xiv). Afterwards, *Singspiele* permanently returned to the court theater only in March of 1795 under the recently appointed director Baron Peter von Braun. By 1795, however, a highly popular tradition of *Singspiele* had been established in the theaters of the Viennese suburbs, especially in Emanuel Schikaneder's Wiednertheater and Karl Marinelli's Theater in der Leopoldstadt, and

Braun's new *Singspiel* company therefore entered into fierce competition with these other theaters.

Throughout the 1780s, Viennese authorities approached the content of the theatrical works produced in the suburban theaters with lesser strictness than those produced at the National Theater.[22] In their recent studies of the late eighteenth-century repertoire of the Leopoldstadt Theater, Beatrix Müller-Kampel and Jennyfer Großauer-Zöbiger have noted inconsistencies between official censorial mandates and the Leopoldstadt repertoire: the Leopoldstadt performances featured a large amount of uncensored improvisation, and numerous critics from the late eighteenth and early nineteenth centuries complained about the censor's lax approach to the Leopoldstadt humor (Müller-Kampel 2010, 130–32; Großauer-Zöbiger 2010, 23–29, 33–35). The *heroisch-komische* operas based on the librettos by Emanuel Schikaneder and produced at the Wiednertheater throughout the 1790s, moreover, feature numerous elements that would have been deemed impermissible due to their immorality by the *Singspiel* company associated with the National Theater in the 1780s (Nedbal 2009b, 140–151).

Braun was probably aware of the fact that the less strictly supervised suburban repertoire with its reliance on crude sexual jokes, risqué plots, and vulgar language was much more popular with audiences than the high-minded *Singspiele* presented at the National Theater in the 1780s. In order to ensure the financial success of his *Singspiel* venture, Braun pursued two contradictory courses of action in that he both distanced himself from the suburban theaters and imitated them. In January of 1795, just a few months before establishing the new permanent *Singspiel* ensemble, Braun wrote a letter to Emperor Francis II in which he described the German-language theater he proposed to establish at the court theater as a national and didactic institution, similar to the one that the bureaucrats and theater personnel hoped to create during Joseph II's reign in the 1780s:

> Mein Plan ist, das Theater zur Schule des Patriotismus zu machen, Ruhe, Zufriedenheit, Liebe gegen Fürsten, Ehrfurcht für die Gesetze durch das Schauspiel zu erwecken und zu verbreiten. Auch nichts, was den Regeln der Sittlichkeit zuwider ist, muß auf der Bühne geduldet werden. Ohne Sittlichkeit läßt sich keine bürgerliche Gesellschaft denken und wer als Hausvater, als Gatte, als Freund, kurz als Mensch, seine Pflichten erfüllt, an diesen wird auch der Monarch einen treuen Unterthan, der Staat einen ruhigen Bürger haben. Wenn also das Theater seiner hohen Bestimmung soll näher gebracht werde, so muß es auch das moralische Gefühl berichtigen, veredeln, erhöhen.
>
> (Irmen 1996, 145)

> My plan is to transform the theater into a school of patriotism, to awaken and spread obedience, satisfaction, love for the rulers, and observance of laws through plays. Nothing that contradicts the rules of morality can be tolerated on a stage. No civil society can exist without morality and those who want to fulfill their duties as fathers,

husbands, friends—in short, as humans—will also become faithful subject of a monarch and peaceful citizens of a state. Thus if theater shall achieve a higher purpose, it must convey, ennoble, enhance the moral sensibility [of its audience].

Braun also complained about the depravity of the suburban stages and the need for them to be supervised more closely by the government:

> Was kann es helfen, daß die Hof-Direktion alle nur im geringsten zweydeutige Stelle sorgfältig wegstreicht, wenn der Schauspieler in der Vorstadt sich nicht einmahl mit einer Zweydeutigkeit befriedigt, sondern si durch Gebehrden und Extemporiren— das zwar verboten doch im Schwange ist—zur offenbaren Zote macht?
>
> (Irmen 1996, 146)

> The court-direction has been cutting out all expressions [from theatrical texts] that are even slightly ambiguous, but how can that change anything, if the actor in the suburbs not only enjoys using these double entendres, but also often presents them with improvised gestures that, albeit forbidden, are extremely popular and that transform these double entendres into explicit obscenities?

In response to Braun's complaints, the emperor issued a note on February 5, 1795, in which he called for a stricter supervision of all theaters, including those in the suburbs. In the following decade the Austrian authorities gradually strengthened their control over the suburban stages (Schembor 2010, 231–236).

Contrary to his critique of the suburban stages, Braun also seems to have attempted to build the repertoire of his new opera company around works that would appeal to audiences frequenting the suburban opera houses. Many works written for the *Singspiel* company at the court theater in the late 1790s abandoned the artistic and moralistic standards that marked many court theater *Singspiele* of the 1780s. The reports about one of the most successful productions by Braun's new *Singspiel* company, Johann Schenk's *Der Dorfbarbier* (1796), illustrate the loosened approach to the content of operatic works. Ignaz Castelli's account of *Der Dorfbarbier*'s early performances at the court theater might as well have referred to a performance in one of the less strictly supervised suburban theaters:

> I cannot describe with precision what a sensation this *Dorfbarbier* and Baumann in it created in those days. It was no longer a performance; it was the crass, comical nature itself. A prompter was not needed, since both principal characters, the barber and Adam [his servant], hardly spoke any words that appeared in the script, instead they extemporized throughout the whole piece. It was a contest between two comedians, a private joke that they played upon one another, and upon which the audience took a great deal of interest. The presentation was filled with ribaldries, but the audience took them well and wanted to have a good laugh for once.
>
> (Rice 2007, 314)

Schenk's opera, moreover, was not the only one that brought extemporizing and crass, sexual humor into the Kärntnertortheater, as an 1802 complaint from Hägelin suggests:

> Die Hoftheatralvizedirektion ist schon aus Kasseabsichten auf den Gedanken verfallen, Stücke von minderem Geschmacke oder Werte manchmal aufführen zu lassen, vermutlich im Kärntnertortheater, um auch das mindere Publikum an sich zu ziehen.... Sie hat daher zwei Spaßmacher von den Vorstadttheatern an sich gezogen, nämlich den Akteur Baumann vom Leopoldstädter und den Spaßmacher Stegmayer vom Wiednertheater....
>
> (Glossy 1915, 14)

> The Court-Theater directors have tried to improve their income by presenting pieces of inferior taste or value, presumably in the Kärntnertortheater, in order to attract the lower-class audiences.... To achieve this goal, they have also hired two comedians from the suburbs, namely the actor Baumann [Adam in *Der Dorfbarbier*] from the Leopoldstadttheater and the comedian Stegmeyer from the Wiednertheater....

Apparently, Braun managed to circumvent the censors in the late 1790s and early 1800s and got away with improvised comedy and sexual jokes, which had largely disappeared from the imperial stages decades ago.

Several elements account for the fluctuating supervision of theatrical content in the late 1790s, both in the suburbs and eventually also at the court theater. As the Austrian scholar Carl Glossy explained, the Viennese authorities feared the spread of the French revolutionary ideals during this period and were willing to compromise on censorship in a quest to provide the audiences with apolitical entertainment in which crass, obscene humor would divert the spectators from thinking too much about pressing social and political issues. Donald Emerson (1968, 22–25) has claimed, moreover, that throughout the 1790s Pergen's Ministry of Police attempted to increase its control of the Viennese theaters but was not successful due to the opposition from other political factions in Vienna. De Alwis and others have shown, furthermore, that "the institution of [theater] censorship was in a state of upheaval" during the early 1800s (De Alwis 2012, 105; Schembor 2010, 225–242). The 1798 *Don Juan*, with its farcical elements and interpolated scenes, must have been a result of this temporarily relaxed supervision and Braun's successful evasion of that supervision. That this relaxation happened at all once again shows that the terms of Viennese censorship continued to be negotiable throughout the late 1790s.

The changing form of Da Ponte's libretto for Mozart's *Don Giovanni* as it was published in Vienna and presented at the city's premier stage between 1787 and 1803, both in Italian and German, hints at the opera's constant involvement with the institution of theater censorship. Yet the exact nature of this involvement was quite complicated and calls for a highly flexible approach to the study of Viennese theater censorship in the time of the French Revolution. As I have shown, the supervision of theaters in Vienna around 1800 was neither all-powerful nor merely restrictive: it was filled with constant negotiations and disagreements, rules and principles were ever-changing, different theaters and different repertoires were subjected to varying levels of control, and the financial interests of theater directors sometimes managed to trump the effectiveness of the state controllers. As some of the demands of Hägelin and his superiors from 1803 show, furthermore, at times a censor's ideals in fact coincided with the creative visions of theatrical authors, such as Da Ponte and Mozart. Censorship therefore represented one of the many processes that went into a work's intellectual and artistic conception and, far from functioning merely as a force of oppression, had a creative potential of its own.

Notes

1. The idea has been widely accepted; see Heartz 1992, 163.
2. For example, in his discussion of the differences between the text in the first printed libretto of *The Magic Flute* and the text in Mozart's autograph, Jan Assmann proposes that the composer decided to leave out certain passages out of concern for the censors (Assmann 2005, 139). Similarly, Nicolas Till (1995, 306) has suggested that the padlock placed by the three Ladies on Papageno's mouth in the opening of *The Magic Flute* represented a symbol of Josephine censorship and police surveillance. Till did not specifically claim that Mozart intended for the padlock to serve as a critique of Viennese censorship, but his interpretation does operate with the notion of restrictive censors and subversive authors.
3. Most recently, for example, Kristina Muxfeldt (2012, 6) proposed subversive hearings for several moments in *Fidelio, Don Giovanni*, and *Die Zauberflöte*, moments in which, as she suggests, the composers and librettists created recipes "for circumnavigating the censors."
4. For a recent biography and re-evaluation of Hägelin's career see De Alwis 2012, 7–73.
5. For more examples of Viennese moralistic adaptations of foreign libretti in the early 1780s, see Nedbal 2009a, 64–107.
6. For an explanation of the Viennese distinction between *opera buffa* as a foreign form of unedifying entertainment and German drama and *Singspiel* as "intimately linked both to the encouragement of good morals and taste in significant portions of the population, and to a sense of nationhood that transcended the old feudal divisions," see Hunter 1999, 9–13.
7. The materials documenting censorship of non-German works after the instituting of the German theater censor in 1770 are sparse. A special censor was responsible for the French plays and Italian operas, but little is known about his activities. At first, the office was held by Johann Theodor von Gontier, who was removed in October 1770 and replaced by August von Wöber. See Zechmeister 1971, 50; and Brosche 1962, 132.
8. As De Alwis (2012, 99) has explained, "enclosed spaces in which couples can hide [and engage in sexual activity] seem to be one of Hägelin's particular concerns."
9. For a discussion of Da Ponte's appointment at the court theater see Hodges 2002, 47. Many thanks to Reinhard Eisendle for suggesting this possibility for interpreting the differences between Da Ponte's and Bertati's librettos. That Da Ponte might have been responsible for supervising the moral content of the Italian operas written for the court theater is indicated in his report on his own conversation with Joseph II regarding the adaptation of *Figaro*. There he mentions that in his preparation of the *Figaro* libretto, he "cut anything that might offend good taste and public decency at a performance over which the

Sovereign majesty might preside." The emperor supposedly responded that he trusted Da Ponte's "wisdom as to morality" (Da Ponte 2000, 129–130) Although this account might be apocryphal, it once again illustrates the possibility that there was no special censor of Italian theatrical texts, that Da Ponte was the sole agent responsible for the moral content of Italian operas, and that the emperor was the ultimate arbiter.

10. In a note from December 22, 1803, Hägelin further comments on his own second review of the *Don Juan* libretto: he says that the libretto was submitted for inspection due to a revision executed in December of 1803, which reduced the number of acts and involved numerous cuts and changes (Glossy 1915, 64).

11. As De Alwis (2012, 104–105) has pointed out, "it is inconceivable that the piece could have been revised, resubmitted, and approved in two days" because the censor was by then living in a village outside of Vienna where he received mail only once a week. It is therefore possible that the changes in the two scenes mentioned in the December 16 note were executed by the censor himself.

12. Large portions of this document were published in Glossy 1897, 298–340. The original was then destroyed in the 1927 fire of the Palace of Justice in Vienna. Recently, De Alwis discovered several handwritten copies of the document containing the passages that Glossy deleted from this edition, and her own edition of the full document is forthcoming with the Don Juan Archiv in Vienna.

13. For extensive recent accounts of the growing disagreements between Hägelin and the other state officials responsible for theater control after 1801, see Schembor 2010, 237–242; and De Alwis 2012, 53–72.

14. Schembor (2010, 230) has noted that Braun would hire secretaries who reviewed the content of German theater works before these were submitted to the censor. Schembor (2010, 237) also discusses cases when Hägelin was in disagreement and criticized the editors/secretaries of the court theater. Perhaps one of these secretaries also revised the *Don Juan* libretto in December of 1803.

15. Like the other edits in Hägelin's hand that can be traced to 1798, the ones in the Hermit scene are minimal, though they clearly follow the principles from his 1795 treatise about avoiding any explicit references to religious practices and texts; for example, Leporello originally addresses the Hermit as "venerable father" (*ehrwürdiger Vater*), which was changed to "venerable man" (*ehrwürdiger Mann*), and his exclamation "God be with me" (*Gott steht mir bey*) was changed to "Heaven be with me" (*Himmel steht mir bey*).

16. One of the revisions that might have come from Hägelin occurs in Leporello's account of his earlier adventure with Donna Elvira. Disguised as his master, Leporello drew Elvira out of her house, but then tried to escape from her. His escape proved difficult, however, since Elvira "*klebte [ihm] am Leibe*" (was glued to [his] body). The reviewer (likely Hägelin himself) changed that phrase into "*hing sich an [ihn]*" (she hung on to [him]), probably to reduce the sexual innuendo. The change corresponds to revisions in the earlier scenes, in which the reviewer(s) sought to diminish the possibility that Elvira and Leporello had sex during their escapade.

17. According to Otto Rommel, the Hermit scene originated in the Italian theater and *commedia dell'arte* in the seventeenth century and eventually made its way into Viennese popular theater, such as a Don Juan puppet play and a *Haus- und Staatsaktion* by Gottfried Prehauser (Rommel 1936, 47–48).

18. Out of the two texts on the original page, only the earlier one appears in the conducting score used in the late eighteenth and early nineteenth-century productions of the German

version of the opera as well as in the prompter's book containing the text of 1798 and the revisions of 1803. The prompter's book does not contain the aria's second version and provides a separate (fourth) version on an inserted sheet—this increases the possibility that the second version was written into the censorial manuscript sometime between 1798 and 1803 and the versions on inserted sheets originated in response to the 1803 censorial request.

19. There is also a significant difference between the texts that are brought back with the heavily accentuated music later in the aria. In Mozart's Italian original, mm. 86–93 set "*Se trovi in piazza qualche ragazza, teco ancor quella cerca menar*" (If in the piazza you find some girl, try to make her come here with you), whereas in the setting of Lippert's text as given by the 1798 conducting score the pounding rhythms accompany a repeat of the list of women "*Englisch und steurisch, schwäbisch und bäurisch, alles nach Gusto, das ist ja schön.*"

20. De Alwis (2012, 103) suggests that this small revision is the only one that comes from Hägelin, though she does not discuss whether it might have been entered in 1798 or 1803.

21. Other surviving materials probably created for the 1798 production (because they contain the original Lippert text) are the conducting score (*Don Juan*, A-Wn, OA.361/2) and the prompter's score (*Don Juan*, A-Wn, OA.361/4). Dexter Edge (2001, 1754) also thinks it is quite likely the conducting score is connected to the 1798 production because its watermarks and copyists place it in the late 1790s or early 1800s. The text in the conducting score does not incorporate any of the later revisions, whereas the prompter's score incorporates revisions, cuts, and changes associated with later nineteenth-century productions of *Don Juan* at the court theater. Edge (2001, 1755) dates the prompter's score to the nineteenth century.

22. See, for example, the discussion of the double standards in evaluating works by Goethe, Schiller, and Shakespeare at the National Theater and the other Viennese stages in the 1780s in Teuber and Weilen 1903, 89.

References

Albrecht, Carol Padgham. 2008. "Music in Public Life: Viennese Reports from the Allgemeine Musikalische Zeitung, 1798–1804." Ph.D. diss., Kent State University.

Assmann, Jan. 2005. *Die Zauberflöte: Oper und Mysterium*. Munich: Carl Hanser Verlag.

Beales, Derek. 2009. *Joseph II*, 2 vols. New York: Cambridge University Press.

Bretzner, Christoph Friedrich. 1776. *Der Irrwisch, oder Endlich fand er sie*. Leipzig: Schneider.

Brosche, Günther. 1962. "Joseph von Sonnenfels und das Wiener Theater." Doctoral diss., Universität Wien.

Da Ponte, Lorenzo. 2000. *Memoires*. Translated by Elisabeth Abbott. Edited by Arthur Livingston. New York: Dover.

De Alwis, Lisa. 2012. "Censorship and Magical Opera in Early Nineteenth-Century Vienna." Ph.D. diss., University of Southern California.

Deutsch, Otto Erich. 1993. "*Don Juan* und die Wiener Zensur." In *Wiener Musikgeschichten*, edited by Gitta Deutsch and Rudolf Klein, 63–69. Vienna: Jugend und Volk.

Edge, Dexter. 2001. "Mozart's Viennese Copyists." Ph.D. diss., University of Southern California.

Einstein, Alfred. 1956. *Essays on Music*. New York: Norton.

Emerson, Donald E. 1968. *Metternich and the Political Police: Security and Subversion in the Hapsburg Monarchy (1815–1850)*. The Hague: Martinus Nijhoff.
Giger, Andreas. 1999. "Social Control and the Censorship of Giuseppe Verdi's Operas in Rome (1844–1859)." *Cambridge Opera Journal* 11, no. 3: 233–265.
Glossy, Carl. 1897. "Zur Geschichte der Wiener Theaterzensur I." *Jahrbuch der Grillparzer Gesellschaft* 7: 238–340.
Glossy, Carl. 1915. "Zur Geschichte der Theater Wiens I. (1801–1820)." *Jahrbuch der Grillparzer Gesellschaft* 25: 1–323.
Großauer-Zöbiger, Jennyfer. 2010 "Das Leopoldstädter Theater (1781–1806): Sozialgeschichtliche und soziologische Verortungen eines Erfolgsmodelles." *Zeitschrift für Literatur- und Theatersoziologie* 1: 5–55.
Hadamowsky, Franz. 1966. *Die Wiener Hoftheater (Staatstheater), 1776–1966: Verzeichnis der aufgeführten Stücke mit bestandsnachweis und täglichem Spielplan*, vol. 1. Vienna: Prachner.
Heartz, Daniel. 1992. *Mozart's Operas*. Berkeley: University of California Press.
Hodges, Sheila. 2002. *Lorenzo da Ponte: The Life and Time of Mozart's Librettist*. Madison, WI: University of Wisconsin Press.
Holquist, Michael. 1994. "Corrupt Originals: The Paradox of Censorship." *PMLA* 109, no. 1: 14–25.
Höyng, Peter. 2003. *Die Sterne, die Zensur und Vaterland: Geschichte und Theater im späten 18. Jahrhundert*. Vienna: Böhlau.
Hunter, Mary. 1999. *The Culture of Opera Buffa in Mozart's Vienna: A Poetics of Entertainment*. Princeton: Princeton University Press.
Irmen, Hans-Josef. 1996. *Beethoven in seiner Zeit*. Zülpich: Prisca.
Izzo, Francesco. 2007. "Verdi, the Virgin, and the Censor: The Politics of the Cult of Mary in *I Lombardi alla prima crociata* and *Giovanna d'Arco*." *Journal of the American Musicological Society* 60, no. 3: 557–597.
Müller-Kampel, Beatrix. 2010. "Kasperl unter Kontrolle: Zivilisations- und politiksgeschichtlichen Aspekte der lustigen Figur um 1800." *Zeitschrift für Literatur-und Theatersoziologie* 1: 105–134.
Muxfeldt, Kristina. 2012. *Vanishing Sensibilities: Schubert, Beethoven, Schumann*. New York: Oxford University Press.
Nedbal, Martin. 2009a. "Morals across the Footlights: Viennese Singspiel, National Identity, and the Aesthetics of Morality, 1778–1814." Ph.D. diss., Eastman School of Music.
Nedbal, Martin. 2009b. "Mozart as a Viennese Moralist: *Die Zauberflöte* and Its Maxims." *Acta Musicologica* 81, no. 1: 123–157.
Rice, John. 2007. "German Opera in Vienna around 1800: Joseph Weigl and *Die schweizer Familie*." In *Oper im Aufbruch: Gattungskonzepte des deutschsprachigen Musiktheaters um 1800*, edited by Marcus Chr. Lippe, 313–322. Kassel, Germany: Bosse.
Rommel, Otto. 1936. *Die Romantisch-komischen Volksmärchen*. Leipzig: Reclam.
Schembor, Friedrich Wilhelm. 2010. *Meinungsbeinflussung durch Zensur und Druckförderung in der Napoleonischen Zeit*. Vienna: Österreichische Gesellschaft zur Erforschung des 18. Jahrhunderts.
Stephanie der Jüngere, Johann Gottlieb. 1781. *Das Irrlicht, oder: Endlich fand er sie*. Vienna: Logenmeister.
Teuber, Oscar and Alexander von Weilen. 1903. *Das K. K. Hofburgtheater seit seiner Begründung. Die Theater Wiens*, vol. 2. Vienna: Gesellschaft für Vervielfältigende Kunst.

Theaterzettel Burgtheater. 1798, 1799, and 1803. Vienna: Österreichisches Theatermuseum, 773-043-D Th.

Thurn, Rudolf Payer von, ed. 1920. *Josef II. als Theaterdirektor: Ungedruckte Briefe und Aktenstücke aus den Kinderjahren des Burgtheaters*. Vienna: Heidrich.

Till, Nicholas. 1995. *Mozart and the Enlightenment: Truth, Virtue, and Beauty in Mozart's Operas*. New York: Norton.

Volek, Tomislav. 1987. "Prague Operatic Traditions and Mozart's *Don Giovanni*." In *Mozartův Don Giovanni v Praze*, edited by J. Kristek, 21–91. Prague: Divadelní ústav.

Weidinger, Hans Ernst. 2012. "*Il Dissoluto punito*: Untersuchungen zur äußeren und inneren Entstehungsgeschichte von Lorenzo da Pontes & Wolfgang Amadeus Mozarts *Don Giovanni*." Ph.D. diss., Universität Wien.

Woodfield, Ian. 2010. *The Vienna Don Giovanni*. Rochester, N.Y.: The Boydell Press.

Zechmeister, Gustav. 1971. *Die Wiener Theater nächst der Burg und nächst dem Kärntnertor von 1747 bis 1776*. Vienna: Böhlau.

CHAPTER 9

THE DEPOLITICIZED DRAMA

Mozart's Figaro *and the Depths of Enlightenment*

LAURENZ LÜTTEKEN
TRANSLATED BY LEE ROTHFARB

Mozart's *Le nozze di Figaro*: Problems of the Genesis

Le Nozze di Figaro is the only work by Wolfgang Amadé Mozart for which there is at least indirect evidence of having been affected by the practice of censorship as manifested in Joseph II's Vienna. However, the process itself is documented only indirectly, as is the entire history of the origins of the "opera buffa" (as Mozart himself writes in the autograph *Verzeichnüß*), or *commedia per musica* (as in the first edition of the libretto). (A summary of the pertinent sources by Ludwig Finscher are in NMA, VII-XXI.) But on closer examination this link to the practice of censorship turns out to be one in a series of unique features that distinguish this work from all other stage projects that Mozart realized or at least planned in Vienna. Only *Figaro* is based on a contemporary literary model, on an attention-grabbing and successful play. Only *Figaro* derives directly from a French dramatic work, though probably in German translation. Only *Figaro* employs the text of an influential literary figure, who in his carefully planned piece wanted to bring together aesthetic and political stances and therefore prefaced it with an expansive foreword. And only of *Figaro* is it documented, through a disclosure by Da Ponte, that the choice of subject goes back to Mozart himself. As early as 1783 he declared in a letter to his father that in searching for suitable operatic material he had read libretto after libretto:

> *ich habe leicht 100--Ja wohl mehr büchlen durchgesehen--allein ich habe fast kein einziges gefunden mit welchem ich zufrieden seyn könnte;--wenigstens müsste da und dort vieles verändert werden.--und wenn sich schon ein dichter mit diesem abgeben*

will, so wird er vieleicht leichter ein ganz Neues machen.--und Neu - ist es halt doch immer besser.

I have easily perused 100—indeed even more—booklets, yet I found almost not a single one that could satisfy me;—at least much would have to be changed here and there.—And if there is a poet willing to put up with this, he might perhaps more easily write something completely new.—And what is new is just always better. (MBA 3, 267–269)

And indeed, disregarding the two fragments written in the same year, *L'Oca del Cairo* and *Lo sposo deluso*,[1] the first work completed after this statement was *Le Nozze di Figaro*—the single opera, moreover, that originated without an actual commission.

Thus as sparsely as the exact history of the opera's origin is documented (Heartz 1986–1987), this series of unique features is remarkable. The connection with the practice of censorship turns out to be not just its central aspect but rather to some extent its vanishing point. In Mozart scholarship to date, this aspect plays only a very subsidiary role or has been utilized mainly for superficial political argument, which is why it will receive greater attention in the following discussion. Accordingly, a rereading of the known material lies at the center, in order to check for the possibility of, and evidence for, other, divergent conclusions, that is, to gain a new interpretative approach. This procedure is not without risks. However, there is no alternative to it, because the only explicit documents that may perhaps have existed—and even that is by no means certain—could have been among the files of the Imperial and Royal Censor's office. These were almost completely destroyed in the fire at the Vienna Law Court in 1927 (the remaining holdings apparently were destroyed in the last months of World War II). As there was no courtly commission for the opera—that much is certain—no official documents exist from the time before its premiere. Even Mozart's correspondence sheds no light in this regard. The first reference is in a letter of Leopold to his daughter dated November 3, 1785 (MBA 3, 439). Not until the performances themselves is the documentation somewhat more detailed. Only the late recollections of the singer Michael Kelly (1826) and of Lorenzo Da Ponte (1829) contain the few bits of information upon which scholarship still has to rely.

Three aspects of the work's genesis mentioned by Da Ponte turn out to be particularly significant. First is Mozart's choice of the stage play *La folle journée* by Pierre Augustin Caron de Beaumarchais—a finding that has always been given credence in the research, and with good reasons. The second factor mentioned by Da Ponte concerns the extraordinarily quick working out of the score, which perhaps required more than the claimed six weeks, but certainly only a very short span of hectic bustle, which, besides, is documented in Leopold's letters. The complicated work process, which can be reconstructed at least in part, indicates further that the composer made alterations to the design of the text up until the end (Tyson 1986–1987). The third factor mentioned by Da Ponte concerns permission for performance. The astonishing fact that, from the start, it was not a matter of a commission for the collaboration appears all the more interesting if we consider the choice of subject. Da Ponte had averred in his *Memoire* that he was able to convince the emperor to permit the performance, which after the ban on the stage play was not undisputed. Da Ponte's disclosure has been repeatedly disputed in research on Mozart as evidence that the librettist only wanted to draw attention to himself. However, there is no real cause for such doubts, particularly since securing such permission would indeed have been the responsibility of the court stage writer, Da Ponte, whose office could grant him direct access to the emperor. In contrast to a commissioned work, the release from censorship could not follow standard procedure.

The conflict with the censor's office goes back to the reception in Vienna of Beaumarchais's drama. After prolonged delays, the second part of his Figaro trilogy, *La folle journée ou le Mariage de Figaro*, was first performed publicly on April 27, 1784, at the Comédie Française in Paris. The reactions were euphoric not just in France (Kim 1996, 162–165), and soon there were efforts toward productions and translations of the play in other countries. Arriving from Pressburg, the director Emanuel Schikaneder, together with his theater company (led jointly with Hubert Kumpf), was in residence in Vienna from the fall of 1784, where they performed at the Kärntnertortheater from November 5 to February 6, 1785 (Sonnek 1999, 60–62). They began with *Die Entführung aus dem Serail*, and the entire program, through the inclusion of large-scale operas, was obviously tailored to the demands of the royal residence. In February the ensemble unexpectedly disbanded. Kumpf returned to Pressburg, and Schikaneder remained alone in Vienna. During its three-month presence, the ensemble enjoyed the emperor's particular favor, who apparently attended the performances regularly. Thus the *Wiener Zeitung* reported on December 22, 1784: "Der unläugbarste Beweis von der Güte und Ordnung, durch welche sich diese Gesellschaft auszeichnet, ist, Se. Majestät der Kaiser selbst, welche ihre Vorstellungen schon öfters mit Seiner Gegenwart zu begnadigen geruheten, auch bey dieser Oper [Haydns *La fedelta premiata*, L.L.] mit dem ganzen Hofe zugegen war" ("The indisputable proof of the quality and decorum distinguishing this ensemble lies with His Majesty the Emperor himself, who has repeatedly honored their performances with his presence and who also attended this opera [Haydn's *La fedeltà premiata*] with the entire court").[2]

Schikaneder had become interested in Beaumarchais's plays as early as the 1770s. In 1778 he performed *Eugénie* in Augsburg and Stuttgart, and in 1780 *Le Barbier de Seville* in Salzburg, translated by Friedrich Wilhelm Großmann, and with music by Friedrich Ludwig Benda in 1776 and published as a vocal score in 1779 (Sonnek 1999, 27, 33, 47). On February 3, 1785, shortly before the end of the season, *La folle journée* was to be presented. Apparently, the performance was completely unexpectedly subjected to censorship, as can be inferred from the reports in the press. On February 2, 1785, one day before, the following announcement appeared in the *Wienerblättchen*:

> *Herr Rautenstrauch hat das in Paris mit so ausserordentlichem Beyfall aufgenommene Lustspiel les Noces de Figaro kürzlich ins Deutsche übersetzt: Morgen wird selbiges von der Gesellschaft des Herrn Schikaneder und Kumpf zum ersten Mal aufgeführt werden, wobey der von dem hiesigen Publico immer mit Vergnügen gesehene Schauspieler Herr Kronstein in der Rolle des Figaro erscheinen wird. Man erräth leicht, wie neugierig*

ein grosser Theil unserer Theaterfreunde seyn müsse, zu sehen, ob dieses Stück auch auf deutschem Grund und Boden ein so entschiedenes Glück, wie in Frankreich, machen werde

Mr. Rautenstrauch recently translated into German the comedy les Noces de Figaro, which met such extraordinary acclaim in Paris. It will be performed tomorrow for the first time by the company of Mr. Schikaneder and Kumpf, Mr. Kronstein appearing as Figaro, the actor who is always received with great enjoyment by our audiences. One can easily guess how curious a large part of our theater devotees must be to see whether this play will have such clear good fortune on German territory as it had in France.[3]

Two days later, however, in the same paper we read of the play's cancellation: "Das von H. Schikaneder verheißene Lustspiel: Die Hochzeit des Figaro, ist gestern nicht aufgeführt worden und hat selbiges, nach der dem Publiko in dem gestrigen Anschlagzettel mitgetheilten Nachricht, die Censur, zwar zum Drucke aber nicht zur Vorstellung erhalten" ("The comedy announced by Mr. Schikaneder, The Marriage of Figaro, was not performed yesterday. According to news made public in yesterday's placard, its performance but not its printing was censored").[4] At the end of the month the same paper published a brief announcement of the printed translation: "Uiber Figaro. Nach der französischen Ausgabe der Hrn. Brüder Gay und der deutschen Übersetzung des Hrn. Rautenstrauch, ... Wir wollten dessen schon gleich nach seiner Erscheinung erwähnen, als wir aber vernommen, daß es von der Schikaneder- und Kumpfischen Gesellschaft deutscher Schauspieler sollte aufgeführt werden, so hielten wir unser Urtheil zurück, um es zugleich auf die Aufführung auszubreiten. Doch das Stück ward verboten, und die Vorstellung mußte also unterbleiben" ("On Figaro. After the French edition of the brothers Gay and the German translation by Mr. Rautenstrauch, ... We had intended to take note of this translation right after its appearance, but when we noticed that it was to be performed by the ensemble of German actors under Schikaneder and Kumpf, we withheld our judgment in order to lay it out it in connection with the performance. But the piece was prohibited and the performance thus had to be abandoned").[5]

The solution, imposed at the last second, so to speak, and apparently at Joseph II's personal instigation, was therefore ambivalent: prohibition of the performance, release of the printed text. The translator, Johann Rautenstrauch (1746–1801), was one of the most influential and uncompromising, indeed fiercest literary protagonists of the Josephine Enlightenment: author of numerous writings and pamphlets and for a while (before Joseph's accession to the throne) editor of the literarily important Vienna *Realzeitung*, as well as publisher of the *Scheyßereien*, one of the most unconventional literary projects of the entire eighteenth century. His translation was published in Vienna at the end of January 1785, as can be gathered from the chronology of newspaper reports. In the same year, 1785, five further editions of German texts can be verified, published in Kehl, Prague, Leipzig, Munich, and Berlin—except for the first, all apparently originating with performances. The translations themselves and their chronology have so far not been investigated.[6] Mozart is known to have owned a copy of the text, curiously not the

Vienna version by Rautenstrauch, however, as scholarship has assumed until now. For in the estate catalogue the title *Der lustige Tag* is noted (which corresponds to the version published in Kehl), while Rautenstrauch's version is titled *Der närrische Tag* (Deutsch 1961, 510). Mozart apparently never saw the piece on stage before composing it, unless he attended one of the rehearsals of Schikaneder's and Kumpf's company, nor did he use the translation made in Vienna.

It stands to reason, then, that Mozart's version was the Kehl translation, which appeared anonymously but had been authorized by Beaumarchais. That point is not insignificant because, in contrast to Rautenstrauch's, it contains a German version of Beaumarchais's extensive preface. Of course that fact further complicates the situation. While the performance of the comedy was prohibited, Rautenstrauch's version was released. Yet this version was not used by the composer. Furthermore, it is entirely unclear which version Da Ponte used: the French original, a German translation, or a mixture of all these. In any case, the first Italian translation appeared after 1785. Da Ponte reports in his memoirs, moreover, that Mozart suggested this project a few days after Schikaneder's performance was banned. Therefore, he must already have known the text at the time, and also must have been aware of the risk he was taking with the suggestion. Apparently, the plan was considered a kind of secret project, which was to be recommended to the emperor only after its completion. The emperor's personal approval preceded the premiere on May 1, 1786, at the Royal Opera, followed by the anger of those who, with some justification, saw in these events the court procedures disregarded. Moreover, the ban on the performance of the drama and the release of the opera were directly contrary to one another.

The Text of Beaumarchais

If we consider this background, the whole set of circumstances surrounding Mozart's *Figaro* appears in need of renewed explanation. The point of departure has to be Beaumarchais's drama. As already noted, the comedy was first performed on April 27, 1784, at the Comédie Française. It was one of the greatest successes not only of the author but of eighteenth-century theater overall. The pre-history of this production is long and complicated. In 1767, in his *Essai sur le genre dramatique sérieux* Beaumarchais already settled up with French tragedy in the tradition of Racine, and pointedly intervened in an ongoing aesthetic debate. Only theater that addressed current class conflicts could be valid as timely, while the miraculous and the improbable should no longer play a role in theater. Initially, the author was not thinking of comedy, for with *Eugénie* he produced a domestic tragedy. Only after its failure did he turn to comedy, and in that genre he achieved great renown beginning with *Le Barbier de Seville*, which in its second run in 1775 was a brilliant theatrical success. The sequel, announced already in the preface to the first edition, revealed the plan to write several dramas, ultimately a trilogy. *La folle journée*, the second piece, was probably completed by 1778. However, a protracted and increasingly bitter conflict followed with the censor's office, staged with mounting insistence and effectiveness. Ultimately, the work acquired the status of a political symbol, not least because Louis XVI himself had commented negatively on it.

Until the moment of its eventually attained and sanctioned premiere, which was announced as a major event, the play's effect in the semi-public literary and intellectual circles of Paris occurred, so to speak, under the radar. A number of readings took place beginning in 1778, ultimately in September 1781 a private reading at the Comédie Française (Kim 1996, 26–28. The initial conflict with the censor's office was expanded ever more systematically not least because Beaumarchais assured himself of increasingly high-ranking advocates at the readings. Altogether the author provoked at least six rounds of censorship until, after a letter to Louis XVI, he finally received approval for performance (Kim 1996, 59ff., 117–120). The play, which was long since known, thus turned into a political matter of the highest rank, not least because of Figaro's grand monologue in the third scene of act five. The success was overwhelming, with seventy-three repeat performances at the Comédie Française, virtually unprecedented, and it earned the participants considerable profits (Brown 2006, 107–108). But the author delayed the official publication considerably for reasons that cannot be precisely traced. Even though permission to publish the play was available in March 1784, that is, shortly before the first production, two identical editions were first published early in 1785: in Paris (by Ruault) and in Kehl (by the literary society), where Beaumarchais had placed his Voltaire edition (Kim 1996, 266–269). The Kehl edition was available in January 1785, and since Kehl belonged to Baden at that time (i.e., not to France), the author may have been concerned about simultaneously publishing a German translation. We may thus assume that this version was available at the same time, at the beginning of the year 1785.

The long-standing conflict with the French censor's office ensured the play the highest level of attention, far beyond Paris and France. Considering the reception of French authors in Josephine Vienna, the play's presence even there is not surprising. Further, Beaumarchais was not unknown there. In August 1774 he had visited the royal residential city under scandalous circumstances, allegedly on a secret mission that ended in arrest, however, three days after his arrival (on August 19, 1774) and after an audience with Maria Theresia. Joseph von Sonnenfels (1732–1817), who at this time was already a professor at Vienna University (since 1763) and a theater censor (since 1770), acted as mediator (Arneth 1868, 18–20). Sonnenfels was doubtlessly one of the most influential figures in Josephine Vienna, particularly in the world of theater and censorship. It is not known how the relationship between Sonnenfels and Beaumarchais unfolded after this encounter. We may at least assume, with high probability, Sonnenfels's heightened interest in the texts and dramatic works of the French author.

However, as is evident from the above-quoted note in the *Wienerblättchen* of February 28, 1785, for his planned *Figaro* performance Schikaneder did not make any use of the version authorized by the poet, to which in early February he most likely had no access yet. Rather, he turned to one of the numerous free versions that, in addition to a number of adaptations, imitations, and sequels, began to flood the French market in the second half of 1784 (Kim 1996, 326–328. It was a version by the brothers Gay, who ran a French bookstore in Vienna, were key in conveying French literature to Austria and Hungary, and occasionally collaborated with the publisher Johann Thomas von Trattner. That version appeared in 1785; a precise date of publication cannot be established, but the note in the *Wienerblättchen* confirms that it must have been available before Rautenstrauch's translation appeared, that is, probably in January of 1785. Considering the tight network of literary circles in Vienna, it is certain that for his translation Rautenstrauch already owned the manuscript at an earlier point, indeed that plans for the performance originated jointly with Schikaneder, Rautenstrauch, and the brothers Gay. Against that background, the conflict with the censor's office becomes even more conspicuous. For the edition of the brothers Gay—a version whose textual foundation is wholly unclear—must have already passed through censorship by the time Schikaneder and Rautenstrauch requested approval of their plans. This may explain why Rautenstrauch promptly received permission to publish his version. The process may have been automatic. The prohibition of the performance, on the other hand, becomes all but inexplicable against this background because the piece had, in fact, already passed censorship twice. We will return to this matter below.

Information on Lorenzo Da Ponte's connections to the literary world of his time remains rather vague. That applies to life in Vienna, which was dominated by his office as court poet of the theater. How he established contact with Johann Rautenstrauch, for example, or with Joseph von Sonnenfels—with whom he shared Jewish heritage—remains unknown. Nor do we know whether he had a personal connection to Beaumarchais. Considering the wealth of *Figaro* versions already available at the beginning of 1785, the plan of an opera based on yet another adaptation at first does not appear unusual. But the well-founded assumption that Mozart owned the translation published in Kehl indicates that for their adaptations both intended to—and indeed did—use the authorized text by Beaumarchais. Accordingly, they differ from Rautenstrauch, who only used an apocryphal version. Against this background, the differences between drama and opera are all the more remarkable. These differences have been examined repeatedly and in the end can be reduced to two main aspects (cf. Ruf 1977, 72–76). First, Da Ponte primarily used only a skeleton of the plot. Apparently, however, the two considered precise knowledge of Beaumarchais's text as important. That attitude also holds for the abbreviation to four acts, for already in 1784 three- and even one-act versions were circulating. However, having four acts, highly unusual in opera buffa, apparently derives directly from the original. The second aspect concerns the quality of the cuts made in the play, for example in the extended monologue of the fifth act. Since other passages, no less politically explosive, were preserved, it is significant that here, too, the cuts were made directly to Beaumarchais's original and not to a version that had already been altered. A third aspect, often overlooked in the research, should certainly be highlighted as well. For the text contains, quite unusually, a preface which, as mere fact, recalls the extended preface with which Beaumarchais introduced his own comedy, and about which we must assume Mozart and Da Ponte knew.

Josephine Vienna, Freedom of the Press, and Censorship

The astonishment concerning the circumstances surrounding the censoring of Beaumarchais's performance and the release of the opera increases further when we consider the larger context. Joseph II assumed sole power after Maria Theresia's death in 1780. He immediately decided both to accelerate and to radicalize the implementation of reforms in the spirit of a controlled enlightenment. In the first year of his reign the emperor already introduced a series of frantically passed innovations that led in the early 1780s to far-reaching transformations of the state and society. Already the year 1781 is marked by several important changes: the Edict of Tolerance granted full civil rights to each confession; the "Judenpatent" was to enable the integration of the Jews into the new centralized state; serfdom was abolished; and the new pension laws strengthened a new, central class of civil servants. Finally, the abolition of church property followed in the subsequent year. Of particular significance for intellectual life in Vienna, along with fundamental reforms in the school and educational system, were the new censorship rules enacted on June 11, 1781. Government supervision, henceforth to be executed by a censor's office with the status of a court commission, was reduced to a minimum (Plattner 2008, 67–68. The third article of the act in particular granted liberties almost unparalleled in Europe: "Kritiken, wenn es nur keine Schmähschriften sind, sie mögen treffen, wen sie wollen, vom Landesfürsten an bis zum Untersten, sollen ... nicht verboten werden" ("Critiques, so long as they are not libelous ... will not be prohibited, no matter at whom they are directed, from the territorial ruler to the lowest individual").[7] In only a few places in Europe were there efforts to go beyond this, for example in the archbishopric of Salzburg, where the authorities even considered abolishing censorship (Klueting 2008, 47–49. In Vienna the censors' board consisted initially of nine, ultimately only six full-time censors, two of whom in each case had to pass judgment independent of each other (Olechowski 2007). In 1782 the commission was merged with the study commission, and the clergy, in 1780 still predominant in the procedure, was at that time replaced entirely by secular civil servants and writers (Bodi 1977, 1). The index of prohibited books published in 1784 contains just nine hundred titles, in contrast to the five thousand of its predecessor, and the majority of prohibitions were pornographic titles, writings of the radical French Enlightenment, and devotional literature.

Precisely this far-reaching liberalization of censorship fundamentally altered intellectual life in Vienna. The city was permeated by journalistic controversies on all communal topics, and in that manner literature and music could first become the subject of public debate. Special significance accrues to this new form of publicity not only because of the accompanying emergence of a new public discourse—one whose limitations were of course soon reached owing to its de facto illimitability. Rather, the new publicity may have fundamentally altered the practice of censorship, and probably also overtaxed it after a short time. With almost unimaginable frequency, a comparatively small literary-intellectual elite debated publicly on matters of government, the sciences and the arts, and in this way literature (and with it music) now became matters of State. When in the spring of 1781 Mozart moved to Vienna—at first reluctantly—he must immediately have recognized these new possibilities for mooring himself publicly. The words of posthumous fame addressed to his father that Vienna "is a glorious place and for my line of work the best place in the world" (04.04.1781, MBA 3, 101–103;) date from this time, and probably refer to his first experiences in that incomparable environment around 1780. Mozart's plan to build a new life in Vienna under these auspices may have arisen under the impression of that reality, launched, moreover, by an especially spectacular public breach with a clerical authority in the anti-clerical environment of the Josephine Enlightenment.

Mozart was not the only profiteer in this new situation, not even the only musical one. In 1785 Vincente Martín y Soler arrived in Vienna, attracted by the opportunities the city offered. He too came with no institutional affiliation, which was achieved only in 1787 with the prestigious call to St. Petersburg. Among the literary profiteers was not only Johann Rautenstrauch but also Joseph von Sonnenfels, who as censor became institutionally involved in the Josephine Enlightenment. One special characteristic of this environment was the admission of active writers into the censor's office—prominently in the case of Aloys Blumauer (1755–1807) and Joseph von Retzer (1754–1824), who in 1782 were both appointed to the censor's commission by its director Gottfried van Swieten. In this way writers became the censors of writers, which may have nullified censorship in the strict sense, or in any case reduced it to personal conflicts. However, the attractiveness of the Josephine state was not limited to intellectuals from the imperial state, as confirmed by the prominent example of the Venetian molded Lorenzo Da Ponte, who in 1782 travelled from Dresden to Vienna, hardly by coincidence. Moreover, if we consider the dates alone of birth of all of the important figures in this context—Blumauer in 1755, Retzer in 1754, Da Ponte in 1749, Rautenstrauch in 1746, Schikaneder in 1751, Martín y Soler in 1754, Mozart in 1756—we discover that the attractiveness of the Josephine reforms must have been especially strong for the members of a certain generation.

Mozart's plan to establish himself as a composer without a fixed position, financed only by concerts, opera commissions, and exorbitantly high teaching honorariums, was facilitated—if not indeed occasioned—by the unique situation in Vienna in the 1780s. Characteristic of this society was not only a high degree of class permeability, which Mozart exploited programmatically in his academies, but also an intense way of informal exchange, which was reflected in salons and social gatherings, and reached a certain formal level in the freemason circles. There was practically no member of the literary-intellectual elite in Josephine Vienna who did not belong to a Masonic lodge. Viennese society therefore offered its leading elite and intellectual eminences nearly unlimited freedom, and even treatises that were officially still censored—like those of La Mettrie—were apparently available and obtainable without major efforts. Theater censorship had a noticeable impact on the practice of the court stages, particularly concerning a dramatic reform imposed from above, so to speak, by Sonnenfels. It was a matter here not so much of content as of adjusting the genre's poetics. Beyond the court theater, however, this censorship remained more or less ineffective, because the buffoon, often attacked by proxy, remained ever present. This situation was directly significant for Viennese journalism, whose verbal wit quite naturally presupposes familiarity with this type of theater. Considering these background factors, the prohibition of the *Figaro* performance at the Kärntnertortheater seems incomprehensible. The French and German adaptations (thus also the authorized versions from Kehl) were available in Vienna, and in 1784 the work itself had cleared quite different censorship hurdles in Paris, so that there were certainly no diplomatic or familial concerns to consider. Since Joseph himself had repeatedly intervened in theater politics and, moreover, had frequently attended performances of the Schikaneder and Kumpf troupe, the ban on *Figaro* appears to go back exclusively to him personally, and thus not to a conflict between theater and book censorship. On January 31, 1785, the emperor wrote to the minister of police, Johann Anton Count Pergen:

> *Ich vernehme, dass die bekannte Komedie le Mariage de Figaro in einer deutschen Übersetzung für das Kärntnerthortheater angetragen seyn solle; da nun dieses Stück viel Anstössiges enthält; so verstehe Ich mich, dass der Censor solches entweder ganz verwerfen, oder doch solche Veränderungen darinn veranlassen werde, dass er für die Vorstellung dieser Piece und den Eindruck, den sie machen dürfte, haften werde könnte.*

> I hear that the popular comedy le Mariage de Figaro is proposed for the Kärntnertortheater in a German translation; yet since this piece contains much that is offensive, I understand that the censor will either reject it entirely or will surely arrange for such alterations to be made so that he could take responsibility for the performance of this piece and the impression it might make.[8]

Joseph's directive had the desired result insofar as the censors in charge, who must have previously released the piece, prohibited the performance. However, the release for printing could no longer be reversed, and it appears that decision was no longer an item of revision. Further, it is unclear whether Joseph had actual knowledge of the text or judged only by hearsay. In no case could he have known Beaumarchais's original, at most an adaptation. The term "offensive" is particularly tricky. It can refer to the political or moral sphere, but its aesthetic meaning is more likely intended. The emperor, influenced by Sonnenfels, was always concerned with the refinement of the stage according to the Enlightenment, and so could have had misgivings against the work in that regard. Johann George Sulzer's *Allgemeine Theorie der Schönen Künste* even contains a separate entry which leans toward such an interpretation: "Das Anstößige gehört unter die wichtigsten Fehler, besonders deswegen, weil es die *Täuschung*, die so oft der vornehmste Grund der guten Würkung eines Werks ist, gänzlich zernichtet. Es beleidiget die Vorstellungskraft so sehr, daß man gezwungen wird, das Auge von dem beleidigenden Gegenstand wegzuwenden" (Sulzer 1771, 74; "The offensive is one of the weightiest mistakes, particularly because it utterly destroys illusion, which so often is the noblest reason for a play's beneficial impact. It offends the imagination to such a degree that one is forced to avert one's eyes from the offending object"). Accordingly, Joseph's interference could well have related to theater aesthetics, that is, to the concern that imperial efforts for reform, in the sense of regulating dramatic art, would be centrally affected. It is not possible to say whether Beaumarchais's pre-history in Vienna and his arrest played a role here, but it appears quite probable that they were.

Since the cancellation of the play was one of the rare examples of censorship that was publicly noticeable, the effect may have been considerable. Yet in view of all of the arguments adduced so far, the motivation for it is not to be sought in the work's political explosiveness, for from 1781 on, in view of class criticism, much more drastic writings were published in Vienna, among others Rautenstrauch's *Scheyßereien*. It is therefore much more likely that the emperor had reservations concerning the comedy itself (or in any case some of its proponents in Vienna, above all Rautenstrauch). Accordingly, the effect of the prohibition may have been the opposite of what was intended, for the public announcement seems to have greatly promoted the sale of the printed versions, both French and German. In any case, the ban unexpectedly provided the play with publicity comparable to that in Paris, though arising from completely different motives. The explosiveness of the reaction to the play appears to have fascinated Mozart from the start, but it was the dramaturgic explosiveness, so to speak, of a publicly conducted aesthetic debate. In Mozart's version there is not a single indication of concealed political motivations. Mozart was thus enthusiastic about the comedy itself, and his effort to turn it into an opera must have secured him the greatest possible publicity in Vienna—enhanced by the fact that it was not even an imperial commission.

Comedy and Psychological Drama

Summarizing the facts so far, one arrives at a complex picture. After a six-year, ever more involved debate with the Paris censor's office, Beaumarchais's *La folle journée* was an absolutely sensational success in April 1784. Treatments and adaptations played everywhere, including Vienna. There, a French version and, at about the same time, a German translation by Rautenstrauch of that version appeared even before Beaumarchais's authorized edition (or possibly simultaneously with it). The two volumes must have been available by January of 1785. The performance of Rautenstrauch's version planned for early February by the theater company of Emanuel Schikaneder and Hubert Kumpf was prohibited literally at the last moment following the emperor's directive. In view of the Viennese censorship practice, political motives for this prohibition may be excluded. Rather, we may suppose reasons of stage aesthetics, though it is unclear to what extent Joseph II had concrete knowledge of the work. Immediately after the potentially scandalous announcement of the ban, Mozart decided to ask Da Ponte for a libretto based on Beaumarchais's original. With this opera project it was not a matter of a commission, so the censor's office was not prompted in advance. Yet Mozart used neither the French arrangement published in Vienna nor Rautenstrauch's version, but most probably the German translation authorized by Beaumarchais—hence deliberately chose the complete text. Da Ponte will at least have been acquainted with this edition as well. To what extent he consulted the French original cannot be determined.

Beaumarchais's text contains an important preface, with which, we can assume, Mozart was familiar. In this preface, in dispute with the censor's office, the author develops a theory of comedy, which was for him based on theatrical decorum. (Beaumarchais 1785d, preface, 5–54). True comedy should draw "alle seine Gemählde aus unsern Sitten, und alle seine Subjekte aus der gewöhnlichen menschlichen Gesellschaft" (Beaumarchais 1785d, 9; "all its portrayals from our manners, and all its subjects from common human society"). This characteristic should distinguish comedy from tragedy, and Beaumarchais always emphasizes the morality of this kind of theater, which could and should dispense with the miracles and the horrors of tragedy. Moreover, it is thus the prerogative of comedy to portray manners exactly as they are: "Die nützliche und wahrhaftliebende Comedie ist kein lügenhaft Lob, keine prahlerische akademische Rede" (Beaumarchais 1785d, 12; "Useful and authentic comedy is no deceitful praise, no pretentious academic speech"). This reasoning is remarkable because it remains aesthetical, and politics does not become discernible even as a subtext. Beaumarchais does insist upon the social function of theater, but not in the political sense that was claimed in the subsequent reception of *Figaro*.

Mozart seems to have understood the aesthetics of comedy as a challenge, for it is remarkably close to his own concept of opera buffa. The idea that musical theater would present involved characters of "ordinary human society" seems to have captivated him. The version that he initiated and accomplished jointly with Da Ponte takes up precisely this point: the almost complete elimination of superficial political elements in favor of the psychological drama of the characters involved. This approach was certainly no concession to potential censors, for on Viennese stages much more radical political messages could be presented, for example in Da Ponte's *Bertoldo*. Mozart apparently envisioned in Beaumarchais's comedy the ideal model for musical theater as he conceived of it, and it ultimately differed from the tradition to the extent that Beaumarchais's comedy differed from that of French theater. The differences, outwardly apparent in the great length, in the numerous main characters, and in its four acts, led to a proportionate justificatory preface in the edition of the libretto. There, we find talk of "the new kind of stage play" ("der neuen Art des Schauspiels," Da Ponte 1786, 2), that is, of an innovative approach to the genre, which Beaumarchais had pursued as well.

The suppression of superficial political elements thus does not represent an adaptation to ostensible Viennese realities but rather the systematic realization of this plan. The portrayal of human conditions on stage certainly necessitated music because—here the central music-aesthetic paradigm shift around 1780—only music is able to credibly represent for the listener the imprecise, indistinct, and volatility of these conditions. Precisely this, though, leads to a theatrical compression that reaches far beyond the drama. An essential characteristic of Mozart's and Da Ponte's *Figaro* lies in the unqualified intensification of the Aristotelian unities of place, time, and plot, because the representation on stage no longer recognizes any gap at all. Represented time and the time of representation become fully identical, and their expansion in the sense of a psychological portrayal is due solely to music. This approach does evoke the opera buffa tradition, yet also, as it were, a distancing from it. Even the overture turns out to be a kind of inversion of a traditional opera beginning: *piano* against *forte* instead of *forte* against *piano*, an arpeggiated triadic figure (the typical opening of an orchestral *tutti*) in the strings against the response of the full orchestra, and so on. The jarring element of this new approach was certainly perceived, for *Figaro* was not a work of immediate but rather of a slow, increasing success, which emerged virtually explosively only in the especially unconstrained social environment of Prague, which was particularly receptive to such conceptions.

Yet all this was more or less overshadowed by the censorship affair that affected the play. The first performance of the opera on May 1, 1786, therefore, required the emperor's permission. Only two pieces of evidence document the process. In Da Ponte's memoirs there is talk of the emperor consenting—quickly—after the poet described his adaptation and the magnificence of Mozart's music. Since no commission was involved, Mozart not only played scenes for the monarch, but Joseph attended at least one rehearsal. On July 11, 1786, a review signed with "Fr." appeared in the *Wiener Realzeitung*, which may stem from the actor Johann Friedel (ca. 1751–1789). There, with a quotation from the *Barbier de Seville*, the author once again addresses the practice of censorship:

> 'Was in unsern Zeiten nicht erlaubt ist, gesagt zu werden, wird gesungen.' Könnte man nach Figaro sagen. Dieses Stück, das man in Paris verbothen, und hier als Komödie sowohl in einer schlechten als in einer guten Uebersetzung aufzuführen nicht erlaubt hat, waren wir endlich so glücklich als Oper vorgestellet zu sehen. Man sieht, daß wir besser daran sind als die Franzosen.

> 'What in our times may not be said, is sung.' One could say with Figaro. This piece, which was forbidden in Paris and was not allowed on stage here as a comedy, both in a bad and a good translation, we were finally lucky enough to see performed as an opera. Our lot, we see, is better than that of the French. (*Wiener Realzeitung*, July 1, 1786, Mozart-Dokumente, 243–244)

But precisely this report, in which the advantages of enlightened Vienna compared with Paris are obviously being defended, lays claim to the prohibition solely as a sensation, and probably deliberately contrary to the facts. For in Paris the piece had long since been successful on stage, and in Vienna printed editions could still be regularly purchased.

Especially in his Vienna years, Mozart was anxious for performances effective with the public, beginning with his separation from the archbishop of Salzburg. His decision for *Figaro* coincides so strikingly with the prohibition of the stage play that coincidence can be ruled out. The factually inapposite review in the *Realzeitung*, the most important literary critical journal in Vienna, documents that this connection was noticed. Yet this complicated situation suggests an explanation that deviates from previous interpretations. The connection to censorship may well be understandable as the triggering and, ultimately, overall distinctive feature of Le Nozze di Figaro. However, that distinctiveness does not aim at political discord but rather at a new, different type of comedy in which music assumed a new function. This is the actual, the strong link to Beaumarchais's comedy. Prevailing over censorship, coupled with prevailing over a commission, constituted the spectacular exterior, the outer surface of the drama, set in motion by a composer who, around 1785, appeared to succeed in virtually everything, and who proclaimed it time and again to the public. Circumventing an, at the least, threatening imperial ban on a performance provided the opera with the potency of a sensation that also surrounded Beaumarchais's play. The political dimension, so significant in Paris, must have seemed rather uninteresting in libertine Josephine Vienna, in view of a public that was accustomed to something quite different. Mozart apparently was not interested in that dimension or only in the sense as set out in Beaumarchais's *Vorrede*. More important to him, as it seems, was to weed out what the emperor claimed as "offensive" in that deep aesthetic sense in order to present the opera, that is, the music, as the true representational form of comedy.

However, that claim makes Le Nozze di Figaro of Da Ponte and Mozart paradigmatic in every respect. *Figaro* was not merely the self-representation of the successful composer on the opera stage but rather the definition of a wholly new genre. This claim of an innovative genre imprinted Mozart's creative output during the first years in Vienna on various levels—in the string quartet, the piano concerto, and the serenade—and now it had reached the stage. All normal mechanisms of opera production were rooted out, and Da Ponte indicates in his memoirs the degree of the intrigues that this dual staging provoked. It also involved a completely new kind of collaboration between librettist and composer. Prevailing over censorship—nearly impossible in Vienna in the early 1780s because it had almost ceased to exist as a noticeable factor—in a way triggered the drama. For a composer who wanted to strategically position himself, this was a sensation-begging by-product. The contact with censorship thus explains the many unusual characteristics of *Figaro* in a fundamental way, but not in a political sense. For the pioneer of a new musical theater, this was just another, if initial, challenge to highlight the utterly exceptional nature, the unique quality of his creativity. As the basis of a new form of musical theater, this playful contact with censorship makes Le Nozze di Figaro not merely a characteristic product of the Josephine Enlightenment, but rather its incomparable paradigm.

Notes

1. Plans for at least two further projects are still traceable: a setting of Goldoni's *Servitore di due Padroni* (in a German translation by Johann Nepomuk Binder von Krieglstein), and a carnival pantomime based upon motifs of the commedia dell'arte (March of 1783, transmitted fragmentarily, KV 446/416^d). The music of *Der Schauspieldirektor* does not really belong to this context.
2. *Wiener Zeitung*, 1784, Wednesday, December 22, 1784, Suppl. No. 102, 2905; quoted in Sonnek 1999, 61.

3. *Das Wienerblättchen*, Wednesday, February 2, 1785; quoted in Sonnek 1999, 61–62.
4. *Das Wienerblättchen*, Friday, February 4, 1785; quoted in Sonnek 1999, 61.
5. *Das Wienerblättchen*, Monday, February 28, 1785; quoted in Sonnek 1999, 62.
6. In his translation Friedrich Ludwig Huber remarks ironically: "Zu meiner Entschuldigung für Manche, die verdrüßlich ausrufen möchten: Wieder eine deutsche Uebersetzung des Figaro! Sey es gesagt, daß diese Uebersetzung angekündigt und angefangen war, ehe noch einer von den tausend und aber tausend Uebersezzern des heil. Röm. Reichs an diese Arbeit vielleicht nur gedacht hatte" (Beaumarchais/Huber 1785, fol. A2r.; "I have to apologize for those people exclaiming: Again a German translation of Figaro! But I have to confess that this translation has been announced and started in a moment when none of the thousands and thousands of translators in the Roman Empire has even thought of their work").
7. Zensurordnung für Österreich u.d.E. 1781; quoted in: https://www.univie.ac.at/medienrechtsgeschichte/Zensurverordnung1781.pdf (edition of the complete document).
8. Joseph II, letter to Count Pergen, March 31, 1785; quoted in Payer von Thun 1920, 60.

References

Arneth, Alfred Ritter von. 1868. *Beaumarchais und Sonnenfels*. Vienna: Braumüller.
Bales, Derek. 1987–1988. *Joseph II: In the Shadow of Maria Theresia 1741–1780*. 2 vols. Cambridge and London: Cambridge University Press.
Beaumarchais, Pierre-Augustin Caron de. 1785a. *La folle journée, ou, Le mariage de Figaro. Comédie en cinq actes et en Prose*. Strasbourg and Vienna: Frères Gay.
Beaumarchais, Pierre-Augustin Caron de. 1785b. *Der närrische Tag oder die Hochzeit des Figaro. Ein Lustspiel in 5 Aufzügen. Übersetzt von Johann Rautenstrauch*. Vienna.
Beaumarchais, Pierre-Augustin Caron de. 1785c. *Der tollste Tag oder Figaro's Hochzeit, ein Lustspiel in fünf Aufzügen. Aus dem Französischen des Herrn von Beaumarchais. Nach der aechten Ausgabe übersezt*. [von Friedrich Ludwig Huber, Dessau and Leipzig: Göschen].
Beaumarchais, Pierre-Augustin Caron de. 1785d. *Der lustige Tag oder Figaro's Hochzeit. Ein Lustspiel in fünf Aufzügen. Aus dem Französischen übersezt. Aechte, vom Herrn Verfasser einzig und allein genehmigte, vollständige Ausgabe*. Kehl, Germany: Müller.
Bodi, Leslie. 1977. *Tauwetter in Wien. Zur Prosa der österreichischen Aufklärung 1781–1795*. Frankfurt am Main: Fischer.
Bolt, Rodney. 2006. *The Librettist of Venice: The Remarkable Life of Lorenzo Da Ponte, Mozart's Poet, Casanova's Friend, and Italian Opera's Impresario in America*. New York: Bloomsbury.
Brown, Gregory S. 2006. *Literary Sociability and Literary Property in France, 1775–1793. Beaumarchais, the Société des auteurs dramatiques and the Comédie Française*, Studies in European Cultural Transition, vol. 33. Aldershot, UK, and Burlington, Vt.: Ashgate.
Da Ponte, Lorenzo. 1786. *Preface to Hochzeit des Figaro. Ein Schauspiel in Musik in 4. Aufzügen aus dem Französischen herausgezogen. Aufgeführt in dem k.k. Nationaltheater. Im Jahre 1786*. Vienna: Kurzböck, s. d.
Da Ponte, Lorenzo. 1807. *Storia compendiosa dell'a vita di Lorenzo da Ponte scritta da lui medesimo*. New York: Riley.
Da Ponte, Lorenzo. 1819. *An Extract from the Life of Lorenzo da Ponte, with the History of Several Dramas written by him, and among others Il Figaro, Il Don Giovanni, & La Scuola Degli Amanti set to Music by Mozart*. New York: da Ponte.

Da Ponte, Lorenzo. 1823–1827. *Memorie di Lorenzo da Ponte, da Ceneda. Scritte da Esso.* 4 vols. New York: Gray & Bunce,.

Da Ponte, Lorenzo. [1829] 1960. *Memorie di Lorenzo da Ponte da Ceneda. Scritte da Esso. Seconda edizione corretta e amplicata con note dell'autore e l'aggiunta d'un volume.* 3 vols. New York: Gray & Bunce; ed. Cesare Pagnini, Milan: Rizzoli.

Deutsch, Otto Erich. 1961. *Mozart. Die Dokumente seines Lebens.* Wolfgang Amadeus Mozart: Neue Ausgabe sämtlicher Werke, vol. 10, no. 34. Leipzig: Deutscher Verlag für Musik (Mozart-Dokumente).

Ellis, S[tewart] M[arsh]. 1930. *The Life of Michael Kelly, Musician, Actor, and Bon Viveur, 1762–1826.* London: Gollancz.

Glossy, Carl. 1897. "Zur Geschichte der Wiener Theaterzenrsur." *Jahrbuch der Grillparzer-Gesellschaft* 7: 238–340.

Gnau, Hermann. 1911. *Die Zensur unter Joseph II.* Strasbourg: Singer.

Goertz, Harald. 1988. *Mozarts Dichter Lorenzo Da Ponte. Genie und Abenteurer.* Munich: Piper.

Grau Tanner, Miriam. 2006. "L'Ape musicale oder die Selbstständigkeit Lorenzo da Pontes in Wien." In *Lorenzo Da Ponte. Aufbruch in die neue Welt*, edited by Werner Hanak, 87–97. Ostfildern, Germany: Hatje Cantz.

Hadamowsky, Franz. 1979. "Ein Jahrhundert Literatur- und Theaterzensur in Österreich." In *Die österreichische Literatur. Ihr Profil an der Wende vom 18. zum 19. Jahrhundert (1750–1830)*, edited by Herbert Zeman, 1:289–305. Graz: Akademische Druck- und Verlagsanstalt.

Heartz, Daniel. 1986–1987. "Constructing 'Le nozze di Figaro.'" *Journal of the Royal Musical Association* 112, no. 1: 77–98.

Hodges, Sheila. 2002. *Lorenzo Da Ponte. The Life and Times of Mozart's Librettist.* Madison: University of Wisconsin Press.

Hunter, Mary K. 1999. *The Culture of Opera Buffa in Mozart's Vienna: A Poetics of Entertainment.* Princeton: Princeton University Press.

Kim, Sae-Hwan. 1996. "Analyse d'un succès. 'Le mariage de Figaro' de Beaumarchais. 1778–1793." Diss., Université François Rabelais, Tours.

Klueting, Harm. 2008. "Salzburg und die Aufklärung." In *Mozarts Lebenswelten. Eine Zürcher Ringvorlesung 2006*, edited by Laurenz Lütteken and Hans-Joachim Hinrichsen, 31–53. Kassel: Bärenreiter.

Lütteken, Laurenz. 2004. "Mozart, Prag und die Aufklärung. Eine Problemskizze." *Acta Mozartiana* 51: 59–68.

Morton, Brian N., and Donald C. Spinelli. 1988. *Beaumarchais. A Bibliography.* Ann Arbor, MI: Olivia and Hill.

Mozart, Wolfgang Amadeus. 1963. *Briefe und Aufzeichnungen. Gesamtausgabe.* Edited by Wilhelm A. Bauer and Otto Erich Deutsch. Vol. 3. Kassel: Bärenreiter (MBA).

Mozart, Wolfgang Amadeus. 1973. *Le Nozze di Figaro.* Edited by Ludwig Finscher. Wolfgang Amadeus Mozart: Neue Ausgabe Sämtlicher Werke, vol. 2, nos. 5–6. Kassel: Bärenreiter.

Olechowski, Thomas. 2007. "Zur Zensur am Ende des 18. Jahrhunderts. Dichter als Zensoren." In *Aloys Blumauer und seine Zeit*, Jahrbuch der Österreichischen Gesellschaft zur Erforschung des 18. Jahrhunderts, vol. 21, edited by Franz M. Eybl, Wynfried Kriegleder and Johannes Frimmel, 135–143. Bochum, Germany: Winkler.

Payer von Thun, Rudolf. 1920. *Joseph II. als Theaterdirektor. Ungedruckte Briefe und Aktenstücke aus den Kinderjahren des Burgtheaters.* Vienna and Leipzig: Heidrich.

Plattner, Irmgard. 2008. "Josephinismus und Bürokratie." In *Josephinismus als aufgeklärter Absolutismus*, edited by Helmut Reinalter, 53–96. Vienna: Böhlau.

Reinalter, Helmut. 2008. "Der Josephinismus als Variante des aufgeklärten Absolutismus und seine Reformkomplexe." In *Josephinismus als aufgeklärter Absolutismus*, edited by Helmut Reinalter, 2–16. Vienna: Böhlau.

Ruf, Wolfgang. 1977. *Die Rezeption von Mozarts "Le nozze di Figaro" bei den Zeitgenossen*, Beihefte zum Archiv für Musikwissenschaft 16. Wiesbaden: Steiner, 1977.

Sashegyi, Oskar. 1958. *Zensur und Geistesfreiheit unter Joseph II*. Budapest: Akad. Kaidó.

Sonnek, Anke. 1999. *Emanuel Schikaneder. Theaterprinzipal, Schauspieler und Stückeschreiber*. Schriftenreihe der Internationalen Stiftung Mozarteum Salzburg, vol. 11. Kassel: Bärenreiter.

Sulzer, Johann George. 1771. *Allgemeine Theorie der Schönen Künste in einzeln, nach alphabetischer Ordnung der Kunstwörter auf einander folgenden, Artikeln abgehandelt*. Vol. 1. Leipzig: Weidmanns Erben & Reich.

Tyson, Alan. 1986–87. "Some Problems in the Text of 'Le nozze di Figaro': Did Mozart Have a Hand in Them?" *Journal of the Royal Musical Association* 112, no. 1: 99–131.

Tyson, Alan. 1988. "The 1786 Prague Version of Mozart's Le Nozze di Figaro." *Music and Letters* 69: 83–96.

Wagner, Hans. 1977. "Die Zensur in der Habsburgermonarchie (1750–1810)." In *Buch- und Verlagswesen im 18. und 19. Jahrhundert*, edited by Herbert Georg Göpfert, 28–44. Berlin: Carmen.

Wangermann, Ernst. 2004. *Die Waffen der Publizität. Zum Funktionswandel der politischen Literatur unter Joseph II.*, Schriftenreihe des Instituts für Österreichkunde. Wien: Verlag für Geschichte und Politik; München: Oldenbourg.

Wolf, Norbert Christian. 2007. "Von 'eingeschränkt und erzbigott' bis 'ziemlich inquisitionsmäßig': Die Rolle der Zensur im Wiener literarischen Feld des 18. Jahrhunderts." In *Zensur im Jahrhundert der Aufklärung. Geschichte—Theorie—Praxis*, edited by Wilhelm Haefs and York-Gothart Mix, 305–330. Das achtzehnte Jahrhundert, Supplementa, vol. 12. Göttingen: Wallstein.

Zelle, Carsten. 2008. "Was ist josephinische Aufklärung—in der Literatur." In *Mozarts Lebenswelten. Eine Zürcher Ringvorlesung 2006*, edited by Laurenz Lütteken and Hans-Joachim Hinrichsen, 132–158. Kassel: Bärenreiter.

CHAPTER 10

THE CURIOUS INCIDENT OF *FIDELIO* AND THE CENSORS

ROBIN WALLACE

IN Arthur Conan Doyle's story "Silver Blaze," Sherlock Holmes famously drew the attention of Scotland Yard's Inspector Gregory to "the curious incident of the dog in the night-time." The curious incident, of course, was that the dog did nothing in the night-time. The oft-told story of *Fidelio* and the censors may very well hinge on a similar paradox with curious implications of its own. That the "incident" is known at all is mainly due to two letters written by Beethoven's librettist Joseph Sonnleithner. In the first, dated 2 October 1805 and addressed to the imperial royal police (Brandenburg 1996, 266–267 [no. 237]), Sonnleithner complained that the opera had been returned to him, three days earlier, as unsuitable for performance. He gave five reasons why the production should be allowed to continue, and asked to be informed as to what changes would be necessary. The following day he wrote to Philipp von Stahl, a high-ranking police official (267–269 [no. 238]), asking for his assistance. Though the written response has not survived, it came quickly. On 5 October Sonnleithner was informed that the opera could be performed if the "harshest scenes" ("*grobsten Scenen*") were changed (Brandenburg 1996, 269 [no. 239]; Biberhofer 1921, 117).

It is a common misperception that this brush-up with the police delayed the first performance of the opera, which took place on 20 November 1805. In all likelihood, though, the postponement of the initial performance date of 15 October was due solely to "the mechanics of getting the music composed, copied and rehearsed." (Thayer 1967, 386). *Thayer's Life of Beethoven*, in the definitive edition revised and edited by Elliott Forbes, also suggests, somewhat implausibly, "On October 5th, the ban was lifted after some changes had been made in the most harsh scenes" (Thayer 1967, 386). Within three days of Sonnleithner's original letter of protest, in other words, changes are supposed to have been made and the opera approved for performance.

Could Sonnleithner have been advised of the necessary changes, made them, and received permission from the censors within three days? Even Willy Hess (1986, 55), the most indefatigable researcher on the early versions of the opera, acknowledges that the "untrimmed" ("*unfrisiert*") text, while it would be interesting to see, exists only hypothetically. Thus, it is entirely possible that not only did the censors fail to delay the performance, but that no changes were actually made. Nor did the censorship issue crop up again, either at the ill-fated 1806 revival, nor at the more significant one that took place in 1814.

Nevertheless, this near non-event has contributed significantly to the prevailing interpretation of *Fidelio, oder Die eheliche Liebe* (the official title from the 1805 performances on) as a political opera. Paul Robinson (1996, 5) writes, "*Fidelio* has long enjoyed a visceral appeal for people on the left as the opera that most fully embodies the ideal of a pacified existence." He goes on to point out, though, that Beethoven's politics, and the political content of the opera, are far more elusive than such a simple analysis suggests. Jean-Nicolas Bouilly's *Léonore, ou L'amour conjugal*, on which Sonnleithner's libretto was based, was actually inspired by opposition to the French Revolution, or at least to the Reign of Terror. Beethoven, meanwhile, has long been suspected of having been, in Virgil Thomson's words, "an old fraud who just talked about human rights and dignity but who was really an irascible, intolerant, and scheming careerist" (Thomson 1981, 204). His ambivalence toward Napoleon and the ideals of the French Revolution is well known, and in fact the 1814 revival of *Fidelio* took place at precisely the point when his public popularity was at its peak due to his musical celebration of Wellington's victory over Napoleon's forces at Victoria. Later that year, *Fidelio* "became the first opera given for the assembled dignitaries of the Congress of Vienna … forging an almost official link between Beethoven's operatic celebration of freedom and the great diplomatic enterprise that fashioned post-Napoleonic Europe" (Robinson 1996, 148).

There is thus a crowning irony in the fact that the paradigmatic opera of political liberation took its present form, and acquired its present status, precisely at the time of what is widely regarded as a triumph of reactionary politics, particularly in Austria. The irony, though, may very well begin with an exaggerated emphasis on a comparatively trivial episode during the work's inception nine years earlier. This essay will explore the implications of re-examining the episode, its consequences, and its relevance to our current understanding of the opera as a political work.

The Background of the Story

Since fashions in opera can change even more quickly than those in other kinds of music, it is worth spending some time reviewing the context in which Sonnleithner's text for *Fidelio* took shape. From this perspective, the opera was neither new nor particularly provocative: it was one of the most conventional topics that Beethoven could have chosen.

Fidelio is a late example of the "rescue opera," a genre that was widely popular in the late eighteenth century and remained so briefly at the beginning of the nineteenth. The best known today of the many earlier works of this type is Mozart's *Die Entführung aus dem Serail* (*The Abduction from the Seraglio*), the first opera that he wrote for the Viennese stage. By far the most successful in its own time, though, was Cherubini's *Les Deux Journées* of 1800. It was first performed in Vienna on 13 August 1802 (*Allgemeine musikalische Zeitung* 5, 25ff.) and, under the title *Der Wasserträger* (and sometimes also as *Graf Armand* or *Die Tage der Gefahr*), it continued to be widely heard in the German-speaking countries into the 1840s and beyond. Its libretto, which was also written by Bouilly, tells a story that is not only cut from the same mold as that of *Fidelio*, but is in some respects nearly identical to it. Both are ostensibly based on events that took place during the Reign of Terror. Both hinge on a dramatic scene in which a wife emerges from disguise to defend her husband. In *Les Deux Journées* her actual name is Constance. Both feature a host family of a lower social class with a daughter named Marceline (spelled with a final "a" in *Les Deux Journées*). In both Bouilly texts, the lower class characters slur words together in a way that marks them immediately as socially inferior to the primary actors.

Both of Bouilly's versions were first performed at the Théâtre Feydeau in Paris, where the audience must have noticed the resemblance. Crucially, both feature a government official who abuses his power. In *Les Deux Journées* it is Cardinal Mazarin, and the action takes place in the seventeenth century in France, while Bouilly's *Léonore* and its subsequent adaptations are set in Spain and the villain is the governor of the prison. Sonnleithner may have used this resemblance to try to confuse the Viennese censors; the fourth reason he gave for lifting the ban on the work's performance was that it was set in the sixteenth century, a fact that he had "forgotten" to mention on the title page. (In fact, the time of the action of *Fidelio/Léonore* is never specified by Bouilly or anybody else.)

For Bouilly, then, it can be said that the libretto of *Les Deux Journées* constituted a second draft of the *Léonore* material, presented in a way that was perhaps more dramatically effective but no less politically charged. One of the main differences is that the later story places far less emphasis on the themes of wifely fidelity and marital love. This is significant because the *first* argument that Sonnleithner presented to the Viennese censors for allowing the opera to be performed was that the empress, Marie Therese, had assured him that no opera text had ever pleased her more than that of Bouilly's *Léonore, ou L'amour conjugal*.

In his informative study of Marie Therese's activities as a patron of music, John Rice (2003, 10–11) has established that the empress was especially dedicated to the theme of marital fidelity. He believes that she played a crucial role in the creation of two Italian operas on the *Léonore* theme—those by Paer (*Leonora*) and Mayr (*L'amor coniugale*)—and, on the basis of Sonnleithner's comment, suggests that she was "at the nexus of a web connecting the three Léonore operas of 1804–05" (257). Indeed, Beethoven's version was initially to have premiered on the empress's name day, 15 October. If Rice's speculation is correct, there can be no doubt that Marie Therese chose the story because of the theme of marital fidelity. In every other regard there is little reason to prefer it to that of *Les Deux Journées* or countless other rescue operas.

The empress also had a predilection for the so-called *sotterraneo* scene (Rice 2003, 94). The *sotterraneo* was a large-scale scene complex set underground, and was also commonplace in operas of the late eighteenth and early nineteenth centuries. Often, as in *Fidelio*, the setting was a dungeon. Stephen Meyer (2002, 481) has written, "the popularity of the prison scene seems to have increased significantly from 1790 to 1815 ... such scenes were featured in dozens of operas during these decades." Though not all underground opera scenes are set in prisons—and, of course, not all prisons are underground—the dungeon seems to have had a special appeal as a place of horror and mystery. Meyer suggests that in operatic prison scenes, "as in so much of eighteenth- and early nineteenth-century literature, our attention is directed away from external action toward the internal drama within the prisoner's soul" (478). This is certainly true of the scene that opens act 2 of *Fidelio*, but in historical perspective this scene was hardly a novelty. Indeed, the most venerable of all operatic stories, that of Orpheus, deals with a spousal descent into a kind of underground prison and an attempted rescue (480). What distinguishes the *Fidelio* scene, according to Meyer, is the fact that, in the 1814 revision, it uses music in a unique way to signal transcendence—the oboe solo that begins the final section of Florestan's aria thus serves the same function as does the portrait of Leonore that inspires and comforts him in Bouilly's original (514). In this view, then, the 1814 version is less political and more "internal" than the earlier version.

The Theme of Marital Love

If the empress appreciated the story of *Fidelio* primarily for its portrayal of wifely fidelity and conjugal love, so did contemporary critics. After the 1805 performances, the Viennese correspondent of the *Allgemeine musikalische Zeitung* describes the subject of the opera as follows:

> A man having been unjustly and suddenly dragged off to a dungeon through the fierce vindictiveness of his enemy and languishing there under fierce treatment, his death must now hide the shameful deed forever, since here and there something of the crime is beginning to be made known. However, his loving wife (Fidelio) has followed him into prison as the warden's apprentice, has been able to win the trust of the tyrant and finally rescues her husband. The daughter of the warden falls in love with Fidelio and causes thereby a rather commonplace episode. (Senner, Wallace, and Meredith 2001, 173)

Despite the reference to Pizarro as a "tyrant," it is clear that this writer saw the story in terms of individual human relationships rather than politics. Pizarro is Florestan's "enemy," his imprisonment a "shameful deed" and a "crime." Fidelio/Leonore, the only character mentioned by name, is portrayed as the hero of the action, her rescue of her husband as its consequence. In short, the writer presents *Fidelio oder die eheliche Liebe* (he is careful to cite the full title) as a rescue opera whose distinguishing feature is a strong female lead and a theme of conjugal love.

Meanwhile, the critic of *Der Freymüthige*, also citing the full title, described the work only as "a story of liberation of the kind that has come into fashion since Cherubini's

Les Deux Journées" (Senner, Wallace, and Meredith 2001, 176). The reviews of the 1806 and 1814 revivals, while much more enthusiastic about the music, barely mention the story, although the *Zeitung für die elegante Welt* stated in 1806: "It is incomprehensible how the composer could have resolved to enliven this empty shoddy piece of work by Sonnleitner [*sic*] with beautiful music" (179).

One of the most significant contributions to Beethoven's reception in general is Amadeus Wendt's lengthy 1815 essay on *Fidelio* (the title is now given in its shortened form) in the *Allgemeine musikalische Zeitung*. Here is Wendt's brief summary of the plot:

> The story of the opera is that of a noble woman who rescues her husband, who has been overthrown by a court intrigue and placed in the deepest dungeon as a state prisoner as a result of the inhuman revenge of the governor of the state prisons, from assassination, through which the governor strives to remove him from the sight of the minister who is visiting the prison, and who naturally brings about poetic justice in the end. By means of the confidence, which, disguised as a young man, she has won from the dungeon master she finally discovers her husband after great exertion. (Senner, Wallace, and Meredith 2001, 203)

Wendt goes on to point out, "This subject . . . is *outwardly*, that is, in relation to dramatic and scenic *variety*, very deficient; *inwardly*, however, that is, in regard to the active description and elaboration of the situations that occur that is *possible* here by means of poetry and music, it is endlessly fruitful" (203).

Some qualifications need to be made. Wendt had heard, in Leipzig, what he believed to be the original version of the opera (it was actually a makeshift three-act adaptation of the 1806 *Fidelio*). He suggested that one reason for its initial failure was that people in Vienna were already acquainted with the subject "to the point of saturation" through Paer's *Leonora* (Senner, Wallace, and Meredith 2001, 202). He was obviously wrong about this as well, since *Leonora* was not performed in Vienna until March 1806 and was not performed publicly there until February 1809 (Robinson 1996, 34). However, his comment implies that, far from finding the subject controversial, he found it commonplace; this perception, in fact, supports one of the central themes of his essay, which is that Beethoven's music alone creates the dramatic unity that makes the work outstanding.

Fidelio and German Nationalism

One theme that does emerge strongly from the early reviews is that of German nationalism. Reviewing a 1829 performance in Dresden, Richard Otto Spazier wrote, in the longwinded style typical of such appeals:

> Whoever knows the circumstances under which the German opera in Dresden has had to operate since its inception, in competition with a rival, which for many years had monopolized the interest of the public, but otherwise enjoying support and

patronage, with no means seeming too costly, no task too great for its maintenance, and which thus tried, successfully, to keep as much as possible within its possession, so that German art was always forced to clothe itself with those rags that the other had left behind and, as has rightly been said elsewhere, had to run like a humble beggar in pursuit of an arrogant rich man in its own fatherland: whoever knows the situation will rightly take phenomena like [the success of the *Fidelio* performance] as harbingers of a new dawn, which now, thanks to the persistent efforts of the men who influence the dissemination of art in Germany, is beginning to break forth upon the long overclouded artistic sky of a city gifted with quite rich resources. (Senner, Wallace, and Meredith 2001, 258)

As distasteful as such comments may appear in historical hindsight, it is worth emphasizing that in context they are often associated with progressive political thinking, and thus militate against the idea that an "almost official link" existed between Beethoven's opera and the conservative legacy of the Congress of Vienna. If the Congress represented a reaction against the revolutionary fervor that had swept Europe during the previous two decades, a strong reflection of its conservatism was seen in the cross-cultural nature of the newly formed Austrian empire, which by its very existence ignored the rising tide of nationalist sentiment that was to transform Europe over the next century. As Henry Kissinger writes in his classic reappraisal of the Congress of Vienna:

In 1919, the Austro-Hungarian Empire disintegrated not so much from the impact of the war as from the nature of the peace, because its continued existence was incompatible with national self-determination, the legitimizing principle of the new international order. It would have occurred to no one in the eighteenth century that the legitimacy of a state depended on linguistic unity. It was inconceivable to the makers of the Versailles settlement that there might be any other basis for legitimate rule. Legitimizing principles triumph by being taken for granted. (Kissinger 1956, 265)

By the early twentieth century, in other words, Spazier's vehement nationalism would have seemed mainstream, while in context it was revolutionary.

This point can be sustained by comparing the stunning success of the revived *Fidelio* with the parallel trajectory of the "Posse" *Unser Verkehr* by Karl Borromäus Alexander Sessa (1786–1813). First performed in Breslau in 1813, this notoriously anti-Semitic farce premiered in Berlin on 2 September 1815. There it shared the stage of the royal opera house with *Fidelio*, which first appeared there the following month—a fact that explains Clemens Brentano's statement in the *Berlinische Nachrichten von Staats-und gelehrten Sachen* of 17 October that *Fidelio* had appeared "without much noise, without prior proclamation, for this is none of our business (*unser Verkehr*)" (Senner, Wallace, and Meredith 2001, 223).

Sessa's play was a vicious satire of the attempts of German Jews to fit into mainstream culture. It was precisely the question of linguistic unity that was at stake. By broadly satirizing the way that even assimilated Jews spoke German, the play mocked their pretensions to have left their former identity behind (Grossman 2000, 148, 150–152). Its performance in Berlin had encountered the determined opposition of Prussian Chancellor Karl August von Hardenberg, who had also been one of the leading diplomats at the Congress of Vienna (Hertz 2007, 141). Hardenberg doubtless saw it as a direct rebuke to the Emancipation Edict of 1812, which for the first time had made Prussian Jews citizens. Thus, unlike *Fidelio*, Sessa's play faced determined censorship at the very highest level of authority and was only performed due to sustained public demand. *Unser Verkehr* remained controversial, and Ferdinand Alois Wurm (some sources give his name as Albert Wurm or even Albert Wurms), whose highly provocative portrayal of the character Jakob intensified the play's anti-Semitism, was quickly sentenced to a year in prison and banished from Berlin. (Senner, Wallace, and Meredith 2001, 231; *Allgemeine musikalische Zeitung* 17, 840).

In this case, the "conservative" legacy of the Congress of Vienna stood in direct opposition to the mounting German nationalism that would eventually make that legacy, and the diplomatic order on which it depended, obsolete. The attempts of Spazier and others to celebrate *Fidelio* as a nationalist work need to be read in this context. They show that, contrary to the claims of an "almost official link" with the Congress, *Fidelio* quickly became a powerful symbol of German cultural and linguistic identity. In the years of the *Vormärz*, this made it, at least potentially, a revolutionary work—though not in a way that appeals to twenty-first-century sensibilities.

The Austrian Police

The context in which the Austrian police attempted to censor *Fidelio* in 1805 is also more complicated than is commonly understood. Austria under Metternich has the reputation of having been a police state, and Beethoven already complained in 1794 to Franz Gerhard Wegeler, "You can't speak too loudly here, or the police give you a place to stay" (Brandenburg 1996, 26 [no. 17]; my translation). Lewis Lockwood (2006, 480) refers to a Viennese civil servant who recorded in his diary the yearning that many Viennese felt, on the arrival of the French, for "the times of the unforgotten Joseph II," when "free thought ... [was] relieved of its fetters."

Donald Emerson (1968, 7) has made it clear, however, that it was Joseph II himself whose "torrent of imperial efforts incidentally tossed up a new police system while he displaced the old provincial Estates in favor of his own administrators whose organization he passionately strove to systematize and strengthen." In 1793, three years after Joseph's death, his "Police Ministry was definitively incorporated into the Hapsburg government ... to guard the security of Austria at war then with revolutionary France" (Emerson 1968, 1). Johann Anton, Count von Pergen (1725–1814), used his considerable skills to consolidate this ministry, so that "by 1787 all the provincial arms had emerged for the centralized police system by which [he] sought to surpass the other great states of Europe" (11).

Joseph's successor, Leopold II, tried to reverse this process, turning "from the Count's simple concentration on the security of the state to new emphasis on individual security and public welfare." Leopold's disregard for Pergen's consolidation of police power led to the latter's resignation in 1791, but he was reinstated by Leopold's successor Francis II (later Emperor Francis I) the following year in the midst of growing concern over the threat posed by revolutionary France (Emerson 1968, 18, 22). Thus, during Beethoven's first years in Vienna, a pitched battle was underway between Pergen, the great proponent of centralized police authority, and highly influential opponents who feared the kind of power that Pergen sought to obtain. That battle had begun under Joseph II well before the French Revolution, which only served to intensify it.

It was not until 1801, though, that the Police Ministry was entrusted with censorship powers (Emerson 1968, 27). By the time *Fidelio* appeared four years later, Pergen had retired permanently, removing the most effective police advocate from the field. The following year, his successor was described by "an informed critic . . . as a man who could not achieve the goals of higher state police: an inconceivable weakling who lacked will, tact, sagacity, and education" (Emerson 1968, 27).

In other words, the Police Ministry that attempted to censor *Fidelio* in 1805 was not the all-powerful entity of the Metternich years; it was more of a bungling, wounded giant poised between the power of the newly created imperial state and that of implacable enemies who sought to make the most of the situation. It is hardly surprising, therefore, that Sonnleithner was able to pull strings behind the backs of the police and win approval for the opera. The fact that the police were unaware of the empress's interest in and support for this very story is symptomatic of the often difficult role they had to play in competing for imperial favor.

The Congress of Vienna

By the time the opera was revived in 1814 the political situation was, of course, very different. The threat of Napoleon had been contained, but the one posed to the established order by revolution was as strong as ever—a fact that Napoleon's dramatic escape from Elba and return to Paris would illustrate the following year. The long years of war had institutionalized the role of the centralized police force begun by Joseph II and made possible the truly oppressive censorship that would shortly begin under Metternich.

In this context, it is traditional to read the changes that Treitschke and Beethoven made to *Fidelio* as a capitulation. As is widely known, the opera was altered so that the dramatic uncertainty of the earlier ending, which took place in the dungeon, is resolved in a triumphant scene on the parade ground of the prison, in which it is announced that the king has set all the prisoners free. Thus, the benevolence of monarchy is affirmed while an entire people—it is easy to see the prisoners as representing Austria under Napoleon—is liberated. The presumptive historical precedent, the storming of the Bastille, is turned on its head, with the prisoners being set free *by* the state rather than *from* it. This change presumably made the censorship issue moot: even though a state minister still abuses his power, it is beyond question that, as Sonnleithner had claimed in 1805, he is only exercising private vengeance.

Such a reading, though, becomes problematic when viewed with the benefit of historical hindsight. If the opera indeed confirmed the conservative goals of the Congress of Vienna and reinforced the role of traditional monarchy, then its "visceral appeal for people on the left" is clearly based on a profound misunderstanding. It is hard to believe, however, that the more subversive implications of the liberation scene could have been completely overlooked in 1814. With the abundance of rescue operas during the preceding decades, audiences were predisposed to understand the genre in a broader context of progressive politics. Meyer has written:

> Even in the absence of overt statements or gestures, the political meanings of operatic imprisonment are impossible to ignore. Indeed, in these decades European culture was so saturated with narratives and images of imprisonment that it would have been difficult for audiences not to regard the prisons in which the tenors and sopranos languish as miniature versions of the Bastille or Bicetre ... Familiarity with the sources upon which rescue operas were based strengthened the tendency to read the operatic prison through the lens of politics. (Meyer 2002, 483)

It would have been highly unusual for that lens to reveal a simple reaffirmation of the pre-Napoleonic status quo.

The Congress of Vienna, though, was also more complex and contradictory than is often recognized. As mentioned earlier, it stood in opposition to the kind of German nationalism that encouraged the virulent anti-Semitism of the later nineteenth century. A serious attempt was also made at the Congress to end the international slave trade, which is often seen as a crucial step toward its eventual abolition (Nicolson 1946, 209–214). The settlements reached at the Congress mark an important precedent for all later international peacekeeping systems, including the League of Nations and the United Nations, which came into existence after similarly cataclysmic wars. As Richard Langhorne explains, the Congress's reputation rose in the 1930s when it became evident that the Treaty of Versailles had failed due to the exclusion of Germany from the negotiations. By contrast, the full inclusion of France at Vienna had helped to guarantee a solution that maintained the balance of power for a century through what is often called the Concert of Europe (Langhorne 1986, 313–314). During the 1950s, against the background of this changing perspective, Henry Kissinger made a highly influential attempt to rehabilitate Metternich's reputation as a statesman and peacemaker.

Thus, it is entirely fair to associate the Congress with "hopeful new beginnings," and even, as Robinson (1996, 148) also suggests, with "fundamental political transformation." It is also easy to understand why the opera's more revolutionary implications were downplayed during the years of the *Vormärz*, when "revolution" was the enemy of the international order in the same sense that communism was in the later twentieth century (Langhorne 1986, 316). As is so often the case with major political events and great works of art, both the Congress and *Fidelio* pointed in multiple directions at once.

Ironically, then, the fact that the opera avoided censorship in 1814 may be largely a result of the hopeful political climate in which it re-emerged, which focused attention on its optimism rather than on its revolutionary political pedigree. But there are other, as yet unconsidered, possibilities as well.

Schröder-Devrient and the Theme of Marital Love

The fact that the opera's political content remained secondary through much of the nineteenth century is often attributed to the influence of Wilhelmine Schröder-Devrient, who first sang the role of Leonore in 1822 and quickly became identified with it. As Robinson writes:

> Schröder-Devrient's performance was geared to convey a single passion: Leonore's unstinting devotion to her husband. She anxiously examined the faces of the prisoners as they entered the courtyard; she embraced Florestan rapturously at the moment of rescue; and in the final tableau, according to Chorley, "there was something subduing in the look of speechless affection with which she at last undid the chains of the beloved one, saved by her love." (Robinson 1996, 150)

The implication here is that Schröder-Devrient neutralized the opera's revolutionary politics by focusing on the secondary theme of marital love. In this view, the rediscovery of *Fidelio* as a political opera did not occur until the twentieth century.

We have already seen, however, that this "secondary" theme is the only one discussed in any depth by early reviewers, and that Marie Therese's interest in it may well have motivated Beethoven to write the opera and helped to overcome the censors' objections. Did the twentieth century simply invent the idea that *Fidelio* had always been a political opera, causing the censorship episode to acquire more significance than it really deserves? Or is it possible that modern critics, like Conan Doyle's Inspector Gregory, are missing something obvious but unremarkable?

Meyer (2002, 484) hints at this latter possibility when he writes, "the operatic prisons of the late eighteenth and early nineteenth centuries manifest a more broadly disseminated tendency to cast political drama in terms of interpersonal relationships." Meyer cites Lynn Hunt's book *The Family Romance of the French Revolution*, which, while it does not refer to *Fidelio* directly, certainly suggests a strong connection between the opera's political themes and its central story about wifely virtue and heroism. Hunt's thesis is that French writers—particularly novelists—of the late eighteenth century used stories about family relationships to work out their understanding of the changing nature of political power. In particular, mounting distrust of royal authority was reflected in a large number of stories in which the traditional "good father" was almost entirely absent, forcing children to take a much more active and creative role in defining their place in the world (Hunt 1992, xiii). (The Freudian term "family romance" refers to what Freud saw as a widespread tendency to deny one's true parents and replace them with imaginary ones more gratifying to a patient's self-image, usually because they have a higher social standing.)

In a fascinating final chapter, Hunt shows how the family was then rehabilitated in post-revolutionary stories in ways that legitimized the new order while also reflecting crucial changes in the ways that authority and legitimacy were understood:

> Fathers were restored as rightful heads of the family, but only if they were willing to take on new roles as nurturers and guides rather than unfettered tyrants. Women were to confine themselves to motherhood, but motherhood was given greater value, and many questions remained about just what mothers should know. . . . The new forms of social organization did not simply incarnate the power of the father; they instituted a fragile, unstable, constantly shifting equilibrium between the individual and the family. (191)

Significantly for our understanding of *Fidelio*, one of the crucial forms in which that equilibrium was explored during the 1790s was the emerging genre of the melodrama. First appearing as a distinctive form with the abolition of the royal theaters in January 1791, melodrama was at the peak of its popularity when Bouilly's *Léonore* appeared in 1798 (Hunt 1992, 181–183). Although Bouilly's version, unlike Beethoven's opera, did not include a melodrama, it had most of the standard characters of the new genre: "the persecuted innocent, the traitor, the tyrant and the liberator were all stock types taken from the pantomime tradition" out of which the melodrama sprang (Hunt 1992, 183). The chronology is significant because such stories became prominent in the years immediately after the Reign of Terror, when the excesses of rapid, radical political change were fully apparent.

Situated in political and historical context, then, Bouilly's play is a clear, if perhaps partly unconscious, response to contemporary events. Florestan, the man of reason, has no effective father figure to protect him against the arbitrary vengeance of his immediate enemies. It falls to his wife to take on the unaccustomed role of protector and vindicator. In doing so, she of course steps out of her accustomed gender role and literally "wears the pants" for much of the opera. Her actions, however, also affirm the significance of marriage as a force of social stability in whose maintenance wives have an expanded but still limited role. Leonore the revolutionary and Leonore the Biedermeier housewife are, paradoxically, one and the same.

With this understanding, we can draw some intriguing conclusions about the censorship incident and its historical significance. Far from being an arbitrary and external event, it mirrors the "internal" action of the opera with remarkable symmetry. The Viennese police force, which attempted to censor the work, was acting not as a proxy for the state, but, much like Pizarro, as a rogue agent plagued by insecurity about its role. The work's vindicator, who had stood by it from the first, was the wife of the powerful but remote Emperor Francis I, busy carving out for herself a new, if underappreciated, role as a patroness of the arts. The empress admired this story above all others because she no doubt saw in its heroine a character with whom she felt a deep affinity: a woman who exercised her power to influence history through and because of her identity as a wife. Both Marie Therese and Leonore were responding to historically determined ambiguities in their roles as women, and were doing so reconstructively, by affirming the relevance of those roles at a time when traditional authority had been largely discredited.

At the time of the opera's revival the empress was dead, and royal authority—now imperial authority—was well on the way to being legitimized again. It is conventional to read the changes made to the opera's story in 1814 as a bow to this new reality, but it might be more accurate to see them as springing from a common source: the deep desire to see social stability restored on lasting post-revolutionary terms. This desire, which was implicit in Bouilly's original story, had no convincing historical embodiment in 1805—certainly not in the person of Napoleon, who was still a highly destabilizing figure—and so no such embodiment was suggested, either by Bouilly or by Sonnleithner. By 1814 the prominent figure of the benevolent monarch was not simply convenient but was directly conceivable as an object of both conservative and progressive political goals: conservative in that it restored order, but progressive in that it did so, ostensibly at least, on more enlightened terms. Though the historical record in Austria did not immediately bear out these more liberal expectations, they might have seemed highly plausible to Beethoven and Treitschke in 1814. Thus, the "internal" modifications that they made to the story were just as clear a reflection of political reality as was Bouilly's original. By this reading, *Fidelio* in both versions was a political opera both inside and out.

Conclusions

Our examination of this "curious incident," then, has indeed helped to solve a few mysteries about *Fidelio*, its reception, and its political meaning. To summarize:

- The efforts of the Viennese police to censor *Fidelio* in 1805 did not have the backing of the imperial government and collapsed almost immediately when the empress's name was invoked.
- The opera's two themes—those of political liberation and wifely fidelity—were strongly linked at the historical moment when the opera was written.
- Likewise, the external effort at censorship and its failure mirror these internal themes to a surprising extent.
- The changes made to the story of *Fidelio* in 1814 are an accurate reflection of the ways in which popular understanding of the role of authority figures—both in the

family and in society at large—had been changed, and those figures rehabilitated, in the decade since the premiere.
- The political legacy of the Congress of Vienna at least partially vindicates this view of authority. In Austria that legacy led to oppression and increased censorship, but the Congress also provided a bulwark against the darker forces of nationalism that remained in place throughout a century of significant political progress.
- The prevailing later nineteenth-century view of *Fidelio* as an opera about marital fidelity does not cancel its political significance. Rather, it suggests that the opera was understood, at least in part, as a parable about how traditional power relationships can change to fit changing circumstances.

Finally, we can surmise that the re-emergence of *Fidelio* in the twentieth century as an overtly political opera simply reflects the obsolescence of the marital theme, which could no longer be understood in progressive political terms at a time when traditional authoritarian power structures, now incapable of being rehabilitated, were instead being swept away.

Beethoven's reputation as a political progressive has no doubt helped the opera's political theme remain relevant to twentieth- and twenty-first-century audiences. Ironically, however, changing circumstances have made the later version, which is now solidly anchored in the standard repertory, appear less political than its predecessors. As this summary has suggested, it was neither more nor less political; it was simply a reflection of a different political reality. Since the protagonist in this version was vindicated by the state, there was obviously no reason for the state to censor it. It remained for the twentieth century to witness abuses of power that once again cast the state's very legitimacy into doubt. Thus, people in our own time have needed to believe in a censored *Fidelio* that was subversive enough to challenge state power in a fundamental way. That *Fidelio* is largely our creation, not Beethoven's.

References

Allgemeine musikalische Zeitung. 50 vols. Leipzig: Brietkopf und Härtel, 1798–1848. (References to *Fidelio* are catalogued in the index volume).
Biberhofer, Raoul. 1921. "Beethoven und das Theater." In *Ein Wiener Beethoven-Buch*, edited by Alfred Orel, 108–131. Vienna: Gerlach und Wiedling.
Brandenburg, Sieghard, ed. 1996. *Ludwig van Beethoven: Briefwechsel Gesamtausgabe*, Vol. 1. Munich: G. Henle.
Emerson, Donald E. 1968. *Metternich and the Political Police: Security and Subversion in the Hapsburg Monarchy (1815–1830)*. The Hague: Martinus Nijhoff.
Grossman, Jeffrey A. 2000. *The Discourse on Yiddish in Germany: From the Enlightenment to the Second Empire*. Rochester, N.Y.: Camden House.
Hertz, Deborah. 2007. *How Jews Became Germans: The History of Conversion and Assimilation in Berlin*. New Haven, Conn.: Yale University Press.
Hess, Willy. 1986. *Das Fidelio-Buch*. Winterthur, Switzerland: Amadeus.

Hunt, Lynn. 1992. *The Family Romance of the French Revolution*. Berkeley: University of California Press.

Kissinger, Henry A. 1956. "The Congress of Vienna: A Reappraisal." *World Politics* 8, no. 2: 264–280.

Langhorne, Richard. 1986. "Reflections on the Significance of the Congress of Vienna." *Review of International Studies* 12: 313–324.

Lockwood, Lewis. 2006. "Beethoven's *Leonore* and *Fidelio*." *Journal of Interdisciplinary History* 36, no. 3: 473–482.

Meyer, Stephen. 2002. "Terror and Transcendence in the Operatic Prison, 1790–1815." *Journal of the American Musicological Society* 55, no. 3: 477–523.

Nicolson, Harold. 1946. *The Congress of Vienna, a Study in Allied Unity: 1812–1822*. New York: Harcourt, Brace.

Rice, John A. 2003. *Empress Marie Therese and Music at the Viennese Court, 1792–1807*. Cambridge: Cambridge University Press.

Robinson, Paul. 1996. *Ludwig van Beethoven:* Fidelio. Cambridge Opera Handbooks. Cambridge: Cambridge University Press.

Senner, Wayne, Robin Wallace, and William Meredith, eds. 2001. *The Critical Reception of Beethoven's Compositions by His German Contemporaries*, Vol. 2. Translated by Robin Wallace. Lincoln: University of Nebraska Press.

Thayer, Alexander Wheelock. 1967. *Thayer's Life of Beethoven*. Revised and edited by Elliott Forbes. Princeton, N.J.: Princeton University Press.

Thomson, Virgil. 1981. *A Virgil Thomson Reader*. Boston: Houghton Mifflin.

Tusa, Michael C. 2000. "Beethoven's Essay in Opera: Historical, Text-Critical, and Interpretative Issues in *Fidelio*." In *The Cambridge Companion to Beethoven*, edited by Glenn Stanley, 200–217. Cambridge: Cambridge University Press.

III
CENSORSHIP IN TRANSITIONAL GOVERNMENTS

CHAPTER 11

"YEARS IN PRISON"

Giuseppe Verdi and Censorship in Pre-Unification Italy

FRANCESCO IZZO

"YEARS IN PRISON"

ON May 12, 1858, Giuseppe Verdi wrote a letter to his close friend, the Milanese countess Clarina Maffei. He was hardly in the best of moods: "From *Nabucco* onward I haven't had, one can say, an hour of peace. Sixteen years in prison!" (Oberdorfer 1981, 230–231).[1] Few expressions from Verdi's correspondence surface more frequently in biographies and scholarly discussions of the celebrated opera composer than the final words of this passage: "years in prison" (*anni di galera*). And none, perhaps, are as consistently decontextualized and misinterpreted. This expression is often taken to indicate Verdi's growing impatience with a variety of obstacles and restrictions that he had to face during the early years of his career—from tight deadlines to singers' demands. A visitor to the music division of any research library will have no trouble finding biographies of the composer, histories of opera, and histories of music in which entire chapters or sections devoted to the composer are entitled "years in prison." The words are typically used to refer to the period of Verdi's activity between his debut with *Oberto, conte di San Bonifacio* in 1839 and the late 1840s (*Luisa Miller* [1848]) or early 1850s (*Il trovatore* and *La traviata* [1853]). Very few authors take the trouble to mention—let alone explain— that the composer himself had talked about "*sixteen* years in prison" (an important exception is Gossett 2010).

What, then, did Verdi mean by those words? We cannot be entirely sure. An important clue, however, comes from the date of the letter: in May 1858, Verdi was facing severe difficulties with his *Gustavo III*, planned for the Teatro San Carlo in Naples and blocked by the censors. After various modifications, the opera saw the light of day only the following year in Rome as *Un ballo in maschera*. It was an intense and protracted struggle, in which ultimately the composer, as we shall see, had to accept substantial changes to the plot and the text. Against this backdrop, it seems probable that "*anni di galera*" referred specifically to theatrical censorship, which for him had been a prison of sorts, consistently restricting his creative freedom since the time of *Nabucco* (1842).

Most of Giuseppe Verdi's operas up to that point had been composed for Italy, which since the end of the Napoleonic wars and the 1815 Restoration had been politically fragmented into a number of states. The northeastern part of the peninsula, Lombardy-Venetia, was a kingdom under the direct control of the Austrian Empire; the northwest and the island of Sardinia formed the Kingdom of Sardinia, under the house of Savoy; several duchies under Austrian rule occupied portions of the Po valley and all of Tuscany; central Italy was controlled by the Pope; and the Bourbons ruled over the Kingdom of the Two Sicilies, which included the southern part of the peninsula and Sicily. It was only in 1861, two years after the premiere of *Un ballo in maschera*, that—following the defeat of the Austrian Empire in the Second War of Italian Independence—most of these states were annexed to the Kingdom of Sardinia, leading to the formation of the Kingdom of Italy. The political unification of the peninsula was completed in 1870, with the end of the temporal power of the Catholic Church and the annexation of the Papal States to Italy. In this period of Italian history, commonly referred to as the Risorgimento, each state was under absolute rule, with political authorities closely monitoring every aspect of culture and society. To be sure, no freedom of press existed, and artistic expression was routinely subjected to censorship. The theater was the prime site for censorial control: new and old plays and librettos had to obtain official approval prior to reaching the stage. Dramatists and poets who worked for Italian theaters understood the system full well, and often tried to anticipate and avoid potential problems with subject matter, dramatic situations, and verbal expressions that could trigger censorial intervention. Nonetheless, problems often arose. The censors often raised their eyebrows and lowered the nibs of their pens, striking out single words or entire passages, providing comments, and providing alterations. Their responses varied between requests for minor revisions and outright prohibitions. The latter were rare, however. The authorities typically sought to strike a balance between preventing the use of materials that could be deemed offensive or subversive while making sure that theatrical life did not come to a halt. Theatrical texts in nineteenth-century Italy often tell a story of compromise between what was originally intended and what was actually published or performed.

The history of operatic censorship in nineteenth-century Italy concerns first and foremost the texts of librettos. Why then, one might ask, devote a chapter of this handbook to a composer rather than a librettist or the opera libretto in general? Two reasonable answers may be given. First: many of Giuseppe Verdi's operas of the 1840s and 1850s are widely known and can be used as case studies to explore broadly the workings of operatic censorship in pre-unification Italy. Second, and more important: to a greater extent than his predecessors, Giuseppe Verdi exerted considerable control over all aspects of the creation and production of his operas; after his earliest works, he typically chose the subject matter himself, he had specific ideas about how to turn literary sources into operas, and he provided his librettists with detailed instructions; although, like the censors themselves, he aimed to make his operas performable, he became increasingly unyielding during the second decade of his career. By the time he wrote to Clarina Maffei in May 1858 he clearly felt that censorship was not merely an integral factor of the creative process, but a confinement of his creative freedom.

CREATING (AND CENSORING) A NEW OPERA: SUBJECT, WORDS, AND MUSIC

In mid-nineteenth-century Italy, when plans began to unfold for a new opera, one of the preliminary concerns was to choose a subject that would not incur radical censorial opposition. Quite frequently, the impresario submitted to the authorities a summary of the subject prepared by the librettist. It was only after receiving approval (or requests for alterations) that the librettist would draft the poetry, which was then sent to the censors for detailed examination and final approval, normally while the composer worked on the music. For example, the choice of Victor Hugo's play *Hernani* as the subject for Verdi's *Ernani* (1844), his first opera for Venice, was not made lightly. The librettist, Francesco Maria Piave felt that a political plot that included a conspiracy against an absolute monarch, Charles V of Spain, could have caused difficulties (Lavagetto 2010, 26). A decade earlier, Vincenzo Bellini had considered an opera on the same subject, but set it aside for fear that the censors would not allow it, and in 1837 the Milanese censors had prohibited *Hernani* and other works by Hugo.

It was Verdi who persuaded Piave (Conati 1983, 75–79). The young composer's confidence in regard to the subject for *Ernani* is remarkable. Following the astounding success of *Nabucco* and *I lombardi alla prima crociata* (1843), he clearly felt that he could negotiate favorable conditions on various fronts. Indeed, the management of La Fenice in Venice agreed to a substantial fee and allowed Verdi to be involved in the casting. Furthermore, it is possible that the censors were more lenient toward him than they would have been with another composer. According to one of Verdi's early biographers, the previous year the Milanese authorities had turned a blind eye on objections to *I lombardi alla prima crociata* raised by the local archbishop, outraged at the depiction of "processions, churches, the valley of Jehosaphat, a conversion, and a baptism" (Pougin 1881 48). Out of sympathy for the young and brilliant composer, the director of police, Count Carlo Giusto Torresani Lanzfeld, allowed the opera to be performed as it was originally conceived, requiring only that the invocation "Ave Maria" at the beginning of Giselda's prayer in act 1 be changed to the less liturgical "Salve Maria." This change was made at a late stage, and in the autograph manuscript one can see how the word "Ave" in Verdi's hand was changed to "Salve" with the addition of the letters "S" and "l." Whereas we cannot be certain that the authorities in Milan and Venice granted Verdi a preferential treatment, there is ample evidence that in 1849 Verdi's privileged status prompted the Roman censors to permit the inclusion of a problematic religious text in *La battaglia di Legnano* (Giger 1999, 250–251).

Despite his ostensible confidence, several years after *Ernani*, Verdi still seemed somewhat surprised that the Venetian censors had allowed this subject. On April 28, 1850, he wrote to Piave: "I would have another subject that, if the police wanted to allow it, would be one of the greatest realizations of modern theater. Who knows! They allowed *Ernani*, and they might allow this one as well, and here there would be no conspiracies" (Abbiati 1959, 2: 59).[2] Verdi was correct in indicating that this new subject was less problematic than *Ernani* from a political standpoint. But he had good reasons to worry about censorial opposition: as he and Piave began to work on the new project, drawing on another play by Victor Hugo, *Le Roi s'amuse* and provisionally entitled *La maledizione* (The curse), it became clear that changes would have to be made. Verdi plowed ahead, despite worrisome signals sent from the management of La Fenice. On August 24 he wrote to the superintendent, Carlo Marzari: "The doubt that *Le Roi s'amuse* may not be allowed puts me in great difficulty. I was assured by Piave that there were no obstacles to that subject, and I, confiding in the poet, began to study it, to think through it deeply, and in my mind the idea, the *tinta musicale* [musical color] was found" (Lavagetto 2010, 44).[3]

Verdi's reference to *tinta musicale* is of great significance. What emerges from his words is that his musical ideas were intimately connected to the subject of the new opera, and that an alteration of the latter would impact on his musical creativity. The flow from the subject to the poetry and to the music itself appears to be uninterrupted. His words leave little doubt that Verdi was concerned about the possible censorship of *La maledizione* not only because of the subject itself but also because of its musical implications.

The magnitude of the censorial opposition to this opera became fully apparent on November 21, 1850, when the military governor of Venice, Karl von Gorzkowski, ordered to forbid the representation of this subject on the Venetian stage. The words attributed to him in a letter from the Central Direction of Police were harsh to say the least:

> [The Military Governor] deplores that the poet Piave and the celebrated Maestro Verdi could not choose another field in which to display their talents than that of a disgusting immortality and obscene triviality which is the subject of the libretto entitled *La maledizione*. . . . His Excellency has thus chosen to forbid absolutely its performance, and wants that at the same time I advise this Presidency [of La Fenice] that they should abstain from further insistence in this regard.[4] (Lavagetto 2010, 48)

The changes that the authorities required were such that they destroyed the essence of the plot as we know it today: the jester's physical deformity was to be suppressed, the curse was to disappear not only from the title but also from the plot, the king was not to be found in the inn scene, and Gilda's body was not to be placed in a sack. Piave hastened to draft a libretto, entitled *Il duca di Vendome* (the text is published in Lavagetto 2010, 147–179), which transposed the time and place of the action and introduced numerous other changes in accordance with censorial requirements. On December 14, Verdi's reaction, in another important letter to Marzari, was thoroughly negative, and reiterated how the subject and the words were indissolubly connected to his musical thought: "I chose precisely this subject for all of these qualities, and if these original traits are taken away, I can no longer make music for it. If they tell me that my notes can be used also with this drama, I will respond that I do not understand this argument, and I will say frankly that my notes, be they beautiful or ugly, are never written by accident and that I always take care to give them a character" (Cesari and Luzio 1913, 111).[5] It was only by the end of the month that a compromise was reached, leading to the creation of the opera under the title of *Rigoletto*. And one should make no mistake: even after the details of the plot were agreed upon, the authorities continued to scrutinize the text of the opera through the compositional process. One late change to the poetry of the opera occurred at the beginning of act 3, when the Duke arrives at Sparafucile's inn. In the uncensored poetry, the Duke asks Sparafucile for "tua sorella e del vino" (your sister and some wine), still legible in Verdi's autograph manuscript, whereas all printed sources transmit a more veiled request: "una stanza e del vino" (a room and some wine).

It is, in a way, the fine line that separates the idealism from the pragmatism, the artistic rigor from the concreteness that define Verdi's attitude toward censorship during the 1850s. In some of his letters, as we have seen, he appears intransigent, frustrated, or overtly defiant. On January 5, 1851, for example, just as light began to appear at the end of the tunnel for *Rigoletto*, Verdi wrote to his publisher Ricordi in regard to a revival of *Stiffelio*:

> Returning to *Stiffelio*, if one absolutely wanted to perform it, it would be necessary first of all that the censors were persuaded that in that libretto there is nothing against politics or against religion, and that they left the original libretto with all its words and the respective staging; and that [the opera] were performed with no alteration and no castration and with every possible effort on everyone's behalf.[6] (Cesari and Luzio 1913, 112)

To anyone who is even superficially interested in language analysis, the word "castration" will speak volumes. Two years later, on January 1, 1853, his words to his friend De Sanctis suggest that he actually took pleasure in choosing a controversial subject: "For Venice I am doing *La Dame aux camélias*, which will probably be called *La traviata*. A subject of our own age. Another would not have done it because of the costumes, the period, and a thousand other silly scruples. But I am doing it with every pleasure" (Abbiati 1959, 2: 189).[7] Notoriously based on the story of the Parisian courtesan Marie Duplessis (1824–1847) mediated through the novel and play by Alexandre Dumas *fils*, *La Dame aux camélias*, *La traviata* encountered relatively few obstacles in Venice, where for the world premiere the authorities merely demanded that the action be removed from its contemporaneous nineteenth-century setting and transferred to "around 1700." Its poetry, however, was subjected to a number of substantial alterations once it reached different Italian stages (Buia 1990).

It was *Un ballo in maschera*—Verdi's last opera composed for an Italian opera house prior to the unification—that caused by far the greatest difficulties. David Rosen

(1999–2000) has told the story in great detail. The libretto, initially adapted from a French text by Eugène Scribe for Daniel François Esprit Aubert, *Gustave III* (1833), dealt with the true story of the murder of Gustavus III of Sweden at a ball in Stockholm in 1792. With his librettist, Antonio Somma, Verdi worked in earnest on the new opera, then called *Gustavo III*, drafting a great deal of the music. But the Neapolitan authorities stepped in aggressively. As they had done on various occasions during the Risorgimento (for example in 1834 with Donizetti's *Maria Stuarda*), they objected to the onstage representation of the assassination of a sovereign and demanded a change of status for the main character. Furthermore, they called for a change of time and setting for the action, and requested various other alterations to the story. Somma and Verdi readily came up with a new version of the story, now set in seventeenth-century Pomerania and called *Una vendetta in Domino*. This did not satisfy the censors, however, who called for a transposition of the story to fourteenth-century Florence against the backdrop of the conflict between Guelphs and Ghibellines. This version was to be called *Adelia degli Adimari*, but Verdi firmly refused it. A lawsuit ensued, and it is at this point that the composer wrote the letter to Clarina Maffei with which this chapter begins. The contract with Naples was finally cancelled, and Verdi offered *Gustavo III* to Rome. There, too, the censors had their objections, and an agreement was finally reached, involving the notorious transposition of the plot from eighteenth-century Gothenburg to colonial Boston; Gustavus III became the governor of Boston and was nobly assassinated by knife instead of by vile gunshot. The opera finally premiered on February 17, 1859, as *Un ballo in maschera*.

The musical implications of the censorship of *Gustavo III* are particularly complex. There is ample evidence that while negotiations were underway in Naples, Verdi had not only begun to think of *tinta musicale*, but also produced a draft of the entire opera in short score (what Verdi scholars typically call a "continuity draft" [Jensen 2004, 263]). Based on that draft, Philip Gossett has in fact produced a hypothetical reconstruction of *Gustavo III* as it presumably would have been without the intervention of the censors in Naples. The reconstruction is discussed by Gossett (2006, 491–513), and a commercial recording conducted by Maurizio Barbacini is available (Verdi 2003a). Furthermore, in recent times it has become customary to perform *Un ballo in maschera* with the locale moved to eighteenth-century Sweden and the names of the principal male characters changed from Riccardo to Gustavo, and Renato to Anckarström, respectively. This is not the venue to discuss the significance and specific artistic merits of the musical differences between the hypothetical *Gustavo III* and *Un ballo in maschera*. But we should be aware that those differences exist and that, even where we might be persuaded that *Un ballo in maschera* is better thought through, more refined, and, ultimately, a better piece, the thinking, the refinement, and the "improvement" were triggered by the radical act of censorship that took place in Naples. In addition, it is important to realize that in the process, there were musical materials that were lost (for example, an early version of "Eri tu che macchiavi quell'anima," the aria sung by Anckarström/Renato in act 3) or substantially modified (for example, the orchestral prelude that opens the opera, or the ensuing chorus "Posa in pace").

A mere two months after the world premiere of *Un ballo in maschera*, on April 27, 1859, the Second War of Italian Independence broke out in northern Italy. Within a few months, the war resulted in the end of Austrian domination in substantial portions of the Italian peninsula. Lombardy and several duchies were rapidly liberated and annexed by plebiscite to the Kingdom of Sardinia, under the house of Savoy. The process continued with the annexation of Southern Italy in 1860 and the formal foundation of the Kingdom of Italy on March 17, 1861. One of the effects of the liberation and unification was the lifting of censorship. While the process of unification continued through the 1860s, with the annexation of Venetia in 1866, and finally the end of the temporal power of the Roman Church and the annexation of the Papal States in 1870, Verdi fulfilled commissions only for opera houses outside of Italy—*La forza del destino* (1862) for Saint Petersburg, the revision of *Macbeth* (1865) and *Don Carlos* (1867) for Paris, and *Aida* for Cairo (1871). Although *La forza del destino* had to be modified once it reached Rome, where its title changed to *Don Alvaro*, never again did Verdi have to face difficulties of the magnitude he had experienced with *Rigoletto* or *Un ballo in maschera*. His "years in prison" had ended.

Work and Event: After-the-Fact Censorship

Verdi's reactions to censorial intervention during the gestation of several of his pre-unification operas are significant not only as expressions of his stubborn personality, strong creative will, and opposition to authoritarian rulers, but also, more broadly, as indications of how he had come to regard the musical and verbal texts of his operas as fundamentally stable. In other words, his attitude toward censorship is closely connected with his contemporaneous efforts to gain greater authority over all aspects of operatic production, from casting to publication and royalties. This should not lead to rushed conclusions. What we have seen thus far is a composer profoundly convinced that subject matter and poetry have a strong impact on musical choices, but also one who stretched his bargaining power to its limit (to the point, in the case of *Un ballo in maschera*, of changing venue and city when his requirements were not met) but usually reached agreements or compromises with the authorities ensuring the production of his works.

Nonetheless, Verdi knew all too well that while he could try to achieve a good degree of control over the creation of a new opera, the destiny of his works beyond their creation and world premiere was much more difficult to control. Although the letter of January 5, 1851, cited previously expresses the need to perform *Stiffelio* with no alterations, in fact the opera, which deals with the adultery of a protestant minister's wife, was heavily censored during the 1850s: on various occasions it was performed with a radically different plot under the title of *Guglielmo Wellingrode*, and in 1857 Verdi himself ended up reworking the opera into *Aroldo*. It is only in recent times that *Stiffelio* has been recognized an important work (in many ways superior to *Aroldo*), properly restored to its original version, and made available in an excellent critical edition by Kathleen Kuzmick Hansell (Verdi 2003b).

The remake of *Stiffelio* into *Aroldo* demonstrates how Verdi could be eminently practical and choose what he regarded as the lesser of two evils: rather than having his work circulate in heavily altered (castrated, to use his word) versions over which he had no control, he prepared a new performable version himself. The case of *Aroldo* is the most extreme, but not the only one. Several years earlier, he was able to foresee and preempt censorial opposition to his *La battaglia di Legnano*: on September 24, 1848, while he was intent on the composition of this opera, he wrote from Paris to his librettist, Salvadore Cammarano: "I entrust myself to you; in the meantime, keep sending me the libretto you have begun and tell me: in the event that the censors were not to permit it, do you believe that by changing the title, the locale, etc., we'll be able to retain all or most of the poetry?" (Mossa 2001, 51).[8] In order to make sense of this letter and its contrast with the far less obliging attitude of the correspondence concerning *Rigoletto*, one needs to understand the plot and circumstances of *La battaglia di Legnano*. The action unfolds against the backdrop of the 1176 battle in which the Lombard League faced and defeated the army of the Holy Roman Empire led by Frederick Barbarossa, whose rule over Lombardy was thus broken. Such an explicitly patriotic subject had been intended as a celebration of the 1848 revolutions that shook much of Italy and temporarily freed several of its states, including Lombardy-Venetia, of their absolute rulers. Its premiere performance at the Teatro Argentina on January 27, 1849, greeted with great enthusiasm by the audience, was an homage to the independent republic established there by Giuseppe Mazzini. When Verdi wrote to Cammarano in late September, however, it was already clear to him that the Italian revolutions were destined to fail. In Northern Italy, indeed, the situation had already taken a turn for the worse: the Austrian army, after spending several months in a deadlock in the strongholds of the Lombard-Venetian "Quadrilateral" (Peschiera, Verona, Legnago, and Mantua), on July 25 had defeated the Piedmontese army at Custoza, and on August 6 had entered Milan to little resistance. In this scenario, Verdi understood all too well that the opera had practically no chance of circulating undisturbed, and began to think of ways of allowing its circulation beyond the specific occasion of its premiere performance. His prediction was correct, and during the 1850s the opera circulated as *L'assedio di Arlem* (The siege of Harlem), a version that removed the action from twelfth-century Lombardy and placed it in the context of the Spanish-Flemish conflict during the Eighty-Years' War. The opening chorus of the people of Northern Italian cities in *La battaglia di Legnano*, which begins with the cheerful cry "Viva Italia!" (Long live Italy!), became a chorus of Flemish people singing "Viva Olanda!" (Long live Holland!). It was only after the conclusion of the second war of Italian independence that the uncensored version of the opera resurfaced in various Italian cities and that *L'assedio di Arlem* disappeared.

The censorship of *La battaglia di Legnano* was clearly dictated by political factors and is emblematic of the types of concern that informed the decisions of the authorities in the repressive climate after the failed revolutions of 1848–1849. Any reference to patria (homeland) became problematic, especially in association with scenes of oppression and with calls to action. When *Macbeth* was revived in Milan in 1849, for example, the opening words of the chorus of Scottish exiles, "Patria oppressa" (Oppressed homeland) were changed to "Noi perduti" (We are lost), and the cabaletta "La patria tradita" (The betrayed homeland) began with "La fede tradita" (The betrayed faith). And works that, like *La battaglia di Legnano*, depicted Italians of any epoch and region rising against foreign oppressors were met with firm opposition. Such is the case of *Les Vêpres siciliennes*, composed for the Paris Opéra and premiered there in 1855. Eugène Scribe's libretto, which describes the real-life Sicilian rebellion against French occupiers that took place during Easter week in 1282, was bound to raise concerns with the Italian authorities, and Scribe himself, with Verdi's approval, suggested preparing an Italian translation that relocated the action to seventeenth-century Portugal, with the title of *Giovanna de Guzman* (Chusid 1998, 3). In this case, as with *L'assedio di Arlem*, the composer never wrote against the recasting of the libretto. Just as the uncensored *La battaglia di Legnano* took to the stage again after the unification, however, so did *Les Vêpres siciliennes*, which entered the Italian repertoire in a more literal translation, *I vespri siciliani*—with the time, the locale, and indeed the title unchanged.

The practical needs of operatic production, as well as the hectic pace at which Verdi's operas circulated in different Italian states, where the priorities of the authorities could be radically different, meant that the composer had no chance of retaining control over the alterations that were made to his operas. To be sure, those alterations were often made not only without his consent but also without his awareness. Changes were often superficial and involved only the replacement of individual words—such as "*patria*" in the Milanese revival of *Macbeth*—or brief passages of poetry. In Rome, the papal authorities routinely required the replacement of any words or expressions that suggested associations with religion. "*Dio*" (God) was always changed into "*cielo*" (heaven); references to prayer and the liturgy were removed; and Latin words were translated—for instance, the celebrated "*Miserere*" (have mercy) in the final act of *Il trovatore* (1853) became "*Ah pietate*," an Italian expression with the same meaning but without the association to the Latin text of Psalm 51.

In some instances cuts were deemed necessary, and this affected the music as well as the drama: Giselda's prayer to the Virgin in *I lombardi alla prima crociata* was sometimes omitted (Izzo 2007, 580), and when *I masnadieri* (1847) reached the Papal States, the ecclesiastical authorities suppressed an entire scene in the final act, in which a protestant priest, Moser, confronts the villain, Francesco, on religious matters involving divine punishment and forgiveness (Verdi 2000, liii).

But in some instances, the changes were pervasive, affecting not only passages of the poetry but also the locale, character names, and often the whole plot. The recasting of *Stiffelio* into *Guglielmo Wellingrode* mentioned previously (discussed in detail in Dionisi Ascari 1987) is a case in point. The action shifted from the early 1800s to the beginning of the fifteenth century, and the protagonist changed from Stiffelio, a Protestant preacher, into Guglielmo, the prime minister of a German prince, thus eliminating the religious thread from the plot. Even more remarkable are the remakes of the libretto for *Rigoletto* that circulated during the 1850s. As we have seen, the transposition of the plot of *Le Roi s'amuse* to Mantua, with the King transformed into a duke, had appeased the Venetian authorities. But when the opera began to circulate, various other issues arose. Aside from minor alterations that appear in virtually every libretto printed for performances across the Italian peninsula, three versions had different titles and new locations and times: in Rome in the fall 1851, the opera was given as *Viscardello*, set in Boston; at the Teatro Nuovo in Naples in 1853 it appeared as *La figlia di Perth*, its plot loosely based on Walter Scott's *The Fair Maid of Perth*; and in 1855, again in Naples but at the Teatro San Carlo, it was staged as *Lionello*, set in Verona. The latter two versions were prepared by Emanuele Bardare, who had worked on the libretto for *Il trovatore* after the death of Salvadore Cammarano. The countless alterations that appear in these versions have been discussed in various studies (in particular Chusid 1998 and Lavagetto 2010). A close reading of selected passages from *Viscardello*, however, reveals all the transformative power of censorship, showing the extent to which a plot could be disfigured without changing its overall structure and, therefore, without altering the music. (The original poetry and translations are quoted or abridged from Verdi 1977. The passages from *Viscardello* are cited from Verdi n.d.)

One can well imagine that the moral issues that emerge from the original plot of *Rigoletto* would have worried the ecclesiastical authorities of the Papal States, beginning with the unashamed misogyny and apology for infidelity in two of the Duke's arias, "Questa o quella per me pari sono" in act 1 and, famously, "La donna è mobile" at the beginning of act 3. In "Questa o quella," the Duke famously spells out his quintessential libertinism:

Questa o quella per me pari sono	For me, this woman or that is the same
A quant'altre d'intorno mi vedo;	As the many others I see around me;
Del mio core l'impero non cedo	I don't surrender the rule of my heart
Meglio ad una che ad altra beltà.	More easily to one beauty than to another.
La costoro avvenenza è tal dono	Their loveliness is like a gift
Di che il fato ne infiora la vita;	With which fate bedecks life;
S'oggi questa mi torna gradita,	If today this woman pleases me,
Forse un'altra doman lo sarà.	Perhaps tomorrow it will be another.
La costanza, tiranna del core,	Fidelity, the tyrant of the heart,
Detestiamo qual morbo crudele,	We detest, like a cruel disease,
Sol chi vuole si serbi fedele,	Let only those who wish remain faithful;
Non v'ha amor, se non v'è libertà.	There is no love, if there is no freedom.
De' mariti il geloso furore,	I deride the jealous fury of husbands,
Degli amanti le smanie derido;	And the ravings of lovers;
Anco d'Argo i cent'occhi disfido	I defy even Argus's hundred eyes
Se mi punge una qualche beltà.	When some beauty tickles me.

The message is altogether different in *Viscardello*. The Duke (who now, incidentally, rules over Nottingham, not Mantua) is in love with one woman whom he intends to marry, and that explains his indifference to other women. Although he is believed to be unfaithful, he is in fact true to his love. He may be a man "di tempra vivace e leggera" (with a lively and light temper), but he clearly means no harm:

Questa o quella per me pari sono	For me, this woman or that is the same
A quant'altre d'intorno mi vedo;	As the many others I see around me;
Del mio core l'impero sol cedo	I only surrender the rule of my heart
Non ad esse ma ad altra beltà.	Not to them, but to another beauty.
La costoro avvenenza è tal dono	Their loveliness is like a gift
Che di molti fa lieta la vita;	Which makes happy the life of many;
Ma sol una mi torna gradita,	But only one woman pleases me,
Lei sol amo e mia sposa sarà.	I love only her and she will be my bride.
Altri i dolci misteri del core,	Let others unravel and detest the heart's
Schiuda e sprezzi qual morbo crudele,	Mysteries, like a cruel disease,
Mentre ognuno mi stima infedele,	While everyone believes me unfaithful,
Io mi piaccio serbar fedeltà.	I like to keep my fidelity.
Degli amanti il geloso furore,	I deride the jealous fury of lovers,
Degli amanti le smanie derido;	And the ravings of lovers;
Ch'io ben d'Argo i cent'occhi disfido	I defy even Argus's hundred eyes
Se mi accende una pura beltà.	When a pure beauty ignites me.

"La donna è mobile," too, changes radically. The original text reads as follows:

La donna è mobile	Woman is fickle
Qual piuma al vento,	Like a feather in the wind,
Muta d'accento	She changes her words
E di pensiero.	And her thoughts.
Sempre un amabile	Always a lovable
Leggiadro viso,	And pretty face,
In pianto o in riso,	Weeping or laughing,
È menzognero.	Is lying.
È sempre misero	The man's always wretched
Chi a lei s'affida,	Who believes in her,
Chi le confida	Who recklessly entrusts
Mal cauto il core!	His heart to her!
Pur mai non sentesi	And yet one who never
Felice appieno	Drinks love on that breast
Chi su quel seno	Never feels
Non liba amore!	Entirely happy!

In *Viscardello*, again, the Duke detaches himself from the concepts of the initial lines of the poetry. Not all women are fickle, and a beautiful woman is "often" (i.e., not "always") lying. The final four lines change radically: the sensual image of a man drinking love on a woman's breast disappears, replaced by the more spiritual concept of happiness that can only be achieved trough the "faith and love" of a woman:

La donna è mobile	Woman is fickle
Qual piuma al vento,	Like a feather in the wind,
Muta d'accento	She changes her words
E di pensier.	And her thoughts.
Spesso un amabile	Often a lovable
Leggiadro viso,	And pretty face,
In pianto o in riso,	Weeping or laughing,
È menzogner.	Is lying.
È spesso misero	The man's often wretched
Chi a lei s'affida,	Who believes in her,
Chi le confida	Who recklessly entrusts
Mal cauto il cor!	His heart to her!
Pure di vivere	And yet one
Lieto sol crede	Can only live happily
Chi da lei chiede	If he asks of her
Fede [ed] amor.	Faith and love.

With the Duke now an example of moral rectitude, the appearance of Monterone loses much of its dramatic power. And, as mentioned previously, a curse was off limits on the Roman stage. The original words in Piave's libretto are among the most powerful in the entire opera (which originally, let's not forget, was to be entitled *La maledizione*):

Rigoletto (*al Duca contraffacendo la voce di Monterone*)	**Rigoletto** (*to the Duke, imitating the voice of Monterone*)
Ch'io gli parli.	Let me speak to him.
(*Si avanza con ridicola gravità.*)	(*He comes forward with mock gravity.*)
Voi congiuraste contro noi, signore;	You plotted against us, Sir.
E noi, clementi in vero, perdonammo...	And we, truly clement, forgave you...
Qual vi piglia or delirio, a tutte l'ore	What folly now seizes you, to make you
Di vostra figliaa reclamar l'onore?	Complain at all hours about your daughter's honor?
Monterone (*guardando Rigoletto con ira sprezzante*)	**Monterone** (*looking at Rigoletto, with contemptuous wrath*)
Novello insulto! Ah sì, a turbare,	A new affront! Ah yes, I'll come
Sarò vostr'orgie... verrò a gridare	To disturb your orgies... I'll come to shout
Fino a che vegga restarsi inulto	As long as I see the terrible insult
Di mia famiglia l'atroce insulto;	To my family remain unavenged;
E se al carnefice pur mi darete.	And even if you give me to the executioner,
Spettro terribile mi rivedrete,	You'll see me again, a terrible specter,
Portante in mano il teschio mio,	Carrying my own skull in my hand,
Vendetta a chiedereal mondo, a Dio.	To ask vengeance of the world, of God!

Duca	**Duke**
Non più, arrestatelo.	No more, arrest him!
Rigoletto	**Rigoletto**
È matto!	He's mad!
Borsa, Marullo, Ceprano	**Borsa, Marullo, and Ceprano**
Quai detti!	What words!
Monterone (*al Duca e Rigoletto*)	**Monterone** (*to the Duke and Rigoletto*)
Ah, siate entrambi voi maledetti!	Ah, may you both be cursed!
Slanciare il cane a leon morente	To unleash the dog on a dying lion
È vile, o Duca...	Is cowardly, o Duke...
(*a Rigoletto*)	(*to Rigoletto*)
E tu, serpente,	And you, serpent,
Tu che d'un padre ridi al dolore,	Who laugh at a father's grief,
Sii maledetto!	Be cursed!
Rigoletto (*da sè, colpito*)	**Rigoletto** (*to himself, stricken*)
(Che sento, orrore!)	(What do I hear? Oh, horror!)

In *Viscardello*, Monterone (renamed the Count of Mornand) is annoyed that the Duke has withdrawn the marriage promise made to his daughter, but there is no indication that the young woman has been dishonored: "*onore*" (honor) is replaced by "*dritto*" (right). The good Duke, of course, hosts not orgies but dances, "God" becomes "heaven," and uncomfortable references to incarceration and an executioner are removed:

Viscardello (*al Duca contraffacendo la voce di Mornand*)	**Viscardello** (*to the Duke, imitating the voice of Monterone*)
Ch'io gli parli.	Let me speak to him.
(*Si avanza con comica gravità.*)	(*He comes forward with mock gravity.*)
Voi pur sorgeste contro noi, signore,	You rose against us, Sir,
E noi, clementi in vero, abbiam taciuto...	And we, truly clement, remained silent...
Qual vi piglia or delirio, in suon d'afflitto	What folly now seizes you, with a plaintive
Di vostra figlia reclamar il dritto?	Sound, to reclaim your daughter's right?
Mornand (*guardando Viscardello con ira sprezzante*)	**Mornand** (*looking at Viscardello, with contemptuous wrath*)
Novello insulto! Ah sì, a turbare	A new affront! Ah yes, I'll come
Sarò le danze... verrò a gridare	To disturb your dances... I'll come to shout
Che alla mia figlia il senno invola	For your false wedding promise
D'imen la vostra falsa parola;	Is taking my daughter's sanity away;
E fossi in polvere pur io cangiato,	And even if you turn me to dust,
Spettro terribile vi sarò allato,	I'll be at your side, a terrible specter,
Chiedente ognora con labbro anelo	Asking at all times with ardent lips,
Un fulmin vindice al mondo e al cielo.	A vengeful thunderbolt of the world and heaven!

Duca	**Duke**
Non più, scacciatelo.	No more, chase him away!
Viscardello	**Viscardello**
È matto!	He's mad!
Coro	**Coro**
Quai detti!	What words!
Mornand	**Mornand**
Sì, per voi pena dal ciel s'aspetti!	Yes, let us await your punishment from heaven!
Slanciare il cane a lion morente	To unleash the dog on a dying lion
È vile, o Duca...e tu, serpente,	Is cowardly, o Duke... And you, serpent,
Tu che d'un padre ridi al dolore,	Who laugh at a father's grief,
Trema, s'hai figli!	Be cursed!
Viscardello	**Viscardello**
Che sento, orrore!	What do I hear? Oh, horror!

Other characters, too, change radically. Sparafucile, who in *Rigoletto* is an assassin who kills in exchange for financial remuneration, in *Viscardello* holds personal resentment against the Duke, and for this reason is already planning to kill him. No money changes hands between him and Viscardello. Sparafucile's sister, Maddalena, also becomes perfectly respectable. She happens to be the woman with whom the Duke has been in love all along, and when the two meet onstage in act 3, the latter addresses her as a "gentile vergine" (gentle virgin). And other details are changed throughout the libretto. One particularly amusing example is the reference to Gilda and the Duke's first encounters in church. It does not surprise that for the Roman censors the church was no place for romantic encounters, and in *Viscardello* Gilda reminisces: "Tacqui che un giovin / Ne seguiva al parco" (I didn't say that a young man followed us to the park).

Viscardello is indeed a text that will upset those who are familiar with the opera and who see a great deal of its dramatic strength fade before their eyes. Verdi was not amused, as he indicated to his publisher, Ricordi, in a letter of October 11, 1851:

> In Rome too, *Rigoletto* went to the devil! With the alterations and mutilations that have been made it is impossible to obtain any success. The public wants interesting [subject matter]. The authors do everything possible to find it. If the censors take it away *Rigoletto* is no longer my work. With different words, with different locales, I would not have made the music of *Rigoletto*. On the playbill in Rome they should have said: "*Rigoletto*, poetry and music by Don..." and here the Censor's name..."[9] (Lavagetto 2010, 75)

Yet, as an exercise in rhetoric, it is admirable in its own right. The attention to detail with which the censors altered a large percentage of the poetry, without affecting verse lengths and other aspects that would have required substantial musical emendations, is indeed striking, and Verdi is certainly correct in attributing them at least some degree of authorship.

Rigoletto was not the last opera whose plot and title changed in censored versions not sanctioned by Verdi. In 1854, *La traviata* began to circulate under the title of *Violetta*,

VIOLETTA

Libretto di Francesco Maria Piave

MUSICA DEL MAESTRO CAV.

GIUSEPPE VERDI

Officiale della Legion d'Onore

MILANO
DALL' I. R. STABILIMENTO NAZIONALE PRIVILEGIATO DI
TITO DI GIO. RICORDI

FIGURE 11.1 Title page for La traviata under the censored title of VIoletta (Ricordi edition).

with productions at Florence, Rome, and Naples. The word "traviata," along with the subject matter, had to be eliminated due to moral concerns. In this version, still printed by Ricordi with Francesco Maria Piave's name on the title page (Figure 11.1), the heroine intones her cabaletta at the end of act 1 not to the well-known incipit "Sempre libera"

DON ALVARO

LIBRETTO IN QUATTRO ATTI

DI F. M. PIAVE

PER MUSICA

DEL MAESTRO CAVALIERE

GIUSEPPE VERDI

UFFICIALE DELLA LEGION D'ONORE

EC. EC.

DA RAPPRESENTARSI

NEL NOBIL TEATRO DI APOLLO

LA STAGIONE DI CARNEVALE 1862 IN 63.

ROMA

Tip. di G. Olivieri al Corso 336

con permesso

FIGURE 11.2 Title page for La forza del destino under the censored title of Don Alvaro (Rome 1862).

(forever free) but to "Innocente ognor" (forever innocent), and in her act 3 aria she refers to herself not as "traviata," but as "afflitta." And as late as 1862, when most of Italy was already independent and unified and Verdi's years in prison had effectively ended, in Rome the first version of *La forza del destino* had to be given as *Don Alvaro* (Figure 11.2). Once more, the censors wiped out the wealth of religious imagery that filled the opera, along with numerous details that they deemed morally offensive. As we have seen, the composer at that point had been feeling for a long time that when his operas underwent such pervasive changes under the strokes of the censor's pen they were no longer his "work." The "event" of individual productions in many cases took precedence, however, and in that crucial phase of Italian history, Verdi's music was known and loved also thanks to those texts, which were "mutilated" and "castrated" but immensely fascinating for the opera lover and historian, shedding light retrospectively on what Verdi and his librettists sought to achieve as artists, and the forces they reckoned with.

Conclusion

In recent decades, textual research conducted in conjunction with the critical edition of Verdi's operas, an ongoing joint effort by Ricordi and the University of Chicago Press, has unearthed an abundance of evidence concerning the working of censorship. A great deal has been done to return the texts of many operas to what the composer and his librettists had originally intended. As mentioned previously, before "La donna è mobile" we now often (albeit not always) hear the Duke sing the correct words, "Tua sorella e del vino." And in the past few years it has become possible to hear Joan of Arc pray to the Virgin Mary, rather than to a vague supernatural entity, "speme del mondo" (hope of the world), in her entrance aria in *Govanna d'Arco* (1845) (Verdi 2007). Furthermore, thanks to the pivotal work of Andreas Giger, we know who Verdi's censors in Rome were and what they sought to achieve (Giger 1999; Giger 2010). And it is becoming increasingly possible today to read librettos, as it were, through the eyes of mid-nineteenth-century censors, and to determine inductively or deductively how they may have intervened on texts for which we only have the final product.

I have argued at the beginning that Giuseppe Verdi's thorough involvement in the creative process of his works makes him a central figure in the discourse on censorship in pre-unification Italy. His attitude toward, and relationship with, censorship in pre-unification Italy, however, is both unique and highly representative of broader trends. We must bear in mind that operas by composers who dominated the world of Italian opera before Verdi, including Vincenzo Bellini and Gaetano Donizetti, had had their share of difficulties. And there is no reason to believe that the censors of the 1840s and 1850s kept a closer eye on Verdi than they did on his contemporaries. Just at the outset of Verdi's career, for example, a seemingly innocuous comic work, Donizetti's *La Fille du régiment* (1840), was significantly altered once it reached the Italian stage in order to avoid depicting the military invasion of a territory of the Austrian empire (Izzo 2004).

It would be wrong to assume that the composer carried the burden by himself. It is clear from his exchanges with poets and impresarios that other parties with a vested interest in the production of a new opera had much to be concerned about when it came to their relations with the authorities. And it would be wrong to assume that Verdi was the only one who sought to express himself freely in a repressive climate. In 1860, as soon as it became viable to comment publicly on the censorial practices of pre-unification Italy, the critic Francesco Regli did so in regard to Temistocle Solera, the librettist of choice of Verdi's early years: "Solera, even under the pressure of censorship, always wrote as an Italian, and in every opera of his the patriotic element dominates in the first degree"[10] (Regli 1860, 504).

Above all, the examples discussed in this chapter shed light on the negotiations with the authorities that took place before and during the actual production of a new work, and the remarkable alterations that could be made after the score had left Verdi's desk. On those alterations, Verdi had little or no jurisdiction. He spoke out, sometimes vehemently, in his letters, but the show had to go on. And on it went—despite the censors, but also, to a point, because of them. Censorship is not to be viewed merely as repression, but also as process, and this perspective informs the discussion in these pages. The shared objective for artists and authorities was to allow all operas, new or otherwise, to reach the stage in a variety of contexts and climates.

Notes

1. "Dal Nabucco in poi non ho avuto, si può dire, un'ora di quiete. Sedici anni di galera!"
2. "Avrei un altro soggetto che se la polizia volesse permettere sarebbe una delle più grandi realizzazioni del teatro moderno. Chi sa! Hanno permesso l'*Ernani* potrebbe permettere anche questo, e qui non ci sarebbero congiure."
3. "Il dubbio che *Le Roi s'amuse* non si permetta mi mette in grave imbarazzo. Fui assicurato da Piave che non eravi ostacolo per quel sogetto, ed io fidando nel suo poeta, mi misi a studiarlo, a meditarlo profondamente e l'idea, la tinta musicale erano nella mia mente trovate."
4. "[Il governatore militare] deplora che il poeta Piave ed il celebre Maestro Verdi non abbiano saputo scegliere altro campo per far emergere i loro talenti che quello di una ributtante immo'ralità ed oscena trivialità qual è l'argomento del libretto intitolato *La Maledizione* [...] Eccellenza sua ha quindi trovato di vietarne assolutamente la rappresentazione, e vuole che in pari tempo io renda avvertita codesta Presidenza di astenersi da ogni ulteriore insistenza in proposito."
5. "Scelsi appunto questo sogetto per tutte queste qualità, e questi tratti originali, se si tolgono, io non posso più farvi musica. Se mi si dirà che le mie note possono stare anche con questo dramma, io rispondo che non comprendo queste ragioni, e dico francamente che le mie note o belle o brutte che siano non le scrivo mai a caso e che procuro sempre di darvi un carattere."
6. "Tornando a *Stiffelio*, se si vuole assolutamente eseguire bisognerebbe prima di tutto che la Censura si persuadesse che nulla avvi in quel libro nè contro la politica nè contro la religione, e lasciasse il libretto originale con tutte le parole e la *mise en scene* rispettiva; che si eseguisse senza nessuna alterazione nè castrazione e con tutto l'impegno possibile per parte di tutti."

7. "A Venezia faccio *La Dame aux camelias* che avrà per titolo, forse, *Traviata*. Un sogeto [*sic*] dell'epoca. Un altro forse non l'avrebbe fatto per i costumi, pei tempi, e per mille altri goffi scrupoli... Io lo faccio con tutto il piacere."
8. "Mi raccomando a voi; intanto continuate a mandarmi il dramma incominciato e ditemi: caso mai le Censure nol permettessero credete voi che si potrà cambiando titolo, località etc.... ritenere tutta o quasi tutta la verseggiatura?"
9. "Anche a Roma *Rigoletto* è andato al diavolo! Colle alterazioni e mutilazioni ridicole che si sono fatte è impossibile qualunque esito. Il pubblico vuole interesse: gli autori fanno il possibile per trovarne: se i censori lo levano il *Rigoletto* non è più opera mia. Con altre parole, con altre posizioni, io non avrei fatto la musica del *Rigoletto*.—Nel Manifesto a Roma doveva dirsi: "*Rigoletto, poesia e musica di Don* ..." e qui il nome del Censore..."
10. "Il Solera, anche sotto la pressione della Censura, scrisse sempre italianamente, ed in ogni suo melodramma domina in primo grado l'elemento patrio."

References

Abbiati, Franco. 1959. *Giuseppe Verdi*. 4 vols. Milan: Ricordi.

Antolini, Bianca Maria, Arnaldo Morelli, and Vera Vita Spagnuolo, eds. 1994. *La musica a Roma attraverso le fonti d'archivio: Atti del convegno internazionale Roma 4–7 giugno 1992*. Lucca, Italy: LIM.

Banti, Alberto M. 2000. *La nazione del Risorgimento: Parentela, santità e onore alle origini dell'Italia unita*. Turin: Einaudi.

Black, John. 1984. "Code of Instructions for the Censorship of Theatrical Works: Naples 1849." *Journal of the Donizetti Society* 5: 147–150.

Buia, Anna. 1990. *Un così eroico amore: Genesi e diffusione censurata del libretto de 'La Traviata.'* Milan: Associazione Amici della Scala.

Calzolari, Monica. 1994. "La censura nella Roma pontificia dell'Ottocento: Il ruolo predominante della Direzione Generale di Polizia." In *La musica a Roma attraverso le fonti d'archivio: Atti del convegno internazionale Roma 4–7 giugno 1992*, edited by Bianca Maria Antolini, Arnaldo Morelli, and Vera Vita Spagnuolo, 287–298. Lucca, Italy: LIM.

Cataldi, Renata. 1994. "La censura sugli spettacoli nella Roma pontificia dell'Ottocento: Le licenze del cardinal vicario." In *La musica a Roma attraverso le fonti d'archivio: Atti del convegno internazionale Roma 4–7 giugno 1992*, edited by Bianca Maria Antolini, Arnaldo Morelli, and Vera Vita Spagnuolo, 299–320. Lucca, Italy: LIM.

Cesari, Gaetano, and Alessandro Luzio, eds. 1913. *I copialettere di Giuseppe Verdi*. Milan: n.p.

Chusid, Martin. 1998. "On Censored Performances of *Les vêpres siciliennes* and *Rigoletto*: Evidence from the Verdi Archive at New York University." *Verdi Newsletter* 25: 3–19.

Commons, Jeremy. 1983. "Un contributo ad uno studio su Donizetti e la censura napoletana." In *Atti del 1º Convegno Internazionale Donizettiano*, edited by Pieralberto Cattaneo. 2 vols. 1: 65–106. Bergamo, Italy: Azienda Autonomo di Turismo.

Conati, Marcello. 1983. *La bottega della musica: Verdi e La Fenice*. Milan: Il Saggiatore.

Degrada, Francesco. 1984. "A Note on Censorship." In *Verdi's "Macbeth": A Sourcebook*, edited by David Rosen and Andrew Porter, 56–58. New York: W.W. Norton.

Di Stefano, Carlo. 1964. *La censura teatrale in Italia*. Rocca San Casciano, Italy: Cappelli.

Dionisi Ascari, Diana. 1987. "Da *Stiffelio* a *Guglielmo Wellingrode*: gli interventi della censura." In *Tornando a Stiffelio*, edited by Giovanni Morelli, 129–139. Florence: Olschki.
Fairtile, Linda B. 1997. "Censorship in Verdi's *Attila*: Two Case Studies." *Verdi Newsletter* 24: 5–7.
Fubini, Mario. 1971. "Un mito del Risorgimento: La Lega lombarda." In *Romanticismo italiano: Saggi di storia della critica e della letteratura*, 157–188. Bari, Italy: Edizioni Laterza.
Fulcher, Jane. 1987. *The Nation's Image: French Grand Opera as Politics and Politicized Art*. Cambridge: Cambridge University Press.
Giger, Andreas. 1999. "Social Control and the Censorship of Giuseppe Verdi's Operas in Rome (1844–1859)." *Cambridge Opera Journal* 11, no. 3: 233–265.
Giger, Andreas. 2010. "Behind the Police Chief's Closed Doors: The Unofficial Censors of Verdi in Rome." *Nineteenth-Century Music Review* 7, no. 2: 63–99.
Gossett, Philip. 1990a. "Becoming a Citizen: The Chorus in *Risorgimento* Opera." *Cambridge Opera Journal* 2, no. 1: 41–64.
Gossett, Philip. 1990b. "Censorship and Self-Censorship: Problems in Editing the Operas of Giuseppe Verdi." In *Essays in Musicology: A Tribute to Alvin Johnson*, edited by Lewis Lockwood and Edward Roesner, 247–257. Philadelphia: American Musicological Society.
Gossett, Philip. 2005. "Le 'edizioni distrutte' e il significato dei cori operistici nel Risorgimento." *Saggiatore musicale* 12: 339–387. Translated into English as "'Edizioni distrutte' and the Significance of Operatic Choruses during the Risorgimento." In Victoria Johnson, Jane F. Fulcher, and Thomas Ertman, eds. *Opera and Society in Italy and France from Monteverdi to Bourdieu*, 181–242. Cambridge: Cambridge University Press, 2007.
Gossett, Philip. 2006. *Divas and Scholars: Performing Italian Opera*. Chicago: University of Chicago Press.
Grantaliano, Elvira. 1994. "La censura nella Roma pontificia dell'ottocento: Tipologie ed esempi." In *La musica a Roma attraverso le fonti d'archivio: Atti del convegno internazionale Roma 4–7 giugno 1992*, edited by Bianca Maria Antolini, Arnaldo Morelli, and Vera Vita Spagnuolo, 321–336
Ipson, Douglas Leon. 2011. "'Giuriamo per la patria': The Operatic Oath Scene in Revolutionary Rome, 1846–1849." Ph.D. diss., University of Chicago.
Izzo, Francesco. 2004. "Comedy between Two Revolutions: Opera Buffa and the Risorgimento, 1831–1848." *Journal of Musicology* 21, no. 1: 127–174.
Izzo, Francesco. 2007. "Verdi, the Virgin, and the Censor: The Politics of the Cult of Mary in *I Lombardi alla prima Crociata* and *Giovanna d'Arco*." *Journal of the American Musicological Society* 60, no. 3: 557–597.
Jensen, Luke. 2004. "An Introduction to Verdi's Working Methods." In *The Cambridge Companion to Verdi*, edited by Scott L. Balthazar, 257–268. Cambridge, UK: Cambridge University Press.
Jones, Derek. 2001. *Censorship: A World Encyclopedia*. 4 vols. London: Routledge.
Kimbell, David R.B. 1981. *Verdi in the Age of Italian Romanticism*. Cambridge: Cambridge University Press.
Lavagetto, Mario. 2010. *Un caso di censura: Il "Rigoletto."* 2nd ed. Milan: Bruno Mondadori.
Marvin, Roberta M. 2001. "The Censorship of Verdi's Operas in Victorian London." *Music and Letters* 82, no. 4: 582–610.
Mossa, Carlo Matteo, ed. 2001. *Carteggio Verdi-Cammarano (1843–1852)*. Parma, Italy: Istituto Nazionale di Studi Verdiani.
Mugayar Kuhl, Pablo. 1998. "Censura y autocensura: G. Martinelli y la ópera en Portugal en el siglo XVIII." In *La abolición del arte*, edited by Alberto Dallal, 317–337. Mexico City: Universidad Nacional Autónoma de México (Instituto de Investigaciones Estéticas).

Oberdorfer, Aldo. 1981. *Giuseppe Verdi: Autobiografia dalle lettere*. 3rd rev. ed., with annotations and additions by Marcello Conati. Milan: Rizzoli.

Ponzo, Giovanni. 1980. *Le origini della libertà di stampa in Italia (1846–1852)*. Rome: Giuffré Editore.

Pougin, Arthur. 1881. *Giuseppe Verdi: Vita aneddotica*. With notes and additions by Folchetto [Giacomo Caponi]. Milan: Ricordi.

Regli, Francesco. *Dizionario biografico dei più celebri poeti ed artisti melodrammatici . . . che fiorirono in italia dal 1800 al 1860*. Turin: Enrico Dalmazzo.

Rizzuti, Alberto. 2001. "Music for a Risorgimento Myth: Joan of Arc 1789–1849." Ph.D. diss., University of Chicago.

Rosen, David B. 2007. "'Si ridesti il leon di Castiglia la fiamma sopita': Ricordi's Censored Libretto of *Ernani* and Some Vicissitudes of the Conspiracy Scene." *Verdi Forum* 34: 9–27.

Rosen, David B. 1999–2000. "A Tale of Five Cities: The Peregrinations of Somma's and Verdi's Gustavo III (*and Una vendetta in dominò and Un ballo in maschera*) at the Hands of the Neapolitan and Roman Censorship." *Verdi Forum* 26–27: 53–66.

Rosselli, John. 1984. *The Opera Industry in Italy from Cimarosa to Verdi: The Role of the Impresario*. Cambridge: Cambridge University Press.

Rubsamen, Walter H. 1946. "Political and Ideological Censorship of Opera." *Papers of the American Musicological Society*, edited by Otto Kinkeldey and Gustave Reese, 30–42. Philadelphia: American Musicological Society.

[Ruffini, Giovanni]. 1853. *Lorenzo Benoni, or Passages in the Life of an Italian*. Edinburgh: Th. Constable & Co.

Verdi, Giuseppe. n.d. *Viscardello: Melodramma in tre atti*. Milan: Ricordi.

Verdi, Giuseppe. 1977. *Seven Verdi Librettos*. Translated by William Weaver. New York: W.W. Norton.

Verdi, Giuseppe. 1983. *Rigoletto*. Critical edition by Martin Chusid. The Works of Giuseppe Verdi [WGV]. Series I: 17. Chicago and Milan: University of Chicago Press and Ricordi.

Verdi, Giuseppe. 2000. *I masnadieri*. Critical edition by Roberta Montemorra Marvin. The Works of Giuseppe Verdi [WGV]. Series I: 11. Chicago and Milan: University of Chicago Press and Ricordi.

Verdi, Giuseppe. 2003a. *Gustavo III*. CD Recording. Hypothetical reconstruction by Philip Gossett. Conducted by Maurizio Barbacini. Genoa: Dynamic.

Verdi, Giuseppe. 2003b. *Stiffelio*. Critical edition by Kathleen Kuzmick Hansell. The Works of Giuseppe Verdi [WGV]. Series I: 16. Chicago and Milan: University of Chicago Press and Ricordi.

Verdi, Giuseppe. 2007. *Giovanna d'Arco*. Critical edition by Alberto Rizzuti. The Works of Giuseppe Verdi [WGV]. Series I: 7. Chicago and Milan: University of Chicago Press and Ricordi.

Werr, Sebastian. 2008. "'Tutta immorale, ed orrenda': Hugo, Romani, Donizetti e la censura italiana." In *D'une scène à l'autre. L'opéra italien en Europe*, edited by Damien Colas and Alessandro di Profio, 273–278. Liège, Belgium: Mardaga.

CHAPTER 12

MICRONARRATIVES OF MUSIC AND (SELF-) CENSORSHIP IN SOCIALIST YUGOSLAVIA

ANA HOFMANN

> Yes, that's me! I banned "Juga"! It could have been the editor himself, but he consulted me. This time it's my personal taste and attitude. I prohibited the song and because of that I am responsible. I would allow Silvana with any other song, but with this one—no![1]

THIS chapter engages with the issue of music censorship in socialist Yugoslavia. It attempts to highlight the complexity of censorial practices, drawing on new academic writings that move away from reducing and simplifying the concept of censorship to restrictive technology and move toward understanding the complexity of this category (Jansen 1991; Holquist 1994; Burt 1994; Butler 1998; Müller 2003). The "new censorship" debate challenges the common understanding of censorship as a set of regulatory and institutionalized interventions and, instead, treats it as a complex of intellectual practices within a particular social-historical context (Boyer 2003, 539). Critical approaches interrogate the binary relation between the "the censor" and "the censored," challenge their fixed positions, and recognize a variety of different agents involved in censorial activities rather than a single institution or authority. They also challenge the censorship/free-speech binary, successfully showing that all cultural products are generated by processes of regulation and selection (Fish 1994).

The binary discourse of repression versus freedom is best reflected in the scholarly accounts on censorship in "totalitarian," "closed" state-socialist societies. After the fall of socialism in Eastern Europe, official records and archival materials became available throughout the region, spurring increased interest in censorial practices among both scholars and the wider public (Müller 2003, 3). The censorship mechanisms of the "newly democratized" countries were widely discussed from the oppression-liberation perspective, attaching to censorship an a priori negative and pejorative meaning. Focusing on state regulatory practices, the studies explored official records and described censorial institutions, regulations, and practices. This focus went along with theorizing Eastern European cultural production as rigidly imposed and controlled by the state or as the product of reception, surveillance, and appropriation of Western culture. Censorship in the state-socialist societies thus has been seen through the opposition between state officers (functionaries, nonprofessionals) and dissidents (subversive elements such as free-minded intellectuals and artists) who fought against the official ideology or compromised with the regime (see Pettan 1998). The public sphere was seen as dominated by restrictive practices, while private or semiprivate spaces were seen as the only niches for free, uncensored activities. Mainly understood as authoritarian regulatory practices exercised by institutions, the censorship in socialist societies was usually regarded as taking place after the production or act of expression, while the censored person/piece was treated as a passive object.[2]

In contrast to the existing views, this chapter proposes more nuanced and dynamic interpretations of censorial practices in socialist societies and tries to bring to light a whole range of specificities that destabilize the binary positions of authoritarian censor and free dissident. It draws on new studies that go beyond the Cold War dualism of neoliberal, free-market capitalism on the one hand and state socialism on the other, while recognizing the diversity within socialist societies.[3] My main aim is to propose a more nuanced view of the complexity of censorial norms and to show that cultural production—not only under socialism but in societies in general—operates both implicitly, through internalized forms of censorship as discussed by Freud and Lacan, and explicitly, through the application of external norms such as institutional restrictions. As a main material for my examination, I use the official (state and scholarly) narratives and media discourses, providing a framework for discussing and analyzing the complexity of socialist music censorship.[4] However, access to the formal documents did not prove to be helpful since the official policy of the former Yugoslavia guaranteed absolute freedom of all artistic and cultural activities. In order to retain the image of Yugoslavia as a liberal socialist state within the international realm, censorship was never mentioned in legal documents, and consequently any traces of it being practiced were very difficult to find. On the other hand, after the break up of Yugoslavia, in keeping with the general tendency of revisionist reinterpretation of the socialist past, studies of censorial activities were colored by the narratives of "communist prosecutors" or "cultural crimes," denying the existence of any kind of free, uncontrolled spaces of cultural production in Yugoslavia.

Yugoslav Culture Politics

In the declared multiethnic or multinational state of Yugoslavia, with its specific form of socialism,[5] policymakers exhibited ambivalent attitudes toward the concepts of nation and religion. Nations were constitutive parts of the multinational country, so the concept of nation was not abandoned or banned but rather integrated into the broader concept of Yugoslav identity. This led to Yugoslavia's inherent instability, for issues of ethnicity and national identity appeared to be a central political problem up to the disintegration of the state (Naumović 2008, 219). In the context of such complex and sensitive identity politics, the country adopted the official policy of "brotherhood and unity," aiming to achieve a balance among the ethnic and regional cultures. In general, emphasis was put on persuasion rather than coercion, which meant encouraging people to understand and embrace their ideology for themselves rather than forcing them to do so (Vuletić 2010, 114).

Though it is not my intention to romanticize Yugoslavia as a "unique case,"[6] it is nevertheless important to mention that in the field of popular music production, Yugoslavia was an exception in comparison to other Eastern-bloc countries. Liberalization of the music market started already in the 1950s, when a state-centralized model was abandoned in favor of liberalization of many segments of political, economic, public, and cultural life (Naumović 1996, 56). Therefore, beginning in the 1950s, when the first phase of "revolutionary romanticism" ended, officials did not consider it useful to forbid the "old" patterns of entertainment through administrative regulations:

> The folklore groups should not be administratively banned or transformed into some kind of "rhythm groups" (*ritam sekcije*), even though stylized performances of folk dances can further develop many elements of our folk dances. New folk dance groups should not be established and favored in the urban environments (for example through the festivals). Other contents of amateur work should be developed.[7]

Regarding religion, despite the declared fight against it in the first post-WWII years, party officials chose to slowly replace religious holidays rather than restrict them. In place of the old religious holidays, they insisted upon the establishment of new village holidays connected with the revolutionary past, such as the First of May, the Day of the Republic or the New Year, the day of the village, the day of the foundation of the local school, the day of the village's electrification or the building of a canal for irrigation:[8] "Through the culture-educational activity we simultaneously tried to gradually suppress religious holidays and to attach various manifestations of culture and sports to existing holidays" (AJ-142). Rather than treating traditional celebrations as a threat to the state's multicultural politics, socialist officials tended to consider the customs, music, and dances connected to some religious holidays as means of entertainment and expression deeply rooted in the everyday lives of the people: "But church gatherings (*crkveni sabori*), *slava*,[9] and various entertaining village dances from the ancient times are not only the outcome of some backward influence or a result of wider intention for their perseverance, but in great part a desire for amusement and expression" (AJ-142).

In the early postwar years, the censorship of Western popular music was inconsistent: "cultural politics was confused and unconsolidated, and party leaders even expressed contradictory attitudes among themselves" (Vuletić 2010, 75). In the early 1960s the popular culture industry established itself through a spreading network of local public radio stations (by the late 1960s there were also private ones) and the growth of the Yugoslav record industry.[10] By the mid-1960s, the record industry became an important economic field.[11] The authorities justified the growth of the record industry with an argument that new means of education and cultural production, such as the gramophone record, should follow the living standard of the Yugoslav working people and satisfy emerging cultural needs: "The gramophone record [was viewed] as a cultural heritage, as an indispensable tool in spreading and developing musical culture and education in general" (Gavarić 1973, 154).[12] Popular music thus served not only as an economic field and valuable cultural product but also as one of the country's most important cultural exports and a mark of the success of the Yugoslav liberal-socialist project (Vuletić 2008). For other countries of the former Eastern bloc, Yugoslav popular music served as a specific "window to the West."[13]

The 1970s were marked by a very complex political and social climate and extremely dynamic changes in the field of Yugoslav cultural policy. In 1971 the so-called "quasi confederate phase" in Yugoslav history started with the Slovenian "Road Affair" and the Croatian nationalist mass movement (Naumović 2008, 220). Demands for national independence, conflicts between the republics, and growing tensions between national cultural elites resulted in legal regulation of certain types of censorship and restriction for the first time in Yugoslav history. The same year, at the Congress of Cultural Action (*Kongres kulturne akcije*), which took place in the Serbian town of Kragujevac, a new, restrictive political line in the official cultural policy was announced, followed by administrational measures against "noncultural," "noneducational," and "low-grade" cultural products. The Tenth Congress of SKJ (*Savez komunista Jugoslavije,* or the League of Communists of Yugoslavia), held in Belgrade in May 1974, announced a struggle against all features of nationalism and all kinds of cultural "kitsch"[14] and *šund* (art trash) as a response to the overall intellectual crises and national tensions (Đokić 1974, 174). "Low-quality cultural genres" including magazines, books, movies, and commercial music genres such as *novokomponovana narodna muzika* (newly composed folk music, or NCFM) were declared to be particularly problematic.[15]

Campaign Against "Šund"

As mentioned, institutional censorship in Yugoslavia was never publicly acknowledged, and there was never any government body established for the task of monitoring cultural production. In the absence of such a centralized institution or bodies, censorial practices were often hidden behind other regulatory strategies. The most efficient way to keep music production under control was to deny or dispute the artistic quality of particular pieces. Although such actions were an inseparable part of music production from its very beginning, starting in 1971 the so-called Law Against *Šund* (art trash), formalized these practices. This law, with the unwieldy title "Law on

Amendments to the Republican Tax on Retail Goods" (*Zakon o izmenama i dopunama o republičkom porezu na promet robe na malo*), was inaugurated on December 29, 1971, only within the Socialist Republic of Serbia. It was announced as an attempt to end "unregulated cultural politics" and growing nationalism in all fields by introducing a stricter policy as a return to the ideological roots of Marxism. Presented to the public as part of the "cultural revolution," the Congress of Cultural Action proclaimed a war against all cultural products promoting imperialist and/or bourgeois propaganda. The changes in tax policy involved introducing a republic tax of 31.5 percent on cultural products (in the case of music, gramophone records), which was added to the federal one of 12.5 percent. It was not centralized and each municipality in Serbia had an opportunity to increase the percentage of additional tax up to 50 percent.[16] The music products that were not perceived to be of "artistic quality" were proclaimed as *šund* and charged additional tax. So-called *šund* committees were established in the main state radio-television stations—in the case of Serbia, at the radio-television station of Belgrade—with the aim of assessing the quality of recordings and making decisions about which should get the *šund* label. Committees consisted of editors, music experts, journalists, and public intellectuals.

Apart from tax policy, which can be considered as a kind of "soft censorship," a negative assessment of a certain piece of music by proclaiming it as *šund* was enough to ban it in the media or prevent it from being recorded. The main argument was that the censored content did not share a universal "artistic quality": "That meant that if a cultural product (a gramophone record, for example) was given the label of *šund*, you could immediately place it in a closet—that nobody would want to buy it and it would be three times more expensive."[17] In accordance with official rhetoric and public discourse, the main goal was to give "high culture" the opportunity to compete with commercial and widely available cultural products.

However, as was the case for the cultural policy in general, the law against *šund* left many issues unregulated, avoiding a strict definition of *šund* and not specifying exactly which people or agencies were responsible for dealing with problematic cultural products (according to the law, the main responsible body should be "a republican governing body in charge of cultural affairs").[18] The public reactions to the law were accordingly contentious. The opponents of the law immediately pointed to the problem of leaving *šund* undefined by declaring just what should be considered valued cultural products: "Šund-law was passed before the definition of *šund*!" (*Nin* 1122, 1972). They also warned the policymakers that *šund* was an organic part of the mass culture in industrial society that could be neglected or eliminated. Particularly strong were the voices of those who criticized the hypocrisy of the law and the cultural policy in general, claiming that this act actually legitimized *šund* and elevated its status instead of reducing it: "by the law you can produce and consume *šund* but for that privilege you have to pay additionally" (*Nin* 1114, 1972.).[19] Some intellectuals expressed fear of using the *šund* campaign to prosecute all potential new, fresh, and avant-garde cultural practices (*Nin* 1005, 1970). Proponents of the law, on the other hand, claimed that this easy-listening, entertaining music was much more dangerous for society since it promoted social inactivity, passivity, and a lack of interest in social reality, an effect considered particularly harmful for younger generations (*Nin* 1122, 1972). In this regard, this law was an attempt to suppress the productions of commercial culture, which started gaining enormous popularity, and NCFM was one of the main targets.

Why did socialist cultural policy have a more restrictive attitude toward music genre that was seen merely as entertainment not intended for transmitting any kind of political message? The contentious attitudes toward NCFM stemmed from its commercial nature, associated with capitalist modes of cultural production.[20] This genre was developed under grass-roots entrepreneurial conditions (Vidić Rassmussen 2002, xxiv) within a capitalist business model including managers, agents, record companies, and the open promotion of consumerism. Additionally, much of the musical activity took place in an unregulated space of *kafana*,[21] which made it much less financially controlled than genres of "entertainment music" or Yugoslav rock (see Hofman 2015). Even though this music genre had its roots in traditional folklore, it was not considered an authentic musical form as it lacked the educational and "enlightening" elements that were one of the main postulates of the socialist cultural policy. While "institutionalized folklore" was a preferred genre for the representation of patriotic content in the public sphere, its commercial version, newly composed folk music, was not.

Therefore, the law against *šund* provided a perfect ground for exercising the so-called soft censorship and facilitating control over this cultural production. A few months after ratification of the law, radio stations hesitated to transmit commercial folk songs and gave preference to more "profound" and "cultured" music genres like classical music and opera: "Recently, and definitely under the influence of the Congress of Cultural Action, we tried to eliminate everything which is tasteless from our program (of Radio Belgrade) (*Nin* 1097, 1972.) However, after the initial attempts to implement the conclusions of the Congress of Cultural Action and the law against *šund*, the media returned, cautiously at first and then more freely, to the previous repertoire policy as they realized that elitism did not bring in any money and that "in the end, they had to live on something" (*Nin* 1122, 1972). Nevertheless, the law against *šund* served as a fertile ground for the editors, who usually played it safe and did not release musical pieces that could be potentially seen as problematic, particularly ones that addressed sensitive political topics.

Two Songs of Yuga

One of the first victims of the law against *šund* was the song "Jugo moja, Jugo" performed by the famous female folk singer Silvana Armenulić. As Petar Luković writes, Silvanu Armenulić was an entertainment icon of the 1970s. Her career brought new approaches and new listeners of NCFM across Yugoslavia in comparison to other NCFM singers whose music was still much more regionally oriented (such as Lepa Lukić, also popular in that time yet who was considered a performer solely of Serbian-style traditional music) (Luković 1989). She introduced a new public image for folk music stars by wearing modern designer dresses more typical for singers of entertainment music (Hofman 2010, 153), driving cars, and in general bringing an "urban" style to the image of folk singers.[22] The song "Jugo moja, Jugo" was planned to be a first NCFM song about Yugoslavia and a potential informal anthem. The scenario was designed absolutely in accordance with the socialist cultural model described above—lyrics came from the working people and the performer was chosen by free voting organized by the magazine *TV Revija*: the magazine got a letter from Milenija Radovanović, a Yugoslav guest-worker ("gastarbeiter") from Munich, Germany, with the lyrics of a patriotic song about Yugoslavia. Radovanović was ill and needed money for medical treatment in Germany, so the magazine started a charitable project to find appropriate music to accompany the lyrics that would involve all readers of the magazine, poets, singers, and musicians. In the end, the readers voted for the Yugoslav singer who should perform this song, which had already been predicted to be extremely popular and reach "gold record" status. Lyrics addressed the nostalgia for a homeland:

> My Juga, full of everything,
> I left all my dearest in you:
> a husband, children,
> the whole family and everyone else that I loved.
> My Juga, my homeland,
>
> I'll be longing for you forever.
>
> Oh, if I can get a clod of native soil
> to put it on my weary chest!
> I cry, I cry and my heart hurts,
> everything I like is faraway.
> Here, there is a money and everything is rich
> but Juga is my real gold.
>
> Six months are sad and long
> until I return to my dear Juga.
> My Juga, my dearest flower,
> you are the most beautiful country in the world.
>
> Jugo moja, puna svega dosta
> u tebi mi sve najdraže osta:
> muž i deca i rodbina cela
> i svi drugi koje sam volela.
> Jugo moja, rodni zavičaju,
> ja za tobom večno ću da žalim.
> Oj, da mi je grumen rodne grude
> na umorne grudi da ga stavim!
> Plačem, plačem i srce me boli
> daleko je sve što tamo volim.
> Ovde para i sve je bogato

al' je Juga moje pravo zlato.
Šest meseci tužni su i dugi

dok ja pođem mojoj dragoj Jugi.
Jugo moja, moj najdraži cvetu,
najlepša si ti zemlja na svetu.

The lyrics were emotional, even sentimental in some parts, and reflected the diasporic longing for the homeland. Readers flooded the magazine with suggestions for a potential performer. Since Armenulić's fans were the most persistent and numerous, it was decided that she would perform "Juga." She immediately recorded the song as a single record published by Jugoton in 1971 and went abroad on tour to perform to Yugoslav guest-workers in Western Europe. The first performances of "Juga" in Denmark and West Germany were a real spectacle: people cried and sang along with her. Fellow musicians were full of praise for Armenulić: prominent songwriter Arsen Dedić stated that Yugoslavia had been waiting for years for this kind of song. Armenulić herself was much more cautious: "I am afraid of this song, this is a huge responsibility. I have never sung a song with so much soul" (Luković 2008). She was aware that this was the first NCFM song carrying a patriotic message.

And her caution was warranted: after the first concerts, the music editors of Radio-Television of Sarajevo (RTV Sarajevo) first asserted that this song did not have any poetic quality. They claimed that it was cheap manipulation of the audience's emotions, and banned Armenulić from singing "Juga" at concerts they organized. RTV Belgrade then joined in the action against the song, and soon it was banned in all the media. Nor could the record company Jugoton advertise the single through paid commercials. In the end, the song was formally banned by Mira Čonkić-Radović, an expert on "music issues" at RTV Belgrade because of its banal lyrics. As Borivoje Ilić, the editor at Radio Belgrade and president of the Committee for Listening to Folk Songs, explained, this restrictive action over "Juga" was a part of the new shift in cultural policy in Serbia and the more restrictive measures introduced by the Congress of Cultural Action (Luković 2008). Silvana was a scapegoat of this new policy.

Toma Zdravković, a famous *kafana* singer,[23] faced similar censorship for his song

"Jugoslavijo" from 1978:

You are so wonderful, my country,
as a garden full of flowers,
Yugoslavia, Yugoslavia.
Green are your fields,

your peaceful rivers and mountains,
Yugoslavia, Yugoslavia.

Refrain:

My country is the most beautiful for me,
there are my brothers, all my comrades.

> It's wonderful summer when rose turns red,
> and when autumn comes and grapes.
>
> How you would not be pretty
>
> when many lives are given for you,
> Yugoslavia, Yugoslavia?
> They died with the song on their lips,
> wept and sang,
> Yugoslavia, Yugoslavia.
>
> Bas si divna zemljo moja,
> kao basta puna cveća,
> Jugoslavijo, Jugoslavijo.
> Zelena su tvoja polja,
> mirne reke i planine,
> Jugoslavijo, Jugoslavijo.
>
> Refrain:
>
> Moja je zemlja najlepsa za mene
> u njoj su braća, drugovi moji svi.
> Divno je leto kad ruža pocrveni
> a jesen dođe kada grožđe zri.
> Kako ne bi bila lepa
> kad su mnogi život dali
> Jugoslavijo, Jugoslavijo,
> sa pesmom su umirali,
> plakali su i pevali
> Jugoslavijo, Jugoslavijo.

Even though the editors of the radio and TV stations allowed its recording and it was not formally banned, the song was proclaimed *šund* and never broadcast in the media. The main problem was Zdravković's low profile as a *kafana* performer. His song "O, Old Man, Old Man,"[24] dedicated to the president of socialist Yugoslavia Josip Broz Tito's birthday and which he planned to record in 1979, experienced a slightly different fate, reverse of the two previous cases: since the song touched an even more delicate topic in a particularly sensitive time of Tito's weakness (Tito died in 1980), the editors rather prevented Toma from recording the song as they did not want to risk the possibility of having to ban the song. According to Marko Lopušina, this song was evaluated at a party meeting, where it was decided that it was a "kitschy and tasteless glorification of the president" (Lopušina 1991).

> O, Old Man, Old Man, lives long, lives long.
> Fly pigeons over the blue sea,
>
> take on your wings my heart's greeting.
> Old Man lives long with a song in his heart,

let us share the good and evil with him.
O, Old Man, Old Man, lives long, lives long.
O, Stari, Stari, o živi, živi.

Poletite golubovi preko sinjeg mora,
na krilima odnesite pozdrav srca mog,
nek nam Stari dugo živi s pesmom u srcu,
nek sa nama deli i dobro i zlo.
O, Stari, Stari, o živi, živi.

Toma Zdravković was advised to change the text before the record could be released. He opted for the strategy that was usually taken when it came to problematic content—he changed just one word, renaming the song "Mother's Birthday" and changing the exclamation from "Old Man" to "Mother." Regarding this substitution, Zdravković himself said:

> If that song about Tito was made by Konjović,[25] it would go through without problems (*to bi prošlo iz cuga*), but if it is composed by one Toma Zdravković it does not! [...] Obrad Jovović from Jugoton and I have decided to put on the other side of the record the song "Yugoslavia"; because of the seriousness of topic it did not make sense to put "Ljiljana" or "Bouquet of White Roses." After all, I changed the name of the song to "Mother" and it still lives within the people. All of that hurt me a lot, because I had honest and patriotic intentions and see how badly they responded."[26]

All these cases show how the censorial practices operated in accordance with unwritten norms and practices. They also highlight the specificities of censorial methods when dealing with the music's ability to simultaneously convey a variety of potential interpretations, multiple layers of meaning and ambiguity at the same time easy to be (mis)understood and manipulated. In addition, presented cases witness the importance of looking at the censorial practices through the lenses of cultural valuation particularly in relation to "good" and "bad" forms of popular culture (Čvoro 2014, 38) masked under the "ideological innapropriety." Therefore the process was twofold: the argument of artistic quality was used in order to fight against potential subversive content while exercising "ideological rightness" was often a euphemism for supressing commercial popular music genres.

New Post-Socialist Censorship?

In the previous sections I described the attempts of Yugoslav officials to promote an individualized, subjective approach to censorship without strict rules and institutional supervision. Authors were often left to decide for themselves what to do with their work, which kept censorship practices in the realm of the informal. Court actions were very rare and officials rarely discussed the merits or demerits of particular pieces or ensembles (Ramet 1999b, 136). Thus, a range of censorial activities were carried out under an unwritten law, which left plenty of space for interpretation, improvisation, and subjective impressions. Although there existed special committees for culture, arts, and publishing; editorial and artistic councils; and groups for assessing ideological correctness—still, many of the restrictions and bans depended on the affinities, courage, and capricious feelings of a particular person at a particular moment.

Yugoslav cultural critics defined this so-called "editorial censorship" as a specific form of Yugoslav-invented "self-managed censorship,"[27] where the responsibility for ideological supervision was transferred from institutions to individuals (Golubović 1990, 24). It was usually the editor who was considered responsible for determining limits, often in agreement with the authors. The editors thus were the main keepers of the ideological, moral, and political correctness of a particular cultural product, with the result that much of the censorial activity happened in a kind of limbo, in the interplay of official, interpersonal, and subjective spheres. With editors being eager to keep their own positions and careers, this type of personalized approach opened a space for more careful, detailed, and efficient censorial mechanisms. On the other hand, editors' decisions were frequently based on their personal interests and moral dilemmas. Very often they tried to find a balance between their personal moral beliefs and what they thought would be the politically and socially approved stance. These people were given the difficult task of negotiating between their own attitudes and artistic preferences on the one hand and public opinion and official doctrine on the other. In many cases, they worked together with the artists and helped them revise the "problematic" piece in accordance with the norms (Đogo 1990, 20). In this way they kept their positions safe but also often appeared to be the main agents responsible for introducing fresh, new ideas. In order to prevent a work from being banned, they opted for the appearance of accidental printer errors (for instance, by erasing some words in lyrics or on the cover), which enabled many potentially subversive pieces to see daylight. Furthermore, very often the censor and the censored came from the same background, were friends, or even exchanged their roles at different times, factors that rendered the dynamics of censorship even more complex. Thus "editorial censorship" involved constant conscious (self-)censorship.

After the break up of Yugoslavia, the newly founded states claimed to be free from totalitarianism and repression, finally having cultural production free from state control. The *šund* label in the post-Yugoslav era started to be recognized as one of the main markers of a dissident position and resistance against the repressive socialist regime. In (re)writing their biographies, many musicians were proud to highlight that the socialist authorities had banned their music. However, in contrast to their rock colleagues, the NCFM performers rarely mentioned being banned. On the other hand, some members from *šund* committees have claimed that the law against *šund* actually helped in improving the existing music production, by forcing composers and performers to maintain a minimum of artistic and educational standards. They do not interpret these strategies as a kind of state restriction but as necessary policies that discouraged distributors and other agents involved in the music market from exclusively bending to market demand

and instead put them under the influence of experienced professionals. In addition, these policies provided a space for independent, less commercial music production to develop, survive, and operate relatively free of market pressures. However, members of *šund* committees all express their awareness that censorship in the name of art was part of the official cultural policy and a reflection of the existing power relations, which, in the end, did not result in serious changes in the production of music ("Ispovijest Člana Šund—Komisije," *Justarnji List* [January 21, 2006]).

In the post-socialist reality marked by commercialization of public culture, rampant consumerism, domination of big media companies, the emergence of new political and economic elites, and a general crisis of social values, other ways of controlling cultural production—apparently unmotivated by ideology—have been established. With the current dominance of globalized music corporations, *šund* committees appear to be just a relic of foregone socialist times. The democratic market has become the main censorial agent, with or without awareness that it actually may be the most censorious agent of all while also being the hardest to monitor. Today, post-Yugoslav music markets seem to be more centralized than ever, with two domestic labels dominating production of NCFM in Serbia ("Grand Production" and "Production of Gramophone Records of RTV of Serbia") on the one hand, and global music labels that have adapted to corporate regulation of the music industry on the other. "Market censorship" renders artists fully dependent on the general taste of the public and sales rates, leaving them with relatively less artistic freedom. And again, the editors are motivated by the ideology of "expanding sales," which results in a number of censorial actions taken by various agents. They endorse Bourdieu's idea that the more effective the process of regulation and repression is, the less apparent it becomes, as it begins to appear as the natural "way of the world" (Bourdieu 1991, 138).

Notes

1. Statement of Mira Čonkić-Radović, an expert for "music issues" in the Radio-Television of Belgrade, Serbia (Luković 2008).
2. For critique of such approaches see Yurchak 2006 and Hofman 2013.
3. See Goldman 2002; Crowley and Reid 2002; Haney 2002.
4. I consulted resources from the Archive of Yugoslavia, leading popular music magazines during the socialist period, and personal archives of people involved in the research.
5. The Yugoslav concept of self-management was introduced in the 1950s as a way of reducing state control over the economy and enabling decision-making by the workers themselves. Socially owned companies were supervised by worker councils, which were made up of all employees and decided issues concerning the division of labor, general production methods, scheduling, customer care, and so on.
6. The case of Yugoslavia is already recognized by scholars as "exceptional" and "famous for its contradictions" (Ramet 1999a, 90).
7. Archive of Yugoslavia, League of Communists of Yugoslavia, thereafter: AJ-142, The Report on the Plenary of SSRNJ—Socijalistički savez radnog naroda Jugoslavije or the Socialist Alliance of Working People of Yugoslavia 1959, F-616.

8. Replacement of existing community rituals and celebrations by the new tendency to institutionalize cultural activities was often met with disapproval in the villages.
9. *Slava*, also called *krsna slava* or *krsno ime*, is a celebration on the day of a family's patron saint, celebrated annually by each household separately.
10. According to official reports, first attempts to establish a record industry started already in the early 1950s (in Serbia in 1952). The first gramophone records started to be produced in 1959 (AJ-475, Fifth Congress of the Association of Music Artists, 5–7.11.1965).
11. In 1965 over 10 milion records were produced in Yugoslavia (ibid.).
12. Up to 1987, there were eleven record and cassette companies, with the major two in Zagreb (Jugoton) and Belgrade (Production of Gramophone Records Radio-Television Belgrade, PGPRTB), which released 75 to 80 percent of the music marketed in Yugoslavia (Vidić Rasmussen 2002, 178).
13. Particularly in the 1980s, it was used as a symbol of rebellion against communist regimes, when not only Yugoslav rock bands but also folk singers started performing freely at the stadiums as a specific indicator of democratization of these societies.
14. The phenomenon of "kitsch" in the local context included all kinds of artistic works considered aesthetically impoverished and morally dubious (Ivanović 1973, 191).
15. The literal translation of the term *novokomponovana narodna muzika* introduced by Ljerka Vidić Rasmussen (see Vidić Rasmussen 2002).
16. Administrational measures through extra taxes were applied first on the so-called *šund* literature. In one of the most bizarre occurrences, during the Congress of Cultural Action, some magazines and editions, comics, and pulp literature were burned in public. In 1972, after measures against the popular press, in the law against *šund* regulated other culture fields as well (movies, books, music).
17. "Ispovijest Člana Šund-Komisije," Justarnji List (January 21, 2006).
18. A special committee of seventeen people was founded for the purpose of reconsidering cases in which cultural products were proclaimed as *šund* by mistake. This committee would meet on a regular basis (*Nin* no.1122, 1972).
19. This caused a blackmarket for publications across the republic borders, since in other republics (such as Bosnia and Hercegovina) *šund* magazines were much cheaper.
20. For more on introducing a "neoclassical" liberal economy into Yugoslavia, see Bockman 2011.
21. The main performance setting for NFCM was the *kafana* (or private party), a space that remained marginalized from the official sphere while at the same time being the preferred setting for the everyday consumption of music. As a kind of cultural niche, it was much less controlled than other performance settings such as concerts or festivals. For specific place politics associated with the *kafana*, see Hofman 2010, 155.
22. Silvana Armenulić was one of the icons of NCFM and the most popular female star from late 1960s until the mid 1970s, when she died in a car accident (in 1976).
23. The *kafana* has been a central space for informal socialization, networking, and entertainment, in rural, semi-urban, and urban environments from the eighteenth century onward. Offering a specific mode of sociability, the *kafana* has been a place where people can drink alcoholic beverages, eat, listen to music, dance, and have a good time in the company of friends. Until the mid-twentieth century, the clientele consisted mainly of men, while in the more recent period it has included all types of people from diverse backgrounds. Live music has been one of the most important elements, which marked the specific mode of

entertainment taking place in the *kafana*. Being a *kafana* singer was considered a low-prestige profession.
24. Tito's partisan nickname used during the Second World War.
25. A famous Yugoslav composer of Serbian origin.
26. Toma Zdravković, http://www.titomanija.com.ba/index.php?option=com_content&task=view&id=13&Itemid=26.
27. The Yugoslav concept of workers' self-management was introduced in the 1950s as a way of reducing state control over the economy and enabling decision-making by the workers themselves. Socially owned companies were supervised by worker councils, which were made up of all employees and decided issues concerning the division of labor, general production methods, scheduling, customer care, and so on.

References

Bockman, Johanna. 2011. *Markets in the Name of Socialism: The Left-Wing Origins of Neoliberalism*. Stanford, CA: Stanford University Press.

Bourdieu, Pierre. 1991. *Language and Symbolic Power*. Translated by John B. Thompson. Edited by Gino Raymond and Matthew Adamson. Oxford: Polity Press.

Boyer, Dominic. 2003. "Censorship as a Vocation: The Institutions, Practices, and Cultural Logic of Media Control in the German Democratic Republic." *Comparative Studies in Society and History*, 45, no. 3: 511–545.

Burt, Richard, ed. 1994. *The Administration of Aesthetics: Censorship, Political Criticism and the Public Sphere*. Cultural Politics 7. Minneapolis: University of Minnesota Press.

Butler, Judith. 1998. "Ruled Out: Vocabularies of the Censor." In *Censorship and Silencing: Practices of Cultural Regulation*, ed. Robert C. Post, 247–259. Los Angeles: Getty Research Institute for the History of Art and the Humanities.

Crowley, David, and Susan E. Reid, eds. 2002. *Socialist Spaces: Sites of Everyday Life in the Eastern Bloc*. Oxford: Berg.

Čvoro, Uroš. 2014. *Turbo-folk Music and Cultural Representations of National Identity in Former Yugoslavia*, Surrey and Burlington: Ashgate.

Đokić, Radoslav. 1974. "Stvaralaštvo i sloboda (Tribina X kongresa)." *Kultura* 24: 170–175.

Đogo, Gojko. 1990. "Censorship", *Književna kritika* 3–4 (May–June): 20–23.

Fish, Stanley. 1994. *There's No Such Thing as Free Speech*. Oxford: Oxford University Press.

Gavarić Dragoljub. 1973. "Kulturna delatnost bez kulturne politike." *Kultura* 23: 154–165.

Goldman, Wendy Z. 2002. *Women at the Gates: Gender and Industry in Stalin's Russia*. Cambridge: Cambridge University Press.

Golubović, Zagorka. 1990. "O samoupravnoj cenzuri." *Književna kritika* 3–4 (May–June): 23–24.

Haney, Lynne. 2002. *Inventing the Needy: Gender and the Politics of Welfare in Hungary*. Berkeley: University of California Press.

Hofman, Ana. 2010. "Kafana Singers: Popular Music, Gender and Subjectivity in the Cultural Space of Socialist Yugoslavia." *Narodna umjetnost* 47, no. 1: 141–161.

Hofman, Ana. 2013. "Ko se boji šunda još? Muzička cenzura u Jugoslaviji" [Who Is Afraid of Schund? Music Censorship in Yugoslavia.] In *Socijalizam na klupi: Jugoslovensko društvo očima nove postjugoslavenske humanistike* [Socialism on bench: Yugoslav society through the lenses of new post-Yugoslav humanities], edited by Lada Duraković and Andrea Matošević, 280–316. Pula, Zagreb: Srednja Evropa.

Holquist, Michael. 1994. "Corrupt Originals: The Paradox of Censorship." *PMLA* 109, no. 1: 14–25.
"Ispovijest Člana Šund-Komisije," *Justarnji List* (January 21, 2006). http://www.jutarnji.hr/ispovijest-clana-sund-komisije/13019/ (accessed 13.3.2014).
Ivanović, Narodna. 1973. Muzika između folklora I kulture masovnog društva. *Kultura* 23: 166–196.
Jansen, Sue Curry. 1991. *Censorship: The Knot That Binds Power and Knowledge.* New York: Oxford University Press.
Lopušina, Marko. 1991. *Crna knjiga: cenzura u Jugoslaviji 1945–91.* Belgrade: Fokus.
Luković, Petar. 1989. *Bolja prošlost: Prizori iz muzičkog života Jugoslavije 1940–1989.* Belgrade: Mladost.
Luković, Petar. 2008. "Bolja prošlost: Silvana Armenulić (2). Embargo na smrt." *E-Novine,* October 11. http://www.e-novine.com/index.php?news=17804.
Müller, Beate. 2003. "Censorship and Cultural Regulation: Mapping the Territory." *Critical Studies* 22, no. 1: 1–31.
Naumović, Slobodan. 1996. "Identity Creator in Identity Crisis: Reflections on the Politics of Serbian Ethnology." *Anthropological Journal of European Cultures* 8, no. 2: 39–128.
Naumović, Slobodan. 2008. "Brief Encounters, Dangerous Liaisons and Never-Ending Stories: The Politics of Serbian Ethnology and Anthropology in the Interesting Times of Yugoslav Socialism." In *Studying People in the People's Democracies II: Socialist Era Anthropology in South East Europe,* edited by Vintila Mihailescu and Ilia Iliev i Slobodan Naumović, 211–260. Halle Studies in the Anthropology of Eurasia, vol. 17. Berlin: LIT Verlag.
Pettan, Svanibor. 1998: "Music and Censorship in Ex-Yugoslavia—Some Views from Croatia." Paper presented at the first Freemuse world conference in Copenhagen, November 20–22. http://www.freemuse.org/sw26648.asp.
Ramet, Sabrina P. 1999a. "In Tito's Time." In *Gender Politics in the Western Balkans: Women and Society in Yugoslavia and the Yugoslav Successor States,* edited by Sabrina Ramet, 89–105. University Park: Pennsylvania State University Press.
Ramet, Sabrina P. 1999b. *Balkan Babel: The Disintegration of Yugoslavia from the Death of Tito to the War of Kosovo.* Boulder, CO: Westview.
Vidić Rasmussen, Ljerka. 2002. *Newly Composed Folk Music of Yugoslavia.* New York: Routledge.
Vuletić, Dean. 2008. "Generation Number One: Politics and Popular Music in Yugoslavia in the 1950s." *Nationalities Papers* 36, no. 5: 861–879.
Vuletić, Dean. 2010. *Yugoslav Communism and the Power of Popular Music.* PhD diss., Columbia University.
Yurchak, Alexei. 2006. *Everything Was Forever, Until It Was No More: The Last Soviet Generation.* Princeton, NJ: Princeton University Press.
Archival ResourcesArchive of Yugoslavia, League of Communists of Yugoslavia, funds: 507, VIII-1—Central Committee of the League of Communists of Yugoslavia, Minutes from the Commission Meetings. 475, Fifth Congress of the Association of Music Artists, 5–7.11.1965.
Magazines*NIN* no. 1005, April 12, 1970; no. 1114, May 14, 1972; no. 1122, July 9, 1972.
Estrada year 1, October 1963; year 4, December 1968.
DiscographyArmenulić, Silvana. 1971. *Jugo moja, Jugo,* Jugoton. Single record. SY-11886
Zdravković, Toma. 1972. *O, majko, majko,* Jugoton. Single record. SY 22146
Zdravković, Toma. 1978. *Jugoslavijo.* Jugoton. Single record. SY 23419

CHAPTER 13

POPULAR MUSIC AS A BAROMETER OF POLITICAL CHANGE
Evidence from Taiwan

NANCY GUY

In a much-cited passage from his book *Noise: The Political Economy of Music* the economist Jacques Attali (1985, 11) declares:

> Music is prophecy. Its styles and economic organization are ahead of the rest of society because it explores, much faster than material reality can, the entire range of possibilities in a given code. It makes audible the new world that will gradually become visible, that will impose itself and regulate the order of things; it is not only the image of things, but the transcending of the everyday, the herald of the future. For this reason musicians, even when officially recognized, are dangerous, disturbing, and subversive; for this reason it is impossible to separate their history from that of repression and surveillance.

In this chapter, I aim to show that a review of more than two decades of popular music in Taiwan supports Attali's bold claim.[1] I assert that the innovative musical creations of the late 1980s through the 1990s heralded the regime change of May 2000, which ended the Chinese Nationalist Party's (also known as Kuomintang, or KMT) fifty years of unbroken, and often iron-fisted, rule in Taiwan. However, seeds foretelling the troubles that the newly-elected Democratic Progressive Party (DPP) administration would face sprouted the morning of President Chen Shui-bian's inauguration with pop star A-Mei's singing of the national anthem of the Republic of China (ROC).

China banned A-Mei (a.k.a. Zhang Huimei), then one of the world's most widely listened to singers of Mandarin pop, immediately following her performance. Quickly absorbing China's message, other Taiwanese performers, who also had their eyes on the enormous Chinese market, turned their backs firmly on President Chen, who was believed by Beijing to be forwarding a Taiwanese independence agenda. A number of high-profile pop artists soon released songs that incorporated sonic symbols of China and themes compliant with the "greater China" ideology favored by authorities in China.

President Chen Shui-bian's inauguration marked a sea change in Taiwan. This change was reflected in musical production, which, as I argue here, rather quickly foreshadowed the next major shift in the island's political and economic orientation. Chen would spend eight years as an embattled president. At the end of his second term, Taiwan elected pro-China, Nationalist Party candidate Ma Ying-jeou to the presidency. With Ma's election came the strengthening of all manner of ties to China. Those listening critically to the island's popular music could have heard this critical "reorientation" toward China coming, which amounted to a renunciation of dreams for an independent nation of Taiwan.

An obvious criticism of the notion that music heralds change is that its prophetic accuracy is typically proclaimed in hindsight. Sociologist Jon Cruz (1999, 64) believes music is not intrinsically prophetic and asserts, it is "the social movements, upon which music rides that matter." Attali's and Cruz's divergent positions seem to be locked in a chicken-or-egg conundrum. Rather than aiming to prove definitively that a particular song launched a social movement, or vice versa, I aim to show that music acts as a barometer of coming political change, if it is listened to with discerning ears and interpreted within a framework sensitive to the popular zeitgeist.

Through music, listeners (and performers, of course) are able to try on differing identities, personae, and emotional states. How does it feel to embrace and take pride in a distinctly local Taiwanese lifestyle and cultural practice? Listening to "Drifting Down to Tamsui" as performed by Jinmen Wang (a.k.a. King of Jinmen) and Li Binghui allowed for the emotional embodiment of this sense. The Labor Exchange's efficacious protest song, "If the Dam Can be built, then Shit Can be Eaten," could incarnate the spirit of an indignant, Taiwan-loving environmentalist in its listeners, if only for a moment. Most everyone is familiar with the practice of indulging a melancholic mood through music. Perhaps no other activity can more readily enable you to feel—to the depths of your soul—the pain of a broken heart than listening to a deeply sad song. In all of these cases, musical expression acts as a vehicle for defining and strengthening not only emotion but also attitude and identity, including ethnic affiliation and political orientation. Through music, attitudes and worldviews become visceral and experiential long before political and social change can fully normalize such visions.[2]

The power of music to both monitor and propel change has been noted by philosophers and governmental institutions since ancient times. One of the most frequently cited passages from the ancient West is found in Plato's *Republic*: "any musical innovation is full of danger to the whole State, and ought to be prohibited ... when modes of music change, the fundamental laws of the State always change with them" (Plato 1907, 248). Ancient Greek ideas about music are remarkably similar to those developed by early Chinese philosophers. The *Analects* and the *Book of Rites* (Liji) both associate Confucius with the idea of music as an instrument of moral education. Commenting on ancient Chinese classics, Kenneth J. DeWoskin (1982, 29) observes that the "perception of music as a spontaneous expression of public sentiment or barometer of the spiritual condition of the people was pervasive."[3] The Music Bureau (Yuefu) of the Western Han dynasty (206–25 B.C.) put this notion into real-world practice with its systematic collection of folk songs from throughout the empire. Since music was believed to reflect "the mood of the times," bureau officials listened to and analyzed songs as a means of measuring the state's efficacy (Perris 1983, 12). Jumping ahead two thousand years, though illustrating a fundamentally similar attitude towards music and the state, Anthony Y. F. Fung (2007, 427) contends that in contemporary China, popular music not only acts as a "political yardstick" for appraising the political ideologies of the time, but also "presages" and reflects the "control and measures" that the authorities employ in the interest of restraining the oppositional ideologies.

If music acts as a measuring device (as in DeWoskin's "barometer" or Fung's "yardstick") for political, social, and even economic change, how do we evaluate what popular music in Taiwan has forecast over the last twenty years? In pursuing this question, I am not seeking a cause-and-effect relationship. Nor am I aiming to determine which has more efficacy—music or social movement—as does Cruz. Turning the clock back to 1988 puts us conveniently at the year after the lifting of martial law. The late 1980s and early 1990s witnessed a surge in musical creativity and experimentation in popular music not seen in Taiwan since the 1930s. Before jumping straight into an analysis of the scintillating music of this period, a very brief overview of Taiwan and of developments in Taiwan's pop music world, so far as they relate to political change, is necessary.

The Peoples and Politics

With the arrival in the late 1940s of approximately 1.5 million émigrés who followed Chiang Kai-shek and his Nationalist government from mainland China to Taiwan, Taiwan society came to be viewed as being comprised of four distinct ethnic groups. For many years, a rather volatile divide existed between the Nationalist arrivals, who hailed from all over mainland China and were known collectively as "*waishengren*" ("outside province people"), and the "*benshengren*" ("people of this province"). *Benshengren* and their ancestors came to Taiwan from mainland China before 1945, the year that administration of the island shifted from Japan to the Republic of China (then under the control of the Chiang's Nationalist regime). The *benshengren* group is comprised of two culturally distinct groups who also share a somewhat contentious history. The largest of these are the Hoklo, whose ancestors migrated to Taiwan from southern Fujian, and whose language is typically referred to as "Taiwanese" in English. Also belonging to the *benshengren* group are the Hakka people, whose ancestors migrated to Taiwan primarily from southeastern Guangdong province. Taiwan aborigines, who are Austronesian and lived in numerous distinct tribes before Chinese immigrants came to dominate the island in the early nineteenth century, comprise yet another group.[4] Currently, there are fourteen officially recognized aboriginal groups who together make up less than two percent of Taiwan's overall population. *Benshengren* (including both Hoklo and Hakka populations) comprise about eighty-five percent while *waishengren* are about fourteen percent of the island's population.[5]

Political party allegiance in Taiwan is often, but not always, associated with ethnicity. *Waishengren* generally form the Nationalist Party's base, though some *benshengren* also vote with the "pan-blue" coalition. The Nationalist Party represents the cornerstone of the "pan-blue" coalition, which includes other parties that favor a similar pro-China stance. The Democratic Progressive Party, which leans towards Taiwan independence, is central to the "pan-green" coalition. The vast majority of green supporters are of Hoklo heritage.

Musical Antecedents

Up to and through the 1970s, a number of songs, each with its own complicated genealogy of meaning, had become associated with the democratization movement and the struggle for Taiwan's self-determination. Some date from the 1930s (for instance, "A Flower in the Rainy Night" [雨夜花] and "Longing for the Spring Breeze" [望春風]), the 1940s ("Mending Broken Nets" [補破網]), and others from as late as the 1960s ("Hometown at Dusk" [黃昏的故鄉]). Today all of these are considered Hoklo classics and are heard in many different settings (both overtly political and not), including concert halls, political rallies, and karaoke clubs. Over time, these classics, which are currently referred to as "old Taiwanese songs" (*lao Taiyu ge*), came to be viewed as carrying a fundamentally melancholy quality.

The old Taiwanese songs employed by democratization activists in the 1970s, typically express a passive, victimized persona.[6] The mid 1970s, however, witnessed the composition of songs sung in Mandarin that stood apart from these "classic" musical expressions of resistance. Singer/songwriter Lee Shuangtze's "Beautiful Formosa" (美麗島) and "Young China" (少年中國), for example, communicated a determined and empowered sensibility. Pro-democracy activist Linda Arrigo observed, "'Mending Broken Nets' and other early songs have a rather depressing tone about them although 'Broken Nets' is also a little activist, (i.e., we must repair the nets for our future).[7] 'Beautiful Formosa' is notable for its upbeat style, very positive, no more victim role" (e-mail correspondence with author, June 24, 2007).

Lee Shuangtze was an important voice during the fermentation of the campus folksong movement of the 1970s.[8] Lee is colorfully remembered for his call to liberate Taiwan's music from American and Japanese influences when, during a live performance in 1976, he threw down his Coke bottle and shouted, "We must sing our own songs!" While many of the Movement's songs were simple expressions of life and love, some powerfully reflected political concerns of the time. The ROC's rapidly increasing diplomatic isolation prompted young people to question their identity. Was their home ultimately in China or in Taiwan? Lee's songs "Beautiful Formosa" and "Young China" explored both answers to this question. Aboriginal singer Hu Tefu, who is sometimes called "Taiwan's Bob Dylan" for his singing of protest songs during the 1960s and 1970s, premiered "Beautiful Formosa" at Lee Shuang-tse's funeral in 1977. The song quickly gained popularity with students and political activists and became their virtual anthem. It was banned following the violent clash in December 1979 between prodemocracy activists and police known as the Formosa incident.[9] As the singer most closely associated with "Beautiful Formosa," Hu Tefu found himself blacklisted from radio and TV (Baker 2006, 18). Ironically, "Young China" was also banned as KMT censors feared the song promoted a pro-(Communist) China sentiment.

No overview of popular music history in Taiwan, with special reference to social relevance and political critique, is complete without mention of Luo Dayou, who over his more than a quarter-century-long performing career, attained iconic status in Taiwan, Hong Kong, and mainland China. Luo's artistic innovations include both textual and musical innovations. Luo introduced an "edgier" aesthetic to Taiwan's popular music and is often credited with being the earliest innovator of Chinese rock and roll. In terms of lyric content, Luo engaged in social and political criticism that was virtually unprecedented in its directness. His musical critiques focused on issues that were rooted in the specifics of life in Taiwan. For example, "Lugang, Small Town" (鹿港小鎮)—which is the opening track of his first album *Pedantry* (之乎者也), released in 1982—expresses angst over modern, urban life by contrasting the small fishing village of Lugang (with its famous Matsu temple) with neon-lit, urban Taipei.

Modernist alienation is a persistent theme throughout much of Luo's career. The title track of his second album *Masters of the Future* (未來的主人翁), released in 1983, equates urban living with dangerous technological developments (such as, the "sky polluted by the games of technology," "computer-dependent children," silent spring) and contrasts these with elements of the natural environment (such as, green grass, the earth, blue sky).[10] His once banned "Super Citizens" (超級市民), from his third album *Home* (家), released in 1984, gives very specific, place-bound examples of Taiwan's environmental degradation and rising crime levels. Luo sings of Taipei's garbage floating down the Tamsui River, bars on the windows of highrise apartments that keep out rats but not burglars, and gunfire reverberating along Kaohsiung's Liuhu Road. Luo's criticism is direct and cutting, as it illustrates places and circumstances well known to people in Taiwan. It is linked thematically to Taiwan's emerging civil society and strengthening social movements. In this sense, Luo daringly opened a path to the expressive renaissance of the late 1980s and 1990s.

Heralding Regime Change

As I asserted in this chapter's opening, I believe that popular music of the late 1980s and 1990s foretold the regime change of the year 2000. Taiwan's increasingly free political environment allowed for the expression of sentiments long banished from public discourse in forms long pushed to the cultural fringes. One bold artistic step led to the next. As musicians created throughout the decade, the vision of a Taiwan dominated by local culture (as opposed to mainland-Chinese derived and identified), forms of expression, and political leadership came into clearer and clearer focus. Earlier songs of protest, with their melancholy tunes and passive positionality, gave way to more proactive, upbeat, and aggressive sounds. Below, I organize popular music trends and innovations from this period into five overlapping categories: (1) the Hoklo popular music revival; (2) intensification of music as criticism; (3) exploration of local epistemologies of music making; (4) sounding of a multicultural strategy; and (5) embracing long-disparaged cultural elements.

The Hoklo popular music revival

It is beyond the scope of this chapter to detail the various factors that led to the stagnation in Hoklo song creativity and productivity in the forty or so years prior to the 1980s. Hoklo, often referred to in English as Taiwanese, is the native language of the majority of Taiwan's populace. Language has long been a battleground for political tensions between "native" Taiwanese and the KMT government and its supporters who fled to Taiwan along with Chiang Kai-shek in the late 1940s. Suffice to say that KMT government restrictions on the hours per day allotted to non-Mandarin broadcasts, the banning of specific Hoklo songs, and a pervasive attitude that cast "local" or *bensheng* cultural production as inferior to Mandarin or mainland-Chinese-derived expressions, combined to siphon capital and talent away from the composition of Hoklo popular song. One of the artistic consequences of this draining away of resources was a decrease in the composition of original songs. In the 1950 through the 1970s, the setting of Hoklo texts to Japanese or Western melodies was practiced widely, though by no means exclusively. One of the best known and enduring songs to emerge from this practice is "Hometown at Dusk" (黃昏的故鄉) whose Hoklo words were written by singer/lyricist Wen Hsia and set to a Japanese melody. With tonal languages such as Hoklo, word meaning is easily obscured if melodic contours are not made to accommodate linguistic tone. In the early 1980s, songwriters once again turned their attention to the importance of the relationship between melody and linguistic tone. "Who Knows My Heart" (心事誰人知), written by Cai Zhennan and recorded by Shen Wencheng, is often credited with launching the Hoklo pop revival (Liu 1998, 96–97; Gao 2007a). Released in 1982 and sold underground at night markets, the song became hugely popular, outliving government censorship (Gao 2007b). According to music critic Wang Chen-yi, this song, "which depicts a man's endless struggle and subtly alludes to the collective state of mind in an oppressed society . . . represented a major shift toward a stronger linkage between melody and lyrics" (quoted in Gao 2007a). Other songs released within several years of "Who Knows My Heart" were also key in revitalizing Hoklo pop music, including Hong Ronghong's "A Little Umbrella" (一支小雨傘; 1982), Jiang Hui's "Farewell

Coast" (惜別的海岸; 1984), Chen Hsiao-yun's "Dancing Girl" (舞女; 1985), and Ye Qitian's "Fighting to Win" (愛拼才會贏; 1985).

The songs in this first wave of the Hoklo pop revival, though taking greater care in text setting, did not deviate from what had become typical Hoklo pop performance conventions. These included the use of *nakashi*-style arrangements and Japanese *enka*-style vocal techniques and ornamentations. In other words, they maintained the musical aesthetic of the Hoklo pop of previous generations (that is, the 1950s–70s). The first major move away from this marginalized musical style came with Jiang Hui's 1992 hit album *My True Feelings Come Out after Drinking* (酒後的心聲). Released on Diangjiang Records, a label best known for its Mandarin albums, Jiang's album was attractively packaged and well-marketed. It sold about one million copies and is credited with being the first Hoklo pop album to attract Taiwan's white-collar listening audience en masse. Jiang Hui, often dubbed the Queen of Taiwanese Music, was the perfect candidate for moving Hoklo into the mainstream. She had already enjoyed an unusually high degree of media recognition for a singer of Hoklo songs. For example, in 1984 she was named one of the top ten most popular singers by the influential *Variety Show 100*. Of the top ten, Jiang was the only one to have made her career singing in Hoklo rather than Mandarin. From that time forward, Jiang "was at the forefront of an important trend that brought Taiwanese-dialect songs into the popular music market" (Wester 1994, 14).

In summary, the 1980s witnessed a revitalization of Hoklo song due in part to a strengthening of the artistic product through greater attention to the text–tone relationship. The main question is, what prompted these creative advancements at this point in time? Taiwan's rapidly growing economy represented a key factor. Members of Hoklo pop's long-standing audience (that is, blue-collar workers) were finding themselves with greater disposable income. At the same time, government censors were gradually loosening restrictions. Jiang Hui's 1992 album represented a massive breakthrough as Hoklo pop moved into the respectable mainstream; thus, it inspired the creative efforts of other Hoklo lyricists, composers, and performers. These elements combined to significantly brighten the prospects for the Hoklo pop market and to raise the status of Hoklo pop generally.

Intensification of music as criticism

Widely noted as a seminal work, the album titled *Songs of Madness* (抓狂歌) opened a new chapter in Taiwan's popular music history. Released in 1989 by a consortium of musicians working under the subversive name Blacklist Workshop, the album "changed the ecology of Taiwanese dialect music," according to Landy Chang, the former president of Magic Stones Records (quoted in Her 2000, 19). Multiple elements combined to make *Songs of Madness* an extraordinary work for its time. Perhaps foremost was its breaking away from the melancholic tone that had dominated postwar Hoklo pop music (Jiang 1996, 65).[11] This album's casting aside of the passive, victimized stance led the way for further daring musical, social, and political moves. Other elements that made *Songs* *of Madne*ss exceptional were its: (1) pointed criticism of the Nationalist government; (2) predominate use of Hoklo;[12] (3) colorful and detailed depiction of contemporary life in Taiwan, particularly in urban Taipei; and (4) musical innovations such as the use of rap-style text delivery and extended, nonformulaic song forms (Figure 13.1).

I take "A Democracy Bumpkin" (民主阿草) as illustrative of the above points. Significantly, this piece "claims the distinction" of being one of the last songs officially banned by the ROC Government Information Office (Schweig 2013, 93). The lyrics of "Democracy Bumpkin" narrate the experience of several "country bumpkins" who have traveled to the urban capital to take in the sites. While out for a morning stroll near Ximending (Taipei's historic entertainment district which borders the section of Taipei housing central government offices, including the Presidential Palace and Legislative Yuan) they come upon civilian and military police sporting full riot gear. The bumpkins

FIGURE 13.1 Blacklist Workshop's 1989 release *Songs of Madness*.

© Rock Records Co., Ltd., All Rights Reserved.

ask a policeman if they are preparing to take back the mainland (the words "take back the mainland" [反攻大陸] are spoken in heavily accented Mandarin). The policeman tells them to hurry home or they might find themselves in jail. A man next to them laughs at their naiveté and introduces himself as a member of the DPP. He explains that he has come to protest against the old political system, complaining that the National Assembly is filled with shameless men who are so old that they can barely breathe. Even when offered money, they will not retire. Next they encounter a group of war veterans who had come with Chiang Kai-shek to Taiwan and have been in Taiwan for forty years, working like oxen, with their only compensation being promissory notes for land in China, to be awarded once the mainland is regained. Here, the narration is broken up by five repetitions of the line "I want to protest" (我要抗議; rapped clearly in Mandarin). The lyrics close with a statement and a question: "It's now the seventy-eighth year of the Republic of China . . . Are we going prepare for war and take back the mainland?"

The song is a direct, colorful, and cutting attack on the farcical National Assembly whose elderly members were last elected to office in 1947, when the ROC was still based in mainland China.[13] Insisting that all of China's provinces must be represented, the National Assembly was essentially frozen in time since the Communist rebellion made it impossible for new representatives to be elected in China. It was only after the lifting of martial law in July 1987 that this obvious ploy on the part of the KMT regime to impede both democratization and Taiwanization could be safely criticized.

Musically, "Democracy Bumpkins" opens as a funeral dirge for the Republic of China with the first full phrase of the ROC national anthem being belted out by an out-of-tune band. This small ensemble's sound is unmistakably that of the kind of brass, woodwind, and percussion group one might hear at a Taipei funeral parlor. The Blacklist Workshop's message could not be more clear. The national anthem is heard again in the final instrumental passage, after the last line of text is rapped. This time it is played heroically by a full cello section, though the musical irony continues as the Valkyrie leitmotiv from Wagner's *Der Ring des Nibelungen* is played by synthesized brass instruments twice over the top of the anthem's melody. Following the second statement of the Valkyrie theme, drums enter and introduce the final section of the song which is best described as patterned noise or chaos.

The musical feature most often mentioned in reviews of *Songs of Madness* is its introduction of rap-style text delivery to Hoklo musical expression. The lyrics of "Democracy Bumpkin" are rapped throughout. All but a few words are in Hoklo. Another of the song's innovative musical features is its form, which takes seven minutes and twenty-six seconds to unfold. The text, which narrates its story with only one full stanza of repetition, is complemented by three extended instrumental sections. This piece is a significant advancement in terms of not only its direct criticism of the Nationalist regime (in both textual and musical terms), but also in its moving Hoklo popular song away from decades-old musical conventions in terms of song form (usually strophic), length, and instrumental accompaniment.

Another vital voice of musical dissent of the 1990s was Zhu Yuexin (also known as Jutoupi, literally "pig-head-skin"). Like the Blacklist Workshop, Zhu's first commercial releases were produced by Crystal Records. Crystal Records was at the center of the so-called Wax Club, an organization formed in 1986 in reaction to Taiwan's overly commercialized and, ultimately, dull mainstream pop music. The initial motivation of the Wax Club founders was to use Crystal Records to distribute foreign "indie" music. The Club's greatest achievement, however, was in providing a recording opportunity for Taiwan's own innovative artists.[14]

While each of these artists found his or her own particular musical niche, Zhu Yuexin specialized in social and political satire. These, he often communicated by playing on textural ironies (such as peculiar pronunciation conventions that are associated with stereotypes of Taiwan's various ethnic groups and socioeconomic classes) which he underscored through his pastiche-like compositional practice. Literary scholar Jiang Wenyu (1996, 74) proclaimed Zhu's "funny rap" to be the most courageous experiment with language in Taiwan's popular music history. As an example of the subversive nature of Zhu's work, I briefly examine his song "Long Live Punk'N'Funk" (中華民國萬萬歲) from his 1994 hit album *Pig-head-skin's Funny Rap: I'm Insane* (豬頭皮的笑魁唸歌：我是神經病). "Long Live the Republic of China" is a direct translation of the song title, but I retain Zhu's own translation (Figure 13.2).

A first glance at Zhu's liner notes for "Long Live Punk'N'Funk" yields a perplexing cross between a scholarly paper and a comic book. Zhu is pictured wearing a flowered shower cap, thick glasses, a suit jacket and dress shirt (with rolled-up sleeves), a tie, cropped pants, and Japanese-style thong slippers. Meanwhile, the different text stanzas are labeled as A1, A2, B1, B2, and so on. These are then referenced with notes that clarify and translate the text (from Hoklo to Mandarin and Mandarin to Hoklo). Zhu is also meticulous in crediting, translating, and elaborating on the sources of his sampled materials. These translations and explanations highlight the fact that ironies of language and (mis)pronunciation are central in communicating Zhu's message.

In his first stanza, Zhu takes "Long Live the Republic of China" (and the sentiment this idiom represents) and raps about the ways in which Nationalist ideology has placed the ROC at the center of life in Taiwan. The second stanza—in the form of a vignette in which a dopy teacher instructs students in Mandarin on various forms of taxes—plays on the near homonyms "sui" (歲; meaning "long life") and "shui" (稅; meaning "tax").[15] Through his intentional conflation of these words, Zhu implies that it is mainly through the imposition of ten thousand forms of tax that the ROC has meaning in people's lives. In the last of the song's eight stanzas, Zhu plays further with homonyms and nonstandard Mandarin, which is typically associated with local Hoklo pronunciation of the national language (for instance, a failure to distinguish retroflex sounds such as /sh/ from nonretroflex sounds such as /s/). The play on words is found at the last syllable of the first half of each of the four lines. From these subtle shifts in pronunciation, the listener can easily comprehend the short distance separating deference and disdain.

中華民國萬萬歲　　我個人認為啊
Zhong hua min guo wan wan **sui** (long life) wo ge ren ren wei a
Long live the ROC

FIGURE 13.2 Zhu Yuexin's 1994 release *Pig-head-skin's Funny Rap: I'm Insane*.

© Rock Records Co., Ltd., All Rights Reserved.

中華民國亂亂睡　　國家建設要更好啊
Zhong hua min guo luan luan **sui**[16] (sleep) guo jia jian she yao geng hao a
The ROC chaotically, chaotically sleeps.

中華民國快快碎　　誠實納稅不可少啊
Zhong hua min guo kuai kuai **sui** (shatter) cheng shi nei tuo bu ke xiao a
May the ROC quickly shatter

中華民國 walk this way　　are you gonna go my way?
Zhong hua min guo walk this way are you gonna go my way?
ROC, walk this way.

　　Musically, Zhu crafts his song to give a strong sense of impatience and forward momentum. With its very fast tempo (which increases from the initial 126 beats per minute to an allegro agitato of 132 beats per minute), this piece races towards its final defiant statement; ultimately, Zhu is pushing towards the shattering of the Republic of China. The sense of rushing is not only accomplished through a quickening tempo, but also through an overlapping of phrases. Basically, each line of text is set to eight beats. For the first two stanzas, a new line begins on the first beat following the last (eighth) beat of the previous line. This pattern is disrupted, though, when the first line of the third stanza begins before the last line of the second stanza finishes. With this premature entry of the key phrase "Long live the Republic of China," the established pattern is broken and weight is shifted from the syllables "Zhonghua Mingguo" (Republic of China) to "wan wan sui" (long live). This overlapping of phrases occurs again when the last stanza begins before the seventh stanza ends. Thus, the song lurches ever forward to its final damning lines.

Overall, Zhu's work, as exhibited in this piece, is irreverent. He is direct in his criticism of the government; he presents caricatures of widely recognized types of people (old mainlanders with heavily-accented Mandarin, working class Hoklo speakers, and so on); and he is clearly pushing for the termination of the Republic of China. In the song's introduction, a sampled excerpt spoken in American-accented English says, "This one is going to change the course of history." In an endnote, Zhu writes, "I hope that our song can change the history of popular music in the Republic of China. We needn't have wild ambitions about changing all of history; that would be too arrogant" (希望我們這個歌可以改變中華民國的音樂史啦 不用野心大到整個力歷史 太臭屁).

Zhu's work, as illustrated by "Long Live Punk'N'Funk," was significant not only in opening new creative avenues for musical expression within the field of Taiwanese pop music, but also in providing a frame through which key aspects of life in Taiwan could be glimpsed. Zhu's tact was to reveal and disempower through parody. By listening to the interactions of Zhu's caricatures of stereotyped personalities (all of whom had a particular place in social and political hierarchies on Nationalist Taiwan), the comic vignettes in which they engaged could be understood as constructed (that is, not inevitable) and, ultimately, deconstructable. With the present depicted with such unforgiving clarity, a new, post-ROC Taiwan could be imagined.

Exploration of local epistemologies of music making

In her writing on Hong Kong, Rey Chow (1998, 152) observed that nativism, as a form of resistance against the dominant colonial culture, is inevitable in the postcolonial aftermath. As Taiwanese creative artists worked to move Taiwan towards a postcolonial (that is, post-Chinese Nationalist) state, one avenue they took was to explore local musical forms such as folk singing, Taiwanese opera, and aboriginal song. Chow writes disparagingly of what she terms "nostalgic root-searching," as she believes that rooting through the past in a quest for identity reduces the multiplicity of the present in the name of a long-lost (mythic) origin (162). One must ask, though, as urban-based musicians sought to find a voice for the expression of life in post-martial law Taiwan, where were they to turn? What musical languages were available for this "self-writing" project? As discussed above, some artists, including Zhu Toupi and members of the Blacklist Workshop, adapted foreign idioms such as American rap, while others continued to work in familiar styles such as *enka*-derived Hoklo pop. For others, the living remnants of traditional Hoklo expression provided another obvious resource.

Chen Ming-chang drew inspiration from musics such as Taiwanese opera, *nanguan* opera, *beiguan*, and *budaixi*, which he had heard as a child growing up in Beitou, a northern suburb of Taipei. Chen says that two factors were instrumental in driving him to ask, "What is Taiwanese music?" and "What is my Taiwanese music?" (Guo 2005, 100–101). First was his profound reaction to hearing Chen Da, a recent folk music legend.[17] While Chen Ming-chang had composed songs in Mandarin during the campus folksong movement, after hearing Chen Da's performance, he suddenly realized that his own earlier creations neither expressed feelings for the land (*tudi*) nor did they in any way reflect on local culture (*bentu wenhua*). Second was his disbelief and anger at only learning of the February 28, 1947, uprising in his late twenties.[18] Chen took it as his mission to ensure the transmission of Taiwan's history.

The first Hoklo song that Chen Ming-chang wrote was "Immigration from Mainland to Taiwan" (唐山過台灣), which tells of the early immigrants' gratitude to the gods for overseeing their safe passage from China to Tamsui and other named places in Taiwan (Guo 2005, 101). He recorded this song on his highly acclaimed second solo album, *An Afternoon Drama* (下午的一齣戲), released in 1990. The piece opens with a *dizi* (horizontal bamboo flute), which continues to provide a countermelody above the plucked string accompaniment to his singing. The plucked strings (guitar and mandolin) play in a heterophonic texture reminiscent of that heard in traditional Taiwanese opera. The mood shifts for a reprise of the third stanza as the bubbling plucked strings give way to a gentle accompaniment dominated by *erhu* (two-stringed bowed lute) with supporting violin, viola, and cello lines.

On this album, Chen not only pays homage to Taiwan history, but also to two masters of local performing traditions. He does so both through his text and musically by incorporating sounds (in the form of instrumental timbres) and textures (the use of heterophony rather than homophony, which is common in Western-derived forms) characteristic of local performing traditions. Chen Ming-chang dedicates the song "Chen Da" (紅目達仔) to the master singer of melodies from Taiwan's southernmost area of Hengchun. In his notes, which take the form of background stories for each of the songs (that is, scenes in this "afternoon drama"), Chen Ming-chang reminisces about attending a performance by Chen Da in a Western restaurant in Taipei. Chen Da sat on the stage wearing a ill-fitting Western suit as his listeners sat before him eating steak. Chen Ming-chang recalls the great distance that separated the audience members' lifestyle from Chen Da's music.

The album's final track "Bamboo Poem" (竹枝詞) is dedicated to the elderly *nanguan* teacher Jin Zhishi (金枝師). In the description preceding the song text, Chen sets a wistful mood as he describes how the illiterate master teacher now only finds performing opportunities once or twice a month. The master says that his art will die with him. In the note following the song text, Chen writes that it was only once he was in his thirties that he began to understand that "music will decay and die away with our flesh" (音樂是會隨肉體腐化而死亡). The main instrumental accompaniment is provided by traditional instruments, including *pipa* (a four-stringed plucked lute which is an essential instrument in the *nanguan* ensemble), *xiao* (an end-blown vertical flute whose delicate sound is also featured in *nanguan* music), *erhu*, hand-held cymbals, and several drums. The only Western instruments are piano, acoustic guitar, and electric guitar, which are all played unidiomatically. For example, rather than playing chords or scale-like patterns as in Western music, the piano plays only a two-note pattern (the two notes are not simultaneities) at cadential points. With this through-composed song, Chen heavily employed a musical epistemology that has more in common with heterophonic musics such as *nanguan* and Taiwanese opera than with Western pop, which typically employs homophonic textures and strophic form.

As Chen Ming-chang strove to answer the questions of "What is Taiwanese music?" and "What is *his* Taiwanese music?" he did not simply borrow sounds that were immediately identifiable as traditional to use as symbols of Taiwaneseness. Instead, he drew upon musical epistemologies (that is, ways of knowing music, or the processes through which music is created and performed) employed by the practitioners of the native traditions he grew up hearing. He integrated these into his own compositional practice creating pieces that do not neatly fit into any preexisting form or genre, but which are unmistakably of Taiwan.

Sounding of a multicultural strategy

In the 1980s, the pan green camp began to assert a vision of Taiwan as a multicultural (多元文化主義) society comprised of four equally important ethnic groups: aboriginal, Hoklo, Hakka, and mainland Chinese. This view was a corrective to the hierarchical policy of Chinese nationalism expounded by the KMT; a policy that ranked mainland Chinese culture at the top followed by Hoklo and Hakka cultures, with aboriginal cultures at the bottom (Wang 2004, 304–305). By the early 1990s, the DPP was creating polices based on the multicultural model with two main objectives in mind. First was to address the inequality inherent in the KMT's policy of Chinese nationalism. Second was to bolster the notion of Taiwan as a unique society with distinctly non-Han Chinese roots. Central to this premise was Taiwan aboriginal culture and the possibility that many of Taiwan's *benshengren* had aboriginal (i.e., non-Chinese) ancestors. This notion gained traction. Anthropologist Michael Stainton reported that in 1997 a Taiwanese scientist (whom Stainton did not name) asserted in an e-mail discussion group that as many as 60% of Taiwanese are descendants of aborigines (1999, 41). As people explored their possible Austronesian ancestry, they naturally became curious about aboriginal culture, including music.

While aboriginal singers had gained mainstream attention in the past, the environment in the mid-1990s was ripe for aboriginal artists to become major stars. The singer to reach the greatest popularity was A-Mei, a member of the Puyuma tribe. In her first album, released in 1996, she was joined in the recording studio by her mother and sisters who sang several phrases of a traditional Puyuma melody in the title hit song "Sisters" (姐妹). This along with her concert attire, especially in the early years of her career, indicated that her aboriginal identity was key to her marketing. Another singer to gain a good deal of attention from politicians, especially Chen Shui-bian, was Kuo Ying-nan, a master singer from the Amis tribe. He became a national symbol when his voice was used, without his knowledge or consent, as integral element in the international megahit "Return to Innocence" released by Enigma in 1993 (Guy 2002b). This song was used as a theme song for the 1996 Centennial Olympics.

Other aboriginal singers were snapped up by record companies who were eager to cash in on the surge of interest in indigenous music. When aboriginal performers and songs using Hoklo "swept away contenders" in the 11th annual Golden Melody Awards held in April 2000, the *Taipei Times* reported that "despite all the glam and glitz ... the main theme" of the award ceremony "was somewhat serious, focusing on Taiwan's cultural and musical identity" (*Taipei Times*, 29 April 2000). Aboriginal music in particular, and the wonder and interest it inspired in the mid to late 1990s, made the DPP's vision of Taiwan as a multicultural society "real" and visceral in a way that little else could have.

Embracing long-disparaged cultural elements

It is well known that for many decades KMT authorities suppressed and disparaged local Taiwan languages, customs, and culture, including the performing arts. With the lifting of martial law in 1987 and the dismantling of sedition laws, opposition politicians made increasing attacks on the policies that had institutionalized the disparity between (pre-1949 mainland-derived) national culture and local culture.[19] By the early 1990s, local politicians openly debated their mainlander colleagues in Hoklo, a language whose use had been forbidden in schools and other public places. In fact, opposition politicians were so successful in changing the terms of their debate that a number of KMT politicians took up formal study of Hoklo lest they be rendered speechless. The political battle to end discriminatory policies was complemented, at the societal level, by an embracing of long-denigrated local languages and cultural practices.

As I have discussed above, the 1980s and 1990s witnessed a revival of Hoklo popular music, including daring artistic experimentation that drew on both foreign and local sources and musical idioms. Another fascinating phenomenon, which was clearly one facet of a growing "Taiwan consciousness," was the (re)claiming of deeply marginalized local musics. The 1991 release on the Crystal Record label of the two-CD set titled *Sounds from Taiwan's Underclass* (來自台灣底層的聲音) represented an early effort to acknowledge and embrace native performing traditions that existed well beyond the periphery of middle class respectability. Not unlike the characters that populate the writings of nativist (*xiangtu*) authors, these musics are coded unmistakably as Taiwanese. The CD was compiled by a small group of academics, fieldworkers, and documentary filmmakers and included a variety of musics such as *nakashi*, Hakka mountain songs, the music of *cheguzhen* rituals, Hengchun folk songs, and plains aboriginal song. *Sounds from Taiwan's Underclass, Vol. 2*, followed in 1996 with an equally eclectic mix of aboriginal pop, *nakashi*, and electrified *beiguan* music. While these two releases reached a relatively small audience, two of the *nakashi* musicians, Wang Yingtan (王英坦; also known as the King of Jinmen [金門王]) and Li Binghui (李炳輝), featured on the second volume became pop music sensations.

Nakashi is a syncretic though uniquely Taiwanese music, which is believed to have originated in Taiwan's port cities of Keelung (Jilong) and Tamsui (Danshui) in the early 1900s. Japanese sailors came ashore bringing their instruments and songs. In the context of teahouses, local musicians eventually melded Hoklo lyrics and melodies with this sailor music while maintaining the foreign accompaniment of guitars and accordions. Before they became nationally recognized pop icons, Wang Yingtan and Li Binghui, both blind musicians, earned their livings as *nakashi* musicians playing in seedy bars and restaurants in the former port city of Tamsui, and in the hot spring, pleasure quarters of Beitou.

Wang and Li's break came when Chen Ming-chang, with his interest in tapping into Taiwan's unique musical resources, envisioned producing an album featuring them and their *nakashi* music. Chen wrote the music and lyrics for the album's title song "Drifting Down to Tamsui" (流浪到淡水) while rock sensation Wu Bai and his band China Blue arranged it. While the two releases of *Sounds from Taiwan's Underclass* presented marginalized musics lifted directly from their performing contexts, Wang and Li's *nakashi* music, as produced by Magic Stone Records, was professionally arranged and recorded. Through this process, Chen Ming-chang oversaw the packaging of this lower-class music in a form that middle-class listeners could identify with and embrace. When the album was released in 1997, it "took the local music scene by storm" reaching the top of local pop charts (Phipps 2002). Album sales surpassed 700,000 units within two months of its releases. Landy Chang, then the president of Magic Stone Records, admitted that he had not expected the album to sell more than 30,000 to 50,000 units; he had cautioned company executives not to spend too much on producing or promoting it.

With the creation of this album, Chen Ming-chang articulated and added to the nativist zeitgeist prevalent on the eve of the 2000 presidential election. As journalist Pat, Her (2000, 19) observed the album *Drifting Down to Tamsui* "seemed to many people to come as close as music could come to the soul of what it meant to be Taiwanese at the close of the twentieth century." What did it mean for this music to represent Taiwaneseness? What did Taiwaneseness sound and look like as represented by Li and Wang? A glimpse at Wang, the King of Jinmen, offers a few answers. Wang personifies the familiar, persevering victim figure, not unlike characters in Huang Chunming's stories such as Bai Mei in "A Day for Watching the Sea." Wang lost his eyesight and his left hand when as a teenager he found a detonator on a street in his native Jinmen (also known as Kinmen) that blew up as he was playing with it. Wang's injuries, therefore, resulted directly from the Nationalists' ongoing conflict with the Chinese Communists, who shelled the offshore island on a regular basis until 1979. Looking a little deeper into Wang's biography shows that his parents gave him up for adoption; this no doubt resonated with the theme of Taiwan as the "orphan of Asia." Despite all of these trials and tribulations, Wang—who strums his guitar with a pick strapped to his maimed left wrist—became an accomplished musician, albeit beyond the fringes of respectable society. For educated, middle-class listeners, there was a certain authenticity to Wang and his music. In the face of multiple colonizations and discrimination, "authentic Taiwanesness" had been maintained by Wang, Li, and others peopling the underclass.

Relevant to the sea change which followed Chen Shui-bian's inauguration, Landy Chang (then president of the Magic Stone label) mused in 2002 that Wang and Li's meteoric rise to fame of 1997 would probably not be repeatable in the early 2000s. He surmised that "the sense of Taiwanese-ness is not as strong anymore . . . With the DPP in power and martial law lifted, there is little call for Taiwanese-ness. It's like nobody cares about such things anymore" (Phipps 2002).

In this section, I have discussed only a small fraction of the popular music that nourished and drew nourishment from a virtual renaissance that took shape over the late 1980s and 1990s as Taiwanese explored local history and cultural practices. The move towards nativism or localization that sweep across Taiwan during this period was essentially an efficacious social movement. The musical creativity that formed as part of this zeitgeist was not insignificant in the push towards the unprecedented regime change in the year 2000. Through this musical practice, the future could be viscerally imagined.

Singer A-Mei Signals a Tide Change

It is not only through the sound of music, but also through the public actions of prominent musicians that social, economic, and political change is signaled. Certain elements of a passage from Attali's *Noise* resonate strongly with the circumstances that Taiwanese pop singers, particularly those who record primarily in Mandarin, have been forced to negotiate at the turn of the millennium. How they negotiate these competing forces, and the choices they make as they weigh one power against another, is not lost on their audience members. Writing about the period in which European musicians earned their keep through court patronage, Attali writes that the musician was:

> economically bound to a machine of power, political or commercial, which paid him a salary for creating what it needed to affirm its legitimacy. Like the notes of tonal music on the staff, he was cramped, channeled. A domestic, his livelihood depended on the goodwill of the prince. (17)

The case of A-Mei's performance of the "Republic of China National Anthem" at Chen Shui-bian's first inaugural ceremony in May 2000, laid bare the power dynamics present in contemporary Taiwan's political and economic environments.[20] If, as a musician, A-Mei's livelihood depended on the goodwill of the "prince," her actions following the inaugural ceremony signaled that her prince resided in Beijing and not in Taipei. Most pop artists, like other good capitalists, gravitate towards commercial power. In the case of China, access to this commercial power is granted only after loyalties are proven, as A-Mei discovered. Other performers quickly learned from her case. Behaviors similar to A-Mei's could be observed in many different commercial corners throughout Chen Shui-bian's eight years in the presidency.

The ceremonial events marking Chen Shui-bian's inauguration were large-scale spectacles in which music, dance, and poetry narrated the past, reaffirmed the present, and offered a vision for the future. Breaking with the usual practice of inviting a (Western) operatically trained singer to perform the national anthem, the new Chen administration invited A-Mei, a pop star of Taiwan aboriginal descent, to perform this highly symbolic song. At the time of the inauguration, A-Mei was arguably the most popular female singer of Mandarin pop alive. Her fame extended across the Taiwan Straits to China as well to the rest of the Mandopop-listening world. Musically, her performance of the anthem went well. As the ceremony organizers expected, A-Mei brought a fresh, and even hopeful, sound to this old Nationalist Party song.[21]

Unfortunately for A-Mei, Chen's inaugural ceremony was being carefully scrutinized in China. Immediately following her singing of the anthem, the Communist Party's propaganda department ordered all state-owned media to halt the dissemination of advertisements featuring the Taiwanese star. Coca-Cola, which had hired A-Mei to endorse Sprite, was notified the day prior to Chen's inauguration that its multimillion-dollar advertising campaign featuring her must be withdrawn (Dickie and Kynge 2000, 14). Initially, A-Mei was banned from entering the Chinese mainland for a period of three years.[22]

China's ban sent A-Mei's career into free fall. Since approximately ninety-five percent of the CDs sold in China are pirated copies, the main opportunities for recording artists to gain a piece of the Chinese market are through concert appearances and product promotions (Fung 2007, 434). In assessing A-Mei's situation in early 2001, *Newsweek* magazine's Mahlon Meyer (2001, 37) adeptly observed that:

> A-mei's Mei's tale, writ large, is also Taiwan's . . . For Beijing, the muzzling of A-mei is just another way of dimming Taiwanese hopes for independence. But if she can resurrect her career despite Beijing's ban, her example may encourage the island's youth to believe they needn't give into Chinese pressure.

A-Mei's career never returned to its pre-inaugural heights. And A-Mei did not stand up to China's pressure. Instead, she made every effort to appear apolitical. Eventually, she even denied making the decision to sing for Chen's inauguration (Wang and Chang 2004). She said her recording company had made it for her. When invited to sing the national anthem again at the October 2000 ROC National Day celebration, she refused.

A little more than a year after her banning, Chinese authorities invited A-Mei back to China. Two months prior to the issuing of the invitation, she sang at a benefit performance in Hong Kong that was attended by the PRC Vice Minister for Health. This was taken as a sign of her coming rehabilitation. Reporting on the event, the *South China Morning Post* cited her as saying, "I just hope to perform on the mainland as soon as possible . . . I am not a politician, but a singer with innocent beliefs" (Lau 2001, 3). A-Mei's first return performance was in Beijing at a prefight concert for China's first hosting of a World Boxing Association match. Upon learning the news, A-Mei said, "I'm a person that likes to sing, concerts are very important to me, it's wonderful singing for my fans, it doesn't matter if it's in Taiwan or China. So long as it's a place with Chinese people (*huaren*), I like to sing there" (Zhu 2001).

The rehabilitation of her concretizing career in China was not without its trials. In June 2004, protestors—who accused her of being a "green performer" and supporting Taiwan independence—forced the cancellation of a concert in Hangzhou. Several months later, protestors in Beijing demanded that she sing China's national anthem, "March of the Volunteers." She didn't sing the anthem, though she did break down and wept on stage (Bishop 2004, 4). Nevertheless, A-Mei continues to seek the good favor of Beijing officials. For example, she recorded an English-language song, "Forever Friends," which she submitted for consideration for the Beijing Olympics opening ceremony. Olympic organizers reported that the song was one of their top five candidates, "despite Chang's [sic.] checkered past in China" (Lin 2008).

It was ironic for China to cast A-Mei as a Taiwan independence supporter by virtue of her singing at Chen Shui-bian's inauguration. She had never shown support for Chen or his Democratic Progressive Party. In fact, while A-Mei pleads ignorance of political matters, she had ties to the most pro-China, pro-unification faction in Taiwan. She was the performer of the theme song for the UFO radio station that was established by Jaw Shau-kong, the founder of the pro-China New Party. With its strongly pro-unification stance, the New Party occupied the opposite side of the political spectrum from Chen Shui-bian's DPP. This is unimportant, though, as the Chinese authorities were employing a well-worn tactic: "kill one to warn a hundred."

And, warn it did. Other performing artists quickly gleaned from A-Mei's experience that to keep their careers afloat in China, they needed to distance themselves from President Chen Shui-bian and anything that could be construed as connecting them to him or his administration. For example, in early June 2000, in a *United Daily News* report on Taiwan pop artists' upcoming concert tours in China, singer Zhang Xinzhe was cited as saying, in clear reference to A-Mei's situation, "Luckily, when it comes to important occasions, no one thinks of me. This turns out to have been very fortunate indeed!" (Keng 2000). Artists avoided officially sponsored events like the plague. For the first New Year's Eve celebration of Chen's term, Sony Music Entertainment and MTV Asia were vying for the chance to produce the show that would be staged in front of the Presidential Palace. Late in the bidding process, the government announced the condition that President Chen would join the performers on stage for the countdown to midnight. Sony immediately withdrew from the bidding because it did not want to risk having its artists, who included Coco Lee, the boy band F4, David Huang, and Harlem Yu, banned in China (Kearns 2001).

In "normal countries" (to borrow former Taiwan President Lee Teng-hui's notion of *zhengchang guojia*), an invitation to sing the national anthem at state-sponsored events is considered an honor (Lee 2002). After the A-Mei incident, however, many performers viewed such invitations with trepidation. They imposed their own self-censorship in line with cues from China. An article reporting on the National Day celebration in 2004 opened, "No pop star has volunteered to sing the national anthem during this year's Double Ten National Day celebration" (Ko 2004). According to a *Taipei Times* editorial published on October 21, 2004, both superstars Jay Chou and Jolin Tsai declined invitations to perform at the event. In the end, no professional singers stepped forward to sing the anthem; instead, two athletes who had competed in the 2004 Olympics sang the anthem.

The 2008 inaugural celebration for newly elected President Ma Ying-jeou provides a fascinating shift in attitudes towards singing for state ceremonies. Ma is a KMT member and is widely viewed as being China-friendly and pro-unification. A month before Ma's inauguration, the incoming administration's core advisors leaked to the press that they had been overwhelmed by performers' requests to sing the national anthem. It was simply impossible for them to choose one from among the many qualified artists vying for the honor to perform. To avoid hurt feelings, they chose to invite a children's chorus to sing this important song (Qiu 2008). Nevertheless, the morning's inaugural event was star-studded with top pop artists, including Wang Lee-hom, Wu Bai and China Blue, Jiang Shuna, and Feng Feifei, all taking the stage (Zhongyangshe 2008). It is clear that the many performers (which in addition to pop artists also included Peking opera performers, a *budaixi* troupe, Cloudgate Dance Theatre, and a group of aboriginal singers, among others) who eagerly participated in Ma's inaugural celebration did not fear reprisal from China.

Through their actions, such as distancing themselves from Chen Shui-bian and embracing Ma Ying-jeou, pop artists publicly signal with crystal clarity that the "machine of power" to which they are bound sits across the Straits in China. By making an example of A-Mei, Beijing demonstrated that the Chinese market cannot be accessed without the goodwill of Chinese authorities. A-Mei's reaction to her banning in China foretold Chen Shui-bian's future. Chen would fail in nation-building. Any gesture in that direction was met with Chinese threats to capitalist interests.

Sounding Greater China

In the aftermath of China's banning of A-Mei, quite a few pop stars associated with Taiwan have managed to be quite successful in creating works that attract huge audiences in China. Many of these works also extend the ideology of Chineseness (or "greater China" ideology) promoted by Chinese state authorities (Fung 2007, 435). Anthony Fung adeptly observes that mainland authorities have moved from shunning pop music to actively molding it to "co-opt the people and public culture" (435). While Fung writes specifically about China, I would assert that his argument, like the power of Chinese authorities, extends to Taiwan.

Fung points to Jay Chou, who has been one of the most popular singers in China and Taiwan since the early 2000s, as exemplifying this trend. Through his masterful combining of Chinese-sounding melodies, which are often played on Chinese instruments, and Mandarin poetic texts performed in rap and R&B vocal styles, Jay creates a sonic image that is identifiably Chinese, modern, and "cool." For example, his song "Nunchaku" (雙截棍), released in 2001, opens with distorted electric guitars and a heavy rock sound. Several lines of Jay's rapped text are punctuated by the unmistakable timbre of a Peking opera gong. In a break between stanzas, an *erhu* enters playing a wistful melody. In the video that accompanies the song, Jay wears a tight-fitting tank top that accentuates his sculpted muscles. In several scenes, he twirls the *nunchaku* weapon (*shuang jie gun*) in a virtuosic martial arts pattern. Jay visually punctuates his vocal delivery of the rapped text by alternating hip-hop gestures and Chinese martial arts movements. When the album containing this song was current, Jay frequently brought his live concerts to a climax with his *nunchaku* routine. Jay's use of these martial art routines can be viewed as patriotically Chinese in their invocation of the image of the legendary martial arts master Bruce Lee, who, in his classic movie *The Chinese Connection*, "fought the Japanese and publicly declared that Chinese are not the 'Sick Men of Asia'" (Fung 2007, 435). This song and its video exemplifies Chou's melding of sonic and visual elements, some of which are coded as Chinese, in the creation of a persona that is strong, global, yet unmistakably Chinese. As Anthony Fung observes: "Jay Chou nowadays, with the support from [mainland] Chinese authorities and various state-corporations, is sublimated into an icon of Chineseness—apolitical and yet unifying the new generation for the nation" (ibid.). For observers in Taiwan, Jay presents a positive image of the possibilities of a future-looking greater China through both his artistic creations and the smooth management of his career in China.

Born in the United States to parents from Taiwan, Wang Lee Hom's fame extends to all corners of the Mandopop world. Like Jay Chou's work, Wang draws heavily on R&B vocal mannerisms, hip-hop-style text delivery and accompaniment, and elements of traditional Chinese music. Here I focus on Wang Lee Hom's song "Heroes of the Earth" (蓋世英雄) which was released in late 2005. Wang organically weaves iconically Chinese musical sounds into his original composition. For example, Peking opera gongs and drums are an integral part of the hip-hop rhythmic accompaniment. He also includes several passages performed by an authentic Peking opera singer. These are central to Wang's hopeful message of a rising greater China: "Fierce power spreads through the north China plain; the King raises the signal fire. Massive strength sways the mountains, rivers, and sky; vast power returns triumphantly."[23]

Wang sings of his travels from Shanghai, to Beijing, with a stop in Taipei, and back to Hong Kong. As part of his stated "purpose" of bringing "chinked-out" to the world, Wang marvels at the world's growing interest in China, and he repeats, this time in English, his message of change coming through his new music:

> they wanna know about us; we been around for ages; a couple thousand years; a bunch of pioneers; just artists and scholars makin' noise it was loud and clear; hey yo, the future's here the revolution's near.

Wang expresses his eagerness for the future, which, he raps, is on the brink of being realized. Expressing a sentiment consonant with early philosophers' conceptions of music as a harbinger of change, Wang exclaims in Mandarin: "Only with a new breakthrough can a new song style bring forth a new ultimate hero."

The new hero arises from Chinese cultural resources. His sound is that of the *wusheng* (the martial male role type in Peking opera): "Turn the volume up as loud as it'll go, the sound you hear is once again a *wusheng*." According to Wang, the future will be delivered through new music. The essence of this epoch-making music is the integration of hip-hop (which is coded as a global music of resistance) and traditional Chinese opera (and all it symbolizes, such as thousands of years of Chinese culture). Wang's song is a confident expression of Attali's notion of music heralding change.

On May 20, 2008, when Wang Lee Hom performed this song at President Ma Ying-jeou's inaugural ceremony, he was joined on stage by four Peking opera *wusheng* actors and six dancers. Wang revised the text of the Peking opera segment of "Heroes of the Earth" by replacing the words that outlined his name in the 2005 release (Ba, Wang, Lee, Hom) with words that paid tribute to Ma Ying-jeou (Zhi, Ma, Ying, Jeou) (NOWnews 2008).[24] When he came to the phrase, "The ultimate hero is here," he sang especially loudly, thus emphasizing Ma's heroic status as the leader to bring forth a new world (Zhongyangshe 2008).

Conclusion

Regardless of the method employed or medium of interpretation, predicting political change is an uncertain science. Listening for the heralding quality of music is perhaps more of an art than a science. Since the end of the 1960s, the rational actor model and its variants have dominated social and political analyses; until fairly recently theories of social movements and collective action gave emotion little notice (Goodwin, Japser, and Polletta 2001, 5). In his book *The Political Brain: the Role of Emotion in Deciding the Fate of the Nation*, psychology professor Drew Westen (2007, xv) asserts that "the political brain is an emotional brain." As a music scholar, my subject deals explicitly with the expression of emotion and the experiential aspects of cultural meaning. The study of music allows the attuned listener to gain a sense of how things are playing out in the hearts of those on the ground.

The primary challenges of listening to music as a herald of change derive from two key uncertainties. The first is data selection. Of the thousands of popular songs released over the twenty years surveyed here, how can I be sure that I have picked the most *prophetic* ones? Hindsight is helpful, of course, but what about predicting future change? Like the officials who staffed the Music Bureau of the Western Han, I listen for resonances between music and the observable world. There is also the question of time frame. The hopeful songs of the 1990s heralded the regime change of 2000, but they could not predict the sea change that followed A-Mei's singing of the national anthem.

This change came abruptly. The fallout from A-Mei's performance was profound and predictive of Taiwan's coming acceptance of closer relations with China (as exhibited in Ma Ying-jeou's 2008 and reelection in 2012). The promise of economic prosperity (which would only come on China's terms) trumped the drive for self-determination and dreams of permanent sovereignty. True to the musical antecedents to his election, over his eight years in office, President Ma greatly bolstered Taiwan's relations with China through more economic ties, increased tourism links, and the signing of a significant trade pact.

Finally, one might ask, was Ma Ying-jeou the ultimate hero Wang Lee Hom sang about in 2005 or was Wang's original vision broader in view? Perhaps Ma Ying-jeou's election to the presidency was just the first stage of a larger and longer process. As with all acts of interpretation, only time will reveal the accuracy and full focus of Wang Lee Hom's vision and this musicologist's interpretation of it.

Notes

1. I presented earlier versions of this paper at the UCLA Center for Chinese Studies, the University of South Carolina Conference on Taiwan Issues, and in the Department of Music at the Chinese University of Hong Kong. I thank Helen Rees, Marc Moskowitz, and Yu Siu Wah for their comments and suggestions as I worked through this material.
2. Music is, in fact, often an integral part of the social aspect of movements (see Eyerman and Jamison 1998). Given the dominance of rational actor models of analysis, it is not surprising that music and other forms of performative expression went unnoticed by the vast majority of scholars of social movement until fairly recently. Music lies within the realm of emotion, and this is precisely the aspect ignored by scholars seeking rational explanations for participant motivation.
3. These themes were subsequently canonized in the early Han in the "Book of Music" chapter of the *Book of Rites* and in the "Treatise on Music" (Yueji) from the *Records of the Grand Historian* (Shiji).
4. While the word "tribe" has become politically incorrect in some circles, the scholarly and popular literature focusing on Taiwan aboriginal peoples continues to employ this term. For example, "tribe", "tribespeople", and "tribal" are used throughout the article, "Minority, Not Minor", published in the June 2001 issue of the *Taipei Review* (an official publication of the R.O.C. Government Information Office). I retain this usage in my own writings (see also Wang 2000, 237; Chiu 1995, 128).
5. Population percentages are taken from Copper 1999, 11–12.
6. Some of these songs are still invoked at rallies and demonstrations. For an extended analysis of the use of "A Flower in the Rainy Night" by two different campaigns during the Taipei and Kaohsiung mayoral races in December 2002, see Guy 2008.
7. Shortly after Nationalist censors lifted the ban on "Mending Broken Nets" in 1977, opposition activists began employing the song during their political activities (Yang 2004). Guests at a banquet held in celebration of the founding of the *Formosa Magazine* back in September 1979 reportedly sang "Mending Broken Nets" (Chen and Zhang 2006). Folk musician and legislator Qiu Chuizhen recalls that he sang three songs the evening of the 1979 Formosa incident: "Mending Broken Nets," "A Flower in the Rainy Night," and

"Longing for the Spring Breeze" (Lu 1997, 480). As punishment for singing during this pro-democracy rally turned riot, Qiu spent four years in jail.

8. Lee Shuang-tse's death in a tragic drowning accident in 1977 came just as he was becoming one of the most articulate musical voices in the artistic quest for Taiwan identity.

9. The Formosa incident (also known as the Kaohsiung incident, since it took place in the southern city of Kaohsiung) marked the climax in a year of conflicts between opposition activists and KMT censors, police, and hired thugs. After the rally-turned-riot broke up, KMT forces systematically rounded up, jailed, and in some cases, tortured, the demonstration's key participants. The event is widely viewed as a "pivotal event in modern Taiwanese history" because ultimately it galvanized the opposition against KMT authoritarian rule (Rubinstein 1999, 441).

10. This theme persisted in Luo's songs after he moved his base of operation to Hong Kong. See for example, his songs "The Year to Say Farewell" (告別的年代), released in 1989), and "Queen's Road East" (皇后大道東), released in 1991 and sung in Cantonese. Rey Chow (1998, 165–66) includes English translations of both songs' lyrics, along with textual analysis in her book *Ethics after Idealism*.

11. It is essential to note that Hoklo popular music has not always been perceived as melancholy. The conflation of this music with the notion of Taiwanese people, and hence, their cultural expressions, being sad or tragic (*bei-ai*) is a relatively recent phenomenon dating from the postwar period. Plenty of Hoklo songs from the 1930s were very upbeat. How these songs have been remembered and how their postwar meanings are constructed are processes that deserve sustained scholarly attention.

12. Of the albums nine tracks, only three include Mandarin. Mandarin is sung in the chorus of "Mad" (抓狂; track 2). A few key phrases of Mandarin are heard in "A Democracy Bumpkin" (民主阿草; track 7). The song "Taxi" (計程車; track 6) is sung in both Mandarin and Hoklo with spoken vignettes in Hoklo.

13. Based on the premise that all of China's provinces be represented in the National Assembly this legislative body was essentially frozen in time since the Communist occupation of China made it impossible for new representatives to be elected in mainland provinces. When assemblymen passed away, substitutes, such as the second-place winners of the 1947 election, filled their seats. The first full election in Taiwan of the National Assembly was not held until 1991. Prior to this election, the National Assembly was comprised of elderly members who were last elected to office in 1947 when the ROC was still based in the mainland.

14. Crystal Records also organized the Taipei New Music Festival (台北新音樂節), which ran from 1987 to 1990. The festival, coupled with the label, resulted in the nurturing of some of the most daring musical experimentations of the time. This scene gave birth to what became known as Taiwan New Music (現代台灣歌謠). The artists who performed at the Taipei New Music Festival, recorded for Crystal Records, and ultimately created New Music included not only Zhu Yuexin and the Blacklist Workshop but also Wu Bai and China Blue, Lin Qiang, Chen Ming-chang (who was also a member of the Blacklist Workshop), and the punk band Double X, to name a few.

15. With proper Mandarin pronunciation, the word for "tax" should be pronounced as *shui*, not *sui* as it would typically be pronounced with a strong Hoklo accent.

16. With proper Mandarin pronunciation, the word for "sleep" should be pronounced as *shui*, not *sui*.

17. In 1967, as part of the large-scale effort to collect, record, and preserve Taiwan's indigenous music (including Hoklo and Hakka folk music as well as aboriginal music), ethnomusicologist Hsu Tsang-houei "discovered" Chen Da in Hengchun in rural southern Taiwan. When he was first recorded by Hsu, Chen Da was already sixty-two years old, he had no relatives, and he was essentially homeless, living in a windowless hovel made of dirt. Chen Da was illiterate and had worked as a laborer in his youth. In the decade following Hsu Tsang-houei's first meeting with Chen Da, Hsu invited Chen to Taipei several times where he performed in public and made a recording. He was recognized as the foremost bearer of the improvisatory Hoklo folksong form known as *Hengchun diao*. Chen Da died in a traffic accident in 1981 at the age of seventy-six.
18. When control of Taiwan was awarded to Chiang Kai-shek and his Republic of China government at the end of World War II, people in Taiwan were initially elated to learn that they would be freed of their Japanese colonizers. However, due to communication difficulties (for example, few Taiwanese understood the Chinese national language, Mandarin; few Nationalist officials or soldiers could speak Hoklo, the majority language in Taiwan) and a sizable cultural gap which had formed as a result of fifty years of Japanese colonization, among other factors, relations between the Taiwanese and the Nationalists quickly soured. Tensions exploded into violence on February 28, 1947, continued for weeks, and spawned the White Terror Period, which lasted for decades. The Nationalist military suppression of the February 28 uprising was brutal; an estimated eighteen thousand to twenty-eight thousand people died in the struggle (Copper 2003, 64). The ROC government vehemently denied that the uprising had taken place until 1995 when Taiwan-born President Lee Teng-hui publically apologized to the victims' families.
19. For example, Peking opera was termed "national opera" (國劇) beginning in the mid-1960s in Taiwan. As a *national* form, the central government maintained at least four full-time professional Peking opera troupes and two training schools through the mid-1990s. Over the same period, the central government provided no such support for Taiwanese opera. Beginning in the late 1980s, opposition politicians began their attack against Peking opera by first questioning its moniker "national opera." By 1996 state support for Peking opera troupes and schools was cut by more than half. For greater detail, see Guy 2005.
20. For more on the various meanings ascribed to the ROC national anthem at the turn of the millennium, see Guy 2002a.
21. The song now known as the "Republic of China National Anthem" won first prize in a contest to select the official Nationalist Party song back in 1928. Dr. Sun Yat-sen wrote the lyrics and first delivered them in a speech at the 1924 opening ceremony of the Whampoa Military Academy in Guangzhou, China. The anthem's music was composed by Cheng Mao-yun. Incidentally, the song was honored as the world's best anthem in 1936 at the Berlin World Olympics. It was finally adopted as the official anthem of the ROC in 1943 (ROC Government Information Office).
22. A-Mei was not the only performer to be censured by Beijing for participating in Chen's celebration. Rock star Wu Bai and his band China Blue performed during the massive concert held at Taipei's Chiang Kai-shek Memorial Hall Square on the evening of May 20. The *United Daily News* reported on May 24, 2000, that as punishment for his participation in the inaugural concert, Wu Bai was stripped of his award for Best Popular Male Singer from Taiwan, which he was scheduled to receive in Shanghai in June 2000 at the MTV Music Festival (co-organized by MTV and the Chinese Central Television Company).

23. In Wang's original Chinese lyrics, the first syllable of each phrase (indicated in bold here) outlines his name with the adjective *ba* (meaning "hegemonic") preceding "Wang Lee Hom": 霸氣傲中原 王者揚烽煙 力拔山河天 宏威征凱旋.
24. As with the original interpolation of Wang Lee Hom's name into the text, the interpolation of Ma Ying-jeou's name is also preceded with a complimentary term. In this case, Ma's name is preceded by *zhi* (智) meaning "talented and wise."

References

Attali, Jacques. 1985. *Noise: The Political Economy of Music*. Translated by Brian Massumi. Minneapolis: University of Minnesota Press.

Baker, Diane. 2006. "Kimbo Digs Deep for the 'Strong Songs' that Define Him." *Taipei Times*, June 4, 18.

Bishop, Mac William. 2004. "A-Mei Just Can't Please Anybody." *Taipei Times*, August 3, 4.

Chen Zhiping and Zhang Yating. 2006. "Xi fan wei quan jin dao bian: dou chang bu po gang" [Former Anti-authoritarians aim to depose Chen: Everyone sings 'Mending Broken Nets']. *Lianhebao* [United Daily News], 13 Sept.

Chow, Rey. 1998. *Ethics after Idealism: Theory, Culture, Ethnicity, Reading*. Bloomington, IN: Indiana University Press.

Copper, John. 2003. *Taiwan: Nation-State or Province?* Boulder: Westview Press.

Cruz, Jon. 1999. *Culture on the Margins: The Black Spiritual and the Rise of American Cultural Interpretation*. Princeton, NJ: Princeton University Press.

DeWoskin, Kenneth J. 1982. *A Song for One or Two: Music and the Concept of Art in Early China*. Ann Arbor: Center for Chinese Studies, University of Michigan.

Dickie, Mure, and James Kynge. 2000. "Beijing Calls the Tune for Coca-Cola Advert." *Financial Times*, May 25, 14.

Eyerman, Ron, and Andrew Jamison. 1998. *Music and Social Movements: Mobilizing Traditions in the Twentieth Century*. Cambridge: Cambridge University Press.

Fung, Anthony Y. H. 2007. "The Emerging (National) Popular Music Culture in China." *Inter-Asia Cultural Studies* 8, no. 3: 425–437.

Gao, Pat. 2007a. "Songs from the Roots." *Taiwan Review* 57, no. 4. (April). http://taiwantoday.tw/fp.asp?xItem=24039&CtNode=2229.

Gao, Pat. 2007b. "Music, Interrupted." *Taiwan Review* 57, no. 11 (November). http://taiwantoday.tw/ct.asp?xItem=24780&ctNode=2198&mp=9.

Goodwin, Jeff, James M. Jasper, and Francesca Polletta, eds. 2001. *Passionate Politics: Emotions and Social Movements*. Chicago: University of Chicago Press.

Guo Lijuan. 2005. *Baodao gesheng* [Taiwan song], vol. 2. Taipei: Yushanshe chuban.

Guy, Nancy. 2002a. "'Republic of China National Anthem' on Taiwan: One Anthem, One Performance, Multiple Realities." *Ethnomusicology* 46, no. 1: 96–119.

Guy, Nancy. 2002b. "Trafficking in Taiwan Aboriginal Voices" In *Handle with Care: Ownership and Control of Ethnographic Materials*, edited by Sjoerd R. Jaarsma, 195–210. Pittsburgh: University of Pittsburgh Press.

Guy, Nancy. 2005. *Peking Opera and Politics in Taiwan*. Urbana and Chicago: University of Illinois Press.

Guy, Nancy. 2008. "Feeling a Shared History through Song: 'A Flower in the Rainy Night' as a Key Cultural Symbol in Taiwan." *TDR: The Drama Review* 52, no. 4: 64–81.
Her, Kelly. 2000. "Songs from the Heart." *Taipei Review* 50, no. 4: 14–23.
Jiang Wenyu. 1996. "Cong 'zhua kuang' dao 'xiao kui': liuxing gequde yuyan xuanzhe zhi yuyan shehuixue fenxi [From 'madness' to 'funny rap'. . .]." *Zhongwai wenxue* 25, no. 2: 60–81.
Kearns, Patrick. 2001. "China Fears Give Sony Stage Fright." *Taipei Times*, December 27.
Keng Xuan. 2000. "Taiwan geshou dalu kaichang [Taiwan singers perform in China]." *Lianhebao* [United Daily News], June 8.
Ko Shu-ling. 2004. "Organizers Promise an Eventful Double Ten Day." *Taipei Times*, October 5.
Lau, Shirley. 2001. "Taiwanese Singer Hopes for End to Ban." *South China Morning Post*, June 2, 3.
Lee, Teng-hui. 2002. *Maixiang Zhengchang guojia: Taiwan zhutixingde zhuixun* [Becoming a 'normal country': The quest for a Taiwan-centered frame of reference]. Taipei County: Caituan Quncehui.
Lin, Vivi. 2008. "Once-banned Taiwan Singer Eyes Games Opening Ceremony." *China Post*, February 2.
Liu Guowei. 1998. *Taiwan sixiang qu* [Taiwan's thought in song]. Taipei: Huafeng wenhua.
Lu Hsiu-lien. 1997. *Chongshen Meilidao* [Recalling Meilidao]. Taipei: Qianwei chubanshe.
Meyer, Mahlon. 2001. "The Muzzling of A-Mei" *Newsweek* 15 January, 37–38.
NOWnews. 2008. "Ma shang ren: Wang Lihong chang Gai Shi Ying Xiong [Ma takes office: Wang Lee Hom loudly sings 'Heroes of the Earth']." *NOWnews*, May 20. http://www.nownews.com/2008/05/20/11445-2277639.htm.
Perris, Arnold. 1983. "Music as Propaganda: Art at the Command of Doctrine in the People's Republic of China." *Ethnomusicology* 27, no. 1: 1–28.
Phipps, Gavin. 2002. "Final Nail in the Coffin for Nakashi" *Taipei Times*, 29 June.
Plato. 1907. *The Dialogues of Plato*, vol. 2. Translated by B. Jowett. New York: Charles Scribner's Sons.
Qiu Liling. 2008. "520 jiuzhi dadian: xiaoxuesheng chang gouge [May 20 Inaugural Ceremony: Elementary students will sing the national anthem]." *Lianhebao* [United Daily News], April 20.
ROC Government Information Office. 2000. Accessed July 6. www.oop.gov.tw/roc/nisituat/enisitua.htm.
Rubinstein, Murray A. 1999. "Political Taiwanization and Pragmatic Diplomacy: The Eras of Chiang Ching-kuo and Lee Teng-hui, 1971–1994." In *Taiwan: A New History*, edited by Murray A. Rubinstein, 436–480. Armonk, NY: M.E. Sharpe.
Schweig, Meredith. 2013. "The Song Readers: Rap Music and the Politics of Storytelling in Taiwan." PhD diss, Harvard University.
Stainton, Michael. 1999. "The Politics of Taiwan Aboriginal Origins" In *Taiwan: A New History*, ed. Murray A. Rubinstein, 27–44. Armonk, NY: M.E. Sharpe.
Wang, Hsiao-wen and Chang, Yun-ping. 2004. "A-mei blasted for Not Taking a Stand" *Taipei Times*, 7 Aug.
Wang, Li-jung. 2004. "Multiculturalism in Taiwan" *International Journal of Cultural Policy*, 10(3): 301–318.
Westen, Drew. 2007. *The Political Brain: the Role of Emotion in Deciding the Fate of the Nation*. New York: PublicAffairs.
Wester, Michael. 1994. "The Queen of Taiwanese Music." *Free China Review* 44, no. 6: 14.

Yang Kelong. 2004. "Bu Po Gang" (Mending Broken Nets). In *Taiwan wenhua shidian* (Taiwan culture encyclopedia), edited by Lin Rengqian, et al., p. 814. Taipei: Shida renwen zhongxin.

Zhongyangshe [Central news agency]. 2008. "520 jiudian biaoyan: Wu Bai gaochang, Feng Feifei chang zhangsheng xiangqi" [May 20 inaugural performance: Wu Bai sings spiritedly, Feng feifei sings 'zhangsheng xiangqi'] *Lianhe xinwengang*, May 20.

Zhu Liqun. 2001. "Amei 'jing' chi fusu [A-Mei's 'luster' is restored]." *Minshengbao*, March 12.

CHAPTER 14

MUSIC AND CENSORSHIP IN VIETNAM SINCE 1954

BARLEY NORTON

In 2011, tensions between Vietnam and China flared up over the long-disputed sovereignty of the Spratly Islands and territorial boundaries in the East China Sea. An incident on May 26, in which a Chinese vessel is reported to have cut the cables of a Vietnamese oil exploration ship 120 kilometers off Vietnam's south-central coast, sparked widespread anti-Chinese street protests across Vietnam.[1] Although large-scale public demonstrations are not usually permitted in Vietnam, the authorities allowed regular rallies to be organized in Vietnam's major cities from June to August 2011. The street protests were peaceful, but in September the government decided they had to stop, partly due to fears that the rallies were being used to "stir up dissent against communist rule."[2] To prevent further demonstrations, the police employed strong-arm tactics, using violence to arrest and disperse protestors. Many activists continue to express their anger about the government's foreign policies and the treatment of protestors on Internet blogs, but large public demonstrations are no longer tolerated.

In response to the crackdown on the demonstrations, the singer Việt Khang wrote two songs—"Anh là ai?" ("Who Are You?") and "Việt Nam tôi đâu?" ("Where is My Vietnam?")—which expressed his feelings about the actions of the authorities.[3] Musically these songs are in the style of mainstream Vietnamese pop-style ballads: they have slow-paced, gentle vocal melodies, and Việt Khang's warm, coaxing voice seems to implore the listener to sing along. The lyrics, however, boldly question the security forces' actions and portray the protestors as true patriots who are defending the nation against Chinese aggression. The song "Who Are You?" for example, includes the following lyrics:

> May I ask, who are you?
> Why arrest me? What have I done wrong?
> May I ask, who are you?
> Why beat me mercilessly?

> May I ask, who are you?
> To stop me from protesting on the streets.
> Our people have endured so much for the love of our country.
>
> May I ask, where are you from?
> To prevent me from opposing the Chinese invaders.
> ...
> I cannot sit quietly while Vietnam falls and as my people sink into a thousand years of darkness.
> I cannot sit quietly to see my children grow up without a future; where will their roots lie when Vietnam no longer exists in the world?[4]

Việt Khang uploaded his songs on YouTube and they soon went viral. According to Internet blogs, Việt Khang was initially detained on September 16, shortly after the songs were posted on the web, and was formally arrested on December 23, 2011. A "Free Việt Khang" movement was established by Vietnamese communities in the United States, and a petition concerning human rights, which includes a reference to Việt Khang, was submitted to the US government.[5] After spending over ten months in detention, Việt Khang was brought to trial on October 30, 2012. Charged with conducting propaganda against the state under Article 88 of the penal code, Việt Khang was given a four-year prison sentence followed by two years of house arrest.[6]

Any activity that challenges the primacy of the Vietnamese Communist Party or opposes the one-party nation state is forbidden in Vietnamese law, and the prosecution of Việt Khang highlights the draconian forms of punishment that musicians in Vietnam are likely to face if they are deemed to oppose the government's policies. Given this situation, it is not surprising that few Vietnamese musicians have directly challenged the authority of the party by writing songs with lyrics that overtly challenge the government's policies or actions.

The popular music scholar Martin Cloonan (2003, 17) has suggested that music censorship operates on three main levels: "prior restraint, restriction and suppression." In Vietnam, music censorship is most commonly achieved through prior restraint and restriction: officially, music must be approved in advance by state censors connected to the Ministry of Culture before it is publicly performed, broadcast, or released as a recording.[7] The suppression of music and musicians, which includes the imprisonment of individual musicians like Việt Khang, is less routine and is typically a last resort when the censorship system of prior restraint and restriction has proved ineffective. Even though Việt Khang's music has managed to gain quite a large audience internationally through the Internet, the reach of his songs among the general populace in Vietnam is still restricted by way of omission from mainstream state-controlled media.

Acts of music censorship are assertions of power. They are carried out within a field of power relations in which musical aesthetics intersect with the political, the ideological, and the social (see also Nooshin 2009). To discuss music censorship is to discuss the meanings that accrue to music and how these meanings are negotiated, controlled, contested, and resisted. Authoritarian states that employ government agencies to deliberately and systematically suppress, prohibit, and restrict music seem to offer the most clear-cut examples of censorship. The censorship of music in Vietnam, however, as in other authoritarian states, is rarely straightforward and cannot be reduced to the overt actions of state censors. As John Street (2012, 14) notes, in authoritarian regimes, "censorship is often routinized—usually becoming a form of self-censorship—and operated by a concatenation of functionaries in the security services, the broadcasting organizations and in the propaganda departments." In contemporary Vietnam, the control of musical expression by the state censors is not total or absolute, the prohibition of music is rarely done in an open, transparent way, and there is often confusion about what is or is not permitted and why. Party decrees on culture and the arts set the general tone, but specifics are often left vague and are open to interpretation. This approach not only spreads confusion but also encourages self-censorship. Typically, musicians have to second-guess what might be censored, and this encourages them to err on the side of caution. Censors in the Ministry of Culture and the directors of the state-run radio and television companies, record labels, and publishing houses are also often not clear about what they should or should not permit.[8] Such ambiguity can lead to arbitrary decisions, which are usually not fully explained or justified, and this fosters a climate of caution and restraint. As Martin Scherzinger (2007, 95) astutely points out in relation to the restriction of music in the United States after 9/11, "it is the silent and invisible acquiescence of the cautious and compromised artist that ultimately registers the extent of genuine political power." Such internalized censorship, which permeates the social realities and mindset of musicians, is often hard to pinpoint, but is all too familiar to many of the Vietnamese musicians with whom I have discussed censorship.

The literature on music censorship in liberal, capitalist societies has addressed how the censorship of music is often bound up with the workings of the market. Cloonan (2003, 15), for instance, defines censorship in quite broad terms as "the process by which an agent (or agents) attempts to, and/or succeeds in, significantly altering, and/or curtailing, the freedom of expression of another agent with a view to limiting the likely audience for that expression," in order to promote the argument that censorship may arise from "market-based decisions within the music industry" as well as from the actions of official or state censorship agencies. Cloonan argues that forms of omission—for instance, decisions by private media companies not to release or broadcast certain songs on grounds of taste or a perceived lack of interest from audiences—may constitute a form of censorship. Although market economic reforms have been introduced in Vietnam since 1986, the state has retained a tight hold over all official media. Unauthorized and bootleg recordings (by both Vietnamese and international artists) are widely available for purchase at retail outlets and markets, but Vietnam does not have a large market-driven music industry comparable to those found in liberal democracies, so the importance of private companies in relation to censorship is limited. Nonetheless, when public debate about music censorship in Vietnam has been permitted, issues of musical aesthetics and taste feature prominently. An important consideration for censors and media commentators in contemporary Vietnam, for instance, is whether popular culture supports or undermines traditional values and therefore whether it is morally suitable for Vietnamese audiences. As is often the case with music censorship around the world, the lyrics of songs are typically the primary concern for censors in Vietnam, but the way in which music is performed and issues relating to musical aesthetics are also often an important consideration.

This chapter traces the complex history of music censorship in Vietnam since 1954 and is organized chronologically.[9] The first section provides an overview of music censorship from 1954 to 1975, when Vietnam was divided into North and South along the 17th parallel. In the northern Democratic Republic of Vietnam (DRV) the government led by the Vietnamese Communist Party quickly moved to establish ideological control over the performing arts, and it was quite effective at using music for propaganda purposes. In contrast, control over musical expression in the American-backed Republic of Vietnam (RVN) in the south was less absolute, and as a result the musical culture that developed was more diverse and multifaceted in regard to its ideological content. For instance, the musical movement known as "Sing for Our Compatriots to Hear," which arose in the RVN in the late 1960s, was closely linked to antiwar student protests. The second section considers the period following the end of the Vietnamese-American war in 1975, when the country was reunified under the leadership of the Vietnamese Communist Party until the Renovation policy, known as *đổi mới*, was introduced in 1986. Music censorship after 1975 was extremely severe. As part of the effort to mold the more commercially oriented culture of the south into the form of the socialist north, the Vietnamese Communist Party implemented "purification" campaigns that sought to eradicate the musical culture of the former RVN. The third section discusses the limits of cultural freedom in the reform era after 1986, focusing on the rock musician Trần Tiến and his band Black and White. It also considers how anxieties about the forces of globalization have affected the government's cultural policies. In the reform era, the censorship of popular music has often been intertwined with concerns about morality, and prerevolutionary forms of music, which were previously banned, are being promoted in order to bolster national cultural identity. Prior to the conclusion, the final section of the chapter considers the impact of technology since the late 1990s, focusing on Vietnamese rap and the potential of the Internet to bypass conventional systems of state censorship. While the overview of music censorship in this chapter does not aim to be comprehensive in its coverage of Vietnamese musical traditions and styles, it gives a broad perspective by referring to many different types of music that cut across genre boundaries. Popular musical styles in Vietnam have very different historical trajectories compared with traditional genres, yet all areas of musical activity have been subject, in different ways, to varying degrees of censorship.

MUSIC, WAR, AND CENSORSHIP 1954–1975

Following the victory of Việt Minh forces against French troops at the battle of Dien Bien Phu in April 1954, the newly established communist government in the DRV underwent a root and branch restructuring of cultural and social life. The Vietnamese Communist Party's cultural policy, as outlined by party ideologues such as Lê Duẩn and Trường Chinh during the 1950s and 1960s, was that the arts should serve the ideological interests of the party, the nation, the socialist revolution, and the fight for the unification of the country (Hồ Chí Minh et al. 1976). The aim was to forge a new, "scientific" musical culture that appealed to the "masses" and was imbued with "socialist content and national character." Under the umbrella of the Ministry of Culture, musical activities were coordinated and organized by the Department of Arts, and an extensive network of music troupes and schools was established throughout the DRV. The Vietnam National Music School, the forerunner of today's Vietnam National Academy of Music, opened in 1956, the Musicians' Union was founded in 1957, and state-run music troupes were established in northern Vietnam during the late 1950s and 1960s. These included music theater troupes for the three major genres of *chèo* (folk theater), *tuồng* (classical opera), and *cải lương* (reformed theater) and other groups like "music and dance troupes" (*đoàn ca múa*), which specialized in performing new compositions and "modern national music" (*âm nhạc dân tộc hiện đại*). These troupes and institutions continue to form the backbone of state-supported musical activity to this day.

The music performed by state-run troupes in the DRV conformed to strict ideological criteria. Music was considered to be an "ideological weapon" (*vũ khí tư tưởng*) to propagate the ideals of the new socialist society and to support the war effort. By the early 1960s, the Communist Party had managed to exert a high level of control over all aspects of culture, but the socialist cultural revolution did meet some resistance from leading intellectuals. Kim Ninh's detailed examination of the politics of cultural transformation in northern Vietnam from 1945 to 1965 highlights the complex process through which the party's ideological position on culture and the arts was established (Ninh 2002). A key moment of intellectual dissent, known as the Nhân Văn–Giai Phẩm Period, occurred in 1956 when a group of intellectuals argued for more intellectual freedom and criticized the restrictions that were being placed on artists by the party. The main leaders of Nhân Văn–Giai Phẩm were writers like Hoàng Cầm and Trần Dần, but the musicians Tử Phác and Văn Cao were also associated with the group. At the end of 1956 the journals *Nhân Văn* (Humanism) and *Giai Phẩm* (Works of Beauty) were closed down and the intellectuals who had voiced their criticisms were punished. This included members of the group being placed under house arrest and being forced to undergo self-criticism sessions (Ninh 2002, 121–163). Others were dismissed from their jobs and could only work again if they publicly reformed their views. The composer Văn Cao, for instance, was excluded from the Musicians' Union and forced to publish a self-criticism (Gibbs 2007, 152–153). Following this brief period of dissent, the Ministry of Culture, founded in 1955, tightened its control over cultural activities.

As the war escalated in the mid 1960s, the primary focus was on harnessing music and the other arts to help "resist the Americans and save the country" (*chống Mỹ cứu nước*). In 1966, for instance, the Youth Song movement (Phong Trào Thanh Niên Ca Hát) was established across the DRV to encourage youth to join the armed struggle (Norton 2013). This movement was conceived as a grass roots movement, with songs to be sung at impromptu performances throughout the country. To support the war effort, numerous small music groups, known as *đoàn văn công*, were formed, some of which were connected to military units. These small music collectives traveled around the country performing different types of music—such as folk songs (*dân ca*) and popular songs (*ca khúc*) with revolutionary lyrics—to entertain, encourage, and strengthen the resolve of the troops and workers. In response to the bombing raids in the North by American planes, which began with the Flaming Dart and Rolling Thunder campaigns in 1965, the slogan "Song Drowns Out the Sound of Bombs" (*Tiếng hát át tiếng bom*) was coined, and this became synonymous with the Youth Song movement (see People's Army Publishing House 1968). Songs like "Hanoi Dien Bien Phu" ("Hà Nội Điên Biên Phủ") and "Sleepless Nights in Hanoi" ("Hà Nội những đêm không ngủ") by Phạm Tuyên, for instance, aimed to combat the psychological impact of the US bombing offensive by bolstering unity and morale (Norton 2013, 103-104).

Although the cultural infrastructure established by the Communist Party in the DRV dominated musical activity in the 1960s and early 1970s, there were some pockets of resistance. In 1967, for instance, an organization known as the Democratic Antiwar Peace Force was established, and according to a report by the Minister of Public Security at the time, this group frequently met to sing forbidden "yellow music" (*nhạc vàng*) and to discuss revolutionary propaganda (Nguyen 2012, 155). In late December 1967, the leaders of this movement were arrested and were sentenced to fifteen years imprisonment for "reactionary" activities that "spread distortions about Party and state policies" (Nguyen 2012, 156). Apart from those involved in the Democratic Antiwar Peace Force, there were other enthusiasts of yellow music in the DRV. One of the most prominent of these was the singer Phan Thắng Toán, known as Hairy Toan. From 1965 onward, Hairy Toan was the lead singer in bands that performed prohibited "pre-war" music and foreign love songs at weddings and parties, but in 1968 he was arrested along with six other band members. When this group of musicians was eventually put on trial in 1971, they were accused of "disseminating depraved imperialist culture and counter-revolutionary propaganda" and sentenced to long jail sentences (Nguyen 2012, 196-198).[10] Even though these musicians later claimed they did not have a political agenda and were only motivated by their love for yellow music, their imprisonment illustrates the extent to which party leaders were determined to crack down on musical activity which they thought would undermine people's commitment to socialism and resolve for war.[11] The long sentences metered out on musicians like Hairy Toan, who was not released until 1980, served as a warning to other musicians: conform to the party line or be incarcerated.

As part of the socialist transformation of cultural life in the DRV, many forms of traditional music—including the music-theater forms *chèo*, *tuồng*, and *cải lương*—were reformed and used for propaganda purposes by state-run troupes. Of these theater forms, *chèo* folk theater had the strongest popular following in northern Vietnam, and this made it particularly potent as a vehicle for mass propaganda. The primary purpose of new plays written in the mid 1960s—such as *Liberation Women* (Cô giải phóng) by Út Tịch and *Road to the Battlefield* (Đường về trận địa) by Hoài Giao and Tào Mạt—was to convey information about the war. Such plays were known as "news chèo" (*chèo thông tấn*) and were performed for soldiers on the frontline as well as at theaters and festivals (Trần Việt Ngữ 1996, 500–502).

While a number of important genres were reformed, some traditional forms of music were discouraged or prohibited because the Communist Party considered them to be unsuitable for the new socialist society. Such genres included the *ca trù* chamber music and *chầu văn* mediumship music, among others. For different reasons, the traditional performance contexts of *ca trù* and *chầu văn* were prohibited and largely curtailed. This resulted in *ca trù* being largely excluded from the public sphere and prerevolutionary *chầu văn* songs could only be performed at clandestine mediumship rituals. In the case of *chầu văn*, however, some of the main melodies were revised and sung with new lyrics by *chèo* troupes to make them suitable for promoting socialism on the "revolutionary stage".

Typically, *ca trù* is performed by a small chamber ensemble consisting of a female singer, who also plays a percussion instrument called the *phách*, a lutenist who plays the three-stringed *đàn đáy* lute, and a drummer who plays a small "praise drum" (*trống chầu*).[12] During the Nguyễn dynasty (1802–1945), *ca trù* was performed in village festivals and was also patronized by scholars who wrote refined literary poems to be sung by *ca trù* performers. Due to such connections with the feudal elite, the party considered *ca trù* to be inappropriate for the new socialist society. In the first half of the twentieth century, *ca trù* also became a popular form of performance in "singing bars" in Hanoi and other urban areas in northern Vietnam. Aside from being places to appreciate *ca trù* music, these singing bars became known for prostitution, drugs, and gambling. Communist rhetoric argued that *ca trù* had been "corrupted" by colonialism (Đào Trọng Từ 1984, 26), and the singing bars were closed down after 1954. Apart from secret, private performances and a few exceptions when special public performances were permitted, *ca trù* was silenced from the late 1950s until the 1980s.[13]

After the end of the Vietnamese-American war in 1975, the most famous *ca trù* singer, Quách Thị Hồ, recorded several songs with revolutionary socialist lyrics, but the music was never reformed to suit the musical aesthetics of the new socialist society. Unlike other forms of traditional music, it was difficult to change the music of *ca trù* without destroying the genre's distinctive qualities. For instance, *ca trù* is characterized by irregular, free rhythm, whereas revolutionary music typically had a fast, regular pulse to evoke the collective spirit and "happiness" of socialism. In a recording made by the Voice of Vietnam Radio in 1980, Quách Thị Hồ sings a patriotic text called "Many Springs" ("Những mùa xuân"), but the music and highly ornamented vocal style of *ca trù* is not altered. "Many Springs" charts the "resplendent" springs of Vietnamese history and repeatedly praises the party. The final lines of the text are as follows:

> In the eightieth spring [1980] we are even more resplendent,
> With the Party, the rough road has the scent of flowers,
> Our Vietnam has written more songs,
> More music for the generations, more heroic pages of history,

Celebrate that Vietnam is 35 years old,[14]
Celebrate our Party's fiftieth birthday,
Our people's army sings a song of unity.

In contrast to *ca trù*, which was discouraged because of associations with the feudal elite and prostitution, *chầu văn* was prohibited due to its religious context. Traditionally, *chầu văn* is performed throughout rituals known as *lên đồng*, in which a medium is possessed by a sequence of spirits from a large pantheon. *Chầu văn* songs are performed throughout *lên đồng* by a small ensemble, which in northern Vietnam typically consists of two to five male musicians who sing and play instruments such as the two-stringed moon lute (*đàn nguyệt*) and a set of percussion instruments. For each spirit possession, a distinctive sequence of songs—which I have previously referred to as a "songscape"—is performed, evoking the presence of the spirit (Norton 2009).

The practice of mediumship was condemned as "superstition" and was banned as part of a vigorous antisuperstition campaign that sought to eliminate "backward customs and habits." The practitioners of superstitious rituals were portrayed in the campaign as liars and swindlers who profited financially from holding rituals. Belief in the ability of the spirits to cure illness and to alleviate misfortune was ridiculed in the propaganda because it was seen to have "no basis in reality" and was "completely unscientific" (Truth Publishing House 1982, 19; see also Malarney 2002). This campaign greatly diminished the number of *lên đồng* that took place, but it did not eliminate them entirely. Even during the height of the campaign during the 1960s and 1970s, some mediums continued to hold small-scale *lên đồng* in secret, despite the threat of punishment, and even imprisonment, if they were caught. To avoid being noticed by the authorities, *lên đồng* were often arranged in remote rural areas or late at night. One musician from Hanoi told me that he was twice held at the police station in the early 1980s, the first time for five days and the second time for twenty days, for performing at *lên đồng*.

In its prerevolutionary form, *chầu văn* was deemed to be incompatible with revolutionary socialist ideology. To transform it from a "superstitious product" to a "cultural product," a new form of revolutionary *chầu văn* was created by music theater troupes—such as the *chèo* troupe in Nam Định province, south of Hanoi—in the 1960s. One of the main ways in which *chầu văn* was adapted to become revolutionary was through the use of new song texts that erased any reference to mediumship. In place of traditional song texts that describe and praise the character and deeds of the spirits, poems with socialist and patriotic themes were used. Chu Hà's "The Moon Remembers Uncle Ho" ("Vầng trăng nhớ Bác") is a typical example of the songs texts used for revolutionary *chầu văn*:

Looking at the moon I remember the smiling face of uncle Ho,
Seeing the clouds reminds me of his gray hair,
The wind is like his young hands stroking the beard of the revered and loved uncle Ho.
. . .
Moon, people are busy on the military training ground,

> Visit the compassionate soldiers,
> Visit the villages of the homeland,
> Where the people are, the moon will follow.
> Follow the footsteps of uncle Ho and write a people's poem;
> A happy poem full of the sentiments of uncle Ho.

Revolutionary *chầu văn* did not just consist of changes to the song text used; the music was also transformed in order to suit the new socialist aesthetic. Key musical changes included: ignoring the ritual conventions of the songscapes performed during *lên đồng* by arranging songs into new suites that often built to a rousing dramatic climax; choosing a few lively and happy songs and excluding songs with sad sentiments; performing songs at a much faster tempo; and changing the vocal style (for example, many revolutionary *chầu văn* suites were performed by a female singer or a group of female singers in unison in a style more reminiscent of *chèo* than *chầu văn*, which is typically performed by male musicians).

In the overview above, I have highlighted the extent to which musical culture in the DRV was transformed and censored. The situation in the southern Republic of Vietnam was different. In general terms, censorship of the press and other media in the RVN oscillated between periods of relative freedom and phases when the government attempted to silence critics. As David Marr (2003) notes, there were severe crackdowns on the press and intellectuals toward the end of Ngô Đình Diệm's presidency (from 1960 to 1963, when Diệm was killed) and at the start of Nguyễn Văn Thiệu's term as president in 1967. As the political and military situation in South Vietnam deteriorated in the late 1960s and early 1970s, it became increasingly difficult for the regime to exert control over the media and dissenting voices. But even during crackdowns, when critics of the government were jailed and newspapers were closed down, intellectuals were still able to "publish experimental fiction and poetry in small circulation journals," and "many groups were still able to use mimeographic machines to circulate provocative information" (Marr 2003, 275).

More historical research is needed to provide a detailed understanding of the diverse musical culture that existed in the RVN. However, the situation concerning censorship of popular song in South Vietnam was broadly similar to that described by Marr in regard to literature and journalism. As Schafer (2007, 620) points out, officially, written permission was required from the Office for Coordination of Art Works, a division of the Ministry of Information, before songs could be circulated, yet many unapproved songs were performed and unauthorized songbooks were published. Compared with the DRV, popular music in the RVN was less tightly controlled, so songwriters had greater scope to experiment with different musical styles and to express diverse feelings about the war. While patriotic and anticommunist songs that expressed support for the RVN government and army were encouraged, the regime was unable to silence dissent. To give an impression of the kinds of popular song that managed to evade the censors, here I will briefly discuss the antiwar songs of one of Vietnam's most famous songwriters, Trịnh Công Sơn (1939–2001), and the musical movement known as "Sing for Our Compatriots to Hear" ("Hát cho đồng bào tôi nghe").

On January 30, 1968, the army of the northern DRV and the guerrilla forces of National Liberation Front (NLF) launched the Tet Offensive, which consisted of a series of coordinated attacks against targets across the RVN. As part of the Tet Offensive, the old imperial city of Hue was attacked and held by communist forces for nearly a month before South Vietnamese and American troops regained control of the city. In the fierce fighting in Hue, thousands of civilians, as well as troops, were massacred and the city itself was reduced to ruins. Trịnh Công Sơn was in his hometown of Hue during the Tet Offensive and he witnessed the devastation firsthand. In direct response to the horrific loss of life, Trịnh Công Sơn wrote several songs, including "Singing on the Corpses" ("Hát trên những xác người") and "Song for the Corpses" ("Bài ca cho những xác người"). Such songs have been dubbed antiwar (*phản chiến*) because of their humanist and pacifist stance.[15] Rather than writing songs that glorified the war, Trịnh Công Sơn wrote sentimental songs about the pain and suffering of war, about the desire for peace, and about lost love and human fate (see Norton 2013, 108-116). The lyrics of "Singing on the Corpses" describe corpses strewn around after the battle and the confused reaction of bereaved women. The final lines are as follows:

> Afternoon by the mulberry groves,
> Singing on the corpses.
> I have seen, I have seen,
>
> Trenches filled with corpses.
> A mother claps to welcome war,
> A sister cheers for peace.
> Some people clap for more hatred,
> Some clap to repent.

In "Singing on the Corpses" there is a tension between the meaning of the lyrics and the expressivity of the melody, which contributes to the song's emotional impact. The song consists of melancholic, arch-shaped vocal phrases that use the "minor" hexatonic scale (C, D, E♭, F, G, B♭). The reassuring, arch-shaped vocal melody is reminiscent of a melancholic lullaby, but the consoling music contrasts starkly with the bleak lyrics about death and the confused human responses to war.

Songs like "Singing on the Corpses"—as well as many other antiwar songs that were published in songbooks like *Songs of Golden Skin (Ca Khúc Da Vàng)* (1966–1967) and *Prayer for Vietnam (Kinh Việt Nam)* (1968)—became immensely popular in South Vietnam and created what has been referred to as the "Trịnh Công Sơn phenomenon" (see Schafer 2007). During the late 1960s and early 1970s, Trịnh Công Sơn performed his songs with the singer Khánh Ly across South Vietnam, including regular performances at the Quán Văn club in Saigon.[16] The format of their performances was reminiscent of the 1950s and 1960s folk song revival in the United States: they both sang to a rhythmic strummed guitar accompaniment played by the songwriter himself. In addition to live performances, Trịnh Công Sơn's songs became popular as a result of Khánh Ly's recordings and the printing of songbooks, which enabled amateur musicians to learn his songs.

As Trịnh Công Sơn's fame grew, the RVN regime became concerned about the impact of the Trịnh Công Sơn phenomenon, and in 1969 a decree was issued banning the circulation of his songs (Schafer 2007, 611, 620). The ban, however, proved ineffective as Khánh Ly's recordings were still widely circulated and Trịnh Công Sơn moved from one printing press to another to ensure that he could still self-publish his songbooks (Trịnh Công Sơn 1989, 462).

Trịnh Công Sơn did not associate himself with a particular musical movement or political faction. However, other songwriters in South Vietnam like Tôn Thất Lập, Trần Long Ẩn, Trương Quốc Khánh, and Miên Đức Thắng were active in the antiwar movement, "Sing for Our Compatriots to Hear." This student-led movement held street demonstrations, public debates and performance events at university campuses that voiced opposition to the RVN regime and the American military presence in the late 1960s and early 1970s. At the first major event organized by the movement—the "Quang Trung Tet Festival" held in Saigon in early 1968 just before the Tet Offensive—Tôn Thất Lập's song "Sing for my people to hear" ("Hát cho dân tôi nghe") was sung in unison by a chorus of over two hundred students (personal communication. Tôn Thất Lập, August 2012). "Sing for my people to hear" has march-like rhythms—it has a strong 2/4 meter, dotted rhythms and regular four-bar phrases—and a rousing melody that uses the pentatonic scale, G, B♭, C, D, F. The song begins with the words:

> Sing so the people hear, the sound of singing unfurls the flag each day.
> Sing in the autumn nights, while fires burn the enemy's camps.
> A sombre song in the night, thousands of arms rise up.
> Sing for the workers, to break their chains like a dispersing cloud.
> Sing for the farmers, to put aside their ploughs and follow the call.
>
> Each day the people freely rise up to break the chains of slavery.
> Each day we stand undaunted together with our compatriots.
> Take back the river water for growing rice in the green fields.
> Take back the cities, hands rise up for peace.

In an interview I conducted in August 2012 with Tôn Thất Lập, the recognized leader of the "Sing for Our Compatriots to Hear" movement, he estimated that about 10,000 people participated in the movement's first event, even though the police tried to block the roads to stop people from gathering. The movement grew as more people became disillusioned with the war, especially after the devastation caused by the Tet Offensive. At a street protest held in September 1970, Tôn Thất Lập said that the police fired flares from helicopters, threw tear gas grenades to disperse the crowd, and arrested him along with 179 fellow students.[17] The students were released a few days later after going on a hunger strike, but while in prison they continued to sing in defiance. In my interview with Tôn Thất Lập he recalled that, during the time when he was imprisoned, the head of the police bureau called him in to his office and said angrily, "You can do whatever you want, but I forbid singing!" In Tôn Thất Lập's view the police chief had reprimanded him in this way because he was "afraid of the power of song" (sợ sức mạnh của tiếng hát).

Despite suppressing demonstrations and imprisoning students, the authorities were unable to stem the wave of protests. The movement attracted a broad base of support, not only from students but also from Buddhist and Catholic groups, and this made it difficult for the authorities to prevent street demonstrations. Many of the students were sympathetic to the NLF, but according to Tôn Thất Lập, "Sing for Our Compatriots to Hear" was a broad based coalition, which incorporated many different viewpoints and was not controlled by the NLF. The songs performed by the NLF's Liberation Music Groups were also different in tone from those sung by students. While NLF songs often referred directly to the armed struggle and had a more aggressive, military style, the lyrics of the songs performed at student demonstrations concentrated on urging others to join them on the streets, on expressing love of the homeland and the people, and on voicing people's yearning for peace and independence.[18] Partly due to this lack of militancy, it was difficult for the RVN authorities to justify using excessive force to quash the "Sing for Our Compatriots to Hear" movement.

Music Censorship in the Socialist Republic of Vietnam after 1975

On April 30, 1975, the North Vietnamese army took Saigon, and this marked the end of the war. With official reunification in 1976, the country was renamed the Socialist Republic of Vietnam (SRV) under the leadership of the Vietnamese Communist Party. After 1975 the communists sought to impose the model of socialist society developed in the DRV and to eliminate the culture and way of life of the market-oriented society in the former RVN. As Philip Taylor (2000) has discussed, the musical culture of South Vietnam—particularly music that was pejoratively referred to as yellow music (nhạc vàng)—was derided by party cadres as "neocolonial poison," which needed to be eradicated.

In an article titled "What is Yellow Music?" published in 1976, the scholar Tô Vũ suggests that the term yellow music should not be thought of as referring to a discrete genre of music. Rather, he argues that the term refers to particular musical and lyrical characteristics that can be found across different genres. Lyrically, he gives examples of yellow songs that have "weakening romantic" (lãng mạn ủy mị) and "melancholic" (tình sầu) words (Tô Vũ 1976, 44). Musically, he characterizes yellow music during the time of the "American-puppet" (Mỹ ngụy) regime as being:

> sorrowful and sobbing, or extremely gloomy and desolate. The melodies of yellow music have moments that are interminably low and languid, like drops of sad,

persistent rain, and other moments of torturous lament like continuous blasts of wind. (Tô Vũ 1976, 45)

The "negative effect" of listening to such music, Tô Vũ contends, is that it "spreads pessimism" and "saps the will," which is especially damaging in the "context of striving to revive the country after war" and is contrary to the business of building "a cheerful and happy way of life" (Tô Vũ 1976, 46).

While Tô Vũ considers the aesthetics of yellow music, in another article published in 1976 the critic Cửu Long Giang condemns the musical culture of the RVN as "reactionary" (*phản động*). According to Cửu Long Giang, the United States and the RVN's "puppet regime" used "anti-communist music and lustful and depraved music" as a form of "psychological warfare" to oppress the people and to encourage them "to take up arms against and kill one's compatriots" (2003 (1976), 598). Cửu Long Giang credits such reactionary music with having a profound effect on the people of South Vietnam and concludes by declaring that the "depraved" music of US neocolonialism must now be "wiped out" (2003 (1976), 602).

Articles like the one by Cửu Long Giang articulate the rationale for the purging of music that took place after 1975. As part of a string of campaigns to "eliminate the cultural vestiges of the former regime" (Taylor 2000, 104), all music deemed yellow or reactionary was banned. This encompassed virtually all the popular music that existed in the former RVN, including the music of Vietnamese bands that played US-influenced rock music (see Gibbs 2008b). The performance of yellow music was strictly prohibited, the state took control of the distribution and broadcasting of music, and records, tapes, and songbooks were systematically collected and destroyed. An official report on the progress of "purification" in South Vietnam, first published in 1981 in the official *Communist Magazine*, notes that 5,000 songs with "bad content" were seized from "dimly lit" coffee houses in Precinct 5 of Ho Chi Minh City alone (Tran Tho 1982, 10). The reports states that by June 1981, 151,200 books, 41,723 music recordings, and 53,751 song scores and paintings had been seized in Ho Chi Minh City, and that smaller amounts of material had been confiscated in other cities across Vietnam, including 1,216 music tapes in Hanoi (Tran Tho 1982, 10).

As well as the confiscation of "unhealthy" cultural products, individuals who were deemed to be responsible for "counter-revolutionary crimes" were arrested and could be imprisoned for up to twelve years.[19] Many musicians who were famous for performing yellow music fled the country; those that remained were likely to be sent to re-education camps. In place of the decadent culture of the former RVN regime, musicians were encouraged to compose "red music" (*nhạc đỏ*) such as "political songs" (*ca khúc chính trị*) that had nationalist, revolutionary, and socialists themes (see Đặng Trung 1988). Although political songs aimed to rouse the masses to support the new socialist society and to strengthen national pride, there seems to have been limited enthusiasm for such songs, especially among the youth. For instance, a speech by Võ Văn Kiệt (1981, 20)—given at a conference on "art for the masses" in 1981 when he was Secretary of the Party Committee in Ho Chi Minh City—acknowledges that more needed to be done to raise the quality of "youth songs" in order to satisfy young people's craving for "the new."

The stagnancy of popular culture and the lack of enthusiasm for the political songs of the late 1970s and early 1980s among Vietnamese youth were sufficiently severe for a conference to be held in 1982 on the topic of "Youth—Music—Our Time" ("Tuổi Trẻ—Âm Nhạc—Thời Đại"). At this conference, senior figures in the Musicians' Union and the performing arts debated how to develop a vibrant popular song culture that would be embraced by young people. The government had eliminated poisonous neocolonial influences, but having purged these elements, what kind of popular songs should musicians compose? A topic that provoked much debate at the conference was the issue of rhythm. In particular, delegates discussed how to compose songs with "lively" (sôi động) rhythms, without resorting to imitating popular music from the West. For instance, Đỗ Nhuận, the general secretary of the Musicians' Union, opined in his conference speech:

> I do not oppose learning from European arrangements of "light music" (nhạc nhẹ) but I do not agree to imitating rock and disco music, which is spreading out from the capitalist West, in a servile manner. I do not oppose jazz rhythms, but I do not agree with a style of jazz drumming that is like smashing up wood... with the sound of drums drowning out the rest of the ensemble in the way it is fashionable today, and I do not agree with picking up things from tapes and records that distort the hearing of the youth. (Đỗ Nhuận 2003 (1982), 793)

To avoid resorting to aping popular music from the West, which would mean succumbing to the "culture of American enslavement" (nền văn hóa nô dịch Mỹ), Đỗ Nhuận argued that the best way to enliven Vietnamese popular song was to "exploit the rhythm of the nation," by which he meant that songwriters should utilize rhythms found in traditional Vietnamese music (2003 (1982), 792).

Despite such attempts by cultural cadres to suggest new ways to reinvigorate popular song by drawing on traditional rhythms, in the early 1980s it was still incumbent on songwriters to compose political songs that would "educate" the youth. This situation did not change until after 1986 when the Renovation policy was introduced.

Music and the Renovation Policy

The introduction of the Renovation policy or đổi mới at the Sixth Party Congress in 1986 was primarily aimed at introducing reforms to invigorate the failing postwar economy, but đổi mới also extended to the cultural sphere. In the area of culture, Resolution 5 of the party's politburo entitled "Renovating and enhancing the leadership and management of the literature, arts and culture to a higher stage of development," signaled a shift toward greater creative freedom. For instance, Resolution 5 states, "Freedom of creativity is a vital condition for creating true values in culture, literature and the arts and for developing talents."[20] After the Sixth Party Congress, Nguyễn Văn Linh, who was General Secretary of the party's Central Executive Committee and a key architect of the Renovation policy, elaborated further on the party's new policies. At a meeting with a group of writers in October 1987, for instance, he listened to and reflected upon their grievances. In his speech at the meeting, Nguyễn Văn Linh frankly acknowledges that "the leadership of the Party in the field of culture and arts lacks democracy, and is authoritarian and imposing" and that "the literature of many writers is still banned."[21] Going against the previous orthodoxy that cultural works should always promote a "rosy" (tô hồng) picture of life, Nguyễn Văn Linh encouraged writers to criticize negative aspects of society including corruption, excessive bureaucracy, and the harassment of people. Emboldened by such comments, intellectuals and artists began to adopt a more critical stance. Writers such as Dương Thu Hương, Nguyễn Huy Thiệp, and Bảo Ninh, for instance, wrote controversial novels and short stories that criticized everyday realities and the changes that were taking place in Vietnamese society, and offered a reassessment of the past (see Healy 2000). Such works included Bảo Ninh's novel *The Sorrow of War* (*Nỗi Buồn Chiến Tranh*), which reflects critically on the war, and Dương Thu Hương's novel *Paradise of the Blind* (*Những Thiên Đường Mù*), which highlights the personal tragedies that resulted from the land reform programs in the 1950s.

In the field of popular music, the songwriter Trần Tiến was one of the first to take advantage of the shift in cultural policy. In 1987 Trần Tiến formed the rock band Black and White (Đên Trắng) and on November 12 the band performed a program called "Conversation '87" ("Đối Thoại '87") in Ho Chi Minh City. A newspaper review of this first concert reported that the audience response was very enthusiastic: songs were greeted with rapturous applause and some audience members were moved to tears (Nguyễn Thanh Đức 1987). Reflecting on "Conversation '87" in an interview I conducted with Trần Tiến in 2011, he said the atmosphere at the concert was akin to a street demonstration, and that after the second performance he was accused by the city authorities of "inciting a riot" and was arrested. Trần Tiến was detained by the authorities overnight and, according to him, he was "saved" from further detention by the politician Nguyễn Văn Linh, who backed him by publicly declaring, "Trần Tiến's music incites patriotism, it does not incite riots." Although Trần Tiến was released, he was prevented from performing any more concerts, and on November 21 the People's Committee of Ho Chi Minh City sent out an official communiqué banning Black and White and forbidding other groups to perform the songs. The stated reasons for the ban were that Black and White's songs had "bad content," which had caused "public discontent."[22]

One of the songs that caused the most controversy in Black and White's program was the song "Naked '87" ("Trần Trụi '87").[23] The song includes the following lyrics:

> I have seen my Vietnamese friends selling goods on the streets in Russia.
> My friends beg on the streets of America.
> Friends in the homeland trick each other because of poverty.
> Does this cause you pain?

> I have seen mothers who in the past greeted the troops,
> And brought rice for the soldiers,
> Mothers who now wander around as beggars on train coaches.
> Does this cause you pain? Does this cause you pain?
>
> Please don't always sing songs that praise.
> Songs with dull lyrics have lulled our glorious homeland, which is full
> of pride, into forgetting about food, clothing and roses.
>
> The soldiers who fell,
> Never thought they would see,
> Our homeland today,
> Full of beggars, whose screaming breaks our hearts.
>
> Please do not say false things!
> Where are the hands that did grueling work in the past?
> Now we are all together, let's build our country,
> For freedom, for food and clothing, for roses!

"Naked '87" is a passionate rock ballad that speaks out against the use of music as party propaganda. The lyrics challenge the system of censorship which only permits "false" songs that "praise" the new society and ignore the severe hardships that people were suffering in the postwar "subsidy period" (*thời bao cấp*). Trần Tiến's vocal delivery is full of heartfelt anguish and seems to encapsulate the disillusionment that many Vietnamese felt during the postwar economic depression. The reflections in the song lyrics on the impoverished position of those who gave so much for the war—including the "mothers" whose sons fought in the war—are given added weight by the fact that Trần Tiến is a war veteran. In the song, the exodus of Vietnamese refugees to the United States after 1975 and the dire circumstances of Vietnamese working in the Soviet Union are exposed as a sign of lost pride.

In the spirit of the Renovation policy, Trần Tiến offers a candid view of life in postwar Vietnam that is far removed from party rhetoric. With songs like "Naked '87," and others such as "Rock Clock" ("Rock Đồng Hồ"), Trần Tiến aims to "truthfully" reflect people's realities and sentiments.[24] Although the public concerts by Black and White, which stimulated such emotion and excitement among the audience, were hastily stopped, Trần Tiến did perform songs from the "Conversation '87" program on one more occasion at the Musicians' Union in Hanoi on January 11, 1988. Importantly, this performance was not for the general public: it was for other professional musicians and was followed a few days later by a meeting during which members of the union shared their opinions about the concert. So even though "Conversation '87" was banned, it did receive serious critical attention, and two prominent scholars Tô Ngọc Thanh (2003 (1988)) and Tú Ngọc (2003 (1988)) published articles that discussed the merits and pitfalls of Trần Tiến's songs. Both of these articles offer positive reflections on Trần Tiến's attempt to make popular song relevant to real life, but they also criticize his songs for overemphasizing feelings of sadness and loneliness. Tô Ngọc Thanh, for example, praises Trần Tiến for composing songs that tackle "negative phenomena" and spring from the "feelings of the heart" (2003 (1988), 166), but he chastises him for misrepresenting society and for not providing a clearer perspective on the social problems raised in the songs.

Even though Trần Tiến's songs stimulated debate among professional musicians about their social role as artists, the Black and White band were not permitted to perform publicly or release recordings. Shortly after the "Conversation '87" controversy, Trần Tiến went to the Soviet Union for several months to participate in a "Rock for Democracy" tour, which featured musicians from across the communist world. Trần Tiến told me that he was not officially permitted to travel to the Soviet Union, but he managed to do so because he was helped by a friend in the border security team at the airport in Hanoi. On his return to Vietnam, Trần Tiến continued to write songs that addressed social issues, but none have been as contentious as those he performed with his band "Black and White" (Gibbs 2008a).

Despite the shift in party policy toward the arts that occurred as part of the Renovation policy, the "Conversation '87" controversy demonstrates that the cultural liberalization was in fact quite limited. The authorities were sufficiently worried about the social impact of Trần Tiến's music to harass him and prohibit his music. The same pattern of restriction occurred in the literary sphere. When the Renovation policy was announced, writers initially seized the opportunity to publish more critical works, but politicians soon became concerned that writers were becoming too outspoken. In the late 1980s and early 1990s, the party reassessed its line on creative freedoms and cracked down on writers who they thought had overstepped the mark: the work of the most outspoken writers was banned, some like Dương Thu Hương were imprisoned, and others were "harassed and persecuted" (Healy 2000, 43).

As Vietnam introduced further market reforms during the 1990s, the government became increasingly concerned about declining morale standards, especially among the younger generation. Despite high rates of growth and decreasing levels of poverty during the 1990s (Haughton et al. 2001), the gap between rich and poor widened and the levels of crime, drug addition, and prostitution increased. Anxiety about morality led the government to initiate a campaign against "social evils" (tệ nạn xã hội) at the end of 1995. One of the targets of the campaign was the karaoke bars that had sprung up in urban areas. Prostitution and drug taking had become commonplace in bars offering "hugging karaoke" (karaoke ôm), in which girls could be hired by clients to join them in private rooms. In February 1996, regulations about karaoke rooms were introduced, and subsequently many bars were raided (Olsen 2008).

The censorship of popular music on moral grounds has extended beyond karaoke. In a high profile case, an album called Nhật Thực (Solar Eclipse) featuring the famous pop singer Trần Thu Hà, encountered problems with the censors in 2001 because of sexual references in the lyrics. All the songs on the album, which were composed by Ngọc Đại, use poems by the young female poet Vi Thùy Linh. The poems had already been published in Vietnam, but an official responsible for authorizing the album's release at the Department of Performing Arts, Lê Nam, demanded that some "vulgar lyrics" (*ca từ dung tục*) be "corrected."[25] At an extraordinary meeting in Hanoi, where prominent musicians and officials discussed the album, Lê Nam argued that the lyrics of several songs did not conform to Vietnamese cultural values and the state's requirement of "ensuring purity in the lyrics of popular song."[26] Lyrics thought to be too risqué included: "My body goes crazy when it is held in your arms" and "Suddenly in front of me, the skirt of a nun flew up."[27] While such lines may seem extremely mild by Western standards, they were deemed sufficiently vulgar to be censored. When I discussed the censorship of *Nhật Thực* with the album's composer, Ngọc Đại, in 2011, he said that the lyrics were "uncharming" (*vô duyên*) and "coarse" (*thô bỉ*) after they had been censored, but he had to comply with the censors' demands or otherwise the album would not be approved. After several months of delay and modifications to the titles of songs as well as lyrics, the album was authorized for release, yet only seven of the thirteen songs performed in the live concerts were permitted on the album. This difference highlights a common tactic of restriction: the album was subject to more rigorous censorship than the live performances because it had the potential to reach a wider audience than the concerts. In the Vietnamese press *Nhật Thực* was hailed as a significant landmark in the development of popular music and the album sold tens of thousands of copies, a larger number in the Vietnamese context.

Apart from the issue of morality, Communist Party policy toward the arts since the 1990s has focused on promoting national cultural identity. Globalization, understood negatively as an unstoppable flood of foreign culture, technology, and mass media, is seen by many cultural nationalists as a threat to indigenous cultural forms and values (Vietnamese Institute for Musicology 2004). Fears that traditional music will disappear are being voiced with increasing urgency and the preservation of cultural identity has moved center stage. In response to concerns about the detrimental influence of foreign culture, in 1998 the party issued Resolution 5 on "Building and Developing a Progressive Vietnamese Culture Rich in National Identity" (Ministry of Culture 1999). This policy was a major turning point because it laid the foundations for the preservation of cultural heritage in order to promote national identity. In this new framework, prerevolutionary traditions that were previously prohibited, including *ca trù* and *châu văn*, are being promoted as cultural heritage. For instance, in 2009 the Ministry of Culture successfully nominated "*Ca trù* singing" for inscription on UNESCO's Intangible Cultural Heritage "Urgent Safeguarding List." While the change in cultural policy in the late 1990s marked a dramatic shift in regard to traditional music, the promotion of intangible cultural heritage by the state raises thorny issues concerning the representation, ownership, and stewardship of prerevolutionary music traditions. As I have argued elsewhere (Norton 2014), state discourse on intangible cultural heritage has led to traditional music forms like *ca trù* being defined primarily in nationalist terms, which serves to limit and control *ca trù*'s musical meanings. The promotion of intangible cultural heritage in the reform era does not, therefore, signal the end of censorship. Rather it has resulted in attempts to incorporate prerevolutionary musical forms into the cultural infrastructure of the state and to control the meanings ascribed to traditional culture.

Censorship, the Internet, and Vietnamese Rap

Vietnam is one of the most restricted countries in the world in terms of Internet access. The state-run Internet service providers systematically and routinely filter sites, and in 2011, Reporters Without Borders listed Vietnam as an "internet enemy."[28] Despite claims by the government that Internet filtering is needed to prevent access to elicit sexual material, few pornographic websites have been blocked. Instead, Internet filtering in Vietnam focuses on "politically and religiously sensitive sites that could challenge the state's one-party system," especially those sites that have Vietnamese-language content.[29]

Given the Vietnamese government's emphasis on blocking websites with contentious political and religious content, it is perhaps not surprising that music, which has not been granted official approval, can easily be accessed on the Internet. For instance, many unauthorized songs from the past—such as pre-1975 yellow music, Trịnh Công Sơn's antiwar songs, and Trần Tiến's "Conversation '87" songs—can be heard on mp3 file-sharing sites that are hosted in Vietnam, as well as international sites like YouTube.[30] Contemporary musicians have also taken advantage of the Internet. In addition to Việt Khang, other songwriters such as Tuấn Khanh have released songs on the Internet in order to bypass state censorship.[31]

In addition to providing an alternative method for music distribution, the rise of the Internet in Vietnam since the late 1990s has greatly increased access to, and awareness of, popular music from around the world, particularly from the West and other parts of Asia like South Korea. Exposure to a vast array of music on the Internet, as well as through cable television and other new media technology, has stimulated many young Vietnamese musicians to experiment with new styles of popular music and to incorporate influences from diverse styles including jazz, pop, rock, and rap. Of all the recent new developments in Vietnamese popular music, the rap scene is probably the most reliant on the Internet. Indeed, it would be hard to imagine hip hop gaining roots in Vietnam without the worldwide web, not least because Vietnamese rap exists to a great extent in the virtual world of cyberspace. Although break dance crews practice on the streets of major cities and regularly organize competitions and others events, live rap events are less frequent, and Vietnamese rap is mainly mediated in cyberspace. The reasons for this are linked to censorship: most Vietnamese rap would not pass the censors because of its "dirty" (bẩn) lyrical content, yet censors have not prevented its circulation on Internet rap forums. In terms of music production, the worldwide web has also been a crucial resource: drum loops and other samples downloaded from the Internet are a ubiquitous feature of Vietnamese rap tracks.

The first rap track to use Vietnamese language was "Vietnamese Gangs." This track was originally released in 1997 and features rap by two Vietnamese Americans based in Portland, Oregon: Thai (who raps in English) and Khanh Nho (who raps in

Vietnamese).[32] From its origins in the Vietnamese diaspora in the United States, it took a few years before rap music became established in Vietnam. It was not until 2002 that the first rap collective, known as Da Rapclub, emerged in Hanoi. The rappers in this collective, such as LK, Eddy Viet, Young Uno, Lil' BK, Chip Nho, and Ca Chep, became the main hub of "Northside rap," a term that refers broadly to rap from northern parts of Vietnam. "Southside rap" from Ho Chi Minh City and other cities in southern Vietnam became prominent in 2006, when a hip-hop collective called FanHipHop (FHH) was established by a rapper called VTA. In addition to the Northside/Southside polarity, which has parallels with the East Coast/West Coast division in US rap, the English terms *overground* and *underground* are often used to distinguish between two sides of the Vietnamese rap scene. Mirroring the distinction between commercial versus "real" rap in the United States and elsewhere, the overground/underground dichotomy is typically equated with a series of other oppositions: commercial/noncommercial, inauthentic/authentic, false/real, superficial/sincere. A few rap artists have managed to go overground by pairing up with famous pop singers. Following the model of R&B songs in the United States, some rappers have collaborated with famous pop singers and have performed "clean" rap—mainly about love and romance—on mainstream pop songs for television broadcast. The southern rapper Tiến Đạt (also known as Mr. Dee), for example, became well known in the mid 2000s for rapping on commercial tracks with female pop divas like Thanh Thảo and Ngô Thanh Vân. Despite some rappers going overground, most of the Vietnamese rap scene exists underground and is excluded from the state-controlled broadcast media and performance venues. Many of the Vietnamese rappers I have spoken to expressed frustration about the lack of opportunities for them to gain exposure in the mainstream media, which greatly hindered their attempts to become professional artists.

An important part of Vietnamese underground rap is oriented around battles, in which a rapper "disses" another rapper, who in turn responds with an "answer" rap. Such battling may be quite trivial, even silly. Nonetheless, battling has played an important role in the development of Vietnamese rap because it is a competitive, combative medium through which rappers hone their skills and vie for status. One of the interesting dimensions of battling in Vietnam has also been the way it has been a forum of combative exchange between Vietnamese rappers in different places, both within Vietnam and in the Vietnamese diaspora, particularly in Germany and the United States.[33] "Diss" raps have caused considerable controversy in Vietnam because of the frequent use of foul language, and this is partly responsible for public perceptions that rap is a negative Western import associated with gang culture that is incompatible with Vietnamese values.

One notorious example of a rap battle between Northside rappers took place between Khanh, a rapper from the port city of Hai Phong approximately ninety kilometers southeast of Hanoi, and two rappers from the Hanoian "Da Rapclub" crew, Lil' BK and Chip Nho. Khanh's rap "Hanoi Stars" ("Hà Nội Sao") started the battle with a slow snarling rap in Vietnamese that uses coarse language and threats of violence toward Lil' BK and Chip Nho over a minimal two-bar keyboard riff and a slow drum beat (about 92 beats per minute).[34] In the rap, which is entirely in Vietnamese except for a few references to English slang, Khanh unleashes a torrent of abuse, including homophobic and other sexual insults. Playing with the names of the two Hanoi rappers, Khanh accuses the "handsome" Lil' BK of being gay (with the line "Is it Lil' BK or Lil' B 'Gay'?") and he refers to Chip Nho as "*chim nhỏ*," which is slang for "small dick." In Khanh's characterization, Lil' BK and Chip Nho are vain Hanoian upstarts who fantasize about being famous like Eminem, whereas he portrays himself as ruthless gangster with a rough disheveled appearance who controls the criminal gangs along Highway 5 (the road that runs from Hanoi to Hai Phong). Toward the end of the rap, Khanh invokes the memory of President Hồ Chí Minh or "Uncle Ho." The following is a translation from Vietnamese of the final lines of the rap:

> I bow down and apologize to Uncle Ho,
> Who is resting peacefully in the sky.
> Uncle Ho has passed away and only crazy idiots are left.
> Please come down from heaven Uncle and witness.
> I will execute the two traitors,
> Who ran away to America to become prostitutes,
> Who rap like two crazy idiots.
> Your music is stolen [i.e., not your own] and your voice sounds like dick,
> Yet you dream that you rap like Eminem.
> Look into the mirror and what do you see,
> Eminem or just two dogs?
> Dogs sitting eating children's shit on the side of the road,
> Yeah, Five Tigers will live forever.

After the end of the Vietnamese-American war in 1975, there was an exodus of refugees from Vietnam, and in Khanh's rap, the reference to "traitors" who "ran away to America" is clearly loaded with this historical context. Khanh taunts Lil' BK and Chip Nho by saying that they are just weak imitators of US rappers like Eminem, whereas he pays homage to Uncle Ho and presents himself as authentically Vietnamese.

There have been several answer raps to "Hanoi Stars," including a track by Lil' BK and Chip Nho called "Hai Phong Stars" ("Hải Phòng Sao"), which is also in Vietnamese with only occasional references to English words.[35] The track begins with a conversation that is a mocking imitation of two hapless boys from Hai Phong who are talking about how they cannot find their way to Hanoi. After the introduction, the backing track abruptly changes to the faster drum break and sax riff on Eminem's "Without Me," followed by a lively, upbeat rap, which pokes fun at Khanh's attempt to shock with his foul language and portrays Khanh as a poor, ignorant country boy. In both "Hanoi Stars" and "Hai Phong Stars," sharp disparities in wealth, style, and opportunity, which are a feature of the ever increasing rural-urban divide, are a central theme.

Rap tracks like "Hanoi Stars" and "Hai Phong Stars" have contributed to anxieties about the detrimental effects of globalization on Vietnamese youth. In order to stem the negative influence of culture from abroad, the Ministry of Culture would no doubt wish to stop such rap battles. However, they do not seem to have attempted to filter the websites where rap battles are circulated.[36] This may be simply because it is practically impossible to effectively censor such sites. Due to the lack of serious political content, it is also likely that rap is not a priority for the authorities and they may just dismiss rap battles as juvenile name-calling. Whatever the rationale, as long as rap battles are restricted to the virtual world of cyberspace and do not surface in the "real" public sphere, the censors seem unconcerned. Nonetheless, the circulation of uncensored rap tracks on the Internet has enabled young Vietnamese to express themselves, at least to their peers, in ways that are far removed from anything that is permitted in the official media, and this would seem to indicate the increasing inability of the state to entirely control cultural expression in the way it has done in the past. Prior to the Internet, black-market recordings—mainly tapes smuggled in from abroad—were circulated in Vietnam, but the dissemination of illegal music was much more restricted than it has been since digital technology became widespread. The Internet undoubtedly offers great potential as a tool for bypassing state censorship. Its power, however, is limited: without official permission to broadcast on the state-run media and to perform publicly, it is still hard for musicians to reach a large audience.

Conclusion

In his book *Music and Politics*, John Street argues that "music *embodies* political values and experiences, and *organizes* our response to society as political thought and action. Music does not just provide a vehicle for political expression, it *is* that expression" (2012, 1, emphases in original). The complicated history of censorship in Vietnam since 1954, which I have sketched in this chapter, offers numerous examples of the ways in which music might be understood, following Street, as constituting political experience, organization, thought, and action. The extent to which the authoritarian regimes that have existed in Vietnam since 1954 have sought to control and censor musical expression would seem to indicate an awareness of how deeply music is implicated in political agency and embodies political values.

During the Vietnamese-American War music was not just a vehicle for political propaganda. Rather, musical mobilization was itself a form of political mobilization. In the DRV, musical-political mobilization was evident in the performances of state-run troupes and musical movements like "Song Drowns Out the Sound of Bombs," which embodied the values of revolutionary socialism and the ideology of a just war of resistance against foreign invaders. Traditional musics like *ca trù* that were not well suited for ideological reform were largely silenced. In keeping with the Vietnamese Communist Party's use of music as an "ideological weapon," many music troupes were interconnected with the army: music troupes regularly performed for troops and musicians formed music collectives within army units. Resistance to the use of music as an ideological weapon was exercised by some musicians in the DRV who performed yellow music, but musicians who deviated from the party line, like Hairy Toan and his band, were imprisoned. In the RVN, state-condoned music embodied political values such as anticommunism, but the government was unable to prevent political opposition galvanizing around the "Sing for Our Compatriots to Hear" movement. This musical movement seems to have spurred a large number of students to be politically engaged and to organize demonstrations; it provided a forum for the youth to think through their oppositional stance toward the RVN regime and the war and to articulate their feelings of disillusionment. The political agenda of Trịnh Công Sơn's immensely popular antiwar songs was not so overtly oppositional to the regime as the "Sing for Our Compatriots to Hear" movement, yet the authorities tried to prevent their circulation because, rather than glorifying the heroism of the RVN troops, they encapsulated people's powerful emotional responses to the tragedy of war and their yearning for peace.

After the end of the war in 1975, the Vietnamese Communist Party placed a high priority on eradicating all music deemed antithetical to the development of a new socialist society. In order to do this, the authorities thoroughly purged the musical culture of South Vietnam. In the post-1975 period, however, the disconnect between the official rhetoric of a rosy socialist utopia as expressed in state-condoned political songs and the realities of postwar hardship undermined music's social relevance. The initiation of the Renovation policy in 1986 provided opportunities for some musicians like Trần Tiến to compose songs that were critical of some aspects of postwar socialist society and spoke to people's everyday concerns. The limits of creative freedom in the early Renovation period were made clear by the restrictions placed on Trần Tiến and the banning of his rock band, Black and White. After seeming to give artists greater scope to adopt a more critical stance in the first flush of the Renovation policy, the party quickly moved to reassert control over the public sphere and to limit dissent. Since the 1990s, the forces of globalization have contributed to a gradual process of cultural liberalization, but anxieties over standards of morality and the erosion of national cultural identity have increased. Popular music continues to be subjected to censorship on moral grounds, and previously prohibited traditional musical forms are now being harnessed to bolster national cultural identity. Technological change and access to the Internet has challenged the state's ability to control all forms of musical expression and underground rap battles that bypass the conventional system of state censorship have been unleashed in cyberspace. While experimentation with different forms of musical expression is not encouraged, it is increasingly tolerated. The Communist Party, however, is still quick to punish musicians who are seen to be a political threat, as demonstrated by the imprisonment of Việt Khang discussed at the start of this chapter. As in the past, songwriters in contemporary Vietnam who dare to write lyrics that directly challenge the authority of the party or its policies face extremely serious consequences.

Notes

1. See http://www.bbc.co.uk/news/world-asia-pacific-13592508 (accessed August 2012).
2. See http://www.bbc.co.uk/news/world-asia-pacific-14574075 (accessed August 2012).
3. Việt Khang's recordings of "Anh là ai?" and "Việt Nam tôi đâu?" can be heard at http://www.youtube.com/watch?v=iqkZuoo7IIE&playnext=1&list=PLCA7AD6EDA464798A&feature=results_main and http://www.youtube.com/watch?v=_KEPmduvlAg respectively (accessed September 2012).
4. All translations from Vietnamese in this chapter are my own.
5. For details about the petition and the US government's response, see: https://petitions.whitehouse.gov/petition/stop-expanding-trade-vietnam-expense-human-rights/53PQRDZH (accessed October 2012).
6. http://www.voanews.com/content/two-vietnamese-musicians-jailed-for-anti-state-propaganda/1535821.html (accessed October 2012). Alongside Việt Khang, another musician, Trần Vũ Anh Bình, was also charged under Article 88 and was given a six-year prison sentence.
7. Officially, musicians must submit detailed information, including a full transcript of song lyrics, about the items they will perform prior to any public performance to the local bureau of the Ministry of Culture for approval. The music industry is also largely controlled by state-run companies (such as Dihavina, Ho Guom Audio, Phuong Nam) and officially recordings must be given a stamp of approval prior to distribution. The content of programs on the state-run media—including radio and television—is also carefully vetted before broadcast.
8. Some of the contradictions and confusion about the censorship of popular songs are discussed in the 2004 newspaper article by Cao Minh Hiền and Dạ Ly titled "Pop Song... Censored and Not Censored!" ("Chuyện ca khúc... duyệt và không duyệt!"), http://vietbao.vn/Van-hoa/Chuyen-ca-khuc-duyet-va-khong-duyet/45122599/181/; and Minh Thi's 2006 article, "The Censorship of Popular Song: Still Causes Confusion" ("Kiểm duyệt ca khúc: Vẫn còn nhiều sự nhập nhằng"), http://vietbao.vn/Van-hoa/Kiem-duyet-ca-khuc-Van-con-nhieu-su-nhap-nhang/65051073/107/ (accessed October 2012).
9. By referring to 1954 as an approximate start of this account, I do not mean to suggest that censorship is a post-1954 development. Rather, 1954 is taken as a nominal starting point due to fact that it marked the beginning of the postcolonial period and is therefore a significant turning point in the history of Vietnam.
10. I am grateful to Jason Gibbs for alerting me to the pre-1975 "yellow music movement" in the DRV. An English translation of a newspaper article that reported the trial of Phan Thắng Toán and other members of his band, which was originally published in Vietnamese Hà Nội Mới on January 12, 1971, can be downloaded from the Vietnam Center and Archive website at http://www.virtual.vietnam.ttu.edu/ (accessed December 2012).
11. See Nga Pham's 2010 article "Risking Life for Pop Music in Wartime Vietnam," http://www.bbc.co.uk/news/10312758 (accessed December 2012).
12. Video performances of ca trù by the Ca Trù Thái Hà Ensemble can be seen at: http://www.gold.ac.uk/music/catru/. See Norton 2005 and 2014 for further information about ca trù.
13. According to Chu Hà, there were a few ca trù performances and radio broadcasts in the 1960s and 1970s including a performance at the Temple of Literature in Hanoi during the Lunar New Year in 1962, which President Hồ Chí Minh attended. Chu Hà 1980, 59, 124.

14. The text refers to the thirty-five years since Hồ Chí Minh's declaration of independence in 1945. The Vietnamese Communist Party (formerly called the Vietnamese Labor Party) was founded in 1930.
15. See Bửu Chỉ 2005 (2001) and Schafer 2007.
16. Recordings of performances by Trịnh Công Sơn and Khánh Ly at the Quán Văn club can be heard at http://www.tcs-home.org/ (accessed August 2012).
17. The songwriter Miên Đức Thắng was also arrested and put on trial for performing his songs at demonstrations, and his arrest on September 27, 1968, is reported in an article in *Le Monde* by Mirielle Gansel (1972). In the article, Gansel praises the struggles of the "Sing for Our Compatriots to Hear" movement, and she points out that the poems and songs had endured despite violent oppression, prohibition, and censorship.
18. For a collection of the main songs of "Sing for Our Compatriots to Hear" movement see Youth Publishing House (2000). See also Tôn Thất Lập and Nguyễn Phú Yên (2012).
19. According to the report in the *Communist Magazine*, 107 people were arrested as a result of the crackdown on "reactionary and decadent cultural, artistic and literary products" (Tran Tho 1982, 11).
20. Nhân Dân, December 5, 1987, 1. See also Healey 2000, 42–43.
21. See http://www.viet-studies.info/NhaVanDoiMoi/NguyenVanLing_NoiChuyenVanNgheSi.htm for a full transcript of Nguyễn Văn Linh's speech (accessed July 2010).
22. I obtained a copy of the communiqué (Thông Báo) banning Black and White from Trần Tiến in 2011. The communiqué is numbered 988 and is signed by Trần Văn Tài, the Vice-Director of the Central People's Committee of Ho Chi Minh City.
23. A version of "Naked '87" sung by Trần Tiến with guitar accompaniment can be heard at: http://www.nhaccuatui.com/nghe?M=x78nUx3-Az (accessed August 2011).
24. For further discussion about the song "Rock Clock" ("Rock Đồng Hồ"), see Hiebert 1991 and Gibbs 2008a, 169–182.
25. See http://giaitri.vnexpress.net/tin-tuc/gioi-sao/trong-nuoc/toa-dam-ve-ca-tu-dung-tuc-trong-album-nhat-thuc-1872597.html (accessed November 2014).
26. See http://giaitri.vnexpress.net/tin-tuc/gioi-sao/trong-nuoc/toa-dam-ve-ca-tu-dung-tuc-trong-album-nhat-thuc-1872597.html (accessed November 2014).
27. In Vietnamese the two lines that were censored are "*Những điên mê trên thân thể em trong tay anh thập tự*" and "*Bỗng chiếc váy trên mình tu nữ bay thốc.*" The second of these lines does, however, appear on the 2009 CD recording of the song "Cây nữ tu" by Ngọc Đại's new band Đại Lâm Linh. For further information about Ngọc Đại and Đại Lâm Linh see the film I directed about the group called *Hanoi Eclipse: The Music of Dai Lam Linh* and the accompanying film study guide, http://www.der.org/films/hanoi-eclipse.html. Incidentally, I was informed by email in October 2012 that the censors had barred the screening of *Hanoi Eclipse* at the first International Anthropological Film Festival, held in Ho Chi Minh City in November 2012. Despite my requests for further information, the reasons why the censors would not allow the screening were not given.
28. See http://en.rsf.org/vietnam-vietnam-12-03-2012,42048.html (accessed September 2012). Internet filtering is in line with the tight control of journalism in Vietnam: on the 2011–2012 World Press Freedom Index, Vietnam is ranked 172 out of 179 (with only Bahrain, China, Iran, Syria, Turkmenistan, North Korea, and Eritrea ranked lower); see http://en.rsf.org/IMG/CLASSEMENT_2012/CLASSEMENT_ANG.pdf.

29. These quotations are from a detailed report on internet filtering in Vietnam in 2005–2006; see http://opennet.net/studies/vietnam (accessed October 2012).
30. At the time of writing (October 2012) the mp3 file sharing site http://www.nhaccuatui.com hosted by the NCT corporation in Ho Chi Minh City seems to have one of the widest and least restricted selections of Vietnamese music. Based on casual searching, other sites like Zing (http://hn.nhac.vui.vn/ and http://mp3.zing.vn/) seem to offer a more limited selection of music.
31. For example, in 2007 the musician Tuấn Khanh released his album *Bụi Đường Ca* on the Internet in order to avoid having to submit the album to the censors. See http://tranquanghai.info/p1130-vn%3A-nhac-si-tuan-khanh-dua-nhac-len-internet,-tranh-kiem-duyet.html (accessed August 2012). Like Việt Khang, Tuấn Khanh has written songs like "Vietnamese Heart" ("Trái Tim Việt Nam") protesting against Chinese actions in the East China Sea.
32. "Vietnamese Gangs" can be heard at: http://www.youtube.com/watch?v=lor3q0Koby4&feature=player_embedded (accessed August 2012).
33. For example, there have been numerous battles between Southside rappers, like VTA, and rappers who are part of a collective known as Genius Viet Rap (GVR), like Lee7 and Andree. The GVR collective is active in Vietnam, but some members have roots in the Vietnamese diaspora in Germany.
34. "Hà Nội Sao" can be heard at: http://www.youtube.com/watch?v=BU_SazR6nlQ (accessed August 2012).
35. One version of Lil' BK and Chip Nho's rap can be heard at: http://rappervn.net/music/download-1550-Hai_Phong_Sao_ft_Chip_Nho.html (accessed November 2014).
36. See for example http://rappervn.net/music/ (accessed August 2012).

References

Bửu, Chỉ. 2005 (2001). "Về Trịnh Công Sơn và những ca khúc phản chiến của anh." In *Trịnh Công Sơn: Cuộc đời, âm nhạc, thơ, hội họa, suy tưởng*, edited by Trịnh Cung and Nguyễn Quốc Thái, 1-4-26. Ho Chi Minh City: Nhà Xuất Bản Văn Hóa Sài Gòn.

Chu, Hà. 1980. "Hát cửa đình Lỗ Khê." In *Hát cửa đình Lỗ Khê*, 28–125. Hanoi: Sở Văn Hóa Thông Tin, Hội Văn Nghệ Hà Nội.

Cloonan, Martin. 2003. "Call That Censorship? Problem of Definition." In *Policing Pop*, edited by Martin Cloonan and Reebee Garofalo, 13–29. Philadelphia: Temple University Press.

Cửu, Long Giang. 2003 (1976). "Âm nhạc phản động." In *Hợp tuyển tài liệu: Nghiên cứu lý luận phê bình âm nhạc Việt Nam thế kỷ XX, tập 5B*, 597–602. Hanoi: Viện Âm Nhạc.

Đặng, Trung. 1988. *Ca khúc chính trị và tuổi trẻ*. Hanoi: Nhà Xuất Bản Thanh Niên.

Đào Trọng, Từ. 1984. "Renaissance of Vietnamese Music." In *Essays on Vietnamese Music*, 96–161. Hanoi: Foreign Languages Publishing House.

Đỗ, Nhuận. 2003 (1982). "Hội thảo 'Tuổi trẻ—âm nhạc—thời đại'—tham luận của nhạc sĩ Đỗ Nhuận." In *Hợp tuyển tài liệu: Nghiên cứu lý luận phê bình âm nhạc Việt Nam thế kỷ XX, tập 1*, 789–793. Hanoi: Viện Âm Nhạc.

Gansel, Mireille. 1972. Poésie et résistance. *Le Monde*, February 11.

Gibbs, Jason. 2007. "The Music of the State: Vietnam's Quest for a National Anthem." *Journal of Vietnamese Studies* 2, no. 2: 129–174.

Gibbs, Jason. 2008a. *Rock Hà Nội và Rumba Cửu Long: Câu chuyện âm nhạc Việt Nam*. Hanoi: Nhà Xuất Bản Trí Thức.

Gibbs, Jason. 2008b. "How Does Hanoi Rock? The Way to Rock and Roll in Vietnam." *Asian Music* 39, no. 1: 5–25.
Haughton, Dominique, et al., eds. 2001. *Living Standards during an Economic Boom: The Case of Vietnam*. Hanoi: Statistical Publishing House.
Healy, Dana. 2000. "Literature in Transition: An Overview of Vietnamese Writing in the Renovation Period." In *The Canon in Southeast Asian Literatures*, edited by D. Smyth, 41–50. Richmond, Surrey: Curzon.
Hiebert, Murray. 1991. "Singing Between the Lines." *Far Eastern Economic Review* (February 21): 30–31.
Hồ, Chí Minh, et al. 1976. *Về văn hóa nghệ thuật*. Hanoi: Nhà Xuất Bản Văn Hóa.
Malarney, Shaun Kingsley. 2002. *Culture, Ritual and Revolution in Vietnam*. London: Routledge Curzon.
Marr, David. 2003. "A Passion for Modernity: Intellectuals and the Media." In *Postwar Vietnam: Dynamics of a Transforming Society*, edited by H. V. Luong, 257–295. Lanham, Md.: Rowman & Littlefield Publishers, Inc.
Ministry of Culture. 1999. *Xây dựng và phát triển nền văn hóa Việt Nam tiên tiến đậm đà bản sắc dân tộc: Thực tiễn và giải pháp*. Hanoi: Bộ Văn Hóa Thông Tin.
Nguyen, Lien-Hang T. 2012. *Hanoi's War: An International History of the War for Peace in Vietnam*. Chapel Hill: University of North Carolina Press.
Nguyễn, Thanh Đức. 1987. Âm nhạc vào cuộc: Xem chương trình 'Đối thoại 87.' *Tuổi trẻ* (November 14).
Ninh, Kim N. B. 2002. *A World Transformed: The Politics of Culture in Revolutionary Vietnam, 1945–65*. Ann Arbor: University of Michigan Press.
Nooshin, Laudan. 2009. "Prelude: Power and the Play of Music." In *Music and the Play of Power in the Middle East, North Africa and Central Asia*, edited by L. Nooshin, 1–31. Aldershot, UK: Ashgate.
Norton, Barley. 2005. "Singing the Past: Vietnamese Ca Tru, Memory and Mode." *Asian Music* 36, no. 2: 27–56.
Norton, Barley. 2009. *Songs for the Spirits: Music and Mediums in Modern Vietnam*. Urbana and Chicago: Illinois University Press.
Norton, Barley. 2013. "Vietnamese Popular Song in '1968': War, Protest and Sentimentalism." In *Music and Protest in 1968*, edited by Beate Kutschke and Barley Norton, 97–118. Cambridge: Cambridge University Press.
Norton, Barley. 2014. "Music Revival, Ca Trù Ontologies, and Intangible Cultural Heritage in Vietnam." In *The Oxford Handbook of Music Revivals*, edited by Caroline Bithell and Juniper Hill, 158-179. New York: Oxford University Press.
Olsen, Dale A. 2008. *Popular Music of Vietnam: The Politics of Remembering and the Economics of Forgetting*. New York: Routledge.
People's Army Publishing House. 1968. *Tiếng hát át tiếng bom*. Hanoi: Nhà Xuất Bản Quân Đội Nhân Dân.
Schafer, John C. 2007. "The Trịnh Công Sơn Phenomenon." *The Journal of Asian Studies* 66, no. 3: 597–643.
Scherzinger, Martin. 2007. "Double Voices of Musical Censorship after 9/11." In *Music in the Post-9/11 World*, edited by Jonathan Ritter and J. Martin Daughtry, 91–121. New York: Routledge.
Street, John. 2012. *Music and Politics*. Cambridge: Polity.
Taylor, Philip. 2000. "Music as a 'Neocolonial Poison' in Postwar Southern Vietnam." *Crossroads: An Interdisciplinary Journal of Southeast Asian Studies* 14, no. 1: 99–131.

Tô, Ngọc Thanh. 2003 (1988). "Suy nghĩ thêm về chương trình Đối Thoại 87 của Trần Tiến." In *Hợp tuyển tài liệu nghiên cứu lý luận phê bình âm nhạc Việt Nam thế kỷ XX, tập 5B*, 160–166. Hanoi: Viện Âm Nhạc.

Tô, Vũ. 1976. "Nhạc vàng là gì?." *Văn hóa nghệ thuật* 57: 43–46.

Tôn, Thất Lập and Nguyễn Phú Yên. 2012. "Hát cho đồng bào tôi nghe". In *Tham luận hội thảo yêu nước thanh niên sinh viên học sinh 1954–1975*, 107–112. Da Nang: Bộ Giáo Dục và Đạo Tạo.

Tran, Tho. 1982. "Wiping Out Decadent Culture: A Cultural Commissar's Official Report on the Progress of 'Purification' in South Vietnam." *Index on Censorship* 11, no. 3: 9–11.

Trần, Việt Ngữ. 1996. *Về nghệ thuật chèo*. Hanoi: Viện Nghiên Cứu Âm Nhạc.

Trịnh, Công Sơn. 1989. "Phác thảo chân dung tôi." In *Đời và nhạc*, edited by Lê Giang and Lư Nhất Vũ, 455–482. Ho Chi Minh City: Nhà Xuất Bản Tổng Hợp Hậu Giang.

Truth Publishing House. 1982. *Bài trừ mê tín dị đoan*. Hanoi: Nhà Xuất Bản Sự Thật.

Tú, Ngọc. 2004 (1987). "'Đối Thoại 87'—Một cách tiếp cận cuộc sống." In *Hợp tuyển tài liệu nghiên cứu lý luận phê bình âm nhạc Việt Nam thế kỷ XX, tập 5B*, 156–160. Hanoi: Viện Âm Nhạc.

Tú, Ngọc, et al. 2000. *Âm nhạc mới Việt Nam: Tiến trình và thành tựu*. Hanoi: Viện Âm Nhạc.

Vietnamese Institute for Musicology. 2004. *Âm nhạc dân tộc cổ truyền trong bối cảnh toàn cầu hóa*. Hanoi: Viên Âm Nhạc.

Võ, Văn Kiệt. 1981. *Một số vấn đề về văn hóa văn nghệ hiện nay của thành phố chúng ta*. Ho Chi Minh City: Nhà Xuất Bản Văn Nghệ.

Youth Publishing House. 2000. *Hát cho đồng bào tôi nghe*. Ho Chi Minh City: Nhà Xuất Bản Trẻ.

IV

CENSORSHIP IN TOTALITARIAN STATES

CHAPTER 15

MIGUEL ÁNGEL ESTRELLA

(Classical) Music for the People, Dictatorship, and Memory

CAROL A. HESS

It is the evening of September 26, 1987. After a seven-year military dictatorship, democratic rule has prevailed in Argentina for almost four years. Argentine pianist Miguel Ángel Estrella has just walked onto the stage of the Teatro Colón in Buenos Aires before an audience of three thousand (Camps 1987, 2). The seven-tiered, acoustically perfect theater in neo French-Renaissance style is a bastion of "universal" culture, an ideal Buenos Aires elites have ardently defended in an ongoing tussle over artistic expression. Rejecting folkloric nationalism as fit only for "puerile and folkloric spirits," as characterized in the 1930s by Juan Carlos Paz, Latin America's first serialist composer, intellectual elites have traditionally taken universal culture to mean that of Europe, inclining especially toward France (Paz 1936, 80). In fact, Estrella's recital was a tribute to Nadia Boulanger, who had died in October 1979 and who, as we shall see, was one protagonist in Estrella's story, which blends the local and the cosmopolitan in some striking ways.

The bulk of the program perfectly complemented both the setting and the occasion. On the program were "Soeur Monique" and "La Bandoline" by François Couperin, "Le cou cou" and "L'hirondelle" by Louis-Claude Daquin, and some short works by Rameau. In addition to these French miniatures, Estrella played Five Little Preludes (J. S. Bach) and the C-Major Prelude and Fugue from Book II of the *Well-Tempered Clavier*, a Scarlatti sonata, and a Gigue and Passacaglia by Handel; he also included the imposing Sonata in E-flat Major, Hob. XVI: 52 by Haydn. On the second half were Beethoven's "Waldstein" sonata, op. 53, the *Fantasy Impromptu* by Chopin, op. 66, and three etudes by the same composer, op. 25 no. 2, and op. 10 nos. 9 and 12 (the "Revolutionary"). In the midst of this tribute to the European tradition, however, Estrella also paid homage to Argentine music, offering "Triste en la," from Julián Aguirre's *Aires Nacionales* and an arrangement of "Chakai Manta," a well-known chacarera, a folkloric dance with alternations of 3/4 and 6/8, often involving percussive effects in the guitar accompaniment. Another Argentine work was explicitly political. *Canción sin verano* (Song without Summer), by Juan "Tata" Cedrón, is based on a poem by the recently deceased Julio Cortázar, which deals with exile and "the silenced voices of friends." Having left Argentina for political reasons in 1951, Cortázar had watched the Dirty War—torture, imprisonment, and "disappearance" of those perceived as dissidents— from France and mourned in verse that "summer was no more" in Argentina, now "a land of ashen sun and a gray moon." Nonetheless, one day, the poet declared, "the wheat would rise on the pampa of liberty."

Another political move, which launched the concert, relied not on national but universal culture. Estrella began with a Bach chorale, unusual in and of itself in a piano recital. Introit-like and in four parts, the chorale (the Buenos Aires press does not specify which) was intended as a gesture of thanksgiving, as Estrella explained to the audience from the stage via a microphone. He was grateful, he announced, not only for being able to play in his own country but for Argentina's return to democracy. Throughout the rest of the recital, he commented on various aspects of the music, seeking "total communication with the public," as a sympathetic reviewer put it (Camps 1987, 2).

Estrella's gratitude was genuine. Ten years earlier he had been held captive in a clandestine house of torture in Uruguay, an environment so twisted that proper names or names of commonplace objects denoted the sinister tools plied there: an electroshock machine might be called "Susana" while the *pileta* ("swimming pool" or "sink" in American Spanish) was a bowl filled with urine and feces in which a prisoner's face was repeatedly dunked. From that nightmare, Estrella was transferred to a prison some sixty kilometers from Montevideo known as Libertad (liberty), in this instance, not a cruel euphemism but the actual name of the town in which the prison was located. A supporter of Juan Domingo Perón, Estrella had taught and performed in rural Argentina on the premise that the masterworks of the Western canon belonged to all citizens, not just elites. He later recalled to various interviewers the reproach of one of his torturers, later identified as Colonel José Nino Gavazzo. "'You'll never play the piano again,' that individual would hiss, adding, 'because you're no guerilla fighter, you're something worse: with your piano and your big fat smile you win over the shit [*la negrada*] of society and make them believe they can listen to Beethoven'" (Bonasso 2003, 18). An important detail here is the term "*negrada*." Although literally translated as "niggers," "*la negrada*" can refer generally to lower socio-economic classes of other races, the venom toward which the word "shit" seems most aptly to convey, even as it effaces the all-too obvious racist overtones. Thus, in addition to being formally charged with subversion, sedition, and terrorist activities—the actual extent of his political activities is discussed below—Estrella was also seen to threaten existing class structures by promoting the masterworks of the Western canon.

During the Cold War, when military regimes throughout Latin America were supported to varying degrees by the United States government, folk and popular musicians were frequently tagged "Marxist subversives" (Kornbluh 2003; McSherry 2005). In Brazil, Chico Buarque, Caetano Veloso, and Gilberto Gil (later Minister of Culture in the administration of Luiz Inácio Lula da Silva) were imprisoned and subsequently exiled for their politically provocative imaginations, manifested in song and theatrical displays (Veloso 2002, 216–217). Especially vulnerable were singers associated with *nueva canción*, whose lyrics of protest often sparked massive audience participation. In Argentina, Mercedes Sosa was searched and arrested on stage at a 1979 concert in La Plata; she subsequently moved to France. Most grotesque was the torture and murder of Víctor Jara, a fervent supporter of Salvador Allende, whose government Augusto Pinochet overthrew in 1973 with the aid of the CIA; Pablo Neruda (1904–1973) mourned Jara's fate as the equivalent of "killing a nightingale" (Urrutia 2002, 18). These artists and many others challenged authority through song, either using subtle imagery or more direct means. In "Preguntas por Puerto Montt," for example, Jara identified by name the Chilean Minister of the Interior responsible for ordering an overwhelming police presence on squatter families in the city of Puerto Montt in 1969, resulting in widespread death and injury (Schechter 1999, 429). Other *nueva canción* artists attacked the Vietnam war and the "American way of life," which many believed US multinationals and mass culture—including that purveyed by Walt Disney—were trying to implant in Latin America (Taffet 1997, 91–103; Dorfman and Mattelart 1975). To the broad public, these musical activists were the face of resistance to the Dirty War.

As for classical music in Latin America, by the time Estrella came of age most composers were under the spell of the avant-garde. In Argentina alone there was the Centro Latinoamericano de Altos Estudios Musicales (CLAEM, or Latin American Center of Advanced Musical Studies) in Buenos Aires, the most highly regarded program for new music in South America; the CLAEM, in turn, was a branch of the Instituto Torcuato di Tella, founded in 1958 as a center for avant-garde art. The same year, Francisco Kröpfl founded, under the auspices of the Architecture School of the University of Buenos Aires, the Estudio de Fonología, the first electroacoustic studio in Latin America attached to an academic institution. In 1959 in Córdoba, three hundred kilometers north of Buenos Aires, another such studio was established. Like their counterparts in *nueva canción*, some avant-garde composers actively resisted the Dirty War, both through direct political action or "revolutionizing" traditional musical parameters.

Estrella resisted this high-modernist ferment, remaining loyal to Beethoven, Haydn, Bach, Couperin, Scarlatti, and Chopin, a repertory that, unlike *nueva canción*, ostensibly posed little threat to the regime. Yet the remarks attributed to his torturer, cited above, suggest otherwise. As such, his story prompts several questions about this grim chapter in the history of Latin American music, which US scholars are only beginning to explore. How, if at all, do Estrella and his traditionalist repertory relate to the ongoing debate among composers and critics over socially engaged music (*música comprometida*)?[1] What are the historical antecedents of this debate and how do they inform present-day reactions to the status of either the avant-garde or the Western canon in *música comprometida*? Perhaps most important, how might scholars in the United States, especially those mindful of the love-hate relationship between their country and Latin America, seek to understand Estrella's story? In this essay, I propose to contextualize Estrella's experience in light of these broader issues.

Classical Music for the Masses and its Polemics: Estrella in History

Since the late nineteenth century, classical (i.e., art music) composers have debated music's role in periods of social upheaval. A central concern is the extent to which the Western canon constituted but a remnant of bourgeois culture, begging to be supplanted by new forms of expression. In determining what sort of new music was to rise out of the ashes of revolution, some argued for folk tunes, dance rhythms, or other elements familiar to oppressed constituencies. Others, especially members of the avant-garde, believed that only by "revolutionizing" form, harmony, texture, or instrumentation could composers mirror in their works the overthrow of existing social models. With regard to the Western canon itself, its revolutionary potential was up for grabs, depending largely on context and presentation.

In the first half of the twentieth century, composers and political leaders tested these ideas. José Vasconcelos, Minister of Education in the aftermath of the Mexican Revolution, was convinced that the masses could be uplifted through the masterworks of the European canon. Accordingly, the ministry sponsored public concerts, many in parks or other unrestricted spaces. As Vasconcelos later recalled, the newly reorganized Sinfónica Nacional presented (free of charge) "the complete series of Beethoven, the symphonies of Chaikovski, Brahms, Mozart, selections by Wagner, Debussy and Saint-Saëns, works of Strauss, the 'Unfinished' by Schubert . . . Berlioz and others" (Vasconcelos 1926, 1261). Vasconcelos's compatriot and contemporary Carlos Chávez not only shared these beliefs but was convinced of the astuteness and sensitivity of this largely working-class audience. In 1939, by which time Chávez had made his mark in the United States, he wrote an essay for *The New York Times*. Its title, "Music in a Mexican Test Tube," conveys the experimental nature of the post-revolutionary cultural program (Chávez 1939, SM5). He enthuses over a state-subsidized, ten-year run of workers' concerts presented by the Orquesta Sinfónica de México, which, like Vasconcelos's concerts, were often "out-of-concert-hall" experiences (Beckles Willson 2009a). The inaugural event, held at the Centro Social y Deportivo Venustiano Carranza, attracted all ages, including numerous children and workers in "faded overalls" or otherwise "shabbily dressed." Other free concerts, organized in collaboration with trade-union leaders, were held at the Palacio de Bellas Artes. Again, some audience members showed up barefoot while others sported worn but freshly laundered white shirts, a gesture Chávez found to be "as fine a compliment as an audience has ever paid an orchestra." Concerts were well attended. "People swarmed in to listen," Chávez recalled, "their eyes fixed on the orchestra; their heads and bodies barely stirred," behavior quite different from that of the easily distracted "regular cultivated subscription audience." For Chávez, this unaffected and spontaneous reaction was the bedrock of Mexico's post-revolutionary cultural renaissance, namely, that "art must be . . . universal in its foundations and reach the vast majority of the people." Further, Chávez notes, this "untutored and inexperienced" public possessed discriminating taste. On one occasion, a Haydn symphony that "experienced ears find charming and irresistible" made no impact whatsoever. When a Stravinsky work was played (Chávez does not identify it) the workers applauded enthusiastically, "as if they had been brought up on a diet of nothing but dissonance, atonality, and rhythms that changed with bewildering uncertainty." Despite its material poverty, clearly this public was innately sophisticated—at least, as Chávez told it to *The New York Times* at a moment when similar artistic projects in the United States were being realized under the Works Progress Administration.

More than once, Stravinsky's music was seen to speak for the masses, as if defying the composer's own elitism. The long-awaited Madrid premiere of *The Rite of Spring* in December 1932 prompted a near-delirious reaction in Republican Spain, with many critics applauding not so much Stravinsky's score as the wisdom of the people, who evidently listened to its complexities "with an interest and emotion seldom equaled," as one reviewer declared. Another attributed this reaction to the music's freedom "from all intellectualism, from any dialectical gesture of salon-style elegance," through which "the great Russian himself, without knowing it, has been a spokesman, a herald of the revolution" (Hess 2001, 284–286). Clearly, if the masses were capable of embracing both the European canon and modern music, it was only natural that politically minded composers target this constituency as performers. For decades, workers' choruses such as the Orfeó Català of Barcelona performed European masterworks, along with folk songs. In Vasconcelos's Mexico, such choruses were sometimes founded in the poorest "most miserable" neighborhoods of the "entirely miserable" Mexican capital, as Vasconcelos himself put it (Vasoncelos 1926, 1265). One composer who tapped into this performing force was Hanns Eisler, who famously quarreled with Schoenberg over what he considered the undue complexity of new music. Eisler's own mild brand of modernism emerged in his *Massenlieder* style, the meter shifts, harmonic surprises, and angular, sometimes unpredictable, melodic turns of which were imitated in the United States where workers' choruses had thrived since the waves of immigration at the turn of the twentieth century. Aaron Copland, for example, composed "Into the Streets May First!" in 1934 while associated with the New York-based Composers' Collective. Worker-performers might also confront the modernist idiom in the *Lehrstücke* of Hindemith and Weill or in the political theater of Marc Blitzstein.

Among those who addressed the political merits of modern music was Charles Seeger. Rejecting the power structure embedded in "bourgeois" concert life, Seeger developed his short-lived concept of proletarian music, that is, revolutionary "content" realized via "the forward looking technic [sic] of contemporary art music" composed with "the people" in mind. Indeed, although he insisted that workers would "not have any trouble" performing musically complex works (Seeger 1934, 125), Seeger (who ultimately embraced folk music) nonetheless advised composers to be judicious in their technical demands, wondering aloud if Copland's "Into the Streets May First!" would "ever be sung on the picket line" (Crist 2005, 29; Seeger 1939). For this stance, Seeger was attacked by the communist journalist Mike Gold, who argued that while "a new content often demands a new form," audiences would rightly complain if "the new form gets so far ahead of all of us that we can't understand its content" (Hess 2008, 331). Common ground was established when Seeger excoriated artists who perpetuated the status quo, targeting "the liberal composer who has sat in his ivory tower and said, whether or not there is a class struggle, music has nothing to do with it . . . broadcasting negative propaganda (tacit approval) for the social system that gives him a tower and allows him to sit in it" (Seeger 1934, 126). Decades later in Latin America, Ernesto (Che) Guevara addressed the artist's obligations in similar terms. Acknowledging that some might take "artistic experimentation as the definition of freedom," he nonetheless attacked avant-garde artists who indulge in mere formalist escapism as little more than "docile servants of official thought . . . 'scholarship students' who live at the expense of the state—practicing freedom in quotation marks" (Guevara 1989, 11–13).

If some fervently believed in "the wisdom of the people," others saw an unbridgeable rift between the uneducated public and the educated elites. Embodied in the complexity, abstraction, and profoundly anti-mimetic qualities of modern art, this rift was energetically debated in Latin America during the early part of the twentieth century vis-à-vis the ideas of Spanish philosopher José Ortega y Gasset. Famously arguing that the "new art" (*el arte nuevo*) was not only unpopular but *anti*-popular, Ortega encapsulated some of the agendas just surveyed, especially persuasive given that the adjective "popular" in Spanish refers not merely to approbation (popularity) but also means "of the people." The title of Ortega's best-known essay on this subject, "The Dehumanization of Art," encapsulates the new art's incapacity to serve any social (human) end. "A work of art is nothing but a work of art," Ortega asserts, echoing debates in late-nineteenth century Vienna over absolute music. "New art," bound to the principles of "disinterested" aesthetic contemplation, was thus inimical to political utterance (Ortega 1968, 14).

Such an aesthetic stance, rudely dividing elites and masses, is of course eminently political, and Latin Americans have explored Ortega's work as such. Some elites adapted the attitude of Victoria Ocampo, who, in founding the Argentine journal *Sur* (in some ways modeled on Ortega's own *Revista de Occidente*), maintained that the intellectual should reflect on "the eternal questions of culture and knowledge" and remain largely aloof from politics (King 1986, 39). Yet as Vicky Unruh observes, Latin American vanguards have tended to invest Ortegan dehumanization with a meaning at odds with that intended by its creator (Unruh 1994, 23–26). Far from pursuing the realms of "disinterested" contemplation—rejecting the ivory tower described by Seeger or the "docility" of "official thought" against which Che warned—several Latin American modernists took "new art" as a point of departure for social action, arguing that it should embrace *confrontation* between art and experience. "Experience" could of course be political. For the Peruvian Marxist José Carlos Mariátegui (1894–1930), Ortega had gotten it only half right. Although the new art was an important concept, Mariátegui maintained, art that did nothing more than introduce new techniques was "decadent," given its preoccupation with merely "formal conquests" rather than social engagement (Mariátegui 1986, 182). Neruda, too, rejected the idea that "a work of art is nothing but a work of art." In a 1935 essay on "poetry without purity," Neruda opposed *poésie pure* to a poetry "penetrated by sweat and smoke, redolent of urine and the lily," all signs of "the confused impurity of human beings" (Neruda 1986, 243). For others, political engagement (*compromiso*) was the defining element of Latin American modern art, one that separated it from Europe. In 1927, the Peruvian poet Magda Portal (1900–1989) urged artists to reject "the vanquished '-isms' of Europe," brandishing in capital letters the slogan "HUMANIZATION OF ART," with its "double mission of aesthetics and life" (Portal 1988, 208). As these essayists responded to Ortegan ideals, the principles of confrontation and engagement they advocated gained ground in several areas of Latin American life. An obvious example is the work of Paulo Freire, the Brazilian educational philosopher whose best-known work, *The Pedagogy of the Oppressed* (1968), confronted the unequal distribution of intellectual opportunity, a position similar in many ways to Estrella's.

Twentieth-century, left-leaning Latin American composers have taken several approaches to these issues. Silvestre Revueltas, for example, sought to deliver a revolutionary message to a mass audience via a traditional symphonic format in his *Homenaje a Federico García Lorca*, composed in 1936 in honor of the slain Spanish poet. (Lorca himself believed that peasants and workers were innately receptive to the classics, having founded the traveling theater program La Barranca to bring the works of Lope de Vega and Calderón de la Barca to Spain's rural poor.) Traveling under the auspices of LEAR (League of Revolutionary Writers and Artists) at the height of the Spanish Civil War, Revueltas was applauded in Madrid and Barcelona for writing music that the "unsophisticated public . . . knows how to assimilate with refined instinct" (Hess 1997, 286). Others asserted their aesthetic-political stance through modernist anti-nationalism. In Brazil, during the first regime of Getúlio Vargas, the entity Grupo Musica Viva centered around the German-born Schoenberg adherent Hans-Joachim Koellreuter, Brazil's first serialist. Musica Viva's manifesto denounces the "egocentric and individualistic currents" of musical nationalism. As Gerard Béhague has noted, any attempt to establish a Brazilian dodecaphonic school also defied the ideology of *brasilidade* Vargas had trumpeted (Béhague 1979, 279). In Cuba, modernist composers were often explicit: José Ardévol, whose 1969 book repeatedly refers to "the triumph of the [communist] revolution," wrote two cantatas, the serialist *Che comandante* and *La Victoria de Playa Girón*, which contains aleatoric passages (Ardévol 1969, 100). In Chile during the Allende years, composers such as Gustavo Becerra, Sergio Ortega, and Luis Advis experimented with the *cantata popular*. Decidedly *anti*-modernist, that genre sought to unite the world of *nueva canción* and the cantata, as in Luis Advis's *Santa María de Iquique* of 1969, which combines trio-sonata textures and recitative-like passages with various folk forms, such as the *cueca*, while commemorating the 1907 massacre of nitrate workers in northern Chile. Joan Jara (Víctor Jara's widow) later recalled the discussion such works prompted, raising many of the same questions Seeger had pondered. Could classical forms express the voice of the masses? Were "elite," conservatory-trained composers qualified to evoke the plight of ordinary workers (Jara 1984, 196)?

Such debates continue today. In a spirited essay of 2008, Argentine composer Graciela Paraskevaídis contrasts the long tradition of politicized music with the relative scholarly silence on Latin American music during the latter part of the twentieth century, when composers' political convictions were tested as perhaps never before. Drawing on the work of the Mexican Marxist theorist Leopoldo Zea, Paraskevaídis argues that to accept any model at all is to accept subordination and that history itself is a succession of fractured models. *Música comprometida* must therefore reject tradition, whether from recent or distant musical history. Neither are merely setting a few texts by Neruda or incorporating symbolic references to the same sufficient to constitute *música comprometida*. Electroacoustic music, however, is especially well suited to resisting stylistic subordination and confronting political injustice, as demonstrated in Rafael Aponte-Ledée's *En memoria a Salvador Allende* or Hilda Dianda's . . . *después el silencio*, for example. Other works Paraskevaídis considers in her important essay commemorate the life of Che Guevara (*Ñancahuasú* by César Bolaños, *¡Volveremos a las montañas!* by Gabriel Brnčić) and the 1973 coup in Chile (*Cantata de Chile*, by Leo Brouwer, *Biografía mínima de Salvador Allende* by Juan Orrego-Salas, and *Chile 1973* by Gustavo Becerra). Non-Latin American composers, too, have honored the victims of political oppression in Latin America. James Tenney of the United States composed *Fabric for Che* for digital fixed media (electronic tape) in 1967, the year the CIA expedited Che's death in the mountains of southern Bolivia. Luigi Nono composed works inspired by the Dirty War, including *Y entonces comprendió* (dedicated to Che) and *Como una ola de fuerza y de luz*, on the death of a Chilean militant (Paraskevaídis 2008, 5). The best-known such composition in Europe and the United States is surely *36 Variations on "The People United Will Never Be Defeated!" by Sergio Ortega and Quilapayún* by US composer Fredric Rzewski of 1975 (Madsen 2003, 9; Hess 2013, 171–186). A large-scale virtuosic work in a time-honored traditional form that commemorates the Allende years and the victims of the coup, Rzewski's variations have been attacked from various sides of the political spectrum. Although Paraskevaídis acknowledges that Rzewski "expresses his solidarity and pays homage to the tortured and the disappeared," for her the work falls short, as Rzewski has "let himself be seduced by a musical model that is hardly revolutionary," resulting in an "oxymoron" (Paraskevaídis 2008, 7). The *New York Times* critic John Rockwell, on the other hand, upholds the values of capitalist society and apolitical music in his comments on the work, faulting not only Rzewski but Cornelius Cardew and Christian Wolff for failing to make "much of an impact on the working classes, or on the third-world masses, or on China, or whomever it is they are ostensibly celebrating in their music" (Rockwell 1983, 93). Thus the lines of debate are drawn: form, tradition, and intent all jostle for priority in the ideological mix.[2]

For performers, too, the Western canon is seen either as an unfit model for socially engaged music or as a vehicle for challenging existing social structures. The celebrated Venezuelan Youth Symphony, merely one ensemble in the network of orchestras throughout Venezuela known as *El Sistema*, draws most of its players from slums or poor rural areas. Like the West-Eastern Divan Orchestra, founded in 1999 by Daniel Barenboim and Edward Said to unite Israeli and Palestinian musicians, it concentrates almost solely on the Western canon. (To be sure, some see this emphasis as "tension between repertoire . . . and marketing" [Beckles Willson 2009b, 319]). Carlos Sedan, director of one of the orchestra's schools in Sarria (one of Caracas's poorest neighborhoods), credits the ensemble with bringing "the sounds of Beethoven to the masses," thus destroying "the myth that you have to be from the upper classes to play the violin" ("Venezuelan Youths Transformed by Music" 2005). This outlook is summed up in the orchestra's rubric "*Tocar y luchar*," which urges its members "to play and to fight." Clearly Estrella's campaign to bring Beethoven to the masses can be summed up with the same pithy slogan.

Classical Music and the "Pedagogy of the Oppressed"

Born in 1937, Miguel Ángel Estrella spent his early childhood in Vinará, a rural town in Tucumán province. He later described it as a "Macondo" (Estrella 1985, 33), the fictional town created by Gabriel García Márquez that has come to symbolize third world Latin America, the poverty of which is enveloped in a profound sense of the magical and the absurd. As a boy, Estrella sang constantly and taught himself to play various folk genres on the guitar. He especially responded to the folk singer Atahualpa Yupanqui, whose songs of exploitation and the day-to-day agonies of the rural poor Estrella considers a "synthesis of collective memory and personal experience" that transform "daily realities into poetry" (Estrella 1985, 82). His parents were working-class, leftist, anti-clericalists who forbade him from taking the obligatory class in Catholic dogma in school. Miguel Ángel's insistence at age twelve on being baptized in the church thus came as rather a surprise. By then, the family had left "Macondo" for San Miguel de Tucumán, the provincial capital. There they lived next door to a convent from which music was frequently heard. Estrella decided to become a musician and began playing the piano on his own, since he felt that Tucumán had little to offer in the way of instructors or classes.

At age eighteen, and mindful of the gaps in his training, Estrella entered the National Conservatory of Music in Buenos Aires. He and some of his fellow students agitated for curricular reform, finding its "academicism" and "colonialism" oppressive, as he later noted. Seeking stimulation outside the conservatory, Estrella chose his own models, which ranged from Villa-Lobos (for his synthesis of classical and vernacular idioms) and, perhaps surprisingly, the anti-folkloric Paz (for his iconoclasm). These youthful explorations helped shape Estrella's evolving belief that the supposed boundaries between vernacular and classical music were "fictitious and self-interested" (Estrella 1985, 86). All the while, he worked at his piano playing, counting Adolfo Mindlin, Orestes Castronuovo, Erwin Leuchter, and Celia de Bronstein among his teachers. He also enjoyed some success. In 1959, he entered a contest and was so nervous that he asked the jury if he could play a zamba (a folkloric dance in a slow three) to relax before beginning the "real" repertory. Surprised by his request, the jury acquiesced and he delivered a prize-winning performance.

Estrella once claimed that he had been a Peronist "for as long as he could remember"; as a child, he was entranced by "Evita," Perón's first wife, María Eva Duarte (Estrella 1985, 49). Perón came to power in 1946 on the heels of a military coup, which he partly expedited. Still a force in Argentine political life today (and still controversial), Peronism has always been difficult to define. At its height in the 1940s and early 1950s, Perón's principal support came from workers and the rural poor, known as the *descamisados*: literally, the "shirtless ones" (they removed their shirts to perform manual labor). This base was cultivated in large part through Evita's charity projects and her personal charisma. Under Perón, women were also given the right to vote. Yet Perón the populist also suppressed civil liberties in the universities, thus appealing to some authoritarians and pseudo-fascists, many of whom had supported the Axis during the Second World War. From its beginnings, Peronism was also staunchly anti-US, a sentiment the radical left nurtured as well. Alliances also shifted: the Argentine Catholic Church, one of the more conservative in Latin America, initially supported Perón but later broke with his government after conflicts arose over the legalization of divorce and prostitution. Defining anti-Peronism is equally difficult, since it has been embraced by Catholics and non-Catholics, civilians and the military, right and left.

Having watched Evita in newsreels, Estrella was "in love" with her when she visited Tucumán province. This reaction was hardly unnatural in an era when many workers illuminated her image in their homes with a lit candle, befitting her status as "Santa Evita," as some called her. Her words during that visit remained engraved in Estrella's memory: "I will die fighting for the right of each one of you to freely choose your destinies," Evita declared (González Toro 2000, 54). He also recalls the reception some of the upper-middle-class ladies of Tucumán had prepared for her, table after table of fine pastries. But Evita pointed out to her hosts that while they enjoyed fine food every day, others were unfamiliar with such delicacies. She then opened the doors of the establishment to admit a multitude of children, mostly poor, into "the sanctuary of the bourgeoisie" (Estrella 1985, 52).

As for Peronism and the Western canon that Estrella embraced, there would seem to be little relationship, since Peronism has never enjoyed a particularly strong association with elite culture. A party slogan, "*¡Alpargatas sí, libros no!*" (itself a response to early anti-Peronist demonstrations by students) is part of Argentina's collective memory. (Alpargatas, or espadrilles, are the footwear of the lower classes [López 1975, 410]; Estrella recalls that in Vinará they were so common that "one would almost never see a *campesino* wearing shoes" [Estrella 1985, 59].) The history of Peronism and intellectuals bears out this antagonism. Cortázar, for example, left Argentina because of Perón and Alberto Ginastera's difficulties with the regime are well known, if inadequately documented. Nicolas Shumway traces such tensions to Argentina's beginnings. In 1838, not two decades after independence from Spain, the author Esteban Echeverría published the short story "El matadero" (The slaughterhouse), portraying the despot Manuel Rosas, hated by intellectuals, as an indiscriminate murderer. Echeverría also observes the crazed mob that beats to death a refined youth, detailing its barbarism, bloodthirstiness, and physical ugliness. Over a century later, Perón awakened the skepticism of

Argentine elites, who in principle supported democracy but feared mob rule, the lower classes, and the massification of culture (Shumway 1991, 143). Some intellectuals and artists allied themselves with Perón, however, especially those who believed that culture should arise from popular utterances rather than "colonialism," as Flavia Fiorucci has noted (Fiorucci 2002; Surra 2003). The government's occasional gesture on behalf of culture reinforced these loyalties. Much the way Evita invited workers to receptions in the homes of the bourgeoisie, she and Perón flung open to workers the doors of the Teatro Colón. Not only did the emblematic theater serve as a site for political speeches and rallies, but a series of free concerts for workers was administered by Evita and her staff (Albino 2009, 12–23).

In June 1955, when Estrella was eighteen, the Argentine air force bombed the Plaza de Mayo, the principal square in Buenos Aires, killing over three hundred and ousting Perón, who went to Spain in exile (Evita had died in 1952). The ensuing military regime presided over a polarized country. Two democratically elected presidents followed, but in 1966 General Juan Carlos Onganía (whom the United States was quick to recognize) effected a military coup. As inflation raged and university students avidly read Marx, Perón was increasingly seen as a beacon throughout the 1960s and his return was eagerly awaited. Peronism, however, splintered into two groups: the more conservative *justicialistas* and a radical wing, which included the *montoneros*, the party's militants.

Estrella experienced post-Perón Argentina in other ways. Once he tried to attend a concert at the Colón with his future wife, Martha: "We bought the least expensive tickets . . . I was wearing pants and a modest pullover. Without beating around the bush and with an audacious smile, the usher said to me: 'Get out, kid . . . the Teatro Colón is no longer open to *descamisados* and [*la negrada*]" (Estrella 1985, 95). Nonetheless, it was during the 1960s and 1970s that Estrella became convinced that music, like shelter, food, and medical care, was part of an ordinary citizen's rights. Declaring, "I'm a child of Evita and I believe that the people should receive the best," he stamped this ideal with Peronism, effectively replicating Evita's opening of the Colón by taking the Western canon to rural Argentina (Calderaro 2000, 4). His concerts seem to have been informal and didactic: he would often comment on the music and solicit reactions from the public, sometimes playing a composition more than once. Like Chávez's audiences in post-revolutionary Mexico, Estrella's compatriots responded with alacrity and honesty. On one occasion, he played the opening of Beethoven's Sonata in C Minor, op. 13 (the "Pathétique") for a group of workers. When he asked them to give it a name, one responded "the lights are out" (Calderaro 2000, 4). On another, he was in his house playing Brahms and a crowd gathered in the street. Another time, a listener was disappointed upon learning that he would never be able to meet Bach, whose music, with its immediacy and infectious rhythms, had so affected him.

At times Estrella struggled over the concessions his career seemed to require. By November 1960 he and Martha were married; he was soon supporting two children as well. On a grant in Paris in 1964, he studied with Marguerite Long, who insisted that he make proper connections at receptions, teas, and other events Estrella found utterly stultifying. (A far happier experience was his work with Boulanger when he returned to

France four years later; like many Boulanger students Estrella has expressed gratitude for her rigor and her desire to cultivate each student's individual voice.) Martha, by her husband's account a fine singer, was also a committed leftist who upbraided him whenever he wavered from his ideals. A domestic battle ensued, for instance, when he accepted an engagement to play in the presence of Onganía, whom she scathingly dubbed a "military gorilla" (Bonasso 2003, 18). Estrella's conviction that the Western canon was the "lost property" of the masses grew ever more firm, however. Rejecting the rights of the "oligarchy" to classical music, as he put it, Estrella, like Chávez, remained confident of his public's openness and lack of preconceptions (Caillabet 2004, 32). Estrella also denounced the conservatory system, which, he maintained, prepares students to play in the Colón or the Salle Pleyel but solely for listeners who can afford tickets. By performing in backwaters, mental hospitals, or jails as a socially committed musician (*músico social*), Estrella learned skills the conservatory failed to teach him. His concerts emphasized Bach, Mozart, Beethoven, Chopin, Schumann, French baroque masters, Scarlatti, and Ravel, and represented only occasionally twentieth-century music (Messiaen, Bartók). From time to time, he performed Argentine music: Ginastera, Aguirre, Carlos Guastavino, early works of Antonio Tauriello, and arrangements of Yupanqui or folkloric music. Conspicuously absent were works created through "radical" or "revolutionary" musical techniques.

In 1972, Perón returned to Argentina and, in September 1973, won the presidency with some 60 percent of the vote. His second wife, Isabel, a former nightclub dancer, was his vice president. But by the time Perón died in July 1974, he had largely disappointed the left and Isabel, now in charge, lacked the charisma of her predecessor and was widely viewed as incompetent. As for Estrella, besides his musical campaign he was active in several political organizations. These included the FOTIA, the union of sugar workers in Tucumán, and the Jotapé (Juventud Peronista), the Peronist youth organization, which emerged from the *justicialista* wing of the party. By his own admission, he indulged in some rather silly pranks, such as writing subversive messages on napkins in cafes and then reinserting them in napkin holders for unsuspecting diners to discover (Sánchez 1992, 28). At no point, as he would repeatedly insist in the ensuing years, did he join the *montoneros*, which in any case, were losing steam by the late 1970s. In 1975, Martha, his wife and collaborator for social justice, died of cancer, leaving Estrella with two small children and a sense of overwhelming loss.

Months later, on March 24, 1976, Argentina suffered another military coup, known in the Orwellian language of its perpetrators as the National Reorganization Process. A firsthand witness of the period, Jacobo Timerman, editor-in-chief of the Buenos Aires daily, *La Opinión*, was one of the few who advocated dialogue and due judicial process among seemingly intractable factions. He describes the political landscape at this critical moment. There were

> rural and urban Trotskyite guerrillas, right-wing Peronist death squads; armed terrorist groups of the large labor unions, used for handling union matters; paramilitary army groups, dedicated to avenging the murder of their men; para-police groups of

both the Left and the Right vying for supremacy within the organization of federal and provincial police forces; and terrorist groups of Catholic rightists organized by cabals who opposed Pope John XXIII's propositions to reconcile the liberal leftist Catholic priests seeking... rapprochement between the Church and the poor.

Timerman adds, "these, of course, were only the principal groups of organized or systematized violence" coexisting in Argentina (Timerman 1981, 13).

No one was prepared for the Dirty War, the state-sponsored purge of left-wing guerillas, pro-Perón terrorists, and whoever appeared to support them. As is well known, many were abducted, tortured, and killed ("disappeared") simply because they exercised freedom of speech or assembly, or because they practiced suspect professions such as university teaching, journalism, psychiatry, or community work; liberal priests and Jews were targets as well. All were seen to threaten the status quo. Some in the military even believed that Argentina, misunderstood by the rest of the world, was the site of World War III, itself a sacred struggle between left-wing terrorists and defenders of traditionalist Christian "civilization." Timerman, tortured and imprisoned in 1977, has reflected on the totalitarian mind, with its fear of science, Freud, Jews, and intellectuals, and its resistance to "subtlety, contradiction or complexity." The guiding principle, Timerman concludes, was simply, "what you don't understand you destroy" (Timerman 1981, 104). Of course, it is impossible to know if intellectuals were considered threatening because of their work or because they often openly supported the left (Plotkin 2001, 218–219). Anyone inquiring as to the whereabouts of a *desaparecido* (one who has been "disappeared") would be subject to a futile bureaucratic chase. Like the "unpersons" in Orwell's *1984*, a *desaparecido* was ultimately nullified, as if he or she had never existed. Precise numbers of the disappeared vary widely, with Amnesty International estimating between 15,000 and 20,000 in Argentina alone (Brysk 1994). If the face of resistance was the *nueva canción* singer, the face of the demand for accountability—for memory—has been the Mothers (and Grandmothers) of the Plaza de Mayo. Since 1977, after fruitless and repeated inquiries on the status of family members, these women have stationed themselves in Buenos Aires's Plaza de Mayo every Thursday afternoon at 3:30. Silently holding photographs of their missing sons and daughters and wearing the white bandanas that became emblematic of their cause, the Madres have added their steely hope to Argentina's convulsive political landscape.

Almost immediately, Estrella suffered a series of punishments, as promised by an article in the Buenos Aires daily *La Prensa* for anyone who "by any means, diffuses, divulges or spreads propaganda or images through illicit associations or individuals or through groups dedicated to subversion or terrorism" (Ministry of Education 2009). His concerts began to be curtailed or even canceled, since his habit of speaking from the stage was seen as potentially subversive. Once, being told that a certain concert venue was unavailable, he was invited to play in the "Casa de Gobierno" instead. (According to one account, he did in fact play there.) Another time, an inadequate piano was delivered to a hall in which he was scheduled to play a concerto. All the while, the massive campaign of torture, imprisonment, and disappearance was generating fear and evasiveness in the public mind. "Por algo será" was the phrase often uttered when an individual was disappeared—"there must be some reason." Reactions among the population at large ranged from silent compliance to rashness.

Friends began warning Estrella that he was in danger, and he thought seriously of leaving the country. In August 1977, he moved to Montevideo as a temporary measure, having received an offer to teach in Panama. He subsequently turned down the offer, however, persuaded to do so by his children, who wanted to remain close to Buenos Aires. To be sure, there was plenty of danger in Uruguay, which was also under a dictatorship. Having established a reputation there, Estrella reasoned, quite naively as he later acknowledged, that "his prestige as a pianist would give [him] a certain immunity" (Estrella 1985, 191–208). Warnings intensified to the point that he asked for an official report on his status. Although that document certified nothing unusual, a government contact advised him to leave, as Uruguayan officials were now following their Argentine counterparts in denying him performances. In late 1977 Estrella was hired to teach in Mexico and Canada during the coming year. All that remained was to pack up his house in Montevideo, where he was living with his son Javier (age fourteen) and daughter Paula (age eleven), two Argentine friends, and his secretary Raquel. They planned to spend Christmas in Buenos Aires with Martha's family and from there depart for Mexico.

In mid-December, however, an old friend showed up on Estrella's doorstep. Carlos Valladares, a *montonero* and music lover, reported over dinner at Estrella's house that his mother, wife, and son had all been "disappeared." Estrella invited him to stay overnight; Valladares refused out of concern for the family's safety. Of course, the house was being watched. When Valladares was apprehended shortly thereafter, he promptly swallowed a cyanide pill. The two children were quickly farmed out to neighbors. Guilty largely of showing poor judgment—for having welcomed a *montonero* into his home without apparent thought for his family—on December 15, Estrella was taken by the authorities, along with the other adults in the household.

Naturally, the military saw things differently. A report in the Uruguayan press announced that "*montoneros* are in [the] country" as are "elements thereof" (*El Día* 1977). Estrella is by no means the main topic of the report. Rather, his name is buried in a lengthy narrative of weapons and strategies: explaining that the infrastructure of a *montonero* cell had been broken up, the paper displays photos of a submachine gun and two Browning 9mm pistols, presumably shipped in from Argentina, and munitions, along with the suitcase used to conceal them. Given the *montoneros*' skill in making weapons, the report continued, along with their "fanaticism" and the international support they enjoyed from "Marxist-Leninist" groups worldwide, the recent capture was billed as a tour de force on the part of the Uruguayan security forces. Certainly the reader has no way to verify whether the guns in the photo are really the recovered weapons or if a staff photographer hastily assembled a few props under pressure from the Uruguayan military. Other press documents show Estrella's photo, along with his identity number, and describe his association with the "seditious group" while listing his profession as "concert pianist"; another report, far briefer, frames Estrella's story by announcing his capture in paragraph one and concluding with mention of his studies with Boulanger

(*El País* 1977, 18; *La Opinión* 1977, n. p.). The latter report also notes that, according to a military source, Yehudi Menuhin was inquiring about Estrella and rails against "campaigns of calumny and lies about our own reality" that have repeatedly misled the international community.

As noted, Estrella was taken to a clandestine house of torture. There he spent some six days, which included torture of the "classic kind" and a woman in spike heels repeatedly jumping up and down on his hands (Estrella 1985, 221). As his torturers inflicted their physical and psychological wounds, Estrella, sustained by his faith, shouted *Padrenuestros* at the top of his lungs. He also used his musician's ear: hooded and blindfolded during his capture and torture, he later remarked that he came to identify twenty-two different voices, among them, that of Colonel Gavazzo. As Timerman points out, the prisoner's relationship with his or her torturer may be the only "exercise of [the prisoner's] human condition," however perverse (Timerman 1981, 38). This "exercise," which Gavazzo initiated, centered not only on the "crime" of leading *la negrada* to believe it was capable of listening to Beethoven but of withholding this music from its rightful public. As Colonel Gavazzo reportedly told him, "you were made to play for us" but "you chose *la negrada*" (Camps 1987, 2). Thus the totalitarian mind, resistant to complexity and eager to destroy what it does not understand, had, at least according to Estrella's narrative, made room in its stunted perception of human behavior for classical music.

Meanwhile, an international campaign waged by Boulanger, Menuhin, Pierre Boulez, Henri Dutilleux, Iannis Xenakis, and others began. Based in Neuilly, France, the Comité de Soutien de Miguel Angel Estrella was engineered by one Yves Hagenauer, a French industrialist whom Estrella and Martha had met in Paris in 1969. Hagenauer seems to have left no stone unturned. He prepared press releases on Estrella's behalf and presented the case to the United Nations, UNESCO, the Red Cross, the Vatican, Amnesty International, and other entities. He expedited the release on the Erato label of a recording Estrella had made in 1971 for Radio France to raise funds for the pianist's children. He also obtained the signed contracts for Estrella's teaching appointments in Canada and Mexico, thus debunking the notion that Estrella intended to organize terrorists in Montevideo (Estrella 1985, 248). Eventually these efforts began to bear fruit. After his transfer to Libertad prison, Estrella was given a silent keyboard, which he could use for about an hour a day. He was also moved to a better cell, where he received a French lawyer, François Cheron. Finally, in February 1980, after a hearing that lasted around two hours, Estrella and his three companions, held for "subversive associations and attacks on the constitutions," were free, although expelled from the country. Whatever international censure Estrella's torture had aroused, for the Uruguayan press he was still a *montonero*, however. As an editorial of February 14 states, "the *montonero* Estrella has his pianist's hands tinged with the blood spilled by his crimes, kidnappings, assaults, and attacks by explosives. With this, there is plenty to judge him. Not as a pianist but as a terrorist" (*El País* 1980).

Two days later Estrella landed at Orly and the rest of his career took on a dream-like quality. In 1982, he founded Musique Espérance, a global version of his work in rural Argentina. As he tells it, the organization, which eventually had fifty-five affiliates in

Europe, the Americas, the Middle East, and Africa, depends on "no political affiliation nor subsidies," with members paying for their own travel (González Toro 2000, 54; Camps 1990). In 1985 he was named to the Legion of Honor (together with Vladimir Horowitz) and in 1988 became ambassador to UNESCO, an honor bestowed on him in Paris in the presence of François and Danielle Mitterand and which he continues to hold today (*Clarín* 1988, 4). In June 1989 he was awarded an honorary doctorate from University of Lille, and in 2000, recognized as a "*pianista social*," he received the ACNUR prize (Alto Comisionado de las Naciones Unidas para los Refugiados) for "outstanding humanitarian labor" (*La Hora Popular* 1989; *La República* 2000, n. p.). He began concertizing again, sometimes with folk musicians such as flutist Raúl Mercado, who played with Mercedes Sosa (*La Hora Popular* 1989, n. p.). He also performed internationally. In November 1984, he played at that bastion of music and left-leaning politics, the New School for Social Research in New York, in a benefit for Musique Espérance, with proceeds earmarked for the "Grandmothers of the Plaza de Mayo" and the "Detainees' Parents Support Committee" in South Africa. *New York Times* critic Will Crutchfield acknowledged that, although Estrella was "no Paderewski," he was nonetheless "a real pianist who would be well worth listening to apart from his mission." Summarizing Estrella's political difficulties, Crutchfield notes that only a "dangerously effective propagandist" would have paid such a "harrowing price" as the torture Estrella underwent. In a twisted variant of the mentality described above—*por algo será*—Crutchfield blithely affirms, "this is what Mr. Estrella must have been" (Crutchfield 1984, C12).

Whoever researches the history of Latin American music in the latter part of the twentieth century will confront not only compositions, events, and biographies, but the memories of those who lived this period. In light of still-open wounds, conflicting views will inevitably emerge. Several comments in Estrella's account of his experiences could be questioned, for example. He remarks that in February 1977 he decided to stay in Montevideo because "several Uruguayan artists and composers told him: 'all the musicians are gone, the country is empty and we need someone like you to work with young pianists'" (Estrella 1985, 201). In fact, "all the musicians" were not gone. Four students of one of Uruguay's most important composers, Héctor Tosar (an associate of Copland, Koussevitsky, and Milhaud and twice a Guggenheim fellow), established Núcleo Música Nueva, an organization that exists to this day; among its founding members, Coriún Aharonián resisted the dictatorship especially vigorously (Aharonián 2002). This fact also casts doubt on Estrella's contention that "everyone on the left was in prison or in exile" (Estrella 1985, 211; Paraskevaídis 2009). Estrella himself has struggled with his legacy in Latin America. If others, such as Veloso or Chico Buarque, returned to their native countries after exile, he never took this step. As the review by Crutchfield just cited suggests, Estrella the pianist is often described as "the pianist who was a political prisoner" or the "pianist who was tortured," with less sensational accounts referring to "Estrella, founder of Musique Esperance" or "defender of rights of man to include music for all" instead of to his actual musical abilities (*La República* 2000, n. p.; Caillabet

1992, n. p.). The 1987 concert mentioned at the outset of this essay was sandwiched into the Colón's schedule just before the main event (a production of *Salomé*) and seems to have been covered by only one Buenos Aires daily. Five years later, despite the honors he had accrued, Estrella bluntly told a reporter for a Uruguayan paper, "I don't exist in Argentine music," adding, "my quarrel with those who marginalize me isn't as great as the sorrow I feel at not being able to share my experiences with my Buenos Aires public" (*La República* 1992, n. p.). Nonetheless, a 2009 tribute published in Buenos Aires—a scrapbook-style series of anecdotes and testimonials (some fictionalized) interspersed with lengthy extracts of Estrella's own words—challenges the suggestion that his torturers succeeded in silencing him in his native land (Biondi 2009).

For researchers interested in memory additional complications arise. Some Latin Americans advocate "moving forward," that is, bracketing, if not suppressing, the memory of collective tragedy so as not to unleash waves of social instability by revisiting the ravages of the past. This was largely the approach taken by president Raúl Alfonsín, who presided over the restoration of democracy in Argentina in 1983. Others seek historical clarity, including punishment for the perpetrators, who must first be identified. "*Tienen nombre y apellido*"—they have a first and a last name—is the phrase one often hears. Any account offered will be subject to fundamental questions of memory and conflicting versions of the "official story," to borrow the name of the powerful 1985 movie dealing with the dictatorship and its casualties. In informal conversations on Estrella, for example, I have encountered enthusiastic accounts of his playing, which inspired some listeners to musical idealism. Other informants simply note his importance while others roundly declare, "*nunca fue gran pianista*" (He was never a great pianist), suggesting that Estrella was little more than a *poseur*.

The power of lived moments may also haunt the researcher. As a Fulbright lecturer in Buenos Aires in 2005, I regularly attended films and lectures at the "Free University" organized by the Madres and their supporters. On June 16 of that year, an important decision of the Supreme Court hit the press: the laws that for over twenty years protected the architects of the dictatorship and their lackeys were now deemed unconstitutional. This momentous event, along with the fiftieth anniversary of the bombing of the Plaza de Mayo in 1955, would be commemorated that evening. In the main hall of the Free University, the first two rows of seats were roped off. I soon found out the reason: minutes before the event was to begin, a contingent of elderly women entered the hall, each wearing the white bandana. As that unlikely revolutionary force filed in, the crowd rose, applauding loud and long. One does not forget such a noisy surge of gratitude nor the moist eyes in the room.

A few nights later, I was at one of Buenos Aires's cafés, the historic Tortoni, where Jorge Luis Borges, Carlos Gardel, and other luminaries have sipped coffee. I was chatting with an Argentinian acquaintance only slightly younger than most of the Madres and an impassioned leftist. She mentioned that she had an exchange student from California in her home. "You Americans!" she sputtered. "You all want to romanticize the Madres!" They hadn't even come up in our conversation. "Why," she continued, "they're a bunch of hypocrites! Starting that goddam university!" "Well," I ventured, correctly sensing that

I was stepping into a minefield. "Perhaps what we in the U.S. 'romanticize,' as you put it, is the *spirit* of the Madres. The idea that nonviolence can effect change." Rolling her eyes heavenward, my acquaintance snorted and I ventured no further. On another occasion, I lunched with a paralegal in her mid-thirties who lamented what she described as her "total ignorance" of the most recent dictatorship, confessing that she had gone to school both with children of *montoneros* and children from military families, and that no one had ever said anything about the political reality of the moment. We of the United States who attempt to make sense of these accounts may well see ourselves as stereotypically naïve American tourists when we visit this realm of silence, needless death, and the prejudices of our own government.

This essay, with its modest goal of contextualizing Estrella's activities, leaves open the debates over music's political content outlined above. Just as some reject the very notion of *música comprometida*, others promote it by denouncing subordination to existing models or traditional forms. Others reject the taint of the ivory tower by accompanying themselves on the guitar in vast soccer stadiums, prompting outpourings of popular song from the masses. Others, such as Rzewski, confront aesthetic and political bias to convey events in Latin America to a worldwide public. Obviously, the Western canon, hailed since the nineteenth century as transcendent, timeless, and "autonomous," can be as politically charged as many a more explicit repertory. Surely it is part of the fraught tale of Latin American musical politics in the twentieth century.

Notes

1. I wish to thank the numerous Argentine friends and colleagues for sharing with me their impressions of Estrella. I am especially grateful to Graciela Paraskevaídis, who provided me the great majority of the press sources consulted for this essay from her personal archive, discussed music and dictatorship with me, and commented in detail on a draft of this essay. Special thanks are also due Kevin Bartig and Marcie Ray for their careful reading of an earlier draft and to Edgardo Raul Salinas for clarification on several terms in Argentine Spanish. When possible, I cite English translations for the major sources I discuss. Any errors, of course, are my own.

    As the Chilean musicologist Daniel Party notes, there is no direct English translation for "*música comprometida*," a broad term for music that is "politically or socially engaged," and, as Party points out, often "born of resistance, protest, and dissent" (Party 2009, 671–684; see http://sites.google.com/site/dparty/publications-1/beyondprotest). Neither are the terms "art" or "classical" music (or the frequently used alternative, "concert music" or the Spanish "*música culta*") satisfactory although in this essay I rather unenthusiastically opt for "classical."

2. However we view such polemics, it is worth pointing out that in the Colossus of the North, whose public is notoriously ignorant of both Latin America and its government's machinations there, Rzewski's variations have brought home to many a listener Nixon and Kissinger's role in bringing Pinochet to power; indeed, scarcely a scholar or critic of the work fails to mention the CIA (Pollack 1992, 383; Wason 1988, 113).

References

Aharonián, Coriún. 2002. "Héctor Tosar (1923–2002), muerte de un gran compositor." *Revista Musical Chilena* 56, no. 197, 81–84. http://www.scielo.cl/scielo.php?pid=S0716-27902002019700005&script=sci_arttext.

Albino, Graciela. 2009. "La revolución abrió las puertas del Teatro Colón a los obreros." In *Movimiento Obrero Argentino: De los trabajadores para los trabajadores*, edited by Mario O'Donnell, 13–23. Buenos Aires: UPCN.

Ardévol, José. 1969. *Introducción a Cuba: La música*. Havana: Instituto del Libro.

Rachel Beckles, Willson. 2009a. "Whose Utopia? Perspectives on the West-Eastern Divan Orchestra." *Music and Politics* 3, no. 2. http://www.music.ucsb.edu/projects/musicandpolitics/archive/2009-2/beckles_willson.html

Rachel Beckles, Willson. 2009b. "The Parallax Worlds of the West-Eastern Divan Orchestra." *Journal of the Royal Musical Association* 134, no. 2: 303–331.

Béhague, Gerard. 1979. *Music in Latin America: An Introduction*. Englewood Cliffs, New Jersey: Prentice-Hall.

Biondi, Hugo, with Adolfo Fonsalido. 2009. *Estrella, tú que miraste*. Buenos Aires: Corregidor.

Bonasso, Miguel. 2003. "El pianista Miguel Ángel Estrella recuerda la tortura en Uruguay." *Página* 12, October12, 18.

Brysk, Alison. 1994. "The Politics of Measurement: The Contested Count of the Disappeared in Argentina." *Human Rights Quarterly* 16: 676–692.

Calderaro, Romina. 2000. "Voy a seguir siendo solidario," *Página* 12, November 4, 4.

Caillabet, Carlos. 1992. "Paysandú Miguel Ángel Estrella," *Mate Amargo*, October 7, n. p.

Caillabet, Carlos. 2004. "Un retorno sin hollín." *Brecha*. September 3, 32.

Camps, Pompeyo. 1987. "Estrella: la música y el humanismo." *Clarín*, September 29, 2.

Camps, Pompeyo. 1990. "Ocho años de música y esperanza." *Clarín*, May 19, n. p.

Chávez, Carlos. 1939. "Music in a Mexican Test Tube." *New York Times*, July 2, SM5.

Crist, Elizabeth. 2005. *Music for the Common Man: Aaron Copland During the Depression and War*. New York: Oxford University Press.

Crutchfield, Will. 1984. "Music: Estrella, Pianist," *The New York Times*, November 12, C12.

"Desbaratan en Uruguary un intento montonero." 1977. *La Opinión*, December 23.

"Desmantelaron actividades de la guerrilla montonera." 1977. *El Día*, December 23, 1977, n.p.

Dorfman, Ariel, and Armand Mattelart. 1975. *How to Read Donald Duck: Imperialist Ideology in the Disney Comic*. Translated by David Kunzle. New York: International General.

"El caso Estrella." 1980. *El País*, February 14.

Estrella, Miguel Ángel. 1985. *Música para la esperanza: conversaciones con Jean Lacouture*. Buenos Aires: Ediciones de la Flor.

"Estrella es ahora embajador." 1988. *Clarín*, November 26, 4.

"Estrella junto al Castillo." 1989. *La Hora Popular*, December 23, n.p.

Fiorucci, Flavia. 2002. "Los marginados de la Revolución: los intelectuales peronistas (1945, 1955)." In *Proceedings of the 2. Congresso Brasileiro de Hispanistas*. São Paulo. http://www.proceedings.scielo.br/scielo.php?script=sci_arttext&pid=MSC0000000012002000300023&lng=en&nrm=iso

González Toro, Alberto. 2000. "Premio de la ONU al pianista argentino Miguel Ángel Estrella." *Clarín*, November 4, 54.

Guevara, Ernesto (Che). 1989. *Socialism and Man in Cuba*. Translator and editor unidentified. New York: Pathfinder.

Hess, Carol A. 1997. "Silvestre Revueltas in Republican Spain: Music as Political Utterance." *Latin American Music Review 18*, no. 2: 278–296.

Hess, Carol A. 2001. *Manuel de Falla and Modernism in Spain, 1898–1936*. London and Chicago: University of Chicago Press.

Hess, Carol A. 2008. "Competing Utopias? Musical Ideologies in the 1930s and Two Spanish Civil War Films." *Journal of the Society for American Music 2*, no. 3: 319–354.

Hess, Carol A. 2013. *Representing the Good Neighbor: Music, Difference, and the Pan American Dream*. New York: Oxford University Press.

"'Honoris causa' por Estrella." 1989. *La Hora Popular*, June 3.

"Integrantes de la base 'Montonera' Procesados." 1977. *El País*, December 27, 18.

Jara, Joan. 1984. *An Unfinished Song: The Life of Victor Jara*. New York: Tickner & Fields.

King, John. 1986. *Sur: A Study of the Argentine Literary Journal and Its Role in the Development of a Culture, 1931–1970*. Cambridge: Cambridge University Press.

Kornbluh, Peter. 2003. *The Pinochet File: A Declassified Dossier on Atrocity and Accountability*. New York and London: The New Press.

López, Alfredo. 1975. *Historia del movimiento social y la clase obrera argentina*. Buenos Aires: A. Peña Lillo.

Madsen, Jessica. 2003. "Music as Metaphor: A Study of the Political Inspiration Behind Frederic Rzewski's *36 Variations on 'El Pueblo Unido Jamás Será Vencido!'* (The People United Will Never Be Defeated!), a Chilean Nueva Canción by Sergio Ortega and Quliapayún." DMA document, University of Cincinnati.

Mariátegui, José Carlos. 1986. "Arte, revolución y decadencia." In *Las vanguardias literarias en Hispanoamérica (manifiesto, proclamas y otros escritos)*, edited by Hugo J. Verani, 204–206. Mexico City: Fondo de Cultura Económica.

McSherry, J. Patrice. 2005. *Predatory States: Operation Condor and Covert War in Latin America*. Lanham, Md.: Rowman & Littlefield Publishers.

"Miguel Ángel Estrella: la marginación porteña." 1992. *La República*, 16 September.

Ministry of Education of the Nation (Argentina). 2009. "Día Nacional de la Memoria por la Verdad y la Justicia." http://www.me.gov.ar/efeme/24demarzo. (accessed December 27, 2009).

Neruda, Pablo. 1986. "Sobre una poesía sin pureza." In *Las vanguardias literarias en Hispanoamérica (manifiesto, proclamas y otros escritos)*, edited by Hugo J. Verani, 266–267. Mexico City: Fondo de Cultura Económica, 1986.

Ortega y Gasset, José. 1968. *The Dehumanization of Art and Other Essays on Art, Culture, and Literature*. Translated by Helene Weyl. Princeton, N.J.: Princeton University Press, 1968.

Paraskevaídis, Graciela. n.d. "Algunas reflexiones sobre música y dictadura en América Latina." www.gp-magma.net/pdf/txt_e/sitio-MusyDicfinal2008.pdf.

Paraskevaídis, Graciela. 2009. Interview, with author. Buenos Aires. 28 June. 2009.

Paz, Juan Carlos. 1936. "Bach y la música de hoy." *Sur* 17 (February), 80.

Party, Daniel. 2009. "Beyond 'Protest Song': Popular Music in Pinochet's Chile (1973–1990). In *Music and Dictatorship in Europe and Latin America*, edited by Roberto Illiano and Massimiliano Sala. Turnhout: Brephols Publisher, 671-684.

Plotkin, Mariano Ben. 2001. *Freud in the Pampas: The Emergence and Development of Psychoanalytic Culture in Argentina*. Stanford, Calif.: Stanford University Press.

Pollack, Howard. 1992. *Harvard Composers: Walter Piston and His Students from Elliott Carter to Frederic Rzewski*. Metuchen, N.J.: The Scarecrow Press.

Portal, Magda. 1988. "Andamios de Vida." In *Manifestos, proclamas y polémicas de la vanguardia literaria hispanoamericana*, edited by Nelson Osorio. Caracas: Ayacucho, 206-209.
"Premió a pianista que fue preso politico en Uruguay." 2000. *La República* 22, December, n. p.
Rockwell, John. 1983. *All American Music: Composition in the Late Twentieth Century*. New York: Alfred A. Knopf.
Sánchez, Matilde. 1992. "Música para la esperanza." *Clarín*, September 27, 28.
Schechter, John M., ed. 1999. *Music in Latin American Culture: Regional Traditions*. New York: Schirmer Books.
Seeger, Charles. 1934. "On Proletarian Music," *Modern Music 11*, no. 3: 121–127.
Seeger, Charles. 1939. "Grass Roots for American Composers." *Modern Music 16, no. 3*: 143–149.
Shumway, Nicolas. 1991. *The Invention of Argentina*. Berkeley: University of California Press.
Surra, Roberto. 2003. *Peronismo y cultura*. Buenos Aires: Corregidor.
Taffet, Jeffrey F. 1997. "'My Guitar is Not for the Rich': The New Chilean Song Movement and the Politics of Culture." *The Journal of American Culture 20*, no.2: 91–103.
Timerman, Jacobo. 1981. *Prisoner Without a Name, Cell Without a Number*. Translated by Tony Talbot. New York: Alfred A. Knopf.
Unruh, Vicky. 1994. *Latin American Vanguards: The Art of Contentious Encounters*. Berkeley: University of California Press.
Urrutia, Matilde. 2002 (1986). *Mi vida junto a Pablo Neruda*. Reprint. Buenos Aires: Seix Barral.
Vasconcelos, José. 1957–1961 (1926). "Indología." In *Obras completas, 1069–1303*. vol. 2. Mexico City: Libreros Mexicanos Unidos.
Veloso, Caetano. 2002. *Tropical Truth*. Translated by Isabel de Sena. Edited by Barbara Einzig. New York: Alfred A. Knopf.
"Venezuelan Youths Transformed by Music." 2005. *BBC News World Edition*. November 28. http://thewe.cc/weplanet/news/americas/venezuela/revolution_youth_venezuela.htm.
Wason, Robert. 1988. "Tonality and Atonality in Frederic Rzewski's Variations on 'The People United Will Never Be Defeated!'" *Perspectives of New Music 26, no. 1*: 108–143.

CHAPTER 16

A CASE STUDY OF BRAZILIAN POPULAR MUSIC AND CENSORSHIP

Ivan Lins's Music during Dictatorship in Brazil

THAIS LIMA NICODEMO

IVAN Lins is a Brazilian songwriter whose career began in the late 1960s. He is still recording and performing nowadays, and his work began drawing attention during Brazil's military regime, which lasted from 1964 until 1985. His musical production during the period was of a critical nature, challenging the authoritarian regime, and also achieved significant commercial success. Since the late 1970s, the government repression agencies included Lins in the list of major "suspects" of the musical scene, alongside other Brazilian popular music songwriters, such as Chico Buarque and Milton Nascimento (Napolitano 2004, 108). His songs were often censored and his performances were frequently observed, as can be perceived from the assessment of the many documents on the matter available at Brasilia's Arquivo Nacional (National Archive).[1]

Since the late 1950s, Brazilian artists and intellectuals established a strong relationship with left-wing thought. This network of values, in which the greatest emphasis was given to the concepts of people and nation, was constantly resignified and gained space in the cultural production of the 1960s and 1970s (Ridenti 2005, 81–84). These artists and intellectuals sought amid the popular culture the bases to support a social revolution based on concepts of developmentalism and the national popular. Their ideals, often considered utopian, were grounded on the understanding of art as capable of increasing one's awareness of reality and therefore contributing to a social revolution (Hollanda 2004, 23). The artistic production that emerged from this context strongly influenced that of the 1960s and 1970s (Napolitano 2007, 85–86), when developmentalism and the national popular remained in the foreground and evolved to acquire new meanings.

Lins's work in the 1970s can be understood as part of a group of work by Brazilian artists whose creation was marked by a set of values that flourished in the years prior to the military coup. As such, in order to discuss his musical production, the meanings thereof, and its relationship with the regime's repression forces, it is first necessary to further understand the historical context of the years preceding the coup that implemented the military dictatorship.

Pre-Coup Context and Culture as a Symbolic Place of Resistance

In 1961, after the resignation of President Jânio Quadros, vice-president João Goulart became chief of state until 1964. After seven months in office, Quadros left the presidency in a state of severe political and economic crises, on the verge of a possible civil war (Gáspari 2002a, 46). In this context, Goulart ruled Brazil under an imposed parliamentary regime, which significantly limited his power (Dreifuss 1981, 130). Following the reestablishment of the presidential system via a plebiscite conducted in January 1963, João Goulart fully assumed the government and put into practice the so-called *reformas de base* (base reforms), which would lead to a series of transformations in several sectors of society, and whose main purpose was to decrease Brazil's social inequality (Dreifuss 1981, 131–132).

The production of politically engaged art in Brazil's intellectual and cultural circles gained relevancy during Goulart's government, backed by the strengthening of rural movements during the period as well as the effects of international popular revolutions, such as the Cuban Revolution in 1959 and the Vietnam War, which was being fought at the time (Ridenti 2010, 89–90). For instance, artists connected to music, theater, film, and literature came together through the creation of an organization supported by the União Nacional dos Estudantes (National Students Association) called Centro Popular de Cultura (Popular Culture Center) in 1961. They aimed to raise awareness among people with their work by using elements of both national and popular culture in order to promote a social revolution (Hollanda 2004, 21–23). Such ideas further echoed in 1960s musical production, amid the transformations of a period marked by the pursuit of social equality and political liberty, permeated by a feeling of national identity (Naves 2010, 39–41).

As the measures adopted by President João Goulart were increasingly and effectively oriented toward both urban and agrarian reforms, they became a threat to conservative eyes. With the growing political tension and economic crisis, the military conspiracy against the president intensified and was soon transformed into a coup supported by segments of civil society, the Catholic Church, multinational companies, and the American government, thus resulting in the military coup of 1964 (Alves 1985, 23). The military resorted to the coup "apparently to free the country from corruption and communism, and to restore democracy" (Fausto 1999, 465); however, the regime lasted for twenty-one years and became evermore authoritarian. Institutional bases were created to adopt repressive measures against opponents of the regime, including the removal of officials from office and the suspension of political rights under the excuse that such measures were necessary for the sake of "National Security," and this became the doctrine used by the Brazilian military government to legitimize the "imposition of a control and domination system" (Alves 1985, 26).

The military regime soon began to watch over public space so as to politically demobilize society (Napolitano 2004, 104). In 1964, a complex repression system was established based on this logic through the creation of the Serviço Nacional de Informações (National Information Service), centralizing the information of the government's repression and surveillance agencies, thereby fighting subversion and attempting to prevent any activities deemed disturbing to public order (Magalhães 1997, n. p.).

The coup melted down the left's expectations of a possible social revolution in Brazil (Ridenti 2000, 46). However, unlike what happened to other segments such as the student organizations and trade unions, which were promptly dissipated by the military regime, popular music (which already had a sense of political involvement) gained strength as a symbolic space of opposition to the authoritarian regime while further consolidating itself as a key aspect in the process of establishing the cultural industry in the country by means of its relation with television and the growing music industry (Schwarz 1978, 62–67). This relationship reached its zenith in the music festivals—the music programs hosted by television networks at theaters and gyms, in which artists competed with their songs and audiences actively participated. These events played an important role in the initial process of increasing the popularity of television in Brazil and reflected "a simulacrum of popular involvement and freedom of expression when the country was increasingly dominated by political authoritarianism" (Napolitano 2007, 93).

Nonetheless, the cultural media were under constant watch, for they were seen as spaces in which so-called "communists" and "subversive people" circulated. The acronym MPB was coined during the second half of the 1960s, standing for Brazilian popular music (from *música popular brasileira*, in Portuguese), and this music was constantly guarded with suspicion, especially with regard to the works and activities of artists connected to music festivals and the academic environment, whose concerts attracted a great number of people, mostly from the middle classes (Napolitano 2004, 105).

By late 1968 the authoritarian nature of the military regime was further hardened by the enactment of the so-called *Ato Institucional no. 5* (Fifth Decree), which granted extraordinary powers to the President of the Republic, such as subjecting National Congress to forced recess, impeachment of representatives, suspension of political rights, and dismissal of public servants from office. Additionally, censorship and repression increased, including by means of imprisonment and torture (Fausto 1999, 480).

Although musical censorship was warrented by the Constitution since the 1930s, it gained strength during the military dictatorship, especially by the late 1960s and early 1970s, whereby it was legally modified according to the surveillance criterion that guided the regime (Carocha 2007, 35). If, at first, artists and intellectuals had remained relatively untouched by more extreme forms of oppression, they were directly affected during this period of severe repression (Schwarz 1978, 63). The intensification of the regime led several artists and intellectuals into exile, as was the case of MPB artists such as Caetano Veloso, Gilberto Gil, Geraldo Vandré, and Chico Buarque.

Ivan Lins and Brazilian Popular Music (MPB)

The artistic rise of songwriter Ivan Lins occurred amid the music festivals in the late 1960s. This period was marked by an intense coercion practice by the government, which contributed to the deflation of the current cultural scenario. Lins was first known as a songwriter mainly for his predominantly romantic songs, written together with lyricist Ronaldo Monteiro de Souza. His repertoire was largely connected to soul music, then popular in the Brazilian music industry. Lins was subject to censorship from 1973, as he gradually shifted his work from soul music to so-called protest songs, which contained statements against the military regime and revealed a greater Brazilian musical identity through the use of national and regional rhythms. These changes also secured greater prestige to the artist in the culture industry and among MPB's audience and critics. Though Lins had hit the commercial jackpot with his soul music, he was not exactly praised by segments of the musical scene, represented by artists, the music business, critics, and MPB consumers (Nicodemo 2012, n. p.).

As previously mentioned, though the MPB repertoire had multiple musical and poetic meanings, it consolidated itself around certain common concepts, such as the ideas of a "participant intentionality," "freedom," and "social justice," defined according to the trend set by the culture-consuming public, especially the intellectualized "middle classes" (Napolitano 2002a, 2–3). Considering these factors, it is possible to say that Lins only managed to find his place in the MPB circle once he began composing songs that were closer to some specific poetic and musical standards of the protest songs. Hence, in a way, Lins and other MPB composers were not only subject to official censorship, as implemented by the military regime, but also to a different type of censorship put into practice by the specialized critics and intellectuals, who expected artists' works to be imbued with political meaning that challenged both society and the authoritarian regime (Lopes 2008, 9). These expectations are clear in the declarations of musical producer Mariozinho Rocha in an interview with Lins (Lins 1972, 12):

> Mariozinho Rocha: You only write about love? . . . there are things other than love that happen in any social class. Why do you concentrate your efforts on this easier, cheesier subject?
>
> Ivan Lins: I believe this is very important for me, for it is what I feel like talking about, do you understand?

There is a clearly hostile tone in Rocha's question, when he calls Lins's choice of writing love songs "easier," calling the artist's attention to the social context faced in Brazil. In turn, Lins attempts to defend himself by appealing to the concept of free speech. One may see Rocha's question as contradictory, for he was an acclaimed musical producer, engaged by multinational record companies and widely known among the artists of MPB, which nevertheless was one of the top-selling products in Brazil's cultural industry (Dias 2000, 58–59). From this standpoint, would it be relevant to judge Lins for his allegedly "easier" choice?

After being criticized by different groups of intellectuals and press members, and following the substantial drop in the sale of his albums (Scoville 2008, 122), Lins redirected his production. It is possible to see that since his album *Modo Livre*, recorded in 1974, the artist consolidated a repertoire of critical songs, including themes such as the lack of freedom of expression and the control and vigilance imposed on society by the regime. If Lins's romantic songs of the early 1970s were generally approved by censorship, as can be seen in the analyzed documents from the Arquivo Nacional, his new repertoire was soon to be gradually vetoed by the regime.

Censorship and Ivan Lins's Songs

Prior to recording albums, artists or labels had to submit the songs to the Divisão de Censura de Diversões Públicas (Censorship Division of Public Entertainment). Three different censors then assessed the songs. If any lyrics were forbidden, songwriters were allowed to modify them, either according to their own terms or based on the suggestions often provided by the censors, and the relevant decisions could be appealed (Carocha 2007, 47–58). Given this process, below are examples of songs by Lins that were vetoed, with special attention given to the arguments the censors included in the reports available in the National Archive as well as to the relationship established between artists, the music industry, and the censors.

The first example refers to the words to "Não Há Porque" (There Is No Reason),[2] a song written by Lins and Ronaldo Monteiro de Souza, which was submitted to censorship in 1973. This song illustrates the transition period in Lins's work, which was marked by the pursuit of a critical agenda:

Não há porque fantasiar essa vida	There's no reason to dress up this life
Quem quiser discordar eu vou desconfiar	Whoever wants to disagree I'll distrust
Quem vier debochar	Whoever comes to make fun
Cuidado que o barco pode virar	Watch out for the boat might overturn
No estádio esse meu time só me põe doente	In the stadium that time of mine just makes me sick
Eu esbarro em minhas dívidas diariamente	I bump into my debts daily

Na esquina quero amor e vejo o mal presente	On the corner I want love and I see the evil present
Só me esqueço quando tomo um copo de aguardente	I only forget when I have a glass of booze
O escândalo se abafa, isso é prudente	The scandal is smothered, this is prudent
Nas escadas o degrau não é pra toda gente	On the stairs the step isn't for everyone
A estrada dessa vida é coisa pra valente	The road of this life is something for the valiant
Do estado desse mundo Deus está ciente	Of the state of this world God is aware
Na espreita sobrevivo até comicamente	In ambush I survive even comically
Os efeitos vêm a público amargamente	The effects become public bitterly
Um estranho ao me ver percebe claramente	The stranger upon seeing me perceives clearly
Nas entranhas uma dor que fere lentamente	In my entrails a pain that wounds slowly
O espanto me domina tão tragicamente	The fright dominates me so tragically
A espécie dessa vida é morte que se sente	The nature of this life is death that one feels
A espera se renova em todo poente	The expectation gets renewed in every sunset
Qual espuma eu fico fraco, mas eu vou em frente	Like foam I live weak, but I go forward

As most songs on the same 1975 album *Chama Acesa*, "Não Há Porque" was written as a samba. It is possible to notice that partners Lins and Souza, who would mostly write love songs and dance music, transitioned to a musical language which had more Brazilian rhythms, thereby coming closer to the musical style connected to protest songs. Additionally, the lyrics have a strong melancholic and aggressive poetic language. The main character of the lyrics describes his emotional state in terms of an oppressive context, referring to the presence of evil, of somebody watching him, of a pain that hurts and a fear that takes over him. The song combines elements of daily life, such as the speaker's economic debts and his bad reaction to a soccer match, with subjective feelings motivated by the reality that surrounds him. Though veiled, the song brings to light the state of repression experienced in Brazil.

The lines "On the corner I want love and I see the evil present," "The scandal is smothered, this is prudent," and "The nature of this life is death that one feels" reveal that Lins and his partner were attempting to draw attention to real-life situations that frequently took place in Brazilian society. The song portrayed and denounced the condition of fear in which many individuals lived during the repression years. Tortures and assassinations were disguised, omitted, and unlawfully perpetrated by government agencies under the excuse of fighting subversion and armed revolutionary forces. As Elio Gáspari has noted, "It was not only dangerous to be against the regime—it was even risky to mention what took place in the dungeons" (2002b, 225). In view of the foregoing, the lyrics to Lins's song are critical of and contrary to the authoritarian regime and were vetoed by the censor, as can be seen in the opinion of censor Gilberto Pereira Campos,[3] issued in August 1973:

> Time Period: Current
> Genre: Political
> Language: Normal
> Topic: Social
> Message: Negative
> Plot: Subversively detracts society's values
> Conclusion: Considering the core of the [song's] idea of subversive nature, which goes against national interest... I advise... THE NON-LIBERATION of the text presently assessed.

In view of the foregoing, it is clear that the censor uses a technical model for his opinion, whereby songs are classified according to specific parameters. According to historian Alexandre Fiuza, Brazilian censorship implemented this type of assessment, in which songs were generally categorized according to genre—such as "protest songs," "romantic songs," "lyrical songs," "songs with double meanings," "political songs," or "obscene songs"—so as to clearly mark which songs were likely to be censored (Fiuza 2006, 87).

The aforementioned opinion clearly reveals that the censor interprets the song as being subject to prohibition, for it was considered up-to-date, political, social, negative and subversive. It thus appears that the censor justified prohibition as an issue of "national security," by claiming that the song "goes against national interest." His assessment is likely a result of the accusatory tone of the song.

When we compare the lyrics of the song Lins originally recorded with the version submitted to censorship, we see that the song had already been revised by the writers themselves, and it is unclear whether these changes were voluntary or required by the censors, in which case they may have rendered the approval of the song easier. According to the submitted document, the original title of the song was "Não Há Porque Negar a Verdade" (There's No Reason to Deny Truth), identical to the opening line of the lyrics, but this was replaced by "Não há porque fantasiar essa vida" (There's no reason to dress up this life). It is also noteworthy that the original line, "Work is nothing but a salary, a constant burden," was replaced by "I bump into my debts daily" in the recorded version. Censors would usually suggest minor changes to the lyrics in order to approve them for recording purposes. This practice reveals the influence censors had in the process— they could intervene with their personal opinion on a given work, thereby widening the scope of their role, which was thus no longer limited to the veto power (Carocha 2007, 59).

Below is the second assessment, issued in September 1973, of censor Paulo Leite de Lacerda,[4] whose opinion seems to reinforce the same attributes seen in the prior assessment:

> This is in reference to a musical composition that marks a clear protest against certain situations to which man is subject. Precisely for this reason, the message is inappropriate and inconvenient for this period in time. As such, I believe the poem assessed hereunder should not be approved.

Considering the censor's observation that this song is contrary to "situations to which man is subject," he seems to acknowledge that the lyrics refer to concrete problems, and this is precisely why he believes the song is inappropriate for the time. It is also worthy of attention that both censors' opinions reflect an effort to politically demobilize society by preventing the circulation of a song that could include a message against the authoritarian regime.

In 1974 Lins recorded the song "Abre Alas," his first song with lyricist Vitor Martins, who remained his main partner until the 1990s. The song was deemed the milestone of his politically engaged phase. Though it is perhaps less evident, the lyrics for "Abre Alas" also address issues similar to those seen in the previously mentioned song, "Não Há Porque":

Abre alas pra minha folia	Make way for my revelry
Já estará chegando a hora	It will soon be time
Abre alas pra minha bandeira	Make way for my banner
Já estará chegando a hora	It will soon be time
Apare teus sonhos que a vida tem dono, ela vem te cobrar	Trim your dreams, life has an owner, and it'll come after you
A vida não era assim, não era assim	This was not how life was like, how life was like
Não corra o risco de ficar alegre pra nunca chorar	Don't run the risk of being happy to never cry
A gente não era assim, não era assim	This is not what we were like, what we were like
Ecosta essa porta, que a nossa conversa não pode vazar	Shut the door, this conversation cannot be heard
A vida não era assim, não era assim	This was not how life was like, how life was like
Bandeira arriada, folia guardada pra não se usar	Banners low, revelry kept down and set aside
A festa não era assim, não era assim	This is not what the party was like, what the party was like

MPB composers and lyricists would often resort to metaphorical language as a strategy to overcome censorship. This strategy seems to have been quite successful specifically in the case of "Abre Alas." Though the censor did make certain observations, the song was approved for recording. Below is the opinion of censor Eugênia Costa Rodrigues,[5] issued in March 1974: "Having been assessed for recording, besides the most highlighted 'double sense' of the last paragraph, it does not carry meanings of greater political dimensions. . . . The present lyrics was approved." In this song, recorded in the form of a samba on the album *Modo Livre* in 1974, the composer uses the metaphor of carnival to cry out for freedom, represented by revelry. The title itself is a reference to a widely known carnival song written in 1899 by Chiquinha Gonzaga,

"Ó Abre Alas." The expression *abre alas* (make way), is used for "make way" for the merrymaker in carnival. Nonetheless, in Lins's song, "make way" can also be understood as a form of protest, in the sense that it is necessary to make way for freedom. This message becomes even clearer when the narrator speaks of trimmed down dreams, the risk of being happy, a conversation that cannot be heard, and how life didn't used to be like this. It once again shines a light on the state of repression implemented in Brazil by the military regime. Then the narrator cries out for freedom: "Make way for my revelry / It will soon be time." The censor who issued the opinion noticed the existence of a double meaning, but concluded that the song did not carry meanings of greater political dimensions. Comparing the assessment of "Não Há Porque" to that of "Abre Alas" clearly reveals, on the one hand, that censorship criteria were sometimes subjective and contradictory and, on the other, that it was possible to approve lyrics by means of poetical maneuvers.

Several MPB composers, including Chico Buarque—one of the artists who suffered the most at the hands of the censors—used the theme of carnival as a metaphor for a moment of revolt (Napolitano 2004, 113). An example of this is his song "Quando o Carnaval Chegar" (When Carnival Comes), which was part of the score of the eponymous film directed by Cacá Diegues and was recorded on the album *Quando o Carnaval Chegar*: "E quem me ofende, humilhando, pisando / pensando que eu vou aturar / Tô me guardando pra quando o carnaval chegar" (And he who offends me, humiliating and stepping on me / believing I will take this any longer / I'll spare myself for when carnival comes). The narrator carries the burdens of an oppressive context and waits for the day when carnival or revolt comes so he can fight back.

In turn, Lins used this theme in other songs, such as "Palhaços e Reis" (lyrics by de Souza), recorded on the album *Chama Acesa*; "Não tem Perdão" (lyrics by de Souza); and "Rei do Carnaval" (lyrics by Pinheiro), recorded on the album *Modo Livre*. Below are the verses to "Rei do Carnaval":

O rei chegou	The king has come
E atrás dele o povo inteiro	And behind him came the people
E o rei mandou	And the king ordered
Nem ligar pro rei guerreiro	Don't mind the warrior king
E o povo em bando	And the people, in a crowd
Fez-se chamar e a seu comando	Were called upon and under his command
A cidade iluminou	The city was lit
O rei chegou	The king has come
Porque o povo é o rei primeiro	Because the people are kings first
E o rei mandou	And the king ordered
Porque era fevereiro	Because it was February
E o povo em bando	And the people, in a crowd
Saiu na rua cantando	Took the streets, in a shout
Quando o dia clareou	Upon the dawn of a new day,

Apesar de passageiro	Though ephemeral,
Seu reinado eternizou	Immortalizing their reign
Mas é que o mal do rei	But the king's evil
É o bem que o rei jurou	Is the good he swore to
Através dos carnavais	Every carnival
Mas é que o mal do rei	But the king's evil
É o bem que o rei jurou	Is the good he swore to
E um rei não volta atrás	And a king won't take back his words
O rei chegou	The king has come
Mas pra nosso desespero	But much to our despair
O rei mandou	The king ordered
E era a voz do rei guerreiro	And it was the warrior king's voice
E o povo em bando	And the people, in a crowd
Desta vez voltou chorando	Now came back in tears
Porque tudo se acabou	Because all was now over

Lyricist Paulo César Pinheiro used a narrative poem about a king who brings peace to the life of a people, and another king, a warrior king who puts an end to such peace. It is also possible to interpret these characters as a single one: a king who proves to be democratic at times, despotic at others. The lyrics use carnival as background for the narrative: peace comes in February, which is the month of carnival, when the people are on the streets singing, and the day rises; upon the warrior king's arrival, the people leave in tears and it is all over. Once again, carnival is used as a metaphor for the moment of freedom.

Below is the interpretation of censor Maria Luiza Barroso Cavalcante,[6] who prohibited the lyrics, in her opinion issued in March 1974:

> The main idea behind the song is to highlight the role of "King Momo" as a myth, given his popular appeal. Additionally, the author makes a clear connection between this "king" and a "warrior king"; the former asks the people to move away from the latter and to lead him to the carnival. However, as put by the author, the illusion comes to an end upon the arrival of the "warrior king," which, according to the verses of the last stanzas, brings sadness to the people. Though identifying this "warrior king" with the figure of the President of the Republic . . . is far-fetched, this interpretation is nevertheless possible in view of political oppositions. The lyrics nonetheless have double and obscure meanings, whereby I do not believe they should be approved, especially considering the content of the last stanza.

The censor associates the king in the song with the mythological figure of "King Momo," symbol of carnival revelry, and reinforces the possible association between the figure of the warrior king and the president of the republic, who at the time was General Emílio

Garrastazu Médici, whose rule was the most repressive of the entire military dictatorship. If double meaning arising out of allegory had favored the approval of "Abre Alas," in the case of "Rei do Carnaval" it was the reason behind the prohibition of the song. The second assessment, by censors José do Carmo Andrade and Rony Camargo Ruas[7] in March 1974, reinforces the observations of the previous analysis, taking the symbolism into account to back the veto: "I noticed the existence... of symbolical language, thereby providing for different interpretations; considering Brazil's current political moment, I believe it typifies a severely harmful connotation for the Maximum Authority of the Nation."

Based on the version of the lyrics submitted to censorship and included in the consulted reports, it is clear that from the poetical standpoint, it is different from the version recorded in the 1974 album *Modo Livre*. Prior to the censorship assessment, the lyrics included stanzas that perhaps rendered the relationship between the events of the narrative and the military regime more evident. The original title was "O Rei Chegou, o Rei Mandou" (The King Is Here, the King Has Ordered), which could attribute a greater sense of authoritarianism to the image of the king. The song's third stanza was almost entirely changed—these are the original lyrics:

Se o rei fosse verdadeiro	If the king were honest
Não teria successor	There would be no successor
Mas é que o mal do rei	But the king's evil
É o bem que o rei jurou	Is the good he swore to
E um rei não volta atrás	And a king won't take his words back
Mas é que o mal do rei	But the king's evil
É o bem que o rei trocou	Is the good he exchanged
Pela máscara da paz	For the mask of peace

Based on these stanzas, it would even be possible to compare the attitudes of the kings in the song to those of certain generals who governed Brazil under the military regime. For the sake of clarification, the first president to take office following the 1964 coup was General Castelo Branco, who promised to reestablish democracy in Brazil; however, the president "passed on a divided nation to the hands of his successor, elected by 295 people" (Gáspari 2002a, 125). Hence, the previously mentioned stanzas seem to describe such events: a ruler who uses the "mask of peace" to make his promises, and a ruler after whom, had his promises been fulfilled, "there would be no successor." It is possible to apply the same comparison to the subsequent president, General Costa e Silva, who promised the opening of the regime to politicians but the continuation thereof to the military (Gáspari 2002a, 276).

In the foregoing cases, the songs "Não Há Porque" and "Rei do Carnaval" were forbidden by censorship because their lyrics were deemed to have political content. It is notable that though subject to minor changes, the critical nature of both songs nevertheless remained perceivable. Nonetheless, they were approved and released in albums: the first one was recorded in 1975, and the second one in 1974. It is worth mentioning that the record labels often mediated the relationship between artists, their songs, and the censorship mechanism. The labels that managed the careers of many prestigious MPB artists, such as Lins, Chico Buarque, and Caetano Veloso, were multinational companies that opened branches in Brazil following the economic policy used since the 1964 coup. The state conducted a process of internalization of capital and of significant investment in the culture industry, backed by the idea of "national integration." The compatibility between the interests of the business segments, which aimed at "market integration," and of the military regime, led to the substantial development of the culture industry in Brazil during the 1960s and 1970s (Ortiz 2006, 118). Considering the economic relevance of the music companies in the Brazilian market, and because MPB was one of its main products, the interest of both parties—record labels and the government alike—in approving the songs and releasing the albums in order to move the economy was clear. From this perspective, it is possible to understand why songs that were initially vetoed would subsequently be recorded, despite the veto and their supposedly inappropriate content.

Popular Song and Political "Opening"

A period of slow political opening began in Brazil with the term served by General Ernesto Geisel, in 1974. The president intended to gradually restore democracy, though in a conservative fashion, without allowing the opposition to come to power. Despite such expectations, the repressive agencies still had control and continued to act violently and with autonomy, as can be seen in the words of historian Boris Fausto (1999, 490):

> The repression agencies took over power, thereby producing negative reflexes in the hierarchy of the armed forces. A lower-ranking official could control information, decide on the life or death of a person according to his insertion in the repression mechanism, without his superior in the military hierarchy being able to oppose him.... In order to reestablish hierarchy, it was necessary to neutralize the hard core of the military, decrease repression and gradually promote "the return of the military to the headquarters.

Torture, people "disappearing," killings by government repression agencies, vigilance, and censorship remained in effect while: the government oscillated between permission and coercion (Gáspari 2004, 34). If press censorship underwent a period of gradual relaxation, musical censorship remained in full force (Carocha 2007, 78).

Lins's songs were rolled out precisely when Brazil's political opening process had already begun. This aspect could have contributed to the understanding that though embedded with critical content toward the regime, the songs were nevertheless recorded. However, although Lins was not subject to more drastic censorship measures, this was not the case of other contemporary songwriters who recorded their work and who also were critical of the government. This is the case of Chico Buarque: in 1973, during the regime's strongest period of repression, his play *Calabar* was forbidden, as was his album *Chico Canta*, released in the same year and removed from circulation (Napolitano 2003, 123). Also in 1973, three songs Milton Nascimento included on the album *Milagre dos Peixes* were prohibited, at which point he decided to record them instrumentally only (Garcia 2000, 138–39). Some years later, amid the "opening" period, in 1976, composer Taiguara had his album *Imyra, Tayra, Ipy* collected from stores and his show prohibited (Fiuza 2011, n. p.). It is therefore clear that when compared to Lins, other songwriters were far more persecuted by censorship mechanisms.

It is nevertheless clear that, though not a constant censorship target, Lins's songs were still monitored by authorities, despite the opening process of President Geisel's government. The song "Um Fado," recorded in 1977 on the album *Somos Todos Iguais Nesta Noite*, is a good example. Rejected by the censors, its lyrics describe a state of desperation, based on references to Portugal:

Nenhuma esperança à vista	There is no hope in sight
Nada virá do horizonte	Nothing will come from the horizon
Não haverá mais conquistas	There will be no more achievements
E nem quem as conte	Or anyone to tell them
Mulheres gastaram as contas	Women wasted the beads
Do terço em salve-rainhas	Of the rosary in Hail-Maries
Contando nos dedos os filhos	Counting on their fingers the children
Que faltam nas vinhas	Who are missing in the vineyards
Pra enxugar tantos olhos	To dry so many eyes
Fizeram muitos moinhos	They made a lot of mills
Mas o vento foi pouco	But there was little wind
E os olhos do povo	And the eyes of the people
Mancharam as vestes de vinho	Stained the garments with wine
Nenhuma esperança à vista	No hope in sight
Não haverá mais conquistas	There won't be any more conquest
Não, navegar não é preciso	No, navigating isn't necessary
Viver é preciso	Living necessary[8]

From a musical standpoint, the song is written in the Portuguese style, as a *fado*, and with respect to the poetry, it refers to the characteristics of Portugal, such as the vineyards, the wine, the mills, and the Catholic faith. These specificities are used allegorically in reference to life in Brazil, to the lack of freedom, to the mothers waiting in vain for their missing sons whose lives were lost to the regime. It is noteworthy that democracy was being reestablished in Portugal at the time, with the end of the dictatorship that lasted forty-one years, in 1974; hence, Portugal's freedom represented a relief for

Brazilian society. Below is the assessment of the lyrics to "Um Fado," set out in the opinion of censor Sônia Maria Galo Mendes,[9] on January 10, 1977:

> The lyrics' subject matter hereof have a clear negative sense for its political connotation, portraying the deception and lack of hope of a people with the possibility of witnessing the change of a system of popular oppression.
> In view of the foregoing..., I believe the work should be vetoed.

The censor realized that the metaphor of hopelessness of a people living under oppression might transmit a negative and political idea relative to Brazil's authoritarian regime, though there was already a glimpse of civil liberty at the time (in 1977). Specifically in relation to this song, the only perceivable change to the lyrics between the document sent to the censor and the recorded version is the title: originally "Fado das Contas" (Fado on Beads), it was changed to "Um Fado." This is one more example in which a song was deemed inappropriate because of its critical content, but was nevertheless recorded as part of a top-selling album.[10]

Following the pathway of political opening, in late 1978 President Geisel annulled the decrees that violated the Constitution, thereby increasing the scope of civil freedom. In this context, in the period from 1977 through 1980, Lins released the albums *Somos Todos Iguais Nesta Noite, Nos Dias de Hoje, A Noite,* and *Novo Tempo.* On these albums, Lins consolidated his partnership with lyricist Vitor Martins, with songs for which the duo is frequently remembered, having achieved significant commercial success and critical acclaim. The albums' repertoire proved to be the result of a production marked by ideas of freedom, emphasizing the perspective of imminent political opening and freedom.

As has been previously mentioned, culture played an important role of resistance to the repression imposed by the military regime. Lins's songs, like cultural production as a whole during this time, gradually promoted "messages of hope of better days, ethics of peace and justice, human rights and democracy, values which became more central to the leftist political culture following the defeat of armed resistance, in the early 70s" (Napolitano 2002b, 2). It is notable that since the late 1960s, several left wing organizations involved in armed resistance were organized with the purpose of taking over the government. This factor became the excuse for the crimes perpetrated by the government agencies for political demobilization against the left; the armed groups were practically exterminated by the regime, by means of assassinations, use of torture, and general imposition of fear. In the meantime, in the early 1970s, certain international press sectors and the Catholic Church published and disclosed information on the tortures and assassinations denied by the Brazilian government, thus revealing to the world what the Brazilian press and society had to otherwise silence in the country (Gáspari 2002b, 275–278).

Aside from being both musically and poetically in line with the values that circulated in the cultural media in his songs, Lins also resorted to imagery to prove his stand, having used his own mock prisoner portrait as the cover of the album *Nos Dias de Hoje.* As can be seen in Figure 16.1, the imagery simulated his imprisonment for political reasons,

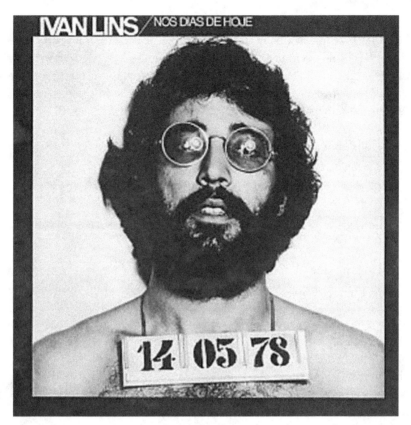

FIGURE 16.1 Cover of the album *Nos Dias de Hoje*.

which never actually happened, adding strong symbolism to the album. In so doing, Lins clearly marked the political connotation of both his work and his image as a public person, and also "reported" the repressive arbitrary acts of the regime to its opponents; this can also be seen in the artist's own description of this album cover, in an email sent to the author on June 23, 2013:

> Adman and artist José Carlos Mello Menezes, who was widely known in Rio de Janeiro, created the cover. The idea behind it was exactly as portrayed in the picture, I had a police record, as if I had been arrested for being against the regime and had thus become a dangerous person. The content of the album reveals the reason why: some of the songs were almost censored, but finally approved thanks to the work of EMI's lawyers, using certain maneuvers . . . By "almost" I mean that the lawyers analyzed them before having them personally delivered to the censors, duly defended. Additionally, the title reflected the reality of the time: nowadays we run the risk of being arrested and of having a criminal record for being against the regime. Note that the light on my glasses reflects the reflectors, as if I were in an interrogation room. It was all on purpose.

The artist's declaration reveals significant issues not only with respect to his work but also in relation to censorship of the artists, and the cultural industry. The album cover could have sufficed to justify the prohibition of the album; additionally, the song "Cartomante" (Fortuneteller) (Lins / Martins), whose first line is the title of the album *Nos dias de hoje* (Nowadays), has a strong sense of denunciating both the repression of and the opposition to the military regime, as can be seen in lines such as:

Nos dias de hoje é bom que se proteja	You better watch out for yourself nowadays;
Não ande nos bares, esqueça os amigos	Don't roam around bars, forget your friends
Não pare nas praças, não corra perigo	Don't hang around parks, don't run any risks
Não fale do medo que temos da vida	Don't speak of our fear of life;
Nos dias de hoje não lhes dê motive	Don't give them any reason, nowadays
Porque na verdade eu te quero vivo	For the truth is, I want you alive.

However, taking into account Lins's words, it is clear that the label EMI and the artist used preconceived strategies to prevent censors from acting: even before the songs were prohibited, they had already prepared professional defenses, via their lawyers, to promote the approval of the songs. As historian Alexandre Fiuza has explained, legal cases sent by artists and labels to the censorship services favored the construction of meanings that flourished in the musical discourse of popular song, by means of both tacit and implied language of opposition against the authoritarian regime, which was often a successful strategy to have the songs approved (Fiuza 2006, 21). It is also worth mentioning the words of lawyer João Carlos Müller, counsel to labels PolyGram and EMI-Odeon, on the negotiations with the censors:

> I was in charge of rendering the activities of the musical industry feasible.... For instance, a composer brought six songs to me. I would then say, "Write a really violent one." The material was taken to the censors, who would veto the most violent one first, and would already get ready to veto the next one. This is when I would step in and say: "... you've already vetoed one, are you really going to veto another song?" I mean, these are negotiation tricks, they have nothing to do with ideology.[11]

It is therefore clear that the labels would engage lawyers exclusively for the purposes of negotiating with censors, as in the foregoing case. The lawyer also described another strategy used to get past censors, which consisted of having songwriters write something that would first be vetoed, for the sake of negotiation. As the lawyer himself has mentioned, it was not ideological issues that were at stake but, rather, the interests of the labels. From this perspective, it is necessary to once again take into account the thin line that separated any work's political engagement from the interests of the music industry, and the limits of censorship. The significant commercial success of Lins's albums, released in the second half of the 1970s, reveals his appraisal in a market segment in which "engaged" songs were also a highly profitable product. They were integrated into the production and consumption systems of major multinational companies (Ridenti 2010, 98).

Still, with respect to the relation between censorship and the album *Nos Dias de Hoje*, it is worth noting an episode described by lyricist Vitor Martins.[12] According to Martins, specifically in his case, the approval process for songs was generally conducted exclusively by the record labels and the censors, without the involvement of the artist. He also claimed he usually did not have to change the words to his vetoed songs in order to ensure approval. He had a peculiar experience, however, with the song "Cartomante" (Lins / Martins) and censorship; in the 1970s, Lins and Martins started a music editing company through which they collected the royalties for their songs. When "Cartomante" was submitted to the censors it was initially vetoed; Martins says the song was ultimately approved after he promised to have it published by EMI-Odeon rather than by his own publishing company. In other words, the song was approved following negotiations between the censorship agency and the record label, which would gross even more sales with the hit, not only as recorded by Lins but also thanks to the original recording by Elis Regina on the album *Transversal do Tempo*, which was also a huge sales hit.[13]

It is noteworthy that since the mid-1970s, Lins began to actively participate in events promoted by left-wing organizations, such as student and labor organizations. There are confidential documents available at the Serviço Nacional de Informações (SNI), at the Arquivo Nacional, reporting his participation in such events. It is clear that these documents created a logic to promote suspicion, as described by Napolitano (2004, 104):

> The obsession with surveillance as a means to prevent any "subversive" acts, especially with respect to what the manuals on the National Security Doctrine referred to as "subversive propaganda" and "psychological warfare against democratic and Christian institutions," eventually created a logic of suspicion or "persecutory ethos."

Lins's performance and his statements during concerts and to the media were constantly under surveillance, up to the fall of the military regime in 1985. The surveillance agencies believed these acts were part of some sort of conspiracy, even if there were no grounds for such interpretation. For instance, in a magazine article on his concert at the Intituto de Educação, in Rio de Janeiro, the author says Lins's microphone and lights were cut out during the performance, because of the disapproving implications of his speech (Chrysóstomo 1977, 125). In 1978, he was included in the list of "dangerous" persons, in one of SNI's reports, after having criticized the government in an interview given to the newspaper *O Diário* in the city of Ribeirão Preto.[14] When a concert was to be held in May 1982 at the gym of the União Campograndense de Estudantes (Student Union of the City of Campo Grande), references to Lins were made in the SNI documents in the following terms: "Subject: political-subversive connotation of musical concert—Ivan Lins"; "Said concert is being organized by persons connected to leftist organizations and to members of the Brazilian Communist Party."[15] The document included a list of all the sponsors of the event. By so doing, the government had already produced a negative record of an event that had not even taken place. As Napolitano (2004, 107) has affirmed, these documents "reveal the agents' conclusions that there was a perpetual conspiracy orchestrated by 'subversive' political groups that used the culture industry to launch a 'psychological war.'"

Final Considerations

In 1979 General Batista Figueiredo became president and continued the political opening process in Brazil. In August 1979 the head of state enacted the amnesty law, whereby political crimes were forgiven, suspended political rights were restored, political exiles were allowed to return to the country, and public liberties increased. The law, however, also pardoned agents who tortured and killed during the regime. Though the dictatorship ended in 1985, censorship remained in effect until 1988, albeit in a reduced capacity.

During the period marked by political opening, Lins and his partners, especially Vitor Martins, managed to translate the dark mood of the most repressive period of the military regime into their songs, without setting aside hope and the sensation of having overcome the recent trauma, based on a perspective of freedom. To this end, as has been noted by Napolitano (2010, 390), Brazilian popular song "not only dialogued with the authoritarian context and the struggles of civil society, but also helped, from the poetical and musical standpoint, to give a meaning to the social experience of resistance to the military regime."

The purpose of this chapter has been to further understand the relationships between censorship and musical production, based on the works of a highly acclaimed MPB artist during the military regime in Brazil. Through his songs, the assessed documents, and the artists' statements, it is possible to explore the range of conflicts and ambiguities revealed in the relationship between music, politics, and the culture industry. As part of Brazil's popular music production, Ivan Lins's work played a substantial role of symbolic resistance to the authoritarian regime and contributed to the consolidation of an ideal shared by artists and audiences alike. These characteristics were also strongly integrated to the market system, thereby revealing the specificities and contradictions behind the production of politically engaged Brazilian popular music.

Notes

I would like to thank the Fundação de Amparo à Pesquisa do Estado de São Paulo—FAPESP (São Paulo Research Foundation) for supporting this research, and Christina Rostworowski da Costa for her precious help translating this paper, including lyrics, censor documents, and citations, originally in Portuguese. I would also like to thank Ivan Lins and his writing partner Vitor Martins, who kindly contributed the testimonials provided for the paper.

1. The documents consulted are available at the Arquivo Nacional (National Archive), in Brasília and Rio de Janeiro, at Fundo: Divisão de Censura de Diversões Públicas (Fund: Division of Public Entertainment Censorship) and Fundo: Serviço Nacional de Informações (Fund: National Information Service). It is worth noting that some of the Brazilian military dictatorship's documents were recently released for public consultation, such as the Fundo Serviço Nacional de Informações (National Information Service Fund), available since 2006, thereby substantially contributing to knowledge of this period in Brazilian history.
2. Translation of the original lyrics in Portuguese according to Sternberg (1998, n. p.).
3. Report No. 6968/73, by censorship technician Gilberto Pereira Campos, August 29, 1973.
4. Report No. 7305/73, by censorship technician Paulo Leite de Lacerda, September 4, 1973.
5. Report No. 25571, by censorship technician Eugênia Costa Rodrigues, March 20, 1974.
6. Report No. 13536/74, by censorship technician Maria Luiza Barroso Cavalcante, March 8, 1974.
7. Report No. 13537/74, by censorship technicians José do Carmo Andrade and Rony Camargo Ruas, March 8, 1974.
8. Translation of the original lyrics in Portuguese according to Sternberg (1998, n. p.).
9. Report No. 064, by censorship technician Sonia Maria Galo Mendes, January 10, 1977.
10. According to data obtained from the Associação Brasileira de Produtores de Disco—ABPD (Brazilian Association of Record Producers), verified from September 1 to 7, 1977, and from August 25 to 31, 1977, by the Instituto Paulista de Pesquisa de Mercado—IPPM (São Paulo Market Research Institute), *Somos Todos Iguais Nesta Noite*, ranked among the top ten best-selling national LPs in São Paulo and Rio de Janeiro.
11. Leonardo Cavalcanti, "Estrevista com João Carlos Müller: Estava Ali Para Resolver," *Correio Braziliense*, April 25, 2010. http://www.correiobraziliense.com.br/app/noticia/brasil/2010/04/25/interna_brasil,188552/entrevista-com-joao-carlos-muller-estava-ali-para-resolver.shtml
12. Vitor Martins. In an interview with the author, April 29, 2013.
13. According to data obtained from the Instituto Brasileiro de Opinião Pública e Estatística—IBOPE (Brazilian Institute of Public Opinion and Statistics), (*Pesquisa de Vendas de discos. Relatório semanal sobre vendas de discos*, Rio de Janeiro, January–November 1978. AEL, Universidade Estadual de Campinas), in August 1978, the album *Nos Dias de Hoje* ranked thirteenth among the best-selling cassettes, and the album *Transversal do Tempo*, ranked fifteenth among the best-selling LPs in Rio de Janeiro.
14. Declaration No. 1370-B/78, DOPS SP, September 19, 1978, SNI Fund.
15. Declaration No. 160/116/ACG/82, 116 ACG/SNI, May 13, 1982, SNI Fund.

References

Alves, Maria Helena Moreira. 1985. *Estado e Oposição no Brasil (1964–1984)*. Petrópolis: Editora Vozes.

Carocha, Maika Lois. 2007. *Pelos versos das canções: um estudo sobre o funcionamento da censura musical durante a ditadura militar brasileira (1964–1985)*. MM thesis, Universidade Federal do Rio de Janeiro.

Chrysóstomo, Antônio. 1977. "Livre do Sucesso." *Revista Veja* (São Paulo), August 10.

Dias, Márcia Tosta. 2000. *Os Donos da Voz—Indústria Fonográfica Brasileira e Mundialização da Cultura*. São Paulo: Boitempo Editorial.

Dreifuss, René Armand. 1981. *1964: A conquista do Estado: ação política, poder e golpe de classe*. Petrópolis: Editora Vozes.

Fausto, Boris. 1999. *História do Brasil*. São Paulo: Edusp.

Fiuza, Alexandre Felipe. 2006. Entre um samba e um fado: a censura e a repressão aos músicos no Brasil e em Portugal nas décadas de 1960 e 1970. PhD diss., Universidade Estadual Paulista.

Fiuza, Alexandre Felipe. 2011. "Canção no exílio: trajetória, sons e política no Cone Sul." Paper presented at VI Congresso Internacional Roa Bastos: Arquivos de Fronteira. UNILA. Foz do Iguaçu, September 28–30. http://www.nelool.ufsc.br/simposio2011/cancao_no_exilio.pdf

Garcia, Luiz Henrique Assis. 2000. *Coisas que ficaram muito tempo por dizer: o Clube da Esquina como formação cultural*. MM thesis, Universidade Federal de Minas Gerais.

Gáspari, Elio. 2002a. *A Ditadura Envergonhada*. Vol. 1. Coleção As Ilusões Armadas, São Paulo: Companhia das Letras.

Gáspari, Elio. 2002b. *A Ditadura Escancarada*. Vol. 2. Coleção As Ilusões Armadas, São Paulo: Companhia das Letras.

Gáspari, Elio. 2004. *A Ditadura Encurralada*. Vol. 3. Coleção O Sacerdote e o Feiticeiro, São Paulo: Companhia das Letras.

Hollanda, Heloisa Buarque de. 2004. *Impressões de Viagem: CPC, vanguarda e desbunde: 1960/70*. Rio de Janeiro: Aeroplano.

Lins, Ivan. 1972. "O que caiu no golpe do Olimpiá." Interview with Julio Hungria, Henfil, Mariozinho Rocha. *O Pasquim*, no. 174: 9–12.

Lopes, Andrea Maria Vizzotto Alcântara. 2008. "As canções de Gonzaguinha e Ivan Lins e o conceito de engajamento." Paper presented at the conference XIX Encontro Regional de História da Associação Nacional de História, Universidade de São Paulo. São Paulo, September 8–12. http://www.anpuhsp.org.br/sp/downloads/CD%20XIX/PDF/Autores%20e%20Artigos/Andrea%20Lopes.pdf

Magalhães, Marionilde B. 1997. "A lógica da suspeição: sobre os aparelhos repressivos à época da ditadura militar no Brasil." *Revista Brasileira de História* 17, no. 34: 203–220. http://www.scielo.br/scielo.php?pid=S0102-01881997000200011&script=sci_arttext

Napolitano, Marcos. 2002a. "A música popular brasileira (MPB) dos anos 70: resistência política e consumo cultural." In *Anais do IV Congreso de la rama latino- americana del IASPM*. Mexico City. http://musica.universidadarcis.cl/wm/descarga/aud1brasil/MPB%20anos%2070%20-%20Marcos%20Napolitano.pdf

Napolitano, Marcos. 2002b. "O 'Tesouro Perdido': a resistência no campo da cultura (Brasil 1969/1976)." Paper presented at the Colloquium A banalização da violência: a atualidade do pensamento de Hannah Arendt, Universidade Federal do Paraná. Curitiba, October 14–18. http://pt.scribd.com/doc/96821915/Artigo-Napolitano-h-arent

Napolitano, Marcos. 2003. "Hoje preciso refletir um pouco: ser social e tempo histórico na obra de Chico Buarque de Hollanda—1971/1978." *História (São Paulo)* 22, no. 1: 115–134. http://www.scielo.br/pdf/his/v22n1/v22n1a05.pdf

Napolitano, Marcos. 2004. "A MPB sob suspeita: a censura musical vista pela ótica dos serviços de vigilância política." *Revista Brasileira de História* 24, no. 47: 103–126.

Napolitano, Marcos. 2007. *A síncope das idéias: a questão da tradição na música popular brasileira*. São Paulo: Editora Fundação Perseu Abramo.

Napolitano, Marcos. 2010. "MPB: a trilha sonora da abertura política (1975/1982)." *Estudos Avançados* 24, no. 69: 389–404.
Naves, Santuza Cambraia. 2010. *Canção popular no Brasil*. Rio de Janeiro: Civilização Brasileira.
Nicodemo, Thais Lima. 2012. "Ivan Lins: um 'ator móvel' na MPB dos anos 1970." *Revista Brasileira de Estudos da Canção* 24, no. 47: 103–126. http://rbec.ect.ufrn.br/index.php/Ivan_Lins_um_ator_móvel_na_MPB_dos_anos_1970
Ortiz, Renato. 2006. *A Moderna Tradição Brasileira: Cultura Brasileira e Indústria Cultural*. São Paulo: Editora Brasiliense.
Ridenti, Marcelo. 2000. *Em busca do povo brasileiro*. Rio de Janeiro: Record.
Ridenti, Marcelo. 2005. "Artistas e intelectuais no Brasil pós-1960." *Tempo Social (Universidade de São Paulo)* 17, no. 1: 81–110. http://www.scielo.br/pdf/ts/v17n1/v17n1a03.pdf
Ridenti, Marcelo. 2010. *Brasilidade Revolucionária*. São Paulo: Editora UNESP.
Schwarz, Roberto. 1978. *O pai de família e outros estudos*. Rio de Janeiro: paz e Terra.
Scoville, Eduardo Henrique Martins Lopez de. 2008. *Na barriga da baleia: a Rede Globo de Televisão e a música popular brasileira na primeira metade da década de 1970*. PhD diss., Universidade Federal do Paraná.
Sternberg, Janet. 1998. "The Songs of Ivan Lins as Political Propaganda." Unpublished manuscript kindly provided by the author.

Discography

Buarque, Chico. *Quando o Carnaval Chegar*. 1972. Phonogram/Philips, 6349038, 33⅓ rpm.
Buarque, Chico. *Chico Canta*. 1973. Phonogram/Philips, 6349093, 33⅓ rpm.
Lins, Ivan. *Modo Livre*. 1974. RCA/BMG, 1030092, 33⅓ rpm.
Lins, Ivan. *Chama Acesa*. 1975. RCA/BMG, 1030154, 33⅓ rpm.
Lins, Ivan. *Somos todos iguais nesta noite*. 1977. EMI-Odeon, XEMCB7023, 33⅓ rpm.
Lins, Ivan. *Nos Dias de Hoje*. 1978. EMI-Odeon, 064422808, 33⅓ rpm.
Lins, Ivan. *A Noite*. 1979. EMI-Odeon, 064422849, 33⅓ rpm.
Lins, Ivan. *Novo Tempo*. 1980. EMI-Odeon, 064422872, 33⅓ rpm.
Nascimento, Milton. *Milagre dos Peixes*. 1973. EMI-Odeon, XSMOFB3762, 33⅓ rpm.
Regina, Elis. *Transversal do tempo*. 1978. Phonogram, 6349384, 33⅓ rpm.
Taiguara. *Imyra, Tayra, Ipy*. 1976. EMI-Odeon, XSMOFB389, 33⅓ rpm.

CHAPTER 17

ALBAN BERG'S "GUILT" BY ASSOCIATION

PATRICIA HALL

AFTER the premiere of Alban Berg's opera *Wozzeck* in Berlin on December 14, 1925, the music critic Paul Zschorlic wrote: "Leaving the State Opera House *Unter den Linden* last evening, I had the feeling that I was not leaving a public institute of art but a public madhouse. On the stage, in the orchestra, in the stalls: a lot of madmen ... *Wozzeck* by Alban Berg was the battle-cry—the work of a chinaman from Vienna. For these massed attacks and convulsions of instruments had nothing to do with European music and its development (Reich 1965, 61).

By 1933, by which time *Wozzeck* had achieved undisputed success, Berg was fighting a different battle: when Hitler assumed the leadership of Nazi Germany, the works of many atonal composers, whether Aryan or not, were banned from performance in Germany. Nonetheless, Berg attempted, under the harshest physical and economic conditions imaginable, to finish his next opera *Lulu*. Various handwritten documents show that while Berg detested the Nazi party, he also calculated how he could survive as a composer in this political environment. He tabulated the number of conductors performing *Wozzeck* who were Jews versus Aryans. He provided documentation that proclaimed both he and his wife as Aryans. In a letter to the conductor of the Berlin State Opera, he defined himself as a German composer, even though he was born and lived his entire life in Austria. Perhaps most significantly, while he immediately excluded a stereotypical Jewish character from the plot of *Wozzeck*, in *Lulu* he included a corrupt banker, who in his autograph score he describes in anti-Semitic language.

One of Berg's many eccentricities was his habit of saving seemingly every letter he received, and every scrap of paper that he wrote on, including musical sketches, drafts of letters, calendars, and other personal documents. This results in a lengthy document trail, in which it is possible, more than other composers who weren't Jewish but were persecuted during the Third Reich, to see the effects of this censorship on his artistic output and his life. This chapter will examine these documents held in the Austrian

National Library to show how Berg plotted to survive as an artist in an increasingly threatening political atmosphere.

The authors of *Musik und Drittes Reich* avoided the term "epoch" for the years 1933–1945, explaining that the effect of the Third Reich on music began much earlier and lasted much later (Drüner and Günther 2012, 10). One can see, for example, that the comments of some music critics during the Berlin premiere of *Wozzeck* in December 1925, anticipate those Berg would receive nearly ten years later.

TRIERISCHE LANDESZEITUNG, TRIER

> Atonality is slowly beginning to be a danger to our German cultural music, and it is high time that those still healthy progressive thinking musicians in Germany give everything to energetically confront this sinister movement. If jazz bands and nigger tunes invade our German cultural music, atonal hubbub on the other, both working off texts with no foundation, then the situation is indeed serious (ÖNB Musiksammlung F 21 Berg 3213/108).

VÖLKISCHER KURIER, MÜNCHEN

"The atonal composers, meaning the Jews, are encroaching more and more onto the State Opera by evoking artificial successes through all means, by feigning more successes to the press, to appeal to them. Over the long or short run the Berlin State Opera will thus become an experimental stage on which lobbyists will luxuriously flower" (ÖNB Musiksammlung F 21 Berg 3213/104).

Nonetheless, during the years 1925 through 1932, *Wozzeck* was performed 163 times, 130 of these performances taking place in Germany. In our first document (Figure 17.1), Berg has meticulously tabulated each performance of *Wozzeck*, including the city in which it was performed, the date of the performance, and the number of times in each performance cycle (ÖNB Musiksammlung F 21 Berg 3213/3). These compilations no doubt served to remind Berg that despite his current rejection as an artist in Nazi Germany, he had for eight years been a success by any artistic standard.

In April 1933, Berg first learned of cancellations of *Wozzeck* in Germany from Hans Heinsheimer, head of the Opera Division at Universal Edition. Berg's heated response, including a handwritten draft in which "Reichsdeutscher" is underlined in blue, "Deutsch-Österreichischer" in green, and *arischer* in red pencil, is typical of the period:

> That Büchner is one of the greatest German-Aryan playwrights, hardly needs mentioning; and I, too, as you'll see from the enclosed family tree, am neither Jew nor

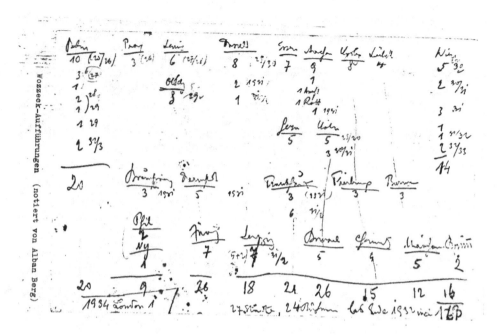

FIGURE 17.1 Berg's Compilation of *Wozzeck* Performances (ÖNB Musiksammlung F 21 Berg 3213/3).

Used with the kind permission of the Musiksammlung of the Austrian National Library.

foreigner, rather, as far back as I can follow with the documents that are available to me at this time, 5/8 imperial German and 3/8 German-Austrian heritage, and up to four generations back, also without exception and comprehensively Aryan race; whereby the assumption appears justifiable, that my relatives who lived 200 years before (that is, the parents and grandparents descended from empirial Bavarian civil servants and military officials, as well as the Prussian-Schliesian and Bavarian borderland forbears on my mother's side) would also not be of Jewish descent (ÖNB Musiksammlung F 21 Berg 1473/272/4).

In later letters, Berg consistently identifies himself as a German rather than Austrian composer, and brings attention to the number of Aryan versus Jewish conductors he has worked with in productions of *Wozzeck*. In a letter dated April 20, 1934, to Heinz Tietjen, director of the Prussian State Theatre, he writes:

> It's no accident that all of the interest my music has attracted, indeed that the positioning of my creative work within contemporary output has emanated from Germany, where in fact all my greatest works were premiered. The objection, that this is the result of Marxist politics in post-war years, or even that it could be seen as a Jewish affair, can be refuted in that—to name only one work—among the approximately twenty German theatre managers (Directors) who at that time took on my opera *Wozzeck*, and among the equally many masters who performed it, among

these more than three dozen leading personalities of German theatre and music—there were a scant half-dozen non-Aryans.

And that among the Aryan conductors and musical directors of the *Wozzeck* stages from Aachen to Königsberg, today almost all are active on German stages and many moreover remain in the top and very top positions. My international recognition makes it impossible to supply a motive, that one calls the music I write somewhat romantic, or Slavic or oriental or in some other way exotic, in a word un-German.

And as clear and irrefutable as it is that music like mine could have originated only in a German country—equally clear and irrefutable is the difference in every measure between art that is based on centuries-old German music tradition, and the art of every other country and race. (ÖNB Musiksammlung F 21 Berg 1473/272/4). Berg's letter is accompanied by a chart (Figure 17.2) in which he lists the Jewish versus Aryan conductors and directors for past performances of *Wozzeck*.[1]

Given Berg's anti-Semitic tone in his letters, it becomes less surprising that this attitude also infiltrated his opera. In Berg's *Wozzeck* sketches from 1917, he immediately omits the scene with the Jewish merchant containing offensive stereotyping (Hall 2011, 27). While it would have been nearly impossible to omit the character of the corrupt banker in *Lulu* it was not the inclusion but Berg's added anti-Semitic annotations to the score that so offended Schoenberg. In his letter to Universal Edition he angrily notes that Berg added the terms "judeln" to his libretto, where the Banker "lapses more and more into Yiddish" (Perle 1985, 283). By these, and other similar annotations, Berg made the Jewish identity of the Banker overt, when he could have simply made him "a Banker."

A final blow comes when Berg is informed that *Lulu*, the opera he is now struggling to complete, will also be banned in Germany. In May 1934 he again sends a family tree to Wilhelm Furtwängler, conductor of the Berlin Philharmonic, who responds:

> You don't have to prove to me that you are a German composer. I know you, know your music for some time, and would think nothing of taking on *Lulu*, if it weren't for the text, which because of the public feeling here in Germany seems impossible to me at the moment. It doesn't have anything to do issues of race—Wedekind was also an Aryan—rather merely because the *Erdgeist* tragedy cannot be performed in today's Germany at all, or at least not with a successful outcome.
>
> That you're widely considered to be a Jew—which you clearly aren't—shouldn't surprise you, by the way. It's related to your close relationship with Arnold Schoenberg, whose most prominent student you are considered (ÖNB Musiksammlung F 21 Berg 755/1-3).

Berg's final strategy was to repackage his unfinished opera *Lulu* by extracting passages to be played as orchestral excerpts—a technique he had used to great advantage with *Wozzeck*. Only the third movement out of five, "Das Lied der Lulu," is sung, thus essentially neutralizing the Wedekind text. Berg aptly refers to his "Symphonische Stücke aus der Oper *Lulu*" as his "propaganda suite," and fills it with some of the most romantic, Wagnerian-sounding passages of the opera. Still, the only conductor who consented to

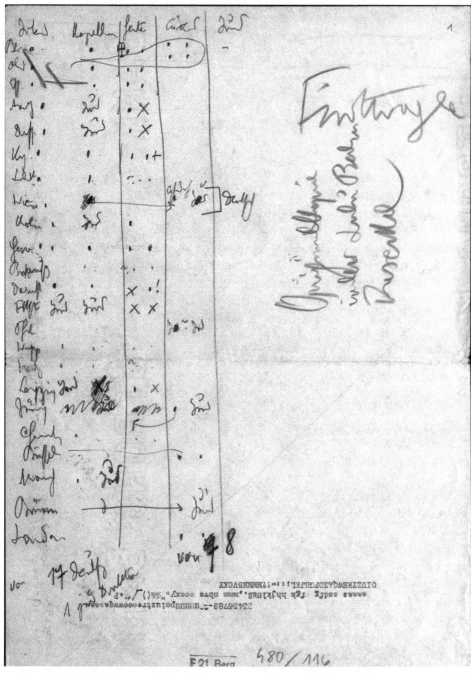

FIGURE 17.2 Berg's Compilation of Jewish Conductors and Directors for German Performances of *Wozzeck* (ÖNB Musiksammlung F 21 Berg 480/116). Used with the kind permission of the Musiksammlung of the Austrian National Library.

perform it in Nazi Germany was Berg's fellow Austrian and close friend Erich Kleiber, who also premiered *Wozzeck* in Berlin nearly ten years earlier.

The comments of music critics, now working for officially sanctioned newspapers in the Third Reich, give us insight into the peculiar atmosphere at the premiere of these pieces on November 30, 1934. These comments are available to us because Berg retained a clipping service and assiduously gathered these reviews into scrapbooks.

DIE MUSIK, BERLIN, ALFRED BURGARTZ

"The new work of Alban Berg that Erich Kleiber premiered on November 30th, in the second symphony concert of the Berlin State Opera, is five symphonic pieces: a concert arrangement of the Lulu opera. How spun into his workshop, how uninvolved in today's events must a composer be, who writes an opera and today takes up material by Wedekind. And even if Wedekind appeals to him, why Lulu? Lulu was the fantasy apparition of Bohemians, which never really was the idol of shadowy late romantics. A Lulu has never existed—we would have to disown our mothers, our sisters, as at best, slime from the sewer" (ÖNB Musiksammlung F 21 Berg 3130/38).

In fact, Berg chose his libretto at the end of the 1920s, long before the creation of the Third Reich. Moreover, he included jazz elements and ragtime that would have been appropriate to the 1920s. But a second reviewer makes it clear that it is not just the Wedekind text that is problematic.

ANGRIFF, BERLIN, G. SCHULTZE

"Before the war, Wedekind, in his dramas threw the accusations of a shattered society in your face. And in the tragedy "Lulu" we learn the path of suffering of a tart. Presented very refined, psychologically. We have other problems to occupy us. We have other ideals, other than the disintegration of a person's soul, other than the disintegration of a decadent strata of society, to watch and to be sentimentally amused by it.

And now a composer comes along and makes an opera out of this material. His style is romantic. However, in this dreamy music that conveys an unheard of refined tension, the sensational flashiness dominates again and again. Muted trumpets blare, siren-like violin melodies flatter, the percussion drones brutally with bang and boom, and woodwinds sweetly whisper. The core of this music is rotten and inappropriate for the times. It's for this reason that Berg's music is problematic, no matter how brilliant the façade might be" (ÖNB Musiksammlung F 21 Berg 3130/31).

It is also common knowledge among the reviewers that—no matter how romantic sounding the final product—Berg has utilized Schoenberg's twelve-tone method.

Nachtausgabe, Berlin

"Alban Berg, in February a fifty-year-old, Viennese by birth, but with a heritage from the German Reich, has remained true to his style of the time, and to his declared Schoenberg discipleship. For clarity, one must explain what twelve-tone music actually means. It's the complete declaration of war against the tradition from Bach to Wagner and with that against the development of Western music. While the strength and emotional force of past music rests on the major and minor scales (particularly on three main tones—cadence), in twelve-tone music, twelve emancipated tones are always varied according to a specific principle of ordering" (ÖNB Musiksammlung F 21 Berg 3130/35).

A final reviewer, Paul Zschorlich, widens the context of the concert in mentioning a similar attempt by Wilhelm Furtwängler to include modern music in his concert:

> In the same moment that the quarrel about Hindemith that led to Furtwängler's resignation had burned out, General Director Erich Kleiber found it appropriate to pour oil on the fire and to perform fragments of the opera Lulu by the Austrian Alban Berg. He shouldn't wonder if he feels pressured after all this.... An unknown singer, Lilli Claus, who appeared before the public in a scarlet dress, conveyed perfectly the decadent sensuality of her part. That is frankly a questionable complement.... It was delectable to watch the audience on this occasion. I noticed no less than eleven people around me with their head leaned against their hands, apparently trying desperately to detect the deep meaning of Alban Berg's music. These heavy laborers trick themselves into looking for something that's not there. Many were caught up in this auto-suggestion, and that's easily explained, in that the typical Kleiber audience, in which, as usual, the percentage of Jewish listeners is unmistakably strong, had turned up at this festivity. (ÖNB Musiksammlung F 21 Berg 3130/54)

It would seem then, that Berg's many precautions in preparation for this premiere were to no avail: as the composer of *Wozzeck*, Schoenberg's most prominent student and the adaptor of a text by Wedekind, his rejection in Nazi Germany was almost guaranteed. Moreover, features of Berg's music—his exotic orchestration and use of jazz idioms—further assured complaints from the German press.

Yet in the reviews in papers of other nationalities, particularly of countries that would fight or be overtaken by Nazi Germany, Berg's premiere became a cause célèbre for a composer who was still resisting the cultural constraints of the New Germany.

Herbert F. Peyser, who published a review of the concert in *The New York Times*, interviewed Berg in his home a few days before the concert, and seemed particularly fascinated by the political implications of this concert in Nazi Germany:

> Erich Kleiber could hardly have picked a more psychological moment for the first performance of extracts from Alban Berg's still uncompleted opera "Lulu." With the country in a state of ferment over Paul Hindemith, with Furtwaengler under

attack for daring to defend him, it took courage to sponsor within the four walls of Hermann Goering's Staatsoper the latest production of the author of "Wozzeck."

Mr. Kleiber had this courage and his valor was becomingly rewarded. For almost fifteen minutes after the novelty he was cheered, applauded and recalled. The orchestra and an imported soprano shared in the ovation. The composer was not present, but if he had been he would undoubtedly have tasted the savor of glory. However, let there be no mistake. One has to read more these days in the applause lavished by German audiences on infrequent modern works than mere enjoyment of the music or endorsement of the performance. Demonstrations of the sort have an edge of hysteria and recall the times when Italians shouted "Viva Verdi" and meant something else.

. . . A moving glimpse, these fragments, of what may, peradventure, be a modern masterwork! Mr. Kleiber put his heart's blood into the performance and, thanks to the foresight of the composer, a capable young operetta soprano from Vienna, Lillie Claus, was ready to spring into the breach and save the performance when Maria Cebotari did not appear (ÖNB Musiksammlung F 21 Berg 3130/46).

Kleiber, like Furtwängler, would resign his post as general director of the Berlin State Opera. Unlike Furtwängler, however, he would leave Germany.

Along with Berg's rejection as an artist, was its effect on his income. Berg's statements of gross income, also retained among his documents, plunge from a high of 22,000 ATS in 1932, to 6,923.60 ATS in 1934 (ÖNB Musiksammlung F 21 Berg 3022-3026).

A draft of a letter to Leo Schidrowitz in 1935, gives us details about the specific living conditions Berg endured because of this loss of income. Staying at the Waldhaus, his summer home in Carinthia, Berg writes: "Shall I be even clearer and divulge that it's for these reasons that we've stayed here, where we can live a lot more cheaply than in Vienna. That it's no pleasure to endure this beastly cold, surrounded by ice and snow, with single panes, without a water supply" (Musikhandschriftensammlung, Wiener Stadt—und Landesbibliothek, MH 14261/c). In many letters he refers to the Waldhaus as his "concentration camp."

His calendar for the last year of his life, 1935, has many annotations dealing with death and financial obligations. In addition to the anniversaries of Gustav Mahler's and Emil Hertka's death, he records the exact time of Mutzi's death (Alma Mahler's daughter) as ¼ 4, 22. IV.

Figure 17.3 shows his tabulations of every expected expense in the next six months, as well as his anticipated income, including the $500 he would receive from Louis Krasner for composing the Violin Concerto, his last complete work. During this period he was also contributing support of 100 ATS per month to his sister, and 200 ATS per month to institutionalize his mentally ill brother-in-law, who in 1930 cut off the end of his little finger as an offering to Kaiser Franz Joseph. Berg calculates that he has approximately 2000 ATS to live on during each three-month period (ÖNB Musiksammlung F 21 432/31).

Berg's wife, Helene Berg, has often been blamed for his death. Rather than incurring medical expenses, she occasionally treated Berg's chronic abscesses using sterilized

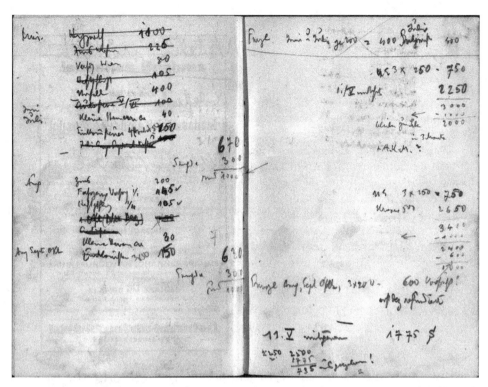

FIGURE 17.3 Berg's Compilation of Expenses and Income for the Remaining Months of his Life (ÖNB Musiksammlung F 21 Berg 432/31).

Used with the kind permission of the Musiksammlung of the Austrian National Library.

scissors. However, a typescript in the Austrian National Library written by Helene Berg reveals critical details about this final illness. The location of the infected abscess—even after two exploratory surgeries necessitating a transfusion—was discovered too late to prevent general sepsis[2]:

> Alban Berg suffered frequently during his lifetime from boils—during the First World War acutely, later always isolated abscesses. In his letters to me he reported about them in detail. In Summer-Fall 1935 several small boils appeared <u>at the same time</u> that were healed by Chief Physician Dr. Engstler in Velden. At the time Alban worked feverishly on *Lulu* and the Violin Concerto, although he didn't feel well. In November, back in Vienna, he suffered a mild heart attack that was remedied by Dr. Friedmann within a few hours. From then on he *swore* upon Dr. Friedmann's therapy, and when he developed a larger abscess at the base of his spinal column, Dr. Friedmann treated it with Solux radiation and painkilling morphine suppositories. Suddenly Alban got a 40-degree fever! In response to my <u>7:00 AM</u> telephone call Dr. Friedmann didn't arrive until <u>6:00</u> in the afternoon!

He examined the abscess that he had treated and that was in a state of healing, verified that the wound was uninfected and in the process of healing, and suspected that the high fever could have resulted from it, but rather, must have another cause. I was afraid, however, that he was trivializing Alban's condition. He advised me to take Alban to the hospital the next day; he had a good friend there who would "have a look at him." That night was so bad that I ordered an ambulance for him at 6:00 AM. That was December 17th. Alban was "thoroughly" examined, but no one thought to examine him <u>rectally</u> as well. (As a result of the morphine tablets, however, he had no pain.) After three days both buttocks had been cut a hand's breadth deep, (because of a red spot, that he probably got from lying on the hard bed) <u>without finding the slightest thing</u>! Alban lost so much blood from this unnecessary operation that a blood transfusion became urgently necessary. I was present during his examination. Professor Dr. Hess was the first to examine him rectally, and found an abscess in the rectum. But it was already too late. The poison had infiltrated the hemoroidal blood vessels and through them was carried into the entire body. (The latter was reported to me by our longstanding doctor and friend of the Nahowski family, Medical Specialist Doctor Martin.) Even a 24-hour IV could no longer save him. Alban insisted that I had to swallow a strong sleeping remedy in front of him. But I didn't sleep, I held him in my arms until the end (ÖNB Musiksammlung F 21 Berg 433/69).

In the last days of his life, the annotations in Berg's calendar are by Helene Berg. She writes, "Fieber (fever) on Friday, December the 13th, "letzte Stunden" (last hours) on December 14th and 15th, Friedmann, the doctor she consulted, on the 16th, and "Spital" (hospital) on the 17th, the day Berg was taken to the Rudolfstiftung in the 3rd district." A final annotation (Figure 17.4) marks the day he died, a small cross between December 23rd (coincidentally his number of fate) and the 24th.

If Berg had survived a few years longer, he would have witnessed not only the Anschluss, but his inclusion in the Degenerate Music exhibition that began in Düsseldorf and eventually traveled to Vienna. Moreover, Universal Edition would be purged not only of its remaining Jewish composers, but of its Jewish employees, including the director, Yella Hertzka, and head of opera publishing Hans Heinsheimer. Unlike many composers who were persecuted during the Third Reich, however, Berg's music flourished after World War II, to the point that *Wozzeck* is today considered the most famous twentieth-century work in the opera repertoire.

Berg's many personal documents have allowed us a fuller and more accurate picture than is often possible with other composers who were persecuted during the Third Reich. The title of my paper alludes to Berg's assumed guilt as a student of Schoenberg. However, these documents also show that Berg had a bit of guilt of his own, in that he was self-promoting to the point of aligning himself with Nazi Germany, at least as it existed in the 1933–1935 period. But the documents also make clear Berg's desperation as a result of Germany's censorship of performances of *Wozzeck*, Berg's primary source of income as a composer. While some composers might emigrate under these circumstances, Berg's premature death preempted even this possibility, leaving us his last opera

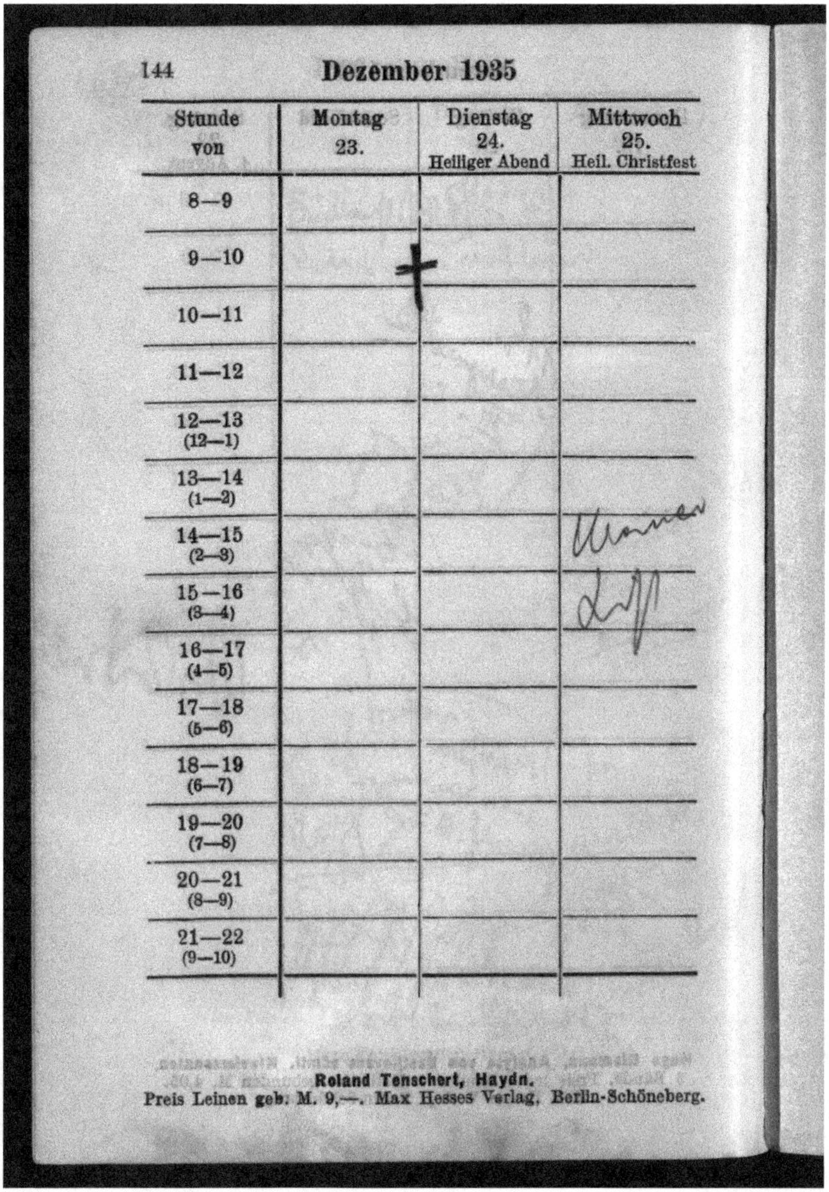

FIGURE 17.4 Cross annotated in Berg's Calendar by Helene Berg for December 24th (ÖNB Musiksammlung F 21 Berg 432/31).

Used with the kind permission of the Musiksammlung of the Austrian National Library.

Lulu unfinished until forty-four years later. A final telling quote from a letter to Webern in 1933 emphasizes the ambiguity of Berg's position: "Ever since I've been *here*, I can't get rid of the fear that the Nazis will take over here too, that is, our government *won't* be strong enough to stop it" (Hilmar 1985, 15).

Notes

I would like to thank Lee Rothfarb for his invaluable help translating the German passages in this article.

1. Transcribed in Herwig Knaus, *Alban Berg. Hanschriftliche Briefe, Briefentwürfe und Notizen. Aus den Bestanden der Musiksammlung der Österreichischen Nationalbibliothek* (Florian Noetzel, Wilhelmshaven, 2004), p. 79.
2. See also Steiger (2013, 327).

References

Drüner, Ulrich, and Georg Günther. 2012. *Musik und "Drittes Reich" Fallbeispiele 1910 bis 1960 zu Herkunft, Höhepunkt und Nachwirkungen des Nationalsozialismus in der Musik.* Vienna: Böhlau.

Hall, Patricia. 2011. *Berg's* Wozzeck. New York: Oxford University Press.

Hall, Patricia. 1996. *A View of Berg's 'Lulu' Through the Autograph Sources.* Berkeley: University of California Press.

Hilmar, Ernst. 1985. "Alban Berg's Selbstzeugnisse zu Entstehung und Aufführbarkeit der Oper *Lulu*. In *Alban Berg "Lied der Lulu": Faksimile-Ausgabe der Anton V. Webern gewidmeten autographen Partitur.* Vienna: Wiener Stadt- und Landesbibliothek.

Knaus, Herwig. 2004. *Alban Berg. Handschriftliche Briefe, Briefentwürfe und Notizen. Aus den Beständen der Musiksammlung der Österreichischen Nationalbibliothek.* Wilhelmshaven, Germany: Florian Noetzel.

Perle, George. 1985. *The Operas of Alban Berg, Volume Two, 'Lulu.'* Berkeley: University of California Press.

Reich, Willi. 1965. *Alban Berg.* New York: Vienna House.

Steiger, Martina. 2013. *Briefe der Freundschaft: Alban Berg—Erich Kleiber.* Vienna: Seifer.

CHAPTER 18

SLOW DISSOLVES, FULL STOPS, AND INTERRUPTIONS

Terezín, Censorship, and the Summer of 1944

MICHAEL BECKERMAN

Prelude

On June 22, 1944, an extraordinary concert took place in the Terezín (Theresienstadt) concentration camp in Czechoslovakia (Figure 18.1).

Flanked by Hugo Wolf's Michelangelo songs and Dvorak's Gypsy Melodies and preceded directly by Beethoven's *An die ferne Geliebte*, Pavel Haas's *Four Songs From Chinese Poetry* received its premiere, performed by bass Karel Berman with Rafael Schachter at the keyboard. Viktor Ullmann, about whom you will read more later, wrote one of his most enthusiastic reviews:

> Once one has heard them, one would not want to miss Haas' topical songs so full of life, and live with them in intimate relationship. For only this way can new art succeed in the course of time: it becomes house music and an indispensable friend, like a good book, like everything that one acquires with practice. An especially lucky hit is the graceful, bright, and rhythmically pulsating second song of the cycle, which turns up later once more in the fourth song as the Coda of the whole work and brings it to conclusion. However, even these earnest songs, yearning for home—in which the first and third are linked with each other by an *idee fixe* of four tones that returns as an *ostinato* or *cantus firmus* in manifold metamorphoses—are the result of an impressive, genuine, and still progressive inspiration. (Karas 1985, 83)

FIGURE 18.1 Concert Program, June 22, 1944.

Haas's cycle appeared in the middle of the concert and we may begin our musical exploration by looking at a moment in the very middle of one of the middle songs of his cycle. The text of the song, "Far Away Is the Moon of Home," is rich in images of nature and yearning:

Far Away Is the Moon of Home

The moon grows from the black darkness of the sea,
in that far land it is blossoming too.
Love is lamenting its dream.
It waits for a far off evening.

The moon shines ever brighter through my tears.
I put on nighttime clothes, rime-frost chills so much.

> My hands, hands that are empty
> Saying everything.
>
> Oh sleep give me a dream
> Give me a dream of going back to my home
> Sleep, you cannot give me a dream,
> my yearning keeps me awake.

As one might imagine in a place like Terezín, homesickness could be a literal disease, even though, or perhaps especially because, many of the prisoners were only a short distance from their actual dwelling places. Ullmann spoke of a leitmotiv of four notes, and they are there, but it is the allusions called forth by those pitches, and their role in what might be termed a local Terezín dialect that is so compelling. We find this out only in an interlude in the song. Hidden here is a reference to perhaps the oldest musical figure that can be associated with the Czechs, the famous "Svatý Vaclave," or St. Wenceslaus hymn (see Velek 2008 for an exhaustive treatment of this melody). It was not the first time Haas used it in his work, and it may function here as a symbol of the homeland that has been lost (Figure 18.2).

With those four notes and this concert, summer began in Terezín and it would be difficult to imagine a stranger place than Terezín in the summer and early autumn of 1944.

FIGURE 18.2 St. Wenceslaus Hymn Quotation.

On Censorship

The opening of this study, and the material that directly follows this section, offer a detailed look at what I argue to be the effects of censorship on creative musical work, involving both the materials of composition (the proliferation of quotations, for example) and structural considerations (the placement of significant material in the center as an act of hiding). But teasing out just why these musical features are characteristic of Terezín and how artists operate under censorship is rather treacherous.

Censorship turns out to be one of those things that we understand best when we do not have to define or explain it. Who exactly told Pavel Haas what he could and could not do when he composed his Chinese songs? If we cannot answer this clearly why should we speak of censorship? After all, if I decide not to speak out at a faculty meeting because I do not want to risk the dean's disapproval, can I legitimately speak of being censored? This kind of "self-censoring" is a far cry from being told explicitly that I am not allowed to speak because of my opinion, isn't it? Or is our sense that we know censorship when we see it misplaced?

Shortly after the 1989 Velvet Revolution in Czechoslovakia, the writer Ivan Klima gave a talk titled "The Unexpected Benefits of Oppression." Klima claimed, somewhat perversely, that censored writers enjoyed extraordinary conditions under the Communists. In his view, writers were banned not because of what they wrote in Czechoslovakia at that time but because of who they *were*; and once prohibited, a writer could not publish anything under his or her own name, whether it was a nondescript fairy tale or an antigovernment screed. A paradoxical sense of freedom resulted. There was no need to watch one's language carefully. Because there was complete censorship, there was no censorship: censored writers could do exactly as they liked.

While one could argue that it is only the "official" censorship that fully deserves the name, many would agree that what we might call "secondary censorship" raises more fundamental questions. Regimes of terror do not really need to do much in the way of censoring. A few garrotings, a hanging here and there and the population quickly gets the idea of what is permissible and takes it upon themselves to create standards accordingly. While working within the extremely narrow limits proscribed by a totalitarian government might encourage certain forms of ingenuity, it is doubtless also enervating and unnerving. In this study we shall refer to any place where "speakers" have legitimate fears that certain kinds of expression can bring them severe harm as a *censoring environment*. It is understood that there is no precise definition of what this is and how it works, and yet we may agree that Terezín was an environment where censorship of various kinds, from black-lined postcards to self-censorship, became part of the fabric of life.

Of course, literary censorship, of the kind discussed by Klima, is one thing while its musical equivalent is another. In fact, aside from the censorship we described in Communist Czechoslovakia, where a person rather than a product is banned, musical censorship has historically been practiced primarily on the basis of style (jazz, say, or *Entartete Musik* under the Nazis), level of dissonance (from the Council of Trent to dodecaphony), use of subversive musical quotations (do not quote the Internationale in Franco's Spain!), or use of lyrics that are either considered obscene (Run DMC) or politically dangerous (Schulhoff's Eighth Symphony chorus of "Marx, Lenin, Stalin!").

And yet the circumstances under which various kinds of musical censorship are practiced are rarely clear-cut. It is a truism that contemporary Shostakovich reception owes a great deal to the assumption that the composer is trying to speak so as to fly under the censors' radar, that he is working in a *censoring environment*; but even now there are opposing views about just what he was doing, why he made certain choices, and what role this has in our readings of his works. With Haas's Chinese songs the words allow us to make a connection between homesickness and a musical figure, the St. Wenceslaus Chorale. But when we take away the lyrics, can we claim with certainty that a particular moment in a piece is subversive and somehow a response to censorship? For more on this question, let us return to northern Czechoslovakia in 1944.

Terezín

A former garrison town designed like a fortified star, Terezín had become what we might call a ghetto, prison, or concentration camp, with a population that may have reached seventy-five thousand, but at least fifty thousand during the war years.[1] Originally intended as a place to put prominent Jews too conspicuous to simply disappear, it became two other things as well. The first was simply a transit point to the camps further east, playing a role in the Final Solution; the second was more ingenious and complicated. Considering the growing alarm in certain European and world circles about the fate of the Jews, Terezín became a potent propaganda tool. And in this capacity it reached its apex in the summer of 1944. Because the Nazis had gradually allowed a cultural life to exist in Terezín, and because of its appearance as something like a normal town (at least compared to Auschwitz and Dachau), it was ideal for such a purpose. Beginning in the fall and winter of 1943–1944 a campaign of beautification commenced, and this was intensified in the spring of 1944 in anticipation of a visit by the Red Cross. Because the camp had been beautified in anticipation of this visit, the Nazis also decided to make a propaganda film beginning in August, showing the idyllic conditions under which the Jews lived in the Protectorate. It is these special conditions, among others, that make Terezín an ideal laboratory in which to examine the issues of censorship and self-censorship and their effects on musical composition.

Let us then try to imagine Terezín in the summer of 1944. From one vantage point, it may have appeared idyllic, yet it was a Potemkin village where inmates lived in desperate fear of deportation. Culture was important, but so was disease and starvation (hundreds died every day during certain periods). The summer was a time of warmth and time outdoors, but also a time of rampant bedbugs and oppressive heat, as noted in several of the surviving diaries. The Red Cross arrived on June 23, one day after the performance of Haas's Chinese songs. The visit was a charade. Most likely the inspectors were completely fooled, although one of them would later claim that they gave the camp a clean bill of health only in the hope that the Nazis would continue to let packages through to the inmates. As usual with Terezín, nothing was clear, and what people said may or may not be what happened. Many prisoners were devastated by the Red Cross response. Shortly after the Red Cross visit, a group of artists was arrested for making realistic rather than idealized images of the camp, at least in part to show the world what was really happening in Terezín (Green 1978, 95ff.). All the artists were taken to the Small Fortress, interrogated, beaten, and tortured; only two survived. Meanwhile, news comes of the Allied landings during this period, so there was a potent mix of hope and despair, desperation and fear and also some weird sense of normalcy. Throughout August and into September, the Nazis shot a propaganda film, directed, at least at the beginning, by the famous German actor Kurt Gerron. Filming was over on September 11, and within a few weeks the camp was emptied of almost all its long-term inhabitants, most of whom were immediately gassed upon their arrival at Auschwitz. Several works of instrumental music completed during this period raise potent questions about censorship and the nature and limits of musical expression.

Dramatis Personae

The four protagonists of this particular drama would hardly make any obvious group in another context. The oldest, by one year, was Viktor Ullmann, born in 1898 in Teschen (now Cesky Tesin) to parents who had converted to Catholicism (Schultz 2008). A pupil of Schoenberg, Zemlinsky, and later Alois Hába, Ullmann directed an opera company in Usti nad Labem, wrote music criticism, and composed. A committed "Anthroposophist," who followed the teaching of Rudolf Steiner, he operated a philosophical bookstore in Stuttgart until 1933 when he moved to Prague. Hans Krása, born in 1899, was a German-speaking Czech who was part of the emerging generation of young composers. He also fell under the influence of Zemlinsky and studied with Albert Roussel in Paris, absorbing the cheeky music of *Les Six* (Červinková 2003). His opera *Betrothal in a Dream* and his *Symphony for Small Orchestra* brought him a good deal of local and international attention. Pavel Haas (b. 1899), whose Chinese songs we have already encountered, came from a Moravian Jewish family and was a leading pupil of Leoš Janáček (Peduzzi 2005). His opera *The Charlatan* was a great success in Brno in 1938, and he was working on a large symphony when he was deported to Terezín. Finally, the youngest of the group by almost twenty years was Gideon Klein (b. 1919), a gifted pianist and promising composer also from Moravia (Slavicky 1996). Between them they had a wide palette of styles, from the various looks of Czech national music to atonality and serialism, and from Hába's quarter-tone music to jazz, blues, and neoclassical approaches.

While in the camp, these four, along with several others, functioned somewhat as a musical school. According to various memoirs, Klein and Krása were particularly close despite the difference in ages. There are also stories that Klein had a galvanizing effect on Haas, who arrived at the camp depressed (though this has been disputed by Haas's biographer Lubumir Peduzzi). Ullmann acted as a kind of dean, active both as a composer and music critic, penning a series of concert reviews, one of which we have already sampled.

Dances and Lullabies

The most popular piece of new music performed in the camp was undoubtedly Krása's children's opera *Brundibar*, and for many today this work symbolizes not only Terezín but also something about the Holocaust more broadly. However, Krása's compositional style had an edge not always obvious from looking at this opera, and it was on full display that summer in a series of compositions. Let us begin with a moment from Krása's *Tanec* (Dance) (see Figure 18.3).

This moment is akin to a slow dissolve in a film, moving to a different scene, perhaps some kind of dream sequence, or at least something removed from the normal reality of things. Marked *ruhig*, it has the character of a lullaby, and indeed, it bears some similarity to Smetana's lullaby from *Hubicka*, a seminal piece for Czech composers, and of course, shares its opening pitches with the famous lullaby by Brahms.

The first question we might raise is just what a lullaby is doing in the middle of a composition titled *Dance* that opens in this manner (see Figure 18.4).

A second question is why the above example is followed by a passage that sounds like a musical equivalent of some kind of earnest direct speech (see Figure 18.5). We may also note that this theme is marked *zart* when it first appears and thereafter *espressivo* and *molto espressivo*, suggesting a certain insistence and reaching out.

We will return to this after considering the resonance of *Tanec* in another composition by Krása. *Tanec* is undated. Joza Karas (1985) gives 1943 as the time of composition (and this is also the date given in the printed score), but this is almost certainly wrong. In her latest edition of Krása's biography, Blanka Červinková (2003, 241) has revised the date to 1944. Two important reasons for accepting the later date involve its relationship to the composer's *Passacaglia and Fugue*, completed, according to notations on the manuscript, on August 7, 1944, and thus Krása's final composition. Further dating issues involve the very fact that *Tanec* is a string trio.

One of the things that suggests some symbolic significance of *Tanec* is that both the *Passacaglia* and the *Fugue* reference it in ways that do not seem to be a matter of any classic organic outgrowth, but rather some kind of conscious plan. While the appearance of *Tanec* in the *Fugue* seems harmonious and triumphant or even Dionysian at the very end, it acts in the *Passacaglia* as something of an unprepared and unexpected irritant appearing first in variation 6 and then in variations 10 and 11 (see Figure 18.6).

If *Tanec* is some kind of meaningful thorn in the side of the *Passacaglia and Fugue*, what does *Tanec* itself signify, and what is the lullaby doing in its center? While making

FIGURE 18.3 Krasa's *Tanec*, transition.

FIGURE 18.4 *Tanec*, opening theme.

FIGURE 18.5 *Tanec*, middle.

FIGURE 18.6 Caption Krasa, *Passacaglia*, var. 6.

firm statements about such things is problematic (there are always reasons for things that we cannot know and always a chance we are missing something critical), we may note that the lullaby becomes something of a Terezín staple, with both an undeniably literal role and one that is symbolic on multiple levels. Traditionally, the lullaby is a comfort song, binding parent to a child. And in a place with so many orphans and so much pain and suffering, certainly lullabies provided comfort. Several of the loveliest compositions written or arranged in Terezín were lullabies, from Ilse Weber's exquisite "Wiegala" to the heartbreaking lullaby from *Brundibar*, where children imagine their mothers imagining them all grown up.

In *Tanec* we see a pattern: the outer dance conceals two inner worlds of lullaby and dramatic speech. It is not our fate to ever be able to speak precisely about this dramatic speech, but we may note that the lullaby has historically a connection with that sleep of sleeps, death itself, whether in Schubert's "Death and the Maiden" or Mussorgsky's *Songs and Dances of Death*. This aspect of the lullaby is also suggested by Klein's darkening arrangement.

These kinds of associations alone would make Krása's slow dissolve to lullaby a potent Terezín symbol, of both comfort and death, and lend some special quality to whatever it is that is being "said" in the declamatory passage (and we will have more to say about declamatory musical speech when we reach Klein's Trio).

It is my view, ultimately shared by Krása's biographer Blanka Červinková, that *Tanec* was actually written during the summer of 1944, probably as a companion piece to the *Passacaglia and Fugue*, or perhaps it preceded it by a month or two. Otherwise it is difficult to account for the presence of three string trios appearing suddenly after several years in Terezín. And if the two trios by Krása are connected, then the reemergence of *Tanec* in the *Passacaglia and Fugue* may suggest just what kind of dance this is and further suggest the relationship between fear, censorship, and musical form. We will revisit the core of this piece toward the end of this study when we consider Gideon Klein's final composition.

Ullmann's Jupiter

In the famous coda to the Finale of Mozart's "Jupiter" Symphony the main themes of the movement seem to orbit around each other in a kind of classic balance, cycling in timeless perfection. One of the most remarkable passages written in Terezín, or anywhere else for that matter, is a moment in Viktor Ullmann's final composition, his Piano Sonata no. 7, that seems to channel this Mozartian model. Completed on August 22, 1944, the sonata probably postdates two other significant Terezín compositions by Ullmann: the remarkable melodrama *Die Weise von Liebe und Tod des Cornets Christoph Rilke* (The Lay of the Love and Death of Cornet Christopher Rilke) and the *Emperor of Atlantis*.[2] The moment I want to explore comes from the final fugal variation of the final movement of the sonata (see Figure 18.7).

FIGURE 18.7 Ullmann, Piano Sonata no. 7, final movement, quotations.

Here is another "non-transition transition," a kind of full stop. While Mozart's "quodlibet" moment is not, to our knowledge, based on actual songs nor does it imply "real world" elements, when the world of the *Fugue* comes to a halt in Ullman's composition it is filled with characters. First Bach himself enters in his solmization guise (see the "musical name" spelled out above). Underneath in the bass line are fragments of the movement's main theme, a Zionist composition by Yehuda Sharett on a poem by Rachel. This is followed immediately by a clear quotation of that potent Czech war song "Ye Who Are God's Warriors," a Hussite song from the fifteenth century *Jistebnice cancional*, in the upper part at m. 140.

Folded in to this mix is an idea that is at once clear and obscure. We can see in the lower voice a passage all in half notes beginning at m. 141. According to some sources this is a quotation of the chorale "Nun danket alle Gott," which was associated with German victory celebrations. There is a small problem in identifying the precise source. It turns out that there is no ascending fifth in the chorale as there is in Ullmann's example. Such an interval can be found in the chorale "O Lamm Gottes unschuldig," but the rhythm is different. Since Ullmann is quoting the Czech song literally, why not quote the chorale literally if a particular one has symbolic value? Could the passage refer to the inner phrase of "Ein Feste Burg," or perhaps to the idea of "choraleness," and why are all these strung together? And as if combining four such things was not enough, there is a likely relationship between the Rachel tune and the Slovak national anthem.

What does it all mean? Is it a moment of defiance, or perhaps simply an attempt to give an image of Terezín, where Zionists and Communists, Czech assimilationists and deep believers in German culture are thrust together? Does "Old Bach" come to admonish, or does he ride to the rescue, reasserting himself in the face of false prophets of the German spirit? Could the musical image be Ullmann's life passing before his eyes, or a tribute to his beloved anthroposophy? Or are all these things but pretexts that allow Ullmann to create some remarkable music? While such passages are definitely interpretable, perhaps they are most powerful when, mirroring the action and modes of combination, we allow different possibilities to percolate around us.

Yet even as we do so, we may find this a classic type of work written in a *censoring environment*. Crushing its shards together in the middle of the *Fugue* with enormous force, it is almost a literal representation of the kinds of "geological" pressures brought to bear on the structure of the composition.

INTERPOLATION 1: ULLMANN IN THE MIDDLE

It was customary for people throughout Europe, and also in Terezín, to enter various greetings, comments, aphorisms, and poems in the guestbooks at particular homes. Fritz Janowitz, was one of the prominent people in the camp and the "block elder," or supervisor, of the Magdeburg barracks, and in his guestbook for January 3, 1944, we find the following short composition (see Figure 18.8).

Recently discovered by Dr. Anna Hajková, it gives thanks by turns serious, pompous, and humorous to the block elder, and after some serious contrapuntal entries at the beginning ends in a cadence right out of a Bach chorale. While this composition is hardly something Ullmann would have wanted to hide from the Nazi authorities, it does still have some of the qualities of art in a censoring environment. Not only is the composer giving thanks to the block elder for some favor (perhaps he had been given better lodgings), he also places his own name in the middle of this little composition, followed by his address (Block F, or B.F., uses the musical notes B-flat, F).

A FINAL SCREAM 1

Now we turn to the final composition written in the summer and early fall of 1944. Surely it is not incidental that both Klein and Krása, close friends, end up writing trios as their final works. Lubomir Peduzzi suggests that Klein's Trio is modeled on Haas's *Study*

FIGURE 18.8 (a) Viktor Ullmann's Musical Thank You part 1. (b) Viktor Ullmann's Musical Thank You part 2.

for Strings (known best from its appearance in the propaganda film), and there are certain similarities. But Klein probably knew Krása's work as well, and it may have played a role in the composition of his own trio.

Interpolation 2: Thoughts About History

The previous paragraph illustrates the seductiveness of historical arguments: Klein *probably* knew; Peduzzi *suggests* that Klein studied the Haas score, and so on. As historians we often follow the behavior of addicts; that is, we make up stories to justify our habit of making up stories. In other words, it is probably about time that we admitted that so-called clear documentary evidence only gives us points in historical space. Any attempt to connect those points is fiction, more or less. So it is actually only when we seem most certain about the past that it becomes clear that we do not know what we are talking about.

Klein's Trio is the only composition we know of that was actually written during the time of the transports in late September and October 1944, although it was probably begun in late August since the completion date of the first movement is listed as early September. From this work I will choose one moment, in this case, not a dissolve or a pause, but an interruption (Figure 18.9).

This passage comes from the fifth variation in Klein's middle movement, whose subject is a Moravian folk song called "The Kneždub Tower." The variation starts softly, *Andante mesto, mf* and additionally is marked *con espressione* and *con sordino*. It is both a free augmentation of the theme and probably a reference to two parts of the Verdi *Requiem*, both the opening of the *Requiem* and the "Libera me." At the beginning, the characteristic anapestic regional rhythm of the theme is absent, and just as it reappears it is cut off by the extravagantly marked passage in the cello we have shown above.

FIGURE 18.9 Cello Solo *"Con gran espressione"*.

When we moved from Haas's Chinese songs to the Krása Trio we made an amazing traversal from a world where certain things seem evident, for example the relationship between the text of the song and the musical materials, to a place (textless music) where nothing seems so certain. And yet, there are ample reasons for assuming that these composers are trying to speak in instrumental music, to convey ideas with the kind of specificity perhaps not usually associated with it. Let us rerun this traversal once again using Klein's own composition. In 1943 Klein composed a madrigal for five voices on a text by Hölderlin. In the following passage an ensemble descends to a quick pause, and into that comes a single lamenting voice, "Here I am nothing, and live unhappily." We may note that the dramatic recitation of the text is preceded by a two-voice "lamenting" figure of a descending minor second (Figure 18.10).

Let us compare this with the *Con gran espressione* section of the Trio (Figure 18.11).

The lead-up is identical, even to the pitches used. But not only are they amplified by an ascending sequence, but the solo utterance is more dramatic, coming as an interruption, a classic mode of disruption. It cannot wait to say what it must say. And we must also

FIGURE 18.10 Klein Madrigal on a text by Hölderlin.

FIGURE 18.11 Comparison of Madrigal and Trio.

note that the speech melody of this passage differs from that in the madrigal. The term "speech melody" is not here used incidentally. The *sospirando* sighs in the upper strings are quotes from Janáček's Second String Quartet, one of *his* final works and one in which he most conspicuously tries to speak in music.

And we might also note a kinship between Klein's line and the "declaimed" passage in the middle of Krása's *Tanec* (see Figure 18.5 above). This moment, and the movement that surrounds it, and the movements that surround that raise potent questions.

Just what kind of communication is music in this context? Is Klein's cello solo an autobiographical moment, a confession? A last will and testament? A message in a bottle? Is it an example of using the local situation to stimulate new artistic designs? Is Klein's expressive cello interruption a scream, or is it, in the way it forces the cellist to writhe in a certain frenzy, a kind of prediction for the future? And does it somehow convey the ultimate frustration of a composer who is allowed to create, but with the proviso that his works will be used to show that the Jews were treated well by the Nazis? We can say many things about this music, but if we practice our own form of resistance—that is, if we resist the temptation to try to know things that cannot be known—we might begin to understand that it is possible the music knows things the composer does not really know, and faces things the composer cannot yet face.

The Web of Culture: Knowledge or Belief?

It has become something of an article of faith in both musicology and ethnomusicology that there exists a relationship between music and the culture from which it emerges. Thus in this case we might begin by assuming that there is a connection between the kind of music written in Terezín and the censoring environment in which it was conceived. But as with so many other pieties, this is neither a simple matter nor is it readily demonstrable. One of the reasons it is an article of faith is that it works best as a matter of belief rather than as something requiring scientific proof. Yet we may still ask on what level this relationship takes place. For the more the relationship is thought to exist on a general level, the less any single example may be invoked. And as with all such things, if we insist on finding evidence of highly specific types, we could conclude that some pieces are more a product of their culture than others, and ultimately we might be left with the absurdity that certain pieces do not adequately reflect the world from which they came and end up finding them somehow wanting.

And yet, we may at least try to characterize the world of Terezín and wonder in which ways, if any, the music of that time and place encapsulates this character. In this spirit we might conclude that starting in 1943 Terezín had become a Potemkin village, one in which hope and energy mixed effortlessly with lassitude, terror, and anxiety—a world where people are thrust together in an unplanned and unplannable mix, a kind of cultural black box which emits no light and absorbs none either. It was also a dynamic intellectual and artistic stew with a particularly rich school of composition, filled with gifted figures who crossed many stylistic, national, philosophical, religious, and political lines. It would be my contention, in brief, that we can hear the camp in this music, or at least get as much of a sense of the place as from any other source.

What are then the characteristics of this culture? I would suggest that in many cases the inmates dealt with the Potemkin village aspect by creating musical analogues to it, or what I call *reverse Potemkin villages*, where a seemingly harmless facade covers something quite subversive. Thus this place is, in response to a broad and overarching censorship, a culture of secrets and perhaps even musical sabotage, where the goal of a work is to subvert and undermine the official (i.e., Nazi) view of the culture, much the same way the Terezín painters created secret art that documented the reality of the Terezín experience.

Because one tends to hide musical secrets in the middle rather than the beginning or end of a work, Terezín music becomes a culture of middles. And toward the end of the period, as suggested by the Klein schematic, the middles get more and more bloated, and they must bear more and more the weight of censorship, terror, and oppression. Terezín was also a place of the harshest contrasts: "The presentation of a cabaret on the one hand, and on the other, old people dying," as Gonda Redlich wrote in his diary, and the interruptions, and juxtapositions in Ullmann, Krása, and Klein reflect this (Friedman 1992). And because the inmates are shut in and cannot get out, the place has a claustrophobic quality to it; Terezín is like a faulty air-conditioner running on recirculated air, with no venting to the outside. Thus we find quotation and collage used not only for the purpose of conveying a series of parallel "sabotaging" meanings but also because these people are locked in together, endlessly quoting each other and what snippets they can remember of the outside. In a discussion about this music, the author and Terezín survivor Zdenka Fantlová noted the important role memory plays in these compositions. Whether Haas and Ullmann remember certain tunes or Krása remembers his own *Tanec*, recall is central here. Finally, the three pieces of instrumental music we encountered involve variations, and despite the high quality of these works, there is perhaps something fractured about the genre, offering shards rather than conventional wholes.

JUST MORE MUSIC?

But even after all this we may ask: is Terezín music like other music, or is there something special about it? Does censorship really play a major role in fundamental musical choices? Are the contexts of Ullmann, Klein, Haas, and Krása qualitatively different than those of Beethoven, Schumann, Dvořák, and Ives? To be flip, we might note that although these Terezín composers lived in an atmosphere of dread and even terror, probably nothing was more terrifying than being in Beethoven's head at any time. And if we were to decide that the Terezín composers were either very much like or quite unlike the above composers, would this supposed truth be more a matter of belief or science? In academic life we must ask this question. Because in the absence of anything like scientific evidence for our propositions, the pose of authority often masks cult-like and uncritical thinking. In other words, it is when we lack such evidence that we must be the most careful.

No matter what we end up concluding about censorship, we must of course realize that the composers in Terezín faced an unbearable ethical paradox. To compose, knowing all the while that your works will be used to obliterate the sufferings of you and your people, is almost too painful to contemplate; and yet remaining silent is no victory either. That these composers sought to use forms, genres, styles, quotations, pastiche, collage, and other techniques to reach out of the work and communicate something about their experience in this terrible place is not provable, but seems probable.

Interpolation 3: Haas Again

There are two famous musical moments from Terezín captured on film, both readily available in a simple Internet search. The most notorious is the scene from *Brundibar* with a clip of Terezín children singing the final chorus. The second is a fragment from Haas's *Study for Strings*, composed in the camp and performed for the propaganda film. The conductor, Karel Ancerl, survived, and commented on the charade, noting that the players were actually wearing wooden shoes, which were concealed from the camera by flower pots (Lagus et al. 1968). Though this piece had been written before the summer of 1944, it has its own strange reference in the middle, one that is worth mentioning and has never before been investigated. Haas's big hit before the war was the opera *The Charlatan*, based on a conflation of several legends—Czech and German—about an itinerant doctor. Leaving aside for future investigation the connection suggested in this 1938 work between fascist dictators and the charlatan himself, I would like to focus on one moment.

In Act 1 the travelers come across a place where a village had been before. Titled "Here stood a village," Haas creates an eerie soundscape in the upper registers. Surely this is the sound world we hear in the very middle of the *Study for Strings*, unprepared and in its distance and weirdness unpreparable. And its anomalous presence in the midst of another dancelike work—this one anchored in Moravian folk song—as a kind of unprepared interruption, suggests that the vanished village in this case is Terezín. The town has consumed itself.

Closing Up

The early fall in Terezín brought a change in weather and the High Holy Days, and Klein continued to work on his Trio during this period. At some point after the middle of September, another round of large-scale transports was announced. While there is not a single shred of evidence that those sent "east" knew their ultimate fate (as we now know theirs), it was at best a moment of disruption, deep sadness, and for many, genuine terror. In late September and early October 1944, while Klein was completing the Trio's final movement, thousands of long-term residents of Terezín, including almost all of the so-called "prominents," piled into trains, many, like Philip Manes, thinking they were on a six-week work detail after which they would be returned to Terezín. Klein's concluding movement, the last piece to be written in Terezín, is almost a caricature of reverse Potemkinism; seemingly a charming burlesque (and so marked in the score), it references Ravel, Josef Suk, and Schubert's song, "Gretchen am Spinnrade."

Finally, on October 16, nine days after the Trio's completion, the four composers were themselves transported east. The three older men were immediately gassed. Klein survived until January 1945 when, shortly after his camp, Furstengrübe, was liberated by the Red Army, he either died in one of the so-called Death Marches, or more likely, was shot when a group of SS officers retook the camp. It is thought that he enjoyed a few uncensored hours before the end.

Notes

1. It is not the goal of this study to make strenuous arguments about terminology. Most scholars of the period would consider Terezin a "ghetto," and its official name under the Nazis was "Ghetto Theresienstadt." That it also functioned as a *concentration camp* (a group of people brought together from many different places and kept in servitude), a *transit camp* serving as a holding pen before transports to the east is difficult to dispute.
2. Dating in Terezín is treacherous, as can be the case with any composition. What actually does a "date of completion" signify? It might be contiguous with the date of composition, but it could be considerably later, just as the "date of composition" might be hours, weeks, or years later than the date of conception. For example, Ullmann's melodrama has a dedication from late September, but the work was almost certainly finished before that. Klein's Trio also has dating that may or may not correspond to the moment of composition.

References

Agamben, Giorgio. 2002. *Remnants of Auschwitz: The Witness and the Archive*. New York: Zone Books.
Amery, Jean. 1980. *At the Mind's Limits*. Bloomington: Indiana University Press.
Anidjar, Gil. 2003. *The Jew, the Arab*. Stanford, Calif.: Stanford University Press.
Arendt, Hannah. 1994. *Eichmann in Jerusalem: A Report on the Banality of Evil*. New York: Penguin.
Bauer, Yehuda. 2001. *Rethinking the Holocaust*. New Haven: Yale University Press.
Berenbaum, Michael, and Abraham J. Peck, eds. 2002. *The Holocaust and History: The Known, The Unknown, The Disputed, and the Reexamined*. Bloomington: Indiana University Press.
Blatter, Janet, and Sibyl Milton, eds. 1981. *Art of the Holocaust*. New York: Rutledge.

Borowski, Tadeusz. 1976. *This Way for the Gas, Ladies and Gentlemen*. New York: Penguin.
Cole, Tim. 1998. *Selling the Holocaust: From Auschwitz to Schindler*. London: Routledge.
Evans, Richard. 2001. *Lying About Hitler: History, Holocaust and the David Irving Trial*. New York: Basic Books.
Finkelstein, Norman. 2000. *The Holocaust Industry*. London: Verso.
Fonseca, Isabel. 1995. *Bury Me Standing: The Gypsies and Their Journey*. New York: Knopf.
Frank, Anne. 1998. *The Diary of Anne Frank: The Critical Edition*. Edited by David Barnouw and Gerrold van der Stroom. New York: Doubleday.
Goldhagen, Daniel. 1996. *Hitler's Willing Executioners*. New York: Knopf.
Gilbert, Shirli. 2005. *Music in the Holocaust*. Oxford: Oxford University Press.
Greif, Gideon. 2005. *We Wept Without Tears*. New Haven: Yale University Press.
Laks, Szymon. 1989. *Music of Another World*. Evanston, Ill.: Northwestern University Press.
Lanckoronska, Countess Karolina. 2007. *Michelangelo in Ravensbruck: One Woman's War Against the Nazis*. Cambridge, MA: Da Capo.
Lang, Berel. 2000. *Holocaust Representation: Art within the Limits of History and Ethics*. Baltimore: Johns Hopkins University Press.
Langbein, Hermann. 2004. *People in Auschwitz*. University of North Carolina Press, 2004. See esp. "The Muselmann," 89–105.
Langer, Lawrence L. 2006. *Using and Abusing the Holocaust*. Bloomington: Indiana University Press.
Levi, Primo. 1989. *The Drowned and the Saved*. New York: Vintage. See esp. "The Gray Zone," 36–69.
Levi, Primo. 1993. *Survival in Auschwitz*. New York: Touchstone.
Levi, Primo. 2005. *The Black Hole of Auschwitz*. Cambridge: Polity Press.
Levi, Neil, and Michael Rothberg. 2003. *The Holocaust: Theoretical Readings*. New Brunswick: Rutgers University Press.
Lewy, Gunther. 2000. *The Nazi Persecution of the Gypsies*. Oxford: Oxford University Press.
Lipstadt, Deborah. 1994. *Denying the Holocaust*. New York: Plume.
Malvinni, David. 2004. *The Gypsy Caravan: From Real Roma to Imaginary Gypsies in Western Music and Film*. New York and London: Routledge.
Moricz, Klara. 2008. *Jewish Identities: Nationalism, Racism and Utopianism in Twentieth-Century Music*. Berkeley: University of California Press.
Ng, Wendy. 2002. *Japanese American Internment During World War II: A History and Reference Guide*. Westport, CT.: Greenwood Research Guide.
Novick, Peter. 1999. *The Holocaust in American Life*. Boston: Houghton Mifflin.
Painter, Karen. 2007. *Symphonic Aspirations: German Music and Politics, 1900–1945*. Cambridge, Mass.: Harvard University Press.
Polansky, Paul. 1998a. *Black Silence: The Lety Survivors Speak*. Prague and New York: G plus G.
Polansky, Paul. 1998b. *Living Through it Twice: Poems of the Romany Holocaust (1940–1997)*. Prague: G plus G.
Rosenberg, Otto. 1999. *A Gypsy in Auschwitz*. London: London House.
Segev, Tom. 1991. *The Seventh Million: The Israelis and the Holocaust*. New York: Henry Holt.
Shandley, Robert R., ed. 1998. *Unwilling Germans: The Goldhagen Debate*. Minneapolis: University of Minnesota Press.
Shermer, Michael, and Alex Grobman. 2000. *Denying History*. Berkeley: University of California Press.
Sofsky, Wolfgang. 1999. *The Order of Terror: The Concentration Camp*. Princeton, N.J.: Princeton University Press.

Steinweis, Alan. 1993. *Art, Ideology, & Economics in Nazi Germany*. Chapel Hill: University of North Carolina Press.
United States Holocaust Museum. 1997. *Hidden History of the Kovno Ghetto*. Boston: Bullfinch Press. See also the accompanying CD "Hidden History: Songs of the Kovno Ghetto."
Velek, Viktor. 2008. "Die St. Wenzelsche Musiktradition von ihrem Anfang bis 1848" (The St. Wenceslaus Music Tradition from its Inception to 1848," PhD dissertation, University of Vienna.

Articles

Agamben, Giorgio. 2003. "What Is a Camp?" In *The Holocaust: Theoretical Readings*, edited by Neil Levi and Michael Rothberg, 252–256. New Brunswick, N.J.: Rutgers University Press.
Bock, Gisela. 2003. "Racism and Sexism in Nazi Germany." In *The Holocaust: Theoretical Readings*, edited by Neil Levi and Michael Rothberg, 160–168. New Brunswick, N.J.: Rutgers University Press.
Fackler, Guido. 2007. "Music in Concentration Camps 1933–1945." Translated by Peter Logan. *Music and Politics* 1, no. 1.
Goldenberg, Myrna. 1996. "Lessons Learned from Gentle Heroism: Women's Holocaust Narratives." *Annals AAPSS* 548 (November): 78–93
Habermas, Jurgen. 1998. "Goldhagen and the Public Use of History: Why a Democracy Prize for Daniel Goldhagen?" In *Unwilling Germans?*, edited by Robert R. Shandley, 263–273. Minneapolis: University of Minnesota Press.
Joffe, Josef. 1998. "'The Killers Were Ordinary Germans, Ergo the Ordinary Germans Were Killers': The Logic, The Language and the Meaning of a Book That Conquered Germany." In *Unwilling Germans?*, edited by Robert R. Shandley, 217–227. Minneapolis: University of Minnesota Press.
Levinas, Emmanuel. 2003. "Ethics and Spirit." In *The Holocaust: Theoretical Readings*, edited by Neil Levi and Michael Rothberg, 241–245. New Brunswick, N.J.: Rutgers University Press.
Lyotard, Jean-Francois. 2003. "The Differend." In *The Holocaust: Theoretical Readings*, edited by Neil Levi and Michael Rothberg, 257–263. New Brunswick, N.J.: Rutgers University Press.
Reemstma, Jan Philipp. 1998. "Turning Away from Denial: *Hitler's Willing Executioners* as a Counterforce to 'Historical Explanation.'" In *Unwilling Germans?*, edited by Robert R. Shandley, 255–262. Minneapolis: University of Minnesota Press.
Ringelheim, Joan. 1985 "Women and the Holocaust: A Reconsideration of Research." *Signs: Journal of Women in Culture and Society* 10, no. 4: 741–761.
Zalmanoff, Rabbi Samuel. 1948. *Sefer Hanigunim*. New York: Shulsinger Brothers.

Terezín

Adler, H. G. 1960. *Theresienstadt, 1941–1945*. Tubingen: Mohr.
Beckerman, Michael. 2007. "Postcard from New York—Trio From Terezín." *Music and Politics* 1, no. 1: 1–9.
Berkley, George E. 1993. *Hitler's Gift: The Story of Theresienstadt*. Boston: Branden Books.
Bondy, Ruth. 1989. *"Elder of the Jews": Jakob Edelstein of Theresienstadt*. New York: Grove Press.
Bor, Josef. 1978. *The Terezín Requiem*. Translated by Edith Pargeter. New York: Avon Books.
Červinková, Blanka. 2003. *Hans Krása: život a dílo skladatele*. Prague: Tempo.

Fleischmann, Karel. 1987. *Karel Fleischmann: Life and Work*. Prague: State Jewish Museum.
Friedman, Saul S., ed. 1992. *The Terezín Diary of Gonda Redlich*. Lexington: University Press of Kentucky.
Green, Gerald. 1978. *The Artists of Terezín*. New York: Schocken Books.
Karas, Joza. 1985. *Music in Terezín 1941–1945*. New York: Beaufort Books.
Karel, Rudolf Iltis, Walter Hacker, et al. 1968. *Theresienstadt*. Vienna: Europe-Verlag.
Lederer, Zdenek. 1983. *Ghetto Theresienstadt*. New York: Fertig.
Makarova, Elena, Sergie Makarov, and Victor Kuperman, eds. 2004. *University Over the Abyss*. Jerusalem: Verba Publishers.
Neimark, Anne E. 1986. *One Man's Valor: Leo Baeck and the Holocaust*. New York: E.P. Dutton.
Peduzzi, Lubomir. 1993. Pavel Haas: život a dílo skladatele. Brno: Muzejní a vlastivědná společnost v Brně.
Peduzzi, Lubomir. 2005. *Musik im Ghetto Theresienstadt*. Brno: Barrister and Principal.
Schultz, Ingo. 2008. *Viktor Ullmann*. Kassel: Barenreiter, 2008.
Schwertfeger, Ruth. 1989. *Women of Theresienstadt: Voices from a Concentration Camp*. Oxford and New York: Berg.
Slavicky, Milan. 1996. *Gideon Klein: A Fragment of Life and Work*. Prague: Helvetica Tempora.
Spies, Gerty. 1997. *My Years in Theresienstadt: How one Woman Survived the Holocaust*. Amherst, N.Y.: Prometheus Books.
Troller, Norbert. 1991. *Theresienstadt: Hitler's Gift to the Jews*. Chapel Hill: University of North Carolina Press.

Music and Censorship

Brown, Steven, and Ulrik Volgsten, eds. 2006. *Music and Manipulation: On the Social Uses and Social Control of Music*. New York and London: Berghahn Books.
Chirambo. Reuben. 2006. "Traditional and Popular Music, Hegemonic Power and Censorship in Malawi: 1964–1994." In *Popular Music Censorship in Africa*, edited by Martin Cloonan and Mark Drewett, 109–126. London: Ashgate.
Cloonan, Martin. 1995. "Popular Music and Censorship in Britain: An Overview." *Popular Music and Society* 19, no. 3: 75–104.
Cloonan, Martin. 1996. *Banned! Censorship of Popular Music in Britain: 1967–92*. Hampshire, UK: Ashgate.
Cloonan, Martin. 2004. "What is Music Censorship? Towards a Better Understanding of the Term." In *Shoot the Singer! Music Censorship Today*, 3–5. London: Zed Books.
Cloonan, Martin, and Mark Drewett, eds. 2006. *Popular Music Censorship in Africa*. London: Ashgate.
Cloonan, Martin, and Rebee Garofalo, eds. 2003. *Policing Pop*. Philadelphia: Temple University Press.
Corpe, Marie, ed. 2004. *Shoot the Singer! Music Censorship Today*. London: Zed Books.
Craig, Dylan, and Nomalanga Mkhize. 2006. "Vocal Killers, Silent Killers: Popular Media, Genocide, and the Call for Benevolent Censorship in Rwanda." In *Popular Music Censorship in Africa*, edited by Martin Cloonan and Mark Drewett, 39–52. London: Ashgate.
Dewhirst, Martin, and Robert Farrell, eds. 1973. *The Soviet Censorship*. Metuchen, NJ: Scarecrow Press. (Includes a chapter on self-censorship.)
Eyre, Banning. 2004. "Playing with Fire: Manipulation of Music and Musicians in Zimbabwe." In *Shoot the Singer! Music Censorship Today*, 94–105.

Hill, Trent. 1992. "The Enemy Within: Censorship of Rock Music in the 1950s." In *Present Tense: Rock & Roll Culture*, edited by Anthony DeCurtis, 39–72. Durham, N.C.: Duke University Press.

Jones, Steve. 1991. "Ban(ned) in the U.S.A.: Popular Music and Censorship." *Journal of Communication Inquiry* 15, no. 1: 73–88. http://stevejones.me/pubs/1991/BannedUSA.pdf

Korpe, Marie, Ole Reitov, and Martin Cloonan. 2006. In "Music Censorship from Plato to the Present." In *Music and Manipulation: On the Social Uses and Social Control of Music*, edited by Steven Brown and Ulrik Volgsten, 239–263. New York and London: Berghahn Books.

Martin, Peter. 2006. "Music, Identity and Social Control." In *Music and Manipulation: On the Social Uses and Social Control of Music*, edited by Steven Brown and Ulrik Volgsten, 57–73. New York and London: Berghahn Books.

Mazo, Margarita. 1996. "The Present and the Unpredictable Past: Music and Musical Life of St. Petersburg and Moscow Since the 1960s." *International Journal of Musicology* 5: 371–400.

Moreno, Joseph J. 2006. "Orpheus in Hell: Music and the Holocaust." In *Music and Manipulation: On the Social Uses and Social Control of Music*, edited by Steven Brown and Ulrik Volgsten, 264–286. New York and London: Berghahn Books.

Nuzum, Eric. 2001. *Parental Advisory: Music Censorship in America*. New York: Perennial.

Nuzum, Eric. 2004. "Crash Into Me, Baby: America's Implicit Music Censorship Since 11 September." In *Shoot the Singer! Music Censorship Today*, 149–159. London: Zed Books.

Rothstein, Robert. 1980. "The Quiet Rehabilitation of the Brick Factory: Early Soviet Popular Music and Its Critics." *Slavic Review* 39, no. 3: 373–388.

Schwarz, Boris. 1972. *Music and Musical Life in Soviet Russia 1917–1970*. London: Barrie Jenkins.

Taruskin, Richard. 2001. "Music's Dangers and the Case for Control." *New York Times*, December 9, 2:1.

Thram, Diane. 2006. "ZVAKWANA!—ENOUGH! Media Control and Unofficial Censorship of Music in Zimbabwe." In *Popular Music Censorship in Africa*, edited by Martin Cloonan and Mark Drewett, 71–90. London: Ashgate.

Wallis, Roger. 2006. "The Changing Structure of the Music Industry: Threats to and Opportunities for Creativity." In *Music and Manipulation: On the Social Uses and Social Control of Music*, edited by Steven Brown and Ulrik Volgsten, 287–314. New York and London: Berghahn Books.

Web Resources

ACLU: Brief Timeline on Censored Music http://www.aclu.org/free-speech/brief-timeline-censored-music

Freemuse: The World Forum on Music and Censorship www.freemuse.org
- Excellent website with links to banned musicians plus current news
- Produces free reports on various places (available as PDF download), including:
  - "A Little Bit Special: Censorship and the Gypsy Musicians of Romania," by Garth Cartwright (2001).
  - "Can You Stop the Birds from Singing: The Censorship of Music in Afghanistan" by John Baily (2001).
  - "Singing in the Echo Chamber: Music Censorship in the U.S. after September 11" by Eric Nuzum (2006).
  - "Hidden Truths: Music, Politics, and Censorship in Lukashenko's Belarus" by Lemez Lovas and Maya Medich (2007).

CHAPTER 19

SELLING SCHNITTKE
Late Soviet Censorship and the Cold War Marketplace

PETER J. SCHMELZ

"And from the very moment when they first
saw God's light, / they began to distinguish
black from white, / and they became ecstatic and hurried to declare that
this here is white, / while that is black"

—Gennadiy Aygi, from the cycle "Silence" (*Tishina*)[1]

"In the early nineties, when anyone who would be considered liberal tried to boast a history of repression."

—Masha Gessen, *Dead Again: The Russian Intelligentsia after Communism*, 71.

"It's complicated. But it's been complicated for a long time—Russian literature, that is. It's an international brand. Like Russian vodka or Kalashnikov."

—Vladimir Sorokin (2007)[2]

"With a straight face, the Soviets advised the German disk firms that 'We believe in competition. We don't like monopolies or exclusive deals.' "

—Omer Anderson, "Red Countries Lifting Curtain on Classical Product to West," *Billboard*, January 15, 1966, 56.

SOVIET censorship resists easy summary. Despite, or perhaps because of this difficulty, during the Cold War Americans and Western Europeans evinced a special fascination for the topic; they attempted to emphasize their freedom by dissecting the lack of freedom in the USSR. In a 1973 symposium report titled *The Soviet Censorship*, a typical Cold War product funded by the Radio Liberty Committee of New York and the Institute for the Study of the USSR of Munich, Germany (both in turn funded by the US government through the CIA), the chapter headings nevertheless give some sense of the vast scope of the matter and its resulting complications: "Self-Censorship," "The System of

Formal Censorship," "The Unofficial Censorship," "Censorship of Music," "Censorship in the Soviet Cinema," "Censorship and Science," and "Evading the Censor" (Dewhirst and Farrell 1973). Defining the term "censorship" proves exceedingly complicated, then and now, because of Cold War clichés, and because governmental control of the arts in the Soviet Union was fundamentally paradoxical: multifaceted and one-dimensional, all-encompassing and evadable. Censorship persisted almost to the end on all levels of Soviet society, even the most personal—the internal mind of the individual—but it varied from field to field, discipline to discipline, sometimes from individual to individual. Thus censorship in the USSR needs to be very carefully and dispassionately described and delineated. No longer can it be understood in sensationalistic, Manichean terms—despite the still powerful tendency poet Gennadiy Aygi pinpoints in the first epigraph to this chapter.

The very recent nature of the post-Stalin period (from 1953 to 1991), together with the yet potent traces of the Cold War—and especially the tendency to overdramatize governmental restrictions—make untangling its peculiar censorship structures deeply problematic. Many participants from the time are still living (often bearing grudges, guilty consciences, or both), and the documentary record remains incompletely researched. Nonetheless, generalizations can be made based upon oral testimony, archival holdings, and other primary and secondary sources. Like any Soviet topic, studying musical censorship during the final decades of the USSR requires weighing multiple strands of sometimes contradictory evidence, always allowing for the fact that contradictions were part and parcel of the Soviet experience.

Rather than tackling the censorship structures of post-Stalin Soviet music wholesale, the present chapter focuses on composer Alfred Schnittke (1934–1998); his own ongoing, evolving interactions with Soviet political and aesthetic strictures; and the representation and interpretation of those interactions abroad, particularly in the United States and the United Kingdom. The choice is not random: Schnittke serves as an ideal case study for the increasingly complex, globalized musical economy in which late Soviet censorship played such a prominent role, especially during the final decades of the Cold War, and after. Although the history traced below is very recent, enough time has passed that it has become strangely unfamiliar. Its multiple changes—political, social, geographic, and technological—reward historically informed reexamination.

Schnittke and his advocates often highlighted his travails under the Soviet regime. In the early 1990s, just after the collapse of the USSR, a *New York Times* reporter quoted Schnittke as saying, "I have long suffered in Russia because I have not one drop of Russian blood." In the same article, cellist Mstislav Rostropovich more colorfully "suggested that Mr. Schnittke's case was 'like a dog: if you always beat a dog, he is not coming back to the place where he was beaten. In Moscow all of Schnittke's life, they beat him'" (Rockwell 1992). Schnittke, like many of his colleagues and many of his fellow citizens, undeniably suffered greatly under the Soviet system in ways difficult for outsiders to comprehend. Nevertheless, Rostropovich exaggerates.

By the time this article appeared in 1992, the occasion being the world premiere of Schnittke's opera *Life with an Idiot* (*Zhizn' s idiotom*) at the Netherlands Opera, Schnittke resided in Hamburg, Germany, and was being celebrated and honored around the world. Listeners scrutinized his works, and especially *Life with an Idiot*, hoping to descry Russian intentions immediately after the collapse of the Soviet Union. In an important 1992 appraisal of the composer, critic Alex Ross observed, "Schnittke has become wildly trendy," and also noted what he called the "current Western cult of Schnittke." "Audiences . . . listen to [Schnittke] eager for clues to the Russian enigma, and in that respect they are not disappointed" (Ross 1992; also Larner 1989). Ross was not alone. Claire Polin also called Schnittke "perhaps a seer for our day," declaring, "he remains, too, a representative of the current Russian condition" (Polin 1994, 14). As we shall see, the sentiment that Schnittke remained iconicly Russian, while also symbolizing a more general, worldwide moment, became a critical commonplace in the early 1990s.

The anxious interest in the "Russian enigma" that Ross, Polin, and others convey was provoked by the collapse of the USSR and the end of the Cold War. But the interest had emerged while the Cold War was still raging. Richard Taruskin underscores the role that the conflict played in spurring Schnittke's Western reception, pointing out that the "Shostakovich debates, and Schnittke's special status among his contemporaries, were perhaps the last musical symptoms of the cold war" (Taruskin 2005, 5:471). Censorship played a key part, as a sense of redressing Soviet wrongs fueled the Western interest in Schnittke. Pianist Vladimir Feltsman, famously blocked from emigrating from the USSR for eight years, observes, "The fact that many non-conformist artists had difficult times with authorities and had been accused of formalism, modernism, cosmopolitism, and other 'mortal sins,' was very helpful for the development of their reputations and careers in the west. Let's not forget—it was a Cold War" (Feltsman 2003).

We may combine Taruskin's and Feltsman's observations and take them a step further: censorship, Shostakovich, and the Cold War formed the interconnected foundation of the Schnittke "brand." The term "brand" is not chosen lightly. Russian music, like the Russian literature that controversial author Vladimir Sorokin describes in the epigraph above, has long been a potent brand, and Schnittke acted as a powerful, contemporary reinvention of that brand.[3] By the early 1990s, Schnittke had become a prominent—prestigious, if not notorious—musical name, whose multiple connotations were interlaced with continuing Cold War anxieties. By the mid-1990s he had become the most recorded of contemporary composers; he also was, as critic Michael Walsh summarized, "against all odds . . . among the most commissioned of living composers" (Bambarger 1998; Moore 1994; Walsh 1994).

Perhaps surprisingly, as Ross and Polin indicate, the Cold War helped Schnittke even after it ended. While the conflict threatened to lose its relevance for popular culture, and Hollywood filmmakers looked elsewhere for stock villains, Schnittke's relevance and repute continued to mount. Although the censorship of Schnittke's music in the USSR had effectively ended by the late 1980s, censorship proved central to his Western image well into the 1990s, even up to (and after) his death in 1998. The Western (American and European) romanticized conception of life behind the Iron Curtain was founded on the myth of the suffering, dissenting artist and its aesthetic corollary, summarized by Taruskin, that "the better Soviet artists were dissident in direct proportion to their perceived artistic standing" (Taruskin 2005, 470–471). The better the artist, the more dissident he must be (and vice versa). Such skewed logic fueled the resurgence of interest in Shostakovich following the 1979 American publication of his fraudulent memoirs, which purported to reveal his lifelong, closet opposition to the Soviet regime (Volkov 1979). The myth of the suffering artist also drove the Western response to Schnittke and, indeed, the Western reception of all postwar Soviet "avant-garde" (or "unofficial") music.

Taruskin (2005, 464) further observes that "a romantic aura of martyrdom" suffused discussions of Schnittke in the late 1980s and throughout the 1990s. Much of these discussions were penned by sympathetic Russians, like his biographer Alexander Ivashkin, who writes:

> For many years in the 1970s and 80s Schnittke's music was the most sincere and expressive language of Russian culture and Russian life, explaining or reflecting everything in a more perfect way than could any verbal language. Soviet officials somehow understood this, which was why Schnittke's music was always subject to such harsh censorship. (Ivashkin 1996, 169)

These seemingly credible reports were repeated and amplified in the many obituaries for the composer that appeared in widely distributed American and British publications following his death in August 1998, as in *Billboard*: "Schnittke's progressive, provocative mix of the sardonic and sincere caused his music to be officially banned in the Soviet Union for years" (Bambarger 1998). Or in *Time*: "Blacklisted by the Soviet Composer's Union for his nonconformity, Schnittke supported himself for years by writing movie scores" (Gray 1998). Or the BBC News, whose subheading blared: "Symphony banned" (Anonymous 1998b).

This chapter investigates the "harsh censorship" Schnittke was reportedly subjected to, the blacklists and the bans, as well as his "romantic aura of martyrdom" and how it came to, in Taruskin's words, "dominate reportage" both East and West during the fading twilight of the Cold War. Of particular interest are the various agents who helped Schnittke gain a worldwide following, from Gidon Kremer and the Kronos Quartet, to Nicolas Slonimsky, the Soviet copyright agency VAAP (All-Union Agency for the Protection of Authors' Rights or Vsesoyuznoye agentsvo po okhraneniye avtorskikh prav), the BIS record label, and countless critics from Russia, America, and Europe. The history below focuses on major moments and major figures in Schnittke's reception during the 1980s and 1990s. It assumes a transnational perspective—Soviet, European (especially the United Kingdom), and American—for during this period Soviet music, particularly unfamiliar Soviet music, garnered an increased presence on the world stage, transmitted on a variety of media from radio to LPs and eventually compact discs.[4] The argument, in short, traces the development of Schnittke's "brand": how Schnittke's censorship (actual and imagined) translated into prominence, and ultimately prestige, with its accompanying markers, monetary and otherwise, including performances, recordings, commissions, festivals, and prizes. In some respects, this survey is preliminary: many of the detailed financial ramifications of the branding—commission rates and other such details—remain confidential. Yet long overdue is an assessment of Schnittke's exceptional position among contemporary composers in the late 1980s and into the 1990s and its implications, both financial and otherwise.

Finally, this discussion develops a larger turn within musicology, a shifting of the spotlight from the composer and the idea of the autonomous artwork to the actors (performers, producers, impresarios, critics, and listeners) who affect how music is shaped and received, bought and sold—how reputations (and careers) are made (and sometimes unmade) (see Becker 1982; DeNora 1995; Cherednichenko 2002, 39–50; Kildea 2002; Taruskin 2005; Gelbart 2007; Thornton 2008; Jakelski 2009; Vazsonyi 2010; Piekut 2014; Schmelz 2015b). The totality of the multifaceted process is key, for no matter how artfully Schnittke crafted his music, or how steadily his agents advocated his music, ultimate success hinged upon listeners and critics willing to buy, in senses literal and metaphorical. And buy they did. What they thought they were buying and why remain to be answered. The answers to these questions reveal which aspects of Schnittke's work attracted both fame and notoriety, in the end helping to enrich our overall sense of his music and its many meanings, both past and present.

The Spectrum of Censorship: From *Nagasaki* to *Seid nüchtern und wachet* . . .

In a society in which censorship (and self-censorship) permeated all levels, one can quickly assemble a laundry list of real and perceived slights for (almost) any figure. Schnittke is no exception. Before turning to the Western reception of Schnittke, then, the composer's own interactions with the authorities must be discussed. These interactions suggest the range of censorious acts in the late Soviet period.

In the USSR censorship permeated the structures of musical dissemination from top to bottom, from the Central Committee and the Ministry of Culture; the state's primary censorship apparatus, or Glavlit (Chief Directorate for the Protection of State Secrets in the Press, Glavnoye Upravleniye po Okhrane Gosudarstvennïkh tain v Pechati); the Union of Composers; the purse strings of the Union, or Muzfond (Muzïkal'nïy fond USSR); and the various concert organizations (such as, Goskontsert, Roskontsert, Moskontsert, or the Moscow or Leningrad Philharmonics—not to be confused with the orchestras in those cities); to individual concert halls or other concert venues (Bogdanova 1995; Schwarz 1983; Schmelz 2009c). Orders were typically handed down from the highest levels of the Soviet governmental apparatus but also could be taken proactively by individuals lower in the hierarchy, attempting either to sycophantically predict what higher-ups might think or to defensively forestall or soften detrimental actions from above. The Union of Composers thus had some room to maneuver on its members' behalf (Tomoff 2006, 3 and 301; Khrennikov and Rubtsova 1994, 18). Percussionist

Mark Perkasky said, "It was a nightmare to understand where and what you could perform—it was very complicated. It would seem that the Baltic states were free, in opposition. Nothing of the sort. The leaders, wanting to gain favor with Moscow and be good, they banned on their own initiative" (Schmelz 2009c, 193). Some actions were more underhanded than others, as when lexicographer Nicolas Slonimsky attempted to contact Igor Blazhkov during a US-sponsored visit to Kiev in 1962. Slonimsky was deliberately told that the young conductor was out of town, when in fact Blazhkov had never left, but was instead eagerly awaiting Slonimsky's call (Slonimsky 2002, 217; Blazhkov 2011).

Despite the freedom of actors lower in the hierarchy, the top never completely relinquished control and could intervene whenever it chose. Alla Bogdanova writes of the decision to allow the extremely belated premiere of Shostakovich's opera *Katerina Izmailova* in 1962 (its earlier incarnation, *Lady Macbeth of the Mtsensk District*, having been banned in 1936): "Also characteristic are the strictness and detail of the phased nature of the party control over all the details of both the composition itself and also its future production on the stage" (Bogdanova 1995, 371). While total control over all the details was the aim, the results often fell far short. As we will see, the competing bureaucratic bodies meant that numerous loopholes existed. Consequently, by the late 1960s, and into the 1970s and 1980s, the situation had become very fluid. Instead of a monolithic system, censorship in the USSR must be understood in a much wider sense, on a continuum ranging from top-down dictates to acts undertaken without direct command from above; from outright bans to smaller, still annoying interventions. The blunt term censorship fails to capture the entire spectrum of artistic control in the USSR.

Schnittke's conservatory composition *Nagasaki* serves as a prime example of the contradictions within the Soviet censorship apparatus and within the Soviet bureaucracy more generally. Initially the work was criticized rather severely by the Union of Composers. In fact, subsequent accounts of Schnittke's life often recount this episode as the beginning of his suffering (e.g., Anderson 1998; Anonymous 1998a). Yet not long after the work was revised by Schnittke it was recommended, with Shostakovich's blessing, for recording by Moscow Radio. *Nagasaki* was subsequently broadcast both domestically and abroad (in Japan) to mark the occasion of the 15th anniversary of the atomic bombing of Hiroshima (Schmelz 2009a). Tapes were also officially disseminated. In an undated letter to Blazhkov, likely from the early 1960s, West German music writer Fred Prieberg (1928–2010) stated: "In exceptional cases the Composers Union is of assistance; for instance, they sent a tape copy of Schnitges [sic] 'Nagasaki' not regarding the fact that this composition had to undergo strong criticism and cannot be classified" (original in English) (See also Schmelz 2015a, 206).

"Blacklist" is a misnomer. It seems there was never any explicit order prohibiting the performance of all Schnittke's works. Rather, decisions were made on a case by case basis, depending upon the venue, occasion, and performers, among other factors. Schnittke never obtained a number of domestic performances comparable to such successful Soviet composers from his generation as Rodion Shchedrin, nor was he allowed to travel abroad with any frequency. Nonetheless, his music was heard, both at home and abroad, especially near the end of the 1960s and into the 1970s. He even received favorable reviews in *Sovetskaya muzïka* for his Second Violin Sonata, "Quasi una Sonata," and his First String Quartet, among other compositions. The First Quartet in particular received a number of auditions in the late 1960s thanks to its dedicatees, the Borodin Quartet (Schmelz 2002, 391–396). Valentin Berlinsky, the group's cellist, recalled that Schnittke "was an odious name, a name that was often pronounced abusively at the Congresses of the Union of Composers," but that the Borodin Quartet encountered no real problems when they wanted to play Schnittke's composition. "There were no difficulties," Berlinsky remembered, "Only there were recommendations ... that maybe you shouldn't [play it], but all the same we did what we wanted to do" (Schmelz 2002, 394). The Borodin Quartet even recorded Schnittke's work, and it subsequently appeared on the 1970 (rereleased 1976) Melodiya-Ariola-Eurodisc LP set *Contemporary Composers in the USSR*, alongside his Violin Concerto no. 2 and Piano Sonata no. 1.

Despite the number of performances Schnittke enjoyed in the late 1960s, we must be wary of supporting long-time Union of Composers leader Tikhon Khrennikov's disingenuous contention that "no-one censored [avant-garde composers], they were simply performed less than other composers" (Khrennikov 2000, 255). When Kremer tried to perform one of Schnittke's violin sonatas (likely no. 2) in Riga after he won the 1970 Tchaikovsky Competition, he received a telegram that bluntly read: "Schnittke doesn't suit us. Play Beethoven instead" (Dyer 1992).

Cellist Mstislav Rostropovich, in many respects a poster-child for Soviet repression and control, suggested the vagaries of Soviet censorship in his famous October 31, 1970, "open letter" to *Pravda* and three other Soviet papers: "In 1948 there were lists of banned works. Today verbal bans are preferred, in the form of suggestions that 'an opinion exists, stating that such and such is not recommended....' But it is impossible to ascertain from whom that OPINION originates" (quoted in Wilson 2008, 355–356). Rostropovich's exasperation stemmed primarily from the apparent capriciousness of the censoring. At the time he wrote the letter in the early 1970s, there evidently were no lists of banned works. Rather, opinions circulated on all levels of the system, occasionally fueled by more specific directives.

A case in point: Under the auspices of the Leningrad Philharmonic concert organization during the mid- to late 1960s, the transplanted Ukrainian conductor Blazhkov and other sympathetic musicians and administrators often performed more difficult works, including Andrey Volkonsky's *Suite of Mirrors* and Edison Denisov's *Sun of the Incas* and *Laments*. Both Blazhkov and the head of the Small Glinka Hall, Irina Nikolayevna Semyonova, were fundamental in arranging these concerts (Schmelz 2009c, 198; Blazhkov 2009a). Ultimately, higher authorities were unable to continue ignoring them. The final straw seems to have been an overly ambitious May 6, 1968, concert featuring works by Luigi Nono (*Polifonia-monodia-ritmica*), Arnold Schoenberg (Three Small Pieces for Chamber Orchestra [1910]), Anton Webern (Five Pieces for Orchestra, op. 10), and Edison Denisov (*Laments*).

After an informant reportedly approached the Ministry of Culture, a document was prepared on June 20, 1968, by the Directorate of Musical Institutions of the Ministry of Culture USSR (Upravleniya muzïkal'nïkh uchrezhdeniy Ministerstva kul'turï SSSR), then headed by Zaven Gevondovich Vartanyan (1907–1974). Titled "On insufficiencies in the repertoire of the Leningrad Philharmonic" (*O nedostatkakh repertuara Leningradskoy filarmonii*), this document declared that the "Philharmonic's propaganda of works by representatives of the Western musical 'avant-garde' and their followers among Soviet composers deserves the most serious criticism," before rattling off a list of taboo music that had been included on programs in Leningrad from 1966 to 1968, among them "formalistic, decadent works by P. Boulez, A. Schoenberg, Ch. Ives, E. Varèse, K. Penderecki, and also E. Denisov, V. Silvestrov, A. Volkonsky, and the most scholastic, formalistic works of A. Schnittke." (The compositions by Schnittke in question included the Music for Piano and Chamber Orchestra [November 9, 1966] and the String Quartet no. 1 [January 13, 1968].) Vartanyan also singled out Blazhkov's conducting and other activities on behalf of both the Western and Soviet avant-gardes.

A decree that responded and acted upon these charges quickly followed from the Ministry of Culture, signed by Yekaterina Furtseva on June 21, 1968. Blazhkov was dismissed as part of the subsequent shakeup; he ultimately returned to a conducting post in Kiev (see also Schmelz 2015a, 212–213). In the aftermath, First Deputy Minister of Culture of the USSR, the musicologist Vasiliy Kukharsky (b. 1918), produced a *Sovetskaya muzïka* article borrowing the language from the original report but heightening its rhetoric. Kukharsky fumed at Blazhkov and concluded with a warning:

> I want to underscore that government organs of culture will reject the aggressive attempts of devotees of the avant-garde to break through to a wider concert stage, to occupy a constant place there. No one, neither organizationally nor materially, intends to support the sickly sweet imitations of "avant-gardism," its decadent aesthetic norms and technological regulations, its antisocialism. (Kukharskiy 1968, 7)

The specific decree resulted in a vague yet threatening command from a Soviet arts official that further fueled the "opinions" Rostropovich found so vexing. Caryl Emerson aptly observes that "in Russia's ideologically weary society of the 1960s, where censorship was as much a matter of inertia as of positive control over content, the setting of an official precedent ... was ... the crucial first step" (Emerson 1997, 91).

Such warnings, such setting of official precedent, occurred periodically throughout the 1960s and into the 1970s and later, but Soviet officials grew more tolerant of new music. Willing parties—arts officials, concert hall managers, performers, and composers—found ways to work within and around the system. A key example, and a turning point in Schnittke's own career, was the premiere of his First Symphony in February 1974 in the closed city of Gorky. This concert received approval from the highest levels, with Russian Union of Composers head Rodion Shchedrin's go-ahead itself scrutinized by officials in the Central Committee (Schmelz 2009c, 304). The decision to allow the performance came as a revelation to Schnittke. He concluded in a mid-1970s interview "that no kind of total conspiracy against me existed in secret circles.... There were also people, who if they wanted something done, then it was wonderfully carried out." In the same interview, Schnittke also noted that several works by such supposedly "banned" composers as Volkonsky, Denisov, and Sofia Gubaidulina were published by the official Sovetskiy kompozitor publishing house in the 1970s. "Because that was possible," he said, "it indicates that no one ever gave any kinds of central directives about this matter" (Schmelz 2009c, 189–190).

In his December 1983 memoir of the 1960s and 1970s, artist Il'ya Kabakov includes what he calls a "graph of hope and fear." According to this graph, "fear" rose gradually from 1957, peaking in 1974 before falling precipitously from 1974 to 1976, slowly rising again until 1983. "Hope," in contrast, rose sharply from 1957 to 1963, when it collapsed immediately, only very gradually rising from 1963 to 1983, because, in Kabakov's words, "as it seems to me, they [hopes] were always equal to zero" (Kabakov 2008, 86). Kabakov's primary references are the visual arts, namely the Manezh exhibition of late 1963, and the so-called "bulldozer exhibition" of 1974, but his general impressions of "hope" and "fear" from the late 1950s to the early 1980s are instructive for our understanding of government control of all the arts during this period and immediately after, into *perestroika* and the eventual end of the Soviet system.

The key factor is the stability (both perceived and actual) that emerged in the mid-1970s, most evident in Kabakov's sense of the leveling off of fear. As he put it, "but then fear was a bit less, or more truthfully, it remained exactly the same, but the impression was created that they would let 'unofficial artists' remain 'as they were' until an undetermined time" (Kabakov 2008, 86). Isolated, exceptional moments, such as the two art exhibitions that Kabakov singles out, drew much attention, and, as with the Manezh exhibition or the premiere of Schnittke's First Symphony, often involved the highest levels of the Soviet bureaucracy. But on a day to day basis, the unofficial artists, composers, and performers were allowed to remain more or less "as they were," with freedoms haltingly emerging—and sometimes fading—as the 1970s passed into the 1980s. Pianist Aleksey Lyubimov confidently summarized the situation:

> [The officials] understood that it was impossible to settle with that [new music], that it was going forward and it was impossible to ban everything. Therefore they didn't ban it, they limited it: only in some institutes or in some kinds of proportions. For example, it was impossible to perform an entire concert of Schoenberg, but two or three things were possible (Schmelz 2009c, 194).

"All in all," he observed, "situations were always found when it was possible to play any composition. As a rule you did it once or twice. In my concerts across the country I could play some kinds of pieces many times, but not often large pieces for ensembles" (Schmelz 2009c, 207).

Over the 1970s, Schnittke's reputation slowly grew, abetted by a softening in his style witnessed in works such as the Piano Quintet (1976). At the same time, anecdotal and archival evidence reveals that Schnittke's name continued to raise eyebrows among officials. It helped motivate the closing of the electronic music studio in the Scriabin House-Museum in Moscow in the mid-1970s. An official communication noted that the studio had attracted a "narrow group of composers (Schnittke, Gubaidulina, Denisov and others)." A Melodiya administrator reacted negatively to a proposed LP of electronic compositions, reportedly declaring, "Since Schnittke's name is there I won't even listen to it!" "I know that all concert organizations were warned not to include performances of [Schnittke's, Gubaidulina's, and Denisov's] music in their repertoire," composer Stanislav Kreichi recalled, "even if a well-known performer wanted to play it" (Schmelz 2009b, 269).

Although suspect for internal release, Melodiya found Schnittke suitable for export. His music appeared with some regularity on LPs released under a joint agreement with Ariola-Eurodisc, among them the 1970/1976 recording featuring the Borodin Quartet playing his string quartet. Many featured violinist Gidon Kremer, including three recorded in 1977 (not long after the closing of the Scriabin studio): a set of violin duos with Kremer and his former wife Tatyana Grindenko, containing Schnittke's "Moz-Art"; a pairing of Mahler's Piano Quartet in A minor with Schnittke's Piano Quintet (Yuriy Bashmet, Grindenko, and Aleksey Lyubimov also appeared on this LP); and a release of Sibelius's Violin Concerto alongside Schnittke's First Concerto Grosso, this last presenting Kremer and Gindenko as soloists with the London Symphony conducted by Gennadiy Rozhdestvensky (Kremer 2003, 228–229; Kremer 2006, 481–482). The Sibelius record turned more than a few Americans on to Schnittke (Sachs 2009; Rhein 1979).

The agreement between Melodiya and Eurodisc had been negotiated and signed in 1965 (the year after Melodiya's founding), and quickly turned into a very profitable venture for Eurodisc—and presumably for Melodiya as well. A 1966 article declared, "The Melodia magic has rubbed off on the entire Ariola Eurodisc repertoire" (Anderson 1966). By late 1974, the catalog held two hundred albums in a variety of genres: "symphonic music, concertos, chamber music, opera and folklore" (*Billboard* 1974). This successful collaboration also set the stage for similar agreements between Melodiya and other foreign record labels, including with Capitol in the United States (signed in 1966).

A major brouhaha erupted in the Soviet press in March 1978 over a planned staging of Chaikovsky's *Queen of Spades* to be directed in Paris by the renowned Taganka Theater head Yuriy Lyubimov, with new entr'actes composed by Schnittke. But Schnittke did not long suffer: both his foreign and domestic careers were just taking off. A year later (1979) matters had relaxed enough that Schnittke's name was absent from a key speech critical of leading avant-garde Soviet musical figures delivered by Khrennikov, although at the time Schnittke reported that his "relations with Khrennikov are strained" (Schwarz 1983, 631 and 623–626).

By the end of the 1970s, despite Kreichi's recollection above, well-known performers were able to program Schnittke's music with some success, even in larger venues in Moscow. Violinist Oleh Krysa (b. 1942) recalled that in the late 1970s and early 1980s concerts of Schnittke's music were "not officially difficult [to arrange], not officially prohibited. But the officials often tried to stop such concerts, or tried to make it more difficult to perform. Sometimes he was in trouble. But any time a new piece appeared, it sold out immediately." He added, "Everything became easier with Gorbachev, of course" (Krysa 2010).[5]

Kremer proved a powerful champion, launching Schnittke's international recording presence with a series of LPs pairing Schnittke's music with that of well-known composers such as Mahler, Beethoven, Paganini, and Stravinsky. These included the Melodiya exports mentioned above but also extended to deals with Philips and Eurodisc alone (Kremer 2003, 226–27). Sometime after 1977, VAAP even produced a brochure for distribution touting Schnittke's music in glowing terms, complete with quotations from *Sovetskaya muzïka* and other official publications (**see example 19.1**). Nonetheless, until the early 1980s, VAAP often impeded efforts to perform his compositions. As Joel Sachs recalled, it often succeeded in "just being obstructive" when approached by Westerners about obtaining performing materials (Sachs 2009; also Huckerby 1980).

In 1980 Schnittke apparently refused to join the Secretariat of the Union of Composers, although he had become a member of its Board (Pravleniye) the previous year. Khrennikov reportedly retaliated by preventing him from traveling to several foreign performances of his music, with the 1981 premiere of his Third Symphony in Leipzig, East Germany, the notable exception (Ivashkin 1996, 162–164). Even so, Schnittke's unique, "protected" position among his cohort became part of the conventional wisdom, at least among foreign observers. In a 1981 article American historian Harlow Robinson remarked that the "rather Mephistophelean Mr. Shnitke" was the "composer of the avant-garde most palatable to the official Soviet musical establishment" (Robinson 1981; Rhein 1982).[6] In 1982 Schnittke, Denisov, and Gubaidulina even achieved a landmark performance at the Large Hall of the Moscow Conservatory (on April 15) and a subsequent release of a live recording of the concert in a 3-LP Melodiya boxed set, both clear markers of their official acceptance.

The previous year a detailed, sympathetic profile of Schnittke appeared at long last in *Sovetskaya muzïka*, albeit not without some behind-the-scenes hassles (Savenko 1981). Svetlana Savenko, the musicologist who authored the profile, explains the situation:

> Of course, by 1981 Schnittke was, as before, under suspicion: For the Secretariat of the Union of Composers and, it follows, for Soviet power he was foreign, "not one of us" ["ne nashiy"], his compositions were performed almost exclusively thanks to musicians, the most important of whom was Kremer... The situation changed radically only during the time of Gorbachev, by the end of the 1980s.

"You may ask," Savenko continues, "How then did the very commission for an article profiling him arise if Schnittke continued to remain 'objectionable'?" Her answer reveals much about the vicissitudes of Soviet power in the early 1980s:

> The times had nonetheless changed, Schnittke's (unofficial) authority was already very great, and the "top" already had begun to play up to Schnittke, and in 1979 they even selected him to be on the Board ["Pravleniye"] of the Union of Composers

EXAMPLE 19.1. Schnittke VAAP Brochure, late 1970s. Box 228, Folder 72 (Biographical Materials: Schnittke, Alfred), Nicolas Slonimsky Collection, Music Division, Library of Congress, Washington, D.C.

USSR.[7] That was a sign for the leaders of the journal: a profile has been proposed for a member of the Board, the hierarchy was clear. But to somehow praise him was still impossible! Yes, such are Soviet dialectics (Savenko 2011).

Schnittke's achievements and recognition notwithstanding, obstacles still arose. "Soviet dialectics" still held sway. In Spring 1983, conductor Gennadiy Rozhdestvensky attempted to schedule the world premiere of Schnittke's Faust cantata, *Seid nüchtern und wachet . . .* based not on Goethe, but on the Faust story of Johann Spies from 1587. According to Rozhdestvensky, the Moscow Philharmonic had flexibility in determining its programs, but this came at a cost:

> The possibilities that the Moscow Philharmonic would include or exclude this or that composition from its schedule were unbounded. At the same time, it was possible for several symphonic concerts at the Large Hall of the Conservatory to be canceled thanks to the sudden appearance of an "order from above" introducing a (ten-day) festival ["dekada"] of the art of the republic of Tuva or something of the sort (Rozhdestvenskiy 2001, 188).

By the early 1980s censorship had relaxed but remained extremely unpredictable.

Rozhdestvensky noted that the "first official ban"—the prohibition on performing Schnittke's cantata—came over the phone on May 20, 1983, mere days before the scheduled concert on May 24. This was not a complete surprise. Conductor Valeriy Polyansky recalls that Rozhdestvensky had already warned him of problems with the hall before the very first rehearsal with Alla Pugachova, the Soviet pop diva originally meant to sing the role of Mephistopheles. After this rehearsal, Rozhdestvensky informed the musicians, "it was the first and last rehearsal: there won't be a concert; it was forbidden by the powers that be" (Polyanskiy 2003, 259).[8] In the call informing Rozhdestvensky of this decision, the director of the Moscow Philharmonic, a man with the ironic name (given the circumstances) Avangard (i.e., "Avant-garde," or "vanguard," meant in the sense of Soviet sloganeering) Alekseyevich Fedotov, claimed, among other things, that the cantata's text was too "mystical" ("misticheskiy"). (Rozhdestvensky quipped that his parents should have named him "Arrière-garde" [Rozhdestvenskiy 2001, 194].) The texts proved so dangerous in fact that Polyansky was told by the director of printing at the Ministry of Culture that "your programs have been confiscated [arestovanï] by the KGB, and they must be destroyed" (Polyanskiy 2003, 259).

There were apparently few written communications concerning the cancellation. "The bosses did not like sending letters. Why? A printed document might turn out to be dangerous," Rozhdestvensky observed. "Better to call on the telephone." Fedotov's rejection stunned Rozhdestvensky because the work already had been approved by the Presidium of the Board of the Moscow organization of the Russian Union of Composers at the request of another bureaucrat within the Moscow Philharmonic organization, S. I. Bodrenkov. The Presidium's chairman Boris Terent'yev (1913–1989) declared that the Union of Composers "did not object to its performance, especially since this work was completed by a talented and capable author and presents artistic interest." The cantata also had been vetted independently by the Purchasing Commission of the Ministry of Culture of the USSR (Zakupochnoy komissii Ministerstva kul'turï SSSR), which in April had authorized VAAP "at last, after countless requests from the Austrians" (Rozhdestvensky's words) to send the score to Vienna for performance and publication by Universal Edition. Yet Fedotov had company. Strangely, on May 20 one of VAAP's bureaucrats apparently received a "dressing down" (*mïlil sheyu*) from Yuriy Konstantinovich Kurpekov, the head of the Section on Music in the Central Committee, for sending the Schnittke score to Universal Edition. The VAAP bureaucrat responded by presenting Kurpekov the letter of support from the Purchasing Commission of the Ministry of Culture. Not so easily swayed, Fedotov dug in his heels. During another phone call, he refused to acknowledge the approval of the Union of Composers, telling Rozhdestvensky: "I don't take orders from the Union of Composers. Let them play the cantata at the Moscow Autumn festival, it's an experimental festival!" (Rozhdestvenskiy 2001, 189). The cantata was indeed performed at this festival later that year on October 23, 1983, although problems still arose: a specific mention of Heaven and God in the text needed to be excised (Ivashkin 1996, 179–180; Polyanskiy 2003, 262). The world premiere occurred in Vienna on June 19, 1983 (Foulds 1983). (Schnittke later incorporated it as the third act of his opera *Istoriya Doktora Ioganna Fausta*, completed just over a decade later in 1994.)

This rather confusing sequence of events reveals Schnittke's prominence at the time, but also suggests the convoluted bureaucracy affecting programming decisions. Rozhdestvensky's and Polyansky's accounts involve the conductor, the composer, the Moscow Philharmonic (the concert organization), the Russian Union of Composers, various departments within the Ministry of Culture of the USSR, VAAP, and the Section on Music of the Central Committee, all acting with some independence and their own (sometimes disputed) sense of their position in the hierarchy of power and control. In the end, the incident demonstrates both the excessive subservience paid to the decisions made at the "top" of this hierarchy, and the related (sometimes excessive) reluctance of those lower down to make potentially controversial decisions, even in the absence of explicit directives—or despite positive ones. Furthermore, the entire process was extremely underhanded: Fedotov alleged that his call about the cantata's cancellation came so late because he did not have Rozhdestvensky's telephone number. Meanwhile, he claimed in writing that the cantata could not be performed for technical reasons: Schnittke had not followed proper procedures for auditioning and scheduling. Such frustrations were numerous, leading Rozhdestvensky to exclaim: "And people always ask me, 'Why did Schnittke have four strokes?'" (Rozhdestvenskiy 2001, 195).

Maintaining his increasingly multinational career became easier for Schnittke once travel restrictions were lifted following Gorbachev's rise to power in 1985. (His first, near-fatal stroke in late July 1985 thus came at a particularly inopportune time.) Yet now that overt censorship had all but ceased, the petty rivalries and jockeying for position that had always characterized the Union of Composers rose to the forefront (Tomoff

2006, 268–299). Schnittke and his close associates found them particularly chafing, given his worldwide recognition near the end of the Soviet period. He might have been able to travel, but his jealous overseers refused to provide him the respect his status had led him to expect. Previous disputes over canceled concerts or prohibited travel turned into complaints over a lack of first-class seats on aircraft and his unsatisfactory housing (Ivashkin 1996, 196; Larner 1989).

Nevertheless, by this point governmental restrictions had weakened, and, in fact, Schnittke received a Russian State Prize in 1986. Although perhaps more indicative of American than Soviet attitudes, he also was among the 125 guests invited to the so-called reciprocal dinner held on May 31, 1988, at the US ambassador's home in Moscow in conjunction with the Reagan-Gorbachev summit. Reportedly he sat at the same table as Gorbachev, a report partially corroborated by the proposed seating chart (McBurney 1988; Crist 2009, 169–171; Crist 2011). (Among the others listed at the table were Nancy Reagan, Senator Robert Dole, and the well-known writers Andrey Voznesensky and Tatyana Tolstaya.) "The situation in the Soviet Union is much better now than it was 15 years ago," Schnittke told an American critic in 1988. "These days my work is performed quite frequently, and by our best musicians. I can't complain" (Kozinn 1988).

Official recognition (by either American or Soviet authorities) mattered little, for now Schnittke became more or less an independent operator. In 1988 he began efforts to quit the increasingly antiquated VAAP, reasoning that he could make more money by joining a German equivalent, GEMA (Society for Musical Performing and Mechanical Reproduction Rights, Gesellschaft für musikalische Aufführungs- und mechanische Vervielfältigungsrechte) (Ivashkin 1996, 196). VAAP usually commanded a large share of royalties; novelist Anatoliy Rybnikov's agreement to publish *Children of the Arbat* in English ceded 20 percent of his compensation to the agency (Dudar 1988; Muravina 1991, 427–428). Schnittke officially joined GEMA only on January 1, 1990 as VAAP's monopoly officially began to erode (Kusterer 2011; Duffek 2011; Muravina 1991; Elst 2004, 359–361).[9] Rozhdestvensky conducted a complete survey of Schnittke's symphonies in Moscow in 1990, receiving glowing press and inspiring discussions of the "Schnittke phenomenon" (Pantiyelev 1990, 81). Yet after being awarded a fellowship in 1989 to live in West Berlin for a year, the composer became a resident of Germany in Autumn 1990, leaving the Soviet censorship behind for the freedoms and rewards of the West.

Marketing Censorship

Schnittke's improving fortunes in the USSR form only one part of the story; how Western listeners framed those fortunes, the other. From the start censorship pervaded the Western familiarization with Soviet "avant-garde" music, as it was frequently called. One of the earliest performances of a composition by an "unofficial" Soviet composer became itself, in a sense, censored. On March 13, 1964, at an International Society for

Contemporary Music concert at the New School in New York, pianist Paul Jacobs performed a Soviet twelve-tone composition whose author was deliberately kept anonymous. The program listed only: Suite for Piano (1961) by a "Contemporary Soviet 12-tone composer (Name withheld)." (**See example 9.2.**) "The atmosphere [was] definitely cloak and dagger," critic Theodore Strongin recalled three years later. "Even the pianist, Paul Jacobs, didn't know the composer's name. The composer had to be protected. He had written his piece in the 12-tone technique, a system too avant-garde to be accepted by the Establishment in the Soviet Union" (Strongin 1967). The "piece" in question drew from Ukrainian composer Valentin Silvestrov's *5 Pieces* and *4 Signs* (5 p'es and 4 znaka), composed in 1961 (Paul Jacobs Collection; Schwarz 1983, 487n and 442). Previously Volkonsky's *Musica Stricta* was considered to be the first Soviet twelve-tone composition performed in the United States; but Jacobs' performance of Silvestrov's music occurred two years earlier (Taubman 1966).

Cloak-and-dagger elements affected the American and European reception of Soviet music for some time. The transmission of information—scores and recordings primarily—was greatly aided by a series of visitors to the USSR, among them the American Joel Spiegelman who studied from late 1965 through early 1966 at the Gnesin Institute in Moscow; he returned with "17 advanced scores" (Taubman's words 1966; Spiegelman 2009). Other visitors used the diplomatic pouch or their diplomatic contacts at the US Embassy to secrete scores. Conductor Joel Sachs obtained a cache of music from an individual with diplomatic contacts who was living in Moscow in the late 1970s. This individual (who surprisingly still wishes to remain anonymous) had befriended Schnittke, Gubaidulina, Pärt, and several Ukrainian composers (including Silvestrov), and was able to take many of their scores and recordings to the United States (Sachs 2009; Rhein 1982). Sometimes the smuggling went in the opposite direction. A Symposium on Soviet Avant-Garde Music was held February 20–21, 1967, at Indiana University, Bloomington. One of the participants, Richard Cameron-Wolfe (later on the faculty of SUNY–Purchase), recalled in 1989, "we performed several pieces and the recordings were smuggled back into the Soviet Union, and the composers [including Schnittke and Denisov] had an opportunity to hear their music" (Greene 1989).

Even visitors from closer to the USSR had to be wary. Conductor Kurt Masur, a resident of Leipzig, East Germany, visited Schnittke in the mid-1970s to offer a commission commemorating the new Gewandhaus. According to Masur, Schnittke "advised me, first come at midnight because we probably won't be observed." When Masur returned to East Germany, he discovered that they had been observed after all: "Consequently, then Minister of Culture of the GDR, Hans-Joachim Hoffmann [1929–1994], summoned me to Berlin and needed to reprimand me: 'It has been established that you have met with the dissident Schnittke'" (Forner 2002, 215). Yet once Hoffmann had ascertained the reason for Masur's visit to the "dissident" composer, everything was settled. Schnittke even attended the premiere of the resulting commission, his Third Symphony (see also Yaeger 2013).

Schnittke largely required others to disseminate and propagandize his music. This differs from a composer such as Benjamin Britten, who, as Paul Kildea has demonstrated,

THE INTERNATIONAL SOCIETY FOR CONTEMPORARY MUSIC

in collaboration with

THE NEW SCHOOL FOR SOCIAL RESEARCH

presents

a concert of chamber music

PROGRAM

**STRING QUARTET (1962) . . . . PETER MAXWELL DAVIES

FRANKLIN STRING QUARTET
Joseph Schor, violin   Jacob Glick, viola
Ernestine Briesmeister, violin   Donald Anderson, cello

FOUR SONGS, OP. 12 (1917)
FIVE CANONS ON LATIN TEXTS, OP.16 (1924)
THREE SONGS, OP.25 (1934) . . . . ANTON WEBERN

BETHANY BEARDSLEE, soprano
ROBERT HELPS, piano
ARTHUR BLOOM, clarinet
STANLEY WALDEN, bass clarinet

**THIRD STRING QUARTET (1920) . . . . NICOLAS ROSLAVETZ

FRANKLIN STRING QUARTET

INTERMISSION

**SUITE FOR PIANO (1961) . . . . Contemporary Soviet 12-tone composer
(Name withheld)

PAUL JACOBS, piano

***VARIANTS FOR SOLO CLARINET (1963) . . . . WILLIAM O. SMITH

Performed by the composer

TRIO FOR FLUTE, CELLO & PIANO (1963) . . . . . . CHARLES WUORINEN

HARVEY SOLLBERGER, flute
ROBERT MARTIN, cello
CHARLES WUORINEN, piano

***COMPOSITION FOR NINE INSTRUMENTS (1961) . . . . ROBERT TAYLOR

CONTEMPORARY CHAMBER ENSEMBLE
ARTUR WEISBERG, conductor

**First American performance
***First performance anywhere   Admission -- $2.50 (Students - $1.25)

NEW SCHOOL AUDITORIUM
66 West 12th Street
FRIDAY EVENING, MARCH 13, 1964, at 8:30 P.M.

NEXT CONCERT -- Friday, April 17, 1964
NEW YORK WOODWIND QUINTET plays SCHOENBERG * LEEDY * PISTON * BLACKWOOD

EXAMPLE 19.2 Program for March 13, 1964 ISCM concert at the New School for Social Research. New York Public Library, Paul Jacobs Collection.

EXAMPLE 19.3 Alfred Schnittke discography sent to Nicolas Slonimsky, 1982 or 1983. Box 228, Folder 72 (Biographical Materials: Schnittke, Alfred), Nicolas Slonimsky Collection, Music Division, Library of Congress, Washington, D.C.

"was involved in these new market articulators from their beginnings—often influencing their shape and potency" (Kildea 2002, 4). Schnittke played a more subsidiary role in the propagandizing of his own music, at least until the late 1980s. He certainly provided information about himself to Westerners (or had it sent through associates), as he did a work-list and discography to Nicolas Slonimsky in 1982 or 1983 (**see example 9.3**) (Slonimsky 2002, 288). Yet because of Schnittke's constrained position within the Soviet Union, he was much more indebted than Britten to performers and others pushing his music on both sides of the Iron Curtain. In some respects, he was also indebted to Soviet governmental agencies, which, as we have seen, helped disseminate his compositions via radio or through agencies such as VAAP or Melodiya.

Schnittke became most definitely marketed in the early stages of the 1980s. Censorship initially enhanced the establishment of Schnittke's "brand," lending him greater prominence and cachet. Although it is difficult (and often misleading) to attempt quantifying prestige, and although the specific economic ramifications of this marketing remain to be fully detailed, statistics can help begin tracking Schnittke's increasing prominence (Straus 1999; Shreffler 2000). The most solid indication of his rising stock came at the end of the 1980s with several notable (and sizable) prizes and commissions, among them the Austrian State Prize for European Composers (Österreichischer Staatspreis für europäische Komponisten) in 1991 (then 200,000 Austrian schillings; about $17,600), Japan's Praemium Imperiale in 1992 (then 15 million yen; about $122,000), and, the same year (the first of its existence), Russia's non-governmental "Triumph" (*Triumf*) prize, sometimes called the "Russian Nobel" (then about $50,000), which Schnittke donated to one of the institutes where he was treated for his strokes (Kretova 1993; Irina Schnittke 2011a).[10] The culmination arrived late: in 1998 he received the Gloria/Slava Award selected by Rostropovich and worth $250,000 (Zolotov 1998).

Schnittke's long string of commissions began in the late 1970s and early 1980s. In 1978 he was commissioned by Southwest German Radio to write an orchestral work, *Passacaglia* (1979–1980), for 8,000 West German Marks (about $13,000 in 2011 dollars) (Juilliard Manuscript Collection). Offers soon followed from the Leipzig Gewandhaus— Symphony no. 3—and the Salzburg Festival—*(K)ein Sommernachstraum* (commissioned in 1983, premiered in 1985). The number of commissions grew steadily, culminating with five alone in 1994: Philharmonisches Staatsorchester Hamburg for *Symphonic Prelude*; the Stockholm Concert Hall Foundation for Symphony no. 8; The Royal Liverpool Philharmonic Society for the orchestral *For Liverpool*; the International Bach Academy Stuttgart for Lux Aeterna, part of the collectively authored *Requiem of Reconciliation*; and the London Sinfonietta for a cantata that Schnittke never completed. By the early 1990s he already had more commissions than he could handle. In 1989, the Library of Congress's Elizabeth Sprague Coolidge Foundation offered Schnittke $15,000 (about $28,000 in 2011 dollars) to write a new work for piano and chamber orchestra, to be performed by the Continuum ensemble in October 1992 (LaVine 2011). Schnittke never fulfilled the commission, focusing instead on the presumably more lucrative commissions that followed immediately on its heels from the Carnegie Hall Corporation for the Cleveland Orchestra (Concerto Grosso no. 5, premiered 1991), the National Symphony and Mstislav Rostropovich (Symphony no. 6, premiered 1993), and the New York Philharmonic (Symphony no. 7, premiered 1993).[11]

These commissions mark Schnittke's transition from obscurity to accolades. But the mechanisms and ramifications of the early shaping of Schnittke's reputation, before the offers came pouring in, are most evident in the actions of two central proponents of Schnittke's music: Gidon Kremer and the Kronos Quartet. Each naturally emphasized different compositions and garnered varying reactions. These reactions point to the burgeoning image of Schnittke in the West, an image founded on dissent but touching on larger issues affecting art music in the 1980s, foremost among them the tensions between the dueling avant-gardes of the time, the friction between modernism and postmodernism. Censorship consistently formed an undercurrent. Not every critic mentioned it in every review, but, like the ubiquitous references to Schnittke as "the heir to Shostakovich," it frequently percolated to the surface.

The key incongruity remains: Schnittke's fame soared, fueled by censorship, just as censorship (and the USSR itself) vanished. Schnittke himself seems to have contributed (wittingly or not): compare the statements he made to Kozinn in 1988 ("I can't complain") and to Rockwell in 1992 ("I have long suffered in Russia") (see also Schnittke and Ivashkin 1994, 176). It would be too easy to read the first as a typically guarded instance of Soviet-speak, the second his true feelings. But both appear genuine, with the second betraying the complexities of the changing situation: Schnittke's emigration, the end of the USSR, his awareness of his growing cultural capital, and his bitterness at his belated recognition. His second statement recalls the post-Soviet "boasting" of repression in Gessen's epigraph above.

Besides Kremer and the Kronos Quartet, one important strand of reception stands out: academic interest in Soviet "new music." This interest underscored the 1967 American festivals of Soviet music at which works by Denisov, Silvestrov, Schnittke, and others were performed (Schmelz 2009c, 172). It can best be summarized by comments made by *New York Times* reporter Harold Schonberg when he visited Kiev and inquired after the local avant-garde (including composers Silvestrov, Leonid Hrabovsky, Volodymyr Zahortsev, and Vitaly Hodzyats'ky). Schonberg told the official "old-school composers" to whom he was first introduced: "We in the United States ... were familiar with their type of music, whereas the Russian avant-garde was an unknown quantity to us. That was why I was especially interested in hearing the new kind of Russian music" (Schonberg 1967, 180).

Curiosity spurred this seemingly apolitical reception, often fueled by comparing the Soviet avant-garde to other new music developments in the West. Thus a *Musical Quarterly* review of Schnittke's Music for Piano and Chamber Orchestra from the 1967 Bloomington festival spoke only of the music, judging that "his talent as a composer is unquestionable. However, one fault of great consequence emerges: he paces climaxes poorly." The review also faulted Schnittke, as many Western reviews of new Soviet music did, for being derivative: "Similar features, as well as the over-all sound, can be found in a more familiar work [!] such as Maderna's Serenata No. 2" (Brody and Oncley 1968, 91).

The new music world's infatuation with the Soviet "avant-garde" extended into the 1980s, thanks to groups such as New York's Continuum ensemble. Several landmark concerts by this organization, among them one featuring Soviet avant-garde composers (including Schnittke) and another devoted to Schnittke alone, took place in the early 1980s. The January 11, 1981, ad for the Continuum ensemble concert on January 17, 1981, says it all. Its headline asks in large bold font—"Avant-garde music from the USSR?"—only to be answered, in slightly smaller but more excited text: "A sensational revelation! Stunning music scarcely heard." The title of the concert followed: "USSR—Unveiling the Avant-garde." It featured "Major works by Schnittke & Gubaidulina; Denisov, Grabovsky, Silvestrov, Part [*sic*]."

Unexpectedly, a preview of this concert by Harlow Robinson discounted the political. "In the end," he wrote, "The music of the Soviet avant-garde will, of course, stand or fall on musical, not political, values." Robinson concluded with a similar statement by the ensemble's conductor Joel Sachs: "Our purpose is not to promote the idea of a heroic people working in the face of adversity, but simply to show the New York audience that this music is important and should enter the repertory" (Robinson 1981; also Rhein 1982). At a November 1983 Continuum concert again featuring Soviet composers (Schnittke among them), the group "argued . . . that our view of present-day Soviet composition is vague and distorted . . . . Distorted, because the image of totalitarian repression cannot explain the diversity and liveliness of the actual music being created in the Soviet Union, much of it available through official channels" (Rockwell 1983).

Such balanced, informed statements were atypical for the broader reception of new Soviet music, and especially of Schnittke's compositions. More standard were declarations such as that made by Edward Rothstein over a decade later, writing what many had been thinking for some time about both Schnittke's political stance and his debt to Shostakovich—the dissenting Shostakovich of *Testimony*: "Mr. Schnittke's music often seems to embody playful dissent, carrying on the coded opposition to official culture that Shostakovich brought to his music" (Rothstein 1993). A *Washington Post* review of the 1983 Vienna premiere of Schnittke's Faust Cantata emphasized its censorship, calling it "one of Moscow's biggest music scandals of recent years" (Foulds 1983). Stephen Pettitt, writing in the London *Times* about a 1982 performance of Schnittke's Violin Concerto no. 3, opined, "its melancholy is the cry of a nation, perhaps, as well as an individual trapped by tyranny" (Pettitt 1982). Others fixated on his opposition in other ways, as in a *Guardian* overview that pointedly (if bizarrely) commented on Schnittke's "dissident-length hair" (Larner 1989).

Kremer and Schnittke the Prankster

Gidon Kremer was one of the main engines driving the early reception of Schnittke in Europe and the United States. His own Cold War story of emigration and defection led to multiple overviews of him and his repertoire throughout the 1980s (Blau 1980; Rich 1986; Kremer 2003, 239–257). Kremer's largesse extended beyond Schnittke to Gubaidulina and Pärt; and the original *Moskovskaya troitsa*—that is, Denisov, Gubaidulina, and Schnittke (solidified by the aforementioned 1982 concert)—metamorphosed into Kremer's new, more geographically decentered triumvirate.

Kremer achieved notoriety early on for programming some of Schnittke's more outlandish, and in many ways exceptional, compositions, among them his deconstruction of *Silent Night* (Stille Nacht) and his cadenzas for Beethoven's Violin Concerto in D. First premiered in Salzburg in 1977, and recorded for release in 1980, the Beethoven cadenzas raised Schnittke's profile even as they provoked critics to question his seriousness as a composer (Kremer 2003, 232–233). "These cadenzas might be rationalized as a contemporary composer's gloss of the material," Alan Kozinn remarked, "or, as one colleague put it, akin to 'painting a moustache on the Mona Lisa'" (Kozinn 1983). "Were these cadenzas really typical of this avant-garde composer?" *Gramophone* reviewer Bryan Crimp asked Kremer in 1981. In response, Kremer defended Schnittke as "one of the most gifted and interesting composers of our time," pithily defining Schnittke's polystylism as "unfamiliar notes by known composers and familiar notes by unknown composers" (Crimp 1981, 36). Kremer provided a useful overview of the cadenza in the first movement, while forcefully justifying the work's seriousness:

> In Beethoven's case we only have an idea of his cadenza—from the version of the concerto for piano and orchestra—in which he used timpani. So you will find in Schnittke's cadenza the timpani as well as, of course, Beethoven's own themes. But you will also find a collage of many familiar extracts from other violin concertos; not just fragments for fun but a very serious work with the themes of three centuries! Not so much a cadenza as a composition (Crimp 1981, 36).

As Schnittke himself explained, the quoted works included excerpts from Berg's Violin Concerto (among them its own quotation of Bach's chorale "Es ist genug"), as well as from Shostakovich's First Violin Concerto and Bartok's two violin concertos. Rather than a loose pastiche, as his critics averred, Schnittke contended that the compositional "work was very difficult." Mixing metaphors from tailoring, bookkeeping, and carpentry, he focused on the general process: "I united those 'scraps of cloth' without carrying forward ["transport"]: in order that they meshed and spliced together thematically, tonally and texturally, it demanded colossal exertion. . . . It was its own kind of an attempt to build a 'house without nails'" (Schnittke and Shul'gin 1993, 73–74). As is so often the case, Schnittke's compositional (and precompositional) efforts remained inaudible, and Kremer often provided more philosophical explications of the cadenzas for critics, as he did to Alan Rich in 1986: "We suddenly find ourselves within the Beethoven Violin Concerto but also in our own century. That builds up a tension, not to destroy Beethoven's music but to show that we are far away from this beauty" (Rich 1986).

Because the cadenzas accompanied a canonic Beethoven composition, the stakes were especially high. The coupling thus proved beneficial for Schnittke's flourishing fame. His experience proves the old chestnut: much of the press was quite bad, and his status rose nonetheless. Another *Gramophone* reviewer censured Schnittke, declaring, "These two [new cadenzas] have been composed by Alfred Schnittke, an avant-garde composer whose occupation I can easily believe suits him well. I wish he would return to that occupation if it means he will keep his hands off Beethoven." "The version is not recommended as a whole because of the cadenza," he concluded (Macdonald 1982, 26). *Gramophone*'s conservative reviewers predictably launched a vendetta against Schnittke's cadenzas. A subsequent review of the CD release of the Kremer recording (with Neville Marriner and the Academy of St. Martin-in-the-Fields) vented: "Schnittke's [cadenzas] are a vulgar interruption in Beethoven's music" (Harvey 1983). In 1982 Robert Layton referred to them as "odious" and "a disfiguring element in Kremer's new record" (Layton 1982), while a later *Gramophone* review from February 1984 commented on "those tasteless cadenzas by Alfred Schnittke" (1984; also Kenyon 1983).

The *New York Times* was kinder. On a 1985 list of the top one hundred classical CDs aimed at newcomers to the still-novel medium, John Rockwell included Kremer's recording of Beethoven's Violin Concerto with the Schnittke cadenzas but no work by Schnittke himself (Rockwell 1985). Bernard Holland had defended them two years previously (Ashby 2010, 77–78; citing Holland 1983). Michael Walsh applauded the cadenzas at greater length in *Time*: "Schnittke's adventurous interludes are a modern commentary on Beethoven's themes and provide a welcome, if at first startling, respite from the usual cadenzas by Joseph Joachim and Fritz Kreisler. This is avant-garde Beethoven with a vengeance that causes the listener to sit up and pay attention to the music. It's about time" (Walsh 1984). Schnittke already drastically divided critics and listeners. By the mid-1980s, despite attempts to defend his avant-garde, high-art credentials, in some quarters he grew notorious for his "trashings of the classics" (Glass 1986). (Kremer recorded the concerto again in 1993, this time with his own arrangement of Beethoven's cadenza from his piano transcription of the concerto [Beethoven 1993].)

Beyond the wide dissemination of his name, a crucial component of Schnittke's reputation had been established: he was a joker. Schnittke himself embraced the role: "Sometimes I'm tweaking the listener," he declared to Kozinn in 1988. In 1990 a conservative Boston critic commented on the "outrageous jokes (many of them successful) and dour poignancies (of questionable sincerity) of Alfred Schnittke's Viola Concerto, a boisterous, wasteful mess of a piece" (Buell 1990a). Yet the criticisms also accompanied—and arguably provoked—a wider sampling of his compositions, including such works as the Concerto Grosso no. 1; the Second Violin Sonata ("Quasi una Sonata"); and the Piano Quintet.

Listeners and critics became transfixed by his more serious side, and his prestige grew accordingly, bolstered by the advocacy of prominent critics. "Alfred Schnittke is a contemporary Soviet composer who is hardly known outside of his homeland," Edward Rothstein remarked poetically in a preview of the January 9, 1982, Continuum concert in New York. "But like Coleridge's Ancient Mariner," he continued, "once his voice is heard, it cannot be ignored. He fixes a listener with a glittering eye and holds him fast until he has had his say. There is no easy way out of the world he weaves" (Rothstein 1982). "In Memoriam," the orchestral version of the Piano Quintet, especially captured critics' attention. After hearing the New York Philharmonic perform the work in September 1985, Donal Henahan declared that the "esteem in which [Schnittke] is held in avant-garde circles is not misplaced" (Henahan 1985).

The Kronos Quartet and the Postmodern Schnittke

By the second half of the 1980s the two threads of Schnittke's reception spurred by Kremer and the Beethoven cadenzas—avant-garde versus tradition—became engaged with other anxieties about the future of new (and old) music then entangling the Kronos Quartet. As we have seen, Schnittke himself often drew criticism, but as the Kronos Quartet championed his music, Schnittke was buffeted by the critical reactions to their own unique brand. Familiar (uninformed) preconceptions about life behind the Iron Curtain persisted. "As so often with Schnittke, you got the feeling that a lot of it was an avant-garde dressing-up game, a sort of guilty pleasure coming from a place (the Soviet Union) where such things are still pretty new and scary," Richard Buell wrote in 1990 of a Kronos performance of Schnittke's String Quartet no. 2. Buell concluded that at this Boston Kronos concert, "A complacent mindlessness was being encouraged . . . , and with a vengeance. Really, the most fearless, challenging thing the Kronos could have done would have been to play a Schubert string quartet" (Buell 1990b).

Kronos included Schnittke's String Quartet no. 3 on their 1988 CD *Winter Was Hard*, which featured works ranging from the safe (Samuel Barber's *Adagio*) to the soothing (Pärt's *Fratres*) to the audacious (John Zorn's *Forbidden Fruit*) (see **example 9.4**). Kremer had been a prolific champion, but with Kronos—"as close to a pop supergroup as you'll find in classical music"—Schnittke entered another level of popularity (Gates 1998). A critic raved about their marketing prowess:

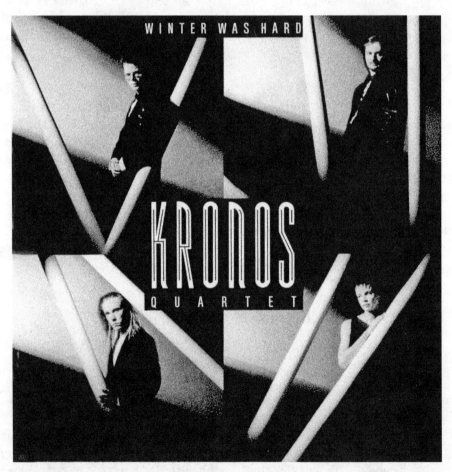

EXAMPLE 19.4 Kronos Quartet, *Winter Was Hard*, Electra/Nonesuch CD 9 79181-2 (1988).

Kronos is big business now, with three best-selling CDs, a radio series, nearly 70 US concert appearances this season, three tours of Europe and a trip to Japan. Who would have believed it—a string quartet, of all things, even if they do dress like rock stars, and a string quartet specializing in contemporary music. (Dyer 1988)

Another critic noted, "their last two albums—*Kronos Quartet* and *White Man Sleeps* (both on Elektra/Nonesuch)—stayed on Billboard's charts for nearly a year and peaked well inside the top 10.[12] Moreover, they have earned nearly unanimous plaudits from classical-music critics, possibly a first for post-modernism" (Kaplan 1988). Postmodernism was the key here, for in the late 1980s that term was achieving popularity in the United States beyond academic circles. Schnittke, especially for conservative critics like Buell, called forth strong reservations about the new aesthetic's musical manifestations.

The Kronos Quartet openly embraced this new aesthetic; they were even referred to as the "first postmodern quartet" (Swed 1989b). Their releases, including *Winter Was Hard*, were "packaged almost like a pop release" (Swed 1989a), and their audiences were "unusually catholic." Tim Page, reviewing a 1987 Kronos concert in New York featuring Schnittke's String Quartet no. 2, observed that at the concert "Elliott Carter, the distinguished modernist composer, sat next to the unusually venturesome rock musician Sting. The two may or may not be aware of each other's work, but this listener would wager that many members of the audience have enjoyed music by both men." Page, like others, seemed suspicious of their attire. "Despite their Haight-Ashbury cum Jetsons fashions and punk-rock hairdos," he admitted, "the members of the Kronos Quartet have assembled an ensemble of exceptional seriousness and importance" (Page 1987). Kozinn also acknowledged the "quartet's trendy clothes and hair styles," while criticizing their playing as "not especially virtuosic": "By today's standards of quartet playing, the Kronos's failings are many." The programming was the key, their "ability to assemble interesting, cohesive programs that, caveats aside, the players address with evident passion" (Kozinn 1988). They can't play all that well, but at least they're passionate, seems to have been a predominant sentiment, although Page concluded his review by declaring, "Kronos Quartet played magnificently, with lyricism and tragic grandeur." Such disagreements over the ensemble's basic technical competence differed drastically from the rave, adulatory reviews critics usually bestowed upon Kremer (Henahan 1979; Blau 1980).

The dichotomies—or collisions—within Kronos—flash versus substance, and what might be called a posturing popular aesthetic versus the true avant-garde (expressed more pithily as an opposition between low vs. high)—also easily mapped onto Schnittke, making them an ideal match. In his 1989 Kronos review, Kozinn described Schnittke's String Quartet no. 3 as a "time-warp piece" because of its quotations from Lasso and Beethoven. (He missed the quartet's references to Shostakovich.) Kozinn also observed the dichotomy within Schnittke's output: "Mr. Schnittke weaves this rhetorically diverse group [of quotations] into a variegated tapestry that alternates between an eerie, modernistic ambiguity and a crackling, fiery neo-Romanticism" (Kozinn 1989). Swed concurred in his review of *Winter Was Hard*: "The idea [of the CD] seems to be to move from otherworldly minimalism to a more raucous pop-influenced new music that leads to a climactic synthesis in Mr. Schnittke's Third Quartet" (Swed 1989a). Schnittke offered a new option, ideally suited to the contemporary soundscape. Concluding with what became a mantra in Western Schnittke reception over the next decade, Swed called the Third Quartet a "major addition to the repertoire," declaring, "this piece ... is obsessed by Beethoven's 'Grosse Fuge,' fighting it, dissecting it, grafting it onto other musics and styles, and in the process the composer produces a powerful and profound statement about our kaleidoscopic musical environment."

THE BOOM YEARS

Thanks to both Kremer and Kronos, but also a phalanx of other proponents, largely comprised of Russian émigrés, Schnittke's renown boomed in the late 1980s and 1990s. The boom spanned the years between 1988 and 1994, driven by a notable increase in performances (at least in the United States) as well as by recordings and the takeoff of the new format of the compact disc.[13] In the November 1986 *Atlantic*, an American critic described Schnittke as "a Soviet composer of little influence in the West," while the same year a *Washington Post* writer erroneously identified him as an "East German composer" (Davis 1990, 229; Richards 1986). By 1994 he had been profiled or reviewed in *Time* magazine, the *New York Times*, the *New Republic*, the *New Yorker*, and even *USA Today* (Walsh 1994; Taruskin 1992; Ross 1992; Griffiths 1994; Stearns 1994).

Beyond Kremer, Kronos, and Schnittke's other champions, including Mark Lubotsky, Yuriy Bashmet, Kurt Masur, Vladimir Feltsman, and Rostropovich, the small Swedish record label BIS assumed perhaps the greatest importance. The launching of the label's complete Alfred Schnittke Edition in 1987 proved foundational to disseminating his music. According to Swed:

> Perhaps the best indication that Mr. Schnittke can capture a wide audience is the fact that a spectacularly recorded if only decently played recent CD release on the BIS label, of Mr. Schnittke's Concerto Grosso No. 1 (a ravishing work that includes Mr. Cage's prepared piano used with rare individuality), his Oboe and Harp Concerto and his electrifying Piano Concerto, has developed a cult following, and record stores cannot keep it on their shelves (Swed 1988; see also Fanning 1988).

Although this album did not climb the *Billboard* charts as Kronos' releases did, Schnittke's compact disc presence, whether through the BIS complete edition or the myriad artists championing his music, soon grew overwhelming.[14] Paul Griffiths remarked in 1994 that the "only sure hope in [Schnittke's] music—one notes this more bleakly than gaily—is the hope it brings to the record business. With more than forty compact discs devoted to his works, Mr. Schnittke must be the living composer most frequently recorded (Philip Glass would be the nearest contender for that title)" (Griffiths 1994, 92; also Stearns 1994). Evidence supports Griffiths's claims. Between 1987 and the end of 1994, approximately fifty-five compact discs containing Schnittke's music were released, compared to approximately forty for Philip Glass, thirty for Elliott Carter, twenty for Arvo Pärt, and twenty for György Ligeti. (These general totals, while suggestive, say nothing about each composer's actual sales.) And Schnittke's recordings accumulated quickly. In 1989, only five years previous, critic Edward Greenfield observed the "very few Schnittke records listed so far"—around ten were in print by the end of that year (Greenfield 1989).[15]

Although none dominated like Schnittke, many Soviet composers fared well at the time. By the late 1980s, Soviet music stood apart from other contemporary music in the West because of its ubiquity, a result of its perceived profitability for the institutions and individuals performing it. In 1989 Cameron-Wolfe of SUNY Purchase declared that the "real irony of what I'm doing in terms of bringing Soviet music to the United States right now is that it's probably more likely that I can interest a conductor in programming Soviet contemporary music than American music" (Greene 1989). This interest largely stemmed from the recent political changes transforming the USSR. The suppositions Western critics made about the effect of these changes on music often betrayed familiar assumptions about authentic—or authentically repressed—Soviet music. "How long will it take for the utter gloom and cynicism of composers writing in the Brezhnev era to disperse?," a *Gramophone* reviewer asked in 1990. "Alfred Schnittke's Cello Sonata dates from 1978—before the reforms—and it certainly seems to speak for a collective psyche that is groaning under repression and a very negative attitude towards life" (Methuen-Campbell 1990).

Other critics continued to be concerned more with the politics of style than with the direct impact of Soviet politics on style. Representative is John Webb's 1992 overview of Schnittke for *Tempo*, which he concluded with a discussion rife with conventional assumptions about national identity and meaning in Russian and Western music. He traced Schnittke's polystylism to the "German tradition of Mahler, Schoenberg, and Berg," but emphasized that "his music is also distinctly Russian, for the Russian traditions allowed the Mahlerian aesthetic to continue as a living force in a way the Western tradition did not." For Webb this was not a happy combination: "It is from the divergence of these two traditions that my doubts about Schnittke's music stem." He then moved to the crux of the matter, his own deeply held (if indirectly stated) modernist values:

> Although in the West, the reaction against romanticism has long since passed, as has the modernism of the 1950s and 60s, certain attitudes from those times still remain. For many, contemporary music should be an abstract, objective art form. Schnittke's music has a vulgar, heart-on-the-sleeve quality about it. (Some might say it is cheap.) These qualities do not sit easily with abstraction and objectivity (Webb 1992; see also Mann 1980).

Most of Schnittke's fans—the "cult of Schnittke" that Ross, Swed, and Larner noted—had long tired of abstraction and objectivity. They already had resolved what Karol Berger calls the "Cold War of mimesis and abstraction," where mimesis represented the socialist realist products from the East and abstraction the thorny, modernist opuses from the West (Berger 2000, 150–151). Such listeners no longer assumed that the "avant-garde" acted as a "showcase of Western freedoms" (Berger 2000, 151). Instead, they were enthralled by the flexing of freedom they heard in Schnittke's music, the stories it seemed to tell: its familiar narrative pull.

Webb was not alone; reservations about Schnittke persisted. Paul Griffiths, another British modernist, varied in his opinion of Schnittke but found the Requiem to be beneath contempt, for it "turned out to be one of his gruesome, self-destructive journeys into musical horror, banality and tackiness" (Griffiths 1990). Taruskin gave something of a response in his 1992 appraisal of the composer: "The wonder of it all . . . is how often Mr. Schnittke, like Shostakovich before him, manages to skirt the pitfall [of bathos] and bring off the catharsis—a catharsis a mere hairbreadth from blatancy and all the more powerful for having braved the risk. Others listeners may disagree. Black-and-white has never been much of a moral color scheme" (Taruskin 1992, 20). Two years later in the pivotal *Schnittkejahre* of 1994—his sixtieth birthday and the pinnacle of his popularity—another reviewer still questioned the composer's true identity: "The flow of recordings of music by Alfred Schnittke continues unabated. So does the debate about Schnittke: is he a faker, mocker, pasticheur, or genius?" Rather than answering the question, this reviewer touted Schnittke's success: "Schnittke is now one of the world's most often performed and recorded composers, and leading musicians champion his music. That says something!" (Jong 1994). As the Cold War began to recede, Schnitke's inescapable presence encouraged questions to be asked about censorship, but also about belonging and belief, identity and meaning.

Conclusion: The Censor is Dead, Long Live the Censor!

At the end of the USSR, the tides seemed to be turning for Schnittke in Russia. A Russian official, Vladimir Demyanko, told reporter Richard Dyer in 1991, "Now the circumstances are very strange—the music of our composer Alfred Schnittke is better known in the West than it is here" (Dyer 1991). Although this had arguably been true for some time, the most vexing recent problems affecting Russian musical life were emigration and the struggling post-Soviet economy. Like many, Ivashkin bemoaned the exodus of musical talent. "You will not meet Alfred Schnittke and Sofia Gubaidulina in Moscow, Valentin Silvestrov in Kiev, or Gia Kancheli in Tbilisi anymore," he complained. "To reach them, you have to go to Germany or even to the Canary Islands. In fact, one can say that Russian culture exists more now in the West than in Russia itself" (Ivashkin 1992, 543).

Niceties of geographical location mattered little for many Westerners: Schnittke was and forever would be ineluctably Russian (and ineluctably Soviet), no matter how ambivalent the composer himself felt about his own Russianness, especially in statements he made following his emigration. "Schnittke has been a resident of Hamburg since 1990, but his music remains inseparable from his native milieu in its anxiety, its foreboding, its confusion and its fury," Walsh wrote (Walsh 1994). Griffiths concurred, "Though Mr. Schnittke lives in Hamburg, he remains a Russian composer" (Griffiths 1994, 93). In an interview published the same year, Schnittke himself painted a more anguished picture of rootlessness:

> Several years ago I was in Poland. It so happened that exactly there I understood: I am absolutely unnecessary to anyone and I won't have support anywhere. I was unnecessary, firstly, to the Russians, because I look like a Jew. I turned out to be unnecessary to the Polish, because they also relate to that differently. And I understood that I was unnecessary both to them, and to other Germans, because I don't look like a German. And from that moment it became clear to me: there is no consoling answer (Schnittke 1994; also Babak 1990).

Schnittke's ongoing crisis of identity belies the seemingly unshakeable assumptions about musical Russianness—both his brand and the international brand of Russian music—held by Western listeners.

Censorship vanished, but other problems persisted, among them economic. Sofia Gubaidulina declared in 1993,"In Russia we no longer have to endure ideological restrictions, but censorship for material reasons. That's the sad destiny of this country" (Mérigaud 1993, cited in Hamer 1994; also Condee and Padunov 1991, 88–90). Many bemoaned the loss of the old securities provided by the state. In 1990, Kabakov told an interviewer:

> Good Russian art only grew in a specific situation, between Scylla and Charybdis—between the Scylla of total repression and danger and the Charybdis of a crack of freedom under Khrushchev; in the little hole permitted between official art and private life. That was enough for a little bloom of art. And today we have lost our enemy. We can do anything. But what? (Wallich 1991, 83; compare Ivashkin 1992, 81)

While former Soviets were concerned about the economy, the loss of inspirational repression, and a fragmented national identity in the wake of large-scale emigration, Western analysts worried over Schnittke's relevance, aggressively asserting his universality and timelessness just when he seemed the most rooted in time and place. (That he himself felt most uprooted then seems especially poignant.) Borrowing a familiar trope, Michael Walsh linked Schnittke to Shostakovich, emphasizing the rebellious nature of both, while noting his unanticipated pertinence:

> Unlike Shostakovich, who was finally ground down by Stalinism and had to express his rebellion in a private musical code, Schnittke has lived to see the end of overt artistic oppression. Grim as his music can be, it is never hopeless; relentless as it sometimes is, it is never despondent.... As the century staggers to a conclusion, Schnittke suddenly seems to speak for us all (Walsh 1994).

The exploding interest in Schnittke's music after 1991, the increase in commissions and recordings, was not just a matter of redressing past wrongs (past censorship), a type of post-communist affirmative action, although that played an important role, as we have seen.

Critics also expressed genuine interest in understanding the other side and, it seems, themselves. At the end of the Cold War Schnittke had become a musical ambassador. Rather than "tragic prankster" (the title of his *New Yorker* obituary), this arguably represented the most important critical evaluation (Ross 1998). The sentiment became widespread at the time, and it tells us much about the hopes of the early 1990s, the apparent effacing of geographic as well as aesthetic borders at the triumphant end of the decades-long standoff, and the "end of history" for many gloating Americans (Fukuyama [1992] 2006). In 1994 musicologist Glenn Watkins suggestively called Schnittke "an agent provocateur in the dissolution of the Iron Curtain mentality" (Watkins 1994, 410). Already in 1989, Gerald Larner had underscored Schnittke's contemporaneity. Schnittke, Larner commented, is a "composer who speaks with an obviously contemporary voice but who also likes the kind of music we like—Bach, Mozart, Mahler, jazz, rock even—and sees no reason for refusing to indulge us and at the same time to clarify the meaning of his work by alluding to them in one way or another" (Larner 1989). Ross likewise optimistically signaled both Schnittke's immediate relevance, as well as his (paradoxical) timelessness in 1992: "Schnittke represents not only a moment in the history of Russia, but also a moment in the history of music. He will not vanish when his times are up" (Ross 1992, 30).

Almost a decade later, such proponents of Schnittke's music as Feltsman and Krysa report difficulties in programming late Soviet music in America. Those times—the heady early 1990s—*are* up. The number of performances of Schnittke's work appears to have fallen, while that of Shostakovich's and Pärt's remains high (Wagner 2010, 25). Yet Feltsman remarks that when he plays Schnittke he observes "a certain lost look in [listeners'] faces ... for me a very clear sign that something important, something primal, has happened to them." "But," Joseph Horowitz cautions, "it remains possible that, Shostakovich excepted, the [avant-garde Soviet] composers in question [including Schnittke] will prove incompletely exportable from the singular time and place that both spawned and suppressed them" (Horowitz 2003).

Near the end of his 1996 biography of the composer (itself an indicator of Schnittke's standing at the time), Ivashkin addresses these concerns, noting that "today people in Russia prefer to evaluate Schnittke's music from a more objective position, often not linking it with the social or cultural situation from which it emerged." This remains a common Russian response, a rejection of the forced social interpretations of art fostered under the Soviet system and also those appraisals of Schnittke (including Ivashkin's quotation above) that emphasized his "music [as] the most sincere and expressive language of Russian culture and Russian life." "In any case," Ivashkin continues, "Schnittke's music does not need this kind of linking in order to be comprehensible. It absorbs and augments historical meaning. In it we can sense the spiritual efforts of many generations without the experience of these generations being directly referred to or recreated." "The music of Schnittke," he concludes, "in many ways engendered by the Russian tradition . . . , turns out to be not only Russian and local but general and universal" (Ivashkin 1996, 216). Ivashkin presents a great deal of wishful (and double) thinking; yet this need to universalize Schnittke is understandable, if not defensible. American critics shared the impulse; witness Bradley Bambarger (1998) in *Billboard* upon Schnittke's death, neatly summarizing the move from censorship to transcendent universality: "Schnittke's 'polystylism' speaks directly from and to the supersaturated postmodern age, transcending its genesis in the repressive atmosphere of the Soviet Union to provide timeless, universal challenge and reward."

For all the emphasis on Schnittke's timelessness and universality, he, more than many of his generation, became ineluctably linked to a specific time and place. His troubles with the Soviet authorities—often misrepresented or overstated—generated a mystique that vouchsafed the quality of his music over the course of the 1980s, in the USSR as well as in Europe and America. Once that censorship expired, he came unmoored, yet seemed still rooted; in many quarters he was credited with foreseeing, even provoking, the end—of the USSR, of the Cold War, of musical boundaries high and low. Schnittke really did appear to be "Between Two Worlds," the title of a London festival celebrating what would have been his seventy-fifth birthday in 2009.

Yet today he, or more accurately his posthumous reputation, belongs fully to neither, stuck in limbo between past and present, Russia and the West. In 2008 Russian composer Viktor Yekimovsky told American musicologist William Quillen:

> During its time, his music made a phenomenal impression. But now, it doesn't work. Schnittke was connected with his time. . . . It's not abstract music, it's connected to its time. Therefore, today only a handful of Schnittke's works come across as interesting, sound good, like they did before—for example, the Concerto Grosso [No.1]. And the others? They've stopped working (Quillen 2010, 102).

The absence of a seventy-fifth-anniversary tribute to Schnittke in the pages of *Muzïkal'naia akademiya* in 2009 (beyond two articles in the fourth issue) also suggests current attitudes, as does the lack of a festival of his music in Moscow corresponding to the large-scale seventieth birthday observances held there in 2004. In response, Irina Schnittke, his widow, complained: "Who needs Schnittke today?" (Mitta and Murav'yeva 2009). In 1994, on the occasion of a Schnittke Festival in Moscow, an unidentified critic wrote, "We don't yet know how much time it will take for us to stop listening to him as a prophet and to understand him just as a great composer" (Ivashkin 1996,

214). Yet now that his status as prophet has receded, even his greatness itself appears under question in some—but decidedly not all—quarters.

The ex-Soviets who achieved the greatest success with Western audiences—especially Pärt, Gubaidulina, and Silvestrov—first capitalized upon their outsider status but subsequently distanced themselves from that "milieu," replacing it with a less geographically rooted image of mysticism and religiosity. (Denisov and Shchedrin were not so lucky.) Schnittke's place in the history books—and the auction houses (and archives)—appears secure, for as Bambarger (1998) observed, Schnittke represented "one of the late 20th-century's signature voices." A large collection of his manuscripts was auctioned by Sotheby's in 2003 for 106,400 GBP (double its estimated value of 40,000–50,000 GBP) (Sotheby's 2003, lot 155).[16] He prominently features in music histories both Russian and Western (compare Savenko 2008 and Taruskin 2005, 5:464–472).

What will become of Schnittke's brand in twenty-first-century concert halls and recordings now that he is beholden only to the fickle forces of the marketplace remains to be seen. Composers' reputations often sharply decline after death, only to rebound some years later. Suggestively, Schnittke achieved his largest audience in recent years (if not ever) on the soundtrack to director Martin Scorsese's psychological thriller *Shutter Island* (2010), which included the second of his *Four Hymns*. This film seems to separate Schnittke from the times that so thrilled his late Cold War auditors, placing him among diverse avant-garde samples to cultivate what one critic called "an alternate universe for a film that has at its essence an alternate universe" (Swed 2010). Schnittke's newly untethered music complements the soundtrack's revivified strains of musical modernism, framing another spooky tale. With one small catch: Schnittke's music first accompanies the revelation of the film's early Cold War backdrop, reeling him inexorably back.

Notes

1. I am indebted to many individuals for their assistance, especially Igor Blazhkov, Joel Spiegelman, Joel Sachs, Stephen Crist, and Laurel Fay. Generous research help was also provided by Vladic Kostin and David Chapman (Washington University in St. Louis) and Juliet Forshaw, and the gracious staff of the Music Division of the New York Public Library, The Juilliard School (Jane Gottlieb), and the Library of Congress (Kevin LaVine), in addition to Charlotte Sucher of the Austrian Bundesministerium für Unterricht, Kunst und Kultur. I would also like to thank Philip Rupprecht and his graduate seminar, "Post-War Musical Nationalisms," at Duke University for valuable comments and suggestions. Unless otherwise indicated, all translations are mine.

    Translation mine. The original and a different translation are in Kudryavitsky (2006, 2–3).
2. Cited in Emerson (2008, 240).
3. For a different interpretation of late and post-Soviet musical "branding," see Cherednichenko (2002, 39–50).
4. A general overview of Schnittke reception, especially in Germany, can be found in Wagner (2010).

5. Krysa premiered *A Paganini* in Leningrad in 1982, and played in the first performance of the Concerto Grosso no. 3 in Leningrad in 1985.
6. Some authors and editors at this time still preferred to transliterate the Russian form of his name rather than render the German equivalent.
7. This is to be distinguished from the more exclusive Secretariat of the Union, which Schnittke never joined.
8. For Pugachova's side of the story, see Razzakov 2003, 282–283.
9. Schnittke's rights within the USSR were maintained by VAAP and, eventually, RAO, the Russian equivalent. As a comparison, Sofia Gubaidulina renegotiated her agreement with VAAP in 1990 and officially resigned from VAAP only on December 19, 1991, after learning of the impending dissolution of the USSR. See the "Diverse" correspondence folder, Sofia Gubaidulina Collection, Paul Sacher Stiftung.
10. As I was informed by a representative of the Austrian Bundesministerium für Unterricht, Kunst und Kultur, "The only other composers who have been awarded with the same prize were Olivier Messiaen in 1985 and György Kurtag in 1994" (Sucher 2011). See also *Muzïkal'naya akademiya*, no. 2 (2008).
11. The amounts for a majority of his completed commissions remain unknown. Irina Schnittke declined to provide this information (Irina Schnittke 2011b). The Salzburg Festival responded to an inquiry, "We cannot tell you the amount because of data privacy" (Lettowsky 2011). The Kuhmo Festival stated, "Unfortunately, as it is so long ago, the contribution for the composition could not be found" (Eerola 2011). The New York Philharmonic "restrict[s] records that are within the time period of a still living Music Director. In this case that would be Kurt Masur" (Wandel 2011). Given Masur's recent passing (in December 2015), presumably the relevant records will soon be opened. Sikorski was unwilling to provide information about Schnittke's financial situation (Duffek 2011). Further research must await the passage of sufficient time.
12. *Winter Was Hard* first appeared on *Billboard*'s "Top Classical Albums" chart at no. 12 on November 12, 1988. It stayed on the chart for just over thirty-five weeks, reaching no. 5 in late December 1988 and early January 1989.
13. The records of G. Schirmer, the US publisher for most (but not all) of Schnittke's music, are not comprehensive, focusing only on rental scores and leaving chamber and other solo works unaccounted for. The figures cited by Wagner for Schnittke performances as tracked by Schirmer between 2005 and 2010 thus need to be read with caution (Wagner 2010, 25). Nonetheless, the records Schirmer does keep, along with other published and unpublished sources, allow the general contours of Schnittke's performances to be traced.
14. I have been unable to verify Swed's claim. The BIS recording never reached the Billboard "Top Classical Albums" chart, but this does not invalidate the album's purported cult cachet. Record sales data from this period are notoriously unreliable because they were never systematically collected. SoundScan only began tracking actual point of sale data (as opposed to "ranked reports" from selected record stores) in 1991, beginning with pop and country music (Anonymous 1991).
15. Ascertaining the exact number of compact discs available at any one time remains difficult, if not ultimately impossible, dependent upon a variety of unpredictable factors. Thus, the data on compact disc releases in this paragraph must be taken with a certain amount of leeway. They derive from several sources: Schwann catalog listings (http://schwann.odyssi.com/member/sosearch.htm), the Schnittke discographies in Ivashkin 1994 and

Köchel et al. 1994 (290–299), other published discographies (e.g., for Glass), and Worldcat holdings, among others. My Schnittke tally above is conservative: the more comprehensive "CD Discography" in Köchel et al. 1994 contains 101 entries (including many rarities, reissues, or duplicates). A point of reference: according to Arkhiv.com, a useful indicator of CDs currently in print, Schnittke has 209; Glass has 189; John Adams has 88; Elliott Carter has 141; and Arvo Pärt has 214 (consulted April 7, 2011).

16. For reference, a manuscript copy of Beethoven's Ninth Symphony (lot 16), valued between 2 and 3 million GBP, sold at the same auction for 2,133,600 GBP, and the entire sale total was 2,833,816 GBP. The Schnittke manuscripts were subsequently donated to The Juilliard School in New York, where they are now among the holdings of the Juilliard Manuscript Collection.

References

Interviews and Personal Communications

Blazhkov, Igor. 2009a. Telephone interview by author, April 25. Tape recording.
Blazhkov, Igor. 2009b. Telephone interview by author, May 2009. Tape recording.
Blazhkov, Igor. 2011. Email to author, March 24.
Crist, Stephen. 2011. Email to author, March 24.
Duffek, Hans-Ulrich. 2011. Emails to author, April 21 and May 2.
Eerola, Ritva. 2011. Email to author, May 25.
Krysa, Oleh. 2010. Interview with author, October 24.
Kusterer, Erich. 2011. Email to author, April 14.
LaVine, Kevin. 2011. Email to author, May 5.
Lettowsky, Franziska-M. 2011. Email to author, May 5.
Sachs, Joel. 2009. Telephone interview by author, December 14. Tape recording.
Savenko, Svetlana. 2011. Email to author, March 25.
Schnittke, Irina. 2011a. Telephone conversation with author, June 9.
Schnittke, Irina. 2011b. Telephone conversation with author, October 18.
Spiegelman, Joel. 2009. Telephone interview by author, May.
Sucher, Charlotte. 2011. Email to author, April 8.
Wandel, Richard. 2011. Email to author, May 6.

Archives

Alfred Schnittke Materials. The Juilliard Manuscript Collection. The Juilliard School.
Brubeck Collection, 1.H.7.8: Moscow Summit Trip, May 25-Jun 3, 1988—Misc. Ephemerae, Holt-Atherton Special Collections, The University of the Pacific.
Elizabeth Sprague Coolidge Foundation Collection. Music Division, Library of Congress.
Nicholas Slonimsky Collection. Music Division, Library of Congress.
Paul Jacobs Collection. New York Public Library.

Other Primary and Secondary Sources

Anderson, Martin. 1998. "Obituary: Alfred Schnittke." *The Independent (London)*, August 5, 6.

Anderson, Omer. 1966. "Melodia Repertoire Pushing Ariola to All-Time Sales High." *Billboard*, December 24, 46.
Anonymous. 1991. "Billboard Sets Date for Use of SoundScan Chart Data." *Billboard*, May 11, 6.
Anonymous. 1998a. "Obituaries: Alfred Schnittke." *Gramophone, November*, 31.
Anonymous. 1998b. "Russian Composer Alfred Schnittke Dies." *BBC News*, August 3. http://news.bbc.co.uk/2/hi/europe/144527.stm.
Ashby, Arved. 2010 *Absolute Music, Mechanical Reproduction*. Berkeley and Los Angeles: University of California Press.
Bambarger, Bradley. 1998. "Keeping Score [Alfred Schnittke Obituary]." *Billboard*, August 22.
Becker, Howard S. 1982. *Art Worlds*. Berkeley: University of California Press.
Berger, Karol. 2000. *A Theory of Art*. New York: Oxford University Press.
Billboard. 1974. "Ariola/Eurodisc, Melodiya: 10 Years of Cooperation." *Billboard*, December 14, 27.
Blau, Eleanor. 1980. "Soviet Puzzle: 'Greatest Violinist in the World.'" *New York Times*, August 27, C20.
Bogdanova, Alla. 1995. *Muzïka i vlast'*. Moscow: Naslediye.
Brody, James, and Lawrence Oncley. 1968. "Current Chronicle: Bloomington, Indiana." *Musical Quarterly* 54: 87–92.
Buell, Richard. 1990a. "Hear, Hear: Newly-Minted Debussy, Disturbing Elgar." *Boston Globe*, November 6, 55.
Buell, Richard. 1990b. "Kronos Quartet's Skill is Overshadowed by an Overdose of Experimental Effects." *Boston Globe*, September 18, 70.
Cherednichenko, Tat'yana. 2002. *Muzïkal'nïy zapas: 70-ye. Problemï. Portretï. Sluchai*. Moscow: Novoye literaturnoye obozreniye.
Condee, Nancy, and Vladimir Padunov. 1991. "'Makulakul'tura': Reprocessing Culture." *October* 57: 79–103.
Crimp, Bryan. 1981. "Gidon Kremer." *Gramophone*, October, 36–41.
Crist, Stephen A. 2009. "Jazz as Democracy? Dave Brubeck and Cold War Politics." *Journal of Musicology* 26 (2): 133–174.
Davis, Francis. 1990. "Avant-Garde Comrades." In *Outcats: Jazz Composers, Instrumentalists, and Singers*, 227–233. New York: Oxford University Press.
DeNora, Tia. 1995. *Beethoven and the Construction of Genius: Musical Politics in Vienna, 1792–1803*. Berkeley: University of California Press.
Dewhirst, Martin, and Robert Farrell, eds. 1973. *The Soviet Censorship*. Metuchen, N.J.: Scarecrow Press.
Dudar, Helen. 1988. "Moscow Rights: Doing a Book Deal With the Soviets." *Wall Street Journal*, February 23, 28.
Dyer, Richard. 1988. "Kronos Brilliant, But There's the Rub." *Boston Globe*, October 29, 10.
Dyer, Richard. 1991. "Music in Moscow: An Endangered Art." *Boston Globe*, May 27, 35.
Dyer, Richard. 1992. "Violinist Gidon Kremer Shuns Celebrity." *Boston Globe*, April 12, B29.
Elst, Michiel. 2004. *Copyright, Freedom of Speech, and Cultural Policy in the Russian Federation*. Leiden: Martinus Nijhoff Publishers.
Emerson, Caryl. 1997. *The First Hundred Years of Mikhail Bakhtin*. Princeton: Princeton University Press.
Emerson, Caryl. 2008. *The Cambridge Introduction to Russian Literature*. Cambridge: Cambridge University Press.

Fanning, David. 1988. Review of Schnittke, Concerto Gross no. 1, etc. (BIS). *Gramophone*, April, 92.
Feltsman, Vladimir. 2003. "Underground." Liner notes to concert program "Masterpieces of the Russian Underground" (January 28 and February 2, 2003, New York). Accessed January 24, 2010, on Feltsman's website. http://www.feltsman.com/index.php?page=notes#underground.
Flechsig, Amrei, and Christian Storch, eds. 2010. *Alfred Schnittke: Analyse—Interpretation—Rezeption*. Hildesheim: Georg Olms.
Forner, Johannes. 2002. *Kurt Masur: Zeiten und Klänge: Biographie*. Berlin: Propyläen.
Foulds, Diane. 1983. "'Faust' Exults in Exile: Moscow-Banned Oratorio Scores in World Premiere." *Washington Post*, June 20, C6.
Fukuyama, Francis. (1992) 2006. *The End of History and the Last Man*. New York: Free Press.
Gates, David. 1998. "Rebels Without a Pause." *Newsweek*, October 26, 82.
Gelbart, Matthew. 2007. *The Invention of "Folk Music" and "Art Music": Emerging Categories from Ossian to Wagner*. Cambridge: Cambridge University Press.
Gessen, Masha. 1997. *Dead Again: Dead Again: The Russian Intelligentsia after Communism*. London: Verso.
Glass, Herbert. 1986. "Fiddler's Five." *Los Angeles Times*, July 20, 60.
Gray, Tam. 1998. "Milestones [Alfred Schnittke Obituary]." *Time*, August 17.
Greene, Donna. 1989. "Crossing Soviet Musical Boundaries." *New York Times*, September 3, WC3.
Greenfield, Edward. 1989. "Records: New Voice of Russia." *Guardian* (London), August 25.
Griffiths, Paul. 1990. "Clearly a Fine Reading." *Times* (London), September 8.
Griffiths, Paul. 1994. "Schnittke's Seventh." *New Yorker*, March 7, 91–93.
Hamer, Janice Ellen. 1994. "*Sofia Gubaidulina's Compositional Strategies in the String Trio (1988) and Other Works.*" Ph.D. diss., City University of New York.
Harvey, Trevor. 1983. "Review of Beethoven, Violin Concerto in D major, Op. 61." *Gramophone*, August, 27.
Henahan, Donal. 1979. "Violinist: Gidon Kremer Plays in a Different Way." *New York Times*, March 27, C12.
Henahan, Donal. 1985. "Music: The Philharmonic in a Schnittke Premiere." *New York Times*, September 27, C20.
Holland, Bernard. 1983. "Concert: Gidon Kremer With English Chamber." *New York Times*, November 11.
Horowitz, Joseph. 2003. "Where Composers Still Held Sway, From Underground." *New York Times*, January 19.
Huckerby, Martin. 1980. "Arts Diary: BBC Worry." *Times* (London), February 28.
Ivashkin, Alexander. 1992. "The Paradox of Russian Non-Liberty." *Musical Quarterly* 76: 543–556.
Ivashkin, Alexander. 1996. *Alfred Schnittke*. London: Phaidon.
Jakelski, Lisa. 2009. "The Changing Seasons of the Warsaw Autumn: Contemporary Music in Poland, 1960–1990." Ph.D. diss., University of California, Berkeley.
Jong, De. 1994. "Guide to Records." *American Record Guide* 57 (4): 165–166.
Kabakov, Il'ya. 2008. *60–70-ye . . . Zapiski o neofitsial'noy zhizni v Moskve*. Moscow: Novoye Literaturnoye Obozreniye.
Kaplan, Fred. 1988. "Kronos Quartet Spinning and Twisting the World of Music into New Orbits." *Boston Globe*, October 2, 18.
Kenyon, Nicholas. 1983. "Concerts: Lumina: Wigmore Hall." *Times* (London), January 10.

Khrennikov, Tikhon. 2000. "My Conscience Is Clear: Interview with Anders Beyer." In *The Voice of Music: Conversations with Composers of Our Time*, edited by Anders Beyer. Edited and translated by Jean Christensen and Anders Beyer, 253–260. Aldershot, UK: Ashgate.

Khrennikov, Tikhon, and V. Rubtsova. 1994. *Tak eto bïlo: Tikhon Khrennikov o vremeni i o sebe*. Moscow: Muzïka.

Kildea, Paul. 2002. *Selling Britten: Music and the Market Place*. Oxford: Oxford University Press.

Köchel, Jürgen, Hans-Ulrik Duffek, Helmut Peters, Ulrike Patow, and Mark Heyer, et al., eds. *Alfred Schnittke zum 60. Geburtstag: Eine Festschrift*. Hamburg: Sikorski, 1994.

Kozinn, Allan. 1983. "Fresh Insights into Standard Works." *New York Times*, March 13, H32.

Kozinn, Allan. 1988. "An Eclectic Mix, Through a Contemporary Prism." *New York Times*, May 22.

Kozinn, Allan. 1989. "The Kronos Quartet." *New York Times*, February 13, C20.

Kremer, Gidon. 2003. *Zwischen Welten*. Munich: Piper. (Versions of this were incorporated, but also expanded upon in Kremer 2006.)

Kremer, Gidon. 2006. *In@rodnïy artist: Vospominaniya*. Moscow: Novoye literaturnoye obozreniye.

Kretova, Yekaterina. 1993. "V Bol'shom vruchili premii 'Triumf': Triumfatorami stali predstaviteli elitarnoy kul'tury." *Kommersant*, January 9.

Kudryavitsky, Anatoly, trans. and ed. 2006. *A Night in the Nabokov Hotel: 20 Contemporary Poets from Russia*. Dublin: Dedalus Press.

Kukharskiy, Vasiliy. 1968. "V interesakh millionov." *Sovetskaya muzïka*, no. 10, 2–10.

Larner, Gerald. 1989. "Alfred the Great." *Guardian* (London), October 19.

Layton, Robert. 1982. "A Quarterly Retrospect of Orchestral, Chamber and Instrumental Recordings." *Gramophone*, August, 27–28 (225–226).

Macdonald, Malcolm. 1982. "Review of Beethoven Violin Concerto, Kremer, Academy of Saint Martin in the Fields." *Gramophone*, June, 24–27.

Mann, William. 1980. "BBCSO/Rozhdestvensky; Festival Hall/Radio 3." *Times* (London), April 24.

McBurney, Gerard. 1988. "Musical Chairman Knows the Game Backwards." *Guardian* (London), December 13.

Mérigaud, Bernard. 1993. "Des notes surgies du silence," *Télérama*, no. 2247 (February 3): 57.

Methuen-Campbell, James. 1990. Review of Rachmaninov, Cello Sonata in G minor, op. 19, et al. *Gramophone*, April, 90.

Mitta, Aleksandr, and Irina Murav'yeva. 2009. "Al'fred Shnitke: Kod dostupa." *Rossiyskaia gazeta*, November 24.

Moore, D. 1994. *American Record Guide* 57, no. 6 (November): 184.

Muravina, Elena. 1991. "Copyright Transactions with Soviet Authors: The Role of VAAP." *Loyal Entertainment Law Journal* 11, 421–451. Also available at: http://digitalcommons.lmu.edu/elr/vol11/iss2/5

Page, Tim. 1987. "Music: The Kronos Quartet at Weill Hall." *New York Times*, March 15, 62.

Pantiyelev, Grigoriy. 1990. "Pyat' simfoniy Al'freda Shnitke." *Sovetskaya muzïka*, no. 10: 81–87.

Pettitt, Stephen. 1982. "Tyranny Made Music." *Times* (London), August 25, 7.

Piekut, Benjamin. 2014. "Actor-Networks in Music History: Clarifications and Critiques." *Twentieth-Century Music* 11 (2): 191–215.

Polin, Claire. 1994. "The Composer as Seer, but Not Prophet." *Tempo*, no. 190 (September): 13–17.

Polyanskiy, Valeriy. 2003. [Untitled Reminiscences about Schnittke]. In *Al'fredu Shnitke posvyashchayetsya* 3, 256–264. Moscow: Kompozitor.

Quillen, William. 2010. "After the End: New Music in Russia from *Perestroika* to the Present." Ph.D. Dissertation, University of California, Berkeley.

Razzakov, Fyodor. 2003. *Alla Pugachova: Po stupenyam slavï: Dokumental'naya povest'*. Moscow: Yauza/Eksmo.

Rhein, John Von. 1979. "Record Briefs: Lineup for Listening." *Chicago Tribune*, October 14, D24.

Rhein, John Von. 1982. "The Russians Are Coming! Avant-Gardists Hit Town." *Chicago Tribune*, May 23, G8.

Rich, Alan. 1986. "From Russia, With Love." *Newsweek*, May 19, 73.

Richards, David. 1986. "Exiled Director Gets Soviet Overtures; Lyubimov Might Return to Moscow." *Washington Post*, December 25.

Robinson, Harlow. 1981. "The Soviet Avant-Garde." *New York Times*, January 11.

Rockwell, John. 1983. "Music: Continuum, Soviet Bill." *New York Times*, November 3, C18.

Rockwell, John. 1985. "The 100 Best CD Releases—A Selective Discography." *New York Times*, April 21, H26.

Rockwell, John. 1992. "Schnittke's Opera in World Premiere." *New York Times*, April 15.

Ross, Alex. 1992. "Connoisseur of Chaos." *New Republic*, September 28, 1992, 30–34.

Ross, Alex. 1998. "The Tragic Prankster." *New Yorker*, September 7, 90–91.

Rothstein, Edward. 1982. "Evening With a Lively Composer From Soviet." *New York Times*, January 8, C24.

Rothstein, Edward. 1993. "Where East And West Do Not Meet." *New York Times*, February 21.

Rozhdestvenskiy, Gennadiy. 2001. *Treugol'niki: Triptikh*. Moscow: Slovo.

Savenko, Svetlana. 1981. "Portret khudozhnika v zrelosti." *Sovetskaya muzïka*, no. 9, 35–42.

Savenko, Svetlana. 2008. *Istoriya russkoy muzïki XX stoletiya ot Skryabina do Shnitke*. Moscow: Muzïka.

Schmelz, Peter J. 2002. *Listening, Memory, and the Thaw: Unofficial Music and Society in the Soviet Union, 1956–1974*. Ph.D. diss., University of California, Berkeley.

Schmelz, Peter J. 2009a. "Alfred Schnittke's Nagasaki: Soviet Nuclear Culture, Radio Moscow, and the Global Cold War." *Journal of the America Musicological Society* 62 (2): 413–474.

Schmelz, Peter J. 2009b. "From Scriabin to Pink Floyd." In *Sound Commitments: Avant-Garde Music and the Sixties*, edited by Robert Adlington. New York: Oxford University Press.

Schmelz, Peter J. 2009c. *Such Freedom, If Only Musical: Unofficial Soviet Music during the Thaw*. New York: Oxford University Press.

Schmelz, Peter J. 2015a. "Intimate Histories of the Musical Cold War: Fred Prieberg and Igor Blazhkov's Unofficial Diplomacy." In *Music and International History in the Twentieth Century*. Edited by Jessica C. E. Gienow-Hecht, 189–225. New York: Berghahn.

Schmelz, Peter J. 2015b. " 'Shostakovich' Fights the Cold War: Reflections from Great to Small." *Journal of Musicological Research* 34 (2): 91–140.

Schnittke, Alfred [Shnitke, Al'fred]. 1994. "Muzyka v prisutstvii vetra." Interview with S. Maslovyi. *Komsomol'skaya Pravda*, February 4, 12. Cited in *Kompozitor Al'fred Shnitke*, by Valentina Kholopova, 162. Cheliabinsk: Arkaim, 2003.

Schnittke, Alfred [Shnitke, Al'fred], and Aleksandr Ivashkin. 1994. *Besedï s Al'fredom Shnitke*. Moscow: Kul'tura.

Schnittke, Alfred [Shnitke, Al'fred], and Dmitrii Shul'gin. 1993. *Gody neizvestnosti Al'freda Shnitke*. Moscow: Delovaia Liga.

Schonberg, Harold C. 1967. "The World of Music." In *The Soviet Union: The Fifty Years*, edited by Harrison E. Salisbury, 175–198. New York: Harcout, Brace & World.

Schwarz, Boris. 1983. *Music and Musical Life in Soviet Russia*, 2nd enl. ed. Bloomington and Indianapolis: Indiana University Press.

Shreffler, Anne C. 2000. "The Myth of Empirical Historiography: A Response to Joseph N. Straus." *Musical Quarterly* 84 (1): 30–39.

Slonimsky, Nicolas. 2002. *Perfect Pitch: An Autobiography.* Edited by Electra Slonimsky Yourke. Second Expanded Edition. New York: Schirmer, 2002.

Sotheby's. 2003. *Music Including the Paul Wittgenstein Archive,* May 22. http://www.sothebys.com/app/live/lot/LotDetail.jsp?sale_number=L03410&live_lot_id=155.

Stearns, David Patrick. 1994. "Composer Alfred Schnittke Under a Deep, Dark Cloud." *USA Today*, February 14.

Straus, Joseph N. 1999. "The Myth of Serial 'Tyranny' in the 1950s and 1960s." *Musical Quarterly* 83 (3): 301–343.

Strongin, Theodore. 1967. "Concert Examines Group With Names: Soviet Avant-Garde." *New York Times*, May 26, 52.

Swed, Mark. 1988. "Schnittke: At the Summit of Soviet Music." *Wall Street Journal*, June 7, 32.

Swed, Mark. 1989a. "An Eclectic Lineup, Fit for The Kronos." *New York Times*, January 22, H23.

Swed, Mark. 1989b. "Home Entertainment/Recordings; And Keep in Mind." *New York Times*, March 5.

Swed, Mark. 2010. "Critic's Notebook: 'Shutter Island' as a New-Music Haven," *Los Angeles Times Blogs*, February 24, 2010. http://latimesblogs.latimes.com/culturemonster/2010/02/shutter-island-as-a-new-music-paradise.html.

Taruskin, Richard. 1992. "A Post-Everythingist Booms." *New York Times*, July 12, 20 and 24.

Taruskin, Richard. 2005. *The Oxford History of Western Music.* Oxford: Oxford University Press.

Taubman, Howard. 1966. "Compositions of Avant-Garde Music Gaining Influence in Soviet." *New York Times*, February 18, 22.

Thornton, Sarah. 2008. *Seven Days in the Art World.* New York: Norton.

Tomoff, Kiril. 2006. *Creative Union: The Professional Organization of Soviet Composers, 1939–1953.* Ithaca, N.Y.: Cornell University Press.

Vazsonyi, Nicholas. 2010. *Richard Wagner: Self-Promotion and the Making of a Brand.* Cambridge: Cambridge University Press.

Volkov, Solomon. 1979. *Testimony: The Memoirs of Dmitri Shostakovich as Related to and Edited by Solomon Volkov.* Translated by Antonina Bouis. New York: Harper and Row.

Wagner, Hans-Joachim. 2010. "Die Rezeption Alfred Schnittke: Überlegungen zu einer Kontextualisierung." In *Alfred Schnittke: Analyse—Interpretation—Rezeption*, edited by Amrei Flechsig and Christian Storch, 13–28. Hildesheim: Georg Olms.

Walsh, Michael. 1984. "Some Classic Small Packages." *Time*, July 23.

Walsh, Michael. 1994. "The Sound of Russian Fury." *Time*, March 14.

Watkins, Glenn. 1994. *Pyramids at the Louvre: Music, Culture, and Collage from Stravinsky to the Postmodernists.* Cambridge, Mass.: Belknap Press of Harvard University Press.

Webb, John. 1992. "Schnittke in Context." *Tempo*, no. 182 (September): 19–22.

Wilson, Elizabeth. 2008. *Rostropovich: The Musical Life of the Great Cellist, Teacher and Legend.* Chicago: Ivan R. Dee.

Yaeger, Jonathan L. 2013. "The Leipzig Gewandhaus Orchestra in East Germany, 1970–1990." Ph.D. Dissertation, Indiana University.

Zolotov, Andrei., Jr. 1998. "Ill Composer Gets Top Rostropovich Award." *Moscow Times*, March 14.

Discography and Filmography

Babak, M. 1990. *Ia, nemetskii kompozitor iz Rossii . . . Monolog Al'freda Shnitke*. Moscow: Tsentral'naia Studiia Dokumental'nykh Fil'mov (TsSDF; RTsSDF).
Beethoven, Ludwig Van. Violin Concerto in D. Gidon Kremer, Academy of St. Martin-in-the-Fields. Philips CD, 410 549-2 (1982).
Beethoven, Ludwig Van. *Violin Concerto, Romances*. Gidon Kremer, The Chamber Orchestra of Europe. Teldec CD, 9031-74881-2 (1993).
Kronos Quartet. *Winter Was Hard*. Elektra/Asylum/Nonesuch CD, 9 79181-2 (1988).
Schnittke and Mahler. Melodiya-Ariola-Eurodisc LP, 28 384 KK (c1977).
Schnittke, et al. Melodiya-Ariola-Eurodisc LP, 200 083 (c1977).
Schnittke Concerto-Grosso no. 1. Melodiya-Eurodisc S 10 13135-6. Kremer, Grindenko, Rozhdestvensky, London Symphony Orchestra.
Simfonicheskaia muzyka sovetskikh kompozitorov: E. Denisov, S. Gubaidulina, A. Shnitke. Melodiia LP, S10-18758 (1983).
Zeitgenössische Komponisten in der Sowjetunion (Contemporary Composers in the USSR), Lokshin, Owtschinnikow, et al. (includes Schnitke String Quartet no. 1, played by Borodin Quartet. Melodiya-Ariola-Eurodisc 27 393 XGK (1970, 1976).

CHAPTER 20

CURB THAT ENTICING TONE

Music Censorship in the PRC

HON-LUN YANG

The focus of this chapter is music censorship in the People's Republic of China (hereafter the PRC). Music has always played an important role in Chinese society. Seen as the embodiment of dynasty, strength, and power, music was ascribed a political role in past centuries. When the Chinese Communist Party (hereafter the CCP) founded the PRC in 1949, music was called upon for socialist propaganda. Though the notion of censorship did not exist prior to the Reform and Open Policy introduced in 1978, government control was and still is pervasive. The censorship that is used by the government to monitor the nation's musical soundscape can be restrictive or constitutive, overt or covert.[1] This chapter has three objectives: (1) to illuminate censorship's relationship to socialist ideology; (2) to provide some examples of music censorship in the PRC at different phases of its history; (3) to reveal some of the intricacies and complexities in present-day music censorship in the PRC, particularly regarding music censorship on the Internet.

The Ideology of Socialist Music

One Chinese writer, Zeng Suijin, observed that in the first two decades of the PRC, what the government preached and what the people wanted were more or less the same. He states:

> Under the party leadership and encouragement, intellectuals of the literary and art world as well as the general public were infused with patriotism, collectivism, and communism. . . . People were fighting for the noblest cause, filled with confidence and hope for a better future, charged with a combative spirit that helped them overlook current problems. Most of all, they respected and admired their leaders. . . . People composed with deep emotions, they sang with deep passions,

and they listened with great enthusiasm.... This was what the government expected as music was the best way to educate, orient, and unify the people, and to fight the enemy.... It was also the opportunity for the intellectuals to transform and strengthen themselves.... (Zeng 2003, 33).

Zeng's observation and generalization of the sentiments of the period is fair. As the CCP invested heavily in the cultural scene, the nation witnessed a blooming socialist musical scene. While the Chinese Musicians Association was founded during the first meeting of the Chinese Writers Union held in July 1949 (Qu 2002, 1), there was a burgeoning of music conservatories and music organizations. The former were given the task of training a new generation of socialist musicians whereas the latter had the objective of propagating socialist music through performances. Equally prolific was the creative arena, which consisted of a significant repertoire of songs, symphonic and instrumental pieces, and dance and theatrical works by Chinese composers, all glorifying the new nation, the CCP, and its leaders and envisioning a new life (Qu 2002, 2–7).[2]

What Zeng and most Chinese witnessed in the musical arena of the 1950s and early 1960s was not only the triumph of a socialist world view but also strict government control. By the late 1930s and early 1940s, the CCP had mobilized left-wing writers to preach socialist ideologies in music. In their discourses, they called on music, first, to serve as a weapon to rescue the nation from Japanese invasion and fight for class struggle between the proletariat and the bourgeois. Second, they called on music to serve politics while denying its role as a form of self-expression. Third, they required music to follow the compositional approach of "Socialist Realism," which had recently been introduced in China, followed later by the ideologies of "nationalization" and "massification"(Feng 2007). Such artistic theories were first expounded in Mao Zedong's famous 1942 *Talks at the Yan'an Forum* and reiterated in discourses in the next two decades. They were sometimes fine tuned to suit the corresponding political climate of the time; for example, around 1955 Socialist Realism was put on the pedestal, whereas in 1958 Revolutionary Romanticism, Mao's Sinified form of Socialist Realism came to the fore (Yang 2004).

Although Socialist music ideology had a strong appeal in the early history of the PRC, it was not without contention in the music world. But ideological control was inevitable in the PRC, since the state monopolized the means of communication. As pointed out by Sue Jansen (1991), the Marxist-Leninist eschatology is inherently intolerant of heterodox ideas. Since proletarian revolution is taken as the ultimate goal of a historical progress, any intellectual or artistic currents seen as impediments to such a goal must be seen as deviations, signs of the "reactionary" (105). Likewise in the PRC, leading ideologies of the time—whether political or cultural—were to become dogmas often used by those in power as mandates to purge contending ideas or even personal rivals.

The debate between Lü Qi and He Lüting in 1955 was a case in point of ideological differences that turned political. Contending views were treated as a revival of capitalist ideology that had to be punished, the ultimate measure for those with power to silence opposing views, even in music. The two contending schools—the so-called "populist" versus the "cosmopolitan" (Kraus 1989, 29)—were represented by

Lü Qi and He Lüting, respectively. Lü Qi, then the president of the Chinese Musicians Association, emphasized the importance of songs over other musical genres and political messages over technical competence in musical compositions. He Lüting, then the president of the Shanghai Conservatory, emphasized the need to pay attention to the teaching and learning of compositional techniques as well as the benefit of learning from the West. Both had their supporters. The open debate started with He's speech reiterating his stance at the annual meeting of the 1953 Chinese Musicians Association, which was published in the journal *People's Music* (*Renmin Yinyue*) the following year. Supporters of Lü and He wrote to the journal to express their views, but their discourse turned political and belligerent, with each waging a war on the other. He was criticized for withdrawing from politics and real life to indulge in technique; his faults were linked with those of Hu Feng, who had recently been condemned for his "bourgeoisie idealism"—that is, his unwillingness to accept realism as the only literary aesthetic approach. He would have suffered the same fate as Hu Feng—an imprisonment of fourteen years for "anti-revolutionary" and "anti-party" crimes—had Vice Premier Chen Yi not interfered by calling for an end to the dispute and criticizing both sides. Though bloodshed was avoided this time, more ideological wars were to come, culminating in the infamous Cultural Revolution, during which even He could not escape imprisonment and almost all types of music, with the exception of the so-called "modeled works," were banned.[3]

Uprooting the Poison Weeds of the Society

The first musical genre wiped out of the PRC's soundscape was Shanghai pop for its association with jazz, the United States, and old Shanghai, icons of Western capitalistic culture. Dubbed "yellow," Shanghai pop consisted of popular-style songs from the 1930s and 1940s, which were "transmitted through LP records, radio broadcast, or performance at cabaret, the so-called venues of the petit bourgeoisie" (Lian 1957, 35). Shortly after the founding of the regime, the genre came under attack. In an issue of *Renmin Yinyue*, the editor, after reminding readers about the onset of the Korean War, went on to attack American culture and singled out jazz as a type of music that deluded people's reason and conscience. He considered Chinese yellow songs as imitations of jazz that would soon be replaced by revolutionary songs (Anonymous 1950, 7). The majority of love songs were branded yellow since sentiments of love, such as physical desire, melancholy, longing, and unrequited admiration were deemed unhealthy and viewed as propagating the sentiments and lifestyle of the petite bourgeoisie (Zhou 1958, 15). It was feared that they would fool people into forgetting about the cruel reality of the past and indulging in the materialistic life of a selected group (Li 1959, 15).

After the onset of the Anti-yellow Song Campaign in 1957, severe criticisms on the genre and those connected to it wiped out the genre until the mid 1980s. Shanghai pop composers such as Li Jinhui, Liu Xue'an, and Cheng Gexing were all reprimanded for the politically incorrect songs they had composed earlier.[4] Li Jinhui (1891–1967), the forefather of Chinese pop and the first composer to experiment with setting Chinese Mandarin songs to Western pop-style accompaniment in the late 1920s and early 1930s, had to renounce himself several times in public for the yellow songs he had written and the bad effects they had on the masses so as "to follow the party's lead," as he put it in a letter to his brother (Sun 2007, 83). Though he escaped the axe of the anti-rightist movement in 1957, he was not spared by the Cultural Revolution—he died in February 1967, during a cold winter shortly after his home had been raided by the Red Guards. Chen Gexing (1914–1961) and Liu Xue'an (1905–1985) were branded "rightist" in 1957. Chen was sent away to a labor camp in the north where he died three years later (Chen 2003). Liu was labeled "anti-revolutionary, yellow, and a traitor" for more than two decades until he died in 1985, blinded and paralyzed.[5]

As a child growing up in the PRC in the early 1960s, I did not remember Shanghai pop. Blasting from the public speakers and radio were only revolutionary songs, and no one dared to hold onto the LPs of the petite bourgeoisie during the Cultural Revolution, let alone to play yellow music at home, which would be considered a deadly sin. Not until the mid 1980s was there any mention of Li Jinhui and his songs, and more in-depth studies on his works and his position in Chinese music history began to appear only after 2000 (Sun 2007). As the Chinese writer Sun Jinan (2007, 233) observed,

> For quite a long period after the Cultural Revolution, "yellow music" was still a taboo. Even for those who missed and respected Li, due to the sensitivity of the topic, few chose to be engaged with the issue. But time has changed. With the reform and open policy, popular music has become an inevitable part of people's live. It is inevitable to revisit the songs of the 1920s and 1930s and to reconsider the value of "yellow music" and Li Jinhui.

The reappearance of popular music into the PRC's soundscape had to do with the illegal transmission of Hong Kong and Taiwan popular music through cassette tapes smuggled into the PRC territory in the early 1980s. These were then reproduced and disseminated widely in the country (Baranovitch 2003). The phenomenon did raise concerns in the society, and there were attempts to stop the influx of yellow music by both the government and prominent musical figures such as Wu Yongyi, Zhao Feng, and Lü Qi. The line of attack on the genre was not so different from that of the mid-1950s, but the outcome was utterly different (Hanson 2005). Popular-style songs—including songs from Hong Kong and Taiwan, recently revived Shanghai pop songs, as well newly composed songs in similar styles (including the folk-music inspired *xibeifeng*)—fell under the new nomenclature *tongzugequ* and were gradually accepted into the musical soundscape, becoming again the music of the masses in the mid-1980s.[6] At the time, as the central government was more concerned with economic prosperity than public entertainment, hardliners on socialist music had to give way to the "capitalistic taste" of the masses. This change, as one government official affirms in his preface to a recently released book on popular music's cultural meaning in the PRC, was a sign of the triumph of Deng Xiaoping's Reform and Open Policy.[7]

Chinese Rock's Long March

Not only did pop-style songs return to the PRC's soundscape after the Cultural Revolution thanks to the Reform and Open Policy, new genres such as rock and roll also found their way onto Chinese soil. Rock was largely an underground genre until 1986 when Cui Jin, the so-called godfather of Chinese rock, brought the genre to public recognition by singing his song "Having nothing" (*Yiwu suoyou*) at a pop music concert.[8] Cui was seen as having "introduced into post-revolutionary China a whole new ethos that combined individualism, nonconformism, personal freedom, authenticity, direct and bold expression, and protest and rebellion, in short, the essence of Western rock culture" (Baranovitch 2003, 32). But since rock is a genre imbued with the sentiment of rebellion against oppression and conformity, it is no wonder that it never quite overcame its marginalized status in China and has always been treated with caution by the state.[9] Despite a short blooming period from the late 1980s to the early 1990s, the rock music scene in the PRC has been in decline since the mid-1990s, and rockers and rock bands are struggling for survival.

The marginalization of Chinese rock is due to many factors, among them: the June Fourth Incident in Tiananmen Square in 1989, which changed the political as well as cultural climate of the society; the intensified influence of Hong Kong and Taiwan pop music; the rapid spread of karaoke technology; the radical commercialization in all sectors of Chinese society (Baranovitch 2003, 42–53); and last but not least, illegal Internet transmission and state interference. As one Chinese writer remarks:

> Rock is not a genre with government support in the West, but with more than half a century of development, the state would not interfere with its practice. Not only that, but it is even given public space, such as including it at public activities, even at presidential election. But in China, this is not the case. As stipulated by media regulations, singers wearing long hair are not allowed on TV. Rockers who talk to audiences at live concerts run the risk of being banned if what they say is regarded as inappropriate. Because of all these problems, Chinese rock cannot be seen as developing along the same path as Western rock. (Guo 2007, 303)

Indeed, Chinese rock bands enjoy very little commercial success in the PRC and most rockers can't even make their living as full-time band players. Multinational conglomerate music companies, such as EMI, Warner, Sony, and Universal, had in the late

1980s and early 1990s foreseen a blooming PRC rock music scene, which nonetheless never materialized. Rockers such as Cui Jian and He Yong were signed by Western record labels, which finally withdrew their contracts (Guo 2007). State regulation and intervention were among the causes. The band Breathing (*Huxi*), for example, was scheduled to release its first album in 1990 but was stopped by the government due to one of the songs on the album *The Sun is Rising* (*Taiyang chulai le*) being regarded as containing a subversive message (Baranovitch 2003, 216). When the album was released in 1992, the second Chinese rock album after Cui Jian's 1989 *Rock and Roll of the New Long March*, it did not enjoy the enormous success the band thought it would have if it had been released in 1990. Cui Jian also suffered a setback in his rock career. His 1990 concert tour of ten major cities to raise ¥1 million RMB for Beijing to host the Asian Games was terminated halfway through the tour, presumably because he violated a regulation by talking to the audience (Baranovitch 2003, 227–228). Cui Jian stopped giving large-scale public concerts in Beijing after 1993. For twelve years, he only gave large-scale concerts outside Beijing, where he performed only at private venues until 2005.[10] Only in 2013, during his interview with the Hong Kong reporter Patrick Boehler, was the ban explained as being due to his veiled condemnation of the Tiananmen crackdown (December 1). Another rocker, He Yong, disappeared from the rock stage for almost eight years after he was reprimanded for what he said at the Beijing concert in 1996—he asked whether Li Xuli was beautiful after performing his song "Beautiful Girls" (*guniang piaoliang*).[11] He's question must have been considered condescending by certain officials, as Li Xuli was an exemplary communist who was just awarded the honor of Model of the Working People (*laodong mofan*). He was banned for four years. Magic Stone (Moya changpian), a branch of Taiwan's Rock Records and Tapes (Gunshi changpian) that had high hopes for He as well as a number of other rockers and invested heavily in the PRC's rock market, ended up bankrupt (Guo 2007). The band Black Panther, which still struggles to survive after almost two decades, regarded its experience as quintessential to rock music in the PRC, as "it came across a lot of natural disasters as well as human damages." The latter included their music video being banned from TV in 1996 and a scheduled large-scale concert in Xi'an being canceled at the last minute, causing the organizer to lose a lot of money (Guo 2007, 119).

Just like the majority of the Chinese population, the younger generation of rockers is indifferent toward politics. As pointed out in a recent article in *Asian Times* (November 14, 2009), even though the young rockers are aware of the many injustices in Chinese society and know that they should fight for what they believe in, they lack the fire to act on these views. The lyrics of their songs do allude to some of the problems of society but only vaguely, so they fail to directly articulate the root of the problem.[12] The writer of this chapter would perhaps adopt a more sympathetic stance if he/she considered the unique context in which Chinese rock bands negotiate their existence—the various levels of restriction on freedom of expression, which will be explored in the following section. Most important of all, let us not forget that there are still rockers who fight for what they believe in with their music, even at the risk of their own safety.[13]

Music Censors and Censored Music in the PRC

Although the PRC government relaxed its restriction of the forms of entertainment the Chinese public is allowed to enjoy, it did not give up its control over what it regards as good for the public. As Baranovitch (2003, 215) observes:

> in its attempts to maintain its hegemony and control the state nevertheless often actively suppresses voices that do not conform to its own. In the popular music scene, the state uses various methods to silence other voices, the most important of which are censorship of lyrics, restrictions on live concerts, and exclusion from television.

As censorship is a taboo in the PRC, the state has been slow and evasive to admit to such a practice[14] just as in the former USSR, where officially state censorship was found never to have existed (Jansen 1991, 100). In theory, Chinese citizens enjoy as much freedom of speech as people in Western countries. As stated in Article 35 of the Chinese constitution: "citizens of the PRC enjoy freedom of speech, of the press, of assembly, of association, of procession and of demonstration." But in reality there are various laws such as the Prior Restraint Regulation and executive orders and circulars such as the Important Topics and many more issued in recent years to cope with what the state sees as problems. These laws and regulations are above the constitutional rights of the individual. As a result, the public's right to freedom of speech is largely compromised.[15]

At present, more than a few state departments are responsible for implementing music censorship, all with the aim to protect its citizens against "mental contamination" as well as to protect its government against criticism. The earliest censorial agent in the PRC is perhaps the Central Propaganda Department (CPD), which was founded in 1924 shortly after the establishment of the CCP in 1921. Though its original task was to promote communist ideology, it acquired tremendous power through overseeing the ideologies of the country and, more importantly, various state departments to implement the dissemination of proper ideologies. In the area of print, the General Administration of Press and Publication (GAPP) is responsible for granting licenses to all the state and private presses, which bestow the censorial responsibility to the presses' editors to ensure all published content follows the directives of the party. When violations are caught, the editors can be held responsible for repeated violations and run the risk of being fired while the press can be shut down.[16]

The Ministry of Culture is responsible for funding various state-owned performing institutions and granting performance licenses to state and private agents as well as restricting and banning undesirable performances and artists. The State Administration of Radio, Film and Television, a branch of the State Council, is responsible for the content of all radio, television, satellite, and Internet broadcasts to ensure that no undesirable messages reach the masses. The Customs Department is responsible for ensuring that all the items imported into the country, including music CDs and DVDs, are not "harmful to the government, economy, culture, or morals of the PRC."[17] The Internet is supervised by both the Ministry for Information Industry as well as the State Council Information Office.

As one netizen remarked, "In this area, our country's policy is difficult to understand—similar stuff, some are banned, some are not; similar people, some are arrested and some are not."[18] As censorship is not an area open for public discussion, the question of why some music is censored and other music is not always intrigues the public. When certain songs are thought to be banned, there are always netizens who claim they do have a copy, which suggests the lack of consistency and transparency in the government's implementation of censorship.

Although there are no clear guidelines as to what type of music would be censored, it is safe to assume that singers who have provoked the regime in one form or another and songs with lyrics interpreted by the state as containing subversive messages—such as direct criticism of the government and its policies or challenges to the party's legitimacy—would be banned (Baranovitch 2003, 216). Besides, songs rated as vulgar, obscene, rebellious, or satirical and songs poking fun at party leaders or other ethnic groups would also be banned. Furthermore, singers who are seen as violating party taboos or defiant in behavior are banned as well.

Protecting people from moral contamination is a frequent argument for censorship. For example, Anita Mui's famous song "Bad Girl" (*huai nuhai*) was banned in the early 1990s presumably because of the lyrics' explicit reference to sexual transgression—an innocent girl who wants to become bad (Man 2005). The ban has perhaps more to do with Mui's open support of the pro-democracy participants of the June Fourth Incident and the English phrase of the lyrics—"Why, why, tell me why." Officials might fear that Mui would inspire audiences to chant the phrase as a challenge to the regime's legitimacy (Witzleben 1999). In 1995, Mui defied the ban by singing "Bad Girl" in the concert encore, which resulted in the cancellation of all her scheduled concerts and the banning of her further appearances in the PRC (Lin 1995).

Songs by individuals uploaded onto the Internet are routinely screened. As another example of song censorship in 2009, the song "Conquer the World" (*zhengfu shijie*) by a group known as Lekeban has been banned for its frivolous and politically incorrect lyrics—"taking a sticky photo with the ex-party leader Jiang Zemin, picking up French girls, and shooting a Japanese A-grade movie." Another song entitled "Even Pigs Laugh" (*zhu dou xiao*) by the group Hagou has been banned for its "vulgarity and rebellious tone even though it does reflect reality at times."[19]

The implementation of censorship, from the eyes of the outsider, seems to depend on the general political atmosphere of the time as well as other factors including the relationship between the individual and the state officials or the potential publicity value of the individual concerned. The Taiwanese singer Chang Hui-mei, better known as A-mei, for example, has been banned since May 2000 after she sang the national anthem at the inauguration of the Taiwanese president Chen Shui-bian. While she was not allowed to sell records in the PRC and her songs were banned from broadcast on radio stations, all her endorsers had to pull out of her TV commercials. As mentioned in the

Chinese Wikipedia, at a 2004 interview with CCTV, the program host posed the following question to her: "Given that it will affect so many, do you think you have to be more careful about what you do?"[20] Her scheduled 2004 concert in Hangzhou had to be canceled due to the strong sentiments of the rallying protesters. The ban on her music was finally lifted, however. She gave a concert in Shanghai in November 2007 and returned to the PRC in 2009 with a series of concerts in Guangzhou, Shanghai, and Beijing. The improved relationship between the PRC and Taiwan might have played a part in the lifting of the ban. With the return of power to the Nationalist Party, the threat of the Democratic Progressive Party's (DPP) call for independence was gone and the tension between the PRC and Taiwan eased. While A-Mei had been seen as a supporter of the DPP, a political party notorious for its stance in favor of Taiwanese independence, she was seen in 2007 as a Taiwanese cultural icon capable of improving the relationship between the people of the PRC and Taiwan (Jennings 2007).

During supposedly sensitive times of the year, such as prior to the anniversary of the June Fourth Incident, or any major national events, such as the 2008 Summer Olympics, the government would be extremely cautious about granting performance licenses to public concerts so as to avoid any chances of public disruptions and embarrassments that would tarnish the image of the regime. For example, months prior to the Olympics, public concerts were banned and bars and clubs had to obtain licenses for live performances, putting many Beijing musicians in hibernation. On April 26, 2008, the Ministry of Culture announced plans to tighten control over cultural activities and products ahead of the Olympics so as to ensure neither major security accidents nor mass incidents would happen. As confirmed by the Xinhua news agency, Beijing police had ordered the cancellation of several major events, including a popular music festival in May.[21]

As any public performance requires the approval of the Ministry of Culture, the state has strict control over the contents of the performance, which have to be submitted to the Ministry's screening prior to the issuing of the license. But even so, there is no guarantee of smooth sailing even after the license has been granted, as the Ministry of Culture can still interfere by requiring a last-minute change of program or simply calling a halt to a scheduled event. For example, at jazz pianist Harry Connick's Shanghai concert on March 8, 2009, the players were required by officials from the Ministry of Culture an hour before the concert to replace some of the existing pieces with more desirable ones, for which the group did not happen to have the performing charts with them. As a result, the performance delivered was somewhat disappointing to the audience (*TMZ*, March 15, 2008; *Shanghaiist*, March 13, 2008).

Any incident could trigger a tightening of control. For instance, the Icelandic singer Björk's saying the words "Tibet, Tibet" after her song "Declare Independence" at her Shanghai concert on March 2, 2008, has been linked with the subsequent tightening of control on foreign performers,[22] an area where the government had been seeking more power prior to the incident. Curiously, the concert of the band Oasis, which was scheduled on April 3 and 5, 2009, in Beijing and Shanghai respectively, was canceled in March 2009, even though the immigration and licensing processes for the concerts had been completed before tickets were on sale. As for what caused the cancellation, there were two very different explanations. The concert promoters attributed the cancellation to the Ministry of Culture's finding out that lead singer Noel Gallagher had participated in a Free Tibet benefit concert in the United States in 1997 (*BBC News*, March 2, 2009). The Ministry of Culture denied its role in the cancellation. The Chinese organizer, a Mr. Luo (only identified by his last name) from a company named Beijing All Culture Communication Co. Ltd., told the media that the concert was canceled because of his company's financial difficulties.[23]

In the Name of God

We are unlikely to find out the genuine reason behind the cancellation of Oasis's scheduled concert. It is worth pointing out that religious music is another sensitive area carefully monitored by the state. One instance of such censorship was the cancellation of a classical music concert of the Chinese-Canadian composer Huang Anlun scheduled to take place in Beijing on April 17, 2004. A graduate of the Central Conservatory, Huang was invited to take part in a concert entitled "To Glorify China in God's Grace," which was also the title of a large-scale vocal piece with lyrics by the Taiwan poet Chen Weifang. The composer revealed that this work of his was inspired by the generosity shown to the victims of the Taiwan earthquake by the people of the Chinese mainland and Hong Kong. Wang considered the theme of the concert to be patriotic—it glorified god, his country, and its people—and he saw nothing wrong in it. So he attributed the cancellation to the religious connotation of the title of the concert and the unprecedented ticket sales that resulted from some religious organizations purchasing blocks of tickets. These must have raised a red flag, he thought, with the Ministry of Culture, which was cautious about religious groups using the concert as a venue for unlawful gathering. While Huang was disappointed, he admitted that there was very little he could do then.[24]

In 2008 there was another tightening of control over the performance of religious music. In October, as reported by Richard Spencer in the London *Daily Telegraph* (September 30, 2008), foreign performing groups were prevented from performing pieces of a religious nature. For example, at a fundraising concert in honor of the dead in Sichuan's earthquake zone, the Sinfonica Orchestra di Roma was forced to drop its original program featuring Mozart's Requiem and replace it with a program of nonreligious works. The British Academy of Ancient Music was instructed to give *The Messiah* as a concert by invitation only to get around the problem, and ironically, the audience in attendance included members of the Politburo and other senior government officials.

Top officials' caution toward religious music is the byproduct of the atheistic stance of the CCP. In the words of Catherine Sampson writing for the London *Guardian* (October 8, 2008),

> [Christianity] presented people with an alternative authority (God) and an alternative set of rules. . . . Music may speak for itself, and perhaps even party officials have been moved in ways that have alarmed them. In general, however, audiences for

performances of western religious music seem to be there primarily for the musical experience.

During the early years of the PRC's history, all religions were banned and religious practitioners were persecuted. But in the past decades, the regime has adopted a more tolerant attitude toward religious practices,[25] and the rising trend in the study of religious music suggests relaxed control.[26]

According to the observation of the *Daily Telegraph*, there seems to be a divide among China's top leaders regarding the spread of Christianity: "Some regard an explosion in evangelical Christianity across the country as having social benefits, while others regard it as an alien threat to Communist party control" (Spencer 2008). The divide perhaps explains the variable policy toward religious music. The fact that works such as Mozart's Requiem or Handel's *Messiah* were banned as religious music is perhaps a reflection of the Ministry of Culture officials' lack of cultural awareness—these works have been enjoyed by secular audiences since they were written, and they certainly played no part in the transmission of Christianity in China and elsewhere.

A Symphony to Reflect on the Path of Communism

Generally, officials provide no explanations for canceled events, and the Ministry of Culture's decision to stop an event or require changes to the proposed program could be triggered for reasons that appear trivial by Western standards. Such is the case with the Beijing composer Wang Xilin to be discussed in below.[27] Wang Xilin's symphonic music concert was scheduled to be held in Beijing on December 8, 2000, in an event supported by the Ministry of Culture as Wang was the resident composer of the Beijing Symphony Orchestra. The event was canceled just a few days prior to the scheduled performance. The composer presumed that the reason for the cancelation was the statement he made at rehearsal explaining that the impetus of one of the pieces in the concert, his Symphony No. 4, was his reflection on the path and downfall of communism in the twentieth century. Despite Wang's inquiries with officials at the Ministry of Culture in the next two years both in person and in writing regarding the cancellation of his concert, he received no explanation or apology. The Swiss soloist Egidus Streiff, who had commissioned the violin concerto scheduled to be performed also at the concert, was sent home with full pay. He was told the conductor was struck by illness, but his request to visit the conductor and the composer was denied.

It is unclear whether the rationale for canceling Wang's concert was the speech he gave or a message perceived to be embedded in the music. But the case does illustrate the power and will of the government to stop any gesture interpreted as defiant or questioning the legitimacy of the regime. In this case, Wang insisted the cancellation was unjust punishment, as he believed there was nothing wrong in his speech because it did not criticize the government but just reflected on the path of communism as a whole—while it failed in the West, it still prevailed in the PRC.

The cancellation of the concerts of Wang Xilin and Huang Anlun were not high-profile incidents that attracted attention beyond the small classical music circle in the PRC. Since I happened to be in Beijing shortly after both of the incidents, I had the opportunity to hear remarks on the incidents by various musicians I encountered. Naturally, most were sympathetic to the situation but often blamed the composers for their inadequate self-discipline. Wang Xilin was faulted for not keeping his mouth shut at the rehearsal (as instrumental music is, after all, abstract in its meaning without verbal articulation) while Huang Anguo was blamed for his naiveté in articulating the religious aspect of his music. Rather than condemning the practice of government censorship, the majority of Chinese see self-discipline as an acceptable practice by which to avoid stepping beyond the authority's boundaries. This view is what the government has encouraged: self-regulation as the best measure for keeping society in harmony.

Anthony Loewenstein's recent study on Internet censorship in the PRC corroborates my observation. The views expressed by Loewenstein's interviewees bespeak a stance shared by the majority of Chinese in the PRC. Loewenstein (2008, 198–199) writes regarding the response of one of his interviewees:

> Gin painted a Chinese society that had far bigger issues to worry about than internet censorship. He said that life was much freer than ten years ago and the situation was not as black and white as Westerners often portrayed. Books were routinely banned but, if someone really wanted a title, the active black market in books could usually oblige. . . . In perhaps his most perceptive comment, Gin said that censorship worried Western human rights campaigners more than the Chinese themselves.

Another of Loewenstein's interviewees named Hsu remarked, "people just want to get on with their lives," and pointed out that in the PRC, "money had become the new god of industry as long as political content was generally avoided" (200). Unlike people in the West where core values such as democracy and respect for individual rights have been in practice for a much longer period, as Loewenstein's interviewee Gin put it, "Chinese people are still not used to the law protecting them" (199), and complying with authorities is an ingrained part of Chinese culture that could be traced back to the teaching of Confucius.

Wang Xilin and Huang Anguo suffered no further censorial acts from the government. Neither of them was banned from later concerts. Huang Anguo was soon featured at a concert of his works held at the Central Conservatory in December 2005 to celebrate the school's fifty-fifth anniversary, and other concerts of his works were to follow in the next few years. Wang's Symphony No. 4 at last received its premiere in Beijing in April 2005 at a concert devoted to all Wang's works. The 2005 concert proceeded smoothly, though the composer was advised by all his friends not to speak what they considered nonsense at all the related events. Wang's Symphony No. 4 was repeated in the following year at a concert to celebrate the composer's seventieth birthday, though it was entitled "Concert of Works by Wang Xilin—celebrating 50 years of his music composition—dedicated to the memory of Lu Xun to commemorate the 125th anniversary of his birth and the 70th anniversary of his death," presumably to avoid the pitfall of self-aggrandizing.

Each of Wang's two concerts was followed on the next day by a seminar of his works attended by prominent musical figures in Beijing, including the conductor of the Beijing Symphony Orchestra, Tan Lihua, as well as leading composers and professors from the various music conservatories in Beijing. The first seminar was co-hosted by the Central Conservatory and the Beijing Musicians Association, the second by the Beijing Musicians Association alone. Curiously, at the second event, each of the participants was reimbursed ¥500 RMB to cover transportation, which as I was told, was a regular practice, presumably an incentive for participants to take part in such government organized events. There is no doubt that both events were testimony to the Ministry's support of the composer. In fact, the state support Wang received—two concerts devoted exclusively to his works and earlier in 2004 a commission for his Symphony No. 6 with a very handsome fee—would make any composers in the West envious, as one Israel composer who happened to take part at the seminar remarked.

Wang's Symphony No. 4 was a great success both in the PRC and beyond. There are studies on its compositional techniques, though none mentioned the canceled premiere. The score was published by the People's Music Publishing House (Renmin yinyue chubanshe), the regime's leading music publisher, which used to only publish music with explicit socialist themes. Nonetheless, the introductory note the composer invited me to write to accompany the score never got to the printer, the explanation to the composer by the editor of the press being that he failed to receive my approval. The score is scheduled to be published again by another state press in Hunan (Hunan wenyi chubanshe) along with the composer's other works, and I was again invited by Wang to provide an introductory note to the score of his Symphony No. 4. The composer insisted on my mentioning the performance history of the work and his suffering during the Cultural Revolution. I have complied with his instructions, though not without hesitation as I doubt that such a comment will pass the built-in editorial censorship of the press—each publication is overseen by a responsible editor to ensure that its content adheres to the party's directives. While I feel obligated to speak on behalf of the composer, Wang uses my Hong Kong-based outsider position as his voice. I do have concerns about the consequence of "speaking the truth," and I find it extremely frustrating to waste time on projects likely to be censored. Not particularly proud of my stance, I am the more sympathetic to the millions of Chinese who have to live with censorship. If they appear indifferent to outsiders, I suppose it is because they have no choice or they don't know they have other options.

The combination of threat and seduction from the state—that is, both censorship and support—is what Wang Xilin experienced in his career and what Miklos Harszti referred to as the "velvet prison," a system used by post-totalitarian governments in Eastern Europe to keep intellectuals collaborating with the leadership (McCormick

2007, 131). While Wang wanted me to speak on his behalf about his experience, he valued the state support he was enjoying. Just prior to the 2005 commemoration of the June Fourth Incident, when a Hong Kong newspaper did a report on how Wang's Symphony No. 3 was inspired by that event, Wang was upset and asked me to write a protest note to the press asserting that the symphony has nothing to do with the incident. He related to me that he did not want his concert to be canceled, given that it was so hard to have contemporary-style works performed. As McCormick (2007, 132) points out, the velvet prison system works because of the lack of alternatives outside the system and the continuous threat of serious sanctions for those who violate it. In fact, Wang did not consider himself a beneficiary of the system because of his outspokenness and his insistence on not writing "leading melody" works that glorify the regime as many composers do. In a nation like the PRC, the relationship between the individual artist and the state is intricate—the state relies on the individual for its ideological propaganda while the individual takes advantage of the state's resources to advance his or her arts.

The Great Firewall of China

While the advent of Internet technology has changed the music industry, it has created challenges for censors. Though it is believed that the PRC once forbade its citizens from using the Internet, it now has more net users than the United States—228.5 million by March 2008 compared with 217.1 million in America (Loewenstein 2008, 177). Having invested heavily in technologies to block unwanted websites and to track the behavior of users, many of which were provided by Western companies such as Cisco and Microsoft (Loewenstein 2008, 188–191), the PRC is now able to control what its citizens are allowed to see and hear on the superhighway. For example, when our family was in China for vacation during the last few days of December 2009, we faced the power of the great firewall—my daughter was not able to log onto Facebook to chat with her friends, I was prevented from locating a performance on YouTube, and my husband could not access Sina.com to read the news.[28]

To comply with the laws of the PRC, search engines are required to block out sites with politically sensitive materials such as "the three T's"—Tibet, Taiwan, and Tiananmen—whereas Internet providers are required to shut down sites identified by the government as violating the law and to reveal to the authority the identity of the users. While web owners bear the responsibility of maintaining a "legal" and "healthy" Internet by following the executive guidelines laid out by the government, including removing any postings not in accordance in bulletin board systems (BBS) and chat rooms, hundreds and thousands of Internet inspectors are hired to police the highway around the clock so as to catch and punish the violators (Loewenstein 2008; McCormick 2007). As a result, not only news and information but also music does not flow as freely on the Chinese Internet as in the West even though Chinese officials openly denounced such practices. Then, those who have money enjoy more freedom than those who don't. Just when I was blocked from YouTube, a message popped up from a company offering me the service of rerouting my Internet connection to an off-PRC site for the price of $12.99 a month. Presumably, with the technology such service provides, the user can climb over the firewall to visit blocked sites. Taking note of the fast growth of the Internet music scene, which has exceeded that of other areas such as online gaming and trading, the PRC government has wanted to assert more control since as far back as 2006. In May of that year, the Ministry of Culture took action to block unlicensed Internet music sites as well as sites that uploaded music not being screened by the Ministry of Culture.[29] In the following year, a circular entitled "The Ministry of Culture's Opinion on the Development of Internet Music and Management" was issued.[30] The circular, which was an executive order, was supposed to deal with the following problems: (1) the vulgarity of some of the contents of Internet music products; (2) privacy and illegal upload and download, violations of intellectual property rights which disrupt the order of the market; (3) some sites' transmission of unscreened musical products from the West; (4) a small number of products that are harmful to ethnic custom and the stability of society.[31] In addition to providing a clear definition of Internet music and stating the government's encouraging attitude toward developing Internet music with Chinese characteristics, the circular stipulated the need to tighten control over the dissemination of Internet music, requiring music sites to self-screen uploaded local music and submit imported music to the Ministry of Culture for approval. In August 2009 another circular entitled "The Ministry of Culture on strengthening the screening the contents of internet music" reiterated the tightening control.[32] According to the circular, as of January 1, 2010, all Internet music distributors, including Yahoo China, Baidu, and Google, have to submit all imported music, including the songs' lyrics and translations if not in Chinese, to the screening of the Ministry of Culture prior to being put online for distribution. Music from Hong Kong, Taiwan, and Macau is treated as imported music. Chinese Internet music has to be registered and made available for scrutiny when necessary, but approval is not required prior to upload.

With such measures, the state hopes to have better control over what music will be disseminated for its citizens by eliminating illegal sites and unauthorized uploaded materials, some of which could have vulgar or obscene content or be interpreted as containing subversive or merely politically incorrect messages. But as pointed out in a widely disseminated Internet article, requiring website owners to self-screen uploaded music is a daunting task and presumably not a realistic measure due to the volume of the music traffic and the spontaneous nature of Internet transmission. Tracing the sources of uploads would be extremely difficult, and ensuring the accuracy and thoroughness of the screening would require great resources.[33] In response to the 2009 circular, another Internet article raises six questions challenging the practicality of the measures mandated in the circular and also mentions the government's failure to enforce the compliance of all music site providers after the 2007 circular.[34]

Even in the PRC, the Internet is still a relatively free space for music's dissemination. Song writers are able to upload their creations for others to share, presumably spared from the covert censorship of the mores of the society or the concern of the market. Even though the government exerts strong control over the contents of the nation's media, banned songs are still easily accessible for download, as is information about banned singers and performers. A list of banned singers and songs has even been circulated.[35] While it is impossible to verify the reliability of the information, some Internet users do provide seemingly accurate explanations for the banning of songs. Interestingly, the explanations are given in such a way as to evade the filtering technology. For example, one netizen asked at Baidu's BBS why it does not have a site for the singer Hou Dejian, who was once very well known, particularly for his song "The Dragon's Descendent" (*long de zhuanren*). The answer posted is as follows: "The inquirer from 83 should know why. Baidu shields anything political. Hou Dejian made some political mistakes in 1989—he stood on the students' side."[36] The Internet is also a place to share information and views that are banned but have somehow escaped the screening technology as well as the highway police. For instance, a netizen posted on Baidu's BBS a *Wall Street* reporter's interview with Noel Gallagher in which the latter talked about the cancellation of the concert. The netizens who read the note were astonished by the sensitive nature of the content.[37]

Conclusion

To be able to make music and enjoy music is considered a human right, so any unlawful attempt to stop the production and consumption of music is a violation of this right. But in most countries, just as in the PRC, censorship is a legal procedure by which the government keeps away certain undesirable forms of expression, including music. Why do governments exercise censorship? It is because of fear. As George Bernard Shaw pointed out in *Mrs. Warren's Profession*, "All censorships exist to prevent anyone from challenging current conceptions and existing institutions." It is no wonder that music, with its power to provide the masses with a sense of orientation, a means of identification, and a venue for emotional expression (Frith 1987), is an area of concern for both the government and the public. Supporters of censorship believe that it protects the less informed from impending harm, such as the contamination of the mind. But a contending school of thought holds that it is better to leave it to the individual to decide what is best for him or her as well as to protect musicians' right to freedom of expression. There are always debates on the pros and cons of censorship as well as on where and how to draw the line between the interests of both sides. While Western critics generally frown on censorship as a form of control, in the PRC most citizens accept its presence. Actually, 80 percent of the netizens who took part in a poll conducted by the Pew Internet and American Life Project supported censorship, believing that it would protect them from harmful information (Loewenstein 2008, 183). If, after all, the criteria for censorship are largely ideological—that is, informed by a particular value system—there is undoubtedly a need for continuous and constant negotiation and renegotiation of boundaries to ensure that censorship serves more people than it punishes. From the time "yellow music" was banned to the present when Chinese netizens are able to share music files on the Internet, albeit under the scrutiny of the filtering system and the Internet police, the PRC has indeed moved many steps forward in opening up its nation's soundscape.

Notes

1. As pointed out in recent studies on censorship, in addition to repressive censorship that generally involves silencing an opposing expression, there is constitutive censorship such as the taboos and mores of the community as well as the subtle control asserted by corporations and the media, and the underlying construction of psychic and social forces performs the same function of restricting expression and controlling behavior. See for example discussions in Riley 1998 and Müller 2004.

    Note that Chinese names in the main text appear last name first according to Chinese practice, and all English translations from Chinese are by the present author unless specified.
2. For more information on Chinese compositions composed in the 1950s and 1960s, see Liang 2004 as well as Qu 2002.
3. For more information on Chinese music in the Cultural Revolution see, for example, Kraus 1989, Melvin and Cai 2004, and Clark 2008.
4. The relocation of Pathe-EMI to Hong Kong in 1952 opened doors to Shanghai pop composers and singers to relocate to Hong Kong. A handful of composers including Li Houxiang and Yao Min and singers such as Yao Lee, Chang Loo, and Yeh Ming found a home in Hong Kong (Wong 2001, 81). But the composers who stayed behind were patriotic and had faith in the CCP. They were also willing to reform themselves according to the teachings of communism. For more on Shanghai pop, see Jones 2001.
5. Liu's condemnation was due partly, if not entirely, to his being the composer of "When Will You Come Again" (*Heri jun zailai?*), a very popular Shanghai pop song composed in 1938 for the movie *Sanxing banyue*. Because the song was sung by Li Xianglan, a Shanghai pop star of Japanese descent who appeared in a number of Japanese-made movies in the 1940s, it was used as a piece of evidence in Liu's condemnation. Liu's songs were banned in the PRC until 1984 when a Hong Kong pop star sang a song of Liu's at a Beijing concert. See Liu 2001, preface. The publication of *Selected Works of Liu Xue'an* (*Liu Xuean Zuopinxuan*) was initiated and supported by Liu's friends from abroad and in the PRC. The project was received with great enthusiasm partly due to the fact that many who knew Liu felt the injustice done to him and his family.
6. The popular (*liuxing/tongsu*) style of music was officially recognized in 1986 and became a legitimate singing category in the annual state-run CCTV singing competition (Yang 1990, 226).
7. The preface was written by Lin Xiong, who was the top official of the Propaganda Department of the Guangdong province (Chen and Chen 2008). For a discussion of the PRC's economic reform, see for instance Keuth 1989 and Wu 2005.
8. The first Chineses rock band known as "Wenli Mawang" was founded in 1980 with members from Beijing's Second Foreign Language Institute (Guo 2007, 5). For more information on Cui Jin, see Jones 1992, and Cui and Zhou 2001.
9. Music censorship, particularly that of rock music, is also found in other countries such as in the United Kingdom. See Cloonan 1996.

10. The following songs of Cui Jian were included on an unverified list of banned songs in the PRC: "Have Nothing" (Yiwu zuoyou), "A Piece of Red Cloth" (Yikuai hongbu), "The Egg under the Red Flag" (Hongqi xia de dan), "The Last Fire" (Zuihou yichang), and "Nanni Bay" (Nanniwan). These songs are identified on YouTube as banned in the PRC. People I know from Beijing did tell me about the ban of Cui Jian in Beijing, but no details were given regarding the ban and its extent. I interviewed Cui Jian once and he was very cautious about what he said. See Yang 2007.
11. He gave a concert in Hong Kong in 2004 at which he chatted with the audience by asking if Hong Kong's girls are beautiful. His song "Beautiful Girls" is ironically about the materialistic nature of Chinese girls.
12. Cui Jian also noted such a problem as he spoke during an interview with a reporter after his concert in Hong Kong: "I recently found out there are three Chinas—one is ideology, one is economy, one is the emotion, the culture, the history. But the problem I can see is, these three are fighting each other. Most of the young people, they forget about politics, just want the other two" (Boehler 2013).
13. I have come across references to the rocker Huang Wei who insisted on playing in Tiananmen Square on June 4, 2009. He was said to disappear on his way to host his Beijing concert in Tiananmen Square after his farewell Internet concert on May 31, 2009. His act was said to have raised concerns among the government as well as his family members. One local official was said to have lined up corporate sponsorship for his concert and promised to help him issue an album in exchange for his not going to Beijing. But Huang refused and was alleged to have said, "Away from the square, my music loses its life. I refuse this deal." And to the State Security (*guoanbu*) official, he is supposed to have said, "You can arrest me in Beijing, but cannot house arrest me in Wenzhou. Otherwise, I'll do something better than Yang Jie." The news is originally from a source identified as *Xin tongren* June 4, 2009, accessed on January 4, 2010, http://www.ntdtv.com/xtr/b5/2009/06/04/a302519.html. The news has been reposted on various other sites, sometimes to accompany the music video of Huang Wei, and is identified as "banned news in the PRC."
14. The Chinese diplomat Yang Xiokun was reported to have declared, "We don't have software blocking internet sites. I'm not sure why people say these things. We do not have restrictions at all." Quoted in Rowan Callick's article "China's great firewall," *Australian*, March 12, 2007.
15. For a better understanding of the legal aspect of censorship in the PRC, see the website set up by the Congressional–Executive Commission on China, on which a page is devoted to agencies responsible for censorship. http://www.cecc.gov/pages/virtualAcad/exp/expcensors.php, accessed January 5, 2010.
16. For more discussion on how the government controls the press, see McCormick 2007 and Human Rights in China 2004. But locals do have strategies to deal with the rules and regulations of the government. I was once given a volume of music writings from the 1980s on "new-wave music" which was identified as for internal distribution only. As articles published in the 1980s might not pass the censorship standard of the twenty-first century, I was told, such was the strategic solution to the need for such a volume to serve the institution's teaching needs.
17. Based on Article 4 in "Regulations on Customs' Administration of Printed Materials and Audio/visual Materials Imported or Exported by Individual Via Carriage or Post," issued on July 10, 1991.

18. Interestingly, the netizen's remark quoted here, which I downloaded on December 4, 2009, was blocked or removed on January 5, 2010, when I tried to find the URL for the quote. Searching with the exact phrase of Chinese words, I am still able to see its location embedded in a video at the following URL: www.jahu.net/videos/video/CgCBkLkyBS8/. But after I click, I am told the site is not available, and the search engine directs me to a substitute video.
19. The information is from a Chongqing newspaper dated December 20, 2009, which warned Hong Kong people to be careful if they go to sing at karaoke in Chongqing. It was reported that an alarm system connected to the local police station has been set up at all the karaoke centers. When banned songs are picked, the system will alert the local police right away. There are a number of banned songs highlighted in the report, including the two mentioned in the main text of this article. The criticism of these banned songs is supposed to come from the officials. News release of the ban can be found on *Sohunews* dated December 19, 2009, http://news.sohu.com/20091219/n269060638.shtml, accessed on December 1, 2013.
20. The original line is: "*zai hui yinxiang zhemeduoren de qianti zhixia, ni shi bus hi yao geng jinshen, zhiji yingai suo de shi shenme.*"
21. The source of my information is the web page "China tightened control over cultural activities," *Freemuse: Freedom of Musical Expression,* http://www.freemuse.org/sw27231.asp. But when I tried to verify the source by locating the original release of the Xinhua news agent by performing a text search on January 5, 2010, I found that the site was no longer available.
22. A number of such incidents are listed on *Freemuse*: http://www.freemuse.org/sw29562.asp.
23. The Chinese version of explanation is issued by Shanghai Faxin She, posted on q.sohu.com, http://q.sohu.com/forum/20/topic/5277407, accessed on January 5, 2009.
24. All of the information about Huang's incident presented here is based on an article entitled "The cancellation of Huang Anlun's concert" (Huang Anlun yinyuehui quxiao) posted on the site Headphoneclub.com, accessed January 6, 2010, http://www.headphoneclub.com/bbs/viewthread.php?tid=42037. The incident was confirmed by other sources such as people I know.
25. As reported by Amnesty International, there are incidents in which "individuals who practiced their religion outside officially sanctioned channels, including Christians, Muslims, Buddhists and others, faced harassment and persecution." *2009 Annual Report for China,* accessed June 5, 2010, http://www.amnestyusa.org/annualreport.php?id=ar&yr=2009&c=CHN.
26. A bibliographic study registers over fifty entries on the study of religious music by Chinese scholars from the period 1994 to 2004, though the author also admits that there are also unpublished studies for internal circulation only in the area of Christian music in China (Wang 2006).
27. The information in this section of the article is based on my numerous visits, correspondence, phone conversations, and working with the composer and the various related people from 2001 to the present. For more information on Wang's Symphony No. 4, see Yang 2005.
28. As we later find out, these sites have been blocked on and off in the PRC since March 2009. The blocking probably had to do with the trial and conviction of the dissident Lui Xiaobo

just a few days earlier, which had caused protests in Hong Kong as well as public condemnations from international diplomats in Beijing.
29. Based on an article entitled "Interpreting the Ministry of Culture's suggestions on internet music's development and management" posted on the site Sanminwenhuawang, accessed on January 5, 2010, http://whj.smx.gov.cn/ReadNews.asp?NewsID=2436.
30. The circular is posted on the site Zhongguowang china.com.cn, http://www.china.com.cn/policy/txt/2006-12/12/content_7491763.htm, accessed January 5, 2010
31. "Interpreting the Ministry of Culture's suggestions" (see note 29).
32. The circular is available on the Ministry of Culture's website: http://www.ccnt.gov.cn/xxfb/xwzx/whxw/200909/t20090903_73041.html, accessed January 5, 2010.
33. The article is entitled "'Vigilant screening of netizens' self-made music'—three misplacements" ('Yanshen wangmin zhibian yinyue' de sange zuowei), posted on the site Net Ease www.163.com, accessed January 5, 2010, http://comment.culture.163.com/culture_bbs/327I6D6100280004.html.
34. The article is entitled "Ministry of Culture's new policy on net music—six questions" (Wenhuabu wangluoyinyue xinzheng de liuge yiwen), which can be accessed at: http://blog.sina.com.cn/s/blog_4ac308a20100epas.html~type=v5_one&label=rela_prevarticle, accessed on January 5, 2010.
35. The list looks like an internal circular issued in around 2006 to staffs at the Beijing Radio Station regarding what music was to be banned. The circular is scanned and posted on the site ent.aboluowang.com at the following URL: http://www.aboluowang.com/ent/data/2007/0310/article_6215.html, accessed on January 5, 2010.
36. Hou who was of Taiwan origin relocated to the PRC in 1983, the first Taiwanese to have done so. But during the June Fourth Incident, he joined the student leaders at Tiananmen Square, organizing a hunger strike with the students. In 1990, when he was forced to leave the PRC, he chose to move back to Taiwan, where he was arrested for entering without proper documentation rather than treason. In 1992 he emigrated to New Zealand. In 2006 Hou was allowed to return to the PRC. Information gathered from a radio interview at Taiwan in October 2008. The transcription of the interview is available online at http://blog.roodo.com/honeypie/archives/7393767.html, accessed on January 5, 2010. At an interview with *Yangcheng wanbao*, Hou said he planned to write songs in the next few years, suggesting the ending of the ban. The interview is available at the following URL: http://www.ycwb.com/ePaper/ycwb/html/2009-08/08/content_564223.htm, accessed on January 5, 2010.
37. The posting and the responses are available on Baidu's BBS at the following URL: http://tieba.baidu.com/f?kz=568587253, accessed on January 5, 2010.

References

Anonymous. 1950. "The Nation's Music Workers Take Action—Embark onto the Anti-America and Support North Korea Propaganda Campaign to Protect Our Home and Defend Our Country" (quanguo yinyue gongzuojie xingdong qilai, kaizhan gang mei wanchao baojis weiguo de xuanzhuan yundong!). *Renmin Yinyue* 1, no. 4: 7.
Baranovitch, Nimrod. 2003. *China's New Voices: Popular Music, Ethnicity, Gender, and Politics 1978–1997*. Berkeley: University of California Press.
BBC News. 2009. "Oasis China concerts are shelved." March 2.

Boehler, Patrick. 2013. "Young have forgotten politics, says rock rebel." *South China Morning Post*, December 1.

Chen, Gang, ed. 2003. *Chen Gexin's Songs: Rose, Rose I Love You (Gexie Chen Gexin zhi ge: meigui meigui wo ai ni)*. Xianggang: Yuanjing chubanshe.

Chen, Xiaoqi, and Chen Zhihong. 2008. *Chinese Popular Music and Civic Culture (Zhongguo luixing yingyue yu gongmin wenhua)*. Guangdong: Xinshijie chubanshe.

Clark, Paul. 2008. *The Chinese Cultural Revolution: A History*. Cambridge: Cambridge University Press.

Cloonan, Martin. 1996. *Banned! Censorship of Popular Music in Britain: 1967–92*. Hants, UK: Ashgate Publishing Limited.

Cui, Jian, and Zhou Guoping. 2001. *Free Style (Zhiyou fengge)*. Guangxi: Gaungxi shifan daxue chubanshe.

Feng, Changchun. 2007. *The Thoughts of Music in Modern China (Zhongguo jindai yinyue sichao yanjiu)*. Beijing: Renmin yinyue chubanshe.

Frith, Simon. 1987. "Towards an Aesthetic of Popular Music." In *Music and Society*, edited by Richard Leppert and Susan McClary. Cambridge: Cambridge University Press, 133-150.

Guo, Facai. 2007. *Shackles and Freedom: Observation on 1980–2005 Chinese Rock and Roll's Independent Cultural Environment (Jiazuo yu benpao: 1989-2005 zhongguo raogenyue duliwenhua shengtai guancha)*. Hubei: Hubei renmin chubanshe.

Hanson, Anders. 2005 "The Return of Yellow Music." *CHIME* 16/17: 148–179.

Human Rights in China. 2004. *Media Control in China: A Report by Human Rights in China (Zhongguo zhengfu ruhe kongzhi meiti: zhongguo renquan yanjiu baogao)*. New York: Human Rights in China.

Jansen, Sue Curry. 1991. *Censorship: The Knot that Binds Power and Knowledge*. Oxford: Oxford University Press.

Jennings, Ralph. 2007. "Once banned Taiwan pop star re-emerges in China." *Reuters*, September 13.

Jones, Andrew F. 1992. *Like a Knife: Ideology and Genre in Contemporary Chinese Popular Music*. Ithaca, NY: Cornell University Press.

Jones, Andrew F. 2001. *Yellow Music: Media Culture and Colonial Modernity in the Chinese Jazz Age*. Durham, NC: Duke University Press.

Keuth, Y. Y. 1989. *Chinese Economic Reform: Approach, Vision and Constraints*. Canberra: National Centre for Development Studies.

Kraus, Richard C. 1989. *Piano and Politics in China: Middle-Class Ambitions and the Struggle over Western Music*. Oxford: Oxford University Press.

Li, Huanzhi. 1959. "Songs Are to Serve the Politics of Socialism" (Gequ wei shehuizhuyi de zhengzhi fuwu), *Renmin Yinyue* 10/11: 13–16.

Lian, Kang. 1957. "Yellow Songs Are Poison Weeds" (Huangse gegu shi ducao). *Renmin Yinyue* 9: 35–36.

Liang, Maochun. 2004. *Chinese Music of Today: 1949–1989 (Zhongguo dangdai yinyue: 1949-1989)*. Shanghai: Shanghai yinyue chubanshe.

Liang, Maochun. 2008. *Contemporary Chinese Music History: 1949–2000 (Zhongguo jinxiandai yinyueshi: 1949–2000)*. Beijing: Renmin yinyue chubanshe.

Lin, Er. 1995. "Mui Yim-Fong's Tianhe Concert Creates an Explosion" (Mui Yanfang Tianhe yanchang diu zhongbang zadan). *Ming Pao Weekly*, April 2, 43–46.

Liu, Xue'an. 2001. *Selected Works of Liu Xue'an (Liu Xue'an zuopin xuan)*. Beijing: Zhongguo wenlian chubanshe.

Loewenstein, Antony. 2008. *Blogging Revolution*. Melbourne: Melbourne University Press.
Man, Ivy. 2005. "Three Decades of Canto-pop: Hybridization, Consolidation and Innovation." PhD Thesis, University of Liverpool.
McCormick, Barrett L. 2007. "Censorship and Accountability in the Chinese Media." In *China in the Twenty-First Century: Challenges and Opportunities*, edited by Shiping Hua and Sujian Guo. New York: Palgrave Macmillan.
Melvin, Sheila, and Cai Jindong. 2004. *Rhapsody in Red: How Western Classical Music Became Chinese*. New York: Algora Publishing.
Müller, Beate. 2004. *Critical Studies: Censorship & Cultural Regulation in the Modern Age*. Amsterdam: Rodopi.
Qu, Qihong. 2002. *A History of Chinese Music: 1949-2000 (Xin zhongguo yinyue shi: 1949-2000)*. Hunan: Hunan meishu chubanshe.
Riley, Gail Blasser. 1998. *Censorship*. New York: Facts on File, Inc.
Sampson, Catherine. 2008. "Switching Off Church Music in China." *The Guardian*, October 8.
Shanghaiist. 2008. "Harry Connick Jr. concert last Sunday disappointing; Ministry of Culture to blame?" March 13.
Spencer, Richard. 2008. "China bans Western religious music," *Daily Telegraph*, September 30.
Sun, Jinan. 2007. *Li Jinhui and Li-style Music (Li Jinhui yu lipai yinyue)*. Shanghai: Shanghai yinyuexueyuan chubanshe.
TMZ. 2008. "China Fears Harry Connick Jr." March 15.
Wang, Jin. 2006. "A Study on Mainland China's Christian Music 1994-2004" (1994-2004 Zhongguo dalu jidujiao yinyue lilun yanjiu zhongshu). *Yishu baijia* 89, no. 3, 102-103, 124.
Witzleben, Lawrence. 1999. "Cantopop and Mandapop in Pre-Post Colonial Hong Kong: Identity Negotiation in the Performances of Anita Mui Yim-Fong." *Popular Music* 18, no. 2: 240-258.
Wong, Kee Chee. 2001. *The Age of Shanghainese Pops: 1930-1970*. Hong Kong: Joint Publishing (H.K.) Co., Ltd.
Wu, Jinglian. 2005. *Understanding and Interpreting Chinese Economic Reform*. Ohio: Thomson/South-Western.
Yang, Hon-Lun. 2004 "Socialist Realism and Chinese Music." In *Socialist Realism and Music*, edited by Mikuláš Bek, Geoffrey Chew, and Petr Macek, 135-144. Colloquium Musicologicum Brunense 36, 2001. Praha: Bärenreiter-Verlag.
Yang, Hon-Lun. 2005 "'Angry Young Old Man' Wang Xilin's Symphonic Odyssey." *CHIME* 16/17: 34-56.
Yang, Hon-Lun. 2007. "When Rock Meets Classical—A Dialogue on Music Between the Chinese Grandfather of Rock Cui Jian and the Symphonic Master Wang Xilin" (Dang yaogen yushang jiaoxiang—zhongguo yaogen zhifu Cui Jian ji xiaoxiang dashi Wang Xilin dui yinyue zhi fangdanlu). Twenty-First Century, no. 62 (Web version). http://www.cuhk.edu.hk/ics/21c.
Yang, Xiaolu. 1990. "A General Description of Contemporary Chinese *Tongsu* Songs" (Zhongguo dangdai tongsu gequ gaishu). In *An Appreciation Dictionary of Chinese and Foreign Tongsu Songs (Zhongwai tongsu gequ jiangshang cidian)*, edited by Yang Xiaolu and Zhang Zhentao, 225-227. Beijing: Beijing Shijie zhishi chubanshe.
Zeng, Suijin. 2003. *Music of the Chinese Masses (Zhongguo dazhong yinyue)*. Beijing: Communication University of China CUC Publishing House.
Zhou, Yongxiang. 1958. "Examining the Concept of Love in Several Examples of Yellow Songs." (Cong qige lizi kan huangse gegu li de 'aiqing'). *Renmin Yinyue* 5: 15-17.

V
CENSORSHIP IN DEMOCRACIES

CHAPTER 21

CENSORSHIP AND THE POLITICS OF RECEPTION

The Filmic Afterlife of Marc Blitzstein's
The Cradle Will Rock

DAVID C. PAUL

ANY discussion of censorship necessarily entails issues of reception. Suppression of a work, genre, or artist begins with an interpretive act, the decision of a powerful elite that something or someone poses a threat to their interests. Such decisions haunt the "afterlife," to use Walter Benjamin's evocative term, of the censored work and, at first sight, would seem to act as a stabilizing node that counters the dissipative tendencies that are characteristic of the reception process (Benjamin 1996, 254; Samson 1994). Forbiddenness becomes a part of the allure of the work, dominating the interpretive framework of subsequent performers and listeners. Indeed, the existence of *The Oxford Handbook of Music Censorship* is a powerful testimony to our fascination with the subject and its centrality to our readings of the various works, genres, and artists explored in these pages. But, as the case of Marc Blitzstein's *The Cradle Will Rock* reveals, even though censorship leaves an indelible imprint, the significance of that imprint is fluid and open to the same kinds of negotiations involved in conferring meaning on the work itself.

External events conspired to make Blitzstein's opera politically toxic. The work is set in Steeltown, USA, an imaginary fiefdom ruled ruthlessly by steel magnate Mr. Mister until Larry Foreman rallies his proletarian troops behind a closed-shop union. In the weeks leading up to the premiere, scheduled for June 16, 1937, in New York, real-world steel towns had become flashpoints of the labor battle in American industry. Most notoriously, several steelworkers were killed and many others wounded in the so-called Memorial Day Massacre as police attempted to break up a demonstration in Chicago. The *Cradle* production was under the auspices of the Federal Theatre Project (FTP), one of the New Deal artist relief organizations created by the Roosevelt administration. The FTP had already sustained heavy fire from conservative congressmen and, with the upheavals in the steel industry making headlines, a government-supported pro-union opera could not but be incendiary. Fearing the worst, federal authorities withdrew funding—"Censorship under a different guise," as FTP director Hallie Flanagan described it (Flanagan 1965, 202–203). The Maxine Elliott Theatre, where the premiere was supposed to take place, was padlocked and armed guards were posted to ensure that nothing was removed from the premises. Director Orson Welles and producer John Houseman were not to be denied, and, at the eleventh hour, they moved the production twenty blocks uptown to the vacant Venice Theatre. The plan was to have Blitzstein perform the score singlehandedly, delivering all the parts from an upright piano at center stage, since both the musicians and actors unions had ruled that their members were not to participate in the clandestine impromptu production.[1] Nonetheless, several of the actors did perform their parts from where they sat amid the audience, the house spotlight roving across craned heads to illuminate them as they sung (strictly speaking, since they were not on stage, they were not violating union rules). Thus, the censors were circumvented and *Cradle* became a legend in American theater history.

That legend has had a stabilizing effect on productions of *The Cradle Will Rock*, bespeaking a desire to circle back, to attempt to recover the nexus of meanings that crystallized at the moment of censorship. Directors have felt compelled to replicate aspects of the Venice Theatre performance, favoring spare sets, piano accompaniment, and unorthodox placements of actors and musicians. To cite a particularly notable example, John Houseman's 1983 production of *Cradle* was conceived as a revival in the most literal sense of that word. Houseman explained, "We're trying to recreate as much of that famous opening night as we can. I've decided to begin each performance with a 10-minute narrative recounting how the play was originally banned. We're also having a pianist on stage . . . [who] will impersonate Marc [Blitzstein] in his shirt sleeves and red suspenders." For all his reconstructive efforts, however, Houseman conceded that Blitzstein's "excessive love of unions" was dated, and that audiences would find other meanings in the work with more contemporary resonances (Leiter 1983). For Houseman then, the fact of censorship, which he made integral to his production, was separated from the interpretations that had prompted federal authorities to curtail the premiere— interpretations that were very much a response to Blitzstein's pro-union stridency. Two inferences follow from Houseman's comments: first, the meanings censors impose on a work do not exhaust its semantic plenitude and, second, the act of censorship has its own reception history, or afterlife, one that is inextricably entangled with the work it was intended to silence.

To explore the validity of these inferences further, I will examine three screenplays that took up the challenge of translating the events connected with the premiere of *The Cradle Will Rock* to the big screen. The first two, the separate efforts of Ring Lardner Jr. and Orson Welles, were written in the mid-1980s, on the heels of Houseman's revival of *Cradle*. The third screenplay, by Tim Robbins, was completed in the late 1990s, and it was the only one of the three that completed the hazardous voyage to film. Each writer re-enacts the opening night of *Cradle* and addresses the issue of censorship, but the stories they tell are markedly different. Here the potent metaphor of literary critic Hans Robert Jauss is helpful: censorship stood as a distinctive landmark on "the horizon of expectations" as Lardner, Welles, and Robbins approached Blitzstein's work (Jauss 1982, 22). But their vantage points differed and, accordingly, censorship cast different shadows on the surrounding topography. As we shall see, all three screenplays have as much to tell us about American culture of the late twentieth century as they do the New Deal period, when *The Cradle Will Rock* had its premiere.

THE POLITICS OF LABOR AND THE POLTICS OF PERSONALITY IN SCREENPLAYS OF RING LARDNER JR. AND ORSON WELLES

In 1983, the same year as Houseman's revival of *Cradle*, independent film producer Michael Fitzgerald set about transferring the story of the premiere to celluloid. The original impetus had come several years earlier, when he heard a recording of Blitzstein describing the events of that memorable summer night in 1937 (Trainor 1984/85, 32). Fitzgerald's first step was to ask Ring Lardner Jr. to draft a screenplay. Lardner was an obvious choice, not only because of his reputation as a successful screenwriter—he had Academy Awards for *Woman of the Year* (1942) and *M*A*S*H* (1970)—but also because he had direct experience with 1930s radicalism. In addition, Fitzgerald recruited Orson Welles, who had been one of the central protagonists in the drama surrounding *Cradle*'s premiere. The producer initially intended Welles to serve the project in an advisory capacity, but decided to up the ante by offering him the director's chair. Welles prevaricated at first, but found the prospect of revisiting his early career too tantalizing to pass up. Then he set to work on Lardner's script, editing, rewriting, and expanding. The end result was a second script so unlike the first that an exasperated Lardner concluded in an undated memorandum, "they don't relate to or affect each other in any significant way" (Lardner Jr. Papers, folder 97). Welles continued to work on the film, recruiting the cast and organizing shooting locations. Unfortunately, financial backing fell through, and despite Welles's efforts to secure money and support, the project collapsed (Leaming 1985, 512–521). Both completed screenplays do survive, however, and a perusal of their content raises questions about the impact of censorship on a work's reception.

The tone of Lardner's screenplay is set in the first scene, which portrays Blitzstein, in full evangelical fervor, pitching *The Cradle Will Rock* to Welles. "You have to use all the means available to say what's crying out to be said," Blitzstein insists, "Music and theatre together . . . to show the society we live in all its corruption and to change it." Welles is skeptical and Blitzstein admits, "we still may have to go through the mechanics of a revolution after the message has been delivered." He nonetheless insists that *The Cradle Will Rock* "exposes the whole rotten structure of capitalism" (Lardner Jr. Papers, Folder 94). This would seem to be the goal of Lardner's screenplay too, which is a full-throated affirmation of Blitzstein's politics. He tells the story of the controversy over *Cradle* in such a way as to amplify the message that the government had sought to suppress, almost as if the work still suffered the threat of censorship. To shout down the censors, as it were, Lardner takes every opportunity to quote excerpts from the opera, liberally doling out the most political passages in scenes that depict auditions, rehearsals, and performances. The last third of his screenplay, which features the reenactment of the Venice Theatre premiere, presents so much of *Cradle* that many of its pages are simply a reproduction of the original libretto.

Larry Foreman's eponymous number, "The Cradle Will Rock," enjoys particular prominence. Carol Oja has identified it as an example of the mass song style that a group of New York–based composers—Blitzstein, Henry Cowell, and Aaron Copland, among others—had developed earlier in the 1930s to engage the proletariat and stimulate revolutionary aspirations (Oja 1989). It is an aggressive song, with the beat thumped out in the left hand of the piano part. The structure is climactic, a stentorian march (Allegro Marcia) toward the chorus dramatized by the gradual extension of the vocal register through the verse and the chromatic ascent of the pre-chorus. The highpoint comes with Larry Foreman's prognosticative pronouncement, "the cradle will rock," which occurs at the end of the chorus. Here, the voice plummets down an octave from the D# that marks the melodic apex, then draws out the syllables of "Cradle will" over two beats in a manner that departs from Blitzstein's tendency to follow the natural stresses of the language. The harmonic progression that supports the phrase is notable for its strident parallelism (B major moving to A major) and a cadence that pivots on a tritone axis (D to A♭) instead of relying on the expected dominant to tonic progression (Figure 21.1). Typical of the mass song style, the harmony is clear but unorthodox, as if to suggest that the tonal hierarchy among triads needs to be reconfigured—a reconfiguration that serves as a musical analogy to the social revolution demanded by the radical left.

FIGURE 21.1 Mm. 35-41, "The Cradle Will Rock," from Marc Blitzstein's *The Cradle Will Rock*.

Given that "The Cradle Will Rock" serves as the climax of Blitzstein's opera, one might expect that it would appear as the climactic moment of the re-enacted premiere in Lardner's screenplay—and indeed it does. But Lardner seems intent on fixing this song in the memories of his audience, for it makes multiple appearances. In the first third of the screenplay, we are introduced to the song as Blitzstein auditions the work for John Houseman, and then we hear it twice more in the context of scenes depicting rehearsals. Based on the screenplay alone, a reader unfamiliar with *Cradle* could be forgiven for concluding that Larry Foreman figures prominently throughout the opera, rather than appearing toward the end, *deus ex machina*.

At various junctures, Lardner provides glimpses of steel industry turmoil, using conspicuously placed radio broadcasts and newspaper headlines. But, not content to let *Cradle* serve merely as an example of art imitating life, he also outfitted his narrative with two incidents in which the imaginary of Blitzstein's stage impinges more directly on the reality of contemporaneous labor struggles. First, in the scenes depicting the march uptown from the Maxine Elliott to the Venice Theatre, Lardner has *Cradle* ticketholders momentarily join a picket line when they encounter a group of striking workers outside a hotel. Second, at the very end of the screenplay, instead of taking the obvious approach of rolling the credits immediately after recreating the triumphant premiere, Lardner adds a codicil that depicts a later performance of *Cradle*. The place is Bethlehem, Pennsylvania, and the performance comes at the behest of union officials for the benefit of local steel workers. As we learn, the wealthy owners of the local steel plant, in collusion with the news media, have done everything in their power to discourage attendance—even organizing a company picnic for the same day. The film ends with Blitzstein delivering the opening lines of *Cradle*, just as he had done at the Venice Theatre, but before a tiny audience of twelve. Lardner, by confronting us with the realities of a Pennsylvania steel town, dilutes the initial triumph of *Cradle*, implying that victory in the larger battle has yet to be secured.

From the standpoint of political engagement, Welles's screenplay begins promisingly enough, suggesting that it too might take up the provocative themes explored by Lardner. For the opening sequence, Welles envisioned a montage of photographs "recording the desolation, anguish and the curious beauty of Americans standing up straight in the midst of that long storm we remember as the years of our Great Depression" (Welles 1984, 1). The sequence simultaneously embraces the documentary aesthetic characteristic of the 1930s and invokes its most famous example: *Let Us Now Praise Famous Men*, Walker Evans and James Agee's photojournalistic exploration of the plight of Southern sharecroppers. As the photographs fade in and out, the narrator (a part Welles intended for himself) describes the circumstances that gave rise to the FTP.

From the moment the principals are introduced in the next few scenes, however, politics are pushed into the background. The screenplay is best described as a domestic drama that examines the strains and strengths of Welles's marriage to Virginia Nicholson, with the premiere of *Cradle* serving as a picturesque backdrop. What little overt discussion of politics there is, is left mostly to Virginia, whose few brief exchanges with political radicals leave her skeptical. In her first meeting with Blitzstein, for example, the composer asks if she is aware that *Cradle* has a message. Virginia answers in the affirmative, but suggests that there might be other solutions to the problems addressed by the opera. With Virginia serving as a proxy, Welles holds the politics of the *Cradle* milieu at arm's length.

Welles also distances himself from the sights and sounds of Blitzstein's proletarian opera. A reader coming to the screenplay without any familiarity with *The Cradle Will Rock* would be hard-pressed to explain why it provoked the censors' ire. Until nearly the end of the screenplay, the only excerpt that Welles includes is the song "Honolulu," which is the work's most anodyne number. Musically and textually speaking, it is the antithesis of Larry Foreman's "The Cradle Will Rock." While the latter asserts the reality of revolution, "Honolulu" entices with fantasies of exotic women and fast living. Mr. Mister and Editor Daily, who sing most of the song, hope to inveigle Junior Mister into taking a Hawaiian sojourn, thereby sidelining him and his potentially embarrassing peccadilloes. Whereas "The Cradle Will Rock" is restless harmonically and melodically, "Honolulu" is monotonous. The verse oscillates incessantly between tonic and dominant, supporting the tedious repetition of a phrase that is the height of melodic complacency: a simple arpeggiation of the underlying chords (Figure 21.2). The refrain is equally banal, although it does add a predominant chord (G minor ninth) to underscore the feigned enthusiasm of Mr. Mister and Editor Daily as they conjure up their clichéd island fantasy.

FIGURE 21.2 Mm 1-8, "Honolulu," from Marc Blitzstein's *The Cradle Will Rock*.

Even the few politically charged scenes from *Cradle* that did make it into the very end of the screenplay are portrayed in such a way as to mitigate the political content of the opera. Welles crosscuts images of the audience riveted by the unorthodox Venice Theatre performance with a scene outside the theater featuring the triumphant director and his wife. While Larry Foreman issues his pro-union rallying cry, Orson and Virginia affect a reconciliation of sorts and look ahead optimistically: not to a world remade according to the politics of *Cradle*, but to the prospects of Orson's career in the film industry.

Where is censorship in all this? It is just another of the many obstacles that Welles's character has to overcome in his professional and private life. It demands the kind of audacity that emerges as his greatest trait in the screenplay—from requisitioning an off-duty ambulance so that he can race through the crowded streets of Manhattan, to redesigning special effects midway through the run of *Faustus* to accommodate rehearsals for *Cradle* on the same stage. It is his élan that carries the day when the police padlock the Maxine Eliott and the demise of the production seems inevitable.

For Welles then, the screenplay is an opportunity to explore the strengths and shortcomings of his younger self—something he as much as admitted to his biographer Barbara Leaming (1985, 512–514). This objective is entirely at odds with Lardner's screenplay, which gives *Cradle* a new lease on life by capturing its original urgency (the headline aperçus on the labor woes of the steel industry), celebrating its politics (the multiple repetitions of Larry Foreman's revolutionary song), and implying that the threat of censorship remained (the open-ended codicil). The scripts are irreconcilable—irreconcilable as the differences between Welles and Virginia ultimately proved to be.

OLD LEFT LEGACIES AND THE COLD WAR

It is a screenwriter's prerogative to tell a story from whatever vantage point he or she wishes—subject, of course, to pressures from producers and directors. That said, however, there is good reason to expect that Lardner and Welles might have arrived at screenplays that bore closer resemblance to each other than the ones they actually wrote. After all, both men had been enmeshed in the radical politics that yielded *Cradle*.

Lardner's involvement with the far left dates from the period of his undergraduate studies at Princeton University, where he joined the Socialist Club. After his sophomore year in 1934, he embarked on a tour of the Soviet Union, following a precedent set by idealistic Americans intent on seeing the Soviet experiment firsthand. Intourist, the official travel agency established by Stalin, ensured that visitors came away with only positive impressions. Lardner was duly impressed and decided to enroll in a course at the recently established Anglo-American Institute at the University of Moscow. In his memoir, he concedes that he was extraordinarily naïve, and that having accepted what little he saw as corroborating the more affirmative literature on the Soviet Union, proceeded to dismiss anything critical of communism (Lardner Jr. 2000, 47). Returning to New York, Lardner worked briefly as a reporter for the Hearst-owned tabloid the *Daily Mirror*. The human misery he witnessed on the job served to reinforce the Marxist literature he was reading in his spare time. Thus, when Lardner moved to Hollywood in 1935, he was low-hanging fruit for the local branch of the Communist Party. He was rapidly drawn into the endless round of committee work and meetings that were requisite for party members, from serving on the executive board of the Screen Writers Guild to organizing support for the loyalists in the Spanish Civil War.

Welles's reputation as an egocentric auteur, whose most respected films have been studies of the psychological complexities of deeply flawed individuals, has tended to create the impression that he was detached from the political concerns of his contemporaries. But, as a number of scholars have recently pointed out, Welles's projects of the 1930s and 1940s were very much engaged with politics. Cultural historian Michael Denning puts it in the strongest possible terms: "Welles was the American Brecht, the single most important Popular Front artist in theater, radio, and film, both politically and aesthetically" (Denning 1996, 362). One need not go as far as Denning to accept Welles's political credentials. It is clear that from 1935 to 1947, the period that witnessed Welles's transformation from charismatic denizen of the New York theater world to Hollywood celebrity, he was involved in numerous organizations associated with the left end of the ideological spectrum—the New Theatre League, the League of American Writers, and the Sleepy Lagoon Defense Committee among them. When, following *Cradle*, Welles and Houseman set about assembling the Mercury Theatre from the rubble of their FTP outfit, the Houseman-authored manifesto for the new company was published in the *Daily Worker*, organ of the Communist Party (Houseman 1937). Several months later, Welles published his own article "Theatre and the People's Front" in the same venue (Welles 1938). Unlike Lardner, Welles never joined the Communist Party; but he was under surveillance by the FBI, deemed a person of interest for his political activities (McBride 2006, 48–54).

Given the degree of overlap between their social milieus during the 1930s, why is Lardner's screenplay so resolutely political and Welles's so resolutely apolitical? Or, to put the question another way, why does the censorship of *Cradle* receive such different treatments from Lardner and Welles? The answer lies with the vicissitudes of the radical left during the Cold War period and the different paths pursued by Lardner and Welles beginning in the late 1940s and early 1950s, when anti-communist sentiment peaked in the United States. I will track those vicissitudes by the traces they leave in widely consumed media—newspaper articles, books, films, and television programs—delineating a trajectory from condemnation to vindication.

In September 1947, the House Un-American Activities Committee (HUAC) issued forty-three subpoenas to film industry personnel who were to serve as witnesses in an investigation of Communist infiltration into the Screen Writers Guild. Lardner was one of the nineteen witnesses dubbed "unfriendly" by the *Hollywood Reporter* for their declared hostility to HUAC. Of the "unfriendly nineteen," eleven were called to testify. Ten members of the group agreed to a collective legal strategy, but Bertolt Brecht, the eleventh, sought separate counsel, answered the committee's questions, and then departed from the United States. The "Hollywood Ten," a rubric that soon came into common usage, opted instead to invoke the First Amendment, refusing to answer questions on the grounds that their personal beliefs and rights to assembly were protected. When it was Lardner's turn to testify, he was asked the notorious question: "Are you now or have you ever been a member of the Communist Party?"

Lardner famously responded, "I could answer [the question], but if I did, I would hate myself in the morning" (Lardner Jr. 2000, 9). The House of Representatives cited Lardner and the other members of the Hollywood Ten for contempt, and they were subsequently indicted by a federal grand jury. Their trials took place over the following three years and, in each case, returned a guilty verdict. Two of the ten, John Howard Lawson and Dalton Trumbo, appealed the decision, with the others intending to follow suit if the Supreme Court ruled in their favor: it did not. The Hollywood Ten were fined and sentenced to serve time in prison. For Lardner, the whole ordeal, from receiving the subpoena to being released from prison, played out over nearly four years, from September 1947 to April 1951.

Welles, meanwhile, had left the United Sates in November 1947 and was safe from the rising anti-communist tide. Film scholar Joseph McBride, who has made the strongest case for a connection between Welles's departure and the inclement turn of American politics, thinks it likely that Welles would have been caught up in HUAC's second round of Hollywood hearings, beginning in 1951 (McBride 2006, 97). While this is speculative, it seems that Welles was increasingly aware of the danger that came with his past associations, not to mention the repercussions of having modeled the titular character of *Citizen Kane* on William Randolph Hearst, the vindictive conservative newspaper publisher. In 1945, he even went so far as to grant an interview to Hedda Hopper, a gossip columnist of the *Los Angeles Times* who made a regular point of outing "commies" in the film industry. "I'm sick of being called a Communist," he told Hopper, adding, "It's true that I've worked for some of the things the Communist party has advocated. But that was merely coincidental. I'm opposed to political dictatorship" (Hopper 1947). But Welles did not manage to clear his name entirely for he was accorded a lengthy entry in *Red Channels* (1950), an index assembled by three former FBI agents purporting to list the names and activities of individuals exerting "communist influence in radio and television." *Red Channels* served as one of the principal sources of information for anti-communist inquisitors (American Business Consultants 1950).

By 1951, the pole star in the anti-communist firmament was Senator Joseph McCarthy, whose efforts to root out red subversion in government institutions, from the State Department to the army, were regular fare for the front pages of newspapers. This was the era of the blacklist in Hollywood, when the mere hint of an association with the radical left—even in the distant past—meant being barred from the major studios. At the top of the list were, of course, the members of the Hollywood Ten, denounced officially in the so-called Waldorf Statement, which was issued by the major studio executives in early December of 1947 (Ceplair and Englund 2003, 328–331). The path to political absolution for blacklistees new and old was grim: recant publicly and, if called upon to do so, name the names of other individuals involved in the radical left. Lardner chose not to tread that path and, after being released from prison, had to resort to writing scripts pseudonymously for a British television producer.

As far as it is possible to tell, Welles was never denied work on the basis of his past political activities even though he was listed in *Red Channels*. But he did not seek employment in the United States during the height of the McCarthy period. Welles took numerous film roles in Europe, channeling much of his earnings into his own projects. He did return to the United States for three years, beginning in 1956, a period during which he wrote and starred in *A Touch of Evil*. By then, anti-communist fervor had begun to subside: Khruschev had denounced Stalin (although he would send troops to quell the Hungary Revolution in November of 1956), McCarthy had been censured, and HUAC's credibility was declining.

Most accounts of the blacklist tend to trace its unraveling to the beginning of the 1960s, when director Otto Preminger announced publicly that Dalton Trumbo, one of the Hollywood Ten, was the screenwriter for *Exodus* (1960). Kirk Douglas followed suit, crediting the screenplay for *Spartacus* (1960) to Trumbo, who was thereafter hired under his own name. Blacklistees began to trickle back into the Hollywood studios, although only a small fraction of them regained anything like their former professional lives (Ceplair and Englund 2003, 419–420).

Suspicions persisted at first. For example, in the *Los Angeles Times*, conservative columnist and former screenwriter Morrie Ryskind (who had been one of HUAC's "friendly witnesses") responded with vitriol to an episode of *The Defenders* that sympathetically portrayed the plight of the blacklisted. Hollywood communists got what they deserved, he argued, for they had subverted the Screen Writers Guild in the 1930s and 1940s and maintained their own blacklists, actively undermining the careers of those who were not in agreement with their ideology (Ryskind 1964a; 1964b). Robert R. Kirsh, a *Los Angeles Times* book reviewer, opted for a more ambivalent tone in his review of Alvah Bessie's *Inquisition in Eden* (1965), the first published memoir by one of the blacklistees. Kirsh suggested readers might be "repelled by Communist ideology and find the beliefs of the men involved distasteful," but then again, imprisoning the Hollywood Ten went too far. That same year, a *New York Times* article about Bessie and his memoir offered staid neutrality, furnishing criticism of HUAC only in the form of quotations from an interview with the writer himself (Stang 1965).

By the late 1960s, the temper of public discourse had begun to shift. A bellwether was C. Robert Jennings's retrospective article, published in the *Los Angeles Times* Sunday magazine in 1967 and marking the twentieth anniversary of HUAC's Hollywood inquiries. At the outset, Jennings explained that he hoped to galvanize the interest of a generation that had "grown up on a diet of Beatles and Bond." The alliterative popular culture reference was not merely a rhetorical device: the length of his article, which ran to sixteen columns, bespeaks a sense of urgency, a concern that the blacklist period was now so historically distant that it required detailed description in order to impress its significance on younger readers. In contrast with past authors, Jennings sided firmly with the Hollywood Ten. HUAC, he averred, "never found a hair of subversion in a single can of celluloid; and anything they found out about the opinions of people who made those movies was clearly none of their business" (Jennings 1967). Jennings need not have worried about the blacklist being a musty irrelevancy to the readership of the *Los Angeles Times*. His article elicited several letters to the editor, most applauding the publication of the piece and only one excoriating the *Times* for being "shocking in its bias and unfairness" (Julber 1967). A new consensus was emerging and subsequent writers who took up the subject of the blacklist and the activities of HUAC tended to side with Jennings.

That condemnation of the congressional committee should become the norm is hardly surprising in light of the fact that it had recently returned to the spotlight with its ill-considered investigations of the New Left. In 1966, HUAC hearings intended to determine if and how the New Left aided the Vietcong had degenerated into chaos as protestors were dragged from the hearing room kicking and screaming. The *New York Times* reported, "It was a classic contest between the most militant protesters against American policy in Vietnam and Representatives who believe in using Congressional hearings as a weapon against Communism. Both sides seemed pleased at the opportunity for action" (Herbers 1966). Two years later, another subcommittee set out to examine the role played by "Communist and pro-Communist elements" in inciting the riots that had marred the Democratic National Convention in Chicago. Again, protestors showed up turning the hearings into a raucous carnival, and a number of the witnesses, Abbie Hoffman and Jerry Rubin among them, mocked the proceedings at every turn. For a large cross section of the public, the antics of Hoffman, Rubin, and their Yippie brethren were hardly endearing; but their would-be interrogators were equally unappealing. As one reporter wrote, "The Yippies and the HUACs, who might be expected to be strange dinner partners, fed upon one another last week in their mutual quest for publicity" (Hunter 1968).

As HUAC's little remaining stock plummeted, leading to the eventuality of the committee being dissolved in 1975, the prestige of the Hollywood Ten climbed. The 1970s witnessed a flood of articles, films, books, and even plays about the purported victims of HUAC and McCarthy. Among the books were Steven Kanfer's *A Journal of the Plague Years* (1973), Lillian Hellmann's *Scoundrel Time* (1976), and Eric Bentley's *Thirty Years of Treason* (1971), an annotated collection of HUAC hearings that served as the basis of his play *Are You Now or Have You Ever Been?* (1972). Two major Hollywood films depicted the congressional committee antagonistically, *The Way We Were* (1973) starring Barbara Streisand and Robert Redford, and *The Front* (1976) starring Woody Allen.

The volume of material on the subject was such that Hilton Kramer, the *New York Times*' conservative art critic, felt obligated to comment. "A new wave of movies, books and television shows," he complained, "is assiduously turning the terrors and controversies of the late 1940's and 1950's into the entertainment and best-sellers of the 1970's." Kramer disparaged as "revisionist history" the new consensus narrative, according to which "the Cold War was somehow a malevolent conspiracy of the Western democracies to undermine the benign intentions of the Soviet Union." He went further, offering his own thesis about the recent glut of material about the anti-communist inquiries of the early Cold War period. "The point, it seems, is to acquit 60's radicalism of all malevolent consequence, and to do so by portraying 30's radicalism as similarly innocent, a phenomenon wholly benign, altruistic and admirable" (Kramer 1976). In vindicating the Old Left, the New Left validated itself.

Kramer's assertions elicited passionate responses from a number of high-profile American intellectuals, their correspondence dominating the letters page of two subsequent editions of the *New York Times*. Those siding with Kramer included literary critic Alfred Kazin (1976) and historian Arthur Schlessinger Jr. (1976), both of whom were pivotal in shaping the anti-Communist tenets of American liberalism in the 1950s and 1960s (Pells 1985). Schlesinger suggested that Kramer's article should be required reading for anyone born after 1940, a clear dig at the generation that had birthed the New Left. Those against Kramer's views included historians Eric Foner (1976), Ronald Radosh (1976), and Louis Menashe (1976), all of whom were born around 1940, and all of whom defended what Kramer labeled "revisionist history" as a more realistic assessment of anti-Communism and its dangers. Given the active involvement of this trio in New Left causes (Radosh and Menashe even coauthored an early sympathetic study of the teach-in movement), Kramer drew the partisan lines correctly, whatever one might think of his distaste for one side.[2] As Kramer also suggested, at least some members of the New Left were looking for a political heritage on a kind of quest for roots. In 1975 an organization calling itself the New American Movement Media Group and devoted to "radicalizing the media," sponsored a panel discussion of the blacklist in Hollywood. The program issued for the event explained, "We feel strong bonds with the men and women in Hollywood who fought to change the entertainment industry decades ago and were punished for their efforts by the Cold War inquisitions. We want to learn from their struggles and personal experiences" (Kilday 1975).

Beyond the collapse of HUAC and the New Left search for a "usable past," there was a third factor that contributed to the burgeoning books, films, and articles about the blacklist period in the 1970s: Richard Nixon and the Watergate scandal. Nixon cut his teeth as an anti-communist crusader, serving on HUAC during its late 1940s ascendancy and thus playing a bit part in the blacklisting drama. But it was the collapse of the Nixon Whitehouse under the strains of the Watergate scandal that proved to be the salient factor. It cast a pall over the authority of the federal government, fostering the belief that too often moral scruples were sacrificed on the altar of political exigency. A *Los Angeles Times* reporter who attended the aforementioned blacklist panel noted, "Almost all of the individuals interviewed agreed that Watergate had thrown a new light on the period just as it has triggered second looks into the causes of Alger Hiss and Julius and Ethel Rosenberg." Martin Ritt, who directed *The Front* and was among the panel participants, suggested Watergate "showed that the call for law and order came from people who didn't respect law and order when it applied to them" (Kilday 1975). Commenting on the popularity of Bentley's play *Are You Now or Have You Ever Been*, Gale Sondergaard, an actress who had herself been blacklisted, speculated, "I think Watergate has stimulated a great deal of curiosity about other scandals in recent American history. Of course Nixon got his start during the HUAC hearings" (Farber 1975).

By the early 1980s, several scholarly monographs on the subject of the blacklist had been published, notably Larry Ceplair and Steven Englund's *The Inquisition in Hollywood* (1979) and Victor S. Navasky's *Naming Names* (1980), both of which joined the chorus of redemption that had sounded for over a decade. The men and women who had suffered most from the anti-communist purges of the 1940s and 1950s found themselves celebrated as folk heroes. It was not necessarily a validation of their politics, for the patina of age had drained their radicalism of its provocative charge and many of them had long since abandoned the leftmost extremities of the political spectrum. Rather, they were regarded as martyrs for the First Amendment and lauded for standing up to government authority—that authority being very much at low ebb in the years following the downfall of the Nixon administration. For Lardner, this was a period in which he found himself in regular demand as a lecturer, asked to speak about both his experiences as a blacklistee and recent triumphs as a screenwriter.

The kind of celebrity that redounded to Lardner as an alumnus of the Hollywood Ten offers an explanation for his take on the story of *Cradle Will Rock*. The screenplay was an opportunity to revisit the political ferment of the 1930s, and to explore an incident that served as a prelude to HUAC's Hollywood inquisition. The efforts government authorities made to shutter *Cradle* flouted the First Amendment; it was censorship through economic deprivation—budgets revoked, contracts canceled, and careers threatened—exactly the sort of thing with which Lardner had had to cope. His response, as we have seen, was to amplify the message that censors wanted to stifle, ensuring that the First Amendment would be honored even when breached by the powerful. In short, censorship stood as the most pronounced promontory on the horizon of expectations that conditioned Lardner's view of *Cradle*, a consequence of his own experiences with HUAC and the validation that came with the consensus that the anti-communist zealotry of the early Cold War period was a dark chapter in American history.

Not so for Welles. As we have seen, he was in Europe for the years in which anticommunism burned brightest, and, as a result, escaped the stigma associated with the leftist causes and organizations he had been involved with during the 1930s. As a result of his absence, however, he missed out on the aura of victimhood that subsequently settled about those who had been pilloried by anti-communist crusaders. In the eyes of the public, his biography was not defined by early partisanship for the causes of the radical left—a marked contrast with Lardner. Instead, the running narrative about Welles was the encumbrance of a prodigy: he was the genius who had flamed with early promise that was never fully realized. This was the subtext to a question an interviewer asked of Michael Fitzgerald concerning his choice of Welles as director for the *Cradle* film project: "Welles hasn't made a picture that he hasn't produced himself in twenty-seven years. Why?" Fitzgerald conceded that his director had a reputation for "going over budget and not having the capacity to finish things" (Trainor 1984/85). But, he argued, this was a myth perpetuated by Hollywood's tendency to run on received opinion rather than truth. Myth or not, Welles himself was clearly preoccupied with the tensions between an artist and the institutions of financial support to which he or she is beholden. His unfinished film *The Other Side of the Wind*, which he labored over during the 1970s, was about an aging director contending with the changes in an industry that had once venerated him. It is within this context that Welles's screenplay about *Cradle* is best understood. It was not a monument to freedom of speech, as Lardner's was, but an exploration of the obstacles a director needed to overcome en route to a successful production. Censorship was, of course, a big hurdle—but not necessarily more so than the challenges of his personal life. From Welles's vantage point then, censorship was not the defining feature on his horizon of expectations.

Artistic Authenticity and Political Commitment in Tim Robbins's *Cradle Will Rock* (1999)

I have argued that the screenplays of Lardner and Welles differ so significantly because of the ways in which public perceptions of 1930s radicalism shifted over the course of the second half of the twentieth century. One man was fused ineluctably to that era and the other was severed from it, the inquiries of HUAC being the decisive factor. For all their differences, though, the screenplays do share a common feature: neither one identifies any of its characters as members of the Communist Party. Even Lardner, who invests so much in the politics of Blitzstein's proletarian opera, avoids answering for any of his characters the question: "Are you now or have you ever been . . . ?" This is not the case in Tim Robbins's screenplay for the 1999 film *Cradle Will Rock*. Whereas Welles and Lardner shunned the word "communist," Robbins uses it frequently, just one of many indications that his work is the product of a different time. This is not to say that Robbins dispenses it incautiously. To the contrary, even though he was writing in the 1990s, after the dramatic collapse of the Soviet Union, Robbins shows an acute awareness of the heavy semantic freight that "communist" acquired over the Cold War years. Unloading that freight is one of his main items of business, and he accomplishes it in ways that address the issue of censorship.

In the screenplay, the allegation that someone is "red" comes most frequently from Tommy Crickshaw, a disgruntled and somewhat unhinged ventriloquist. Crickshaw is a fictional character who plays a role in one of the many counternarratives Robbins weaves in and around the central account of the *Cradle* premiere. Crickshaw's accusations are always misplaced, as evidenced by the first target of his animus, Hallie Flanagan, tireless director of the FTP. She explains that the organization has hired Crickshaw to teach Vaudeville to a younger generation so that it will be preserved. He responds, "Vaudeville will be around long after you and your Communists are." Crickshaw is subsequently seen haranguing two of his students, addressing them as "communists"; they put up with it for a while but eventually reveal that they are "pink" not "red." That bit of information reinforces a scene in which Welles asks Blitzstein if he is a member of the Communist Party. Blitzstein responds, "Officially, no. I am a homosexual and that excludes me from membership in the party. I am faithful to the ideals of the party" (Robbins 2000a, 15, 48). Robbins has strayed from historical accuracy here: Blitzstein was certainly a card-carrying member of the party, although it is difficult to determine exactly when he joined (Gordon 1989, 167). But this is a screenplay described as a "mostly true story," and

Blitzstein's response serves to underscore a point Robbins makes about the destructive effect of a label that effaces the complexity of human beings.

There are only two characters in the screenplay who are unambiguously identified as communists. The first is Diego Rivera. Again, playing loose with history, Robbins shifts from 1933 to 1937 the events that unfolded after Nelson Rockefeller commissioned Rivera to paint a mural in the lobby of his office building. Rivera is an ambiguous character: on the one hand, he willingly accepts the patronage of Rockefeller when offered a hefty paycheck, on the other, he refuses to alter the mural when Rockefeller objects to the inclusion of the image of Lenin. In the heated exchange between painter and patron, we learn that Rivera does not think highly of Stalin, whom he proposes sarcastically as an alternative. The implicit message is that not all "communists" are the same. The second character identified as communist is Crickshaw's dummy, who has a disturbing habit of taking on a life of his own. In the midst of their last act together, the dummy explains to Crickshaw that he and his brothers "will not rest until all the country is red." He then turns to the audience and announces, "Ladies and gentlemen, this man exploits my labor for his own profits. This capitalist pays me zero, works me whenever he likes. I sleep in a coffinlike apartment" (Robbins 2000a, 119). Crickshaw quits the stage, leaving behind the dummy, who begins to sing the *Internationale*. Spouting slogans and singing the Soviet National anthem, the dummy is the stereotypical communist. The fact that he is a puppet shows up the stereotype for what it is: a hollow, wooden shell, readily manipulated by those who would stoke the fears of the American public in order to advance their own interests. The dummy's presence, along with Robbins's portrayal of Congressional investigations of the FTP conducted by HUAC in its late-1930s infancy, represent a continuation of the consensus about anti-communism that bolstered Lardner's fortunes.

The destruction of the mural and the lockdown of the Maxine Elliot are only the most overt kinds of censorship figuring in the film. Unlike Lardner or Welles, Robbins explores the issue of self-censorship, the ways in which power and money can subvert an artist. The instigators are a trio of wealthy financiers, Nelson Rockefeller, William Randolph Hearst, and an imaginary steel magnate named Gray Mathers. For these men, incarnations of Blitzstein's Mr. Mister, art is a symbol of prestige and a form of capital; it is the coin Mussolini uses to purchase the support of Hearst newspapers and the steel he needs for his army from Mathers. Rockefeller possesses a genuine interest in art, but only insofar as it poses no threat to the kind of power he represents. The most notable scene featuring the tycoon triumvirate is set at a costume ball, all three wearing eighteenth-century garb in an obvious evocation of the Ancien Régime and its power structure. Rockefeller, still smarting from what he sees as the betrayal of Rivera, is consoled by Mathers and Hearst, who talk about how they might shape the future direction of art. It will be "nonpolitical" Mathers says, and Rockefeller agrees, "Yes, abstract. Colors, form, not politics." Rockefeller will fund it and Hearst will use his newspapers to "hail it as the next new thing. We will canonize the artists, make them rich" (Robbins 2000a, 125). Here, Robbins takes a jab at the post–World War II avant-garde and the valorization of abstract expressionism. Art as an end in itself—art for art's sake, as one of Blitzstein's songs is titled—is a cop-out that plays into the agenda of a moneyed elite intent on depoliticizing art. It is, in effect, a form of self-censorship.

In the final montage of the film, one of its most memorable moments, Robbins suggests that the problems of power and patronage persist. Juxtaposed with scenes re-enacting *Cradle*'s opening night and the razing of Rivera's mural, a funeral procession wends its way toward Broadway. At the front of the cortège, Crickshaw's dummy is carried in a coffin, his pallbearers a contingent of Vaudevillians. A sign is held aloft pronouncing the Federal Theatre "killed by an act of congress." When the procession arrives at Times Square, the camera swings up and out to reveal the film crew, the extras, and the lights of modern-day Broadway, aglitter with advertisements. This is, of course, an example of Brechtian *Verfremdungseffect*, when the curtain is drawn to reveal the machinery that creates cinematic illusions. But it is also a clear indictment of modern-day Broadway and its rampant commercialism, where compromise is the rule rather than the exception.

Ultimately, Robbins's film champions a kind of politically committed artistic authenticity that is exemplified by two of *Cradle*'s actors, Olive Stanton and Aldo Silvano. Both of them remain dedicated to *Cradle* despite the cost it exacts on their personal and professional lives. Stanton, who begins the film alone and homeless, finds security in the relationship she develops with actors' union representative John Adair. But when the union rules that *Cradle*'s actors cannot perform because the production has lost its FTP sanction and Welles and Houseman do not have the funding to pay union rates, Adair forbids Stanton from having anything to do with the Venice Theatre production. Stanton defies her lover, losing him and the roof over her head, but saves the production and catapults it into theater history: it is her small voice, entering on cue as Moll, that relieves Blitzstein of the onerous task of performing the show by himself and, at the same time, sets the precedent for the riveting spectacle of the actors delivering their parts from wherever they stand or sit amidst the audience. Silvano, a fictional character who takes Howard da Silva's place as the actor playing Larry Foreman, is part of a family that has recently emigrated from Italy. When his relatives reveal their enthusiasm for Mussolini, Silvano refuses any further financial support from them. His wife suggests that he runs the risk of putting his kids in the soup lines and he responds, "What would that teach them, to take my parents' money? That it's alright to believe in something or have pride but if you're just a little bit hungry, sell it?" (Robbins 2000a, 90). Silvano's principled stand is vindicated by his triumphant performance as Larry Foreman.

OLD LEFT LEGACIES IN THE AGE OF GLOBALIZATION

In confronting political issues head on, Robbins's screenplay bears more resemblance to Lardner's than Welles's. However, the many counternarratives—the destruction of Diego Rivera's mural in Rockefeller Center, the death of Vaudeville, the ascendancy of

HUAC—deflect attention away from the pro-union politics that are central both to *The Cradle Will Rock* itself and the Lardner screenplay. Robbins's sprawling epic of a film illustrates once more how differently a story (even one involving censorship) can be told. And, once again, we will have to look to Robbins's own background and his experience of the American left for an explanation.

The impetus for his film, Robbins has explained, came from reading Hallie Flanagan's *Arena*, an account of her experience as the director of the Federal Theatre Project for the four years of its existence. Robbins had little previous knowledge of the Works Progress Administration (WPA) arts organizations when he encountered Flanagan's book in the mid-1990s, but it is hardly surprising that it struck him with the force of revelation. The so-called "Culture Wars" echoed the conflict that had brought down FTP and its sister organizations. Ever since the early 1980s, a constituency of conservative commentators and politicians had advocated "defunding" the National Endowment for the Humanities (NEH) and the National Endowment for the Arts (NEA), the Great Society successors to the arts organizations of the New Deal era. They gained ground by arguing that many of the artists and academics who received moneys from the NEH and NEA contravened the values of normal Americans (Jensen 1995). Communism was no longer the bête noire it had been in the 1930s; instead, the right was exercised by the sexual content in some of the art funded by the organizations (Robert Mapplethorpe's photography and Karen Finley's performance art, for example) and the cancerous spread of "political correctness," which, they argued, led to supporting projects simply on the basis of the minority status of an artist or scholar. When the 1994 elections swept a Republican majority into Congress, the budgets of both the NEH and NEA were drastically cut. It was not exactly the 1930s redux, but there were enough similarities for Flanagan's experience to resonate with a reader of Robbins's New Left predilections.

Throughout *Arena*, Flanagan argues that art should be accessible to the average person, should speak a language intelligible to them, and, in doing so, should reaffirm American democracy. In the closing section of her book, which functions as something of a eulogy for the Federal Theatre, she presents this credo:

> Either the arts are not useful to the development of the great numbers of American citizens who cannot afford them—in which case the government has no reason to concern itself with them; or else the arts are useful in making people better citizens, better workmen, in short better-equipped individuals—which is, after all, the aim of democracy—in which case the government may well concern itself increasingly with them. Neither should the theatre in our country be regarded as a luxury. It is a necessity because in order to make democracy work the people must increasingly participate; they can't participate unless they understand; and the theatre is one of the great mediums of understanding (Flanagan 1965, 372).

For Flanagan, theater was leaven not luxury; it was transformative and a vital part of community life, engaging with those issues that pressed most urgently upon its audience.

Robbins's career has been shaped by his involvement with artists and arts organizations imbued with this belief. His earliest acting experience was with the Theatre for the New City, a Greenwich Village group passionately devoted to programming that addressed the community, a quintessential product of the New Left. Topical urban issues—tenants' rights, homelessness, the immigrant experience—were standard fare for the Theatre for the New City, as were affordable or free performances. Robbins participated in the "political street vaudevilles" that were part of the company's summer endeavors (Agee 1990). Moving to the West Coast, where he enrolled in the theater program at UCLA, Robbins helped found the Actors' Gang, a theater troupe committed to unorthodox productions, community engagement, and at times, political agitation. With celebrity redounding to him after playing a major role in *Bull Durham*, Robbins emerged as one of the most prominent members of the Hollywood left.

Given Robbins's background and political sympathies, the appeal of *Cradle* and its milieu is fairly obvious. To account for the particular way in which he tells the story of the premiere, however, we will have to look a bit more closely at the state of the left in the 1990s. Robbins opens up a window on the subject in a letter he wrote to the *New York Times*, rebutting the negative film review he received from the paper. Walter Goodman (2000), the reviewer, criticized the film for replicating the black and white moral universe of Blitzstein's piece of operatic agitprop: "working stiffs are set against millionaire bosses and their fascist consorts." Robbins retorted that the problem lay not with the film, but with Goodman's discomfort with the "alternate account of official history" it presented, specifically the suggestion "that the United States was complicit in the rise of Hitler and Mussolini." Moreover, Goodman was wrong to dismiss Blitzstein's work as the stale and irrelevant remnants of Popular Front politics. Invoking Larry Foreman's climactic speech as his parting shot, Robbins (2000b) opined, "The protests in Seattle took the Goodmans of the world by surprise, and as much as they try to write it off as an anomaly, Seattle may be the beginning of an irreversible storm."

Robbins was referring to the demonstrations that rocked the World Trade Organization Ministerial Conference that took place in Seattle in November 1999. Those demonstrations were the culmination of the loosely concerted organization of multiple groups with multiple grievances against "globalization": labor unions angered by the loss of jobs to overseas workers, environmentalists concerned about the ease with which corporations could set up shop in countries with lax environmental regulations, organizations that objected to doing business with governments that habitually violated human rights, and anarchists hell-bent on, well, anarchy. The protests met with heavy-handed police action, and newspapers across the country carried images of officers attempting to disperse the crowds with pepper spray, tear gas and, when it came to it, truncheons. Redolent of the protests of the 1960s and 1930s, these images and the stories that accompanied them garnered the antiglobalization movement an unprecedented level of public attention. In addition, they served as a lens that brought into focus the simmering discontent on the left with the triangulation policies of the Clinton administration, particularly its pursuit of deregulation and trade agreements that benefited big business interests at the expense (according to movement activists) of ordinary people. That discontent would also lead many on the left, Robbins among them, to vote for Ralph Nader in 2000, an expression of their disgust with the compromises made by the Democratic Party (Robbins 2001).

The linkage Robbins establishes between Blitzstein's pro-union rallying cry and the demonstrations of the antiglobalization movement is significant. The various blocs of protestors might have different objectives in mind, but they shared a sense that political leaders were all too willing to sacrifice principle for expediency and that "compromise" often stood for capitulation to the interests of big business. The problem was selling out—self-censorship to appease the powerful. Everyone has his price, Mr. Mister declares, an idea that is amplified in Robbins's screenplay by his three tycoons and their plans to buy off avant-garde artists. But, insofar as there was a coherent message emerging from the antiglobalization protests, it was that some things were not for sale. This too was the central point of Robbins's film: the heroes are Stanton and Silvano who remain true to their convictions even when it endangers their livelihood.

Conclusion

Lardner, Welles, and Robbins are (or were) all men of the left, insiders in the Hollywood film industry, and ostensibly telling the same story, yet they arrived at narratives that dramatize censorship in vastly different ways. Their screenplays reveal that just as the meaning of *Cradle* was not exhausted by the one censors imposed on it, the significance of censorship is open to multiple interpretations and can serve a number of agendas. To generalize, censorship occupies a shifting place in the complex of meanings that a work accrues in its afterlife, despite the apparent semantic singularity of the censor's act. It is the task of reception history to untangle this complex—a task I have attempted to accomplish here for Blitzstein's *The Cradle Will Rock* by examining the legacy of 1930s radicalism for the American left in the latter half of the twentieth century. The stories Lardner, Welles, and Robbins tell shed light on their own circumstances and political allegiances, warmed by the glow of that summer night in 1937, when *The Cradle Will Rock* made theater history.

Notes

1. The premiere was supposed to feature a large ensemble cast supported by a forty-four-person chorus and a twenty-eight-piece orchestra, and elaborate sets that were born across stage on a fleet of illuminated, glass-bottomed wagons that Welles himself had designed.
2. Radosh's politics have since shifted to the right, a response in part to the experience of becoming a pariah to the radical left when his research led him to conclude (reluctantly) that Julius Rosenberg was indeed a spy (Radosh 2001). Radosh's most recent book, a

collaborative effort with his wife Allis, revisits the Hollywood blacklist and attempts to strip away the layers of mythology. The Radoshes are in agreement with Kramer: though the blacklist went too far, its victims were not guiltless dupes of the Soviet Union (Radosh and Radosh 2005).

REFERENCES

Agee, J. 1990. "Two-Coast Man." *Newsweek* 116, no. 20 (November 12): 80.
American Business Consultants. 1950. *Red Channels: The Report of Communist Influence in Radio and Television*. New York: Counterattack.
Benjamin, Walter. 1996. "The Task of the Translator." In *Walter Benjamin: Selected Writings*, edited by Marcus Bullock and Michael William Jennings, 1:253–263. Cambridge, Mass.: Harvard University Press.
Ceplair, Larry, and Seven Englund. 2003. *The Inquisition in Hollywood: Politics in the Film Community, 1930–1960*. Urbana and Chicago: University of Illinois Press.
Denning, Michael. 1996. *The Cultural Front: The Laboring of American Culture in the Twentieth Century*. London: Verso.
Farber, Stephen. 1975. "A Play about HUAC Stirs Hollywood." *New York Times*, September 7.
Flanagan, Hallie. 1965. *Arena: The History of the Federal Theatre*. New York: Benjamin Blom.
Foner, Eric. 1976. Letter to the Editor. *New York Times*, October 17.
Goodman, Walter. 2000. "A Visionary Who Deserves a Fuller Portrait." *New York Times*, January 9.
Gordon, Eric A. 1989. *Mark the Music: The Life and Work of Marc Blitzstein*. New York: St. Martin's Press.
Herbers, John. 1966. "War Foes Clash with House Unit; 17 Are Arrested." *New York Times*, August 17.
Hopper, Hedda. 1947. "Orson Welles Sets Own Schedule and It's Tough." *Los Angeles Times*, July 27.
Houseman, John. 1937. "Again—A People's Theatre; the Mercury Takes a Bow." *New York Daily Worker*, September 18.
Hunter, Marjorie. 1968. "HUAC and the Yippies Do Their Thing." *New York Times*, October 6.
Jauss, Hans Robert. 1982. *Toward an Aesthetic of Reception*. Translated by Timothy Bahti. Minneapolis: University of Minnesota Press.
Jennings, C. Robert. 1967. "The Hollywood 10, Plus Twenty." *Los Angeles Times*, September 3.
Jensen, Richard. 1995. "The Culture Wars, 1965–1995: A Historian's Map." *Journal of Social History* 29.
Julber, Eric. 1967. Letter to the Editor. *Los Angeles Times*, September 16.
Kazin, Alfred. 1976. Letter to the Editor. *New York Times*, October 17.
Kilday, Greg. 1975. "Blacklisting Comes Out of the Shadows." *Los Angeles Times*, September 9.
Kirsh, Robert R. 1965. "One of the 'Hollywood Ten' Appeals to Public Opinion." *Los Angeles Times*, April 2.
Kramer, Hilton. 1976. "The Blacklist and the Cold War." *New York Times*, October 3.
Lardner, Ring, Jr. *Papers*. Margaret Herrick Library, Los Angeles.
Lardner, Ring, Jr. 2000. *I'd Hate Myself in the Morning*. New York: Thunder's Mouth Press.
Leaming, Barbara. 1985. *Orson Welles: A Biography*. New York: Viking Penguin.

Leiter, Robert. 1983. "A New Look at the "Cradle" that Rocked Broadway." *New York Times*, May 1.

McBride, Joseph. 2006. *What Ever Happened to Orson Welles? A Portrait of an Independent Career.* Lexington: University of Kentucky.

Menashe, Louis. 1976. Letter to the Editor. *New York Times*, October 17.

Navasky, Victor S. 1980. *Naming Names.* New York: The Viking Press.

Oja, Carol J. 1989. "Marc Blitzstein's The Cradle Will Rock and Mass-Song Style of the 1930s." *Musical Quarterly* 73, no. 4: 445–475.

Pell, Richard H. 1985. *The Liberal Mind in a Conservative Age.* New York: Harper & Row.

Radosh, Ronald, and Allis Radosh. 2005. *Red Star Over Hollywood.* San Francisco: Encounter Books.

Radosh, Ronald. 1976. Letter to the Editor. *New York Times*, October 17.

Radosh, Ronald. 2001. *Commies: A Journey Through the Old Left, the New Left, and the Leftover Left.* San Francisco: Encounter Books.

Robbins, Tim. 2000a. *Cradle Will Rock.* New York: Newmarket Press.

Robbins, Tim. 2000b. Letter to the Editor. *New York Times*, January 23.

Robbins, Tim. 2001. "What I Voted For." *Nation*, August 6.

Ryskind, Morrie. 1964a. "Straight Goods on Filmland Reds." *Los Angeles Times*, January 29.

Ryskind, Morrie. 1964b. "Taking a Look at the Red Record." *Los Angeles Times*, March 4.

Samson, Jim. 1994. "Chopin Reception: Theory, History, Analysis" In *Chopin Studies 2*, edited by John Rink and Jim Samson, 1–17. Cambridge: Cambridge University Press.

Schlessinger, Arthur. Jr. 1976. Letter to the Editor. *New York Times*, October 17.

Stang, Joanne. 1965. "20 Years after the Hollywood 10." *New York Times*, July 4.

Trainor, Richard. 1984/85. "O'Connor, Lowry, Huston and Welles." *Sight and Sound* 54, no. 1: 31–33.

Welles, Orson. 1938. "Theatre and the People's Front." *New York Daily Worker*, April 15.

Welles, Orson. 1984. *The Cradle Will Rock.* University of California, Santa Barbara Library. Duplicated typescript.

CHAPTER 22

PETE SEEGER'S PROJECT

DICK FLACKS

PETE Seeger, the modern American troubadour, is today one of the most honored and celebrated performers in the United States. In 1994 President Clinton awarded him the National Medal for the Arts (the highest honor given to artists by the US government). In that year he was a recipient of the Kennedy Center lifetime achievement honor. His ninetieth birthday on May 3, 2009, provided the occasion for a huge Madison Square Garden celebratory concert featuring a wide array of popular musicians singing his songs and honoring his influence. A letter of appreciation from President Obama was read to those assembled. In January 2009 Seeger participated in the Obama inaugural concert at the foot of the Washington Monument.

The Madison Square Garden concert culminated several years of adulation bestowed on Seeger by the popular music industry. In the nineties, Seeger was awarded a lifetime Grammy and admitted into the Rock and Roll Hall of Fame. His visibility was considerably enhanced by Bruce Springsteen's international concert tour and recording project called The Seeger Sessions, featuring material drawn from Seeger's folksong repertory. A documentary film biography called *Pete Seeger: The Power of Song* was released on public television and in theaters in 2007. There was an ongoing campaign to get him nominated for the Nobel Peace Prize. A long adulatory essay on Seeger appeared in *The New Yorker*, and an extended version is now out as one of three biographies published in 2009 (Wilkinson 2006 and Wilkinson 2009). In addition to that essay by Alec Wilkinson, there is a biographical narrative by the historian Allan Winkler and a major revised updating of David Dunaway's "official" biography originally published in 1981 (Winkler 2009; Dunaway 2008).

This recognition is certainly deserved given Seeger's influence on American music and the nature of his life story. Yet central to that story is that he is one of the least well known famous persons in America. For example, I use protest music a lot in my teaching about social movements; over the years, I've found that fewer than 5 percent of my students can identify Seeger (and this is probably a higher proportion than one would find in a sample of the wider public). The attention he has received in recent years has undoubtedly increased his name recognition, but that recognition does not match his cultural importance.

This paradox goes to the heart of what his life was about. Seeger was marginalized because of his politics. His relative obscurity is largely due to his virtual exclusion from the commercial mass media. There is, however, a further paradox: the exclusion and censorship he experienced enhanced his ability to fulfill his particular artistic and political project. Seeger's marginalization was rooted in his lifelong commitment to the American Left. That commitment is something he was born and raised to have. His father, the noted composer and musicologist Charles Seeger, was an important figure in left-wing cultural expression even before Pete's birth in 1919. He lost his position as professor of music at Berkeley because of outspoken opposition to World War I despite his pathbreaking work as a composer and musicologist. Alongside his professional accomplishments, Charles Seeger tried to construct links between music and political consciousness. In the early depression years Charles helped form the Composers' Collective (whose membership included Marc Blitzstein, Aaron Copland, and other young radical musicians) whose goal was to create a new music for revolutionary workers. They began as radical modernists but eventually turned to the preservation and reinvigoration of folk and vernacular musics as an alternative to commodified mass culture (Dunaway 2008).

Seeger grew up immersed in the Left, and the cultural Left in particular. He joined the Young Communist League during his brief time at Harvard and was a Communist Party member (according to Dunaway) during most of the 1940s. Although he stopped formal membership in the party in the late 1940s, he remained one of the star cultural figures of the communist-oriented Left for many years after that.

David Dunaway, who has written the most authoritative biography of Seeger, suggests that when he was a party member, Seeger was sometimes at odds with party discipline. In the 1930s many Communist Party members from comfortable backgrounds felt the need to demonstrate their revolutionary bona fides by slavish conformity to party lines and party demands. Dunaway describes Seeger as restless with such demands, avoiding boring meetings, and alienated by abstract theorizing. Indeed, his dedication to the promotion of folk music was not particularly appreciated by party cultural commissars, who may have preferred that the party line be set to more mainstream popular tunes (Dunaway 2008, 134–135).

But such tensions were submerged by Seeger's public role as a staunchly left-wing performer and activist. His first significant musical project was to help organize a singing group—the Almanac Singers—which, in the late 1930s, aimed to connect music to movements and causes of the day. The Almanacs, who included Woody Guthrie, Lee Hays, Bess Lomax Hawes, and Millard Lampell as members of the fluid collective, pioneered the concept of making songs with topical lyrics on contemporary themes set to traditional folk music tunes and forms. They cultivated a spontaneous, homespun performance style and performed mainly at rallies and benefits related to the labor movement.

The Almanacs' first recording was released in the aftermath of the Nazi-Soviet pact in early 1941. In the years prior to the Pact, the Communist Party was vociferously anti-Nazi and critical of American isolationism in face of the Nazi threat. But the party line radically changed after the Pact, becoming vociferously antiwar. True to this new line, the Almanacs recorded an album of antiwar songs condemning the start of conscription and FDR's military build-up. But one month after the album's release, the Soviet Union was attacked by Hitler, and the American party overnight became a leading advocate of war against the Nazis. Unsold copies of the antiwar album *The Songs of John Doe* were destroyed, and soon after The Almanacs put out an album supporting the war effort. This episode is a tale often used to demonstrate that the CPUSA was Stalin's tool, and that its members were unable to think and act in principled ways. There are some who still cannot forgive Seeger for this display of party-line cultural compliance. Apart from what it suggests about the way the party was able to engineer emotion and expression, the evident self-censorship that all concerned engaged in is disturbing. *Songs of John Doe* was finally made publicly available when it was included in a ten-disc compilation called *Songs for Political Action*, a compilation of all known 78 RPM recordings of political songs released in 1966 by Bear Family Records (Cohen and Samuelson 1996).

The Almanacs were together for about three years, releasing a classic album of union songs and several recordings of traditional folk music. They performed primarily in political contexts—rallies, benefit concerts, and the like—but attempted commercial ventures as well. These included several major network radio programs and nightclub bookings. But the *John Doe* material was soon unearthed by the FBI and various newspapers, causing public questions about the Almanacs' patriotism. The commercial possibilities dried up before they could begin to be realized. Seeger and friends were largely blocked from the cultural mainstream during the war despite their fealty to the war effort.

The Almanacs' collective did not last long, in part because several members, including Seeger and Guthrie, entered military service. While in uniform, Seeger recorded songs of the Spanish Civil War and a number of other topical songs (accompanied by other emerging folksingers including Burl Ives, Josh White, and Sonny Terry) for left-wing labels. He served in the Philippines as an entertainer for wounded GIs, learning quite a bit about how music can work to build collective morale. By war's end, he was certain that making politically relevant music was his life's work.

After the war Seeger's energies turned toward organizational entrepreneurship and performing. He sparked the formation of a national network of left-wing music-makers (artists, songwriters, presenters, and so on). "People's Artists" (later called "People's Songs") served as a booking agency, a publisher of song sheet newsletters and song books, and a support framework for advancing a popular music relevant to political action. In the immediate postwar period leftists were hopeful that the dynamism of the labor movement of the 1930s would continue and that the social democratic logic of the New Deal would be maintained by the post-FDR government. Seeger imagined that his people's music network would be wedded to the rising unions and other social movements and that there would be fertile ground for growing a leftward popular culture.

These hopes proved illusory. Instead, the Cold War against the Soviet Union and communism defined official policy and increasingly penetrated the political culture. A bitter split occurred in the union movement and the Left on the communist issue in the context of the emerging Cold War. Many liberal and labor leaders sought to exclude communists and their sympathizers from their organizations and alliances. The presidential candidacy of former vice president Henry Wallace on a third-party ticket, which was supported by the Communist Party in 1948, was a major source of division among liberals. The People's Song project provided a soundtrack for the Wallace campaign, but the total failure of that candidacy and the increasing tempo of the red scare thoroughly marginalized the network Seeger had worked hard to build.

Seeger's passion for building alternative institutions like People's Artists was rooted in the cultural Left's longstanding ambivalence about the mainstream culture industry. Those who, like Charles Seeger and Alan Lomax, in the 1930s wanted to create a popular music rooted in American folk traditions, thought that by so doing they would foster alternatives to mass culture dominated by commercial media. Woody Guthrie frequently expressed disdain for commercial music, and his legend, dramatized in the fictionalized film biography *Bound for Glory*, celebrated his deliberate refusal to accept radio network contracts and nightclub dates. The Almanacs and the postwar People's Artists thought they could create a noncorporate, social movement–based apparatus to reach popular audiences, and those hopes were in some ways fulfilled (by a plethora of record labels, community radio stations, and the like). On the other hand, the Almanacs, from the beginning, were not averse to commercial opportunity; they and Woody Guthrie did land spots on network radio and in nightclubs. Yet each time such commercial breakthroughs happened, press uproars about their politics soon followed, and consequently such bookings declined.

Seeger undoubtedly recognized that he could be politically freer by working on the margins rather than in the mainstream of the culture industry. Despite this, however, he continued to try to find avenues for mainstream opportunity. Seeger's most promising such venture was the effort by the Almanacs' successor group, The Weavers, to work commercial venues. The quartet was born out of the People's Artists/Henry Wallace cultural left, but was discovered and signed by Gordon Jenkins of Decca Records (one of the largest record labels of the 1940s and 1950s). Jenkins produced a series of Weavers' hits (several of these among the biggest selling singles of the era), and they were booked into many of the leading club and concert venues. The Weavers uncomfortably complied with their handlers' demands that they steer clear of the causes and organizations they had been used to working for, but it was not long before right-wing entrepreneurs of the emerging red scare went after them, largely because of Seeger's long association with communist politics. An FBI informant named them as communists before the House Un-American Activities Committee (HUAC), and the charge was echoed in news media and nurtured by organs of the blacklist. Soon, major concert bookings were canceled, club dates were dropped, radio and television appearances were no longer forthcoming, and their Decca recording contract was terminated.

Some two years after they had burst on the scene, the Weavers' commercial recording and live performance career was over. Their story typified the workings of the McCarthy era cultural blacklist: a symbiotic relationship between government agencies like the FBI and HUAC with a network of professional anti-communist organizations who publicly branded entertainers and artists. Those so identified were usually given the opportunity to denounce their past politics and inform on others whom they had known. Refusals to recant led to quite complete erasure from the main entertainment media.

Seeger was among those most thoroughly erased in the 1950s. But he realized that there were niches and circuits where he could continue to perform and find audiences. With his wife Toshi Seeger as manager, he embarked on a perpetual tour of America's college campuses, progressive children's camps, and left-wing sponsored benefits, where he honed a solo performance style and repertory that defined him as a musician. At the same time, he discovered that he could win an army of young fans and that the relatively accessible and uncensored space provided by college campuses and surviving left-wing cultural institutions could counter the effects of mainstream censorship. In these venues he was carrying on the ancient role of the troubadour, bringing the news through song, inspiring interest among young people in traditional musics, and becoming a model of the autonomous popular artist.

It was undoubtedly a hard row to hoe. There were many occasions when bookings were canceled because of political pressure or fear. And of course income from his appearances was decidedly modest, the road was lonely, and touring meant long periods of separation from his growing family. Still, it was in his struggle to survive the blacklist that Pete Seeger found his calling. From the time he started to perform in the late 1930s, Pete Seeger seems quite consciously to have constructed his work as a project rather than a career. For Seeger, the word "career" suggests that one is orienting one's life toward personal success, climbing a ladder of accomplishment and fame. Seeger instead set out to channel his ambition toward social and cultural change and, more than most politically minded performers, to try to exorcise his strivings for personal recognition.

Seeger's commitment to his project was embodied in a particular performance style, which he perfected in his years of exile from mass media. The key for him was not to display his talent and skill, nor to thrill or entice an audience. It was instead to bring songs to people so that they could make them their own. Every Seeger performance was centered on group singing. Simply getting a mass audience to sing was an achievement, but he aimed further—to teach new songs and to foster unrehearsed singing in harmony. He became a master at this.

Seeger did not, to my knowledge, lay out a full-fledged theory to explain his passion to promote mass singing. But such a theory was implicit in his performances: there is an empowering effect in the very sound of a singing assembly; there is a persuasive effect that can come when audience members sing lyrics expressing a political perspective or commitment; there is a sense of mutual validation when a crowd of people sing together in an attitude of resistance. And, once you sing a song, there is a good chance that you will be able to reproduce it by and for yourself, with no need for the professional performer to evoke it. Seeger's father Charles had expressed, when Pete was a teenager, the wish for a mode of musical performance that had the ability to "aid in the welding of the people into more independent, capable, and democratic action" (quoted in Wilkinson 2009, 124). That definition was undoubtedly a fundamental guideline for the performance style Seeger created in the face of the blacklist.

Indeed, one might argue that the blacklist necessitated this style: as a political being Seeger could not be content with finding audiences who appreciated his performances. He felt the need to somehow fight back against the blacklist. He came to the view that resisting the blacklist effectively meant creating an artistic alternative to the popular mainstream and helping it grow: to inspire a new generation of performers, to foster forms of expression and taste that went counter to the popular—and have these take hold despite censorship. In this aim, as we will see below, he was successful.

Meanwhile, the Weavers eventually overcame the blacklist to some degree as the decade went on. In late 1955 their manager Harold Leventhal was able to book them for a holiday concert in Carnegie Hall. It was an event widely seen as a direct challenge to the blacklist, and the concert quickly sold out. A live recording of the event released by the new Vanguard label was a best seller. For many on the Left, attending the concert and buying the recording provided a simple way to flaunt censorship. The revival of the Weavers suggested not only that the blacklist was not monolithic but also that it might be weakening its hold.

The Weavers continued to perform and record for several years thereafter, but Pete Seeger left the group soon after the Carnegie Hall concert. By then, he had carved out a distinctive role for himself and preferred not to work the conventional show business path that defined the Weavers. Moreover, he was receiving new political threats. Just months before the Carnegie Hall event, Seeger had been subpoenaed to testify before the House Un-American Activities Committee. Most who came before that body had refused to testify about their membership in the Communist Party and other political involvements on the constitutional grounds provided by the Fifth Amendment (which declares that no person can be forced to bear witness against themselves). Seeger decided not to "take the Fifth" but to declare simply that congressional efforts to force disclosure about political beliefs were improper (the so-called "First Amendment stance"). This was courageous since the only legally recognized grounds for declining to answer such questions was self-incrimination. As a result of his stance, Seeger was declared to be in contempt of Congress, a criminal offense. While awaiting trial on the charge, his travel was restricted, and his political visibility made it even harder to get performance opportunities. On the other hand, in the late 1950s his audiences at live concerts were growing, and he made literally dozens of albums for Folkways records.

Seeger's trial on the contempt charge took place five years after his original congressional appearance. He was convicted and sentenced to ten years in prison to run concurrently (so that the actual time served would have been a year and a day). That conviction bolstered Seeger's reputation as a voice of dissent and an exemplar of courageous protest. Then, in 1962, a Court of Appeals overturned the conviction on technical grounds. That verdict vindicated Seeger's principled refusal to cooperate with HUAC, further enhancing his stature as a tribune of dissent.

In that same period Seeger was winning audiences and recognition previously denied him. Columbia Records' great producer John Hammond overcame resistance in the corporation and signed Seeger for the Columbia label, thereby promising wide distribution for his recordings. Meanwhile, Seeger was packing big concert venues (although still experiencing canceled bookings and local controversies). At the same time, a pop-centered folk song revival was becoming commercially successful. Weavers imitators, led by the Kingston Trio and, later, Peter, Paul and Mary, sold millions of records. In the early 1950s the Weavers had shown the commercial potential for popularized folk music, but the resulting commodification inevitably cheapened, denatured, and contradicted Seeger's hopes and intentions. By the early 1960s, however, a musical rebellion against pop folk was in the works, as a band of young troubadours, consciously following in Guthrie's and Seeger's footsteps, came on the scene. Bob Dylan, Joan Baez, Phil Ochs, Odetta, and many others performed in new folk clubs, recorded on upstart labels, appeared at civil rights and "ban the bomb" rallies, and dominated the college tours. Seeger and others launched the Newport Folk Festival, which deliberately brought together this new breed of urban folksinger with a wide range of traditional and vernacular performers before audiences in the thousands. This folk music boom was a political as well as cultural phenomenon. The festivals, concerts, and clubs where folk fans congregated were among the prime social spaces for shaping awareness and engagement with the southern civil rights movement and the New Left.

Pete Seeger's belief in the power of song derived in large part from history—the fact that a number of great social movements were fueled by music. There is a tradition of labor song in America, dating from the nineteenth century, and a number of songs from that tradition continue to this day to help define the identities of labor organizers and raise the spirits on the picket line. The Almanacs and People's Songs had been experiments designed to make the US labor movement of the 1930s and 1940s a singing movement—but the results were mixed at best. Seeger's dream of a singing mass movement was much more fully realized in the civil rights struggle of the 1960s.

Music has of course been a central feature of African-American culture from its origins. In the early 1960s, as marchers gathered in churches to prepare to challenge segregation with their very bodies, traditional songs and song styles used in these churches were turned into hymns of solidarity and shared risk-taking (with lyrics adapted for the occasion). Seeger contributed to the development of this freedom singing. It was he who had first made "We Shall Overcome" known to civil rights activists in the 1950s, and his concerts in the early 1960s taught the new freedom songs to mass audiences in the north. He encouraged Bernice Reagon to found the Freedom Singers quartet (modeled on the Almanacs), and he and Toshi managed the group's touring across the country to raise support for the Student Nonviolent Coordinating Committee.

The music of the southern movement was an important factor in forging a moral identification with it among northern students—an identification that led to a flood of volunteers to southern organizing campaigns and manifold support efforts. Seeger was an important enabler of all this and his life project was finding its fulfillment in his work on stage and as an organizer. You can get a feel for that moment by listening to a recording of his concert in Carnegie Hall on June 8, 1963, available on the Columbia label under the title "We Shall Overcome."

The recording captures the way that Seeger was able to transform the concert into a moment of collective history-making, bringing the southern civil rights movement into Carnegie Hall.

Seeger's growing acceptance, vindication, and political ascendancy, however, did not end efforts to censor him. The blacklist remained particularly effective with respect to television. In the early 1960s several network bookings of Seeger were suddenly canceled. The most dramatic story had to do with ABC's development of a folk music show called "Hootenanny." The word "hootenanny" was introduced to the New York folk scene in the early 1940s, after Seeger and Guthrie returned from a trip to Seattle, where they had heard the word used to refer to folk singing parties. The Almanac singers hosted weekly hootenannies to help them pay their house rent. After the war, People's Songs sponsored regular concerts featuring a wide range of performers and called these events hootenannies. Of course, the word was not copyrighted, and ABC was able to commercially appropriate it for their series.

Seeger and his manager Harold Leventhal were led to believe that he would be invited to perform on the show, but they later learned through the grapevine that this was not to be. Seeger's exclusion soon became a public issue. Joan Baez refused to appear at any venue that barred Seeger, and her boycott of the ABC program was joined by several dozen other performers. That the patriarchal figure of urban folk-singing would be banned from a show that capitalized on his work angered large numbers of fans. Seeger personally encouraged some performers to go on the show, arguing that it was a great opportunity to reach young audiences with the songs, but the boycott (and the generally debased quality of the program's content) eventually led to its demise.

In 1963, freed from the travel restrictions tied to his contempt case, Seeger made use of another way to overcome the blacklist. Together with his family, he embarked on a tour of Asia, Africa, and Eastern and Western Europe that lasted nearly a year. In some of those places he was able to reach the mass audience that had been denied to him in the United States. He sang on Indian radio to an audience nearly the size of the American population and taught "We Shall Overcome" to people across the planet (thereby helping to make it the universal freedom anthem). His work and name became better known in some European countries than in the United States.

In the mid-1960s Seeger became actively involved in opposition to the Vietnam War. Some of his earlier antiwar anthems (such as "Where Have All the Flowers Gone") became hugely popular. The events of the decade inspired him to pour increasing energy into writing his own songs, and many of these were antiwar songs. Controversy swirled when he sang war protest songs overseas (including at Moscow University), reviving the frequently reiterated depiction of him as "Moscow's canary." Such episodes seemed to justify the continuing exclusion of Seeger by mainstream commercial outlets.

Television was the main such outlet at the time. Seeger tried various stratagems to break through on TV. He succeeded, using his own savings, in creating a television series called *Rainbow Quest,* which appeared in 1965 on around a dozen UHF channels in New York and other cities, reaching an inevitably miniscule audience. Many of these programs have been released on DVD (and some are excerpted on YouTube). They are a priceless record of the folk revival and feature a number of traditional performers as well as the rising young troubadours.

The network television blacklist of Seeger ended in 1967 when CBS permitted the Smothers Brothers (hosts of the most popular variety show on national television at the time) to feature Seeger before a live audience. Among the songs he sang before that audience was his newly released antiwar ballad, "Waist Deep in the Big Muddy." The song was constructed as a parable about an army platoon in World War II trapped in a muddy swamp under the leadership of a stubborn captain. Its final verse makes the Vietnam connection clear:

> Every time I read the papers
> That old feeling comes on
> We're waist deep in the big muddy
> And the big fool says to push on.

When the program aired, Seeger's performance of that song was censored out (and the cut was crude—Seeger is shown beginning a song with his twelve-string guitar, but the jump shot has him playing a banjo). The edit was done without informing the Smothers Brothers. Media coverage was extensive: before the censorship, press accounts hailed CBS for ending the blacklist; after the Big Muddy episode, many decried what CBS itself admitted was the censoring of political expression.

Some months later, CBS felt compelled to allow Seeger to be invited back; he performed "Big Muddy" as part of a medley of songs about war (which can be viewed on YouTube). A year later the Smothers Brothers show was terminated (perhaps in part because of its propensity to be embroiled in controversy). That January 1968 appearance by Seeger did not usher in a television career for him. In fact, his appearances on commercial television remained quite rare. Years later, in his eighties, he was the subject of an hour-long interview on public television by Bill Moyers. PBS subsequently distributed a feature-length documentary about Seeger and broadcast the Madison Square Garden celebration of his ninetieth birthday. It took some sixty years for Pete Seeger to be able to freely express himself on national television.

Pete Seeger was one of the most censored musicians in American history. He was not prevented from performing, recording, or publishing his work as such but rather was barred from appearing in the primary mass media. His experience is directly related to the rise of commercial mass media as the main means by which musical performance is distributed.

Since the late 1930s there have been concerted efforts to marginalize artists identified as sympathetic to communism. These efforts were facilitated by the collection of files on such sympathizers by the Federal Bureau of Investigation. These files resulted from the work of FBI informants embedded in targeted organizations, who were either paid undercover agents of the FBI or private individuals motivated by patriotism or fear to inform on colleagues. The FBI shared information with the House Un-American Activities Committee and with trusted allies in the news media. HUAC and the press publicized allegations of communist ties, particularly of performers who were having commercial success or visibility. The Almanacs and the Weavers were early targets of this kind.

In the 1950s, during the red scare, a network of private organizations and individuals developed whose business was to systematically publicize names of communists in the entertainment industry, create opportunities for those named to clear themselves through self-abnegation, or create pressure on entertainment executives and corporate sponsors to purge or avoid hiring unrepentant communists and fellow-travelers. Television and radio sponsors and movie studios were pressured by threats of product boycotts, pickets, and the like, and for perhaps a decade the resulting blacklist was effective in barring hundreds of people from regular employment in the entertainment industry.

Seeger began his work as a participant in a large circle of musical creators and performers who identified with the Left. His father had been a leader of the Composers Collective whose ranks included Aaron Copland, Marc Blitzstein, and other composers of note. Many musicians participated in politically oriented cabarets and theater projects. Many jazz musicians performed in clubs and did benefits sponsored by communists. Some world-famous artists were strongly identified with the Communist Party, most notably Paul Robeson, as well as refugees from Nazism including Hanns Eisler and Bertolt Brecht.

Many of these artists were subjects of the blacklist in the 1950s. Some were called to testify by HUAC. Robeson, who was highly celebrated and financially successful, was denied a passport, recording contracts, and concert bookings, and for a period of years he could perform only at black churches. Some of those targeted sought ways to clear themselves in order to be able to work. Many others found a livelihood in teaching and performing at venues provided by the marginal left.

Music-makers are harder to totally silence than are artists who depend on costly technology for production and for distribution and therefore those who control access to such means. Musicians who use simple, portable instruments can find audiences in all kinds of spaces. The technology of recording requires less capital for production and distribution than radio, television, or cinema. Pete Seeger was effectively kept from the mainstream mass media but he was far from silenced. Indeed, the censorship and exclusion he suffered in certain ways enhanced his social impact.

By the end of the 1960s Seeger could take satisfaction that his decision to organize his life around a principled project and reject a "career" had changed history. He, more than any other American artist, had conceived and fostered a tradition of protest song. He helped uncover and did much to popularize songs, drawn from a number of cultural roots, that had significant political consequence. These efforts reshaped the forms and content of popular music. His performances revived the ancient social role of the troubadour—a special kind of intellectual, who uses song to bring news and enlightenment about current events and about the past. But he performed in ways that were intended to empower audience members to sing their own songs, and find capacities for democratic action through that singing.

If Seeger is often portrayed as a victim of blacklisting and censorship, it is nevertheless clear that his long marginalization was necessary for the fulfillment of his project. His refusal to discuss his political allegiances with the House Un-American Activities Committee in 1955 meant that he risked jail time and suffered years of costly litigation, travel restriction, and blacklisting. Yet as a result of the charges and his resistance, he came, says Alex Wilkinson, to "typify the principles of all the brave people he sang about" (Wilkinson 2009, 84).

Over the last century in a number of countries, troubadours have become icons of resistance. Seeger did quite a bit to popularize such heroes. Joe Hill, the wobbly bard whose funeral after his execution for murder was attended by thousands, was one of the sources for the Almanacs. Woody Guthrie's legendary stature in American culture derives in part from Seeger's efforts to make him known. And then, in the 1960s and 1970s, iconic troubadours emerged all over the world: Bob Marley in Jamaica, Víctor Jara in Chile, Vladimir Vysotsky in the Soviet Union, Wolf Biermann in East Germany, Cui Jian in China, and Miriam Makeba in South Africa. Some of these, such as Jara, explicitly used Seeger and Guthrie as models. All were able to achieve iconic stature and profound popular affection as a result of persecution, censorship, and martyrdom. Meanwhile, all over the world, many hundreds of other singers who have taken on the troubadour role have not become heroes and martyrs but have produced work with significance in defining the political culture. Pete Seeger's example had much to do with the revival of this style of musical expression.

The Madison Square Garden birthday celebration on May 3, 2009, featured many contemporary American musicians of this sort. Some, such as Bruce Springsteen and Dave Matthews, have had enormous commercial success, and most of the others who were on stage were better known to a wider public than Seeger himself. Their participation was evidence of the cultural effect of his project. Each of the stars testified explicitly or implicitly to the pull of Seeger's example: to devote something of their work to movements and causes, to question if not defy the political and expressive constraints of the culture industry.

That event was the culmination of several years in which that industry bestowed all kinds of honor on Seeger, while he was showered with the major honors that the federal government offers to cultural figures. A cynic might say that in America political troublemakers are marginalized and suppressed when they are young but are canonized when they are safely old or dead so that we can persuade ourselves that we really are a free country. A further paradox: these very honors may undermine Seeger's standing as a courageous voice of radical dissent.

It is likely, however, that Pete Seeger viewed all this as a vindication of his project, and as a measure of positive change in the American political culture. The blacklist did unravel; a number of court cases, including his own, invalidated many of its mechanisms and practices. Limits were placed on congressional political inquisition and FBI surveillance. Some blacklisted entertainers won major civil suits. At the same time, within the entertainment industry, a good deal of apology and regret has been expressed over the years. On the other hand, it is not clear that the form and content of Seeger's art is still welcome by commercial cultural purveyors.

At the height of the blacklist, Pete Seeger found and made good use of channels of communication outside of the corporate culture industry. Relatively inexpensive recording technology provided means of dissemination; emergent non-commercial FM stations provided an avenue for bypassing commercial broadcasting. His life story indicates that even in the face of censorship an artist's voice on the margins can ripple through the culture with powerful effect.

Today, the Internet, diverse recording technologies, and a proliferation of musical subcultures make traditional forms of censorship and blacklist even less likely to be effective. Still, to the extent that the means of distribution of popular culture remain under the control of mega corporations, Pete Seeger's vision of a democratically empowering music will need to struggle to be heard.

References

Cohen, Ron, and Dave Samuelson. 1996. *Songs For Political Action*. Hambergen, Germany: Bear Family Records.
Dunaway, David King. 2008. *How Can I Keep From Singing?: The Ballad of Pete Seeger*. New York: Villard.
Seeger, Pete. 1989. *We Shall Overcome: Complete Carnegie Hall Concert [Live]*. Sony Records.
Wilkinson, Alec. 2006. "The Protest Singer: Pete Seeger and American Folk Music." *The New Yorker*, April 17, 44–53.
Wilkinson, Alec. 2009. *The Protest Singer: An Intimate Portrait of Pete Seeger*. New York: Knopf.
Winkler, Allan. 2009. *'To everything there is a season': Pete Seeger and the Power of Song*. New York: Oxford University Press.

CHAPTER 23

GOVERNMENT CENSORSHIP AND AARON COPLAND'S *LINCOLN PORTRAIT* DURING THE SECOND RED SCARE

JENNIFER DELAPP-BIRKETT

IN 1953, at the height of the Second Red Scare in the United States, Aaron Copland's music was, in effect, censored when a government official publicly accused the composer of being "un-American" and declared his music unfit for performance at a national celebration. Many members of the concert music community in the United States—especially recent émigrés from Europe—were deeply troubled, recalling the state policies there that had gradually and subtly marginalized musicians who were deemed enemies of the party in power in the years before World War II. "The music of the Coplands and who knows how many others could be stilled in America," music critic Paul Hume wrote ominously in *The Washington Post* (January 18,1953). Although nothing approaching the atrocities of World War II ultimately unfolded in the United States, the music critic's comment was in some ways prescient, for in the early Cold War years, the domestic anti-communist movement in the United States—a shifting but extensive coalition of government and private-sector groups—sought to strip politically disfavored musicians of cultural influence. Copland was one of the targets.

Borne by the public's fears of a communist takeover and intensified by rivalry between the two main political parties, the movement to purge communist ideals from American culture was powerful. Copland easily could have been swept into the same semi-obscurity as the authors, actors, and screenwriters who fell victim to the movement. He was not. But the Second Red Scare took a toll on Copland. It destroyed his flourishing network of artistic support and drained him of time and energy. And, paradoxically, it reinforced the idea that concert music was essentially apolitical, existing on a separate plane from everyday American life—an idea that directly contradicted Copland's previously stated convictions.

Dwight D. Eisenhower was elected president of the United States in November 1952, the first Republican president since Herbert Hoover. The inaugural celebration would last many days, with balls, dinners, and of course the ceremony. One of these events would be a celebratory concert by the National Symphony Orchestra on January 18 in Constitution Hall. In addition to Italian opera arias and works by Beethoven and Mendelssohn, the concert planners programmed some American-written works: music of Samuel Barber and George Gershwin, and Aaron Copland's *Lincoln Portrait*.

Lincoln Portrait is a fourteen-minute-long composition for narrator and symphony orchestra. Copland wrote it in 1942 at the request of conductor André Kostelanetz, who commissioned a series of works honoring "great Americans" (Copland and Perlis 2013, 143-144; Pollack 1999, 356). During the last section of the work, the narrator intones the words of Abraham Lincoln, assembled by Copland with simple connecting prose. The instruments play folk tunes from the Civil War era, set among Copland's own themes and harmonic framework. The tone is serious and respectful, and listeners consistently heard it as such.

The composer himself was by this time a national symbol of American-grown classical music. He had written Hollywood film scores for movies based on American literature—"Of Mice and Men" (1939, after John Steinbeck), "Our Town" (1941, after Thornton Wilder), "The Red Pony" (1948, after Steinbeck), and "The Heiress" (1949, after Henry James)—and for "The North Star," with a script by Lillian Hellman. His Americana-themed ballets *Appalachian Spring* (winner of a 1945 Pulitzer Prize), *Billy the Kid*, and *Rodeo* were popular among modern dance enthusiasts; their suites, along with *Fanfare for the Common Man* and the Third Symphony, were fast becoming staples of the national repertory.

Three days before the inaugural concert, a leading national news agency reported that *Lincoln Portrait* had been removed from the program because the composer was alleged to have a record of "un-American activities." A member of Congress, Representative Fred Busbey, claimed there was substantial evidence that Copland's beliefs and activities made him a potential threat to national security. Busbey's evidence, he said, came from the House Committee on Un-American Activities (HUAC), a Congressional committee to which he belonged that sought to expose and stop anti-American propaganda efforts; after World War II, supporters of communism were HUAC's main target. The inaugural committee agreed that such allegations made it imprudent to program Copland's music, and *Lincoln Portrait* was removed from the program (Copland and Peris, 234–236).

Before January 15, only a small fraction of the voting public would have paid attention to the logistics behind the inaugural events—the ceremonies, the parties, the formal appearances—much less to their musical components. But after the cancellation was announced, readers of *The Washington Post*, the *New York Times*, and every other newspaper that published the Associated Press news wires knew that the composer Aaron Copland stood accused of being un-American.

The incongruity between HUAC's accusations and Copland's public reputation as a prominent composer of American symphonic music demanded explanation, as *Washington Post* music critic Paul Hume immediately stated in an editorial the next day. He noted Copland's exceptional achievements, the patriotic subjects in his oeuvre, and the absurdity of considering *Lincoln Portrait* unsuitable for a national celebration. In response, Busbey enumerated his reasons in remarks preserved in the *Congressional Record* (U.S. Congress, 16 Jan. 1953, 178–80).

Busbey's explanation for censoring *Lincoln Portrait* deserves close attention, for as a summary of Red Scare dogma applied directly to Copland, it touches on five themes that recurred throughout Copland's experience of music and censorship in the decade after World War II: the domestic fight against communism (also known as McCarthyism or the Second Red Scare); the belief that communist thought had infiltrated influential segments of American government and society at large; partisan politics; gender identity; and finally, the view that while composers could be political, music itself was not—a subtle premise that aggravated an estrangement between concert music and everyday American life.

> As I have but a passing knowledge of music, I cannot and do not offer any comments on the quality of Mr. Copland's work.
>
> However, when I learned that this piece of music was to be played at the inaugural concert, I voiced my objections with all the vigor at my command. My objections were based on but one thing—the known record of Aaron Copland for activities, affiliations, and sympathies with and for causes that seemed to me to be more in the interest of an alien ideology than the things representative of Abraham Lincoln....
>
> I do not detract one iota from Copland's musical ability, but I do stand firm in my conviction that the inaugural concert of President-elect Eisenhower is no place for Copland's music.
>
> For nearly 20 years, the Communist Party devoted time and effort to infiltrating the various departments of our Federal Government while the Democrats were in control of the executive branch.... I fought this infiltration of government under the Democratic Party and I assure you I will continue to fight this infiltration under the Republican Party.
>
> Experience has taught us that the real Communist is not always easy to identify, but the same experience has taught us that the nonparty member, or so-called fellow traveler is more easily identified by his record of activities and affiliations. I agree that any person could have been affiliated with or supported one of the many Communist fronts that have mushroomed over a period of years without being aware that he was giving aid and comfort to the Communist Party, but I insist that as the number of such activities or affiliations increase, any presumption of the innocence of such a person must necessarily decrease.
>
> With all the music of fine, patriotic, and thoroughly American composers available to the concert committee of the Inauguration Committee, 1953, I not only questioned the advisability of using music by a composer with the long record of questionable affiliations of Mr. Copland, as reported by the House Committee on Un-American Activities, but protested the use of his music.
>
> I sincerely believe the Republican Party would have been ridiculed from one end of the United States to the other by the press, columnists, and radio commentators if any of Copland's music was played at the inauguration. Whether or not I was justified in the stand I took, I will leave to you, after you have carefully read the record of Aaron Copland, as furnished to me by the House Committee on Un-American Activities.

Here Busbey inserted into the record the names of thirty-four organizations and events that Copland allegedly had supported, each of which now appeared on government watch lists. He closed with the following words:

> Mr. Speaker, I solemnly pledge that I am going to do everything in my power to keep the Republican administration under President Eisenhower from becoming tainted as was the Democratic Party.
>
> There is no room for anyone in Government or either political party where there is any question as to that individual's loyalty and patriotism.
>
> Mr. Paul Hume, music editor of the Washington Post, has missed the point entirely. Mr. Hume seems to think that, because of the fact that Mr. Copland received a Pulitzer prize in 1945, a Guggenheim fellowship and the New York music critics' award, the concert committee should not have canceled his score, A Lincoln Portrait [sic].
>
> The real issue involved is whether the Republican Party should lay itself wide open at the beginning of its administration by permitting music to be played by a composer who has been cited as having been associated in various ways with numerous Communist and Communist-front organizations, each of these organizations having been so designated by either the Attorney General of the United States or the House Committee on Un-American Activities.

When Busbey objected to Copland's "activities, affiliations, and sympathies with and for causes that seemed . . . to be more in the interest of an alien ideology than the things representative of Abraham Lincoln," he referred to international communism, led by the Communist Party of the Soviet Union. Busbey personified the aspirations of the much larger network that comprised domestic anticommunism. He sought a government free from the influence of any communist ideals. He sought to improve his standing with the party in power, namely the Republicans. He sought voter approval (twice in recent years he had been unseated by his opponent after a two-year term in office). Like most political leaders of the day, Busbey recognized that many American voters believed that the Soviet Union could gain control of the United States by influencing the thoughts and values of the populace, starting with cultural and intellectual leaders like Copland.

Busbey fully acknowledged his partisanship, starting and ending his remarks with the claim that the Republican Party alone stood strong against communism. He expected his defeated Democratic opponents to find and publicize any contradiction to the anticommunist campaign platform that had gotten Eisenhower elected—such as having music by an alleged communist sympathizer performed at the inaugural concert. In both his introduction and his conclusion, Busbey gave his "solemn pledge" "to keep the Republican administration from becoming tainted as was the Democratic Party."

Less directly, Busbey's language alludes to another fundamental Red Scare tenet: any departure from heteronormative values compromised the nation's moral strength and ultimately paved the way for a communist takeover. Many believed that any history of homosexual activity turned a person into an irredeemable security risk, forever susceptible to blackmail by foreign agents. The conflation of "communist," "national security risk" and "homosexual" may seem incredible in the twenty-first century, but scholars have documented its widespread impact on government policies and the federal workforce in the 1950s (Johnson 2004). Coded language was crucial for discussing this "unspeakable" subject. Euphemisms like "deviants," "perverts," and "morals problems" were widely used to refer to bisexual or homosexual people. In an oft-cited 1950 speech, Secretary of State Dean Acheson defended the State Department against accusations of effeminacy and underscored its patriotism with words like "clean" and "vigorous" (Johnson 2004, 71–72). Similarly, Busbey used one- and two-syllable words with strong consonants to describe his own actions on behalf of the Eisenhower administration: "vigor," "command," "voiced." For Copland he used multi-syllabic words in which dactylic, feminine rhythms and softer sounds predominated: "sympathies," "activities," "affiliations." Busbey's explicit purpose was to expose Copland's history of (alleged) communist sympathies, but his language shows the gendered subtext that often underlay political accusations of disloyalty in the 1940s and 1950s.

Busbey's immediate purpose was to defend the cancellation of Copland's work against Hume's objections. Yet he also sought to proclaim the operating assumptions of the House Committee on Un-American Activities. He communicated the nation's urgent responsibility to defeat international communism. He charged that communist ideals had corrupted government and cultural leaders in the United States. He touched upon the intense rivalry between the two main political parties in the United States and its effects on censorship issues. In a period noted for its under-the-surface social upheaval, Busbey's language reassured those who sought to re-establish traditional gender norms that he and his party stood for power, strength, and masculine virtues.[1] Lastly, his remarks conveyed his beliefs about the role of music in society. He took the increasingly influential position that in a political context, musical style and quality were irrelevant; it was the affiliations and beliefs of the musicians that needed scrutiny.

As news of the cancellation spread, a wave of support for Copland appeared in the press via editorials, letters to the editor, and news articles. They characterized Busbey's position as artistically ignorant, laughable, petty and political, and even dangerous.

The objection on artistic grounds was that because Copland's music was exceptional in quality, it deserved, at the least, immunity from government suppression. The nation's own citizens and its reputation abroad stood to benefit from the creation of good art within its borders. An underlying assumption was that music ultimately stood on its own, independent of the actions or beliefs of the person who composed it.

Some artistic objectors argued that music and politics were essentially unrelated, and the former should be judged by standards of musical quality alone. Others asserted that Copland's music went beyond a demonstration of skill and artistry. Copland had a unique ability to portray, in classical music, essential aspects of the American spirit. *The Dartmouth* ("Sour Note," January 21) opined, "We would be hard–put . . . to think of a more patriotic American composer than Aaron Copland. Copland's well-received and much-played music is simply saturated with pure Americana. . . . It would be extremely difficult to find a composer who has done more for American culture and whose compositions would be better suited for the Inaugural Concert." The *New York Times* critic

Howard Taubman supported Copland with an article titled "'Portrait' of President Deeply Patriotic—Composer's Stature Not in Doubt" (February 1). Many artistic objectors, assuming a hierarchy between two separate spheres, claimed that it debased the art of music to involve it in political squabbles. In all, they felt music for a state occasion should be chosen for its inspirational tone and its artistic merits. This was the very argument Busbey had dismissed as irrelevant.

The second most frequent response took an internationalist perspective and predicted worldwide ridicule. Others protested that the Republicans had gone to embarrassing lengths: the whole nation looked silly, to itself and others, when it publicly banned the performance of a work by a U.S.-born composer honoring one of the nation's most historically significant presidents. "To bar from the Inaugural Concert [Copland's] music, and especially music about Abraham Lincoln, will be the worst kind of blunder and will hold us up as a nation to universal ridicule," one reader protested in a letter to the *New York Times* (January 18). Another questioned "how . . . Representative Busbey can . . . profess to be contributing something to the struggle against the world menace to freedom" by removing the work from the program (Clark 1953). William Fleming's "The Cold War in Music" points out inconsistencies in Busbey's position: "Has [Rep. Busbey] found out yet that parents are poisoning the minds of the next generation by playing Prokofieff's Peter and the Wolf to them on the phonograph in lieu of telling them a good capitalistic bedtime story?" (Fleming 1953). In *The Nation* Bruce Catton picked up on the partisanship, accusing Republicans of a transparent attempt to portray the Democrats as a party overrun by communistic liberals. He concluded sarcastically, "So the Copland number was not heard, and if this was in the end something less than a fatal blow to the evil designs of the men in the Kremlin, at least it saved the assembled Republicans from being compelled to listen to Lincoln's brooding words" (Catton 1953, 98). *The New Republic* (January 26, 1953) ridiculed the idea of "Wicked Music" and accused Republicans of purely political motivations.

The most serious objection to the *Lincoln Portrait* cancellation was that the United States put itself in the company of totalitarian regimes when it suppressed the music of "disapproved" composers. *The Washington Post* protested,

> The road is clear. It was traveled in Germany, and it is being traveled in Russia today. For there is no other way out of the tangle once you start on the path laid out by the Congressman. Clearly, you must screen all composers . . . and from there it is a quick step to the place where you begin to hear echoes of "capitalist decadence," "bourgeois mouthings," and all the other things the Soviets claim can be heard in the demoralized music of the weakening civilization of the West. The American tenet that a man is innocent until proven guilty has had a rough time lately. . . . It was through such machinery as the Congressman advocates that the music of Mendelssohn and a dozen others was silenced in Germany. It is by such means that the music of the Coplands and who knows how many others could be stilled in America. Can it happen here? (Hume 1953)[2]

The *Washington Star* printed an anonymous letter to the editor from a supporter of the National Symphony that drew an analogy to Hitler's banning of Mendelssohn (January 20, 1953). Hume noted that by Busbey's line of thinking, the Air Force Symphony Orchestra should not have played *Rodeo* the previous week. Indeed, taken to its logical conclusion, Busbey's argument suggested that no government-sponsored group should ever be permitted to perform Copland's music. Hume reported that when this was pointed out to Busbey, he failed to find the suggestion outrageous, replying, "Indeed, that is something we would have to consider" (Hume 1953).

Some of Copland's responses are preserved in a letter written soon afterward to the board of the League of Composers, the organization that had served as something of a musical family to him from the beginning of his career in the 1920s (Oja 2000, 237–251). He wrote, "This was an attack by an elected official on the patriotism of a private citizen who had never been asked questions by anyone, never been shown any lists, never been requested to explain or justify anything. . . ." Indeed, HUAC's representative had denounced Copland in Congress (the legislative branch of the U.S. government) based on an allegation of his links to organizations designated suspicious by the Attorney General, who, as a presidential appointee, was part of the executive branch. Because these allegations were not proven in a court of law, the third component of the federal government's system of checks and balances, the judicial branch, was bypassed, leaving Copland no opportunity to defend himself.[3] It seemed to Copland that members of the U.S. government were secretly gathering information about its artists, then using those findings to publicly denounce them. He alluded to Soviet and Nazi censorship when he wrote, "It is surely a sign of the times that a musical organization like our own should have become involved in an affair such as this" (Copland to League of Composers Board of Directors, 9 Feb. 1953, Aaron Copland Collection [ACCLC] Box 345/7 and Box 427); (Copland and Perlis 2013, 237.

Copland's friend Elie Siegmeister wrote that he was "very indignant over the incident of last week. What the Hell goes on anyway? Will they soon be forbidding Walt Whitman and the Declaration of Independence? It's all so childish and ridiculous that it is unbelievable—except that it happens" (ACCLC, Siegmeister to Copland 1953, Box 262/31; Box 427). Like Copland, Siegmeister was a New York City native and Boulanger composition student who, in the 1930s, began to incorporate populist elements into his music and was subject to anticommunist investigations after World War II. His letter ended by expressing hope that conductors would spearhead an effort to perform as much of Copland's music as possible. Another friend, dance critic Edwin Denby, encouraged the argument that music and politics were separate: "I hope you will find a lot of nice jokes to make, if any one asks you. That you didn't ask to have it put on, since you were a Stevenson man. That you're glad they didn't turn it down for its musical qualities"(ACCLC, Denby to Copland 1953, Box 253/21; Box 427).

Copland's supporters and his Red Scare detractors agreed about one thing: music is—or should be—separate from partisan politics. Busbey claimed that because Copland's political beliefs were suspect, the quality of his music was irrelevant. Copland's supporters claimed that because his music celebrated patriotic subjects, used distinctly American melodies, met high artistic standards, and garnered international respect, his personal political views were simply unimportant. The positions of both sides encouraged a policy of détente between the two cultural spheres: musicians would stay out of politics, and politicians would leave musicians to govern their own realm.

Although the cancellation of *Lincoln Portrait* and the public attack on Copland's patriotism seemed to come without warning, in fact, for many years a network of government and private-sector organizations had been gathering information about him. In Copland's case, five distinct but interdependent elements of the Second Red Scare network converged. Besides the House Committee on Un-American Activities these were the public media, private-sector organizations including the American Legion, the Federal Bureau of Investigation under J. Edgar Hoover, and the Senate subcommittee that was run by Senator Joseph McCarthy. This network relied on lists of names, which they shared to form blacklists, and the practice of "informing." Both practices touched Copland's life, and introduced distrust and guilt by association.[4] The efforts of these five anticommunist entities developed into a self-reinforcing feedback loop that seriously threatened Copland's reputation and career.

Copland had some acquaintance with anticommunist forces before the *Lincoln Portrait* incident. His longtime friend and cousin Harold Clurman had written from California about the Hollywood Ten hearings run by HUAC in 1947, and had urged Copland to support Hanns Eisler, a mutual acquaintance, during Eisler's deportation trial and enforced departure from the United States.[5] And Copland had experienced directly the effects of the anticommunist press and the newly emerging noncommunist left in the months surrounding the March 1949 Cultural and Scientific Conference for World Peace at the Waldorf Astoria Hotel in New York. The Waldorf Peace Conference was one of a series of Peace Conferences staged around the world by the Comintern as forums for intellectuals and cultural leaders to debate ideology in a high-profile setting.[6] Dmitri Shostakovich, back in Soviet favor after a period of harsh official criticism, was a Russian delegate. Copland was one of many progressive intellectuals and artists from the United States in attendance.

The event was something of a media circus, bringing to the fore the widening division in the United States between outspoken anticommunists and those deemed sympathizers, namely anyone unwilling to join them in "fighting Communism." The Hearst press, known for its anticommunist stance and its active cooperation in the anticommunist movement, distributed a wire photo of the two composers in conversation with a caption implying that Copland had special Soviet approval (*Los Angeles Examiner* March 27, 1949). The quantity of newspaper and magazine coverage of the Peace Conference was prodigious. Between mid-February and the end of May more than seventy articles appeared in the *New York Times* alone; the *Christian Science Monitor* ran twenty-one. *Life* magazine (April 4, 1949) ran a five-page photo feature that included a small photo of each individual delegate and the headlines "DUPES AND FELLOW TRAVELERS DRESS UP COMMUNIST FRONTS" and "Red Visitors Cause Rumpus."[7]

In addition to the press, private-sector groups were out in full force. The American Legion ran pickets outside the hotel.[8] A new group of anticommunist intellectual leaders, calling themselves Americans for Intellectual Freedom, attempted to disrupt the conference by asking hostile questions from the floor (Brody 1993; Jumonville 1991). Sidney Hook was an organizer, and a composer acquaintance of Copland named Nicolas Nabokov was part of the group; many were former sympathizers who became disillusioned with communism. They were also called the noncommunist left. The Peace Conference brought to Copland's attention the strength of the anticommunist movement, particularly the press and private-sector organizations. And it brought Copland's name to the attention of anticommunist leaders.

The next month, HUAC issued a report on the conference that ultimately placed Copland on many additional blacklists. Introduced with inflammatory language about the "menace" posed by the Peace Conference, the *Review of the Cultural and Scientific Conference for World Peace* consisted mainly of lists (U.S. Congress 1950. H.R. 1954). The first set of lists—nearly one hundred pages long—named each suspect organization or cause, described its "subversive" nature, and then listed alphabetically the Peace Conference delegates who supported it. A second set of lists grouped the delegates by the number of times they appeared in the first set. Copland had supported twenty-seven organizations; few delegates' names appeared more often.

HUAC kept an index of the personal names mentioned in its reports; this was combined with an index of HUAC hearing transcripts (U.S. Congress House. 1962; and U.S. Congress House. 1970). Each time Copland's name appeared on a new page, even for the same allegation, his entry in the HUAC index got longer. In April 1951, a new House report, *The Communist "Peace" Offensive*, described the Peace Conference as part of a much larger communist effort to win supporters by promoting peace (U.S. Congress 1951. H.R.378). In it were all the lists from the earlier report, and two more that named Copland. His name had arisen in hearings years before the Peace Conference, usually via a clipping from *The Daily Worker* that listed the supporters of some communist-related cause or event, and was presented in a Congressional hearing as evidence of another signer's communist sympathies. By the time Eisenhower won the 1952 election, Busbey would have seen a very long list of document codes and page numbers after Copland's name in the HUAC index.

One of the most popular private-sector blacklists, *Red Channels: The Report on Communist Influence in Radio and Television* (American Business Consultants 1950), relied heavily on HUAC's data. *Red Channels* lists twenty-one allegations under Copland's name (Figure 23.1); the HUAC *Review of the Scientific and Cultural Conference for World Peace* is cited as the source for all but three. The American Legion and other private-sector organizations consulted *Red Channels* when choosing targets for their pickets and letter-writing campaigns, some of which touched Copland (Copland and Perlis 2013, 97–106, 210–212; DeLapp-Birkett 2008, 40–44; DeLapp 1997, 175–176).

Most of the allegations found in HUAC reports and *Red Channels* also appeared in the FBI's file on Copland, which was opened that summer.[9] It was July 5, 1950, when a

FIGURE 23.1 Copland's entry in *Red Channels*.

Hollywood Writers Mobilization, Writers Congress	Co-chairman; member, advisory committee. *House Un-Am. Act. Com., Appendix 9*, pp. 786, 790.
Film Audiences for Democracy, Films for Democracy	Member, Advisory Board. *House Un-Am. Act. Com., Appendix 9*, pp. 729, 730.
National Committee for the Defense of Political Prisoners	Affiliated. *House Un-Am. Act. Com., Appendix 9*, p. 1174.
National Committee for People's Rights	Affiliated. *House Un-Am. Act. Com., Appendix 9*, p. 1179.
Workers Alliance	Sponsor. Federal Acts Council. *House Un-Am. Act. Com., Appendix 9*, p. 1547.
Medical Bureau to Aid Spanish Democracy, Manhattan Chapter	Patron, Benefit Performance and Dance. *House Un-Am. Act. Com., Appendix 9*, p. 1614.

AARON COPLAND
Composer, Writer

	Reported as:
People's Songs	Affiliated. Un-Am. Act. Com. *Review of Scientific and Cultural Conference for World Peace*, 4/19/49, p. 33.
Scientific and Cultural Conference for World Peace	Sponsor and panel speaker. Official program, 3/49. "The effects of the cold war on the artist in the United States were decried by Aaron Copland, American composer, who predicted that, 'the present policies of the American Government will lead inevitably into a third world war.'" *NY Times*, 3/28/49, p. 2.

(References to organizations listed begin page 161.)

39

FIGURE 23.1 Continued

Independent Citizens Committee of the Arts, Sciences and Professions	Affiliated. Un-Am. Act. Com. *Review of Scientific and Cultural Conference for World Peace*, 4/19/49, p. 2.
American League Against War and Fascism	Supporter. Un-Am. Act. Com. *Review of Scientific and Cultural Conference for World Peace*, 4/19/49, p. 7.
Win the Peace Conference	Affiliated. Un-Am. Act. Com. *Review of Scientific and Cultural Conference for World Peace*, 4/19/49, p. 8.
American Committee for Democracy and Intellectual Freedom	Affiliated. Un-Am. Act. Com. *Review of Scientific and Cultural Conference for World Peace*, 4/19/49, p. 21.
American Committee for Protection of Foreign Born	Affiliated. Un-Am. Act. Com. *Review of Scientific and Cultural Conference for World Peace*, 4/19/49, p. 21.
Artists' Front to Win the War	Affiliated. Un-Am. Act. Com. *Review of Scientific and Cultural Conference for World Peace*, 4/19/49, p. 23.
Open letter for Harry Bridges	Signer, 1942. Un-Am. Act. Com. *Review of Scientific and Cultural Conference for World Peace*, 4/19/49, p. 23.
National Committee for the Defense of Political Prisoners	Affiliated. Un-Am. Act. Com. *Review of Scientific and Cultural Conference for World Peace*, 4/19/49, p. 31.
National Federation for Constitutional Liberties	Affiliated. Un-Am. Act. Com. *Review of Scientific and Cultural Conference for World Peace*, 4/19/49, p. 31.
Communist Bookshops	Supporter. Un-Am. Act. Com. *Review of Scientific and Cultural Conference for World Peace*, 4/19/49, p. 35.
Committee of Professional Groups for Browder and Ford, 1936	Affiliated. Un-Am. Act. Com. *Review of Scientific and Cultural Conference for World Peace*, 4/19/49, p. 40.

(References to organizations listed begin page 161.)

40

FIGURE 23.1 Continued

female "confidential informant" told an FBI agent that Copland "has been a member of every communist front which expressed a change of line going from the American League Against War and Fascism down to the Win the Peace Conference" (Copland file [4]). The allegations in HUAC's Peace Conference reports were reissued, supplemented,

Hanns Eisler Concert	Sponsor. Un-Am. Act. Com. *Review of Scientific and Cultural Conference for World Peace*, 4/19/49, p. 43.
National Council of American-Soviet Friendship	Affiliated. Un-Am. Act. Com. *Review of Scientific and Cultural Conference for World Peace*, 4/19/49, pp. 44, 50, 51.
Morris U. Schappes Defense Committee	Affiliated. Un-Am. Act. Com. *Review of Scientific and Cultural Conference for World Peace*, 4/19/49, p. 45.
American-Soviet Music Society	Affiliated. Un-Am. Act. Com. *Review of Scientific and Cultural Conference for World Peace*, 4/19/49, p. 52.
New Masses	Contributor. Un-Am. Act. Com. *Review of Scientific and Cultural Conference for World Peace*, 4/19/49, p. 56.
National Council of the Arts, Sciences and Professions	Signer. Advertisement, "We are for Wallace." *NY Times*, 10/20/48.
"The First of May," mass song	Composer. *Un-Am. Act. Com., Index II*, p. W38.
Dimitri Shostakovich	Signer. Scroll presented to Shostakovich: "We welcome your visit also in the hope that this kind of cultural interchange can aid understanding among our peoples and thereby make possible an enduring peace." *NY Times*, 3/28/49, p. 2.

NORMAN CORWIN
Radio Writer, Director, Producer

Reported as:

Russian War Relief, Inc.	Signer. Statement issued by the Russian War Relief under the caption, "These Eminent Americans Ask Your Help on Behalf of the Russian People." *NY Times*, 10/10/41.

(References to organizations listed begin page 161.)

41

FIGURE 23.1 Continued

repackaged, borrowed, and cited repeatedly not only by HUAC, but also by other government agencies and by private organizations.

Once an alleged subversive's name was lodged in the labyrinthine anticommunist data banks, removing it was nearly impossible.[10] "Naming names" emerged as the most effective way for a person once connected with communism to demonstrate a change in beliefs. Anyone who truly opposed the Cold War enemy, reasoned Red Scare leaders, would not hesitate to expose former associates. While historians continue to disagree about the legality and fairness of these methods, virtually all agree that they were highly effective in dismantling networks of personal and professional relationships—both organized and informal—that brought together Americans of liberal persuasion.

Many of Copland's former associates' names had been appearing in HUAC proceedings (DeLapp 1997, 156). Many years later, Copland's partner Erik Johns recalled, "It was difficult because friends that [Copland] had would go down [to testify] and he wasn't sure what they were going to say.... Except [that] people were losing jobs about it ... it seemed unbelievable, and a burlesque" (Johns 1981). One of Copland's professional acquaintances, Jerome Robbins, had "named names" in a public Congressional hearing, though Copland was not mentioned then, nor were any of their close associates. When Robbins later cleared his name in private meetings with Red Scare leaders, it reportedly strained his relationship with at least one composer.[11] Being a gay man added a layer of concern, as the stigma of being "outed" was high, and conventional wisdom held that homosexuals were particularly susceptible to blackmail (D'Emilio 1998, 41–49; May 1988, 94; Hubbs 2004, 158–59). Copland's collaborative community was fractured by this dynamic (DeLapp-Birkett 2008, 31–62; DeLapp 1997, 154–163).

Four months after the inauguration, Copland's name came to the attention of Senator Joseph McCarthy. In May McCarthy subpoenaed Copland to testify for his notorious Senate subcommittee in Washington, D.C. The outlines of Copland's encounter with McCarthy are now familiar: the Friday evening summons to a hearing on Monday morning, the rush to secure counsel, the one-day extension granted for "reasons of health," and the private hearing on Tuesday, May 26, when he faced aggressive questioning by McCarthy, Roy Cohn, and other members of the committee (U.S. Congress Senate. 1953).

Copland's name had appeared in two contexts that were highly incriminating, in McCarthy's view. Besides the recurring theme of Copland's involvement in the 1949 Peace Conference, McCarthy seized upon Copland's links to Hanns Eisler. Copland had met the German émigré composer in New York in the mid-1930s when both were involved in the workers song movement. As it happened, around that time Eisler visited the Soviet Union and publicly announced that Copland was an American ally in the cause of revolutionary music. Now, nearly twenty years later, McCarthy possessed a translated copy of Eisler's remarks, and used them as the closing flourish to the May 1953 hearing.

> THE CHAIRMAN: Did you agree with the statement by Eisler that "Revolutionary music is now more powerful than ever. Its political and artistic importance is growing daily."
> MR. COPLAND: That is a vague statement. I don't know what he means by "revolutionary music."

Copland was certainly familiar with Eisler's views on music's role in a communist society; Eisler had defined "revolutionary music" in *Modern Music*, which Copland read avidly (Eisler 1935). He and Eisler had attended meetings of the Composers Collective at about the same time, both had authored articles in the same issue of the communist periodical *Music Vanguard*, and workers' songs composed by Copland and Eisler had appeared together in the *Workers Song Book No. 2*. Yet under McCarthy's reductive questioning, Copland's main objective was to distance himself from Eisler and from current Soviet aesthetics. So when McCarthy continued to press him, Copland categorically denied any connection between politics and music, doggedly sticking with the present tense.[12]

> THE CHAIRMAN: Do you agree with [Eisler] that there is a political importance in music?
> MR. COPLAND: I certainly would not. What the Soviet Government has been trying to do in forcing their composers to write along lines favorable to themselves is absolutely wrong. It is one of the basic reasons why I could have no sympathy with such an attitude (U.S. Congress 1953, 96–97).

Copland managed to get through the private hearing without naming names himself. When asked for the names of people he saw at the Peace Conference he evaded the question, and finally agreed to send additional information after checking his records at home. Ultimately, as Perlis reports, he wrote, "I have read over the *New York Times* account of the fine arts panel of the conference ... I do not personally remember having seen anyone at the conference who is not listed in those published reports" (Copland and Perlis 2013 239, ACCLC Box 427).

Copland left the May 26 hearing with the understanding that he would soon be called back for a second hearing open to the public and the media. From the moment the hearing ended, Copland's counsel checked the media daily for signs that a second, public hearing was being planned. When Congress approved funding for the Fulbright Exchange Program on August 3, a second hearing became less likely. Nonetheless, hundreds of leaves of correspondence, drafts, notes, and bank records in his personal files attest to the heavy cost to his attention and time (Copland and Perlis 2013, 242-243; ACCLC Box 427).

Copland's bureaucratic workload and legal fees were compounded later that fall when the U.S. Passport office "tentatively disapproved" the passport renewal application Copland had submitted in August (ACCLC Box 427). He was considering three European engagements: participation in an international music festival organized by Nicolas Nabokov, serving on a committee headed by Nadia Boulanger to select the next Olympic hymn, and a conducting engagement in Spain (Copland and Perlis 2013, 241,257). Copland had not previously clashed with the State Department, who had consistently promoted his music and financed his travels abroad. But at the beginning of the Eisenhower administration the State Department was under pressure to persuade Congress, who allocated their budget, that its stance against both communism and homosexuality was sufficiently tough (Johnson 2004, 118–46; D'Emilio 1998, 46–47). At about the same time, new legislation gave the Secretary of State "unlimited discretion" to approve or deny passports, as Copland's attorneys reminded him after the initial disapproval was received (ACCLC Box 427).

Thus Copland began a substantial new project: compiling a dossier in support of his patriotism. At his attorney's instruction, he assembled a list of the anticommunist causes he had supported, sought letters from prominent persons vouching for his pro-American beliefs, and wrote a detailed letter that covered points his attorneys had supplied, including the direct assertion that he did not intend to advance communist or Soviet doctrine while abroad (ACCLC Box 427). His attorneys added their own lengthy argument for the renewal of Copland's passport, and then hand-delivered the documents to the passport office on October 16. Nearly two months later, Copland's passport was returned to him with a six-month renewal (ACCLC Box 427).

These documents, preserved at the Library of Congress, reveal the subtle and persistent pressure that encouraged Copland and others to disassociate their music from the rest of American life. "Music probably has no political content," Copland's attorneys wrote in their letter to the Passport Office. Even if it did, they continued, the nationalist subjects in much of Copland's music demonstrate that "his entire effort has been to enrich American culture in the field of music at a time when the communist line is that America is materialistic and without culture" (ACCLC Box 427). In his own letter, Copland, too, emphasized a division between music and politics, characterizing his involvement in alleged front activities as incidental to his musical concerns. "I have never attended any purely political meetings of any kind," he wrote. "My experience [at the Peace Conference] convinced me that the Conference was a manoeuvre of those in control to advance communist doctrine, and I determined not to do anything in the future that could possibly be interpreted as aiding their cause. I have since March 1949 rigorously confined myself to purely musical matters" (ACCLC Box 427).

Such comments reinforced an outlook Copland had protested throughout his career: namely, that American audiences failed to consider concert music an integral part of their society. In his 1952 book *Music and Imagination*, he chided his readers when he wrote, "audiences still prefer to think of the musical creator as a man closeted with his idea, unsullied by the rough and tumble of the world around him," and he denounced the "musical museum" that had developed as a result (Copland 1952, 47; DeLapp 2000, 108–121). Just a year or two later, Copland and his attorneys found themselves not only denying the cultural meanings that had surrounded many of his works' origins, but supporting the view that music and political concerns were essentially and fundamentally disconnected. Missing from their statements is any acknowledgement that, in previous decades, the Communist Party in the United States sponsored numerous activities in musical spheres, and that Copland's communities of personal and artistic support—friends, acquaintances and romantic interests, sponsors and artistic collaborators—formed to a large extent around the progressive and communist-influenced belief that music was, and should be, an agent for social change (DeLapp 1997, 67–85; Crist 2005).

Copland's attorneys engineered a remarkably successful outcome to what might have been a disaster, with Copland unable to leave the country and insinuations swirling in the public media. Nonetheless, from May 22 well through the end of 1953, Copland's creative activities were edged out by the project of defending his loyalty. The opera he had begun in 1952 languished, not to be completed until the night before its April 1954 premiere. A commission he had accepted for a work commemorating the Juilliard School of Music's fiftieth anniversary stalled; and Copland wrote no more film scores for Hollywood. Instead, he produced hundreds of pages of annotated lists, personal statements, and legal correspondence. Crowding his schedule were trips to Washington, meetings with lawyers, and sorting through twenty years' accumulation of personal records to check the accuracy of each allegation.

Engagements were canceled and invitations withdrawn: a concert at the Hollywood Bowl for which Copland was to conduct his own music was canceled when board members objected to his alleged affiliations(Copland and Peris, 2013, 241). The University of Alabama specifically invoked Busbey's remarks when canceling Copland's appearance there; the University of Colorado hid its reasons for canceling a planned talk by Copland until a local pro-labor newspaper uncovered the same motive (Copland and Perlis 2013, 241). New lecture and conducting invitations slowed considerably that year.

By the end of 1953, the consequences of the Red Scare were clear. Copland's time for creative activities had been severely curtailed, his previously fruitful collaborative network was damaged by the blacklisting and naming dynamic, and he was pushed into stating that music was separate from daily life, particularly from contemporary American politics. The rhetoric and tactics of Second Red Scare pressed Copland into denying that music could have any ideological purpose; that it stood apart from the daily events of history; that music was merely an individual's expression of feeling and had no connection with political beliefs.

Did the Red Scare change the *sound* of Copland's music? I believe it did, within limited parameters. What the public heard of Copland's music was unchanged. The familiar folk-inspired music continued to circulate on concert stages, in movie theaters, on records, and over the airwaves. But Copland's *new* compositions increasingly tended to emphasize the abstract, modernist aspects of his creative impulse.

Copland was aware that tonal or neo-tonal music with nationalistic overtones was strongly encouraged by the Union of Soviet Composers, and modernist—especially twelve-tone—music had been harshly denounced. Such falsely dichotomized oppositions were endemic to the times, he lamented in a speech at the 1949 Peace Conference, stating that "Communism vs. the Profit System" paralleled in some ways the rivalry between the modernist Schoenberg and Shostakovich, and that such dualisms were best resolved rather than escalated.[13] Copland's old acquaintance Nicolas Nabokov, who attended the conference as an uninvited representative of the anticommunist left—and other musicians—reinforced this dichotomy. Readers of the New York newspapers understood that Shostakovich had repeatedly been censored for writing modernist music, that he had rehabilitated his reputation with his Fifth Symphony and had recently won the Stalin Prize for the socialist cantata *Song of the Forests* (Thomson 1948a,b and 1949; DeLapp 1997, 50–54). Ideological subtexts to mid-century concert music were recognized by both composers and listeners at this time (Thomson 1948a,b; Crist 2005, 10–13, 181, 191; Gentry 2011, 315–320, 327). Copland's 1950 *Quartet for Piano and Strings*, which he called his first work to "consciously use" a twelve-tone technique, was, as I have argued elsewhere, a musical response to this "false dichotomy" (DeLapp 1997, 59–66, 94–112; DeLapp-Birkett 2008, 31–62).[14]

Not surprisingly, Busbey, HUAC, and McCarthy were unconcerned with debates about compositional techniques and musical style. They repeatedly failed to pursue questions about how a composer's aesthetic might communicate or reflect political ideals. Despite the influence of communism on the Americanism of the 1930s, and the corollary that had led modernist composers like Copland to write accessible new music for general audiences, neither McCarthy, nor HUAC, nor the private-sector anticommunists recognized this connection. Aside from an FBI informant's insinuation that the title of Copland's "Abraham Lincoln Symphony" followed "the [Communist] change of line," among nonmusicians Copland's music "for the common man" was not presented as evidence of communist—or even liberal—sympathies.

While the Second Red Scare was harmful to Copland and his career, it would be misleading to portray him solely as a victim. He was not beholden to a single employer and so was less vulnerable to the kind of economic penalties faced by blacklisted screenwriters or academics. He acknowledged the injustices of his situation privately (Copland and Perlis 2013, 239-240), but wasted little time cataloging them or seeking revenge. He continued to compose, teach, write, and speak according to the opportunities that remained open to him. He ceased public expression of his own political views—apart from firmly denouncing the well-publicized Soviet attempts to control their composers' output (Copland 1952, 75–77). His consistent professionalism and self-control served him well: by refraining from engaging his opponents on their own terms, he offered no new fuel for public debate.

Copland undoubtedly benefited from the ineffable, multivalent nature of musical meaning. Music without an obviously political, verbal message couldn't easily be shown to embody Marxist ideology, even when that influence was (or had been) present to some degree. Copland used this to his advantage. From the 1949 Peace Conference onward he emphasized when possible those aspects of his oeuvre and philosophy that many considered antithetical to communism: the personal, individual nature of creativity, and the abstract, modernist aspects of his musical language. He stressed that his commitment to socio-musical engagement predated the Popular Front. In a 1952 lecture at Harvard, he said that his "conviction" that "the two things that seemed always to have been so separate in America—music and the life about me—must be made to touch," had arisen in the early 1920s during his student years in France (Copland 1952, 97–98). Far from disavowing his populist compositions as politically tainted, he supported their performance at a wide variety of patriotic events, and let listeners discern their own meanings.

Despite the best efforts of Busbey, Hoover, and the American Legion, Copland's name never became synonymous with communism among the music-loving public. By the time Red Scare rhetoric permeated the listening public's consciousness, Copland's music had already captured their affection. His populist works and his growing body of accessible writings *about* music had convinced the American people that he was on their side. Elected officials had to please the public, and ultimately couldn't afford to disparage him publicly.

Paradoxically, it was by embracing the position that music "probably has no political content" that Copland was able once again to make an important international contribution on behalf of his country.[15] Just seven years after *Lincoln Portrait* was publicly removed from the presidential inaugural concert, Copland traveled to Russia as a State Department–funded cultural ambassador, a role he assumed often over the next twenty years (Ansari 2011, 335–364). By encouraging the view that concert music *was* essentially disconnected from ideology and daily life in the United States, Copland allowed his "music for the people" to shed the progressive, socialist aspects of its origins and to serve as a nonpartisan symbol of American musical culture at home and abroad.

Notes

1. The 1950s' alleged social conformity is challenged in W. T. Llahmon Jr. 2002 and Jamison and Eyerman 1995. Concerning gender, Joanne Meyerowitz (1993) famously complicated Betty Friedan's picture of oppressive domesticity in "Beyond the Feminine Mystique."
2. Hume quotes from an infamous 1948 Soviet decree that created widespread international controversy. Contemporaneous reactions published in the Unites States include Nabokov 1948a; 1948b; 1949; Thomson 1948a; 1948b; 1949; Cazden 1948, 11, 19; and Norton 1948. For an authoritative discussion of this period in Soviet music censorship, see Fay 2000, 154–158.
3. The list of subversive organizations was started in 1947 during President Truman's administration to help employers comply with an executive order that banned Communist Party members and sympathizers from federal employment.
4. On the social and professional consequences of blacklisting, see Navasky 2003, 333–346; Ceplair and Englund 2003, 254–298, 379–386.
5. On Copland's interactions with Eisler, see DeLapp 1997, 88–92; and Bick 2001, esp. 32–34, 59–61. On Eisler reception in the United States after 1947, seeCalico 1998, 120–136. For a German account of HUAC's interest in Eisler, see Hermand 2006.
6. On Copland's involvement in the Peace Conference, see Copland and Perlis, 2013, 183–84; and DeLapp 1997, 94–98. See alsoGentry 2011. An abridged version of Copland's speech appears in Gillmor 1949, 90–91. Copland's remarks are now published in Kostelanetz 2003, 128–132. Studies treating the Waldorf Peace Conference from different angles include Jumonville 1991, 1–48; Wellens 2002, 8–10; Saunders 1999, 45–56; and Lieberman 2000, 59–72. Written just months after the conference, Singer (1950, 258–270) gives a preliminary analysis and eyewitness account of the press coverage of the conference.
7. In phrasing that Busbey later echoed, the caption described the participants as "ranging from hard-working fellow travelers to sot-headed do-gooders who have persistently lent their names to organizations labeled by the U.S. Attorney General or other government agencies as subversive." These delegates were dangerous, the caption claimed: the Communist Party carefully cultivated them to lend credibility to their ideological infiltration of American society.
8. Founded after World War I, The American Legion, a private-sector veteran's organization recognized by the U.S. Government as a patriotic organization, during the Cold War mobilized its nearly three million members to "fight communism." See O'Neil 1948, 16–17, 42–44.

9. As an agency within the Justice Department, which was part of the executive branch, in practice the Federal Bureau of Investigation wielded power far in excess of its official status under the legendary direction of J. Edgar Hoover.
10. Some did succeed, through a variety of means. One could meet privately with anticommunist leaders, usually with the paid assistance of a guide with the right connections. Former communists could publish articles expressing remorse for their past associations, participate in "overtly anti-communist actions," circulate petitions for anti-communist causes, or submit confessional letters to anti-communist organizations. For a good summary of name clearing, see Schrecker 2002, 91–92.
11. Jerome Robbins, who "had wanted to collaborate with Copland since 1944" (Pollack 1990, 486), cleared his name privately with former FBI agent John Kirkpatrick in April 1950, but Edward Scheidt of the FBI's New York office concluded that Robbins might still be a Communist sympathizer because he was "evasive" and avoided incriminating friends. The public hearing was March 23, 1951. Lawrence 2001, 158–160, 167; Jowitt 2004, 176–177.
12. The 1948 decree by the USSR's composers' union received a fair amount of public critique in the United States, and sees significant treatment in Copland's *Music and Imagination*. On Copland and the Peace Conference, see also Copland and Perlis 2013, 233–235
13. Since Stravinsky was commonly named as Schoenberg's stylistic opponent, Copland's substitution of Shostakovich, a Soviet citizen, underscored the political aspects of his comparison. That "Communism vs. the Profit System" had parallels in the composers' world would have been reinforced by his acquaintance Nicolas Nabokov, who was about to produce two anti-communist concerts in Europe with covert funding from the CIA; see Saunders 1999 and Wellens 2002.
14. In making these points, I contend not that partisan politics offer the sole, or even primary, explanation for Copland's artistic choices, but merely that they are one significant component in a nuanced understanding of them. I do seek to overturn the persistent Cold War–era assumption that American "classical" music and U.S. politics coexisted without shaping each other in any significant way.
15. Strengthened during the postwar period, the legacy of this perceived separation between "classical" music and everyday life in the United States is manifest in twenty-first-century debates about state and public support for contemporary composers. A significant number of cultural leaders, listeners, and even music scholars in the United States seem convinced that symphonic music is primarily a European import, essentially peripheral to American national identity.

References

Aaron Copland Collection [ACCLC]. *Music Division, Special Collections*. Library of Congress. Washington, D.C.

American Business Consultants. 1950. *Red Channels: The Report of Communist Influence in Radio and Television*. New York: Counterattack.

Ansari, Emily Abrams. 2011. "Aaron Copland and the Politics of Cultural Diplomacy." *Journal of the Society for American Music* 5, no. 3: 335–364.

Bick, Sally M. 2001. "Composers on the Cultural Front: Aaron Copland and Hanns Eisler in Hollywood." Ph.D. diss., Yale University.

Brody, Martin. 1993. "'Music for the Masses': Milton Babbitt's Cold War Music Theory." *Musical Quarterly* 77: 161–192.

Calico, Joy H. 1998. "'The Karl Marx of Music': Hanns Eisler Reception in the United States after 1947." In *Hanns Eisler: 's müsst dem Himmel Höllenangst werden*, edited by Maren Köster, 120–136. Hofheim, Germany: Wolke.

Catton, Bruce. 1953. "Maharajah in the White House." *The Nation*, January 31.

Cazden, Norman. 1948. "What's Happening in Soviet Music?" *Masses & Mainstream*, April.

Ceplair, Larry, and Steven Englund. 2003. *The Inquisition in Hollywood: Politics in the Film Community, 1930–1960*. Urbana and Chicago: University of Illinois Press.

Clark, Roy E. 1953. Letter to the editor. *Washington Post*, January, 20.

Copland, Aaron. 1952. *Music and Imagination*. Cambridge, Mass.: Harvard University Press.

Copland, Aaron. 1953. Letter to [League of Composers] Board of Directors, February 9. Aaron Copland Collection, Library of Congress.

Copland, Aaron, and Vivian Perlis. 1989, revised 2013. *The Complete Copland.*. Hillsdale, NY.: Pendragon Press.

Crist, Elizabeth B. 2005. *Music for the Common Man: Aaron Copland during the Depression and War*. New York and Oxford: Oxford University Press.

D'Emilio, John, 1998. *Sexual Politics, Sexual Communities*. Chicago: University of Chicago Press.

DeLapp, Jennifer. 1997. "Copland in the Fifties: Music and Ideology in the McCarthy Era." Ph.D. diss., University of Michigan.

DeLapp, Jennifer. 2000. Fighting the Musical Museum: Aaron Copland's Music and Imagination. In *The Arts, Community, and Cultural Democracy*, edited by Lambert Zuidervaart and Henry Luttikhuizen, 108–121. New York: St. Martin's Press.

DeLapp-Birkett, Jennifer. 2008. "Aaron Copland and the Politics of Twelve-Tone Composition in the Early Cold War United States." *Journal of Musicological Research*, 27: 31–62.

Eisler, Hanns. 1935. "Reflections on the Future of the Composer." *Modern Music* 12 (May–June): 180–206.

Fay, Laurel. 2000.*Shostakovich: A Life*. New York: Oxford University Press.

Federal Bureau of Investigation. 1950–. Aaron Copland file HQ 100-370562. Duplicated, redacted photocopies.

Fleming, William. 1953. "The Cold War in Music." *Post–Standard*, February 1.

Gentry, Philip. 2011. "Leonard Bernstein's The Age of Anxiety: A Great American Symphony during McCarthyism." *American Music* 29, no. 3: 308–310.

Gillmor, Daniel S., ed. 1949. *Speaking of Peace: An Edited Report of the Cultural and Scientific Conference for World Peace, New York, March 25, 26 and 27, 1949 under the Auspices of National Council of the Arts, Sciences and Professions*. New York: National Council of the Arts, Sciences and Professions.

Hermand, Jost. 2006. "Gerhart Eisler, Ruth Fischer-Eisler, Hanns Eisler und Bertolt Brecht: Die vier 'Deutschen' vor dem House Committee on Un-American Activities." In *Musik-Avantgarde: zur dialektik von vorhut und nachhut—eine gedankensammlung für Günter Mayer zum 75. geburtstag*, 144–153. Oldenburg, Germany: BIS.

Hubbs, Nadine, 2004. *The Queer Composition of America's Sound: Gay Modernists, American Music, and National Identity*. Berkeley: University of California Press.

Hume, Paul. 1953. "Music Censorship Reveals New Peril." *The Washington Post*, January 18.

Jamison, Andrew, and Ron Eyerman, eds. 1995. *Seeds of the Sixties*. Berkeley: University of California Press.

Johns, Erik. 1981. Interview with William Owen. Oral History, American Music Archive, Yale University.

Johnson, David K. 2004. *The Lavender Scare: The Cold War Persecution of Gays and Lesbians in the Federal Government*. Chicago: University of Chicago Press.

Jowitt, Deborah. 2004. *Jerome Robbins: His Life, His Theater, His Dance*. New York: Simon & Schuster.

Jumonville, Neil. 1991. *Critical Crossings: The New York Intellectuals in Postwar America*. Berkeley: University of California Press.

Kostelanetz, Richard, ed. 2003. *Aaron Copland: A Reader*. 2003. New York: Routledge.

Lawrence, Greg. 2001. *Dance with Demons: The Life of Jerome Robbins*. New York: G. P. Putnam's Sons.

Lieberman, Robbie. 2000. *The Strangest Dream: Communism, Anticommunism, and the U.S. Peace Movement, 1945–1963*. Syracuse, N.Y.: Syracuse University Press.

Llahmon, W.T., Jr. 2002. *Deliberate Speed: The Origins of a Cultural Style in the American 1950s*. 2nd ed. Cambridge, Mass.: Harvard University Press.

May, Elaine Tyler. 1988. *Homeward Bound*. New York: Basic Books.

Meyerowitz, Joanne. 1993. "Beyond the "Feminine Mystique": A Reassessment of Postwar Mass Culture, 1946–1968." *Journal of American History* 27, no. 4: 1455–1482.

Nabokov, Nicolas. 1948a. "The Music Purge." *Politics*, Spring.

Nabokov, Nicolas. 1948b. "The Atonal Trail: A Communication." *Partisan Review*, May.

Nabokov, Nicolas. 1949. "Russian Music after the Purge." *Partisan Review*, May.

Navasky, Victor S. 2003. *Naming Names*. New York: Hill and Wang.

Norton, Mildred. 1948. [Untitled column]. *Los Angeles Daily News*, April 5.

Oja, Carol. 2000. *Making Music Modern*. Oxford: Oxford University Press.

O'Neil, James F. 1948. "How You Can Fight Communism." *American Legion Magazine*, August, 16–17, 42–44.

Pollack, Howard. 1999. *Aaron Copland: The Life and Work of an Uncommon Man*. New York: Henry Holt.

"Red Visitors Cause Rumpus." 1949. *Life* 26 (April 4): 14.

Saunders, Frances Stonor. 1999. *The Cultural Cold War: The CIA and the World of Arts and Letters*. New York: The New Press.

Schrecker, Ellen. 2002. *The Age of McCarthyism: A Brief History with Documents*. 2nd ed. Boston: Bedford Books of St. Martin's Press.

Singer, Henry A. 1950. "An Analysis of the New York Press Treatment of the Peace Conference at the Waldorf-Astoria." *Journal of Educational Sociology* 23, no. 5: 258–270.

"Sour Note." 1953. *The Dartmouth* (Hanover, N.H.), January 21.

Thomson, Virgil. 1948a. "Composers in Trouble." *New York Herald Tribune*, February 22.

Thomson, Virgil. 1948b. "Soviet Aesthetics." *New York Herald Tribune*, May 2.

Thomson, Virgil. 1949. "Russians Recover." *New York Herald Tribune*, February 27.

U.S. Congress. 1950. *House Report No. 1954: Review of the Scientific and Cultural Conference for World Peace*, April 26, 81st Congress (originally released April 19, 1949). Washington, DC: United States Government Printing Office.

U.S. Congress. 1951. *House Report No. 378: The Communist "Peace" Offensive*, April 25, 82nd Congress (originally released April 1). Washington, DC: United States Government Printing Office.

U.S. Congress. 1953. *Congressional Record*, Appendix. 83rd Cong., 1st sess., 16 January. Washington, DC: United States Government Printing Office.

U.S. Congress. Senate. 1953. Testimony of Aaron Copland, 48–97. In *State Department Teacher-Student Exchange Program*, hearings by the Senate Committee on Government Operations, Permanent Subcommittee on Investigations, 83rd Congress, 1st session, 26 May. Typewritten transcript.

U.S. Congress. House of Representatives. 1962. *Cumulative Index to Publications of the Committee on Un-American Activities: 1938–1954*. Washington, DC: United States Government Printing Office.

U.S. Congress. House of Representatives. 1970. *Supplement to Cumulative Index to Publications of the Committee on Un-American Activities: 1955–1968*. Washington, DC: United States Government Printing Office.

Wellens, Ian. 2002. *Music on the Frontline: Nicolas Nabokov's Struggle Against Communism and Middlebrow Culture*. Burlington, Vt.: Ashgate.

"Wicked Music." 1953. *New Republic*, January 26.

CHAPTER 24

"A DAY IN THE LIFE"

The Beatles and the BBC, May 1967

GORDON THOMPSON

On Friday, May 19, 1967, British papers carried news that the British Broadcasting Corporation had chosen the Beatles to represent the UK in the first global television broadcast. A spokesperson, explaining the BBC's choice for the June 25 "Our World" telecast, commented that the band members represented "the best of their kind" and that the corporation saw them as "particularly British" (Bell 1967, 22). Ironically, the very same day, an internal memo reveals that even before EMI had released the group's next album, *Sgt. Pepper's Lonely Hearts Club Band*, the BBC had decided to ban the final track, "A Day in the Life," because internal censors believed that the recording "could encourage a permissive attitude to drug-taking" (Fox 1967a).[1]

The national broadcaster had banned recordings by other artists; but this represented the first time they had blocked something by Britain's recently MBE-honored economic heroes. Composers Lennon and McCartney initially skirted the assertion, only much later admitting that the song did contain an oblique drug reference. Problematically, BBC officials failed to identify the offending passages, leaving the Beatles and the press guessing as to what had drawn the ban. The innocuous wordplay of the Beatles' previous songs had skirted censorship and, while audiences would arrive at a variety of interpretations for the lyrics, Lennon and McCartney believed that "A Day in the Life" had met contemporary standards. But the BBC's decision questioned more than words; in the context of other events, this purging of a musical item from a program constituted a confrontational salvo between generations and cultures.

By the mid-sixties, the BBC had grown from its initial role as an addendum to the post office (the first radio broadcasts were telegraph transmissions) into a powerful media corporation at the dawn of the age of globalization. With expanding international travel via commercial jet airliners and the initiation of satellite communications, the national broadcaster found its audience increasingly able to compare British programming with that of the rest of the Western world. Moreover, the Beatles had played a significant role in making British popular music commercially successful in an increasingly transnational market.

Domestically, the BBC's legal monopoly on radio in the United Kingdom came under attack in the sixties as so-called "pirate" radio stations began anchoring ships in the waters surrounding the island nation and occupying former gunnery platforms (leftovers from the Second World War) in the Thames Estuary. These privately owned offshore commercial stations followed relatively lenient guidelines in their content policies, sold advertising, and perhaps most importantly made popular music the core of their programming. The BBC, by contrast, closely limited how many hours a week it allocated to pop and continued to follow in intent if not in detail a broad set of guidelines from the 1940s that defined what met the threshold of appropriateness. Later that summer, Parliament would pass the Marine, &c., Broadcasting (Offenses) Act 1967 to terminate offshore broadcasting, which effected the immediate closing of over twenty stations (a clear act of censorship). The "pirates" simply filled a cultural and economic vacuum; but when a governmental organization determines when, how, and what a population might hear and see, disruptive forces like offshore radio stations introduce instability into a system that abhors change.

The corporation had taken as its charge the edification of the nation and—when faced with diminishing audiences, growing competition, and a youth culture it only partially understood—scrambled in a futile effort to reconcile the network's mission with the confusing reality confronting it. When the BBC decided to protect the British public from "A Day in the Life," they drew attention to the factors driving their decision.

The Challenge of the "Contemporary Limits on Decency and Good Taste"

When EMI, the corporation that distributed the Beatles catalogue, dropped the Sex Pistols from its roster in 1977, the chairman, Sir John Read, justified the action as following the "contemporary limits of decency and good taste" (Cloonan 2003, 15). The admission that these standards were in a state of change ("contemporary") reveals much about the psychology and challenges faced by both producers and broadcasters. Ten years before that decision, the BBC faced a similar problem in the rapidity with which youth culture generated language and accorded meaning to the music and art it created and patronized. The semiotic difficulty lay in recognizing when the meaning of symbols (including words) had changed, especially in the context of popular music where metaphor plays such a powerful role in commercial value. A phrase might have one set of benign meanings among some parts of the population and quite another interpretation by members of other groups. For example, when Ian Whitcomb sang "You Really Turn Me On" in May 1965, audiences interpreted the phrase as implying physical and emotional attraction. Two years later, to say you wanted to "turn someone on" had quite a different meaning among a growing number of people.

Semioticians such as Jean-Jacques Nattiez (1990) have argued that we project meaning on the world, such that when we sense something, we assign an interpretation to that experience. In the case of artistic expression, the artist (dancer, painter, musician, and so on) may intend an interpretation for his or her creation that audiences may or may not entirely share. The exchange hardly occurs in a vacuum. We live in a symbolic world where culture provides interpretive tools to help us create meanings based on our experiences. Consequently, the more that artists and their audiences mutually possess a cultural language, the richer will be their shared experience of the symbolic. Idiosyncratic interpretations by an individual may make what he or she has encountered personally meaningful; but shared interpretations result in socially meaningful experiences.

Numerous factors influence the interpretation process. Gender, class, race, age, education, and nationality are only some of the factors involved in how we understand artistic expression. When we encounter something new, we sometimes experience cognitive disequilibrium and attempt to reconcile what we perceive with what we already think we know. The everyday reality of common culture allows for a broad exchange of information through shared interpretation, significantly accommodating cultural communication in areas such as commercial trade. However, the specialized reality of a select social group such as a band involves coded language; a musical quotation, for example, might serve as an in-joke and refer to a specific shared experience. In the mid-sixties perhaps the most celebrated of specialized realities belonged to the Beatles, whose fame enforced a circumscribed and relatively isolated world limited to the four musicians and their immediate associates.

Societal subgroups will have their own coding practices, often to thwart translation of their specialized reality by other groups. For example, when Liverpudlian slang became fashionable among some British teens in 1963 and 1964, they were able to communicate in ways that excluded adults, not only in their understanding of the jargon, but also in the appropriateness of the very use of this language. Comedy skits abound during this era based solely on the inappropriateness of adults aping the language of teens. Even though adults may have uttered the same words, the meaning changed through the specific social context of the language.[2]

When censors—governmental or private—interpret for society, they attempt to place themselves between the object and the observer with the intention of imposing their meaning and their values on audiences. In the sixties, when issues such as personal freedom and the right to challenge authority flourished in the demographic anomaly of the postwar baby boom, such intervention naturally met resistance.

The BBC and Its Mission: Class and Education

When the British Broadcasting Company formed in the 1920s, its founders had in mind something rather different than the competitive commercial licenses that flourished in the United States. Indeed, London's traditional elite juxtaposed British identity to most things American, and the geographical and cultural differences between the two nations meant that broadcasting would arrive at contrasting solutions. Perhaps more importantly, Britain sought to place control of broadcasting in the hands of a governmental body, which by definition meant upper-middle-class bureaucrats. The amalgamation of several fledgling British telecommunications companies in 1922 under founder John Reith came as an extension of the Royal Mail. Over its first few years, the BBC attracted a surprising number of subscribers who paid license fees in order to be able to use their radios.[3] By 1926 the Royal Mail had issued over two million licenses, a number that continued to grow over the following decades (Briggs 1961, 18).

In May 1926 the nine-day general strike stranded Britain without newspapers, positioning the BBC as the primary source of information, a situation that the government of Conservative prime minister Stanley Baldwin (and chancellor of the exchequer Winston Churchill in particular) sought to manage. Consequently, the next year, on January 1, a royal charter established the British Broadcasting Corporation and took the potential for political control of the broadcaster away from Parliament and placed it under the crown. Parliament would hold the purse strings, but the BBC answered to a board chaired by (now Sir) John Reith (Briggs 1961, 18)

Reith began with the goal of providing the "best of everything to the greatest number of homes," a directive that left unarticulated what constituted and who defined "best" (BBC, n.d.). With a monopoly on broadcasting in the UK, the Board of Governors saw an opportunity to set the tenor of intellectual discourse in the nation and, consequently, its aesthetic tastes; however, as ownership of radio sets expanded and listener demographics grew more diverse, lower-middle-class and working-class families came to dominate the audience.

Between 1962 and 1967, the BBC operated three domestic services: the Home Service (which provided regional programming), the Light Programme (popular entertainment), and the Third Programme (the heart of the BBC's educational mission). The very title of the Light Programme implied the inferiority of a service that provided listeners with only a small window for commercial popular music. The corporation often operated as though it were broadcasting either to an Oxbridge elite (with plays, symphonies, and debates between scholars and politicians on the Third Programme) or to the masses (with programs on subjects like farming and housekeeping).

The BBC had long experienced competition from Radio Luxembourg, situated in the tiny nation nestled between France, Belgium, and then West Germany. This commercial station operated one of the most powerful transmitters in Europe and broadcast many programs specifically for British listeners. Record companies like EMI and even music publishers bought time to run radio programs that they had produced in the UK, even if the weather occasionally impaired reception of the station's broadcasts. But the anchoring of the MV *Caroline* off Britain's east coast in March 1964 and the subsequent commencement of broadcasts by Radio Caroline marked the beginning of the rise of independent offshore stations that briefly and significantly challenged the BBC's authority.

Over the next three years, listeners tuned away from the national broadcaster to listen to nonstop pop with a decidedly hipper accent and less rigid set of controls.

The government reacted to this perceived infringement on their authority (and that of the upper classes) by passing the Marine, &c., Broadcasting (Offences) Act 1967 on July 14, primarily on the pretext that these stations sometimes took wavelengths reserved for ship communications. August 1967 would see offshore broadcasters fold overnight (with the exception of Radio Caroline which fought the ruling by anchoring in the waters of the semi-independent Isle of Man). By way of compensation to the listening public, the BBC reorganized and opened a new radio channel devoted to popular music. In September 1967, the BBC renamed their services Radios 1, 2, 3, and 4, with Radio 1 begrudgingly giving popular music a limited but more prominent place (see Annan 1977, 11–12.)

The "Green Book"

The BBC's unique status positioned it between the responsibility of serving British audiences and the power of the government. During World War II, Churchill's government placed severe restrictions on radio broadcasts, with the service sometimes conveying coded messages to agents in German-occupied Europe. Earlier in 1933, the government had even pressured the corporation to cancel a series of talks on India (Briggs 1965, 129). As a rule of thumb, the governors of the network sought to avoid controversy, which included eschewing editorial statements (128–132). Thus, when the BBC discussed censorship, it had a very specific practice in mind that focused on national welfare, including physical and mental health and social wellbeing. By 1949 Michael Standing (with assistance from others) had developed the *BBC Variety Programmes Policy Guide for Writers and Producers* (unofficially known as the "Green Book") to establish Britain's standards for broadcast taste (Took 1981, 86). The language of the *Guide* effectively reveals attitudes that would guide decisions long after the document had ceased to be officially operational.

In this internal document, the corporation clearly understood its power of influence on listeners, which justified the considerable weight of its assumed "responsibility for a high standard of taste." Further defining this aesthetic policy, Standing reasoned that, because of the diversity of their potential audience, they had to avoid "vulgarity, political bias," and matters of "questionable taste." Specifically on "matters of taste," the BBC wished to set a "standard that will be accepted by most rational people" (Took 1981, 86). Strategically, "rational people" remained undefined, but in practice this group would be identical with the corporate framers of the *Guide*.

The *Guide* assigns "responsibility for enforcing" these standards to the producers of their programs, equating them with censors who must know the "Corporation's general attitude towards the subject and of the detailed rules which have been drawn up during some 25 years' practical experience" (Took 1981, 86). Of course, the producers had to walk a delicate line between what the corporation demanded and what audiences wanted, setting up inevitable conflicts of interest. The reference to "25 years' practical experience" clearly indicates that the BBC's standards derived from the past and not the present.

For entertainment, the authors of the *Guide* specifically prohibited references to lavatories, effeminacy in men, honeymoon couples, chambermaids, fig leaves, prostitution, women's underwear, marital infidelity, and religion. Writers could refer to alcohol consumption, as long as they did so "in strict moderation" and could justify its inclusion only on "entertainment grounds." Of course, the BBC forbade, except in a "serious dramatic setting," the use of expletives, such as "God, Good God, My God, Blast, Hell, Damn, Bloody, Gorblimey," and "Ruddy." They recommended instead the substitution of "innocuous expressions" (Took 1981, 89). Thus, the BBC set the rules of engagement for the next twenty years.

The BBC and Music

The very British issues of class and race emerge in curious arenas, including music. Notably, Standing found the word "Niggers" unacceptable unless a producer referred to a proper title, such as "Nigger Minstrels."[4] Furthermore, the *Guide* treats the Western classical music tradition as an almost sacred entity, banning the "jazzing" of any works in this repertoire (Took 1981, 90). This rule from the *Guide* clearly was in effect in March 1961, when the BBC banned Nero and the Gladiators' version of Grieg's "In the Hall of the Mountain King" from broadcast. Reflecting the corporation's class-conscious reverence for hierarchy and without irony, Standing instructed producers in doubt about the acceptability of a musical performance to take the consultation of a "higher authority."

As the first bête noir on the BBC's list of questionable entertainment, the songs and jokes of the music hall presented a serious challenge to the *Guide*'s standards of taste. The working-class tradition had flourished in the nineteenth century, gaining an even broader audience in the early twentieth century. Nevertheless, the potpourri of song, dance, acrobatics, magic, and risqué humor that constituted a typical music hall program hardly represented Reith's idea of the "best of everything."

By the 1940s, however, the institution of the music hall was on the wane, its most successful stars having made the transition to film, which provided a cheaper and more domesticated alternative to the theater. George Formby perhaps represented the most notable among the transitional music hall stars, and his song "When I'm Cleaning Windows"—from the film *Keep Your Seats Please* (1936)—seems to have served as the template for some of the BBC's standards. The corporation possibly responded to the popularity of the song with contempt, especially when the king made Formby an Officer of the Order of the British Empire in 1946 for his entertainment of the troops during the war and when Stalin awarded him the Order of Lenin for the laughter he brought people.

"When I'm Cleaning Windows" takes the voice of a workman as he variously views honeymooning couples, disrobing actresses, a bootlegger, and flirting chambermaids. Indeed, this song and others seemed to run the gamut of the BBC's forbidden topics. The corporation as a matter of principle rejected other Formby songs with titles such as "The Wedding of Mr Wu" (1933), "Hindoo Man" (1937), "The Wash House at the Back" (1935), and "Fanlight Fanny" (1935). In particular, the BBC objected to the phallic innuendos of songs about his trademark banjo-uke (or banjolele) and his northern origins, such as "With My Little Ukulele in My Hand," which Decca Records withdrew at first in 1933, and "With My Little Stick of Blackpool Rock" (1937), which resulted in an official BBC request for rewritten lyrics.

Unlike the radio, the limited broadcast range of television meant that the government entertained the idea of independent networks; but the BBC's standards applied here as well. The ban on George Formby's material remained in place such that, in November 1963, BBC TV prevented British country rocker Joe Brown from performing "My Little Ukulele" on *The Billy Cotton Band Show*. Shortly afterwards the independent television networks also removed Brown from the shows *Thank Your Lucky Stars* (ABC) and *Five O'Clock Club* (AR-TV). Three and a half years later in January 1967, the BBC would cut seven minutes of discussion about the Game's "The Addicted Man" from the popular program *Juke Box Jury* because of the song's descriptions of drug use.

Second on the list, the corporation frowned upon "Americanisms," particularly in the use of American slang and accents by singers, and wished to emphasize that producers were to favor British music wherever possible. Nothing less could be expected of a national broadcaster. Their ally among publishers had been the Dance Music Policy Committee so that the corporation felt sure that sheet music had already been vetted; but, by the mid sixties, record sales had left printed music in the dust and the committee ceased to exist.

The BBC now increasingly operated on a global stage where their audiences compared their standards to those of other countries whose broadcasters sometimes seemed to hold a stricter line. By 1967 the Rolling Stones could get away with "Let's Spend the Night Together" in Britain; but in the United States, Ed Sullivan would force them to change the lyrics to "let's spend some time together." Only a few months later, the Troggs found their song "I Can't Help Myself" banned from British television shows on both the BBC and the independent networks; but Australia totally blacklisted the disc even for sale (Altham 1966). In each case, the BBC found other countries and programs to hold even more prejudicial standards than their own, leading to an internal dialogue questioning whether they needed to tighten their standards.

The Beatles and Censorship

During much of 1964, Bob Dylan's music had preoccupied John Lennon, and meeting the American in New York that summer reinforced the influence. In addition to introducing the Beatles to marijuana, Dylan instilled in Lennon the importance of lyrics. In turn, the Beatles' recording of "I Want to Hold Your Hand" had impressed Dylan in part because he had misheard the text, thinking they sang, "I get high" instead of "I can't hide." He wondered how they had gotten the song past the censors and he told them so. Thus, like schoolboys, as the Beatles began to fall under the spell of what they euphemistically called "tea" and played with the notion of slipping things under the noses of officialdom, the phrase "I feel fine" may have had an alternative meaning for them. Paul McCartney, for his part, thought it would become the "catch phrase" for the season (Nicholl 1964, 11).

Over the next few years, they would embrace the idea of duping the most immediate representative of the establishment: their producer George Martin. At first, their attempts were simply naughty adolescent pranks. For example, in 1965 during their sessions for the album *Rubber Soul*, the song "Day Tripper" sought to depict a woman who disingenuously implied interest in sex. McCartney claims that "big teaser" replaced "prick teaser" (someone who took you "half the way there"), a phrase he expected his friends to get but the general public to miss (Miles 1997, 209). Not long after the "Day Tripper" sessions, he and Lennon grew bolder, introducing the word "tit" as part of the backing vocals to Lennon's song "Girl." The producer stopped them at one point and asked, "Was that 'dit dit' or 'tit tit' you were singing?" To which they replied, "Oh, 'dit dit,' George, but it does sound a bit like that, doesn't it?" (Apple 2000, 276.)

Lennon and McCartney also admit that *tripper* had a meaning beyond that of a vacationer, referencing someone who took hallucinogens and providing another inside reference for their coterie (Miles 1997, 209; Apple 2000, 199). Letting a common phrase describing someone who took a day trip overlap with a newer meaning that could slide past corporate gatekeepers represents what McCartney has described as one of the advantages of collaboration, where the partners would push the envelope with a "nudge-nudge, wink-wink" (Miles 1997, 209–210). As they began work on their next album, *Revolver*, their use of drugs emboldened them, and the references now sat hidden in plain sight. For example, in the song "Got to Get You into My Life," McCartney claims that he let the idea of looking for ways to bring a lover into his world stand for his marijuana craving (see Miles 1997, 190). Other drug references, however, should have been much more obvious to the BBC.

On April 1, 1966, near the one-year anniversary of a London dentist's surreptitious spiking of his and George Harrison's coffees with LSD, Lennon visited Barry Miles's Indica Books and picked up a copy of Timothy Leary, Ralph Metzner, and Richard Alpert's *The Psychedelic Experience: A Manual Based on the Tibetan Book of the Dead*. Originally published in 1964, the book gained a broad audience as the use of LSD spread. In its pseudo-mystical prose, Lennon found partial inspiration for one of the most audacious recordings the Beatles would ever attempt: "Tomorrow Never Knows." Leary, Metzner, and Alpert had freely adapted verses from the *Tibetan Book of the Dead*, a Buddhist treatise on the attachment to life and how to prepare for death, the ultimate detachment from worldly obsessions. Lennon's adaptation of *The Psychedelic Experience* included lines like "But listen to the colour of your dreams. It is not living, it is not living," that referenced his visual reactions to LSD while still appearing poetic enough for censors to ignore.

Throughout this period, the Beatles relied on a cooperative press to keep their private lives and thoughts separate from their public personas. Consequently, few dared to interpret the music of the giggly Fab Four as meaning anything but superficial good fun. That was about to change.

"More Popular than Jesus"

In the spring of 1966, as swinging London and its colorful denizens attracted the attention of *Time*, the managing editor of *Datebook* found part of a recent interview with John Lennon to be of particular interest. Articles on the Beatles had boosted sales of the American teen magazine and, with a cover story on the band, he hoped to raise circulation even more. Collaterally, a rapid disintegration of the complex identity that the Beatles management, the media, the fans, and even the musicians themselves had constructed ensued, setting in motion a number of dark forces.

An old friend (she had given them one of their first positive national reviews), the British journalist Maureen Cleave had interviewed Lennon for a series in the *Evening Standard* on the everyday lives of the Beatles and had questioned Lennon about his library and reading habits. He cited books about the variety of humankind's beliefs in the sacred that had led him to an understanding of how ideas had come and gone over time. Notably, he sensed that Christianity, like other religions, had contributed good ideas, but that something else would eventually replace it too. To that end, Lennon asserted, "Christianity will go . . . It will vanish and shrink." As his evidence, he added that currently the Beatles were "more popular than Jesus" and, as a corollary of his theorem, he projected that even rock "n" roll would disappear.

His comments hardly surprised his friends. In the wake of the Second World War, their generation had openly questioned the received wisdom asserting the presence of a supreme deity, even as they sometimes embraced exotic alternatives. Attendance at British churches had dropped precipitously in the postwar years, and by the sixties, these institutions fought a losing ideological battle with sports events and the cinema. For the Beatles, their student conversations in Liverpool and debates with their college friends in Hamburg had shaped a decidedly existentialist worldview. In contrast, teenage fans in North America, particularly in the southern United States, commonly held a rather more conservative, innocent, and insular view of religion.

When *Datebook* published excerpts of the interview on the eve of the Beatles' US tour, it displayed the headline, "I don't know what will go first—rock 'n' roll or Christianity" as one of several quotes on the cover and as the title of the article inside. Soon, two radio stations in the American South saw the marketing possibilities of the statement and loudly banned Beatles recordings before moving on to displays that offered even more theatrical possibilities. Initially, the tempest that swirled around Lennon's comments had the intended effect of focusing attention on the self-righteous zealots who burnt Beatles records in scenes reminiscent of Nazi Germany's book burnings. More menacingly, members of the Ku Klux Klan picketed performances and threatened violence, sending manager Brian Epstein into a frenzy and the Beatles into disbelief. Lennon gave the impression of a deer in the headlights at a Chicago press conference on August 11, 1966, as he tried to satisfy a press corps that smelled blood, saying, "I still don't know quite what I've done."

By the end of the summer's tours, the band felt unhinged. They had received death threats from Japanese militants and physical abuse at the hands of Filipino police, not to mention experiencing extortion at the hands of officials who confiscated every peso the band had earned from two concerts in Manila. After the last Beatles concert (in San Francisco on August 29), George Harrison turned to a British reporter traveling with them and sighed, "Well, that's it. I'm not a Beatle anymore" (Lewisohn 1992, 214).

Harrison soon disappeared to India to study sitar with Ravi Shankar, Lennon headed first to Germany and then Spain to act in the film *How I Won the War*, and McCartney worked on a film score and on his reputation as an eclectic consumer of musics both popular and esoteric. More importantly, their recording contract with EMI expired that fall without even a whimper, and for the first time in years they did not release a recording for the Christmas market. In their absence and at an important juncture in their recording careers, the press began to speculate that their days were numbered and that they would soon release a statement announcing their disbandment. The blush was clearly off the bloom.

"A Day in the Life"

When the Beatles returned to the studio in November 1966 to record, they had no particular deadline and only the most general of themes. They began with Lennon's "Strawberry Fields Forever" before moving on to Paul McCartney's "When I'm Sixty-four" and "Penny Lane." Toward the end of January 1967, however, manager Brian Epstein concluded negotiations with EMI, locking the Beatles into a nine-year recording contract and setting them once more on a record-and-release schedule. To shore up the reputation of the band (and perhaps to appease EMI), Epstein and Martin selected the two best recordings in their current portfolio to release as a single. Unfortunately, "Strawberry Fields Forever" and "Penny Lane" confused reviewers and the public alike, and the disc would be the first Beatles single not to top all of the charts since their very first release, "Love Me Do" in 1962. Momentarily shaken but undeterred, the band and their production crew continued with a song that Lennon had brought to the studio in early January and on which he and McCartney had collaborated.

Lennon began "In the Life of . . . " after the death of Tara Browne—the son of an Irish baron and a Guinness Brewery heir—who had lived a high-profile life in swinging mid-sixties London and had been a friend of the band (Sheff 1981, 163). The previous year Browne and McCartney had been riding mopeds at night in suburban Liverpool when the Beatle hit a hole, went over the handlebars, and chipped his front tooth. No such easy escape awaited Browne in the early morning hours of Sunday, December 18, 1966, when he and model Suki Potier left a friend's house in Earl's Court and headed into London, his small fiberglass Lotus Elan speeding through the streets of South Kensington. Singer Marianne Faithfull has commented that she had recently taken LSD with Browne and that all of their friends commonly drove around London while on the drug (Faithfull

2000, 89). Various reports have the car swerving to miss another vehicle and spinning; but Browne either missed or ignored a stoplight, sending his car crashing into a parked van. The side impact put the driver of the low-slung sports car directly in harm's way. Potier survived; but the twenty-one-year-old father of two soon died from his injuries.

A month later, Lennon found himself in a surreal situation. A habitual reader of newspapers, the musician sat working on a song for their upcoming recording sessions while digesting the coroner's report on Browne's accident. Death had visited Lennon in the past when his uncle, who was also his guardian, died, followed by the deaths of his mother and his friend Stuart Sutcliffe, but Browne was younger than Lennon and seemed to have everything going for him. Indeed, they were much alike: young men with young families living fast lives between their elegant homes and London's clubs and sampling the same drugs.

The song begins by citing the newspaper article and, without naming Browne, references the experience of seeing the gadabout's smiling face in the picture, igniting a flickering memory of happier times. The inquest noted that Browne had failed to stop at a light and that he suffered severe head injuries, facts perhaps referenced in the song's comments about not noticing that the "lights had changed." In a reference to the fleeting and transient nature of fame that must have resonated with Lennon, some people probably seemed unsure whether the Browne that had died was Tara or his father, a member of the House of Lords.

Lennon brought the incomplete song to McCartney's home in St. John's Wood where they sat at a piano in his partner's music room to expand on the ideas. Interestingly, McCartney claims not to have known that Lennon had Tara Browne on his mind, thinking they were describing a politician (Miles 1997, 324). They added a verse about Lennon's experiences making the film *How I Won the War* (which would not see release until the next fall) and, for sheer surrealistic randomness, Lennon and McCartney pulled a news item about road repairs in Blackburn, Lancashire, not far from their Liverpool homes. The article dutifully reported the estimated number of holes (like the one that McCartney had hit the previous year) as around four thousand. Lennon's first draft, reflecting his sarcastic whimsy, also lets slip an obliquely scatological pun, suggesting that the authorities had to count "everyone." But, as the music for the verse changed, he needed to amend that ending, retaining the idea to say that the authorities now knew how many of these holes might be seated in the Albert Hall.

At this point, Lennon knew he needed contrasting material for the chorus and his partner thought he had a bit of music that would fit. In a narrative style McCartney had used in "Eleanor Rigby" and "Penny Lane," the songwriter proposed an up-tempo section with words that suitably narrated the everyday experience of someone rushing off to work. The juxtaposition of McCartney's section with the existing verses suggests that Lennon's material constitutes part of someone's dream, a reading underscored by the last line of this middle section in which the narrator climbs the stairs of the bus, draws on his or her cigarette, and drifts back into his or her somnambulism.

The passage that McCartney later acknowledged could refer to drug use arrived as part of the bridge material commencing first from the end of Lennon's initial verses and before McCartney's chorus and then again from Lennon's last verse to the coda. With Timothy Leary's advocacy and knowing the double meaning of the phrase to "turn on," Lennon slow-trilled McCartney's insertion of "I'd Love to turn . . . you . . . on . . ." (Miles 1997, 325). The music that follows had an intended metaphoric meaning, with McCartney projecting the dramatic orchestral crescendo of rising-pitch chaos (achieved through a conscious imitation of American John Cage's aleatoric composition) to reflect the spirit of Lennon's dream (Miles 1997, 325). That is, the two orchestral transitions in "A Day in the Life" represent McCartney's experience of the psychedelic.

Lennon's wordplay and surrealistic contrasts create a powerful metaphoric amalgam of sound and image that his singing style further enhances. In one more symbolic touch, Lennon had the production crew treat his voice with a strong echo and reverberation while they would eventually choose to leave McCartney's voice dry, sonically emphasizing the distinction between dream and waking states. Lennon, McCartney, and the production crew had created a richly symbolic object loaded with vaguely defined symbols. They seem to have given little thought as to how others would interpret the material.

The Beatles and the BBC

May 1967

Sgt. Pepper's Lonely Hearts Club Band sat completed, awaiting only hot presses to begin producing millions of vinyl copies. And while the band already worked on its next project, the historic nature of the disc they had just completed led to leaks of unofficial pre-release versions of some tracks ("Sgt. Pepper's Lonely Hearts Club Band," "She's Leaving Home," "When I'm Sixty-four" and "A Day in the Life") making their way into the hands of disc jockeys in the United States.

During the "Summer of Love" in 1967, a war broke out in the Middle East, Red Guards set fire to the British embassy in Beijing, and Lyndon Johnson escalated American bombing in Southeast Asia. Earlier in the year, Mick Jagger had threatened to sue the tabloid *The News of the World* for libel, leading the authorities (with probable assistance from the paper) to raid the home of fellow Rolling Stone Keith Richards. The police charged Richards, Jagger, and art dealer Robert Fraser with a variety of drug offenses, bringing them to court on May 10, and providing the tabloid with further fuel for its outrage at the behavior of pop stars. In the United States, perhaps hoping to pick up on some of the previous summer's press-attracting outrage and building on the news from London, a radio station in Los Angeles chose to take offense at what it perceived as drug references in "A Day in the Life." The news reached London almost immediately.

Upon learning of the ban, Dick James, the director of the Beatles' Northern Songs publishing venture, retorted, "I cannot understand how anyone could take exception to 'A Day in the Life.' Certainly this is an unusual song. There is reference to a man smoking, but it is quite innocuous. How anyone could object to it—especially in the

Los Angeles area of all places—is beyond me." Derek Taylor, who lived in Los Angeles but had formerly been an assistant to Beatles manager Brian Epstein, reported that the radio station had dropped the disc because the station director thought he heard Lennon sing, "40,000 holes in my arm," a phrase he presumed to describe heroin use. But knowing that the actual words to the song referred to road repairs, Taylor opined, "Any idea that this may encourage people to use drugs is, to say the least, remote!" (*Disc and Music Echo* 1967a).

Almost two weeks later on Friday May 19, 1967—the day before the Beatles were to appear in a taped special on *Where It's At* hosted by Chris Denning to talk about *Sgt. Pepper's Lonely Hearts Club Band*—Roland Fox, the Assistant Head of Publicity at the BBC, circulated a memo. The note asserted that the corporation had assumed a "pretty liberal attitude" toward contemporary pop in recent years, but after listening to "A Day in the Life" "over and over again," they had decided to exercise their "editorial discretion . . . not to broadcast this particular song." They had concluded that the recording appeared to "go a little too far and could encourage a permissive attitude to drug-taking." He instructed the Radio Publicity Officer and others that they should not volunteer this information, but given the likelihood that the story would break over the weekend, they should use the memo for their talking points (Fox 1967a).

The producers of *Where It's At* consequently removed "A Day in the Life" from the special segment that offshore (Radio London) Liverpudlian disc jockey Kenny Everett had independently recorded. The Beatles and their entourage learned of the banning at Brian Epstein's private press party the day of Fox's memo and the night before the broadcast. A week later *Disc and Music Echo* quoted the line from the memo about drug-taking almost verbatim.[5] With no more details forthcoming from the corporation, the paper approached the Beatles for their reaction. Unsurprisingly, Lennon led the attack, concentrating on the line that he thought might have provoked the censorship and sarcastically declaring that he would like to "meet the man who banned this song of ours. I'd like to turn him on to what's happening. Why don't they charge the Electricity Board with spreading drugs because to get electricity you have to 'switch on?' Hidden meanings, man" (Coleman 1967, 8). Then the songwriter cut to the core of the problem, claiming that the lyrics held no obvious declarations in favor of drug use and that the censors themselves had chosen to interpret the words that way.

The BBC's unspecific ban also confused McCartney who focused on his passage about going upstairs on a bus and having a smoke. He first rhetorically asked, "Does THAT have to be about drugs?" before identifying a specific cigarette brand (something else that the BBC would have banned had it been in the song): "Park Drive."[6] Ultimately, he claimed that the song could have referred to "just about ANYTHING" and that the words described a "dream on the top of the bus" (Coleman 1967, 9).

McCartney put a further spin on the ban by declaring that drugs were obviously on the mind of the censors and that their ban would have a contradictory effect. "It just draws attention to a subject when all the time their aim is to force attention away from it. Banning never did any good."[7] Reflecting on the BBC's vagueness, McCartney professed that the meaning of their declaration was "just beyond me." He then went on to compare the banning of the song with another recent controversy, a failed ban of a film adaptation of Joyce's *Ulysses* (for its use of the word "fuck"), but noted that road repairs in Lancashire were "like images in a dream—that was what we were after" (Coleman 1967, 9).

The BBC's decision to leave their rationale vague created a paranoiac atmosphere that left musicians and producers broadly unsure of whether records crossed the boundary. With the lyrics of songs increasingly surrealistic and employing broad abstract metaphors, the corporation's intentions seemed to be to return pop music to something simpler, but the gates had already opened. Internally, the BBC attempted to show a united face, albeit with some ruffled feathers. Robin Scott, Controller of the Light Programme, which aired *Where It's At*, complained it was a "pity that events overtook us," acknowledging that the statement "effectively constituted a ban on the record." Perhaps referring to an article in the Saturday *Daily Mirror* (Short 1967), he further complains that neither he "nor [the] Gramophone Department[8] nor producer of the programme concerned was aware of what had happened until we read our Saturday morning newspapers" (Scott 1967).

Scott notes, "We obviously have to stick to our guns on this," finding reassurance that Radio Luxembourg had agreed with the decision to ban the recording and that both it and the BBC were writing letters to record companies explaining their stance on songs they perceived as promoting drug use. He concedes, "In the process . . . some offending records will get through and some innocent ones will suffer, but there can be no doubt about the rightness of our intentions." Fox (1967b) shot back a memo in defense of the Publicity Department to the effect that events had not overtaken them and that the Director of Sound Broadcasting had "informed the H.P. [Head of Programming] and A.H.P. [Assistant Head of Programming] about the decision on this particular 'track' at our routine with him on Thursday, May 18.[9] We discussed the wording of a Press Office comment in case the story broke over the weekend." Referencing the press party where the Beatles learned this news, he felt satisfied that he had contacted and warned all of the appropriate people.

The next day (May 25, 1967), the Assistant Director of Sound Broadcasting R. D. Marriott supported Fox in a memo to Scott that expressed surprise "since you both took part in the decision," before going on to explain "matters of central policy."[10] He supported the conclusion to ban the record because of a "consensus of opinion about the dangers of drugs that makes it unlikely that the Press would criticize us." Moreover, with the exception of comments from the Beatles and "our own disc jockey," he notes that the press had been silent. Ominously, he remarks that he understands that the disc jockey (Kenny Everett) "is being dealt with," suggesting that the Beatles were not the only ones censored. Unclear from Marriott's and Scott's correspondence is whether or not Scott had actually been part of the deliberative process.

June 1, 1967

The summer of 1967 saw numerous significant musical releases by artists as diverse as the Kinks ("Waterloo Sunset"), Procol Harum ("A Whiter Shade of Pale"), Traffic

("Paper Sun"), and the Jimi Hendrix Experience ("The Wind Cries Mary"). A significant number of these songs evoked ideas that had listeners deciphering the lyrics and repeatedly listening to recordings to catch even the most insignificant bit of audio symbolism. With the release of the *Sgt. Pepper's Lonely Hearts Club Band*, this hyperactive interrogation of cultural artifacts went into overdrive. Peter Blake's album-cover montage of figures selected by the Beatles as influences (Karl Marx, Stu Sutcliffe, Edgar Allen Poe, etc.), the band costumes, the insert of a cutout mustache, sergeant's stripes, an image presumably of Sgt. Pepper himself, and the lyrics on the back cover all seemed to encourage even the most reluctant student to indulge in analysis. The adolescent audience, whom the Beatles had first attracted in 1963, had matured into students familiar with metaphor and interpretation. Even some teachers had begun choosing Lennon and McCartney's words for class discussion.

In addition to running a "cartoon" depicting the creation of the album, the *New Musical Express* devoted an entire article to descriptions of each track. Allen Evans approached "A Day in the Life" in full narrative mode, creating a complete story line. Notably, when the orchestral crescendo first appears, Evans describes it as "the loudest thunderings of war noises," presumably because it follows Lennon's verse about the English Army (Evans 1967, 4). He also suggests that the wordless bridge material at the end of McCartney's chorus depicts the dream referenced in the last line. Finally, he interprets the second appearance of the orchestral crescendo as "the sounds of war again which swell up and go into the sound of a plane diving, then rumblings and fading as the notes try to die but hang on and on" (4). He makes no mention of drug use or hallucinations.

The Evans interpretation, contemporary with the decisions to ban the recording from airplay in the United States and the United Kingdom for supposed references to drugs, shows that listeners could easily infer other meanings from the music. Even William Mann in the conservative *Times*, acknowledging the BBC's ban, described the drug references in the song as "ambivalent" (Mann 1967, 9).

Censorship and Semiotics

The idea of "process" in culture implies an individual or a group of individuals undertaking a series of decisions and other symbolic acts that result in change, as actors and the consequences of their behavior move from one state or condition to another. Process also suggests a psychological state in which individuals make sense of information. The processes by which the Beatles created and recorded "A Day in the Life" and the processes by which the BBC enacted and then justified a ban represent musical and policy changes that occurred in the context of dichotomous social interactions. That is, in the environment of 1967 pop culture, individuals sought to maximize the advantage of their talent and/or to position themselves socially in order to reap the most rewards from the market, sometimes competing against one another and sometimes bonding to gain greater leverage against others.

In his description of the objects of semiology, Nattiez (1990, 15) describes creative expression as composed of "poietic processes" and its reception and interpretation as consisting of "esthesic processes." The complex symbolic configurations that we analyze (such as the dense lyrical, musical, and sonic recordings emanating from EMI's Studio Two) lie between these two sets of activities. The Beatles and their production team engaged in a poietic process when developing (a) the song's melody, harmonic structure, and lyrics, (b) the performed interpretations of these materials, and (c) the acoustic realization of the performances. Roland Fox and his team at the BBC esthesically interpreted something in this realization as encouraging the use of drugs.

Cloonan (2003, 15) defines censorship as the "process by which an agent (or agents) attempts to, and/or succeeds in, significantly altering, and/or curtailing, the freedom of expression of another agent with a view to limiting the likely audience for that expression." That is, censorship exists when someone or something in a position of power intercedes in the reception of the "traces" of creativity. Both creation and reception relate to the "material reality of the work" (the physical "trace" of the processes that created it), and thus inform how we approach analysis (Nattiez 1990, 15).

In the BBC's decision to ban this one track from the album *Sgt. Pepper's Lonely Hearts Club Band*, a variety of factors influenced their decision-making process. Lennon, McCartney, and their production crew created the "trace" through poietic processes while the BBC and publications like the *New Musical Express* interpreted it through esthesic processes. Roland Fox and others functioned as mediators between the Beatles and audiences whose experience of popular music came primarily through BBC broadcasts. Censorship thus functioned as mediation between audiences in the esthesic process.

Did the BBC curtail the ability of the Beatles to express themselves to their intended audience? Cloonan (2003, 17–19) provides a useful starting point for this discussion by distinguishing three levels of censorship: prior restraint (the prevention of the creation of works "usually based on aesthetic or market considerations, or both"), restriction (limitations on who has access to works), and suppression ("attempts by a government or legal system to enforce a moral and/or political code"). Under these definitions, the BBC's decision to ban the broadcast of "A Day in the Life" represents an ultimately futile attempt at limiting expression.

Although EMI had the power to prevent the Beatles from recording at their studios (prior restraint), they had no interest in surrendering the most economically profitable artists in the world. Indeed, EMI had every financial reason to encourage the band, its production crew, and its management to create a product that would earn the company significant profits. They presumed that in the poietic process, the Beatles and George Martin would self-censor to create a product that would meet their mutual expectations. The company had recently signed a recording contract with the band's management and had subsequently provided them with access to the valuable resource of studio time and personnel, manufactured their most expensive product to date (including its color cover and insert by Peter Blake), and sold the product in their stores. They anticipated an album they could sell, and the Beatles delivered a product that clearly exceeded market expectations.

As for restriction, in an environment where offshore radio stations continued to broadcast the recording, the BBC's ban limited access only to those British listeners who were unwilling or unable to change the station. Indeed, even with the impending closure of the "pirates" by an act of Parliament, patrons could still purchase the disc in stores. Nevertheless, a broadcasting ban on a recording could limit sales.

The BBC's director of sound broadcasting, Frank Gillard, wrote to Sir Joseph Lockwood (chairman of EMI) and nineteen other record company executives to express concern "over the allegations that some pop records contain references to drug taking, and could be construed as giving encouragement to unfortunate habits and perhaps even to vice." The executive feigns compassion for EMI by noting that catching drug references can prove "a very difficult problem . . . , since these references are often obscure and couched in language and jargon not readily understood by ordinary people" (Gillard 1967). The phrase "ordinary people" stands out. Gillard's language carries overtones of class condescension implying that a variety of others—from lower-tier employees to listeners—through the ignorance of their birth and cultural background, would fail to catch the drug references. Illogically, he suggests that "A Day in the Life" could subliminally sway some BBC audiences to use drugs, even though they did not understand the references. Of course, Lennon and McCartney routinely included references that only their friends could understand.

Gillard in his powerful position justified editorial control by referencing the "millions of young people" who listen to BBC programming, underscoring his concern about lyrics that some could interpret as "offensive or even dubious." Echoing parts of the internal correspondence, he reminds Lockwood and other recording executives that the BBC had moved to "liberalize" their position on recordings in recent years, but that he found it "necessary to be particularly vigilant from now on in this matter." He then assured record company executives that, although the BBC might sometimes "penalise an innocent disc . . . , if the axe has to fall at all, it will come down only on the guilty" (Gillard 1967). In other words, even if producers created discs that had no intended references to drugs, the BBC still held the power of interpretation to determine whether or not a recording actually encouraged vice. The letter reminds record company executives of the power of the BBC and of the cultural battle in which he presumes they are reluctant allies.

In terms of suppression, the BBC had the power to ban the disc from its radio and television programs, even if shops continued to carry it, and with legislation pending that would shut down offshore broadcasters, Gillard must have felt some authority underlining his intention of applying a "moral and/or political code." As the gatekeeper of British broadcast culture, the corporation would soon have greater ability to control what people heard on the radio. Indeed, an even more blatant example of suppression lies in the Marine, &c., Broadcast (Offences) Act 1967 itself. With this legislation and with the force of the Royal Navy, the British government completely censored offshore broadcasters, ostensibly on the grounds that they obstructed safety, but in reality because they challenged the authority of the BBC and of the class system itself. Given that the programming of these broadcasters consisted primarily of pop, the act sought to ban any music of which the BBC had not approved.

Deciphering a Ban

The banning of "A Day in the Life" proved a response to the quickly evolving culture of mid-sixties Britain. Fashions and language changed dramatically and rapidly, and metaphors and wordplay grew so thick that conservative institutions like the BBC grasped at interpretation. Individuals at the BBC felt compelled to decide about the appropriateness of the recording, but with abstract musical and lyrical metaphors purposefully obscuring any concrete meaning, they found themselves influenced by contemporary events.

In the second half of the sixties substantial numbers of baby boomers came into adulthood, gaining the right to vote and threatening the authority of an establishment that had ruled Western democracies since the end of the Second World War. Part of the biochemical revolution of the postwar years included the availability of drugs, which spread rapidly and globally through youth culture, championed in part by the behavior of prominent figures such as rock musicians and film stars. The establishment reacted.

The Beatles at this point in their career sought to retain legitimacy among their peers and in the eyes of their audience by pushing the envelope of what the middle class found acceptable. They had successfully evaded external censorship in the past and they felt that the text here successfully stayed on a path that allowed different audiences their own interpretations. EMI, the corporation funding and promoting their product, benefited from the sales of the album, even as they complained to Parliament about pirates not paying royalties. They relied on Lennon, McCartney, and producer George Martin to provide a product that would pass muster with the BBC and the press.

Internally, the BBC sailed stormy waters in the straits between a public that had grown tired of the musically mundane "Light Programme" and a newly invigorated conservative political force demanding a reversal in cultural trends. Emboldened by recent electoral victories in the UK, conservative forces such as the police force and publications like the *News of the World* actively attacked the counterculture, challenging institutions like the BBC to follow suit.

Externally, American culture continued to grow in global influence, undermining and challenging traditional British customs and the cultural hegemony of institutions like the BBC. Consequently, BBC executives found themselves justifying their actions in terms of international forces. For example, when R. D. Marriott pedantically explains banning to Robin Scott (a communication from an administrative superior to an employee commenting on how well he thinks their system works), he cites decisions by Radio Luxembourg and American stations.

The Beatles had long represented a safe and productive resource: an appearance by band members on any program could boost its audience. But the Beatles' position as untouchable icons of the British pop music industry had eroded with attacks by American radio stations in response to Lennon's comments about the relative popularity of the band and Jesus. And the contemporaneous arrest and court appearances of Mick Jagger and Keith Richards on drug charges proved that the establishment could attack pop stars successfully. If the Rolling Stones could be arrested and prosecuted, why not ban the Beatles? And if Parliament could shut down offshore broadcasters, the BBC should be able to exercise a similar decision in taste in regards to a pop song. The tide seemed to be turning and the BBC would not want to be caught in the harbor.

Understanding how the BBC reacted to "A Day in the Life" involves more than a simple argument about whether or not the words of the song refer to drug use. Multivariate factors influenced the cultural environment in which BBC executives interpreted the recording, factors that were to become much more complicated.

Notes

1. Thank you to Nigel Paine (former Chief Executive for Broadcast Training, BBC) and Jessica Hogg (Archives Researcher, BBC Written Archives Centre) for their assistance.
2. The alternative is true of films such as *Austin Powers: International Man of Mystery* (1997), where Mike Myers brings sixties colloquialisms into a world in which they have lost their meaning.
3. In contrast, Americans seem never to have presumed they would be able to monitor who owned and operated radios and who did not, let alone who would be willing to pay for a license.
4. The BBC would repeatedly draw criticism over the years for Blackface minstrel shows, which some producers found perfectly acceptable. For instance, black-faced performers appeared on "The Black and White Minstrel Show," which ran on BBC television from the fifties until the seventies.
5. London's music papers published once a week on Fridays or Saturdays. *The Daily Mirror* (Short, 1967) quoted directly from Fox's memo, while *Disc*'s (May 27, 1967) version replaced "could" with "might." The *New Musical Express* (May 27, 1967) quoted the BBC as saying that the song "could be considered to have drug-taking implications." The Associated Press waited several weeks (June 9, 1967) before quoting the relevant parts of Fox's memo word-for-word.
6. In an interview with *Melody Maker* (May 27), McCartney again cites the passage about going upstairs for a smoke and notes that the ban drew further attention to the album.
7. McCartney would take a similar position later that year when he admitted to having taken LSD, blaming the press for reporting his use.
8. Anna Instone served as Head of Gramophone Programmes. Roland Fox's memo of May 24, 1967, indicates his understanding that they had contacted her the night of Friday, May 19, and that she had expressed the opinion that she was "happy we were all in step."
9. "Head of Programming" possibly refers to Robin Scott, "Controller, Light Programme"; however, Scott indicates that he was unaware of this meeting.
10. Marriott was involved in other instances of censorship. See Whitehead 1989, 43.

References

Altham, Keith. 1966. "Trogg-Men Ridicule Song Ban." *New Musical Express*, October 21, 18.

Annan, Lord. 1977. *Report of the Committee on the Future of Broadcasting*. London: Her Majesty's Stationery Office.

Apple Corps Ltd. 2000. *The Beatles Anthology*. San Francisco: Chronicle Books.

BBC. n.d. "1920." *The BBC Story*. Accessed July 2011. http://www.bbc.co.uk/historyofthebbc/resources/factsheets/1920s.pdf.

Bell, Jack. 1967. "The Greatest TV Show Ever . . . with the Beatles." *The Daily Mirror*, May 19, 22.

Briggs, Asa. 1961. *History of Broadcasting in the United Kingdom: The Birth of Broadcasting*. Oxford: Oxford University Press.

Briggs, Asa. 1965. *History of Broadcasting in the United Kingdom: The Golden Age of Wireless*. Oxford: Oxford University Press.

Cloonan, Martin. 2003. "Call that Censorship? Problems of Definition." In *Policing Pop*, edited by Martin Cloonan and Reebee Garofalo, 13–29. Philadelphia: Temple University Press.

Coleman, Ray. 1967. "The Beatles-Now! They're Back—with a Great New Album . . . Today, They Talk about Themselves in Four Special Interviews." *Disc and Music Echo*, May 27, 8–9.

Disc and Music Echo. 1967a. "Beatles 'Drugs' Song Is Banned." May 6, 16.

Disc and Music Echo. 1967b. "Beatles LP Switch, Song Ban, World TV Show." May 27, 6.

Evans, Allen. 1967. "LP in Full." In *New Musical Express* (May 20): 4.

Faithfull, Marianne. 2000. *Faithfull: An Autobiography*. New York: Cooper Square Press.

Lewisohn, Mark. 1992. *The Complete Beatles Chronology*. New York: Harmony Books.

Mann, William. 1967. "The Beatles Revive Hopes of Progress in Pop Music." *The Times*, May 29, 9.

Melody Maker. 1967. "Beatles Laugh Off BBC Ban: 'It Might Help the LP.'" May 27, 1.

Miles, Barry. 1997. *Many Years from Now*. New York: Henry Holt.

Nattiez, Jean-Jacques. 1990. *Music and Discourse: Toward a Semiology of Music*. Translated by Carolyn Abbate. Princeton, NJ: Princeton University Press.

New Musical Express. 1967. "Beatles—World TV, Drug Song Denial." May 27, 9.

Nicholl, Don. 1964. "Studio 'Error' Stayed on New Beatles Recording." *Disc*, November 28, 11.

Sheff, David. 1981. *The Playboy Interviews with John Lennon and Yoko Ono*. New York: Playboy Press.

Short, Don. 1967. "Beatles Hit Back at BBC Ban on Song." *Daily Mirror*, May 20, 3.

Took, Barry. 1981. *Laughter in the Air: An Informal History of British Radio Comedy*. London: Robson Books.

United Kingdom. 2011. Marine, &c., Broadcasting (Offences) Act 1967. Accessed July. http://www.legislation.gov.uk/ukpga/1967/41/contents/enacted.

Whitehead, Kate. 1989. *The Third Programme: A Literary History*. Oxford: Clarendon Press.

BBC Correspondence (BBC Written Archives Centre)

Fox, Roland (Assistant Head of Publicity, BBC). 1967a. "The Beatles New L.P." BBC internal memo to Radio Publicity Officer; C.P.O. Tel [Chief Publicity Officer, Television]; Tel. Pub. Org. [Television Publicity Office]; D.P.O. [Director, Publicity Office]; Television Press Officer; All Evening Press Officers; and copied to Assistant Director Sound Broadcasting [R.D. Marriott] and H.P. [Robin Scott, Controller, Light Programme], May 19.

Fox, Roland. 1967b. Memo to H.P. ["Head of Programming," Robin Scott, Controller, Light Programme], May 24.

Gillard, Frank (Director of Sound Broadcasting). 1967. "Gramophone Records." Letter to Sir Joseph Lockwood, May 25.

Marriott, R. D. (Assistant Director of Sound Broadcasting). 1967. "The Beatles: 'A Day in the Life.'" BBC internal memo to C.L.P. [Robin Scott, Controller, Light Programme], May 25.

Scott, Robin (Controller, Light Programme). 1967. "The Beatles: 'A Day in the Life.'" BBC internal memo to A.D.S.T. [R. D. Marriott, Assistant Director of Sound Broadcasting], May 22.

VI

CENSORING RACE, GENDER, AND SEXUAL ORIENTATION

CHAPTER 25

COMPOSING IN BLACK AND WHITE

Code-Switching in the Songs of Sam Lucas

SANDRA JEAN GRAHAM

> What is the Negro in the artistic conception of white America? In the brighter light, he is a simple, indolent, docile, improvident peasant; a singing, dancing, laughing, weeping child; picturesque beside his log cabin and in the snowy fields of cotton; naively charming with his banjo and his songs in the moonlight and along lazy southern rivers; a faithful, ever-smiling and genuflecting old servitor to the white folks of quality; a pathetic and pitiable figure. In a "darker" light, he is an impulsive, irrational, passionate savage, reluctantly wearing a thin coat of culture, suddenly hating the white man, but holding an innate and unescapable belief in the white man's superiority; an everlasting alien and irredeemable element in the nation; a menace to Southern civilization; a threat to Nordic race purity; a figure casting a sinister shadow across the future of the country.
>
> – James Weldon Johnson, "Double Audience Makes Road Hard for Negro Authors," *Philadelphia Tribune*, Nov. 29, 1928 (Wilson 1995, 2:410)

"THE minstrel was the first door of entrance opened to Negroes on the American stage," wrote Sam Lucas, who stepped over that threshold himself in 1871. Lucas (1840–1916) was one of the most popular black performers of the late 1870s and 1880s, renowned for his songs, comic ingenuity, pleasing tenor voice, nimble dance steps, and dramatic intensity. He became the first African American to portray the title character in *Uncle Tom's Cabin* on stage (1878) at a time when whites considered the role too difficult for uneducated blacks to read and memorize. He left minstrelsy for variety and vaudeville, where his musical comedy act was a hit on integrated bills. Some sixty years after black men began joining the ranks of blackface minstrels, however, Lucas noted that African American performers were still "compelled to confine themselves to comedy" (Lucas 1915).

Despite that, there were marked differences between the postbellum and turn-of-the-century theatrical landscapes, especially in the northeast: by 1900 blacks produced, wrote, composed, and performed in their own shows; managed their own theaters; and created characters that were rooted in the ideologies and culture of young urban African Americans, even if traces of minstrelsy remained. As the nineteenth century drew to a close, Lucas—approaching the age of sixty—had no interest in retiring or in mounting nostalgic tributes to the minstrel show's heyday, as many old-timers were doing. Instead, he joined the new generation's groundbreaking productions for the legitimate stage, with roles in Bob Cole and Billy Johnson's *A Trip to Coontown* (1898)—the first black full-length musical comedy—and Bob Cole and J. Rosamond Johnson's *Shoo-Fly Regiment* (1906) and *Red Moon* (1908). At the end of his life he reprised the role of Uncle Tom in director William Robert Daly's (white) 1914 silent movie, becoming the only African American to star in the genres of blackface minstrelsy, variety and vaudeville, turn-of-the-century black musical comedy, and film.[1]

When Lucas was working part-time as an entertainer in the early 1870s he was eager for a full-time career in minstrelsy. Several years later, having become a celebrated minstrel, he was just as eager to abandon minstrelsy for the legitimate stage. Music was a major means of achieving this transition. Black minstrels of the postbellum era managed to both comply with and subtly defy the codified stereotypes of minstrelsy, and Lucas was no exception. That tension is illuminated in the styles of songs that Lucas adopted at strategic points in his career. Based on surviving printed music, Lucas wrote (or claimed to have written) over fifty songs, and he was the most celebrated interpreter of several songs composed by others. Most of these songs fall into one of two stylistic categories:

Folk model (black code)	*Parlor song model (white code)*
Form based on the folk spiritual (verse + chorus, internal refrains); lots of textual and melodic repetition	Verse and chorus or strophic form, patterned on Euro-American sentimental, motto, and comic songs
Lyrics in dialect, pastiche quality	Lyrics in standard English; narrative
Themes relating specifically to black life (e.g., eating possum, crossing over to heaven, plantation life)	Themes implying middle- or upper-class white cultural identity (no explicit mention of race)
Modal flavor (frequent use of gapped scales), minor mode, major mode	Invariably major mode
Meter: Quadruple	Meter variable: Duple, triple, compound
Example: Lucas's "De Young Lambs Must Find de Way" (1880)	*Example*: Lucas's motto song "Things That Make a Man Feel Like a Fool" (1885)

In this chapter I analyze the ways in which Lucas's songs deploy ideologically laden codes to signify social constructions of race. His "black-coded" songs had their genesis in minstrelsy, whereas his "white-coded" songs aimed to eclipse the minstrel straits.

(A handful of songs mix codes, which I discuss later in the chapter.) When his songs are considered in the context of his life and career, it becomes clear that Lucas's choice of code when composing a song invokes a deliberate claim to social group affiliation and status, and functions as a way to manage his ambiguous position between sociocultural groups. Lucas stands as an example of the ingenuity required to transcend the restrictions imposed on black entertainers in the last quarter of the nineteenth century. That he succeeded is evident in James Weldon Johnson's testimonial upon Lucas's death in 1916: "He enjoyed the respect of both white and colored members of the profession, and the special love and esteem of those of his own race" (Wilson 1995, 1:127).

LIFE STORIES

Although the lives of white minstrels are fairly well documented (see, for example, Rice 1911), those of black minstrels are not. Not only were black performers considered unworthy of biography during their lifetimes (the exceptions being Fletcher 1954; Simond 1892; and Trotter 1878), but the attempts of later historians were often frustrated by lack of information: blacks born into slavery might not know their year of birth or even their family members, for example, and performers who lived on the road might not appear in censuses. The most generous contemporaneous source on black minstrels was the press, whose accuracy was unreliable. When Lucas began his career in minstrelsy around 1870, for example, entertainment news was littered with puff pieces—long on superlatives and short on description—fashioned by impresarios who were steeped in the sensationalist marketing tactics of P. T. Barnum (1810–1891). The development of a durable black press toward the end of the century (e.g., the *Indianapolis Freeman*, started 1884; *New York Age*, 1887; *Pittsburgh Courier*, 1910) recuperated the life stories of many early black performers. The careful reporting in these newspapers countervailed many of the stereotypes perpetrated by white periodicals, but by that time critical biographical details of many entertainers who had come of age after the Civil War were lost.

As a result, the first half of Lucas's life (until about 1880) remains less distinct than the second half. Fortunately Lucas was an inveterate storyteller and had numerous outlets for his life stories: a biographical sketch that he and his (white) publisher Charles A. White wrote for his *Sam Lucas' Songster* (n.d.; reprinted in his 1881 *Sam Lucas' "Careful Man" Songster*); an autobiographical article he wrote in 1909 ("Sam Lucas' Theatrical Career Written By Himself," published by the *New York Age* in 1916); and a lengthy 1911 interview for *The Sun* ("Long Sam Lucas"). There are valuable secondary sources that mention Lucas written by those who knew him (e.g., Simond 1892; Frohman and Marcosson 1915; Johnson 1930; also Kelly 1974, a reporter from Washington Court House, Ohio, who knew Lucas's descendants), plus modern scholarship that both adds detail and perpetuates inaccuracies (e.g., Holly 1988, a groundbreaking overview that asserts Lucas's surname as Milady, despite lack of evidence). For the most part Lucas's stories about himself seem to be true, taking into account the understandable failings of memory concerning dates and chronology. Embellished or not, the stories he told about his life are significant because they reveal how he wanted others to perceive him, and how he perceived himself. This section presents a selective biography of Lucas culled from primary sources and Lucas's own narratives, with the goal of illuminating his strategy of code-switching, a discussion of which concludes the chapter.

Youth

In most sources, Lucas said he was born in Washington Court House, Ohio, on August 7, 1842 (*Sam Lucas' Plantation Songster*; "Long Sam Lucas" 1911; Lucas 1916). In his songster biographies he says that his parents were slaves belonging to Samuel Cockerill, of Romney, Hampshire County, Virginia (now part of northeastern West Virginia), and that Cockerill was Sam's namesake. Primary sources support this story. According to federal census data from 1840, Cockerill owned forty-five slaves, and he died in late 1841 or early 1842. His will stipulated that his slaves be emancipated upon his death, and he provided $500 for their removal from Virginia so they would not be re-enslaved. If Lucas was born in 1840, as the best evidence from government documents suggests, he would have been between one and two years of age when his family moved from Virginia to a small house on East Street in Washington Court House (population 10,979; founded 1810), the county seat of Fayette County, about seventy miles northeast of Cincinnati.[2] Whether that small house was initially home to anyone other than Lucas and his mother, Malinda, is unclear, although Kelley (1974, 468) mentions brothers in passing. By about 1844 Lucas's mother had married a man named Powell and given birth to a son named Clarence; she died in 1863 (Kelley 1974, 468).

Lucas's rich Virginia accent often struck interviewers as anomalous, since he was supposedly a native Ohioan. He offered this explanation for his southern drawl: "Three or four hundred cullud people had been emancipated and had come up to Ohio befo' I was born. I grew up among 'em, so I suppose I couldn't help talkin' the way they did" ("Long Sam Lucas" 1911). In fact, even the majority of the town's original white residents came from southern states (Allen 1914).

Although Lucas's songster biography says that Sam was "placed in school where he remained for five years" (*Sam Lucas' Plantation Songster*, 3), Lucas clarified in a later interview that his education was informal: "We didn't have schools. I used to go across the fields at night to a lady that taught me my letters and I made out somehow to learn to read and write. But I never had any real education" ("Long Sam Lucas" 1911). (Even the white population in Washington Court House was schooled in homes until the first schoolhouse was built in 1846; Allen 1914, 204). This same interview gives a glimpse of Lucas's earliest musical experiences:

> "As for music and poetry, well! My father [stepfather] wouldn't have whistled a tune if it had cost him his life. But he did love music notwithstandin'. My mother used to

sing but it was only like this, you know." And swaying back and forth in good old camp meeting fashion, Sam sings:
"The Lawd—He—sent His angel down."

This story suggests that thanks to his mother, and perhaps to the surrounding community of ex-slaves, Lucas grew up intimately familiar with spirituals and camp meeting hymns--the very music he drew on for his earliest compositions.

At the conclusion of his schooling Lucas worked as a farmhand and apprenticed to the barber James Jackson (Kelley 1974, 468). Around 1859, when he was nineteen, Lucas moved about twenty miles west to Wilmington (so named because many of its residents came from North Carolina), where he participated in some amateur minstrel entertainments. The early 1860s found him in Cincinnati, where he returned to barbering and began his musical career: "It was while a 'knight of the razor' that my early taste for music developed. I first attracted attention while connected with Hamilton's celebrated Colored Quadrille Band as guitarist and caller" (Lucas 1916). Brothers Dave and Jake Hamilton had a respected ensemble (Simond 1892, 3), and Lucas might have met Dave professionally, for census data reveal that Dave too worked as a barber in the early 1860s. In March 1865 Lucas enlisted as a private in the Union Army, 5th U.S. Colored Infantry. He worked as an assistant ward master in the hospital at Fortress Monroe and was discharged six months later, shortly after the Civil War ended.

The barbershop became a proving ground for Lucas's innate musical and comedic talents. As one reporter noted, "When he got to be a barber in St. Louis [ca. 1870] it was harder for him than for anybody else to shave customers because his clientele was in a chronic state of broad grin" ("Long Sam Lucas" 1911). Lucas was a natural mime, and his excellent memory, sense of humor, and buoyant personality made him a captivating storyteller. Not only did barbering sustain him in the lean times of his early entertainment career, but it gave Lucas a sense of style. In those days, according to black minstrel Tom Fletcher (1873–1954), "colored barbers were the only colored men who were well-dressed. They were usually called dudes. Sam kept that well-dressed tradition all of his life. He always looked like he had just stepped out of a bandbox" (Fletcher 1954, 69). This impression was confirmed by James Weldon Johnson (1930, 90), who described Lucas as "well educated, cultured in his manners, and a neat dresser." Lucas was a handsome man: According to his military records he was tall and lanky (5' 11½"), with brown eyes, light brown skin, and neatly styled hair (Figure 25.1).

Minstrel Days: Voicing "Blackness"

Blackface minstrelsy codified the caricatures of African Americans depicted by James Weldon Johnson in the epigraph to this chapter. The caricatures of the 1870s and 1880s were dominated by the "brighter" light as he described it, but by the era of Jim Crow the "darker" side became more characteristic. "Nevertheless," as Johnson (1930, 93) pointed out, "[minstrel] companies did provide stage training and theatrical experience for a

FIGURE 25.1 Sam Lucas, around age thirty-eight. Detail from the sheet music to "De Day I Was Sot Free," White, Smith & Co., 1878.

(Library of Congress, Music Division).

large number of coloured men.... which, at the time, could not have been acquired from any other source." Therefore, when Lucas's patrons in his St. Louis barbershop prodded, "Why don't you go and be a minstrel yourself?" ("Long Sam Lucas" 1911), that's exactly what he did.

Lucas, a self-taught musician, "could always sing and dance, although he never had a lesson in his life," according to Tom Fletcher (1954, 69). Lucas spent the next couple of years working with black-managed troupes: Lew Johnson's Minstrels in St. Louis, which dissolved after only three weeks; then Jake Hamilton's Minstrel Company in New Orleans; followed by a summer tour in 1871 with Lew Johnson's reconstituted Plantation Minstrels. But Lucas had his eyes set on a troupe that was earning a reputation as the best in the nation: Charles Callender's Georgia Minstrels.[3] He sent Callender (white) a letter of application, and in 1873 Callender invited Lucas to join the troupe in Leavenworth, Kansas, at a salary of four dollars per week (*Sam Lucas' Plantation Songster*; "Long Sam Lucas" 1911).

Callender's company of twenty-four performers included the standard minstrel show roles: an interlocutor (master of ceremonies) and two endmen (Mr. Bones and

Mr. Tambo), supplemented by singers, dancers, sketch artists, and specialty performers. Lucas's first assignment was to sing in the troupe's quartet and fill in generally as needed. Before long, however, Callender promoted Lucas to endman at a salary of ten dollars per week. Lucas's rising popularity was rewarded again with a raise to twenty dollars in 1874, although he was never able to convince Callender to pay him more than that ("Sam Lucas" 1882). In short, in one year Lucas went from the bottom of the bill to the top, becoming one of the troupe's most popular performers ("Long Sam Lucas" 1911). He wore his success with pride, beginning with a gold-headed cane in 1873 that was succeeded in later years by gold medals, rings, and other flashy adornments. "Whatever their salaries," noted historian Robert Toll (1974, 225), "black minstrels, like their white colleagues, dressed like important people," and Lucas delighted in upholding an image of respectability and prosperity.

Lucas took a notable leave of absence during his two-year engagement with Callender to appear as endman with Henry Hart's Colored Minstrels for one season in 1874 (*New York Clipper*, June 6, 1874), which reunited him with banjoist Jake Hamilton. Hart (1839–1866), a violinist and composer, wrote a number of songs for that tour, among them "Daffney Do You Love Me" and "Carve Dat Possum," both sung by Lucas ("Henry Hart" 1879).[4] Lucas took these songs with him when he rejoined the Georgia Minstrels, and his celebrated interpretations resulted in their publication in 1875 by White, Smith & Co. and John F. Perry & Co., respectively, with Lucas credited as lyricist for "Daffney" and as composer and lyricist for "Carve Dat Possum." Lucas's claim to "Possum" set off a public feud with Hart, which was played out in the pages of the entertainment weekly *New York Clipper* (see, for example, Lucas's advertisement of September 4, 1875). Lucas eventually acknowledged Hart as the author ("Henry Hart" 1879), although Lucas's name remained on the sheet music and the song is attributed to Lucas even today.[5]

Several years earlier, the *New York Clipper* had written, "It is believed that Mr. Hart is the first colored man who has attempted musical composition in this country" ("Musical," September 3, 1870). Although Hart was by no means the first African American to compose, this speculation underscores how little the public knew of black composers and suggests that Lucas could have been eager to join Hart in adding "composer" to his growing list of accomplishments. On the other hand, Lucas may have felt entitled to claim authorship based on his idiosyncratic performance of the song. In the nineteenth century it was the performer rather than the composer who was pictured on the cover of sheet music and who "sold" the song; composers, though credited, were often unfamiliar to the purchaser.

The notion of "originality" is complicated with regard to African American popular song of this period. Raised with the norm of orally transmitted and communally created expressive culture, black composers borrowed tunes and texts freely. Musical ownership and copyright became relevant issues only as black musicians started to make a living as entertainers. For example, the tune to Hart's "Carve Dat Possum" comes from the spiritual "Go Down Moses" (the internal refrain "Carve him to the heart" replacing "Let my people go"), and Lucas likely felt he had as much right to this orally transmitted folk song as Hart did. Furthermore, the degree to which printed music reflected the composer's original musical conception is open to question, since many black composers had at best a rudimentary formal education and were self-taught musicians who could not notate their own music.

Lucas claims in one remembrance that by 1873 he had already begun "making up songs on his own account" and that he took these songs with him to Callender ("Long Sam Lucas" 1911). There is no reason to doubt this, although it wasn't until 1879 that a steady stream of sheet music by Lucas began to appear (see Appendix). Since a great many minstrels, white and black, could not read or write music (nor could many band members), vocalists taught their songs to the band by singing the tune and having the band fashion an arrangement. Lucas, however, did it differently:

> An' maybe I wasn't proud when I had my first rehearsal, the rest o' the company sitting out in the regular seats an' watchin' me. You see I'd had my music arranged with parts for the orchestra, which was something nobody in that show had ever thought o' doin'. They'd just stand up befo' the orchestra an' hum. "Teedle dee dee dee, Tumty tum ty tum." An' when I handed round my scores I could see the other members o' the company nudgin' each other an' saying "My gracious! That fellow must be something great." ("Long Sam Lucas" 1911)

From the outset of his professional career Lucas demonstrated an entrepreneurial nature, in this case spending several dollars to hire an arranger and have a score printed up. This undoubtedly facilitated publication when those songs became hits. From 1877 to 1881, sixteen of Lucas's songs were published, all of them closely related in style to "Daffney" and "Possum" (see Appendix; I discuss these in more depth later).

The Quest for Legitimacy: Toward Voicing "Whiteness"

By 1876, observed Lucas, "I had built myself up to the point where I was one of the best all-around entertainers in the business and I could pick out my own shows" (as recalled by Fletcher 1954, 69). Dissatisfied with the constraints of minstrel performance, Lucas left Callender's Georgia Minstrels and joined the Hyers Sisters Dramatic Company. Since 1867 the formally trained vocalists Anna Madah (1855–ca. 1920s) and Emma Louise (1857–1901) Hyers had been earning favorable reviews for their concerts of operatic and art song repertory, supplemented with popular ballads. They impressed audiences and reviewers not only with the range, suppleness, and power of their voices, but with their overall refinement and culture. In 1876 the sisters turned to musical theater, producing and starring in *Out of the Wilderness*, by the white playwright Joseph Bradford (1843–1886). Sam Lucas added star power to the Hyers' company, as did two Georgia Minstrels who appeared with Callender's permission: Wallace King and John W. Luca.

Out of Bondage (as the play was renamed in 1877) was a mélange of minstrel-style comedy, improvisations, spirituals and parlor songs, and dance, floating freely within a loose narrative. The first act takes place in a cabin during slavery and centers on the preparation of a possum for a meal. The second act depicts the arrival of the Union Army during the Civil War and the ensuing emancipation. The youngsters Henry (Lucas), Kaloolah (Emma Hyers), Prince (Wallace King), Narcisse (Anna Hyers), and Jim (A. C. Taylor) decide to go north and seek their fortune while the elders stay behind. The third act takes place five years later in a drawing room up north. The elders have come to visit and are amazed that the young people are educated and earning a living—by singing! The old couple does not at first recognize the northerners, who now speak in standard English and wear evening dress. The drama concludes with a "concert" in the fourth act that demonstrates "the advance in culture during five years at the North" ("Out of Bondage," *Boston Globe*, August 21, 1877), in which Sam Lucas performs a ballad and the company sings "a higher class of music" reminiscent of the Hyers sisters' classical concerts (see Southern 1994 for a facsimile of Bradford's script).

Of the twenty songs in the show, all but four were traditional spirituals (Southern 1994). The exceptions were commercial songs based on the compositional model of folk spirituals, including "Carve Dat Possum" performed by Lucas. A *Boston Globe* reviewer of an August 1877 revival wrote: "the scenery, costumes and inimitable acting of Sam Lucas and Miss Emma gave an entirely new attraction to these quaint music compositions, which have generally been heard in the concert room without these accompaniments" ("Out of Bondage," August 21). The reviewer was referencing concert troupes like the Fisk and Hampton student singers, who sang four-part a cappella arrangements of spirituals but appeared in formal dress and used no props or body movement in performance. By contrast, the Hyers' fourth-act concert, which conveyed the characters' social and economic advancement, consisted of operatic arias and parlor songs, sung in the formal attitude of groups like the Fisk Jubilee Singers. One of these became Sam Lucas's next hit: "Grandfather's Clock" (New York: C. M. Cady, 1876).

"Grandfather's Clock" is credited to the white composer Henry Clay Work (1832–1884), an abolitionist whose best songs were written during the Civil War: "Kingdom Coming" (1862), "Wake Nicodemus" (1864), "Marching through Georgia" (1865). It chronicles the story of a grandfather clock that was purchased on the day that the title character was born, then tick-tocked through the ninety years of the grandfather's life only to stop short, "never to go again, when the old man died." According to Lucas, however, Work's sole contribution to the song was the lyrics to the first verse:

> It was written when I was with the Hyers Sisters [ca. 1876] and this was how it happened. I was here in New York and went around one day to see a man named Henry C. Work, the man who wrote "Wake, Nicodemus!" Just as I was about to leave he pulled out a paper and said: "Here, Sam; here's the first verse for a song. I wrote this one but I can't seem to make anything more out of it. Maybe you can." It was the first verse of "My Grandfather's Clock." . . . I read it and took it away with me, but I didn't do anything with it for some time. Then one morning when we were out on the road I got up from the breakfast table at the hotel where we were stopping and as I turned around there in the corner stood a regular grandfather's clock just like the one in the verse Mr. Work had given me. ("Long Sam Lucas," 1911)

This supposedly inspired Lucas to devise the remaining verses, the last of which described the old man's death:

> You know that folks are superstitious when a clock strikes more than it ought to. They think it's a bad sign somebody goin' to die. So I wrote about the alarm ringin' when it had been dumb for ninety years. An' the neighbors all said jest what they would have said if they'd been the neighbors I'd known: they said death was comin' to that house. An' the clock struck twenty-four—that meant the whole round of a life, you see—and then it stopped. And the old man died....
>
> Yes, I wrote that and I wrote the music. I mean I made it up.... I took the song back to Mr. Work and he published it as his but with my picture on the front of it.... No, I never got a cent for it, except that I had a big success singin' it before anybody else did. The royalties Mr. Work received from that song amounted to thousands of dollars. ("Long Sam Lucas," 1911)

The music publisher Chauncey M. Cady (white) relayed a different version of events. As Cady recalled, Work was impoverished by the 1870s, scraping together a living by writing for periodicals in New York City. Cady ran into Work on the street one day and asked him to write some songs for Cady to publish. Work gave him three in 1876, among them "Grandfather's Clock." The song rescued Work from poverty; in 1879 Cady was paying Work $250 a month in royalties for that title alone.[6]

No matter the extent of Lucas's compositional contributions, there is no denying that it was his imaginative interpretation that popularized the song, as Cady readily admitted. Lucas appeared alone onstage, with the Hyers' vocal ensemble behind him, hidden from view by a curtain. He sang the verses solo, but when it came to the refrain the chorus sounded the "tick-tick-tick-tick" metronomically in the distance, to the audience's great surprise and delight (see for example, Schrader 1897).

Although Lucas's account of the song's composition has the ring of truth, from specific memories of its genesis to the folk belief that excessive ringing signaled impending death, it nonetheless seems unlikely (see also Cuney-Hare 1936, 46–48, who uncritically repeated Lucas's version of events). Despite his remark about royalties, Lucas never risked the kind of public feud with Work over ownership that he had had with Henry Hart over "Possum." By 1911 Lucas was an elder of the profession who had lived with the song for thirty-five years; he had come to regard it as his own. Although Lucas's image did appear on the sheet music in 1877 after he made it a hit (Figure 25.2b), the original edition published in 1876 had a typographical cover (Figure 25.2a). In addition, there is a type of word play absent from Lucas's other song lyrics—even the "white" ones. In verse 3, for example, the grandfather describes the clock in a series of puns (noted in Finson 1994, 130):

> My grandfather said that of those he could hire,
> Not a servant so faithful he found;
> For it wasted no time, and had but one desire—
> At the close of each week to be wound.
> And it kept in its place—not a frown upon its face;
> And its hands never hung by its side . . .

(a)

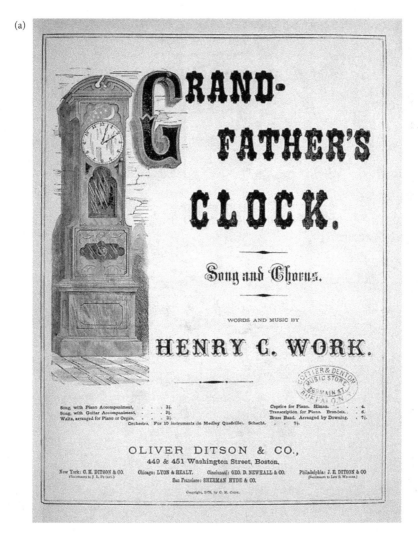

FIGURE 25.2a Original cover of "Grandfather's Clock".

(Library of Congress, Music Division).

Lucas's association with the song persisted until his death, when the James Reese Europe Orchestra played it at his funeral (*New York Age*, January 20, 1916).

Lucas stayed with the Hyers Sisters Combination until April 1878, leaving only because of personal difficulties with the sisters' father, who managed the company. The following month he made history as the first black to portray the title role in *Uncle Tom's Cabin*, in Frohman, Stoddart and Dillon Company's (white) stage production. (Whites in blackface had played the role previously.) He went on to perform Uncle Tom with other companies throughout his life, earning as much as $150 a week. Harriet Beecher Stowe, who wrote the 1852 novel on which stage adaptations were based, saw Lucas portray Uncle Tom and in a letter to the management pronounced his rendition closer to her idea of the character than that of any other actor ("Long Sam Lucas," 1911; see also

(b)

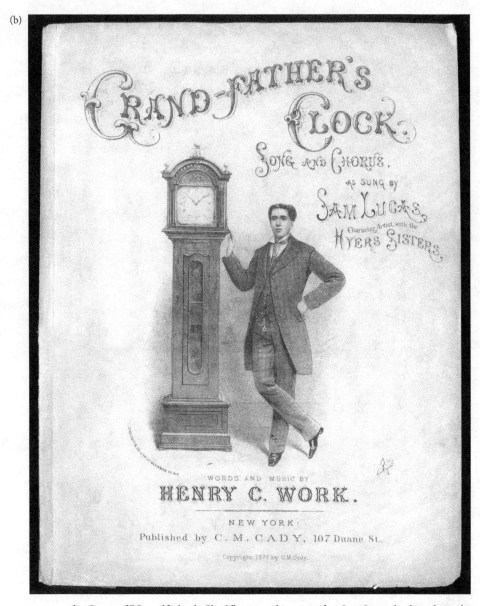

FIGURE 25.2b Cover of "Grandfather's Clock" reissued in 1877 after Sam Lucas had made it a hit (courtesy The Lilly Library, Indiana University, Sam DeVincent Collection of American Sheet Music, Bloomington, Indiana).

Reynolds 2011, 180). "The trouble with most white actors," said Lucas, "is that they play *Uncle Tom* like they would play *Hamlet* or *King Richard*":

> They make him straighten himself up an' look his marster in the eye an' say at the top of his voice 'You may kill me if you like! But I won't do this thing! No! Never!!'

Why ... slaves didn't talk that way to their marster, shoutin' defiance and proclaimin' what they wouldn't do, as if they were sayin' they were just as good or better than their marster. ("Long Sam Lucas" 1911)

Lucas eschewed histrionics in favor of quiet intensity; this restraint is poignantly evident in his final performance in the 1914 silent film.

In 1879 Pauline Elizabeth Hopkins (1859–1930) wrote a play titled *Peculiar Sam, or The Underground Railroad* as a vehicle for Lucas. It was the first play he appeared in that was penned by an African American. After the play failed to impress during an initial tour in the Midwest, Hopkins reduced its four acts to three, changed the title to *The Slave's Escape, or, The Underground Railroad*, and gave it a new premiere in Boston on December 8, 1879. The plot is essentially the same as Bradford's *Out of Bondage*, but Hopkins infuses it with more idealism and makes her characters more multidimensional. For example, the slaves do not wait for the Union army to emancipate them but rather take responsibility for their own freedom by becoming fugitives. The elders accompany the youth north instead of staying behind on the plantation. By the end of the play, safely in Canada where they have been educated, the protagonists represent a more diverse set of professions: schoolteacher, member of Congress, and the requisite singer. Although they speak in standard English, their plantation culture has not been erased, as is evident in the stage directions for the characters to "get happy" during a music and dance number. The play was ideal for Lucas, who got to disguise himself as a number of different characters, invent lots of comic business, sing specialty songs, and dance. But it was ideal in another way as well, for the plot mirrored Lucas's ambitions to be successful in a white world without losing his essential identity.

Lucas rejoined the Hyers Sisters in 1878 and toured with them through the first half of 1880, appearing in *Out of Bondage*, their own racially integrated production of *Uncle Tom's Cabin*, and a burlesque called *Urlina, the African Princess* (also known as *The Princess of Madagascar*). The last was less successful than the others because of a weak libretto, according to a *San Francisco Chronicle* review (March 31, 1879). Even though the Hyers' productions were comic, Lucas regarded them as a higher class of entertainment than minstrelsy and was proud of his leading roles; he referred to them once as "*real* shows, in which I was *starred*. The billing was 'The Hyer Sisters, *starring* Sam Lucas'" (Fletcher 1954, 69–71; emphasis in original).

After his debut as Uncle Tom, Lucas tried to replicate his success in other white dramatic productions. "He played his first theatrical engagement at the Lyceum theatre, in Chicago, in the winter of 1879, producing 'Black Diamonds,' 'Over the Hill to the Poor House,' and 'Uncle Tom'" ("Sam Lucas" 1882). In 1880 the *Omaha Bee* announced that "a new star has arisen—Sam Lucas ... who, supported by a white company, will be seen in a four-act called 'Restored'" ("Musical and Dramatic"), written for him by John P. Addams (white). In 1882 the *Boston Globe* reported that Lucas paid George Russell Jackson (white), who had written lyrics to several of Lucas's songs, $500 cash plus $100 per week royalty for the play *The Professor of Chores*. The 1883 season promised another outing in *Chores*, the production of a new comedy called *The Dude*, and plans to appear in another play by Jackson called *Mingo* (*Boston Globe*, July 1, August 19, and October 28, 1883; *Folio* 22 [July 1882]: 245). In 1888 Lucas and his then wife, Carrie Melvin Lucas, performed their musical specialties in the pier scene of *Under the Gaslight*, a revival of the 1867 melodrama by the celebrated white playwright Augustin Daly (*St. Paul* [MN] *Daily Globe*, February 27, 1888).[7] Despite repeated attempts, Lucas was unable to convert these efforts into a full-time career on the legitimate stage.

In an 1879 blurb the *Washington Post* referred to Lucas as a "retired minstrel" (September 16). His engagement with Sprague's Georgia Minstrels in 1878, apparently motivated by one of the largest salaries ever paid a black performer, was his last in the minstrel semicircle (*Folio* 17 [September 1878]: 334). Although he performed with J. H. Haverly's Minstrels in 1881 and 1882 (Haverly, white, had bought Callender's Georgia Minstrels in 1878), he sang only motto songs in the olio; he was at once a part of, and apart from, the minstrel show. In summer 1883 Callender put together a Monster Colored Minstrel Festival that combined six former troupes (including Callender's and Haverly's troupes, the Hyers sisters, and Lucas's vocal combination). When Callender took the show to San Francisco, however, Lucas was absent, "as his specialty did not answer minstrel purposes" ("July Amusements," *Boston Daily Globe*, July 1, 1883). In other words, Lucas's character songs had become too "white" for minstrelsy. After his last appearance with Haverly's troupe, Lucas told Ike Simond that "he would never black his face again." Simond, writing about ten years later, reflected, "as I have met him in nearly every city of the United States since that time I don't think he ever has" (Simond 1892, 9).

Variety, Vaudeville, and Musical Comedy: Code-switching

As a black musical comedian pursuing a stage career, Lucas had few alternatives to minstrelsy. His stage plays did not sustain him financially, and the role of Uncle Tom, although remunerative, was creatively limiting. His remaining option was variety (and later, vaudeville), which overtook minstrelsy in the 1880s as the preeminent entertainment genre in the United States. Lucas entered variety via two avenues: as an individual act in shows with predominantly white bills, and by staging concerts with his own company of vocalists.

Lucas's individual act combined comic monologues, dance, and white-coded specialty songs, which he infused with memorable characterizations and wit. He once performed his famous motto song "We Ought to Be Thankful for That" in a small town in Indiana, where a bank cashier had recently absconded with the bank funds. Lucas fashioned a verse about the calamity, putting a positive spin on the outcome: "He's skipped with the hoodle / But he's left the bank / And we ought to be thankful for that!" ("Long Sam Lucas," 1911). It delighted the audience and became the fourth verse of the song as published in 1892 (Boston: White-Smith).

Given that Lucas was a variety performer even before leaving minstrelsy, his transfer to the variety stage was seamless. Among the many notable black comedians then before the public, wrote one reporter, no one had Lucas's ambition, energy and education to aspire beyond the stereotyped, big mouthed, bone rattling, heel shuffling, mouth contortioned, conventional minstrel performances. Mr. Lucas, by his gentlemanly demeanor and many noble characteristics has endeared himself to all he has had the opportunity of becoming associated with, and he has a circle of friends which many artists enviously acknowledge. ("Sam Lucas," *Omaha Daily Bee*, February 16, 1882)

This air of cultivation was one that Lucas vigorously pursued both onstage and off. He maintained a lifestyle consistent with his dapper dress and flamboyant accoutrements, giving sumptuous dinners at his Boston residence and entertaining at the private affairs of others. In August 1884 he opened his own social club, the Recherche in New York City, where the fragrance of Havanas "wafted through . . . spacious parlors" that were "fitted up in the most exquisite style" and patronized by "many well-known businessmen" (*New York Age*, August 2, 1884). Like many in his profession he was an Elk (*Chicago Defender*, January 15, 1916), and in New York he was member of The Frogs, a fraternity devoted to advancing the interests of black arts professionals and preserving theatrical history. Lucas was also a church member as an adult, and performed benefits for black churches and benevolent associations, despite the fact that in his early minstrel days even black ministers called him the devil and warned parishioners not to attend his shows ("Long Sam Lucas" 1911).

Lucas had begun his minstrel career as a member of a quartet, and he appeared regularly over the years in small groups of males that sang spirituals, popular songs modeled on spirituals, and parlor songs. As early as 1877 he began publishing commercial songs based on the compositional model of spirituals (see Appendix), a genre I refer to as "commercial spirituals." His publication activity in this genre increased in 1879–1881, when he published at least sixteen commercial spirituals. He performed some of these in plays, but another significant outlet was the so-called sacred concert. Laws at that time prohibited theatrical productions on Sundays, but concerts of sacred music were exempt. Many performers circumvented the ban by offering concerts of secular music that were sacred in name only, or that included a token hymn or two.

In the summer of 1880 Lucas appeared in a variety of sacred concerts that featured jubilee music (meaning traditional spirituals initially, but after 1877 usually meaning commercial spirituals), with the (Pauline) Hopkins' Colored Troubadours, the Hyers sisters, and Haverly's Colored Minstrel Carnival. That fall Lucas was engaged by the Redpath (white) Bureau in Boston as a member of the Redpath Ideal Colored Company, a concert ensemble of African American musical luminaries, among them the prima donna Marie Selika (1849–1937). A sample of one of their programs follows:

Jubilee selections—Ideal quartet
"Oh, What Rapture" (Venzna)—Mme. Marie Selika
Motto songs—Mr. Sam Lucas
"The Sailor's Grave"—(A. Sullivan)—Mr. Wallace King
"Oh, Say, Through Best and Brightest" (Graham)—Mr. Sampson Williams

Jubilee selections—Mr. Sam Lucas and quartet
Beriot's seventh concerto—Mr. Joseph R. Brindis
"We Meet Again" (L. Liebe)—Mr. J. M. Waddy
Jubilee selections—Mr. Sam Lucas and quartet
"Bright Angel from Heaven" (L'Africaine)—Mme. Selika and Mr. King
"Good Night" (Flotow)—Ideal quartet

(*Boston Globe*, December 5, 1883)

Lucas performed both jubilee songs (most likely commercial spirituals) and motto songs: the former associated with black culture, the latter with white, on a bill that was part classical concert, part variety. In 1882 he joined the Slayton (white) Lyceum Bureau's jubilee organization, which conferred additional respectability on his work.

For the next several years (through 1885) Lucas's troupe gave Sunday concerts in greater Boston throughout the summer season while he worked during the week in variety or Tom shows.[8] He formed the Sam Lucas Colored Comic Opera Company and toured the West with his musical comedy *The Dude* for the 1883–1884 season (*Boston Globe*, August 19, 1883; *Columbus* [NE] *Journal*, January 16, 1884). In summer 1885 Lucas was associated with the Star Lecture Course of Redpath's Lyceum Bureau, and in October of that year he came under the management of James Bergen's (white) Star Concert Company, which organized concerts and benefits. According to the *New York Age*, about fourteen hundred people patronized the Bergen Star Concert in New Bedford, Massachusetts, on November 12 (November 21, 1885). Lucas claimed to have been "the first colored man to appear in what is now known as vaudeville as a legitimate variety performer" (Lucas 1916). Although it is impossible to substantiate that claim, he was certainly one of the first.

After some thirteen years, Lucas changed his home base from Boston to New York, where he stayed the rest of his life. In the 1890s New York theater underwent a significant evolution, from large white-managed and black-performed burlesque productions to fledgling musical comedies written, directed, performed, and produced solely by African Americans. Sam Lucas, then in his fifties, participated in almost every stage of this development.

The decade began somewhat retrospectively with Sam T. Jack's (white) Creole Burlesque Company. His *Creole Show* followed the three-part minstrel model, without the blackface and plantation references, and with beautiful women front and center (see Johnson 1930, 95). The company featured fifty beautiful women (twenty "dark-eyed Egyptian beauties" and thirty "Louisiana Creole Queens," according to advertisements); a female conversationalist (i.e., interlocutor, a role filled by Mrs. Lucas); and male endmen (whom Lucas joined in the third part). In addition to song, dance, and comedy the troupe offered a burlesque titled "Beauty of the Nile," assorted specialty acts, tableaux, and an "Amazonian March" that concluded the festivities. Although Jack is credited with the concept, Lucas claimed that the show was his idea, and that he had enlisted Jack's support when they met in Denver in 1889 (Lucas 1916). As he had his whole career, Lucas won favor through well-modulated performances that steered clear of hamming.

"The quiet humor of Mr. and Mrs. Sam Lucas is something seldom met with in the variety ranks," wrote a satisfied reviewer (*Pittsburg* [PA] *Dispatch*, May 5, 1891).

After two years (1893–1895) with his wife in Europe, Lucas returned and spent about six months with Al G. Fields's (white) extravaganza *Darkest America, or From Plantation to Palace*, an "ethnographic" minstrel show that aimed to depict plantation life over a period of some fifty years. Afterward he continued with variety and vaudeville. By then he was known as the "dean of the colored theatrical profession" or, affectionately, "Dad." In fall 1897 he was a principal in Bob Cole and Billy Johnson's *A Trip to Coontown*, "the first full-fledged, critically acknowledged black musical comedy" (Abbott and Seroff 2007, 69), and remained with the show through the 1900–1901 season. Lucas's acting won praise from white and black critics, despite the show's incoherent plot: "Sam Lucas, being an aged man in reality, plays the grand old man of Coontown with an air of perfect ease and reflects much credit on the show" (*Indianapolis Freeman*, October 20, 1900).

Subsequently, Lucas appeared as a supporting player in Ernest Hogan's musical comedy *Rufus Rastus* (1905), Bob Cole and J. Rosamond Johnson's *Shoo-Fly Regiment* (1906), and Cole and Johnson's *Red Moon* (1908), garnering unanimous praise for his performances. The following review of *The Shoo-Fly Regiment* must have given Lucas particular satisfaction: "Bob Cole and Sam Lucas, who would be funny in any color, keep the audience in a roar with their comicalities" (*Pittsburg* [PA] *Dispatch*, November 5, 1907). *The Red Moon* gave Lucas another, deeper kind of satisfaction as well, as a columnist for the *New York Age* relayed:

> "Dad," Sam Lucas, "the Grand Old Man," says he is happy to-day because of the advance of the show business to where it is at present. As far back as 1873–74 he dreamed of heading or being identified with such successful and legitimate musical comedies as "The Red Moon." The members of the Red Moon Company thank "Dad" for the compliment and are proud to be associated with an actor such as Sam Lucas. (C.A.H., "Rays from the Red Moon," *New York Age*, April 1, 1909)

The Red Moon was Lucas's last major theatrical appearance. He officially retired from the stage in 1912 due to recurring health problems (*New York Age*, October 31, 1912), though he returned to vaudeville every now and again, as he was able. In 1914 he made history a final time, in Daly's silent film of *Uncle Tom's Cabin*.

Composing in Black

When Lucas joined Callender's Georgia Minstrels in July 1873, minstrelsy was in the grip of a burgeoning musical trend: jubilee singing, which had been sparked the previous year by the arranged spirituals popularized by the Jubilee Singers of Fisk University. Minstrels began parodying the Fisk singers and their rapidly proliferating imitators, eventually giving birth to a new genre of song based on folk spirituals. These new commercial spirituals, often referred to as "jubilee songs" or "plantation songs" in the minstrel trade, indexed traditional spirituals through form and lyrical tropes (such as "gospel cars," "every day'll be Sunday by and by"). "Typically, the verse of the minstrel song was newly invented, the chorus drew upon or used a slave-song, and the piece concluded with an eight- or sixteen-measure dance chorus," writes Eileen Southern (1996, 173). This recalls George Pullen Jackson's description of folk spirituals as compositions that were "sung to pieces"—that is, composed by patching together repetitions, refrains, and choruses (Jackson 1940, 2). It stands to reason that descendants of that folk tradition who composed commercial songs would follow that same process, particularly if they lacked formal musical training. This explains the compositional style of Georgia Minstrels Jim Grace, Pete Devonear, Billy Kersands, and Sam Lucas—who learned slave songs from his mother.

The earliest published commercial spirituals credited to Lucas ("Possum," "Daffney," and "Hannah Boil Dat Cabbage Down") have secular lyrics set to a folk style of melody (see Appendix). "I'se Gwine in de Valley" broke that mold with religiously themed lyrics. Like "Carve Dat Possum," this song also borrows from "Go Down Moses," this time lyrically: "When I was down in Egypt land / I'se gwine in de valley to meet my Lord; / I heard some talk of the promised Land, / I'se gwine in de valley to meet my Lord." Whereas Lucas's previous commercial spirituals had been written for minstrel performance, "I'se Gwine in de Valley" was written for the Hyers sisters' 1877 production of *Out of the Wilderness*, where it was interspersed with genuine spirituals (*Folio* 16 [January 1877]: 9).

Lucas's commercial spirituals reflect other idiomatic aspects of traditional spirituals. For example, he frequently uses the form of a double verse of sixteen measures, alternating a solo call and an internal choral refrain, plus an eight-measure chorus; "De Young Lambs Must Find de Way" (1880), whose chorus quotes the lyrics to the traditional spiritual "Sheep, Sheep, Don't You Know the Road," models this form (Figure 25.3; see also Graham 2013 for a recording of this song). With its theme of crossing over to heaven and a message urging self-reliant action, its textual and melodic repetition, and its gapped-scale melody, this song could pass as a folk spiritual. Sometimes the folk influence is more removed: Lucas's topical song "I Am Grant and I've Traveled 'Round the World" (1881), about a black alderman, borrows from the melody of "Angel Gabriel," a skillful commercial spiritual by James E. Stewart (white), thereby becoming an imitation of an imitation of a folk spiritual.

Another idiomatic element of Lucas's commercial spirituals is asymmetrical phrase structure. In "Down By de Sunrise" (1884; recorded on Graham 2103), for example, the verse alternates a two-measure solo call with a four-measure internal refrain, resulting in a verse of twenty-four measures. The chorus features a flatted seventh scale degree in the chorus (also found in "Children, I'm Gwine to Shine"), another marker of folk style. These lyrics are minstrelized, describing the frying of ham for a sabbath celebration and, in the third verse, the comic image of "Jackariah" climbing a tree to better view his Lord but losing the opportunity when the limb breaks precipitously. Still, the lyrics index traditional spirituals through the phrases "play on the golden harp" and "glory, I'm a trav'lin."

(a)

FIGURE 25.3 Score of Lucas's "De Young Lambs Must Find de Way" (1880), a black-coded song. Unlike most commercial spirituals, the words are not comic. The refrain lyrics quote the folk spiritual "Sheep, Sheep, Don't You Know the Road".

(Library of Congress, Music Division).

"When We Meet in the Sweet By and By" (1879) exhibits the "continuous cadence," a feature that Theodore Seward found worthy of comment in his transcriptions of the Fisk Jubilee Singers (see, for instance, "Didn't My Lord Deliver Daniel" in Seward 1872).

(b)

FIGURE 25.3 Continued

The refrain runs on directly from the verse instead of pausing to cadence on the last note of the verse melody, which would be more common in Euro-American hymns. This happens again in the middle of the refrain, when the solo connects the two choral responses (Figure 25.4, last measure). Another folk element is a notated melisma in "Every Day'll Be Sunday By and By."

CODE-SWITCHING IN THE SONGS OF SAM LUCAS 579

FIGURE 25.3 Continued

FIGURE 25.3 Continued

A final parallel to folk spirituals concerns the occasional lack of a key center. Since the creation of folk spirituals was not guided by music theory, it sometimes happens that they are not centered on a keynote. As a result, a traditional spiritual might begin in one key area as understood in Western music theory and end in another (e.g., see Allen et al. 1867, nos. 26, 41, 77). One of Lucas's songs, "Gospel Cars," displays this feature, beginning in A minor and ending in D minor.

FIGURE 25.4 The chorus of Lucas's "When We Meet in the Sweet By and By" has a continuous cadence in the last measure.

(Library of Congress, Music Division).

The kinship of Lucas's "black" songs (see Appendix) to folk spirituals is unmistakable: they are all in duple meter, and they variously feature gapped scales, modulation that does not return to the home key, asymmetrical phrases, blue notes, run-on cadences, decorative melismas, call and response, internal refrains, and textual or melodic quotations that exemplify a pastiche compositional approach. Of course, Lucas's songs were required to adhere to a minstrel formula, which meant use of broad dialect, lyrics reflecting white-dictated stereotypes of black experience (such as eating possum, ham, and pigeon wing; or shouting, dancing, and other exuberant scenes from slave life), dim-witted characters, and the inclusion of dance. Nonetheless these songs were topically, stylistically, and performatively specific to real or imagined black experience.

Composing in White

Lucas's "white" compositions consist of motto, topical, and sentimental songs belonging to the cultivated parlor song tradition. Unlike his "black" songs, these display a variety of meters (duple, triple, compound). Their form might be strophic (often with a coda) or verse and refrain, but they do not contain prolonged melodic and textual repetition. Phrases are comprised of 4 + 4 measures without exception. Brief modulations to the dominant or relative minor within the verse are characteristic, as are more adventurous harmonies that introduce chromatic tones, but all songs begin and end in the same key, which is exclusively major mode. Melodies are usually heptatonic and often employ chromatic stepwise movement or chromatic neighboring tones. (In fact one song has such a large range as to be unsingable by amateurs: the waltz song "Starlight on the Sea," 1882, features a two-octave range up to high B-flat and melismas comprised of daunting arpeggios and cascading scale passages.) The lyrics are in standard English and typically avoid racially specific references.

Lucas's white-coded songs focus on universal themes of love and domesticity, or the concerns of upwardly mobile whites (see Figure 25.5, which contrasts the covers of a black-coded and a white-coded song). In this sense, compositional style indexes social groups and activities, so that music becomes a means of social differentiation. Even the comic songs, such as "Things That Make a Man Feel Like a Fool" (1885), are rooted in the white working-class humor of the British music hall as opposed to the black referential humor of the minstrel show (Figure 25.6; recorded on Graham 2013):

> Don't go to get shaved with no hair on your face,
> It will make a man feel like a fool.
> If you lose all the money you bet on a race,
> It will make a man feel like a fool.
> If you take a young lady to see a new play,
> And invite her to supper at a fashionable café,
> Put your hand in your pocket with no money to pay,
> It will make a man feel like a fool.

The comic stance of the hapless working man contrasts with the broad, malaprop-laden humor of minstrel end songs. More importantly, whereas Lucas's black-coded

(a)

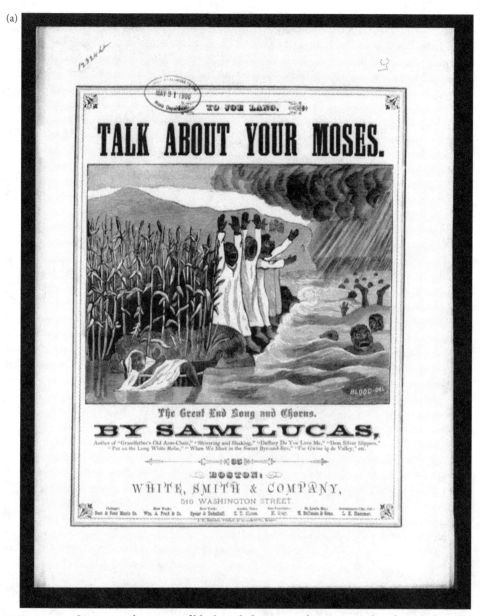

FIGURE 25.5 Images on the covers of black-coded songs tend to contrast sharply with those on the covers of white-coded songs, reinforcing them as mutually exclusive categories. "Talk about Your Moses" exemplifies a black cover, and "Don't You Hear the Baby Crying" a white cover.

(Library of Congress, Music Division).

songs kept African Americans rooted in a timeless past of plantation life where consumption of watermelon and possum, jubilees, and faith in the rewards of heaven were the order of the day, white-coded songs allowed for commentary on contemporary topics. "The Jolly Dude" (recorded on Graham 2013) reflects the latest trends in style;

(b)

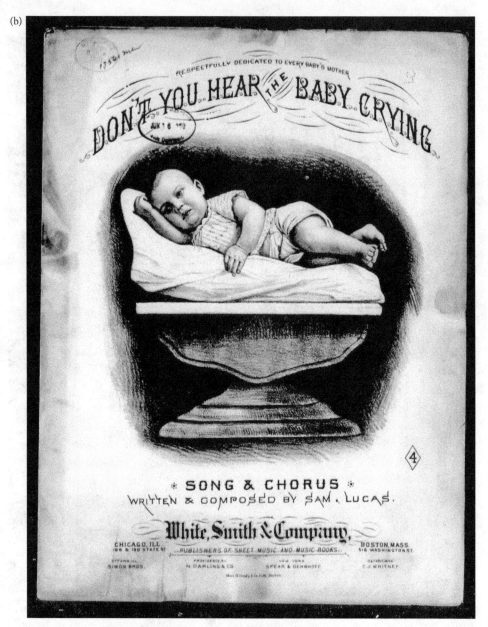

FIGURE 25.5 Continued

"That's What the Little Bird Whispered to Me" (1885) comments on the elections of 1884, better pay for laborers, and women's suffrage; and "You Know the Sort of Fellow I Mean" describes some "funny folk living in this world of ours just now-a-days."

In the pathetic vein (and in the spirit of "imitation is the sincerest form of flattery") are songs about nature and family, such as "Grandfather's Old Arm Chair," an obvious attempt to capitalize on the popularity of Work's "Grandfather's Clock" (it was published the following year). The lyricist is George Russell Jackson, who collaborated with Lucas

FIGURE 25.6 An example of one of Lucas's strophic motto songs from 1885, in compound meter.
(Library of Congress, Music Division).

on several of his white songs. (By contrast Lucas had only one credited collaborator on a jubilee song.)

In fact, Lucas seems to have borrowed as liberally in his white-coded songs as he did in his black-coded songs. One might expect that after his feud with Henry Hart over the authorship of "Carve Dat Possum," he would have given Hart wide berth, but in 1884

Lucas published "My Thoughts Are of Thee," a close imitation of Hart's 1871 song of the same name (featuring the same melody and some identical words). The words to Lucas's "Jeremiah Brown" seem to have originated with an Oswald Allan (see Graham 2013).

SHADES OF GRAY

Lucas wrote a handful of songs that mix black and white codes by setting dialect lyrics to music typical of the cultivated parlor song. The most disturbing of these is a group of "coon" songs published in the mid-1880s that exploit the image of the urban dandy. "De Coon Dat Had de Razor," for example, describes an out-of-control "coon" who

> carved poor Johny's coat tail off,
> Den cut him to de fat;
> He cut his ear clear off his head,
> Den cut his beaver hat.

This slasher story, set to a jaunty march, is an anomaly for Lucas, who disguises his identity as lyricist by crediting the words to "Prof. Wm. F. Quown" (i.e., "coon"; see Finson 1994, 227–228). "Coon's Salvation Army," also a march, lacks the brute image but still manages to insinuate that all blacks steal melons and chickens (verse 3), a theme echoed in "Dar's a Lock on de Chicken Coop Door." The latter song was dedicated to the white minstrel Harry Woodson (born John Archer Shields, 1852–1898) and was possibly a commission. Judging from the small number of these songs and his use of a pseudonym, Lucas had little interest in feeding the public's appetite for such fare.

A few of Lucas's mixed-code songs were "answer" songs to hits written by James Bland (1854–1911), Lucas's friend and colleague from his minstrel days. Lucas replied to Bland's celebrated "Dem Golden Slippers" with "Dem Silver Slippers" (1879), a black-coded song, and "Dem White Kid Slippers" (words by George Russell Jackson, 1883), a mixed-code song. He answered Bland's "De Golden Wedding" (1880) with the mixed-code "Uncle Sam's Silver Wedding" (1881).

FINDING LUCAS'S VOICE

We will never know for sure what kinds of songs Lucas would have chosen to write had he been free of the pressure to conform to the formulas of a racist entertainment model or the desire to escape its constraints. When Lucas joined Callender's in 1873, African American minstrels were still novel, and the white public wanted to revel in the music they took to be an authentic representation of plantation life. The *Memphis*

Daily Appeal (November 22, 1873) summed up the general attitude in advising that Callender

> throw into the programme ... as much as possible of negro peculiarity, as the company understand and so well interpret it, and this at the expense, if necessary, of the entire absence of any of the mere "minstrel" tricks that are so old and so stale. The members have a rich fund of originality that if drawn on more freely, will enable them to do even better things than they have given us yet, especially in song.

Lucas's black-coded songs, stemming musically from black culture but perverted thematically for white pleasure, fit that bill. His novelty songs, however, were too "white" for minstrelsy, as Charles Callender made clear when he dismissed Lucas from the 1883 Monster Colored Minstrel Festival.

By the end of his life, Lucas valued his songs modeled on the white cultivated tradition over his commercial spirituals. Lucas didn't mention his jubilee songs in interviews, preferring instead to talk about "Grandfather's Clock," "Shivering and Shaking Out in the Cold," and his motto songs. Like the characters he played in *Out of Bondage* and *The Underground Railroad*, Lucas "moved north" over the course of his career, leaving behind his black-coded songs for material that allowed him to exercise his creativity without self-inflicted wounds.

Nonetheless, Lucas's metaphorical move north probably would not have happened without his commercial spirituals. Although he performed his sentimental character song "Shivering and Shaking Out in the Cold" in 1873 (recorded on Graham 2013), it was not published until 1878, well after he had won acclaim for the black-coded "Possum" and "Daffney." The large number of jubilee songs he published around 1880 served as an important pivot in his career, as a glance at the Appendix reveals. By interpolating those songs into the Hyers sisters' race-based musicals, and presenting them in concert performances by his own jubilee troupes, Lucas was able to intermingle them with his white character songs. In so doing he linked himself at least superficially to respected jubilee artists like the Fisk and Hampton student singers, whose profits sustained black schools in the South and who were widely regarded as paragons of racial uplift. Over the course of the 1880s, the black-coded songs gradually disappeared from Lucas's repertory as the jubilee craze waned and as Lucas pursued performance opportunities that embraced "cultivated" songs.

When considered in tandem with his career trajectory, it is clear that Lucas's code-switching from black to white underscored the ideologies associated with each musical style: lower to higher class, uneducated to educated, "primitive" to "cultivated," outsider to insider. Code-switching also accompanied his emergence from ensemble member to solo star performer. Ironically, after thirty years in show business Lucas finally found the freedom to perform his "white" motto and character songs in the new century's black musical theater.

Lucas died in a home maintained by the Colored Vaudeville Benevolent Association, supported in his last years by generous friends and a meager pension of nineteen dollars per month. Even at his funeral, officiated by Lucas's cousin, the activist A.M.E. minister Reverdy C. Ransom (1861–1959), Lucas's voice was heard, through a message he had penned the year before he died:

> To my Friends, Brothers and Sisters throughout the Entire World: The curtain has gone down on me for the last time. I have prepared myself to meet Him, the Creator of all of us, and if you will prepare yourself to meet him you will meet me at Heaven's gate, because I will be there. Don't think for a moment that I leave here with regret for in comparison with the troubles of this world mine has been a golden sunshine, and now all is done. (*New York Age*, January 20, 1916)

APPENDIX: CATEGORIZATION OF LUCAS'S COMPOSITIONS

Note: Because Lucas's earliest compositions were published years after their first performance, I order them by earliest known performance and give publication date in brackets. After 1877, all dates refer to year of publication. Recordings and sheet music of songs preceded by an asterisk may be found on Graham (2013).

Year	"Black" songs	"Mixed" songs	"White" songs
1871	Carve Dat Possum [1875] Daffney Do You Love Me? (music: Henry Hart) [1875]		
1873			*Shivering and Shaking Out in the Cold[a]
1877	Hannah Boil Dat Cabbage Down[b] I'se Gwine in de Valley[c]		Grandfather's Old Arm Chair (words: Geo. Russell Jackson)
1878	*De Day I Was Sot Free!		
1879	Dem Silver Slippers Put on My Long White Robe When We Meet in the Sweet Bye and Bye		
1880	De Gospel Cars Oh, I'll Meet You Dar *Talk about Your Moses (White, Smith) *De Young Lambs Must Find de Way		

Year	"Black" songs	"Mixed" songs	"White" songs
1881	Children I'm Gwine to Shine Dem Golden Shoes *Every Day'll Be Sunday By and By (White, Smith) I Done Got Rid of My Burden Meet Me at de Sunrise in de Morning Ole Nicker Demus, "De Ruler ob de Jews" De Ole Ship ob Zion On de Banks by de Ribber Side *What Kind of Shoes You Gwine to Wear I Am Grant and I've Traveled 'round the World	Dis Darkey's Growing Old Uncle Sam's Silver Wedding	*Don't You Hear the Baby Crying? Mother's Calling Baby Home (words: Geo. Russell Jackson) You Know the Sort of Fellow I Mean
1882			Gentle Mary of the Lea *Get Up with the Lark *Jeremiah Brown; or, "That Brown, That Brown" Starlight on the Sea (waltz song) Strolling in the Park in the Moonlight (words: Geo. Russell Jackson)
1883	Ring Dem Heavenly Bells	Dem White Kid Slippers (words: Geo. Russell Jackson)	*The Jolly Dude[d] Pretty Little Kittie (lyrics only; music by Herbert Leslie, white)
1884	*Down by de Sunrise	Coon's Salvation Army Susan Brown's Wedding	My Thoughts Are of Thee
1885	Rasper's Birthday Party	De Coon Dat Had de Razor Dar's a Lock on de Chicken Coop Door	Careful Man Dear Mother Waits for Me[e] The Level-Headed Man[e] That's What the Little Bird Whispered to Me *Things That Make a Man Feel Like a Fool

(continued)

Year	"Black" songs	"Mixed" songs	"White" songs
1887	Come and Row on de Golden Stream (words: J. O'Halloran)		
1886			Good Bye, Annie Darling
1892			Thankful Every Time I'm Thinking of the Golden Past We Ought to Be Thankful for That

^aLucas and Abe Cox sang this song with Callender's Georgia Minstrels in 1873 ("The Georgia Minstrels," *Nashville Union and American*, Nov. 8, 1873). *Folio* (June 1876, 212) has a publication notice for this song, although the earliest sheet music I have located dates from 1878.

^b*Folio* (Feb. 1877, 51) advertises this latest song by Lucas. The earliest sheet music I have located dates from 1878.

^c*Folio* (Jan. 1877, 9) mentions that Lucas performed this song with the Hyers Sisters Troupe, as well as *Shivering and Shaking*. The earliest sheet music I have found dates from 1879.

^dAccording to the advertisement for this song in *Folio* (Oct. 1883, 148), it is sung by Lucas "with great success in his new play."

^eThis title was advertised on sheet music published in 1885, making the date 1885 or earlier.

Acknowledgments

Thanks to Rob Bird for sharing his assiduous research and (unfinished) dissertation on Sam Lucas with me; and the students in Paul LaRue's Research History Classes 2000–2003, Washington Senior High School, Washington Court House, for sharing their collection *Ohio's African American Civil War Heritage*, of which Ben Nichols's essay "Samuel Lucas—Actor, Composer, Member of 5th Regiment United States Volunteer Colored Infantry," was particularly helpful. I'm grateful to Tamar Barzel, John Graziano, Beth Levy, and Jean Snyder for invaluable feedback.

Notes

1. The entertainers discussed in this chapter are black unless otherwise designated.
2. Although no list of Cockerill's slaves survives, it seems certain that this Cockerill was the one who owned Lucas's parents. Lucas gave Virginia as his birthplace and 1840 as his year of birth on his earliest military documents—enlistment and muster rolls from 1865—and a 1912 pension document (National Archives, Records of U.S. Army Continental Commands, 1821–1920, Record Group 393, Compiled Military Service Record of Samuel Lucas, Volunteer Enlistment Form, Mar. 29, 1865; and National Archives, Records of the Veterans Administration, Record Group 15, Pension Application File of Samuel Lucas, Dept. of the Interior, Bureau of Pensions, Nov. 20. 1912). His death certificate states that he was seventy-five when he died in January 1916, which also supports 1840 as his birth year (State of New York, Dept. of Health of the City of New York, Bureau of Records, Standard Certificate of Death,

registered no. 1615). Kelley (1974) also states that Lucas was born on the Cockerill plantation. Lucas's family does not appear in federal census data for Washington Court House or Fayette County from 1840 to 1870. Lucas never mentioned his father; he may not have known him.
3. There were a number of black minstrel troupes using the name "Georgia Minstrels." This one had been founded in 1865 by Charles "Barney" Hicks, an African American whose light skin tone was an asset in competing with white managers. Callender took over the troupe on April 6, 1872, and immediately began enlarging it with the best black talent available (Southern 1996, 167).
4. The scores for most of the songs cited in this chapter can be viewed at "Music for the Nation," the Library of Congress's American Memory website: http://memory.loc.gov/ammem/mussmhtml/mussmhome.html.
5. "Daffney" became a hit among white minstrels as well, who followed the usual custom of applying in writing to Hart for permission to perform it and for a copy of the score.
6. "My Grandfather's Clock," *The Columbian* [Bloomsburg, PA], March 14, 1879, p. 1; Library of Congress, "Chronicling America: Historic American Newspapers," http://chroniclingamerica.loc.gov/lccn/sn83032011/1879-03-14/ed-1/seq-1/. Cady did acknowledge that Lucas was the first to sing and popularize the song.
7. I have been unable to sort out Lucas's marital history. He married in spring 1882 and introduced his "little daughter Nettie" in a Sunday concert in Boston the following year ("Sunday Concert at Park Garden," *Boston Globe*, Aug. 5, 1883), as well as at a private entertainment at his home (*New York Age*, Aug. 25, 1883). According to a letter written by a former wife named Eliza, Lucas left her with a daughter named Marie in the second year of marriage and was gone for three years, sending them only seventy-five dollars in that time (National Archives, Records of the Veterans Administration, Record Group 15, Pension Application File of Samuel Lucas, Dept. of the Interior, Bureau of Pensions, letter dated Nov. 14, 1932). Lucas married Carrie Melvin in August 1886, in Providence, Rhode Island. She played violin, cornet, mandolin, banjo, and guitar, and sang. She and Lucas performed variety and vaudeville under the name Mr. and Mrs. Sam Lucas for about twelve years. They separated in the late 1890s and divorced; she died in 1908 (Southern 1982, 251). According to Lucas's pension application, their daughter Marie was born in 1887 or 1889. I've been unable to confirm the identity of Nettie, Marie's exact date of birth, and whether Eliza was Lucas's first wife. Lucas admitted to having only one wife (Carrie) on his pension papers, and denied that he had been married previously. Marie Lucas, a trained musician, became a successful orchestra leader and performer (trombone, piano) in the early twentieth century.
8. His troupes were fluid in personnel and variable in name: for example, Sam Lucas and His Ideal Colored Jubilee Singers, the Hub Concert Company, the Hub Concert and Jubilee Company.

References

Abbott, Lynn and Doug Seroff. 2007. *Ragged but Right: Black Traveling Shows, "Coon Songs," and the Dark Pathway to Blues and Jazz*. Jackson: University Press of Mississippi.
Allen, Frank M., ed. 1914. *History of Fayette County, Ohio*. Indianapolis: B. F. Bowen & Co.
Allen, William Francis, Charles Pickard Ware, and Lucy McKim Garrison, eds. 1867. *Slave Songs of the United States*. New York: A. Simpson & Co.
Cuney-Hare, Maud. 1936. *Negro Musicians and Their Music*. Reprint. New York: Da Capo Press, 1974.
Daly, William Robert (director). 1914. *Uncle Tom's Cabin*. World Film Corporation, film. (Most of the film can be viewed online at the website "Uncle Tom's Cabin and American Culture," http://utc.iath.virginia.edu/onstage/films/1914/1914hp.html.)

Finson, Jon W. 1994. *The Voices That Are Gone: Themes in Nineteenth-Century American Popular Song.* New York: Oxford University Press.

Fletcher, Tom. 1954. *100 Years of the Negro in Show Business.* New York: Burdge & Co.

Frohman, Daniel and Isaac F. Marcosson. 1915. "The Life of Charles Frohman," parts 1 and 2. *Cosmopolitan* 59 (September and October): 444–457; 564–571.

Graham, Sandra Jean. 2013. "The Songs of Sam Lucas." Annotated recordings (Web). Murfreesboro: Center for Popular Music, http://popmusic.mtsu.edu/lucas/lucas.html.

"Henry Hart." 1879. *The Pacific Appeal,* October 25.

Holly, Ellistine Perkins. 1988. "Sam Lucas, 1840–1916: A Bibliographic Study." In *Feel the Spirit: Studies in Nineteenth-Century Afro-American Music,* edited by George R. Keck and Sherrill V. Martin, 83–103. New York: Greenwood Press.

Jackson, George Pullen. 1940. *Down-East Spirituals and Others.* New York: J. J. Augustin.

Johnson, James Weldon. 1930. *Black Manhattan.* Reprint. New York: Da Capo Press, 1991.

Kelley, B. E. 1974. *Down through the Golden Years: A Volume of Historical Events and Unusual Information . . . in My 13 Years of Column and Feature Writings in the "Record Herald," of Washington C. H., Ohio.* Washington Court House, OH: privately printed.

"Long Sam Lucas: Artist of Negro Minstrelsy." 1911. *The Sun* [New York], October 22.

Lucas, Sam. 1915. "Sam Lucas' Appreciation of the Late Billy Kersands." *New York Age,* August 5.

Lucas, Sam. 1916. "Sam Lucas' Theatrical Career Written by Himself in 1909." *New York Age,* January 13.

"Musical and Dramatic." 1880. *Omaha Daily Bee,* August 30.

Reynolds, David S. 2011. *Mightier Than the Sword:* Uncle Tom's Cabin *and the Battle for America.* New York: Norton.

Rice, Edward Le Roy. 1911. *Monarchs of Minstrelsy, from "Daddy" Rice to Date.* New York: Kenny Publishing Co.

"Sam Lucas: A Chapter from the Life of the Celebrated Comedian and Vocalist." 1882. *Omaha Daily Bee,* February 16.

Sam Lucas' "Careful Man" Songster. 1881. Chicago: White, Smith & Co.

Sam Lucas' Plantation Songster. n.d. Unsigned biographical sketch. Boston: White, Smith & Co.

Schrader, Frederick F. 1897. "My Grandfather's Clock." *The Washington Post,* June 10.

[Seward, Theodore F.] (compiler). 1872. *Jubilee Songs: As Sung by the Jubilee Singers of Fisk University.* New York: Biglow & Main.

Simond, Ike. 1892. *Old Slack's Reminiscences and Pocket History of the Colored Profession, from 1865 to 1891.* Reprint. Bowling Green, OH: Bowling Green University Popular Press, 1974.

Southern, Eileen. 1982. *Biographical Dictionary of Afro-American and African Musicians,* s.vv. "Lucas, Sam"; "Lucas, Carrie Melvin"; "Lucas, Marie." Westport, CT: Greenwood Press.

Southern, Eileen. 1994. *African American Theater.* Nineteenth-Century American Musical Theater, vol. 9. New York: Garland.

Southern, Eileen. 1996. "The Georgia Minstrels: The Early Years." In *Inside the Minstrel Mask: Readings in Nineteenth-Century Blackface Minstrelsy,* edited by Annemarie Bean, James V. Hatch, and Brooks McNamara. Hanover: University Press of New England.

Toll, Robert C. 1974. *Blacking Up: The Minstrel Show in Nineteenth-Century America.* New York: Oxford University Press.

Trotter, James M. 1878. *Music and Some Highly Musical People.* Boston: Lee & Shepard.

Wilson, Sondra Kathryn, ed. 1995. *The Selected Writings of James Weldon Johnson.* Vol. 1, *The "New York Age" Editorials (1914–1923);* and vol. 2, *Social, Political, and Literary Essays.* New York: Oxford University Press.

CHAPTER 26

EXPLORING TRANSITIONS IN POPULAR MUSIC

Censorship from Apartheid to Post-Apartheid South Africa

MICHAEL DREWETT

DURING the apartheid era (1948–1994) South Africa became increasingly notorious for its severe censorship system, affecting all published materials, from books, magazines, pamphlets, and posters to cassettes, records, and later, compact discs. There has been much written about censorship in apartheid South Africa, both on a general level and in relation to popular music in particular.[1] The purpose of this chapter is to specifically explore changes in the field of musical censorship affected by South Africa's transition to democracy. During the apartheid era, censorship took a wider variety of forms than is possible in present-day South Africa, and all of these will be considered in this chapter. The central focus, however, will be on central government mechanisms of music censorship through the former Directorate of Publications and the South African Broadcasting Corporation (SABC), as these state institutions are the official custodians of current regulation and censorship legislation. This chapter demonstrates that while formal mechanisms of censorship have been considerably relaxed since the early 1990s, regulation and censorship mechanisms applicable to popular music are still in place. Musicians undoubtedly experience a great deal of the freedom of expression for which they struggled during the apartheid years, but they cannot do so without constraint. The chapter concludes with a consideration of the current situation and the implications of present legislation for the future.

Popular Music Censorship during Apartheid

In apartheid-era South Africa the state was intricately and deeply involved with the censorship of published materials as part of a struggle to maintain its hegemony. However, formal (bureaucratic) censorship constituted only a minor strategy within its overall system of control. The state relied foremost on repressive apartheid laws and state coercion, which fostered a pervasive censorial environment within which "the distinction between artist as artist and artist as person (was) untenable" (Kunene 1986, 43). A wide range of repressive legislation in South Africa impeded performing artists' freedom of expression, not only legislation aimed specifically at restricting publications. Apartheid laws fundamentally restricted (especially black) musicians by preventing them from freely participating in core aspects of musical creation and performance. For example, musicians of different "racial groups" were prohibited from performing together, black musicians could not live and perform wherever they wanted to, and curfews made evening performances illegal.

Notwithstanding the severity of these laws, the focus of this chapter is on specific censorship mechanisms used by the state in its attempt to prohibit the expression of undesired views expressed by popular musicians. With the exception of police harassment of artists and activists, apartheid state censorship took the form of bureaucratic censorship, centered on the state's apartheid policies and closely related religious-based legitimacy. Importantly, the apartheid state, by forming strategic alliances in its multifaceted struggle to maintain its hegemony founded on capitalism, racism, and Calvinism, by necessity used censorship processes to silence *all* messages that fell outside of the dominant discourse. The moral-political framework outlined in the Publications Act (see below) integrally connected moral, religious, and political criteria so that opposition to the state's stance on any one of these areas implied an attack on the entire hegemonic project.

It is according to this expanded notion of the apartheid project that the apartheid state's chief censor, the Directorate of Publications, approached its mandate of maintaining "order in society" (Van Rooyen 1987, 3). The Directorate of Publications was linked to the Department of Home Affairs, but answerable to Parliament. Operating according to a supposed relative autonomy, the Directorate was not directly answerable to any government ministry. Decisions were carried out by a committee appointed by the Minister of Internal Affairs, and objections were referred to the Publications Appeal Board (PAB), which was also a government-appointed committee designed to set aside or confirm decisions of the Directorate. In terms of the Publications Act of 1974, any member of the public or police or any state official could submit items to be inspected by the Directorate. A committee convened by the Director of Publications would then scrutinize the item and decide whether or not it should be banned. According to the act, a publication or object, film, or public entertainment, or any part thereof would be declared undesirable if it:

1. Was indecent, obscene, or immoral;
2. Was blasphemous;
3. Ridiculed or brought into contempt any inhabitants of South Africa;
4. Was harmful to the relationship between any groups in South Africa;
5. Was threatening to the safety of the state or disturbed peace and good order;
6. Disclosed indecent, obscene, or offensive matters with reference to judicial proceedings.

Thousands of publications were declared "undesirable" and banned by the Directorate of Publications, yet only approximately 120 music albums or seven-inch singles were ever banned (*Index of Objectionable Literature* 1991). A large proportion of these recordings was banned for reasons of indecency, immorality, and blasphemy, deemed offensive to the average member of the public. There was also a concern that such recordings could cause young people (in particular) to be led away from hegemonic moral values. For example, the Directorate banned Celi Bee and the Buzzy Bunch's "Superman" because "the words of this record have obvious sexual implications and as such they are offensive and undesirable. They are designed to stimulate lust and thus are offensive to public morals" (P77/10/57). Political music such as Peter Gabriel's song "Biko," however, was banned because it was regarded as being able to "contribute to a condition that will be harmful to the security of the state" (P80/9/90). An inspection of a cross section of Directorate of Publications decisions reveals that the Directorate was particularly concerned that antiestablishment lyrics, combined with emotive strains of music, could threaten state hegemony—both in making the subversive message more enticing and in inciting listeners into forms of antiestablishment behavior. For example, Roger Lucey's song "You Only Need Say Nothing" (1979) was declared "dangerous" by the Directorate of Publications because: "A climate of grievance and protest is built up, and especially as the words are accompanied with the beat of African rhythm to enhance the impact of the words, the song can incite people toward insurgency and violence which can be dangerous to the safety of the State" (Directorate of Publications 1982). State censors literally feared the potential for music to drum up support for antiestablishment practice, whether on moral, religious, or political grounds.

This fear of musical messages was not only true of Directorate of Publications censors, but also of state censors operating according to a similar hegemonic brief at the SABC. During the apartheid era, virtually all radio stations were owned by the SABC, which gave it extensive control over what South Africans were able to listen to. The SABC made use of a rigorous system to vet all music played on any of its stations. An all-white SABC committee regularly held "record meetings" to scrutinize the lyrics of all music submitted to the SABC for airplay. This committee prohibited thousands of songs from airplay. Music was banned under categories similar to those applied by the Directorate, but in addition, songs that mixed languages were also prohibited from airplay because they disrupted the apartheid state's agenda of separate development.

When the SABC record committee decided to prohibit a piece of music from airplay, "Avoid" was written alongside the song title on the sleeve of the SABC's copy or copies of the album. On some occasions the vinyl itself was defaced: diagonal crosses were often scratched into the vinyl of condemned tracks, so that the needle would jump if a DJ were to disobey the intention behind the "Avoid" stickers on the cover. (Marre and Charlton 1985, 46; author's interview with SABC archivist Cecile Pracher 2000). By eliminating the forbidden image, the censor hoped to regulate society through a form of sonic warfare, rigidly setting up cultural boundaries.

Over time these cultural boundaries became fairly clear to record companies and recording artists wanting to secure airplay on SABC and intent on avoiding the banning of their music by the Directorate of Publications. Falling foul of state censors was almost certain to lead to the financial failure of a musical release. Financial repercussions thus strengthened the influence of state censors, whose decision-making power had a panoptical effect on anyone dependent on radio play and record sales for a living. As a consequence, record companies and even musicians themselves routinely vetted potential songs before finalizing albums for release. Controversial ideas and phrases were often altered or completely dropped. One of the most famous examples of a musician's decision to compromise in this way was Joseph Shabalala of Ladysmith Black Mambazo, who in the early 1970s declared that: "We keep the radio in mind when we compose. If something is contentious they don't play it, and then it wouldn't be known anyway" (Andersson 1981, 87).

Alongside the bureaucratic system of state censorship practiced by the Directorate of Publications and the SABC, the South African Police operated to maintain state hegemony, submitting music to the Directorate, detaining people in possession of banned music, harassing musicians, and interfering with live performances. The police thus gave censorship its teeth, in a repressive sense, not only policing censorship laws but adding the dimension of fear. The worst cases included tear-gassing venues, throwing petrol bombs into musicians' houses, and detaining musicians (for a more detailed account of South African state and record company censorship see Drewett 2003; Gilder 1983; Kerkhof 1986; Page 1986).

The state's incorporation of bureaucratic and repressive means in its attempt to silence what it perceived as the harmful effects of antiestablishment music places music within a context of hegemonic struggle. Although in a minority, a cross section of South African musicians wrote music and performed in opposition to apartheid hegemony. Some of these musicians simply expressed the way they felt about issues, including injustices in South African society, while others had greater ambitions, attempting to contribute toward social change in the form of a new democratic political dispensation. While some of these latter musicians, such as Mzwakhe Mbuli, were political activists, others, such as the members of Bayete, Sabenza, and Stimela, aligned themselves with progressive organizations, supporting their causes but not becoming active committee members. Whatever the lyrical aspirations of these musicians, Simon Frith's (1996,

164) caution that there is "no empirical evidence that song words determine or form listeners' beliefs and values" (see also Negus 1996, 192) needs to temper any claims about the potency of popular music as a catalyst of social change. The importance of popular music protest, however, was in musicians' circumvention of censorship structures in order to be heard. Each instance of counterhegemony—each song, each performance— represented the refusal of musicians to relinquish a desire for a freer society. Their contributions were important in "communicating a vision of what the world could be like to others" (Eyerman and Jamison 1998, 172). This message certainly came through, not only in the lyrical and musical messages, but also in the very act of contesting the dominant apartheid discourse.

The significance of resistance music in terms of the broader political movement, regardless of the immediate effects of its lyrics on its audience, emphasizes the strategic value of apartheid censorship in attempting to silence resistant messages. In the face of severe repression and censorship, fighting censorship became a priority for many musicians. This is clearly borne out by the way in which the South African Musicians' Alliance (SAMA) was formed around the need for musical expression. SAMA focused its efforts around the three basic freedoms central to the work of any musician: the freedom of association, the freedom of expression, and the freedom of movement. SAMA fought strongly for these freedoms by not only resisting apartheid restrictions but also trying to find ways for progressive South African musicians to play outside South Africa despite the cultural boycott. Senior members of SAMA were generally opposed to a blanket cultural boycott. The feeling was that if the apartheid government could propagate its ideas and values through popular music, so too should progressive musicians use the arena of popular music to counter those ideas with alternatives. For this reason the relaxation of political restrictions in 1990 was important to musicians, not only as South African citizens, but as musicians, in allowing them to express themselves musically.

Censorship Procedures in a Period of Transition

It certainly did not take long for the general political climate in South Africa to affect the censorship of popular music terrain. Before the end of 1992 the Directorate of Publications had officially unbanned a number of political recordings as a result of submissions from record companies—such as "Biko" (1980) by Peter Gabriel (P92/07/33), "Equal Rights" (1977) by Peter Tosh (P92/07/32), and "Jabula in Amsterdam" (1977) by Jabula (P92/07/46)—and had ceased banning political material even when it was submitted. As early as 1989 the Directorate decided not to ban the Simple Minds' "Street Fighting Years" (1989) even though the album included the overtly political songs "Biko" and "Mandela Day" (P89/6/32). Only three music albums were banned in the period between 1990 and 1994. These were Guns n' Roses' *Use Your Illusion I* and *II* (1991) on the grounds of obscenity and Diamanda Galas's *The Litanies of Satan* (1982) on religious grounds.

However, it took the SABC longer to follow. The SABC's record committee, who carried out censorship on behalf of the SABC, had always been overzealous in its banning of music from the airwaves. As Cecile Pracher, manager of the SABC record library stated:

> Many other sections in the SABC, especially the news departments, were highly politicised and often had visits from intelligence, but we did our work so efficiently no-one had to interfere, neither intelligence nor the publications board... bothered us.
>
> (Reitov 1998, 84)

Certainly, as indicated earlier, the SABC banned thousands more songs than did the Directorate of Publications. Regularly songs passed by the Directorate of Publications were banned by the SABC. This included songs from the Simple Minds' *Street Fighting Years* (1989), which the SABC banned from airplay but, as noted above, the Directorate decided not to ban. Even in November 1990 the SABC sent out a memorandum reinforcing the ban of various songs from Mzwakhe Mbuli's Change Is Pain (1986) album, despite the Directorate of Publications' decision to unban the album in June of that year (P90/06/16).

It seems that the conservative SABC Record Committee, through its mere existence, carried on censoring well into the 1990s for the sake of having a job to do. In the post-1994 election period, it became clear that it was no longer permissible for the committee to ban songs for political reasons, yet the committee only unbanned Jennifer Ferguson's political songs in May 1995. The committee continued to meet into 1996, banning songs on the basis of offensive language, sexually explicit content, and other controversial issues. Only when the workings of the committee hit news headlines in 1996 did the SABC decide to review its approach to censorship and dissolve the committee. In May 1996, national media reported on the banning of tracks by South African musicians David Kramer, Valiant Swart, and Nataniël. The songs were banned because "they 'were in bad taste' and could 'cause offence'" (Underhill 1996). One of the songs banned was David Kramer's "Bloemfontein Blues" (1996), which simply stated that Bloemfontein was the "kakkest [Afrikaans for 'shittiest'] place" he'd ever been. SABC's Govin Reddy stated that he was personally opposed to these songs being banned, but that the SABC was still caught up in old policies, which were being reformulated at the time. The result of the reformulation was a more relaxed internal censorship policy. Cecile Pracher, Manager of the SABC Record Library in 2000 stated: "There is virtually no formal censorship practiced by the SABC regarding lyrics of songs on CD. Record Librarians indicate on CDs when unacceptable words or content appear as part of the lyrics, and it is up to the announcer or DJ, to decide whether the song is to be played, or not" (personal correspondence with author 2000).

Accordingly, radio stations and individual DJs (SABC and independent) had to answer solely to the newly formed Broadcasting Complaints Commission of South Africa (BCCSA) rather than to the Censorship Committee (see below). Furthermore, during the same period the new democratic government oversaw a deregulation of the airwaves. As a result the SABC operated far fewer radio stations, and there was a concomitant growth of independent commercial and community stations. These stations are equally answerable to the BCCSA.

Censorship Processes in the Post-1994 Era

In an attempt to make a clear break from the censorship practices of the apartheid government, the new African National Congress (ANC) government sought to introduce a more democratic approach to dealing with published material including recorded popular music. The deregulation of the airwaves was an important move in that direction, as was the decision to establish the BCCSA and the introduction of the Film and Publication Board (FPB) to replace the Directorate of Publications. The underlying philosophy of all these new approaches to broadcasting and publishing was to shift control from government to the South African population more generally. The BCCSA and FPB attempted to distance themselves from the "censorship" and rather embrace "regulation" as a guiding philosophy.

The BCCSA was established as an independent body in 1993 "to promote freedom of speech, the free flow of information, and the maintenance of high standards of broadcasting in South Africa" (BCCSA 2004). Accordingly all complaints to do with broadcast material were to be directed to the Commission, rather than the individual radio stations. This procedure was an attempt at ensuring the "speedy and cost effective settlement of complaints" (BCCSA 2004) against members of the National Association of Broadcasters of South and Southern Africa (NAB). The onus was placed on individual DJs and radio stations to avoid breaking the Commission's code of conduct, according to which the electronic media shall not:

> present material which is indecent or obscene or harmful or offensive to public morals, which is offensive to religious convictions or feelings of a section of the population, which is likely to harm relations between sections of the population or is likely to prejudice the safety of the state or the public order.
>
> (BCCSA 2004)

Nor should the electronic media "without due care and sensitivity, present material which contains brutality, violence or atrocities" (BCCSA 2004). In addition, the electronic media is warned to "exercise due care and responsibility in the presentation of programmes where a large number of children are likely to be part of the audience" (BCCSA 2004). Where controversial issues are aired these need to be of "public importance," and "reasonable efforts" need to be made "to fairly present significant points of view" in the same program or similar program soon afterwards.

Given that most daytime and early evening radio and television programs could feasibly have any number of children as an audience, these regulations mean that content deemed "intended for adult audiences" must be aired during a "watershed period" between 9:00 P.M. and 5:00 A.M. (BCCSA 2004). Alternatively the broadcaster can play so-called clean versions of controversial material, as the commercial music station 5FM has chosen to do, by playing versions in which the record company has bleeped out controversial words, as is the case with Eminem songs.[2] In an overt form of censorship, record companies regularly supply broadcasters with two versions of songs with controversial lyrics: one "clean" version and one as originally released. This form of self-censorship on behalf of record companies seems to leave the censorship decision up to the broadcaster, although the record companies who do this are clearly complicit.[3]

The watershed requirements outlined in the BCCSA constitution, however, reveal how terminology used in the constitution is open to subjective interpretation and consequently relies heavily on the whims of BCCSA panel members. Take for example the statement that "with the advancement of the watershed period progressively less suitable material may be shown and it may be that a programme will be acceptable for example at 23h00 that would not be suitable at 21h00" (BCCSA 2004). What, exactly, is permissible at 9:00 P.M. but not at 11:00 P.M. and who decides this, is open to wide interpretation, a situation very reminiscent of apartheid-era censorship. Indeed, the chairperson of the BCCSA, Jacobus Van Rooyen, is the former chairman (*sic*) of the (apartheid-era) Publications Appeal Board, and he was instrumental in drawing up the constitution of the BCCSA. Van Rooyen's legal expertise and experience in the area of censorship led to an invitation, in 1993, from the National Association of Broadcasters to set up the Broadcasting Complaints Commission. In 1994, the newly elected ANC government asked Van Rooyen to draft a new Publications Act, based on the notion of harm (see below). Although he relinquished the chairpersonship of the Press Council, Van Rooyen went on to chair the Broadcasting Complaints Commission, a position he still holds (author's interview with Van Rooyen 1998).

An insightful exposition of the BCCSA ties to apartheid censorship thinking is found in the BCCSA code as cited above. Many of the items listed as material to be avoided by broadcasters are remarkably similar to definitions of "undesirable" publications as stipulated in the Publications Act Number 42 of 1974 (listed above). This fact is rather disturbing, given that this act did not meet the requirements of the new constitution, in part because it employed vague terminology and was overly regulatory (Film and Publication Board 2004). While the BCCSA inspects popular musical messages on the electronic media, music in general is evaluated (if necessary) by the FPB, which replaced the apartheid-era Directorate of Publications as a result of the Films and Publications Act, Number 65 of 1996. This act paved the way for the new board, which came into full effect in June 1998 (FPB 2004).

Both the BCCSA and FPB make decisions on publications only on receipt of complaints, and both base their decisions on Section 16 of the Constitution of South Africa, according to which the right to the freedom of speech is upheld but does not extend to propaganda for war, incitement of imminent violence, or the advocacy of hate speech based on race, ethnicity, gender, or religion, "and that constitutes incitement to cause harm" (Constitution of South Africa).

The FPB insists that it simply classifies material and does not act as a censor. In other words, if any material (other than child pornography, which is covered by Section 27 of the Films and Publications Act) is seen to intrude on other freedoms, it will not be banned but will be age restricted. According to the FPB (2004):

> the difference between classification and censorship is not simply a matter of semantics. Censorship, in essence, involves the control of what others may see or read. Classification, on the other hand, involves the regulation of films and publications by means of the imposition of age restrictions and the provision of information on the basis of which choices about what to see or read may be made.

This would suggest that in all instances other than child pornography adults should be able to listen to popular music and view the sleeve in which it is packaged. The FPB tried to capture this new approach to publications through the adoption of the slogan "We inform, you choose" (FPB 2004). However, this slogan ignores the fact that the FPB does have the ability to impose an XX rating on certain publications (hate speech based on religion) and thus, even according to its own definition, practices censorship. Furthermore, while adults are allowed freedom of choice, the same does not apply to those younger than eighteen, in particular teenagers under the age of eighteen who can be denied the ability to purchase age-restricted music.

Importantly, "bona fide literature, drama, documentaries, scientific materials, and except in the case of child pornography, art, are exempted from the application of the Act" (FPB 2004). Only in the cases where children are concerned is the board able to apply age restrictions to "disturbing or harmful materials" relating to "issues of sexuality, violence and religion" (FPB 2004). How exactly "harm" is defined and how it is caused are not clearly stipulated in the act, allowing for a strong element of subjectivity to enter the classification process of films and publications.

Despite the scope for the FPB to restrict the sale of materials on the basis of harmful content, the board did not restrict the sale of any music in the initial euphoric atmosphere of South Africa's new democracy. During these early years of democracy most political music tended to be celebratory with a few musicians raising questions about lack of government delivery, corruption, and broader social issues such as sexual inequality, HIV/AIDS, and imperialism. While not having any significant bearing on public opinion, such musical endeavors reaffirmed the new democracy's commitment to freedom of expression. However, the release of Mbongeni Ngema's song "AmaNdiya" in March 2002 led to the first instance in which the FPB restricted a music item.

"Ama-Ndiya"—Mbongeni Ngema

Ngema's "Ama-Ndiya" (2002), co-written with Hugh Masakela, confronts the issue of relations between Africans and Indians in Durban. The song features Ngema singing (in Zulu) to the backing of the Committed Artists female singers. He calls on leading public figures to tackle the issue of the ill treatment and exploitation of Africans by Indians in the Durban region. It includes lines such as "We struggle so much here in Durban, because Indians have dispossessed us" and "Black people buy from Indians yet Indians do not like to build schools for black children, they don't even like the children of black people." The song opens with Ngema providing an introductory voice-over stating, "This song represents the way many African people feel about the behavior of the Indian people in this country. It is intended to begin a constructive discussion that will lead to a true reconciliation between Indians and Africans" (Ngema 2002). From the outset Ngema has claimed that the song in part reflects his views about unacceptable behavior practiced by Indians, but not all the lyrics represent his own views. Some of the sentiments are those of ordinary Africans "at taxi ranks, soccer matches, shebeens and many other places" (Ngema, quoted in "Ngema song" 2002).

In responding to a complaint from the South African Human Rights Commission (SAHRC), the BCCSA banned the song from South African airwaves. The BCCSA argued that the song promoted hate speech against Indians and constituted incitement to harm (BCCSA 2002). In reaching this decision, Chairperson Van Rooyen claimed that the commission took cognizance of the fact that the song was a form of art and as such "should be afforded the protection which section 16 (1) grants to the right to artistic creativity." He argued, however, that the BSSCA needed to "determine where art ends and hate speech commences" (BCCSA Case Number 2002/31, 7). For the BCCSA, the striking nature of the melody and singing simply heightened the effect of the hate speech in the song, and certainly did not give cause for the song to be provided the sanctity an art form merits according to the Constitution.

The FPB took a similar view, deciding that the song advocated hate speech. As with the BCCSA, the FPB interpreted Ngema's call for Africans to confront Indians about their economic practices as a call to confront and thereby harm Indians. Given that the FPB "unfortunately" (as they worded it, FPB 2002) did not have the right to completely ban a song based on racial hate speech, they imposed the strongest measure possible, prohibiting the sale of the album to persons under the age of eighteen years. However, had the option been available, the board would have opted for an XX rating whereby the song would have been banned from distribution in South Africa. The FPB justified their decision to restrict the sale of the album on the basis that "the song, judged as a whole, advocated hate speech based on race and constitutes incitement to cause harm" (FPB 2002).

After "Ama-Ndiya" was banned from airplay and sales of the album were restricted to those who were eighteen and older, Ngema (author's interview 2004) commented,

> It was an eye-opener to a lot of people that that song was banned. Because people thought censorship was gone. It has made people very wary of the fact that it now means that they cannot criticize this government. The very government that was fighting for the liberation of the press—free press, free expression, free everything. Can this be the government, can it really be the government that will condone censorship? I don't know why the censorship is still there. And I think it should be dismantled.

The censorship of Ngema's song indeed raised a few eyebrows. It was the first song to suffer official censorship in post-1994 South Africa, in a country proud of its liberal constitution and concomitant freedom of expression. Indeed, various critics thought that the BCCSA and FPB based their decisions on simplistic understanding of cause and effect, where it is simply taken for granted that listening to Ngema's song could lead Africans to physically confront and harm Indians. Ngema (author's interview 2004) rightly ridiculed this view, saying,

> It's a stupid argument because what that means is that Zulu people are very stupid people. They can just listen to a song and pick up arms and go and kill. And I think it's an insult to the Zulu race [sic]. And in fact if that was the case—since the song was banned from the airwaves people have been buying it to this day—why haven't they picked up arms?

Neither the BCCSA nor the FPB supported their claims linking music lyrics to harm with argument or evidence. They seem to be satisfied that hate speech in itself is harmful, and on that basis censored or regulated the song, depending on how one defines censorship.

Censorship and Hate Speech

The problem confronting official regulators (and potential censors) such as the BCCSA and FPB is that absolute freedoms cannot exist for the simple reason that we cannot all have the right to do whatever we want to do without impinging on others' corresponding freedoms to do what they want to do and their rights to be protected from harm. Jim McGuigan (1992, 202) notes that many forms of restriction on freedom of expression exist in order to protect certain rights of individuals, organizations, and states (the same can be said, to varying degrees, of freedom of association and movement). He argues that "absolute freedom of expression is a principle of intolerance," given that the notion of free speech "is used to justify all manner of oppressive discourse, most notably sexist and racist discourses" (1996, 157).

Free expression, however, does not necessarily entail the acceptance of all discourses that emerge within the context of that freedom. Such a position rejects McGuigan's argument that supporting absolute freedom of speech justifies oppressive discourse.

On the contrary, freedom of speech allows oppressive discourses to be heard but also allows for counterstatements and arguments to be made, in an ongoing contest in which critical discourse is encouraged. This position is supported by Gary Baines (2006, 67) who, in discussing the "Ama-Ndiya" case, argues,

> hate speech is not the real problem. The conditions that create a receptive audience for hate speech—ignorance, inequity, and fear—constitute the problem. To address these is much more difficult than attempting to silence the voices that remind us, by example, that problems exist... Banning inhibits the exchange of ideas and information which is the lifeblood of democracy. Thus hate speech must be recognized as a legitimate and valuable form of symbolic expression in society—not because it is true or sound, but because it identifies discontent, injustice, inequities. To deny voices, even those voices that are vile, disgusting, and hateful, is itself an act of contempt.

The dangers of banning the message should not be underestimated. Censorship, Christopher Merrett (1994, 213) argues, "can be a form of protection, allowing fascist ideas to fester in the gloom of the banned book cupboard rather than being destroyed in the fresh air of intellectual debate." Clearly, this is not an easy stance to assume. Unlike censorship, which involves an absence of critical thinking on the part of society, intellectual debate requires the public to actively participate in governance, considering a wide variety of ideas and deciding how best to justify their own reactions to these. Given South Africa's dark totalitarian past, this would appear to be preferable to a state-supported form of "defensible" censorship whereby the state censors get to defend censorship according to their own agenda.

More recently, censorship battles in South Africa have shifted from censorship boards to courts of law. In March 2010, a Johannesburg court declared it illegal to sing the anti-apartheid song "Ayesaba amagwala [The cowards are afraid]" on the grounds that it incited hatred toward white South Africans (Schmidt et al. 2010, 181). The song includes the controversial line "Dubula Ibhunu" which means "Kill the Farmer" but more widely understood as "kill the white Afrikaaner." However, these instances of silencing music have related to singing songs in public, and not to recordings of the songs. As such, the court rulings relate to singing as an act of speech. In this case, the songs are regarded as hate speech and have been silenced as speech acts. It is not clear what would happen were these songs to be recorded and released in the marketplace. Given the ruling on Ngema's "Ama-Ndiya" though, it would seem that the BCCSA and FPB would act similarly, banning these songs from airplay and restricting the sale of the music in retail outlets. While censorship is no longer a common occurrence in South Africa, the mechanisms do exist to prevent people from freely singing and listening to whatever they want to.

Conclusion

As a result of the demise of the apartheid government and the acceptance of a democratic constitution, South Africa has clearly progressed from an extremely censorial and controlled musical terrain to one that allows far greater freedom. Certainly, South Africa's Truth and Reconciliation process of the mid-to-late 1990s reflects the need for openness and honesty as South Africans attempt to move toward social equality. Growth cannot happen in a context of repression. Even songs such as Ngema's allow negative views to be aired, and subsequently to be debated and discussed. Out of such critical reflection South Africans can work toward better relations, if they are to avoid moving toward a totalitarian system where certain views are simply not permitted. As much as South Africa has embraced a democratic system, the mere existence of censorship boards and mechanisms of censorship means that when certain people hear music that offends them, rather than dealing with the issues raised by the musicians, they simply appeal to the censors to repress the music, almost as if wishing it away, without confronting the underlying issues dealt with by the lyrics. The Ngema incident and more recent ones suggest that there is still a way to go before censorship processes lose their legitimacy (based on false arguments about cause and effect as they are) so that South Africans can constructively deal with problems raised in the lyrics of popular music.

Notes

1. See, for example, Andersson 1981; Brink 1985; Byerly 1996; Coetzee 1996; Coplan 2000; Denselow 1989, 186–202; Drewett 2003, 2004a, 2004b, 2005, 2006, 2008; Drewett and Clegg 2006; Gilder 1983; Gordimer 1988, 1990; Hepple 1960; Hope 1987; Horn 1979; Kerkhof 1986, 1989; Korpe and Reitov 2010; Marcus 1984, 1987; Marre and Charlton 1985; Merrett 1982, 1994; Page 1986; Reitov 1998; Stewart 1990, 1986; Street 1986, 19–23; Tlali 1984; Van Rooyen 1987.
2. See for example Eminem's "Business" (2002). See BCCSA Case No: 2003/49 for discussion of this song's airplay status.
3. On occasion the pressure to edit material to meet broadcasters' format and lyrical requirements comes in the form of direct requests from the broadcasters. For example in the late 1990s Radio Highveld refused to play the Egyptian Nursery's "God's Window" (1998) because it included a section of French rap in the middle. The station had a policy of not playing rap. They approached Benjy Mudie (author's interview 1998) of the band's record company and asked him to supply an alternate version of the song without the rap. The band refused to comply.

References

Andersson, Muff. 1981. *Music in the Mix: The Story of South African Popular Music*. Johannesburg: Ravan Press.
Baines, Gary. 2006. "Racist Hate Speech in South Africa's Fragile Democracy: The Case of Ngema's 'AmaNdiya.'" In *Popular Music Censorship in Africa*, edited by Michael Drewett and Martin Cloonan, 53–70. London: Ashgate.
Brink, Andre. 1985. *Literatuur in die Strydperk*. Cape Town: Human and Rousseau.
Broadcasting Complaints Commission of South Africa (BCCSA). 2002. Case Number 2002/31 SABC-"Ngema Song." Accessed November 3, 2014, http://bccsa.co.za/index.php?option=com_content&view=article&id=355:case-no-31-2002-ukhozi-fm-hate-speech&catid=23&Itemid=2.

Broadcasting Complaints Commission of South Africa (BCCSA). 2003. Case Number 2003/49 5fm (SABC)—Eminem Song—Religious. Accessed November 3, 2014, http://bccsa.co.za/index.php?option=com_content&view=article&id=317:case-no-49-2003-5fm-hate-speech&catid=23&Itemid=2.

Broadcasting Complaints Commission of South Africa (BCCSA). 2004. BCCSA Constitution. Accessed November 3, 2014, http://bccsa.co.za/index.php?option=com_content&view=article&id=12&Itemid=26.

Byerly, Ingrid. 1996. "The Music Indaba: Music as Mirror, Mediator and Prophet in the South African Transition from Apartheid to Democracy." PhD dissertation, Duke University.

Coetzee, J.M. 1996. *Giving Offense: Essays on Censorship*. Chicago: University of Chicago Press.

Coplan, David. 2000. "Popular Music in South Africa." In *The Garland Handbook of African Music*, edited by R. Stone, 333–354. New York: Garland Publishing.

Denselow, Robin. 1989. *When the Music's Over: The Story of Political Pop*. London: Faber and Faber.

Directorate of Publications. 1982. P82/9/115. File on Roger Lucey's *The Road is Much Longer*.

Drewett, Michael. 2003. "Music in the Struggle to End Apartheid: South Africa." In *Policing Pop*, edited by M. Cloonan and R. Garofalo, 153–165. Philadelphia: Temple University Press.

Drewett, Michael. 2004a. "Aesopian Strategies of Textual Resistance in the Struggle to Overcome the Censorship of Popular Music in Apartheid South Africa." In *Censorship and Cultural Regulation in the Modern Age*, edited by B. Müller, 189–207. Amsterdam: Rodopi Press.

Drewett, Michael. 2004b. "Remembering Subversion." In *Shoot the Singer!*, edited by M. Korpe, 88–93. London: Zed Books.

Drewett, Michael. 2005. "'Stop this Filth': The Censorship of Roger Lucey's Music in Apartheid South Africa." In *SAMUS: South African Music Studies* 25: 53–70.

Drewett, Michael. 2006. "The Cultural Boycott Against South Africa: A Case of Defensible Censorship?" In *Popular Music Censorship in Africa*, edited by Michael Drewett and Martin Cloonan, 23–38. London: Ashgate.

Drewett, Michael. 2008. "Packaging Desires: Album Covers and the Presentation of Apartheid." In *Composing Apartheid*, edited by G. Olwage, 115–135. Johannesburg: Wits University Press.

Drewett, Michael, and Clegg, Johnny. 2006. "Why Don't You Sing About the Leaves and the Dreams? Reflecting on Popular Music Censorship in Apartheid South Africa." In *Popular Music Censorship in Africa*, edited by Michael Drewett and Martin Cloonan, 127–136. London: Ashgate.

Eyerman, Ron, and Jamison, Andrew. 1998. *Music and Social Movements*. Cambridge: Cambridge University Press.

Film and Publication Board (FPB). 2002. "Report to the Deputy Minister: Classification of the Mbongeni Ngema song 'Ama-ndiya' by the Film and Publication Board.". Accessed July 15, 2004, http://www.fpb.gov.za/documents/history.htm.

Film and Publication Board (FPB) 2004. "From Censorship to Classification." Accessed July 15, 2004, http://www.fpb.gov.za/documents/history.htm.

Frith, Simon. 1996. *Performing Rites: Evaluating Popular Music*. Oxford: Oxford University Press.

Gilder, Barry. 1983. "Finding New Ways to Bypass Censorship." *Index on Censorship* 1: 18–22.

Gordimer, Nadine. 1988. "Censorship and the Artist." *Staffrider* 7, no. 2:10–16.

Gordimer, Nadine. 1990. "Censorship and its Aftermath." *Index on Censorship* 7:14–16.

Hepple, Alex. 1960. *Censorship and Press Control in South Africa*. Johannesburg: Alex Hepple.

Hope, Christopher. 1987. "Notes From the Scaffold: South African Censorship Then and Now." *Index on Censorship* 10: 15–17.

Horn, Peter. 1979. "The Right to Censor." In *Dead in One's Lifetime—Art in Apartheid Society*, 44–61. Cape Town: NUSAS.

Index of Objectionable Literature 1991 Update. 1991. Pretoria: Jacobsens.

Kerkhof, Ian. 1986. "Music and Censorship in South Africa." *Rixaka: Cultural Journal of the African National Congress* 2: 27–31.

Kerkhof, Ian. 1989. "Music in the Revolution." *Keskidee: A Journal of Black Musical Traditions* 2: 10–21.

Korpe, Marie, and Reitov, Ole. 2010. "Banned: A Guide to Music Censorship. *Index on Censorship* 39, no. 3: 34–45.

Kunene, Daniel. 1986. "Holding the Lid Down: Censorship and the Writer in South Africa." In *South African Literature: Liberation and the Art of Writing*, edited by W. Schäfer and R. Kriger, 41–59. Bad Boll, Germany: Evangelische Akademie.

Marcus, Gilbert. 1984. "Blacks Treated More Severely." *Index on Censorship* 6:14–21.

Marcus, Gilbert. 1987. "The Gagging Writs." *Reality* 19, no. 3: 8–10.

Marre, Jeremy, and Charlton, Hannah. 1985. "Rhythm of Resistance: The Black Music of South Africa." In *Beats of the Heart: Popular Music of the World*, 34–52. London: Pluto Press.

McGuigan, Jim. 1992. *Cultural Populism*. London: Routledge.

McGuigan, Jim. 1996. *Culture and the Public Sphere*. London: Routledge.

Merrett, Christopher. 1982. "Political Censorship in South Africa: Aims and Consequences." *Reality* 14, no. 2: 3–6.

Merrett, Christopher. 1994. *A Culture of Censorship: Secrecy and Intellectual Repression in South Africa*. Cape Town: David Phillip.

Negus, Keith. 1996. *Popular Music in Theory*. Cambridge: Polity Press.

Page, Phillip. 1986. "Forbidden Music: Songs Against Apartheid." *Ear Magazine of New Music* 10, no. 4 (May–June): 4, 5, 27.

Reitov, Ole. 1998. "Only Doing My Duty: Interview with Cecile Pracher." *Index on Censorship* 27, no 6: 83–85.

Schmidt, Natasha, Ángel García, Ed Gillett, David Paton, Pete Ward, and Kathie Wu. 2010. "Index." *Index on Censorship* 39, no. 3: 176–182.

South African Human Rights Commission. 2002. "Comment on Mbongeni Negam's 'Amandiya.'" Accessed July 15, 2004, http://www/sahrc.org.za/mbongeni_ngeams_amandiya.htm.

Stewart, Peter. 1986. "On the Cultural Boycott." *Reality* 18, no. 6: 3–5.

Stewart, Peter. 1990. "Beyond the Mythology of Censorship in South Africa." *Reality* 22, no. 4: 16–20.

Street, John. 1986. *Rebel Rock: The Politics of Popular Music*. Oxford: Basil Blackwell.

Tlali, Miriam. 1984. "Remove the Chains." *Index on Censorship* 6: 22–26.

Underhill, Glynnis. 1996. "David Livid, Radio Boss Red-Faced at Song Ban." *Argus* 11, no. 12 (May).

Van Rooyen, Jacobus. 1987. *Censorship in South Africa*. Cape Town: Juta.

Government Acts

Constitution of the Republic of South Africa, Act 108 of 1996.

Film and Publication, Act 65 of 1996.

Publications Act, 42 of 1974.

Directorate of Publication Files

P77/10/57 File on "Superman"—Celi Bee and the Buzzy Bunch.
P80/9/90 File on "Biko"—Peter Gabriel.
P89/6/32 File on *Street Fighting Years*—Simple Minds.
P90/06/16 File on *"Change is Pain"*—Mzwakhe Mbuli.
P92/07/32 File on *"Equal Rights"*—Peter Tosh.
P92/07/33 File on "Biko"—Peter Gabriel.
P92/07/46 File on *"Jabula in Amsterdam"*—Jabula.

Author's interviews

Mudie, Benjy. Sandown, Johannesburg, September 10, 1998.
Ngema, Mbongeni. Pretoria, May 14, 2004.
Pracher, Cecile. Personal correspondence, March 17, 2000.
Pracher, Cecile. Johannesburg, September 19, 2000.
Van Rooyen, Jacobus. Pretoria, September 11, 1998.

Discography

Bee, Celi & the Buzzy Bunch. 1977. "Superman." RCA.
Egyptian Nursery. 1998. *New Anthem*. Fresh Music.
Eminem. 2002. *The Eminem Show*. Aftermath Records.
Gabriel, Peter. 1980. "Biko." Charisma Records.
Galas, Diamanda. 1982. *The Litanies of Satan*. Mute-Restless.
Guns n' Roses. 1991. *Use Your Illusion 1*. Geffen Records.
Guns n' Roses. 1991. *Use Your Illusion 2*. Geffen Records.
Jabula. 1977. *Jabula in Amsterdam*. De Anti-apartheids Beweging.
Kramer, David. 1996. *Klassic Kramer*. Blik Music.
Mbuli, Mzwakhe. 1986. *Change is Pain*. Shifty Records.
Ngema, Mbongeni. 2002. *Jive Madlokovu!!!* Universal Music.
Simple Minds. 1989. *The Street Fighting Years*. Virgin Records.
Tosh, Peter. 1977. *Equal Rights*. CBS.

CHAPTER 27

RAP MUSIC AND RAP AUDIENCES REVISITED

How Race Matters in the Perception of Rap Music

TRAVIS L. DIXON

RESEARCH on rap music has turned from a lack of attention to an alarmist examination of the genre. In the 1980s rap music was seldom studied by scholars in the academic community (Dixon and Linz 1997). Today rap has increasingly been considered a troubling form of musical expression related to a number of negative psychological outcomes (Barongan and Hall 1995; Johnson et al. 1995a, 1995b; Johnson et al. 2000; McLeod et al. 1997). These perceptions have often led to censorship efforts (Dixon and Linz 1997). Although it is clear that rap and other forms of music do periodically contain misogynist and violent themes (Jones 1997; Smith 2005), research has not thoroughly addressed how rap music audiences respond to these themes. Furthermore, rap research has not fully identified which factors may moderate or mediate the negative effects associated with exposure to the music.

In the current paper, I first detail how both lay critics and social scientists have suggested that censorship might be the best course of action for the music. Afterwards, I report on a program of research designed to examine the themes contained in rap music and investigate the effects of exposure to rap with special attention given to the nature and composition of rap music audiences. Few studies have investigated whether rap musicians and fans can exercise adequate control over the rap product that is distributed, and this program of research was designed to do just that. Before I describe this program of research, however, I offer a review of some of the early studies of rap. Afterwards, I discuss some of the more recent rap investigations that have been dominated by research on negative effects and then describe how concerns about the genre have led to censorship efforts.

A Widening Interest in Rap

Although rap music was born in the 1970s, most critics and scholars acknowledge that it became a significant musical force in the 1980s (Powell 1991; Rose 1991). Rap was almost immediately criticized for its "street" message and origins (Binder 1993). At the same time it was hailed for its commercial success (Stephens 1991). Early on, most media scholars simply ignored rap. Quantitative scholars specializing in media effects were especially quiet during this era, even though many such scholars had claimed in other contexts that the examination of music as mass communication was important (Dixon and Linz 1997).

Most communication scholars did not change course and begin to study rap music until the early 1990s. Much of this new research focused on the cultural roots of rap music (Binder 1993; Kuwahara 1992; Pressley 1992; Rose 1991, 1994). These scholars made two interesting observations. First, they claimed that rap music was a form of cultural expression. Second, they stated that understanding rap was rooted in understanding the cultural underpinnings of the music.

Blaming the Messenger: Research on Misogynist and Violent Rap Themes

Starting sometime around the mid-1990s, media effects scholars and critics ceased to be primarily concerned with the cultural aspects of rap. Instead, they turned their attention to the impact of rap music on audience members. This scholarship focused on misogynist and violent lyrics in rap.

Effects of Exposure to Violent Rap Lyrics

There is a long history of research on the effects of violent television on behavior. Media effects researchers have documented that violent television has a number of psychological effects on viewers. These include desensitization to actual acts of violence, learning aggressive behaviors, and increased fear of victimization (Harris 1999; Huessman and Miller 1994). These media effects scholars quickly applied this theorizing to rap music. After all, rap music had been accused by critics for some time of containing excessively violent themes (Lynxwiler and Gay 2000; Armstrong 1993).

These studies revealed several interesting trends. The strongest findings suggested that violent themes in rap music can prime other violent thoughts (Harris 1999; Hansen 1995). Johnson et al. (1995a, 1995b) tested whether such a priming process would lead rap music to encourage black teens to engage in violent behavior and drug selling. They found that teens exposed to violent rap music expressed greater acceptance of the use of violence and reported that they would likely engage in violence in the future. In addition, black teens exposed to rap videos were more likely to support the illegal acquisition of wealth.

Other studies have suggested that rap music has become so associated with violence that exposure to rap alone conjures images of aggressive behavior. For example, Ballard et al. (1999) found that antisocial rap lyrics were less likely to inspire prosocial behaviors than antisocial country or pop lyrics. They concluded that the media might link rap fans with a lack of adaptive behavior. Another study by Rubin et al. (2001) found that rap listeners showed more aggression and distrust of authority than non-rap listeners.

Rap music and Misogyny

In addition to the contention that violent themes in rap increase aggressive behavior and attitudes, many effects scholars and critics have also claimed that rap music perpetuates misogyny. In fact many scholars note that some rap lyrics attempt to objectify, devalue, or subjugate African American women through insulting and subordinating words such as "bitch" and "ho" (Henderson 1996; Pinn 1996; Watts 1997; Powell 1991; Rose 1994). Some of these scholars have suggested that black women have historically been convenient targets on which black men release their aggression (Pinn 1996, 1999). Content analyses have provided some support for the notion that much of the most popular rap music appears to contain objectionable lyrics (Ballard et al. 1999).

Rap researchers have gone beyond identifying the misogynist themes and have investigated whether this type of music may lead to a number of negative psychological outcomes. For example, Gan et al. (1997) found that exposure to rap laden with sexual imagery fostered distinctly unfavorable evaluations of black women. Barongan and Hall (1995) discovered that misogynous music facilitates sexually aggressive behavior. In addition, a study by Johnson et al. (1995a, 1995b) revealed that women who viewed rap videos of women in sexually subordinate roles showed greater acceptance of violence than those who were not exposed to such videos. A study by Wester et al. (1997) also uncovered that even men unfamiliar with rap music culture who are briefly exposed to sexually violent rap music become more likely to believe that men and women have adversarial relationships.

Censorship, Perceived Negative Effects, and Racial Stereotyping

Partly based on perceptions of rap's violence and misogyny, critics began to assail rap music and other controversial forms of R&B during the 1990s. One of the primary incidents that led to this criticism included the 2 Live Crew, a rap group based out of Miami, Florida. In June of 1990, the album *As Nasty As They Wanna Be* by the 2 Live Crew was declared legally obscene by a federal court judge. This represented the first time that a musical recording was declared legally obscene by a federal jurist (Dixon and Linz 1997). The judge used his own interpretation of the level of community tolerance without impaneling a jury.

The 2 Live Crew Story

The Broward County sheriff received a citizen's complaint about the recording on January 1, 1990, from Jack Thompson, a conservative politician who had a vendetta against 2 Live Crew for supporting his rival in a local state race (Campbell 1991). After listening to several of the songs on the album that were purchased from Hammond records, the sheriff transcribed the lyrics to some of the songs and presented them to a Broward county judge who said that there was probable cause that the record was obscene (Campbell 1991; Clark 1990). With the judge's ruling in hand, the sheriff proceeded to send written notices to record store owners informing them that selling the album could be a violation of obscenity law.

Almost immediately, most stores in the county stopped selling the record. 2 Live Crew brought civil suit against the sheriff for violating their civil rights on March 19, 1990. They claimed that the record was not obscene and that the sheriff's action constituted a prior restraint of speech (Campbell 1991; Clark 1990). On March 27, Sheriff Navarro filed a separate action to have the album declared obscene. On June 6, the federal judge in the civil suit ruled that the sheriff's action did constitute a prior restraint and was illegal but that the record was indeed obscene. On June 10, the 2 Live Crew was arrested for performing their lyrics at an adults-only club. A jury of their peers later acquitted them of any wrongdoing (Baker 1993; Campbell 1991).

Explaining Negative Reactions to Rap Music

In a previous study, my coauthor and I attempted to understand whether censorship of the 2 Live crew specifically and rap in general was rooted in ignorance of rap's cultural roots. In addition, we sought to understand whether racial animus against blacks also drove those negative reactions (Dixon and Linz 1997). In our study we uncovered evidence that a better understanding of rap music's cultural elements and historical roots made listeners more tolerant of the genre and less likely to censor. Specifically, we found that cultural factors such as appreciation of linguistic exaggeration and African American humor were related to tolerance for controversial rap music. In addition, political attitudes regarding sexual freedom and beliefs about rap's contribution to societal degradation were also predictive of tolerance for rap. We did not find direct evidence that racism, stereotyping, or racial animus contributed to reactions to rap. We concluded at the time that this might be a measurement problem.

Our suspicions regarding the limitations of our study regarding stereotyping were later confirmed by the results of another study conducted by Fried (1999). She undertook two studies. In the first, she provided lyrics to participants where a photo of either a black or white artist was pictured. In the second study, she had participants read a violent lyrical passage that was described as a rap song, folk song, or country song. She found that participants wanted to censor and reduce the sales of the items when the passage was described as rap and the artist was pictured as black. This suggests that negativity toward rap is driven by a racialized perception of the genre. This racialized perception was confirmed by yet another study described below.

Rap has become deeply associated with aggressive behavior, misogyny, and blackness. McLeod et al. (1997) observed that controversy around rap is tied to the belief that these associations exist. In addition, these associations were seen as harmful to hypothetical consumers of the music. They found that the perception of potential harm from exposure to rap led to greater calls of censorship of the musical genre.

Understanding the Rap Message and Rap Audience

Although several studies appear to document that rap music contains violent and misogynist themes and that these themes can have an impact on viewers, the vast majority of this research does not fully investigate the intricacies of the rap audience. Moreover, the calls for censorship seem premature and misinformed about the nature of media effects. In addition, the general content of rap music is a "moving target" with many iterations and various sub-genres and styles. In other words, the rap audience and the content of rap are extremely complex phenomena that require much more in-depth study. One of the deficiencies of prior rap research is its focus on white audience members or black adolescents exclusively. In addition, there are several complexities regarding the rap audience demographically and culturally that must be considered. After examining each of these below, I provide background on a program of research I have engaged in designed to address these problems.

Prior Work on the white Rap Audience

Almost all of the research regarding the effects of rap music have focused on whites (Ballard et al. 1999; Barongan and Hall 1995; McLeod et al. 1997; Eveland and McLeod 1999; Fischoff 1999). A few studies have examined African Americans, but most of these have focused on African American teens (Johnson et al. 1995a, 1995b; Johnson et al. 2000; Hakanen 1995). This is significant because there is some evidence to suggest that the rap audience itself is diverse and includes whites and blacks, teens and middle-aged adults (Gladney 1995; Haines 1999; Rose 1994).

However, it is understandable why whites have received so much attention in prior research. First, whites purchase more rap music than African Americans. Second, whites have very little contact with blacks. As a result, they might use the content as a surrogate for contact with African Americans (Haines 1999; Stephens 1991). Third, white rap consumption may influence rap music's marketing and promotion patterns. For example, Haines (1999) has observed that the popularity of so-called gangsta rap coincided with an increase in white consumption of rap music. Some whites have even appropriated rap as an expression of rebellious resistance. A few critics have called whites who engage in such appropriation "culture vultures" (Haines 1999; Stephens 1991). These three reasons suggest that it is important to understand white audience members' reaction to the music. However, focusing too much on white audience members may limit our understanding of rap and its effects. We explore some of these issues below.

Blacks and Black Culture as Central to Rap Culture

The focus on white audience members draws attention away from the fact that rap music was created by the black community and continues to be associated with black culture (Dixon and Linz 1997; Rose 1994). Below I argue that two issues are important with regard to the centrality of blacks within the culture of rap music. The first has to do with the extent to which African Americans are the central producers of the music. Second, it is important to examine the various constituencies that make up the black rap audience and consider how they might be engaged in deconstructing and/or consuming the messages of the songs.

As suggested earlier, African Americans play a unique role in the creation of rap. Most performers in rap music are black. This would suggest that they have a tremendous amount of influence over the music. However, there has been some contention over whether black performers have the ability to affect the content of their music. Some of this controversy is related to the issue of who controls the distribution of rap recordings. Some have framed this issue as a battle between independent labels (also known as "indies") and major labels (Gladney 1995). Some observers contend that the independent labels allow hip-hop artists to pursue alternative commercial venues in order to maintain authenticity. Either African Americans or whites who are trying to create a niche market typically run these labels. However, major labels encourage commercial gain that retards the development of valid cultural expression (Gladney 1995).

The Complex Black Rap Audience

The rap audience itself has many different elements. One element that has been understudied is black women performers and audience members (Conrad, Dixon, and Zhang, 2009; Zhang, Dixon, and Conrad, 2010). As suggested above, a number of studies suggest that some rap music contains misogynist themes and that such themes can have a negative psychological effect on rap consumers. However, we need to understand the extent to which black women performers and audience members use the music to challenge sexist assumptions regarding black women. For instance, bell hooks (1994) has suggested that black women are perpetually negotiating "the gaze" that relegates them to sexualized and subordinate positions in relation to men. Black women who find it disempowering often resist this gaze. Furthermore, some women have not only resisted this gaze but have created an alternative gaze by which they try to make onlookers see them in a new light.

Rap music videos may allow some female artists to find alternative ways to present themselves (Roberts 1994). For example, Roberts (1994) observed that rap artist Queen Latifah draws upon African musical and cultural tradition to critique sexism and racism in her music. McLean (1997) observed, for instance, that African American and Latina females actively used rap music to construct sexual expression that did not subordinate them to men.

Overall, this section has suggested several things. First, whites have received a tremendous amount of attention by those studying the impact of rap music. Second, rap themes are complex and influenced by various market forces along with black culture. Third, the rap audience itself is complex. Black women represent one aspect of this audience that must receive more attention in future work. Particularly important is the issue of how black women contend with sexism and objectification.

Advancing a Research Program on Rap Music and Rap Audiences

In this section I outline a research program designed to address some of the shortfalls of past research. Specifically, a two-pronged research program needs to be undertaken that utilizes a number of methods. First, content analyses will track both rap music themes and outlets.

Second, all facets of the rap audience, with special attention directed toward women, will be investigated.

Understanding Rap Themes

As mentioned above, rap music contains a number of themes. Several studies have been conducted on rap music's effects, but only a small number of studies have actually studied rap's themes, and most of them are dated. In order to address this concern, my research team and I conducted a large-scale content analysis of rap music videos. A comprehensive analysis that examines both positive and negative themes occurring in rap music is rare. Some previous research suggests that there are several negative themes that dominate rap. These themes include sex, violence, materialism, and misogyny.

Research has also found several positive messages as well including expression of culture, community unity, political awareness, and disaffection toward mainstream society. Up to this point, however, there has been much disagreement about the frequency with which these themes air. No analysis has considered that both of these themes may be occurring at the same time. Our research team undertook a study designed to extend this research by looking for both positive and negative messages in current rap music (Conrad et al. 2009). In addition, three more issues were the focus of the content analysis work.

First, rap music is often linked to black male identity, which may lead to an increase in themes of sexism and misogyny for women (hooks 1992). This suggests that there are important gender issues to consider in an examination of rap music. Second, unlike in other music genres, the majority of rap artists are black (Kubrin 2005). Black individuals often face issues of colorism in media whereby individuals with lighter skin may be given advantages over those with darker skin (Kurbrin 2005; Dixon and Maddox 2005; Oliver et al. 2004). However, the effect of Afrocentric features and skin-tone on the success of individuals in rap music has never been analyzed. Third, we examined the body image of women portrayed in rap music videos. Previous content analyses of body images have generally focused on mainstream media where the majority of female models are white (Fouts and Burggraf 2000; Silverstein et al. 1986; Wiseman et al. 1990). However, little is known about the nature of body images presented in the media geared toward black audiences. The purpose of these studies is to address this gap in the literature by examining the female body images in rap music videos.

We undertook this analysis by having four independent coders analyze the annual countdowns of the cable outlets for music videos (BET, MTV, and VH1) in a rigorous content analysis. Our coders were diverse, and we held ourselves to high standards of assessing reliability and validity. The results of this study have implications for better understanding the images in rap music videos. First, the analysis of controversial themes found that current rap music videos have emphasized themes of materialism and misogyny. Second, men and women perpetuate these themes differently. While male characters are significantly more likely to perpetuate a variety of themes, female characters only perpetuate themes of objectification. Third, the results of this study show that females in rap music videos are more likely than males to have Eurocentric features. Furthermore, thin female characters in the videos were prevalent and overrepresented compared to the real population. Moreover, when the music videos were high in themes of *materialism, love,* or *sex,* women were more likely to have smaller body sizes. In contrast, when the videos were high in themes of *political awareness* women were more likely to have larger body sizes. We used the above findings from the content analysis to begin to explore the potential effects of this content on viewers. However, we resisted focusing on white viewers. Instead, we examined the reactions of black viewers, specifically black women, to assess whether cultural perspectives influenced rap perceptions.

Understanding the Rap Audience

We believe that more studies should be done on black audience members to understand (1) what impact rap music has on them and (2) what kinds of meanings they take away from the music. For instance, we need to understand how the audience actively critiques the music rather than just how they are affected by the music. In order to accomplish this, my research team and I undertook two surveys. One of them was designed to assess black audience members' perceptions of misogyny and Afrocentricity within rap and to measure whether their self-concept was influenced by rap music consumption (Dixon et al. 2009). The second survey examined the responses of black women to determine whether rap music consumption influenced their perceptions of body image (Zhang et al. 2009). I report on the major findings below.

We asked approximately 140 black college students on a predominately white campus to respond to an online survey. The survey questions addressed three important constructs concerning the relationship between black audience members and rap content: collective self-esteem, misogynistic images, and the perpetuation of Eurocentric features in rap videos. First, we found that the collective self-esteem of African American audience members was positively related to their consumption of rap music. Second, viewing more misogynistic videos appears to be related to a decreased belief that rap music degrades women. Third, for black consumers who have stronger Afrocentric features, viewing videos with Afrocentric rather than Eurocentric standards of beauty is related to increased identification with the video. These findings tell us in some respects that priming operates below consciousness for certain perceptions such as misogyny. At the same time, rap audiences use the music for their own purposes, to increase their self-concept and to identify with rap music characters that share their skin-tone.

In our complementary survey we asked over one hundred black females to take part in a survey that assessed the relationship between body image and rap consumption. Findings from previous studies have suggested a weaker association between media exposure and negative body image among black women than among white women. However, the complexity of this association remains less clear, particularly because most studies have examined only mainstream media. The present study extends the literature by exploring the relationship between exposure to thin ideals in black-oriented programming (in this case, rap music videos) and young black women's body image perceptions, specifically addressing the moderating role of ethnic identity.

No significant relationships were found between exposure to rap music videos and body image. In other words, the amount of exposure to rap videos laden with images of predominantly black, thin women was not directly related to how black women perceived their own body images. Instead, the influence of exposure was shaped by black female viewers' level of identification with their culture. Specifically, for black women with stronger ethnic identity, viewing rap videos that idealize thinness seemed to promote healthier body images; while for black women with weaker ethnic identity, viewing these same videos appeared to correlate with poorer body images. The implication of this study is that ethnic identity is an important moderator of negative effects of rap music for African American women.

Conclusion

Although we are still in the infancy of rap music research, we are beginning to make progress on many fronts, both in terms of investigating rap content and in terms of understanding effects. As new media technology begins to transform the ways in which we receive rap content, this literature review provides a useful understanding of the content and consequences of digesting the music. Moreover, what we do know is that censorship of the genre appears to be an overreaction to the actual content and effects of the music. Specifically, there are four things we can take from this program of research.

First, controversial themes persist in the music but the music itself continues to undergo change, especially with the advent of new technology. Violence has subsided while misogyny has risen as a theme. Moreover, independent artists now can use the Internet to distribute less popular "positive" themes, though they are not a substantial part of the popular rap genre. Our team has turned our focus to the impact of Internet distribution on the production and reception of rap music themes.

Second, the research program has established that rap music can definitely have negative effects on people's thoughts and potential actions. Specifically, controversial rap themes can encourage an acceptance of misogyny and violence. Although a few researchers have advanced the notion that the impact of "negative" themes may differ by race, we know that negative themes can influence both black and white audience members.

Third, although there is the potential for negative themes to influence members of different racial groups, the effects of rap music may differ by cultural experience. In other words, racial identification was a strong moderator of effects of potentially harmful themes. Those with a greater racial awareness rejected Eurocentric images including thin-body ideals. So although some rap themes can negatively influence black audiences, the story is more complicated because audiences are smarter than we give them credit for.

Fourth, it appears that the way forward goes through the path of media literacy and empowerment instead of censorship. Those who can proficiently critique the production of rap and the controversial themes contained in the music become the most able to resist the potentially negative effects of rap consumption. Those most concerned about these potential negative effects need to focus on providing education and support for alternate rap platforms so that audiences can better empower and equip themselves in the twenty-first century.

References

Armstrong, Edward G. 1993. "The Rhetoric of Violence in Rap and Country Music." *Sociological Inquiry* 63, no. 1: 64–83. doi: 10.1111/j.1475-682X.1993.tb00202.x.

Baker, Houston A., Jr. 1993. *Black Studies, Rap, and the Academy*. Chicago: University of Chicago Press.

Ballard, Mary E., Alan R. Dodson, and Doris G. Bazzini. 1999. "Genre of Music and Lyrical Content: Expectation Effects." *Journal of Genetic Psychology* 160, no. 4: 476–487. doi: 10.1080/00221329909595560.

Barongan, Christy, and Gordon C. Nagayama Hall. 1995. "The Influence of Misogynous Rap Music on Sexual Aggression against Women." *Psychology of Women Quarterly* 19, no. 2:195–207. doi: 10.1111/j.1471-6402.1995.tb00287.x.

Binder, Amy. 1993. "Constructing Racial Rhetoric: Media Depictions of Harm in Heavy Metal and Rap Music." *American Sociological Review* 58, no. 6: 753–767. doi: 10.2307/2095949.

Campbell, Emily. 1991. "Obscenity, Music and the First Amendment: Was the Crew 2 Lively?" *Nova Law Review* 15, no. 1:159–240.

Clark, Anne L. 1990. "As Nasty As They Wanna Be: Popular Music on Trial." *New York University Law Review* 65, no. 6: 1481–1531.

Conrad, Kate, T. L. Dixon, and Yuanyuan Zhang. 2009. "Controversial Rap Themes, Gender Portrayals and Skin Tone Distortion: A Content Analysis of Rap Music Videos." *Journal of Broadcasting & Electronic Media* 53, 134–156. doi: 10.1080/08838150802643795.

Dixon, T. L., and Daniel G. Linz. 1997. "Obscenity Law and Sexually Explicit Rap Music: Understanding the Effects of Sex, Attitudes, and Beliefs." *Journal of Applied Communication Research* 25, no. 3: 217–241. doi: 10.1080/00909889709365477.

Dixon, T. L., and K. B. Maddox. 2005. "Skin Tone, Crime News, and Social Reality Judgments: Priming the Stereotype of the Dark and Dangerous Black Criminal." *Journal of Applied Social Psychology* 38, 1555–1570. doi: 10.1111/j.1559-1816.2005.tb02184.x.

Dixon, T. L., Yuanyuan Zhang, and Kate Conrad. 2009. "Self-Esteem, Misogyny, and Afrocentricity: An Examination of the Relationship between Rap Music Consumption and African American Perceptions." *Group Processes and Intergroup Relations* 12, no. 3: 345–360.

Eveland, William P., Jr., and Douglas M. McLeod. 1999. "The Effect of Social Desirability on Perceived Media Impact: Implications for Third-Person Perceptions." *International Journal of Public Opinion Research* 11, no. 4: 315–333. doi: 10.1093/ijpor/11.4.315.

Fischoff, Stuart P. 1999. "Gangsta' Rap and a Murder in Bakersfield." *Journal of Applied Social Psychology* 29, no. 4: 795–805. doi: 10.1111/j.1559-1816.1999.tb02025.x.

Fouts, G., and Burggraf, K. 2000. "Television Situation Comedies: Female Weight, Male Negative Comments, and Audience Reactions." *Sex Roles* 42, 925–932.

Fried, Carrie B. 1999. "Who's Afraid of Rap: Differential Reactions to Music Lyrics." *Journal of Applied Social Psychology* 29, no. 4: 705–721. doi: 10.1111/j.1559-1816.1999.tb02020.x.

Gan, Su-lin, Dolf Zillmann, and Michael Mitrook. 1997. "Stereotyping Effect of Black Women's Sexual Rap on White Audiences." *Basic & Applied Social Psychology* 19, no. 3: 381–399. doi: 10.1207/15324839751037020

Gladney, Marvin J. 1995. "The Black Arts Movement and Hip-Hop." *African American Review* 29, no. 2: 291–301. doi: 10.2307/3042308.

Haines, Rebecca J. 1999. "Break North: Rap Music and Hip-Hop Culture in Canada." In *Politics and Public Policy: Case Studies in Canadian Diversity*, edited by Harold Troper and Morton Weinfeld, 54–88. Toronto: University of Toronto Press.

Hakanen, Ernest A. 1995. "Emotional Use of Music by African American Adolescents." *Howard Journal of Communications* 5, no. 3: 214–222. doi: 10.1080/10646179509361664.

Hansen, Christine Hall. 1995. "Predicting Cognitive and Behavioral Effects of Gangsta Rap." *Basic & Applied Social Psychology* 16, no. 1: 43–52. doi: 10.1207/s15324834basp1601&2_3.

Harris, Richard Jackson. 1999. *A Cognitive Psychology of Mass Communication*. 3rd ed. Mahwah, NJ: Lawrence Erlbaum Associates.

Henderson, Errol A. 1996. "Black Nationalism and Rap Music." *Journal of Black Studies* 26, no. 3: 308–339. doi: 10.1177/002193479602600305.

hooks, bell. 1994. *Outlaw Culture: Resisting Representations*. New York: Routledge.

Huessman, L. R., and L. S. Miller. 1994. "Long-Term Effects of Repeated Exposure to Media Violence in Childhood." In *Aggressive Behavior*, edited by L. R. Huessman, 153–186. New York: Plenum Press.

Johnson, James D., Mike S. Adams, Leslie Ashburn, and William Reed. 1995a. "Differential Gender Effects of Exposure to Rap Music on African American Adolescents' Acceptance of Teen Dating Violence." *Sex Roles* 33, nos. 7–8: 597–605. doi: 10.1007/BF01544683.

Johnson, James D., Lee Anderson Jackson, and Leslie Gatto. 1995b. "Violent Attitudes and Deferred Academic Aspirations: Deleterious Effects of Exposure to Rap Music." *Basic & Applied Social Psychology* 16, nos. 1–2: 27–41. doi: 10.1207/s15324834basp1601&2_2.

Johnson, James D., Sophie Trawalter, and John F. Dovidio. 2000. "Converging Interracial Consequences of Exposure to Violent Rap Music on Stereotypical Attributions of Blacks." *Journal of Experimental Social Psychology* 36, no. 3: 233–251. doi: 10.1006/jesp.1999.1404.

Jones, Kenneth. 1997. "Are Rap Videos More Violent? Style Differences and the Prevalence of Sex and Violence in the Age of MTV." *Howard Journal of Communications* 8, no. 4: 343–356. doi: 10.1080/10646179709361765.

Kubrin, C. 2005. "Gangstas, Thugs, and Hustlas: Identity and the Code of the Street in Rap Music." *Social Problems* 52, 360-378. doi: 10.1525/sp.2005.52.3.360.

Kuwahara, Yasue. 1992. "Power to the People Y'all: Rap Music, Resistance, and Black College Students." *Humanity and Society* 16, no. 1: 54–73.

Lynxwiler, John, and David Gay. 2000. "Moral Boundaries and Deviant Music: Public Attitudes Toward Heavy Metal and Rap." *Deviant Behavior* 21, no. 1: 63–85. doi: 10.1080/016396200266388.

McLean, Polly E. 1997. "Age Ain't Nothing But a Number: A Cross-Cultural Reading of Popular Music in the Construction of Sexual Expression among At-Risk Adolescents." *Popular Music & Society* 21, no. 2: 1–16. doi: 10.1080/03007769708591665.

McLeod, Douglas M., William P. Eveland, and Amy I. Nathanson. 1997. "Support for Censorship of Violent and Misogynic Rap Lyrics: An Analysis of the Third-Person Effect." *Communication Research* 24, no. 2: 153–174. doi: 10.1177/009365097024002003.

Oliver, M.B., R.L. Jackson, N.N. Moses, and C.L. Dangerfield. 2004. "The Face of Crime: Viewers' Memory of Race-Related Facial Features of Individuals Pictured in the News." *Journal of Communication* 54, 88-104. doi: 10.1111/j.1460-2466.2004.tb02615.x.

Pinn, Anthony B. 1996. "'Gettin' Grown': Notes on Gansta Rap Music and Notions of Manhood." *Journal of African-American Men* 2, no. 1: 61–73.

Pinn, Anthony B. 1999. "'How Ya Livin'?': Notes on Rap Music and Social Transformation." *Western Journal of Black Studies* 23, no. 1: 10–21.

Powell, Catherine Tabb. 1991. "Rap Music: An Education with a Beat from the Street." *Journal of Negro Education* 60, no. 3: 245–259.

Pressley, Arthur. 1992. "Rap Music by Black Male Artists: A Psychotheological Interpretation." *Western Journal of Black Studies* 16, no. 2: 92–97.

Roberts, Robin. 1994. "'Ladies First': Queen Latifah's Afrocentric Feminist Music Video." *African American Review* 28, no. 2: 245–257.

Rose, Tricia. 1991. "'Fear of a Black Planet': Rap Music and Black Cultural Politics in the 1990s." *Journal of Negro Education* 60, no. 3: 276–290. doi: 10.2307/2295482.

Rose, Tricia. 1994. *Black Noise: Rap Music and Black Culture in Contemporary America*. Hanover, NH: University Press of New England/Wesleyan University Press.

Rubin, Alan M., Daniel V. West, and Wendy S. Mitchell. 2001. "Differences in Aggression, Attitudes toward Women, and Distrust as Reflected in Popular Music Preferences." *Media Psychology* 3, no. 1: 25–42. doi: 10.1207/S1532785XMEP0301_02.

Silverstein, B., L. Perdue, B. Peterson, and E. Kelly. 1986. "The Role of the Mass Media in Promoting a Thin Standard of Attractiveness for Women." *Sex Roles* 14, 519-532.

Smith, Stacy L. 2005. "From Dr. Dre to Dismissed: Assessing Violence, Sex, and Substance Use on MTV." *Critical Studies in Media Communication* 22, no. 1: 89–98. doi: 10.1080/0739318042000333743.

Stephens, Gregory. 1991. "Rap Music's Double-Voiced Discourse: A Crossroads for Interracial Communication." *Journal of Communication Inquiry* 15, no. 2: 70–91. doi: 10.1177/019685999101500205.

Watts, Eric K. 1997. "An Exploration of Spectacular Consumption: Gangsta Rap as Cultural Commodity." *Communication Studies* 48, no. 1: 42–58. doi: 10.1080/10510979709368490.

Wester, Stephen R., Cynthia L. Crown, Gerald L. Quatman, and Martin Heesacker. 1997. "The Influence of Sexually Violent Rap Music on Attitudes of Men with Little Prior Exposure." *Psychology of Women Quarterly* no. 21, no. 4: 497–508. doi: 10.1111/j.1471-6402.1997.tb00127.x.

Wiseman, C.V., J.J. Gray, J.E. Moismann, and A.H. Ahrens. 1990. "Cultural Expectations of Thinness in Women: An Update." *International Journal of Eating Disorders* 11, no. 1: 85–89.

Zhang, Yuanyuan, Travis L. Dixon, and Kate Conrad. 2009. "Rap Music Videos and African American Women's Body Image: The Moderating Role of Ethnic Identity." *Journal of Communication* 59, no. 2: 262–278.

Zhang, Y., T. L. Dixon, and K. Conrad. 2010. "Female Body Image as a Function of Themes in Rap Music Videos: A Content Analysis". *Sex Roles* 62, 787–797. doi: 10.1007/s11199-009-9656-y.

CHAPTER 28

DEATHS AND SILENCES

Coding and Defiance in Music about AIDS

PAUL ATTINELLO

CREATORS and performers of music that reflects the experiences of the AIDS crisis are inevitably praised for their courage—as is generally implied, in the face of oppression and resistance. Although in most cases such music, and such public discussions, have rarely been subject to actual external censorship, the social mechanisms that lie at the roots of social or political control have continued to operate. The reasons for this will be evident—despite changes in sexual and social discourses across an era of vastly increased freedoms, traditional shames and rages do not vanish but remain in the cultural and personal psyche. Because of all this, music about AIDS is filled with a volatile, self-conscious mixture of caution and defiance, provocation and obscurity; in fact, many works foreground implicit feelings of transgression, sometimes more definitely than other aspects of the disease's impact. And, in a few cases—especially those associated with avant-garde music and art, and therefore with expectations of breaking through perceived cultural boundaries—actual social or political censorship has occurred, if briefly and locally.

Of course, associations with the gay community are often more of a concern than attitudes toward a more general sexuality, or toward illness or death. Those associations have also created dissension among those who have lived with AIDS as well as those who have supported them—for instance, the formerly unspeakable nature of AIDS in North American black communities resulted largely from the taboo on any appearance of an alignment with the gay community. Anti-gay rhetoric associated with AIDS appears in Africa to this day, despite other potentially embarrassing associations that can be made. Of course, the status of the gay community has changed—and partly as a result of all these events: just as anti-Jewish rhetoric was banished from socially accepted behavior after the Holocaust, so acceptable middle-class conversation has permitted markedly less anti-gay rhetoric since the 1980s.

Because those who are unacquainted with the cultural and artistic responses to AIDS are often surprised by their number, range, and complexity, it is worth outlining the larger context of the discussion.

Music and AIDS

Because AIDS treatments have gradually retreated from the apocalyptic to the mundane, people no longer seem as strongly compelled to make art about AIDS as they did between 1983 and 1996. That period saw the creation of a great deal of AIDS-related work—many novels and memoirs, with detailed, tragic personal narratives; various approaches to theater, emphasizing the confrontational, the instructional, or the hallucinatory; poetry, much of it narrative, and often more immediate than might be expected; and of course a vast array of visual arts, including installations and street art of many kinds. However, there does seem to have been a somewhat smaller response to AIDS in music than in some of the other arts; it also seems that the music that does exist, across all its genres, is frequently more oblique and cautious in its presentation of strongly charged material, such as political slogans or medical terminology.

Reasons why all the genres of music seem less political than comparable production in the other arts would obviously include commercial calculations in the popular music industry and obedience to the norms of polite social reserve in classical music institutions. And, of course, many songs and reinterpretations designed for benefit performances tend to avoid specifics; this makes sense, as their purpose is to generate an uncontroversial empathy that encourages people to give money. I think, however, a more generous explanation also applies—that music often works better as an expression of feeling states than it does as a vehicle for articulating a political stance or describing a contemporary situation. I do not, of course, intend for such an explanation to apply to all music—I don't credit musical universals myself, and there are always musical works and activities functioning outside the boundaries of the merely typical. However, we do have a lot of ingrained musical habits, many of them linked to sentiment and the creation of feelings—ultimately, the love song is a more central genre for music than the romance novel is for literature. Therefore, though the typical construction of music related to AIDS often reflects a certain social or political timidity, I suggest this may be because it is intended to convey more private, subtle, or complex feelings than the shouting of slogans would allow.

The music I have collected represents most of the major genres on sale in record stores—classical, avant-garde, popular vocalists and groups, musicals, film scores, and so on. Interestingly, examples within each genre tend to present tropes and ideas related to AIDS that are fairly consistent within that genre, but there is far less similarity across the genres. For instance, the approach of classical chamber music tends to be mournful but politely coded, while hip-hop assertively tries to educate the black community with blunt commands. Some genres are differentiated by the emotions they try to convey—film scores tend to offer a diffuse atmosphere of sadness and foreboding, while punk songs are usually charged with defiant rage or savage abuse. Such similarities and contrasts can be seen as a simple confirmation of social construction theory; they also suggest where there are channels of communication between musical communities in the late twentieth and early twenty-first centuries.

A simplified cultural history of AIDS, especially as it has impacted artistic expression, would begin with the first public awareness in 1981, followed by a handful of early works—both music and theater address the crisis for the first time in 1983. The middle and late 1980s were experienced as a widening crisis, with an enormous expansion of artistic responses; between 1987 and 1995 dramatic concerns about personal death and large-scale disaster shifted back and forth across various experiences, political and medical blunders and triumphs, and of course a range of developing medications. The late 1990s saw a greatly increased global consciousness of the ways the crisis struck different parts of the world; even now there remain, however, very different attitudes between urban and rural communities, as well as between "northern" and "southern" nations and between more and less technologically developed cultures. It is interesting to note the large psychosocial shift in 1996 around the advent of protease inhibitors: although, obviously, AIDS/HIV remains a world crisis, there has certainly been a shift in the conversation toward the pragmatic and immediate and away from the transcendent passions and anxieties associated with death, fear, and the end of the world. This has had more impact on music since the late 1990s than on most other aspects of culture.

For this chapter, I will focus on classical, popular, and avant-garde musics of the Anglophone West. It would be productive to also look at other parts of the world, as many of them involve very different cultural and musical contexts. For instance, a wide range of responses in music, film, art, and even cultural theory in France, especially by Parisian artists and intellectuals, often reflect the idea, too shocking to be widely considered in Anglo-Germanic art works, that a person with AIDS could knowingly infect someone else out of selfishness or anger. The many cultures and situations across sub-Saharan Africa also show varying attitudes toward openness and secrecy around AIDS in their differing contexts (Barz and Cohen 2011).

Classical Reticence

Classical—or, more often, broadly neoromantic—works composed about AIDS were largely written for performance by chamber and orchestral musicians for audiences that would attend conventional classical performances. The most famous—the first volume of the *AIDS Quilt Songbook* (1992), Corigliano's Symphony no. 1, and associated works—are perhaps the best examples of the kind of music that seems to be written inside a cloud of mild equivocation, one that reflects the expectations of a particular class identity. It also reflects a geographical identity: many of these works are associated with Carnegie Hall and Lincoln Center audiences, and it is worth noting that a large number of other classical works (the second volume of the *AIDS Quilt Songbook* and other ungrouped songs associated with it, plus numerous songs, cantatas, and choral and instrumental works written later and in other locations) show less self-conscious propriety than these first and most famous works.

Of course, reading this as propriety—or equivocation, circumlocution, even a kind of internalized censorship—is always an interpretation. The poetry of the 1980s and early 1990s varies in directness for various stylistic and historical reasons. In any case, it is clear that many East Coast poets of the time, especially those chosen for the anthology *Poets for Life* (Klein 1989), which was a source for many texts used in the *AIDS Quilt Songbook*, tended either to focus on image as metaphor or to use fairly oblique rhetorical styles.[1] Thus, we would have to consider, for instance, the beginning of Susan Snively's "Fury," used for Donald Wheelock's song of the same name:

> I have a poisoned hand,
> I have a bitter voice.
> I look death in the face,
> I have no choice.

Intense, visceral imagery, immediate and experiential: but, unlike language used in literature, theater, and a wide range of visual art around the same time, there are no direct references to AIDS, HIV, or their associated terms and conditions; as the remainder of the poem becomes more imaginative (developing the personification of death, invoking the ill and those who might help them), it becomes even less specific. Ultimately, if the "poisoned hand" is interpreted without preconceptions, it might not even be connected to illness. Another poem, "blues for an imaginary valentine," includes the phrase "long-time companion" (which clearly refers to the *New York Times* circumlocution for gay partners); otherwise it might be about any kind of partner left behind by death (*AIDS Quilt Songbook* 1993, iv, 1–14).

Perhaps these expectations are too strict; or, to be fair, perhaps the texts only seem overly cautious in comparison with the assertive directness of the other arts (such as the dramatic graphic designs and art works associated with ACT UP, the concrete references and events in literature and dramatic works, and so on). Of course, some of the songs, even from the first volume of the *AIDS Quilt Songbook*, are more direct than the above examples. Interestingly, most of these resulted in less neoromantic musical styles, such as the satiric jazz references composed by David Krakauer to accompany the specifically medical terms of Melvin Dixon's "80s Miracle Diet":

> Cocktails of Perrier with a twist of AZT,
> Bactrim broiled with bacon bits
> Egg lipid quiche for lunch. (*AIDS Quilt Songbook* 1993, v, 37–41)

On the other hand, we might feel uneasy over John Harbison's choice of a 1971 translation of Kabir's poetry by Robert Bly for "The Flute of Interior Time." The publicity value of including all these famous names in the *AIDS Quilt Songbook* is obvious, but the poem is not about any kind of loss, illness, or death, though its ecstatic paean to love does offer an existential or transcendent comfort and connects the suffering of the present with centuries-old experiences. This particular song might be seen to resemble Burt Bacharach's "That's What Friends Are For" (discussed below)—comforting, but also relatively vague and far from the point. In any case, there is an enormous distance between the Harbison and, for instance, Elizabeth Brown's setting of Marie Howe's "A Certain Light," which includes concrete references, an intimacy with medication and illness, an arrestingly concrete person with AIDS on the verge of death, and a comparable reference to transcendental love and hope (*AIDS Quilt Songbook* 1993, viii, ix, 75–77, 92–100).

Naturally, some songs in the *AIDS Quilt Songbook* are more hermetic or oblique than others. Hans Werner Henze's *Requiem* (1994) is deeply expressive but mute about the disease itself; David Del Tredici's later songs, which are ruthlessly confessional about sexuality, AIDS, and alcoholism, are comments on the larger context (Del Tredici 2001). And of course some of the more oblique songs, and those written or composed before the appearance of AIDS, blend in simply because we concentrate on felt and implied meaning, while the context and surrounding songs supply the specifics; direct reference might be superfluous or unnecessarily aggressive and might even get in the way of the emotional and experiential authenticity of a given song.

In the same context of famous works associated with New York classical institutions, John Corigliano's Symphony no. 1 can be seen as slightly coded rather than entirely direct. The expressive, labeled materiality of the symphony stands in contrast to the choral movement "Of Rage and Remembrance," which includes a memorial text by the playwright William Hoffman, including names chosen by "members of the chorus who have lost friends and wish to remember them." These names do not appear in the orchestral version reasonably enough, but we can consider the tradition of choral symphonies, especially for an innovative modernist/neoromantic like Corigliano. The texted work (a reconstruction of the work of mourning done by the AIDS Memorial Quilt itself) was written earlier, as a sort of draft for the symphony, and then became the invisible structure for the rhythmic detail of the final version of the third movement.[2] Does the transformation of the texted work into an instrumental work represent a kind of silencing, or not?

Popular Spin

We may be on firmer ground when we examine songs by popular artists. In many cases the references and packaging are even less direct than in classical works. Consider for instance Janet Jackson's (1998; 1999) "Together Again," which not only is free of any direct reference to AIDS but even has a cheerful up-tempo style. The song's lyrics are tagged in the CD booklet with a small red ribbon, which is unambiguous if not particularly assertive, and the cheerful style is a deliberate choice that reflects the character of the friend memorialized in the song. Yet in the *Velvet Rope* concert tour this song became the basis for a non-narrative dance number not connected to AIDS in any way. This approach contrasts strongly with, for instance, Madonna's (1992a; 1992b) emphatic lyrics and articulation for "In This Life" which confronts the audience much more directly with a contemporary, material reality.

Many songs by major popular artists are as oblique as the one by Janet Jackson, which makes sense in a context of commercial sales. A related problem appears in music written specifically to raise money for AIDS charities, such as Burt Bacharach's famous "That's What Friends Are For," in which lines such as "I'm glad I got the chance to say" and repetitions of "always" and "forever more" can suggest final communications and transcendence, but they are not specific (Warwick 1989). Ultimately, even the grandest of AIDS benefits cannot generate as much money for either AIDS organizations or for famous musicians' administrative entourages as can months (or years, in the case of the Bacharach) of radio play and CD sales; as a result, many popular songs are clearly designed to be relatively innocuous in order to encourage the broadest possible consumption. This also applies to songs such as Bruce Springsteen's "Streets of Philadelphia," the introduction to the 1993 film *Philadelphia*. Although the film was celebrated as an example of Hollywood finally making a public statement about AIDS, there was a great deal of studio concern over its subject matter before its successful premiere. Perhaps this is why—despite brief references in the lyrics to wasting away, blood turning black, and a faithless kiss—Springsteen's song, and the film segment under it, seem to be more about the poor and disenfranchised than they are about AIDS.

I have written elsewhere about two more complex examples, James Taylor's "Never Die Young" and Tori Amos's "Not the Red Baron" (Attinello 2006). In the first case, there is no proof that the song is related to AIDS, despite some suggestive lyrics:

> You could see them on the street on a Saturday night
> Everyone used to run them down
> They're a little too sweet, they're a little too tight
> Not enough tough for this town
>
> We couldn't touch them with a ten-foot pole
> No, it didn't seem to rattle at all
> They were glued together body and soul
> That much more with their backs up against the wall (Taylor 1988)

In the case of the Tori Amos (1996) song, although references to gay men, AIDS, and (transcendent) death are more definite, it is not until we hear the final references to "red ribbons" that we can bring the dense cloud of metaphors and references into focus. In fact, considering that Amos is not shy about controversy or her audiences, it would be surprising if there was any kind of self-censorship involved, but complex aesthetic construction to create a mysterious transcendence does obscure the song's relation to AIDS.

Of course a tangled network of popular sales, rebellious defiance, the expression of personal feelings, and artistically heavy coding operates in so many popular songs that it is hard to arrive at simple classifications. Matthew Tift's position is that musicians such as Prince, Salt'n'Pepa, and TLC all produced songs where AIDS was strongly suggested but not named, while songs by U2, Elton John, Liz Phair, and Janet Jackson were more specific. I might draw the lines between concealed and direct references slightly differently, but there are certainly different levels of coding and openness in these songs, as there is always pressure from the music industry's superstructure to silence certain materials. Tift (2007, 125; quoting Gaar 2002, 325) mentions a statement made by Janet Jackson about an album created before the appearance of AIDS: ". . . outside forces even influenced Janet Jackson: in the process of making her album *Rhythm Nation 1814* [released 1989], Jackson said that she 'had been advised that her use of 'socially conscious themes' in her material would have a negative impact on . . . sales.'" Although Tift looks for concrete evidence of censorship, he can only be sure that "Few musical responses to HIV/AIDS on the Billboard charts [i.e., the "Hot 100" of current popular music] referred to AIDS explicitly." Ultimately, Tift (2007, 98–141) is most interested in TLC's successful "Waterfall," which is admittedly coded (both the lyrics and video mention sex, sudden change/illness, "three letters" [HIV], and death):

> She give him loving that his body can't handle,
> but all he can say is, "Baby, it's good to me."
> One day he goes and takes a glimpse in the mirror,
> but he doesn't recognize his own face.
> His health is fading and he doesn't know why.
> Three letters took him to his final resting place. (TLC 1994)

So-called alternative musicians, like the avant-garde artists mentioned below, are (and can afford to be) more defiant about projecting radical identification or a more rebellious point of view. Although they rarely have the same financial pressures as major popular artists, their audiences are generally more interested in and receptive to implicit rebellion. Fred Maus has spoken about coding in music of the B-52s and the Pet Shop Boys,[3] pointing out subtle suggestions of feelings and situations, most of which can be ignored by radio audiences.

Other, angrier, musicians have created songs that imply that they exist in opposition to implicit rebellion—The JAMS' disturbing transformation of 'All You Need is Love' or Willie Colón's invasion of the closeted salsa world, as well as songs in the series begun by the Red Hot organization in 1980, create their tone out of a battle to exist which perhaps can no longer be documented.

Avant-Garde Aggression

Perhaps the ambiguous messages issued by high-profile classical and popular artists only seem so in comparison with the directness of the avant-garde. As some parts of the 1980s and 1990s avant-garde were more involved with visual artists and political demonstrations than were other musical genres, they would have been more influenced by stronger and more direct statements—it would feel strange to leave a meeting where everyone discussed marches, infection rates, medications, ACT-UP, funerals, lesions, and government plots to go into a music studio and create allusive or oblique work.

It may seem ahistorical to group experimental musics from various backgrounds into a broadly defined avant-garde, but there is a distinct advantage: in the 1980s and early 1990s, when most of the music about AIDS was being written, the lines between experimental popular musics and experimental chamber/orchestral musics were disintegrating. Although there were signs of a weakening distinction between popular and classical in experimental musics several decades earlier, in this decade such distinctions began to seem pointless—crossover styles by Diamanda Galás, Bob Ostertag, and David Wojnarowicz, and many others were distinguished by their degree of radical experimentation, not by their generic roots. The concept of an avant-garde also made sense in a context of censorship or self-suppression; although popular and classical styles continued to connect to avant-gardes at various technical levels, the characteristic that remained important for an avant-garde was its socially rebellious nature. It may thus come as no surprise that avant-garde musicians who created work about AIDS deliberately attempted to test cultural and aesthetic boundaries and, in at least one instance, have been subject to actual political censorship.

Diamanda Galás is the most important, and perhaps the most complex, artist in this area. Galás's multifarious background—which includes youthful training as a classical piano prodigy; radically hazardous personal, chemical, and sexual experiences; collaborations with European avant-garde composers such as Xenakis and Globokar; rapid education in experimental performance art; extensive work with electronics; and collaborations with jazz, rock, and metal musicians—makes her impossible to easily categorize, except in the way suggested above: that she has always focused on the most extreme and experimental aspects of each of these styles. Her active testing of boundaries became especially evident when she crossed from her earliest compositions (where the rebellious edge is embedded in complex musical and poetic references that would seem abstract to large audiences) to the major works of the late 1980s, most of which are heavily focused on the problem of AIDS, in response to her brother's death in 1986. Thus, if the early *Wild Women with Steak Knives* (1982) was shocking, it was nevertheless eclipsed by the massive *Masque of the Red Death* (1989) and the *Plague Mass* (1991).

As Galás's performances have become gradually more fragmented, including many sections from her longer works that were detached from their original general titles and links, her association with goth and metal subcultures has come to seem more important than her earlier associations with classical and avant-garde musicians. However, her assertive intellectual politics continue, as does the testing of boundaries: the title of her collection of texts and photographs, *The Shit of God* (1996), is a case in point. Galás's work is shocking not only because of its charged explorations of the visceral, the violent, and the extraordinarily degraded, but also because of its precision—compared to most popular musicians, her ability to etch precise and complex vocal microtones and dense bass piano clusters makes her work exceptionally confrontational for many audiences.

But Galás also speaks about her work and its context, and in a highly articulate way—she has repeatedly asserted that much of the rhetoric and representation around AIDS is censored—erased, reduced, distorted, covered over.[4]

David Wojnarowicz, who died in 1992, was more of a visual artist than a musician, although he engaged with a great deal of writing and performance art. He did collaborate on musical projects, most of which are preserved on the CD *ITSOFOMO* ("In the Shadow of Forward Motion"; Wojnarowicz and Neill 1992.). Wojnarowicz's approach to performance lined up with a lot of visual and performance art of the 1980s in using raw or altered graphics, bold techniques, direct statements, and unmistakably political accusations. His own work is distinguished by remarkable openness about abuse, drugs, and prostitution—his identification with the rejected culminated in his work about AIDS. His *AIDS Ragtime* is a case in point—Ben Neill's sardonically dissonant, irregular dance rhythms, and bizarre trumpet licks accompany a powerful bullhorn-style text on government lies, sources of infection, and anti-gay violence. The intent of the voice is clearly to provoke a response, either in the audience or in any government stooges who might be listening. According to Wojnarowicz and Neill, the full version of *ITSOFOMO* "is nearly an hour long and includes four videotapes, Wojnarowicz' spoken texts, and music by Neill. *ITSOFOMO* has been performed and exhibited internationally and includes the same footage that Wojarowicz used in the film *Fire in My Belly*."[5]

Eighteen years after his death, Wojnarowicz was again in the news as his work was subject to real censorship; Galás was also involved, as her music was used for his video "Fire in My Belly." In 2010 the National Portrait Gallery in Washington, D.C., removed the video from an exhibition in response to an intense attack by Christian and right-wing organizations. The case, which was discussed in the press[6] and resulted in protests as well as immense publicity for the video, was complicated by the fact that this is a publicly funded museum—a familiar problem in the world of visual arts and AIDS over the past three decades, as museums and publicly funded organizations have seen much more censorship than music. Galás responded to the situation with a text she had written to be read at a demonstration but which was published on the Internet instead.[7] She points out the dense knot of cultural and religious problems that stand behind this censorship—the Catholic Church ban on condoms (thus invalidating much safer-sex education), the government's weak response to AIDS, and so on. She quotes her own musical settings of Leviticus which focus on the word *unclean*, with all of its associations for people with AIDS, and brings her accusations into focus by reminding us of the immediacy of death. This censorship was of course aimed at the video images rather than at the music; but it does indicate the complicated responses to art about AIDS in the public arena.

Bob Ostertag has interspersed subtly complex electronic and experimental works with aggressively political pieces related to AIDS and gay-bashing, some of which involved Wojnarowicz. *All the Rage*, for string quartet and electronics with voice, is explosively violent—Ostertag (1993) taped a San Francisco riot in 1991, then combined it with an intense text by Sara Miles.[8] The composer says it has been played in places where he wouldn't have expected to hear it, which suggests more openness than we might expect. A "lost" work by Ostertag, *Spiral*, was based on Wojnarowicz's (1992) final writings. The image of turning into glass as he dies resulted in a work performed on glass instruments:

> But ultimately there were very few performances. On the way back to San Francisco from a concert in Brussels, United Airlines lost the instruments. When the cases finally showed up days later, they had been dropped so forcefully that the glass rods inside had not merely broken but shattered into glass dust. That was effectively the end of Spiral, though I am not sure this is such a bad thing. The destruction of the glass was poetic, the perfect end, actually. The music was never recorded. All that is left is some dust, some photos, and some memories. I think of Spiral less as a musical composition than as a ritual in which I engaged to mark David's passing, and the darkest time of the epidemic in this country. (Ostertag 2009)

And perhaps that is another reason it can be difficult to focus on censorship around music about AIDS: death and our own evanescence have caused more things to be lost than directed effort could ever manage to erase.

Zappa: First and Strangest

The earliest musical work I have discovered that refers to AIDS went through a process that reflects the problems of popular and avant-garde musics, plus a few peculiar twists of its own. Frank Zappa created a kind of Broadway musical that parodied a lot of things, including musicals themselves. This project went through a series of false starts, never achieving a live staged performance (in this it was similar to other musicals created by him); but the show's initial idea, that strange creatures were created by government experiments on blacks and homosexuals in prison, appears in a prologue that already existed in 1983–1984. Zappa's intention was evidently to create a show that had some shocking elements, but the sexually explicit aspect became, as it were, overblown when publisher Larry Flynt invited him to present a preview of the work as a nude photo shoot for *Hustler* magazine.[9]

This tangled nexus of pornography, Broadway, and collaborative commercial gambles apparently did not reflect a strong commitment on Zappa's part. As the project went down its strange bypaths, actual performances became less and less probable—especially in an era of relatively weak financial support for new musicals, between the late 1960s and the appearance of megamusicals in the mid-1980s. If the original intent was to create various rebellious shocks by overlapping racial, sexual, and commercial references, the *Hustler* photo shoot gave the whole project a pornographic reputation that would have lost it any remaining chance of financial support. Of course, from Zappa's point of view, government-funded infection of rejected minorities and sexually outrageous imagery were equally good points of attack, but of course in American culture they would fall into very different categories of social (dis)approval.

In any case, the text of the prologue to *Thing-Fish* does create a nexus of hilariously offensive outrage, including its parodic Amos "n" Andy language:

> Once upon a time, musta been 'round October, a few years back, in one o' dose TOP SECRET LABMO-TORIES de gubbnint keep stashed away underneath Virginia, an EVIL PRINCE, occasion'ly employed as a part-time THEATRICAL CRITICIZER set to woikin' on a plot to de systematic GENOCIDICAL REMOVE'LANCE of all unwanted highly-rhythmic individj'lls an' sissy-boys! De cocksucker done whiffed up a secret POTIUM ... an' right 'long wid it, de ATROCIOUS IDEA dat what he been boilin' up down deah jes' mights be de FINAL SOLUTIUM to DE WHITE MAIN'S BOIDENN, ef yo' acquire my drift ... Well, we were sure he had a GOOD THING GOIN' ... but, dere was always de possobility dat somethin' might fuck up, so, he planned to have a little test, jes' to check it all out befo' he dump't it in de wat-tuh supply. Sho'tly denafter, wit HIGH-LEVEL GUBNINT COROBBERATIUM, he arranged to have a good-will visit to SAN QUENTIM, 'long wit some country-wes-tin mu-zishnin's, 'n sprinkle a little bit of it on some of de boys in deah (since dey done used a few of 'em befo' when dey was messin' wit de ZYPH'LISS). So, heah dey come with de POTIUM, dump 'nit all in de mash potatoes! Den dey wen' up to de warden's office fo' some HOT TODDY, watchin', a little football while dey's waitin' to see what gone happen! Fact o' de matter were: NOTHIN' HAPPENED, so dey went off'n dribbled it in a special shipnint of GALOOT CO-LOG-NUH dat went out 'bouts NOVEMBER! Next thing y'know, fagnits be droppin' off like flies ... 'long wit a large number of severely-tanned individj'lls, pre-zumnably of HAY'CHEN EXTRAKMENT! But NOT DE BOYS IN DE REST HOME! Oh no! Mixin' de shit wit de mash potatoes done SMOOTHED IT OUT a little, so's it wouldn't KILL yo' ass, BUT, it sho' would make y'ugly! 'N ef y' was already UGLY, ti'd make yo ass MEAN 'n UGLY ... 'n ef you was already MEAN 'n UGLY, it'd turn ya into a strange, UNKNOWN KREETCHUH, never befo' seen on BROADWAY! Thass right! It'd turn ya' into a 'MAMMY NUN'! Head like a potato ... lips like a duck ... big ol' hands, puffin' up! BIG ONES! Science! Me-jev'l re-LIJ-mus costumery all over yo' BODY! Yow! Oh yeah! Mmm-hmm! (Zappa 1984)

And so, as a student once said to me, "yet again, Zappa got there first." In 1983 he managed to create a remarkable, quasi-musical (but not *entirely* musical, as it is spoken voice over chaotically lively rhythmic background) tour de force of paranoia and satire, summing up the disoriented panics of the time in humorous form. It is admittedly hard to decide whether AIDS is central to *Thing-Fish*, or just a jumping-off point for its polymorphously perverse satire; but its inclusivity (as so many different people are simultaneously insulted) and its sensitivity to the underlying paranoia created around AIDS remains remarkable (as well as hilarious).

Finale Ultimo

In the end, I find myself discussing censorship in relation to music and the AIDS crisis with some ambivalence. Measured against other art forms, and against the general rhetoric around AIDS, many musical works seem cagey, almost bowdlerized, yet there are acceptable cultural, psychological, and aesthetic reasons for most of the elisions. There are also plausible political and commercial reasons, and those are the reasons that we, as products of twentieth- and twenty-first-century thought, generally find less forgivable. What is difficult is to be sure of the intentions or discussions that led to the choices made in many of these works. Perhaps, ultimately, it is most sensible to view this music in terms of what its details suggest: that, whatever plausible justifications might be applied to any given case, the generally constrained rhetoric of most musical works related to AIDS is itself a cultural signal, and a cultural proof: that, for reasons outlined above, a large number of musicians responding to the AIDS crisis were willing to march in the parade but were unwilling to walk in front—and, perhaps, unwilling to walk within the sight of cameras, of bystanders, or of the people they thought they were trying to support.

Acknowledgement

Thanks to Ryan Hepburn and Bob Ostertag, who discussed ideas for this chapter.

Notes

1. This is distinct from the relatively direct language common in American poetry from the 1950s through the 1970s—it is possible to see such directness in texts used for later classical music on the West Coast and in the Midwest, but that may have seemed outmoded in New York in the 1980s; at the other extreme, there appears to be little Language Poetry or Ashbery-esque postmodernism written about AIDS.
2. The choral work is included in the second recording (Corigliano 1996). Mark Adamo's note on the genesis of the work should be taken seriously; as Corigliano's partner, he was presumably present while these works were written.
3. Maus, Fred. "Narrative and Identity in Three Songs about AIDS." In *Musical Narrative since 1900: Musical Meaning and Interpretation*, edited by Michael Klein and Nicholas Reyland (Bloomington: Indiana University Press, 2013), 254–271; Maus, Fred. "Three Songs about Privacy, by R.E.M." Journal of Popular Music Studies, 22, no. 1 (2010): 2–31.
4. There are examples of this in most of her interviews, as well as in numerous performances; for instance, a concert video includes a tirade against Benetton for their use of a picture of a person with AIDS as a way of symbolizing sympathy in an advertisement (Galás 1993a).
5. Wojnarowicz and Neill, video excerpt with comments. http://www.youtube.com/watch?v=BPf8gHJ13D0.
6. The *New York Times* summed up the situation in December 2010. Holland Cotter, "As Ants Crawl Over Crucifix, Dead Artist Is Assailed Again." http://www.nytimes.com/2010/12/11/arts/design/11ants.html?_r=1.
National Coalition against Censorship, "Against Censorship: *Fire in my Belly* by David Wojnarowicz, Diamanda Galás" [press release]. December 2, 2010.
7. "Diamanda Galás Responds to the Smithsonian's Removal of David Wojnarowicz's Work." *Washington City Paper*, December 3, 2010. http://www.washingtoncitypaper.com/blogs/

artsdesk/visual-arts/2010/12/03/diamanda-galas-responds-to-the-smithsonians-removal-of-david-wojnarowiczs-work/.
8. The text by Miles stood in for one expected from Wojnarowicz, who was too ill to complete it.
9. *Hustler*, April 1984. The LP was released on December 21, 1984, eventually followed by a CD pressing. However, the show was explained in an interview on the *David Letterman Show* on October 31, 1983, which puts it well ahead of other musical works about AIDS. It's interesting that Zappa describes the show by repeating parts of the opening monologue—perhaps the performed version was based on his explanation, instead of the reverse.

References

The large number of musical works directly concerning AIDS is often surprising to those who have not engaged with the topic. This list includes the most important of generally available materials and overviews, with works especially related to censorship.

AIDS Quilt Songbook. 1992. Los Angeles: Harmonia Mundi, compact disc.

AIDS Quilt Songbook [score]. 1993. London: Boosey & Hawkes.

Amos, Tori. 1996. *Boys for Pele*. New York: Atlantic, compact disc.

Attinello, Paul. 2006. "Closeness and Distance: Songs about AIDS." In *Queering the Popular Pitch*, edited by Sheila Whiteley and Jennifer Rycenga. New York: Routledge.

Barz, Gregory, and Judah Cohen, eds. 2011. *The Culture of AIDS in Africa: Hope and Healing through Music and the Arts*. New York: Oxford University Press.

Colón, Willie. 1999. "El Gran Varón," on *Ritmo Latina: Salsa*. Sony, compact disc.

Corigliano, John. 1996. *Of Rage and Remembrance* [and] Symphony no. 1. New York: BMG Entertainment, compact disc.

Del Tredici, David. 2001. *Secret Music: A Songbook*. New York: CRI, compact disc.

Gaar, Gillian. 2002. *She's a Rebel: The History of Women in Rock & Roll*. New York: Seal Press.

Galás, Diamanda. 1993a. *Judgment Day*. Chicago: Atavistic Video, VHS.

Galás, Diamanda. 1993b. *Masque of the Red Death: A Plague Mass in Three Parts*. New York: Mute Records, compact disc.

Galás, Diamanda. 1996. *The Shit of God*. New York: High Risk.

Heartbeats: New Songs from Minnesota for the AIDS Quilt Songbook. 1994. St. Paul, MN: Innova, compact disc.

Henze, Hans Werner. 1994. *Requiem: Nine Sacred Concertos for Piano Solo, Trumpet Concertante and Chamber Orchestra*. London: Sony Classical, compact disc.

Jackson, Janet. 1998. *The Velvet Rope: Special Edition*. [N.p.]: Virgin Records, compact disc.

Jackson, Janet. 1999. *The Velvet Rope Tour: Live in Concert*. Chatsworth, CA: Image Entertainment, compact disc.

JAMS [= KLF]. 1988. *History of the JAMS aka The Timelords*. New York: TVT Records, compact disc.

Klein, Michael, ed. 1989. *Poets for Life: Seventy-Six Poets Respond to AIDS*. New York: Crown Publishers.

Madonna. 1992a. *Erotica*. Los Angeles: Maverick Recording, compact disc.

Madonna. 1992b. *The Girlie Show: Live Down Under*. Burbank, Calif.: Warner Reprise, DVD.

Ostertag, Bob. 1993. *All the Rage*. Performed by the Kronos Quartet. New York: Elektra, compact disc.

Ostertag. 2009. *Creative Life: Music, Politics, People and Machines.* Urbana: University of Illinois Press.
Philadelphia. 1993. London: Tristar Home Entertainment, 2004, DVD.
Red Hot Organization. *Red Hot + Blue.* 1990. New York: King Cole, Inc, compact disc. [The first in a long series of benefit compact discs and videos in various genres.]
Springsteen, Bruce, et al. 1993. *Music from the Motion Picture* Philadelphia. New York: Sony Music Entertainment, compact disc.
Taylor, James. 1988. *Never Die Young.* New York: Columbia Records, compact disc.
Tift, Matthew. 2007. "Musical AIDS: Music, Musicians, and the Cultural Construction of HIV/AIDS in the United States." D. Mus. diss., Madison: University of Wisconsin.
TLC. 1994. *CrazySexyCool.* LaFace Records, compact disc.
Warwick, Dionne. 1989. *Greatest Hits 1979–1990.* New York: Arista, compact disc.
Wojnarowicz, David. 1992. *Memories that Smell like Gasoline.* San Francisco: Artspace Books.
Wojnarowicz, David, and Ben Neill. 1992. *ITSOFOMO.* San Germano, Italy: Robi Droli, compact disc.
Zappa, Frank. 1984. *Thing-Fish.* Salem, MA: Rykodisc, 1995, compact disc.

CHAPTER 29

TEACHING SILENCE IN THE TWENTY-FIRST CENTURY
Where are the Missing Women Composers?

ROXANE PREVOST AND KIMBERLY FRANCIS

"If you are a woman and you want to be a composer, you should marry rich."

In September 2000, I sat excitedly in my very first seminar in upper-level composition. Only after proving my proficiency in counterpoint, orchestration, set-theory, and harmony was I allowed to enter this final course, and so it was with great anticipation and pride that I awaited the words of the award-winning Master Teacher assigned to pass on to us his pearls of wisdom. The professor began with this fundamental piece of advice: "if you are a woman, and you want to be a composer, you should marry rich. The same can be said of men, to a degree, but this especially applies to women." It was spoken as nothing more than a matter of fact and no effort was made to suggest whether this reality was just or not. Instead, all eleven of us in that room that first day—eight men and three women—learned that there were two sets of rules for professional composers that divided us along gendered lines. The dynamic decidedly shifted in our class from that point forward. Though not directly caused by his words—which were simply a symptom of a larger problem—only two of the three women present with me that day finished the final course, and neither of us remains in the field of composition now.

THIS story, shared by a colleague, is simply one example among many of the prejudices women continue to face in the field of composition in the twenty-first century. Although women composers have gained recognition in recent years in the domains of performance, grants, publishing, and recordings, the number of active contemporary women composers remains small in comparison to their male counterparts. Considering that more women currently undertake university studies than men, it is remarkable that composition remains a field dominated by men, begging the question: where are all the missing women composers?

This chapter examines the multiple factors that may lie behind this reality from three vantage points. First, we consider the notion that the language of modernist music is a gendered discourse. We explore Catherine Parson Smith's influential argument that the use of sexual linguistics—that is, the contrast between a mode of writing associated with the dominant, or male, voice versus the other, or female, discourse—has proven detrimental to women artists during the modernist era. We present supporters and detractors of this theory while also considering the various contexts that gave rise to the political positioning of the musical language of modernism and the tradition these variables have helped to establish.

Secondly, we consider the role precedent plays in the acceptance of women composers. While male composers generally study with other men and have a long history on which to draw, women artists do not typically have this lineage. The problem is intensified by the canon of works studied in undergraduate analysis classes and analyzed in peer-reviewed music theoretical literature. Women composers are usually excluded and, as a result, their works are often perceived as being of inferior quality and not worthy of discussion. Although there are exceptions—for instance Clara Schumann—the role traditionally assigned to women composers has been that of the mediocre artist who writes for pleasure. Recently, some women have broken the barrier and an increasing number of courses engage with topics concerning women and music, but tradition still comes into play. In this chapter, we examine in greater detail different ways in which the fields of musicology and music theory have reacted to this situation, as well as different strategies scholars have employed and continue to explore to address this imbalance.

Thirdly, we discuss the role of societal stereotypes, which are themselves imbedded within quotidian relationships and remain tacit, yet ever so effective. We explore where women composers are positioned within society, as well as other factors that closely relate to societal conditions affecting the reception of women composers' music. We briefly examine how stereotypes about artistic women affect not only the creativity and output of women composers, but also their professional behavior. We conclude our study by offering new strategies to overcome the obstacles we identify, posing expanded solutions to the following questions: How is it that societal prejudices and pedagogical content influence the fields in which composers' music is received? And, since more women composers than ever before hold positions at post-secondary institutions today thereby creating a legacy for younger students, and since scholars have opened up new discourses concerning creative women, why are there still so few recognized contemporary women composers?

The Gender Dynamics of Musical Modernism

The development of musical modernism in North America and Western Europe has been decidedly marked by gendered rhetoric. In her widely influential article, "A Distinguishing

Virility': Feminism and Modernism in American Art Music," Catherine Parsons Smith (1994) makes the argument that the compositional language of modern music is inherently prohibitive to women. She borrows from the work of literary scholars Sandra M. Gilbert and Susan Gubar, who convincingly theorize that the development of modernist literature was indelibly linked to gender politics. In their text *No Man's Land: The Place of the Woman Writer in the Twentieth-Century*, Gilbert and Gubar (1988) identify two discursive categories used in modernism's "sexual linguistics": a *materna lingua*, or a "mother tongue," spoken by all in domestic situations and outside of the academy, and a *patrius sermo*, a form of language learned only by entering higher education. Gilbert and Gubar argue that the *patrius sermo* of the nineteenth century was Latin, but that as women gained greater access to education, the *patrius sermo* lost its prestige and exclusionary power. Increasingly, male and female writers were using the same materials, and in some cases, such as with the works of Charlotte Brontë and Jane Austen, women were arguably surpassing men in both the realms of critical and popular success. The desire to reinscribe a sense of privilege into the literature of the avant-garde, coupled with the threat that women might overtake the field—a fear exacerbated by the simultaneous advances made by the feminist movement—led male authors such as Ezra Pound, T. S. Eliot, and James Joyce to reappropriate and complicate the *materna lingua*, transforming it into a new *patrius sermo*. In so doing, these men created a style that we now consider the definition of literary high modernism. Women authors, among them Virginia Woolf, Zora Neale Thurston, and Edna St. Vincent Millay, reacted to this discourse by creating their own politically loaded literary techniques, and thus modernism in the field of literature carried with it this "war of words" as authors battled over the politics of gender identities through literature.

Smith maps the concepts of *materna lingua* and *patrius sermo* onto the development of music of the modernist period in North America and Western Europe. She argues that musical materials common during the high Romantic period—or the use of chromatically inflected tonality—were themselves a sort of *materna lingua* by the turn of the twentieth century. This was also a time when women had entered professional music spheres in unprecedented numbers as teachers, performers, composers, and patrons. This female presence was especially true in the United States, to the point that conductor Walter Damrosch remarked, "I do not think there has ever been a country whose musical development has been fostered so almost exclusively by women as America" (Oja 2003, 201).

In reaction to this, Smith argues, male composers in fields as diverse as the American ultra-moderns, the Italian futurists, the French neo-classicists, and the German-Austrian serialists established new *patrii sermones* that could then exclude women from participating in the development of classical music. She cites the highly misogynistic rhetoric surrounding this music and its increasingly specialized technical issues as factors that lead to the sharp decline in women's public participation in music circles after 1920, especially in the United States. Today, it remains true that serialism, neo-romanticism, and computer-assisted music are the dominant modes of composition, often carrying with them masculine connotations. Composers who write using these types of procedures are generally more successful with performances and recordings of their works, while those writing in a discourse that opposes the dominant one are far less likely to be recognized because their music does not fall within this accepted norm.

Ellie Hisama has complicated Smith's assertions, arguing that there were indeed women composers, such as Ruth Crawford Seeger, Marion Bauer, and Vivian Fine, who found modernist techniques satisfying for their own compositional goals. She affirms that simply because "male composers . . . wished to ascribe to modernism stereotypically masculine characteristics is not sufficient reason to claim that modernist music actually *is* a male preserve . . . Smith does not demonstrate the inherent misogyny of music matter itself—that is, pitch, rhythm, and other elements of structure" (Hisama 2001, 10–11). Moreover, Hisama argues that it is difficult to map Gilbert and Gubar's conclusions about a specific sexual syntax on to the matter of musical modernism because its historic development was so different from that of its literary counterpart.

We agree with Hisama that it is difficult to assert that the content or structures of musical modernism are essentially misogynist—a sort of anti-*écriture féminine*, if you will. Simultaneously, we cannot dismiss the misogynist context in which these notes, techniques, and structures were and are created, taught, performed, published, and received. The key lies somewhere between Smith's and Hisama's observations—a balance between interrogating content and context. Modernism's multiple outlets and facets have indeed provided some women with the freedom of expression inherent to their musical vision. At the same time, the classroom, where these techniques were developed and are currently passed on, was and remains to a degree today, a space that privileges men. Furthermore, the system that comprises everything beyond the act of composing—the concert hall, the critic's column, the publisher's catalogue, the foundations' grants—remains a hostile place for women composers, and this can serve as a means to deter or stifle their participation in the field of composition. Before elaborating on the reception and perception of women composers within society, we explore the absence of role models for women composers as well as the implications of established canons of musical works in academic and performance settings.

IDENTIFYING TRADITIONS, ESTABLISHING LEGACIES

One factor that has served to detrimentally affect women artists is a sense of isolation from any kind of lineage or tradition. Indeed, many young women composers find themselves without a female role model or a tradition to which they belong. Without this heritage, women composers may struggle with the notion of precedence. In *Gender and the Musical Canon*, Marcia Citron (1993, 67) argues that ameliorating this situation, and creating a historical lineage for women composers, does not have a simple answer:

> Which past does the female creator relate to: some neutral or universal past, or a female past? Perhaps she might want to relate to more than one tradition. But if one of them is a female tradition the problem is that there is still no fully formed female

tradition to relate to. Music by women is performed occasionally but still has not acquired the status of a meaningful tradition. As statements by many women composers suggest . . . relating to a neutral past can mean marginalization and subordination to the ideologies of dominant culture, which is male culture. This may be especially true given that women are socialized in dominant culture. In fact, there is no such thing as a neutral, universal past; every past represents a later reconstruction that selects what it wishes to emphasize.

It is this sense of isolation that Citron argues may exacerbate a sense of insecurity among some women composers, creating a milieu in which they experience creative anxiety. She writes, "Many female composers of art music have expressed an anxiety of authorship. . . . The anxiety often translates into ambivalence: contradictory statements or actions about one's relationship to the creative process. The ambivalence usually indicates a lack of confidence" (54). Women composers then face a challenge in connecting themselves with past traditions, and a key factor to improving their position rests in establishing a revised canon. Given a firmer grounding in the past, more women may claim a place in the present. This is a reality scholars and composers alike have begun to confront by documenting the activities of women composers throughout history. Understanding the current state of literature on women's history and the communities of women composers that have been established to date will help to explain where the disparities remain and possible reasons for the continued gap between women and men in the field of professional composition. Because of the broad array of creative communities globally, we have chosen to focus this part of our chapter primarily on scholarship and communities based in and around the United States.

Concurrent to women's unprecedented participation in professional music spheres, the early twentieth century also saw the publication of some of the first biographical anthologies concerned with women in music (Elson 1903; Elson 1918). Yet, after 1920, interest in such publications either by authors or by publishers seems to have disappeared. By 1930, women faced criticism from public comments launched against them by male composers such as Charles Ives and critics such as Paul Rosenfeld, who attacked women for the feminization of American music and the inferior quality of their musical abilities and taste (Oja 2003; Tick 1993). Carol Neuls-Bates has also demonstrated that, during the middle of the modernist period, men invoked science to try to explain why there were no great female composers. In particular, she points to the influential behavioral psychologist Carl Seashore, who wrote in 1940, "[admittedly] women have a rich and free imagination, but it is . . . of a less sustained order, while men's achievement in creative work is often attributed to greater capacity for creative power." He further declared that women were far too attracted by the institution and subsequent confines of marriage, stating, "marriage, as a career in itself, then invites music as an avocation. . . . Married women may not have produced great compositions, but they have produced great composers" (Neuls-Bates 1996, 301). Similar sentiments were echoed by perhaps the most prominent woman teacher of the modernist era, Nadia Boulanger, who was notoriously discouraging of the creative aspirations of her women students (Rosenstiel

1982). As modernist aesthetics—particularly serial techniques and computer-generated music—gained ground in the United States during the Cold War era, music's connections to science and masculinity became of the utmost importance. Early McCarthyism, as Nadine Hubbs (2004) has trenchantly argued, was laden with misogynistic, homophobic, and racist conceptions of what classical music ought to be, and who ought to be composing it—a factor in stifling women's further advancement in academic training as composers and exacerbating the sense of isolation from a particular woman-centered legacy.

These conditions began to change in 1975, the year designated by the United Nations as International Women's Year. In collaboration with other events held during this time, the College Music Society hosted the first conference on the Status of Women (Neuls-Bates 1996, 325). This same year, women composers' organizations took shape, the first being the International League of Women Composers (ILWC), founded by Nancy van der Vate. The initial executive board included exceptional women composers from all over the world including van der Vate, Radie Britain, Clair Plin, Marga Richter, Donna Robertson, and Pauline Oliveros (Beath 1991, 1). In an interview from 1981, van der Vate clearly outlined her motivation for forming the IWLC: she strongly believed that "as women, we simply have not had access to the same opportunities as men" (Neuls-Bates 1996, 327). More precisely, the IWLC worked to "redress the imbalance between men and women composers in the areas of orchestral performance, commissions, and recordings" (Beath 1991, 1). The International League was also devoted to providing a network of communication for both composers and those interested in performing their works. It was designed to maintain a sense of community support among its members, and affect an increasingly strong liaison between women composers and the rest of the musical world. Beyond advocating for increased concert performances of women's music, the ILWC also supported female student composers through competitions and sponsored a series of lecture recitals over the radio.

A year after the creation of the ILWC, the American Women Composers Association (AWCA) was founded by Tommie E. Carl. This separate organization was designed to promote music by women composers in the United States (Neuls-Bates, 1996, 361). The AWCA provided recording resources for members and established a tape and score library. Members of this organization also began to lobby successfully for concerts of women's music at such high-profile locations as the Kennedy Center, Carnegie Hall, and the National Museum for Women in the Arts. Working in tandem with the ILWC and the AWCA was the International Congress on Women and Music, established by Jeannie Pool in 1979. This association served as a means to formally organize conferences and meetings for women in music while also maintaining a library of related literature, now housed at California State University, Northridge. In 1995 all three of these bodies merged to form the International Alliance for Women and Music (IAWM). After the merger, the newsletters of these various groups were collapsed into two major scholarly journals dedicated specifically to women in music: the *International Alliance for Women and Music Journal* and *Women and Music*.

The work of these groups has led to some success. In 1983 Ellen Taaffe Zwilich was the first woman to win the Pulitzer Prize for music with her *Symphony No. 1* (Neuls-Bates 1996, 331). She was also the first woman awarded a doctorate in composition from Julliard, an accomplishment she achieved in 1975 (Neuls-Bates, 1996, 331). In 1990 Joan Tower received the Grawemeyer Prize, the first granted to a composing woman, and nine years later, violinists Nadja Salerno-Sonnenberg, Pamela Frank, and Sarah Chang received the Avery Fisher Prize, the first time it was ever awarded to women artists (Ammer 2001, 58–59). These and other groundbreaking accomplishments are signs that the work of associations like the ILWC and the AWCA have contributed to the exposure and successful championing of both women composers and performers.

FEMINISM AND THE ACADEMY: CHALLENGING THE CANON

The push to incorporate feminist thought into the academy took longer to flourish, and it first gained ground in the field of musicology. Beginning in 1980, scholarly anthologies concerning biographical accounts of women composers and women's musical careers began to appear in print. With these texts, women's historical involvement with creative traditions was no longer relegated to isolated, exceptional circumstances; slowly, a canonical tradition began to take shape. Furthermore, from 1991 to 1994 four watershed publications—Susan McClary's *Feminine Endings: Music, Gender, and Sexuality*; Ruth Solie's *Musicology and Difference*; Marcia Citron's *Gender and the Musical Canon*; and Phillip Brett, Elizabeth Wood, and Gary C. Thomas's *Queering the Pitch*—were published. These texts ignited a firestorm of academic debate that marked the beginning of attempts by the scholarly community to interrogate the roles of gender, sexuality, and minority identities in the structure of the canon, the place of women's music, and public perceptions of the *Kleinmeister*. Attempts to critically indict traditions of misogyny, racism, and homophobia within the musicological canon eventually became recognized as a legitimate form of scholarly inquiry.

These efforts have directly resulted in the increased presence of women composers in history textbooks on the Western canon, albeit still in decidedly small numbers compared to men. Another healthy sign that feminist musicologists are gaining ground is that authors now include women as part of the main narrative in their textbooks, no longer relegating them to parenthetical, token discussions of women composers. There is still the need to increase the number of examples within texts that draw on women's music as well as a need to add greater value to those elements of music-making that women have been fundamentally involved with, including teaching, patronage, and review writing. Finally, there has yet to be a textbook on the Western canon written exclusively by a woman. Given that an author's life experiences and personal narrative goals would greatly inflect a book of this kind, one could imagine that a history of

Western music written from a woman's point of view would offer a potentially different narrative than those currently in print.

Conversely, despite this improving state of affairs in musicological spheres, the discipline of music theory still struggles with incorporating women into its canon. This is most apparent in the distinct lack of women's music represented in theory textbooks. Of all the texts produced post-1975 for the purposes of studying tonal music analysis, orchestration, and counterpoint, most exclude examples of music written by women. It is only with recent publications that we begin to see the inclusion of women composers' music in tonal theory textbooks (Clendinning and Marvin 2005; Gauldin 2004; Kostka and Payne 2000; Roig-Francolí 2003). Those books that extend as far as the post-tonal era often reference Ruth Crawford Seeger's music, especially her *String Quartet* (1931), but otherwise, few women are discussed. As with textbooks on tonal music, it is the recent publications that discuss music by women composers. In his second edition (2000) of *Introduction to Post-Tonal Theory*, Joseph N. Straus provides two works by Ruth Crawford Seeger, while his third edition (2005) now includes the same works by Crawford Seeger, in addition to works by Sofia Gubaidulina, Thea Musgrave, and Ellen Taaffe Zwilich. Although these recent publications offer repertoire that is more inclusive, the representation of women composers remains relatively small. For students of composition, this presents a decidedly contradictory message that music theorists are now beginning to interrogate more thoroughly.

In her article "Cognitive Dissonance: Should Twentieth-Century Women Composers be Grouped with Foucault's Mad Criminals?" Rosemary Killam provides a thorough, poststructural critique of the underrepresentation of women composers in the music theory canon. She considers this to be largely the result of how music theory programs developed in the United States during the 1960s. Killam cites the rallying cry put out by Milton Babbitt during the 1950s as a major catalyst for the current structure of music theory programs. Babbitt denounced the effects of public opinion on music composition, aligning himself entirely with the academy, and strongly encouraging other composers to do likewise. This led in many instances to the indelible link between modernist art music composition and the academy. Simultaneously, there was a striking decrease in the percentage of women faculty members within higher-level institutions. This, Killam (1997, par. 22) argues, "may have had unintended consequences on the education of younger contemporary composers and theorists, who may have had minimal opportunities to study theory and composition with women composers/theorists." Killam believes that this lack of women mentors and opportunities to study the music of women artists caused later theorists to avoid including music with which they were unfamiliar, or for which there was no established music-theoretical canon, in their own textbooks and classrooms. Thus, precedence played a large role in setting the stage for the present lack of women's music in theory and analysis textbooks, perpetuating an imbalance both in the matter of academic literature and in the demographics of faculty positions in upper-level institutions.

Marcia Citron's work elaborates on the way this self-perpetuating cycle has resulted in the current canon. Citron highlights as a main problem the often detrimental "male modes of discourse" or "patterns that grow out of ideology and acculturation in Western society," which have served as the overwhelming basis for those who hold positions of critical authority. Professional musical criticism, argues Citron, has been established as the purview of men, or has been driven by a specifically male viewpoint. The limitations of this lens therefore generate a limited outcome, similar to the male-dominated spheres described by Killam. As Citron (1993, 181) explains, "internalized musical values from male predecessors and contemporaries . . . form a pre-evaluative context for the structuring of [critical] discourse." Thus, the act of criticism, of authoritatively assigning value to musical matter, has often been controlled by parameters derived from the male experiential model. If we agree that gender affects our lives profoundly, and therefore how we experience, discuss, and relate to music, then it would also stand to reason that the exclusion of women's perspectives, and women's works, has limited the canon and the modes of musical expression currently in use.

By continuing to promote certain pieces and repertoire as representative of the best works, canons not only promote certain repertoire but also give the impression that this repertoire is of the highest quality, diminishing the value of those works not considered. Moreover, as Citron argues, canons influence both those in academia and those who are involved with the marketing and promotion of music, such as music critics, concert promoters, record producers, and music publishers. And so these tacit canonical assumptions can have wide-reaching and quite pernicious effects, particularly if they remain unquestioned, on the level of the subtext. As Citron (1993, 193) writes, "Canon formation is a complex process that exerts great power in shaping and perpetuating attitudes toward valuation and hence what gets enshrined as masterpieces."

Our perception as listeners and our expectations of how works are to be positioned within the canon are often influenced by the critic's comments or observations. We interpret works within a cultural framework and, as such, we may be convinced to change our interpretation if new information arises. Lucy Green has proven through studies that our response will most likely change if we discover that the work we are studying or listening to was composed by a woman. Her conclusions are worth citing at length:

> Both sides of the masculine delineation of music—the assumption of the male classical composer bequeathed to us by history, and the cerebral, masculine connotation of composition—are still in operation. I have argued that musical delineations are not closed unto themselves, but that they affect our perception of inherent meanings. In the face of the twofold masculine delineation of music, what happens when we do discover a women's mind behind the music is that her femininity then enters the delineation as an unusual and noticeable fact, which conflicts with the delineation of mental capacity arising from composition. From that position, delineated femininity acts to alter our attitude towards the inherent meanings of the music. We are then liable to judge the woman composer's handling of inherent meanings in terms of our idea of her femininity. It is not that there is anything feminine about the inherent meanings, but that the idea of femininity filters our response to them. The fact that some critics have been able to hold on to their conviction that women cannot

compose is not, then, the result of pure prejudice: it is something which they apparently learned from their experience of music itself. I would therefore suggest that it is something which is difficult for everyone, and this must include myself, to resist.

(Green 1997, 107)

Music theorists exert much influence over these canonical formations and their subsequent delineations of masculinity or femininity. They decide what their students will analyze and how this will resonate with what they learn in music history courses and the music they perform in lessons and ensembles. The selection of specific exemplars in anthologies reinforces the valuation of an elite group of compositions. It sends the message that, of all of the works written in a particular historical period, this one in particular must be studied in order for the student to gain a better understanding of music from that time. To borrow Citron's (1993, 201) words again:

> The "great pieces" paradigm, underlying the notion of anthologized works, exerts tremendous power. A tacit assumption is that anthologized works embody high quality and exemplify the important stylistic and historical points that students should know. In varying proportions, each composition is deemed significant in its own right and representative of other works of like-minded values. Furthermore, inclusion implies that its composer as an individual and as part of the diachronic succession delineated via other exemplars merits historical recognition. It suggests that the work and composer exemplify a style that influenced others; for works after 1800 add innovative and original.

Works commonly selected to be part of the canon gain recognition as works of high quality, while pieces that are omitted, by default, are perceived as being of inferior quality. Since few music anthologies include works by women composers, their music is often excluded from classroom analysis and the perception is that women write works that are not as interesting or as valuable in comparison to those of their male counterparts. Music analysis and skills courses, the bread and butter of a composer's training, therefore continue to present a decidedly myopic and discouraging state of affairs that reinforces the stereotype that women's music lacks craft. Thus, we return to the problem of women's music being provincial or crippled by notions of dilettantism when compared to the music of Bach, Mozart, Beethoven, and Wagner. Currently, there is no theory textbook that even distinguishes which Schumann—Clara or Robert—they are referencing in their texts. Instead, the surname is left unqualified, once again reiterating the notion that the male is the default. In the theory classroom, women are still confronted with a world where there is no precedent for them outside of the masculine tradition. Theirs is to choose whether to continue on and create this tradition themselves from scratch, or remain one of the many whose life in music will not extend into the canon of musical works.

Furthermore, the canonical restrictions impose control over the work of music theorists beyond the classroom as well. Scholars of music theory, both male and female, often strategically turn to music written by male composers in order to publish in peer-reviewed journals. These journals seldom accept studies that consider the music of women composers, further reinforcing a limited canon that excludes the feminine. As Killam (1997, par. 20) argues:

> What analyses have been published in music theory journals, written by men theorists about compositions by women, utilizing twelve-tone and set theory? There are multiple examples of the converse: women theorists, in their published analysis, have dutifully and skillfully applied current analytical techniques to men's compositions. Would there have been such outrage against McClary's analyses if she had centered on women's compositions, instead of the "canonized" men's compositions which she frequently analyzes?

Many factors come into play to account for the exclusion of women composers in the music theory canon. In his article "The Canons in the Musicological Toolbox," Randel (1992, 17) argues that one reason music by women composers is excluded is that it was composed for a different audience than the one that promoted a canon of works:

> Music by women composers ... was composed by (and perhaps for) people different from—foreign to—those who officiated at the canonizations that have dominated us. We cannot expect to understand any new repertory other than the traditional ones if we are not prepared to invent new methods appropriate for its study. The canon of Western art music as we know it was formulated by a body of specific individuals, all of who happen to have been men. Until we interrogate that face—and them—we cannot suppose it either an accident *or* a phenomenon of dispassionate nature that this canon includes only the works of men.

Not surprisingly, most women theorists opt to submit studies that focus on music that is part of the canon in order to publish, but, even then, they remain underrepresented in the acceptance rate of articles to the Society for Music Theory journals *Music Theory Spectrum* and *Music Theory Online* relative to their membership in the Society.

Asserting a criticism of the "work concept" and thereby creating space not only for the validation of the lives of women composers but also of their actual music is something theorists have recently started to address. Three such examples include Joseph N. Straus's recent large-scale study of *The Music of Ruth Crawford Seeger* (1995) and the anthology *Music by Women for Study and Analysis* (1993), and Harold and Sharon Krebs's examination of Josephine Lang's life and works in *Josephine Lang: Her Life and Songs* (2006). What makes Straus's study of Crawford Seeger's music particularly noteworthy is his concluding chapter, which addresses the social context of her life as a way to bring nuance to some of his analytical findings. This innovative approach allows for the interaction of biography and analysis that brings forth unique insights concerning the music that he examines. Although publications of these types have begun to appear, few theoretical texts on music of the twentieth and twenty-first centuries focus on the works of women composers, and this is a situation that scholars of music theory must address in order to improve the current canon imbalance.

The issue of women's inclusion or exclusion in canons, classrooms, and concert halls is a complex one, the solutions for which do not rest entirely within the academy. Further extending our reach, we would also like to address how academia's permeable boundaries allow institutionally sanctioned canonical constructs to influence and be influenced by society at large. These factors play an essential role in informing the biases both students and professors bring to bear on the pedagogical experience and therefore affect women's training as composers.

Society and Cultural Factors

Society and cultural environment have played a significant role in the perception of women as creative artists. The common belief that women are associated with the body and emotions, while men are associated with the mind and logic, still resonates with social conditioning in certain cultures, including that of North America. Given these covert views on men and women's behavioral proclivities, Jill Halstead proposes that associating the field of composition with men instead of women is itself contradictory. She argues that this biological determinist theory presents a conflicting set of stereotypes concerning composition that ought to be addressed:

> These [prejudices] reinforce the common belief that men are "by nature" logical, profound, technical and ambitious, whereas women are "by nature" intuitive, refined and caring.... Yet, even if such ideas proved to be true (and based on unchangeable sex differences), the arts and music [remain] depicted as areas of "natural feminine" interest, [but] they have been (and still are) staunchly male-dominated. By this reasoning, "natural interest" on the part of women would seem to have no basis in "natural" ability, unless it is directly related to their reproductive role!
>
> (Halstead 1997, 36)

Stereotypes, therefore, suggest that women, though "naturally" or biologically drawn to the arts, rarely have the actual abilities to achieve professional success in this arena. Prejudices such as this are rarely articulated explicitly, yet their subversive presence has had a lasting effect in creating professional obstacles for women that men fail to face.

Further complicating women's position in contemporary professional music spheres is the notion that women are socialized to be "nurturing" and men "ambitious." Recent studies have asked how it is that these dichotomies are the product of social conditioning, rather than being determined biologically, such as was asserted by Seashore in the quote cited earlier in this chapter. Scholars are now beginning to consider how the conditioning of women to avoid conflict may also set them up for failure in the fractious environments found in music theory and composition circles. In her work, Killam cites research of Gilligan, Ruddick, and others that shows that women, particularly in the United States, are culturally conditioned to avoid conflict and to resolve disagreements whenever possible. Killam then postulates that this may be a possible reason why women composers are less successful in the male-dominated, highly aggressive world of twentieth- and twenty-first-century art music. Killam (1997, par. 13) explains:

> Women may be reluctant to participate in the heated verbal printed exchanges that have occurred in the dialectics defining compositional practices and their appropriate theoretical approaches. Many women composers and theorists display these characteristics.... In addition, when women composers and theorists do attempt to participate in these exchanges, our colleagues may perceive us as operating outside the traditional cultural roles of women and discount our opinions.

If Killam's conclusions are correct, and we believe that for many women they are, women composers and theorists are faced with a two-sided problem. They may either choose to engage with professional conflict by using a dominant discourse that may alienate them and cause them to be perceived as over-aggressive or antisocial, or they may choose to continue to approach professional conflict through the subservient position, a more culturally comfortable vantage point yet one that can prove professionally inefficacious.

Thus the nature of classical music composition, itself a highly competitive and arguably fractious field, may itself seem intimidating or hostile to women. Obviously not all women feel this way, and there are departments and institutions where this is not the case, but these are the exception not the rule. Moreover, social conditioning is so often dismissed as a personal obstacle to be surmounted: women simply need "tougher skin," those who truly want careers in the creative arts will be able to work around the uncomfortable environment. But it is worth considering what would happen if we made a concerted effort to change this ethos. It is worth imagining if in changing this, we might not only help nurture an environment that is friendlier to women but also create a space that is more inclusive in general, more creatively productive, and more intriguing to the general public. True, this would perhaps lead classical music down a path upsettingly divergent from the one suggested by Milton Babbitt, but we believe that inclusivity is not entirely a dirty word, that it would not hamper the quality of people's compositions, and that in addition to being more enticing to women, it might actually bring about healthier change to the field of classical music as a whole.

Concluding Thoughts

Although progress has been achieved in the past twenty years, much remains to be done if creative women are to be accepted as "composers" rather than "women composers." The classification of "woman musician," instead of simply, "musician" differentiates and to some extent segregates female artists, rendering them a novelty, or an inferior class of artist. In *Unsung: A History of Women in American Music*, Christine Ammer (2001, 311), however, argues that this separation is necessary until more grounds are gained in the equal opportunities for all musicians. Only when women have an equal presence within the canon will the "woman composer" label lose its usefulness. For Virginia Caputo, this is not simply a question of redefining which composers become part of the accepted canon; rather, it is a question of examining the assumptions and criteria that make up the canon itself. She argues for an approach that questions the paradigms that lie beneath the surface of canons, limiting our ability to engage with a diverse array of musical expression. In Caputo's words: "rather than focusing on finding a place for music by women in the canon, we should begin to rethink the ways certain assumptions about women, gender, women's music, as well as notions of style, genre, process, and periodization, permeate the assumptions that organize our thinking" (1995, 31–32). For Caputo, the solution is not one that can be entirely fixed by simply wedging women composers into our textbooks and onto our concert programs. This solution is only a band-aid that will not have long-standing results unless accompanied by greater questioning of the larger issues behind canon formation. Caputo (1995, 32) argues that we need to fundamentally question the system that has continued to exclude women artists, the "categories and paradigms in place that sustain the power/knowledge nexus that naturalizes the canon and its categories, keeping universal meanings and valuation of music intact, thus obscuring music by women from audible positions."

Randel echoes this viewpoint by asserting that we should question the canon and its formation rather than simply shoehorning women composers into larger historical narratives through affirmative action. He proposes that not only students but also teachers and listeners stand to benefit from the recovery of women's otherwise silent voices, but adds that without a trenchant criticism of the underlying prejudices that have sanctioned exclusionary practices, we are destined to replicate, in Randel's words, the "gender-related implications of what has enshrined the canon that we propose to expand" (1992, 17). Without this kind of interrogation, well-intentioned acts of historical recovery will remain susceptible to devaluation based upon the unspoken rules that police the margins of the canon. For longer-lasting, longer-reaching results, Randel argues, we must "challenge . . . traditional criterion. For this criterion, which is formulated only vaguely if at all, has been the ultimate weapon—not least because of its vagueness—in the male-produced, male-dominated arsenal that has so long kept women out" (17). By reexamining the canon and its formation, we can better contextualize the factors that have led to the current canonical paradigms and challenge assumptions taken for granted in the past.

Addressing the current gender imbalance in the field of modernist composition will require a multitude of strategies. First, we will have to undo the prejudices that make so many in the field of musical production hostile to women and that consequently make many women feel distant from the techniques of such mediums as serialist, electronic, and aleatoric musical composition. Second, it is imperative that we celebrate and promote those mechanisms that have served to support successful women artists in the past and currently. This will require much work on the part of musicologists and historians to recover the stories of women's creative activities, redefine how women artists of the past secured agency for themselves, and reconfigure our models of cultural production so that they include those sources of power that are so often exploited by women but not currently considered in our histories.

Thirdly, we must begin to revise the music-theoretical canon. Moreover, we propose that the analysis of works incorporated into this expanded canon by women composers be twofold: technical and contextual. Some technical aspects will overlap between works by different women and men composers and similar analytical techniques will be useful to draw insightful conclusions for both. We must then be careful not to focus solely on the matter of music itself, so as to avoid simply reinforcing a narrow criterion of excellence and risk excluding any work that failed to conform to certain technical limitations. Green (1997, 114) highlights the problem that "successful" women composers are often praised for technical traits that parallel those of male composers: "Only the most successful woman composer, whose music conforms to contemporary definitions of what music should be, has been judged on the basis of the inherent meanings of her music. She has then been recognized as an honorary man, her femininity, her real woman's achievement, remaining unsung." Like Citron, we propose that women composers' works also be analyzed in the context of their gender and its representation in society. To use Citron's (1993, 58–59) words:

> In general, we might conclude that the main reason a woman composes is the same reason a man chooses to compose: women have something to express, and expressing it in musical terms is important. But *how* a woman expresses herself can be linked with aspects of her gender and their intersection with cultural and aesthetic convention.

As previously mentioned, theorists, such as Straus and Krebs, have begun to explore new analytical methodologies that take into account the intersections between gender and cultural, societal, and aesthetic conventions. Other theorists, such as Susan McClary (1991), Ellie Hisama (1995), and Laurel Parsons (1999), also offer fascinating analyses of women composers. Furthermore, taken together, these scholars have shown that traditional tools need not be entirely discarded in order to analyze women composers' works. But, they have blended with these traditional tools new methodologies sensitive to the unique and interesting aspects of women composers' music that require a dialogue with gender and cultural issues to be fully explored. This type of new, methodologically innovative research needs to be championed more in the field in order to bring about increased visibility for women composers and to promote the notion that their music too has craft.

If our objective is to stimulate heightened awareness of the music of women composers, more resources must become available for classroom study. Although there are some anthologies entirely devoted to the works of women composers (Briscoe, Straus), we would argue that more publications like this are needed and that standard theory textbooks should include music of both female and male composers. Otherwise, the "woman composer" label will remain. Killam cleverly includes a full course syllabus with a repertoire of pieces and suggested readings at the end of her article. With more courses on women composers offered at the university level, we should expect the number of pedagogical resources to increase, but it is in the compulsory music theory courses that we most need to expose students to music written by women.

Much progress has been done in the recognition of women as composers in the past three decades. As Green argues, the level of sexual discrimination against women composers has decreased, although at some level it still prevails. She credits feminist activism with expanding opportunities for women and also believes a changing social climate has allowed women improved access to education and professional positions. These changes, in Green's (1997, 105) words, have "at least [diminished] the normative masculine delineation of music in contemporary society." But she remains concerned that the "assumption that the composer is a man is still far from unreasonable."

The problem lies in large part with how women composers are still perceived within our contemporary society. The situation will only ameliorate itself when we value the music of composers through a more inclusive set of parameters rather than those set by a limited canon of works. Halstead (1997, 248) comments on this as well, writing that "women's continued under-representation in musical composition is part of a much wider complex social and cultural phenomenon where many groups, including women, are systematically undervalued socially, economically and intellectually." For scholars like Halstead and Green, it is this larger systematic discrimination that must be undone before there will be equality among men and women artists, and women will cease to face unjust professional obstacles.

Solving the gender imbalance in the field of art music composition will require complex approaches, not only because the problem has so many roots, but also because no one solution will speak to all women. We must, as a discipline, interrogate the complex sexual linguistics of modernist musical discourse. We must continue to develop a heritage for women to look back on and celebrate those strategies through which women claimed agency in the past and the creative solutions that they exploited to achieve professional success. We must reconsider the role the academy continues to play, particularly in the fields of music theory and composition, bringing women's music into the textbooks, onto recordings, and into the concert hall. Additionally, we need to consider how these changes in the academy interact with conditions outside of it. Institutions of higher learning need to stand in enhanced dialogue with external organizations. They need to expand their focus; encourage those students taking courses to reach out to high school communities, radio programs, or concert halls; and start offering preconcert talks on women's music, radio programming lists that incorporate works by women, or workshops that bring the idea of women's music beyond the walls of the academic classroom. Communities of women composers such as the IAWM should invest more in student outreach, perhaps even creating satellite student groups within universities and conservatories, and taking the collective power of women artists and bringing it to those most vulnerable to institutional biases. Together, these diverse solutions will bring about further change to the canon, the concert hall, and the recording studio, and help to empower, instead of silence, women's voices.

Anthologies and Collections on Women and Music (listed chronologically):

Year	Bibliographic Information
1903	Elson, Arthur. *Woman's Work in Music*
1918	Elson, Louis Charles. *Women in Music*
1948	Drinker, Sophie. *Music and Women: The Story of Women and Their Relationship to Music*
1980	LePage, Jane Weiner. *Women Composers, Conductors, and Musicians of the Twentieth Century*
1981	Handy, D. Antoinette. *Black Women in American Bands and Orchestras*
1981	Ammer, Christine. *Unsung: A History of Women in American Music*[a]
1982	Neuls-Bates, Carol. *Women in Music: An Anthology of Source Readings from the Middle Ages to the Present*[b]
1982	Placksin, Sally. *American Women in Jazz, 1900 to the Present: Their Words, Lives, and Music*
1983	Green, Mildred Denby. *Black Women Composers: A Genesis.*
1983	Tick, Judith. *American Women Composers Before 1870*[c]
1986	Bowers, Jane, and Judith Tick, eds. *Women Making Music*
1987	Briscoe, James R. *Historical Anthology of Music by Women*
1987	Koskoff, Ellen, ed. *Women and Music in Cross-Cultural Perspective*[d]
1988	Jezic, Diane Peacock. *Women Composers: The Lost Tradition Found*[e]
1991	Pendle, Karin. *Women and Music*[f]
1991	McClary, Susan. *Feminine Endings: Music, Gender, and Sexuality*[g]
1992	Kivy, K. Linda. *Canadian Women Making Music*
1993	Citron, Marcia. *Gender and the Musical Canon*[h]
1993	Marshall, Kimberly, ed. *Rediscovering the Muses: Women's Musical Traditions*
1993	Solie, Ruth, ed. *Musicology and Difference*
1993	Straus, Joseph N. *Music by Women for Study and Analysis*
1994	Brett, Phillip, Elizabeth Woods, Gary Thomas. *Queering the Pitch: The New Gay and Lesbian Musicology*[i]
1994	Cook, Susan, and Judy Tsou. *Cecilia Reclaimed: Feminist Perspectives on Gender and Music*
1994	Fuller, Sophie. *The Pandora Guide to Women Composers: Britain and the United States 1629-Present*
1997	Briscoe, James R. *Contemporary Anthology of Music by Women*
2006	Hinkle-Turner, Elizabeth. *Women Composers and Music Technology in the United States: Crossing the Line*

[a] 2nd ed. in 2001.
[b] 2nd ed. in 1996.
[c] 2nd ed. in 1995.
[d] Reprint in 1989.
[e] 2nd ed. 1994.
[f] 2nd ed. in 2001.
[g] Reprint with new introduction in 2002.
[h] Reprint in 2000.
[i] 2nd ed. in 2006.

References

Ammer, Christine. 2001. *Unsung: A History of Women in American Music*. 2nd ed. Portland, Oreg.: Amadeus Press.

Beath, Betty. 1991. "International League of Women Composers." *The International League of Women Composers Journal* 1–2.

Bowers, Jane, and Judith Tick, eds. 1986. *Women Making Music: The Western Art Tradition, 1150–1950*. Urbana and Chicago: University of Illinois Press.

Brett, Phillip, Elizabeth Wood, and Gary C. Thomas, eds. 2006. *Queering the Pitch: The New Gay and Lesbian Musicology*. 2nd ed. New York: Routledge.

Briscoe, James R. 1987. *Historical Anthology of Music by Women*. Bloomington: Indiana University Press.

Briscoe, James R. 1997. *Contemporary Anthology of Music by Women*. Bloomington: Indiana University Press.

Caputo, Virginia. 1995. "Silent Canons: Places For Music By Women." In *With a Song in Her Heart: A Celebration of Canadian Women Composers*, 23–33. Windsor, Ontario: Humanities Research Group.

Citron, Marcia. 1993. *Gender and the Musical Canon*. New York: Cambridge University Press. Reprint, 2000.

Clendinning, Jane Piper, and Elizabeth West Marvin. 2005. *The Musician's Guide to Theory and Analysis*. New York and London: W. W. Norton & Company.

Cook, Susan, and Judy Tsou, eds. 1994. *Cecilia Reclaimed: Feminist Perspectives on Gender and Music. With a foreword by Susan McClary*. Urbana and Chicago: University of Illinois Press.

Drinker, Sophie. 1948. *Music and Women: The Story of Women and Their Relationship to Music*. New York: Coward-McCann.

Elson, Arthur. 1903. *Woman's Work in Music*. Boston: L. C. Page & Company.

Elson, Louis Charles. 1918. *Women in Music*. New York: University Society Incorporated.

Fuller, Sophie. 1994. *The Pandora Guide to Women Composers: Britain and the United States 1629–Present*. London: HarperCollins.

Gauldin, Robert. 2004. *Harmonic Practice in Tonal Music*. 2nd ed. New York and London: W. W. Norton & Company.

Gilbert, Sandra M., and Susan Gubar. *No Man's Land: The Place of the Woman Writer in the Twentieth Century*. Vol. 1, *The War of the Words* (1998). Vol. 2, *Sexchanges* (1989). Vol. 3, *Letters from the Front* (1994). New Haven, Conn.: Yale University Press.

Green, Lucy. 1997. *Music, Gender, Education*. Cambridge: Cambridge University Press.

Green, Mildred Denby. 1983. *Black Women Composers: A Genesis*. Boston: Twayne Publishers.

Halstead, Jill. 1997. *The Woman Composer*. Aldershot, UK: Ashgate.

Handy, D. Antoinette. 1981. *Black Women in American Bands and Orchestras*. London: Scarecrow Press.

Hinkle-Turner, Elizabeth. 2006. *Women Composers and Music Technology in the United States: Crossing the Line*. Burlington, Vt.: Ashgate.

Hisama, Ellie M. 1995. "The Question of Climax in Ruth Crawford's String Quartet, Mvt. 3." In *Concert Music, Rock, and Jazz Studies Since 1945: Essays and Analytical Studies*, edited by Elizabeth West Marvin and Richard Hermann, 285–312. Rochester, N.Y.: University of Rochester Press.

Hisama, Ellie M. 2001. *Gendering Musical Modernism: The Music of Ruth Crawford, Marion Bauer, and Miriam Gideon*. Cambridge: Cambridge University Press.

Hubbs, Nadine. 2004. *The Queer Composition of America's Sound: Gay Modernists, American Music, and National Identity*. Berkeley: University of California Press.

Jezic, Diane Peacock. 1994. *Women Composers: The Lost Tradition Found*. 2nd ed. Edited by Elizabeth Wood. New York: Feminist Press.

Killam, Rosemary N. 1997. "Cognitive Dissonance: Should Twentieth-Century Women Composers be Grouped with Foucault's Mad Criminals?" *Music Theory Online* 3, no. 2.

Kivi, K. Linda. 1992. *Canadian Women Making Music*. Toronto: Green Dragon Press.

Koskoff, Ellen, ed. 1987. *Women and Music in Cross-Cultural Perspective*. New York: Greenwood Press. Reprint, 1989.

Kostka, Stephen, and Dorothy Payne. 2000. *Tonal Harmony with an Introduction to Twentieth-Century Music*. 4th ed. New York: McGraw-Hill.

Krebs, Harald, and Sharon Krebs. 2006. *Josephine Lang: Her Life and Songs*. New York and Oxford: Oxford University Press.

LePage, Jane Weiner. 1980. *Women Composers, Conductors, and Musicians of the Twentieth Century*. London: Scarecrow Press.

Marshall, Kimberly, ed. 1993. *Rediscovering the Muses: Women's Musical Traditions*. Boston: Northeastern University Press.

McClary, Susan. 2002. *Feminine Endings: Music, Gender, and Sexuality*. Reprint with new introduction. Minnesota: University of Minnesota Press.

Neuls-Bates, Carol. 1996. *Women in Music: An Anthology of Source Readings from the Middle Ages to the Present*. 2nd ed. Boston: Northeastern University Press.

Oja, Carol. 2003. *Making Music Modern: New York in the 1920s*. New York: Oxford University Press.

Parsons, Laurel. 1999. "Music and Text in Elisabeth Luytens's Wittgenstein Motet." *Canadian University Music Review* 20, no. 1, 71–100.

Pendle, Karin, ed. 2001. *Women and Music: A History*. 2nd ed. Bloomington: Indiana University Press.

Placksin, Sally. 1982. *American Women in Jazz, 1900 to the Present: Their Words, Lives and Music*. New York: Wideview Books.

Randel, Don Michael. 1992. "The Canons in the Musicological Toolbox." In *Disciplining Music: Musicology and Its Canons*, edited by Katherine Bergeron and Philip V. Bohlman, 10–22. Chicago and London: University of Chicago Press.

Roig-Francolí, Miguel A. 2003. *Harmony in Context*. New York: McGraw Hill.

Rosentiel, Leonie. 1982. *Nadia Boulanger: A Life in Music*. New York: W.W. Norton & Company.

Smith, Catherine Parsons. 1994. "'A Distinguishing Virility': Feminism and Modernism in American Art Music." In *Cecilia Reclaimed: Feminist Perspectives on Gender and Music*, edited by Susan C. Cook and Judy S. Tsou, 90–106. Urbana and Chicago: University of Illinois Press.

Solie, Ruth A., ed. 1993. *Musicology and Difference: Gender and Sexuality in Music Scholarship*. Berkeley: University of California Press.

Straus, Joseph N. 1993. *Music by Women for Study and Analysis*. New York: Prentice-Hall.

Straus, Joseph N. 1995. *The Music of Ruth Crawford Seeger*. Cambridge and New York: Cambridge University Press.

Straus, Joseph N. 2000. *Introduction to Post-Tonal Theory*. 2nd ed. (3rd ed., 2005) Upper Saddle River, N.J.: Prentice Hall.

Tick, Judith. 1993. "Charles Ives and Gender Ideology." In *Musicology and Difference: Gender and Sexuality in Music Scholarship,* edited by Ruth A. Solie, 83–106. Berkeley: University of California Press.

Tick, Judith. 1995. *American Women Composers Before 1870.* 2nd ed. Rochester, N.Y.: University of Rochester Press.

CHAPTER 30

VEILED VOICES

Music and Censorship in Post-Revolutionary Iran

AMENEH YOUSSEFZADEH

THROUGHOUT Iranian history, music, like many other literary and artistic expressions, has often been subject to control and censorship by autocratic regimes, religious fanatics, and even families. Generating pleasure and emotion as well as mobilizing people, music's power over both the performer and the listener makes it a sensitive subject from the point of view of authorities. The prophet Khezr when asked for his opinion on music replied, "It is the slippery stone on which only the feet of the learned stand fast."[1]

The 1978–1979 revolution in Iran, which established a theocratic Islamic Republic, brought about major political, social, and cultural changes. Soon after the revolution, many forms of music and entertainment were banned from public life. Women could no longer sing solo or dance before an audience which included men (a restriction that still applies for media broadcasting, live performance, and films). Also forbidden were Iranian and Western popular music and all music that was judged to be arousing and vulgar. While some of the restrictions have been lifted or eased gradually, others are still in place.

Although the Koran does not contain any explicit statements against music, Islam, like many other monotheistic religions, has emphasized the power of music and the importance of controlling it. The legitimacy of listening to music has been the subject of endless controversy among Islamic jurists and theologians since the early Islamic period. The real source of the dispute has often been the association of music with worldly pleasures such as wine drinking and sensual enjoyment.[2] Since the establishment of the Islamic Republic, music has been the subject of fierce political and religious debate. Members of the government and religious establishment are conscious of and worried about the powers of music on the human mind (see Youssefzadeh 2000, 40–41).

Up to the beginning of the twentieth century, musicians in the service of kings, princes, and aristocrats were obliged to perform for them exclusively. If they could please their patrons, they were sometimes rewarded with gold; if not, they lost favor and were punished.[3] One of the earliest anecdotes is the story of the Sassanian king

Bahrām Gur (r. 421–438) and his female harpist, Āzāde, recounted in *Shahname* or "The Book of Kings," the Iranian national epic by Ferdowsi (940 CE–1020 CE). In this story, Āzāde expresses sympathy for the hunted gazelles instead of praising Bahrām's skill as a hunter. Offended, he flings her to the ground and lets his camel trample her. Another anecdote from the late nineteenth century concerns a prominent composer and master of classical Persian music, Darvish Khān (1872–1926), one of the last court musicians in the Qājar period (1785–1925). He had to take refuge in the British embassy because his patron, a Qājar prince, had ordered his fingers cut off after he performed for other nobility to supplement his income (Caron and Safvate 1966, 220–221).

During times when religious authorities came into power, music seems to have been one of the first artistic expressions to be repressed. For example, in the late Safavid (r. 1501–1722) period when the *ulamā* (religious authorities) gained power at court, music was banned at court and in all social gatherings (Babayan 1996, 117; Matthee 2000, 145–146).

MUSIC AND CENSORSHIP IN THE PRE-REVOLUTIONARY PERIOD

The Persian term *sānsur* (censor),[4] borrowed from the French, started to be used after the establishment of the Imperial Printing Office during the reign of Nāser al-Din Shah Qājar (r. 1848–1896) for the control of publications (see F. Milani 1985, 325–326; and Karimi-Hakkak 1992, 135–142). During that time, although classical music was cultivated and flourished at court, religious authorities forbade Muslims to trade in music such as selling instruments. These transactions were mostly carried out by religious minorities, in particular Jews and Armenian Christians.[5] In public, musicians had to hide their instruments under their cloaks because of zealots who might smash them (Chehabi 1999, 144–145).

The Constitutional Revolution (1905–1911) reduced the influence of kings and nobility as well as that of the religious authorities. Poetry, music, journalism, and political writings flourished during that period. A type of rhythmic song (*tasnif*) became a much-appreciated genre. Often addressing and criticizing political and social events (for instance, encouraging womens' rights, and condemning religious and political autocracy), they also served as vehicles for mobilizing pro-revolutionary sentiment. An important musician and poet of that period is ʿĀref Qazvini (d. 1934), known as the bard of the revolution. His famous line, "from the blood of the youth of the homeland tulips spring," appeared on walls all over Iran during the 1978–1979 revolution.

Under the reign of the two Pahlavi kings, Rezā Shah (r. 1926–1941) and Mohammad Rezā Shah (r. 1941–1979), Iran experienced rapid secularization and vast increases in the power of the state. One of Rezā Shah's most radical reforms was to ban the veil in public in 1936.[6] Up to that time women had been veiled and segregated in public. The lifting of the veil allowed for more open and public performances by women. The great singer Qamar al Moluk Vaziri (1905–1959)—often compared to her Egyptian contemporary, Umm Kulthum (1898–1975)—was the first woman to perform in public without a veil.[7]

The Pahlavi period, especially the last two decades of the reign of Mohammad Rezā Shah, was characterized by rapid modernization and Westernization, which led to important economic, social, and cultural changes. Twentieth-century Iran witnessed the opening of Western-style theaters, concert halls, and conservatories of both Persian and Western classical music. Female singers were at the forefront of musical life during that period. They were performing all genres of music: Persian classical and popular music, Western classical music, and Westernized pop music.

However, in a male-dominated society like Iran, it was not always easy for a woman to choose music as profession. There are many accounts of female singers who were restrained from performing by their husbands or fathers. One example is 'Ozrā Ruhbakhsh, who, while her father was alive, described herself as a "nightingale in a cage." "When my father died, I was finally free" (Khāleqi, 2002, 2: 142–143). She was one of the first female singers (along with Qamar al Moluk Vaziri) to perform on phonograph records produced in the capital Tehran, and one of the first to perform on the radio, which began broadcasting in 1940.

In an autocratic state, political life under the Pahlavis was controlled, opposition suppressed, and censorship was applied vigorously to publications, broadcasting, and all artistic productions.[8] Poetry, the most important component of Persian classical music, was regarded with suspicion. This has often led Persian poets to use symbolic and allegorical language to express themselves. For example, one of the most celebrated *tasnif* of the first half of the twentieth century was "*Morqe sahar*" (the bird of dawn).[9] It has since been performed regularly by many classical musicians. Often, in different political situations, this *tasnif* has been censored (only a part of it was allowed) because it recounts the unfortunate situation of a bird in a cage and his hope for freedom, a situation with which people usually identified.

At the end of the Pahlavi regime more than five hundred poetry books were on the list of forbidden books (Rajabzadeh 2001, 28–31). For music, as is often the case, the essential target of censorship were lyrics on sensitive subjects such as political and social criticism and on antireligious themes, but not of the music per se.[10] For example, several popular singers of the 1970s known for their social and political criticism, such as Farhad and Dariush, were banned from performing (see Shay 2000, 85; Hemmasi 2010, 70–93).

Although under the Pahlavis Iran was a secular state, religious holidays were strongly respected. Music was not allowed to be heard publicly on certain religious holidays including Moharram and Safar. Even the music schools such as conservatories and the music department of Tehran University were closed down (see Nettl 1978, 153; Blum 1978, 41).

However, Bruno Nettl observed that there was a large variety of music that could be heard in Tehran in the late 1960s:

> The resident of Tehran is surrounded by a large variety of musics. On the radio, on television, in concert halls, music halls, and discotheques, on the streets, at private

gatherings and weddings, and on records he is exposed to a universe of sound. He can hear Western music ranging from Beethoven, Vivaldi, and electronic music, on the one hand, to popular music of the 1950s and 1960s including American rock, Latin American dances, and European chansons, on the other. He can hear Persian classical music (most frequently in a style developed during the 20th century) as well as folk and popular music from various regions of Iran... (1970, 183)

This sonic environment changed dramatically soon after the 1979 revolution.

MUSIC AND CENSORSHIP IN POST-REVOLUTIONARY IRAN

The revolution, which forced Mohammad Rezā Shah to leave Iran, was initially a political reaction against the authoritarianism of the monarch's regime, seen as subservient to Western power, principally to the United States. It was a multi-party and multi-ideological revolution. Many prominent contemporary classical Persian musicians participated in the revolution by composing and performing revolutionary songs.[11] The monarchy, however, was replaced by a theocracy. Iranians were soon disillusioned as clerics took power, imposing religion as the sole authority for legal, cultural, economic, and political aspects of society.

The political system of the Islamic Republic combines religious autocracy (*welayat-e faqih*: authority of the religious jurist) with institutions modeled on Western political democracies. For example, the laws passed by the National Assembly do not take effect unless approved by the Guardian Council (*Shorā-ye negahbān*: a kind of constitutional court composed entirely of religious men). This body reviews all the laws and interprets whether or not political decisions are in accordance with Islamic principles. Based on its view of sharia, Islamic law, this court is in a position to make decisions regarding censorship and reject any aspects that do not respect these principles.[12] In the evolution of the politics of the Islamic Republic, we can distinguish four periods concerning Iranian society and thus, its culture and music: (1) the revolutionary period from 1979 to 1989 (the Ayatollah Khomeini era); (2) the reconstruction period from 1989 to 1997 (President Hashemi Rafsanjani era); (3) the political development from 1997 to 2005 (President Mohammad Khātami era); (4) the conservative/controversial period from 2005 to 2013 (President Mahmud Ahmadinejād era).

The revolutionary period (1979–1989)

The revolutionary period began with the establishment of the Islamic Republic in 1979 and the appointment of Ayatollah Khomeini as the supreme spiritual leader, and lasted until his death in 1989. The decade of Khomeini's rule was marked by eight years of war with Iraq (1980–1988) and an increasing regulation of behavior and ideological controls over the population: sexes in public were segregated, dress codes for both men and women were introduced,[13] theaters and cinemas were closed, and music and entertainment in public and in the media were banned. Music and cinema were condemned for what was perceived to be the influence of the Pahlavi Westernization projects and the US cultural domination. Already back in the early 1940s, Khomeini had criticized Reza Shah's reforms and "harmful" changes, one of which was the introduction of music and theater into public life (see Najmabadi 1987, 209).

Ayatollah Khomeini's first remarks about music upon his return from exile in February 1979 addressed the question of radio and television: "Music is like a drug; whoever acquires the habit can no longer devote himself to important activities.... We must eliminate music because it means betraying our country and our youth. We must completely eliminate it."[14] As a result, all concerts, and especially radio and television broadcasts of foreign and Iranian classical and popular music, were banned. Women vanished from the musical scene. For a while, revolutionary and patriotic songs and hymns performed by men were the only genres of music allowed to be broadcast. Music was not meant to entertain, but to mobilize. The government, moreover, launched a massive propaganda program of Islamic ideology and revolutionary narratives into the mass media such as radio, television, newspapers, and public sermons. Religious Shiite ceremonies constituted the major public performances during the 1980s (Keddie 2010, 443). Singers who specialized in singing laments and narratives about Shiite holy men (called *nowhekhān* and *maddāh*), became stars of the "Sound and Image of the Islamic Republic," the new name of the former Iranian Radio and Television. One such star, Hāj Mohammad Sādeq Ahangari, also called Ahangarān, was famously known as Khomeini's "nightingale."[15] The texts of their pieces made frequent references to the martyrdom of Imām Hoseyn and his family and their tragic death at Karbalā in 680.[16] Moreover, during the war with Iraq, many musicians all over Iran from different ethnic groups and languages were commissioned to compose songs with themes such as praise for the martyrs, the revolution, and the mobilization.[17] In this period it was not even safe to carry a musical instrument in public. Revolutionary guards (*pāsdārān*, a paramilitary force deployed since 1979) would often raid houses looking for alcohol, cards, and forbidden cassettes, which they would confiscate, and the owner of the house would often be taken into custody.[18] In small towns and villages, these forces would organize raids to collect and destroy musical instruments.

As a reaction against the Westernization of the imperial regime, the cultural revolution of 1980–1983 aimed to "Islamize" the institutions and cleanse them of "subversive" elements. This led to the closing of all universities, research centers, music schools, and conservatories. Many professors and students were dismissed; several of them subsequently emigrated.[19] During these repressive times, many musicians also emigrated to Europe and the United States. For example, many pop singers, especially women, went into exile, mostly in the United States. In Los Angeles, an active Iranian diaspora has since been established.[20] Others who stayed in Iran either performed secretly or were forced to remain silent.

Although the musical institutions and departments were officially closed, music continued to be performed in private. Ironically, the attempts to abolish music in public life led to an increase in music making within family circles by all generations and sexes of all social classes. Moreover, despite these measures, all genres of music were widely available through black market cassettes and satellite television channels.[21] People continued to do in private what was prohibited in public.

The reconstruction period (1989–1997)

The reconstruction period following the end of the Iran-Iraq war in 1988 and the death of Ayatollāh Khomeini in 1989 gave rise to a desire for change, as well as to an opening up toward the outside world. Ayatollāh Ali Khāmene'i was appointed Supreme Leader and Ali Akbar Hāshemi Rafsanjāni became president.[22] After the economic decline caused mostly by the eight-year Iran-Iraq war, Rafsanjāni began a slow social reform, which contributed to a more open cultural environment, implemented some economic reconstruction, and improved Iran's foreign relations. Furthermore, at the end of his life, Khomeini had begun to loosen the morality codes. Some films previously banned were released and hundreds of new journals and magazines soon appeared. In 1989 Khomeini had issued a *fatwa* (a religious decree establishing the licit or illicit character of a given act) authorizing the purchase and sale of instruments "serving a licit purpose."[23] The same year, the music department at Tehran University reopened and classes were permitted again. The level of instruction, however, had declined due to the emigration of many teachers and early retirement of others.

Little by little, music slowly started to be broadcast again, and concerts also began to take place. A key musical event during this period was the concert of the famous vocalist and classical musician Mohammad Rezā Shajariān held on December 1988, in celebration of the end of the Iran-Iraq war. Performed in Tehran's most prestigious opera house, the Tālār-e Vahdat, six performances were originally scheduled. During one of the concerts, over two thousand people requested a piece called *Bidād*. (During 1992, 142–143).[24] "Bidād," meaning "injustice or oppression," is based on the poetry of the great fourteenth-century poet Hāfez who, in this poem, asks "what happened to friends?"[25] For Shajariān, it was a political statement: "Bidād was a complaint that we had because of the circumstances that took place after the revolution. The whole work was basically a criticism of the situation . . . " (Shajariān cited by Simms and Koushkani 2012, 35).[26] However, after the third night, the concert hall security canceled the rest of the programs, saying that the unexpected audience turnout far exceeded the number of seats available (During 1992).

In 1989, Hoseyn Alizādeh, the prominent composer and master of classical Persian music, founded an ensemble called "*Hamāvāyān*" (singing together) in which, along with Persian classical instruments, he used a chorus of both male and female vocalists.[27] "I wanted to reintroduce women's voices in public," he explained.[28] According to Alizādeh, women's voices without lyrics can be considered to be like an instrument, and thus are acceptable.[29] While solo female singing continue to be prohibited to male audiences, choral singing is not, since it becomes impossible to clearly identify an individual woman's voice. Many artists inside and outside Iran have expressed their concern about this prohibition. The Iranian-American artist Shirin Neshat (b. 1957) in her video installation, "Turbulent" (1998), shows two screens facing each other. In one, a man, the artist Soja Azari, sings for an audience in a full hall; in the other, a women, the vocalist and composer Sussan Deyhim, sings for an empty hall.[30]

To monitor and control artistic and cultural productions, the Ministry of Culture and Islamic Guidance (often called simply *Ershād*, "Guidance") issued new regulations. All productions to be released commercially, such as music (CD, cassettes, concerts) and films, had to go through several stages to be approved for a permit (*mojavvez*) for their production.[31] According to Article 24 of the constitutional law of the Islamic Republic (approved in 1988): "The publications and press are free to express their views, only if they are not disturbing the foundation of Islam or public rights" (Rajabzādeh 2001, 5).

For music, the control division (*bakhsh-e nezārati*) of the Music Division of Ershād, has had the responsibility of controlling the musical productions. First the lyrics have to be approved by the Council for the Authorization of Poems (*Shora-ye mojavvez-e she'r*), then the Council of Evaluation of Music (*Shora-ye karshenasi-ye musiqi*) has to inspect the music. Finally, the Cultural Council (*Sho'rā-ye Farhangi*) has to approve the final production. Each division has its own criteria and also shares a set of general criteria (for both music and lyrics), quoted below:

1. Should not have an association with pleasure and debauchery (*lahv*)
2. Should not inspire atheism
3. Should not criticize the Islamic order (*nezām*) and religious authorities
4. The content of music and words should have solidity (*estehkām*)
5. From the point of view of the society, music and lyrics should reinforce the spirit of national unity
6. Should guide the youth and the whole society to a bright future and an atmosphere of hope[32]

Certainly, some of these criteria seem vague; no wonder that the situation of music and its acceptance remain ambiguous. Another responsibility of *Ershād* is to issue permits for musical organizations, such as music classes, cultural centers, printing houses, concerts halls, etc.[33]

It should be noted that even though the Ministry of Culture and Islamic Guidance is responsible for all the tasks cited above, other authorities can sometimes disregard its decisions and authorizations. One such authority is the Friday prayer leader (*Imām Jom'e*), who had been appointed for each city after the 1979 revolution. His great power permits him to cancel a concert, close down a music center, and the like. For example, in 1995 a poetry evening (*Shab-e she'r*) was organized in Quchān, a city in north Khorasan, where Kurdish poets and musicians from Khorasan were to appear. The Quchān Ershād had supported the event, yet the performance was interrupted by the Friday imām who declared, "I don't see such a crowd during prayers."[34] Sometimes, one hears of concerts that are canceled at the last moment for unknown reasons even though they have a permit.

Another factor contributing to the reintroduction of music in public life came in September 1992, when Ayatollāh Khāmene'i launched a campaign against "cultural aggression from the West." Ultimately, this initiative restored a certain degree of legitimacy to Iranian musical traditions, both classical and the music of the different regions of Iran, since the authorities came to view them as a valid and valuable expressions of Iran's national identity. Since then, the country's cultural policy has been based on the following directives: "The preservation and propagation of our noble culture as a barrier against cultural aggression"; "The exaltation of our national identity"; and "The preservation of [these musical traditions] to support and uphold our Nation's culture." This sort of liberalization led to an increased production of audio recordings of Persian classical music, which from 1988 to 1998 grew by 80 percent (Youssefzadeh 2005, 432).

Moreover, both of the two major organizations dealing with music, the Music Division of the Ministry of Culture and Islamic Guidance and the Arts Division of the Islamic Propaganda Organization, have sponsored festivals and concerts in the capital city of Tehran as well as in most of the provinces. Most of the events have been organized by the Ministry of Culture and Islamic Guidance and commemorate political, military, and religious events. Indeed, the Islamic Republic has established a series of commemorative days and events of remembrance in order to reinforce national and communal identities, such as "The Week of Unity" (*Hafte-ye Vahdat*) for the anniversary of the Prophet; "The Week of Holy Defense" (*Hafte-ye defā'e moqaddas*), commemorating the beginning of the Iran-Iraq war; and *Fajr* (Dawn), marking the anniversary of the revolution. The Fajr Music Festival, a ten-day celebration in the capital and other regions of Iran, has been the most significant musical event since its inauguration in 1986.[35] During the first three years of its existence, the musical pieces reflected the atmosphere of the country, with titles such as *Zālem Emerika* (America the Oppressor) and *Rāh-e khun* (The Way of Blood). Later, the emphasis was on the traditional repertoire. However, lyrics with moral and religious content were (and continue to be) favored over love songs.[36] The masters of Persian classical music rarely participate in these sponsored festivals, which they see as propaganda for the regime.

Some of the rhythmic instrumental pieces in the repertoire of both Persian classical music (called *radif*) and popular entertainment music (*motrebi*), such as *reng* (a dance piece) and *chāhar mezrāb* (meaning four beats), were considered by authorities to be vulgar and arousing.[37] Some vocal techniques such as *tahrir*, a sort of melismatic yodeling characteristic of Persian classical singing, were also considered to be illicit (During 1984, 12).

The Period of Political Development (1997 to 2005)

A period of political development began with the landslide election of President Mohammad Khātami in 1997. A reformist cleric and modernist, Khātami planned to create a more open and moderate cultural policy.[38] During his electoral campaign he promised greater freedom, sovereignty of the people, support for greater rights for women and youth, and emphasis on civil society. His minister of Culture and Islamic

Guidance, Ata'ollah Mohajerani, eased restrictions on the press (allowing many reformist newspapers to open), book publications, and music. Two of the most significant developments regarding music during Khātami's period were the lifting of the ban on certain types of pop music and the issuing of permits for the public performance of women, but only for all-female audiences.[39]

During the first years of the revolution, pop music produced by exiled musicians, called *Losānjelesi* (because most of it was produced in Los Angeles, California), was heard only through illegally imported recordings that circulated in Iran. Even though anyone caught listening to or owning one of these recordings was subject to fines and even imprisonment, this music always had a vast audience. Following the lifting on the ban on pop music, the Sound and Image of the Islamic Republic *(Sedā o Simā)* became the supporter of the "new pop" *(pop jadid)* as it is called. Many pop singers became famous because of performing in broadcasts made under the auspices of this organization. One of the best-known is Mohammad Esfahāni. A former member of the Revolutionary Guards, he said, "With the help of *Sedā o Simā* we can compete with the *pop-e Losānjelesi* (pop music produced in Los Angeles).[40] Dr. Esfahāni, as he is called because he studied medicine, gave a concert in 2003 in "Iran Hall," the large hall of the Ministry of the Interior. It was the first concert given in this hall, holding over four thousand people.[41] Other pop singers who became famous thanks to *Sedā o Simā* are 'Ali Rezā Asār and Khashāyar Etemādi. Both usually use lyrics drawn from the mystical poets such as Rumi (thirteenth century) or Hāfez (fourteenth century) mostly associated with classical music.[42] Some people refer to this music as "mystical pop." However, the dance rhythm characteristic of the pop music of the Iranian diaspora is lacking in their works (Fatemi 2000, 329; Shay 2000, 61–87). In a concert by Etemādi, as reported by Fatemi (2000), a member of the audience complained: "*Aghā Khashi! Ye tarāne-ye shad* (Mr. Khashi, a happy song!)."

Many young people started to form new bands, which led to a new grass-roots popular music. One of the first pop bands to be formed in the post-1997 period was the band Arian, which achieved great success. Arian was the first band to include women as back-up vocalists, as instrumentalists, and as composer/lyricists (see Nooshin 2009, 245–268).

In 2002, the growth in the production of pop music was astonishing; 50 percent of the permits issued by *Ershād* were given to pop music, and fifty-one pop music concerts were programmed for the spring of the same year.[43]

We should note that in any concert, regardless of the musical genre (classical or popular), there has been a strict control on the behavior of both the performers and the audience. Any moving or clapping to the music is considered un-Islamic and can have consequences; for instance a person can be removed from the concert. This how the Iranian scholar and bestselling author Āzar Nafisi describes a concert that she attended in Tehran in the early 1990s:

> The group consisted of four young Iranian men, all amateurs, who entertained us with their rendition of the Gipsy Kings. Only they weren't allowed to sing; they could

only play their instruments... The players were solemn. Since it was almost impossible to play with no expression at all, their expressions had become morose. The lead guitarist seemed to be angry with the audience; he frowned, trying to prevent his body from moving—a difficult task, since he was playing the Gipsy Kings. (Nafisi 2003, 301)

In any institutions, cultural centers, universities, or governmental offices, a security office called *Herāsat* (meaning "guarding" or "custody") is in charge of the control of the people's behavior.

Since 1997, the state has sponsored several festivals and concerts for and by women. A section dedicated to both classical and regional Iranian music has been added to the Fajr Festival. Another, the annual Jasmine Festival (*Jashnvāreh-ye Gol-e Yās*), which began in 1999, celebrates the birthday of Hazrat Fātemeh, the daughter of the prophet Mohammad and the most important female figure in Shiite Islam. It is divided into different sections, including classical (both Iranian and Western music), regional, and pop music (see DeBano 2009, 229–244).

During the Kh presidency a discourse on civil society emerged. In 1999, the House of Iranian Music (*Khāne-ye Musiqi*) was established in Tehran, to provide a syndicate for musicians. It was the first time that a trade union for music and musicians had been founded in Iran. Since its foundation, this organization has tried to voice musicians' needs. In 2000, *Ershād* spared from censorship control most of the recognized masters of classical Persian music, who have since that time been able to present their works on the market without any permit. Also, the export formalities regarding the taking of musical instruments and recordings out of the country have been eliminated.[44]

Although, as mentioned earlier, *Sedā o Simā* (Sound and Image of the Islamic Republic) was instrumental in advancing the careers of several pop musicians, it was (and continues to be) heavily criticized by both musicians and critics. Since the revolution, this organization has been in the hands of the conservatives and under the direct supervision of Ayatollāh Khāmene'i, the Supreme Leader. As one of the biggest producers and consumers of music (for use in advertising, as background music, during and between programs, and so on), it has its own censorship unit, the "Sound and Image Division," to evaluate music and lyrics and to decide which kind of music is authorized and which is not.

Iranian Television has six channels; one is oriented toward cultural activities. Even today, when a concert of traditional music is broadcast, everything is done to hide the instruments themselves. For instance, large vases of flowers are used to obscure the instruments, or the camera will only show the faces of the performers. For many musicians and critics, "not showing the instrument is like an insult to the musicians."[45] Other genres such as marches and hymns continue to be broadcast on special occasions.

Apart from the popular music promoted by Iranian media, many young artists have been involved in several varieties of musical genres, such as rock, heavy metal, jazz, and rap, known collectively as "underground rock" or "alternative music."[46] Although few of them have managed to get permits to give concerts or to publish CDs, their music can be heard thanks to international communication networks such as satellite programs, video tapes, and the Internet, where it can be downloaded from numerous web sites.[47]

The second term of the Khātami presidency (2001–2005) was marked by the never-ending internal struggles between the two major sections of the government, the reformists and the conservatives, and by a government crackdown on cultural freedom. Most reform measures passed by the Parliament were rejected by the Guardian Council (Keddie 2010, 456–457).[48] Even the Arts Division of the Islamic Propaganda Organization, which is under the supervision of the Guide, Khāmene'i, was criticized for not performing its mission, the propagation of Islamic values:

> The activities in music and art have always been used by the enemy to destroy the identity and the culture of the people, that is why they have to be kept under close watch. The centers of music have become centers of immorality for illicit and immoral activities for young girls and boys.[49]

In 2001, a book was authorized to be published on women and music in which the author, using different historical sources, established that the Prophet himself is said to have enjoyed music as performed by singing girls. It was banned and the author became *mamnu'ol qalam*: no longer allowed to publish.[50]

The Ahmadinejād Era (2005–2013)

In 2005, when the conservative President Mahmud Ahmadinejād succeeded President Khātami, a new regime of censorship commenced. His minister of culture, Mohammad Hosseyn Safār Harandi, a conservative figure and editor-in-chief of the newspaper *Keyhān*, one of the most conservative state journals, criticized the cultural politics of the prior president. Censorship became more restrictive; getting permission to publish books, recordings, or performance became much more difficult. In June 2009, when Ahmadinejād was reelected, strong public protest and demonstrations took place because the election was widely regarded as fraudulent. Called the Green Movement, the protesters demanded the removal of Ahmadinejād. Many people were arrested, tortured, and killed. Many Iranian musicians in Iran and all over the world wrote and performed songs in support of this popular movement and against the violent crackdown of the government. Moreover, the revolutionary and religious songs, such as *Irān sarāye omid* (Iran the house of hope) and *Sepide damid* (The dawn appeared) of the prominent singer Shajariān, had been continuously broadcast since the beginning of the revolution on special occasions without his approval. He protested, asking the *Sedā o Simā* not to broadcast his songs. "When I sang *Sepide damid*," he explained,

> it was to express the resurrection (*hālat-e rastākhiz*), that was the state of the people back then. Now they broadcast it when Khomeini is shown descending the stairs of

the airplane at Tehran Airport [February 1, 1979 after fourteen years in exile]. I sang this for the state of people, not for a single person!⁵¹

Many concerts that had obtained permits to perform were canceled. One of the most significant was the concert in July 2010 of the classical singer Hesāmeddin Sarāj in Kermanshāh, in Western Iran. Before the concert, the militia (*basiji*) were in front of the hall with chains and prevented people from going into the hall.[52] According to Keddie (2010, 460), the Revolutionary Guards and Basiji militia (the supporters of Ahmadinejād) include many who volunteered to go to the front during the Iran-Iraq war and are not happy with the cultural liberation under the previous presidents (Rafsanjāni and Khātami). These men "want a return to egalitarian and strict Islamic policies of the early revolutionary years."

Ahmadinejād's cultural crackdown encouraged a new emigration of artists. Many artists in Iran and outside of the country have voiced their concerns about the restriction on music. The Iranian-Kurdish filmmaker Bahman Qobadi, in his film "No One Knows About Persian Cats" (2009), shows the difficulties that young musicians have to endure in starting a band. The film, which was produced without government authorization, was banned and its filmmaker and the musicians went into exile after the film was shown at the Cannes Film Festival in 2009. Two of Qobadi's other films such as *Marooned in Iraq* (2002) and *Half Moon* (2007), also deal with the restrictions upon music and musicians.

Conclusion

Music is still an object of controversy in Iran and its role is still contentious, partly because the political and economic situation itself is constantly evolving. Its acceptance remains ambiguous, and it is still the object of variable restrictions. The prohibition of a solo female singing for a male audience is only one of many. Musical instruments are still not shown on television. Many alternative bands are not allowed to give concerts or release their CDs. The culture is still under close watch; as the Guide of the Revolution, Khamenei said, in July 2010, "crossing the red lines of moral, religious, and cultural matters is very harmful."[53] According to the Friday prayer leader of Tehran, Ayatollāh Seyed Ahmad Khātami (not to be confused with former president Mohammad Khātami): "The danger of cultural indulgence and negligence is as dangerous as political indulgence and negligence. Here is an Islamic Iran and there is no room for the singers of Los Angeles."[54]

The Islamic Republic, however, seems to have failed to root out what are called "Western cultural values." The extremely literate younger generation, the largest segment of the population, are clearly attracted to values that are not uniquely Western but rather universal: self-determination and freedom of expression. Since the end of the twentieth century, in the context of political and social reform and the emancipation of women and youth, women have managed to play a more active role throughout society and on the musical scene.[55] Today, we can hear Iranian female singers in major international festivals and concerts, performing in front of mixed-gender audiences.

Iranian musicians prefer to perform abroad since at home they have to struggle to get all the required authorizations. Private teaching and concerts in homes remain common.

Apart from governmental or religious restrictions, there is also self-censorship. Musicians, like other artists, are continually pushing against the boundaries that have been set up for them. However, they need to be very calculating. As Mehrdad Oskouei, a prominent documentary filmmaker, said: "In the end, people have to be flexible. I think about how far I can go" (*New York Times*, May 7, 2011).

NOTES

1. Cited by Robson (1938, 5). Robson uses "audition" in his translation but it's understood in the sense of listening to music.
2. On the theological debates on music, see Robson 1938, al-Faruqi 1985, and Farmer 1994.
3. The Abbasid Caliph, Hārun al-Rashid, was so pleased with his Persian court musician, the outstanding Ebrāhim Mawseli (742–803), that he made him a rich man (Farmer 1994, 116–117).
4. The other term used is the Arabic word *momayyezi*, which means to control.
5. The prohibition was put in place when the Safavids came to power (Loeb 1972, 4). More information about Jewish musicians in Iran in the nineteenth and twentieth centuries can be found in Chaouli *Les musiciens Juifs en Iran, aux XIXe et XXe siècles* (2006).
6. The police were ordered to be harsh with women wearing the veil. It was acceptable for the veil to be replaced by a European-style hat (Nashat 2004, 22).
7. She performed in 1924 even before the ban was lifted (Chehabi 2000, 151–166).
8. For example, to possess a book by Maxim Gorky could cost the owner seven years in prison. Some of Shakespeare's plays, such as *Richard the Third, Macbeth*, and *Hamlet*, were not allowed to be performed since they feature the death of a king (Rajabzādeh 2001, 28–31; N. Cram Cook 1949, 407–408). However, during the time when Mohammad Mosaddeq was prime minster (1951–1953) and the government and people campaigned for the nationalization of oil resources, publications and the press flourished up until the 1953 coup. At that time the press was again suppressed and a new security police, the Organization of State Security and Information (known as SAVAK), was founded in 1957 (Rajabzādeh 2001, 27; Karimi-Hakkak 1992, 135–142).
9. The poem, by one of the most prominent Iranian poets of the twentieth century, Malek al-Sho'arā Bahār (d. 1951), was set to music by Morteza Neydavood (1900–1990). Many of Bahār's poems were censored in both the pre-revolutionary and the post-revolutionary periods, in the latter because he supported women's freedom and criticized religious fanaticism in his work.
10. The Ministry of Information (raised to full cabinet status in 1964) had, through its various divisions, responsibility for control over all broadcasting and publication enterprises, both at home and abroad.
11. This participation was short lived. Prominent musicians, such as the singer Mohammad Rezā Shajarian, soon became disenchanted with the government's policies. (See Simms and Koushkani 2012, 11 and 26).
12. On the legal system of the Islamic Republic, see Vogel 2010, 306–313. On the power of the clerics in Iran, see Digard, Hourcade, and Richard 1996, 200–203.

13. Men were not allowed to wear ties and had to grow beards, and women were required to cover the hair and the body. On the political and economic situation during the revolutionary period see Keddie 2003, 240–262.
14. Khomeini's statement was published by the *Keyhān* in 1979 in an article called "Radio and Television Must Strengthen the Young" (See Youssefzadeh 2000, 38).
15. His songs introduced each commentary about the war, so he was heard every day, at peak viewing hours, just before the evening news (Adelkhah 1991, 25).
16. See a video of Ahangarān singing about Imam Hoseyn: http://www.youtube.com/watch?v=7k5MpusW83U&feature=related
17. Iran is a multiethnic state where non-Persian groups constitute almost half of the country's population. There are a number of Turkic-speaking peoples as well as Kurds, Baluchis, Lors, and Arabs who have distinct musical practices. For more information on different genres of music in Iran, see Blum 2002, 823–838. For revolutionary songs in the repertoire of Khorasani bards, see Youssefzadeh 2008, 281–289.
18. Later, one could get away with paying a fine or a bribe. For a description of a similar situation in Afghanistan, see Baily (2009, 153–154).
19. While the universities reopened after three years, their music departments continued to be closed until 1989.
20. On Iranian popular music in Los Angeles, see Hemmasi (2010, 148–208).
21. On satellite television in Iran, see Barraclough (2001, 25–48).
22. The first decade of the Islamic Republic witnessed three presidents, the first two with very short terms: Abol-Hassan Banisadr (January 1980–June 1981), Mohammad-'Ali Rajā'i (July 1981–August 1981) 'Ali Khamene'i (1981–1989).
23. See Youssefzadeh 2000, 39.
24. This song was first available in 1985 on a cassette album "*Bidād (Homayun)*." *Bidād* is a melody type or *gushe* in the mode or *dastgāh* of Homayun.
25. The first line of the poem says: "We don't see friends in anyone, what happened to friends? / How did friendship end? What happened to friends?" Hāfez probably wrote this poem during a period when the fundamentalist Mobarez al-din Mozaffarid ruled his native town Shiraz (1353–1358). Fanatically religious, he forbade wine and music and ordered all to be "severely sober" (see Davis 2012, xiv).
26. For an analysis of the piece see Simms and Koushkani 2012, 35–46.
27. The traditional performance of classical Persian music features a solo vocalist accompanied by one or more instruments. Alizādeh's CD "Raz-e No" ("A New Secret"), including three singers (two women and one man), was released in 1998 (Tehran: Mahoor Institute of Culture and Art).
28. Personal communication with Alizādeh, Tehran, February 2002.
29. Alizādeh first used womens' voices without lyrics in film scores. He composed many scores for films such as *Gabbeh* (1996), by Mohsen Makhmalbaf, and *Half Moon* (2006) by Bahman Ghobādi.
30. Turbulent was awarded a Golden Lion at the 1999 Venice Biennale.
31. For an analysis of censorship rules in cinema, see Naficy 1992, 173–208.
32. Quoted from the statement the Ministry of Culture and Islamic Guidance gave to the publishing houses; I thank the Mahoor Institute of Art for letting me have a copy of the statement.
33. For more detailed rules on the control of music see Youssefzadeh 2000, 44–48.
34. The influence of the leaders of Friday prayers continues into the present era. In 2008, the cultural center of the city of Bojnurd, the capital of northern Khorasan, where music

classes as well as concerts were organized, was closed down because the Friday leader of the city decided that the music was illicit (*harām*) (personal communication with the musical director of Bojnurd's Ershād, Bojnurd, July 2010).
35. There have also been Fajr festivals for Film, Theater, and Poetry.
36. Prior to the festivals, musicians had to provide Ershad with their bibliographies, concert programs, samples of recordings, and the transcriptions of the lyrics (if not in Persian, their translations).
37. For a further explication of these terms (*radif, reng,* and *chāhar mezrāb*) see *Encyclopedia Iranica,* free access on line.
38. Khātami held various posts before becoming president. In 1983 he became Minister of Culture and Islamic Guidance, a post he held until 1992. During his term he encouraged the easing of censorship of printed material and the expansion of Iranian cinema.
39. For a definition of "pop" music in Iranian context, see Nooshin 2005b, 262n2. The tradition of an all-female orchestra performing for an all-female audience is common in nineteenth-century Iran and is existed in many parts of the Middle East and North Africa. See Caton 2002, 140; Ciucci 2005, 188–89; Jones 1987, 81.
40. Interview with Mohammad Esfahāni, in *Hayāt-e Now,* August 13, 2002/1381.
41. In *Yās-e Now,* 2003/1382, no. 186.
42. They use instruments such as electronic keyboards and guitars as well as instruments such as the *daff,* a frame drum often associated with Sufi music.
43. In *Hambastegi,* August 15, 2002/1381.
44. All recordings and instruments taken out of the country had to have an authorization from Ershad, which was presented to customs inspectors.
45. Mohammad Eftekhāri, "atāye andak o jafāye besiyār," *Faslnāmeye musiqi-ye Māhur* 3, 1378/1999.
46. See Nooshin 2005a, 231–72; 2005b, 463–97.
47. Iran has the world's fourth largest number of bloggers, and access to the web and to illegal satellite television is widespread (Keddie 2010, 460)
48. At the end of Khātami's first term in 2000, Mohajerani, his minister of culture, was forced to resign, but his successor Ahmad Masjed Jamei continued Khātami's policy.
49. *Jomhuri Eslāmi* mordād 1381/August 2002.
50. The book is by a female author, Toka Maleki: *Women and Music in Iran: From Mythological Times to Today,* Tehran: Ketāb-e Khorshid, 2001 (See Youssefzadeh 2004, 129–135).
51. Documentary film on M. R. Shajarian, produced by BBC Persian, http://www.youtube.com/watch?v=lBWQGqW9vy8.
52. *Sharq,* 20 tir 1389/11, July 2010.
53. *Khorasan,* 1389/4 July 2010, no. 1759
54. This declaration came following the rumor that *Ershād* had issued a permit for a performance by an Iranian singer from Los Angeles, *Aftāb Yazd,* 11 July 2010, no. 2957.
55. Female literacy rose from 36 percent in 1976 to 72 percent in 1996; in universities 60 percent of the students are women.

References

Adelkhah, Fariba. 1991. "'Michael Jackson ne peut absolument rien faire': Les pratiques musicales en République Islamique d'Iran." *Cahiers d'études sur la Méditerranée orientale et le monde turco-iranien* 11: 23–41.

al-Faruqi, Lois Ibsen. 1985. "Music, Musicians, and Muslim Law." *Asian Music* 17, no. 1: 3–36.

Babayan, Kathryn. 1996. "Sufis, Dervishes and Mullahs: The Controversy over Spiritual and Temporal Dominion in Seventeenth-Century Iran." In *Safavid Persia*, edited by Charles Melville, 117–138. London: I.B. Tauris & Center of Middle Eastern Studies University of Cambridge.

Baily, Johan. 2009. "Music Censorship in Afghanistan 1973–2003." In *Music and the Play of Power in the Middle East, North Africa and Central Asia*, edited by Laudan Nooshin, 143–163. Farnham, UK: Ashgate.

Barraclough Steven. 2001. "Satellite Television in Iran: Prohibition, Imitation and Reform." *Middle Eastern Studies* 37, no. 3: 25–48

Blum, Stephen. 1978. "Changing Roles of Performers in Meshhed and Bojnurd, Iran." In *Eight Urban Musical Cultures: Tradition and Change*, edited by Bruno Nettl, 19–95. Urbana: University of Illinois Press.

Blum, Stephen. 2002. "Iran: An Introduction." In *The Garland Encyclopedia of World Music: The Middle East* 6, edited by Virginia Danielson, Scott Marcus, and Dwight Reynolds, 823–838. New York: Routledge.

Caron, Nelly, and Dariouche Safvate. 1966. *Iran*. Paris: Buchet/Chastel.

Caton, Margaret. 2002. "Performance Practice in Iran: Radif and Improvisation." In *The Garland Encyclopedia of World Music: The Middle East* 6, edited by Virginia Danielson, Scott Marcus, and Dwight Reynolds, 129–143. New York: Routledge.

Chaouli, Alain. 2006. *Les musiciens Juifs en Iran, aux XIXe et XXe siècles*. Paris: L'Harmattan.

Chehabi, Houchang. 2000. "Voices Unveiled: Women Singers in Iran." In *Iran and Beyond, Essays in Middle Eastern History in Honor of Nikki R. Keddie*, edited by Rudi Matthee and Beth Baron, 151–166. Costa Mesa, Calif.: Mazda Publishers.

Chehabi, Houchang. 1999. "From Revolutionary *Tasnif* to Patriotic *Surud*: Music and Nation-Building in Early Twentieth-Century Iran." *Iran* 37: 143–154.

Ciucci, Alessandra. 2005. "Les musiciennes professionnelles au Maroc." *Cahier de Musiques traditionnelles* 18: 18–200.

Cook, Nilla Cram. 1949. "The Theater and Ballet Arts of Iran." *Middle East Journal* 3, no. 4: 406–420.

Davis, Dick. 2012. *Faces of Love, Hafez and the Poets of Shiraz*. Washington, D.C.: Mage Publication.

DeBano, Wendy S. 2009. "Singing against Silence: Celebrating Women and Music at the Fourth Jasmine Festival." In *Music and the Play of Power in the Middle East, North Africa and Central Asia*, edited by Laudan Nooshin, 229–244. Farnham, UK: Ashgate.

During, Jean. 1984. "La Musique Traditionnelle Iranienne en 1983." *Asian Music* 15, no. 2: 11–31.

During, Jean. 1992. "L'Oreille Islamique. Dix Années Capitales de la Vie Musicale en Iran: 1980–1990." *Asian Music* 23, no. 2: 135–164.

Farmer, Henry George. 1994 (1929). *A History of Arabian Music to the XIIIth Century*. London: Luzac Oriental.

Fatemi, Sasan. 2000. "Le chanteur silencieux. Un aperçu général de la vie musicale en Iran." *Cahiers d'études sur la Méditerranée orientale et le monde turco-iranien* 29: 321–333.

Hemmasi, Farzaneh. 2010. *Iranian popular music in Los Angeles: Mobilizing media, nation, and politics*. PhD diss. Columbia University.

Jones, L. JaFran. 1987. "A Sociohistorical Perspective on Tunisian Women as Professional Musicians." In *Women and Music in Cross-Cultural Perspective*, edited by Ellen Koskoff, 69–83. Urbana: University of Illinois Press.

Karimi-Hakkak, Ahmad. 1992. "Censorship (*sānsūr*) in Persia." In *Encyclopædia Iranica* 5, edited by Yārshāter. Costa Mesa, Calif.: Mazda Publishers.

Keddie, Nikki R. 2003. *Modern Iran, Roots and Results of Revolution.* New Haven, Conn.: Yale University Press.

Keddie, Nikki R. 2010. "Culture and Politics in Iran since the 1979 Revolution." In *The New Cambridge History of Islam*, edited by Michael Cook and Robert W. Hefner, 6:438–472. Cambridge: Cambridge University Press.

Khāleqi, Ruhollāh. 1381/2002 (1954). *Sargozashte musiqi-ye Iran* [The history of Persian music]. Vol. 2. Tehran: Mo'asese-ye fahango-honari Mahoor.

Loeb, Laurence D. 1972. "The Jewish Musician and the Music of Fars." *Asian Music* 4, no. 1: 3–14.

Matthee, Rudi. 2000. "Prostitutes, Courtesans, and Dancing Girls: Women Entertainers in Safavid Iran." In *Iran and Beyond. Essays in Middle Eastern History in Honor of N. R. Keddie*, 121–150. Costa Mesa, Calif.: Mazda Publishers.

Milani, Farzaneh. 1985. "Power, Prudence, and Print: Censorship and Simin Danashvar." *Iranian Studies* 18, nos. 2–4: 325–347.

Naficy, Hamid. 1992. "Islamizing Film Culture." In *Iran: Political Culture in the Islamic Republic*, edited by S. K. Farsoun and M. Mashayekhi, 173–208. London: Routledge.

Nafisi, Azar. 2003. *Reading Lolita in Tehran: A Memoir in Books.* London: Random House.

Najmabadi, Afsaneh. 1987. "Iran's Turn to Islam: From Modernism to a Moral Order." *Middle East Journal* 41, no. 2: 202–217.

Nashat, Guity. 2004. Introduction to *Women in Iran: From 1800 to the Islamic Republic*, edited by Lois Beck and Guity Nashat, 1–36. Urbana: University of Illinois Press.

Nettl, Bruno. 1978. "Persian Classical Music in Tehran: The Processes of Change." In *Eight Urban Musical Cultures: Tradition and Change*, edited by Bruno Nettl, 146–185. Urbana: University of Illinois Press.

Nettl, Bruno. 1970. "Attitudes towards Persian Music in Tehran, 1969." *The Musical Quarterly* 56, no. 2: 183–197.

Nooshin, Laudan. 2005a. "Underground, Overground: Rock Music and Youth Discourses in Iran." In "Music and Society in Iran," edited by Wendy DeBano and Ameneh Youssefzadeh, special issue *Iranian Studies* 38, no. 3: 463–497.

Nooshin, Laudan. 2005b. "Subversion and Counter Subversion: Power, Control, and Meaning in the New Iranian Pop Music." In *Music, Power, and Politics*, edited by Annie J. Randall, 231–272. London: Routledge.

Nooshin, Laudan. 2009. "'Tomorrow is Ours': Re-imagining Nation, Performing Youth in the New Iranian Pop Music." In *Music and the Play of Power in the Middle East, North Africa and Central Asia*, edited by Laudan Nooshin, 245–268. Farnham, UK: Ashgate.

Rajabzādeh, Ahmad. 1380/2001. *Momayyezi-e ketāb: pazhuheshi dar 1400 sanad-e momayyezi-e ketāb dar sāle 1375* [Book's permit: Research in 1400 documents about book's censorship]. Tehran: Kavir.

Robson, James. 1938. *Tracts on Listening to Music.* London: Royal Asiatic Society.

Shay, Anthony. 2000. "The 6/8 Beat Goes On: Persian Popular Music from Bazm-e Qajariyyeh to Beverly Hills Garden Parties." In *Mass Mediations: New Approaches to Popular Culture in the Middle East and Beyond*, edited by Walter Armbrust, 61–87. Berkeley: University of California Press.

Simms, Rob and Koushkani, Amir. 2012. *Mohammad Reza Shajarian's Avaz in Iran and Beyond, 1979–2010.* New York and Toronto: Lexington Books.

Vogel, Frank E. 2010. "A Case Comparison: Islamic Law and the Saudi and Iranian Legal Systems." In *The New Cambridge History of Islam*, edited by Michael Cook and Robert W. Hefner, 6: 296–313. Cambridge: Cambridge University Press.

Youssefzadeh, Ameneh. 2000. "The Situation of Music in Iran since the Revolution: The Role of Official Organization." *British Journal of Ethnomusicology* 9, no. 2: 35–61.

Youssefzadeh, Ameneh. 2004. "Singing in a Theocracy: Female Musicians in Iran." In *Shoot the Singer!: Music Censorship Today*, edited by Marie Korpe, 129–135. London: Zed Books.

Youssefzadeh, Ameneh. 2005. "Iran's Regional Musical Traditions in the Twentieth Century: A Historical Overview." In *Music and Society in Iran*, edited by Wendy DeBano and Ameneh Youssefzadeh, special issue *Iranian Studies* 38, no. 3: 417–439.

Youssefzadeh, Ameneh. 2008. "Singing the Martyrs: Revolutionary and Patriotic Songs in the Repertoire of the Khorasani Bards." In *Musical Culture and Memory*, edited by Tatjana Markovic and Vesna Mikic, 281–289. Belgrade: Department of Musicology, Faculty of Music, University of Arts in Belgrade.

Index

Note: Page references followed by an "*e*" indicate example; "*f*" indicate figure; "*t*" indicate table.

"Abre Alas" (Lins/Martins), 362–63, 365
Acheson, Dean, 515
Acosta, José, 99
Acquired Immune Deficiency Syndrome (AIDS). *See* AIDS
Adamo, Mark, 634n2
Addams, John P., 571
Adenauer, Konrad, 138
Admonitio generalis, 11
Advis, Luis, 339
aesthetic compromise
　Gregorian chant as, 7–8
　for Roman church, 11
Æthelwold (bishop), 47
Afternoon Drama (Chen Ming-chang), 287–88
after-the-fact censorship, 243–51, 251f–252f, 253
Agee, James, 481
Agnus Dei, 50, 56, 62
Aguirre, Julián, 333–34
Ahangari, Hāj Mohammad Sādeq, 661
Aharonián, Coriún, 348
Ahmadinejād, Mahmud, 667–68
AIDS, 634n1
　avant-garde music and, 629–32
　classical music and, 625–27
　in comedy, 632–33
　music and, 623–25, 633–34
　popular music and, 627–29
AIDS Quilt Songbook, 625–27
AIDS Ragtime (Wojnarowicz), 631
Alard, Charles, 157
Alfonsín, Raúl, 349
Alizādeh, Hoseyn, 662–63, 670n27, 670n29
Allan, Oswald, 586

Allegemeine Theorie der Schönen Künste (Sulzer), 212–13
alleluias, 48
　for chants, 30–31
　Per signum sancte crucis, 25, 27*e*, 28
Allende, Salvador, 335
All-Night Vigil (Rachmaninoff), 112–13, 115–16
All the Rage (Ostertag), 631–32
"All You Need is Love" (The JAMS), 629
the Almanac singers, 500–502, 505–6, 508
Alpert, Richard, 542
"Ama-Ndiya" (Ngema), 601–4
A-Mei, 275–76, 289, 291–94, 296–97, 299n22
　in PRC, 460–61
American culture. *See* United States
American Women Composers Association, 642
Amerindians. *See* indigenous people
Ammer, Christine, 649–50
Amos, Tori, 628
Ancerl, Karl, 406
Anderson, Omer, 413
Andrade, José do Carmo, 365
Anglophone West, 625
Anglo-Saxon manuscripts, 47
"Anh là ai?" (Việt Khang), 303–4
An l'2440 (Mercier), 154
Anthologies list, 653
anti-communism, 642. *See also* House Un-American Activities Committee; *Red Channels*
anti-Semitism
　in Austria, 229
　as censorship subjects, 146–47
　in Germany, 378–80
Anti-yellow Song Campaign, 455–56, 469

apartheid, 593–97, 599–601, 604–5.
    See also South Africa
Appalachian Spring (Copland), 512
appeals, 194–95
Appleton, Thomas, 76
Aquitaine, 9
Aquitaine manuscripts. *See also* graduals
    chants for, 18–21, 19t–20t
    Gallican prayers for, 24–25
    origins of, 28
Aquitainian mass Propers (religion), 22–25
Aragón, Agustín de (Jesuit), 101
Aran, Zalman, 132, 137
archaism, 28
Ardévol, José, 339
Arena (Flanagan), 493
Argentina
    censorship in, 333–35, 348–50
    classical music in, 336–41
    folk music in, 344
    National Reorganization
        Process in, 344–48
    "pedagogy of the oppressed" in, 341–48
    religion in, 345
    theater in, 343
Arian (band), 665–66
Armenulić, Silvana, 264–66, 271n22
Arnolfini, Giovanni, 57–58
Aroldo (Verdi), 243–44
Arouet, François-Marie. *See* Voltaire
Arrigo, Linda, 278
Artaud, Antonin, 168
artistic integrity, 490–92
Asār, Ali Rezā, 665
As Nasty As They Wanna Be (2 Live
    Crew), 611–12
L'assedio di Arlem (Verdi), 244–45
Assmann, Jan, 197n2
atonality, 378
Attali, Jacques, 275–76, 291–92
Attinello, Paul, 3
Aubert, Daniel François Esprit, 242
audiences, 609–18
Austen, Jane, 639
Austria. *See also* Vienna
    anti-Semitism in, 229
    censorship in, 227–28

Italy and, 244
police in, 227–28
avant-garde music, 629–32
"Ave Maria," 95, 239
"Ayesaba amagwala," 604
Aygi, Gennadiy, 413–14
Azari, Soja, 663

B-52s, 629
Babbitt, Milton, 644
Babington plot of 1586, 79–80
Bach, J. S., 122–24
Bacharach, Burt, 627–28
Bad Girl (Mui), 460
Baez, Joan, 505–6
Bahār, Malek al-Sho'arā, 669n9
"A balad intituled the dekaye of the Duke"
    (Elderton), 74–75
Balbulus, Notker, 29
Baldwin, Stanley, 538
ballads, 73–74, 77. *See also* broadside ballads
Un ballo in maschera (Verdi), 237–38, 241–43
Bambarger, Bradley, 443–44
"Bamboo Poem" (Chen Ming-chang), 287–88
Barbacini, Maurizio, 242
Barbarossa, Frederick, 244
Le Barbier de Séville (Beaumarchais), 167–69,
    205, 207, 215
Bardare, Emanuele, 246
Barenboim, Daniel, 143–46, 148n29, 340–41
Barnum, P. T., 561
baroque-ness, 95–96
baroque style, 96
Barroso Cavalcante, Maria Luiza, 364
Bartlet, M. Elizabeth C., 156–58
La battaglia di Legnano (Verdi),
    239–40, 244–45
Bauer, Marion, 640
BBC. *See* British Broadcasting Company
*BBC Variety Programmes Policy Guide for
    Writers and Producers*, 539–40
B-Br 5777 (manuscript), 58
the Beatles, 535, 549–53
    BBC and, 546–49
    censorship and, 541–46
Beaumarchais, Pierre-Augustin Caron de
    comedy for, 159, 166–70

for Mozart, 213–15
in Vienna, 204–10
"Beautiful Formosa" (Lee), 278–79
"Beautiful Girls" (Cui Jian), 470n11
Becerra, Gustavo, 339
Beckerman, Michael, 3
Beethoven, Ludwig van, 221–23, 225–28, 230–33. *See also Fidelio*
Begin, Menachem, 132, 140
Béhague, Gerard, 339
beiguan music, 290–91
Bellini, Vincenzo, 239, 253
Benda, Friedrich Ludwig, 205
Benedict XIII (Pope), 51
Ben-Gurion, David, 138
Benjamin, Walter, 477
benshengren, 277–78, 288
Bent, Margaret, 52
Ben-Zeev, Noam, 146
Berezovsky, Maxim, 123
Berg, Alban, 377–80, 379f, 381f, 382–87, 385f, 387f
Berg, Helene, 384–86
Berger, Karol, 440
Berlinsky, Valentin, 419
Berlin State Orchestra, 145
Bertoldo (Da Ponte), 214
Bessie, Alvah, 486
Bidād, 662, 670n24
Biermann, Wolf, 509
"Biko" (Gabriel), 595, 597
The Billy Cotton Band Show, 541
Billy the Kid (Copland), 512
bishops
 Æthelwold, 47
 Bishop's Ban, 70
 Dunstan, 47
 Jewel, 73–74
 John of Syracuse, 39
 Oswald, 39
 Sardinha, 100
Bishop's Ban, 70
Björk, 461
black code. *See* racism
black culture, 611–12, 614, 616–17, 624
blacklists, 502–7, 509–10, 528. *See also* House Un-American Activities Committee
Blacklist Workshop, 281–83, 282f, 298n14
Black Mambazo, 596
blackness, 563–66, 564f
Black Panther (band), 458
Blake, Peter, 549, 550
Bland, James, 586
Blazhkov, Igor, 418–20
Blitzstein, Marc, 477–82, 490–92, 494–95, 500, 508
"Bloemfontein Blues" (Kramer, D.), 598
Blumauer, Aloys, 211
Bly, Robert, 626–27
Bod74 (chant), 9, 13–15, 15t–16t, 17, 23
Bodrenkov, S. I., 425
Boehler, Patrick, 458
Bogdanova, Alla, 418
Bolshevik coup, 111
Bonaparte, Napoleon, 222, 228–29, 232
books, 153
Borodin Quartet, 419, 422
Bortniansky, Dmitry, 123
Bouilly, Jean-Nicolas, 222–24, 231
Boulanger, Nadia, 333, 525, 641–42
Bound for Glory (film), 502
Branco, Castelo, 365
Braun, Peter von (Baron), 193–96, 198n14
Brazil
 censorship in, 359–66, 372
 culture in, 356–58
 politics in, 366–72, 369f
 popular music in, 355–56, 358–59, 366–72, 369f
 regimes in, 356–58
Breathing (Huxi), 458
Brecht, Bertolt, 484, 508
Bret, Antoine, 155, 167–68
Brett, Phillip, 643
Bretzner, Christoph Friedrich, 176–77
Brezhnev, Leonid, 109
Britain, Radie, 642
British Broadcasting Company (BBC)
 BBC Variety Programmes Policy Guide for Writers and Producers, 539–40
 the Beatles and, 546–49
 censorship and, 535–41, 550–53
Britten, Benjamin, 428, 430
Briusova, Nadezhda, 112–13

broadside ballads
"A balad intituled the dekaye of the Duke" (Elderton), 74–75
as cautionary tales, 74–75
Doctor Stories Stumblinge into Englonde (Elderton), 69–70, 72
"Earl of Morton" (Elderton), 76–77
in Elizabethan era, 69–71
Elizabeth in, 75–76
fiction in, 76–77
"Greensleeves," 69, 77, 82
"Ladie Nurse" (Elderton), 76–77
narrative devices for, 75–77
"A newe Ballade, declaryng the daungerous shootyng of the Gunne at the Courte" (Elderton), 75–76
Bronsein, Celia de, 341
Brontë, Charlotte, 639
Brotherhood of the Merchant Adventurers, 58
the brothers Gay, 209
Brown, Elizabeth, 627
Brown, Joe, 541
Brown, Wendy, 158
Browne, Tara, 544–45
Brundibar (Krása), 395, 398
Buarque, Chico, 358, 363, 366–67
Buell, Richard, 436–37
Bull Durham (film), 494
Busbey, Fred, 512–19, 527–28, 529n7
Byrd, William, 78–83
Byrd/Tallis Patent of Monopoly, 78–83

Cady, Chauncey M., 568
Cage, John, 546
cải lương, 307–8
Cai Zhennan, 280
Ca Khúc Da Vàng, 312
Calabar (Buarque), 367
Callender, Charles, 564–65, 572, 586–87
Cameron-Wolfe, Richard, 428, 439
Cammarano, Salvadore, 244, 246
Campion, Edmund, 80–81
Campos, Gilberto Pereira, 360–61
Canción sin verano (Cedrón), 334
"The Canons in the Musicological Toolbox" (Randel), 647
cantors, 7–8

Caputo, Virginia, 650
Cardew, Cornelius, 340
Cardiel, Joseph (Jesuit), 91, 96–97, 104n6
Carl, Tommie E., 642
Carmina Burana (Orff), 139
Carolingian Europe, 10
Carolingian interventions, 29
Carter, Elliot, 437, 439
"Cartomante" (Lins/Martins), 370–71
"Carve Dat Possum" (Hart), 565–68, 576, 585–86
Castelli, Ignaz, 195
Castronuovo, Orestes, 341
Catholic church, 245–51, 251f–252f, 253, 631
Elizabeth (Queen) and, 73, 78, 81–82
ca trù, 309–10, 320, 324, 326n13
Catton, Bruce, 516
CCP. *See* Chinese Communist Party
Cecil, William, 72–73
Cecil Bee and the Buzzy Bunch, 595
Cedrón, Juan ("Tata"), 334
celebrations, 94–95
censorship. *See also* Iran; Old Regime; political censorship; self-censorship; Taiwan; Vietnam; Yugoslavia
after-the-fact censorship, 243–51, 251f–252f, 253
after apartheid, 599–601
during apartheid, 593–97
appeals in, 194–95
in Argentina, 333–35, 348–50
artistic integrity and, 490–92
in Austria, 227–28
Bach and, 122–24
BBC and, 535–41, 550–53
the Beatles and, 541–46
of Berg, A., 377–80, 379f, 381f, 382–87, 385f, 387f
of books, 153
in Brazil, 359–66, 372
by Catholic church, 245–51, 251f–252f, 253, 631
in China, 292–94
coded language and, 514–15, 537
of comedy, 167–70, 195–96
of communication, 156
in courts, 612

criticism as, 259–60, 268–70
cultural censorship, 138–39
in Czechoslovakia, 400, 402, 405–7
for disc jockeys, 595–99
of *Don Giovanni* (Mozart), 175–79
drunkenness and, 97–98
editorial censorship, 269–70
in education, 527
Elizabethan censorship, 70–71, 82–83
of *Fidelio* (Beethoven), 227–30
film and, 479–83
flattery and, 79–80
in Germany, 177–78, 197n7
globalization and, 492–95
gossip against, 154–55
governmental forces for, 69–72, 210–13, 593–97
Green Book for, 539–40
hate speech and, 602–5
the Holocaust and, 132–33
homosexuality and, 524
in Hungary, 180
ideology of, 392–93, 468–69, 469n1
internal censorship, 135–44
the Internet and, 321–25, 328n31, 471n18, 471n28
Islam and, 657, 660–61, 663–69
in Israel, 131–33, 139–44
by Jesuits, 91–94
by KMT, 279–81, 283, 288–89
for the Leningrad Capella, 114–16, 126n12
marital love and, 224–25, 232–33
market censorship, 270
for Mozart, 175, 203–4, 206–7, 209
musical instruments and, 97–98, 121–22
by Nazi regime, 377–80, 379f, 381f, 382–87, 385f, 387f, 517
of opera, 157–58, 186t–187t, 191t–192t, 239–43, 253–54
patriotism and, 515–18
of popular music, 261–62
in PRC, 453, 459–62, 468–69
of press, 210–13
Publications Act for, 594–95
of rap music, 609–18
scandals as, 93
semiotics and, 536–37, 549–53

of *Singspiele*, 193–96, 197n6
of songs, 156–57
in South Africa, 604–5
in Soviet-bloc, 465–66
in Soviet Russia, 109–10, 413–17, 427–28, 429e–430e, 430–33, 440–44, 459
symbolism and, 537
by ulamā, 658
in United States, 477–79, 495, 503–4
of vaudeville, 157
in Vienna, 175–78, 203–7, 214–16, 229–30, 426
Vienna Congress for, 226–30
in Vietnam war, 306–14
voluntary censorship, 144–47
YouTube and, 304, 466–67, 470n10
censorship subjects. *See also* classical music
anti-Semitism as, 146–47
audiences and, 609–18
child pornography as, 601
Christianity as, 114–15
communism as, 357
counterhegemony as, 597
"A Day in the Life" (Beatles) as, 535–36, 546–53
drugs as, 541–42, 546–49, 553
in England, 539–40
eroticism as, 96–99, 176–78, 185
folk music as, 2, 261–62
gender as, 3
ideas as, 154–56, 210–11, 596
jazz music as, 455
journalistic ballads as, 73–74
Judaism as, 378–80, 404
King Momo as, 364–65
Lincoln Portrait (Copland) as, 512–13, 516, 518, 529
Nazi regime as, 143–44
Nhân Văn–Giai Phẩm as, 307
nueva canción as, 335
race as, 3
religion as, 2, 180
satire as, 70
sexual orientation, 3
sonorous expressions as, 97–98, 103
in South Africa, 595, 601
šund as, 262–70, 271n16, 271nn18–19

censorship subjects (*cont.*)
  themes as, 615–16, 618
  vulgarity as, 466–67, 600
  Wagner as, 131–33
  Western music as, 109–10, 123–25, 657, 661–62, 664
  women as, 185, 187–88, 246–51, 253
  yellow music as, 308, 314–16, 321, 455–56, 469
Ceplair, Larry, 488–89
"A Certain Light" (Brown, E./Howe), 627
Červinková, Blanka, 395, 398
Chama Acesa (Lins), 360
Les champion des dames (Le Franc), 51
Chang, Sarah, 643
Change Is Pain (Mbuli), 598
Chang Hui-mei. *See* A-Mei
chant books, 48
chants. *See also* Gallican chants; Gregorian chants; Roman chants
  alleluias for, 30–31
  in Aquitaine, 9
  for Aquitaine manuscripts, 18–21, 19*t*–20*t*
  archaism in, 28
  Christological emphasis in, 21, 25
  communions for, 32
  graduals for, 29–30
  for Holy Cross mass, 8, 17–18, 25
  for indigenous people, 89–90
  introits for, 29
  liturgical transformation of, 8
  melodic patterns in, 25, 26*e*–27*e* 28
  neumatic patterns in, 25, 26*e*–27*e* 28
  offertories for, 31
  prosa for, 32
  standardization of, 9–10
The Charlatan (Haas), 394, 406
Charlemagne, 7, 11
Charles the Bold, 58
Charles V (King), 239
Charlevoix (Jesuit), 100
Chaussepierre, Coqueley de, 168
châu văn, 310–11, 320
Chávez, Carlos, 336–37
Chelouche, Moshe, 134
Chen Da, 287, 299, 299n17
Cheng Gexing, 456

Chen Hsia-yun, 280–81
Chen Ming-chang, 287–88, 290–91
Chen Shui-bian, 275–76, 289, 291–94, 460
Chen Weifang, 462
Chen Yi, 455
chèo, 307–11
Cheron, François, 347
Cherubini, Luigi, 223
Chiang Kai-shek, 277, 280, 283, 299, 299n18
Chico Canta (Buarque), 367
child pornography, 601
China. *See also* People's Republic of China; Taiwan
  Anti-yellow Song Campaign in, 455–56, 469
  censorship in, 292–94
  ideology in, 276
  "March of the Volunteers," 293
  Music Bureau (Yuefu) in, 277
  opera in, 294–96, 299n19
  popular music in, 294–96
  "Republic of China National Anthem," 291–92, 299n21
  United States and, 455
  Vietnam and, 303–4
Chinese Communist Party (CCP), 453–54, 459, 462, 469
The Chinese Connection (film), 295
Chip Nho, 322–23
choirbooks
  in Continental Europe, 62–63
  in England, 63–64
  Kyries in, 57–58
Chopin, Frédéric, 1
Chow, Rey, 286–87
Christe eleison. *See Kyrie eleison*
Christian funereal liturgies, 101
Christianity
  as censorship subjects, 114–15
  heathenism and, 90
  indigenous music for, 87, 98
  readaptation of, 99–102
Christ ist erstanden (German Leise), 62
Christological emphasis, 21, 25
Chu Hà, 310–11
churches, 125n3
Churchill, Winston, 538

Citizen Kane (Welles), 485
Citron, Marcia, 640–41, 643–46, 651
clandestine literature, 154
classical music
    AIDS and, 625–27
    in Argentina, 336–41
    in Czechoslovakia, 398–400, 399f
    as "pedagogy of the oppressed," 341–48
    in United States, 530nn14–15
clean versions, for music, 600
Cleave, Maureen, 543
Clegg, Cyndia Susan, 71, 77
Clinton, Bill, 499
Cloonan, Martin, 2, 304–6
Clurman, Harold, 518
Coates, Albert, 111
Cockerill, Samuel, 562, 590n2
coded language, 514–15, 537
code-switching, 572–75, 587. *See also* racism
"Cognitive Dissonance: Should Twentieth-Century Women Composers be Grouped with Foucalt's Mad Criminals?" (Killam), 644
Cold War, 260, 334–35. *See also* Soviet Russia
    Reagan-Gorbachev Summit for, 427
    for Schnittke, A., 414–17
    for United States, 483–90, 492–95, 502–5, 511–19, 520f–523f, 522–29, 642
"The Cold War in Music" (Fleming), 516
Cole, Bob, 560, 575
Collmann, Herbert L., 71
Colón, Willie, 629
Colored Quadrille Band, 563
Colwell, Thomas, 69–70
comedy
    AIDS in, 632–33
    for Beaumarchais, 159, 166–70
    in black culture, 612
    blackness in, 563–66, 564f
    censorship of, 167–70, 195–96
    Forains for, 157
    in France, 159, 163–70, 207–8
    in Italy, 164
    in music, 582
    psychological drama and, 213–16
    race in, 563–66
    in Vienna, 207–9, 213–16

    Zappa for, 632–33
commercial spirituals. *See* spirituals
Committee on Arts Affairs, 117
communication. *See also* gossip
    censorship of, 156
    non-verbal, 165–66
communions
    for chants, 32
    Per signum crucis, 25, 26e, 28
communism. *See also* Cold War; House Un-American Activities Committee; Soviet Russia; Vietnam
    CCP for, 453–54, 459, 462, 469
    as censorship subjects, 357
    jazz music and, 508
    in media, 518–19
    in music, 400
    politics in, 460
    in PRC, 463–66
    Red Channels and, 485–86, 519, 520f–523f
    red music in, 315–16
    RVN for, 306, 311–15, 325
    socialism and, 483–90
    Soviet-bloc for, 121–22
    in United States, 500–502, 530n10
    Workers Song Book No. 2, 525
Concert of Europe, 229
"Concert of Works" (Wang Xilin), 464–65
A Conference about the next succession to the crowne of England (Doleman), 81–82
Confucius, 276–77
Congress, of Vienna. *See* Vienna
Čonkić-Radović, Mira, 266
Connick, Harry, 461
"Conquer the World" (Lekeban), 460
Constantine the Great, 28
Contemporary Composers in the USSR, 419
content of salvation, as theological motifs, 21–23
Continental cantus firmus mass (religion), 61–62
Continental Europe
    choirbooks in, 62–63
    England compared to, 50–51
    English music in, 52, 53t–55t, 55–56
    Kyries in, 46–47
    manuscripts in, 51–52, 64

Continental mass (religion), 61–64, 61t, 63t
Continental mass-motet cycles, 61t, 62
Continental sources, English mass cycles (religion) in, 53t–55t, 55–56
"Conversation '87" (Trần Tiến), 318–19, 321
"De Coon Dat Had de Razor" (Lucas, S.), 586
coon songs, 586
Cooper, Emil, 111
Copland, Aaron, 337, 480, 500, 508
   as un-American, 511–19, 520f–523f, 522–29
Corigliano, John, 626–27, 634n2
Correspondance littéraire (Grimm), 154–55
Cortázar, Julio, 334, 342
Corwin, Norman, 523f
Costa e Silva, Artur, 365
cotiguazús, 98
counterhegemony, 597
Couperin, 333
Cowell, Henry, 480
"The Cradle Will Rock" (Foreman), 480–82, 480e
The Cradle Will Rock (opera/song/screenplay/film). See Blitzstein; Lardner; Robbins, Tim; Welles
Crébillon, Claude-Prosper Jolycot de (junior), 167–68
Crébillon, Prosper Jolycot de, 166
Credos, 50, 56
Creole Show (Jack), 574
Crimp, Bryan, 433
criticism
   as censorship, 259–60, 268–70
   in history, 225–26
   music as, 281–86, 282f, 285f, 596–97
cross and eucharist, as theological motifs, 21, 23
the cross characterized, as theological motifs, 21, 24
crucifixion imagery, 28
Crutchfield, Will, 348–49
Cruz, Jon, 276–77
Crystal Records, 283–84, 285f, 289–90, 298n14
Cui Jian, 457–58, 470nn10–12, 509
cultural censorship, 138–39
cultural revolutions, in Russia, 113–16
cultural unification, 10
culture

black culture, 611–12, 614, 616–17, 624
   in Brazil, 356–58
   Czechoslovakia and, 404–5
   in England, 552–53
   ethnicity and, 260–61
   history and, 404–5
   political censorship and, 623
   in regimes, 289–91
   stereotypes in, 638
   women and, 648–49
   in Yugoslavia, 260–62
Cunctipotens genitor deus (Kyrie), 47
Cuperus, Gisbertus, 160–61, 161f
Curtis, Gareth, 56
Cửu Long Giang, 315
Czechoslovakia
   censorship in, 400, 402, 405–7
   classical music in, 398–400, 399f
   culture and, 404–5
   dances in, 395, 396f–397f, 398
   dramatis personae in, 394–95
   history and, 402–4, 402f–403f
   the Holocaust in, 393–94, 404–6
   lullabies in, 395, 396f–397f, 398
   music in, 389–91, 390f–391f
   Nazi regime in, 393–94, 404

"Daffney Do You Love Me" (Hart), 565–66, 591n5
Daly, William Robert, 560
La Dame aux camélias (Dumas), 241
Damiens, Robert-François, 153
Damrosch, Walter, 639
dances, 395, 396f–397f, 398
Da Ponte, Lorenzo, 204–5, 207, 209, 211, 213–16
Daquin, Louis-Claude, 333
Da Rapclub, 322–23
Dariush (singer), 659
Darkest America, or From Plantation to Palace (Field), 575
Darnton, Robert, 154, 156–58, 170
Davidenko, Alexander, 115
"A Day in the Life" (Beatles), 535–36, 546–53
"Day Tripper" (Beatles), 542
De Alwis, Lisa, 179, 196, 197n8, 198n11
"Death and the Maiden" (Schubert), 398

Declaration of the Rights of Man and of the Citizen, 153
"Declare Independence" (Björk), 461
Dedić, Arsen, 266
Degtyarev, Stepan, 117
Delapp-Birkett, Jennifer, 3
De l'Esprit (Helvétius), 154
Del Tredici, David, 627
"A Democracy Bumpkin," 282–83, 298n12
Demyanko, Vladimir, 440
Denby, Edwin, 517
Denisov, Edison, 419, 423
Denning, Chris, 547
Denning, Michael, 484
de Sartines, Antoine Gabriel, 167–68
Desfontaines, Abbé Pierre-Françoise, 168
Deutsch, Otto Erich, 180, 184
Les Deux Journées (Cherubini), 223
Devereux, Robert, 80–81
Deyhim, Sussan, 663
Diderot, Denis, 153, 156
Diegues, Cacá, 363
Dien Bien Phu, battle of, 306–7
Dinur, Ben-Zion, 137
Dirty War. *See* Argentina; National Reorganization Process
disc jockeys, 595–99
"'A Distinguishing Virility': Feminism and Modernism in American Art Music" (Smith, C. P.), 638–40
Dixon, Melvin, 626
Dixon, Travis L., 3
DJs. *See* disc jockeys
Doctor Stories Stumblinge into Englonde (Elderton), 69–70, 72
Dole, Robert, 427
Doleman, R., 81–82
Dom Jaun (Marinelli), 184
Don Alvaro (Verdi), 252f, 253
Don Giovanni (Mozart), 175–79, 186t–187t, 190t–191t
Đỗ Nhuận, 316
Donizetti, Gaetano, 253
Don Jaun (Strauss), 137–38
Don Juan (Mozart)
   Don Giovanni (Mozart) compared to, 186t–187t, 190t–191t

in Vienna, 176, 179–85, 181f, 183f, 186t–187t, 187–89, 188f, 190t–191t, 192–97
"Don't You Hear the Baby Crying" (Lucas, S.), 584f
D'Orbugny, Alcides, 103–4
Der Dorfbarbier (Schenk), 195–96
Douglas, Kirk, 486
"Down By de Sunrise" (Lucas, S.), 576
Doyle, Arthur Conan, 221
"The Dragon's Descendant" (Hou Dejian), 468
dramatis personae, 394–95
Drewett, Michael, 3
Drifting Down to Tamsui, 290
"Drifting Down to Tamsui" (Wang), 276
drugs
   as censorship subjects, 541–42, 546–49, 553
   in music, 541–42, 545–49, 610–11
drunkenness, 97–98
DRV. *See* northern Democratic Republic of Vietnam
Dubos, Abbé Jean-Baptiste, 162
The Dude (Lucas, S.), 571, 574
Du Fay, Guillaume, 59, 63–64
Dulce Lignum (chant), 17–18, 24
Du Lorens, Jacques, 160–61
Dumas, Alexandre, 241
Dunaway, David, 500
Dunstan (bishop), 47
Dunstaple, John, 51, 64
Dunway, David, 499
Dương Thu Hương, 319
Duplessis, Marie, 241
duplicity, by Jesuits, 99–102
Duverger, Christian, 99
Dyer, Richard, 440
Dylan, Bob, 505, 541

"Earl of Morton" (Elderton), 76–77
Easter, 104n6
Eastern Europe. *See* Yugoslavia
East Francia, 40
Echeverría, Esteban, 342
economics, of rap music, 613–15, 617
Edict of Tolerance, 210
editorial censorship, 269–70

education
  BBC for, 537–41
  censorship in, 527
  in Iran, 670n19, 670n34
  race and, 562–63
  women in, 641, 643–48
Egypt, 158–63, 161f
Egyptian Nursery, 605n3
Eichmann, Adolf, 137–38
"80s Miracle Diet" (Dixon, M.), 626
Einstein, Albert, 175
Eisendle, Reinhard, 197n9
Eisenhower, Dwight D., 512–15, 519, 525
Eisler, Hanns, 508, 518, 523f, 524–25
Elderton, William, 69–78, 82
"Eleanor Rigby" (Beatles), 545
Eliot, T. S., 639
Elizabeth (Queen), 71
  Babington plot of 1586 against, 79–80
  in broadside ballads, 75–76
  Catholic church and, 73, 78, 81–82
  Essex for, 81
  patents for, 78
Elizabethan ballads. See broadside ballads
Elizabethan censorship, 70–71, 82–83
Elizabethan era
  admonitions in, 71–72
  broadside ballads in, 69–71
  Byrd/Tallis Patent of Monopoly in, 78–83
  messages in, 77
  via media (middle way) in, 82
Emerson, Caryl, 420
Emerson, Donald, 196, 227
Eminem, 600
Emperor of Atlantis (Ullmann), 398
England. See also British Broadcasting Company
  Babington plot of 1586 in, 79–80
  censorship subjects in, 539–40
  chant books in, 48
  choirbooks in, 63–64
  Continental Europe compared to, 50–51
  culture in, 552–53
  executions in, 75
  hierarchy in, 537–41
  liturgical reform in, 48–49
  liturgical traditions in, 59–60
  Marine, &c., Broadcasting (Offenses) Act 1967 in, 536, 538–39, 551–52
  politics in, 72–73, 78–79
  privy council in, 69–73, 75–77
  Protestants in, 72
  religion in, 72, 543–44
  treason in, 82
English Church, 47–48
English festal mass (religion), 63
English Kyries
  Continental mass (religion) and, 61–64, 61t, 63t
  for feasts, 63
  history of, 47–52, 49t, 53t–55t, 55–58
  Latin Kyries compared to, 47–52, 49t, 53t–55t, 58–61, 63
  as motets, 60–62, 61t
  schemes for, 59–60
English manuscripts, 56
English mass cycles (religion), 53t–55t, 55–56, 62
English music
  in Continental Europe, 52, 53t–55t, 55–56
  Latin texts in, 79
English reformation, 52
Englund, Steven, 488–89
the Enlightenment, 210–11, 215–16
Die Entführung aus dem Serail (Mozart), 205, 222–23
Epstein, Brian, 543–44
"Equal Rights" (Tosh), 597
Ernani (Verdi), 239–40
eroticism, 96–99, 176–78, 185
Escandón (Jesuit), 101
Esfahāni, Mohammad, 665
Essex (Earl), 80–82
Estrella, Martha, 343–44
Estrella, Miguel Ángel, 333–35, 339, 341–50
Etemādi, Khashāyar, 665
ethnicity, 260–61
Eugénie (Beaumarchais), 167, 205
European art, 87–88
European music, 88
evangelization
  of indigenous people, 87–88
  of music, 90
Evans, Allen, 549

Evans, Walker, 481
"Even Pigs Laugh" (Hagou), 460
Everett, Kenny, 547–48
Evita. *See* Perón, María Eva
Exaltation feast, 14, 17
executions, 75

F22 (chant), 14–15, 15*t*–16*t*, 17
Fabric for Che (Tenney), 340
Facebook, 466
Fairclough, Pauline, 2
Faithfull, Marianne, 544–45
Falconet, Maurice, 161
Fallows, David, 128n49
The Family Romance of the French Revolution (Hunt), 230–31
Fanfare for the Common Man (Copland), 512
Fantlová, Zdenka, 405
"Far Away Is the Moon of Home" (Haas), 390–91
Farce and Fantasy (Isherwood), 157
Farhad (singer), 659
fascicle manuscripts, 56
Fātemeh, Hazrat, 666
fatwas, 662
feasts
  English Kyries for, 63
  Exaltation feast, 14, 17
  Finding feast, 14, 17
  Gallican style for, 8
  for indigenous people, 93–94
  Kyries for, 49
  for the Virgin Mary, 49–51, 92
Federal Republic of Germany. *See* Germany
Fedotov, Alekseyevich, 425–26
Feininger, Laurence, 62
Felix Kon Higher Music School, 114
Feltsman, Vladimir, 415, 442
Feminine Endings: Music, Gender, and Sexuality (McClary), 643
feminism, 638–40, 643–48, 650–51
Ferdowsi (poet), 657–58
festivals
  gourds in, 100
  for indigenous people, 92–94
  in Israel, 145
  liturgical routines compared to, 95
  for Society of Jesus, 94–95
fiction
  in broadside ballads, 76–77
  propaganda in, 82–83
Fidelio (Beethoven)
  censorship of, 227–30
  German nationalism and, 225–27
  history of, 221–22
  marital love in, 224–25, 232–33
  politics of, 230–33
  story of, 222–24
fidelity. *See* marital love
Field, Al G., 575
Figueiredo, Batista, 372
La Fille du régiment (Donizetti), 253
film. *See also specific films*
  censorship and, 479–83
  in United States, 490–92
Finding feast, 14, 17
Finding of the Cross, 14–15, 15*t*–16*t*, 17
Fine, Vivian, 640
Finley, Karen, 493
Fiorucci, Flavia, 343
Fire in My Belly (Wojnarowicz), 631
firewalls. *See* the Internet
Fitzgerald, Michael, 479, 489
Fiuza, Alexandre, 361
Five O'Clock Club (television show), 541
Flacks, Dick, 3
Flanagan, Hallie, 477–78, 493
flattery, 79–80
Fleming, William, 516
Fletcher, Tom, 563–64
Der fliegende Holländer (Wagner), 142–43
"The Flute of Interior Time" (Harbinson), 626–27
Flynt, Larry, 632
folk music. *See also* spirituals
  in Argentina, 344
  as censorship subjects, 2, 261–62
  chèo as, 307–11
  HUAC and, 484–93, 502–4, 507–9
  NCFM, 262–66, 269–70
  politics and, 502–4
  in Russia, 112
  The Weavers for, 502–5
  xibeifeng as, 456

La folle journée (Beaumarchais). *See*
    Le Mariage de Figaro
Foner, Eric, 488
Forains, 157
Forbes, Elliot, 221
Foreman, Larry, 480–83, 494
Formby, George, 540–41
La forza del destino (Verdi), 252f, 253
Four Hymns (Schnittke, A.), 444
Four Songs From Chinese Poetry (Haas),
    389–93, 390f, 403
Fox, Roland, 547–48, 550, 553n8
Le Franc, Martin, 51
France
    comedy in, 159, 163–70, 207–8
    enlightenment in, 210
    *The Family Romance of the French
        Revolution* (Hunt), 230–31
    Forains in, 157
    French Revolution in, 222, 231
    Germany compared to, 170
    Kyries in, 50
    literature in, 209
    Old Regime in, 153–54, 156–60,
        163, 166, 170
    privilège in, 153
    Reign of Terror in, 223, 231
    self-censorship in, 162–63, 212
Francis, Kimberly, 3
Francis I (Emperor), 232
Francis II (Emperor), 182–83,
    194–95
Frank, Pamela, 643
Frankish liturgical books, 12t, 13
Fraser, Robert, 546
freedom of expression, 640
freedom of speech, 603–4
Freedom Singers quartet, 505
Freemuse, 1
Freire, Paulo, 339
French Revolution, 222, 231
Friedal, Johann, 215
Frolova-Walker, Marina, 118
Fung, Anthony Y. F., 277, 294–95
Furtseva, Yekaterina, 420
Furtwängler, Wilhelm, 134, 380, 383–84
"Fury" (Snively/Wheelock), 626

Gabriel, Peter, 595, 597
Gaillard, Gabriel Henri, 168
Galás, Diamanda, 597–98, 630–31, 634n4
Gallagher, Noel, 461–62, 468
Gallican chants, 29
    for mass, 9, 12t
    for Pippen III, 11
    Roman chants compared to, 9
    Roman texts compared to, 13–14
Gallican liturgies, 11, 12t, 13
Gallican musico-liturgical practice, 13
Gallican prayers, 24–25
Gallican style
    for cantors, 7–8
    for feasts, 8
    Roman style compared to, 21
Gallican texts, 25
Galo Mendes, Sônia Maria, 368
Gáspari, Elio, 360
Gavazzo, José Nino, 334, 347
Geisel, Ernesto, 366–68
gender
    as censorship subjects, 3
    *Feminine Endings: Music, Gender,
        and Sexuality* (McClary), 643
    in music, 638–40
    segregation of, 98–99
Gender and the Musical Canon (Citron),
    640–41, 643
Germany. *See also* Nazi regime;
    Vienna; Wagner
    anti-Semitism in, 378–80
    censorship in, 177–78, 197n7
    France compared to, 170
    Kristallnacht in, 131, 133–34
    nationalism in, 225–27
    NCFM in, 266
    Russia and, 441
    Soviet-bloc and, 431
Gerron, Kurt, 394
Gessen, Masha, 413
Gil, Gilberto, 358
Gilbert, Sandra M., 639–40
Gillard, Frank, 551
"Gimn likovaniya" (Rodionov), 123
Ginastera, Alberto, 342
Giovanna de Guzman (Verdi), 245

"Girl" (Beatles), 542
Glass, Philip, 438–39
globalism, 140
globalization
    AIDS in, 625
    censorship and, 492–95
Globokar, 630
Glorias, 50, 55–56, 61
Glossy, Carl, 196
Gnesin, Mikhail, 115, 127n23
Godefroy, Jeanne, 157
God of Silence. *See* Harpocrates
"Go Down Moses" (song), 576
"God's Window" (Egyptian Nursery), 605n3
Goebbels, Joseph, 134
Gold, Mike, 337–38
Gonzaga, Chiquinha, 362–63
Goodman, Walter, 494
Gorbachev, Mikhail, 422–23, 426–27
Gorzowski, Karl von, 240
Gossett, Philip, 242
gossip, 154–55
"Got to Get You into My Life" (Beatles), 542
Goulart, João, 356
gourds
    in festivals, 100
    for music, 97
governmental forces, for censorship, 69–72, 210–13, 593–97
graduals
    for chants, 29–30
    Pa776, 9, 14, 18–21, 19*t*–20*t*, 25
    Pa903, 9, 14, 18–21, 19*t*–20*t*, 25
Graham, Sandra, 3
"Grandfather's Clock" (Work), 567–69, 569*f*–570*f*, 584, 587
Greek invocations, 55, 65n3
    of Kyries, 40–42, 41*e*
    melodic patterns in, 40–42, 40*e*–45*e*, 44–47
Green, Lucy, 645–46, 651–52
Green Book, 539–40
Greenfield, Edward, 439
"Greensleeves" (ballad), 69, 77, 82
Gregorian chants, 13
    as aesthetic compromise, 7–8
    neo-Gregorian chants, 25, 26*e*–27*e* 28
Gregorian manuscripts, 18, 29

Gregory the Great, 39
Gregory VII (pope), 48
Gregory XII (Pope), 51
Grétry, André-Ernest-Modeste, 156–57
Grieg, Edvard, 540
Griffiths, Paul, 438–40
Grimm, Frédéric-Melchior, 154–55
Grindenko, Tatyana, 422
Großauer-Zöbiger, Jennyfer, 194
Großmann, Friedrich Wilhelm, 205
Guaraní Reductions of 1649, 94–95
Gubaidulina, Sofia, 421–23, 432–33, 440–41, 445n9, 644
Gubar, Susan, 639–40
Guevara, Ernesto ("Che"), 338, 340
Guglielmo Wellingrode (Verdi), 243–46
Gulag camps, 114
Gulf War, 143–44
Guns n' Roses, 597–98
Gustavo III (Verdi), 237–38, 242
Guthrie, Woody, 500–501, 505, 509
Guy, Nancy, 2
the Gypsy Kings, 665–66

Haas, Pavel, 389–94, 390*f*, 400, 402–3, 405–6
Habermas, Jürgen, 158
Hāfez (poet), 665, 670n25
Hägelin, Franz Karl, 176–85, 187–89, 196–97, 198n10, 198nn15–16
    manuscripts for, 181*f*, 183*t*, 188*f*
Hagenauer, Yves, 347
Hagou, 460
"Hai Phong Stars"
    (Lil' BK/Chip Nho), 323–24
Hairy Toan, 308
Hajková, Anna, 400
Hakka people. *See* Taiwan
Half Moon (Qobadi), 668
Halstead, Jill, 648, 652
Hamāvāyān (chorus), 662–63
Hamilton, David, 563
Hamilton, Jake, 563, 565
Hamm, Charles, 56, 62–64
Hammer, Paul C., 81
Hammond, John, 504–5
Hanani, Avi, 148n15
Hanley, William, 155

"Hanoi Dien Bien Phu" (Phạm Tuyên), 308
"Hanoi Stars" (Khanh), 322–23
Harandi, Mohammad Hosseyn Safâr, 667
Harbinson, John, 626–27
Hardenberg, Karl August von, 227
Harpocrate (Pannard), 158–59, 163–68, 170
Harpocrates (Egyptian god), 158–63, 161*f*
Harrison, George, 542, 544. *See also* the Beatles
Harszti, Miklos, 465–66
Hart, Henry, 565, 568, 585–86
hate speech, 602–4
Haverly, J. H., 572
"Having Nothing" (Cui Jian), 457
Hawes, Bess Lomax, 500
Hays, Lee, 500
Hearst, William Randolph, 485
heathenism, 90
hegemony, 103–4
Heifetz, Jascha, 137
Heinsheimer, Hans, 378, 386
The Heiress (James), 512
Helena (Saint), 17–18
He Lüting, 454–55
Helvétius, Claude Adrien, 154
Henahan, Donal, 435
Heraclius, 17
Hernani (Hugo), 239
"Heroes of the Earth" (Wang Lee Hom), 295–96
heroisch-komische opera, 194
Hertzka, Yella, 386
Hesbert, 12*t*, 13
Hess, Carol, 2–3
Hess, Willy, 221–22
He Yong, 458
Hicks, Charles Barney, 591n3
hierarchy
  in England, 537–41
  in Society of Jesus, 92
  in Soviet-bloc, 426
Hiley, David, 47
hip-hop, 616–18, 624. *See also* rap music
Hirschfeld, Ariel, 144
Hisama, Ellie, 640, 651
Hiss, Alger, 488

historical references, as theological motifs, 21, 23–24
history
  of AIDS, 623–25
  criticism in, 225–26
  culture and, 404–5
  Czechoslovakia and, 402–4, 402*f*–403*f*
  of English Church, 47–48
  of English Kyries, 47–52, 49*t*, 53*t*–55*t*, 55–58
  of *Fidelio* (Beethoven), 221–22
  of Iran, 660–68
  of Italy, 238
  of rap music, 610
  of Taiwan, 277–78
  Unsung: A History of Women in American Music (Ammer), 649–50
  of Vietnam, 303–6
  women in, 640–43, 650–51, 653
  of Yugoslavia, 262
Hitler, Adolf, 135, 143, 377
HIV. *See* AIDS
Ho Chi Minh, 323, 327n14
Hoffman, Abbie, 487
Hoffman, Hans-Joachim, 428
Hoffman, William, 627
Hofmann, Ana, 2
Hogan, Ernest, 575
Hoklo popular music, 278–81, 298n11
Holland, Bernard, 435
Hollywood, 512–15, 517–19, 520*f*–523*f*, 522–25, 528
the Holocaust, 146. *See also* Nazi regime
  censorship and, 132–33
  in Czechoslovakia, 393–94, 404–6
Holquist, Michael, 176
Holy Cross mass (religion), 8, 17–18, 25
Homanaje a Federico Gacía Lorca (Revueltas), 339
Home (Luo), 279
homosexuality, 524
Hong Ronghong, 280–81
Hon-Lun Yang, 3
"Honolulu" (song), 482, 482*e*
Hook, Sidney, 519
hooks, bell, 615
Hoover, Edgar J., 518, 528, 530n9
Hoover, Herbert, 512

Hopkins, Pauline Elizabeth, 571
Hopper, Hedda, 485
Horowitz, Joseph, 442
Horowitz, Vladimir, 348
Hothby, John, 57–58
Hou Dejian, 468, 472n36
Houseman, John, 478–79, 481, 484, 492
House Un-American Activities
    Committee (HUAC)
  folk music and, 484–93, 502–4, 507–9
  in Hollywood, 512–15, 517–19, 520f–523f, 522–25, 528
Howard, Thomas (Duke), 74–75
Howe, Marie, 627
How I Won the War (film), 544–45
Höyng, Peter, 176
Hsu Tsang-houei, 299n17
HUAC. *See* House Un-American
    Activities Committee
Huang Anguo, 464
Huang Anlun, 462, 464, 471n24
Huang Chunming, 290–91
Huang Wei, 470n13
Hubbs, Nadine, 642
Huber, Friedrich Ludwig, 217n6
Huberman, Bronislaw, 134
Hu Feng, 455
Hugo, Victor, 239
Hume, Paul, 511–13, 515, 517, 529n2
Hungary, 180
Hunt, Lynn, 230–31
Hussein, Sadam, 143
Hustler magazine, 632, 635n9
Hu Tefu, 279
hybridization, 99–102
Hyers, Anna Madah, 566–69
Hyers, Emma Louise, 566–69
hymns
  Four Hymns (Schnittke, A.), 444
  "Kaddish," 143
  St. Wenceslaus Hymn, 391, 391f

"I Can't Help Myself" (Troggs), 541
ideas, 154–56, 210–11, 596
ideology
  of censorship, 392–93, 468–69, 469n1
  in China, 276

musical weapons in, 307
in PRC, 453–55
of Stalinism, 527–28
"If the Dam Can be Built, the Shit Can be
    Eaten," 276
"Immigration from Mainland to Taiwan"
    (Chen Ming-chang), 287
immorality, 180–82
Imyra, Tayra, Ipy (Taiguara), 367
Les Indes galantes (Rameau), 166
indigenous music, 87–88, 92, 98
indigenous people
  chants for, 89–90
  Easter for, 104n6
  evangelization of, 87–88
  feasts for, 93–94
  festivals for, 92–94
  hegemony for, 103–4
  hybridization of, 99–102
  Jesuits and, 88, 96–97
  mission towns for, 89
  motets for, 90
  musical instruments for, 101–2, 104n4
  sexual relations for, 98–99
  as slaves, 94–95
  Spain and, 91
  stereotypes of, 91
indigenous performance, 98
Inquisition in Eden (Bessie), 486
The Inquisition in Hollywood
    (Ceplair/Englund), 488–89
Instone, Anna, 553n8
internal censorship, 135–44
International League of Women
    Composers, 642
International Society for Contemporary
    Music, 428, 429e
the Internet
  censorship and, 321–25, 328n31,
    471n18, 471n28
  in Iran, 671n47
  PRC and, 460, 466–68, 471n18, 471n28
"In the Hall of the Mountain King"
    (Grieg), 540
"In This Life" (Madonna), 628
"Into the Streets May First!"
    (Copland), 337

Introduction to Post-Tonal Theory (Straus), 644
introits, for chants, 29
IPO. *See* Israel Philharmonic Orchestra
Ippolitov-Ivanov, Mikhail, 114
Iran
    education in, 670n19, 670n34
    history of, 660–68
    the Internet in, 671n47
    music in, 657–60, 668–69
    politics in, 664–67
    popular music in, 665, 671n39
    in pre-revolutionary period, 658–60
    reconstruction period for, 662–64
    religion in, 670n17
    revolutionary period for, 660–62
    United States and, 660–61, 664
    women in, 659, 662–63, 668–69, 669n6, 670n13, 671n55
Das Irrlicht (Bretzner), 176–78, 193
Isherwood, Robert, 157
Islam, 657, 660–61, 663–69. *See also* Iran
Israel
    censorship in, 131–33, 139–44
    cultural censorship in, 138–39
    festivals in, 145
    Germany and, 133–35
    globalism in, 140
    Gulf War for, 143–44
    internal censorship in, 135–44
    the Knesset in, 131–33, 136–37, 141–42, 145–46
    nationalism in, 141
    politics in, 135–36
    television in, 142–43
    voluntary censorship in, 144–47
    Yishuv for, 134–35
Israel Philharmonic Orchestra (IPO), 133–38, 142–43
Italy. *See also* Verdi
    Austria and, 244
    comedy in, 164
    history of, 238
    Kyries in, 46
    opera in, 239–43
    police in, 239
    pre-unification in, 243–51, 251f–252f, 253–54
    Second War of Independence for, 243
ITSOFOMO (compilation album), 631
Ivashkin, Alexander, 416, 440–43
Ives, Burl, 501
Ives, Charles, 641
"I Want to Hold Your Hand" (Beatles), 541–42
Izzo, Francesco, 2

"Jabula in Amsterdam" (Jabula), 597
Jack, Sam T., 574–75
Jackson, George Pullen, 576
Jackson, George Russell, 571, 584–85
Jackson, James, 563
Jackson, Janet, 627–29
Jacobs, Paul, 427–28
Jagger, Mick, 546, 553. *See also* the Rolling Stones
Jamei, Ahmad Masjed, 671n48
James, Dick, 546–47
James VI (King), 76–77
The JAMS, 629
Janáček, Leoš, 394, 404
Janowitz, Fritz, 400
Japan, 418
Jara, Joan, 339
Jara, Víctor, 335, 509
Jauss, Hans Robert, 478–79
Jaw Shau-kong, 293
Jay Chou, 294–95
jazz music
    as censorship subjects, 455
    communism and, 508
Jenkins, Gordon, 502
Jennings, C. Robert, 486–87
"Jeremiah Brown" (Lucas, S.), 586
Jesuits. *See also* priests; *specific Jesuits*
    baroque style for, 96
    celebrations for, 94–95
    censorship by, 91–94
    duplicity by, 99–102
    expulsion of, 102–4
    indigenous people and, 88, 96–97
    indigenous performance and, 98
    propaganda by, 88–94
    rulebooks for, 92–93

Jesus Christ, 25
Jewel, John (bishop), 73–74
Jiang Hui, 280–81
Jiang Wenyu, 284
Jiang Zemin, 460
the Jimi Hendrix Experience, 548–49
Jinmen Wang ("King of Jinmen"), 276, 290–91
Jin Zhishi, 287–88
Joachim, Joseph, 435
John, Elton, 629
John of Syracuse (Bishop), 39
Johns, Erik, 524
Johnson, Billie, 560, 575
Johnson, James Weldon, 559, 561, 563–64
Johnson, J. Rosamond, 560, 575
John XXIII (Pope), 51
Jolin Tsai, 294
"The Jolly Dude" (Lucas, S.), 583–84
Joseph II (Emperor), 193, 197n9, 205, 210, 212–13
    police and, 227–28
Josephine Lang: Her Life and Songs (Krebs, H./Krebs, S.), 647
journalistic ballads, 73–74
Joyce, James, 639
jubilee songs, 573–74, 575–78, 577f–581f, 582
Judaism, 378–80, 404
"Jugo moja, Jugo" (Armenulić), 264–66, 268
"Jugoslavijo" (Zdravković), 266–67
Juke Box Jury (television show), 541
Jupiter (Mozart), 398–99

Kabakov, Il'ya, 421
Kabir (poet), 626–27
"Kaddish" (hymn), 143
kafana, 264, 266–67, 271n21, 271n23
Kalinin, S., 123
Karas, Joza, 395
Kastner, Israel (Rudolf), 137
Katerina Izmailova (Shostakovich), 418
Kazin, Alfred, 488
Keep Your Seats Please (film), 540
Khāmene'i, Ali (Ayatollah), 662–64, 666–67
Khān, Darvish, 658
Khánh Ly, 312–13
Khanh Nho, 321–22

Khātami, Mohammad, 664–67, 671n38, 671n48
Khātami, Seyed Ahmad (Ayatollah), 668
Khezr (prophet), 657
Khomeini (Ayatollah), 660–62
Khrennikov, Tikhon, 419, 422–23
Khrushchev, Nikita, 109, 486
Kildea, Paul, 428, 430
Killam, Rosemary, 644–45, 647–49, 651–52
Kim Ninh, 307
King, Wallace, 566–67
"Kingdom Coming" (Work), 567
King Momo, 364–65
Kingston Trio, 505
Kinh Việt Nam, 312
the Kinks, 548–49
Kirkpatrick, John, 530n11
Kirsh, Robert R., 486
Kissinger, Henry, 229
kitsch, 262, 267, 271n14
Kleiber, Erich, 380, 382–83
Klein, Gideon, 394–95, 398, 400, 402–7, 402f–403f
Klein's Trio, 400, 402–4, 402f–403f, 406–7
Klima, Ivan, 392
Klimov, Mikhail, 111–13, 116, 118, 122, 124
KMT. *See* Kuomintang
the Knesset, 131–33, 136–37, 141–42, 145–46
Knogler, Julian (Jesuit), 100–101
Kochanski, Halik, 1
Koellreuter, Hans-Joachim, 339
Kon, Felix, 127n18
Koran. *See* Islam
Korngold, Haim, 148n14
Korpe, Marie, 2
Koussevitsky, Sergey, 111
Kozinn, Alan, 433, 435, 437
Krakauer, David, 626
Kramer, David, 598
Kramer, Hilton, 487–88
Krása, Hans, 394–95, 400, 402–5, 402f–403f
Krasner, Louis, 384
Krebs, Harold, 647, 651
Krebs, Sharon, 647, 651
Kreichi, Stanislav, 422
Kreisler, Fritz, 435
Kremer, Gidon, 419, 422–23, 431–35

Kristallnacht, 131, 133–34
Kronos Quartet, 431–32, 435–38, 436e
Kröpfl, Francisco, 335
Krysa, Oleh, 422–23, 442, 445n5
Kudryatseva, E. P., 117
Kukharsky, Vasiliy, 420
Kulthum, Umm, 659
Kumpf, Herbert, 205–6, 212–13
Kuomintang (KMT), 298n9
    censorship by, 279–81, 283, 288–89
    in Taiwan, 275
Kuo Ying-nan, 289
Kurpekov, Yuriy Konstantinovich, 426
Kyrie eleison, 39–42, 40e–45e, 44–46, 59
Kyries, 39. *See also* English Kyries; Latin Kyries; Old Hall Manuscript
    in Anglo-Saxon manuscripts, 47
    in choirbooks, 57–58
    in Continental Europe, 46–47
    Cunctipotens genitor deus, 47
    for feasts, 49
    in France, 50
    Greek invocations of, 40–42, 41e
    in Italy, 46
    Latin verses in, 40–41, 41e, 46
    for mass (religion), 46–47
    Melnicki, 45e, 46
    Missa Caput, 58, 60–64
    Missa Hilf und gib rat (motet), 53t–55t, 57
    Missa Quem malignus spiritus, 64
    Sarum use for, 49, 49t
    singing of, 40–42, 40e–45e, 44–47
    tropes in, 47–49
Kyrie Vatican, 44–45, 44e
Kyrie verses, 60
Kyrie XIV, 42e–43e, 44–46
Kyrie XVI, 39–40, 40e

Labrador, Sánchez (Jesuit), 97
Lacerda, Paulo de Leite, 361–62
"Ladie Nurse" (Elderton), 76–77
Lady Macbeth of the Mtsensk District (Shostakovich), 418
Laments (Denisov), 419
Lampell, Millard, 500
Landy Chang, 281, 290–91
Lang, Josephine, 647

Langhorne, Richard, 229
Lanzfeld, Carlo Giusto Torresani, 239
Lardner, Ring, Jr., 478–81, 483–85, 489–93, 495
Larner, Gerald, 442
Latin Kyries, 46, 65n3
    English Kyries compared to, 47–52, 49t, 53t–55t, 55–61, 63
    as motets, 62
Latin texts
    in English music, 79
    for Russian music, 118, 125n3
    for Western Music, 110
Latin verses, 40–41, 41e, 46
Leaming, Barbara, 483
Leary, Timothy, 542, 546
Lê Duẩn, 307
Lee, Bruce, 295
Lee Shuang-tse, 278–79, 298n8
Lehar, Franz, 131, 142
Lekeban, 460
Lê Nam, 319–20
the Leningrad Capella
    censorship for, 114–16, 126n12
    setlists for, 117, 119–20, 126n9
    in Soviet Russia, 111–13, 117–22
Leningrad Philharmonia, 111–13, 115–16, 120–21, 125n6, 126n11
Lennon, John, 535, 541–47, 549–53. *See also* the Beatles
Lenoir, Jean Charles Pierre, 168
Leonora (Paer), 223, 225
Léonore, ou L'amour conjugal (Bouilly), 222–23, 231. *See also Fidelio*
Leopold II (King), 228
"Let's Spend the Night Together" (Rolling Stones), 541
Let Us Now Praise Famous Men (Evans, W./Agee), 481
Leuchter, Erwin, 341
Leventhal, Harold, 504, 506
Liber de arte contrapuncti (Tinctoris), 51
Li Binghui, 276, 290–91
librettos, 175. *See also* Beaumarchais; opera
Liebestod (Wagner), 142
Das Lied von der Erde (Mahler), 136
Life with an Idiot (Zhizn's idiotom) (Schnittke, A.), 414–15

Ligeti, György, 439
Li Houxiang, 469n4
Li Jinhui, 456
Lil' BK, 322–23
Lincoln, Abraham, 512–14, 516
Lincoln Portrait (Copland), 512–13, 516, 518, 529
Lins, Ivan, 335–56, 358–66
    politics and, 366–72, 369f
Lin Xiong, 469n7
Lippert, Friedrich Karl, 179–80, 181f, 184–85, 188–89, 190t–191t
    manuscripts by, 186t–187t
litanies
    Kyrie eleison as, 39–42, 40e–45e, 44–46, 59
    Kyrie XVI, 39–40, 40e
    The Litanies of Satan (Galás), 597–98
The Litanies of Satan (Galás), 597–98
literary historians, 70–71
literature, 209
liturgical chants, 10
liturgical prayers, 21–24
liturgical reform
    Carolingian interventions for, 29
    in England, 48–49
    for Roman church, 10–11
liturgical routines, 95
liturgical traditions, 59–60
liturgical transformation, 8
Liturgy (Tchaikovsky), 112–13, 116
Liu Xue'an, 456, 469n5
Livingston, Carol, 71
Li Xianglan, 469n5
Li Xuli, 458
localism, 13
Lockwood, Joseph, 551
Lockwood, Lewis, 227
Loewenstein, Anthony, 464
Lomax, Alan, 502
Long, Marguerite, 343
"Long Live Punk'N'Funk" (Zhu), 284–86
Lorca, Federico García, 339
Lotanis. *See* gourds
Louis XIV (King), 153
Louis XV (King), 153, 155
Louis XVI (King), 208
"Love Me Do" (Beatles), 544
Lozano (Jesuit), 97

Luca, John W., 566
Lucas, Carrie Melvin, 572, 591n7
Lucas, Malinda, 562
Lucas, Sam, 562, 564f, 569f–570f, 573–74, 590n2
    compositions by, 588–90
    marriage for, 572, 591n7
    racism and, 559–61, 563–72, 575–78, 577f–581f, 580–88, 583f–585f
Lucey, Roger, 595
"Lugang, Small Town" (Luo), 279
Lui Xiaobo, 471n28
Lukić, Lepa, 264
Luković, Petar, 264–65
lullabies, 395, 396f–397f, 398
Lulu (Berg, A.), 377, 380, 382, 385–87
Lunacharsky, Anatoly, 111–13, 126n7
Luo Dayou, 279, 298n10
Lü Qi, 454–56
Lu Xun, 465
Lyubimov, Aleksey, 421–22

Madonna, 628
Maffei, Clarina, 237, 239
The Magic Flute (Mozart), 197n2
Magnificat (Bach), 117–18
Mahler, Gustav, 136–37
Makeba, Miriam, 509
La maledizione (Verdi), 240, 248
Malesherbes, Chrétien-Guillaume de Lamoignon de, 155, 168
"Mandela Day" (Simple Minds), 597
Manes, Philip, 407
Mann, William, 549
manuscripts
    Anglo-Saxon manuscripts, 47
    Aquitaine manuscripts, 18–21, 19t–20t, 24–25, 28
    B-Br 5777, 58
    in Continental Europe, 51–52, 64
    English manuscripts, 56
    fascicle manuscripts, 56
    Gregorian manuscripts, 18, 29
    for Hägelin, 181f, 183t, 188f
    by Lippert, 186t–187t
    Old Hall Manuscript, 52, 55–57, 64
    Sextuplex manuscripts, 18

"Many Springs" (Quách Thị Hồ), 309–10
Mao Zedong, 454
Mapplethorpe, Robert, 493
"Marching through Georgia" (Work), 567
"March of the Volunteers," 293
Margaret of York, 58
Le Mariage de Figaro (Beaumarchais), 167–69, 178, 207–8, 213–16
Mariátegui, José Carlos, 338
Marin, François Louis Claude, 167–68
Marine, &c., Broadcasting (Offenses) Act 1967, 536, 538–39, 551–52
Marinelli, Karl, 184
marital love, 224–25, 232–33
market censorship, 270
Markevitch, Igor, 141
Marley, Bob, 509
Marooned in Iraq (Qobadi), 668
Marr, David, 311
Marriott, R. D., 548, 552, 553n10
Martin, George, 542, 550, 552
Martins, Vitor, 362–63, 370–72
Martín y Soler, Vincente, 211
Marville, Claude Henri Feydeau de, 166
Mary Queen of Scots, 74, 77, 79–80
Marzari, Carlo, 240–41
Masakela, Hugh, 602
*M*A*S*H* (film), 479
Masque of the Red Death (Galás), 630
mass (religion). *See also* rite of mass
    Aquitainian mass Propers, 22–25
    Continental cantus firmus mass, 61–62
    Continental mass (religion), 61–64, 61*t*, 63*t*
    Continental mass-motet cycles, 61*t*, 62
    English festal mass, 63
    English mass cycles, 53*t*–55*t*, 55–56, 62
    English music for, 52
    for Finding of the Cross, 14–15, 15*t*–16*t*, 17
    Gallican chants for, 9, 12*t*
    Holy Cross mass, 8, 17–18, 25
    Kyries for, 46–47
    mass-motet cycles for, 62
    movements for, 51
    rite of mass (religion), 13
    Roman mass (religion), 12*t*
    Romano-Frankish mass Proper texts, 14, 28
Masters of the Future (Luo), 279

Masur, Kurt, 428, 445n11
matachines (dance), 104n2
"El matadero" (Echeverría), 342
Matthews, Dave, 509
Maus, Fred, 629
Ma Ying-jeou, 276, 294, 296–97, 300n24
Mazzini, Giuseppe, 244
Mbuli, Mzwakhe, 596–98
McBride, Joseph, 485
McCarthy, Joseph, 485–86, 518, 524–25, 528
McCartney, Paul, 535, 542–52, 553nn6-7. *See also* the Beatles
McClary, Susan, 643, 651
McGuigan, Jim, 603–4
McKitterick, Rosamond, 10–11
media
    communism in, 518–19
    in South Africa, 599–600
    violence and, 610–11
Médici, Emilío Garrastazu, 364–65
medieval West, 10
Mehta, Zubin, 139–41, 144–45, 148n14
Die Meistersinger von Nürnberg (Wagner), 133–34, 142
Melamed, Avraham, 140, 143
Melnicki Kyrie, 45*e*, 46
melodic patterns
    in chants, 25, 26*e*–27*e* 28
    in Greek invocations, 40–42, 40*e*–45*e*, 44–47
    speech melody as, 403–4
Menashe, Louis, 488
Mendelssohn, Felix, 137, 512, 516–17
Menezes, José Carlos Mello, 369, 369*f*
Menuhin, Yehudi, 347
Mercado, Raúl, 348
Mercier, Louis-Sébastien, 154, 156
Merovingian Gaul, 13
Merrett, Christopher, 604
Messiah (Handel), 463
Metternich, Klemens von, 227–29
Metzner, Ralph, 542
Meyer, Mahlon, 292
Meyer, Stephen, 224
Michael, Andrew, 162
Microsoft, 466
middle way, 82

Miên Đức Thắng, 313, 327n17
Milagre dos Peixes (Nascimento), 367
Miles, Barry, 542
Miles, Sara, 631–32, 635n8
Millay, Edna St. Vincent, 639
Minato, Nicolò (count), 160
Mindlin, Adolfo, 341
Minstrel music. *See* Lucas, Sam
Mishory, Gilead, 142
misogyny
    in anti-communism, 642
    in music, 610–11, 613, 640
Missa Caput (Kyrie), 58, 60–64
Missa Hilf und gib rat (motet), 53t–55t, 57
Missale francorm, 9
Missale gothicum, 9
Missa Quem malignus spiritus (Kyrie), 64
Missa Sancti Iacobi (Du Fay), 59
The Mission (film), 87
mission art
    baroque-ness of, 95–96
    European art compared to, 87–88
mission culture, 89–90, 94–96
mission ethnogenesis, 104n1
mission towns, 89
mitotes, 99
Mitterand, Danielle, 348
Mitterand, François, 348
Modo Livre (Lins), 359, 362–63, 365
Mohajerani (Ayatollah), 664–65, 671n48
Molotov-Ribbentrop pact, 118
monopolies, 79–83
"The Moon Remembers Uncle Ho"
    (Chu Hà), 310–11
Morley, Thomas, 81–82
"Morqe sahar" (song), 659
Mosaddeq, Mohammad, 669n8
Moscow Conservatory, 114, 128n24
motets. *See also* Kyries
    Continental mass-motet cycles, 61t, 62
    English Kyries as, 60–62, 61t
    for indigenous people, 90
    Latin Kyries as, 62
    mass-motet cycles, 62
    Missa Hilf und gib rat, 53t–55t, 57
    scholarship for, 57
movements, for mass (religion), 51

Moyers, Bill, 507
Mozart, Wolfgang Amadeus, 177, 179, 211–16
    censorship for, 175, 203–4, 206–7, 209.
    See also specific works
MPB. *See música poular brasileira*
Mravinsky, Yevgeny, 121
Mr. Dee, 322
Mr. Warren's Profession (film), 468
Mudie, Benjy, 605n3
Mui, Anita, 460
Müller, João Carlos, 370
Müller-Kampel, Beatrix, 194
multicultural strategies, 288–89
Mundy, John, 80–81
Musgrave, Thea, 644
music. *See also* classical music; folk music;
    opera; popular music; Western music
    AIDS and, 623–25, 633–34
    Anglophone West in, 625
    Anthologies list, 653
    atonality in, 378
    avant-garde music, 629–32
    beiguan music, 290–91
    ca trù, 309–10, 320, 324, 326n13
    châu văn, 310–11, 320
    churches for, 125n3
    clean versions for, 600
    code-switching in, 572–75, 587
    comedy in, 582
    communism in, 400
    as criticism, 281–86, 282f, 285f, 596–97
    in Czechoslovakia, 389–91, 390f–391f
    drugs in, 541–42, 545–49, 553, 610–11
    English music, 52, 53t–55t, 55–56, 79
    eroticism in, 96–99
    European music, 88
    evangelization of, 90
    feminism in, 643–48
    gender in, 638–40
    gourds for, 97
    Hoklo popular music, 278–81, 298n11
    as ideological weapon, 307
    indigenous music, 87–88, 92, 98
    in Iran, 657–60, 668–69
    in Japan, 418
    jazz music, 455, 508
    jubilee songs, 573–74, 575–78, 577f–581f, 582

music (*cont.*)
    kafana for, 264, 266–67, 271n21, 271n23
    making of, 286–88
    misogyny in, 610–11, 613, 640
    in mission culture, 94–96
    música comprometida, 335, 340, 350, 350n1
    nakashi music, 290–91
    for Nazi regime, 131–32
    NCFM, 262–66, 269–70
    parlor songs in, 582
    for patriotism, 525–26
    politics and, 296–97, 316–20, 324–25, 526, 529, 624–25, 629–32
    for priests, 92–93
    punk music, 624–25
    racism and, 559–61, 563–72, 575–78, 577f–581f, 580–88, 583f–585f
    rap music, 321–24, 609–18
    R&B, 611–12
    red music, 315–16
    rock music, 457–58, 469n8
    in Russia, 442
    sacred songs in, 122–23
    Shanghai pop music, 455–57, 469n4
    socialism and, 453–55
    socialist realism in, 454
    Soviet-bloc and, 121–22, 417–18
    in Soviet Russia, 417–23, 424e, 425–27, 433–38, 436e
    spirituals in, 573–74, 575–78, 577f–581f, 582
    superstition in, 99–100
    tinta musicale, 240, 242
    as tradition, 102–3, 104n7
    United States and, 308
    urban planning and, 90–91
    in Vietnam, 321–25
    violence in, 610–11
    women and, 93, 96–97, 637–38, 649–53
música comprometida, 335, 340, 350, 350n1
musical instruments
    censorship and, 97–98, 121–22
    for indigenous people, 101–2, 104n4
musical modernism, 638–40, 650–51
Musical Thank You (Ullmann), 401f
Music and Imagination (Copland), 526, 530n12
Music and Politics (Street), 324

música poular brasileira (MPB), 357–59, 362, 363, 366, 372
Musica Stricta (Volkonsky), 428
Music Bureau (Yuefu), 277
musicians
    patents for, 78
    RAPM for, 113–16, 126n17, 127n27
    self-censorship for, 2, 79, 550–51
"Music in a Mexican Test Tube" (Chávez), 336–37
The Music of Ruth Crawford Seeger (Straus), 647
Musicology and Difference (Solie), 643
music videos, 617
Musik und Drittes Reich (book), 378
Myaskovsky, Nikolay, 114
"My Little Ukulele" (Formby), 541
"My prime" (Mundy), 80
"My Thoughts Are of Thee" (Lucas, S.), 585–86
My True Feelings Come Out after Drinking (Jiang Hui), 281

Nabokov, Nicolas, 519, 525, 530n13
Nader, Ralph, 495
Nafisi, Āzar, 665–66
Nagasaki (Schnittke, A.), 418
nakashi music, 290–91
"Naked '87" (Trần Tiến), 317–18
Naming Names (Navasky), 488–89
"Não Há Porque" (Lins/Souza), 359–63, 365–66
Napoleon, 222, 228–29, 232
Nardini, Luisa, 2
Narkompros, 110–11, 124, 126n8
narrative devices, 75–77
Nascimento, Milton, 367
Nataniël, 598
nationalism
    in Germany, 225–27
    in Israel, 141
    in Soviet Russia, 527–28
National Liberation Front, 312, 314
National Reorganization Process, 344–48
National Socialism. *See* Nazi regime
Nattiez, Jean-Jacques, 536–37
Navarro, Nick, 612

Navasky, Victor S., 488–89
Nazi regime
　censorship by, 377–80, 379f, 381f, 382–87, 385f, 387f, 517
　as censorship subject, 143–44
　in Czechoslovakia, 393–94, 404
　IPO against, 135–38
　music for, 131–32
　race laws by, 134
　Soviet Russia and, 500–501
NCFM. *See* newly composed folk music
Nedbal, Martin, 2
Ñeezú, 96
Neill, Ben, 631
Neo-Gregorian chants, 25, 26e–27e 28
Nero and the Gladiators, 540
Neruda, Pablo, 335, 338–39
Neshat, Shirin, 663
Nettl, Bruno, 659–60
Neuls-Bates, Carol, 64
neumatic patterns, 25, 26e–27e 28
"Never Die Young" (Taylor, J.), 628
"A newe Ballade, declaryng the daungerous shootyng of the Gunne at the Courte" (Elderton), 75–76
newly composed folk music (NCFM), 262–66, 269–70
Neydavood, Morteza, 669n9
Ngema, Mbongeni, 601–5
Ngọc Đại, 320
Ngô Đình Diệm, 311
Ngô Thanh Vân, 322
Nguyễn Văn Linh, 315–16
Nguyễn Văn Thiệu, 311
Nhân Văn–Giai Phẩm, 307
Nhật Thực (Trần Thu Hà), 319–20
Nicodermo, Thais Lima, 2–3
Nienguirú, Don Alonso, 95
Nietzsche, Friedrich, 137
Nixon, Richard, 488
Nobrega, Manuel de (Jesuit), 100
"Nocturne No. 20 in C Sharp Minor, Opus Posthumus" (Chopin), 1
Noise (Attali), 291–92
No Man's Land: The Place of the Woman Writer in the Twentieth Century (Gilbert/Gubar), 639–40

Nono, Luigi, 340, 419
non-verbal communication, 165–66
No One Knows About Persian Cats (Qobadi), 668
Norfolk (Duke), 74–75
northern Democratic Republic of Vietnam (DRV), 306–8, 311–12, 314. 324–25, 326n10
Northern Rising, 74
Norton, Barley, 2
Nos Dias de Hoje (Lins), 368–71, 369f
"Not the Red Baron" (Amos), 628
Noverre, Jean-Georges, 166
Noyelle, Carlos (Jesuit), 101
Le Nozee di Figaro (Mozart/Da Ponte), 167, 203–4, 214–16
nueva canción, 335
"Nunchaku" (Jay), 295

"O, Old Man, Old Man" (Zdravković), 267–68
"Ó Abre Alas" (Gonzaga), 362–63
Oasis (band), 461–62
Oberto, conte di San Bonifacio (Verdi), 237
Ocampo, Victoria, 338
Ochs, Phil, 505
de Ockeghem, Jehen, 60–61
Odetta, 505
offertories
　for chants, 31
　Protege domine, 25, 26e, 28
Of Mice and Men (Steinbeck), 512
Old Hall Manuscript, 52, 55–57, 64
Old Regime, 153–54, 156–60, 163, 166, 170
Oliveros, Pauline, 642
Onganía, Juan Carlos, 343
opera. *See also* Berg, Alban; *The Cradle Will Rock; Fidelio;* specific operas
　censorship of, 157–58, 186t–187t, 191t–192t, 239–43, 253–54
　in China, 294–96, 299n19
　heroisch-komische opera, 194
　in Italy, 239–43
　politics in, 165
　rescue opera, 222–24
　self-censorship for, 178–79
　tuồng as, 307–8

Les Oracles d'Harpocrate, ou le dieu du silence à la foire (Pannard). *See Harpocrate*
Orfeó Català (chorus), 337
Orff, Carl, 131, 139, 142, 148n15
Ortega y Gasset, José, 338
Orthodox liturgy, 124–25
orthodoxy, 109
Ortiz, José Antonio, 103
Oskouei, Mehrdad, 669
Ostertag, Bob, 630–32
Oswald (bishop), 47
Our Town (Wilder), 512
Out of Bondage (Hyers, A. M./Hyers, E. L.), 566–67, 571, 587
Out of the Wilderness (Hyers, A. M./Hyers, E. L.), 566–67, 576

Pa776 (gradual), 9, 14, 18–21, 19*t*–20*t*, 25
Pa903 (gradual), 9, 14, 18–21, 19*t*–20*t*, 25
Paer, Ferdinando, 223, 225
Page, Tim, 437
Pahlavi regime, 659–60
Palestine Symphony Orchestra, 131
"Palhaços e Reis" (Lins/Souza), 363–64
Pange lingua (chant), 24
Pannard, Charles-François, 158–59, 163–68, 170
pantomime, 166–67
"Paper Sun" (Traffic), 548–49
Paraskevaídis, Graciela, 339–40, 350n1
Parker, William, 72–73
parlor songs, 582
Parsons, Laurel, 651
Pärt, Arvo, 439, 442
Party, Daniel, 350n1
Passacaglia (Schnittke, A.), 431
Passacaglia and Fugue (Krása), 395, 397*f*, 398
patents, 78–83
patriotism
  censorship and, 515–18
  music for, 525–26
Patterson, Annabel, 78–79
Pauke, Florian (Jesuit), 100
Paul, David, 3
Paul the Deacon, 29
Paz, Juan Carlos, 333, 341

Peculiar Sam, or The Underground Railroad (Hopkins), 571, 587
"pedagogy of the oppressed," 341–48
The Pedagogy of the Oppressed (Freire), 339
Peduzzi, Lubomir, 400, 402
Pegen, Johann Anton von, 227
"Penny Lane" (Beatles), 544–45
People's Republic of China (PRC). *See also* China
  censorship in, 453, 459–62, 468–69
  communism in, 463–66
  ideology in, 453–55
  the Internet and, 460, 466–68, 471n18, 471n28
  religion in, 462–63
  rock music in, 457–58, 469n8
  Shanghai pop music in, 455–57
  Taiwan and, 456, 460–61, 472n36
Pepin the Short, 2, 7
Peramás (Jesuit), 90
perestroika, 112, 421
Perkasky, Mark, 417–18
Pernety, Antoine-Joseph, 162
Perón, Isabel, 344
Perón, Juan Domingo, 334, 342–44
Perón, María Eva (née Duarte), 342–43
Per signum crucis (communion), 25, 26*e*, 28
Per signum sancte crucis (alleluia), 25, 27*e*, 28
Persons, Robert, 81
Peter, Paul, and Mary (band), 505
Pete Seeger: The Power of Song (film), 499
Pet Shop Boys, 629
Pettitt, Stephen, 433
Peyser, Herbert F., 383–84
Phair, Liz, 629
Phạm Tuyên, 308
Phan Thắng Tzán ("Hairy Toan"), 308
Philadelphia (film), 628
Philip II (King), 73
The Pianist (film), 1
Piano Sonata no. 7 (Ullmann), 398–400, 399*f*
Piave, Francesco Maria, 239–41, 248, 251, 251*f*
Pig-head-skin's Funny Rap: I'm Insane (Zhu), 284–86, 285*f*
Pinherio, Paulo César, 364
Pinochet, Augusto, 335, 350n2
Pippen III, 11, 29

Pippin III, 10
Piquet, Christophe, 156
Pirioby, Cristobal, 103
Plague Mass (Galás), 630
Planchart, Alejandro, 2
plantation songs. *See* spirituals
Plato, 276
playwrights, 192–93
Plin, Clair, 642
poetry, 74, 659
Poets for Life, 626
police
    in Austria, 227–28
    in Italy, 239
    in South Africa, 596
Polin, Claire, 415
The Political Brain: the Role of Emotion in Deciding the Fate of the Nation, 296
political censorship, 71, 80, 158, 177–78, 180. *See also* South Africa
    culture and, 623
    in Vienna, 214–16, 229–30
The Political Economy of Music (Attali), 275
politics
    in ballads, 77
    in Brazil, 366–72, 369f
    in communism, 460
    of culture, 260–62
    in England, 72–73, 78–79
    of *Fidelio* (Beethoven), 230–33
    folk music and, 502–4
    in Iran, 664–67
    in Israel, 135–36
    Lins and, 366–72, 369f
    music and, 296–97, 316–20, 324–25, 526, 529, 624–25, 629–32
    Music and Politics (Street), 324
    in opera, 165
    popular music and, 275–77
    of silence, 158–59, 163, 167
    in songs, 169–70
    in Taiwan, 277–78, 294–97
    in theater, 169–70
    in United States, 479–83, 500–501, 509–10, 513–14
Polyansky, Valeriy, 425
polyphonic repertory, 50–51, 62–63

Da Ponte, Lorenzo, 175, 177–79, 197n9
Pool, Jeannie, 642
popular music. *See also* Taiwan
    AIDS and, 627–29
    antecedents of, 278–79
    in Brazil, 355–56, 358–59, 366–72, 369f
    censorship of, 261–62
    in China, 294–96
    Hoklo popular music, 278–81, 298n11
    in Iran, 665, 671n39
    MPB, 357–59, 362, 363, 366, 372
    politics and, 275–77
    in South Africa, 593–97
Portal, Magda, 339
"Posse" *Unser Verkehr* (Sessa), 226–27
post-Carolingian Europe, 10
Potier, Suki, 544–45
Pound, Ezra, 639
Powell, Clarence, 562
Power, Leonel, 51, 64
Pracher, Cecile, 598
Prayer for Vietnam (Kinh Việt Nam), 312
PRC. *See* People's Republic of China
"Preguntas por Puerto Montt" (Jara, V.), 335
Preis, Alexander, 123
Preminger, Otto, 486
the present and eschatology, as theological motifs, 21, 24
press, 210–13
Preto, Ribeirão, 371
pre-unification Italy, 243–51, 251f–252f, 253–54
Prevost, Roxane, 3
Prieberg, Fred, 418
priests, 92–93
Prince (musician), 629
The Princess of Madagascar (Hyers, A. M./Hyers, E. L.), 571
privilège, in France, 153
privy council, 69–73, 75–77
Procol Harum, 548–49
The Professor of Chores (Jackson, G.), 571–72
Pro Musica, 121–22, 124
propaganda
    in fiction, 82–83
    by Jesuits, 88–94
    in Russia, 114–16
prosas, 32

Protege domine (offertory), 25, 26e, 28
Protestants, 72
Psalmes, sonets and songs (Byrd), 80
Pshibïshevsky, Boleslav, 114
The Psychedelic Experience: A Manual Based on the Tibetan Book of the Dead (Alpert/Leary/Metzner), 542
psychological drama, 213–16
Publications Act (South Africa), 594–95
publishing, 80–82
Pugachova, Alla, 425
punk music, 624–25

Qājar, Nāser al-Din Shah, 658
Qazvini, Āref, 658
Qobadi, Bahman, 668
Quách Thị Hồ, 309–10
Quadros, Jânio, 356
"Quando o Carnaval Chegar" (Buarque), 363
"Quasi una Sonata" (Schnittke, A.), 419
Queen Latifah, 615
Queering the Pitch (Brett/Thomas/Wood), 643
Qui Chuizhen, 297n7
Quillen, William, 443

race
  as censorship subjects, 3
  in comedy, 563–66
  education and, 562–63
  in vaudeville, 572–75
race laws, by Nazi regime, 134
Rachmaninoff, Sergei, 112–13, 115–16
racial stereotyping, 611–15
racism
  apartheid for, 594–97
  coon songs, 586
  hate speech and, 602–4
  music and, 559–61, 563–72, 575–78, 577f–581f, 580–88, 583f–585f
  race laws, by Nazi regime, 134
  slavery in, 561–63
Radio Caroline, 538–39
Radio Luxembourg, 538, 548, 552
Radosh, Ronald, 488, 495n2
Radovanović, Milenija, 265
Rafsanjāni, Ali Akbar Hāshemi, 662

Rainbow Quest (television show), 506–7
Rameau, Jean-Philippe, 166, 333
Ramsay, Chevalier, 162
Randel, Don Michael, 647, 650
Ransom, Reverdy C., 588
RAPM. *See* Russian Association of Proletarian Musicians
rap music, 321–24, 609–18
Rautenstrauch, Johann, 205–7, 209, 211, 213
Ravel, Jeffrey, 158
R&B, 611–12. *See also* rap music
Read, John, 536
readaptation, 99–102
Reagan, Nancy, 427
Reagan-Gorbachev Summit, 427
Reagon, Bernice, 505
Recherches curieuses d'antiquité (Spon), 160
recirculation, as theological motifs, 21–22
Red Channels (list), 485–86, 519, 520f–523f, 529n3
Reddy, Govin, 598
redemption, as theological motifs, 21–22
Redlich, Gonda, 405
Red Moon (play), 560, 575
red music, 315–16
The Red Pony (Steinbeck), 512
Red Scare. *See* Cold War
reducciones, 88–89
regimes. *See also* Soviet Russia
  in Brazil, 356–58
  culture in, 289–91
  in Czechoslovakia, 392–93, 404
  Hoklo popular music and, 278–81
  multicultural strategies in, 288–89
  music criticism in, 281–86, 282f, 285f
  music making in, 286–88
  self-censorship and, 305
  in Taiwan, 279–91, 282f, 285f
Regina, Elis, 371
Regli, Francesco, 254
Regularis Concordia, 47
"Rei do Carnaval," 364–66
Reign of Terror, 223, 231
Reith, John, 538
religion. *See also* Catholic church; mass
  in Argentina, 345
  as censorship subjects, 2, 180

in England, 72, 543–44
fatwas in, 662
in Iran, 670n17
in PRC, 462–63
in Soviet Russia, 109–10, 127n19
as tradition, 93–94
in United States, 543–44
renovation policy, 316–20
Republic (Plato), 276
"Republic of China National Anthem," 291–92, 299n21
Republic of Vietnam (RVN), 306, 311–15, 325
Requiem (Mozart), 462–63
Requiem (Werner), 627
rescue opera, 222–24
Retov, Ole, 2
"Return to Innocense" (Kuo), 289
Retzer, Joseph von, 211
revolution. *See* France; Iran
Revueltas, Silvestre, 339
Rezā Shah, 658–59
Rezā Shah, Mohammad (son), 658–60
Rhythm and Blues. *See* R&B
Rhythm Nation (Jackson, J.), 629
Rice, John, 223
Rich, Alan, 434
Richards, Keith, 546, 553. *See also* the Rolling Stones
Richter, Marga, 642
Ridolfi Plot, 74
Rigoletto (Verdi), 241, 244, 246–50. *See also* Viscardello
Der Ring des Nibelungen (Wagner), 142, 283
Rishon Letzion Symphony Orchestra, 142, 145
rite of mass (religion), 13
The Rite of Spring (Stravinsky), 337
Ritt, Martin, 488
Robbins, Jerome, 524, 530n11
Robbins, Tim, 478–79, 490–95
Robertson, Donna, 642
Robeson, Paul, 508
Robinson, Harlow, 423, 432
ROC Government Information Office, 282–84, 286, 298n13
Rocha, Mariozinho, 358–59
Rock and Roll of the New Long March (Cui Jian), 458

"Rock Clock" (Trần Tiến), 318
rock music, 457–58, 469n8
Rockwell, John, 340, 434–35
Rodrigues, Eugênia Costa, 363
Rogation day chants, 13
Le Roi s'amuse (Hugo), 240
the Rolling Stones, 541
Rollins, Hyder, 74
Roman chants, 7–8
   Bod74 as, 14–15, 15t–16t, 17, 23
   F22, 14–15, 15t–16t, 17
   Gallican chants compared to, 9
   in Gregorian manuscripts, 18, 29
   Vat5319 as, 14–15, 15t–16t, 17, 23
Roman church
   aesthetic compromise for, 11
   liturgical reform for, 10–11
Roman liturgies, 11, 12t, 13
Roman mass (religion), 12t
Romano-Frankish mass Proper texts, 14, 28
Roman prayers, 22
Roman style, 21
Roman texts, 13–14
Rommel, Otto, 198n17
Van Rooyen, Jacobus, 600
Rosen, David, 241–42
Rosen, Pinchas, 137
Rosenberg trial, 488, 495n2
Rosenfeld, Paul, 641
Ross, Alex, 415, 442
Rostropovich, Mstislav, 414, 419
Rothstein, Edward, 433, 435
Roussel, Albert, 394
Rozhdestvensky, Gennadiy, 422, 425–27
Ruas, Rony Camargo, 365
Rubber Soul (Beatles), 542
Rubin, Jerry, 487
Rufus Rastus (Hogan), 575
Ruhbakhsh, Ozrā, 659
rulebooks, for Jesuits, 92–93
Rumi (poet), 665
Russia. *See also* Soviet Russia
   Committe on Arts Affairs in, 117
   cultural revolutions in, 113–16
   folk music in, 112
   Germany and, 441
   Gulag camps in, 114

Russia (*cont.*)
  music in, 442
  orthodoxy in, 109
  propaganda in, 114–16
  sacred songs in, 117–22
Russian Association of Proletarian Musicians (RAPM), 113–16, 126n17, 127n27
Russian Choir, 122–23
Russian music, 118, 125n3
RVN. *See* Republic of Vietnam
Rybnikov, Anatoliy, 427
Ryskind, Morrie, 486
Rzewski, Frederic, 340, 350, 350n2

sabotage, 405
Sachs, Joel, 423, 428
sacred songs
  in music, 122–23
  in Russia, 117–22
  in Soviet Russia, 121–23
  in Western music, 109–10
Said, Edward, 340–41
Saint Hilaire, Auguste, 103
Salerno-Sonnnenberg, Nadja, 643
Salieri, Antonio, 167–69
Salt'n'Pepa, 629
Sam Lucas' Songster (White, C.), 561
Sampson, Catherine, 462–63
Sanctus, 50, 56
Sanderling, Kurt, 113, 121
Santa María de Iquique (Advis), 339
Sarāj, Hesāmeddin, 668
Sardinha (bishop), 100
Sarum use, 49, 49*t*
satire, 70
Saurd, Jean Baptiste Antoine, 168
Savenko, Svetlana, 423, 425
Scaccabarabozzi, Origo, 57
scandals, 93
Scheidt, Edward, 530n11
schemes, for English Kyries, 59–60
Schenk, Johann, 195
Scherzinger, Martin, 305
Scheyßereien (Rautenstrauch), 213
Schikaneder, Emanuel, 194, 205–7, 208–9, 212–13
Schirmer, G., 445n13

Schlessinger, Arthur, Jr., 488
Schmelz, Peter, 3, 125n2
Schmid, Martin (Jesuit), 101
Schmidt, Helmut, 132, 140
Schnittke, Alfred, 424*e*, 429*e*–430*e*
  as celebrity, 418–27
  Cold War for, 414–17
  Kremer and, 422–23, 431–35
  Kronos Quartet and, 435–38, 436*e*
Schnittke, Irina, 443, 445n11
Schnittkejahre (Schnittke, A.), 440
Schoenberg, Arnold, 419
scholarship
  for English manuscripts, 56
  for motets, 57
Schönberg, Arnold, 139
Schonberg, Harold, 432
Schröder-Devrient, Wilhelmine, 230
Schumann, Clara, 638, 646
Schumann, Robert, 646
Scorsese, Martin, 444
Scotland
  James VI for, 76–77
  Mary Queen of Scots for, 74, 77, 79–80
Scott, Robin, 548, 552, 553n9
Scribe, Eugène, 242, 245
Seashore, Carl, 641
Sedan, Carlos, 340–41
Seeger, Charles, 337–39, 500, 502–3, 505
Seeger, Peter, 499–510
Seeger, Ruth Crawford, 640, 644, 647
Seeger, Toshi, 503, 505
segregation, of gender, 98–99
Seid Nüchtern und wachet (Schnittke, A.), 425
self-censorship, 212, 259–60, 262–70, 392, 626
  AIDS in, 633–34
  editorial censorship as, 269–70
  in France, 162–63, 212
  for musicians, 2, 79, 550–51
  for opera, 178–79
  regimes and, 305
  in Stalinism, 413–14
  in United States, 483
  in Yugoslavia, 259–60, 262–70
self-management, 269, 270n5, 272n27
Selika, Marie, 573–74
semiotics, 536–37, 549–53

Semyonova, Irina Nikolyaevna, 419
sensuality. *See* eroticism
Sepp, Anton (Jesuit), 90–92
Sergeyev, Alexey, 115
Sessa, Karl Borromäus Alexander, 226–27
setlists, for the Leningrad Capella, 117, 119–20, 126n9
the Sex Pistols, 536
Sextuplex manuscripts, 18
sexual orientation, 3
sexual relations, 98–99
Sgt. Pepper's Lonely Hearts Club Band (Beatles), 535, 546–51
Shabalala, Joseph, 596
Shahname (Ferdowsi), 657–58
Shajariān, Mohammad Rezā, 662, 667–68, 669n11
Shanghai pop music, 455–57, 469n4
Shaw, George Bernard, 468
Shchedrin, Rodion, 418, 420
Sheffi, Na'ama, 2
Shen Wencheng, 280
Sheriff, Noam, 142
Shields, John Archer, 586
Shilansky, Dov, 141
The Shit of God (Galás), 630
"Shivering and Shaking Out in the Cold" (Lucas, S.), 587
Shoo-Fly Regiment (play), 560, 575
Shostakovich, Dmitri, 416, 433, 441–42, 518, 523*f*, 530n13
Shumway, Nicolas, 342–43
Shutter Island (Scorsese), 444
Siegfried Idyll (Wagner), 145
Siegmeister, Elie, 517
Sigismund (King), 51
silence, politics of, 158–59, 163, 167
Il silentio di Harpocrate (Minato), 160
Silent Night (Kremer), 433
"Silver Blaze" (Doyle), 221
Silvestrov, Valentin, 428
Simond, Ike, 572
Simple Minds, 597–98
Sing for Our Compatriots to Hear movement, 311–14, 325
singing, of Kyries, 40–42, 40*e*–45*e*, 44–47

"Singing on the Corpses" (Trịnh Công Sơn), 312–13
Singspiele, 193–96, 197n6
El Sistema, 340–41
Les Six (Roussel), 394
slava, 261, 270n9
slavery, 561–63
slaves, 94–95
The Slave's Escape, or, The Underground Railroad (Hopkins), 571, 587
"Sleepless Nights in Hanoi" (Phạm Tuyên), 308
Slonimsky, Nicolas, 418, 430, 430*e*
Smith, Catherine Parson, 638–40
Smith, Jeremy L., 2
Smothers Brothers, 507
Snively, Susan, 626
Snow, Robert, 62
social conditioning, 649
socialism. *See also* House Un-American Activities Committee
  communism and, 483–90
  music and, 453–55
  in Vietnam, 314–24
  in Yugoslavia, 260–68
socialist realism, 454
Socialist Republic of Vietnam. *See* Vietnam
society. *See* culture
Society of Jesus
  festivals for, 94–95
  hierarchy in, 92
Solera, Temistocle, 254
Solie, Ruth, 643
Somans, Alfred, 78–79
Somma, Antonio, 242
Somos Todos Iguais Nesta Noite (Lins), 367–68
Sondergaard, Gale, 488
"Song for the Corpses" (Trịnh Công Sơn), 312–13
songs
  censorship of, 156–57
  coon songs, 586
  jubilee songs, 573–74, 575–78, 577*f*–581*f*, 582
  parlor songs, 582
  politics in, 169–70
  tasnifs, 658–59
Songs and Dances of Death (Mussorgsky), 398

Songs and psalms (Byrd), 80
Songs for Political Action (the Almanacs), 501
Songs of Golden Skin (Ca Khúc Da Vàng), 312
The Songs of John Doe (the Almanacs), 501
Songs of Madness, 281–83, 282f, 298n12
Songs of the Forests (Copland), 527–28
Sonnenfels, Joseph von, 208–9, 211
Sonnleithner, Joseph, 221–23, 228–29, 232
sonorous expressions, 97–98, 103
Sorokin, Vladimir, 413, 415
Sosa, Mercedes, 335, 348
Sounds from Taiwan's Underclass, 289–90
Sounds from Taiwan's Underclass, Volume 2, 290
South Africa
    after apartheid, 599–601
    censorship in, 604–5
    censorship subjects in, 595, 601
    hate speech in, 602–5
    media in, 599–600
    Ngema for, 601–5
    police in, 596
    popular music in, 593–97
    in transition, 597–99
Souza, Ronaldo Monteiro de, 358–60, 363–64
Soviet avante-garde. *See* Schnittke, Alfred
Soviet-bloc. *See also* perestroika
    censorship in, 465–66
    Germany and, 431
    hierarchy in, 426
    music and, 121–22, 417–18
Soviet Russia
    boom years in, 438–40
    censorship in, 109–10, 413–17, 427–28, 429e–430e, 430–33, 440–44, 459
    the Leningrad Capella in, 111–13, 117–22
    music in, 417–23, 424e, 425–27, 433–38, 436e
    nationalism in, 527–28
    Nazi regime and, 500–501
    Pro Musica in, 121–22, 124
    religion in, 109–10, 127n19
    sacred songs in, 121–23
    Stalinism in, 113–16
    United States and, 514
    xenophobia in, 110
Spain, 91, 337, 339

Spartacus (film), 486
Spazier, Richard Otto, 225–26
speech melody, 403–4
Spencer, Richard, 462–63
Spiegelman, Joel, 428
Spiral (Ostertag), 632
spirituals, 573–74, 575–78, 577f–581f, 582
Spon, Jacob, 160
Springsteen, Bruce, 499, 509, 628
Stahl, Philipp Von, 221
Stalin, Joseph, 483, 486
Stalinism
    ideology of, 527–28
    self-censorship in, 413–14
    in Soviet Russia, 113–16
    against Western music, 119
standardization, 9–10
Standing, Michael, 539–40
Stationer's Company, 70–71
Stationer's Registers, 70
staurology, 18
Steiner, Rudolf, 394
Stephanie, Gottlieb (the Younger), 176–77
stereotypes
    of AIDS, 623
    in culture, 638
    of indigenous people, 91
    of women, 637, 648–49
Stewart, James E., 576
Stiffelio (Verdi), 241, 243–45
Story, John, 72–74
Stow, John, 75
Stowe, Harriet Beecher, 569–71
Straus, Joseph N., 644, 647, 651
Strauss, Richard, 131, 135–39, 141–42, 145–46
Stravinsky, Igor, 337, 530n13
"Strawberry Fields Forever" (Beatles), 544
Street, John, 305, 324
Street Fighting Years (Simple Minds), 598
"Street Fighting Years" (Simple Minds), 597
"Streets of Philadelphia" (Springsteen), 628
Streiff, Egidus, 463
String Quartet (Crawford Seeger), 644
Strohm, Reinhard, 58
Strongin, Theodore, 428
The Structural Transformation of the Public (Habermas), 158

Study for Strings (Haas), 400, 402, 406
St. Wenceslaus Hymn, 391, 391f
Suite of Mirrors (Volkonsky), 419
Sullivan, Ed, 541
Sulzer, Johann George, 212–13
Summer of Love, 546
šund, 262–70, 271n16, 271nn18–19
The Sun is Rising (Taiyang chulai le) (Breathing), 458
Sun Jinan, 456
Sun of the Incas (Denisov), 419
"Superman" (Cecil Bee and the Buzzy Bunch), 595
superstition, 99–100
Sutcliffe, Stuart, 545
Sveshnikov, Alexander, 117–19, 122, 128n24
Swart, Valiant, 598
Swieten, Gottfried von, 211
Sydney, Phillip, 80
symbolism, 537
Symphony No. 1 (Zwilich), 643
"Symphony no. 1" (Corigliano), 626–27
Szenkár, Eugen, 134
Szpilman, Wladyslaw, 1

Taiguara (composer), 367
Taiwan, 297n4, 299n18
    A-Mei for, 291–94
    history of, 277–78
    KMT in, 275
    musical antecedents in, 278–79
    politics in, 277–78, 294–97
    PRC and, 456, 460–61, 472n36
    regimes in, 279–91, 282f, 285f
    ROC Government Information Office in, 282–84, 286
"Talk about Your Moses" (Lucas, S.), 583f
Talks at the Yan'an Forum (Mao), 454
Tallis, Thomas, 78–83
Tanec (Krása), 395, 396f–397f, 398, 404
Tan Lihua, 465
Tannhäuser (Wagner), 142–43
taquis, 99
Tarare (Beaumarchais), 168–70
Taruskin, Richard, 415–16
tasnifs, 658–59
Taubman, Howard, 515–16

Taylor, A. C., 567
Taylor, Derek, 547
Taylor, James, 628
Tchaikovsky, Pyotr, 112–13, 116
television, 142–43
Tenney, James, 340
Tercier, Jean-Pierre, 154
Terent'yev, Boris, 425–26
Terezín. *See* Czechoslovakia
Terry, Sonny, 501
Teuber, Oscar, 193
Thai (singer), 321–22
Thanh Thảo, 322
Thank Your Lucky Stars (television show), 541
"That's What Friends Are For" (Bacharach), 627–28
Thayer's Life of Beethoven (Forbes), 221
theater. *See also* opera
    in Argentina, 343
    cải lương as, 307–8
    non-verbal communication in, 165–66
    pantomime in, 166–67
    politics in, 169–70
    in Vienna, 204–5
"Theatre and the People's Front" (Welles), 484
themes, as censorship subjects, 615–16, 618
theological motifs
    content of salvation as, 21–23
    cross and eucharist as, 21, 23
    the cross characterized as, 21, 24
    historical references as, 21, 23–24
    for liturgical prayers, 21–24
    the present and eschatology as, 21, 24
    recirculation as, 21–22
    redemption as, 21–22
Theresia, Maria (Empress), 176, 208, 210, 223–24, 230–32
Thing-Fish (Zappa), 633, 635n9
"Things That Make Me Feel Like a Fool" (Lucas, S.), 582–84, 585f
Third Reich. *See* Nazi regime
Thomas, Gary C., 643
Thompson, Jack, 612
Thurston, Zora Neale, 639
Tiananmen Square, 457, 470n13, 472n36
Tichborne, Chidiok, 79–81
Tiến Đạt ("Mr. Dee"), 322

Tift, Matthew, 629
Till, Nicolas, 197n2
Till Eulenspiegel, 139
Timerman, Jacobo, 344–45
Tinctoris, Iohannes, 51
tinta musicale, 240, 242
Tito, Josip Broz, 267–68
TLC (band), 629
Tocar y luchar, 341
Toeplitz, Uri, 138
"Together Again" (Jackson, J.), 627–28
Toll, Robert, 565
"Tomorrow Never Knows" (Beatles), 542
Tô Ngọc Thanh, 318–19
Tôn Thất Lập, 313–14
Tosar, Héctor, 348
Toscanini, Arturo, 134
Tosh, Peter, 597
totalitarianism. *See* Stalinism; Yugoslavia
A Touch of Evil (Welles), 486
Tourel, Jennie, 136
Tô Vũ, 314–15
Tower, Joan, 643
tradition
    music as, 102–3, 104n7
    religion as, 93–94
Traffic (band), 548–49
Transversal do Tempo (Regina), 371
Trần Thu Hà, 319–20
Trần Tiến, 317–19, 321, 325
La traviata. *See La Dame aux camélias*
La Traviata (Verdi), 250–51, 251f, 253
treason, 82
Trịnh Công Sơn, 311–13, 321, 325
A Trip to Coontown (play), 560, 575
Tristan und Isolde (Wagner), 139, 142, 145
"Triste en la" (Aguirre), 333–34
the Troggs, 541
tropes, 47–49
Trumbo, Dalton, 486
Trường Chinh, 307
Tuấn Khanh, 321, 328n31
Tú Ngọc, 318–19
tuồng, 307–8
"Turbulent" (Neshat), 663, 670n30
Turner, Victor, 98

"Twilight of the Idols" (Nietzche), 137
2 Live Crew, 611–12

U2, 629
ulamā, 658
Ullmann, Viktor, 389, 394–95, 398–400, 399f, 401f
Ulysses (Joyce), 548
"Um Fado" (Lins), 367–68
Uncle Tom's Cabin (Stowe), 559–60, 569–71, 575
"The Unexpected Benefits of Oppression" (Klima), 392
United States
    American Women Composers Association, 642
    censorship in, 477–79, 495, 503–4
    China and, 455
    classical music in, 530nn14–15
    Cold War for, 483–90, 492–95, 502–5, 511–19, 520f–523f, 522–29, 642
    communism in, 500–502, 530n10
    feminism in, 639
    film in, 490–92
    HUAC in, 484–93, 502–4, 507–9, 512–15, 517–19, 520f–523f, 522–25, 528
    Iran and, 660–61, 664
    music and, 308
    politics in, 479–83, 500–501, 509–10, 513–14
    religion in, 543–44
    Seeger, P., for, 499–510
    self-censorship in, 483
    slavery in, 561–63
    Soviet Russia and, 514
    Unsung: A History of Women in American Music (Ammer), 649–50
    Vietnam and, 307–16, 323
Unruh, Viicky, 338
Unsung: A History of Women in American Music (Ammer), 649–50
Uraguay, 346–47, 346–48
urban planning, 90–91
Urlina, the African Princess (Hyers, A. M. /Hyers, E. L.), 571
Use Your Illusion I (Guns n' Roses), 597–98
Use Your Illusion II (Guns n' Roses), 597–98

USSR. *See* Soviet Russia
Utyesov, Leonid, 115

Valladares, Carlos, 346
Văn Cao, 307
van der Vate, Nancy, 642
Vandré, Geraldo, 358
Vargas, Getúlio, 339
Variations on "The People United Will Never Be Defeated!" by Sergio Ortega and Quilapayún (Rzewski), 340
Vartanyan, Zaven Gevondovich, 419–20
Vasconcelos, José, 336–37
Vat5319 (chant), 14–15, 15t–16t, 17, 23
Vatican editions
  Kyrie XIV from, 42e–43e, 44–46
  Kyrie XVI from, 39–40, 40e
vaudeville, 157, 559, 572–75
Vaziri, Qamar al Moluk, 659
Veloso, Caetano, 358, 366
Una vendetta in Domino (Verdi), 242
Venezuela, 340–41
Verdi, Giuseppe, 237–51, 251f–252f, 253–54
via media (middle way), 82
Vienna
  Beaumarchais in, 204–10
  censorship in, 175–78, 203–7, 214–16, 229–30, 426
  comedy in, 207–9, 213–16
  Don Giovanni (Mozart) in, 175–79, 186t–187t, 190t–191t
  Don Juan (Mozart) in, 176, 179–85, 181f, 183f, 186t–187t, 187–89, 188f, 190t–191t, 192–97
  Edict of Tolerance in, 210
  the Enlightenment in, 210–11, 215–16
  immorality in, 180–82
  Mozart in, 211–13
  playwrights in, 192–93
  Polizeihofstelle in, 182–83
  press in, 210–13
  Singspiele in, 193–96
  theater in, 204–5
Vienna, Josephine, 208, 210–13
Vienna Congress, 226–30
Việt Khang, 303–4, 321, 325

Vietnam
  China and, 303–4
  DRV in, 306–8, 311–12, 314. 324–25, 326n10
  history of, 303–6
  music censorship in, 314–16, 326n7, 327n27
  music in, 321–25
  National Liberation Front in, 312, 314
  rap music in, 321–24
  renovation policy in, 316–20
  RVN in, 306, 311–15, 325
  Sing for Our Compatriots to Hear movement in, 311–14, 325
  United States and, 307–16, 323
  Vietnam war in, 306–14, 326n9
  Youth Song movement in, 307–8
Vietnamese Communist Party, 304
"Vietnamese Gangs" (Thai/Khanh Nho), 321–22
Vietnam National Academy of Music, 307
"Việt Nam tôi đâu" (Việt Khang), 303–4
Vietnam war, 306–14, 326n9
villancicos, 93–94, 104n3
Vinogradov, Victor, 115
violence, 610–11
Violetta (Verdi), 250–51, 251f, 253
Violin Concerto no. 3 (Schnittke, A.), 433
the Virgin Mary, 49–51, 92, 102
Viscardello (Verdi), 246–50
Vi Thùy Linh, 319–20
Volek, Tomislav, 178
Volkonsky, Andrey, 122–24, 419, 428
Voltaire, 153–55, 157, 162, 167, 169–70
voluntary censorship, 144–47
Võ Văn Kiệt, 315–16
Les Voyages de Cyrus (Ramsay), 162
Voznesensky, Andrey, 427
VTA (rapper), 322
vulgarity, 466–67, 600
Vysotsky, Vladimir, 509

Waeber, Jacqueline, 167
Wagner, Richard. *See also* Israel
  censorship against, 131–35
  internal censorship against, 135–44
  voluntary censorship against, 144–47
waisgengren, 277–78
"Waist Deep in the Big Muddy" (Seeger), 507

"Wake Nicodemus" (Work), 567
Walker, Thomas, 64
Die Walküre (Wagner), 145
Wallace, Robin, 2
Walsh, Michael, 415, 435, 441–42
Walsingham, Francis, 80
Wang Chen-yi, 280
Wang Lee Hom, 295–97, 300n23
Wang Xilin, 462–66
Wang Yingtan, 290–91
war. *See specific wars*
Der Wasserträger. See Les Deux Journées
"Waterfall" (TLC), 629
Watergate scandal, 488
"Waterloo Sunset" (Kinks), 548–49
Watkins, Glen, 442
Watson, Thomas, 80
The Weavers, 502–5, 508
Webb, John, 439–40
Weber, Carl Maria von, 134
Weber, Ilse, 398
Webern, Anton, 419
Wegman, Rob, 56
Weidinger, Hans Ernst, 178
Die Weise von Liebe und Tod des Cornets Christoph Rilke (Ullmann), 398
Weiss, Shevach, 141
Welles, Orson, 478–79, 481–86, 489–93, 495, 495n1
Wendt, Amadeus, 225
Wen Hsia, 280
Wenli Mawang, 469
"We Ought to Be Thankful for That" (song), 572
Werner, Hans, 627
"We Shall Overcome" (song), 505–6
Westen, Drew, 296
Western music. *See also* Soviet Russia
    as censorship subjects, 109–10, 123–25, 657, 661–62, 664
    Stalinism against, 119
Wetzel-Hecht Memorandum, 1
Whatey, Andrew, 56
"What is Yellow Music" (Tô Vũ), 314–15
Wheelock, Donald, 626
"When I'm Cleaning Your Windows" (Formby), 540–41
"When I'm Sixty-four" (Beatles), 544
"When We Meet in the Sweet By and By" (Lucas, S.), 577–78, 580, 581f
"When Will You Come Again" (Liu Xue'an), 469n5
"Where Have All the Flowers Gone" (Seeger), 506
Where It's At (television show), 547–48
Whitcomb, Ian, 536
White, Charles A., 561
White, Josh, 501
White, Richard, 104n1
white code. *See* racism
White Man Sleeps (Kronos Quartet), 437
"A Whiter Shade of Pale" (Procol Harum), 548–49
Whitman, Walt, 517
Who's Afraid of Richard Wagner (book), 141
"Why do I use my paper, ink and pen" (Byrd), 80
"Wiegala" (Weber, I.), 398
Wilde, Guillermo, 2
Wild Women with Steak Knives (Galás), 630
Wilkinson, Alec, 499
William the Conqueror, 47–48
"The Wind Cries Mary" (Jimi Hendrix Experience), 548–49
Winkler, Allan, 499
Winter Was Hard (Kronos Quartet), 436–38, 436e, 445n12
Wiser, Hans, 58–62
Wojnarowicz, David, 630–32, 635n8
Wolff, Christian, 340
Woman of the Year (film), 479
women
    American Women Composers Association, 642
    as censorship subjects, 185, 187–88, 246–51, 253
    culture and, 648–49
    in education, 641, 643–48
    feminism for, 638–40, 643–48, 650–51
    in history, 640–43, 650–51, 653
    International League of Women Composers, 642
    in Iran, 659, 662–63, 668–69, 669n6, 670n13, 671n55

misogyny for, 610–11
musical modernism for, 638–40
music and, 93, 96–97, 637–38, 649–53
stereotypes of, 637, 648–49
Wood, Elizabeth, 643
Woodson, Harry, 586
Woolf, Virginia, 639
Work, Henry Clay, 567–69, 569*f*–570*f*
Workers Song Book No. 2, 525
Wozzeck (Berg, A.), 377–80, 379*f*, 381*f*, 382–84, 386
Wu Yongyi, 456

Xenakis, 630
xenophobia, 110
xibeifeng, 456

Yahalom, Shaul, 133
Yang Xiokun, 470n14
Yao Min, 469n4
Yavorsky, Boleslav, 112–13
Yekimovsky, Viktor, 443
yellow music, 308, 314–16, 321, 455–56, 469
Ye Qitian, 280–81
Yishuv, for Israel, 134–35
"Young China" (Lee), 278–79
"De Young Lambs Must Find de Way" (Lucas, S.), 576, 577*f*–580*f*
"You Only Need Say Nothing" (Lucey), 595
"You Really Turn Me On" (Whitcomb), 536
Youseffzadeh, Ameneh, 3
Youth Song movement, 307–8
YouTube, 304, 466–67, 470n10
Yuefu, 277
Yugoslavia
culture in, 260–62
self-censorship in, 259–60, 262–70
self-management in, 269, 270n5, 272n27
Yupanqui, Atahualpa, 341
Yurlov, Alexander, 126n14

Zaft, Yehuda, 145–46
Zappa, Frank, 632–33, 635n9
Zdravković, Toma, 266–68
Zea, Leopoldo, 340
Zeng Suijin, 453–54
Zhang Huimei. *See* A-Mei
Zhang Xinzhe, 293
Zhao Feng, 456
Zhdanov, Andrey, 121
Zhu Toupi, 287
Zhu Yuexin ("Jutoupi"), 283–86, 285*f*
zionism, 400
Zschorlich, Paul, 383
Zweig, Stephan, 142
Zwilich, Ellen Taaffe, 643–44